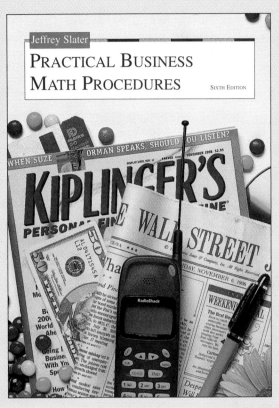

Jeffrey Slater
PRACTICAL BUSINESS MATH PROCEDURES   SIXTH EDITION

- Real-World Applications
- Favorite Features
- Supplements Package
- Alternate Choice

Thank you for using my book in the past and considering this new edition for the future. This Teacher's Edition walkthrough is designed to describe the features that have made **Practical Business Math Procedures** the best-selling business math textbook published. As the author, I believe you should put your energy into the classroom. It is my job to provide the best text and supporting package. I want to hear from you, so here is a toll-free number to my home: **1-800-484-1065 . . . 8980**.

   Getting a college education isn't easy. Students often work full-time to put themselves through school, and I developed and wrote this book and supplements to help you give them every opportunity for success. This edition maintains all the features that have made it successful since its introduction in 1983. These include clear explanations supported by detailed, step-by-step examples; complete coverage at the appropriate level; student-oriented pedagogical tools such as the Chapter Organizer; focus on real business applications; anticipation of student difficulties; accuracy; and unsurpassed teaching support material. Staying on top means constant improvement.

   When I sat down to think about how I could make **Practical Business Math Procedures** even better, I had lots of input to draw from. Feedback from teachers like you, over 40 reviewers and special focus groups, who are gratefully noted in the Acknowledgments page, and my own students gave me advice and suggestions for improvements.

   This Teacher's Edition of the text differs from the student version by including worked solutions to problems printed in red, logos in the margin indicating that teaching acetates are available for those topics, and this walkthrough of key features.

   Let me explain some of these new and retained features on the following pages.

Jeff

Jeffrey Slater

THE SLATER LEARNING SYSTEM

Text
- Money Tip*
- Practice Quiz
- Chapter Organizer
- Critical Thinking Discussion Questions
- Drill Problems
- Word Problems
- Challenge Problems
- Summary Practice Test
- Toll-Free Hotline for students
- A Kiplinger Approach: A Group Project*
- Business Math Scrapbook
- Internet Web site (www.mhhe.com/slater) *
- Appendix A Problems by Learning Unit

Supplements
- Business Math Handbook and Study Guide
- Business Math Internet Resource Guide*
- PowerPoint*
- CD-ROM*
- Overhead Transparencies
- Test Bank
- Computerized Testing
- Instructor's Resource Manual
- Videos
- Excel Workbook and Template Disk
- Business Math Tutorial Software
- Electronic Calculator Guide
- Student Solutions Manual
- Author support—e-mail, toll-free number
- Publisher support—sales representatives, e-mail

*New this edition.

jeffslater@aol.com

REAL-WORLD APPLICATIONS

Instructors asked for an even greater emphasis on the applications of business math in the United States and globally. The Sixth Edition includes references to companies such a Toys "Я" Us, Disney, Sears, Wal-Mart, and Federal Express to illustrate chapter topics. Over 75 actual clippings from *The Wall Street Journal* and 22 *Kiplinger's Personal Finance Magazine* articles give students a more complete view of real-world practices from the business press. New money tips have been added to each chapter opener. (pp. 4, 60, 62)

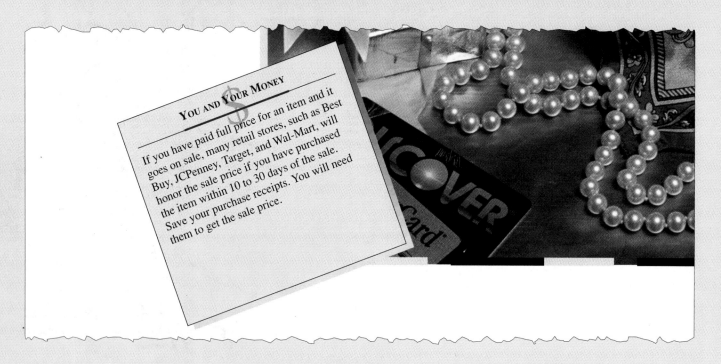

YOU AND YOUR MONEY

If you have paid full price for an item and it goes on sale, many retail stores, such as Best Buy, JCPenney, Target, and Wal-Mart, will honor the sale price if you have purchased the item within 10 to 30 days of the sale. Save your purchase receipts. You will need them to get the sale price.

Money Tips

A KIPLINGER APPROACH

A GROUP PROJECT   Defend or reject the following business math issue based on the *Kiplinger's Personal Finance Magazine* article below:

MY PERSONAL FINANCES

Dr. Glass Does Windows

▶ How Philip Bregstone washes his way to a six-figure income—part-time.   By Marc L. Schulhof

Like many business people, Philip Bregstone counts a laptop computer and a cellular telephone among the tools of his trade. But he doesn't carry a briefcase. He totes a bucket.

As "Dr. Glass," a "boutique window washer" in a tony suburb of Washington, D.C., Bregstone cleans up: His annual gross income hovers around $100,000, a big-city salary that more than satisfies his family's needs—especially because they live in Colorado.

With his wife, Roberta, and 3-year-old son, Jonah, Bregstone spends eight months of the year in Nyland, a "co-housing" community outside Boulder, where the Bregstones own their own home and participate in communal activities. Philip helps raise animals, teaches music and takes care of Jonah while Roberta works as a sign-language interpreter.

But every spring, like the Orioles to Baltimore, they migrate back East for the window-washing season.

HUMBLE BEGINNINGS. Bregstone, 38, launched his business 20 years ago to pay his way through Syracuse University. He spent vacations as Dr. Glass in his hometown of Potomac, Md., and continued the business as a graduate student studying music composition on a full scholarship at the nearby University of Maryland, in College Park.

After moving to Santa Fe, where he spent two years studying the Great Books at St. John's College, Bregstone continued to ply his trade during breaks. "I could fly home for long weekends to wash windows and visit friends," he says. "The work paid for the flight and a rental car." He even opened a branch office in Santa Fe.

When Bregstone finally settled in Colorado, he assumed his business would dry up. Instead, it has doubled. Every March the Bregstones pack up their Subaru and trek to Washington, where they rent an apartment in the shadow of the National Cathedral—usually for less than they charge to rent out their home in Boulder.

Bregstone's first stop is the home of a longtime client who has an extra-large basement, too much furniture and lots of glass. The client stores Bregstone's equipment every winter and lends him furniture for his apartment every summer in exchange for—what else?—annual window washing. (Another client trades Bregstone use of a vacation home near Vail. He washes the windows there, too.)

ON HIS WAY UP. Though most of his tools are simple, "Dr. Glass" maintains his Potomac practice with a boost from technology. When he's in Colorado, calls to his Washington-area phone number are forwarded. He uses a computer to track his finances and appointments. When he's on a ladder 20 feet up, a cell phone keeps him in constant touch with customers and a digital voice recorder enables him to take notes on his calls.

In a given year, Bregstone services roughly half of his 800-customer database, at an average rate of $300 a job (these are big houses). In July the family returns to Colorado, and twice every fall Bregstone flies back to Washington alone to wipe up the last jobs of the season.

Bregstone has mixed feelings about his success. "My high school friends have graduated from law school and become partners while I'm 'just a window washer,'" he says. But life as Dr. Glass is too fulfilling to give up for a button-down career. And besides, "I enjoy washing windows," he says. "You go into a house with dirty windows and you have no money. You leave a few hours later and the windows are clean, you have money, and you get complimented on doing a good job."

In case you were wondering, Dr. Glass's prescription for clean windows is simple: Get a good squeegee. ●

REPORTER: STACY STOVER

KATHERINE LAMBERT

Business Math Issue

In a given year, servicing half of your customer database will lead to lower sales and less customer satisfaction. Philip should consider franchising his business.

1. List the key points of the article and information to support your position.
2. Write a group defense of your position using math calculations to support your view.

McDonald's Franchisees Told About Menu Plans

By a WALL STREET JOURNAL Staff Reporter

ORLANDO, Fla. — McDonald's Corp., acknowledging that its menu needs perking up, plans to improve the taste of several sandwiches and test what it calls "an indulgent bacon cheeseburger" soon.

The fast-food giant also disclosed that it is working on a crispy chicken nuggets item intended to appeal more to adults, and that it will roll out a line of candied ice creams called McFlurry desserts. And, reversing a decision made under pressure from advocates of healthier fare several years ago, McDonald's plans to boost the fat content of its milkshakes.

News of the changes came as the Oak Brook, Ill., company gave its world-wide franchisees a pep talk, following a year of disappointing sales, marketing miscues and domestic management turnover. The franchisees, who are attending McDonald's biennial convention, seemed cheered by word of menu revisions and the way food will be cooked, and gave U.S. Chairman Jack Greenberg a standing ovation.

The likely menu changes appear in part to be a tacit admission of the failure of the highly touted "adult-oriented" Deluxe line, led by the Arch Deluxe hamburger introduced at the convention two years ago. Since then, the fish Deluxe sandwich has been replaced by an updated version of the popular Filet-o-Fish sandwich, and work is under way on the Deluxe chicken sandwich.

FAVORITE FEATURES OF THE BOOK

You can count on all of the key features developed for this book over the years remaining in the sixth edition. I have listened to instructors using the text, as well as my own students, in order to improve the book and make sure it serves you and your students effectively. My goal was to make it as motivating and understandable as possible for both the young, out of high school student and the older, returning student.

Chapter Openers

The chapter openers explain to students where they've been and introduce them to the chapter's topics. By the use of real newspaper clips, students can see the real world applications of business math and make the topics relevant to them.

Teaching Acetates

The transparency logo indicates there is a teaching overhead acetate for the topic shown. This logo appears only in the Teacher's Edition. (p. 64)

TABLE 3.1

Analyzing a bag of M&M's®

Sharon Hoogstraten.

Color*	Fraction	Decimal
Yellow	$\frac{18}{55}$	.33
Red	$\frac{10}{55}$	.18
Blue	$\frac{9}{55}$	.16
Orange	$\frac{7}{55}$	.13
Brown	$\frac{6}{55}$	.11
Green	$\frac{5}{55}$	.09
Total	$\frac{55}{55} = 1$	1.00

*The color ratios currently given are a sample used for educational purposes. They do not represent the manufacturer's color ratios.

Chapter 2 introduced the 1.69-ounce bag of M&M's® shown above. This chapter looks again at this bag of 55 M&M's® in six colors. In Table 3.1 we give the fractional breakdown of the six colors and express the values in decimals. Note that decimals such as .33, .11, and so on have been rounded to the nearest hundredths. Learning Unit 3.1 explains how to round decimals.

We have divided this chapter into two learning units. The first unit discusses rounding decimals, converting fractions to decimals, and converting decimals to fractions. The second unit shows you how to add, subtract, multiply, and divide decimals, along with some shortcuts for multiplying and dividing decimals. Added to this unit is a global application of decimals dealing with foreign exchange rates.

> **THE CHECKOFF:** A basic men's haircut in Japan costs, on average, $48.65, says ECA Windham, New York, which specializes in international relocation. . . .
>
> © 1996 Dow Jones & Company, Inc.

One of the most common uses of decimals occurs when we spend dollars and cents. For example, *The Wall Street Journal,* in "The Checkoff," stated that a basic man's haircut in Japan costs, on average, $48.65. This is a *decimal number.* A **decimal,** then, is a decimal number with digits to the right of a *decimal point,* indicating that decimals, like fractions, are parts of a whole that are less than one. Thus, we can interchange the terms *decimals* and *decimal numbers.* Remembering this will avoid confusion between the terms *decimal, decimal number,* and *decimal point.*

Clear Explanations

Explanations are given in a step-by-step format that is easy to follow and remember, followed by understandable examples. (p. 65)

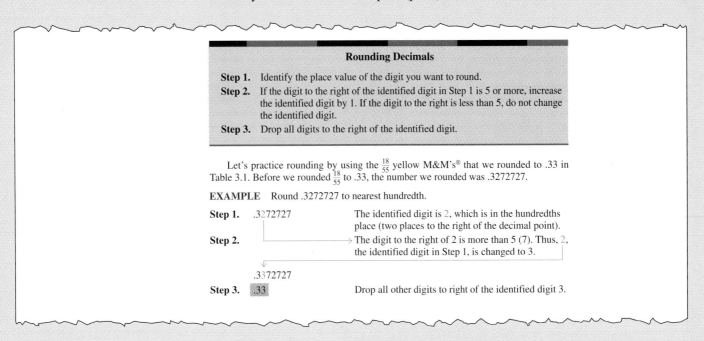

Rounding Decimals

Step 1. Identify the place value of the digit you want to round.

Step 2. If the digit to the right of the identified digit in Step 1 is 5 or more, increase the identified digit by 1. If the digit to the right is less than 5, do not change the identified digit.

Step 3. Drop all digits to the right of the identified digit.

Let's practice rounding by using the $\frac{18}{55}$ yellow M&M's® that we rounded to .33 in Table 3.1. Before we rounded $\frac{18}{55}$ to .33, the number we rounded was .3272727.

EXAMPLE Round .3272727 to nearest hundredth.

Step 1. .3272727   The identified digit is 2, which is in the hundredths place (two places to the right of the decimal point).

Step 2.   The digit to the right of 2 is more than 5 (7). Thus, 2, the identified digit in Step 1, is changed to 3.

.3372727

Step 3. .33   Drop all other digits to right of the identified digit 3.

Functional Use of Color

Functional color-coding was first introduced in the Third Edition of the text. While many books use color, I set out from the beginning to use color to teach. I personally color-coded each element to enhance the learning process. For example, when a student sees a number in red, they know it is a key item they are solving for.

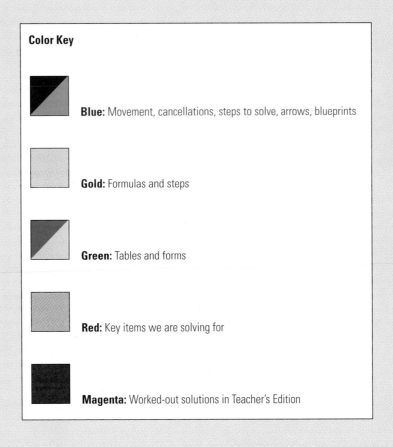

Color Key

Blue: Movement, cancellations, steps to solve, arrows, blueprints

Gold: Formulas and steps

Green: Tables and forms

Red: Key items we are solving for

Magenta: Worked-out solutions in Teacher's Edition

Practice Quizzes follow each Learning Unit in the book. These quizzes provide immediate feedback for students to check their progress and are followed by worked-out solutions. The logo lets students know that videotapes are available along with software tutorials. In these videos I carefully walk students through the material, reinforcing the content. (p. 69)

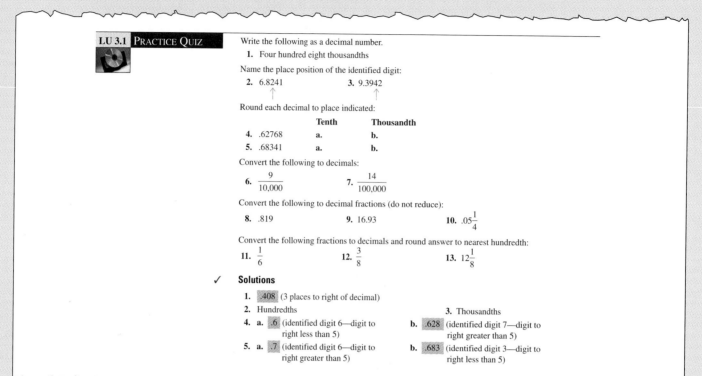

LU 3.1 PRACTICE QUIZ

Write the following as a decimal number.

1. Four hundred eight thousandths

Name the place position of the identified digit:

2. 6.8241

3. 9.3942

Round each decimal to place indicated:

	Tenth	Thousandth
4. .62768	a.	b.
5. .68341	a.	b.

Convert the following to decimals:

6. $\dfrac{9}{10,000}$

7. $\dfrac{14}{100,000}$

Convert the following to decimal fractions (do not reduce):

8. .819

9. 16.93

10. $.05\dfrac{1}{4}$

Convert the following fractions to decimals and round answer to nearest hundredth:

11. $\dfrac{1}{6}$

12. $\dfrac{3}{8}$

13. $12\dfrac{1}{8}$

✓ **Solutions**

1. .408 (3 places to right of decimal)
2. Hundredths
3. Thousandths
4. a. .6 (identified digit 6—digit to right less than 5)   b. .628 (identified digit 7—digit to right greater than 5)
5. a. .7 (identified digit 6—digit to right greater than 5)   b. .683 (identified digit 3—digit to right less than 5)

Blueprint Aid for Dissecting and Solving a Word Problem

Students need help in overcoming their fear of word problems. The first eight chapters (except Chapter 4) provide a "blueprint" format for solving word problems. It shows students how to begin the problem-solving process, gets them actively involved in dissecting the word problem, shows visually what has to be done before calculating, and provides a structure for them to use. Below the blueprints are the steps to solve the problem. The answer is highlighted in red. (p. 74)

How to Dissect and Solve a Word Problem

The Word Problem   May O'Mally went to Sears to buy wall-to-wall carpet. She needs 101.3 square yards for downstairs, 16.3 square yards for the upstairs bedrooms, and 6.2 square yards for the halls. The carpet cost $14.55 per square yard. The padding cost $3.25 per square yard. Sears quoted an installation charge of $6.25 per square yard. What was May O'Mally's total cost?

By completing the following blueprint aid, we will slowly dissect this word problem. Note that before solving the problem, we gather the facts, identify what we are solving for, and list the steps that must be completed before finding the final answer, along with any key points we should remember. Let's go to it!

The facts	Solving for?	Steps to take	Key points
Carpet needed: 101.3 sq. yd.; 16.3 sq. yd.; 6.2 sq. yd. *Costs:* Carpet, $14.55 per sq. yd.; padding, $3.25 per sq. yd.; installation, $6.25 per sq. yd.	Total cost of carpet.	Total square yards × Cost per square yard = Total cost.	Align decimals. Round answer to nearest cent.

Steps to solving problem

1. Calculate the total number of square yards.

$$\begin{array}{r} 101.3 \\ 16.3 \\ 6.2 \\ \hline 123.8 \text{ square yards} \end{array}$$

2. Calculate the total cost per square yard.

$$\begin{array}{r} \$14.55 \\ 3.25 \\ 6.25 \\ \hline \$24.05 \end{array}$$

3. Calculate the total cost of carpet.

$$123.8 \times \$24.05 = \$2,977.39$$

It's time to check your progress.

The Chapter Organizer

This quick reference guide provides students with a complete set of notes, now functionally color coded. Key points, formulas, examples, and vocabulary are included with page references. (p. 101)

Chapter Organizer and Reference Guide		
Topic	**Key point, procedure, formula**	**Example(s) to illustrate situation**
Types of endorsements, *p. 90*	*Blank:* Not safe; can be further endorsed.	Jones Co. 21-333-9
	Full: Only person or company named in endorsement can transfer check to someone else.	Pay to the order of Regan Bank Jones Co. 21-333-9
	Restrictive: Check must be deposited. Limits any further negotiation of the check.	Pay to the order of Regan Bank. For deposit only. Jones Co. 21-333-9

Credit card transactions, *p. 90*	*Manual deposit:* Need to calculate net deposit (credit card sales less returns).
	
	Electronic deposit: Eliminates deposit slips and summary batch header slip.
		Calculate net deposit:
		Credit card sales $55.32
		  62.81
		  91.18
		Credits − 10.16
		  − 8.15
		  $209.31
		  − 18.31
		Net deposit = $191.00

Bank reconciliation, *p. 95*	**Checkbook balance** **Bank balance** + EFT + Deposits in transit + Interest earned − Outstanding checks + Notes collected ± Bank errors − ATM withdrawals − Automatic withdrawals − Check redeposits − NSF checks − Online fees − Overdrafts − Service charges − Stop payments ± Book errors* CM—adds to balance DM—deducts from balance *If a $60 check is recorded as $50, we must decrease checkbook balance by $10.	**Checkbook balance** **Bank balance** Balance $800 Balance $ 632 − NSF 40 + Deposits in transit 416 $760 $1,048 − Service charge 4 − Outstanding checks 292 $756 $ 756
Key terms	ATM (automatic teller machine), *p. 88* Bank reconciliation, *p. 95* Bank statement, *p. 94* Blank endorsement, *p. 89* Check, *p. 88* Check register, *p. 89* Check stub, *p. 89* Credit card, *p. 90* Credit memo (CM), *p. 96* Debit card, *p. 88*	Debit memo (DM), *p. 96* Deposit slip, *p. 88* Deposit in transit, *p. 95* Draft, *p. 88* Drawee, *p. 89* Drawer, *p. 89* Electronic deposit, *p. 91* Electronic funds transfer (EFT), *p. 99* Endorse, *p. 89* Full endorsement, *p. 89*

(Key terms, third column:) Manual deposit, *p. 90*; Merchant batch header slip, *p. 90*; Net deposit, *p. 90*; Nonsufficient funds (NSF), *p. 96*; Outstanding checks, *p. 95*; Overdrafts, *p. 95*; Payee, *p. 89*; Restrictive endorsement, *p. 89*; Safekeeping, *p. 99*; Signature card, *p. 88*

Critical Thinking Discussion Questions

These thought-provoking questions follow the Chapter Organizer and are designed to get students to think about the larger picture and the "why's" of business math. They go beyond the typical questions by asking students to explain, define, create, etc. (p. 150)

Critical Thinking Discussion Questions

1. In converting from a percent to a decimal, when will you have at least 2 leading zeros before the whole number? Explain this concept, assuming you have 100 bills of $1.
2. Explain the steps in rounding percents. Count the number of students who are sitting in the back half of the room as a percent of the total class. Round your answer to the nearest hundredth percent. Could you have rounded to the nearest whole percent without changing the accuracy of the answer?
3. Define portion, rate, and base. Create an example using Walt Disney World to show when the portion could be larger than the base. Why must the rate be greater than 100% for this to happen?

Photos

Over 60 photos are included to stimulate student interest and help students see business math with imagination and enthusiasm. Whether showing cybercafes, Toys "Я" Us expansion into Japan, or inventory being shipped, business math becomes real to them. (p. 73)

Cybercafes

Neurotic about checking e-mail on the road? Relax—there are now cafes with Internet access in virtually every big city (and some small ones). Samples below:

CITY	CYBERCAFE	ON-LINE CHARGES
Albuquerque, N.M.	Webolution Cafe	$4 per half hour (minimum); $7 per hour
Austin, Texas	WWW Cafe Inc.	$3 per half hour; $6 per hour
Berkeley, Calif.	Transbay.net	$5 per half hour; $10 per hour
Nashville, Tenn.	Bean Central	$2 per half hour; $4 per hour
Norman, Okla.	Main Street Cyberhall	$5.40 per half hour; $10.80 per hour

Source: Cybercafes: A Worldwide Guide for Travelers

© 1998 Dow Jones & Company, Inc.

©PhotoDisc.

End-of-Chapter Problems

At the end of each chapter Drill Problems are followed by Word Problems. I've added new problems in each chapter using material from newspapers such as the *Chicago Tribune,* and magazines such as *Nation's Business, Consumer Reports,* and *Smart Money* to help students see the relevance of the material. A disk logo next to a problem indicates an Excel template is available in the Excel Workbook to help solve that problem. Challenge Problems let your students stretch their understanding and ability to solve more complex problems. I've included two per chapter, one of which is new to this edition. A Summary Practice Test concludes the problem section and covers all the Learning Objectives in the chapter. The phone logo reminds students that they can call the student toll-free hotline number at 1-800-338-9708. A first in business math, the hotline allows students to get extra help on these tests. I have recorded tips on how to solve each problem which students can access any time, 24 hours a day, and hear me walk them through the problem they are having difficulty with. In the Fifth Edition we had over 25,000 students call this number for help.

Drill Problems

DRILL PROBLEMS

Identify the place value for the following:

3–1. 7.86328   hundredths

3–2. 158.731   thousandths

Round the following as indicated:

		Tenth	Hundredth	Thousandth
3–3.	.8951	.9	.90	.895
3–4.	.6257	.6	.63	.626
3–5.	6.9245	6.9	6.92	6.925
3–6.	6.8415	6.8	6.84	6.842
3–7.	6.5555	6.6	6.56	6.556
3–8.	75.9913	76.0	75.99	75.991

Word Problems

3–70. The August 1996 *Consumer Reports,* in the "What's the Risk?" article about investing in gold, stated that in 1964 a Ford Mustang sold for $2,500. Gold was valued at $35 per ounce in 1964. How many ounces of gold would it cost to purchase the Ford Mustang? Round up to the next ounce. How does this compare to a $28,000 Ford Mustang today if we assume gold is at $390 per ounce? How many ounces of gold would it take to purchase the Ford Mustang today? Round up to the next ounce.

$2,500 ÷ $35 per oz. = 71.42 = 72 oz. $28,000 ÷ $390 per oz. = 71.79 = 72 oz.   Same amount

3–76. Shelly is shopping for laundry detergent, mustard, and canned tuna. She is trying to decide which of two products is the better buy. Using the following information, can you help Shelly?

Laundry detergent A ✔	**Mustard A**	**Canned tuna A**
$2.00 for 37 ounces	$.88 for 6 ounces	$1.09 for 6 ounces
$2.00 ÷ 37 = $.05	.88 ÷ 6 = $.15	$1.09 ÷ 6 = $.18
Laundry detergent B	**Mustard B** ✔	**Canned tuna B** ✔
$2.37 for 38 ounces	$1.61 for $12\frac{1}{2}$ ounces	$1.29 for $8\frac{3}{4}$ ounces
$2.37 ÷ 38 = $.06	$1.61 ÷ 12.5 = $.13	$1.29 ÷ 8.75 = $.15

3–77. Rick bought season tickets to professional basketball games. The cost was $695.10. The season package included 32 homes games. What is the average price of the tickets per game? Round to the nearest cent. Marcelo, Rick's friend, offered to buy 4 of the tickets from Rick. What is the total amount Rick should receive?

$695.10 ÷ 32 = $21.72 × 4 = $86.88

Challenge Problems

CHALLENGE PROBLEMS

3–87. The following items were charged in Canada to your bank credit card:

1. Harmony Grand Buffet, London, Canada	$40.63
2. Econo Lodge, London, Canada	56.45
3. Teddy's Restaurant, Oshawa, Canada	11.27
4. Charlies Restaurant, Kitchener, Canada	15.98
5. ESSO Gasoline, Spencerville, Canada	18.00

a. Using your text exchange rates, find the amount you should be charged for each item.

b. What should your total bill be? Check your answer.

   a. 1. $ 40.63 × .69594 = $28.28
      2.   56.45 × .69594 = 39.29
      3.   11.27 × .69594 =   7.84
      4.   15.98 × .69594 = 11.12
      5.   18.00 × .69594 = 12.53

   b. $142.33 $99.06

   Check $99.06 × 1.4369 = $142.34 (off 1 cent due to rounding)

Summary Practice Test

SUMMARY PRACTICE TEST

Convert the following decimals to percents: *(p. 137)*

1. .481   48.1%   **2.** .7   70%   **3.** 16.43   1,643%   **4.** 6.00   600%

Convert the following percents to decimals: *(p. 138)*

5. 36%   .36   **6.** 4.85%   .0485   **7.** 900%   9.0   **8.** $\frac{1}{5}$%   .0020

Convert the following fractions to percents (round to nearest tenth percent): *(p. 139)*

9. $\frac{1}{7}$ 14.3%   **10.** $\frac{2}{9}$ 22.2%

Convert the following percents to fractions and reduce to lowest terms as needed: *(p. 139)*

11. $16\frac{1}{4}$% $\frac{65}{4} \times \frac{1}{100} = \frac{65}{400} = \frac{13}{80}$ **12.** 6.2% $6\frac{2}{10}$% $= \frac{62}{10} \times \frac{1}{100} = \frac{62}{1,000} = \frac{31}{500}$

Solve the following problems for portion, base, or rate:

13. Lange Company has a net income before taxes of $85,000. The company's treasurer estimates that 36% of the company's net income will go to federal and state taxes. How much will Lange have left? *(p. 141)*

$85,000 × .64 = $54,400

A Kiplinger Approach

A Kiplinger Group Project at the end of each chapter includes an article from *Kiplinger's Personal Finance Magazine*. Each article presents a business math issue for students to debate and solve. Suggested answers are located in the Instructor's Resource Manual in the Box. This is an excellent tool to develop critical thinking and writing skills. It also provides opportunities for students to become involved in team projects. As stated in the AMATYC standards: "mathematics faculty will foster interactive learning through student writing, reading, speaking, and collaborative activities so that students can learn to work effectively in groups and communicate about mathematics both orally and in writing." (p. 83)

A KIPLINGER APPROACH

A GROUP PROJECT Defend or reject the following business math issue based on the *Kiplinger's Personal Finance Magazine* article below:

TRAVEL
Just the place for terminal workaholics

For less than you'd pay for a crummy airport meal, you can now do some serious work while you're stuck in the terminal.

A Seattle-based company called Laptop Lane is opening private, fully equipped office spaces in airports that travelers may rent for $8.95 per half-hour. Currently available at Cincinnati/Northern Kentucky International Airport and Seattle-Tacoma (and at Atlanta Hartsfield in January), the offices have all the high-tech accouterments of a well-equipped business office, including a T-1 line to the Internet. "You can receive e-mail, participate in a conference call, get a fax and surf the Net all at the same time," says Bruce Merrell, one of Laptop Lane's founders.

And each location is staffed with a real-life "cyberconcierge." Recently, two software-company executives who were pressed for time arrived at the Seattle facility with a lengthy presentation they had worked on en route. The cyberconcierge transferred the file to a desktop computer, printed it on a color laser printer, and made copies in color and black-and-white. She also arranged a limo, so that when the copies were completed the customers walked out of the terminal and into a waiting car. Laptop Lane plans to open facilities in four major airports in 1999.   —LYNN WOODS

Working on the run: Send a fax and surf the Net while you wait at the gate.

ILLUSTRATIONS BY STEVEN GUARNACCIA; CHIEN-CHI CHANG/MAGNUM

Business Math Issue

Laptop Lane will not exist in 10 years. Rental rates at airports are too high.

1. List the key points of the article and information to support your position.

2. Write a group defense of your position using math calculations to support your view.

Business Math Scrapbook

The Business Math Scrapbook provides real-world applications at the end of the chapters. They can be assigned at your discretion to give students an opportunity to apply the chapter theory to real life business situations and to see the importance of what they're learning. (p. 162)

BUSINESS MATH SCRAPBOOK
Putting Your Skills to Work

America's Bestsellers

BRAND	COMPANY	YEAR INVENTED	% OF MARKET (BY VOLUME)
Frosted Flakes	Kellogg	1952	4.6%
Corn Flakes	Kellogg	1898	4.3
Cheerios	General Mills	1941	3.5
Frosted Mini-Wheats	Kellogg	1969	3.5
Raisin Bran	Kellogg	1942	3.1
Rice Krispies	Kellogg	1927	2.7
Honey Nut Cheerios	General Mills	1979	2.7

Sources: Goldman, Sachs & Co.; Information Resources Inc.

A recent Post hit

Project A

Cereal business is $8 billion per year. In dollars, how much does each cereal sell?

$B \times R = P$

$8,000,000,000 \times 4.6\% = \$368$ million
$8,000,000,000 \times 4.3\% = \$344$ million
$8,000,000,000 \times 3.5\% = \$280$ million
$8,000,000,000 \times 3.5\% = \$280$ million
$8,000,000,000 \times 3.1\% = \$248$ million
$8,000,000,000 \times 2.7\% = \$216$ million
$8,000,000,000 \times 2.7\% = \$216$ million

Project B

Prove the 15,000 cut.

$P = B \times R$
$P = 53,500 \times .28$
$P = 14,980$

Compaq to Reduce Digital Work Force By 28% After Deal

By JON G. AUERBACH
And EVAN RAMSTAD
Staff Reporters of THE WALL STREET JOURNAL

Compaq Computer Corp. plans to cut about 15,000 jobs at Digital Equipment Corp., or about 28% of the company's work force, after Compaq's proposed acquisition of Digital is completed, according to people familiar with the matter.

Those numbers are significantly higher than the 10,000 figure Compaq insiders had originally estimated and suggest that Compaq, which is facing its own financial pressures, plans to move aggressively to cut costs at Digital. Since Compaq announced the proposed $9.5 billion acquisition in January, the world's largest personal-computer maker has stumbled due to inventory problems and intense PC price competition.

The layoffs will most likely come from Digital's personal-computer division, some parts of its sales force and some corporate computer operations that overlap with Compaq's business, say people who have heard Compaq's views. Spokesmen for Compaq and Digital declined to comment on the specifics of any reductions. Digital had about 53,500 employees at the end of the last quarter. At its peak in the late 1980s, Digital's work force topped 130,000.

 See text Web site (www.mhhe.com/slater) and *The Business Math Internet Resource Guide.*

SUPPLEMENTS PACKAGE

BUSINESS MATH HANDBOOK AND STUDY GUIDE

Jeffrey Slater

PRACTICAL BUSINESS MATH PROCEDURES

SIXTH EDITION

Contents

Now Includes Calculator Reference Guide

Business Math Handbook and Study Guide

This reference guide contains all tables found in the text and is packaged free with the text. It has a built-in study guide providing self-paced worksheets that review chapter material. The worksheets cover vocabulary, theory, and math applications. A set of 10 extra word problem practice quizzes for each chapter is included. A new section was added on the use of the calculator.

Web Site and Online Learning Center

New Interactive

An exciting Business Math Web site at www.mhhe.com/slater offers interactive environment for teachers and students. The password-protected instructor section contains text updates, supplement information, and teaching support. It includes PageOut—a powerful, easy-to-use tool that allows you to produce professional course Web pages.

The Online Learning Center takes the pedagogical features and supplements of the book and places them online. It includes PowerPoint, The Instructor's Resource Guide, Test Bank, chapter outlines, solutions to all problems, teaching tips, and more. Student material includes practice quizzes, glossary, self-paced worksheets, Internet links, etc.
Included on Student CD-ROM.

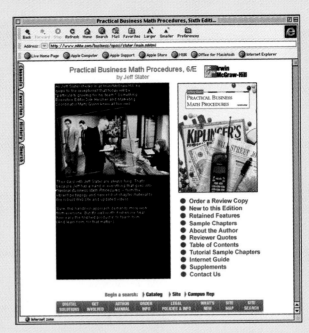

Business Math Internet Resource Guide

New Interactive

The Business Math Internet Resource Guide will take students online and show them and you interesting source materials for business math. Following an introduction on how to use the Internet, each chapter of the book has specific sites listed and a description of what students will find there. There are also projects listed for each chapter relating to the Internet.
Included on Student CD-ROM.

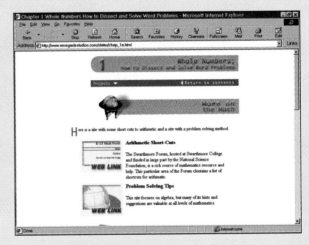

Excel Workbook and Templates

Interactive

The Excel Workbook and Template Disk is available as a shrinkwrapped package with the text. This workbook instructs your students in constructing their own spreadsheets. It includes business topics such as inventory, interest, markup, and annuities using problems from the text. The templates are on disk and are available for selected end-of-chapter problems designated with a disk logo. Students can run these templates as is or add their own data. The disk also includes an interest table feature that allows you to input any percentage rate and terms. The program will then generate table values.
Included on Student CD-ROM.

Tutorial Software

New Interactive

Tutorial Software is new and Windows-based, providing interactive computer assistance for each chapter of the book. It is highly visual, user friendly, and includes True-False, Multiple-Choice, Interactive, and Chapter Terms sections. Students are scored after each response. They can print their results that will give the correct answer to any question they answered incorrectly along with an explanation on how to arrive at the correct solution. The tutorial also includes a pull-down calculator.
Included on Student CD-ROM.

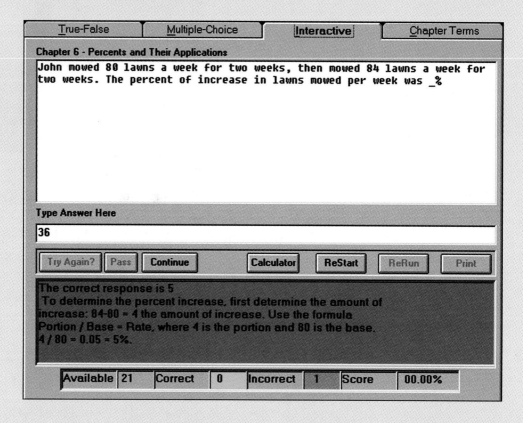

Electronic Calculator Guide with Computer Applications

This manual coordinates **Practical Business Math Procedures** applications with instruction in the 10-key calculator and computer keypad. It also reviews the touch method, includes speed drills, and helps students apply new skills to business math word problems. An introduction to Excel spreadsheets and how to enter data in spreadsheets is included.

Student Solutions Manual

This supplement provides completely worked-out solutions to selected end-of-chapter drill and word problems, plus additional word problems and practice quizzes for student reinforcement.

Videotapes

A complete set of new Videotapes is available for each Practice Quiz in the text. These videos carefully walk students through a review of each Practice Quiz. Brief real applications introduce each chapter segment. You can put these on reserve or encourage your students to bring in blank tapes and make copies to view at home.

Included is a videotape for instructors showing the supplements available with the book and suggestions on how to use them. This is especially helpful for adjunct teachers.

Instructor's Resource Box

This teaching resource contains all the materials you will need to provide the best instruction for your students. These materials reflect my teaching experience of over 30 years. In the Box you will find:

Part A: Instructor's Resource Guide

We've replaced the individual folders with a resource manual that includes:

- Syllabus Preparation
- Self-Paced Syllabus
- Student Progress Chart
- Integrating the Electronic Calculator
- Suggestions for Using Computers and Videos
- Suggestions for Regrouping Chapters
- Internet Organizer for Business Math
- Tips on Teaching Group Activities with *Kiplinger's Personal Finance Magazine*
- Your Course versus Math Anxiety
- Sample Civil Service Exam with worked-out solutions
- Aliquot Parts supplement
- Insight into Proportions supplement
- Excel Template Fact Sheet
- Check Figures for even-numbered end-of-chapter drill and word problems
- Appendix A Solutions (Chapters 13–22)

Each chapter includes:

- Tips from Jeff
- Lecture Outline
- The Pocket Calculator Workshop
- Suggested Solution to Critical Thinking Discussion Questions
- Teacher's Guide to Kiplinger Group Activity
- Five Additional Word Problems not in text
- Worked-Out Solutions to Practice Quiz found in the *Business Math Handbook and Study Guide*
- Vocabulary Crossword with solutions

Part B: Transparency Acetates

- Teaching Transparencies
- End-of-chapter drill problems, word problems, summary practice tests with solutions transparencies (in individual folders)

Comprehensive Testing Package

The Manual of Tests contains six optional exams per chapter in a tear-out version. The computerized testing system featuring the Brownstone/Diploma Software is networkable for LAN test administration. Tests and Quizzes can also be printed for your standard delivery or posted to a Web site for student access. It's available in both Windows and Mac versions.

ALTERNATE CHOICE

Jeffrey Slater

PRACTICAL BUSINESS MATH PROCEDURES
BRIEF SIXTH EDITION

Practical Business Math Procedures, Brief Sixth Edition

The Brief Edition of **Practical Business Math Procedures** is modified, not just shortened. This is the ideal text for a balanced, shorter business math course. The teaching aids have also been revised to ensure your course flows smoothly and all of your teaching objectives are met. The Brief Edition includes Chapters 1–12 from the Sixth Edition, with modifications to Chapter 8.

PRACTICAL BUSINESS MATH PROCEDURES

TEACHER'S EDITION

Jeffrey Slater
North Shore Community College
Danvers, Massachusetts

Sixth Edition

Irwin
McGraw-Hill

Boston   Burr Ridge, IL   Dubuque, IA   Madison, WI
New York   San Francisco   St. Louis
Bangkok   Bogotá   Caracas   Lisbon   London   Madrid   Mexico City   Milan
New Delhi   Seoul   Singapore   Sydney   Taipei   Toronto

McGraw-Hill Higher Education

A Division of The McGraw-Hill Companies

Chapter opening main photos:
Chapter 1: ©PhotoDisc. Chapter 2: ©Michael Dwyer/Stock Boston. Chapter 3: ©PhotoDisc. Chapter 4: ©Andy Sacks/Tony Stone Images. Chapter 5: ©PhotoDisc. Chapter 6: ©PhotoDisc. Chapter 7: ©Superstock. Chapter 8: ©John Coletti/The Picture Cube. Chapter 9: ©PhotoDisc. Chapter 10: ©PhotoDisc. Chapter 11: ©PhotoDisc. Chapter 12: ©PhotoDisc. Chapter 13: ©Bruce Ayres/Tony Stone Images. Chapter 14: ©PhotoDisc. Chapter 15: ©Greg Vaughn/Tony Stone Images. Chapter 16: ©Black Sheep Stock Photography. Chapter 17: ©Peter Langone/ Tony Stone Images. Chapter 18: ©PhotoDisc. Chapter 19: ©PhotoDisc. Chapter 20: ©Leverett Bradley/Tony Stone Images. Chapter 21: Courtesy American Stock Exchange/Photography by Alan M. Rosenberg. Chapter 22: ©PhotoDisc.

All additional chapter opening photos: ©PhotoDisc.

Wall Street Journal articles republished by permission of Dow Jones, Inc. via Copyright Clearance Center, Inc. All Rights Reserved Worldwide.

Kiplinger's articles reprinted by permission of *Kiplinger's Personal Finance Magazine*. Chapter 1: November 1998. Chapter 2: July 1998. Chapter 3: December 1998. Chapter 4: August 1998. Chapter 5: June 1998. Chapter 6: November 1998. Chapter 7: November 1998. Chapter 8: September 1998. Chapter 9: November 1998. Chapter 10: October 1998. Chapter 11: October 1998. Chapter 12: May 1998. Chapter 13: May 1998. Chapter 14: December 1998. Chapter 15: December 1998. Chapter 16: January 1999. Chapter 17: June 1998. Chapter 18: March 1998. Chapter 19: January 1998. Chapter 20: July 1998. Chapter 21: December 1998. Chapter 22: December 1998.

PRACTICAL BUSINESS MATH PROCEDURES

1 2 3 4 5 6 7 8 9 0 DOW/DOW 9 0 9 8 7 6 5 4 3 2 1 0 9

ISBN 0-07-366064-7 (student's edition)
ISBN 0-07-366065-5 (teacher's edition)
ISBN 0-07-229861-8 (brief student's edition)
ISBN 0-07-229862-6 (brief teacher's edition)

Vice president/Editor-in-chief: *Michael W. Junior*
Publisher: *Jeffrey J. Shelstad*
Executive editor: *Richard T. Hercher, Jr.*
Senior developmental editor: *Gail Korosa*
Freelance developmental editor: *Loretta Scholten*
Marketing manager: *Zina Craft*
Senior project manager: *Susan Trentacosti*
Senior production supervisor: *Lori Koetters*
Design team leader: *Michael Warrell*
Cover photo: *Sharon Hoogstraten*
Senior photo research coordinator: *Keri Johnson*
Photo researcher: *Corrine L. Johns*
Senior supplement coordinator: *Cathy L. Tepper*
Compositor: *GAC Indianapolis*
Typeface: *10/12 Times Roman*
Printer: *R. R. Donnelley & Sons Company*

Library of Congress Cataloging-in-Publication Data

Slater, Jeffrey (date)
    Practical business math procedures / Jeffrey Slater. — 6th ed.
      p. cm.
    Includes bibliographical references and index.
     ISBN 0-07-366064-7 (student). — ISBN 0-07-366065-5 (teacher's)
     1. Business mathematics—Problems, exercises, etc. I. Title.
HF5694.S57 2000
650'.01'513—dc21   99-15438

http://www.mhhe.com

Dedicated to:

Shelley—my best pal

Abby and Mike

Russ and Claire

Maggie, Molly, Gracie, and Amber

—Love, Jeff

NOTE TO STUDENTS

Preview of Special Features

Before looking at how to succeed in each chapter, let's look at some special features.

1. **The toll-free, 24-hour hotline.** This toll-free number for students allows you to call anytime and get extra help on any of the 22 summary practice tests located at the end of each chapter. As the author, I have recorded messages on how you should solve each problem. Think of this hotline as a pre-exam tune-up. The toll-free number is 1-800-338-9708.

2. **Group activity: A Kiplinger approach.** In each chapter you can debate a business math issue I raise based on a *Kiplinger's Personal Finance Magazine* article that is presented. This is great for critical thinking, as well as improving your writing skills.

3. *The Wall Street Journal* **newspaper.** This newspaper insert helps explain how to read *The Wall Street Journal,* as well as show how business math relates to it. The newspaper is page-referenced to the text and is helpful for those who have never followed stocks, bonds, and mutual funds.

4. *Business Math Handbook and Study Guide.* This reference guide contains all the tables found in the text. It makes homework, exams, etc. easier to deal with than flipping back and forth through the text. The *Handbook* also features a built-in study guide that provides self-paced worksheets that review each chapter's vocabulary, theory, and math applications. A set of 10 extra word problems for each chapter is included. Also included is a calculator reference guide with advice on how to use different calculators.

5. **Blueprint aid boxes.** For the first eight chapters (not in Chapter 4), blueprint aid boxes are available to help you map out a plan to solve a word problem.

6. **Videotapes.** There is a complete set of videotapes that review all the practice quizzes in the text.

7. **The Business Math Tutor.** This software is a tutorial that guides you through the entire text. It is highly visual and user friendly.

8. **Spreadsheet templates.** Excel® templates are available for selected end-of-chapter problems. You can run these templates as is or enter your own data. The templates also include an interest table feature that enables you to input any percentage rate and any terms. The program will then generate table values for you.

9. **Business Math Internet Resource Guide.** This Guide lists Web sites covering topics from each chapter, as well as descriptions of what you can expect to find at each site. It is referenced on the Scrapbook page in the text and includes group projects you can work on using the exciting possibilities of the Web.

10. **New CD-ROM.** The CD packaged with the text includes practice quizzes, tutorials, links to the Web sites listed in the Business Math Internet Resource Guide, and the Excel® templates mentioned above.

11. **The Slater Business Math Web site.** Visit the site at www.mhhe.com/slater and find the Internet Resource Guide with hot links, tutorials, practice quizzes, and other materials useful for the course.

How to Read and Use the Book

The colors in this text have a purpose. You should read the description below, then look at several pages to see how it works.

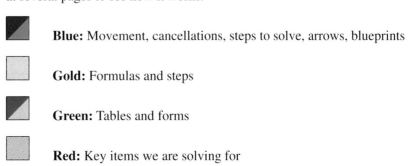

Blue: Movement, cancellations, steps to solve, arrows, blueprints

Gold: Formulas and steps

Green: Tables and forms

Red: Key items we are solving for

Chapters	Each chapter is broken down into learning units. Each learning unit covers a key concept or a small group of concepts. Be sure to look at the You and Your Money feature.
Learning Objectives	At the beginning of each chapter you'll find a list of learning objectives. Each is page referenced.
Practice Quizzes	At the end of each learning unit is a practice quiz, followed by solutions. These provide you with immediate feedback on your understanding of the unit. These are all solved on videotapes. Check with your instructor for availability.
Chapter Organizer	At the end of each chapter is a quick reference guide called the Chapter Organizer. Key points, formulas, and examples are provided. A list of vocabulary terms is also included. All have page references. (A complete glossary is found at the end of the text.) Think of the chapter organizer as your set of notes.
Critical Thinking Discussion Questions	Factual, as well as thought-provoking, questions appear after the chapter organizer.
Problems	At the end of each chapter is a complete set of drill and word problems. Check figures for the odd-numbered problems are located in Appendix B.
Challenge Problems	The last two word problems in each chapter let you "stretch" your business math skills. These are harder and require more effort.
Additional Homework Assignments by Learning Unit	At the end of the text in Appendix A is a complete set of drill and word problems arranged by learning unit. These can be used for additional reinforcement. Your instructor may ask you to turn these in. Check figures for the odd-numbered problems are shown in Appendix B. On the inside back cover of the book is a table showing page references for each assignment.
Summary Practice Test	This is a test before the test. All questions are page referenced back to the topic so you can check your methods. The test is a combination of drill and word problems. Check figures for *all* practice tests are in Appendix B. Remember: There is a toll-free hotline to review these tests at 1-800-338-9708.
Business Math Scrapbook	At the end of each chapter you will find actual clippings from *The Wall Street Journal* and various other publications. These articles will give you a chance to use the theory provided in the chapter to apply to the real world. It allows you to put your math skills to work.
Cumulative Reviews	At the end of Chapters 3, 8, and 13 are word problems that test your retention of business math concepts and procedures. Check figures for *all* cumulative review problems are in Appendix B.

Jeffrey Slater

ACKNOWLEDGMENTS

Academic Experts	Company/Application(s)	
Alec Beaudoin	McDonald's Corp.—*Business decision making; fractions, taxes, statistics*	Kellogg Corp.—*Solving for portion*
Bridget Bell		Compaq Computer Corp.—*Solving for portion*
Maureen H. Bessette	Tootsie Roll Industries, Inc.—*Dissecting and solving a word problem*	Air India—*Discounts*
Evelyn Bookout	Christies International PLC.—*Division shortcuts*	Toys "Я" Us—*Discounts*
Donald F. Boyer		IBM—*Freight charges*
Nelson Collins	*Kiplinger's Personal Finance Magazine— Group projects at end of each chapter*	Avon Products, Inc.—*Discounts*
Ron Cooley		Nucor Corp.—*Discounts*
Charles Darth	Airbus Industrie—*Division shortcut*	Cotter & Company (True Value)—*Retail*
Helen Davis	M&M Mars Co.—*Fractions; decimals; percents; conversions*	Campbell Soup Co.—*Markdowns*
Patricia Dennis		Wal-Mart Stores Inc.—*Markdowns*
Acie Earl	Reebok International Ltd.—*Adding and subtracting fractions*	Kmart—*Markdowns*
DiAnna Eason		Victoria's Secret—*Retail*
Steve Feins	Procter & Gamble Co.—*Multiplying and dividing fractions*	United Airlines—*Payroll*
Alex George		Northwest Airlines—*Payroll*
Jordan Greer	Time Warner Inc.—*Fractions*	Grand Union Co.—*Notes*
Cheryl Honore	Home Depot Inc.—*Fractions*	Fidelity—*Annuities*
Sharon Johnson	ECA Windam, New York—*Decimals*	American Express Co.—*Cost of credit cards*
Tracey L. Johnson	New York Stock Exchange—*Decimals; stocks*	
Gwendolyn Jones		Bestfoods—*Income statement*
Arlene Luhman	Dow Jones & Company, Inc.— *Scrapbooks; foreign currency*	Fuji Photo Film Co.—*Income statement*
Douglas Mace		General Motors Corp. Thailand— *Inventory*
Patricia Madison Manninen	MasterCard—*Banking; debit cards; installments*	
Leland Mansuetti		Prudential Insurance Co.—*Insurance; E-trade; online trading*
Kathy Marino	Visa—*Banking; installments*	
Joyce Mathews	Hawaiian Airlines—*ATMs*	Charles Schwab & Co.—*Online trading*
Jean McArthur	U.S. Treasury—*Internet; Treasury bills*	QVC—*Median*
Debbie McConkey	Blockbuster Video—*ATMs*	Philadelphia Suburban Bank Corp.— *Frequency distributions*
Marilyn McGahon	Citicorp—*Banking*	
Jeff Morford	Nike—*Solving for the unknown*	Logan International Airport—*Graphs*
Kathy C. Nickell	Adidas—*Solving for the unknown*	Burger King—*Statistics*
Evelyn L. Plummer	Walt Disney Co.—*Equations; statistics*	Pizza Hut—*Statistics*
Lou Procoprio	Hershey Foods Corp.—*Equations*	Taco Bell—*Statistics*
Glen Rabb	Coca-Cola Co.—*Percents; financial reports*	Wendy's International, Inc.—*Statistics*
Helen Seery		KFC—*Statistics*
Jim Setterstrom	PepsiCo, Inc.—*Percents; financial reports*	Hardee's—*Statistics*
Betty Taylor		Subway—*Statistics*
Jann Underwood	JCPenney Co.—*Percents; financial reports*	Dairy Queen—*Statistics*
Vicki Vorrell		Domino's—*Statistics*
Jeffrey Waybright	Circuit City Stores, Inc.—*Percent increase and decrease*	Gap—*Statistics*
Keith Weidkamp		
Nancy Weller	Nissan Motor Corp. USA—*Percent increase and decrease*	
Ron Weston		
Steve Wong		
Daniel Wrentmore		
Larry Ziegler		

CONTENTS

BECAUSE MONEY MATTERS . . .
SUBSCRIBE TO *KIPLINGER'S*
AT SPECIAL STUDENT RATES!

Every month, more than three million Americans turn to *Kiplinger's Personal Finance Magazine* for advice and information about how to manage their money. How to save it. Spend it. Invest it. Protect it. Insure it. And make more of it.

If it affects you and your money, then you'll find it in the pages of *Kiplinger's*. From our annual ranking of the nation's best mutual funds to our yearly rating of new automobiles we provide you with a different kind of investment publication.

We make it easy for you to subscribe with the lowest rates available to students and educators. Just provide your name and address below. Make checks payable to *Kiplinger's Personal Finance Magazine.* Or, if you prefer we will bill you later.

_____
Student's Name

_____   _____
Address   Apt. #

_____   _____   _____
City   State   Zip

(____)_____
Phone

Term: One year for $12.97

After completing the form, please mail it to: *Kiplinger's Personal Finance Magazine,* P.O. Box 3291, Harlan, Iowa 51593-2471.

1

WHOLE NUMBERS; HOW TO DISSECT AND SOLVE WORD PROBLEMS

LEARNING UNIT OBJECTIVES

LU 1.1   Reading, Writing, and Rounding Whole Numbers

- Use place values to read and write numeric and verbal whole numbers *(p. 5)*.
- Round whole numbers to the indicated position *(pp. 6–7)*.
- Use blueprint aid for dissecting and solving a word problem *(pp. 7–8)*.

LU 1.2   Adding and Subtracting Whole Numbers

- Add whole numbers; check and estimate addition computations *(pp. 9–10)*.
- Subtract whole numbers; check and estimate subtraction computations *(pp. 11–12)*.

LU 1.3   Multiplying and Dividing Whole Numbers

- Multiply whole numbers; check and estimate multiplication computations *(pp. 13–15)*.
- Divide whole numbers; check and estimate division computations *(pp. 15–17)*.

Business decision making usually involves numbers. These numbers frequently answer questions such as: How much? How many? How soon? How far? How low? People of all ages make business decisions based on the answers to number questions.

Companies often use numbers to measure their market-share performance and make future policy decisions. The following *Wall Street Journal* clipping illustrates how sales numbers influenced the change in the business strategy of McDonald's.

McDonald's Franchisees Told About Menu Plans

By a WALL STREET JOURNAL *Staff Reporter*
ORLANDO, Fla. — McDonald's Corp., acknowledging that its menu needs perking up, plans to improve the taste of several sandwiches and test what it calls "an indulgent bacon cheeseburger" soon.

The fast-food giant also disclosed that it is working on a crispy chicken nuggets item intended to appeal more to adults, and that it will roll out a line of candied ice creams called McFlurry desserts. And, reversing a decision made under pressure from advocates of healthier fare several years ago, McDonald's plans to boost the fat content of its milkshakes.

News of the changes came as the Oak Brook, Ill., company gave its world-wide franchisees a pep talk, following a year of disappointing sales, marketing miscues and domestic management turnover. The franchisees, who are attending McDonald's biennial convention, seemed cheered by word of menu revisions and the way food will be cooked, and gave U.S. Chairman Jack Greenberg a standing ovation.

The likely menu changes appear in part to be a tacit admission of the failure of the highly touted "adult-oriented" Deluxe line, led by the Arch Deluxe hamburger introduced at the convention two years ago. Since then, the fish Deluxe sandwich has been replaced by an updated version of the popular Filet-o-Fish sandwich, and work is under way on the Deluxe chicken sandwich.

In addition to the information in this article, McDonald's plans to upgrade its food preparation. This includes installing "flash-toasting" equipment, a new sandwich assembly process, and computerized gear that transmits orders from the counter to the cooking area. The food will be tastier, fresher, and hotter.

Companies often follow a general problem-solving procedure to arrive at a change in company policy. Using McDonald's as an example, the following steps illustrate this procedure:

Problem Solving Procedure That Companies use.

Step 1.	State the problem(s).	Disappointing sales due to marketing mistakes and management turnover.
Step 2.	Decide on the best method(s) to solve the problem(s).	Menu revisions; improve relationships with franchisees; tastier, fresher, and hotter food through a new computerized system.
Step 3.	Does the solution make sense?	Acknowledges recent trends to tastier adult foods that are fresher and hotter.
Step 4.	Evaluate results.	As market share to adults increases, company earnings will increase.

As you can see, numbers—for McDonald's, a year of disappointing sales numbers—are the foundation of business decision making. Your study of numbers begins with a review of basic computation skills that focuses on speed and accuracy. You may think, "But I can use my calculator." Even if your instructor allows you to use a calculator, you still must know the basic computation skills. You need these skills to know what to calculate, how to interpret your calculations, how to make estimates to recognize errors you made in using your calculator, and how to make calculations when you do not have a calculator. (How to use a calculator is explained in *Business Math Handbook*.)

The United States uses the *decimal numbering system,* or *base-10 system.* Your calculator gives the 10 single-digit numbers of the decimal system—0, 1, 2, 3, 4, 5, 6, 7, 8, and 9. The center of the decimal system is the decimal point. *Whole numbers* are to the left of the decimal point; *decimal numbers* (discussed in Chapter 3) are to the right of the decimal point. This chapter discusses reading, writing, and rounding whole numbers; adding and subtracting whole numbers; and multiplying and dividing whole numbers.

LEARNING UNIT 1.1   Reading, Writing, and Rounding Whole Numbers

World's Busiest Airports

RANK	CITY (AIRPORT)	1996 TOTAL PASSENGERS
1	Chicago (O'Hare Int'l)	69,133,189
2	Atlanta (Hartsfield Atlanta Int'l)	63,344,730
3	Dallas/Ft. Worth Airport, (Dallas/Fort Worth Int'l)	58,034,503
4	Los Angeles (Los Angeles Int'l))	57,974,559

© 1998 Dow Jones & Company, Inc. Source: Airports Council International.

We often use whole numbers in business calculations. For example, look at *The Wall Street Journal* clipping "World's Busiest Airports." As you might expect, the world's busiest airport is O'Hare International Airport in Chicago. In 1996, O'Hare had a total of 69,133,189 passengers. This number—read as sixty-nine million, one hundred thirty-three thousand, one hundred eighty-nine—is a *whole number*. Now let's begin our study of whole numbers.

Reading and Writing Numeric and Verbal Whole Numbers

The decimal number system is a *place-value system*. We can write any whole-number amount with the 10 digits of the decimal system because the position, or placement, of the digits in a number gives the value of the digits.

To determine the value of each digit in a number, we use a place-value chart (Figure 1.1) that divides numbers into named groups of three digits, with each group separated by a comma. To separate a number into groups, you begin with the last digit in the number and insert commas every three digits, moving from right to left. This divides the number into the named groups (units, thousands, millions, billions, trillions) shown in the place-value chart. Within each group, you have a ones, tens, and hundreds place.

In Figure 1.1, the numeric number 1,605,743,891,412 illustrates place values. When you study the place-value chart, you can see that the value of each place in the chart is 10 times the value of the place to the right. We can illustrate this by analyzing the last four digits in the number 1,605,743,891,412:

$$1,412 = (1 \times 1,000) + (4 \times 100) + (1 \times 10) + (2 \times 1)$$

So we can also say that in the number 745, the "7" means seven hundred (700); in the number 75, the "7" means 7 tens (70).

To read and write a numeric number in verbal form, you begin at the left and read each group of three digits as if it were alone, adding the group name at the end (except the last units group and groups of all zeros). Using the place-value chart in Figure 1.1, the number 1,605,743,891,412 is read as one trillion, six hundred five billion, seven hundred forty-three million, eight hundred ninety-one thousand, four hundred twelve. You do not read zeros. They fill vacant spaces as placeholders so that you can correctly state the number values. Also, the numbers twenty-one to ninety-nine must have a hyphen. And most important, when you read or write whole numbers in verbal form, do not use the word *and*. In the decimal system, *and* indicates the decimal, which we discuss in Chapter 3.

By reversing the above process of changing a numeric number to a verbal number, you can use the place-value chart to change a verbal number to a numeric number. Remember that you must keep track of the place value of each digit. The place values of the digits in a number determine its total value.

FIGURE 1.1

Whole-number place-value chart

	Trillions				Billions				Millions				Thousands				Units		
	Hundred trillions	Ten trillions	Trillions	Comma	Hundred billions	Ten billions	Billions	Comma	Hundred millions	Ten millions	Millions	Comma	Hundred thousands	Ten thousands	Thousands	Comma	Hundreds	Tens	Ones
			1	,	6	0	5	,	7	4	3	,	8	9	1	,	4	1	2

Rounding Whole Numbers

Many of the whole numbers you read and hear are rounded numbers. Government statistics are usually rounded numbers. The financial reports of companies also use rounded numbers. All rounded numbers are *approximate* numbers. The more rounding you do, the more you approximate the number.

Rounded whole numbers are used for many reasons. With rounded whole numbers you can quickly estimate arithmetic results, check actual computations, report numbers that change quickly such as population numbers, and make numbers easier to read and remember.

Numbers can be rounded to any identified digit place value, including the first digit of a number (rounding all the way). To round whole numbers, use the following three steps:

Rounding Whole Numbers

Step 1.   Identify the place value of the digit you want to round.
Step 2.   If the digit to the right of the identified digit in Step 1 is 5 or more, increase the identified digit by 1 (round up). If the digit to the right is less than 5, do not change the identified digit.
Step 3.   Change all digits to the right of the rounded identified digit to zeros.

EXAMPLE 1   Round 9,362 to the nearest hundred.

Step 1.   9,362   The digit 3 is in the hundreds place value.
Step 2.   → The digit to the right of 3 is 5 or more (6). Thus, 3, the identified digit in Step 1, is now rounded to 4. You change the identified digit only if the digit to the right is 5 or more.

9,462

Step 3.   9,400   Change digits 6 and 2 to zeros, since these digits are to the right of 4, the rounded number.

By rounding 9,362 to the nearest hundred, you can see that 9,362 is closer to 9,400 than to 9,300.

EXAMPLE 2   Round 67,951 to the nearest thousand.

Step 1.   67,951   The digit 7 is in the thousands place value.
Step 2.   → Digit to the right of 7 is 5 or more (9). Thus, 7, the identified digit in Step 1, is now rounded to 8.

68,951

Step 3.   68,000   Change digits 9, 5, and 1 to zeros, since these digits are to the right of 8, the rounded number.

By rounding 67,951 to the nearest thousand, you can see that 67,951 is closer to 68,000 than to 67,000.

We can use *The Wall Street Journal* clipping "Annual Housing Costs in Selected Cities" to illustrate rounding to the nearest thousand. Note that the annual cost of housing in New York is $61,449 and in Hong Kong, $132,892. Now round these numbers to the nearest thousand as shown above, and you can say, "The annual cost of New York housing is $61,000, but in Hong Kong, the annual cost of housing is $133,000."

Annual Housing Costs in Selected Cities

Bombay, India	$70,459
Duesseldorf, Germany	28,868
Hong Kong, China	132,892
London, England	58,770
Madrid, Spain	31,916
New York, NY	61,449

© 1998 Dow Jones. Source: Runzheimer International.

As you can see, numbers rounded to the nearest thousand can either be substantially less than the actual number, as in the New York annual housing cost, or a little more than the actual number, as in the Hong Kong annual housing cost.

Now let's look at **rounding all the way.** To round a number all the way, you round to the first digit of the number (the leftmost digit) and have only one nonzero digit remaining in the number.

EXAMPLE 3   Round 7,843 all the way.

Step 1.   7,843   Identified leftmost digit is 7.

Step 2.   ⟶ Digit to the right of 7 is greater than 5, so 7 becomes 8.

8,843

Step 3.   8,000   Change all other digits to zeros.

Rounding 7,843 all the way gives 8,000.

Remember that rounding a digit to a specific place value depends on the degree of accuracy you want in your estimate. For example, 24,800 rounds all the way to 20,000 because the digit to the right of 2 is less than 5. This 20,000 is 4,800 less than the original 24,800. You would be more accurate if you rounded 24,800 to the place value of the identified digit 4, which is 25,000.

Before concluding this unit, let's look at how to dissect and solve a word problem.

How to Dissect and Solve a Word Problem

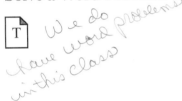

As a student, your author found solving word problems difficult. Not knowing where to begin after reading the word problem caused the difficulty. Today, students still struggle with word problems as they try to decide where to begin.

Solving word problems involves *organization* and *persistence*. Recall how persistent you were when you learned to ride a two-wheel bike. Do you remember the feeling of success you experienced when you rode the bike without help? Apply this persistence to word problems. Do not be discouraged. Each person learns at a different speed. Your goal must be to FINISH THE RACE and experience the success of solving word problems with ease.

To be organized in solving word problems, you need a plan of action that tells you where to begin—a blueprint aid. Like a builder, you will refer to this blueprint aid constantly until you know the procedure. The blueprint aid for dissecting and solving a word problem looks like this:

Blueprint Aid for Dissecting and Solving a Word Problem

The facts	Solving for?	Steps to take	Key points

Now let's study this blueprint aid. The first two columns require that you *read* the word problem slowly. Think of the third column as the basic information you must know or calculate before solving the word problem. Often this column contains formulas that provide the foundation for the step-by-step problem solution. The last column reinforces the key points you should remember.

It's time now to try your skill at using the blueprint aid for dissecting and solving a word problem.

Tootsie Roll Industries, Inc.

BANNER YEAR

Annual Report 1997

Courtesy Tootsie Roll Industries, Inc.

The Word Problem   On the 100th anniversary of Tootsie Roll Industries, the company reported sharply increased sales and profits. Sales reached one hundred ninety-four million dollars and a record profit of twenty-two million, five hundred fifty-six thousand dollars. The company president requested that you round the sales and profit figures all the way.

Study the following blueprint aid and note how we filled in the columns with the information in the word problem. You will find the organization of the blueprint aid most helpful. Be persistent! You *can* dissect and solve word problems! When you are finished with the word problem, make sure the answer seems reasonable.

The facts	Solving for?	Steps to take	Key points
Sales: One hundred ninety-four million dollars. *Profit:* Twenty-two million, five hundred fifty-six thousand dollars.	Sales and profit rounded all the way.	Express each verbal form in numeric form. Identify leftmost digit in each number.	Rounding all the way means only the left-most digit will remain. All other digits become zeros.

Steps to solving problem

1. Convert verbal to numeric.
    One hundred ninety-four million dollars ——————————————→ $194,000,000
    Twenty-two million, five hundred fifty-six thousand dollars ——————→ $ 22,556,000
2. Identify leftmost digit of each number.

    $194,000,000 $22,556,000
3. Round.   ↓   ↓
                           $200,000,000 $20,000,000

Note that in the final answer, $200,000,000 and $20,000,000 have only one nonzero digit.

Remember that you cannot round numbers expressed in verbal form. You must convert these numbers to numeric form.

Now you should see the importance of the information in the third column of the blueprint aid. When you complete your blueprint aids for word problems, do not be concerned if the order of the information in your boxes does not follow the order given in the text boxes. Often you can dissect a word problem in more than one way.

LU 1.1 PRACTICE QUIZ

At the end of each learning unit, you can check your progress with a Practice Quiz. If you had difficulty understanding the unit, the Practice Quiz will help identify your area of weakness. Work the problems on scrap paper. Check your answers with the worked-out solutions that follow the quiz. Ask your instructor about specific assignments and the videotapes available for each chapter Practice Quiz. A complete set of drill and word problems follows each chapter.

Appendix A at the end of the text contains additional drill and word problems for the learning units. In the inside back cover of the text is a page reference guide you can use to find the additional learning unit drill and word problems in Appendix A.

1. Write in verbal form:
    a. 7,948   **b.** 48,775   **c.** 814,410,335,414
2. Round the following numbers as indicated:

Nearest ten	Nearest hundred	Nearest thousand	Rounded all the way
a. 92	**b.** 745	**c.** 8,341	**d.** 4,752

3. Kellogg's reported its sales as five million, one hundred eighty-one thousand dollars. The company earned a profit of five hundred two thousand dollars. What would the sales and profit be if each number were rounded all the way? (*Hint:* You might want to draw the blueprint aid since we show it in the solution.)

✓   **Solutions**

1. **a.** Seven thousand, nine hundred forty-eight
    b. Forty-eight thousand, seven hundred seventy-five
    c. Eight hundred fourteen billion, four hundred ten million, three hundred thirty-five thousand, four hundred fourteen
2. **a.** 92 = 90   **b.** 745 = 700   **c.** 8,341 = 8,000   **d.** 4,752 = 5,000

3. Kellogg's sales and profit:

The facts	Solving for?	Steps to take	Key points
Sales: Five million, one hundred eighty-one thousand dollars. *Profit:* Five hundred two thousand dollars.	Sales and profit rounded all the way.	Express each verbal form in numeric form. Identify leftmost digit in each number.	Rounding all the way means only the left-most digit will remain. All other digits become zeros.

Steps to solving problem

1. Convert verbal to numeric.
   Five million, one hundred eighty-one thousand —————————————→ $5,181,000
   Five hundred two thousand —————————————————————→ $ 502,000
2. Identify leftmost digit of each number.

    $5,181,000 $502,000

3. Round.   ↓   ↓

    $5,000,000 $500,000

LEARNING UNIT 1.2   Adding and Subtracting Whole Numbers

is the opposite of

Remember McDonald's at the beginning of the chapter? You have become a successful executive for McDonald's and must attend business conferences all over the world. Your next trip is to Hong Kong and Paris, France. You want to find out the difference between the average daily cost in Hong Kong and the average daily cost in Paris, France. From *The Wall Street Journal* clipping "1997 Overseas Business Travel Costs," you see that the average daily cost for Hong Kong is $474; for Paris, France, $377. Subtraction will give you the difference:

1997 Overseas Business Travel Costs

LOCATION	To Hong Kong and Paris PER DIEM TOTAL
Hong Kong	$474
Tokyo, Japan	440
Moscow, Russia	392
Buenos Aires, Argentina	383
Paris, France	377
Rio de Janeiro, Brazil	286

© 1998 Dow Jones & Company, Inc. Source: Runzheimer International.

Difference in daily costs

Hong Kong: $474
Paris, France: − 377
                  $ 97

Now you know that to attend a conference in Hong Kong, you will need to allow $97 more a day than for your Paris, France, conference.

This unit teaches you how to manually add and subtract whole numbers. When you least expect it, you will catch yourself automatically using this skill.

Addition of Whole Numbers

To add whole numbers, you unite two or more numbers called **addends** to make one number called a **sum,** or total. The numbers are arranged in a column according to their place values—units above units, tens above tens, and so on. Then, you add the columns of numbers from top to bottom. To check the result, you re-add the columns from bottom to top.

Adding Whole Numbers

Step 1. Align the numbers to be added in columns according to their place values, beginning with the units place at the right and moving to the left (Figure 1.1).

Step 2. Add the units column. Write the sum below the column. If the sum is more than 9, write the units digit and carry the tens digit.

Step 3. Moving to the left, repeat Step 2 until all place values are added.

EXAMPLE

		2 1 1			**Alternate check**

Adding top to bottom → 1,362 / 5,913 / 8,924 / 6,594 ↑ Checking bottom to top

22,793

Alternate check
Add each column as a separate total and then combine. The end result is the same.

1,362
5,913
8,924
6,594
___
13
18
2 6
20
___
22,793

How to Quickly Estimate Addition by Rounding All the Way

In Learning Unit 1.1, you learned that rounding all the way gives quick arithmetic estimates. Using *The Wall Street Journal* clipping "Market Rents," note how you can round each number all the way and the total will not be rounded all the way. Remember that rounding all the way doesn't replace actual computations, but it is helpful in making quick commonsense decisions.

Market Rents

Monthly rents for luxury four-bedroom apartments in neighborhoods where foreign expatriates typically live. All prices are in U.S. dollars.

Rounded all the way

1	Beijing*	$13,200	→ $10,000
2	Hong Kong	13,000	10,000
3	Tokyo	12,800	10,000
4	Shanghai*	10,000	10,000
5	Moscow	9,000	9,000
6	Seoul	8,500	9,000
7	London	7,800	8,000
8	Ho Chi Minh City	7,200	7,000
9	Singapore	7,100	7,000
10	New York	6,000	6,000

$86,000

*Three-bedroom, furnished apartment
Source: Corporate Resources Group, New York

Rounding all the way means each number has only one nonzero digit.

Note: Final answer has more than one nonzero digit, since it is not rounded all the way.

Horizontal and Vertical Addition

Frequently, companies must use both horizontal and vertical additions. For example, manufacturers often need weekly production figures of individual products and a weekly total of all products. Today, many companies use computer spreadsheets to determine various manufacturing figures. The following example shows you how to do horizontal and vertical addition manually.

EXAMPLE

Production report: Units produced						
	Monday	Tuesday	Wednesday	Thursday	Friday	Total
Sneakers	400 +	300 +	170 +	70 +	450 =	1,390
Boots	650 +	180 +	190 +	210 +	220 =	1,450
Loafers	210 +	55 +	98 +	112 +	310 =	785
Totals	1,260 +	535 +	458 +	392 +	980 =	3,625

Besides production reports, payroll records often require horizontal and vertical addition.

The totals of the vertical and horizontal columns check to the grand total of 3,625.

Subtraction of Whole Numbers

Subtraction is the opposite of addition. Addition unites numbers; subtraction takes one number away from another. In subtraction, the top (largest) number is the **minuend.** From the minuend, you subtract the **subtrahend,** which gives you the **difference** between the two numbers.

Subtracting Whole Numbers

Step 1. Align the minuend and subtrahend according to their place values.

Step 2. Begin the subtraction with the units digits. Write the difference below the column. If the units digit in the minuend is smaller than the units digit in the subtrahend, borrow 1 from the tens digit in the minuend. One tens digit is 10 units.

Step 3. Moving to the left, repeat Step 2 until all place values in the subtrahend are subtracted.

Student Centers

States with the highest projected increase in full-time college enrollment.

	1997 ENROLLMENT	2007 ENROLLMENT
Utah	78,964	118,514
Alaska	22,748	31,352
Nevada	56,114	74,580
Arizona	159,972	209,076
New Mexico	60,112	75,627

Source: Woods & Poole Economics, Census Bureau, American Demographics

© 1997 Dow Jones & Company, Inc.

EXAMPLE The numbers for this example were taken from the Nevada numbers for 1997 college enrollment and projected 2007 college enrollment shown in *The Wall Street Journal* clipping "Student Centers." You can use subtraction to determine the enrollment increase expected in 2007.

$$
\begin{array}{r}
\overset{6\ 14\quad 7\ 10}{7\cancel{4},5\cancel{8}\cancel{0}} \leftarrow \text{Minuend (the larger number)} \\
-56,114 \leftarrow \text{Subtrahend} \\
\hline
18,466 \leftarrow \text{Difference}
\end{array}
$$

Check
$$
\begin{array}{r}
56,114 \\
+18,466 \\
\hline
74,580
\end{array}
$$

Starting at the rightmost column of the minuend and subtrahend in the above example, you can see that you cannot subtract 4 units in the subtrahend from 0 units in the minuend. You need more units. To the left of the 0 units are 8 tens. You can take 1 ten from the 8 tens to give you 10 units. To do this, cross out the 8 and write 7 above it. Now you have 10 units, and $10 - 4 = 6$. Moving left to the tens column, $7 - 1 = 6$. Next, moving left to the hundreds column, $5 - 1 = 4$. Moving left again, you have the thousands column. Since you cannot subtract 6 thousands from 4 thousands, you must borrow again from your neighbor on the left—ten thousands. One ten thousands is 10 thousands. So you cross out the 7, which represents 7 ten thousands, and insert a 6 above the 7. Add the 1 ten thousands, which is 10 thousands, to your 4 thousands and you have 14 thousands, $14 - 6 = 8$. Move left once more to the hundred thousands column and subtract, $6 - 5 = 1$. You have your answer—the difference between the 1997 college enrollment and the 2007 college enrollment is 18,466.

Below the subtraction example is the check for the subtraction indicating that the 18,466 difference is correct. Checking subtraction requires adding the difference (18,466) to the subtrahend (56,114) to arrive at the minuend (74,580).

How to Dissect and Solve a Word Problem

Accurate subtraction is important in many business operations. In Chapter 4 we discuss the importance of keeping accurate subtraction in your checkbook balance. Now let's check your progress by dissecting and solving a word problem.

The Word Problem Hershey's produced 25 million Kisses in one day. The same day, the company shipped 4 million to Japan, 3 million to France, and 6 million throughout the United States. At the end of that day, what is the company's total inventory of Kisses? What is the inventory balance if you round the number all the way?

The facts	Solving for?	Steps to take	Key points
Produced: 25 million. *Shipped:* Japan, 4 million; France, 3 million; United States, 6 million.	Total Kisses left in inventory. Inventory balance rounded all the way.	Total Kisses produced − Total Kisses shipped = Total Kisses left in inventory.	Minuend − Subtrahend = Difference. Rounding all the way means rounding to last digit on the left.

Steps to solving problem

1. Calculate the total Kisses shipped.

4,000,000
3,000,000
6,000,000
‾‾‾‾‾‾‾‾‾‾
13,000,000

2. Calculate the total Kisses left in inventory.

25,000,000
−13,000,000
‾‾‾‾‾‾‾‾‾‾
12,000,000

3. Rounding all the way.

Identified digit is 1. Digit to right of 1 is 2, which is less than 5. *Answer:* 10,000,000.

LU 1.2 PRACTICE QUIZ

1. Add by totaling each separate column:
8,974
6,439
6,941

2. Estimate by rounding all the way (do not round the total of estimate) and then do the actual computation:
4,241
8,794
3,872

3. Subtract and check your answer:
9,876
−4,967

4. Jackson Manufacturing Company projected its year 2000 furniture sales at $900,000. During 2000, Jackson earned $510,000 in sales from major clients and $369,100 in sales from the remainder of its clients. What is the amount by which Jackson over- or underestimated its sales? Use the blueprint aid, since the answer will show the completed blueprint aid.

✓ **Solutions**

1.		2. **Estimate**	**Actual**	3.		**Check**
	14	4,000	4,241		9,876 ←	4,909
	14	9,000	8,794		−4,967	+4,967
	2 2	4,000	3,872		‾‾‾‾	‾‾‾‾‾
	20	‾‾‾‾‾	‾‾‾‾‾		4,909	9,876
	‾‾‾‾	17,000	16,907			
	22,354					

(3. with carry marks: 8 18 6 16 over 9,876)

4. Jackson Manufacturing Company over- or underestimated sales:

The facts	Solving for?	Steps to take	Key points
Projected 2000 sales: $900,000. *Major clients:* $510,000. *Other clients:* $369,100.	How much were sales over- or underestimated?	Total projected sales − Total actual sales = Over- or underestimated sales.	Projected sales (minuend) − Actual sales (subtrahend) = Difference.

Steps to solving problem

1. Calculate total actual sales.

$510,000
+ 369,100

$879,100
2. Calculate over- or underestimated sales. $900,000
− 879,100

$ 20,900 (overestimated)

LEARNING UNIT 1.3   Multiplying and Dividing Whole Numbers

Opposite of

Recall from Learning Unit 1.2 that in planning your next business trip for McDonald's, you used subtraction to determine the difference between the average daily cost in Hong

©PhotoDisc.

Kong and the average daily cost in Paris, France. You found that it costs $97 more to stay for a day in Hong Kong than it costs to stay for a day in Paris, France. Your superior has informed you that the Hong Kong conference would be 3 days longer than the Paris conference. Now you want to know how much more it will cost to stay in Hong Kong for 3 days compared to staying in Paris.

How are you going to find the cost of staying 3 days longer in Hong Kong? You could take the daily difference in cost between Hong Kong and Paris, France—$97—and add it three times, which would give you a total cost of $291. You could also use a shortcut and multiply $97 by 3—the number of days longer that you must be in Hong Kong. Before you could add $97 three times or multiply $97 × 3, your math whiz friend said, "The cost of the 3-day longer stay is $291 because $291 divided by 3 is $97."

This unit will sharpen your skills in two important arithmetic operations—multiplication and division. These two operations frequently result in knowledgeable business decisions.

Multiplication of Whole Numbers—Shortcut to Addition

From calculating your 3-day longer stay in Hong Kong, you know that multiplication is a *shortcut to addition.* Here is another example:

$$6 \times 4 = \boxed{24} \qquad \text{or} \qquad 6 + 6 + 6 + 6 = \boxed{24}$$

Before learning the steps used to multiply whole numbers with two or more digits, you must learn some multiplication terminology. To explain this terminology, let's multiply a larger figure.

Note in the following example that the top number (number we want to multiply) is the **multiplicand.** The bottom number (number doing the multiplying) is the **multiplier.** The final number (answer) is the **product.** The numbers between the multiplier and the product are **partial products.** Also note how we positioned the partial product 2090. This number is the result of multiplying 418 by 50 (the 5 is in the tens position). On each line in the partial products, we placed the first digit directly below the digit we used in the multiplication process.

EXAMPLE	418 ⟵ Top number (multiplicand)	
	× 52 ⟵ Bottom number (multiplier)	
Partial	836	2 × 418 = 836
products	20 90	50 × 418 = +20,900
	21,736 ⟵ Product answer ⟶	21,736

We can now give the following steps for multiplying whole numbers with two or more digits.

Multiplying Whole Numbers with Two or More Digits

Step 1. Align the multiplicand (top number) and multiplier (bottom number) at the right. Usually, you should make the smaller number the multiplier.

Step 2. Begin by multiplying the right digit of the multiplier with the right digit of the multiplicand. Keep multiplying as you move left through the multiplicand. Your first partial product aligns at the right with the multiplicand and multiplier.

Step 3. Move left through the multiplier and continue multiplying the multiplicand. Your partial product right digit or first digit is placed directly below the digit in the multiplier that you used to multiply.

Step 4. Continue Steps 2 and 3 until you have completed your multiplication process. Then add the partial products to get the final product.

Checking and Estimating Multiplication

We can check the multiplication process by reversing the multiplicand and multiplier and then multiplying. Let's first estimate 52×418 by rounding all the way.

EXAMPLE

$$
\begin{array}{r}
50 \\
\times\, 400 \\
\hline
20{,}000
\end{array}
\quad\longleftarrow\quad
\begin{array}{r}
52 \\
\times\, 418 \\
\hline
416 \\
52 \\
20\,8 \\
\hline
21{,}736
\end{array}
$$

By estimating before actually working the problem, we know our answer should be about 20,000. When we multiply 52 by 418, we get the same answer as when we multiply 418×52—and the answer is about 20,000. Remember, if we had not rounded all the way, our estimate would have been closer. If we had used a calculator, the rounded estimate would have helped us check the calculator's answer. Our commonsense estimate tells us our answer is near 20,000—not 200,000.

Before you study the division of whole numbers, you should know (1) the multiplication shortcut with numbers ending in zeros and (2) how to multiply a whole number by a power of 10.

Multiplication Shortcut with Numbers Ending in Zeros

Step 1. When zeros are at the end of the multiplicand or the multiplier, or both, disregard the zeros and multiply.

Step 2. Count the number of zeros in the multiplicand and multiplier.

Step 3. Attach the number of zeros counted in Step 2 to your answer.

EXAMPLE

$$
\begin{array}{r}
65{,}000 \\
\times\, 420 \\
\hline
\end{array}
\qquad
\begin{array}{r}
65 \\
\times\, 42 \\
\hline
1\,30 \\
26\,0 \\
\hline
27{,}300{,}000
\end{array}
\qquad
\begin{array}{r}
3 \text{ zeros} \\
+\, 1 \text{ zero} \\
\hline
4 \text{ zeros}
\end{array}
\qquad
\begin{array}{l}
\text{No need to multiply rows} \\
\text{of zeros.} \\[4pt]
\begin{array}{r}
65{,}000 \\
\times\, 420 \\
\hline
00\,000 \\
1\,300\,00 \\
26\,000\,0 \\
\hline
27{,}300{,}000
\end{array}
\end{array}
$$

> ## Multiplying a Whole Number by a Power of 10
>
> **Step 1.** Count the number of zeros in the power of 10 (a whole number that begins with 1 and ends in one or more zeros such as 10, 100, 1,000, and so on).
>
> **Step 2.** Attach that number of zeros to the right side of the other whole number to obtain the answer. Insert comma(s) as needed every three digits, moving from right to left.

EXAMPLE 99×10　$= 99\underline{0}$　$= \boxed{990}$　←——— Add 1 zero

99×100　$= 9,9\underline{00}$　$= \boxed{9,900}$　←——— Add 2 zeros

$99 \times 1,000 = 99,\underline{000} = \boxed{99,000}$ ←——— Add 3 zeros

When a zero is in the center of the multiplier, you can do the following:

EXAMPLE

$$
\begin{array}{r}
658 \\
\times\ 403 \\
\hline
1\ 974 \\
263\ 2\square \\
\hline
\boxed{265,174}
\end{array}
$$

$$
\begin{array}{rr}
3 \times 658 = & 1,974 \\
400 \times 658 = & +\ 263,200 \\
\hline
& \boxed{265,174}
\end{array}
$$

Division of Whole Numbers

Division is the reverse of multiplication and a timesaving shortcut related to subtraction. For example, in the introduction to this learning unit, you determined that it would cost $291 more to stay 3 days in Hong Kong compared to Paris. If you subtract $97 (the difference between the average daily cost of Hong Kong and Paris) three times from $291, you get zero. You can also multiply $97 by 3 to get $291. Since division is the reverse of multiplication, like your math whiz friend, you can now say $291 ÷ 3 = $97.

In division you find how many times one number (**divisor**) is contained in another number (**dividend**). The result, or answer, is the **quotient.** When the divisor (number used to divide) doesn't divide evenly into the dividend (number we are dividing), the result is a **partial quotient,** with the leftover amount called the **remainder.** In later chapters we will see remainders expressed as fractions.

The following example illustrates *even division.*

EXAMPLE

$$
\begin{array}{r}
\boxed{18} \quad \leftarrow\!\!\!-\!\!\!-\!\!\!- \text{ Quotient} \\
15\overline{)270} \quad \leftarrow\!\!\!-\!\!\!-\!\!\!- \text{ Dividend} \\
\underline{15} \\
120 \\
\underline{120}
\end{array}
$$

Divisor ——→

In this example, 15 divides into 27 once with a remainder of 12. We bring the 0 in the dividend down to 12, resulting in 120 divided by 15 equals 8 with no remainder—even division. The example that follows illustrates *uneven division with a remainder.*

EXAMPLE

$$
\begin{array}{r}
\boxed{24\ \text{R1}} \quad \leftarrow\!\!\!-\!\!\!-\!\!\!- \text{ Remainder} \\
7\overline{)169} \\
\underline{14} \\
29 \\
\underline{28} \\
1
\end{array}
$$

Check

$(7 \times 24) + 1 = 169$

Divisor $\times$ Quotient + Remainder = Dividend

Note the check method in the above example. Checking a problem gives assurance that you have calculated correctly.

Because the divisor in the even division example above had more than one digit, we call it *long division.* In the uneven division example, the divisor had only one digit. This is *short division.*

When the divisor has one digit (short division), you can often do the division mentally. Note the following examples:

$$
\begin{array}{cc}
\textbf{EXAMPLES} & \boxed{108} \quad\quad \boxed{16\ R6} \\
& 8)\overline{864} \quad\quad 7)\overline{118}
\end{array}
$$

Next, let's look at the value of estimating division.

Estimating Division

Before actually working a division problem, estimate the quotient by rounding. This estimate helps check the answer. The example that follows is rounded all the way. After you make an estimate, work the problem and check your answer by multiplication.

EXAMPLE

	$\boxed{36\ R111}$	**Estimate**	**Check**
	$138)\overline{5,079}$	50	138
	$\underline{4\ 14}$	$100)\overline{5,000}$	$\times\ 36$
	939		828
	$\underline{828}$		$\underline{4\ 14}$
	111		$4,968$
			$\underline{+\ 111}$ ← Add remainder
			$5,079$

Now let's turn our attention to division shortcuts with zeros.

Division Shortcuts with Zeros

Wagner Baseball Card Draws $640,500 at Auction

NEW YORK (AP) – A 1910 Honus Wagner baseball card, considered the Holy Grail of baseball collectibles, sold at auction Saturday for $640,500.

The winning bidder wasn't identified by the auction house, **Christies International PLC.** The final price was above the $400,000-$600,000 presale estimate of what the card might fetch.

© 1996 Dow Jones & Company.

During the last 20 years, collecting baseball cards has again become popular. With this popularity comes an increase in value. Note the sale of the Wagner baseball card in *The Wall Street Journal* clipping "Wagner Baseball Card Draws $640,500 at Auction."

If a group of 10 investors paid $640,500 for the Wagner card, what did each investor pay?

$$
\frac{\$64,050}{10)\$640,500} \leftarrow \text{Amount each investor pays}
$$

The steps that follow explain the shortcut used in the above division.

Division Shortcut with Numbers Ending in Zeros

Step 1. When the dividend and divisor have ending zeros, count the number of ending zeros in the divisor.

Step 2. Drop the same number of zeros in the dividend as in the divisor, counting from right to left.

Note the following examples of division shortcut with numbers ending in zeros. Since two of the symbols used for division are ÷ and $)\overline{}$, our first examples show the zero shortcut method with the ÷ symbol.

EXAMPLES

One ending zero

Dividend Divisor

Drop 1 zero in dividend

$$
\begin{aligned}
95,000 \div 10 &\longrightarrow 95,00\underline{0} = \boxed{9,500} \\
95,000 \div 100 &\longrightarrow 95,0\underline{00} = \boxed{950} \leftarrow \text{Drop 2 zeros} \\
95,000 \div 1,000 &\longrightarrow 95,\underline{000} = \boxed{95} \leftarrow \text{Drop 3 zeros}
\end{aligned}
$$

In a long division problem with the $)\overline{}$ symbol, you again count the number of ending zeros in the divisor. Then drop the same number of ending zeros in the dividend and divide as usual.

EXAMPLE   6,5<u>00</u>)88,0<u>00</u> ⟵ Drop 2 zeros

```
                                              13 R35
                                           65)880
                                             65
                                            230
                        65)880 ⤶            195
                                             35
```

You are now ready to practice what you learned by dissecting and solving a word problem.

How to Dissect and Solve a Word Problem

The blueprint aid that follows will be your guide to dissecting and solving the following word problem.

The Word Problem   Dunkin' Donuts sells to four different companies a total of $3,500 worth of donuts per week. What is the total annual sales to these companies? What is the yearly sales per company? (Assume each company buys the same amount.) Check your answer to show how multiplication and division are related.

The facts	Solving for?	Steps to take	Key points
Sales per week: $3,500. *Companies:* 4.	Total annual sales to all four companies. Yearly sales per company	Sales per week × Weeks in year (52) = Total annual sales. Total annual sales ÷ Total companies = Yearly sales per company.	Division is the reverse of multiplication.

Steps to solving problem

1. Calculate total annual sales. $3,500 × 52 weeks = $182,000

2. Calculate yearly sales per company, $182,000 ÷ 4 = $45,500

Check
$45,500 × 4 = $182,000

It's time to try the Practice Quiz.

 **LU 1.3 PRACTICE QUIZ**

1. Estimate the actual problem by rounding all the way, work the actual problem, and check:

   Actual   **Estimate**   **Check**

   3,894
   × 18

2. Multiply: **3.** Multiply by shortcut method:

   77,000   95 × 10,000
   × 1,800

4. Divide by rounding all the way, complete the actual calculation, and check, showing remainder as a whole number.
   26)5,325

5. Divide by shortcut method:
   4,000)96,000

6. Assume General Motors produces 960 Chevrolets each workday (Monday through Friday). If the cost to produce each car is $6,500, what is General Motors' total cost for the year? Check your answer.

✓ **Solutions**

1. Estimate	Actual	Check
4,000	3,894	8 × 3,894 = 31,152
× 20	× 18	10 × 3,894 = 38,940
80,000	31 152	70,092
	38 94	
	70,092	

2. $77 \times 18 = 1,386 + 5$ zeros $=$ 138,600,000   **3.** $95 + 4$ zeros $=$ 950,000

4.

Rounding	Actual	Check

Rounding
$$166 \text{ R}20$$
$$30\overline{)5,000}$$
$$\underline{3\,0}$$
$$2\,00$$
$$\underline{1\,80}$$
$$200$$
$$\underline{180}$$
$$20$$

Actual
$$204 \text{ R}21$$
$$26\overline{)5,325}$$
$$\underline{5\,2}$$
$$125$$
$$\underline{104}$$
$$21$$

Check
$26 \times 204 = 5,304$
$$\underline{+\ \ 21}$$
$$5,325$$

5. Drop 3 zeros $= 4\overline{)96}$ $\boxed{24}$

6. General Motors' total cost per year:

The facts	Solving for?	Steps to take	Key points
Cars produced each workday: 960. *Workweek:* 5 days. *Cost per car:* $6,500.	Total cost per year.	Cars produced per week $\times$ 52 = Total cars produced per year. Total cars produced per year $\times$ Total cost per car = Total cost per year.	Whenever possible, use multiplication and division shortcuts with zeros. Multiplication can be checked by division.

Steps to solving problem

1. Calculate total cars produced per week. $5 \times 960 = 4{,}800$ cars produced per week

2. Calculate total cars produced per year. $4{,}800$ cars $\times$ 52 weeks $= 249{,}600$ total cars produced per year

3. Calculate total cost per year. $249{,}600$ cars $\times$ \$6,500 $=$ \$1,622,400,000
(multiply $2{,}496 \times 65$ and add zeros)

Check

$1{,}622{,}400{,}000 \div 249{,}600 = \$6{,}500$ (drop 2 zeros before dividing)

Chapter Organizer and Reference Guide		
Topics	**Key point, procedure, formula**	**Example(s) to illustrate situation**
Reading and writing numeric and verbal whole numbers, p. 5	Placement of digits in a number gives the value of the digits (Figure 1.1). Commas separate every three digits, moving from right to left. Begin at left to read and write number in verbal form. Do not read zeros or use *and*. Hyphenate numbers twenty-one to ninety-nine. Reverse procedure to change verbal number to numeric.	462 $\longrightarrow$ Four hundred sixty-two 6,741 $\longrightarrow$ Six thousand, seven hundred forty-one
Rounding whole numbers, p. 6	1. Identify place value of the digit to be rounded. 2. If digit to the right is 5 or more, round up; if less than 5, do not change. 3. Change all digits to the right of rounded identified digit to zeros.	643 to nearest ten 4 is in tens place value. 3 is not 5 or more. Thus, 643 rounds to 640.
Rounding all the way, p. 7	Round to first digit of number. One nonzero digit remains. In estimating, you round each number of the problem to one nonzero digit. The final answer is not rounded.	468,451 $\longrightarrow$ 500,000 The 5 is the only nonzero digit remaining.

Adding whole numbers, p. 9	1. Align numbers at the right.
	2. Add units column. If sum more than 9, carry tens digit.
	3. Moving left, repeat Step 2 until all place values are added.
	
	Add from top to bottom. Check by adding bottom to top or adding each column separately and combining.
		65
		47
		112 12 Checking sum of each digit
		    10
		    112

Subtracting whole numbers, p. 11	1. Align minuend and subtrahend at the right. 2. Subtract units digits. If necessary, borrow 1 from tens digit in minuend. 3. Moving left, repeat Step 2 until all place values are subtracted. Minuend less subtrahend equals difference.	**Check** 685 193 -492 $+492$ 193 685

Multiplying whole numbers, p. 13	1. Align multiplicand and multiplier at the right.
	2. Begin at the right and keep multiplying as you move to the left. First partial product aligns at the right with multiplicand and multiplier.
	3. Move left through multiplier and continue multiplying multiplicand. Partial product right digit or first digit is placed directly below digit in multiplier.
	4. Continue Steps 2 and 3 until multiplication is complete. Add partial products to get final product.
	
	Shortcuts: (a) When multiplicand or multiplier, or both, end in zeros, disregard zeros and multiply; attach same number of zeros to answer. If zero in center of multiplier, no need to show row of zeros. (b) If multiplying by power of 10, attach same number of zeros to whole number multiplied.
		223
		$\times 32$
		446
		$6\ 69$
		$7{,}136$
		
		a. 48,000 48 3 zeros 524
		   $\times 40$ 4 $+1$ zero $\times 206$
		   1,920,000 $\longleftarrow$ 4 zeros 3 144
		   104 8
		   107,944
		
		b. $14 \times 10 = 140$ (attach 1 zero)
		   $14 \times 1{,}000 = 14{,}000$ (attach 3 zeros)

Dividing whole numbers, p. 15	1. When divisor is divided into the dividend, the remainder is less than divisor.
	2. Drop zeros from dividend right to left by number of zeros found in the divisor.
	
	Even division has no remainder; uneven division has a remainder; divisor with one digit is short division; and divisor with more than one digit is long division.
		1. 5 R6
		   $14\overline{)76}$
		    70
		    6
		2. $5{,}000 \div 100 = 50 \div 1 = 50$
		   $5{,}000 \div 1{,}000 = 5 \div 1 = 5$

Key terms	Addends, *p. 9* Difference, *p. 11* Dividend, *p. 15* Divisor, *p. 15* Minuend, *p. 11*	Multiplicand, *p. 13* Multiplier, *p. 13* Partial products, *p. 13* Partial quotient, *p. 15* Product, *p. 13*	Quotient, *p. 15* Remainder, *p. 15* Rounding all the way, *p. 7* Subtrahend, *p. 11* Sum, *p. 9*

**Critical Thinking
Discussion Questions**

1. List the four steps of the decision-making process. Do you think all companies should be required to follow these steps? Give an example.

2. Explain the three steps used to round whole numbers. Pick a whole number and explain why it should not be rounded.

3. How do you check subtraction? If you were to attend a movie, explain how you might use the subtraction check method.

4. Explain how you can check multiplication. If you visit a local supermarket, how could you show multiplication as a shortcut to addition?

5. Explain how division is the reverse of multiplication. Using the supermarket example, explain how division is a timesaving shortcut related to subtraction.

DRILL PROBLEMS

Add the following:

1–1.   97
   56
  153

1–2.   790
  552
1,342

1–3.   88
  88
176

1–4.   66
  92
158

1–5.   4,592
8,415
13,007

1–6.   59,481
51,411
70,821
181,713

1–7.   78,159
15,850
19,681
113,690

Subtract the following:

1–8.   96
− 18

    8 16
9̸6̸
− 18
  78

1–9.   90
− 58

    8 10
9̸0̸
− 58
  32

1–10.   287
− 199

   1 17 17
2̸8̸7̸
− 199
  88

1–11.   8,900
− 7,200
1,700

1–12.   9,800
− 8,900
900

1–13.   1,622
− 548
1,074

Multiply the following:

1–14.   44
× 9
396

1–15.   510
× 61
510
30 60
31,110

1–16.   900
× 300
270,000

1–17.   677
× 503
2 031
338 5□
340,531

1–18.   309
× 850
15 450
247 2
262,650

1–19.   450
× 280
36 000
90 0
126,000

Divide the following by short division:

1–20. $\dfrac{105}{5)\overline{525}}$

1–21. $\dfrac{90}{9)\overline{810}}$

1–22. $\dfrac{41}{4)\overline{164}}$

Divide the following by long division. Show work and remainder.

1–23.   86 R4
6)520
48
40
36
4

1–24.   143 R49
62)8,915
6 2
2 71
2 48
235
186
49

Add the following without rearranging:

1–25. 99 + 106 = 205

1–26. 1,055 + 88 = 1,143

1–27. 666 + 950 = 1,616

1–28. 1,011 + 17 = 1,028

1–29. Add the following and check by totaling each column individually without carrying numbers:

	Check
8,539	16
6,842	16
9,495	17
24,876	23
	24,876

Estimate the following by rounding all the way and then do actual addition:

	Actual	Estimate			Actual	Estimate
1–30.	7,900	8,000	**1–31.**		6,980	7,000
	8,486	8,000			3,190	3,000
	4,900	5,000			7,819	8,000
	21,286	21,000			17,989	18,000

Subtract the following without rearranging:

1–32. $180 - 77 = 103$ **1–33.** $950 - 870 = 80$

1–34. Subtract the following and check answer:

$$
\begin{array}{r}
8\ 10\ 9\ 9\ 11 \\
591,001 \quad\quad 59\!\!\not{1},\!\not{0}\!\not{0}\!\not{1} \longleftarrow \\
- 375,956 \quad\quad - 375,956 \\
\hline
215,045
\end{array}
\qquad
\begin{array}{r}
215,045 \\
+ 375,956 \\
\hline
591,001
\end{array}
$$

Multiply the following horizontally:

1–35. $13 \times 8 = 104$ **1–36.** $84 \times 8 = 672$ **1–37.** $27 \times 8 = 216$ **1–38.** $17 \times 6 = 102$

Divide the following and check by multiplication:

1–39.
$$
\begin{array}{r}
19\ \text{R21} \\
45\overline{)876} \\
45 \\
\hline
426 \\
405 \\
\hline
21
\end{array}
$$
Check
$45 \times 19 = 855$
$\quad\quad + 21\ (\text{R})$
$\quad\quad\overline{\quad 876 \quad}$

1–40.
$$
\begin{array}{r}
42\ \text{R18} \\
46\overline{)1,950} \\
1\ 84 \\
\hline
110 \\
92 \\
\hline
18
\end{array}
$$
Check
$46 \times 42 = 1,932$
$\quad\quad + 18\ (\text{R})$
$\quad\quad\overline{\quad 1,950 \quad}$

1–41. Add the following columns horizontally and vertically:

Production Report								
	Monday	Tuesday	Wednesday	Thursday	Friday			
Software packages	290	96	157	24	40	=	607	
Laptops	359	68	44	77	30	=	578	
Video	192	41	22	44	18	=	317	
Computer monitors	49	17	51	66	50	=	233	
	890 +	222 +	274 +	211 +	138	=	1,735	

Using data in Problem 1–41, answer the following:

1–42. What was the total difference in production on Monday versus Friday?
$890 - 138 = 752$

1–43. If two weeks ago production was 6 times the total of this report, what was total production?
$1,735 \times 6 = 10,410$

Complete the following:

1–44.
$$
\begin{array}{r}
9,200 \\
- 1,510 \\
\hline
7,690 \\
- 700 \\
\hline
6,990
\end{array}
$$

1–45.
$$
\begin{array}{r}
3,000,000 \\
- 769,459 \\
\hline
2,230,541 \\
- 68,541 \\
\hline
2,162,000
\end{array}
$$

1–46. Estimate the following problem by rounding all the way and then do the actual multiplication:

	Actual	Estimate
	870	900
	× 81	× 80
	870	72,000
	69 60	
	70,470	

Divide the following by the shortcut method:

                                                    850   700

1–47. $1{,}000\overline{)850{,}000}$ $1\overline{)850}$ **1–48.** $100\overline{)70{,}000}$ $1\overline{)700}$

     Drop 3 zeros.   Drop 2 zeros.

1–49. Estimate actual problem by rounding all the way and do actual division:

Actual	**Estimate**
12 R610	12 R600
$695\overline{)8{,}950}$	$700\overline{)9{,}000}$
6 95	7 00
2 000	2 000
1 390	1 400
610	600

WORD PROBLEMS

1–50. On August 1997, *Smart Money* reported an increase in the number of U.S. cable subscriber households from seven-teen million, five-hundred thousand subscribers in 1980 to sixty-five million, four hundred thousand subscribers in 1996. How many more subscribers were there in 1996 compared to 1980? Express your final answer in numeric form.

         ^{5 14 14}
        6̶5̶,4̶00,000 (1996)
  − 17,500,000 (1980)
     47,900,000

1–51. On January 18, 1998, the *Chicago Tribune* reported on the cost of theme parks in southern California. The costs of attending the four parks are as follows:

    Disneyland: adults, $38; children ages 3 to 11, $28
    Universal Studios: adults, $36; children ages 12 and younger, $26
    Knott's Berry Farm: adults, $35; children, $25
    Six Flags Magic Mountain: adults, $35; children, $17

You plan to take your spouse and two children, ages 4 and 5, on a vacation to southern California and would like to attend all four theme parks. What would be your total cost for your family if you attended all four parks?

	Adults (2)		**Children (2)**		
Disneyland:	$38		$28		
	× 2		× 2		
	$76	+	$56	=	$132
Universal Studios:	$36		$26		
	× 2		× 2		
	$72	+	$52	=	124
Knott's Berry Farm:	$35		$25		
	× 2		× 2		
	$70	+	$50	=	120
Six Flags:	$35		$17		
	× 2		× 2		
	$70	+	$34	=	104
					$480

1–52. On January 18, 1998, Jim Mateja wrote an article for the *Chicago Tribune* on the price of collector cars. A Bugattie Type 57 convertible bought by a Japanese investor 2 years ago for two million dollars was sold to a U.S. investor for seven hundred thousand dollars. How much more did the Japanese investor pay for the Bugattie than the U.S. investor? Express your answer in numeric form.

        ^{1 10}
  $2̶,0̶00,000
  − 700,000
  $1,300,000

1–53. On January 18, 1998, the *Chicago Tribune* ran an article titled "Hyundai Pins Hopes on Exports." Hyundai hopes to increase the number of vehicles sold abroad from 601,851 last year to 690,000 units. What will be the increase in the number of cars sold this year compared to last year?

$$
\begin{array}{r}
{\scriptstyle 8\,9\;\;9\,9\,10} \\
690{,}000 \\
-\;601{,}851 \\
\hline
88{,}149
\end{array}
$$

1–54. Members of a local bank plan a company picnic. A pizza (provided by Domino's) will serve 4 people. If the members expect 640 people to attend, how many pizzas will they need? Each pizza costs \$6. What is the total cost of the pizzas?

$$
\begin{array}{r}
160 \\
4\overline{)640} \\
\underline{4}\qquad\qquad 160 \times \$6 = \$960 \\
24 \\
\underline{24} \\
0
\end{array}
$$

1–55. A Goodyear tire store bought 860 tires from its manufacturer for \$25 per tire. What is the total cost of the store's purchase? If the store can sell all the tires at \$48 each, what will be the store's gross profit, or the difference between its sales and costs (Sales − Costs = Gross profit)?

Cost = 860 × \$25 = \$21,500   Sales = 860 × \$48 = \$41,280

$$
\begin{array}{ll}
\$41{,}280 & \text{Sales} \\
-\;21{,}500 & \text{Cost} \\
\hline
\$19{,}780 & \text{Gross profit}
\end{array}
$$

1–56. On January 18, 1998, the *Chicago Tribune* ran an ad for a new 1998 Dodge Caravan. The list price was \$19,619. The ad stated that there was a \$3,270 discount, a \$750 factory rebate, and a \$400 college graduate rebate. What would be the final price for the Dodge Caravan?

$$
\begin{array}{ll}
{\scriptstyle 5\,11} & \\
\$19{,}\cancel{6}\cancel{1}9 & \$3{,}270 \\
-\;4{,}420 & +\;750 \\
\hline
\$15{,}199 & +\;400 \\
& \hline \\
& \$4{,}420
\end{array}
$$

1–57. Frank Consales bought 4,800 shares of Gillette Company stock. He held the stock for 6 months. Then Frank sold 175 shares on Monday, 290 shares on Tuesday and again on Thursday, and 600 shares on Friday. How many shares does Frank still own? The average share of the stock Frank owns is worth \$18 per share. What is the total value of Frank's stock?

$$
\begin{array}{ll}
4{,}800 & \text{shares bought} \\
-\;1{,}355 & \text{shares sold} \qquad\qquad 175 + 290 + 290 + 600 = 1{,}355 \text{ shares sold} \\
\hline
3{,}445 & \longrightarrow 3{,}445 \text{ shares} \times \$18 = \$62{,}010
\end{array}
$$

1–58. On January 21, 1998, the Chicago *Sun-Times* ran the following ad from Option Home Lending asking, "Which Option Do You Prefer?"

Option A: Your current situation		or	Option B: You can pay this monthly	
Mortgage	\$663		Mortgage	\$958
Home equity loan	205		Home equity loan	Zero
Visa card	216		Visa card	Zero
Discover card	197		Discover card	Zero
MasterCard	189		MasterCard	Zero

According to this ad, how much would you save by using Option B?

$$
\begin{array}{r}
\$\;\;663 \\
+\;205 \\
+\;216 \\
+\;197 \\
+\;189 \\
\hline
\$1{,}470 \\
-\;958 \\
\hline
\$\;\;512
\end{array}
$$

1–59. At Lane Community College, Angel Roy received the following grades in her Accounting 101 class: 85, 80, 75, 90, 65, and 90. Angel's instructor, Professor Clark, said he would drop the lowest grade. What is Angel's average?

$85 + 80 + 75 + 90 + 90 = 420 \div 5 = 84$ average

1–60. Amy Hoyt, professor of business, has 15 students in Accounting I, 27 in Accounting II, 19 in Introduction to Computers, and 24 in Introduction to Business. What is the total number of students in Professor Hoyt's classes? If 16 students withdraw, how many total students will Professor Hoyt have?

$\begin{array}{r} 85 \\ - \ 16 \\ \hline 69 \end{array}$ $(15 + 27 + 19 + 24)$

69 students

1–61. Ron Alf, owner of Alf's Moving Company, bought a new truck. On Ron's first trip, he drove 1,200 miles and used 80 gallons of gas. How many miles per gallon did Ron get from his new truck? On Ron's second trip, he drove 840 miles and used 60 gallons. What is the difference in miles per gallon between Ron's first trip and his second trip?

$1,200 \div 80 = 15$ miles per gallon
$840 \div 60 = 14$ miles per gallon   Difference = 1 mile per gallon

1–62. Service Merchandise reduced its $145 Sharpe calculator by $28. What is the new selling price of the calculator? If Service Merchandise sold 2,100 calculators at the new price, what were the store's calculator dollar sales?

$\begin{array}{r} \$145 \\ - \ 28 \\ \hline \$117 \end{array}$ $\times 2,100 = \$245,700$

1–63. Randy's Bookstore has 350 business math texts in inventory. During the month, the bookstore ordered and received an additional 1,950 texts; it also sold 988 texts. What is the bookstore's inventory at the end of the month? If each text costs $44, what is the end-of-month inventory cost?

$350 + 1,950 = 2,300$ $\begin{array}{r} 2,300 \\ - \ 988 \\ \hline 1,312 \end{array}$ end-of-month inventory

$1,312 \times \$44 = \$57,728$

1–64. Cabot Company produced 2,115,000 cans of paint in August. Cabot sold 2,011,000 of these cans. If each can cost $18, what were Cabot's ending inventory of paint cans and its total ending inventory cost?

$\begin{array}{r} 2,115,000 \\ - \ 2,011,000 \\ \hline 104,000 \end{array}$ paint cans $\times \$18 = \$1,872,000$

1–65. Long College has 30 faculty members in the business department, 22 in psychology, 14 in English, and 169 in all other departments. What is the total number of faculty at Long College? If each faculty member advises 30 students, how many students attend Long College?

$30 + 22 + 14 + 169 = 235$ faculty
$235 \times 30 = 7,050$ students

1–66. O'Toole's Buffet had 90 customers on Sunday, 70 on Monday, 65 on Tuesday, and a total of 310 on Wednesday to Saturday. How many customers did O'Toole's Buffet serve during the week? If each customer spends $9, what were the total sales for the week?

$90 + 70 + 65 + 310 = 535$ customers
$\begin{array}{r} \times \ \$9 \\ \hline \$4,815 \end{array}$

If O'Toole's Buffet had the same sales each week, what were the sales for the year?
$\$4,815 \times 52 = \$250,380$

1–67. Longview Agency projected its year 2001 sales at $995,000. During 2001, the agency earned $525,960 sales from its major clients and $286,950 sales from the remainder of its clients. How much did the agency overestimate its sales?

$\begin{array}{r} \$995,000 \\ - \ 812,910 \\ \hline \$182,090 \end{array}$ $(\$525,960 + \$286,950)$

1–68. Jim Floyd works at U.S. Airways and earned $61,000 last year before tax deductions. From Jim's total earnings, his company subtracted $1,462 for federal income taxes, $3,782 for Social Security, and $884 for Medicare taxes. What was Jim's actual, or net, pay for the year?

$\begin{array}{r} \$61,000 \\ - \ 6,128 \\ \hline \$54,872 \end{array}$ $(\$1,462 + \$3,782 + \$884)$

1–69. Levitz Furniture received the following invoice amounts from suppliers. How much does the company owe?

Per item			
15 paintings	$125	=	$ 1,875
32 rockers	69	=	2,208
20 desk lamps	55	=	1,100
95 coffee tables	139	=	13,205
			$18,388

1–70. Jole Company produces beach balls and it operates three shifts. It produces 5,000 balls per shift on shifts 1 and 2. On shift 3, the company can produce 6 times as many balls as on shift 1. Assume a 5-day workweek. How many beach balls does Jole produce per week and per year?

 10,000 balls (shifts 1 and 2)   200,000
$+$ 30,000 balls (shift 3) $\times\ 52$

 40,000 balls per day   10,400,000 balls per year
$\times 5$

 200,000 balls per week

1–71. On January 18, 1998, the *Chicago Tribune* ran an article on the holiday expeditions of Salt Lake City, Utah. A bicycle trip to the San Rafael Swell at the edge of Colorado Plateau in Utah would cost $560 for the 4-day trip of 100 miles. Bicycle rental is an additional $90. What would be the cost per day if you used your own bicycle?

140
$4)\overline{\$560}$
$\underline{4}$
16
$\underline{16}$
0

1–72. Moe Brink has a $900 balance in his checkbook. During the week, Moe wrote the following checks: rent, $350; telephone, $44; food, $160; and entertaining, $60. Moe also made a $1,200 deposit. What is Moe's new checkbook balance?

 $ 900
$+ 1,200$

 $2,100
$\underline{- 614}$ ($350 + $44 + $160 + $60)

 $1,486

1–73. Herman's, an athletic sports shop, bought and sold the following merchandise:

	Cost	Selling price
Tennis rackets	$ 2,180	$ 2,910
Tennis balls	60	160
Bowling balls	950	2,151
Sneakers	7,210	12,810
	$10,400	$18,031

What was the total cost of merchandise bought by Herman's? If the shop sold all merchandise, what were the sales and the resulting gross profit (Sales − Costs = Gross profit)?

 Sales $18,031
$-$ Costs $\underline{- 10,400}$

$=$ Gross profit $ 7,631

1–74. John Purcell, the bookkeeper for Roseville Real Estate, and his manager are concerned about the company's telephone bills. Last year the company's average monthly phone bill was $34. John's manager asked him for an average of this year's phone bills. John's records show the following:

January	$ 34	July	$ 28
February	60	August	23
March	20	September	29
April	25	October	25
May	30	November	22
June	59	December	41
	$228		$168

What is the average of this year's phone bills? Did John and his manager have a justifiable concern?
$228 + $168 = $396 ÷ 12 = $33
No justifiable concern.

1–75. In August 1997, *Smart Money* compared the cost of golfing at various locations in the United States. Pebble Beach is the home of the country's highest daily greens fee—$275. If you were to golf at Pebble Beach one day per week, what would be your total cost for 1 year of golfing at Pebble Beach?

$ 275
× 52
550
13 75
$14,300

1–76. On Monday, Wang Hardware sold 15 paint brushes at $3 each, 6 wrenches at $5 each, 7 bags of grass seed at $3 each, 4 lawn mowers at $119 each, and 28 cans of paint at $8 each. What were Wang's total dollar sales on Monday?

$45 + $30 + $21 + $476 + $224 = $796
(15 × $3) + (6 × $5) + (7 × $3) + (4 × $119) + (28 × $8)

1–77. While redecorating, Morris Company used 125 square yards of commercial carpet. The total cost of the carpet was $3,000. How much did Morris pay per square yard?
$3,000 ÷ 125 = $24 per square yard

1–78. Washington Construction built 12 ranch houses for $115,000 each. From the sale of these houses, Washington received $1,980,000. How much gross profit (Sales − Costs = Gross profit) did Washington make on the houses?

$1,980,000
− 1,380,000   ($115,000 × 12)
$ 600,000

The four partners of Washington Construction split all profits equally. How much will each partner receive?
$600,000 ÷ 4 = $150,000

CHALLENGE PROBLEMS

1–79. The August 1997 issue of *Smart Money* listed the portfolio of Robert Kleinschmidt. Part of the portfolio included 53 shares of Motorola at $70 per share, 30 shares of International Business Machines with a total value of $2,670, and $2,500 total value of Knightsbridge Tankers at a price of $25 per share. **(a)** What is the total value of the Motorola shares? **(b)** What would be the price per share of the International Business Machines stock? **(c)** How many shares does Robert Kleinschmidt have of Knightsbridge Tankers?

a. $ 70
× 53
210
3 50
$3,710 total value

b. $89 price per share
30)$2,670
2 40
270
270
0

c. 100 shares
$25)$2,500

1–80. Pat Valdez is trying to determine her 2001 finances. Pat's actual 2000 finances were as follows:

Income:		Assets:	
Gross income	$69,000	Checking account	$ 1,950
Interest income	450	Savings account	8,950
Total	$69,450	Auto	1,800
		Personal property	14,000
Expenses:		Total	$26,700
Living	$24,500	Liabilities:	
Insurance premium	350	Note to bank	4,500
Taxes	14,800		
Medical	585	Net worth	$22,200 ($26,700 − $4,500)
Investment	4,000		
Total	$44,235		

Net worth = Assets − Liabilities
(own)   (owe)

Pat believes her gross income will double in 2001 and her interest income will decrease $150. She plans to reduce her 2001 living expenses by one-half. Pat's insurance company wrote a letter announcing that insurance premiums would triple in 2001. Her accountant estimates her taxes will decrease $250 and her medical costs will increase $410. Pat also hopes to cut her investment expenses by one-fourth. Pat's accountant projects that her savings and checking accounts will each double in value. On January 2, 2001, Pat sold her automobile and began to use public transportation. Pat forecasts that her personal property will decrease by one-seventh. She has sent her bank a $375 check to reduce her bank note. Could you give Pat an updated list of her 2001 finances? If you round all the way each 2000 and 2001 asset and liability, what will be the difference in Pat's net worth?

Income:			Assets:		
Gross income	$138,000	($69,000 × 2)	Checking account	$ 3,900	($1,950 × 2)
Interest income	300	($450 − $150)	Savings account	17,900	($8,950 × 2)
Total	$138,300		Personal property	12,000	$\left(\$14,000 - \frac{1}{7} \text{ of } \$14,000\right)$
Expenses:			Total	$33,800	
Living	$ 12,250	($24,500 ÷ 2)	Liabilities:		
Insurance premium	1,050	($350 × 3)	Note to bank	4,125	($4,500 − $375)
Taxes	14,550	($14,800 − $250)	Net worth	$29,675	
Medical	995	($585 + $410)			
Investment	3,000	$\left(\$4,000 - \frac{1}{4} \text{ of } \$4,000\right)$			
Total	$ 31,845				

	2000	2001		
Checking account	$ 2,000	$ 4,000		
Savings account	9,000	20,000		
Automobile	2,000	0		
Personal property	10,000	10,000		
Total	$23,000	$34,000	$30,000 = 2001	
Liabilities	5,000	4,000	−18,000 = 2000	
Net worth	$18,000	$30,000	$12,000	

Total estimated difference is $12,000 in favor of 2001.

SUMMARY PRACTICE TEST

1. Translate the following verbal forms to numbers and add. *(p. 5)*
   a. Two thousand, three hundred eighty-two   2,382
   b. Six million, thirteen   6,000,013
   c. Eighteen thousand, six hundred ninety-five   18,695
2. Express the following number in verbal form. *(p. 5)*   6,021,090

   6,828,491 Six million, eight hundred twenty-eight thousand, four hundred ninety-one

3. Round the following numbers. *(p. 6)*

Nearest ten	Nearest hundred	Nearest thousand	Round all the way
a. 48	**b.** 694	**c.** 8,190	**d.** 18,975
50	700	8,000	20,000

4. Estimate the following actual problem by rounding all the way, work the actual problem, and check by adding each column of digits separately. *(pp. 7, 10)*

Actual	Estimate	Check
1,510	2,000	9
6,985	7,000	18
7,994	8,000	2 3
———	———	14
16,489	17,000	———
		16,489

5. Estimate the following actual problem by rounding all the way and then do the actual multiplication. *(pp. 13, 14)*

Actual	Estimate
7,595	8,000
× 605	600
———	———
37 975	4,800,000
4 557 00	
———	
4,594,975	

6. Multiply the following by the shortcut method. *(p. 14)*
   $824,951 \times 1,000 = 824,951,000$

7. Divide the following and check the answer by multiplication. *(p. 15)*

```
              Check
   288 R50      288
64)18,482     ×  64
   12 8        ————
   ———         1,152
    5 68      17 28
    5 12      ————
    ———       18,432
     562      +  50
     512      ————
     ———      18,482
      50
```

8. Divide the following by the shortcut method. *(p. 16)*
   $700 \div 70 = 70 \div 7 = 10$

9. Melody Flynn bought a $99 calculator that was reduced to $46. Melody gave the clerk a $100 bill. What change will Melody receive? *(p. 11)*
   $\$100 - \$46 = \$54$

10. Tina Long plans to buy a $21,600 Chrysler van with an interest charge of $4,000. Tina figures she can afford a monthly payment of $600. If Tina must pay 40 equal monthly payments, can she afford the van? *(p. 15)*
    $\$21,600 + \$4,000 = \$25,600 \div 40 = \$640$ No.

11. Lou Dobbs has the propane tank at his home filled 12 times per year. The tank has a capacity of 200 gallons. Assume **(a)** the price of propane fuel is $2 per gallon and **(b)** the tank is completely empty each time Lou has it filled. What is Lou's average monthly propane bill? Complete the following blueprint aid for dissecting and solving the word problem. *(pp. 13, 17)*

The facts	Solving for?	Steps to take	Key points
Tank filled 12 times per year Tank holds 200 gallons Cost is $2 per gallon	Average monthly propane bill	Total gallons used × Price per gallon = Total cost of propane	Average cost is total cost divided by 12 months in a year.

Steps to solving problem

1. Calculate total number of gallons. $200 \times 12 = 2,400$ gallons
2. Calculate total cost of propane.   2,400 gallons $\times \$2 = \$4,800$
3. Calculate average monthly bill. $\$4,800 \div 12 = \$400$

A KIPLINGER APPROACH

A GROUP PROJECT Defend or reject the following business math issue based on the *Kiplinger's Personal Finance Magazine* article below:

FAMILY FINANCES

Who Needs a Safe-Deposit Box?

▶ **Maybe not you. A home safe is more convenient—and cheaper, too.** By Stephanie Gallagher

Digital-age bank customers don't spend much time in bank lobbies anymore. So why cool your heels waiting for admission to the bank's vault, where you've stashed your valuables in a 3- by 5- by 18-inch metal box? Although a safe-deposit box is a safe place to keep birth certificates, deeds, insurance policies, rare coins and other hard-to-replace possessions, a good home safe can be cheaper and more convenient—and no less secure.

A bank vault may withstand fires, explosions, burglaries and floods, but none is "fireproof, bombproof, waterproof or burglarproof," admits Joyce McLin, executive director of the American Safe Deposit Association. During the 1993 Midwest floods, for example, water seeped into the vault of one Missouri bank and damaged the contents of some safe-deposit boxes. (Keep your documents in sealed plastic bags, McLin advises.)

Such events are rare. But when they do happen, federal deposit insurance won't bail you out, and the bank may not, either—even if it carries liability insurance against its own negligence. "If the bank has alarm equipment in place and has met all the building codes," it would be hard to prove it was negligent, McLin says. So on top of the $30 to $75 a year you pay for your safe-deposit box, you should probably add a rider to your homeowners policy—at $8 to $15 a year—to cover the contents.

A CONVENIENT ALTERNATIVE. For the price of a safe-deposit box plus insurance for four or five years, you could buy a decent home safe that will last a lifetime—and that you can access outside of bankers' hours. Because your valuables are stored right in your home, you could keep more frequently used papers, such as airline tickets and brokerage statements, in it. You could also quickly lock up loose valuables when repair people, cleaning people or babysitters come into your home.

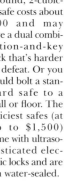

And should the contents be damaged or stolen despite your precautions, they'd be covered under your ordinary homeowners policy.

Expect to spend $150 or so at a hardware or home-supply store for a standard 1-cubic-foot home safe, which holds a lot more than a safe-deposit box. The box should be rated by Underwriters Laboratories for fire protection—a one-hour rating means that the safe can withstand 1,300-degree Fahrenheit heat for an hour. Home safes in that price range are not watertight, so heed the plastic-bag advice at home, too.

Burglary is the one peril that will keep some worried folks from parting with their safe-deposit boxes. A typical 1-cubic-foot safe weighs less than 100 pounds and has a combination lock that a sophisticated burglar could conquer. If you have a security-alarm system, you probably have enough theft protection. If you don't, you may want to spend more for a bigger, heavier safe that would be even harder for a thief to carry away: A 160-pound, 2-cubic-foot safe costs about $300 and may have a dual combination-and-key lock that's harder to defeat. Or you could bolt a standard safe to a wall or floor. The priciest safes (at up to $1,500) come with ultrasophisticated electronic locks and are often water-sealed.

EDWIN FOTHERINGHAM

Business Math Issue

The home safe will completely replace the need for a safe-deposit box.

1. List the key points of the article and information to support your position.
2. Write a group defense of your position using math calculations to support your view.

Higher Math

What college will cost, and the monthly savings needed to pay for it

YEARS UNTIL STUDENT BEGINS COLLEGE	SCHOOL YEAR (FALL)	PROJECTED FOUR-YEAR TOTAL COST* (PUBLIC)	PROJECTED FOUR-YEAR TOTAL COST* (PRIVATE)	MONTHLY SAVINGS (PUBLIC)	MONTHLY SAVINGS (PRIVATE)
1	1998	$45,569	$96,957	$3,636	$7,736
2	1999	47,847	101,805	1,833	3,900
3	2000	50,239	106,895	1,231	2,620
4	2001	52,751	112,240	930	1,979
5	2002	55,389	117,852	749	1,593
6	2003	58,158	123,745	628	1,336
7	2004	61,066	129,932	541	1,151
8	2005	64,120	136,428	476	1,012
9	2006	67,326	143,250	425	904
10	2007	70,692	150,412	384	817
11	2008	74,226	157,933	350	745
12	2009	77,938	165,830	322	685
13	2010	81,835	174,121	298	634
14	2011	85,296	182,827	277	590
15	2012	90,223	191,968	259	551
16	2013	94,734	201,567	243	517
17	2014	99,470	211,645	229	487
18	2015	104,444	222,228	216	460
19	2016	109,666	233,339	205	435
20	2017	115,150	245,006	194	413

Project A

Assume you would like to send your child to college in the year 2010. How much must you save per year for her or him to go to **(a)** a private college and **(b)** a public college? **(c)** How much more expensive is the cost of a four-year private education than a four-year public education?

a. Private college:
$634 × 12 = $7,608

b. Public college:
$298 × 12 = $3,576

c. $174,121
$-81,835$
$ 92,286

Airbus Nears $4 Billion Order From Airlines

By FREDERIC M. BIDDLE
Staff Reporter of THE WALL STREET JOURNAL

Airbus Industrie has reached a preliminary agreement to sell 100 jetliners valued at about $4 billion to a group of Latin American airlines, signaling a major victory for Airbus in a region long dominated by archrival **Boeing** Co., people familiar with the matter said.

If the agreement is translated into firm purchases for Airbus, which some industry officials expected as early as next month, it would be the largest single order placed by Latin carriers and the second largest snared by the European consortium anywhere in the world. It also marks the emergence of a new strategy in which smaller airlines band together to leverage more-favorable terms in buying aircraft.

The preliminary agreement covers nearly a dozen airlines controlled by Chilean carrier **LanChile** and two fast-grow-

Project B

Calculate the price per plane using the shortcut method.

$$\frac{\$4,000,000,000}{100} = \$40,000,000$$

 See text Web site (www.mhhe.com/slater) and *The Business Math Internet Resource Guide.*

You and Your Money

Do you spend $50 per month on lottery tickets, hoping to make a big win? You may not want to bet on the lottery when you know that on average, you will only get $\frac{1}{2}$ of what you bet back. If you invest $50 every month for lottery tickets, 40 years later, after pouring $24,000 into the lottery, you will have on average just $50 left.

2

FRACTIONS

LEARNING UNIT OBJECTIVES

LU 2.1 Types of Fractions and Conversion Procedures

- Recognize the three types of fractions *(pp. 34–35)*.
- Convert improper fractions to whole or mixed numbers and mixed numbers to improper fractions *(pp. 35–36)*.
- Convert fractions to lowest and highest terms *(pp. 36–37)*.

LU 2.2 Adding and Subtracting Fractions

- Add and subtract proper fractions with the same or different denominators *(pp. 38–40)*.
- Find the least common denominator (LCD) by inspection and prime numbers *(pp. 40–41)*.
- Add and subtract mixed numbers with the same or different denominators *(pp. 41–43)*.

LU 2.3 Multiplying and Dividing Fractions

- Multiply and divide proper, improper, and mixed numbers *(pp. 45–47)*.
- Use the cancellation method in the multiplication and division of fractions *(pp. 45–46)*.

Sharon Hoogstraten

M&M's® Chocolate Candies have been a favorite treat for years. They come in different colors—yellow, red, blue, orange, brown, and green. Do you know how many of each color are in a bag of M&M's®? You probably have never stopped to sort the colors and count them.

The 1.69-ounce bag of M&M's® shown here contains 55 M&M's®. In this bag, you will find the following colors:[1]

18 yellow	9 blue	6 brown
10 red	7 orange	5 green

The number of yellow candies in a bag might suggest that yellow is the favorite color of many people. Since this is a business math text, however, let's look at the 55 M&M's® in terms of fractional arithmetic.

Of the 55 M&M's® in the 1.69-ounce bag, 5 of these M&M's® are green, so we can say that 5 parts of 55 represent green candies. We could also say that 1 out of 11 M&M's® is green. Are you confused?

For many people, fractions are difficult. If you are one of these people, this chapter is for you. First you will review the types of fractions and the fraction conversion procedures. Then you will gain a clear understanding of the addition, subtraction, multiplication, and division of fractions.

LEARNING UNIT 2.1 Types of Fractions and Conversion Procedures

This chapter explains the parts of whole numbers called **fractions.** With fractions you can divide any object or unit—a whole—into a definite number of equal parts. For example, the bag of 55 M&M's® shown at the beginning of this chapter contains 6 brown candies. If you eat only the brown M&M's®, you have eaten 6 parts of 55, or 6 parts of the whole bag of M&M's®. We can express this in the following fraction:

$$\frac{6}{55}$$

6 is the **numerator,** or top of the fraction. The numerator describes the number of equal parts of the whole bag that you ate.

55 is the **denominator,** or bottom of the fraction. The denominator gives the total number of equal parts in the bag of M&M's®.

Before reviewing the arithmetic operations of fractions, you must recognize the three types of fractions described in this unit. You must also know how to convert fractions to a workable form.

Types of Fractions

Burger World

Why You Won't Find Any Egg McMuffins For Breakfast in Brazil

McDonald's Expects Growth From Overseas, but a Visit To Rio Is Quite Revealing

They'll 'Fall Right Into Line'

By RICHARD GIBSON and MATT MOFFETT
Staff Reporters of THE WALL STREET JOURNAL

SALVADOR, Brazil — People here love Americana, and no symbol of it is better-known than the Golden Arches of McDonald's Corp. Yet many millions of Brazilians have never tasted a Big Mac. Salvador, a coastal city of nearly three million, has just 11 McDonald's restaurants, one-tenth as many as equally populous Chicago.

© 1997 Dow Jones & Company, Inc.

Do you plan to visit Salvador, Brazil, in the future? If you enjoy a McDonald's Big Mac, you may have to go to a Brazilian restaurant for your hamburger. Note that *The Wall Street Journal* clipping "Why You Won't Find Any Egg McMuffins for Breakfast in Brazil" states that Salvador—a city of nearly 3 million—has only 11 McDonald's restaurants. If you have ever looked for a McDonald's in the equally populous Chicago, you know that you do not have to look very far. In fact, compared to Chicago, Salvador has only one-tenth as many McDonald's. One-tenth $\left(\frac{1}{10}\right)$ is a proper fraction:

---

[1]The color ratios currently given are a sample only used for educational purposes. They do not represent the manufacturer's color ratios.

Proper Fractions

A proper fraction has a value less than 1; its numerator is smaller than its denominator.

EXAMPLES $\dfrac{1}{10}, \dfrac{1}{12}, \dfrac{1}{3}, \dfrac{4}{7}, \dfrac{9}{10}, \dfrac{12}{13}, \dfrac{18}{55}$

Improper Fractions

An improper fraction has a value equal to or greater than 1; its numerator is equal to or greater than its denominator.

EXAMPLES $\dfrac{13}{13}, \dfrac{7}{6}, \dfrac{15}{14}, \dfrac{22}{19}$

Mixed Numbers

A mixed number is the sum of a whole number greater than zero and a proper fraction.

EXAMPLES $4\dfrac{1}{7}, 5\dfrac{9}{10}, 8\dfrac{7}{8}, 33\dfrac{5}{6}, 139\dfrac{9}{11}$

Conversion Procedures

In Chapter 1 we worked with two of the division symbols ($\div$ and $\overline{)}\,$). The horizontal line (or the diagonal) that separates the numerator and the denominator of a fraction also indicates division. The numerator, like the dividend, is the number we are dividing into. The denominator, like the divisor, is the number we use to divide. Then, referring to the 6 brown M&M's® in the bag of 55 M&M's® $\left(\dfrac{6}{55}\right)$ shown at the beginning of this unit, we can say that we are dividing 55 into 6, or 6 is divided by 55. Also, in the fraction $\dfrac{3}{4}$, we can say that we are dividing 4 into 3, or 3 is divided by 4.

Working with the smaller numbers of simple fractions such as $\dfrac{3}{4}$ is easier, so we often convert fractions to their simplest terms. In this unit we show how to convert improper fractions to whole or mixed numbers, mixed numbers to improper fractions, and fractions to lowest and highest terms.

Converting Improper Fractions to Whole or Mixed Numbers

Business situations often make it necessary to change an improper fraction to a whole number or mixed number. You can use the following steps to make this conversion:

Converting Improper Fractions to Whole or Mixed Numbers

Step 1. Divide the numerator of the improper fraction by the denominator.

Step 2. **a.** If you have no remainder, the quotient is a whole number.

b. If you have a remainder, the whole number part of the mixed number is the quotient. The remainder is placed over the old denominator as the proper fraction of the mixed number.

EXAMPLES

$$\dfrac{15}{15} = 1 \qquad \dfrac{16}{5} = 3\dfrac{1}{5} \qquad \begin{array}{r} 3\ \text{R}1 \\ 5\overline{)16} \\ \underline{15} \\ 1 \end{array}$$

Converting Mixed Numbers to Improper Fractions

By reversing the procedure of converting improper fractions to mixed numbers, we can change mixed numbers to improper fractions.

```
████████        ████        ████████
```

Converting Mixed Numbers to Improper Fractions

Step 1. Multiply the denominator of the fraction by the whole number.
Step 2. Add the product from Step 1 to the numerator of the old fraction.
Step 3. Place the total from Step 2 over the denominator of the old fraction to get the improper fraction.

EXAMPLE $6\frac{1}{8} = \frac{(8 \times 6) + 1}{8} = \frac{49}{8}$ ↙ Note that the denominator stays the same.

Converting (Reducing) Fractions to Lowest Terms

When solving fraction problems, you always reduce the fractions to their lowest terms. This reduction does not change the value of the fraction. For example, in the bag of M&M's®, 5 out of 55 were green. The fraction for this is $\frac{5}{55}$. If you divide the top and bottom of the fraction by 5, you have reduced the fraction to $\frac{1}{11}$ without changing its value. Remember, we said in the chapter introduction that 1 out of 11 M&M's® in the bag of 55 M&M's® represents green candies. Now you know why this is true.

✳ To reduce a fraction to its lowest terms, begin by inspecting the fraction, looking for the largest whole number that will divide into both the numerator and the denominator without leaving a remainder. This whole number is the **greatest common divisor,** which cannot be zero. When you find this largest whole number, you have reached the point where the fraction is reduced to its **lowest terms.** At this point, no number (except 1) can divide evenly into both parts of the fraction.

Reducing Fractions to Lowest Terms by Inspection

Step 1. By inspection, find the largest whole number (greatest common divisor) that will divide evenly into the numerator and denominator (does not change the fraction value).
Step 2. Now you have reduced the fraction to its lowest terms, since no number (except 1) can divide evenly into the numerator and denominator.

EXAMPLE $\frac{24}{30} = \frac{24 \div 6}{30 \div 6} = \frac{4}{5}$

Using inspection, you can see that the number 6 in the above example is the greatest common divisor. When you have large numbers, the greatest common divisor is not so obvious. For large numbers, you can use the following step approach to find the greatest common divisor:

 T

Step Approach for Finding Greatest Common Divisor

Step 1. Divide the smaller number (numerator) of the fraction into the larger number (denominator).
Step 2. Divide the remainder of Step 1 into the divisor of Step 1.
Step 3. Divide the remainder of Step 2 into the divisor of Step 2. Continue this division process until the remainder is a 0, which means the last divisor is the greatest common divisor.

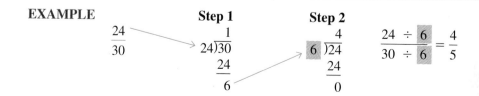

Reducing a fraction by inspection is to some extent a trial-and-error method. Sometimes you are not sure what number you should divide into the top (numerator) and bottom (denominator) of the fraction. The following reference table on divisibility tests will be helpful. Note that to reduce a fraction to lowest terms might result in more than one division.

	2	3	4	5	6	10
Will divide evenly into number if	Last digit is 0, 2, 4, 6, 8.	Sum of the digits is divisible by 3.	Last two digits can be divided by 4.	Last digit is 5 or 0.	The number is even and 3 will divide into the sum of the digits.	The last digit is 0.
Examples	$\dfrac{12}{14} = \dfrac{6}{7}$	$\dfrac{36}{69} = \dfrac{12}{23}$ $3 + 6 = 9 \div 3 = 3$ $6 + 9 = 15 \div 3 = 5$	$\dfrac{140}{160} = \dfrac{1(40)}{1(60)}$ $= \dfrac{35}{40} = \dfrac{7}{8}$	$\dfrac{15}{20} = \dfrac{3}{4}$	$\dfrac{12}{18} = \dfrac{2}{3}$	$\dfrac{90}{100} = \dfrac{9}{10}$

Converting (Raising) Fractions to Higher Terms

Later, when you add and subtract fractions, you will see that sometimes fractions must be raised to **higher terms.** Recall that when you reduced fractions to their lowest terms, you looked for the largest whole number (greatest common divisor) that would divide evenly into both the numerator and the denominator. When you raise fractions to higher terms, you do the opposite and multiply the numerator and the denominator by the same whole number. For example, if you want to raise the fraction $\frac{1}{4}$, you can multiply the numerator and denominator by 2.

EXAMPLE $\quad \dfrac{1}{4} \times \dfrac{2}{2} = \boxed{\dfrac{2}{8}}$

The fractions $\frac{1}{4}$ and $\frac{2}{8}$ are **equivalent** in value. By converting $\frac{1}{4}$ to $\frac{2}{8}$, you only divided it into more parts.

Let's suppose that you have eaten $\frac{4}{7}$ of a pizza. You decide that instead of expressing the amount you have eaten in 7ths, you want to express it in 28ths. How would you do this?

To find the new numerator when you know the new denominator (28), use the steps that follow.

Raising Fractions to Higher Terms When Denominator Is Known

Step 1. Divide the *new* denominator by the *old* denominator to get the common number that raises the fraction to higher terms.

Step 2. Multiply the common number from Step 1 by the old numerator, and place it as the new numerator over the new denominator.

EXAMPLE $\quad \dfrac{4}{7} = \dfrac{\boxed{?}}{28}$

Step 1. Divide 28 by 7 = 4.

Step 2. Multiply 4 by the numerator 4 = 16.

Result:

$$\dfrac{4}{7} = \dfrac{\boxed{16}}{28} \qquad \left(\textit{Note: } \text{This is the same as multiplying } \dfrac{4}{7} \times \dfrac{4}{4}.\right)$$

Note that the $\frac{4}{7}$ and $\frac{16}{28}$ are equivalent in value, yet they are different fractions.

Now try the following Practice Quiz to check your understanding of this unit.

1. Identify the type of fraction—proper, improper, or mixed:

   a. $\dfrac{4}{5}$ b. $\dfrac{6}{5}$ c. $19\dfrac{1}{5}$ d. $\dfrac{20}{20}$

2. Convert to a mixed number (do not reduce):

   $\dfrac{160}{9}$

3. Convert the mixed number to an improper fraction:

   $9\dfrac{5}{8}$

4. Find the greatest common divisor by the step approach and reduce to lowest terms:

   a. $\dfrac{24}{40}$ b. $\dfrac{91}{156}$

5. Convert to higher terms:

   a. $\dfrac{14}{20} = \dfrac{}{200}$ b. $\dfrac{8}{10} = \dfrac{}{60}$

✓ **Solutions**

1. a. Proper
   b. Improper
   c. Mixed
   d. Improper

2. $9\overline{)160}$ = $17\frac{7}{9}$
    $\dfrac{9}{70}$
    $\dfrac{63}{7}$

3. $\dfrac{(9 \times 8) + 5}{8} = \dfrac{77}{8}$

4. a.
   $24\overline{)40}$ $16\overline{)24}$ $8\overline{)16}$
   $\dfrac{24}{16}$ $\dfrac{16}{8}$ $\dfrac{16}{0}$

   $\dfrac{24 \div 8}{40 \div 8} = \dfrac{3}{5}$

   8 is greatest common divisor.

   b.
   $91\overline{)156}$ $65\overline{)91}$ $26\overline{)65}$ $13\overline{)26}$
   $\dfrac{91}{65}$ $\dfrac{65}{26}$ $\dfrac{52}{13}$ $\dfrac{26}{0}$

   $\dfrac{91 \div 13}{156 \div 13} = \dfrac{7}{12}$

   13 is greatest common divisor.

5. a.
   $20\overline{)200}$ $10 \times 14 = 140$ $\dfrac{14}{20} = \dfrac{140}{200}$

   b.
   $10\overline{)60}$ $6 \times 8 = 48$ $\dfrac{8}{10} = \dfrac{48}{60}$

LEARNING UNIT 2.2 Adding and Subtracting Fractions

Reebok Will Offer To Repurchase One-Third of Stock

By JAMES S. HIRSCH
Staff Reporter of THE WALL STREET JOURNAL

Reebok International Ltd., seeking to boost its lagging stock price, said it will offer to repurchase one-third of the company's stock, or 24 million common shares, for as much as $864 million.

This clipping from *The Wall Street Journal* tells you that Reebok will repurchase (buy back) 1 out of 3 $\left(\frac{1}{3}\right)$ of the company's shares of common stock. Since a whole is $\frac{3}{3}$ $\left(\frac{3}{3} = 1\right)$, you can use subtraction to determine that $\frac{2}{3}$ of the stock will not be repurchased. Then you can prove that you are correct by adding $\frac{1}{3}$ and $\frac{2}{3}$.

In this unit you learn how to add and subtract fractions with the same denominators (as in the above example) and fractions with different denominators. Then you are ready to add and subtract mixed numbers.

Addition of Fractions

When you add two or more quantities, they must have the same name or be of the same denomination. You cannot add 6 quarts and 3 pints unless you change the denomination of one or both quantities. You must either make the quarts into pints or the pints into quarts. The same principle also applies to fractions. That is, to add two or more fractions, they must have a **common denominator.**

Adding Proper Fractions with Same Denominators

Adding **like fractions,** which are proper fractions with the same or common denominators, is similar to adding whole numbers.

Adding Proper Fractions with the Same Denominators
Step 1. Add the numerators and place the total over the original denominator.
Step 2. If the answer is a proper fraction, reduce it to lowest terms. If the answer is an improper fraction, change it to a whole or mixed number.

EXAMPLE $\dfrac{1}{7} + \dfrac{4}{7} = \dfrac{5}{7}$

The denominator, 7, shows the number of pieces into which some whole was divided. The two numerators, 1 and 4, tell how many of the pieces you have. So if you add 1 and 4, you get 5, or $\frac{5}{7}$.

Adding Proper Fractions with Different Denominators

To add **unlike fractions** (proper fractions with different denominators), you must first change them to *like fractions.* To do this, find a denominator that is common to all the fractions you want to add. Then look for the **least common denominator (LCD).**[2] The LCD is the smallest nonzero whole number into which all denominators will divide evenly. You can find the LCD by inspection or with prime numbers.

Finding the Least Common Denominator (LCD) by Inspection   The example that follows shows you how to use inspection to find an LCD (this will make all the denominators the same).

EXAMPLE $\dfrac{3}{7} + \dfrac{5}{21}$

Inspection of these two fractions shows that the smallest number into which denominators 7 and 21 divide evenly is 21. Thus, 21 is the LCD.

You may know that 21 is the LCD of $\frac{3}{7} + \frac{5}{21}$, but you cannot add these two fractions until you change the denominator of $\frac{3}{7}$ to 21. You do this by building (raising) the equivalent of $\frac{3}{7}$, as explained in Learning Unit 2.1. You can use the following steps to find the LCD by inspection:

Step 1. Divide the new denominator (21) by the old denominator (7): $21 \div 7 = 3$.

Step 2. Multiply the 3 in Step 1 by the old numerator (3): $3 \times 3 = 9$. The new numerator is 9.

Result:

$$\dfrac{3}{7} = \dfrac{9}{21}$$

Now that the denominators are the same, you add the numerators.

$$\dfrac{9}{21} + \dfrac{5}{21} = \dfrac{14}{21} = \dfrac{2}{3}$$

Note that $\frac{14}{21}$ is reduced to its lowest terms $\frac{2}{3}$. Always reduce your answer to its lowest terms. You are now ready for the following general steps for adding proper fractions with different denominators. These steps also apply to the following discussion on finding LCD by prime numbers.

---

[2] Often referred to as the *lowest common denominator.*

T

Adding Proper Fractions with Different Denominators

Step 1. Find the LCD.

Step 2. Change each fraction to a like fraction.

Step 3. Add the numerators and place the total over the LCD.

Step 4. If necessary, reduce the answer to lowest terms.

Finding the Least Common Denominator (LCD) by Prime Numbers   When you cannot determine the LCD by inspection, you can use the prime number method. First you must understand prime numbers.

Prime Numbers

A **prime number** is a whole number greater than 1 that is only divisible by itself and 1. The number 1 is not a prime number.

EXAMPLES   2, 3, 5, 7, 11, 13, 17, 19, 23, 29, 31, 37, 41, 43

Note that the number 4 is not a prime number. Not only can you divide 4 by 1 and by 4, but you can also divide 4 by 2.

Now let's see how to use prime numbers to find the LCD.

EXAMPLE $\dfrac{1}{3} + \dfrac{1}{8} + \dfrac{1}{9} + \dfrac{1}{12}$

Step 1.   Copy the denominators and arrange them in a separate row.

   3   8   9   12

Step 2.   Divide the denominators in Step 1 by prime numbers. Start with the smallest number that will divide into at least two of the denominators. Bring down any number that is not divisible. Keep in mind that the lowest prime number is 2.

$$2 \, \big/ \, \underline{3 \quad 8 \quad 9 \quad 12}$$
$$ 3 \quad 4 \quad 9 \quad 6$$

   Note: The 3 and 9 were brought down, since they were not divisible by 2.

Step 3.   Continue Step 2 until no prime number will divide evenly into at least two numbers.

   Note: The 3 is used, since 2 can no longer divide evenly into at least two numbers.

$$2 \, \big/ \, \underline{3 \quad 8 \quad 9 \quad 12}$$
$$2 \, \big/ \, \underline{3 \quad 4 \quad 9 \quad 6}$$
$$3 \, \big/ \, \underline{3 \quad 2 \quad 9 \quad 3}$$
$$ 1 \quad 2 \quad 3 \quad 1$$

Step 4.   To find the LCD, multiply all the numbers in the divisors (2, 2, 3) and in the last row (1, 2, 3, 1).

$$\boxed{2 \times 2 \times 3} \times \boxed{1 \times 2 \times 3 \times 1} = \boxed{72} \text{ (LCD)}$$

   Divisors   ×   Last row

Step 5.   Raise each fraction so that each denominator will be 72 and then add fractions.

$$\dfrac{24}{72} + \dfrac{9}{72} + \dfrac{8}{72} + \dfrac{6}{72} = \dfrac{47}{72}$$

$$\dfrac{1}{3} = \dfrac{?}{72} \qquad 72 \div 3 = 24$$
$$\phantom{\dfrac{1}{3} = \dfrac{?}{72} \qquad} 24 \times 1 = 24$$

$$\dfrac{1}{8} = \dfrac{?}{72} \qquad 72 \div 8 = 9$$
$$\phantom{\dfrac{1}{8} = \dfrac{?}{72} \qquad} 9 \times 1 = 9$$

We have summarized the above steps as follows:

Finding LCD for Two or More Fractions

Step 1. Copy the denominators and arrange them in a separate row.

Step 2. Divide the denominators by the smallest prime number that will divide evenly into at least two numbers.

Step 3. Continue until no prime number divides evenly into at least two numbers.

Step 4. Multiply all the numbers in divisors and last row to find the LCD.

Step 5. Raise all fractions so each has a common denominator and then complete the computation.

Adding Mixed Numbers

The following steps will show you how to add mixed numbers:

Adding Mixed Numbers

Step 1. Add the whole numbers.

Step 2. Add the fractions (remember that fractions need common denominators, as in the previous section).

Step 3. Combine the totals of Steps 1 and 2. Make sure you do not have an improper fraction in your final answer. Convert the improper fraction to a whole or mixed number. Add the whole number resulting from the improper fraction conversion to the total whole number of Step 1. If necessary, reduce the answer to lowest terms.

Using prime numbers to find LCD of example

$$
\begin{array}{r|rrr}
2 & 20 & 5 & 4 \\
2 & 10 & 5 & 2 \\
5 & 5 & 5 & 1 \\
\hline
 & 1 & 1 & 1
\end{array}
$$

$2 \times 2 \times 5 = 20 \ LCD$

EXAMPLE

$$4\frac{7}{20} \qquad 4\frac{7}{20}$$

$$6\frac{3}{5} \qquad 6\frac{12}{20}$$

$$+7\frac{1}{4} \qquad +7\frac{5}{20}$$

$$\frac{3}{5} = \frac{?}{20}$$

$$20 \div 5 = \quad 4$$
$$\times 3$$
$$12 \leftarrow$$

Step 1 $\rightarrow 17\frac{24}{20} = 17 + 1\frac{4}{20}$

Step 2 $= 18\frac{4}{20}$

Step 3 $\longrightarrow = \boxed{18\frac{1}{5}}$

Subtraction of Fractions

The subtraction of fractions is similar to the addition of fractions. This section explains how to subtract proper fractions with the same denominators and how to subtract mixed numbers.

Subtracting Proper Fractions with the Same Denominators

To subtract proper fractions with the same denominators, use the steps that follow.

Subtracting Proper Fractions with Same Denominators

Step 1. Subtract the numerators and place the answer over the common denominator.

Step 2. If necessary, reduce the answer to lowest terms.

EXAMPLE $\quad \dfrac{9}{10} - \dfrac{1}{10} = \dfrac{8 \div 2}{10 \div 2} = \boxed{\dfrac{4}{5}}$

$$\uparrow \qquad \uparrow$$
$$\text{Step 1} \qquad \text{Step 2}$$

Subtracting Proper Fractions with Different Denominators

Now let's learn the steps for subtracting proper fractions with different denominators.

> ### Subtracting Proper Fractions with Different Denominators
>
> **Step 1.** Find the LCD.
> **Step 2.** Raise the fraction to its equivalent value.
> **Step 3.** Subtract the numerators and place the answer over the LCD.
> **Step 4.** If necessary, reduce the answer to lowest terms.

EXAMPLE

$$\frac{5}{8} \qquad \frac{40}{64}$$
$$-\frac{2}{64} \qquad -\frac{2}{64}$$
$$\frac{38}{64} = \boxed{\frac{19}{32}}$$

By inspection, we see that LCD is 64. Thus $64 \div 8 = 8 \times 5 = 40$.

Subtracting Mixed Numbers

When you subtract whole numbers, sometimes borrowing is not necessary. At other times, you must borrow. The same is true of subtracting mixed numbers.

> ### Subtracting Mixed Numbers
>
> *When Borrowing Is Not Necessary*
> **Step 1.** Subtract fractions, making sure to find the LCD.
> **Step 2.** Subtract whole numbers.
> **Step 3.** Reduce the fraction(s) to lowest terms.
>
> *When Borrowing Is Necessary*
> **Step 1.** Make sure the fractions have the LCD.
> **Step 2.** Borrow from the whole number.
> **Step 3.** Subtract the whole numbers and fractions.
> **Step 4.** Reduce the fraction(s) to lowest terms.

EXAMPLE Where borrowing is not necessary:

$$6\frac{1}{2}$$
$$-\frac{3}{8}$$

Find LCD of 2 and 8. LCD is 8.

$$6\frac{4}{8}$$
$$-\frac{3}{8}$$
$$\boxed{6\frac{1}{8}}$$

EXAMPLE Where borrowing is necessary:

$$3\frac{1}{2} = \qquad 3\frac{2}{4} = \qquad 2\frac{6}{4}\left(\frac{4}{4} + \frac{2}{4}\right)$$
$$-1\frac{3}{4} = \qquad -1\frac{3}{4} = \qquad -1\frac{3}{4}$$
$$\boxed{1\frac{3}{4}}$$

LCD is 4.

Since $\frac{3}{4}$ is larger than $\frac{2}{4}$, we must borrow 1 from the 3. This is the same as borrowing $\frac{4}{4}$. A fraction with the same numerator and denominator represents a whole. When we add $\frac{4}{4} + \frac{2}{4}$, we get $\frac{6}{4}$. Note how we subtracted the whole number and fractions, being sure to reduce the final answer if necessary.

How to Dissect and Solve a Word Problem

Let's now look at how to dissect and solve a word problem involving fractions.

The Word Problem The Albertson grocery store has $550\frac{1}{4}$ total square feet of floor space. Albertson's meat department occupies $115\frac{1}{2}$ square feet, and its deli department occupies $145\frac{7}{8}$ square feet. If the remainder of the floor space is for groceries, what square footage remains for groceries?

The facts	Solving for?	Steps to take	Key points
Total square footage: $550\frac{1}{4}$ sq. ft. Meat department: $115\frac{1}{2}$ sq. ft. Deli department: $145\frac{7}{8}$ sq. ft.	Total square footage for groceries.	Total floor space − Total meat and deli floor space = Total grocery floor space.	Denominators must be the same before adding or subtracting fractions. $\frac{8}{8} = 1$ Never leave improper fraction as final answer.

Steps to solving problem

1. Calculate total square footage of the meat and deli departments.

$$\text{Meat:} \quad 115\frac{1}{2} = 115\frac{4}{8}$$

$$\text{Deli:} \quad +145\frac{7}{8} = +145\frac{7}{8}$$

$$260\frac{11}{8} = 261\frac{3}{8} \text{ sq. ft.}$$

2. Calculate total grocery square footage.

$$550\frac{1}{4} = 550\frac{2}{8} = 549\frac{10}{8}$$

$$-261\frac{3}{8} = -261\frac{3}{8} = -261\frac{3}{8}$$

$$\left(\frac{2}{8} + \frac{8}{8}\right)$$

$$288\frac{7}{8} \text{ sq. ft.}$$

Check

$$261\frac{3}{8}$$

$$+288\frac{7}{8}$$

$$549\frac{10}{8} = 550\frac{2}{8} = 550\frac{1}{4} \text{ sq. ft.}$$

Note how the above blueprint aid helped to gather the facts and identify what we were looking for. To find the total square footage for groceries, we first had to sum the areas for meat and deli. Then we could subtract these areas from the total square footage. Also note that in step 1 above, we didn't leave the answer as an improper fraction. In step 2, we borrowed from the 550 so that we could complete the subtraction.

LU 2.2 PRACTICE QUIZ

1. Find LCD by the division of prime numbers:
12, 9, 6, 4

2. Add and reduce to lowest terms if needed:

    a. $\dfrac{3}{40} + \dfrac{2}{5}$ **b.** $2\dfrac{3}{4} + 6\dfrac{1}{20}$

3. Subtract and reduce to lowest terms if needed:

    a. $\dfrac{6}{7} - \dfrac{1}{4}$ **b.** $8\dfrac{1}{4} - 3\dfrac{9}{28}$ **c.** $4 - 1\dfrac{3}{4}$

4. Computerland has $660\frac{1}{4}$ total square feet of floor space. Three departments occupy this floor space: hardware, $201\frac{1}{8}$ square feet; software, $242\frac{1}{4}$ square feet; and customer service, _____ square feet. What is the total square footage of the customer service area? You might want to try a blueprint aid, since the solution will show a completed blueprint aid.

✓   **Solutions**

1.

2	/	12	9	6	4
2	/	6	9	3	2
3	/	3	9	3	1
		1	3	1	1

$\text{LCD} = 2 \times 2 \times 3 \times 1 \times 3 \times 1 \times 1 = \boxed{36}$

2. a. $\dfrac{3}{40} + \dfrac{2}{5} = \dfrac{3}{40} + \dfrac{16}{40} = \boxed{\dfrac{19}{40}}$

$\left(\dfrac{2}{5} = \dfrac{?}{40} \atop 40 \div 5 = 8 \times 2 = 16 \right)$

b.

$\begin{array}{r} 2\dfrac{3}{4} \\ +6\dfrac{1}{20} \\ \hline \end{array}$
$\qquad$
$\begin{array}{r} 2\dfrac{15}{20} \\ +6\dfrac{1}{20} \\ \hline 8\dfrac{16}{20} = 8\boxed{\dfrac{4}{5}} \end{array}$
$\qquad$
$\dfrac{3}{4} = \dfrac{?}{20}$

$20 \div 4 = 5 \times 3 = 15$

3. a.

$\begin{array}{r} \dfrac{6}{7} = \dfrac{24}{28} \\ -\dfrac{1}{4} = -\dfrac{7}{28} \\ \hline \boxed{\dfrac{17}{28}} \end{array}$

b.

$\begin{array}{r} 8\dfrac{1}{4} = \quad 8\dfrac{7}{28} = \quad 7\dfrac{35}{28} \\ -3\dfrac{9}{28} = -3\dfrac{9}{28} \quad -3\dfrac{9}{28} \\ \hline 4\dfrac{26}{28} = 4\boxed{\dfrac{13}{14}} \end{array}$
$\quad \leftarrow \left(\dfrac{28}{28} + \dfrac{7}{28} \right)$

c.

$\begin{array}{r} 3\dfrac{4}{4} \\ -1\dfrac{3}{4} \\ \hline \boxed{2\dfrac{1}{4}} \end{array}$
$\qquad$ Note how we showed the 4 as $3\dfrac{4}{4}$.

4. Computerland's total square footage for customer service:

The facts	Solving for?	Steps to take	Key points
Total square footage: $660\dfrac{1}{4}$ sq. ft. Hardware: $201\dfrac{1}{8}$ sq. ft. Software: $242\dfrac{1}{4}$ sq. ft.	Total square footage for customer service.	Total floor space − Total hardware and software floor space = Total customer service floor space.	Denominators must be the same before adding or subtracting fractions.

Steps to solving problem

1. Calculate the total square footage of hardware and software.

$\begin{array}{r} 201\dfrac{1}{8} = \quad 201\dfrac{1}{8} \text{ (hardware)} \\ +242\dfrac{1}{4} = +242\dfrac{2}{8} \text{ (software)} \\ \hline 443\dfrac{3}{8} \end{array}$

2. Calculate the total square footage for customer service.

$\begin{array}{r} 660\dfrac{1}{4} = \quad 660\dfrac{2}{8} = \quad 659\dfrac{10}{8} \text{ (total square footage)} \\ -443\dfrac{3}{8} = -443\dfrac{3}{8} = -443\dfrac{3}{8} \text{ (hardware plus software)} \\ \hline \boxed{216\dfrac{7}{8}} \text{ sq. ft. (customer service)} \end{array}$

LEARNING UNIT 2.3   Multiplying and Dividing Fractions

© Procter & Gamble. Used by permission.

P&G's Joy

By Norihiko Shirouzu

Staff Reporter of The Wall Street Journal

KOBE, Japan—Anyone who thinks Japan doesn't offer opportunities for U.S. consumer products should look at how quickly **Procter & Gamble Co.** has cleaned up in the country's dish-soap market.

Until 1995, P&G didn't sell dish soap in Japan at all. Now it has Japan's best-selling brand, Joy, which commands a fifth of

MARKETING

the nation's $400 million dish-soap market. That's astounding progress, given that the market had appeared to be classically "mature"—both shrinking and dominated by giant Japanese companies.

© 1997 Dow Jones & Company, Inc.

If you visit Japan, you will probably see a familiar dish soap in many Japanese homes—Joy by Procter & Gamble Co. *The Wall Street Journal* clipping "P&G's Joy" states that Joy now commands one-fifth of Japan's $400 million dish soap market. How much is this? One-fifth of $400 million means $\frac{1}{5}$ times $400 million:

$$\frac{1}{5} \times \$400,000,000 = \$80,000,000$$

In this unit you learn how to multiply and divide fractions.

Multiplication of Fractions

Multiplying fractions is easier than adding and subtracting fractions because you do not have to find a common denominator. This section explains the multiplication of proper fractions and the multiplication of mixed numbers.

Multiplying Proper Fractions[3]

Step 1. Multiply the numerators and the denominators.
Step 2. Reduce the answer to lowest terms or use the cancellation method.

First let's look at an example that results in an answer that we do not have to reduce.

EXAMPLE $\frac{1}{7} \times \frac{5}{8} = \boxed{\frac{5}{56}}$

In the next example, note how we reduce the answer to lowest terms.

EXAMPLE $\frac{5}{1} \times \frac{1}{6} \times \frac{4}{7} = \frac{20}{42} = \boxed{\frac{10}{21}}$ Keep in mind $\frac{5}{1}$ is equal to 5.

We can reduce $\frac{20}{42}$ by the step approach as follows:

$$\begin{array}{r} 2 \\ 20\overline{)42} \\ 40 \\ \hline 2 \end{array} \qquad \begin{array}{r} 10 \\ 2\overline{)20} \\ 20 \\ \hline 0 \end{array}$$

We could also have found the greatest common divisor by inspection.

$$\frac{20 \div 2}{42 \div 2} = \boxed{\frac{10}{21}}$$

As an alternative to reducing fractions to lowest terms, we can use the **cancellation** technique. Let's work the previous example using this technique.

---

[3]You would follow the same procedure to multiply improper fractions.

EXAMPLE $\dfrac{5}{1} \times \dfrac{1}{\cancel{6}_{3}} \times \dfrac{\cancel{4}^{2}}{7} = \boxed{\dfrac{10}{21}}$ 2 divides evenly into 4 twice and into 6 three times.

Note that when we cancel numbers, we are reducing the answer before multiplying. We know that multiplying or dividing both numerator and denominator by the same number gives an equivalent fraction. So we can divide both numerator and denominator by any number that divides them both evenly. It doesn't matter which we divide first. Note that this division reduces $\frac{10}{21}$ to its lowest terms.

Multiplying Mixed Numbers

The following steps explain how to multiply mixed numbers:

Multiplying Mixed Numbers

Step 1. Convert the mixed numbers to improper fractions.
Step 2. Multiply the numerators and denominators.
Step 3. Reduce the answer to lowest terms or use the cancellation method.

EXAMPLE $2\dfrac{1}{3} \times 1\dfrac{1}{2} = \dfrac{7}{\cancel{3}_{1}} \times \dfrac{\cancel{3}^{1}}{2} = \dfrac{7}{2} = \boxed{3\dfrac{1}{2}}$

$\nearrow$ $\uparrow$ $\uparrow$

Step 1   **Step 2**   **Step 3**

Division of Fractions

When you studied whole numbers in Chapter 1, you saw how multiplication can be checked by division. The multiplication of fractions can also be checked by division, as you will see in this section on dividing proper fractions and mixed numbers.

Dividing Proper Fractions

The division of proper fractions introduces a new term—the **reciprocal.** To use reciprocals, we must first recognize which fraction in the problem is the divisor—the fraction that we divide by. Let's assume the problem we are to solve is $\frac{1}{8} \div \frac{2}{3}$. We read this problem as "$\frac{1}{8}$ divided by $\frac{2}{3}$." The divisor is the fraction after the division sign (or the second fraction). The steps that follow show how the divisor becomes a reciprocal.

Dividing Proper Fractions

Step 1. Invert (turn upside down) the divisor (the second fraction). The inverted number is the *reciprocal.*
Step 2. Multiply the fractions.
Step 3. Reduce the answer to lowest terms, or use the cancellation method.

Do you know why the inverted fraction number is a reciprocal? Reciprocals are two numbers that when multiplied give a product of 1. For example, 2 (which is the same as $\frac{2}{1}$) and $\frac{1}{2}$ are reciprocals because multiplying them gives 1.

EXAMPLE $\dfrac{1}{8} \div \dfrac{2}{3}$ $\dfrac{1}{8} \times \dfrac{3}{2} = \boxed{\dfrac{3}{16}}$

Dividing Mixed Numbers

Now you are ready to divide mixed numbers by using improper fractions.

Dividing Mixed Numbers

Step 1. Convert all mixed numbers to improper fractions.
Step 2. Invert the divisor (take its reciprocal) and multiply. If your final answer is an improper fraction, reduce it to lowest terms. You can do this by finding the greatest common divisor or by using the cancellation technique.

EXAMPLE $8\dfrac{3}{4} \div 2\dfrac{5}{6}$

Step 1. $\dfrac{35}{4} \div \dfrac{17}{6}$

Step 2. $\dfrac{35}{\overset{}{\underset{2}{4}}} \times \dfrac{\overset{3}{6}}{17} = \dfrac{105}{34} = 3\dfrac{3}{34}$ Here we used the cancellation technique.

How to Dissect and Solve a Word Problem

The Word Problem   Jamie Slater ordered $5\frac{1}{2}$ cords of oak. The cost of each cord is $150. He also ordered $2\frac{1}{4}$ cords of maple at $120 per cord. Jamie's neighbor, Al, said that he would share the wood and pay him $\frac{1}{5}$ of the total cost. How much did Jamie receive from Al?

Note how we filled in the blueprint aid columns. We first had to find the total cost of all the wood before we could find Al's share—$\frac{1}{5}$ of the total cost.

The facts	Solving for?	Steps to take	Key points
Cords ordered: $5\frac{1}{2}$ at $150 per cord; $2\frac{1}{4}$ at $120 per cord. Al's cost share: $\frac{1}{5}$ the total cost.	What will Al pay Jamie?	Total cost of wood × $\frac{1}{5}$ = Al's cost.	Convert mixed numbers to improper fractions when multiplying. Cancellation is an alternative to reducing fractions.

Steps to solving problem

1. Calculate the cost of oak. $5\dfrac{1}{2} \times \$150 = \dfrac{11}{2} \times \overset{\$75}{\underset{1}{\$150}} = \$825$

2. Calculate the cost of maple. $2\dfrac{1}{4} \times \$120 = \dfrac{9}{\underset{1}{4}} \times \overset{\$30}{\$120} = +270$

$\overline{\qquad}$
$\$1,095$ (total cost of wood)

3. What Al pays. $\dfrac{1}{\underset{1}{5}} \times \overset{\$219}{\$1,095} = \boxed{\$219}$

LU 2.3 PRACTICE QUIZ

1. Multiply (use cancellation technique):

   a. $\dfrac{4}{8} \times \dfrac{4}{6}$ b. $35 \times \dfrac{4}{7}$

2. Multiply (do not use canceling; reduce by finding the greatest common divisor):

   $\dfrac{14}{15} \times \dfrac{7}{10}$

3. Complete the following. Reduce to lowest terms as needed.

   a. $\dfrac{1}{9} \div \dfrac{5}{6}$ b. $\dfrac{51}{5} \div \dfrac{5}{9}$

4. Jill Estes bought a mobile home that was $8\frac{1}{8}$ times as expensive as the home her brother bought. Jill's brother paid $16,000 for his mobile home. What is the cost of Jill's new home?

✓ **Solutions**

1. a. $\dfrac{\overset{1}{\underset{2}{\overset{2}{4}}}}{\underset{2}{8}} \times \dfrac{\overset{1}{4}}{\underset{3}{6}} = \boxed{\dfrac{1}{3}}$ b. $\overset{5}{35} \times \dfrac{4}{\underset{1}{7}} = \boxed{20}$

2. $\dfrac{14}{15} \times \dfrac{7}{10} = \dfrac{98 \div 2}{150 \div 2} = \boxed{\dfrac{49}{75}}$

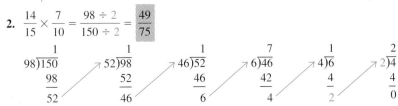

3. a. $\dfrac{1}{9} \times \dfrac{6}{5} = \dfrac{6 \div 3}{45 \div 3} = \boxed{\dfrac{2}{15}}$ **b.** $\dfrac{51}{5} \times \dfrac{9}{5} = \dfrac{459}{25} = \boxed{18\dfrac{9}{25}}$

4. Total cost of Jill's new home:

The facts	Solving for?	Steps to take	Key points
Jill's mobile home: $8\frac{1}{8}$ as expensive as her brother's. *Brother paid:* $16,000.	Total cost of Jill's new home.	$8\frac{1}{8} \times$ Total cost of Jill's brother's mobile home = Total cost of Jill's new home.	Canceling is an alternative to reducing.

Steps to solving problem

1. Convert $8\frac{1}{8}$ to a mixed number. $\dfrac{65}{8}$

2. Calculate the total cost of Jill's home. $\dfrac{65}{\cancel{8}_{1}} \times \cancel{\$16,000}^{\,\$2,000} = \boxed{\$130,000}$

Chapter Organizer and Reference Guide

Topic	Key point, procedure, formula	Example(s) to illustrate situations
Types of fractions, p. 34	*Proper:* Value less than 1; numerator smaller than denominator. *Improper:* Value equal to or greater than 1; numerator equal to or greater than denominator. *Mixed:* Sum of whole number greater than zero and a proper fraction.	$\dfrac{3}{5}, \dfrac{7}{9}, \dfrac{8}{15}$ $\dfrac{14}{14}, \dfrac{19}{18}$ $6\dfrac{3}{8}, 9\dfrac{8}{9}$
Fraction conversions, p. 35	*Improper to whole or mixed:* Divide numerator by denominator; place remainder over *old* denominator. *Mixed to improper:* $\dfrac{\text{Whole number} \times \text{Denominator} + \text{Numerator}}{\text{Old denominator}}$	$\dfrac{17}{4} = \boxed{4\dfrac{1}{4}}$ $4\dfrac{1}{8} = \dfrac{32 + 1}{8} = \boxed{\dfrac{33}{8}}$
Reducing fractions to lowest terms, p. 36	1. Divide numerator and denominator by largest possible divisor (does not change fraction value). 2. When reduced to lowest terms, no number (except 1) will divide evenly into both numerator and denominator.	$\dfrac{18 \div 2}{46 \div 2} = \boxed{\dfrac{9}{23}}$
Step approach for finding greatest common denominator, p. 36	1. Divide smaller number of fraction into larger number. 2. Divide remainder into divisor of Step 1. Continue this process until no remainder results. 3. The last divisor used is the greatest common divisor.	$\dfrac{15}{65} \longrightarrow \begin{array}{r} 4 \\ 15\overline{)65} \\ 60 \\ \hline 5 \end{array} \qquad \begin{array}{r} 3 \\ 5\overline{)15} \\ 15 \\ \hline 0 \end{array}$ $\boxed{5}$ is greatest common divisor.
Raising fractions to higher terms, p. 37	Multiply numerator and denominator by same number. Does not change fraction value.	$\dfrac{15}{41} = \dfrac{?}{410}$ $410 \div 41 = 10 \times 15 = \boxed{150}$
Adding and subtracting proper fractions, p. 39	When denominators are the same (like fractions), add (or subtract) numerators, place total over original denominator, and reduce to lowest terms. When denominators are different (unlike fractions), change them to like fractions by finding LCD using inspection or prime numbers. Then add (or subtract) the numerators, place total over LCD, and reduce to lowest terms.	$\dfrac{4}{9} + \dfrac{1}{9} = \boxed{\dfrac{5}{9}}$ $\dfrac{4}{9} - \dfrac{1}{9} = \dfrac{3}{9} = \boxed{\dfrac{1}{3}}$ $\dfrac{4}{5} + \dfrac{2}{7} = \dfrac{28}{35} + \dfrac{10}{35} = \dfrac{38}{35} = \boxed{1\dfrac{3}{35}}$

Chapter Organizer and Reference Guide (concluded)		
Topic	**Key point, procedure, formula**	**Example(s) to illustrate situations**
Prime numbers, p. 40	Whole numbers larger than 1 that are only divisible by itself and 1.	2, 3, 5, 7, 11
LCD by prime numbers, p. 40	1. Copy denominators and arrange them in a separate row. 2. Divide denominators by smallest prime number that will divide evenly into at least two numbers. 3. Continue until no prime number divides evenly into at least two numbers. 4. Multiply all the numbers in the divisors and last row to find LCD. 5. Raise fractions so each has a common denominator and complete computation.	$\frac{1}{3} + \frac{1}{6} + \frac{1}{8} + \frac{1}{12} + \frac{1}{9}$ $2\,/\,\begin{array}{ccccc}3 & 6 & 8 & 12 & 9\end{array}$ $2\,/\,\begin{array}{ccccc}3 & 3 & 4 & 6 & 9\end{array}$ $3\,/\,\begin{array}{ccccc}3 & 3 & 2 & 3 & 9\end{array}$ $\begin{array}{ccccc}1 & 1 & 2 & 1 & 3\end{array}$ $2 \times 2 \times 3 \times 1 \times 1 \times 2 \times 1 \times 3 = \boxed{72}$
Adding mixed numbers, p. 40	1. Add whole numbers. 2. Add fractions. 3. Combine totals of Steps 1 and 2. If denominators are different, a common denominator must be found. Answer cannot be left as improper fraction.	$1\frac{4}{7} + 1\frac{3}{7}$ Step 1: $1 + 1 = 2$ Step 2: $\frac{4}{7} + \frac{3}{7} = \frac{7}{7}$ Step 3: $2\frac{7}{7} = \boxed{3}$
Subtracting mixed numbers, p. 42	1. Subtract fractions. 2. If necessary, borrow from whole numbers. 3. Subtract whole numbers and fractions if borrowing was necessary. 4. Reduce fractions to lowest terms. If denominators are different, a common denominator must be found.	$12\frac{2}{5} - 7\frac{3}{5}$ $11\frac{7}{5} - 7\frac{3}{5}$ $= 4\frac{4}{5}$ Due to borrowing $\frac{5}{5}$ from number 12 $\frac{5}{5} + \frac{2}{5} = \frac{7}{5}$ The whole number is now 11.
Multiplying proper fractions, p. 45	1. Multiply numerators and denominators. 2. Reduce answer to lowest terms or use cancellation method.	$\frac{4}{7} \times \frac{\overset{1}{7}}{9} = \boxed{\frac{4}{9}}$
Multiplying mixed numbers, p. 46	1. Convert mixed numbers to improper fractions. 2. Multiply numerators and denominators. 3. Reduce answer to lowest terms or use cancellation method.	$1\frac{1}{8} \times 2\frac{5}{8}$ $\frac{9}{8} \times \frac{21}{8} = \frac{189}{64} = \boxed{2\frac{61}{64}}$
Dividing proper fractions, p. 46	1. Invert divisor. 2. Multiply. 3. Reduce answer to lowest terms or use cancellation method.	$\frac{1}{4} \div \frac{1}{8} = \frac{1}{\underset{1}{4}} \times \frac{\overset{2}{8}}{1} = \boxed{2}$
Dividing mixed numbers, p. 46	1. Convert mixed numbers to improper fractions. 2. Invert divisor and multiply. If final answer is an improper fraction, reduce to lowest terms by finding greatest common divisor or using the cancellation method.	$1\frac{1}{2} \div 1\frac{5}{8} = \frac{3}{2} \div \frac{13}{8}$ $= \frac{3}{2} \times \frac{\overset{4}{8}}{13}$ $= \boxed{\frac{12}{13}}$
Key terms	Cancellation, *p. 45* Common denominator, *p. 39* Denominator, *p. 34* Equivalent, *p. 37* Fraction, *p. 34* Greatest common divisor, *p. 36*	Higher terms, *p. 37* Improper fraction, *p. 35* Least common denominator (LCD), *p. 39* Like fractions, *p. 39* Lowest terms, *p. 36*

Mixed numbers, *p. 35*
Numerator, *p. 34*
Prime numbers, *p. 40*
Proper fractions, *p. 35*
Reciprocal, *p. 46*
Unlike fractions, *p. 39*

Note: For how to dissect and solve a word problem, see page 47.

**Critical Thinking
Discussion Questions**

1. What are the steps to convert improper fractions to whole or mixed numbers? Give an example of how you could use this conversion procedure when you eat at Pizza Hut.

2. What are the steps to convert mixed numbers to improper fractions? Show how you could use this conversion procedure when you order doughnuts at Dunkin Donuts.

3. What is the greatest common divisor? How could you use the greatest common divisor to write an advertisement showing that 35 out of 60 people prefer MCI to AT&T?

4. Explain the step approach for finding the greatest common divisor. How could you use the MCI–AT&T example in Question 3 to illustrate the step approach?

5. Explain the steps of adding or subtracting fractions with different denominators. Using a ruler, measure the heights of two different-size cans of food and show how to calculate the difference in height.

6. What is a prime number? Using the two cans in Question 5, show how you could use prime numbers to calculate the LCD.

7. Explain the steps for multiplying proper fractions and mixed numbers. Assume you went to Staples (a stationery superstore). Give an example showing the multiplying of proper fractions and mixed numbers.

DRILL PROBLEMS

Identify the following types of fractions:

2–1. $\dfrac{1}{16}$ Proper

2–2. $11\dfrac{4}{9}$ Mixed

2–3. $\dfrac{14}{11}$ Improper

Convert the following to mixed numbers:

2–4. $\dfrac{49}{9} = 5\dfrac{4}{9}$

2–5. $\dfrac{921}{15} = 61\dfrac{6}{15} = 61\dfrac{2}{5}$

Convert the following to improper fractions:

2–6. $7\dfrac{5}{7} = \dfrac{54}{7}$

2–7. $19\dfrac{2}{3} = \dfrac{59}{3}$

Reduce the following to the lowest terms. Show how to calculate the greatest common divisor by the step approach.

2–8. $\dfrac{16}{38} = \dfrac{16 \div 2}{38 \div 2} = \dfrac{8}{19}$

$$16\overline{)38} \nearrow \quad 6\overline{)16} \nearrow \quad 4\overline{)6} \nearrow \quad 2\overline{)4}$$

with results 2, 32, 6 ; 2, 12, 4 ; 1, 4, 2 ; 2, 4, 0

2–9. $\dfrac{44}{52} = \dfrac{44 \div 4}{52 \div 4} = \dfrac{11}{13}$

$$44\overline{)52} \nearrow \quad 8\overline{)44} \nearrow \quad 4\overline{)8}$$

with results 1, 44, 8 ; 5, 40, 4 ; 2, 8, 0

Convert the following to higher terms:

2–10. $\dfrac{6}{7} = \dfrac{60}{70}$ $70 \div 7 = 10 \times 6 = 60$

Determine the LCD of the following **(a)** by inspection and **(b)** by division of prime numbers:

2–11. $\dfrac{3}{4}, \dfrac{7}{12}, \dfrac{5}{6}, \dfrac{1}{5}$

Inspection 60
$2 \times 2 \times 3 \times 5 = 60$

Check

2	4	12	6	5
2	2	6	3	5
3	1	3	3	5
	1	1	1	5

2–12. $\dfrac{5}{6}, \dfrac{7}{18}, \dfrac{5}{9}, \dfrac{2}{72}$

Inspection 72
$2 \times 3 \times 3 \times 4 = 72$

Check

2	6	18	9	72
3	3	9	9	36
3	1	3	3	12
	1	1	1	4

2–13. $\dfrac{1}{4}, \dfrac{3}{32}, \dfrac{5}{48}, \dfrac{1}{8}$

Inspection 96
$2 \times 2 \times 2 \times 2 \times 2 \times 3 = 96$

Check

2	4	32	48	8
2	2	16	24	4
2	1	8	12	2
2	1	4	6	1
	1	2	3	1

Add the following and reduce to lowest terms:

2–14. $\dfrac{4}{8} + \dfrac{2}{8} = \dfrac{6}{8} = \dfrac{3}{4}$

2–15. $\dfrac{3}{7} + \dfrac{4}{21} = \dfrac{9}{21} + \dfrac{4}{21} = \dfrac{13}{21}$

2–16. $6\dfrac{1}{8} + 4\dfrac{3}{8} = 10\dfrac{4}{8} = 10\dfrac{1}{2}$

2–17. $6\dfrac{3}{8} + 9\dfrac{1}{24} = 6\dfrac{9}{24} + 9\dfrac{1}{24} = 15\dfrac{10}{24} = 15\dfrac{5}{12}$

2–18. $9\dfrac{9}{10} + 6\dfrac{7}{10} = 15\dfrac{16}{10} = 16\dfrac{6}{10} = 16\dfrac{3}{5}$

Subtract the following and reduce to lowest terms:

2–19. $\dfrac{7}{8} - \dfrac{1}{8} = \dfrac{6}{8} = \dfrac{3}{4}$

2–20. $14\dfrac{3}{8} - 10\dfrac{5}{8}$

$$13\dfrac{11}{8}$$
$$-10\dfrac{5}{8}$$
$$\overline{3\dfrac{6}{8} = 3\dfrac{3}{4}}$$

2–21. $12\dfrac{1}{9} - 4\dfrac{2}{3}$

$$12\dfrac{1}{9} = 11\dfrac{10}{9} \left(\dfrac{9}{9} + \dfrac{1}{9}\right)$$
$$-4\dfrac{6}{9} = -4\dfrac{6}{9}$$
$$\overline{7\dfrac{4}{9}}$$

Multiply the following and reduce to lowest terms. Do not use the cancellation technique for these problems.

2–22. $19 \times \dfrac{6}{2} = \dfrac{114}{2} = 57$

2–23. $\dfrac{5}{6} \times \dfrac{3}{8} = \dfrac{15}{48} = \dfrac{5}{16}$

2–24. $8\dfrac{7}{8} \times 64 = \dfrac{71}{8} \times \dfrac{64}{1} = \dfrac{4{,}544}{8} = 568$

Multiply the following. Use the cancellation technique.

2–25. $\dfrac{4}{10} \times \dfrac{30}{60} \times \dfrac{6}{10} = \dfrac{\overset{2}{\cancel{4}}}{\underset{5}{\cancel{10}}} \times \dfrac{\overset{3}{\cancel{30}}}{\underset{\underset{5}{10}}{\cancel{60}}} \times \dfrac{\overset{1}{\cancel{6}}}{\underset{1}{\cancel{10}}} = \dfrac{3}{25}$

2–26. $3\dfrac{3}{4} \times \dfrac{8}{9} \times 4\dfrac{9}{12} = \dfrac{\overset{5}{\cancel{15}}}{\underset{1}{\cancel{4}}} \times \dfrac{\overset{2}{\cancel{8}}}{\underset{3}{\cancel{9}}} \times \dfrac{\overset{\overset{19}{\cancel{57}}}{}}{\underset{\underset{1}{6}}{\cancel{12}}} = \dfrac{95}{6} = 15\dfrac{5}{6}$

Divide the following and reduce to lowest terms. Use the cancellation technique as needed.

2–27. $\dfrac{12}{9} \div 4 = \dfrac{\overset{\overset{1}{\cancel{3}}}{\cancel{12}}}{\underset{3}{\cancel{9}}} \times \dfrac{1}{\underset{1}{\cancel{4}}} = \dfrac{1}{3}$

2–28. $16 \div \dfrac{1}{4} = 16 \times \dfrac{4}{1} = 64$

2–29. $4\dfrac{2}{3} \div 12 = \dfrac{\overset{7}{\cancel{14}}}{3} \times \dfrac{1}{\underset{6}{\cancel{12}}} = \dfrac{7}{18}$

2–30. $3\dfrac{5}{6} \div 3\dfrac{1}{2} = \dfrac{23}{\underset{3}{\cancel{6}}} \times \dfrac{\overset{1}{\cancel{2}}}{7} = \dfrac{23}{21} = 1\dfrac{2}{21}$

WORD PROBLEMS

2–31. On January 22, 1998, the Chicago *Sun-Times* reported that McDonald's Corporation said that about 100 of its expected 300 new U.S. restaurants this year will be built at gas stations. The burger giant seeks cheaper ways to expand in a competitive market. What fraction will be conventional restaurants? Reduce to lowest terms.

$\begin{array}{r} 300 \\ -\ 100 \text{ gas station} \\ \hline 200 \text{ conventional} \end{array}$ $\dfrac{200 \div (100)}{300 \div (100)} = \dfrac{2}{3}$

2–32. The stock of AT&T reached a high of $\$36\dfrac{5}{16}$ per share on Wednesday. At the end of the day, it dropped to $\$35\dfrac{1}{16}$ per share. How much did the stock drop from its high? Reduce to lowest terms.

$\begin{array}{r} \$36\dfrac{5}{16} \\ -35\dfrac{1}{16} \\ \hline \$1\dfrac{4}{16} = \$1\dfrac{1}{4} \end{array}$

2–33. U.S. Airways pays Paul Lose $125 per day to work in security at the airport. Paul became ill on Monday and went home after $\dfrac{1}{5}$ of a day. What did he earn on Monday? Assume no work, no pay.

$\dfrac{1}{5} \times \$125 = \dfrac{\$125}{5} = \$25$

2–34. Brian Summers visited Gold's Gym and lost $2\dfrac{1}{4}$ pounds in week 1, $1\dfrac{3}{4}$ pounds in week 2, and $\dfrac{5}{8}$ pound in week 3. What is the total weight loss for Brian?

$2\dfrac{2}{8} + 1\dfrac{6}{8} + \dfrac{5}{8} = 3\dfrac{13}{8} = 4\dfrac{5}{8}$ pounds

2–35. Ray Miller, who works at Fidelity Investments, received a check for $1,400. He deposited $\dfrac{1}{7}$ of the check in his Citibank account. How much money does Ray have left after the deposit?

$\dfrac{6}{\underset{1}{\cancel{7}}} \times \overset{\$200}{\cancel{\$1{,}400}} = \$1{,}200$

2–36. Lois Milligan worked the following hours as an operator for MCI: $11\dfrac{1}{4}, 5\dfrac{1}{4}, 8\dfrac{1}{2}, 7\dfrac{1}{4}$. How many total hours did Lois work?

$11\dfrac{1}{4} + 5\dfrac{1}{4} + 8\dfrac{2}{4} + 7\dfrac{1}{4} = 31\dfrac{5}{4} = 32\dfrac{1}{4}$ hours

2–37. On January 11, 1998, the *Chicago Tribune* featured an article on the new 1998 Mitsubishi Montero. The EPA mileage in the city was given as 16 miles per gallon. If the tank has a capacity of $19\frac{3}{4}$ gallons, what is the maximum city miles you would be able to travel before the tank would be empty?

$$16 \times 19\frac{3}{4} = \frac{\overset{4}{\cancel{16}}}{1} \times \frac{79}{\cancel{4}} = 316 \text{ miles}$$

2–38. Lester bought a piece of property in Vail, Colorado. The sides of the land measure $115\frac{1}{2}$ feet, $66\frac{1}{4}$ feet, $106\frac{1}{8}$ feet, and $110\frac{1}{4}$ feet. Lester wants to know the perimeter (sum of all sides) of his property. Can you calculate the perimeter for Lester?

$$115\frac{4}{8} + 66\frac{2}{8} + 106\frac{1}{8} + 110\frac{2}{8} = 397\frac{9}{8} = 398\frac{1}{8} \text{ feet}$$

2–39. On January 18, 1998, Menards Lumber Company advertised in the *Chicago Tribune* a sale on rope lighting. You ordered a piece of rope lighting that was 87 inches long and must cut it into $10\frac{7}{8}$-inch sections. How many sections of rope lighting will you have?

$$87 \div 10\frac{7}{8} = \frac{87}{1} \div \frac{87}{8} = \frac{\overset{1}{\cancel{87}}}{1} \times \frac{8}{\underset{1}{\cancel{87}}} = 8$$

2–40. From Home Depot, Pete Wong ordered $\frac{6}{7}$ of a ton of crushed rock to make a patio. If Pete used only $\frac{3}{4}$ of the rock, how much crushed rock remains unused?

$$\frac{1}{4} \times \frac{6}{7} = \frac{6}{28} = \frac{3}{14} \text{ of a ton}$$

2–41. A Coke dispenser held $19\frac{1}{4}$ gallons of soda. During working hours, $12\frac{3}{4}$ gallons were dispensed. How many gallons of Coke remain?

$$\begin{array}{cc} 19\frac{1}{4} & 18\frac{5}{4} \leftarrow \left(\frac{4}{4} + \frac{1}{4}\right) \\ -12\frac{3}{4} & -12\frac{3}{4} \\ \hline & 6\frac{2}{4} = 6\frac{1}{2} \text{ gallons} \end{array}$$

2–42. Katie Kaminski bought a home from Century 21 in San Antonio, Texas, that is $7\frac{1}{2}$ times as expensive as the home her parents bought. Katie's parents paid $16,000 for their home. What is the cost of Katie's new home?

$$\frac{15}{2} \times \$16,000 = \$120,000$$

2–43. Ajax Company charges $150 per cord of wood. If Bill Ryan orders $3\frac{1}{2}$ cords, what will his total cost be?

$$\$150 \times 3\frac{1}{2} = \overset{\$75}{\cancel{\$150}} \times \frac{7}{\underset{1}{\cancel{2}}} = \$525$$

2–44. Bill bought 30 pizzas at Pizza Hut for his son's birthday party. Each guest ate $\frac{1}{3}$ of a pizza. How many guests did Bill have at his son's party?

$$30 \div \frac{1}{3} = 30 \times 3 = 90 \text{ guests}$$

2–45. Marc, Steven, and Daniel entered into a partnership. Marc owns $\frac{1}{9}$ of the company, and Steven owns $\frac{1}{4}$. What part does Daniel own?

$$\frac{4}{36} + \frac{9}{36} = \frac{13}{36} \qquad\qquad 1 - \frac{13}{36} = \frac{23}{36} \text{ for Daniel or } \frac{36}{36} - \frac{13}{36} = \frac{23}{36}$$

2–46. Lionel Sullivan works for Burger King. He is paid time and one-half for Sundays. If Lionel works on Sunday for 6 hours at a regular pay of $8 per hour, what does he earn on Sunday?

$$1\frac{1}{2} \times \$8 = \frac{3}{2} \times \$8 = \$12 \qquad\qquad \$12 \times 6 = \$72$$

2–47. Hertz pays Al Davis, an employee, \$125 per day. Al decided to donate $\frac{1}{5}$ of a day's pay to his church. How much will Al donate?

$$\frac{1}{5} \times \$125 = \$25$$

2–48. A trip to New Hampshire from Boston will take you $2\frac{3}{4}$ hours. Assume you have traveled $\frac{1}{11}$ of the way. How much longer will the trip take?

$$\overset{5}{\underset{1}{\cancel{10}}} \times \overset{1}{\underset{2}{\cancel{11}}} = \frac{5}{2} = 2\frac{1}{2} \text{ hours}$$

2–49. Michael, who loves to cook, makes an apple pie (serves 6) for his family. The recipe calls for $1\frac{1}{2}$ pounds of apples, $3\frac{1}{4}$ cups of flour, $\frac{1}{4}$ cup of margarine, $2\frac{3}{8}$ cups of sugar, and 2 teaspoons of cinnamon. Since guests are coming, Michael wants to make a pie that will serve 15 (or increase the recipe $2\frac{1}{2}$ times). How much of each ingredient should Michael use?

$$\frac{3}{2} \times \frac{5}{2} = \frac{15}{4} = 3\frac{3}{4} \text{ pounds of apples}$$ $$\frac{19}{8} \times \frac{5}{2} = \frac{95}{16} = 5\frac{15}{16} \text{ cups of sugar}$$

$$\frac{13}{4} \times \frac{5}{2} = \frac{65}{8} = 8\frac{1}{8} \text{ cups of flour}$$ $$2 \times \frac{5}{2} = 5 \text{ teaspoons of cinnamon}$$

$$\frac{1}{4} \times \frac{5}{2} = \frac{5}{8} \text{ cup of margarine}$$

2–50. Mobil allocates $1,692\frac{3}{4}$ gallons of gas per month to Jerry's Service Station. The first week, Jerry sold $275\frac{1}{2}$ gallons; second week, $280\frac{1}{4}$ gallons; and third week, $189\frac{1}{8}$ gallons. If Jerry sells $582\frac{1}{2}$ gallons in the fourth week, how close is Jerry to selling his allocation?

$$275\frac{4}{8}$$ $$1,692\frac{6}{8}$$
$$280\frac{2}{8}$$ $$-1,327\frac{3}{8}$$
$$189\frac{1}{8}$$ $$\overline{365\frac{3}{8} \text{ gallons}}$$
$$+\ 582\frac{4}{8}$$
$$\overline{1,326\frac{11}{8} = 1,327\frac{3}{8} \text{ gallons}}$$

2–51. A retail sales class conducted a watch preference survey. The survey showed that $\frac{5}{6}$ of the people surveyed preferred digital watches over traditional styles. Assume 1,800 responded to the survey. How many favored using traditional watches?

$$\frac{1}{\cancel{6}} \times \underset{1}{\overset{300}{\cancel{1,800}}} = 300 \text{ people}$$

2–52. The price of a new Ford Explorer has increased to $1\frac{1}{4}$ times its earlier price. If the original price of the Ford Explorer was \$28,000, what is the new price?

$$1\frac{1}{4} \times \$28,000 = \frac{5}{4} \times \$28,000 = \$35,000$$

2–53. Chris Rong felled a tree that was 299 feet long. Chris decided to cut the tree into pieces $3\frac{1}{4}$ feet long. How many pieces can Chris cut from this tree?

$$299 \div 3\frac{1}{4} = \overset{23}{\cancel{299}} \times \frac{4}{\underset{1}{\cancel{13}}} = 92 \text{ pieces}$$

2–54. Tempco Corporation has a machine that produces $12\frac{1}{2}$ baseball gloves each hour. In the last 2 days, the machine has run for a total of 22 hours. How many baseball gloves has Tempco produced?

$$22 \times 12\frac{1}{2} = \overset{11}{\cancel{22}} \times \frac{25}{\underset{1}{\cancel{2}}} = 275 \text{ gloves}$$

2–55. Irwin/McGraw-Hill publishers stores some of its inventory in a warehouse that has 14,500 square feet of space. Each book requires $2\frac{1}{2}$ square feet of space. How many books can Irwin keep in this warehouse?

$$14,500 \div 2\frac{1}{2} = \overset{2,900}{\cancel{14,500}} \times \frac{2}{\underset{1}{\cancel{5}}} = 5,800 \text{ books}$$

2–56. Alicia, an employee of Dunkin' Donuts, receives $23\frac{1}{4}$ days per year of vacation time. So far this year she has taken $3\frac{1}{8}$ days in January, $5\frac{1}{2}$ days in May, $6\frac{1}{4}$ days in July, and $4\frac{1}{4}$ days in September. How many more days of vacation does Alicia have left?

$$3\frac{1}{8} + 5\frac{4}{8} + 6\frac{2}{8} + 4\frac{2}{8} = 18\frac{9}{8} = 19\frac{1}{8}$$

$$23\frac{2}{8}$$
$$-19\frac{1}{8}$$
$$\overline{4\frac{1}{8}} \text{ days left}$$

2–57. On Monday, IBM Corporation stock gained $\frac{5}{8}$ of a point. The previous closing price on Friday was $119\frac{1}{2}$. What was Monday's closing price?

$$\$119\frac{4}{8}$$
$$+ \quad \frac{5}{8}$$
$$\overline{\$119\frac{9}{8}} = \$120\frac{1}{8}$$

2–58. Shelly Van Doren hired a contractor to refinish her kitchen. The contractor said the job would take $49\frac{1}{2}$ hours. She has worked the following hours:

Monday	$4\frac{1}{4}$	$4\frac{2}{8}$	$49\frac{2}{4}$	$48\frac{6}{4}$
Tuesday	$9\frac{1}{8}$	$9\frac{1}{8}$	$-31\frac{3}{4}$	$-31\frac{3}{4}$
Wednesday	$4\frac{1}{4}$	$4\frac{2}{8}$		$17\frac{3}{4}$ hours to go
Thursday	$3\frac{1}{2}$	$3\frac{4}{8}$		
Friday	$10\frac{5}{8}$	$+ 10\frac{5}{8}$		
		$30\frac{14}{8} = 31\frac{6}{8} = 31\frac{3}{4}$ hours		

How much longer should the job take to be completed?

ADDITIONAL SET OF WORD PROBLEMS

2–59. On January 22, 1998, the Chicago *Sun-Times* reported that MacMillan Bloedel, Canada's largest forestry company, said that it will cut 2,700 of its 13,000 jobs and leave the paper business in a sweeping reorganization. After the cut, what fraction of employees will remain on the job? Reduce to lowest terms.

$$\begin{array}{r} 13,000 \\ - \quad 2,700 \text{ cut} \\ \hline 10,300 \text{ retained} \end{array} \qquad \frac{10,300 \div (100)}{13,000 \div (100)} = \frac{103}{130}$$

2–60. Manny's Produce plans a big sale on apples and received 870 crates from the wholesale market. Manny will bag these apples in plastic. Each plastic bag holds $\frac{1}{7}$ of a crate. If Manny has no loss to perishables, how many bags of apples can be prepared?

$$870 \div \frac{1}{7} = 870 \times 7 = 6,090 \text{ bags}$$

2–61. Frank Puleo bought 6,625 acres of land in ski country. He plans to subdivide the land into parcels of $13\frac{1}{4}$ acres each. Each parcel will sell for \$125,000. How many parcels of land will Frank develop? If Frank sells all the parcels, what will be his total sales?

$$6{,}625 \div 13\frac{1}{4} = 6{,}625 \times \frac{4}{53} = 500 \text{ parcels} \times \$125{,}000 = \$62{,}500{,}000$$

If Frank sells $\frac{3}{5}$ of the parcels in the first year, what will be his total sales for the year?

$$\frac{3}{\cancel{5}} \times \overset{100}{\cancel{500}} = 300 \times \$125{,}000 = \$37{,}500{,}000$$

2–62. A local Wendy's conducted a food survey. The survey showed that $\frac{1}{8}$ of the people surveyed preferred eating pasta over hamburger. If 6,600 responded to the survey, how many actually favored hamburger?

$$\frac{7}{8} \times 6{,}600 = 5{,}775 \text{ people}$$

2–63. Tamara, Jose, and Milton entered into a partnership that sells men's clothing. Tamara owns $\frac{3}{8}$ of the company, and Jose owns $\frac{1}{4}$. What part does Milton own?

$$\frac{3}{8} + \frac{2}{8} = \frac{5}{8} \qquad\qquad 1 - \frac{5}{8} = \frac{3}{8} \text{ for Milton or } \frac{8}{8} - \frac{5}{8} = \frac{3}{8}$$

2–64. On January 18, 1998, the *Chicago Tribune* had an advertising insert from Builders Square Hardware. The insert lists $\frac{1}{2}$-inch by 10-foot PVC conduit on sale. You plan to remodel your home and have measured each room. The conduit you need for each room is $20\frac{1}{4}$ feet, $15\frac{1}{3}$ feet, $12\frac{5}{8}$ feet, and $14\frac{1}{2}$ feet. **(a)** How many feet of conduit will you need to complete the work? **(b)** How many feet will you have left?

a.
$$20\frac{1}{4} = 20\frac{6}{24}$$
$$+15\frac{1}{3} = 15\frac{8}{24}$$
$$+12\frac{5}{8} = 12\frac{15}{24}$$
$$+14\frac{1}{2} = 14\frac{12}{24}$$
$$\overline{61\frac{41}{24} = 62\frac{17}{24}}$$

b. You need to order 7 pieces of 10-foot PVC conduit = 70 feet

$$70 \text{ feet} \qquad = 69\frac{24}{24}$$
$$-62\frac{17}{24} \text{ needed} \qquad -62\frac{17}{24}$$
$$\overline{} \qquad \overline{7\frac{7}{24} \text{ left over}}$$

2–65. A trip to New York from Virginia will take you $3\frac{1}{4}$ hours. If you have traveled $\frac{1}{5}$ of the way, how much longer will the trip take?

$$\frac{\overset{1}{\cancel{4}}}{5} \times \frac{13}{\cancel{4}} = \frac{13}{5} = 2\frac{3}{5} \text{ hours}$$

2–66. Roland Dodge has increased the price of a Dodge truck by $\frac{1}{4}$ from the original price. The original price of the truck was \$13,000. What is the new price?

$$1\frac{1}{4} = \frac{5}{4} \times \$13{,}000 = \$16{,}250$$

2–67. Norman Moen, an employee at Subway, prepared a 90-foot submarine sandwich for a party. Norman decided to cut the submarine into sandwiches of $1\frac{1}{2}$ feet. How many sandwiches can Norman cut from this submarine?

$$90 \div \frac{3}{2} = 90 \times \frac{2}{3} = 60 \text{ sandwiches}$$

CHALLENGE PROBLEMS

2–68. Builders Square Hardware issued a pamphlet (#104) explaining how to build a bookcase with a large shelf on the bottom for magazines. The materials list follows:

4	1 inch × 10 inches × 10 feet	Back and side for 12 pieces, $39\frac{1}{4}$ inches
3	1 inch × 10 inches × 8 feet	Shelves for 3 pieces, $94\frac{1}{2}$ inches
1	1 inch × 12 inches × 8 feet	Top for 1 piece, 96 inches
7	1 inch × 2 inches × 8 feet	Facing for 2 pieces, 40 inches; 4 pieces, 93 inches; 1 piece, 96 inches; 2 pieces, $39\frac{1}{4}$ inches
1	1 inch × 4 inches × 8 feet	Shelf supports for 5 pieces, $11\frac{1}{4}$ inches; 2 pieces, $12\frac{1}{4}$ inches

a. How many inches of lumber will you need for each size lumber?

b. When you are finished, how much lumber in inches will be left?

a.
$$12 \times 39\frac{1}{4} = \frac{\overset{3}{\cancel{12}}}{1} \times \frac{157}{\underset{1}{\cancel{4}}} = 471$$

$$3 \times 94\frac{1}{2} = \frac{3}{1} \times \frac{189}{2} = \frac{567}{2} = \;\;2\overline{)567}^{\;283\frac{1}{2}}$$
$$\underline{4}$$
$$16$$
$$\underline{16}$$
$$7$$
$$\underline{6}$$
$$1$$

$$1 \times 96 = 96$$
$$2 \times 40 = 80$$
$$4 \times 93 = 372$$
$$1 \times 96 = 96$$

$$2 \times 39\frac{1}{4} = \frac{\overset{1}{\cancel{2}}}{1} \times \frac{157}{\underset{2}{\cancel{4}}} = \frac{157}{2} = \;\;2\overline{)157}^{\;78\frac{1}{2}}$$
$$\underline{14}$$
$$17$$
$$\underline{16}$$
$$1$$

$$5 \times 11\frac{1}{4} = \frac{5}{1} \times \frac{45}{4} = \frac{225}{4} = \;\;4\overline{)225}^{\;56\frac{1}{4}}$$
$$\underline{20}$$
$$25$$
$$\underline{24}$$
$$1$$

$$2 \times 12\frac{1}{4} = \frac{\overset{1}{\cancel{2}}}{1} \times \frac{49}{\underset{2}{\cancel{4}}} = \frac{49}{2} = \;\;2\overline{)49}^{\;24\frac{1}{2}}$$
$$\underline{4}$$
$$9$$
$$\underline{8}$$
$$1$$

b.

$$\begin{array}{r} 4 \times 120 = 480 \\ -471 \\ \hline 9 \end{array} \qquad \begin{array}{r} 3 \times 96 = 288 \\ -283\frac{1}{2} \\ \hline +4\frac{1}{2} \end{array} \qquad \begin{array}{r} 1 \times 96 = 96 \\ -96 \\ \hline +0 \end{array} \qquad \begin{array}{r} 7 \times 96 = 672 \\ -80 \\ -372 \\ -96 \\ -78\frac{1}{2} \\ \hline +45\frac{1}{2} \end{array} \qquad \begin{array}{r} 1 \times 96 = 96 \\ -80\frac{3}{4} \begin{cases} -56\frac{1}{4} \\ -24\frac{1}{2} \end{cases} \\ \hline +15\frac{1}{4} \end{array}$$

$$-626\frac{1}{2}$$

$$9 + 4\frac{1}{2} + 0 + 45\frac{1}{2} + 15\frac{1}{4} = 74\frac{1}{4} \text{ inches}$$

2–69. Jack MacLean has entered into a real estate development partnership with Bill Lyons and June Reese. Bill owns $\frac{1}{4}$ of the partnership, while June has a $\frac{1}{5}$ interest. The partners will divide all profits on the basis of their fractional ownership.

The partnership bought 900 acres of land and plans to subdivide each lot into $2\frac{1}{4}$ acres. Homes in the area have been selling for $240,000. By time of completion, Jack estimates the price of each home will increase by $\frac{1}{3}$ of the current value. The partners sent a survey to 12,000 potential customers to see whether they should heat the homes with oil or gas. One-fourth of the customers responded by indicating a 5-to-1 preference for oil. From the results of the survey, Jack now plans to install a 270-gallon oil tank at each home. He estimates that each home will need 5 fills per year. Current price of home heating fuel is $1 per gallon. The partnership estimates its profit per home will be $\frac{1}{8}$ the selling price of each home.

From the above, please calculate the following:

a. Number of homes to be built.

$$900 \div 2\frac{1}{4} = \overset{100}{\cancel{900}} \times \frac{4}{\underset{1}{\cancel{9}}} = 400 \text{ homes}$$

b. Selling price of each home.

$$1\frac{1}{3} \times \$240,000 = \frac{4}{\underset{1}{\cancel{3}}} \times \overset{\$80,000}{\cancel{\$240,000}} = \$320,000$$

c. (1). Number of people responding to survey.

$$\frac{1}{4} \times 12,000 = 3,000 \text{ people}$$

(2). Number of people desiring oil.

$$\frac{5}{6} \times 3,000 = 2,500 \text{ people}$$

d. Average monthly cost to run oil heat per house.

$$270 \times 5 = 1,350 \times \$1 = \frac{\$1,350}{12} = \$112.50$$

e. Amount of profit Jack will receive from the sale of homes.

$$\frac{1}{4} + \frac{1}{5} = \frac{5}{20} + \frac{4}{20} = \frac{9}{20}$$

$$1 - \frac{9}{20} = \frac{11}{20} \text{ for Jack}$$

$$\frac{1}{\underset{1}{\cancel{8}}} \times \overset{\$40,000}{\cancel{\$320,000}} = \$40,000$$

$$\begin{array}{r} \$40,000 \\ \times\ 400 \\ \hline \$16,000,000 \end{array}$$

$$\frac{11}{20} \times \$16,000,000 = \$8,800,000$$

SUMMARY PRACTICE TEST

Identify the following types of fractions. *(p. 35)*

1. $6\frac{7}{9}$ Mixed

2. $\frac{4}{9}$ Proper

3. $\frac{11}{8}$ Improper

4. Convert the following to a mixed number. *(p. 35)*

$$\frac{129}{7} = 18\frac{3}{7}$$

5. Convert the following to an improper fraction. *(p. 36)*

$$8\frac{4}{5} = \frac{40 + 4}{5} = \frac{44}{5}$$

6. Calculate the greatest common divisor of the following by the step approach and reduce to lowest terms. *(p. 36)*

$$\frac{115}{160} = \begin{array}{r} 1 \\ 115\overline{)160} \\ \underline{115} \\ 45 \end{array} \nearrow \begin{array}{r} 2 \\ 45\overline{)115} \\ \underline{90} \\ 25 \end{array} \nearrow \begin{array}{r} 1 \\ 25\overline{)45} \\ \underline{25} \\ 20 \end{array} \nearrow \begin{array}{r} 1 \\ 20\overline{)25} \\ \underline{20} \\ 5 \end{array} \nearrow \begin{array}{r} 4 \\ 5\overline{)20} \\ \underline{20} \\ 0 \end{array} \qquad \frac{115 \div 5}{160 \div 5} = \frac{23}{32}$$

7. Convert the following to higher terms. *(p. 37)*

$$\frac{12}{40} = \frac{?}{280} \qquad 84 \qquad 280 \div 40 = 7 \times 12 = 84$$

8. Find the LCD of the following by using prime numbers. Show your work. *(p. 41)*

$$\frac{1}{2}+\frac{1}{6}+\frac{1}{9}+\frac{1}{3}=\quad \begin{array}{c}2\\3\end{array}\begin{array}{|cccc}2 & 6 & 9 & 3\\1 & 3 & 9 & 3\\\hline 1 & 1 & 3 & 1\end{array}\quad 2\times3\times1\times1\times3\times1=18$$

9. Subtract the following. *(p. 42)*

$$\begin{array}{r}12\frac{6}{10}\\-4\frac{4}{5}\\\hline\end{array}\quad=\quad \begin{array}{r}12\frac{6}{10}\\=-4\frac{8}{10}\\\hline\end{array}\qquad\begin{array}{r}11\frac{16}{10}\longleftarrow\left(\frac{6}{10}+\frac{10}{10}\right)\\-4\frac{8}{10}\\\hline 7\frac{8}{10}=7\frac{4}{5}\end{array}$$

Complete the following using the cancellation technique. *(p. 46)*

10. $\dfrac{8}{12}\times\dfrac{2}{4}\times\dfrac{6}{11}=\dfrac{\overset{2}{\cancel{8}}}{\underset{\underset{1}{\cancel{6}}}{\cancel{12}}}\times\dfrac{\overset{1}{\cancel{2}}}{\underset{1}{\cancel{4}}}\times\dfrac{\overset{1}{\cancel{6}}}{11}=\dfrac{2}{11}$

11. $6\dfrac{4}{7}\times\dfrac{14}{15}=\dfrac{46}{\cancel{7}}\times\dfrac{\overset{2}{\cancel{14}}}{15}=\dfrac{92}{15}=6\dfrac{2}{15}$

12. $\dfrac{4}{5}\div2=\dfrac{\overset{2}{\cancel{4}}}{5}\times\dfrac{1}{\cancel{2}}=\dfrac{2}{5}$

13. A trip to Philadelphia from Boston will take you $6\frac{1}{2}$ hours. If you have traveled $\frac{1}{4}$ of the way, how much longer will the trip take? *(p. 45)*

$$\frac{3}{4}\times\frac{13}{2}=\frac{39}{8}=4\frac{7}{8}\text{ hours}$$

14. Bean Company's new machine produces 180 beanbag chairs per hour. If the machine runs $20\frac{1}{3}$ hours, how many chairs will the machine produce? *(p. 46)*.

$$\frac{\overset{60}{\cancel{180}}}{1}\times\frac{61}{\underset{1}{\cancel{3}}}=3{,}660\text{ chairs}$$

15. A recent taste-testing survey showed that $\frac{2}{7}$ of the people surveyed preferred the taste of veggie burgers over turkey burgers. If 42,000 people were in the survey, how many favored veggie burgers? How many chose turkey burgers? *(p. 45)*

Veggie: $\dfrac{2}{7}\times42{,}000=12{,}000$ \qquad\qquad **Turkey:** $\dfrac{5}{7}\times42{,}000=30{,}000$

16. Mel Bass, an employee of Avis Rent-A-Car, worked $9\frac{1}{2}$ hours on Monday, $3\frac{1}{4}$ hours on Tuesday, $7\frac{1}{2}$ hours on Wednesday, $8\frac{1}{4}$ hours on Thursday, and 8 hours on Friday. How many total hours did Mel work during the week? *(p. 41)*

$$9\frac{2}{4}+3\frac{1}{4}+7\frac{2}{4}+8\frac{1}{4}+8=35\frac{6}{4}=36\frac{1}{2}\text{ hours}$$

17. If the stock of American Airlines was $\$25\frac{5}{16}$ and rose $\$1\frac{1}{4}$ for the day, what is American's closing price? *(p. 41)*

$$\begin{array}{r}\$25\frac{5}{16}\\+1\frac{4}{16}\\\hline \$26\frac{9}{16}\end{array}$$

Defend or reject the following business math issue based on the *Kiplinger's Personal Finance Magazine* article below:

MY PERSONAL FINANCES

Dr. Glass Does Windows

▶ **How Philip Bregstone washes his way to a six-figure income—part-time.** By Marc L. Schulhof

Like many business people, Philip Bregstone counts a laptop computer and a cellular telephone among the tools of his trade. But he doesn't carry a briefcase. He totes a bucket.

As "Dr. Glass," a "boutique window washer" in a tony suburb of Washington, D.C., Bregstone cleans up: His annual gross income hovers around $100,000, a big-city salary that more than satisfies his family's needs—especially because they live in Colorado.

With his wife, Roberta, and 3-year-old son, Jonah, Bregstone spends eight months of the year in Nyland, a "co-housing" community outside Boulder, where the Bregstones own their own home and participate in communal activities. Philip helps raise animals, teaches music and takes care of Jonah while Roberta works as a sign-language interpreter.

But every spring, like the Orioles to Baltimore, they migrate back East for the window-washing season.

HUMBLE BEGINNINGS. Bregstone, 38, launched his business 20 years ago to pay his way through Syracuse University. He spent vacations as Dr. Glass in his hometown of Potomac, Md., and continued the business as a graduate student studying music composition on a full scholarship at the nearby University of Maryland, in College Park.

After moving to Santa Fe, where he spent two years studying the Great Books at St. John's College, Bregstone continued to ply his trade during breaks. "I could fly home for long weekends to wash windows and visit friends," he says. "The work paid for the flight and a rental car." He even opened a branch office in Santa Fe.

When Bregstone finally settled in Colorado, he assumed his business would dry up. Instead, it has doubled. Every March the Bregstones pack up their Subaru and trek to Washington, where they rent an apartment in the shadow of the National Cathedral—usually for less than they charge to rent out their home in Boulder.

Bregstone's first stop is the home of a longtime client who has an extra-large basement, too much furniture and lots of glass. The client stores Bregstone's equipment every winter and lends him furniture for his apartment every summer in exchange for—what else?—annual window washing. (Another client trades Bregstone use of a vacation home near Vail. He washes the windows there, too.)

ON HIS WAY UP. Though most of his tools are simple, "Dr. Glass" maintains his Potomac practice with a boost from technology. When he's in Colorado, calls to his Washington-area phone number are forwarded. He uses a computer to track his finances and appointments. When he's on a ladder 20 feet up, a cell phone keeps him in constant touch with customers and a digital voice recorder enables him to take notes on his calls.

In a given year, Bregstone services roughly half of his 800-customer database, at an average rate of $300 a job (these are big houses). In July the family returns to Colorado, and twice every fall Bregstone flies back to Washington alone to wipe up the last jobs of the season.

Bregstone has mixed feelings about his success. "My high school friends have graduated from law school and become partners while I'm 'just a window washer,'" he says. But life as Dr. Glass is too fulfilling to give up for a button-down career. And besides, "I enjoy washing windows," he says. "You go into a house with dirty windows and you have no money. You leave a few hours later and the windows are clean, you have money, and you get complimented on doing a good job."

In case you were wondering, Dr. Glass's prescription for clean windows is simple: Get a good squeegee. ●

REPORTER: STACY STOVER

KATHERINE LAMBERT

Business Math Issue

In a given year, servicing half of your customer database will lead to lower sales and less customer satisfaction. Philip should consider franchising his business.

1. List the key points of the article and information to support your position.

2. Write a group defense of your position using math calculations to support your view.

BUSINESS MATH SCRAPBOOK

Putting Your Skills to Work

Life Magazine Cuts Third of Editorial Staff In Move by New Editor

NEW YORK (AP)—**Time Warner** Inc.'s Life magazine unit is eliminating about a third of its editorial staff in a reorganization by the monthly's new top editor.

Isolde Motley, who took over as managing editor Jan. 1, decided to lay off 15 editors, reporters and researchers over the past two weeks, a Life spokesman said. The layoffs are effective in March.

In addition, David Friend, assistant managing editor and director of photography, resigned last week. His departure and the layoffs will leave Life with an editorial staff of about 30 people.

Ms. Motley, formerly corporate development editor for Time Warner's Time Inc. unit, took over as Life's managing editor from Jay Lovinger, who was named editor at large. She was the founding editor of two magazines, Martha Stewart Living and This Old House, for Time.

Project A

Prove the $\frac{1}{3}$ figure in the title of this article.

$$\frac{15}{45} = \frac{1}{3}$$

WORKPLACE

Back Corsets Receive Support In UCLA Study

By RHONDA L. RUNDLE
Staff Reporter of THE WALL STREET JOURNAL

Corsets could make a comeback in the workplace as a result of a major new study that finds that they sharply reduce lower-back injuries in workers who lift heavy materials.

The study, by researchers at the University of California at Los Angeles, provides the strongest scientific evidence to date in what has become a simmering workplace-safety controversy. Many employers began discouraging workers from using corsets after a government agency in 1994 said there was no proof that they worked.

The UCLA study, which is to be released today, finds that back-support devices reduced low-back injuries by about one-third in a study of 36,000 **Home Depot** Inc. employees between 1989 and 1994. The study compared the incidence of such injuries before and after the Atlanta-based home-improvement retailer made corsets mandatory for all store employees.

"Back injuries have been with us for years and years and have been a major plague on world-wide industry," says Jess Kraus, a UCLA professor of epidemiology and the study's lead author. "The study found a pretty big effect with a simple countermeasure. It is pretty hard to argue that it is a chance phenomenon."

Low-back injuries account for one-fourth of all workers' compensation claims paid by U.S. employers, costing $11 billion in 1990, according to government estimates.

Project B

Of the 36,000 surveyed, how many had reduced low-back injuries?

$$\frac{1}{3} \times 36,000 = 12,000$$

 See text Web site (www.mhhe.com/slater) and *The Business Math Internet Resource Guide.*

3

DECIMALS

LEARNING UNIT OBJECTIVES

LU 3.1   Rounding; Fraction and Decimal Conversions

- Explain the place values of whole numbers and decimals; round decimals *(pp. 64–65).*

- Convert decimal fractions to decimals, proper fractions to decimals, mixed numbers to decimals, and pure and mixed decimals to decimal fractions *(pp. 66–69).*

LU 3.2   Adding, Subtracting, Multiplying, and Dividing Decimals

- Add, subtract, multiply, and divide decimals *(pp. 70–72).*

- Multiply and divide decimals by shortcut methods *(pp. 73–74).*

- Complete decimal applications in foreign currency *(pp. 72–73).*

TABLE 3.1

Analyzing a bag of M&M's®

Sharon Hoogstraten.

Color*	Fraction	Decimal
Yellow	$\frac{18}{55}$	.33
Red	$\frac{10}{55}$	.18
Blue	$\frac{9}{55}$	.16
Orange	$\frac{7}{55}$	.13
Brown	$\frac{6}{55}$	.11
Green	$\frac{5}{55}$	.09
Total	$\frac{55}{55} = 1$	1.00

*The color ratios currently given are a sample used for educational purposes. They do not represent the manufacturer's color ratios.

Chapter 2 introduced the 1.69-ounce bag of M&M's® shown above. This chapter looks again at this bag of 55 M&M's® in six colors. In Table 3.1 we give the fractional breakdown of the six colors and express the values in decimals. Note that decimals such as .33, .11, and so on have been rounded to the nearest hundredths. Learning Unit 3.1 explains how to round decimals.

We have divided this chapter into two learning units. The first unit discusses rounding decimals, converting fractions to decimals, and converting decimals to fractions. The second unit shows you how to add, subtract, multiply, and divide decimals, along with some shortcuts for multiplying and dividing decimals. Added to this unit is a global application of decimals dealing with foreign exchange rates.

> **THE CHECKOFF:** A basic men's haircut in Japan costs, on average, $48.65, says ECA Windham, New York, which specializes in international relocation. . . .
>
> © 1996 Dow Jones & Company, Inc.

One of the most common uses of decimals occurs when we spend dollars and cents. For example, *The Wall Street Journal,* in "The Checkoff," stated that a basic man's haircut in Japan costs, on average, $48.65. This is a *decimal number.* A **decimal,** then, is a decimal number with digits to the right of a *decimal point,* indicating that decimals, like fractions, are parts of a whole that are less than one. Thus, we can interchange the terms *decimals* and *decimal numbers.* Remembering this will avoid confusion between the terms *decimal, decimal number,* and *decimal point.*

LEARNING UNIT 3.1   Rounding; Fraction and Decimal Conversions

Remember to read the decimal point as and.

In Chapter 1 we stated that the **decimal point** is the center of the decimal numbering system. So far we have studied the whole numbers to the left of the decimal point and the parts of whole numbers called fractions. We also learned that the position of the digits in a whole number gives the place values of the digits (Figure 1.1). Now we will study the

FIGURE 3.1

Decimal place-value chart

Thousands	Hundreds	Tens	Ones	Decimal point	Tenths	Hundredths	Thousandths	Ten thousandths	Hundred thousandths
1,000	100	10	1	and	$\frac{1}{10}$	$\frac{1}{100}$	$\frac{1}{1,000}$	$\frac{1}{10,000}$	$\frac{1}{100,000}$

position (place values) of the digits to the right of the decimal point (Figure 3.1). Note that the words to the right of the decimal point end in *ths*.

You should understand the relationship of the place values of the digits on either side of the decimal point. If you move a digit to the left of the decimal point by place (ones, tens, and so on), you *increase* its value 10 times for each place. If you move a digit to the right of the decimal point by place (tenths, hundredths, and so on), you *decrease* its value 10 times for each place. This is why the decimal point is the center of the decimal system.

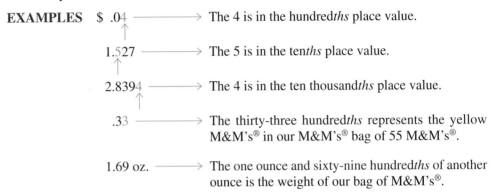

EXAMPLES $ .04 ⟶ The 4 is in the hundred*ths* place value.

1.527 ⟶ The 5 is in the ten*ths* place value.

2.8394 ⟶ The 4 is in the ten thousand*ths* place value.

.33 ⟶ The thirty-three hundred*ths* represents the yellow M&M's® in our M&M's® bag of 55 M&M's®.

1.69 oz. ⟶ The one ounce and sixty-nine hundred*ths* of another ounce is the weight of our bag of M&M's®.

Do you recall from Chapter 1 how you used a place-value chart to read or write whole numbers in verbal form? To read or write decimal numbers, you read or write the decimal number as if it were a whole number. Then you use the name of the decimal place of the last digit as given in Figure 3.1. For example, you would read or write the decimal .0796 as seven hundred ninety-six ten thousandths (the last digit, 6, is in the ten thousandths place).

To read a decimal with four or fewer whole numbers, you can also refer to Figure 3.1. For larger whole numbers, refer to the whole-number place-value chart in Chapter 1 (Figure 1.1). For example, from Figure 3.1 you would read the number 126.2864 as one hundred twenty-six and two thousand eight hundred sixty-four ten thousandths. Remember that the *and* is the decimal point.

Now let's round decimals. Rounding decimals is similar to the rounding of whole numbers that you learned in Chapter 1.

Rounding Decimals

From Table 3.1, you know that the 1.69-ounce bag of M&M's® introduced in Chapter 2 contained $\frac{18}{55}$, or .33, yellow M&M's®. The .33 was rounded to the nearest hundredth. **Rounding decimals** involves the following steps:

Rounding Decimals

Step 1. Identify the place value of the digit you want to round.

Step 2. If the digit to the right of the identified digit in Step 1 is 5 or more, increase the identified digit by 1. If the digit to the right is less than 5, do not change the identified digit.

Step 3. Drop all digits to the right of the identified digit.

Let's practice rounding by using the $\frac{18}{55}$ yellow M&M's® that we rounded to .33 in Table 3.1. Before we rounded $\frac{18}{55}$ to .33, the number we rounded was .3272727.

EXAMPLE   Round .3272727 to nearest hundredth.

Step 1.   .3272727   The identified digit is 2, which is in the hundredths place (two places to the right of the decimal point).

Step 2. ⟶ The digit to the right of 2 is more than 5 (7). Thus, 2, the identified digit in Step 1, is changed to 3.

.3372727

Step 3.   .33   Drop all other digits to right of the identified digit 3.

We could also round the .3272727 M&M's® to the nearest tenth or thousandth as follows:

	Tenth	**or**	**Thousandth**

.3272727 ⟶ .3   .3272727 ⟶ .327

OTHER EXAMPLES

Round to nearest dollar:	$166.39	⟶	$166
Round to nearest cent:	$1,196.885	⟶	$1,196.89
Round to nearest hundredth:	$38.563	⟶	$38.56
Round to nearest thousandth:	$1,432.9981	⟶	$1,432.998

The rules for rounding can differ with the situation in which rounding is used. For example, have you ever bought one item from a supermarket produce department that was marked "3 for $1" and noticed what the cashier charged you? One item marked "3 for $1" would not cost you $33\frac{1}{3}$ cents rounded to 33 cents. You will pay 34 cents. Many retail stores round to the next cent even if the digit following the identified digit is less than $\frac{1}{2}$ of a penny. In this text we round on the concept of 5 or more.

Fraction and Decimal Conversions

In business operations we must frequently convert fractions to decimal numbers and decimal numbers to fractions. This section begins by discussing three types of fraction-to-decimal conversions. Then we discuss converting pure and mixed decimals to decimal fractions.

Converting Decimal Fractions to Decimals

From Figure 3.1 you can see that a **decimal fraction** (expressed in the digits to the right of the decimal point) is a fraction with a denominator that has a power of 10, such as $\frac{1}{10}$, $\frac{17}{100}$, and $\frac{23}{1,000}$. To convert a decimal fraction to a decimal, follow these steps:

Converting Decimal Fractions to Decimals

Step 1. Count the number of zeros in the denominator.

Step 2. Place the numerator of the decimal fraction to the right of the decimal point the same number of places as you have zeros in the denominator. (The number of zeros in the denominator gives the number of digits your decimal has to the right of the decimal point.) Do not go over the total number of denominator zeros.

Now let's change $\frac{3}{10}$ and its higher multiples of 10 to decimals.

EXAMPLES

	Verbal form	Decimal fraction	Decimal	Number of decimal places to right of decimal point
a.	Three tenths	$\frac{3}{10}$	.3	1
b.	Three hundredths	$\frac{3}{100}$	.03	2
c.	Three thousandths	$\frac{3}{1,000}$	.003	3
d.	Three ten thousandths	$\frac{3}{10,000}$	.0003	4

Note how we show the different values of the decimal fractions above in decimals. The zeros after the decimal point and before the number 3 indicate these values. If you added zeros after the number 3, you do not change the value. Thus, the numbers .3 , .30 , and .300 have the same value. So 3 tenths of a pizza, 30 hundredths of a pizza, and 300 thousandths of a pizza are the same total amount of pizza. The first pizza is sliced into 10 pieces. The second pizza is sliced into 100 pieces. The third pizza is sliced into 1,000 pieces. Also, we didn't need to place a zero to the left of the decimal point.

Converting Proper
Fractions to Decimals

Big Board Votes Trades In Decimals

By GREG IP
And PATRICK MCGEEHAN
Staff Reporters of THE WALL STREET JOURNAL

The **New York Stock Exchange**, ending a centuries-old tradition, voted to have its stocks trading in decimals, possibly in as little as a year.

The move by the Big Board will make it the first U.S. exchange to go to decimals. The U.S. is the only major country that doesn't now trade stocks in decimals.

As an interim step, the exchange will begin quoting in 1/16 increments, half the ⅛ increments in which it has traded stocks since the exchange was established in 1792. The move may come by June 23, when necessary upgrades are made to the Inter-

market Trading System, which links the nation's exchanges. But the plan also needs Securities and Exchange Commission approval.

"Decimals will be a key step toward a more global NYSE and prices more easily understood by individual investors than ever-smaller fractions," said the Big Board's chairman and chief executive, Richard A. Grasso. The interim step of 1/16ths would help brokers prepare themselves for decimal-based trading.

The move represents a major shift in stance by the Big Board, which as recently as a few months ago was telling a congressional subcommittee looking at decimals that the exchange saw no net benefit to investors from decimal-based trading.

© 1997 Dow Jones & Company, Inc.

Stock prices have always been quoted in whole numbers and proper fractions. If you look for the price of a particular stock in the newspaper, you will see the price quoted in dollars and a fraction, for example, $25\frac{5}{8}$. For the average investor, this price is confusing. How much of a whole dollar is $\frac{5}{8}$ in cents? As stated in *The Wall Street Journal* clipping "Big Board Votes Trades in Decimals," the New York Stock Exchange has voted to have its stock trading in decimals. The Exchange will begin by quoting stock in $\frac{1}{16}$ increments. This interim step is designed to help brokers prepare for decimal-based trading. Probably by the year 2000, you will hear and read stock prices stated in the same way as your other purchases and sales—in dollars and cents.

How do you convert proper fractions to decimals? Recall from Chapter 2 that proper fractions are a form of division. This makes it possible to convert proper fractions to decimals by carrying out the division.

Converting Proper Fractions to Decimals

Step 1. Divide the numerator of the fraction by its denominator. (If necessary, add a decimal point and zeros to the number in the numerator.)

Step 2. Round as necessary.

EXAMPLES

$$\frac{3}{4} = 4\overline{)3.00} = .75$$
$$\begin{array}{r} 2\,8 \\ \hline 20 \\ 20 \\ \hline \end{array}$$

$$\frac{3}{8} = 8\overline{)3.000} = .375$$
$$\begin{array}{r} 2\,4 \\ \hline 60 \\ 56 \\ \hline 40 \\ 40 \\ \hline \end{array}$$

$$\frac{1}{3} = 3\overline{)1.000} = .\overline{333}$$
$$\begin{array}{r} 9 \\ \hline 10 \\ 9 \\ \hline 10 \\ 9 \\ \hline 1 \end{array}$$

Table 3.2 gives a quick reference for the decimal conversions of common fractions. Note in the example $\frac{1}{3}$ that the 3 in the quotient keeps repeating itself (never ends). We call this a **repeating decimal.** The short bar over the last 3 means that the number endlessly repeats.

Converting Mixed
Numbers to Decimals

A mixed number, you will recall from Chapter 2, is the sum of a whole number greater than zero and a proper fraction. To convert mixed numbers to decimals, use the following steps:

TABLE 3.2   Common fraction to decimal conversions

Fraction	Decimal equivalent	Fraction	Decimal equivalent	Fraction	Decimal equivalent
$\frac{1}{2}$	.50	$\frac{5}{6}$	$.83\frac{1}{3}\ (.83\overline{3})$	$\frac{1}{16}$	$.06\frac{1}{4}\ (.0625)$
$\frac{1}{3}$	$.33\frac{1}{3}\ (.333)$	$\frac{1}{7}$	$.14\frac{2}{7}\ (.143)$	$\frac{3}{16}$	$.18\frac{3}{4}\ (.1875)$
$\frac{2}{3}$	$.66\frac{2}{3}\ (.66\overline{6})$	$\frac{1}{8}$	$.12\frac{1}{2}\ (.125)$	$\frac{5}{16}$	$.31\frac{1}{4}\ (.3125)$
$\frac{1}{4}$	.25	$\frac{3}{8}$	$.37\frac{1}{2}\ (.375)$	$\frac{7}{16}$	$.43\frac{3}{4}\ (.4375)$
$\frac{3}{4}$	.75	$\frac{5}{8}$	$.62\frac{1}{2}\ (.625)$	$\frac{9}{16}$	$.56\frac{1}{4}\ (.5625)$
$\frac{1}{5}$	.20	$\frac{7}{8}$	$.87\frac{1}{2}\ (.875)$	$\frac{11}{16}$	$.68\frac{3}{4}\ (.6875)$
$\frac{2}{5}$	.40	$\frac{1}{9}$	$.11\overline{1}$	$\frac{13}{16}$	$.81\frac{1}{4}\ (.8125)$
$\frac{3}{5}$	.60	$\frac{1}{10}$	.10	$\frac{15}{16}$	$.93\frac{3}{4}\ (.9375)$
$\frac{4}{5}$	.80	$\frac{1}{12}$	$.08\frac{1}{3}\ (.08\overline{3})$	$\frac{1}{20}$	.05
$\frac{1}{6}$	$.16\frac{2}{3}\ (.16\overline{6})$	$\frac{1}{15}$	$.06\frac{2}{3}\ (.06\overline{6})$	$\frac{1}{25}$	.04

Converting Mixed Numbers to Decimals

Step 1.   Convert the fractional part of the mixed number to a decimal (as illustrated in the previous section).

Step 2.   Add the converted fractional part to the whole number.

EXAMPLE

$$8\frac{2}{5} = \textbf{(Step 1)} \quad 5\overline{)2.0} \quad \textbf{(Step 2)}\ 8 + .4 = \boxed{8.4}$$
$$\phantom{8\frac{2}{5} = \textbf{(Step 1)} \quad 5\overline{)}}\ \underline{2\,0}$$

Now that we have converted fractions to decimals, let's convert decimals to fractions.

Converting Pure and Mixed Decimals to Decimal Fractions

A **pure decimal** has no whole number(s) to the left of the decimal point (.43, .458, and so on). A **mixed decimal** is a combination of a whole number and a decimal. An example of a mixed decimal follows.

EXAMPLE   737.592 = Seven hundred thirty-seven and five hundred ninety-two thousandths

Note the following conversion steps for converting pure and mixed decimals to decimal fractions:

Converting Pure and Mixed Decimals to Decimal Fractions

Step 1.   Place the digits to the right of the decimal point in the numerator of the fraction. Omit the decimal point. (For a decimal fraction with a fractional part, see examples **c** and **d** below.)

Step 2.   Put a 1 in the denominator of the fraction.

Step 3.   Count the number of digits to the right of the decimal point. Add the same number of zeros to the denominator of the fraction. For mixed decimals, add the fraction to the whole number.

If desired, you can reduce the fractions in Step 3.

EXAMPLES	Step 1	Step 2	Places	Step 3
a. .3	$\dfrac{3}{}$	$\dfrac{3}{1}$	1	$\dfrac{3}{10}$
b. .24	$\dfrac{24}{}$	$\dfrac{24}{1}$	2	$\dfrac{24}{100}$
c. $.24\frac{1}{2}$	$\dfrac{245}{}$	$\dfrac{245}{1}$	3	$\dfrac{245}{1,000}$

Before completing Step 1 in example **c,** we must remove the fractional part, convert it to a decimal ($\frac{1}{2}$ = .5), and multiply it by .01 (.5 × .01 = .005). We use .01 because the 4 of .24 is in the hundredths place. Then we add .005 + .24 = .245 (three places to right of the decimal) and complete Steps 1, 2, and 3.

d. $.07\frac{1}{4}$	$\dfrac{725}{}$	$\dfrac{725}{1}$	4	$\dfrac{725}{10,000}$

In example **d,** be sure to convert $\frac{1}{4}$ to .25 and multiply by .01. This gives .0025. Then add .0025 to .07, which is .0725 (four places), and complete Steps 1, 2, and 3.

e. 17.45	$\dfrac{45}{}$	$\dfrac{45}{1}$	2	$\dfrac{45}{100} = 17\dfrac{45}{100}$

Example **e** is a mixed decimal. Since we substitute *and* for the decimal point, we read this mixed decimal as seventeen and forty-five hundredths. Note that after we converted the .45 of the mixed decimals to a fraction, we added it to the whole number 17.

LU 3.1 PRACTICE QUIZ

Write the following as a decimal number.

1. Four hundred eight thousandths

Name the place position of the identified digit:

2. 6.8241   **3.** 9.3942
    ↑   ↑

Round each decimal to place indicated:

	Tenth	**Thousandth**
4. .62768	a.	b.
5. .68341	a.	b.

Convert the following to decimals:

6. $\dfrac{9}{10,000}$ **7.** $\dfrac{14}{100,000}$

Convert the following to decimal fractions (do not reduce):

8. .819   **9.** 16.93   **10.** $.05\frac{1}{4}$

Convert the following fractions to decimals and round answer to nearest hundredth:

11. $\dfrac{1}{6}$ **12.** $\dfrac{3}{8}$ **13.** $12\frac{1}{8}$

✓ **Solutions**

1. .408 (3 places to right of decimal)

2. Hundredths   **3.** Thousandths

4. a. .6 (identified digit 6—digit to right less than 5)   **b.** .628 (identified digit 7—digit to right greater than 5)

5. a. .7 (identified digit 6—digit to right greater than 5)   **b.** .683 (identified digit 3—digit to right less than 5)

6. .0009 (4 places)   **7.** .00014 (5 places)

8. $\dfrac{819}{1,000}$ $\left(\dfrac{819}{1 + 3 \text{ zeros}}\right)$ **9.** $16\dfrac{93}{100}$

10. $\dfrac{525}{10,000}$ $\left(\dfrac{525}{1 + 4 \text{ zeros}} \dfrac{1}{4} \times .01 = .0025 + .05 = .0525\right)$

11. .16666 = .17   **12.** .375 = .38   **13.** 12.125 = 12.13

LEARNING UNIT 3.2   Adding, Subtracting, Multiplying, and Dividing Decimals

Mini Bar Madness

While prices for minibar items at all four- and five-star hotels are steep, some are steeper than others:

CITY/HOTEL	COCA-COLA	LOCAL BEER	CHAMPAGNE (1/2 BOTTLE)
Brussels, Sheraton (downtown)	$2.85	$3.45	$32.90
Hong Kong, Grand Hyatt	$5.15	$5.80	$50.38
London, Langham Hilton	$3.30	$5.75	$41.00
New York, Kitano Hotel	$3.50	$5.50	$29.00
Prague, Inter-Continental	$2.60	$3.95	$22.95

Source: Business Traveler magazine

Visiting a minibar in a hotel is expensive. *The Wall Street Journal* clipping "Mini Bar Madness" states that the Grand Hyatt in Hong Kong charges $5.15 for Coca-Cola, $5.80 for local beer, and $50.38 for one-half bottle of champagne. You may wonder if the higher prices charged at minibars are worth the convenience. And if you try to make up for the higher prices by eating more fat-free pretzels, beware. You will pay for the fat-free pretzels in a weight gain. An article in *The Wall Street Journal* states that "there's no such thing as a fat-free pretzel." Pretzels are made from wheat flour and 1 cup of wheat flour contains roughly 2.7 grams of fat, so it is "virtually impossible" to make a pretzel fat-free.

If you visited the Grand Hyatt in Hong Kong and bought 2 Cokes, 1 beer, and 2 one-half bottles of champagne, what would be your total cost?

$$2 \times \$5.15 = \$\ \ 10.30$$
$$1 \times \ \ 5.80 = \ \ \ \ 5.80$$
$$2 \times 50.38 = \ \ 100.76$$
$$\overline{\$116.86}$$

Now you are ready to make calculations involving decimals.

Addition and Subtraction of Decimals

Note how the decimal points in the addition of your purchases at the Hong Kong Grand Hyatt above are aligned. In the following steps, you will see that this is the first step in adding and subtracting decimals.

Adding and Subtracting Decimals

Step 1. Vertically write the numbers so that the decimal points align. You can place additional zeros to the right of the decimal point if needed without changing the value of the number.

Step 2. Add or subtract the digits starting with the right column and moving to the left.

Step 3. Align the decimal point in the answer with the above decimal points.

EXAMPLES   Add 4 + 7.3 + 36.139 + .0007 + 8.22.

Whole number to the right of the last digit is assumed to have a decimal.

```
   4.0000
   7.3000      ← Extra zeros have
  36.1390        been added to make
    .0007        calculation easier.
   8.2200
  55.6597
```

Subtract 45.3 − 15.273.

```
    2 9 10
 45.300
− 15.273
  30.027
```

Subtract 7 − 6.9.

```
  6 10
 7.0
− 6.9
  .1
```

Knowing how expensive it is to have a Coke, beer, and champagne in Hong Kong, we return to the "Mini Bar Madness" clipping and check what these items would cost at the Kitano Hotel in New York. At the New York Kitano Hotel, Coca-Cola is $3.50, local beer is $5.50, and one-half bottle of champagne is $29.00. Adding these items and subtracting the total from the total at the Hong Kong Grand Hyatt, we have a saving of $46.36 in New York:

$$2 \times \$\ 3.50 = \$\ 7.00$$
$$1 \times \quad 5.50 = \quad 5.50$$
$$2 \times \quad 29.00 = \quad \underline{58.00}$$
$$\$70.50$$

$$\overset{11}{\$\cancel{11}6.86} \longleftarrow \text{Hong Kong}$$
$$\underline{- 70.50} \longleftarrow \text{New York}$$
$$\boxed{\$46.36} \longleftarrow \text{Savings}$$

Multiplication of Decimals

When we compared the prices of Coke, beer, and champagne in Hong Kong with the prices in New York, we used multiplication to get the total prices. The steps that follow explain how to do this.

Multiplying Decimals

Step 1. Multiply the numbers as whole numbers ignoring the decimal points.

Step 2. Count and total the number of decimal places in the multiplier and multiplicand.

Step 3. Starting at the right in the product, count to the left the number of decimal places totaled in Step 2. Place the decimal point so that the product has the same number of decimal places as totaled in Step 2. If the total number of places is greater than the places in the product, insert zeros in front of the product.

EXAMPLES

Step 1, Step 2, Step 3

$$8.52 \ (\text{2 decimal places})$$
$$\times \ \ 6.7 \ (\text{1 decimal place})$$
$$5\ 964$$
$$51\ 12$$
$$\boxed{57.084}$$

$$2.36 \ (\text{2 places})$$
$$\times \ .016 \ (\text{3 places})$$
$$1416$$
$$236$$
$$\boxed{.03776} \ \text{Need to add zero}$$

Division of Decimals

If the divisor in your decimal division problem is a whole number, first place the decimal point in the quotient directly above the decimal point in the dividend. Then divide as usual. If the divisor has a decimal point, complete the steps that follow.

Dividing Decimals

Step 1. Make the divisor a whole number by moving the decimal point to the right.

Step 2. Move the decimal point in the dividend to the right the same number of places that you moved the decimal point in the divisor (Step 1). If there are not enough places, add zeros to the right of the dividend.

Step 3. Place the decimal point in the quotient above the new decimal point in the dividend. Divide as usual.

EXAMPLE

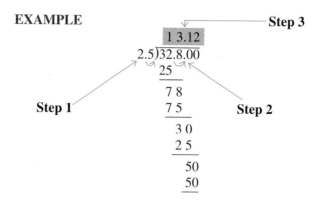

Step 3

Step 1

Step 2

Stop a moment and study the above example. Note that the quotient does not change when we multiply the divisor and the dividend by the same number. This is why we can move the decimal point in division problems and always divide by a whole number.

Decimal Applications in Foreign Currency

Let's assume that you joined the *USA Today* news service. Your cousin from Canada visits you. She is fascinated as she watches you get the latest news on your computer.

Your cousin is thinking about buying a computer. You and your cousin go to Circuit City to shop for computers. You both decide that a $3,500 computer package is the best buy. Your cousin asks, "Considering the foreign exchange rate, what would this computer package cost in Canada?"

Upon returning home, you go to your latest copy of *The Wall Street Journal* and show your cousin a currency cross-rate table similar to the following:

Key Currency Cross Rates

	Dollar	Pound	SFranc	Guilder	Peso	Yen	Lira	D-Mark	FFranc	CdnDlr
Canada	1.4369	2.3992	.95934	.71070	.16925	.01085	.00081	.80028	.23869	....
France	6.0200	10.052	4.0192	2.9775	.70907	.04548	.00339	3.3528	....	4.1896
Germany	1.7955	2.9979	1.1988	.88807	.21148	.01356	.00101	....	.29826	1.2496
Italy	1774.0	2962.0	1184.4	877.44	208.95	13.401	....	988.03	294.68	1234.6
Japan	132.38	221.03	88.383	65.476	15.592	....	.07462	73.729	21.99	92.129
Mexico	8.4900	14.176	5.6683	4.1992	....	.06413	.00479	4.7285	1.4103	5.9086
Netherlands ..	2.0218	3.3758	1.3498	....	.23814	.01527	.00114	1.1260	.33585	1.4071
Switzerland ...	1.4978	2.5009	....	.74083	.17642	.01131	.00084	.83420	.24880	1.0424
U.K.	.59891	....	.39986	.29623	.07054	.00452	.00034	.33356	.09949	.41681
U.S.	....	1.6697	.66765	.49461	.11779	.00755	.00056	.55695	.16611	.69594

Source: Dow Jones

From the first column in the table, your cousin sees that in Canada, the U.S. dollar is worth $1.4369. Multiplying $3,500.00 by $1.4369, she knows that the $3,500.00 Circuit City computer package would cost $5,029.15. How can your cousin check this?

She can check this by looking at the last item, $.69594, in the bottom far right column. This number says that in the United States, the Canadian dollar is worth $.69594. When your cousin multiplies the $5,029.15 Canadian computer package by $.69594, she gets $3,500.00—the cost of the computer package at Circuit City.

$3,500.00 × 1.4369 = $5,029.15 ← Cost in Canada

Check* $5,029.15 × .69594 = $3,500.00 ← Cost in United States

*Off 1 cent due to rounding.

The next section shows you some shortcuts that you can use for multiplying and dividing decimal numbers.

Multiplication and Division Shortcuts for Decimals

If you use e-mail, you may wonder how you can pick up your messages while traveling. *The Wall Street Journal* in its clipping "Cybercafes" tells you that virtually every big city now has cybercafes with Internet access. Do you plan to attend a business conference in

Cybercafes

Neurotic about checking e-mail on the road? Relax—there are now cafes with Internet access in virtually every big city (and some small ones). Samples below:

CITY	CYBERCAFE	ON-LINE CHARGES			
Albuquerque, N.M.	Webolution Cafe	$4 per half hour (minimum); $7 per hour	**Berkeley, Calif.**	Transbay.net	$5 per half hour; $10 per hour
Austin, Texas	WWW Cafe Inc.	$3 per half hour; $6 per hour	**Nashville, Tenn.**	Bean Central	$2 per half hour; $4 per hour
			Norman, Okla.	Main Street Cyberhall	$5.40 per half hour; $10.80 per hour

Source: Cybercafes: A Worldwide Guide for Travelers

©PhotoDisc.

© 1998 Dow Jones & Company, Inc.

Norman, Oklahoma? You and your business associates can visit the Main Street Cyberhall to access the Internet. Assume your group uses 10 hours of Internet time at $10.80 per hour. What is the total cost of the visit? Since this involves a multiple of 10, you can quickly determine the amount by moving the decimal in $10.80 one place to the right. Your total cost will be $108. The shortcut steps that follow show how to quickly solve problems involving multiples of 10.

Shortcuts for Multiples of 10

Multiplication

Step 1. Count the zeros in the multiplier.

Step 2. Move the decimal point in the multiplicand the same number of places to the right as you have zeros in the multiplier.

Division

Step 1. Count the zeros in the divisor.

Step 2. Move the decimal point in the dividend the same number of places to the left as you have zeros in the divisor.

In multiplication, the answers are *larger* than the original number.

EXAMPLE   If the art collector's average trip cost $252.59, what is the total value of 100 trips?

$252.59 × 100 = $25,259.   (2 places to the right)

OTHER EXAMPLES   6.89 × 10 = 68.9   (1 place to the right)

6.89 × 100 = 689.   (2 places to the right)

6.89 × 1,000 = 6,890.   (3 places to the right)

In division, the answers are *smaller* than the original number.

EXAMPLES   6.89 ÷ 10 = .689   (1 place to the left)

6.89 ÷ 100 = .0689   (2 places to the left)

6.89 ÷ 1,000 = .00689   (3 places to the left)

6.89 ÷ 10,000 = .000689   (4 places to the left)

Next, let's dissect and solve a word problem.

How to Dissect and Solve a Word Problem

The Word Problem   May O'Mally went to Sears to buy wall-to-wall carpet. She needs 101.3 square yards for downstairs, 16.3 square yards for the upstairs bedrooms, and 6.2 square yards for the halls. The carpet cost $14.55 per square yard. The padding cost $3.25 per square yard. Sears quoted an installation charge of $6.25 per square yard. What was May O'Mally's total cost?

By completing the following blueprint aid, we will slowly dissect this word problem. Note that before solving the problem, we gather the facts, identify what we are solving for, and list the steps that must be completed before finding the final answer, along with any key points we should remember. Let's go to it!

The facts	Solving for?	Steps to take	Key points
Carpet needed: 101.3 sq. yd.; 16.3 sq. yd.; 6.2 sq. yd. *Costs:* Carpet, $14.55 per sq. yd.; padding, $3.25 per sq. yd.; installation, $6.25 per sq. yd.	Total cost of carpet.	Total square yards × Cost per square yard = Total cost.	Align decimals. Round answer to nearest cent.

Steps to solving problem

1. Calculate the total number of square yards.

2. Calculate the total cost per square yard.

3. Calculate the total cost of carpet.

   It's time to check your progress.

```
  101.3
   16.3
    6.2
  123.8  square yards
$14.55
  3.25
  6.25
$24.05
```
123.8 × $24.05 = **$2,977.39**

LU 3.2 PRACTICE QUIZ

1. Rearrange vertically and add:
   14, .642, 9.34, 15.87321

2. Rearrange and subtract:
   28.1549 − .885

3. Multiply and round the answer to the nearest tenth:
   28.53 × 17.4

4. Divide and round to the nearest hundredth:
   2,182 ÷ 2.83

Complete by the shortcut method:

5. 14.28 × 100   6. 9,680 ÷ 1,000   7. 9,812 ÷ 10,000

8. Could you help Mel decide which product is the "better buy"?

   Dog food A   **Dog food B**
   $9.01 for 64 ounces $7.95 for 50 ounces

   Round to the nearest cent as needed.

9. At Avis Rent-A-Car, the cost per day to rent a medium-size car is $39.99 plus 29 cents per mile. What is the charge to rent this car for 2 days if you drive 602.3 miles? You might want to complete a blueprint aid since the solution will show a completed one.

10. A trip to Mexico cost 6,000 pesos. What would this be in U.S. dollars? Check your answer.

✓ **Solutions**

1. 14.00000
   .64200
   9.34000
   15.87321
   39.85521

2. 28.1549
   − .8850
   27.2699

3.

$$
\begin{array}{r}
28.53 \\
\times\ 17.4 \\
\hline
11\ 412 \\
199\ 71 \\
\underline{285\ 3} \\
496.422
\end{array} = \boxed{496.4}
$$

4.

$$
\begin{array}{r}
771.024 = 771.02 \\
2.83\overline{)218200.000} \\
\underline{1981} \\
2010 \\
\underline{1981} \\
290 \\
\underline{283} \\
7\ 00 \\
\underline{5\ 66} \\
1\ 340 \\
\underline{1\ 132}
\end{array}
$$

5. $14.28 = \boxed{1,428}$ **6.** $9.680 = \boxed{9.680}$ **7.** $.9812 = \boxed{.9812}$

8. **A:** $\$9.01 \div 64 = \boxed{\$.14}$ **B:** $\$7.95 \div 50 = \boxed{\$.16}$ Buy A.

9. Avis Rent-A-Car total rental charge:

The facts	Solving for?	Steps to take	Key points
Cost per day, $39.99. 29 cents per mile. Drove 602.3 miles. 2-day rental.	Total rental charge.	Total cost for 2 days' rental + Total cost of driving = Total rental charge.	In multiplication, count the number of decimal places. Starting from right to left in the product, insert decimal in appropriate place. Round to nearest cent.

Steps to solving problem

1. Calculate total costs for 2 days' rental.
2. Calculate the total cost of driving.
3. Calculate the total rental charge.

$\$39.99 \times 2 = \$79.98$

$\$.29 \times 602.3 = \$174.667 = \$174.67$

$$
\begin{array}{r}
\$\ 79.98 \\
+\ 174.67 \\
\hline
\$254.65
\end{array}
$$

10. $6,000 \times \$.11779 = \boxed{\$706.74}$

Check $\$706.74 \times 8.4900 = 6,000.22$ pesos due to rounding

---

Chapter Organizer and Reference Guide		
Topic	**Key point, procedure, formula**	**Example(s) to illustrate**
Identifying place value, p. 64	$10, 1, \dfrac{1}{10}, \dfrac{1}{100}, \dfrac{1}{1,000}$, etc.	.439 in thousandths place value
Rounding, p. 65	1. Identify place value of digit you want to round. 2. If digit to right of identified digit in Step 1 is 5 or more, increase identified digit by 1; if less than 5, do not change identified digit. 3. Drop all digits to right of identified digit.	.875 rounded to nearest tenth = .9 Identified digit
Converting decimal fractions to decimals, p. 66	1. Decimal fraction has a denominator with multiples of 10. Count number of zeros in denominator. 2. Zeros show how many places are in the decimal.	$\dfrac{8}{1,000} = .008$ $\dfrac{6}{10,000} = .0006$
Converting proper fractions to decimals, p. 67	1. Divide numerator of fraction by its denominator. 2. Round as necessary.	$\dfrac{1}{3}$ (to nearest tenth) $= .3$
Converting mixed numbers to decimals, p. 68	1. Convert fractional part of the mixed number to a decimal. 2. Add converted fractional part to whole number.	$6\dfrac{1}{4}$ $\dfrac{1}{4} = .25 + 6 = 6.25$

Topic	Key point, procedure, formula	Example(s) to illustrate
Chapter Organizer and Reference Guide (concluded)		
Converting pure and mixed decimals to decimal fractions, pp. 68, 69	1. Place digits to right of decimal point in numerator of fraction. 2. Put 1 in denominator. 3. Add zeros to denominator, depending on decimal places of original number. For mixed decimals, add fraction to whole number.	.984 (3 places) 1. $\dfrac{984}{}$ 2. $\dfrac{984}{1}$ 3. $\dfrac{984}{1,000}$
Adding and subtracting decimals, p. 70	1. Vertically write and align numbers on decimal points. 2. Add or subtract digits, starting with right column and moving to the left. 3. Align decimal point in answer with above decimal points.	Add 1.3 + 2 + .4 1.3 2.0 .4 3.7 Subtract 5 − 3.9 $\overset{4\ 10}{\cancel{5}.\cancel{0}}$ − 3.9 1.1
Multiplying decimals, p. 71	1. Multiply numbers, ignoring decimal points. 2. Count and total number of decimal places in multiplier and multiplicand. 3. Starting at right in the product, count to the left the number of decimal places totaled in Step 2. Insert decimal point. If number of places greater than space in answer, add zeros.	2.48 (2 places) × .018 (3 places) 1 984 2 48 .04464
Dividing a decimal by a whole number, p. 71	1. Place decimal point in quotient directly above the decimal point in dividend. 2. Divide as usual.	$\begin{array}{r} 1.1 \\ 42\overline{)46.2} \\ \underline{42} \\ 42 \\ \underline{42} \end{array}$
Dividing if the divisor is a decimal, p. 72	1. Make divisor a whole number by moving decimal point to the right. 2. Move decimal point in dividend to the right the same number of places as in Step 1. 3. Place decimal point in quotient above decimal point in dividend. Divide as usual.	$\begin{array}{r} 14.2 \\ 2.9\overline{)41.39} \\ \underline{29} \\ 123 \\ \underline{116} \\ 79 \\ \underline{58} \\ 21 \end{array}$
Shortcuts on multiplication and division of decimals, p. 73	When multiplying by 10, 100, 1,000, and so on, move decimal point in multiplicand the same number of places to the right as you have zeros in multiplier. For division, move decimal point to the left.	4.85 × 100 = 485 4.85 ÷ 100 = .0485
Key terms	Decimal, *p. 64* Decimal fraction, *p. 66* Decimal point, *p. 64*	Mixed decimal, *p. 68* Repeating decimal, *p. 67* Pure decimal, *p. 68* Rounding decimals, *p. 65*

Note: For how to dissect and solve a word problem, see page 74.

Critical Thinking Discussion Questions

1. What are the steps for rounding decimals? Federal income tax forms allow the taxpayer to round each amount to the nearest dollar. Do you agree with this?

2. Explain how to convert fractions to decimals. If 1 out of 20 people buys a Land Rover, how could you write an advertisement in decimals?

3. Explain why .07, .70, and .700 are not equal. Assume you take a family trip to Disney World that covers 500 miles. Show that $\frac{8}{10}$ of the trip, or .8 of the trip, represents 400 miles.

4. Explain the steps in the addition or subtraction of decimals. Visit a car dealership and find the difference between two sticker prices. Be sure to check each sticker price for accuracy. Should you always pay the sticker price?

DRILL PROBLEMS

Identify the place value for the following:

3–1. 7.86328   hundredths
↑

3–2. 158.731   thousandths
↑

Round the following as indicated:

		Tenth	Hundredth	Thousandth
3–3.	.8951	.9	.90	.895
3–4.	.6257	.6	.63	.626
3–5.	6.9245	6.9	6.92	6.925
3–6.	6.8415	6.8	6.84	6.842
3–7.	6.5555	6.6	6.56	6.556
3–8.	75.9913	76.0	75.99	75.991

Round the following to the nearest cent:

3–9. $1,862.778 $1,862.78

3–10. $4,892.046 $4,892.05

Convert the following types of decimal fractions to decimals (round to nearest hundredth as needed):

3–11. $\dfrac{9}{100}$ .09

3–12. $\dfrac{4}{10}$ .40

3–13. $\dfrac{91}{1,000}$ .09

3–14. $\dfrac{910}{1,000}$ .91

3–15. $\dfrac{64}{100}$ .64

3–16. $\dfrac{979}{1,000}$ .98

3–17. $14\dfrac{91}{100}$ 14.91

Convert the following decimals to fractions. Do not reduce to lowest terms.

3–18. .8 $\dfrac{8}{10}$

3–19. .62 $\dfrac{62}{100}$

3–20. .006 $\dfrac{6}{1,000}$

3–21. .0125 $\dfrac{125}{10,000}$

3–22. .609 $\dfrac{609}{1,000}$

3–23. .825 $\dfrac{825}{1,000}$

3–24. .9999 $\dfrac{9,999}{10,000}$

3–25. .7065 $\dfrac{7,065}{10,000}$

Convert the following to mixed numbers. Do not reduce to lowest terms.

3–26. 6.6 $6\dfrac{6}{10}$

3–27. 28.48 $28\dfrac{48}{100}$

3–28. 6.025 $6\dfrac{25}{1,000}$

Write the decimal equivalent of the following:

3–29. Three thousandths   .003

3–30. Three hundred three and two hundredths   303.02

3–31. Eighty-five ten thousandths   .0085

3–32. Seven hundred seventy-five thousandths   .775

Rearrange the following and add:

3–33. .041,   9.8532,   2.6,   701.3821
713.8763

3–34. .005,   2,002.181,   795.41,   14.0,   .184
2,811.78

Rearrange the following and subtract:

3–35. 7.9 − 4.3 = 3.6

3–36. 7 − 2.0815 = 4.9185

3–37. 3.4 − 1.08 = 2.32

Estimate by rounding all the way and multiply the following (do not round final answer):

3–38. 6.24 × 3.9 = 24.336
Estimate   24 (6 × 4)

3–39. .413 × 3.07 = 1.26791
Estimate   1.2 (.4 × 3)

3–40. 675 × 1.92 = 1,296
Estimate   1,400 (700 × 2)

3–41. 4.9 × .825 = 4.0425
Estimate   4.0 (5 × .8)

Divide the following and round to the nearest hundredth:

3–42. .8931 ÷ 3 = .30

3–43. 29.432 ÷ .0012 = 24,526.67

3–44. .0065 ÷ .07 = .09

3–45. 7,742.1 ÷ 48 = 161.29

3–46. 8.95 ÷ 1.18 = 7.58

3–47. 2,600 ÷ .381 = 6,824.15

Convert the following to decimals and round to the nearest hundredth:

3–48. $\dfrac{1}{8}$ .13 **3–49.** $\dfrac{1}{25}$ .04 **3–50.** $\dfrac{5}{6}$ .83 **3–51.** $\dfrac{5}{8}$ .63

Complete these multiplications and divisions by the shortcut method (do not do any written calculations):

3–52. $96.7 \div 10 = 9.67$ **3–53.** $258.5 \div 100 = 2.585$ **3–54.** $8.51 \times 1,000 = 8,510$

3–55. $.86 \div 100 = .0086$ **3–56.** $9.015 \times 100 = 901.5$ **3–57.** $48.6 \times 10 = 486$

3–58. $750 \times 10 = 7,500$ **3–59.** $3,950 \div 1,000 = 3.950$ **3–60.** $8.45 \div 10 = .845$

3–61. $7.9132 \times 1,000 = 7,913.2$

WORD PROBLEMS

As needed, round answers to nearest cent.

3–62. At a demonstration for a new Compaq Computer, 900 seats were set up. During the demonstration, 60 seats were vacant. In decimals (to nearest hundredth), show how many seats were filled.

$900 - 60 = 840$ $\dfrac{840}{900} = .93$

3–63. Al Fox got 6 hits out of 11 at bats. What was his batting average to the nearest thousandths place?

$\dfrac{6}{11} = .545$

3–64. The October 1997 issue of *Nation's Business* states that proposed changes will increase U.S. postal rates from $.32 to $.33 for a first-class letter. Assuming the proposed changes occur, if you sent 40 Christmas cards this year (at old rate) and plan to send 45 cards next year, what would be your cost this year versus next year? What would be the amount of increase?

$$\begin{array}{r} 40 \\ \times\ \$.32 \\ \hline \$12.80 \text{ this year} \end{array} \qquad \begin{array}{r} 45 \\ \times\ \$.33 \\ \hline \$14.85 \text{ next year} \end{array} \qquad \begin{array}{r} \$14.85 \\ -\ \ 12.80 \\ \hline \$\ 2.05 \text{ increase} \end{array}$$

3–65. Les Vey purchased 16.45 yards of ribbon for the annual fair at the Party Store. Each yard cost 61 cents. What was the total cost of the ribbon?

$16.45 \times \$.61 = \$10.03$

3–66. Douglas Noel went to Home Depot and bought 4 doors at $42.99 each and 6 bags of fertilizer at $8.99. What was the total cost to Douglas? If Douglas had $300 in his pocket, what does he have left to spend?

$$\begin{array}{r} 4 \times \$42.99 = \$171.96 \\ 6 \times\ \ \ 8.99 = \underline{\ \ \ 53.94} \\ \$225.90 \end{array} \qquad \begin{array}{r} \$300.00 \\ -\ 225.90 \\ \hline \$\ \ 74.10 \end{array}$$

3–67. Howard is shopping for a top sirloin beef roast. At market A, a top sirloin roast is $3.998 per pound. At market B, it is $3.813 per pound. How much cheaper is market B?

$$\begin{array}{r} \$3.998 \\ -\ \ 3.813 \\ \hline \$\ .185 \text{ cheaper} \end{array}$$

3–68. Ed Weld is traveling to a comic convention in San Diego by car. His company will reimburse him $.39 per mile. If Ed travels 906.5 miles, how much will Ed receive from his company?

$\$.39 \times 906.5 = \$353.54$

3–69. Mark Ogara rented a truck for the weekend (2 days). The base rental price was $29.95 per day plus $14\frac{1}{2}$ cents per mile. Mark drove 410.85 miles. How much does Mark owe?

$$\begin{array}{r} 2 \times \$29.95 = \$\ 59.90 \\ \$.145 \times 410.85 = \underline{+\ 59.57} \\ \$119.47 \end{array}$$

3–70. The August 1996 *Consumer Reports,* in the "What's the Risk?" article about investing in gold, stated that in 1964 a Ford Mustang sold for $2,500. Gold was valued at $35 per ounce in 1964. How many ounces of gold would it cost to purchase the Ford Mustang? Round up to the next ounce. How does this compare to a $28,000 Ford Mustang today if we assume gold is at $390 per ounce? How many ounces of gold would it take to purchase the Ford Mustang today? Round up to the next ounce.

$\$2,500 \div \$35 \text{ per oz.} = 71.42 = 72 \text{ oz.}$ $\$28,000 \div \$390 \text{ per oz.} = 71.79 = 72 \text{ oz.}$ Same amount

3–71. Lucy King bought a new sweater at Macy's for $189.99. She gave the salesperson two $100 bills. What is Lucy's change? Check your answer.

		Check	$ 10.01
$200.00			+ 189.99
− 189.99			$200.00
$ 10.01 change			

3–72. Russell is preparing the daily bank deposit for his coffee shop. Before the deposit, the coffee shop had a checking account balance of $3,185.66. The deposit contains the following checks:

No. 1 $ 99.50   No. 3 $8.75
No. 2   110.35   No. 4   6.83

Russell included $820.55 in currency with the deposit. What is the coffee shop's new balance, assuming Russell writes no new checks?

$3,185.66
    99.50
  110.35
    8.75
    6.83
+ 820.55
$4,231.64

3–73. On November 17, 1997, the *Chicago Tribune* stated that the NFL standings showed the Green Bay Packers with a .727 win-loss record and the Chicago Bears with a .091 win-loss record. What is the difference in decimals?

.727
− .091
.636

3–74. Christine wants to install wall-to-wall carpeting at home. She needs 110.8 square yards for downstairs, 31.8 square yards for the halls, and 161.9 square yards for the bedrooms upstairs. Christine chose a shag carpet that costs $14.99 per square yard. She ordered foam padding at $3.10 per square yard. The carpet installers quoted Christine a labor charge of $3.75 per square yard. What will the total job cost Christine?

$14.99 + $3.10 + $3.75 = $ 21.84
110.8 square yards + 31.8 square yards + 161.9 square yards =   × 304.5
$6,650.28

3–75. Art Norton bought 4 new Aquatred tires at Goodyear for $89.99 per tire. Goodyear charged $3.05 per tire for mounting, $2.95 per tire for valve stems, and $3.80 per tire for balancing. If Art paid no sales tax, what was his total cost for the 4 tires?

$89.99 + $3.05 + $2.95 + $3.80 = $ 99.79
$99.79 × 4 = $399.16

3–76. Shelly is shopping for laundry detergent, mustard, and canned tuna. She is trying to decide which of two products is the better buy. Using the following information, can you help Shelly?

Laundry detergent A ✔	**Mustard A**	**Canned tuna A**
$2.00 for 37 ounces	$.88 for 6 ounces	$1.09 for 6 ounces
$2.00 ÷ 37 = $.05	.88 ÷ 6 = $.15	$1.09 ÷ 6 = $.18
Laundry detergent B	**Mustard B** ✔	**Canned tuna B** ✔
$2.37 for 38 ounces	$1.61 for 12½ ounces	$1.29 for 8¾ ounces
$2.37 ÷ 38 = $.06	$1.61 ÷ 12.5 = $.13	$1.29 ÷ 8.75 = $.15

3–77. Rick bought season tickets to professional basketball games. The cost was $695.10. The season package included 32 homes games. What is the average price of the tickets per game? Round to the nearest cent. Marcelo, Rick's friend, offered to buy 4 of the tickets from Rick. What is the total amount Rick should receive?

$695.10 ÷ 32 = $21.72 × 4 = $86.88

3–78. A nurse was to give her patients a 1.32-unit dosage of a prescribed drug. The total remaining units of the drug at the hospital pharmacy were 53.12. The nurse has 38 patients. Will there be enough dosages for all her patients?

$\frac{53.12}{1.32}$ = 40.24   Yes.

3–79. Audrey Long went to Japan and bought an animation cell of Mickey Mouse. The price was 25,000 yen. What is the price in U.S. dollars? Check your answer.

25,000 × $.00755 = $188.75
$188.75 × 132.38 = 24,986.73 yen   (Rounded to 25,000 yen)

ADDITIONAL SET OF WORD PROBLEMS

3–80. The oil tank in Gold's Health Club reads 280.90 gallons on January 31. During February, the oil company filled the tank with 112.88 gallons. The club used 210.45 gallons in February. How many gallons of oil are in the tank on February 28?
280.90 + 112.88 = 393.78 − 210.45 = 183.33 gallons

3–81. Tie Yang bought season tickets to the Boston Pops for $698.55. The season package included 38 performances. What is the average price of the tickets per performance? Round to nearest cent. Sam, Tie's friend, offered to buy 4 of the tickets from Tie. What is the total amount Tie should receive?
$698.55 ÷ 38 = $18.38 × 4 = $73.52

3–82. Morris Katz bought 4 new tires at Goodyear for $95.49 per tire. Goodyear also charged Morris $2.50 per tire for mounting, $2.40 per tire for valve stems, and $3.95 per tire for balancing. Assume no tax. What was Morris's total cost for the 4 tires?
$95.49 + $2.50 + $2.40 + $3.95 = $104.34
$104.34 × 4 = $417.36

3–83. In the November 21, 1997, *Downers Grove Reporter,* Aldi Food Store advertised 6 ounces of pecan halves for $1.49 and 16 ounces of walnuts for $2.99. Your recipe calls for 8 ounces of nuts—either pecan or walnuts. What would be the cost using the lowest price for 8 ounces of nuts? Round your final answer to the nearest cent.
$1.49 ÷ 6 = $.2483333 $2.99 ÷ 16 = $.186875 (lowest) $.186875
                                                                    ×   8 oz.
                                                                    ―――――――
                                                                    $1.495   = $1.50

3–84. Steven is traveling to a computer convention by car. His company will reimburse him $.29 per mile. If Steven travels 890.5 miles, how much will he receive from his company?
890.5 × $.29 = $258.25

3–85. Nancy wants to install wall-to-wall carpeting in her house. She needs 104.8 square yards for downstairs, 17.4 square yards for halls, and 165.8 square yards for the upstairs bedrooms. Nancy chose a shag carpet that costs $13.95 per square yard. She ordered foam padding at $2.75 per square yard. The installers quoted Nancy a labor cost of $5.75 per square yard in installation. What will the total job cost Nancy?
$13.95 + $2.75 + $5.75 = $22.45
104.8 square yards + 17.4 square yards + 165.8 square yards = 288 square yards
288 × $22.45 = $6,465.60

3–86. The October 1997 issue of *Nation's Business* reported proposed changes in selected postal rates. For Express mail, a half-pound package would increase to $11.25 and a 2-pound package would increase to $14.95. **(a)** What is the cost per half pound when a 2-pound package is sent? **(b)** If 4 half-pound packages were sent, what would be the total cost? **(c)** What are the total savings in sending a 2-pound package versus 4 half-pound packages? A 2-pound package equals 4 half-pound packages.

  a. $3.7375 or $3.74   **b.** $11.25   **c.** $45.00
         4)$14.95   ×   4   − 14.95
                                     $45.00 $30.05 savings

CHALLENGE PROBLEMS

3–87. The following items were charged in Canada to your bank credit card: U.S. Dollars)
         1. Harmony Grand Buffet, London, Canada $40.63
         2. Econo Lodge, London, Canada   56.45
         3. Teddy's Restaurant, Oshawa, Canada   11.27
         4. Charlies Restaurant, Kitchener, Canada   15.98
         5. ESSO Gasoline, Spencerville, Canada   18.00

  a. Using your text exchange rates, find the amount you should be charged for each item.

  b. What should your total bill be? Check your answer.

    a. 1. $ 40.63 × .69594 = $28.28
          2.   56.45 × .69594 =   39.29
          3.   11.27 × .69594 =   7.84
          4.   15.98 × .69594 =   11.12
          5.   18.00 × .69594 =   12.53
                                     ―――――

    b. $142.33 $99.06

    Check $99.06 × 1.4369 = $142.34 (off 1 cent due to rounding)

3–88. Jill and Frank decided to take a long weekend in New York. City Hotel has a special getaway weekend for $79.95. The price is per person per night, based on double occupancy. The hotel has a minimum two-night stay. For this price, Jill and Frank will receive $50 credit toward their dinners at City's Skylight Restaurant. Also included in the package is a $3.99 credit per person toward breakfast for two each morning.

   Since Jill and Frank do not own a car, they plan to rent a car. The car rental agency charges $19.95 a day with an additional charge of $.22 a mile and $1.19 per gallon of gas used. The gas tank holds 24 gallons.

   From the following facts, calculate the total expenses of Jill and Frank (round all answers to nearest hundredth or cent as appropriate). Assume no taxes.

Car rental (2 days):		Dinner cost at Skylight	$182.12
Beginning odometer reading	4,820	Breakfast for two:	
Ending odometer reading	4,940	Morning No. 1	24.17
Beginning gas tank: $\frac{3}{4}$ full.		Morning No. 2	26.88
Gas tank on return: $\frac{1}{2}$ full.			
Tank holds 24 gallons.			

$\$ \ 79.95 \times 2 = \$159.90 \times 2 \qquad\qquad = \$319.80$

$\$182.12$
$-\ 50.00$
‾‾‾‾‾‾‾
$\$132.12 \qquad\qquad\qquad\qquad\qquad\qquad 132.12$

Breakfast No. 1: $24.17
                   $-\ 7.98$
                   ‾‾‾‾‾‾
                    $16.19 \qquad\qquad\qquad 16.19$

Breakfast No. 2: $26.88
                   $-\ 7.98$
                   ‾‾‾‾‾‾
                    $18.90 \qquad\qquad\qquad 18.90$

$2 \times \$19.95 \qquad\qquad\qquad\qquad\qquad 39.90$

$\$.22 \times 120\ (4{,}940 - 4{,}820) \qquad\qquad 26.40$

$\dfrac{1}{4} \times 24 = 6$ gallons $\times \$1.19 \qquad\qquad \underline{7.14}$

$\qquad\qquad\qquad\qquad\qquad\qquad\qquad\qquad\ \ \$560.45$

 SUMMARY PRACTICE TEST

1. Add the following by translating the verbal form to the decimal equivalent. *(p. 70)*

Three hundred forty-nine and nine hundred four thousandths	349.904
Fifteen and fifty-nine hundredths	15.590
Three and three thousandths	3.003
Seventy-four hundredths	.740
Two hundred three and nine tenths	203.900
	‾‾‾‾‾‾
	573.137

Convert the following decimal fractions to decimals. *(p. 66)*

2. $\dfrac{4}{10}$ .4   **3.** $\dfrac{4}{100}$ .04   **4.** $\dfrac{4}{1,000}$ .004

Convert the following to proper fractions or mixed numbers. Do not reduce to lowest terms. *(p. 68)*

5. .3 $\dfrac{3}{10}$ **6.** 5.76 $5\dfrac{76}{100}$ **7.** .795 $\dfrac{795}{1,000}$

Convert the following fractions to decimals (or mixed decimals) and round to the nearest hundredth as needed. *(p. 67)*

8. $\dfrac{1}{6}$ .17   **9.** $\dfrac{3}{5}$ .60   **10.** $3\dfrac{4}{9}$ 3.44   **11.** $\dfrac{1}{9}$ .11

12. Rearrange the following and add. *(p. 70)*

4.7,   7.45,   9.391,   176.0892,   75.5

$$
\begin{array}{r}
4.7000 \\
7.4500 \\
9.3910 \\
176.0892 \\
75.5000 \\
\hline
273.1302
\end{array}
$$

13. Subtract the following and round to the nearest tenth. *(p. 71)*

$15.966 - 2.59 = 13.4$

14. Multiply the following and round to the nearest hundredth. *(p. 71)*

$8.4295 \times 13.942 = 117.52$

15. Divide the following and round to the nearest tenth. *(p. 71)*

$120,666 \div 4.26 = 28,325.4$

Complete the following by the shortcut method. *(p. 73)*

16. $77.22 \times 1,000 = 77,220$

17. $5,099,169.852 \times 100 = 509,916,985.2$

18. The average pay of employees is $420.55 per week. Leroy Moss earns $462.95 per week. How much is Leroy's pay over the average? *(p. 71)*

$\$462.95 - \$420.55 = \$42.40$

19. Liberty Mutual reimburses Jeff $.29 per mile. Jeff submitted a travel log for a total of 1,500.2 miles. What will Liberty pay Jeff? Round to the nearest cent. *(p. 71)*

$\$.29 \times 1,500.2 = \$435.06$

20. Al Vincent bought 2 new car tires from Firestone for $96.80 per tire. Firestone also charged Al $2.99 per tire for mounting, $2.80 per tire for valve stems, and $4.10 per tire for balancing. What is Al's final bill? *(p. 74)*

$2 \times \$96.80 = \$193.60$

$2 \times \$\ 9.89 = +19.78$ ($\$2.99 + \$2.80 + \$4.10 = \$9.89$)

$\qquad\qquad\quad \overline{\$213.38}$

21. Could you help Mandy decide which of the following products is cheaper per ounce? *(p. 72)*

Canned fruit A	**Canned fruit B** ✔
$.62 for 3 ounces	$.72 for $4\frac{3}{4}$ ounces
$\$.62 \div 3 = \$.2067$	$\$.72 \div 4.75 = \$.1516$

22. Larry Lens bought a watch in Italy for 15,000 lira. What is this in U.S. dollars? *(p. 72)*

$15,000 \times \$.00056 = \$8.40$

$\$8.40 \times 1,774\quad = 14,901.60$ lira   (Rounded to 15,000)

A GROUP PROJECT   Defend or reject the following business math issue based on the *Kiplinger's Personal Finance Magazine* article below:

TRAVEL
Just the place for terminal workaholics

For less than you'd pay for a crummy airport meal, you can now do some serious work while you're stuck in the terminal.

A Seattle-based company called Laptop Lane is opening private, fully equipped office spaces in airports that travelers may rent for $8.95 per half-hour. Currently available at Cincinnati/Northern Kentucky International Airport and Seattle-Tacoma (and at Atlanta Hartsfield in January), the offices have all the high-tech accouterments of a well-equipped business office, including a T-1 line to the Internet. "You can receive e-mail, participate in a conference call, get a fax and surf the Net all at the same time," says Bruce Merrell, one of Laptop Lane's founders.

And each location is staffed with a real-life "cyberconcierge." Recently, two software-company executives who were pressed for time arrived at the Seattle facility with a lengthy presentation they had worked on en route. The cyberconcierge transferred the file to a desktop computer, printed it on a color laser printer, and made copies in color and black-and-white. She also arranged a limo, so that when the copies were completed the customers walked out of the terminal and into a waiting car. Laptop Lane plans to open facilities in four major airports in 1999.   —*LYNN WOODS*

Working on the run: Send a fax and surf the Net while you wait at the gate.

ILLUSTRATIONS BY STEVEN GUARNACCIA; CHIEN-CHI CHANG/MAGNUM

Business Math Issue

Laptop Lane will not exist in 10 years. Rental rates at airports are too high.

1. List the key points of the article and information to support your position.
2. Write a group defense of your position using math calculations to support your view.

BUSINESS MATH SCRAPBOOK
Putting Your Skills to Work

Hint: For 10 Million, Write a 10, Then Six Zeros, Then a Little Dot

By ALBERT R. KARR

Staff Reporter of THE WALL STREET JOURNAL

As small businesses competed in a recent government auction to provide new wireless personal communications services in the area of Norfolk, Va., one bidder seemed to get carried away. PCS 2000, a partnership based in Old San Juan, Puerto Rico, offered $180 million.

Granted, the new wireless phones promise to send low-cost messages, images and data to receivers the size of credit cards or even to Dick Tracy-style wrist-radios. But keeping in mind that a license for the Norfolk PCS market has an estimated value of $30 million—tops— PCS 2000 seemed more than generous when it eclipsed the previous high bid of $16,369,313 from DCR Communications Inc. of Washington, D.C., by $163,630,687.

Even after deducting some small-business credits for which PCS 2000 qualifies, bringing the net bid down to $135 million, the offer ranked Norfolk near the top of 493 wireless-spectrum markets up for grabs in the Federal Communications Commission auction — behind New York, Los Angeles and Chicago but ahead of San Francisco and Philadelphia.

Something seemed wrong — and was it ever. PCS 2000 had misplaced a decimal point. It told the FCC it had really meant to bid $18 million; last week, it canceled the offer. But there is no certainty it can escape so easily. Under FCC rules, which FCC auction chief Kathleen Ham says were "pounded into the bidders" before the auction began, PCS 2000 could face a penalty for backing out. A very big penalty, in fact: the difference between its $135 million net bid and whatever the winning offer turns out to be.

Faced with the prospect of forking over a sum that easily could top $100 million, PCS 2000 officials at first said the mistake was the FCC's, not theirs but now admit it probably was their goof. Ms. Ham says "we're very confident" the commission didn't err. The agency merely takes offers filed by computer, displays them on a screen and even lets bidders print copies; this gives all companies a chance to confirm whether they really want to bid the amounts shown, she explains.

A simple default isn't a way out, either. The FCC then could suspend the company's licenses. So PCS 2000 is seeking a waiver of the penalty, something the FCC has never granted. But there is a hint of relief, Ms. Ham suggests: The agency may be sympathetic if PCS 2000 made a "clear error"—and admits it.

Project A

Explain how this mistake happened. How harsh should the penalty be?

Movie Ticket Costs

U.S. movie ticket prices seem like a bargain compared with the average charge in some major countries.

Movie Ticket Prices Around the World

Japan	$17.19
Switzerland	13.15
Germany	8.93
France	8.85
Australia	8.77
Brazil	7.95
U.K.	7.84
Russia	7.83
Hong Kong	7.55
U.S.	7.07
Singapore	5.30
South Africa	4.15

Source: Business Traveler International

Project B

If a family of 4 (all adults) goes to a movie in Japan and then goes to a movie in the United States, what is the savings from the cost in Japan?

$4 \times \$17.19 = \quad \$68.76$

$4 \times \quad 7.07 = - \quad 28.28$

$\qquad\qquad\qquad \$40.48$

 See text Web site (www.mhhe.com/slater) and *The Business Math Internet Resource Guide.*

CUMULATIVE REVIEW: A Word Problem Approach—Chapters 1, 2, 3

1. The top rate at the Waldorf Towers Hotel in New York is $390. The top rate at the Ritz Carlton in Boston is $345. If John spends 9 days at the hotel, how much can he save if he stays at the Ritz? *(p. 17)*

    $390
    − 345
    $ 45 × 9 = $405

2. Robert Half Placement Agency was rated best by 4 to 1 in an independent national survey. If 250,000 responded to the survey, how many rated Robert Half the best? *(p. 45)*

    $\frac{4}{5}$ × 250,000 = 200,000

3. Of the 63.2 million people who watch professional football, only $\frac{1}{5}$ watch the commercials. How many viewers do not watch the commercials? *(p. 45)*

    $\frac{4}{5}$ × 63,200,000 = 50,560,000

4. AT&T advertised a 10-minute call for $2.27. MCI's rate was $2.02. Assuming Bill Splat makes forty 10-minute calls, how much could he save by using MCI? *(p. 70)*

    $2.27
    − 2.02
    $ .25 × 40 = $10.00

5. A square foot of rental space in New York City, Boston, and Rhode Island costs as follows: New York City, $6.25; Boston, $5.75; and Rhode Island, $3.75. If Compaq Computer wants to rent 112,500 square feet of space, what will Compaq save by renting in Rhode Island rather than Boston? *(p. 70)*

    $5.75
    − 3.75
    $2.00 × 112,500 = $225,000 savings from Boston

6. American Airlines has a frequent-flier program. Coupon brokers who buy and sell these awards pay between 1 and $1\frac{1}{2}$ cents for each mile earned. Fred Dietrich earned a 50,000-mile award (worth two free tickets to any city). If Fred decided to sell his award to a coupon broker, approximately how much would he receive? *(p. 71)*

    If 1 cent: $.01 × 50,000 = $500
    If $1\frac{1}{2}$ cents: $.015 × 50,000 = $750

7. Lillie Wong bought 4 new Firestone tires at $82.99 each. Firestone also charged $2.80 per tire for mounting, $1.95 per tire for valves, and $3.15 per tire for balancing. Lillie turned her 4 old tires in to Firestone, which charged $1.50 per tire to dispose of them. What was Lillie's final bill? *(p. 70)*

    4 × $82.99 = $331.96
    $2.80 + $1.95 + $3.15 = $7.90 × 4 =   31.60
    $363.56 + $6.00 = $369.56

8. Tootsie Roll Industries bought Charms Company for $65 million. Some analysts believe that in 4 years the purchase price could rise to 3 times as much. If the analysts are right, how much did Tootsie Roll save by purchasing Charms immediately? *(p. 13)*

    $65,000,000 × 3 = $195,000,000
                      − 65,000,000
                      $130,000,000

9. Today the average business traveler will spend almost $50 a day on food. The breakdown is dinner, $22.26; lunch, $10.73; breakfast, $6.53; tips, $6.23; and tax, $1.98. If Clarence Donato, an executive for Honeywell, spends only .3̄3̄ of the average, what is Clarence's total cost for food for the day? If Clarence wanted to spend $\frac{1}{3}$ more than the average on the next day, what would be his total cost on the second day? Round to the nearest cent. *(p. 46)*

    $22.26 + $10.73 + $6.53 + $6.23 + $1.98 = $47.73 actual
    $\frac{1}{3}$ × $47.73 = $15.91
    $1\frac{1}{3}$ × $47.73 = $\frac{4}{3}$ × $47.73 = $63.64

    Be sure you use the fractional equivalent in calculating .3̄3̄.

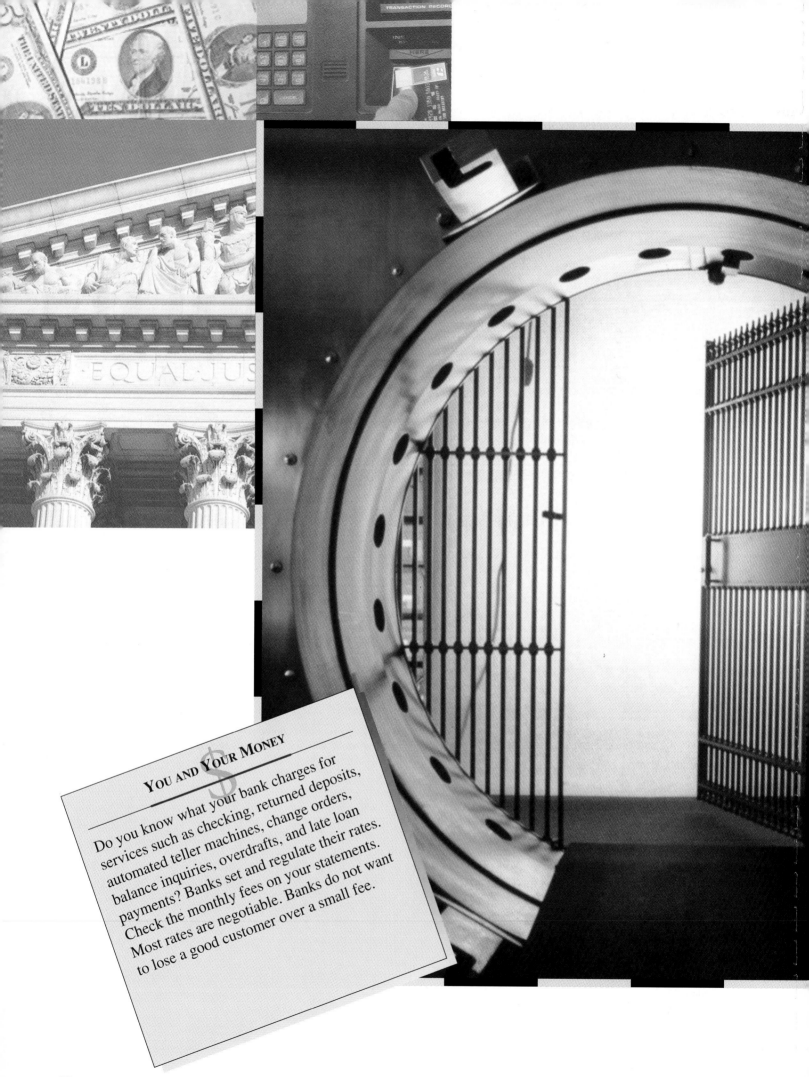

You and Your Money

Do you know what your bank charges for services such as checking, returned deposits, automated teller machines, change orders, balance inquiries, overdrafts, and late loan payments? Banks set and regulate their rates. Check the monthly fees on your statements. Most rates are negotiable. Banks do not want to lose a good customer over a small fee.

4

BANKING

LEARNING UNIT OBJECTIVES

LU 4.1 The Checking Account; Credit Card Transactions

- Define and state the purpose of signature cards, checks, deposit slips, check stubs, check registers, and endorsements *(pp. 88–90)*.
- Correctly prepare deposit slips, write checks, and complete a check register *(pp. 88–90)*.
- Explain how a merchant completes a credit card transaction for manual deposit or electronic deposit *(pp. 90–92)*.

LU 4.2 Bank Statement and Reconciliation Process; Trends in Banking

- Define and state the purpose of the bank statement *(pp. 94–95)*.
- List the steps to complete a bank reconciliation; prepare a bank reconciliation *(pp. 95–97)*.
- Explain the trends in banking *(pp. 98–100)*.

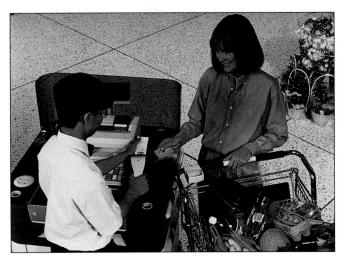

©Telegraph Colour Library/FPG International.

Do you still pay by cash or check for your groceries at the supermarket? Have you noticed that some people now use credit cards to pay for their groceries? This could be because more people are using a credit card company that returns in cash or credit a small percentage of the amount charged during the year. Since so much of a person's income goes for groceries, this is one way to help reduce the grocery bill, or collect more frequent-flier miles.

Another way that you can pay for groceries is by debit card. You have never heard of a debit card? You may have a debit card and do not even know it. **Debit cards** have been called enhanced **ATM (automatic teller machine)** cards or *check cards.* Banks have been issuing enhanced ATM cards as replacements for ATM-only cards. When you use your ATM card to get money from ATM machines, the amount you take out is immediately deducted from your checking account balance. The same is true with a debit card. However, paying by debit cards has some disadvantages.

When you write a check, you have the option of stopping payment on the check. You cannot do this on most debit card transactions. Also, if you use a credit card, you can only be held responsible for $50 of illegal charges, and during the time the credit card company investigates the illegal charges, they are removed from your account. However, with a debit card, this legal limit only applies if you report your card lost or stolen within two business days. After that your liability can increase. During the bank investigation, the amount stolen is not returned to your checking account.

We should add that debit cards are profitable for banks. When shopping, if you use a debit card that does not require a personal identification number, the store pays a fee to the bank that issued the card—usually from 1.4 to 2 cents on the dollar. By the year 2001, it is estimated that 10% of all U.S. consumer transactions will be by debit cards. (See the *Business Math Scrapbook,* page 111, for more details on debit cards.)

This chapter begins with a discussion of the checking account and credit card transactions. You will follow Gayle Jensen as she opens a checking account for Lantz Company and performs her banking and credit card transactions. Pay special attention to the procedure used by Lantz Company to reconcile its checking account and bank statement. This information will help you reconcile your checkbook records with the bank's record of your account. Finally, the chapter discusses how the trends in banking may affect your banking procedures.

LEARNING UNIT 4.1   The Checking Account; Credit Card Transactions

A **check** or **draft** is a written order instructing a bank, credit union, or savings and loan institution to pay a designated amount of your money on deposit to a person or an organization. Checking accounts are offered to individuals and businesses. The business checking account usually receives more services than the personal checking account.

Most small businesses depend on a checking account for efficient record keeping. In this chapter you will follow the checking account procedures of a newly organized small business. You can use many of these procedures in your personal check writing.

Elements of the Checking Account

Gayle Jensen, treasurer of Lantz Company, went to Fleet Bank to open a business checking account. The bank manager gave Gayle a **signature card.** The signature card contained space for the company's name and address, references, type of account, and the signature(s) of the person(s) authorized to sign checks. If necessary, the bank will use the signature card to verify that Gayle signed the checks. Some companies authorize more than one person to sign checks or require more than one signature on a check.

Gayle then lists on a **deposit slip** (or deposit ticket) the checks and cash she is depositing in her company's business account. The bank gave Gayle a temporary checkbook to use until the company's printed checks arrived. Gayle also will receive *preprinted* checking account deposit slips like the one shown in Figure 4.1. Since the deposit slips are in duplicate, Gayle can keep a record of her deposit.

FIGURE 4.1 Deposit slip

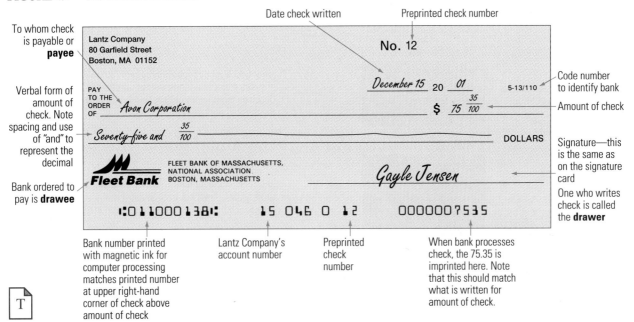

Preprinted numbers in magnetic ink identify bank number, routing and sorting of the check, and Lantz account number.

The 18-22 is taken from the upper right corner of the check from the top part of the fraction. This number is known as the American Bankers Association transit number. The 18 identifies the city or state where the bank is located and the 22 identifies the bank.

FIGURE 4.2 The structure of a check

To whom check is payable or **payee**

Verbal form of amount of check. Note spacing and use of "and" to represent the decimal

Bank ordered to pay is **drawee**

Date check written

Preprinted check number

Code number to identify bank

Amount of check

Signature—this is the same as on the signature card

One who writes check is called the **drawer**

Bank number printed with magnetic ink for computer processing matches printed number at upper right-hand corner of check above amount of check

Lantz Company's account number

Preprinted check number

When bank processes check, the 75.35 is imprinted here. Note that this should match what is written for amount of check.

Writing business checks is similar to writing personal checks. Before writing any checks, however, you must understand the structure of a check and know how to write a check. Carefully study Figure 4.2. Note that the verbal amount written in the check should match the figure amount. If these two amounts are different, by law the bank uses the verbal amount. Also, note the bank imprint on the bottom right section of the check. When processing the check, the bank imprints the check's amount. This makes it easy to detect bank errors.

Once the check is written, the writer must keep a record of the check. Knowing the amount of your written checks and the amount in the bank should help you avoid writing a bad check. Business checkbooks usually include attached **check stubs** to keep track of written checks. The sample check stub in the margin shows the information that the check writer will want to record. Some companies use a **check register** to keep their check records instead of check stubs. Figure 4.3 (p. 90) shows a check register with a ✓ column that is often used in balancing the checkbook with the bank statement (Learning Unit 4.2).

Lantz Company has had a busy week, and Gayle must deposit its checks in the company's checking account. However, before she can do this, Gayle must **endorse,** or sign, the back left side of the checks. Figure 4.4 (p. 90) explains the three types of check endorsements: **blank endorsement, full endorsement,** and **restrictive endorsement.** These endorsements transfer Lantz's ownership to the bank, which collects the money from the person or company issuing the check. Federal Reserve regulation limits all endorsements to the top $1\frac{1}{2}$ inches of the trailing edge on the back left side of the check (Figure 4.4).

Check Stub

It should be completed before the check is written.

No. 12	$ 75 35/100
December 15 20 01	
To Avon Corporation	
For Equipment	

	DOLLARS	CENTS
BALANCE	7,100	00
AMT. DEPOSITED		
TOTAL	7,100	00
AMT. THIS CHECK	75	35
BALANCE FORWARD	7,024	65

FIGURE 4.3
Check register

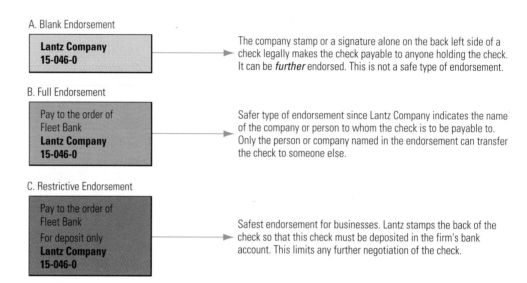

		RECORD ALL CHARGES OR CREDITS THAT AFFECT YOUR ACCOUNT							BALANCE	
NUMBER	DATE	DESCRIPTION OF TRANSACTION	PAYMENT/DEBIT (−)		√	FEE (IFANY) (−)	DEPOSIT/CREDIT (+)		$ 391	68
	2001		$			$	$			
190	4/12	Ranger Co.	55	91					335	77
191	4/17	Longin Co.	39	66					296	11
	4/18	Deposit					412	18	708	29
192	4/22	Flint Utilities	79	33					628	96

FIGURE 4.4
Types of common endorsements

A. Blank Endorsement

> **Lantz Company**
> **15-046-0**

The company stamp or a signature alone on the back left side of a check legally makes the check payable to anyone holding the check. It can be *further* endorsed. This is not a safe type of endorsement.

B. Full Endorsement

> Pay to the order of
> Fleet Bank
> **Lantz Company**
> **15-046-0**

Safer type of endorsement since Lantz Company indicates the name of the company or person to whom the check is to be payable to. Only the person or company named in the endorsement can transfer the check to someone else.

C. Restrictive Endorsement

> Pay to the order of
> Fleet Bank
> For deposit only
> **Lantz Company**
> **15-046-0**

Safest endorsement for businesses. Lantz stamps the back of the check so that this check must be deposited in the firm's bank account. This limits any further negotiation of the check.

After the bank receives Gayle's deposit slip, shown in Figure 4.1, it increases (or credits) Lantz's account by $691.06. Often Gayle leaves the deposit in a locked bag in a night depository. Then the bank credits (increases) Gayle's account when it processes the deposit on the next working day.

Gayle's company handles many credit card transactions. Now let's see how the company records these transactions.

Depositing Credit Card Transactions

On November 1, 2001, Lantz Company will begin using MasterCard and Visa. This should increase its sales and avoid the collection of past-due accounts.

Fleet Bank has given Lantz two options for depositing **credit card** transactions—option 1, manual deposits, and option 2, electronic deposits. Note that although some small companies still use the manual deposit system, most companies favor the electronic system. Now let's study these two systems.

Option 1: Manual Deposits

When Lantz makes a charge sale with the **manual deposit** option, the salesperson fills out a MasterCard or Visa charge slip similar to the one in Figure 4.5, which is for another company. Charge slips give the specific details of the sale.

At the end of *each business day,* Lantz's bookkeeper completes a **merchant batch header slip** and attaches copies of its charge slips. Figure 4.6 shows a sample batch header slip used by another company. Note that the company could list the slips on the form or provide an adding machine tape with the batch header slip. Also note that the total of the charge slips is shown less the total of the credit slips (refunds). The **net deposit** (net amount) is the difference between the total sales and the total credits. At the *end of the statement period,* Fleet Bank charges $3\frac{1}{4}\%$ (this means $3\frac{1}{4}$ cents per dollar) of the net deposit and subtracts this from Lantz's checking account.

FIGURE 4.5

Charge slip

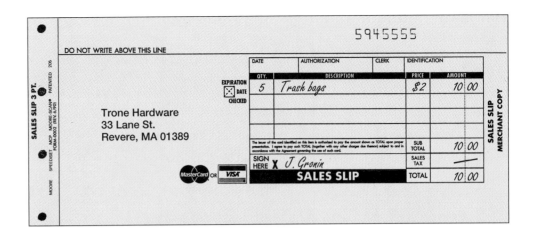

FIGURE 4.6

Merchant batch header slip

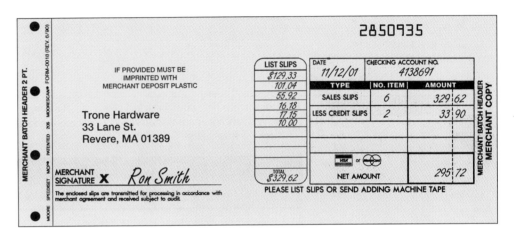

Option 2: Electronic Deposits

Most retail stores use **electronic deposits.** If you use a MasterCard or Visa credit card, you have probably watched the salesperson run your card through an authorization terminal after you have made a purchase. You may also have noticed that some retail stores now use the cash register terminal as a credit card authorization terminal. These authorization terminals not only approve (or disapprove) the amount charged but also add this amount immediately to the store's bank balance—or in our example, to Lantz's bank balance. Charge credits are also immediately subtracted from bank balances. The immediate authorizations and additions to a company's checking account are important advantages of the electronic transaction. Now we go back to Lantz Company to continue the electronic deposit procedure.

Each day Fleet Bank sends Lantz a statement listing its MasterCard and Visa transactions. The bank charges Lantz $2\frac{1}{2}\%$ ($2\frac{1}{2}$ cents per dollar) since it wants to encourage the use of electronic deposits. The statement Lantz receives is similar to the statement in Figure 4.7 (p. 92) for another company. When we work with percents in Chapter 6, you will see how to calculate the amount Lantz pays for using MasterCard and Visa. For now focus on calculating net deposits.

© PhotoDisc.

EXAMPLE   From the following credit card sales and returns, calculate the net deposit for the day.

Credit card sales:	$42.33, $16.88, $19.39, $47.66, $39.18.
Returns:	$18.01, $13.04.
Solution:	Total credit cards sales $165.44
	Less returns − 31.05
	Net deposit $134.39

FIGURE 4.7

Electronic deposit statement

DEPOSIT DETAILS:	CARDHOLDER	DATE	TRAN	AMOUNT	CST–TIME	CODE
	361060558	11/14/01	SALE	15.00	11:55 :36	431011
	336808479		SALE	28.60	12:08 :30	673011
	633615209		SALE	11.28	12:34 :31	934440
	484383		SALE	7.77	14:03 :38	482360
	611445		SALE	17.57	14:12 :48	371224
	343103551		SALE	24.15	15:13 :50	694492
	000115629		SALE	14.74	15:16 :33	378823
	380057254		SALE	16.38	15:33 :18	213011
	288121723		SALE	23.08	16:21 :29	682011
	503999		SALE	9.96	16:27 :41	714593
	309021229		SALE	38.82	16:32 :29	891816
	005291394		SALE	19.93	16:42 :43	731020
	387076		SALE	15.62	16:51 :09	700644
	199011544		SALE	21.00	19:39 :08	001640

	------- SALES -------		------- RETURNS -------		NET DEPOSIT	
	14	263.90	0	.00	263.90	
MASTERCARD	7	147.90	0	.00	147.90	
VISA	7	116.00	0	.00	116.00	

LU 4.1 PRACTICE QUIZ

1. Complete the following check and check stub for Long Company. Note the $9,500.60 balance brought forward on check stub No. 113. You must make a $690.60 deposit on May 3. Sign the check for Roland Small.

Date	Check no.	Amount	Payable to	For
June 5, 2001	113	$83.76	Angel Corporation	Rent

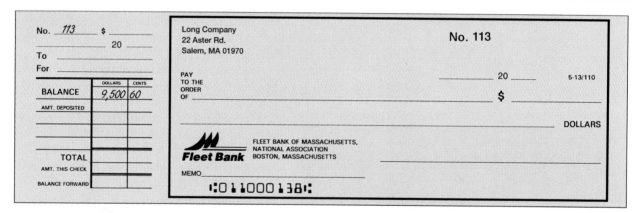

2. From the following information, complete Ryan Company's merchant batch header slip for August 19, 2001. Sign the slip for John Ryan, whose account number is 0139684.

Credit card sales	Credit card returns
$114.99	$14.07
21.15	15.19
72.80	
39.45	

✓ **Solutions**

1.

	DOLLARS	CENTS
No. _113_ $ _83.76_		
June 5 20 _01_		
To _Angel Corp._		
For _Rent_		
BALANCE	9,500	60
AMT. DEPOSITED	690	60
TOTAL	10,191	20
AMT. THIS CHECK	83	76
BALANCE FORWARD	10,107	44

Long Company
22 Aster Rd.
Salem, MA 01970

No. 113

PAY TO THE ORDER OF _Angel Corporation_ $ _83 $\frac{76}{100}$_

June 5 20 _01_   5-13/110

Eighty-three and $\frac{76}{100}$ ——————— DOLLARS

Fleet Bank FLEET BANK OF MASSACHUSETTS, NATIONAL ASSOCIATION BOSTON, MASSACHUSETTS

Roland Small

MEMO _Rent_

⑆011000138⑆ 14 0380 113

2.

LEARNING UNIT 4.2   Bank Statement and Reconciliation Process; Trends in Banking

In a survey by *The Wall Street Journal,* only one-half of the adults surveyed said they balanced their checkbook every month. Almost one-fourth said they never balanced their checkbook. The result of this survey is disappointing. Banks can make mistakes. By balancing your checkbook every month, you also catch your own mistakes.

In this unit Lantz Company reconciles its checkbook balance with the balance reported on its bank statement. You would use the same procedure in reconciling your personal checking account.

Bank Statement

Each month Fleet Bank sends Lantz Company a **bank statement** (Figure 4.8). The statement gives different types of information. We are interested in the following:

1. Beginning bank balance.
2. Total of all account decreases. Each time the bank decreases the account amount, it *debits* the account.
3. Total of all the account increases. Each time the bank increases the account amount, it *credits* the account.
4. Final ending balance.

FIGURE 4.8

Bank statement

Lantz Company			Fleet Bank
80 Garfield St.			Account
Boston, MA 01152			Number 150460

9/30/01 thru 10/29/01   Debits   Credits

DATE	CHECKS•WITHDRAWALS•PAYMENTS		DEPOSITS•INTEREST•ADVANCES	BALANCE
10/1	DM 10.00			16,250.00
10/2	DM 26.00			16,224.00
10/3	360.00			15,864.00
10/4	1,440.00	2,400.00		12,024.00
10/5			2,880.00	14,904.00
10/8	300.00	450.00		14,154.00
10/25			3,960.00	18,114.00
10/28	810.00		1,200.00	18,504.00
10/29	DM 204.00		CM 600.00	18,900.00
10/29			CM 15.18	**18,915.18**

Account Summary

Beginning balance		$16,260.00
Total credits/deposits		8,040.00
Total debits/checks		5,760.00

Other debits	Bank charge	$ 10.00	
	NSF check	204.00	
	ATM withdrawal	26.00	240.00

Other credits	Interest credited	$ 15.18	
	Note collected	600.00	615.18

Ending balance		**$18,915.18**

DM±Deductions
CM±Additions

FIGURE 4.9
Reconciling checkbook with bank statement

Checkbook balance		Bank balance
+ EFT (electronic funds transfer)	− NSF check	+ Deposits in transit
+ Interest earned	− Online fees	− Outstanding checks
+ Notes collected	− Overdrafts	± Bank errors
− ATM withdrawals	− Service charges	
− Automatic withdrawals	− Stop payments*	
− Check redeposits	± Book errors†	

*A *stop payment* is issued when the writer of check does not want the receiver to cash the check.

†If a $60 check is recorded at $50, we must decrease the checkbook balance by $10.

Due to differences in timing, the bank balance on the bank statement frequently does not match the customer's checkbook balance. Also, the bank statement can show transactions that have not been entered in the customer's checkbook. Figure 4.9 tells you what to look for when comparing a checkbook balance with a bank balance. Note the item **overdrafts.** An overdraft occurs when the customer has no overdraft protection and a check bounces back to the company or person who received the check; that is, the customer wrote a check without having enough money in the bank to pay for it (called an NSF check and explained in Step 3 that follows).

To reconcile the difference between the amount on the bank statement and in the checkbook, the customer should complete a **bank reconciliation.** Today, many companies and home computer owners are using software such as Quicken and QuickBooks to complete their bank reconciliation. However, you should understand the following steps for manually reconciling a bank statement.

Reconciling a Bank Statement

Step 1. Identify the outstanding checks (checks written but not yet processed by the bank). You can use the ✓ column in the check register (Figure 4.10) to check the canceled checks listed in the bank statement against the checks you wrote in the check register. The unchecked checks are the outstanding checks.

Step 2. Identify the deposits in transit (deposits made but not yet processed by the bank), using the same method in Step 1.

Step 3. Analyze the bank statement for transactions not recorded in the check stubs or check registers.

Step 4. Check for recording errors in checks written, in deposits made, or in subtraction and addition.

Step 5. Compare the adjusted balances of the checkbook and the bank statement. If the balances are not the same, repeat Steps 1–4.

Lantz keeps a record of its checks and deposits in a check register (Figure 4.10, p. 96). By looking at Lantz's check register, you can see how to complete Steps 1 and 2. The explanation that follows for the four bank statement reconciliation steps will help you understand the procedure.

Step 1. Identify Outstanding Checks

Outstanding checks are checks that Lantz has written but Fleet Bank has not yet recorded for payment when it sends out the bank statement. Lantz's bookkeeper identifies checks No. 115 for $175 and No. 117 for $675 as outstanding by comparing the company's bank statement with its check register.

Step 2. Identify Deposits in Transit

Deposits in transit are deposits that did not reach Fleet Bank by the time the bank prepared the bank statement. The October 29 deposit of $1,000 did not reach Fleet Bank by

FIGURE 4.10

Lantz Company check register

NUMBER	DATE	DESCRIPTION OF TRANSACTION	PAYMENT/DEBIT (−)		√	FEE (IF ANY) (−)	DEPOSIT/CREDIT (+)		BALANCE
		RECORD ALL CHARGES OR CREDITS THAT AFFECT YOUR ACCOUNT						$	16,286 00
114	2001 9/30	ATM	26	00	√				16,260 00
115	10/1	Lowe Co.	175	00					16,085 00
116	10/2	Able Co.	360	00	√				15,725 00
117	10/2	Ajax Co.	675	00					15,050 00
118	10/3	Blue Co.	1,440	00	√				13,610 00
119	10/4	Easter Co.	2,400	00	√				11,210 00
	10/4				√		2,880	00	14,090 00
120	10/7	Long Co.	300	00	√				13,790 00
121	10/7	Utah Co.	450	00	√				13,340 00
	10/24				√		3,960	00	17,300 00
	10/27				√		1,200	00	18,500 00
122	10/28	Last Co.	810	00	√				17,690 00
	10/29						1,000	00	18,690 00

REMEMBER TO RECORD AUTOMATIC PAYMENTS / DEPOSITS ON DATE AUTHORIZED.

the bank statement date. You can see this by comparing the company's bank statement with its check register.

Step 3. Analyze Bank Statement for Transactions Not Recorded in Check Stubs or Check Register

The bank statement shown in Figure 4.8 (p. 94) gives "other debits" that Lantz was not aware of until the company reviewed the bank statement. When a bank debits Lantz's account, the account balance is reduced. Banks inform customers of a debit transaction by a **debit memo (DM).** The following items will result in debits to Lantz's account.

1. *Bank charge:* $10.   The bank charged $10 for printing the checks.
2. *NSF check:* $204.   One of Lantz's customers wrote Lantz a check for $204. Lantz deposited the check, but the check bounced for **nonsufficient funds (NSF).** Thus, Lantz has $204 less than it figured.
3. *ATM withdrawal:* $26.   Lantz withdrew $26 from an automatic teller machine but forgot to update its checkbook for this withdrawal.

The bank statement contained two "other credits" that increased Lantz's account. These are the result of a **credit memo (CM).**

4. *Interest credited:* $15.18.   Since Lantz has a checking account that pays interest, the account has earned $15.18.
5. *Note collected:* $600.00.   As a service to Lantz, the bank acted as a collection agent and received $600 from one of Lantz's customers. Lantz did not know the bank collected this note until it received the bank statement.

Step 4. Check for Recording Errors

If Lantz's bookkeeper had recorded a check for the wrong amount, the checkbook balance would have to be adjusted. For example, if a $30 check were recorded for $10, the checkbook balance would have to be reduced by $20. Also, the bookkeeper could have neglected to record a written check or a deposit. These errors would be caught in the reconciliation process.

Now we can complete the bank reconciliation on the back side of the bank statement, as shown in Figure 4.11. This form is usually on the back of a bank statement. If necessary, however, the person reconciling the bank statement can construct a form similar to Figure 4.12.

FIGURE 4.11

Reconciliation process

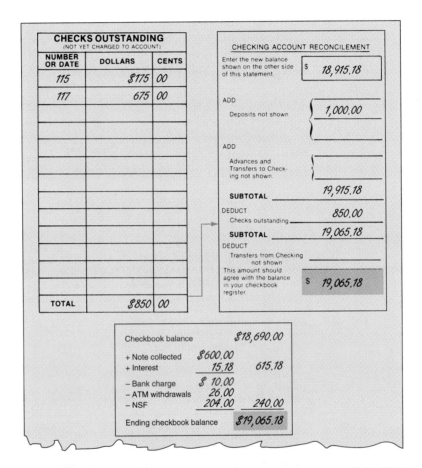

FIGURE 4.12

Bank reconciliation

Lantz Company Bank Reconciliation as of October 31, 2001					
Checkbook balance			**Bank balance**		
Lantz checkbook balance		$18,690.00	Bank balance		$18,915.18
Add:			Add:		
Collection of note	$600.00		Deposit in transit 10/29		1,000.00
Interest	15.18	615.18			$19,915.18
		$19,305.18			
Deduct:			Deduct:		
Check printing	$ 10.00		Outstanding checks:		
NSF check	204.00		No. 115	$175	
ATM withdrawals	26.00	240.00	No. 117	675	850.00
Reconciled balance		$19,065.18	Reconciled balance		$19,065.18

ADDITIONAL EXAMPLE   On December 31, 2001, Bill's Roast Beef had a $5,790.40 checkbook balance. Bill's bank statement showed a $5,981.50 balance. Outstanding checks were No. 101 for $290 and No. 104 for $160. A $221 deposit was in transit. The bank statement showed an NSF check for $40 along with a service charge of $10. For the month, the checking account earned interest of $12.10. Prepare a bank reconciliation.

The following shows the completed bank reconciliation for Bill's Roast Beef:

BILL'S ROAST BEEF
Bank Reconciliation as of December 31, 2001

Checkbook balance			Bank balance		
Bill's Roast Beef checkbook balance		$5,790.40	Bank balance		$5,981.50
Add:			Add:		
Interest earned		12.10	Deposit in transit		221.00
		$5,802.50			$6,202.50
			Deduct:		
Deduct:			Outstanding checks:		
NSF check	$40.00		No. 101	$290	
Bank service charge	10.00	50.00	No. 104	160	450.00
Reconciled balance		$5,752.50	Reconciled balance		$5,752.50

Trends in Banking

Hawaiian Air to Offer Tickets Through ATMs

By a WALL STREET JOURNAL Staff Reporter

HONOLULU—For airline passengers bent on convenience, here is something at least as user-friendly as electronic ticketing: buying plane tickets at an automated teller machine.

Starting March 1, **Hawaiian Airlines** plans to sell tickets for all its interisland flights through Bank of Hawaii's statewide network of 400 ATMs. The program, which requires regulatory approval, is thought to be the first in the nation to use ATMs to sell plane tickets.

Hawaiian Air said both customers and noncustomers of Bank of Hawaii, a unit of **Pacific Century Financial Corp.**, will be able to buy flight coupons through the bank's ATMs 24 hours a day, using cards issued by the bank or a major credit card. The coupons, essentially open tickets, will be available in quantities of one, two, four or eight, will be valid for a year and will cost the same as those purchased from the airline or a travel agency. Customers will need to contact Hawaiian Air to reserve space on their desired flight, the carrier said.

Hawaiian Air, Honolulu, is the nation's 12th-largest carrier and flies within the islands of Hawaii and to the U.S. mainland and the South Pacific.

© 1998 Dow Jones & Company, Inc.

The introductory paragraphs in this chapter introduced you to the debit card—an enhanced ATM card. *The Wall Street Journal* clipping "Hawaiian Air to Offer Tickets Through ATMs" introduces you to an additional use of the automated teller machine. Hawaiian Airlines will sell plane tickets for all its interisland flights through Bank of Hawaii's statewide network of 400 ATMs. Customers will buy flight coupons, which are open tickets, in quantities of one, two, four, or eight. The cost of the coupons will be the same as that for those purchased from the airline or a travel agency. Reservations for particular flights must be made with the airline. This convenience will be available 24 hours per day.

We begin this section with a discussion of the use of electronic fund transfers. You will see how Lantz Company uses electronic fund transfers. Then we discuss the trend of many banks not to return canceled checks. Finally, you will learn about an exciting new Internet feature—online banking.

Electronic Funds Transfer
(EFT)

Treasury Department to Inaugurate:
Internet-Payment Plan Called 'Echeck'

By REBECCA QUICK
Staff Reporter of THE WALL STREET JOURNAL

Old excuse: The check is in the mail. New excuse: The check is in the e-mail.

The U.S. Treasury Department will inaugurate "echeck," a new system for making payments over the Internet, by e-mailing a $32,000 check to GTE Corp. for work on an Air Force contract.

The echeck program, which was announced in 1995, is a cooperative effort backed by the Financial Services Technology Consortium, which includes **International Business Machines** Corp., **Sun Microsystems** Inc., **BankBoston** Corp., **NationsBank** Corp. and **BankAmerica** Corp. The consortium hopes echecks will become a widely accepted method of payment, especially for business-to-business transactions.

"We think this addresses a big void in the business-to-business space," said Mark Greene, vice president of Internet payments at IBM, which built the computer used by the banks involved in the program.

Many existing software packages, such as **Intuit** Inc.'s Quicken, allow consumers to pay bills on-line. But often these programs simply link you to a service that prints out the checks and mails them the old-fashioned way. In some instances, funds are electronically transferred from your account to a creditor.

The echeck program is designed to make it easier for businesses to send money to each other electronically. The problem with most electonic-funds transfer services today is that the payments go straight to a company's bank account, bypassing its traditional accounting system that was designed to handle paper checks. That makes it difficult to track which invoices have been paid.

© 1998 Dow Jones & Company, Inc.

The Wall Street Journal clipping "Treasury Department to Inaugurate Internet-Payment Plan Called 'Echeck'" reports on an e-check program that is designed to make it easier for businesses to send money to one another electronically. This program will increase the value of the Internet.

Electronic bill paying through the Internet has been available to bank customers for several years. As some of you know, this method of bill paying has several advantages. You do not have to write checks, save the envelopes that come with bills, look for stamps, or be concerned that payments will not reach their destination in time to make a deadline. Thus, with the Internet you can transfer money between accounts or checking balances. If you want to make deposits or withdraw funds, however, you must do this by wire, mail, or ATM. Now let's return to Lantz Company.

Lantz is planning to offer to its employees the option of depositing their checks directly into each employee's checking account. This is accomplished through the **electronic funds transfer (EFT)**—a computerized operation that electronically transfers funds among parties without the use of paper checks. ATM technology is possible because of EFT, which is the heart of ATM.

Safekeeping Canceled
Checks

The bank's cost to process and mail canceled checks to customers with their bank statements is substantial. For this reason, many banks no longer return a customer's canceled checks. Instead, banks use a *safekeeping* procedure.

With the **safekeeping** procedure, the banks hold a customer's checks for a period of time (usually 90 days). Then the bank keeps microfilm copies of the checks for at least 1 year and sometimes as long as 7 years. If a customer needs a check, the bank will return the check or a photocopy for a small fee. Some banks provide a picture of the canceled checks in numerical order on a sheet of paper.

Online Banking

With the increased bank mergers, a new era of megabanks has appeared. As a result, to avoid higher banking fees, consumers must keep a higher minimum in checking accounts or participate in other banking options such as savings accounts, bank-sponsored mutual funds, or mortgages. If you want to use banks only for the services you need, you have three choices: credit unions, community banks that have not yet been gobbled up by big banks, and Internet banks.

For many consumers, the refuge from higher fees is the use of online banking—the Internet bank. At the Salem, Massachusetts, Internet bank—Salem Five Cents Bank—you can have a no-minimum-balance checking account, but you are limited to 5 checks per month and 20 online payments. Other Internet banks provide different services, so you must shop for the Internet bank services that best suit your needs.

Internet banking does have disadvantages. If you have checking problems such as a bounced check or missing deposit, you must solve these problems with e-mail or a telephone call. Although Internet banks offer some free ATM withdrawals, you may have to pay a surcharge of about $1 to the bank that owns the ATM. Other disadvantages include time involved in mailing your checks and no cashier's checks.

Let's try the Practice Quiz to check your understanding of this unit.

LU 4.2 PRACTICE QUIZ

Rosa Garcia has received her February 3, 2001, bank statement, which has a balance of $212.80. Rosa's checkbook shows a balance of $929.15. The bank statement showed an ATM fee of $12 and a deposited check returned fee of $20. Rosa earned interest of $1.05. She had three outstanding checks: No. 300, $18.20; No. 302, $38.40; and No. 303, $68.12. A deposit for $810.12 was not on her bank statement. Prepare Rosa Garcia's bank reconciliation.

ROSA GARCIA				
Bank Reconciliation as of February 3, 2001				
Checkbook balance		**Bank balance**		
Rosa's checkbook balance	$929.15	Bank balance		$ 212.80
Add:		Add:		
Interest	1.05	Deposit in transit		810.12
	$930.20			$1,022.92
		Deduct:		
Deduct:		Outstanding checks:		
Deposited check		No. 300	$18.20	
returned fee	$20.00	No. 302	38.40	
ATM	12.00 32.00	No. 303	68.12	124.72
Reconciled balance	$898.20	Reconciled balance		$ 898.20

Chapter Organizer and Reference Guide

Topic	Key point, procedure, formula	Example(s) to illustrate situation
Types of endorsements, *p. 90*	*Blank:* Not safe; can be further endorsed. *Full:* Only person or company named in endorsement can transfer check to someone else. *Restrictive:* Check must be deposited. Limits any further negotiation of the check.	Jones Co. 21-333-9 Pay to the order of Regan Bank Jones Co. 21-333-9 Pay to the order of Regan Bank. For deposit only. Jones Co. 21-333-9

Credit card transactions, *p. 90*	*Manual deposit:* Need to calculate net deposit (credit card sales less returns).
	
	Electronic deposit: Eliminates deposit slips and summary batch header slip.
		Calculate net deposit:
		Credit card sales $55.32
		      62.81
		      91.18
		Credits − 10.16
		     − 8.15
		     $209.31
		     − 18.31
		Net deposit = $191.00

Bank reconciliation, *p. 95*

Checkbook balance	Bank balance	Checkbook balance		Bank balance	
+ EFT	+ Deposits in transit	Balance	$800	Balance	$ 632
+ Interest earned	− Outstanding checks	− NSF	40	+ Deposits in transit	416
+ Notes collected	± Bank errors		$760		$1,048
− ATM withdrawals					
− Automatic withdrawals		− Service charge	4	− Outstanding checks	292
− Check redeposits			$756		$ 756
− NSF checks					
− Online fees					
− Overdrafts					
− Service charges					
− Stop payments					
± Book errors*					
CM—adds to balance					
DM—deducts from balance					

*If a $60 check is recorded as $50, we must decrease checkbook balance by $10.

Key terms

ATM (automatic teller machine), *p. 88*
Bank reconciliation, *p. 95*
Bank statement, *p. 94*
Blank endorsement, *p. 89*
Check, *p. 88*
Check register, *p. 89*
Check stub, *p. 89*
Credit card, *p. 90*
Credit memo (CM), *p. 96*
Debit card, *p. 88*

Debit memo (DM), *p. 96*
Deposit slip, *p. 88*
Deposit in transit, *p. 95*
Draft, *p. 88*
Drawee, *p. 89*
Drawer, *p. 89*
Electronic deposit, *p. 91*
Electronic funds transfer (EFT), *p. 99*
Endorse, *p. 89*
Full endorsement, *p. 89*

Manual deposit, *p. 90*
Merchant batch header slip, *p. 90*
Net deposit, *p. 90*
Nonsufficient funds (NSF), *p. 96*
Outstanding checks, *p. 95*
Overdrafts, *p. 95*
Payee, *p. 89*
Restrictive endorsement, *p. 89*
Safekeeping, *p. 99*
Signature card, *p. 88*

**Critical Thinking
Discussion Questions**

1. Explain the structure of a check. The trend in bank statements is not to return the canceled checks. Do you think this is fair?

2. List the three types of endorsements. Endorsements are limited to the top $1\frac{1}{2}$ inches of the trailing edge on the back left side of your check. Why do you think the Federal Reserve made this regulation?

3. What is the difference between a manual and an electronic deposit of credit card transactions? Do you think credit cards should be used in supermarkets?

4. List the steps in reconciling a bank statement. Today, many banks charge a monthly fee for certain types of checking accounts. Do you think all checking accounts should be free? Please explain.

5. What are some of the trends in banking? Will we become a cashless society in which all transactions are made with some type of credit card?

DRILL PROBLEMS

4–1. Fill out the check register that follows with this information:

2001

June	9	Check No. 510	Home Depot	$ 72.95
	12	Check No. 511	Sears	44.80
	18	Deposit		700.55
	19	Check No. 512	MCI Telephone	109.33
	24	Check No. 513	Dunkin' Donuts	25.77
	29	Deposit		118.85

RECORD ALL CHARGES OR CREDITS THAT AFFECT YOUR ACCOUNT

NUMBER	DATE	DESCRIPTION OF TRANSACTION	PAYMENT/DEBIT (−)	√	FEE (IF ANY) (−)	DEPOSIT/CREDIT (+)	BALANCE $ 795 56
	2001		$		$	$	
510	6/9	Home Depot	72 95				722 61
511	6/12	Sears	44 80				677 81
	6/18	Deposit				700 55	1,378 36
512	6/19	MCI Telephone	109 33				1,269 03
513	6/24	Dunkin' Donuts	25 77				1,243 26
	6/29	Deposit				118 85	1,362 11

4–2. On December 1, 2001, Loo Company has a $7,185.99 checkbook balance. Record the following transactions for Loo Company by completing the two checks and check stubs provided. Sign the checks Jim Leary, Treasurer.

a. December 5, 2001, deposited $189.55.

b. December 5, Check No. 187 payable to Staples Corporation for supplies—$899.18.

c. December 16, Check No. 188 payable to ATT Corporation for equipment—$510.99.

No. 187 $ 899.18
December 5   20 01
To Staples Corp.
For Supplies

	DOLLARS	CENTS
BALANCE	7,185	99
AMT. DEPOSITED	189	55
TOTAL	7,375	54
AMT. THIS CHECK	899	18
BALANCE FORWARD	6,476	36

LOO COMPANY
2 ROUNDY ROAD
ST. PAUL, MN 55113   No. 187

December 5 20 01   5-13/110

PAY TO THE ORDER OF   Staples Corporation $ 899 18/100

Eight hundred ninety-nine and 18/100 _____ DOLLARS

FLEET BANK OF MASSACHUSETTS,
NATIONAL ASSOCIATION
Fleet Bank BOSTON, MASSACHUSETTS   Jim Leary
                                           Treasurer
MEMO   Supplies

⑈011000138⑈   25 11103 187

No. 188 $ 510.99
December 16   20 01
To ATT Corp.
For Equipment

	DOLLARS	CENTS
BALANCE	6,476	36
AMT. DEPOSITED		
TOTAL	6,476	36
AMT. THIS CHECK	510	99
BALANCE FORWARD	5,965	37

LOO COMPANY
2 ROUNDY ROAD
ST. PAUL, MN 55113   No. 188

December 16 20 01   5-13/110

PAY TO THE ORDER OF   ATT Corporation $ 510 99/100

Five hundred ten and 99/100 _____ DOLLARS

FLEET BANK OF MASSACHUSETTS,
NATIONAL ASSOCIATION
Fleet Bank BOSTON, MASSACHUSETTS   Jim Leary
                                           Treasurer
MEMO   Equipment

⑈011000138⑈   25 11103 188

4–3. You are the bookkeeper of Reese Company and must complete a merchant batch header for November 10, 2001, from the following credit card transactions. The company lost the charge slips and doesn't include an adding machine tape. Reese's checking account number is 3158062. The merchant's signature can be left blank. **Credit card sales** are $210.40, $178.99, $29.30, and $82.80. **Credit card returns** are $15.10 and $22.99.

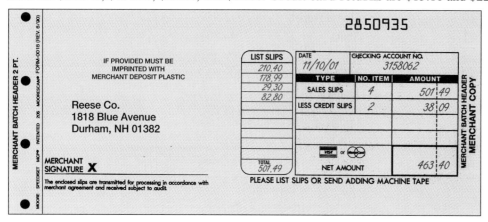

4–4. Using the check register in Problem 4–1 and the following bank statement, prepare a bank reconciliation for Chase Company.

Bank Statement Date	Checks	Deposits	Balance
6/1 balance			$ 795.56
6/16	$72.95		722.61
6/18		$700.55	1,423.16
6/22	25.77		1,397.39
6/30	10.00 SC		1,387.39

Chase's checkbook balance	$1,362.11		Bank balance		$1,387.39
— Service charge	10.00		Add:		
			+ Deposit in transit		118.85
					$1,506.24
			Deduct:		
			— Outstanding checks:	$ 44.80	
				109.33	154.13
Ending checkbook balance	$1,352.11		Ending bank balance		$1,352.11

WORD PROBLEMS

4–5. On May 31, 2001, Ranch Company received a bank statement showing a bank balance of $9,732. Ranch's bookkeeper noticed that the bank collected a $2,400 note. A $500 June 1 deposit was in transit. Outstanding checks for the month were $492. The bank charged a $15 service charge. Ranch forgot to record a $45 withdrawal from the ATM. Could you help Ranch's bookkeeper prepare a reconciliation assuming Ranch has a $7,400 checkbook balance?

Ranch's checkbook balance		$7,400	Bank balance		$ 9,732
Add:			Add:		
Collection of note		2,400	Deposit in transit		500
		$9,800			$10,232
Deduct:			Deduct:		
ATM	$45		Outstanding checks:		492
Service charge	15	60			
Reconciled balance		$9,740	Reconciled balance		$ 9,740

4–6. First National Bank sent Joel Samaha his bank statement showing a $1,861.35 balance. Joel's checkbook showed a $1,763.31 balance. A $244.14 check was outstanding. The bank statement showed a $135.60 NSF check and a $10.50 service charge. Reconcile this bank statement for Joel.

Samaha's checkbook balance		$1,763.31	Bank balance		$1,861.35
Deduct:			Deduct:		
Service charge	$ 10.50		Outstanding check:		244.14
NSF	135.60	146.10			
Reconciled balance		$1,617.21	Reconciled balance		$1,617.21

4–7. On June 8, 2001, Larson Company had the following MasterCard transactions (along with some returns). Sales were $28.96, $210.55, and $189.88. Returns were $11.10 and $29.85. As Larson's bookkeeper you must calculate the net deposit.

Sales $28.96 + $210.55 + $189.88 = $429.39
$$- \ 40.95 \quad (\$11.10 + \$29.85)$$
Net deposit $388.44

4–8. David Denny's August 2, 2001, bank statement showed a balance of $230.12. David's checkbook showed a balance of $1,540.10. David belongs to the YMCA and has his monthly membership fee of $28 paid through his bank. The bank also pays his monthly New York Life Insurance policy of $14.80. The following checks did not clear the bank: No. 612, $210.12; No. 614, $20.40; and No. 615, $123.10. On August 1, David made a $1,623.10 deposit that does not appear on his bank statement. David earned $2.30 in interest. Prepare David Denny's bank reconciliation.

David's checkbook balance		$1,540.10	Bank balance		$ 230.12
Add:			Add:		
Interest		2.30	Deposit in transit		1,623.10
		$1,542.40			$1,853.22
Deduct:			Deduct:		
YMCA automatic withdrawal	$28.00		Outstanding checks:		
N.Y.L.I. automatic withdrawal	14.80	42.80	No. 612	$210.12	
			No. 614	20.40	
			No. 615	123.10	353.62
Reconciled balance		$1,499.60	Reconciled balance		$1,499.60

4–9. Effective June 1, 1997, St. Paul Federal Bank published a list of checking account service charges. Included in the list was a stop payment order fee of $20. Lin Soo wants to balance her checkbook, which shows a balance of $869.58. St. Paul Federal Bank shows a balance of $118.10. The following checks have not cleared the bank: No. 45, $68.50; No. 47, $140.30; and No. 49, $210.12. Lin Soo has a $7 service fee and a $5 NSF fee. The bank pays her $126.10 electric bill through automatic withdrawal. A $1,012.30 deposit does not appear on the bank statement. Prepare Lin Soo's bank reconciliation.

Lin Soo's checkbook balance		$869.58	Bank balance		$ 118.10
Add:			Add:		
			Deposit in transit		1,012.30
					$1,130.40
Deduct:			Deduct:		
Service fee	$ 7.00		Outstanding checks:		
NSF check	5.00		No. 45	$ 68.50	
Stop payment	20.00		No. 47	140.30	
Automatic withdrawal	126.10	158.10	No. 49	210.12	418.92
Reconciled balance		$711.48	Reconciled balance		$ 711.48

4–10. The May 1997 issue of *Money* reported that the California Bank of America will charge you $5.50 in monthly checking fees unless you have your paycheck deposited directly and do not use a teller for routine transactions. Kim Lake, who lives in California, received her bank statement with this $5.50 charge. She also had a $20 overdraft fee, a $5 check redeposit fee, and interest of $1.15. Her bank statement's balance was $206.65, but it did not show the $1,502.80 deposit she had made. Kim's checkbook balance shows $749.90. The following checks have not cleared: No. 480, $630.20; No. 483, $228.10; and No. 485, $130.60. Prepare Kim Lake's bank reconciliation.

Kim's checkbook balance		$749.90	Bank balance		$ 206.65
Add:			Add:		
Interest		1.15	Deposit in transit		1,502.80
		$751.05			$1,709.45
Deduct:			Deduct:		
Service charge	$ 5.50		Outstanding checks:		
Overdraft	20.00		No. 480	$630.20	
Check redeposit	5.00	30.50	No. 483	228.10	
			No. 485	130.60	988.90
Reconciled balance		$720.55	Reconciled balance		$ 720.55

4–11. Roe Company showed a $1,881.54 checkbook balance. The company's bank statement showed a $3,240.00 balance, $21.00 interest earned, and a $14.88 service charge. A $1,279.11 deposit was in transit. Outstanding checks total $1,881.45. In analyzing the bank statement, the bookkeeper noticed the bank collected a $2,100 note. During the month, Roe Company did not deduct a $1,350 check. Prepare a bank reconciliation.

Roe's checkbook balance		$1,881.54	Bank balance		$3,240.00
Add:			Add:		
Interest	$ 21.00		Deposit in transit		1,279.11
Collection of note	2,100.00	2,121.00			$4,519.11
		$4,002.54			
Deduct:			Deduct:		
Service charge	$ 14.88		Outstanding checks:		1,881.45
Error	1,350.00	1,364.88			
Reconciled balance		$2,637.66	Reconciled balance		$2,637.66

4–12. The December 1997 issue of *Kiplinger's Personal Finance Magazine* reported on banking from your home computer. Some banks offer free online banking and bill payment; others charge a flat fee—say $6—to pay 20 bills. (You still pay regular checking account fees.) Wally Wirth uses his home computer for banking and is charged $6. His bank statement also showed $3.00 for check printing, $2.80 for processing 28 checks at $.10 each, and $480.00 for collecting a note. Wally had the following outstanding checks: No. 480, $212.80; No. 483, $416.12; No. 484, $131.08. Wally's bank statement shows a balance of $1,072.00; his checkbook shows a balance of $43.80. A $200 deposit does not appear on the bank statement. Prepare Wally Wirth's bank reconciliation.

Wally's checkbook balance		$ 43.80	Bank balance		$1,072.00
Add:			Add:		
Note collected		480.00	Deposit in transit		200.00
		$523.80			$1,272.00
Deduct:			Deduct:		
Online fee	$6.00		Outstanding checks:		
Check printing	3.00		No. 480	$212.80	
Check processing	2.80	11.80	No. 483	416.12	
			No. 484	131.08	760.00
Reconciled balance		$512.00	Reconciled balance		$ 512.00

4–13. The May 1997 issue of *Money* reported the following checking account fees: $2 to see a real-live teller, $20 to process a bounced check, and $1 to $3 if you need an original check to prove you paid a bill or made a charitable contribution. This past month you had to transact business through a teller 6 times—a total $12 cost to you. Your bank statement shows a $305.33 balance; your checkbook shows a $1,009.76 balance. You received $1.10 in interest. An $801.15 deposit was not recorded on your statement. The following checks were outstanding: No. 413, $28.30; No. 414, $18.60; and No. 418, $60.72. Prepare your bank reconciliation.

Checkbook balance	$1,009.76	Bank balance		$305.33
Add:		Add:		
Interest	1.10	Deposit in transit		801.15
	$1,010.86			$1,106.48
Deduct:		Deduct:		
Teller fee	12.00	Outstanding checks:		
		No. 413	$28.30	
		No. 414	18.60	
		No. 418	60.72	107.62
Reconciled balance	$ 998.86	Reconciled balance		$ 998.86

CHALLENGE PROBLEMS

4–14. Madeleine Paine received her January 4, 2001, bank statement, which showed a $664.34 balance. Her checkbook showed a $478.64 balance. The following transactions occurred: $2.50 check processing fee (25 checks at $.10), $161.86 automatic withdrawal to Peoples Gas, $3.00 teller fee, $20.00 overdraft, $7.50 ATM fee, $20.00 stop payment order, $.75 interest, $1,630 IRS refund check made to bank, $3.00 service fee, $20.00 stop payment fee, $5.00 check redeposit fee, and $4.50 for check printing. A $1,616 deposit is not shown on the bank statement. The following checks were outstanding: No. 102, $280.11; No. 103, $56.94; No. 105, $28.16, and No. 106, $53.10. Prepare Madeleine Paine's bank reconciliation.

Madeleine's checkbook balance		$ 478.64	Bank balance		$ 664.34
Add:			Add:		
Interest	$ .75		Deposit in transit		1,616.00
IRS refund check	1,630.00	1,630.75			$2,280.34
		$2,109.39			
Deduct:			Deduct:		
Check processing fee	$ 2.50		Outstanding checks:		
Automatic withdrawal	161.86		No. 102	$280.11	
Teller fee	3.00		No. 103	56.94	
Overdraft	20.00		No. 105	28.16	
ATM fee	7.50		No. 106	53.10	418.31
Stop payment	20.00				
Service fee	3.00				
Stop payment	20.00				
Check redeposit fee	5.00				
Check printing	4.50	247.36			
Reconciled balance		$1,862.03	Reconciled balance		$1,862.03

4–15. Melissa Jackson, bookkeeper for Kinko Company, cannot prepare a bank reconciliation. From the following facts, can you help her complete the June 30, 2001, reconciliation? The bank statement showed a $2,955.82 balance. Melissa's checkbook showed a $3,301.82 balance.

Melissa placed a $510.19 deposit in the bank's night depository on June 30. The deposit did not appear on the bank statement. The bank included two DMs and one CM with the returned checks: $690.65 DM for NSF check, $8.50 DM for service charges, and $400.00 CM (less $10 collection fee) for collecting a $400.00 non-interest-bearing note. Check No. 811 for $110.94 and check No. 912 for $82.50, both written and recorded on June 28, were not with the returned checks. The bookkeeper had correctly written check No. 884, $1,000, for a new cash register, but she recorded the check as $1,069. The May bank reconciliation showed check No. 748 for $210.90 and check No. 710 for $195.80 outstanding on April 30. The June bank statement included check No. 710 but not check No. 748.

KINKO COMPANY Bank Reconciliation as of June 30, 2001					
Checkbook balance			**Bank balance**		
Kinko's checkbook balance		$3,301.82	Bank balance		$2,955.82
Add:			Add:		
Collection on notes receivable	$400.00		Deposit in transit		510.19
					$3,466.01
Less:					
Collection fee	10.00	390.00	Deduct:		
Error in recording check			Outstanding checks:		
No. 884		69.00	No. 748	$210.90	
		$3,760.82	No. 811	110.94	
			No. 912	82.50	404.34
Deduct:					
NSF check	$690.65				
Service charge	8.50	699.15			
Reconciled balance		$3,061.67	Reconciled balance		$3,061.67

 SUMMARY PRACTICE TEST

1. Blossom Company had the following MasterCard sales for a day: $52.80, $75.99, $69.84, and $149.20. The company also issued two credits for returned merchandise: $14.90 and $28.22. What would be the amount of the net deposit for Blossom Company on its merchant batch summary slip? *(p. 90)*

$52.80 + $75.99 + $69.84 + $149.20 = $347.83
        − 43.12 ($14.90 + $28.22)
Net deposit $304.71

2. Fixmaster Company has a $9,852.66 beginning checkbook balance. Record the following transactions in the check stubs provided. *(p. 89)*

   a. October 10, 2001, check No. 180 payable to MCI Company, $422.88 for telephone expense.

   b. $900 deposit—October 16.

   c. October 22, 2001, check No. 181 payable to Sony Corporation, $655.81 for advertisement.

No. 180	$ 422.88
October 10	20 01
To MCI Corp.	
For Telephone	

	DOLLARS	CENTS
BALANCE	9,852	66
AMT. DEPOSITED		
TOTAL	9,852	66
AMT. THIS CHECK	422	88
BALANCE FORWARD	9,429	78

No. 181	$ 655.81
October 22	20 01
To Sony Corp.	
For Advertisement	

	DOLLARS	CENTS
BALANCE	9,429	78
AMT. DEPOSITED	900	00
TOTAL	10,329	78
AMT. THIS CHECK	655	81
BALANCE FORWARD	9,673	97

3. On March 1, 2001, Jean Company received a bank statement that showed a $7,800 balance. Jean showed a $6,400 checking account balance. The bank did not return check No. 111 for $390 or check No. 116 for $480. A $560 deposit made on February 28 was in transit. The bank charged Jean $20 for printing and $50 for an NSF check. The bank also collected a $1,200 note for Jean. Jean forgot to record a $40 withdrawal at the ATM. Prepare a bank reconciliation. *(p. 95)*

JEAN COMPANY
Bank Reconciliation as of March 1, 2001

Checkbook balance			Bank balance		
Jean's checkbook balance		$6,400	Bank balance		$7,800
Add:			Add:		
Collection of note		1,200	Deposit in transit 2/28		560
		$7,600			$8,360
Deduct:			Deduct:		
Check printing	$20		Outstanding checks:		
ATM	40		No. 111	$390	
NSF check	50	110	No. 116	480	870
Reconciled balance		$7,490	Reconciled balance		$7,490

4. Ron Bytnar banks at St. Paul Federal Bank. Today he received his January 31, 2001, bank statement showing a $1,512.15 balance. Ron's checkbook shows a balance of $894.25. The following checks have not cleared the bank: No 128, $216.50; No. 129, $60.40; and No. 131, $6.80. Ron made a $829.10 deposit that is not shown on the bank statement. He has his $680 monthly mortgage payment paid through the bank. His $1,843.30 IRS refund check was mailed to his bank. Prepare Ron Bytnar's bank reconciliation. *(p. 95)*

RON BYTNAR
Bank Reconciliation as of January 31, 2001

Checkbook balance			Bank balance		
Ron's checkbook balance		$ 894.25	Bank balance		$1,512.15
Add:			Add:		
IRS refund check		1,843.30	Deposit in transit		829.10
		$2,737.55			$2,341.25
Deduct:			Deduct:		
Automatic withdrawal		680.00	Outstanding checks:		
			No. 128	$216.50	
			No. 129	60.40	
			No. 131	6.80	283.70
Reconciled balance		$2,057.55	Reconciled balance		$2,057.55

5. On May 31, 200X, Woody Company's bank statement showed a $8,472.38 bank balance. The bank statement also showed that it collected a $1,300.50 note for the company. A $1,500.10 June 1 deposit was in transit. Check No. 114 for $1,600.11 and check No. 116 for $795.10 are outstanding. Woody's bank charges 30 cents per processed check. This month, Woody wrote 80 checks. Woody has a $6,300.17 checkbook balance. Prepare a reconciled statement. *(p. 95)*

WOODY COMPANY
Bank Reconciliation as of May 31, 200X

Checkbook balance			Bank balance		
Woody's checkbook balance		$6,300.17	Bank balance		$8,472.38
Add:			Add:		
Collection of note		1,300.50	Deposit in transit 6/01		1,500.10
		$7,600.67			$9,972.48
Deduct:			Deduct:		
Check charges (78* × $.30)		23.40	Outstanding checks:		
			No. 114	$1,600.11	
			No. 116	795.10	2,395.21
Reconciled balance		$7,577.27	Reconciled balance		$7,577.27

*Due to two checks outstanding.

A GROUP PROJECT   Defend or reject the following business math issue based on the *Kiplinger's Personal Finance Magazine* article below:

FINANCIAL SERVICES
An ATM on every block—and then some

Automated teller machines are proliferating like rabbits in springtime, and banks are hopping for joy. In the past year the number of ATMs located off bank premises multiplied by 20%, and the typical surcharge for using a cash machine jumped from $1 to $1.50, according to a recent study by the General Accounting Office.

You'll find ATMs at Rite Aid drugstores, Kinko's, Mail Boxes Etc., Sears and even near the visitors center in Grand Canyon National Park. Now Citibank will install ATMs in as many as 3,000 Blockbuster Video stores by the middle of next year.

The GAO study found that surcharges are generally the same regardless of an ATM's location, but occasionally convenience does cost more. For example, Bank One customers pay nothing to use an ATM at the bank but have to fork over $1 when they use a Bank One machine at a Rite Aid or Mail Boxes Etc. store; noncustomers pay a $1.50 fee at all locations. Currently, Citibank ATMs

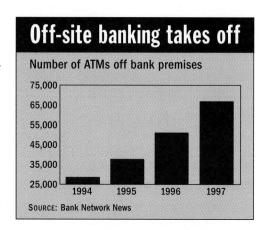

Off-site banking takes off

Number of ATMs off bank premises

SOURCE: Bank Network News

at Blockbuster stores are free to everyone who needs quick cash to rent a movie.

It's only a matter of time before consumers have access to ATMs at home. Already, families at Hickam Air Force Base in Hawaii can hook up to the Internet and download cash from their bank accounts onto a smart card. Banks may pass on an interchange fee of up to $1.50 per transaction.   —C.S

Business Math Issue

Banks should be allowed to charge for ATM use since they provide quick access for customers.

1. List the key points of the article and information to support your position.
2. Write a group defense of your position using math calculations to support your view.

MasterCard Puts $50 Limit on Liability Of Consumers for Stolen Debit Cards

By STEPHEN E. FRANK
Staff Reporter of THE WALL STREET JOURNAL

MasterCard International said it will limit consumers' liability for fraudulent use of stolen debit cards to $50, the legally mandated cap for losses on stolen credit cards. The bank-card association said issuers of its cards will absorb any losses above that level that consumers incur due to debit-card fraud.

The move responds to mounting public concern that users of the increasingly popular debit cards could have their checking accounts cleaned out if their cards are lost or stolen.

Debit cards look and work just like credit cards, but money is deducted instantly from users' checking accounts. The cards have exploded in popularity in recent years, as banks have begun issuing them to customers automatically, in place of traditional automated-teller machine cards. In 1996, alone, the number of MasterCard's MasterMoney brand debit cards in use more than doubled, to 15.6 million; transaction volume totaled $8.7 billion.

MasterCard began issuing debit cards in the early 1980s, but began promoting the cards under the MasterMoney name only three years ago. The Purchase, N.Y., card association controls just over 25% of the U.S. debit-card market, with the rest belonging to **Visa U.S.A.**

MasterCard officials said that in practice, their decision to cap losses merely formalizes the existing policy of the majority of their member banks. Nevertheless, under existing federal law, users of debit cards who do not speedily notify their banks when the cards are stolen are potentially liable for the full loss. Credit-card losses, by contrast, are capped at $50, with card issuers liable for the remainder of any fraudulent card use.

The move was hailed by consumer advocates. "It's great news," said Linda Goldner, president of the National Consumers League, in Washington, D.C. "People are confused with debit and credit cards, and it has been a real problem."

For its part, Visa said its members also "have typically extended protection beyond what is required by law." The San Francisco-based association stopped short of saying it would follow MasterCard's move, but said it would issue a statement soon "regarding potential changes in consumer protection for the Visa check card."

Project A

Do you agree with the $50 limit on liability for stolen debit cards?

Project B

Do you think that banks should all have the same fees and rates?

New Charges Make Banking More Confusing

YOUR
MONEY
MATTERS

By KAREN HUBE
And MATT MURRAY
Staff Reporters of THE WALL STREET JOURNAL

A decade-long flowering of bank fees keeps sprouting new thorns.

Just last week, Citibank announced that it will triple the minimum balance required for unlimited free checking to $6,000 and raise the fee for falling below the level to $9.50 from $7.50.

The move by the giant banking unit of New York's **Citicorp**, which will take effect in late February, is the latest example of the complicated calculations that go into maintaining a bank checking account.

Customers increasingly face a dizzying array of changing charges and balance requirements.

To be sure, banks generally require a smaller minimum deposit to avoid fees than in the past. But customers who drop below the required minimums pay a steeper price.

Perhaps even more annoying to bank customers, banks have been adding automated-teller-machine fees and other charges. Some now charge extra if you want canceled checks mailed back to you.

The Cost of Banking
Average bank fees in 1996

Interest-paying checking accounts	$8.11[1]
Noninterest-paying checking	$6.34[1]
ATM annual fee	$7.94
Using another bank's ATM	$1.10[2]
Overdraft charge	$16.28

[1]Monthly [2]Per transaction
Source: Federal Reserve Board

 See text Web site (www.mhhe.com/slater) and *The Business Math Internet Resource Guide*.

5

SOLVING FOR THE UNKNOWN: A HOW-TO APPROACH FOR SOLVING EQUATIONS

LEARNING UNIT OBJECTIVES

LU 5.1   Solving Equations for the Unknown

- Explain the basic procedures used to solve equations for the unknown *(pp. 115–18)*.

- List the five rules and the mechanical steps used to solve for the unknown in seven situations; know how to check the answers *(pp. 116–18)*.

LU 5.2   Solving Word Problems for the Unknown

- List the steps for solving word problems *(p. 119)*.

- Complete blueprint aids to solve word problems; check the solutions *(pp. 119–21)*.

This letter is based on a true story.

Smith's Decorating Service

Rose Smith
15 Locust Street
Lynn, MA 01915

Dear Professor Slater,

Thank you for helping me get through your Business Math class. When
I first started, my math anxiety level was real high. I felt I had no head for numbers. When
you told us we would be covering the chapter on solving equations, I'll never forget how I
started to shake. I started to panic. I felt I could never solve a word problem. I thought I
was having an algebra attack.

Now that it's over (90 on the chapter on unknowns), I'd like to tell you what
worked for me so you might pass this on to other students. It was your blueprint aids. Drawing
boxes helped me to think things out. They were a tool that helped me more clearly understand
how to dissect each word problem. They didn't solve the problem for me, but gave me the
direction I needed. Repetition was the key to my success. At first I got them all wrong but
after the third time, things started to click. I felt more confident. Your chapter organizers at
the end of the chapter were great. Thanks for your patience – your repetition breeds success –
now students are asking me to help them solve a word problem. Can you believe it!

Best,

Rose

Rose Smith

Are you a TV soccer fan? If you are, you will see more Nike advertisements during the games. *The Wall Street Journal* clipping "Nike Kicks" states that U.S. soccer has joined the sponsorship big leagues. As a soccer sponsor, Nike will pay about $120 million over 8 years to the U.S. Soccer Federation. The clipping goes on to say that this amount will be about 10 times as rich as the federation's current contract with Nike. Do you wonder how much Nike's current contract now pays the U.S. Soccer Federation? To determine this amount, you can use an equation to solve for the unknown.

Nike Kicks

ADVERTISING

By STEFAN FATSIS
Staff Reporter of THE WALL STREET JOURNAL

U.S. soccer is finally joining the sponsorship big leagues.

Nike has agreed to pay about $120 million over eight years to sponsor the U.S. Soccer Federation, the governing body for the top men's, women's and youth teams.

The pact, expected to be announced today in New York, will be about 10 times

as rich as the federation's current contract with Nike and 100 times the size of the federation's pact with its previous shoe sponsor, Adidas of Germany. In fact, Adidas made an 11th-hour effort to get the sponsorship back, according to people familiar with the talks. (An Adidas America spokesman in Portland, Ore., says, "We weren't involved. To our knowledge, there was no 'open to bid.' ")

© 1997 Dow Jones & Company, Inc.

Don't worry. This chapter will show you how to solve equations. You will find that solving for the unknown is important in today's real-world applications.

To introduce you to equations, let's use an equation to find the amount Nike now pays the U.S. Soccer Federation. Since letters are often used to represent unknowns, we will use C as the unknown amount Nike now pays the U.S. Soccer Federation.

10 times some unknown equals $120,000,000. $\dfrac{10C}{10} = \dfrac{\$120,000,000}{10}$

$$C = \boxed{\$12,000,000} \leftarrow \text{What Nike pays for current contract}$$

Learning Unit 5.1 explains how to solve for unknowns in equations. In Learning Unit 5.2 you learn how to solve for unknowns in word problems. When you complete these learning units, you will not have to memorize as many formulas to solve business and personal math applications. Also, with the increasing use of computer software, a basic working knowledge of solving for the unknown has become necessary.

LEARNING UNIT 5.1 Solving Equations for the Unknown

Many of you are familiar with the terms *variables* and *constants*. If you are someone who is continuously on a diet, you know that your weight is a variable. Some days your weight is up; other days it is down. And probably you can never say, "No matter what I eat, my weight is constant." Fortunately, in solving for unknowns, variables and constants are easier to control.

Basic Equation-Solving Procedures

Do you know the difference between an equation and a formula? An **equation** is a mathematical statement with an equals sign showing that a mathematical expression on the left equals the mathematical expression on the right. The numbers and letters within the expressions are called *terms*. The operational signs (such as + or −) within the expressions connect the terms to show a relationship between them. A **formula** is an equation that expresses in symbols a general fact, rule, or principle. Formulas are shortcuts for expressing a word concept. For example, in Chapter 10 you will learn that the formula for simple interest is Interest (I) = Principal (P) × Rate (R) × Time (T). This means that when you see $I = P \times R \times T$, you recognize the simple interest formula. Now we return to our study of basic equations.

As a mathematical statement of equality, equations show that two numbers or groups of numbers are equal. For example, $6 + 4 = 10$ shows the equality of an equation. Equations also use letters as symbols that represent one or more numbers. These symbols, usually a letter of the alphabet, are **variables** that stand for a number. We can use a variable even though we may not know what it represents. For example, $A + 2 = 6$. The variable A represents the number or **unknown** (4 in this example) for which we are solving. We distinguish variables from numbers, which have a fixed value. Numbers such as 3 or −7 are **constants** or **knowns,** while A and $3A$ (this means 3 times the variable A) are variables. So we can now say that variables and constants are *terms of mathematical expressions.*

In solving for the unknown, we place variable(s) on the left side of the equation and constants on the right. The following rules for variables and constants are important.

Variables and Constants Rules

1. If no number is in front of a letter, it is a 1: $B = 1B$; $C = 1C$.
2. If no sign is in front of a letter or number, it is a +: $C = +C$; $4 = +4$.

You should be aware that in solving equations, the meaning of the symbols $+$, $-$, $\times$, and $\div$ has not changed. However, some variations occur. For example, you can also write $A \times B$ (A times B) as $A \cdot B$, $A(B)$, or AB. Also, A divided by B is the same as A/B. Remember that to solve an equation, you must find a number that can replace the unknown in the equation and make it a true statement. Now let's take a moment to look at how we can change verbal statements into variables.

Assume Dick Hersh, an employee of Nike, is 50 years old. Let's assign Dick Hersh's changing age to the symbol A. The symbol A is a variable.

FIGURE 5.1

Equality in equations

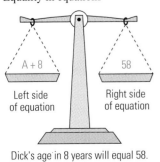

Left side of equation   Right side of equation

Dick's age in 8 years will equal 58.

Verbal statement	Variable A (age)
Dick's age 8 years ago	$A - 8$
Dick's age 8 years from today	$A + 8$
Four times Dick's age	$4A$
One-fifth Dick's age	$A/5$

To visualize how equations work, think of the old-fashioned balancing scale shown in Figure 5.1. The pole of the scale is the equals sign. The two sides of the equation are the two pans of the scale. In the left pan or left side of the equation, we have $A + 8$; in the right pan or right side of the equation, we have 58. To solve for the unknown (Dick's present age), we isolate or place the unknown (variable) on the left side and the numbers on the right. We will do this soon. For now, remember that to keep an equation (or scale) in balance, we must perform mathematical operations (addition, subtraction, multiplication, and division) to *both* sides of the equation.

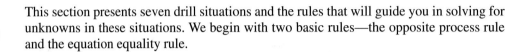

Solving for the Unknown Rule

Whatever you do to one side of an equation, you must do to the other side.

How to Solve for Unknowns in Equations

This section presents seven drill situations and the rules that will guide you in solving for unknowns in these situations. We begin with two basic rules—the opposite process rule and the equation equality rule.

Opposite Process Rule

If an equation indicates a process such as addition, subtraction, multiplication, or division, solve for the unknown or variable by using the opposite process. For example, if the equation process is addition, solve for the unknown by using subtraction.

Equation Equality Rule

You can add the same quantity or number to both sides of the equation and subtract the same quantity or number from both sides of the equation without affecting the equality of the equation. You can divide or multiply both sides of the equation by the same quantity or number (*except zero*) without affecting the equality of the equation.

Drill Situation 1: Subtracting Same Number from Both Sides of Equation

Example
$A + 8 = 58$
Dick's age A plus 8 equals 58.

Mechanical steps
$$A + 8 = 58$$
$$ - 8 \quad\quad - 8$$
$$A = \boxed{50}$$

Explanation
8 is subtracted from *both* sides of equation to isolate variable A on the left.

Check
$50 + 8 = 58$
$58 = 58$

Note: Since the equation process used *addition,* we use the opposite process rule and solve for variable A with *subtraction.* We also use the equation equality rule when we subtract the same quantity from both sides of the equation.

Drill Situation 2: Adding Same Number to Both Sides of Equation

Example
$B - 50 = 80$
Some number B less 50 equals 80.

Mechanical steps
$$B - 50 = 80$$
$$ + 50 \quad\quad + 50$$
$$B = \boxed{130}$$

Explanation
50 is added to *both* sides to isolate variable B on the left.

Check
$130 - 50 = 80$
$80 = 80$

Note: Since the equation process used *subtraction,* we use the opposite process rule and solve for variable B with *addition.* We also use the equation equality rule when we add the same quantity to both sides of the equation.

Drill Situation 3: Dividing Both Sides of Equation by Same Number

Example

$7G = 35$

Some number G times 7 equals 35.

Mechanical steps

$7G = 35$

$\dfrac{7G}{7} = \dfrac{35}{7}$

$G = \boxed{5}$

Explanation

By dividing both sides by 7, G equals 5.

Check

$7(5) = 35$

$35 = 35$

Note: Since the equation process used *multiplication,* we use the opposite process rule and solve for variable G with *division.* We also use the equation equality rule when we divide both sides of the equation by the same quantity.

Drill Situation 4: Multiplying Both Sides of Equation by Same Number

Example

$\dfrac{V}{5} = 70$

Some number V divided by 5 equals 70.

Mechanical steps

$\dfrac{V}{5} = 70$

$5\left(\dfrac{V}{5}\right) = 70(5)$

$V = \boxed{350}$

Explanation

By multiplying both sides by 5, V is equal to 350.

Check

$\dfrac{350}{5} = 70$

$70 = 70$

Note: Since the equation process used *division,* we use the opposite process rule and solve for variable V with *multiplication.* We also use the equation equality rule when we multiply both sides of the equation by the same quantity.

Drill Situation 5: Equation That Uses Subtraction and Multiplication to Solve Unknown

Multiple Processes Rule

When solving for an unknown that involves more than one process, do the addition and subtraction before the multiplication and division.

Example

$\dfrac{H}{4} + 2 = 5$

When we divide unknown H by 4 and add the result to 2, the answer is 5.

Mechanical steps

$\dfrac{H}{4} + 2 = 5$

$\dfrac{H}{4} + 2 = 5$

$\underline{\quad -2 \quad -2 \quad}$

$\dfrac{H}{4} = 3$

$4\left(\dfrac{H}{4}\right) = 4(3)$

$H = \boxed{12}$

Explanation

1. Move constant to right side by subtracting 2 from both sides.
2. To isolate H, which is divided by 4, we do the opposite process and multiply 4 times *both* sides of the equation.

Check

$\dfrac{12}{4} + 2 = 5$

$3 + 2 = 5$

$5 = 5$

Drill Situation 6: Using Parentheses in Solving for Unknown

Parentheses Rule

When equations contain parentheses (which indicate grouping together), you solve for the unknown by first multiplying each item inside the parentheses by the number or letter just outside the parentheses. Then you continue to solve for the unknown with the opposite process used in the equation. Do the additions and subtractions first; then the multiplications and divisions.

Example	**Mechanical steps**	**Explanation**

Example
$5(P - 4) = 20$
The unknown P
less 4, multiplied
by 5 equals 20.

Mechanical steps
$5(P - 4) = 20$
$5P - 20 = 20$
$\underline{+ 20 + 20}$
$\dfrac{\cancel{5}P}{\cancel{5}} = \dfrac{40}{5}$
$P = \boxed{8}$

Explanation
1. Parentheses tell us that everything inside parentheses is multiplied by 5. Multiply 5 by P and 5 by -4.
2. Add 20 to both sides to isolate $5P$ on left.
3. To remove 5 in front of P, divide both sides by 5 to result in P equals 8.

Check
$5(8 - 4) = 20$
$5(4) = 20$
$20 = 20$

Drill Situation 7: Combining Like Unknowns

Like Unknowns Rule

To solve equations with like unknowns, you first combine the unknowns and then solve with the opposite process used in the equation.

Example
$4A + A = 20$

Mechanical steps
$4A + A = 20$
$\dfrac{\cancel{5}A}{\cancel{5}} = \dfrac{20}{5}$
$A = \boxed{4}$

Explanation
To solve this equation: $4A + 1A = 5A$. Thus, $5A = 20$. To solve for A, divide both sides by 5, leaving A equals 4.

Before you go to Learning Unit 5.2, let's check your understanding of this unit.

LU 5.1 PRACTICE QUIZ

1. Write equations for the following (use the letter Q as the variable); do not solve for the unknown:
   a. Nine less than one-half a number is fourteen.
   b. Eight times the sum of a number and thirty-one is fifty.
   c. Ten decreased by twice a number is two.
   d. Eight times a number less two equals twenty-one.
   e. The sum of four times a number and two is fifteen.
   f. If twice a number is decreased by eight, the difference is four.

2. Solve the following:
   a. $B + 24 = 60$
   b. $D + 3D = 240$
   c. $12B = 144$
   d. $\dfrac{B}{6} = 50$
   e. $\dfrac{B}{4} + 4 = 16$
   f. $3(B - 8) = 18$

✓ **Solutions**

1. a. $\dfrac{1}{2}Q - 9 = 14$
   b. $8(Q + 31) = 50$
   c. $10 - 2Q = 2$
   d. $8Q - 2 = 21$
   e. $4Q + 2 = 15$
   f. $2Q - 8 = 4$

2. a. $B + 24 = 60$
      $\underline{ - 24 - 24}$
      $B = \boxed{36}$

   b. $\dfrac{\cancel{4}D}{\cancel{4}} = \dfrac{240}{4}$
      $D = \boxed{60}$

   c. $\dfrac{\cancel{12}B}{\cancel{12}} = \dfrac{144}{12}$
      $B = \boxed{12}$

   d. $\cancel{6}\left(\dfrac{B}{\cancel{6}}\right) = 50(6)$
      $B = \boxed{300}$

   e. $\dfrac{B}{4} + 4 = 16$
      $\underline{\phantom{\dfrac{B}{4}} - 4 - 4}$
      $\dfrac{B}{4} = 12$
      $\cancel{4}\left(\dfrac{B}{\cancel{4}}\right) = 12(4)$
      $B = \boxed{48}$

   f. $3(B - 8) = 18$
      $3B - 24 = 18$
      $\underline{ + 24 + 24}$
      $\dfrac{\cancel{3}B}{\cancel{3}} = \dfrac{42}{3}$
      $B = \boxed{14}$

LEARNING UNIT 5.2   Solving Word Problems for the Unknown

On the first day of your business math class, you count 29 students in the class. A week later, 11 additional students had joined the class. The semester ended with 35 students in attendance. How many students dropped out of class? You can solve this unknown as follows:

> 29 students started the class + 11 students joined the class = 40 total students
>
> 40 total students − $\dfrac{35\ students}{completed\ the\ class}$ = $\dfrac{5\ students}{dropped\ the\ class}$

Whether you are in or out of class, you are continually solving word problems. In this unit we give you a road map showing you how to solve word problems with unknowns by using a blueprint aid. The five steps below will help you dissect and solve these word problems. In Chapters 1 through 3, we also presented blueprint aids for dissecting and solving word problems. Now the blueprint aid focuses on solving for the unknown.

We look at six different situations in this unit. Be patient and *persistent.* The more problems you work, the easier the process becomes. Note how we dissect and solve each problem in the blueprint aids. Do not panic! Repetition is the key. Now let's study the five steps.

Solving Word Problems for Unknowns

Step 1. Carefully read the entire problem. You may have to read it several times.

Step 2. Ask yourself: "What is the problem looking for?"

Step 3. When you are sure what the problem is asking, let a variable represent the unknown. If the problem has more than one unknown, represent the second unknown in terms of the same variable. For example, if the problem has two unknowns, Y is one unknown. The second unknown is $4Y$—4 times the first unknown.

Step 4. Visualize the relationship between unknowns and variables. Then set up an equation to solve for unknown(s).

Step 5. Check your result to see if it is accurate.

Courtesy NIKE.

Word Problem Situation 1: Number Problems   A pair of Nike running shoes at Nike Town were reduced $50. The sale price was $60. What was the original price?

Blueprint aid

Unknown(s)	Variable(s)	Relationship*
Original price	P	P − $50 = Sale price Sale price = $60

*This column will help you visualize the equation before setting up the actual equation.

Mechanical steps

P − $50 = $ 60
  + 50   + 50
————————
P = $110

Check

$110 − $50 = $60
      $60 = $60

Explanation

The original price less $50 equals $60. Note that we added $50 to both sides to isolate P on the left. Remember, $1P = P$.

Word Problem Situation 2: Finding the Whole When Part Is Known   A local Burger King budgets $\frac{1}{8}$ of its monthly profits on salaries. Salaries for the month were $12,000. What were Burger King's monthly profits?

Blueprint aid

Unknown(s)	Variable(s)	Relationship
Monthly profits	P	$\frac{1}{8}P$ Salaries = $12,000

Mechanical steps

$$\frac{1}{8}P = \$12{,}000$$

$$8\left(\frac{P}{8}\right) = \$12{,}000(8)$$

$$P = \boxed{\$96{,}000}$$

Explanation

$\frac{1}{8}P$ represents Burger King's monthly salaries. Since the equation used division, we solve for P by multiplying both sides by 8.

Check

$$\frac{1}{8}(\$96{,}000) = \$12{,}000$$

$$\$12{,}000 = \$12{,}000$$

Word Problem Situation 3: Difference Problems   ICM Company sold 4 times as many computers as Ring Company. The difference in their sales is 27. How many computers of each company were sold?

Blueprint aid

Unknown(s)	Variable(s)	Relationship
ICM	$4C$	$4C$
Ring	C	$\dfrac{-C}{27}$

Note: If problem has two unknowns, assign the variable to smaller item or one who sells less. Then assign the other unknown using the same variable. *Use the same letter.*

Explanation

The variables replace the names ICM and Ring. We assigned Ring the variable C, since it sold fewer computers. We assigned ICM $4C$, since it sold 4 times as many computers.

Mechanical steps

$$4C - C = 27$$

$$\frac{3C}{3} = \frac{27}{3}$$

$$C = \boxed{9}$$

Ring = $\boxed{9}$ computers
ICM = $4(9)$
   = $\boxed{36}$ computers

Check

$$\begin{array}{r} 36 \text{ computers} \\ -\ 9 \\ \hline 27 \text{ computers} \end{array}$$

Word Problem Situation 4: Calculating Unit Sales   Together Barry Sullivan and Mitch Ryan sold a total of 300 homes for Regis Realty. Barry sold 9 times as many homes as Mitch. How many did each sell?

Blueprint aid

Unknown(s)	Variable(s)	Relationship
Homes sold: B. Sullivan M. Ryan	$9H$ $H*$	$9H$ $\dfrac{+H}{300}$ homes

*Assign H to Ryan since he sold less.

Explanation

We assigned Mitch H, since he sold fewer homes. We assigned Barry $9H$, since he sold 9 times as many homes. Together Barry and Mitch sold 300 homes.

Mechanical steps

$$9H + H = 300$$

$$\frac{10H}{10} = \frac{300}{10}$$

$$H = \boxed{30}$$

Ryan: $\boxed{30}$ homes
Sullivan: $9(30) = \boxed{270}$ homes

Check

$$30 + 270 = 300$$

Word Problem Situation 5: Calculating Unit and Dollar Sales (Cost per Unit) When Total Units Are Not Given   Andy sold watches ($9) and alarm clocks ($5) at a flea market. Total sales were $287. People bought 4 times as many watches as alarm clocks. How many of each did Andy sell? What were the total dollar sales of each?

Blueprint aid

Unknown(s)	Variable(s)	Price	Relationship
Unit sales: Watches Clocks	$4C$ C	$9 5	$36C$ $\dfrac{+\ 5C}{\$287}$ total sales

Mechanical steps

$$36C + 5C = 287$$

$$\frac{41C}{41} = \frac{287}{41}$$

$$C = \boxed{7}$$

$\boxed{7}$ clocks

$4(7) = \boxed{28}$ watches

Explanation

Number of watches times $9 sales price plus number of alarm clocks times $5 equals $287 total sales.

Check

$7(\$5) + 28(\$9) = \$287$
$\$35 + \$252 = \$287$
$\$287 = \$287$

Word Problem Situation 6: Calculating Unit and Dollar Sales (Cost per Unit) When Total Units Are Given   Andy sold watches ($9) and alarm clocks ($5) at a flea market. Total sales for 35 watches and alarm clocks were $287. How many of each did Andy sell? What were the total dollar sales of each?

Blueprint aid

Unknown(s)	Variable(s)	Price	Relationship
Unit sales:			
Watches	W*	$9	9W
Clocks	35 − W	5	+ 5(35− W)
			$287 total sales

*The more expensive item is assigned to the variable first only for this situation to make the mechanical steps easier to complete.

Mechanical steps

$9W + 5(35 − W) = 287$
$9W + 175 − 5W = 287$
$4W + 175 \qquad = 287$
$\qquad \underline{- 175 \qquad - 175}$
$\dfrac{4W}{4} \qquad\quad = \dfrac{112}{4}$
$\qquad\qquad\qquad W = \boxed{28}$

Watches $= \boxed{28}$
Clocks $= 35 - 28 = \boxed{7}$

Explanation

Number of watches (W) times price per watch plus number of alarm clocks times price per alarm clock equals $287. Total units given was 35.

Check

$28(\$9) + 7(\$5) = \$287$
$\$252 + \$35 = \$287$
$\$287 = \$287$

Why did we use $35 - W$? Assume we had 35 pizzas (some cheese, others meatball). If I said that I ate all the meatball pizzas (5), how many cheese pizzas are left? Thirty? Right, you subtract 5 from 35. Think of $35 - W$ as meaning one number.

Note in Word Problem Situations 5 and 6 that the situation is the same. In Word Problem Situation 5, we were not given total units sold (but we were told which sold better). In Word Problem Situation 6, we were given total units sold, but we did not know which sold better.

Now try these six types of word problems in the Practice Quiz. Be sure to complete blueprint aids and the mechanical steps for solving the unknown(s).

LU 5.2 PRACTICE QUIZ

Situations

1. An L.L. Bean sweater was reduced $30. The sale price was $90. What was the original price?
2. Kelly Doyle budgets $\frac{1}{8}$ of her yearly salary for entertainment. Kelly's total entertainment bill for the year is $6,500. What is Kelly's yearly salary?
3. Micro Knowledge sells 5 times as many computers as Morse Electronics. The difference in sales between the two stores is 20 computers. How many computers did each store sell?
4. Susie and Cara sell stoves at Elliott's Appliances. Together they sold 180 stoves in January. Susie sold 5 times as many stoves as Cara. How many stoves did each sell?
5. Pasquale's Pizza sells meatball pizzas ($6) and cheese pizzas ($5). In March, Pasquale's total sales were $1,600. People bought 2 times as many cheese pizzas as meatball pizzas. How many of each did Pasquale sell? What were the total dollar sales of each?
6. Pasquale's Pizza sells meatball pizzas ($6) and cheese pizzas ($5). In March, Pasquale's sold 300 pizzas for $1,600. How many of each did Pasquale's sell? What was the dollar sales price of each?

✓ **Solutions**

1.

Unknown(s)	Variable(s)	Relationship
Original price	P*	P − $30 = Sale price
		Sale price = $90

*P = Original price.

Mechanical steps

$P - \$30 = \$\ 90$
$\underline{+ 30 \qquad + 30}$
$P \qquad\ = \boxed{\$120}$

2.

Unknown(s)	Variable(s)	Relationship
Yearly salary	S*	$\frac{1}{8}S$
		Entertainment = $6,500

*S = Salary.

Mechanical steps

$\dfrac{1}{8}S = \$6,500$
$8\left(\dfrac{S}{8}\right) = \$6,500(8)$
$S = \boxed{\$52,000}$

3.

Unknown(s)	Variable(s)	Relationship
Micro	$5C$*	$5C$
Morse	C	$- C$
		20 computers

*C = Computers.

Mechanical steps

$5C - C = 20$

$$\frac{\cancel{4}C}{\cancel{4}} = \frac{20}{4}$$

$C = \boxed{5}$ (Morse)

$5C = \boxed{25}$ (Micro)

4.

Unknown(s)	Variable(s)	Relationship
Stoves sold:		
Susie	$5S$*	$5S$
Cara	S	$+ S$
		180 stoves

*S = Stoves.

Mechanical steps

$5S + S = 180$

$$\frac{\cancel{6}S}{\cancel{6}} = \frac{180}{6}$$

$S = \boxed{30}$ (Cara)

$5S = \boxed{150}$ (Susie)

5.

Unknown(s)	Variable(s)	Price	Relationship
Meatball	M	$6	$6M$
Cheese	$2M$	5	$+ 10M$
			$1,600 total sales

Mechanical steps

$6M + 10M = 1,600$

$$\frac{\cancel{16}M}{\cancel{16}} = \frac{1,600}{16}$$

$M = \boxed{100}$ (meatball)

$2M = \boxed{200}$ (cheese)

Check

$(100 \times \$6) + (200 \times \$5) = \$1,600$

$\$600 + \$1,000 = \$1,600$

$\$1,600 = \$1,600$

6.

Unknown(s)	Variable(s)	Price	Relationship
Unit sales:			
Meatball	M*	$6	$6M$
Cheese	$300 - M$	5	$+ 5(300 - M)$
			$1,600 total sales

*We assign the variable to the most expensive to make the mechanical steps easier to complete.

Mechanical steps

$$
\begin{aligned}
6M + 5(300 - M) &= 1,600 \\
6M + 1,500 - 5M &= 1,600 \\
M + 1,500 &= 1,600 \\
-1,500 \quad\quad & \quad -1,500 \\
\hline
M &= \boxed{100}
\end{aligned}
$$

Meatball $= \boxed{100}$

Cheese $= 300 - 100 = \boxed{200}$

Check

$100(\$6) + 200(\$5) = \$600 + \$1,000$

$= \$1,600$

Chapter Organizer and Reference Guide

Solving for unknowns from basic equations	Mechanical steps to solve unknowns	Key point(s)
Situation 1: Subtracting same number from both sides of equation, p. 116	$D + 10 = 12$ $\quad -10 \quad -10$ $D = \boxed{2}$	Subtract 10 from both sides of equation to isolate variable D on the left. Since equation used addition, we solve by using opposite process—subtraction.
Situation 2: Adding same number to both sides of equation, p. 116	$L - 24 = 40$ $\quad +24 \quad +24$ $L = \boxed{64}$	Add 24 to both sides to isolate unknown L on left. We solve by using opposite process of subtraction—addition.
Situation 3: Dividing both sides of equation by same number, p. 117	$6B = 24$ $\dfrac{\cancel{6}B}{\cancel{6}} = \dfrac{24}{6}$ $B = \boxed{4}$	To isolate B by itself on the left, divide both sides of the equation by 6. Thus, the 6 on the left cancels—leaving B equal to 4. Since equation used multiplication, we solve unknown by using opposite process—division.

Chapter Organizer and Reference Guide (continued)		
Solving for unknowns from basic equations	**Mechanical steps to solve unknowns**	**Key point(s)**
Situation 4: Multiplying both sides of equation by same number, p. 117	$$\frac{R}{3} = 15$$ $$3\left(\frac{R}{3}\right) = 15(3)$$ $$R = \boxed{45}$$	To remove denominator, multiply both sides of the equation by 3—the 3 on the left side cancels, leaving R equal to 45. Since equation used division, we solve unknown by using opposite process—multiplication.
Situation 5: Equation that uses subtraction and multiplication to solve for unknown, p. 117	$$\frac{B}{3} + 6 = 13$$ $$\frac{-6 \quad -6}{\frac{B}{3} = 7}$$ $$3\left(\frac{B}{3}\right) = 7(3)$$ $$B = \boxed{21}$$	1. Move constant 6 to right side by subtracting 6 from both sides. 2. Isolate B by itself on left by multiplying both sides by 3.
Situation 6: Using parentheses in solving for unknown, p. 117	$$6(A - 5) = 12$$ $$6A - 30 = 12$$ $$\frac{+30 \quad +30}{\frac{6A}{6} = \frac{42}{6}}$$ $$A = \boxed{7}$$	Parentheses indicate multiplication. Multiply 6 times A and 6 times -5. Result is $6A - 30$ on left side of the equation. Now add 30 to both sides to isolate $6A$ on left. To remove 6 in front of A, divide both sides by 6, to result in A equal to 7. Note that when deleting parentheses, we did not have to multiply the right side.
Situation 7: Combining unknowns, p. 118	$$6A + 2A = 64$$ $$\frac{8A}{8} = \frac{64}{8}$$ $$A = \boxed{8}$$	$6A + 2A$ combine to $8A$. To solve for A, we divide both sides by 8.

Solving for unknowns from word problems	Blueprint aid	Mechanical steps to solve unknown with check
Situation 1: Number problems, p. 119 U.S. Air reduced its airfare to California by $60. The sale price was $95. What was the original price?	<table><tr><th>Unknown(s)</th><th>Variable(s)</th><th>Relationship</th></tr><tr><td>Original price</td><td>P</td><td>P −$60 =Sale price Sale price =$95</td></tr></table>	$$P - \$60 = \$95$$ $$\frac{+60 \quad +60}{P = \boxed{\$155}}$$ **Check** $$\$155 - \$60 = \$95$$ $$\$95 = \$95$$
Situation 2: Finding the whole when part is known, p. 120 K. McCarthy spends $\frac{1}{8}$ of her budget for school. What is the total budget if school costs $5,000?	<table><tr><th>Unknown(s)</th><th>Variable(s)</th><th>Relationship</th></tr><tr><td>Total budget</td><td>B</td><td>$\frac{1}{8}B$ School = $5,000</td></tr></table>	$$\frac{1}{8}B = \$5,000$$ $$8\left(\frac{B}{8}\right) = \$5,000(8)$$ $$B = \boxed{\$40,000}$$ **Check** $$\frac{1}{8}(\$40,000) = \$5,000$$ $$\$5,000 = \$5,000$$
Situation 3: Difference problems, p. 120 Moe sold 8 times as many suitcases as Bill. The difference in their sales is 280 suitcases. How many suitcases did each sell?	<table><tr><th>Unknown(s)</th><th>Variable(s)</th><th>Relationship</th></tr><tr><td>Suitcases sold: Moe Bill</td><td>8S S</td><td>8S −S 280 suitcases</td></tr></table>	$$8S - S = 280 \text{ (Bill)}$$ $$\frac{7S}{7} = \frac{280}{7}$$ $$S = \boxed{40} \text{ (Bill)}$$ $$8(40) = \boxed{320} \text{ (Moe)}$$ **Check** $$320 - 40 = 280$$ $$280 = 280$$

Chapter Organizer and Reference Guide (concluded)

Solving for unknowns from word problems	Blueprint aid	Mechanical steps to solve unknown with check
Situation 4: Calculating unit sales, p. 120 Moe sold 8 times as many suitcases as Bill. Together they sold a total of 360. How many did each sell?	<table><tr><th>Unknown(s)</th><th>Variable(s)</th><th>Relationship</th></tr><tr><td>*Suitcases sold:* Moe Bill</td><td> 8*S* *S*</td><td> 8*S* +*S* 360 suitcases</td></tr></table>	$8S + S = 360$ $\dfrac{9S}{9} = \dfrac{360}{9}$ $S = \boxed{40}$ (Bill) $8S = \boxed{320}$ (Moe) **Check** $320 + 40 = 360$ $360 = 360$
Situation 5: Calculating unit and dollar sales (cost per unit) when *total units not given*, p. 120 Blue Furniture Company ordered sleepers ($300) and nonsleepers ($200) that cost $8,000. Blue expects sleepers to outsell nonsleepers 2 to 1. How many units of each were ordered? What were dollar costs of each?	<table><tr><th>Unknown(s)</th><th>Variable(s)</th><th>Price</th><th>Relationship</th></tr><tr><td>Sleepers Nonsleepers</td><td>2*N* *N*</td><td>$300 200</td><td>600*N* + 200*N* $8,000 total cost</td></tr></table>	$600N + 200N = 8,000$ $\dfrac{800N}{800} = \dfrac{8,000}{800}$ $N = \boxed{10}$ (nonsleepers) $2N = \boxed{20}$ (sleepers) **Check** $10 \times \$200 = \$2,000$ $20 \times \$300 = \underline{\ 6,000}$ $= \underline{\$8,000}$
Situation 6: Calculating unit and dollar sales (cost per unit) when *total units given*, p. 121 Blue Furniture Company ordered 30 sofas (sleepers and nonsleepers) that cost $8,000. The wholesale unit cost was $300 for the sleepers and $200 for the nonsleepers. How many units of each were ordered? What were dollar costs of each?	<table><tr><th>Unknown(s)</th><th>Variable(s)</th><th>Price</th><th>Relationship</th></tr><tr><td>*Unit cost:* Sleepers Nonsleepers</td><td> *S* 30 − *S*</td><td> $300 200</td><td> 300*S* + 200(30 − *S*) $8,000 total cost</td></tr></table> *When the total units are given, the higher-priced item (sleepers) is assigned to the variable first. This makes the mechanical steps easier to complete.*	$300S + 200(30 - S) = 8,000$ $300S + 6,000 - 200S = 8,000$ $100S + 6,000 = 8,000$ $\underline{\quad - 6,000 \qquad - 6,000}$ $\dfrac{100S}{100} = \dfrac{2,000}{100}$ $S = \boxed{20}$ Nonsleepers $= 30 - 20$ $= \boxed{10}$ **Check** $20(\$300) + 10(\$200) = \$8,000$ $\$6,000 + \$2,000 = \$8,000$ $\$8,000 = \$8,000$
Key terms	Constants, p. 115 Equation, p. 115 Formula, p. 115 Knowns, p. 115	Unknown, p. 115 Variables, p. 115

Critical Thinking Discussion Questions

1. Explain the difference between a variable and a constant. What would you consider your monthly car payment—a variable or a constant?

2. How does the opposite process rule help solve for the variable in an equation? If a Mercedes costs 3 times as much as a Saab, how could the opposite process rule be used? The selling price of the Mercedes is $60,000.

3. What is the difference between Word Problem Situations 5 and 6 in Learning Unit 5.2? Show why the more expensive item in Word Problem Situation 6 is assigned to the variable first.

DRILL PROBLEMS (First of Three Sets)

Solve the unknown from the following equations:

5–1.
$$C + 18 = 50$$
$$\underline{ -18 \quad -18}$$
$$C = 32$$

5–2.
$$A + 19 = 90$$
$$\underline{ -19 \quad -19}$$
$$A = 71$$

5–3.
$$D + 90 = 210$$
$$\underline{ -90 \quad -90}$$
$$D = 120$$

5–4.
$$Q - 60 = 850$$
$$\underline{ +60 \quad +60}$$
$$Q = 910$$

5–5.
$$5Y = 75$$
$$\frac{\cancel{5}Y}{\cancel{5}} = \frac{75}{5}$$
$$Y = 15$$

5–6.
$$\frac{P}{6} = 92$$
$$\cancel{6}\left(\frac{P}{\cancel{6}}\right) = 92(6)$$
$$P = 552$$

5–7.
$$8Y = 96$$
$$\frac{\cancel{8}Y}{\cancel{8}} = \frac{96}{8}$$
$$Y = 12$$

5–8.
$$\frac{N}{16} = 5$$
$$\cancel{16}\left(\frac{N}{\cancel{16}}\right) = 5(16)$$
$$N = 80$$

5–9.
$$4(P - 9) = 64$$
$$4P - 36 = 64$$
$$\underline{ +36 = +36}$$
$$\frac{\cancel{4}P}{\cancel{4}} = \frac{100}{4}$$
$$P = 25$$

5–10.
$$3(P - 3) = 27$$
$$3P - 9 = 27$$
$$\underline{ +9 = +9}$$
$$\frac{\cancel{3}P}{\cancel{3}} = \frac{36}{3}$$
$$P = 12$$

WORD PROBLEMS (First of Three Sets)

Situation 1, p. 119.

5–11. The November 1996 issue of *Ladies' Home Journal* advises you to be a patient shopper. Products sold on TV usually make it to the big stores within 90 to 100 days. The Ab Flex exerciser was reduced by $29.96 from the TV price to the store price of $29.99. What was the TV price of the Ab Flex?

Unknown(s)	Variable(s)	Relationship
TV price	P	P − $29.96 = Store price Store price = $29.99

$$P - \$29.96 = \$29.99$$
$$\underline{ +29.96 = +29.96}$$
$$P = \$59.95$$

Situation 2, p. 120.

5–12. On December 1, 1997, *USA Today* ran an article stating that the Ernie doll was purchased by an Ann Arbor, Michigan, woman for $45, more than $1\frac{1}{2}$ times the original selling price. What did the doll originally sell for?

Unknown(s)	Variable(s)	Relationship
Original price	P	1.5P Selling price = $45

$$1.5P = \$45$$
$$\frac{\cancel{1.5}P}{\cancel{1.5}} = \frac{\$45}{1.5}$$
$$P = \$30$$

Situation 3, p. 120.

5–13. Soo Lin and Hubert Krona sell cars for a Toyota dealer. Over the past year, they sold 150 cars. Soo sells 4 times as many cars as Hubert. How many cars did each sell?

Unknown(s)	Variable(s)	Relationship
Hubert Soo	C 4C	C (30) + 4C (120) 150 cars

$$4C + C = 150$$
$$\frac{\cancel{5}C}{\cancel{5}} = \frac{150}{5}$$
$$C = 30 \text{ (Hubert)}$$
$$4C = 120 \text{ (Soo)}$$

Situation 4, p. 120.

5–14. Nanda Yueh and Lane Zuriff sell homes for ERA Realty. Over the past 6 months they sold 120 homes. Nanda sold 3 times as many homes as Lane. How many homes did each sell?

Unknown(s)	Variable(s)	Relationship
Nanda Lane	3H H	3H (90) + H (30) 120 homes

$$3H + H = 120$$
$$\frac{\cancel{4}H}{\cancel{4}} = \frac{120}{4}$$
$$H = 30 \text{ (Lane)}$$
$$3H = 90 \text{ (Nanda)}$$

Situation 5, p. 120.

5–15. Dots sells T-shirts ($2) and shorts ($4). In April, total sales were $600. People bought 4 times as many T-shirts as shorts. How many T-shirts and shorts did Dots sell? Check your answer.

Unknown(s)	Variable(s)	Price	Relationship
T-shirts	$4S$	$2	$8S$
Shorts	S	4	$+ 4S$
			$600 total sales

$$8S + 4S = 600$$
$$\frac{12S}{12} = \frac{600}{12}$$
$$S = 50 \text{ shorts}$$
$$4S = 200 \text{ T-shirts}$$

Check
$$50(\$4) + 200(\$2) = \$600$$
$$\$200 + \$400 = \$600$$
$$\$600 = \$600$$

Situation 6, p. 121.

5–16. Dots sells 250 T-shirts ($2) and shorts ($4). In April, total sales were $600. How many T-shirts and shorts did Dots sell? Check your answer. *Hint:* Let $S =$ Shorts.

Unknown(s)	Variable(s)	Price	Relationship
T-shirts	$250 - S$	$2	$2(250 - S)$
Shorts	S	4	$+ 4S$
			$600 total sales

$$2(250 - S) + 4S = 600$$
$$500 - 2S + 4S = 600$$
$$-500 \qquad\qquad -500$$
$$\frac{2S}{2} = \frac{100}{2}$$
$$S = 50 \text{ shorts}$$
$$250 - S = 200 \text{ T-shirts}$$

Check
$$200(\$2) + 50(\$4) = \$600$$
$$\$400 + \$200 = \$600$$
$$\$600 = \$600$$

DRILL PROBLEMS (Second of Three Sets)

5–17.
$$20B = 220$$
$$\frac{20B}{20} = \frac{220}{20}$$
$$B = 11$$

5–18.
$$7(A - 5) = 63$$
$$7A - 35 = 63$$
$$\underline{+ 35 \quad +35}$$
$$\frac{7A}{7} = \frac{98}{7}$$
$$A = 14$$

5–19.
$$\frac{N}{9} = 7$$
$$9\left(\frac{N}{9}\right) = 7(9)$$
$$N = 63$$

5–20.
$$18(C - 3) = 162$$
$$18C - 54 = 162$$
$$\underline{+ 54 \quad + 54}$$
$$\frac{18C}{18} = \frac{216}{18}$$
$$C = 12$$

5–21.
$$9Y - 10 = 53$$
$$\underline{+ 10 \quad + 10}$$
$$\frac{9Y}{9} = \frac{63}{9}$$
$$Y = 7$$

5–22.
$$7B + 5 = 26$$
$$\underline{- 5 \quad - 5}$$
$$\frac{7B}{7} = \frac{21}{7}$$
$$B = 3$$

WORD PROBLEMS (Second of Three Sets)

5–23. Macy's reduced its price on men's suits by $110. The sale price was $199.99. What was the original price?

Unknown(s)	Variable(s)	Relationship
Original price	P	$P - \$110 =$ Sale price
		Sale price $= \$199.99$

$$P - \$110 = \$199.99$$
$$\underline{+ 110 \quad +110.00}$$
$$P = \$309.99$$

5–24. Fay, an employee at the Gap, budgets $\frac{1}{5}$ of her yearly salary for clothing. Fay's total clothing bill for the year is $8,000. What is her yearly salary?

Unknown(s)	Variable(s)	Relationship
Yearly salary	S	$\frac{1}{5}S$
		Clothing $= \$8,000$

$$\frac{1}{5}S = \$8,000$$
$$5\left(\frac{S}{5}\right) = \$8,000(5)$$
$$S = \$40,000$$

5–25. Bill's Roast Beef sells 5 times as many sandwiches as Pete's Deli. The difference between their sales is 360 sandwiches. How many sandwiches did each sell?

Unknown(s)	Variable(s)	Relationship
Bill's	$5S$	$5S$ (450)
Pete's	S	$- \;\; S$ (90)
		360 sandwiches

$$5S - S = 360$$
$$\frac{4S}{4} = \frac{360}{4}$$
$$S = 90$$
$$5S = 450$$

5–26. On November 21, 1997, the Chicago *Sun-Times* reported that during the day, Alcoa stock traded at $70 per share. Pete and his partner Al decided to sell 100 shares for a total of $7,000. The stock was purchased for $65 per share ($100 \times \$65 = \$6,500$) for a gain of $500. Pete invested twice as much as Al in the purchasing of the shares. How much should Pete receive and how much should Al receive of the gain? Round to the nearest cent.

Unknown(s)	Variable(s)	Relationship
Pete	$2P$	$2P$
Al	P	$+ P$
		$\$500$

$$2P + P = \$500$$
$$\frac{3P}{3} = \frac{\$500}{3}$$
$$P = \$166.67 \ (\text{Al})$$
$$2P = \$333.34 \ (\text{Pete})$$

5–27. Computer City sells diskettes ($3) and small boxes of computer paper ($5). In August, total sales were $960. Customers bought 5 times as many diskettes as boxes of computer paper. How many of each did Computer City sell? Check your answer.

Unknown(s)	Variable(s)	Price	Relationship
Diskettes	$5P$	$3	$15P$
Boxes of paper	P	5	$+ 5P$
			$\$960$ total sales

$$5P + 15P = 960$$
$$\frac{20P}{20} = \frac{960}{20}$$
$$P = 48 \text{ boxes of paper}$$
$$5P = 240 \text{ diskettes}$$

Check
$$48(\$5) + 240(\$3) = \$960$$
$$\$240 + \$720 = \$960$$
$$\$960 = \$960$$

5–28. Staples sells cartons of pens ($10) and rubber bands ($4). Leona ordered a total of 24 cartons for $210. How many cartons of each did Leona order? Check your answer. *Hint:* Let $P = $ Pens.

Unknown(s)	Variable(s)	Price	Relationship
Pens	P	$10	$10P$
Rubber bands	$24 - P$	4	$+ 4(24 - P)$
			Total = $210

$$10P + 4(24 - P) = 210$$
$$10P + 96 - 4P = 210$$
$$6P + 96 = 210$$
$$- 96 \qquad - 96$$
$$\frac{6P}{6} = \frac{114}{6}$$
$$P = 19 \text{ cartons of pens}$$
$$24 - P = 5 \text{ cartons of rubber bands}$$

Check
$$19(\$10) + 5(\$4) = \$210$$
$$\$190 + \$20 = \$210$$
$$\$210 = \$210$$

DRILL PROBLEMS (Third of Three Sets)

Solve the unknown from the following equations.

5–29.
$$C + 77 - 15 = 160$$
$$C + 62 = 160$$
$$- 62 \qquad - 62$$
$$C = 98$$

5–30.
$$5Y + 15(Y + 1) = 35$$
$$5Y + 15Y + 15 = 35$$
$$20Y + 15 = 35$$
$$- 15 \qquad - 15$$
$$\frac{20Y}{20} = \frac{20}{20}$$
$$Y = 1$$

5–31.
$$3M + 20 = 2M + 80$$
$$- 2M \qquad - 2M$$
$$M + 20 = + 80$$
$$- 20 \qquad - 20$$
$$M = 60$$

5–32.
$$20(C - 50) = 19,000$$
$$20C - 1,000 = 19,000$$
$$+ 1,000 \qquad + 1,000$$
$$\frac{20C}{20} = \frac{20,000}{20}$$
$$C = 1,000$$

WORD PROBLEMS (Third of Three Sets)

5–33. In December 1, 1997, *USA Today* reported that a survey showed that the starting salary for a person with a degree in computer science was expected to be close to $38,000 (rounded to the nearest thousand). This is approximately $1\frac{1}{4}$ times greater than the starting salary of a person with a business degree. What would be the starting salary for a person with a business degree? Round to the nearest thousand.

Unknown(s)	Variable(s)	Relationship
Starting salary for a business degree	S	$1.25S$
		$38,000 for computer degree

$$1.25S = \$38,000$$
$$\frac{1.25S}{1.25} = \frac{\$38,000}{1.25}$$
$$S = \$30,400 = \$30,000$$

5–34. At Maplewood Marine, shift 1 produced 3 times as much as shift 2. Maplewood's total production for June was 6,400 rowboats. What was the output for each shift?

Unknown(s)	Variable(s)	Relationship
Shift 1	$3S$	$3S$ (4,800)
Shift 2	S	$+ S$ (1,600)
		6,400

$$3S + S = 6,400$$
$$\frac{4S}{4} = \frac{6,400}{4}$$
$$S = 1,600$$

5–35. Ivy Corporation gave 84 people a bonus. If Ivy had given 2 more people bonuses, Ivy would have rewarded $\frac{2}{3}$ of the workforce. How large is Ivy's workforce?

Unknown(s)	Variable(s)	Relationship
Total workers	W	$\frac{2}{3}W$
		$- 2$ workers
		84

$$\frac{2}{3}W - 2 = 84$$
$$\underline{\quad\quad +2 \quad +2}$$
$$\frac{2}{3}W = 86$$
$$3\left(\frac{2}{3}W\right) = 86(3)$$
$$\frac{2W}{2} = \frac{258}{2}$$
$$W = 129$$

5–36. Jim Murray and Phyllis Lowe received a total of $50,000 from a deceased relative's estate. They decided to put $10,000 in a trust for their nephew and divide the remainder. Phyllis received $\frac{3}{4}$ of the remainder; Jim received $\frac{1}{4}$. How much did Jim and Phyllis receive?

Unknown(s)	Variable(s)	Relationship
Jim	T	T ($10,000)
Phyllis	$3T$	$+ 3T$ ($30,000)
		$40,000

$$T + 3T = \$40,000$$
$$\frac{4T}{4} = \frac{\$40,000}{4}$$
$$T = \$10,000$$
$$3T = \$30,000$$

5–37. The first shift of GME Corporation produced $1\frac{1}{2}$ times as many lanterns as the second shift. GME produced 5,600 lanterns in November. How many lanterns did GME produce on each shift?

Unknown(s)	Variable(s)	Relationship
Shift 1	$1.5L$	$1.5L$ (3,360)
Shift 2	L	$+ L$ (2,240)
		5,600

$$1.5L + L = 5,600$$
$$\frac{2.5L}{2.5} = \frac{5,600}{2.5}$$
$$L = 2,240$$
$$1.5L = 3,360$$

5–38. Wal-Mart sells thermometers ($2) and hot-water bottles ($6). In December, Wal-Mart's total sales were $1,200. Customers bought 7 times as many thermometers as hot-water bottles. How many of each did Wal-Mart sell? Check your answer.

Unknown(s)	Variable(s)	Price	Relationship
Thermometers	$7B$	$2	$14B$
Hot-water bottles	B	6	$+ 6B$
			Total = $1,200

$$14B + 6B = 1,200$$
$$\frac{20B}{20} = \frac{1,200}{20}$$
$$B = 60 \text{ bottles}$$
$$7B = 420 \text{ thermometers}$$

Check
$$60(\$6) + 420(\$2) = \$1,200$$
$$\$360 + \$840 = \$1,200$$
$$\$1,200 = \$1,200$$

5–39. Ace Hardware sells cartons of wrenches ($100) and hammers ($300). Howard ordered 40 cartons of wrenches and hammers for $8,400. How many cartons of each are in the order? Check your answer.

Unknown(s)	Variable(s)	Price	Relationship
Wrenches	$40 - H$	$100	$100(40 - H)$
Hammers	H	300	$+ 300H$
			Total = $8,400

$$300H + 100(40 - H) = 8,400$$
$$300H + 4,000 - 100H = 8,400$$
$$200H + 4,000 = 8,400$$
$$\underline{\quad -4,000 \quad\quad -4,000}$$
$$\frac{200H}{200} = \frac{4,400}{200}$$
$$H = 22 \text{ cartons of hammers}$$
$$40 - H = 18 \text{ cartons of wrenches}$$

Check
$$22(\$300) + 18(\$100) = \$8,400$$
$$\$6,600 + \$1,800 = \$8,400$$
$$\$8,400 = \$8,400$$

CHALLENGE PROBLEMS

5–40. On November 25, 1997, the Chicago *Sun-Times* ran this article: "Bet on the Lightning. News Item: Illinois announces a new Lotto game, in which odds are 6.1 million to 1 as opposed to 12.9 million to 1. Which means the odds against your winning will be only 10 times greater than being struck by lightning, as opposed to 20 times greater. You don't get offers like this often." What are the odds now being hit by lightning? What were the odds of being hit by lightning?

Unknown(s)	Variable(s)	Relationship
Odds of being hit by lightning	$10L$ $20L$	$10L = 6.1$ $20L = 12.9$

$$10L = 6.1 \text{ million}$$
$$\frac{\cancel{10}L}{\cancel{10}} = \frac{6.1}{10}$$
$$L = .61, \text{ or } 610,000 \text{ to } 1$$
$$20L = 12.9$$
$$\frac{\cancel{20}L}{\cancel{20}} = \frac{12.9}{20}$$
$$L = .645, \text{ or } 645,000 \text{ to } 1$$

5–41. Bessy has 6 times as much money as Bob, but when each earns $6, Bessy will have 3 times as much money as Bob. How much does each have before and after earning the $6?

Unknown(s)	Variable(s)	Relationship
Bessy	$6B$	$6B + 6$
Bob	B	$B + 6$

$$6B + 6 = 3(B + 6)$$
$$6B + 6 = 3B + 18$$
$$\underline{-3B \qquad -3B}$$
$$3B + 6 = 18$$
$$\underline{-6 \qquad -6}$$
$$\frac{3B}{3} = \frac{12}{3}$$
Before: $B = 4$ After: $B = 10$
$\qquad\quad 6B = 24 \qquad\quad 6B = 30$

 SUMMARY PRACTICE TEST

1. Delta Shuttle reduced its round-trip ticket price from Boston to Washington, DC, by $58. The sale price was $189.99. What was the original price? *(p. 119)*

Unknown(s)	Variable(s)	Relationship
Original price	P	$P - \$58 = \text{Sale price}$ Sale price $= \$189.99$

$$P - \$58 = \$189.99$$
$$\underline{+ 58 \qquad + 58.00}$$
$$P \qquad = \$247.99$$

2. On November 23, 1997, the *Daily Herald* reported that the average shopper will spend about $2\frac{1}{5}$ times more for holiday dinners than the $60 spent for holiday decorating, gift wrap, and cards. How much more does the average shopper spend on holiday dinners? *(p. 120)*

Unknown(s)	Variable(s)	Relationship
Amount average shopper spends on holiday dinners	S	$2\frac{1}{5}S$ holiday dinners Holiday decorations, gifts, etc., $60

$$2\frac{1}{5}S = \$60$$
$$\cancel{2\frac{1}{5}}\left(\frac{S}{\cancel{2\frac{1}{5}}}\right) = 60\left(2\frac{1}{5}\right)$$
$$S = \$132$$

3. K Corporation sells 4 times as many GE dishwashers as Wallace Company. The difference between their sales is 180 dishwashers. How many GE dishwashers did each sell? *(p. 120)*

Unknown(s)	Variable(s)	Relationship
K Corporation	$4D$	$4D$
Wallace Co.	D	$\underline{-D}$ 180

$$4D - D = 180$$
$$\frac{3D}{3} = \frac{180}{3}$$
$$D = 60$$
$$4D = 240$$

4. At Lord & Taylor, Joyce Cook and Francis Key sold a total of 870 cosmetic kits. Joyce sold 5 times as many kits as Francis. How many did each sell? *(p. 120)*

Unknown(s)	Variable(s)	Relationship
Joyce	$5C$	$5C$
Francis	C	$+ C$
		$\overline{870}$

$$5C + C = 870$$
$$\frac{\cancel{6}C}{\cancel{6}} = \frac{870}{6}$$
$$C = 145$$
$$5C = 725$$

5. Lang Corporation sells sets of pots ($18) and dishes ($12) at a local charity. On the July 4 weekend, Lang's total sales were $4,884. People bought 3 times as many pots as dishes. How many of each did Lang sell? Check your answer. *(p. 120)*

Unknown(s)	Variable(s)	Price	Relationship
Pots	$3D$	$18	$54D$
Dishes	D	$12	$+ 12D$
			Total = $4,884

$$54D + 12D = 4,884$$
$$\frac{\cancel{66}D}{\cancel{66}} = \frac{4,884}{66}$$
$$D = 74$$
$$3D = 222$$

Check
$$222(\$18) + 74(\$12) = \$4,884$$
$$\$3,996 + \$888 = \$4,884$$
$$\$4,884 = \$4,884$$

6. Pizza Hut sold a total of 1,200 small pizzas ($5) and hamburgers ($6) during Harborfest. How many of each did Pizza Hut sell if total sales were $7,000? Check your answer. *(p. 121)*

Unknown(s)	Variable(s)	Price	Relationship
Hamburgers	H	$6	$6H$
Pizzas	$1,200 - H$	5	$5(1,200 - H)$
			Total = $7,000

$$6H + 5(1,200 - H) = 7,000$$
$$6H + 6,000 - 5H = 7,000$$
$$H + 6,000 = 7,000$$
$$\underline{- 6,000} \qquad \underline{- 6\,000}$$
$$H = 1,000 \text{ hamburgers}$$
$$1,200 - H = 200 \text{ pizzas}$$

Check
$$1,000(\$6) + 200(\$5) = \$7,000$$
$$\$6,000 + \$1,000 = \$7,000$$
$$\$7,000 = \$7.000$$

A GROUP PROJECT   Defend or reject the following business math issue based on the *Kiplinger's Personal Finance Magazine* article below:

INSURANCE
Teens and cars: A high-risk mix

A growing teenage population plus more cars on the road add up to higher auto-insurance premiums for everyone.

The number of 16-year-olds is expected to ratchet up almost every year between now and 2007, as the 73 million children of the echo boom mature. Among drivers, teenagers have the worst accident rate: They're nearly four times as likely to crash as drivers over age 55.

Since 1987 the rise in premiums has slowed, thanks to safer cars and fewer young drivers. Annual rate hikes have been about 2%, compared with double-digit increases in the mid 1980s.

But if accidents pick up significantly, says Sean Mooney of the Insurance Information Institute, "insurance rates will eventually go up for everyone."

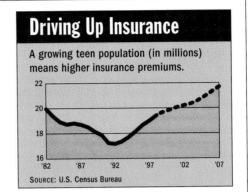

Driving Up Insurance

A growing teen population (in millions) means higher insurance premiums.

SOURCE: U.S. Census Bureau

Teenagers and their families would be among the first to be affected, possibly as early as next year. Teen drivers already pay twice as much for insurance as drivers 25 and older—and those rates are typically for unblemished records.

For their parents, it's a case of *déjà vu.* When baby-boomers were young drivers, auto-insurance premiums raced ahead 50% faster than the overall cost of living.

—*CATHERINE SISKOS*

Business Math Issue

Not all teens should be paying twice as much as older drivers. Good driving records should be rewarded.

1. List the key points of the article and information to support your position.
2. Write a group defense of your position using math calculations to support your view.

BUSINESS MATH SCRAPBOOK
Putting Your Skills to Work

Object of The Week
Toying with History

Artist: *Walt Disney*
Provenance: *artist Ernest Trova*
Estimated Price: *$20,000 to $25,000*
Sold for: *$30,250*

THIS RARE 1920s figure of Mickey Mouse and his pal Horace Horse-collar—an early but short-lived Disney character—sold at auction last month to a Japanese collector after a seven-way bidding war. The price is a shock, especially given the original tag, still attached, imprinted "69¢."

This toy is from the collection of artist Ernest Trova, whose stainless-steel humanoid sculptures are fixtures in several U.S. cities, and who is one of the leading collectors of Disneyana. He paid $6,000 for it in 1989. Tim Luke, who conducted the sale for Bertoia Auctions of Vineland, N.J., says the Japanese toy is one of about five in existence, and adds that unlike other celluloid toys, which are petroleum-based and tend to deteriorate, this one is in mint condition.

But what really makes it valuable is that it documents a lost bit of pop-culture history: Horace Horsecollar never quite caught on with kids, and after Donald Duck debuted, Horace was sent packing.

The high price for this toy wasn't a record for Disneyana, though. A German tin toy of Mickey on a motorcycle brought $88,000 at auction last year.—*Eileen Kinsella*

Project A

How many times (to the nearest thousand) did this toy sell for the original price?

$$\frac{\cancel{\$.69}P}{\cancel{\$.69}} = \frac{\$30,250}{\$.69}$$
$$P = 44,000$$

Project B

Prove the $330 million

$440 − $110 = $330 million

Hershey Foods Corp., branching out beyond its core chocolate products, agreed to acquire the North American confectionery operations of Huhtamaki Oy's Leaf Inc.

The transaction, valued at $330 million, gives Hershey such well-known candy brands as Jolly Rancher, Good & Plenty and Whoppers malted milk balls. Hershey's brands include Hershey's Kisses, Kit Kat and Reese's Peanut Butter Cups.

Under the deal, which is expected to close later this year, Hershey will pay Finland-based Huhtamaki $440 million, plus annual licensing fees, for Leaf's North American business. Hershey will sell Huhtamaki its two European operations — a German praline maker called Gubor and an Italian sugar confectionery company called Sperlari—for $110 million.

 See text Web site (www.mhhe.com/slater) and *The Business Math Internet Resource Guide.*

CLASSROOM NOTES

6

PERCENTS AND THEIR APPLICATIONS

LEARNING UNIT OBJECTIVES

LU 6.1   Conversions

- Convert decimals to percents, percents to decimals, and fractions to percents *(pp. 136–39)*.
- Round percents to the identified digit *(p. 139)*.
- Convert percents to fractions *(p. 139)*.

LU 6.2   Application of Percents—Portion Formula

- List and define the key elements of the portion formula *(pp. 140–41)*.
- Solve for one unknown of the portion formula when the other two key elements are given *(pp. 141–44)*.
- Calculate the rate of percent increases and decreases *(pp. 144–46)*.

Companies frequently use percents to express various increases and decreases between two or more numbers, or to express only an increase or decrease. For example, note the two *Wall Street Journal* clippings "Coke's Market Share Rises to 43.9% as PepsiCo Slips" and "J.C. Penney to Close Stores, Eliminate About 4,900 Jobs." Both clippings express business numbers in terms of percents. PepsiCo Inc.'s share of the $54.7 billion U.S. carbonated soft-drink industry slipped 0.1 of a share point to 30.9%; Coca-Cola Co. gained 0.8 of a share point to 43.9%. Last year it was tough for Pepsi to beat the "Real Thing"—a Coke. J.C. Penney Co. also had a tough year. High costs and weak sales resulted in the plan to close 75 stores and lay off 5% of its management employees.

To use percent increases and decreases, you should first understand the conversion relationship between fractions, decimals, and percents, as explained in Learning Unit 6.1. Then, in Learning Unit 6.2, you will be ready to apply percents to personal and business events.

Photo by Francois Robert/Courtesy The Coca-Cola Company.

LEARNING UNIT 6.1   Conversions

When we described parts of a whole in previous chapters, we used fractions and decimals. Percents also describe parts of a whole. The word *percent* means per 100. The percent symbol (%) indicates hundredths (division by 100). **Percents** are the result of expressing numbers as part of 100. Thus, 30% is 30 parts of 100 parts ($\frac{30}{100}$).

Percents can provide some revealing information. Note the following *Wall Street Journal* clipping, "Very Tough Customers." The percentages of customers in India who own an automobile, have running hot water, have electricity, have a telephone, or own a color TV are compared with the percentages of customers in China and in the United States. When you look at these percentages, it doesn't take long to realize how fortunate we are to live in the United States. For our study in percents, let's concentrate on the automobile ownership comparison.

Out of 100 people living in India, only 2 own an automobile. The figures for China are only slightly higher than those for India, with 3 out of 100 owning an automobile. Now look at the United States. Out

Very Tough Customers Most Indians have low incomes and thus lead spartan lives—even when compared to their neighbors in China, also a developed country. A new Gallup poll of Indian household underscores the changes facing foreign companies in this frugal market.

	OWN AN AUTOMOBILE	HAVE RUNNING HOT WATER	HAVE ELECTRICITY	HAVE A TELEPHONE	OWN A COLOR TV
India	2%	4%	58%	7%	12%
China	3%*	1%	95%	9%	40%
U.S.	90%	98%	99%	97%	97%

*Includes company cars   Source: Gallup India

© 1996 Dow Jones & Company, Inc.

TABLE 6.1

Analyzing a bag of M&M's®

T

Color	Fraction	Decimal (hundredth)	Percent (hundredth)
Yellow	$\frac{18}{55}$	.33	32.73%
Red	$\frac{10}{55}$	.18	18.18
Blue	$\frac{9}{55}$	.16	16.36
Orange	$\frac{7}{55}$	.13	12.73
Brown	$\frac{6}{55}$	.11	10.91
Green	$\frac{5}{55}$	.09	9.09
Total	$\frac{55}{55} = 1$	1.00	100.00%

Note: The color ratios currently given are a sample used for educational purposes. They do not represent the manufacturer's color ratios.

of 100 people living in the United States, 90 own an automobile. Is it any wonder that our highways have become increasingly crowded?

Let's return to the M&M's® example from earlier chapters. In Table 6.1, we use our bag of 55 M&M's® to show how fractions, decimals, and percents can refer to the same parts of a whole. For example, the bag of 55 M&M's® contained 18 yellow M&M's®. As you can see in Table 6.1, the 18 yellow candies in the bag of 55 can be expressed as a fraction ($\frac{18}{55}$), decimal (.33), and percent (32.73%).

In this unit we show you how to make the conversion from decimals to percents, percents to decimals, fractions to percents, and percents to fractions. You also learn how to round percents.

Converting Decimals to Percent

Suppose you have the decimal .48; what would be its equivalent in percent? The decimal .48 in decimal fraction is $\frac{48}{100}$.[1] Since percents are the result of expressing numbers as a part of 100, 48% = $\frac{48}{100}$. So you can conclude that .48 = $\frac{48}{100}$ = 48%. This leads to the following conversion steps:

Converting Decimals to Percents

Step 1. Move the decimal point two places to the right. You are multiplying by 100. If necessary, add zeros. This rule is also used for whole numbers and mixed decimals.

Step 2. Add a percent symbol at the end of the number.

EXAMPLES

$.48 = .48. = \boxed{48\%}$ $.8 = .80. = \boxed{80\%}$ $8 = 8.00. = \boxed{800\%}$

Add 1 zero to make two places.   Add 2 zeros to make two places.

$.425 = .42.5 = \boxed{42.5\%}$ $.007 = .00.7 = \boxed{.7\%}$ $2.51 = 2.51. = \boxed{251\%}$

Caution: One percent means 1 out of every 100. Since .7% is less than 1%, it means $\frac{7}{10}$ of 1%—a very small amount. Less than 1% is less than .01. To show a number less than 1%, you must use more than two decimal places and add 2 zeros. Example: .7% = .007.

---

[1] This is explained in Chapter 3.

Converting Percents to Decimals

To convert percents to decimals, you reverse the process used to convert decimals to percents. The definition of percent states that $48\% = \frac{48}{100}$. The fraction $\frac{48}{100}$ can be written in decimal form as .48. Now you can also conclude that $48\% = \frac{48}{100} = .48$. This leads to the following conversion steps:

Converting Percents to Decimals

Step 1.   Drop the percent symbol.
Step 2.   Move the decimal point two places to the left. You are dividing by 100. If necessary, add zeros.

EXAMPLES

Note that when a percent is less than 1%, the decimal conversion has at least two leading zeros before the whole number .008.

$$.8\% = .00.8 = \boxed{.008} \qquad 8\% = .08. = \boxed{.08} \qquad 82\% = .82. = \boxed{.82}$$

Add 2 zeros to make two places.   Add 1 zero to make two places.

$$82.4\% = .82.4 = \boxed{.824} \qquad 824.4\% = 8.24.4 = \boxed{8.244}$$

Fractional percents such as $\frac{1}{5}\%$ are $\frac{1}{5}$ of 1%. These fractional percents can appear singly or in combination with whole numbers. To convert them to decimals, use the following steps:

Converting Fractional Percents to Decimals

Step 1.   Convert a single fractional percent to its decimal equivalent by dividing the numerator by the denominator. If necessary, round the answer.
Step 2.   If a fractional percent is combined with a whole number (mixed fractional percent), convert the fractional percent first. Then combine the whole number and the fractional percent.
Step 3.   Drop the percent symbol; move the decimal point two places to the left (this divides the number by 100).

EXAMPLES

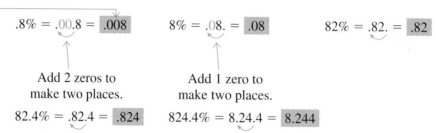

$$\frac{1}{5}\% = .20\% = .00.20 = \boxed{.0020}$$

$$\frac{1}{4}\% = .25\% = .00.25 = \boxed{.0025}$$

$$7\frac{3}{4}\% = 7.75\% = .07.75 = \boxed{.0775}$$

$$6\frac{1}{2}\% = 6.5\% = .06.5 = \boxed{.065}$$

Think of $7\frac{3}{4}\%$ as

$$7\% = \quad .07$$

$$+ \ \frac{3}{4}\% = +\ .0075$$

$$\overline{} \qquad \overline{}$$

$$7\frac{3}{4}\% = \quad .0775$$

Converting Fractions to Percents

When fractions have denominators of 100, the numerator becomes the percent. Other fractions must be first converted to decimals; then the decimals are converted to percents.

Converting Fractions to Percents

Step 1.   Divide the numerator by the denominator to convert the fraction to a decimal.
Step 2.   Move the decimal point two places to the right; add the percent symbol.

EXAMPLES

$$\frac{3}{4} = .75 = .75. = \boxed{75\%} \qquad \frac{1}{5} = .20 = .20. = \boxed{20\%} \qquad \frac{1}{20} = .05 = .05. = \boxed{5\%}$$

Rounding Percents

Rounding percents is similar to rounding whole numbers. Use the following steps to round percents:

Round the same as you would decimals

When using a calculator, you press $\boxed{18} \boxed{\div} \boxed{55} \boxed{\%}$. This allows you to go right to percent, avoiding the decimal step.

Rounding Percents

Step 1. When you convert from a fraction or decimal, be sure your answer is in percent before rounding.
Step 2. Identify the specific digit. If the digit to the right of the identified digit is 5 or greater, round up the identified digit.
Step 3. Delete digits to right of the identified digit.

For example, Table 6.1 shows that the 18 yellow M&M's® rounded to the nearest hundredth percent is 32.73% of the bag of 55 M&M's®. Let's look at how we arrived at this figure.

Step 1. $\frac{18}{55} = .3272727 = 32.72727\%$ Note that the number is in percent! Identify the hundredth percent digit.

Step 2. 32.73727% Digit to the right of the identified digit is greater than 5, so the identified digit is increased by 1.

Step 3. $\boxed{32.73\%}$ Delete digits to the right of the identified digit.

Converting Percents to Fractions

Using the definition of percent, you can write any percent as a fraction whose denominator is 100. Thus, when we convert a percent to a fraction, we drop the percent symbol and write the number over 100, which is the same as multiplying the number by $\frac{1}{100}$. This method of multiplying by $\frac{1}{100}$ is also used for fractional percents.

Converting a Whole Percent (or a Fractional Percent) to a Fraction

Step 1. Drop the percent symbol.
Step 2. Multiply the number by $\frac{1}{100}$.
Step 3. Reduce to lowest terms.

EXAMPLES $76\% = 76 \times \frac{1}{100} = \frac{76}{100} = \boxed{\frac{19}{25}} \qquad \frac{1}{8}\% = \frac{1}{8} \times \frac{1}{100} = \boxed{\frac{1}{800}}$

$$156\% = 156 \times \frac{1}{100} = \frac{156}{100} = 1\frac{56}{100} = \boxed{1\frac{14}{25}}$$

Sometimes a percent contains a whole number and a fraction such as $12\frac{1}{2}\%$ or 22.5%. Extra steps are needed to write a mixed or decimal percent as a simplified fraction.

Converting a Mixed or Decimal Percent to a Fraction

Step 1. Drop the percent symbol.
Step 2. Change the mixed percent to an improper fraction.
Step 3. Multiply the number by $\frac{1}{100}$.
Step 4. Reduce to lowest terms.

Note: If you have a mixed or decimal percent, change the decimal portion to fractional equivalent and continue with Steps 1 to 4.

EXAMPLES $12\frac{1}{2}\% = \frac{25}{2} \times \frac{1}{100} = \frac{25}{200} = \boxed{\frac{1}{8}}$

$12.5\% = 12\frac{1}{2}\% = \frac{25}{2} \times \frac{1}{100} = \frac{25}{200} = \boxed{\frac{1}{8}}$

$22.5\% = 22\frac{1}{2}\% = \frac{45}{2} \times \frac{1}{100} = \frac{45}{200} = \boxed{\frac{9}{40}}$

LU 6.1 | **PRACTICE QUIZ**

Convert to percents (round to the nearest tenth percent as needed);

1. .6666 _____   **2.** .832 _____

3. .004 _____   **4.** 8.94444 _____

Convert to decimals (remember, decimals representing less than 1% will have at least 2 leading zeros before the number):

5. $\frac{1}{4}\%$ _____   **6.** $6\frac{3}{4}\%$ _____

7. 87% _____   **8.** 810.9% _____

Convert to percents (round to the nearest hundredth percent):

9. $\frac{1}{7}$ _____   **10.** $\frac{2}{9}$ _____

Convert to fractions (remember, if it is a mixed number, first convert to an improper fraction):

11. 19% _____   **12.** $71\frac{1}{2}\%$ _____   **13.** 130% _____

14. $\frac{1}{2}\%$ _____   **15.** 19.9% _____

✓ **Solutions**

1. .66.66 = $\boxed{66.7\%}$ **2.** .83.2 = $\boxed{83.2\%}$

3. .00.4 = $\boxed{.4\%}$ **4.** 8.94.444 = $\boxed{894.4\%}$

5. $\frac{1}{4}\% = .25\% = \boxed{.0025}$ **6.** $6\frac{3}{4}\% = 6.75\% = \boxed{.0675}$

7. 87% = .87. = $\boxed{.87}$ **8.** 810.9% = 8.10.9 = $\boxed{8.109}$

9. $\frac{1}{7} = .14.285 = \boxed{14.29\%}$ **10.** $\frac{2}{9} = .22.2\overline{2} = \boxed{22.22\%}$

11. $19\% = 19 \times \frac{1}{100} = \boxed{\frac{19}{100}}$ **12.** $71\frac{1}{2}\% = \frac{143}{2} \times \frac{1}{100} = \boxed{\frac{143}{200}}$

13. $130\% = 130 \times \frac{1}{100} = \frac{130}{100} = 1\frac{30}{100} = \boxed{1\frac{3}{10}}$ **14.** $\frac{1}{2}\% = \frac{1}{2} \times \frac{1}{100} = \boxed{\frac{1}{200}}$

15. $19\frac{9}{10}\% = \frac{199}{10} \times \frac{1}{100} = \boxed{\frac{199}{1,000}}$

LEARNING UNIT 6.2   Application of Percents—Portion Formula

Sharon Hoogstraten.

The bag of M&M's® we have been studying contains M&M's® Plain Chocolate Candies. M&M/Mars also makes M&M's® Peanut Chocolate Candies and some other types of M&M's®. To study the application of percents to problems involving M&M's®, we make two key assumptions:

1. Total sales of M&M's® Plain, Peanut, and other M&M's® Chocolate Candies are $400,000.

2. Eighty percent of M&M's® sales are Plain Chocolate Candies. This leaves the Peanut and other M&M's® Chocolate Candies with 20% of sales (100% − 80%).

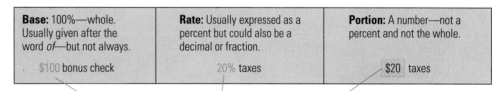

Before we begin, you must understand the meaning of three terms—*base, rate,* and *portion.* These terms are the key elements in solving percent problems.

- **Base (*B*).** The **base** is the beginning whole quantity or value (100%) with which you will compare some other quantity or value. Often the problems give the base after the word *of.* For example, the whole (total) sales of M&M's®—Plain, Peanut, and other M&M's® Chocolate Candies—are $400,000.

- **Rate (*R*).** The **rate** is a percent, decimal, or fraction that indicates the part of the base that you must calculate. The percent symbol often helps you identify the rate. For example, M&M's® Plain Chocolate Candies currently account for 80% of sales. So the rate is 80%. Remember that 80% is also $\frac{4}{5}$, or .80.

- **Portion (*P*).** The **portion** is the amount or part that results from the base multiplied by the rate. For example, total sales of M&M's® are $400,000 (base); $400,000 times .80 (rate) equals $320,000 (portion), or the sales of M&M's® Plain Chocolate Candies. *A key point to remember is that portion is a number and not a percent. In fact, the portion can be larger than the base if the rate is greater than 100%.*

Solving Percents with the Portion Formula

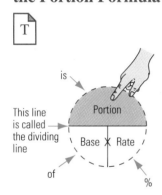

is

This line is called the dividing line

Portion

Base × Rate

of

%

In problems involving portion, base, and rate, we give two of these elements. You must find the third element. Remember the following key formula:

$$\text{Portion } (P) = \text{Base } (B) \times \text{Rate } (R)$$

To help you solve for the portion, base, and rate, this unit shows pie charts. The shaded area in each pie chart indicates the element that you must solve for. For example, since we shaded *portion* in the pie chart at the left, you must solve for portion. To use the pie charts, put your finger on the shaded area (in this case portion). The formula that remains tells you what to do. So in the pie chart at the left, you solve the problem by multiplying base by the rate. Note the circle around the pie chart is broken since we want to emphasize that portion can be larger than base if rate is greater than 100%. The horizontal line in the pie chart is called the dividing line, and we will use it when we solve for base or rate.

The following example summarizes the concept of base, rate, and portion. Assume that you received a small bonus check of $100. This is a gross amount—your company did not withhold any taxes. You will have to pay 20% in taxes.

Base: 100%—whole. Usually given after the word *of*—but not always.	**Rate:** Usually expressed as a percent but could also be a decimal or fraction.	**Portion:** A number—not a percent and not the whole.
$100 bonus check	20% taxes	$20 taxes

First decide what you are looking for. You want to know how much you must pay in taxes—the portion. How do you get the portion? From the portion formula Portion (*P*) = Base (*B*) × Rate (*R*), you know that you must multiply the base ($100) by the rate (20%). When you do this, you get $100 × .20 = $20. So you must pay $20 in taxes.

Let's try our first word problem by taking a closer look at the M&M's® example to see how we arrived at the $320,000 sales of M&M's® Plain Chocolate Candies given earlier. We will be using blueprint aids to help dissect and solve each word problem.

Solving for Portion

The Word Problem Sales of M&M's® Plain Chocolate Candies are 80% of the total M&M's® sales. Total M&M's® sales are $400,000. What are the sales of M&M's Plain Chocolate Candies?

The facts	Solving for?	Steps to take	Key points
M&M's® Plain Chocolate Candies sales: 80%. *Total M&M's® sales:* $400,000	Sales of M&M's® Plain Chocolate Candies.	Identify key elements. *Base:* $400,000. *Rate:* .80. *Portion:* ? Portion = Base × Rate.	Amount or part of beginning Portion (?) Base × Rate ($400,000) | (.80) Beginning whole quantity (often after "of") Percent symbol or word (here we put into decimal) Portion and rate must relate to same piece of base.

Steps to solving problem

1. Set up the formula.   Portion = Base × Rate
2. Calculate portion (sales of M&M's® Plain $P = \$400,000 \times .80$
   Chocolate Candies). $P = \$320,000$

In the first column of the blueprint aid, we gather the facts. In the second column, we state that we are looking for sales of M&M's® Plain Chocolate Candies. In the third column, we identify each key element and the formula needed to solve the problem. Review the pie chart in the fourth column. Note that the portion and rate must relate to the same piece of the base. In this word problem, we can see from the solution below the blueprint aid that sales of M&M's® Plain Chocolate Candies are $320,000. The $320,000 does indeed represent 80% of the base. Note here that the portion ($320,000) is less than the base of $400,000 since the rate is less than 100%.

Now let's work another word problem that solves for the portion.

The Word Problem   Sales of M&M's® Plain Chocolate Candies are 80% of the total M&M's® sales. Total M&M's® sales are $400,000. What are the sales of Peanut and other M&M's® Chocolate Candies?

The facts	Solving for?	Steps to take	Key points
M&M's® Plain Chocolate Candies sales: 80%. *Total M&M's® sales:* $400,000.	Sales of Peanut and other M&M's® Chocolate Candies.	Identify key elements: *Base:* $400,000. *Rate:* .20 (100% − 80%). *Portion:* ? Portion = Base × Rate.	If 80% of sales are Plain, then 20% are Peanut and other M&M's® Chocolate Candies Portion (?) Base × Rate ($400,000) | (.20) Portion and rate must relate to same piece of base.

Steps to solving problem

1. Set up the formula.   Portion = Base × Rate
2. Calculate portion (sale of Peanut and other $P = \$400,000 \times .20$
   M&M's® Chocolate Candies). $P = \$80,000$

In the above blueprint aid, note that we must use a rate that agrees with the portion so the portion and rate refer to the same piece of the base. Thus, if 80% of sales are M&M's® Plain Chocolate Candies, 20% must be Peanut and other M&M's® Chocolate Candies (100% − 80% = 20%). So we use a rate of .20.

In Step 2, we multiplied $400,000 × .20 to get a portion of $80,000. This portion represents the part of the sales that were *not* M&M's® Plain Chocolate Candies. Note that the rate of .20 and the portion of $80,000 relate to the same piece of the base—$80,000 is

20% of $400,000. Also note that the portion ($80,000) is less than the base ($400,000) since the rate is less than 100%.

Take a moment to review the two blueprint aids in this section. Be sure you understand why the rate in the first blueprint aid was 80% and the rate in the second blueprint aid was 20%.

Solving for Rate

The Word Problem   Sales of M&M's® Plain Chocolate Candies are $320,000. Total M&M's® sales are $400,000. What is the percent of M&M's® Plain Chocolate Candies sales compared to total M&M's® sales?

The facts	Solving for?	Steps to take	Key points
M&M's® Plain Chocolate Candies sales: $320,000. *Total M&M's® sales:* $400,000.	Percent of M&M's® Plain Chocolate Candies sales to total M&M's® sales.	Identify key elements. *Base:* $400,000. *Rate:* ? *Portion:* $320,000. $$Rate = \frac{Portion}{Base}.$$	Since portion is less than base, the rate must be less than 100% Portion ($320,000) Base × Rate ($400,000) (?) Portion and rate must relate to the same piece of base.

Steps to solving problem

1. Set up the formula. $$Rate = \frac{Portion}{Base}$$

2. Calculate rate (percent of M&M's® Plain Chocolate Candies sales). $$R = \frac{\$320,000}{\$400,000}$$

$$R = \boxed{80\%}$$

Note that in this word problem, the rate of 80% and the portion of $320,000 refer to the same piece of the base.

The Word Problem   Sales of M&M's® Plain Chocolate Candies are $320,000. Total sales of Plain, Peanut, and other M&M's® Chocolate Candies are $400,000. What percent of Peanut and other M&M's® Chocolate Candies are sold compared to total M&M's® sales?

The facts	Solving for?	Steps to take	Key points
M&M's® Plain Chocolate Candies sales: $320,000. *Total M&M's® sales:* $400,000.	Percent of Peanut and other M&M's® Chocolate Candies sales compared to total M&M's® sales.	Identify key elements. *Base:* $400,000. *Rate:* ? *Portion:* $80,000 ($400,000 − $320,000). $$Rate = \frac{Portion}{Base}.$$	Represents sales of Peanut and other M&M's® Chocolate Candies Portion ($80,000) Base × Rate ($400,000) (?) When portion becomes $80,000, the portion and rate now relate to same piece of base.

Steps to solving problem

1. Set up the formula. $$Rate = \frac{Portion}{Base}$$

2. Calculate rate. $$R = \frac{\$80,000}{\$400,000} \quad (\$400,000 - \$320,000)$$

$$R = \boxed{20\%}$$

The word problem asks for the rate of candy sales that are *not* Plain. Thus, $400,000 of total candy sales less sales of M&M's® Plain Chocolate Candies ($320,000) allows us to arrive at sales of Peanut and other M&M's® Chocolate Candies ($80,000). The $80,000 portion represents 20% of total candy sales. The $80,000 portion and 20% rate refer to the same piece of the $400,000 base. Compare this blueprint aid with the blueprint aid for the previous word problem. Ask yourself why in the previous word problem the rate was 80% and in this word problem the rate is 20%. In both word problems, the portion was less than the base since the rate was less than 100%.

Now we go on to calculate the base. Remember to read the word problem carefully so that you match the rate and portion to the same piece of the base.

Solving for Base

The Word Problem   Sales of Peanut and other M&M's® Chocolate Candies are 20% of total M&M's® sales. Sales of M&M's® Plain Chocolate Candies are $320,000. What are the total sales of all M&M's®?

The facts	Solving for?	Steps to take	Key points
Peanut and other M&M's® Chocolate Candies sales: 20%. *M&M's® Plain Chocolate Candies sales: $320,000.*	Total M&M's® sales.	Identify key elements. *Base: ?* *Rate: .80* *(100% − 20%).* *Portion: $320,000.* $\text{Base} = \dfrac{\text{Portion}}{\text{Rate}}.$	Portion ($320,000) / Base (?) × Rate (.80) (100% − 20%) Portion ($320,000) and rate (.80) do relate to the same piece of base.

Steps to solving problem

1. Set up the formula.

$$\text{Base} = \frac{\text{Portion}}{\text{Rate}}$$

2. Calculate the base.

$$B = \frac{\$320,000}{.80} \longleftarrow \$320,000 \text{ is } 80\% \text{ of base}$$

$$B = \boxed{\$400,000}$$

Note that we could not use 20% for the rate. The $320,000 of M&M's® Plain Chocolate Candies represents 80% (100% − 20%) of the total sales of M&M's®. We use 80% so that the portion and rate refer to same piece of the base. Remember that the portion ($320,000) is less than the base ($400,000) since the rate is less than 100%.

Calculating Percent Increases and Decreases

The Wall Street Journal clipping "April Sales Increased 17% on Gains in Several Lines" reports that Circuit City's sales in April exceeded the company's expectations. The April sales increased 17% from $576.8 million in the year-earlier period to $675.3 million. We will use the Circuit City clipping to introduce the calculation of percent increases and decreases.

The Circuit City clipping gave us the amount that the April sales increased— 17%. Let's assume we do not know the percent amount and see if we can use the portion formula to determine the percent increase, which is the rate (*R*). The portion formula for solving for rate is

$$\text{Rate} = \frac{\text{Portion}}{\text{Base}} \quad \begin{array}{l} \longleftarrow \text{ Difference between old and new sales} \\ \longleftarrow \text{ Old sales} \end{array}$$

$$R = \frac{\$98.5(\$675.3 - \$576.8)}{\$576.8}$$

$$R = \boxed{.1707697, \text{ or } 17\%} \text{ (rounded to nearest whole percent)}$$

As you can see, the 17% increase in Circuit City sales reported in *The Wall Street Journal* is correct. Let's prove the 17% increase with a pie chart.

Using the Circuit City's numbers, the formula for calculating Circuit City's **percent increases** is given below at the left. To calculate **percent decreases,** we use the formula at the right.

Percent of increase $(R) =$ (17%) $\dfrac{\text{Amount of increase } (P)}{\text{Original amount } (B)}$ ($\$98.5$) / ($\$576.8$)	Percent of decrease $(R) = \dfrac{\text{Amount of decrease } (P)}{\text{Original amount } (B)}$

Now you are ready for another example of calculating the rate of percent increase using M&M's®.

Rate of Percent Increase

The Word Problem   Sheila Leary went to her local supermarket and bought the bag of M&M's® shown in Figure 6.1. The bag gave its weight as 18.40 ounces, which was 15% more than a regular 1-pound bag of M&M's®. Sheila, who is a careful shopper, wanted to check and see if she was actually getting a 15% increase. Let's help Sheila dissect and solve this problem.

The facts	Solving for?	Steps to take	Key points
New bag of M&M's®: 18.40 oz. 15% increase in weight. *Original bag of M&M's®:* 16 oz. (1 lb.).	Checking percent increase of 15%.	Identify key elements. *Base:* 16 oz. *Rate:* ? *Portion:* 2.40 oz. $\left.\begin{array}{r} 18.40 \text{ oz.} \\ -\ 16.00 \\ \hline 2.40 \text{ oz.} \end{array}\right\}$ $\text{Rate} = \dfrac{\text{Portion}}{\text{Base}}.$	Difference between base and new weight

FIGURE 6.1
Bag of 18.40-ounce M&M's®

Steps to solving problem

1. Set up the formula.

$$\text{Rate} = \frac{\text{Portion}}{\text{Base}}$$

2. Calculate the rate.

$$R = \frac{2.40 \text{ oz.}}{16.00 \text{ oz.}} \quad \longleftarrow \text{ Difference between base and new weight.}$$
$$\longleftarrow \text{ Old weight equals 100\%.}$$

$$R = 15\% \text{ increase}$$

The new weight of the bag of M&M's® is really 115% of the old weight:

$$\begin{array}{rcl} 16.00 \text{ oz.} & = & 100\% \\ + \ 2.40 & & + \ 15 \\ \hline 18.40 \text{ oz.} & = & 115\% = 1.15 \end{array}$$

We can check this by looking at the following pie chart.

Portion = Base × Rate

18.40 oz. = 16 oz. × 1.15

Why is the portion greater than the base? Remember that the portion can be larger than the base only if the rate is greater than 100%. Note how the portion and rate relate to the same piece of the base—18.40 oz. is 115% of the base (16 oz.).

Now let's see what could happen if M&M/Mars has an increase in its price of sugar.

Rate of Percent Decrease

The Word Problem   The increase in the price of sugar caused the M&M/Mars company to decrease the weight of each 1-pound bag of M&M's® to 12 ounces. What is the rate of percent decrease?

The facts	Solving for?	Steps to take	Key points
16-oz. bag of M&M's®: reduced to 12 oz.	Rate of percent decrease.	Identify key elements. *Base:* 16 oz. *Rate:* ? *Portion:* 4 oz. (16 oz. − 12 oz.). $\text{Rate} = \dfrac{\text{Portion}}{\text{Base}}$.	

Steps to solving problem

1. Set up the formula.

$$\text{Rate} = \frac{\text{Portion}}{\text{Base}}$$

2. Calculate the rate.

$$R = \frac{4 \text{ oz.}}{16.00 \text{ oz.}}$$

$$R = 25\% \text{ decrease}$$

The new weight of the bag of M&M's® is 75% of the old weight:

$$\begin{array}{rcl} 16 \text{ oz.} & = & 100\% \\ - \ 4 & & - \ 25 \\ \hline 12 \text{ oz.} & = & 75\% \end{array}$$

We can check this by looking at the following pie chart:

Portion = Base × Rate

12 oz. = 16 oz. × .75

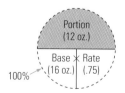

Note that the portion is smaller than the base because the rate is less than 100%. Also note how the portion and rate relate to the same piece of the base—12 ounces is 75% of the base (16 oz.).

LU 6.2 PRACTICE QUIZ

Solve for portion:

1. 38% of 900.
2. 60% of $9,000.

Solve for rate (round to nearest tenth percent as needed):

3. 430 is _____ % of 5,000.
4. 200 is _____ % of 700.

Solve for base (round to the nearest tenth as needed):

5. 55 is 40% of _____.
6. 900 is $4\frac{1}{2}$% of _____.

Solve the following (blueprint aids are shown in the solution; you might want to try some on scrap paper):

7. Five out of 25 students in Professor Ford's class received an "A" grade. What percent of the class *did not* receive the "A" grade?
8. Abby Biernet has yet to receive 60% of her lobster order. Abby received 80 lobsters to date. What was her original order?
9. In 2000, Dunkin Company had $300,000 in doughnut sales. In 2001, sales were up 40%. What are Dunkin sales for 2001?
10. The price of an Apple computer dropped from $1,600 to $1,200. What was the percent decrease?
11. In 1982, a ticket to the Boston Celtics cost $14. In 2000, a ticket cost $50. What is the percent increase to the nearest hundredth percent?

✓ **Solutions**

1. $\underline{342}$ = 900 × .38
   (P) = (B) × (R)

2. $\underline{\$5,400}$ = $9,000 × .60
   (P) = (B) × (R)

3. $\dfrac{(P)430}{(B)5,000}$ = .086 = $\underline{8.6\%}$ (R)

4. $\dfrac{(P)200}{(B)700}$ = .2857 = $\underline{28.6\%}$ (R)

5. $\dfrac{(P)55}{(R).40}$ = $\underline{137.5}$ (B)

6. $\dfrac{(P)900}{(R).045}$ = $\underline{20,000}$ (B)

7. Percent of Professor Ford's class that did not receive the "A" grade:

The facts	Solving for?	Steps to take	Key points
5 "A"s 25 in class.	Percent that did not receive "A."	Identify key elements. *Base:* 25. *Rate:* ? *Portion:* 20 (25 − 5). Rate = $\dfrac{Portion}{Base}$.	Portion (20) Base × Rate (25) (?) The whole Portion and rate must relate to same piece of base.

Steps to solving problem

1. Set up the formula. Rate = $\dfrac{Portion}{Base}$

2. Calculate the rate. $R = \dfrac{20}{25}$

   $R = 80\%$

8. Abby Biernet's original order:

The facts	Solving for?	Steps to take	Key points
60% of the order not in. 80 lobsters received.	Total order of lobsters.	Identify key elements. *Base:* ? *Rate:* .40 (100% − 60%). *Portion:* 80. Base = $\dfrac{Portion}{Rate}$.	Portion (80) Base × Rate (?) (.40) 80 lobsters represent 40% of the order Portion and rate must relate to same piece of base.

Steps to solving problem

1. Set up the formula.

$$Base = \frac{Portion}{Rate}$$

2. Calculate the base.

$$B = \frac{80}{.40} \longleftarrow \text{80 lobsters is 40\% of base.}$$

$$\boxed{B = 200 \text{ lobsters}}$$

9. Dunkin Company sales for 2001:

The facts	Solving for?	Steps to take	Key points
2000: $300,000 sales. *2001:* Sales up 40% from 2000.	Sales for 2001.	Identify key elements. *Base:* $300,000. *Rate:* 1.40. Old year 100% New year + 40 — 140% *Portion:* ? Portion = Base × Rate.	2001 sales Portion (?) Base × Rate ($300,000) (1.40) 2000 sales When rate is greater than 100%, portion will be larger than base.

Steps to solving problem

1. Set up the formula.
2. Calculate the portion.

$$Portion = Base \times Rate$$
$$P = \$300,000 \times 1.40$$
$$\boxed{P = \$420,000}$$

10. Percent decrease in Apple computer price:

The facts	Solving for?	Steps to take	Key points
Apple computer was $1,600; now, $1,200.	Percent decrease in price.	Identify key elements. *Base:* $1,600. *Rate:* ? *Portion:* $400 ($1,600 − $1,200). $Rate = \frac{Portion}{Base}$	Difference in price Portion ($400) Base × Rate ($1,600) (?) Original price

Steps to solving problem

1. Set up the formula.

$$Rate = \frac{Portion}{Base}$$

2. Calculate the rate.

$$R = \frac{\$400}{\$1,600}$$

$$\boxed{R = 25\%}$$

11. Percent increase in Boston Celtics ticket:

The facts	Solving for?	Steps to take	Key points
$14 ticket (old). $50 ticket (new).	Percent increase in price.	Identify key elements. *Base:* $14. *Rate:* ? *Portion:* $36 ($50 − $14). $Rate = \frac{Portion}{Base}$	Difference in price Portion ($36) Base × Rate ($14) (?) Original price When portion is greater than base, rate will be greater than 100%.

Steps to solving problem

1. Set up the formula.

$$\text{Rate} = \frac{\text{Portion}}{\text{Base}}$$

2. Calculate the rate.

$$R = \frac{\$36}{\$14}$$

$$R = 2.5714 = \boxed{257.14\%}$$

Chapter Organizer and Reference Guide		
Topic	**Key point, procedure, formula**	**Example(s) to illustrate situations**
Converting decimals to percents, p. 137	1. Move decimal point two places to right. If necessary, add zeros. This rule is also used for whole numbers and mixed decimals. 2. Add a percent symbol at end of number.	$.81 = .81. = \boxed{81\%}$ $.008 = .00.8 = \boxed{.8\%}$ $4.15 = 4.15. = \boxed{415\%}$
Converting percents to decimals, p. 138	1. Drop percent symbol. 2. Move decimal point two places to left. If necessary, add zeros. For fractional percents: 1. Convert to decimal by dividing numerator by denominator. If necessary, round answer. 2. If a mixed fractional percent, convert fractional percent first. Then combine whole number and fractional percent. 3. Drop percent symbol, move decimal point two places to left.	$.89\% = \boxed{.0089}$ $\quad 8\frac{3}{4}\% = 8.75\% = \boxed{.0875}$ $95\% = \boxed{.95}$ $\quad \frac{1}{4}\% = .25\% = \boxed{.0025}$ $195\% = \boxed{1.95}$ $\quad \frac{1}{5}\% = .20\% = \boxed{.0020}$
Converting fractions to percents, p. 138	1. Divide numerator by denominator. 2. Move decimal point two places to right; add percent symbol.	$\frac{4}{5} = .80 = \boxed{80\%}$
Rounding percents, p. 139	1. Answer must be in percent before rounding. 2. Identify specific digit. If digit to right is 5 or greater, round up. 3. Delete digits to right of identified digit.	Round to nearest hundredth percent. $\frac{3}{7} = .4285714 = 42.85714\% = \boxed{42.86\%}$
Converting percents to fractions, p. 139	Whole percent (or fractional percent) to a fraction: 1. Drop percent symbol. 2. Multiply number by $\frac{1}{100}$. 3. Reduce to lowest terms. Mixed or decimal percent to a fraction: 1. Drop percent symbol. 2. Change mixed percent to an improper fraction. 3. Multiply number by $\frac{1}{100}$. 4. Reduce to lowest terms. If you have a mixed or decimal percent, change decimal portion to fractional equivalent and continue with Steps 1 to 4.	$64\% \rightarrow 64 \times \frac{1}{100} = \frac{64}{100} = \boxed{\frac{16}{25}}$ $\frac{1}{4}\% \rightarrow \frac{1}{4} \times \frac{1}{100} = \boxed{\frac{1}{400}}$ $119\% \rightarrow 119 \times \frac{1}{100} = \frac{119}{100} = \boxed{1\frac{19}{100}}$ $16\frac{1}{4}\% \rightarrow \frac{65}{4} \times \frac{1}{100} = \frac{65}{400} = \boxed{\frac{13}{80}}$ $16.25\% \rightarrow 16\frac{1}{4}\% = \frac{65}{4} \times \frac{1}{100}$ $\qquad = \frac{65}{400} = \frac{13}{80}$
Solving for portion, p. 142		10% of Mel's paycheck of $1,000 goes for food. What portion is deducted for food? $\boxed{\$100} = \$1,000 \times .10$ *Note:* If question was what amount does not go for food, the portion would have been: $\boxed{\$900} = \$1,000 \times .90$ $(100\% - 10\% = 90\%)$

Chapter Organizer and Reference Guide (concluded)		
Topic	**Key point, procedure, formula**	**Example(s) to illustrate situations**
Solving for rate, p. 143	Portion ($100) / Base ($1,000) × Rate (?)	Assume Mel spends $100 for food from his $1,000 paycheck. What percent of his paycheck is spent on food? $$\frac{\$100}{\$1,000} = .10 = \boxed{10\%}$$ *Note:* Portion is less than base since rate is less than 100%.
Solving for base, p. 144	Portion ($100) / Base (?) × Rate (.10)	Assume Mel spends $100 for food, which is 10% of his paycheck. What is Mel's total paycheck? $$\frac{\$100}{.10} = \boxed{\$1,000}$$
Calculating percent increases or decreases, p. 144	Amount of increase or decrease → Portion / Base × Rate (?) ← Original price	Stereo, $2,000 original price. Stereo, $2,500 new price. $$\frac{\$500}{\$2,000} = .25 = \boxed{25\%} \text{ increase}$$ **Check** $2,000 × 1.25 = $2,500 *Note:* Portion is greater than base since rate is greater than 100%. Portion ($2,500) / Base ($2,000) × Rate (1.25)
Key terms	Base, *p. 141* Percent increase, *p. 145*	Percents, *p. 136* Portion, *p. 141* Percent decrease, *p. 145* Rate, *p. 141*

Note: For how to dissect and solve a word problem, see page 142 or page 143.

Critical Thinking Discussion Questions

1. In converting from a percent to a decimal, when will you have at least 2 leading zeros before the whole number? Explain this concept, assuming you have 100 bills of $1.

2. Explain the steps in rounding percents. Count the number of students who are sitting in the back half of the room as a percent of the total class. Round your answer to the nearest hundredth percent. Could you have rounded to the nearest whole percent without changing the accuracy of the answer?

3. Define portion, rate, and base. Create an example using Walt Disney World to show when the portion could be larger than the base. Why must the rate be greater than 100% for this to happen?

4. How do we solve for portion, rate, and base? Create an example using IBM computer sales to show that the portion and rate do relate to the same piece of the base.

5. Explain how to calculate percent increases or decreases. Many years ago, comic books cost 10 cents a copy. Visit a bookshop or newsstand. Select a new comic book and explain the price increase in percent compared to the 10-cent comic. How important is the rounding process in your final answer?

DRILL PROBLEMS

Convert the following decimals to percents:

6–1. .86   86%   **6–2.** .946   94.6%   **6–3.** .9   90%

6–4. 8.00   800%   **6–5.** 3.561   356.1%   **6–6.** 6.006   600.6%

Convert the following percents to decimals:

6–7. 2%   .02   **6–8.** 17%   .17   **6–9.** $45\frac{7}{10}$%   .457

6–10. 75.9%   .759   **6–11.** 119%   1.19   **6–12.** 89%   .89

Convert the following fractions to percents (to the nearest tenth percent as needed):

6–13. $\frac{1}{13}$ = .0769 = 7.7%   **6–14.** $\frac{1}{400}$ = .0025 = .3%

6–15. $\frac{7}{8}$ = .875 = 87.5%   **6–16.** $\frac{11}{12}$ = .9166 = 91.7%

Convert the following to fractions and reduce to lowest terms:

6–17. 4% $4 \times \frac{1}{100} = \frac{4}{100} = \frac{1}{25}$ **6–18.** $18\frac{1}{2}$% $\frac{37}{2} \times \frac{1}{100} = \frac{37}{200}$

6–19. $31\frac{2}{3}$% $\frac{95}{3} \times \frac{1}{100} = \frac{95}{300} = \frac{19}{60}$ **6–20.** $61\frac{1}{2}$% $\frac{123}{2} \times \frac{1}{100} = \frac{123}{200}$

6–21. 6.75% $6\frac{3}{4}$% = $\frac{27}{4} \times \frac{1}{100} = \frac{27}{400}$ **6–22.** 182% $182 \times \frac{1}{100} = \frac{182}{100} = 1\frac{82}{100} = 1\frac{41}{50}$

Solve for the portion (round to nearest hundredth as needed): $P = R \times B$

6–23. 6% of 120

.06 × 120 = 7.2

6–24. 125% of 4,320

1.25 × 4,320 = 5,400

6–25. 25% of 410

.25 × 410 = 102.5

6–26. 119% of 128.9

1.19 × 128.9 = 153.39

6–27. 17.4% of 900

.174 × 900 = 156.6

6–28. 11.2% of 85
.112 × 85 = 9.52

6–29. $12\frac{1}{2}$% of 919
.125 × 919 = 114.88

6–30. 45% of 300
.45 × 300 = 135

6–31. 18% of 90
.18 × 90 = 16.2

6–32. 30% of 2,000
.30 × 2,000 = 600

Solve for the base (round to nearest hundredth as needed): $\frac{P}{R} = B$

6–33. 150 is 130% of __115.38__ $\left(\frac{150}{1.3}\right)$ **6–34.** 36 is .75% of __4,800__ $\left(\frac{36}{.0075}\right)$

6–35. 50 is .5% of __10,000__ $\left(\frac{50}{.005}\right)$ **6–36.** 10,800 is 90% of __12,000__ $\left(\frac{10,800}{.90}\right)$

6–37. 800 is $4\frac{1}{2}$% of __17,777.78__ $\left(\frac{800}{.045}\right)$

Solve for rate (round to nearest tenth percent as needed): $\frac{P}{B} = R$

6–38. __41.6%__ of 190 is 79 $\left(\frac{79}{190}\right)$ **6–39.** __108.2%__ of 85 is 92 $\left(\frac{92}{85}\right)$

6–40. __26%__ of 250 is 65 $\left(\frac{65}{250}\right)$ **6–41.** 110 is __110%__ of 100 $\left(\frac{110}{100}\right)$

6–42. .09 is __4%__ of 2.25 $\left(\frac{.09}{2.25}\right)$ **6–43.** 16 is __400%__ of 4 $\left(\frac{16}{4}\right)$

Solve the following problems. Be sure to show your work. Round to nearest hundredth or hundredth percent as needed:

6–44. What is 160% of 218? $1.60 \times 218 = 348.8$ $P = R \times B$

6–45. 66% of 90 is what? $.66 \times 90 = 59.40$ $P = R \times B$

6–46. 40% of what number is 20? $\dfrac{20}{.4} = 50$ $\dfrac{P}{R} = B$

6–47. 770 is 70% of what number? $\dfrac{770}{.7} = 1{,}100$ $\dfrac{P}{R} = B$

6–48. 4 is what percent of 90? $\dfrac{4}{90} = 4.44\%$ $\dfrac{P}{B} = R$

6–49. What percent of 150 is 60? $\dfrac{60}{150} = 40\%$ $\dfrac{P}{B} = R$

Complete the following table:

Product	Sales in millions 2001	Sales in millions 2002	Amount of increase or decrease	Percent change (to nearest hundredth percent)
6–50. Compaq computers	$295	$460	+ $165	+ 55.93% $\left(\dfrac{\$165}{\$295}\right)$
6–51. Maytag washers	$ 40	$ 35	− $ 5	− 12.50% $\left(\dfrac{-\$5}{\$40}\right)$

WORD PROBLEMS (First of Four Sets)

6–52. At a local Wendy's, a survey showed that out of 8,000 customers eating lunch, 1,600 ordered Diet Pepsi with their meal. What percent of customers ordered Diet Pepsi?

$\dfrac{1{,}600}{8{,}000} = 20\%$ Portion and rate must refer to same piece of the base.

6–53. What percent of customers in Problem 6–52 did not order Diet Pepsi?

$\dfrac{6{,}400}{8{,}000} = 80\%$ Portion and rate must refer to same piece of the base.

6–54. On August 25, 1997, the *Chicago Tribune* reported that the rising cost of nursing homes is forcing families to plan ahead. Nursing home costs have risen roughly 20% in 3 years, to an average of $46,000 per year.

 a. What was the cost of nursing home care 3 years ago? Round to the nearest thousands.

 b. If the same 20% holds true, what will the cost be 3 years from now? Round to the nearest thousands.

a. $\dfrac{\$46{,}000 \ (P)}{1.20 \ (R)} = \$38{,}333.333$

 = $38,000

Portion is larger than base since rate is greater than 100%.

b. $46{,}000 \ (B) \times 1.20 \ (R) = \$55{,}200$

 = $55,000

6–55. Pete Mill, the owner of a Texaco station, bought a used Chevy pickup truck, paying $2,000 down. He still owes 80% of the selling price. What was the selling price of the truck?

$\dfrac{\$2{,}000}{.20} = \$10{,}000$ Rate and portion must relate to same piece of the base. $2,000 is 20% of the base.

6–56. Maria Fay bought 4 Aquatread tires at a local Goodyear store. The salesperson told her that her mileage would increase by 6%. Before this purchase, Maria was getting 22 mpg. What should her mileage be with the new tires?

$22 \times 1.06 = 23.32$ mpg.

Note: Portion is larger than base since rate is greater than 100%.

6–57. Pete Lavoie went to JCPenny and bought a Sony CD player. The purchase price was $350. He made a down payment of 30%. How much was Pete's down payment?

$.30 \times \$350 = \$105$

6–58. Assume that in the year 2000, 800,000 people attended the Christmas Eve celebration at Disney World. In 2001, attendance for the Christmas Eve celebration is expected to increase by 35%. What is the total number of people expected at Disney World for this event?

$800,000 \times 1.35 = 1,080,000$ people

Note: If the rate is greater than 100%, the portion will be larger than the base.

6–59. Pete Smith found in his attic a Woody Woodpecker watch in its original box. It had a price tag on it for $4.50. The watch was made in 1949. Pete brought the watch to an antiques dealer and sold it for $35. What was the percent of increase? Round to the nearest hundredth percent.

$\dfrac{\$30.50}{\$4.50} = 677.78\%$

$\left(\text{The }\$30.50\text{ is } \begin{array}{r} \$35.00 \\ -\ 4.50 \end{array}\right)$

Note: Portion is larger than base since rate is greater than 100%.

Original amount →

6–60. In 2001, the price of an IBM computer rose to $1,200. This is 8% more than the 2000 price. What was the old selling price? Check your answer.

$\dfrac{\$1,200}{1.08} = \$1,111.11$

Portion and rate must refer to same piece of the base.

Check: $\$1,111.11 \times 1.08 = \$1,199.99$ (not quite $1,200 due to rounding)
(B)　　(R)　　(P)

Note: Portion is larger than base since rate is greater than 100%.

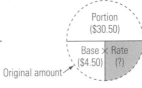

6–61. Christie's Auction sold a painting for $24,500. It charges all buyers a 15% premium of the final bid price. How much did the bidder pay Christie's?

$\$24,500 \times 1.15 = \$28,175$

Portion is larger than base since rate is greater than 100%.

WORD PROBLEMS (Second of Four Sets)

6–62. Out of 5,000 college students surveyed, 2,000 responded that they do not eat breakfast. What percent of the students do not eat breakfast?

$\dfrac{2,000}{5,000} = .40 = 40\%$

Note: Portion and rate refer to same part of base.

6–63. What percent of college students in Problem 6–62 eat breakfast?

$$\frac{3,000}{5,000} = .60 = 60\%$$

Note: Portion and rate refer to same part of base.

6–64. Alice Hall made a $3,000 down payment on a new Ford Explorer wagon. She still owes 90% of the selling price. What was the selling price of the wagon?

$$\frac{\$3,000}{.10} = \$30,000$$

6–65. On December 1, 1997, *USA Today* reported that Visa USA stated that over the last year, the number of Friday and Saturday sales transactions increased 16% to $38.8 million. What were the total sales transactions at this time last year? Round to the nearest million.

$$\frac{\$38.8 \text{ million } (P)}{1.16 \ (R)} = \$33.448275 = \$33 \text{ million}$$

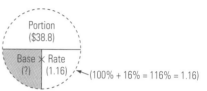

6–66. Jim and Alice Lange, employees at Wal-Mart, have put themselves on a strict budget. Their goal at year's end is to buy a boat for $15,000 in cash. Their budget includes the following:

    40% food and lodging   20% entertainment   10% educational

Jim earns $1,900 per month and Alice earns $2,400 per month. After one year, will Alice and Jim have enough cash to buy the boat?

$100\% - 40\% - 20\% - 10\% = 30\%$

$1,900 \times 12 = \$22,800$

$2,400 \times 12 = \underline{\$28,800}$

                  $51,600 \times .30 = \$15,480$ Yes.

6–67. The price of a Timex watch dropped from $49.95 to $30.00. What was the percent decrease in price? Round to the nearest hundredth percent.

$$\frac{\$19.95}{\$49.95} = 39.94\%$$

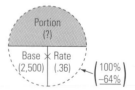

6–68. The Museum of Science in Boston estimated that 64% of all visitors came from within the state. On Saturday, 2,500 people attended the museum. How many attended the museum from out of state?

$2,500 \times .36 = 900$ people from out of state

6–69. Cherokee Stationery pays George Nagovsky an annual salary of $36,000. Today, George's boss informs him that he will receive a $4,600 raise. What percent of George's old salary is the $4,600 raise? Round to the nearest tenth percent.

$$\frac{\$4,600}{\$36,000} = 12.8\%$$

6–70. In 2000, Sweeney Brothers had $550,000 in sales. In 2001, Sweeney's sales were up 35%. What were Sweeney's sales in 2001?

$550,000 \times 1.35 = $742,500

100% old sales

+ 35% new sales

6–71. Blue Valley College has 600 female students. This is 60% of the total student body. How many students attend Blue Valley College?

$\dfrac{600}{.60} = 1,000$

6–72. Dr. Grossman was reviewing his total accounts receivable. This month, credit customers paid $44,000, which represented 20% of all receivables (what customers owe) due. What was Dr. Grossman's total accounts receivable?

$\dfrac{\$44,000}{.20} = \$220,000$

6–73. Massachusetts has a 5% sales tax. Timothy bought a Toro lawn mower and paid $20 sales tax. What was the cost of the lawn mower before the tax?

$\dfrac{\$20}{.05} = \$400$

6–74. The price of a GE microwave oven increased from $600 to $800. What was the percent of increase? Round to the nearest tenth percent.

$\dfrac{\$200}{\$600} = 33.3\%$

6–75. Borders Bookstore ordered 80 marketing books but received 60 books. What percent of the order was missing?

$\dfrac{20}{80} = 25\%$

WORD PROBLEMS (Third of Four Sets)

6–76. At an antique auction, the auctioneer estimated that 30% of the audience was from within the state. Seven hundred people attended the auction. How many out-of-state people attended?

$700 \times .70 = 490$ people from out of state

6–77. On November 17, 1997, the Chicago *Sun-Times* reported that according to the U.S. Census Bureau statistics, more than 1.3 million people in Illinois—about 11% of the population—are without medical insurance. What approximately would be the total population of Illinois? Round to the nearest million.

$$\frac{1.3 \text{ million } (P)}{.11 \ (R)} = 11.818181 = 12 \text{ million}$$

6–78. In 2001, Jim Goodman, an employee at Walgreens, earned $45,900, an increase of 17.5% over the previous year. What were Jim's earnings in 2000? Round to the nearest cent.

$$B = \frac{\$45,900}{1.175} = \$39,063.83$$

6–79. On December 8, 1997, the Chicago *Sun-Times* reported that personal bankruptcy filings nationwide have increased. In 1996, total filings were 1,123,833, compared to 1995 filings of 873,273. How much of a percent increase was there in 1996 compared to 1995? Round to the nearest hundredth percent.

$$\begin{array}{r} 1,123,833 \\ -\ 873,273 \\ \hline 250,560 \text{ increase } (P) \end{array}$$

$$\frac{250,560 \ (P)}{873,273 \ (B)} = 28.69205\% = 28.69\%$$

6–80. In 2001, the price of a business math text rose to $60. This is 4% more than the 2000 price. What was the old selling price? Round to the nearest cent.

$$B = \frac{\$60}{1.04} = \$57.69$$

6–81. Computer Consultants pays Alice Rose an annual salary of $48,000. Today, Alice's boss informs her that she will receive a $6,400 raise. What percent of Alice's old salary is the $6,400 raise? Round to the nearest tenth percent.

$$\frac{\$6,400}{\$48,000} = 13.3\%$$

6–82. Earl Miller, a lawyer, charges Lee's Plumbing, his client, 25% of what he can collect for Lee from customers whose accounts are past due. The attorney also charges, in addition to the 25%, a flat fee of $50 per customer. This month, Earl collected $7,000 from 3 of Lee's past-due customers. What is the total fee due to Earl?

$$\begin{array}{r} \$7,000 \times .25 = \$1,750 \\ 3 \times \$50 = \underline{150} \\ \$1,900 \end{array}$$

6–83. Petco ordered 100 dog calendars but received 60. What percent of the order was missing?

$$\frac{40}{100} = 40\%$$

6–84. Peters Hardware uses MasterCard. MasterCard charges $2\frac{1}{2}\%$ on net deposits (credit slips less returns). Pete made a net deposit of $4,100 for charge sales. How much did MasterCard charge Pete?

$4,100 × .025 = $102.50

6–85. In 2000, Vetron computers had $800,000 in sales. In 2001, Vetron's sales were up 45%. What are the sales for 2001?

$800,000 × 1.45 = $1,160,000

Note: Portion is larger than base since rate is greater than 100%.

WORD PROBLEMS (Fourth of Four Sets)

6–86. Saab Corporation raised the base price of its popular 900 series by $800 to $24,500. What was the percent increase? Round to the nearest tenth percent.

$$\frac{\$800}{\$23,700} = 3.4\%$$

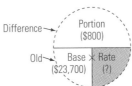

6–87. The sales tax rate is 8%. If Jim bought a new Buick and paid a sales tax of $1,920, what was the cost of the Buick before the tax?

$$\frac{\$1,920}{.08} = \$24,000$$

6–88. Alice Sey bought a new Dell computer system on sale for $1,800. It was advertised as 30% off the regular price. What was the original price of the computer? Round to the nearest dollar.

$$\frac{\$1,800}{.70} = \$2,571$$

6–89. John O'Sullivan has just completed his first year in business. His records show that he spent the following in advertising:

Newspaper	$600	Radio	$650
Yellow Pages	700	Local flyers	400

What percent of John's advertising was spent on the Yellow Pages? Round to the nearest hundredth percent.

$600 + $700 + $650 + $400 = $2,350

$$\frac{\$700}{\$2,350} = 29.79\%$$

6–90. In 2001, Levin Furniture plans to ship furniture overseas for a sales volume of $11.2 million, an increase of 40% from that in 2000. What was the sales volume in 2000?

$$\frac{\$11.2}{1.40} = \$8 \text{ million}$$

6–91. Peg Pouv sold her ski house at Attitash Mountain in New Hampshire for $35,000. This sale represented a loss of 15% off the original price. What was the original price Peg paid for the ski house? Round your answer to the nearest dollar.

$$\frac{\$35,000}{.85} = \$41,176$$

We use .85 so that the p + R refer to the same piece of B

$$\begin{array}{r} 1.00 \\ -\ .15 \\ \hline .85 \end{array}$$

Portion ($35,000)
Base × Rate
(?) (.85)

6–92. Out of 4,000 colleges surveyed, 60% reported that SAT scores were not used as a high consideration in viewing their applications. How many schools view the SAT as important in screening applicants?

$4,000 \times .40 = 1,600$

Portion (?)
Base × Rate
(4,000) (.40)

6–93. On November 30, 1997, the *Chicago Tribune* reported that about 80% of airline tickets—nearly $65 billion worth last year—are issued by travel agents. What were the total sales of airline tickets last year? Round to the nearest billion.

$$\frac{\$65 \text{ billion } (P)}{.80 \ (R)} = 81.25 = \$81 \text{ billion}$$

Portion ($65 billion)
Base × Rate
(?) (.80)

6–94. A major airline laid off 4,000 pilots and flight attendants. If this was a 12.5% reduction in the workforce, what was the size of the workforce after the layoffs?

$$\frac{4,000}{.125} = 32,000 \qquad \begin{array}{r} 32,000 \\ -\ 4,000 \\ \hline 28,000 \end{array}$$

Portion (4,000)
Base × Rate
(?) (.125)

6–95. Assume 450,000 people line up on the streets to see the Orange Bowl Parade in 2000. If attendance is expected to increase 30%, what will be the number of people lined up on the street to see the 2001 Orange Bowl Parade?

$450,000 \times 1.30 = 585,000$

Portion (?)
Base × Rate
(450,000) (1.30)

 CHALLENGE PROBLEMS

6–96. On November 11, 1997, the Chicago *Sun-Times* reported that the following Big Ten basketball coaches with 100 or more wins were compared. Of the top four coaches listed, what were the winning percents for each coach? Overall, what would be the winning percents of the coaches. Round to the nearest hundredth percent.

Gene Keady, Purdue, (405–179)
Bob Knight, Indiana (700–259)
Tom Davis, Iowa (505–269)
Dick Bennett, Wisconsin (395–215)

Portion (Wins)
Base × Rate
(Total) (?)

Gene Keady:

$405 \ (P) + 179 = 584 \ (B)$

$$\frac{405 \ (P)}{584 \ (B)} = 69.34931\% = 69.35\%$$

Bob Knight:

$$\frac{700 \ (P)}{959 \ (B)} = 72.9927\% = 72.99\%$$

Tom Davis:

$$\frac{505\ (P)}{774\ (B)} = 65.24547\% = 65.25\%$$

Dick Bennett:

$$\frac{395\ (P)}{610\ (B)} = 64.754098\% = 64.75\%$$

All coaches:

$$\frac{405 + 700 + 505 + 395 = 2,005\ (P)}{584 + 959 + 774 + 610 = 2,927\ (B)} = 68.50017\% = 68.5\%$$

6–97. Computer Village reported that its sales have increased exactly 22% per year for the last 2 years. This year's sales were $82,500. What were Computer Village's sales 2 years ago? Round each year's sales to nearest dollar.

$$\frac{\$82,500}{1.22} = \$67,623 \text{ sales last year}$$

$$\frac{\$67,623}{1.22} = \$55,429$$

= 122%

Portion = 82,500

Rate = 122%

 SUMMARY PRACTICE TEST

B = $\frac{P}{R}$

Convert the following decimals to percents: *(p. 137)*

1. .481   48.1%

2. .7   70%

3. 16.43   1,643%

4. 6.00   600%

Convert the following percents to decimals: *(p. 138)*

5. 36%   .36

6. 4.85%   .0485

7. 900%   9.0

8. $\frac{1}{5}\%$ .0020

Convert the following fractions to percents (round to nearest tenth percent): *(p. 139)*

9. $\frac{1}{7}$ 14.3%

10. $\frac{2}{9}$ 22.2%

Convert the following percents to fractions and reduce to lowest terms as needed: *(p. 139)*

11. $16\frac{1}{4}\%$ $\frac{65}{4} \times \frac{1}{100} = \frac{65}{400} = \frac{13}{80}$

12. 6.2% $6\frac{2}{10}\% = \frac{62}{10} \times \frac{1}{100} = \frac{62}{1,000} = \frac{31}{500}$

Solve the following problems for portion, base, or rate:

13. Lange Company has a net income before taxes of $85,000. The company's treasurer estimates that 36% of the company's net income will go to federal and state taxes. How much will Lange have left? *(p. 141)*

$85,000 × .64 = $54,400

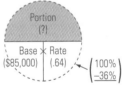

14. Base Corporation projects a year-end net income of $140,000. The net income represents 20% of its projected annual sales. What are Base's projected annual sales? *(p. 144)*

$$\frac{\$140,000}{.20} = \$700,000$$

15. True Value Hardware ordered 300 mowers. When True Value received the order, 15 mowers were missing. What percent of the order did True Value receive? *(p. 143)*

$$\frac{285}{300} = 95\%$$

16. Marika Katz, an employee at Fidelity Investments, receives an annual salary of $75,000. Today, her boss informed her she would receive a $7,000 raise. What percent of her old salary is the $7,000 raise? Round to the nearest hundredth percent. *(p. 145)*

$$\frac{\$7,000}{\$75,000} = 9.33\%$$

17. The price of a U.S. Airways airline ticket from Los Angeles to New York City increased to $600. This is a 20% increase. What was the old fare? *(p. 146)*

$$\frac{\$600}{1.20} = \$500$$

18. Lo Chen earns a gross pay of $550 per week at Office Max. Lo's payroll deductions are 28%. What is Lo's take-home pay? *(p. 141)*

$P = \$550 \times .72$

$P = \$396$

19. Lance Fall is reviewing the total accounts receivable of Paul's Department Store. Credit customers paid $55,000 this month. This represents 20% of all receivables due. What is Paul's total accounts receivable? *(p. 144)*

$$\frac{\$55,000}{.20} = \$275,000$$

A GROUP PROJECT   Defend or reject the following business math issue based on the *Kiplinger's Personal Finance Magazine* article below:

How to Get the Best Exchange Rate

▶ **Go to an ATM with your bank card or debit card—not your credit card.**   By Kimberly Lankford

The last time I was in Canada, I received a very different rate when exchanging cash than I did when using my credit card. What is the best way to exchange money while traveling in foreign countries?
—JAMES PARRISH, *Applegate, Cal.*

You'll probably get the best exchange rate if you withdraw foreign currency from an ATM. If your U.S. bank belongs to the Cirrus network, for example, you'll get the wholesale exchange rate—the same rate that banks get. But you could be charged a fee by your bank as well as by the bank that operates the ATM. Wells Fargo, for example, nicks you $2 for each international transaction, and the Royal Bank of Canada charges $1 for noncustomers who use its machines.

But use your bank card or debit card, not your credit card, at the ATM. Credit card withdrawals are pegged to the wholesale rate plus 1% and are treated as cash advances. So the money starts to accrue interest immediately, and you usually pay a fee of about 2%.

You'll also get the wholesale exchange rate if you buy American Express traveler's checks in foreign currency (available for most major currencies) before you leave the U.S. With Amex traveler's checks you usually pay a 1% fee, but the fee is sometimes waived—such as for American Automobile Association members.

If you exchange your cash for foreign currency in the U.S., you will pay more. Wells Fargo, for example, charges 3% to 4% above the wholesale rate. Foreign-exchange firm Thomas Cook was recently charging a premium of more than 5% plus a $4.95 fee (or 1% of the transaction, whichever is greater).

A lot of travelers get by with a limited amount of cash by charging most purchases to their credit card. MasterCard, Visa and American Express usually charge 1% over the wholesale exchange rate for purchases and

don't add additional fees (although member banks can tack on another 1% to 2%). You also get the wholesale rate for purchases with a debit card—often without the fees.

Call your bank to make sure your ATM, credit or debit card will work where you're going. Cards on international networks—such as Cirrus and Plus—are usually accepted throughout the world.

BEST FUNDS IN A BEAR MARKET
What were the top-performing mutual funds in 1987's down market? Did any of them do well during this summer's stock-market drop?
—A. WILLACEY, *New Bern, N.C.*

All diversified U.S. stock funds still in existence today had negative returns during the 1987 bear market, when the Standard & Poor's 500-stock index tumbled 33.5%. Bond-heavy balanced funds tended to do the best: **Mosaic Equity Balanced** sustained the

least damage, returning –2.4% during the August 25 to December 4, 1987, down market (the fund's annualized return for the three years ending August 31, 1998, was 14.5%).

Of the top 20 performers in the '87 drop, only four were widely held funds that currently have more than $1 billion in assets: **Franklin Income** (–5.8% in the 1987 down market; current three-year annualized return, 8.4%), **Vanguard Wellesley Income** (–7.6%; 13.7%), **Lindner Dividend** (–9.8%; 7.6%) and **Capital Income Builder** (–10.3%; 16.1%).

Only three funds finished in the top 20 in both 1987 and this year's summer sell-off (July 17 to August 31); **Vanguard Preferred Stock** (1.7% in the 1998 down market; three-year annualized return, 10.9%) and market-timers **Rightime Fund** (–0.6%; 6.8%) and **Rightime Blue Chip** (0.8%; 13.6%).

GOODWILL DURING THE NORTHWEST STRIKE
I bought tickets from Northwest Airlines for a vacation to Las Vegas over the Labor Day weekend, and the flight was canceled because of the pilots' strike. I rebooked on US Airways, and Northwest paid for the ticket. Was it required to do that or was that just good PR? —BOB COAD, *Indiana, Pa.*

An airline must refund your money if your flight is canceled and not rebooked. Any steps it takes beyond that are purely to promote good customer relations, says Bill Mosley of the Department of Transportation.

During the strike, which was settled in mid September, the airline gave ticketholders three options, which they could choose in any order: rebook on another airline, reschedule on a Northwest flight after the strike, or get a refund. Northwest managed to rebook a little more than half of its passengers on other airlines and paid any extra cost.

ZOHAR LAZAR

Business Math Issue

Debit cards will replace the credit card in getting the best exchange rate.

1. List the key points of the article and information to support your position.
2. Write a group defense of your position using math calculations to support your view.

America's Bestsellers

BRAND	COMPANY	YEAR INVENTED	% OF MARKET (BY VOLUME)
Frosted Flakes	Kellogg	1952	4.6%
Corn Flakes	Kellogg	1898	4.3
Cheerios	General Mills	1941	3.5
Frosted Mini-Wheats	Kellogg	1969	3.5
Raisin Bran	Kellogg	1942	3.1
Rice Krispies	Kellogg	1927	2.7
Honey Nut Cheerios	General Mills	1979	2.7

A recent Post hit

Sources: Goldman, Sachs & Co.; Information Resources Inc.

Project A

Cereal business is $8 billion per year. In dollars, how much does each cereal sell?

$B \times R = P$

$\$8,000,000,000 \times 4.6\% = \$368$ million
$\$8,000,000,000 \times 4.3\% = \$344$ million
$\$8,000,000,000 \times 3.5\% = \$280$ million
$\$8,000,000,000 \times 3.5\% = \$280$ million
$\$8,000,000,000 \times 3.1\% = \$248$ million
$\$8,000,000,000 \times 2.7\% = \$216$ million
$\$8,000,000,000 \times 2.7\% = \$216$ million

Project B

Prove the 15,000 cut.

$P = B \times R$
$P = 53,500 \times .28$
$P = 14,980$

Compaq to Reduce Digital Work Force By 28% After Deal

By Jon G. Auerbach
And Evan Ramstad
Staff Reporters of The Wall Street Journal

Compaq Computer Corp. plans to cut about 15,000 jobs at Digital Equipment Corp., or about 28% of the company's work force, after Compaq's proposed acquisition of Digital is completed, according to people familiar with the matter.

Those numbers are significantly higher than the 10,000 figure Compaq insiders had originally estimated and suggest that Compaq, which is facing its own financial pressures, plans to move aggressively to cut costs at Digital. Since Compaq announced the proposed $9.5 billion acquisition in January, the world's largest personal-computer maker has stumbled due to inventory problems and intense PC price competition.

The layoffs will most likely come from Digital's personal-computer division, some parts of its sales force and some corporate computer operations that overlap with Compaq's business, say people who have heard Compaq's views. Spokesmen for Compaq and Digital declined to comment on the specifics of any reductions. Digital had about 53,500 employees at the end of the last quarter. At its peak in the late 1980s, Digital's work force topped 130,000.

 See text Web site (www.mhhe.com/slater) and *The Business Math Internet Resource Guide*.

CLASSROOM NOTES

7

DISCOUNTS: TRADE AND CASH

LEARNING UNIT OBJECTIVES

LU 7.1   Trade Discounts—Single and Chain

- Calculate single trade discounts with formulas and complements *(pp. 167–68).*
- Find list price when net price and trade discount rate are known *(p. 168).*
- Calculate chain discounts with the net price equivalent rate and single equivalent discount rate *(pp. 169–71).*

LU 7.2   Cash Discounts, Credit Terms, and Partial Payments

- Explain the freight terms *FOB shipping point* and *FOB destination* and their effect on cash discounts *(pp. 173–74).*
- List and explain typical discount periods and credit periods that a business may offer *(pp. 176–79).*
- Calculate outstanding balance for partial payments *(p. 180).*

Airlines in Asia Offer Personalized Prices By Age, Race, Gender

* * *

Air India Has Its 'Ladies Fare' To Shopping Destinations; Chinese Fliers Are Wooed

By DIANE BRADY
Staff Reporter of THE WALL STREET JOURNAL

HONG KONG — Here's a deal for the chosen few: airline fare discounts based on a traveler's nationality, name, age or gender.

While Asian airlines frequently engage in price wars to fill their planes during slow periods, the practice of targeting ethnic or other groups is relatively new.

Air India recently launched a "ladies' fare" program, offering 33% discounts to women traveling between India and the "shopping destinations" of Dubai, Hong Kong and Singapore. South Korea's **Asiana Airlines** now has special deals for Russian passport holders who fly between Khabarovsk and Seoul, while **Japan Airlines** occasionally offers special deals through its JAL Family Club, restricted to Japanese living abroad.

© 1996 Dow Jones & Company, Inc.

Toys 'R' Us Inc. Warned Manufacturers On Sales to Warehouse Club Discounters

By JOSEPH PEREIRA
Staff Reporter of THE WALL STREET JOURNAL

WASHINGTON — **Toys "R" Us Inc.** acknowledged for the first time that it warned toy manufacturers that it might not carry certain lines of their toys if they were also sold to warehouse clubs that sell at a discount.

The disclosure came at the start of an administrative law proceeding at the Federal Trade Commission, which has accused the company of illegally boosting prices by working to cut off warehouse clubs.

© 1997 Dow Jones & Company, Inc.

The word *discount* makes buyers stop and listen. Consumers have come to look for discounts in many places. *The Wall Street Journal* clipping "Airlines in Asia Offer Personalized Prices by Age, Race, Gender" reports that a "ladies' fare" program was launched by Air India for women shoppers. Women traveling between India and the "shopping destinations" of Dubai, Hong Kong, and Singapore receive a 33% discount. Most fliers watch for the special discounts offered by airlines.

Warehouse club shoppers expect discounts. However, warehouse club shoppers are usually aware that some products are not found in their warehouse club. *The Wall Street Journal* clipping "Toys 'R' Us Inc." reports that Toys "R" Us warned toy manufacturers that it would not carry certain toys if they also sold its toys to warehouse clubs.

This chapter discusses two types of discounts taken by retailers—trade and cash. A **trade discount** is a reduction off the original selling price (list price) of an item and is not related to early payment. A **cash discount** is the result of an early payment based on the terms of the sale.

LEARNING UNIT 7.1   Trade Discounts—Single and Chain

©Alan Abramowitz/Tony Stone Images.

Retailers sell merchandise directly to consumers. The merchandise sold by retailers is bought from manufacturers and wholesalers who sell only to retailers and not to consumers. These manufacturers and wholesalers offer retailer discounts so they can resell the merchandise at a profit. The discounts are off the manufacturers' and wholesalers' **list price** (suggested retail price), and the amount of discount that retailers receive off the list price is the **trade discount amount.**

North Shore Community College Bookstore is a retailer that sells textbooks to students. The bookstore usually buys its textbooks directly from publishers. Figure 7.1 shows a textbook invoice from Irwin/McGraw-Hill Publishing Company to the North Shore Community College Bookstore. Note that the trade discount amount is given in percent. This is the **trade discount rate,** which is a percent off the list price that retailers can deduct. The following formula for calculating a trade discount amount gives the numbers from the Figure 7.1 invoice in parentheses:

FIGURE 7.1

Bookstore invoice showing a trade discount

Invoice No.: 5582

Irwin/McGraw-Hill Publishing Co.
1333 Burr Ridge Parkway
Burr Ridge, Illinois 60521

Date: July 8, 2001
Ship: Two-day UPS
Terms: 2/10, n/30

Sold to: North Shore Community College Bookstore
1 Ferncroft Road
Danvers, MA 01923

	Description	Unit list price	Total amount
50	Managerial Accounting–Garrison/Noreen	$59.99	$2,999.50
10	Marketing–McCarthy	58.66	586.60
	Total List Price		$3,586.10
	Less: Trade Discount 25%		– 896.53
	Net Price		$2,689.57
	Plus: Prepaid Shipping Charge		65.50
	Total Invoice Amount		$2,755.07

Trade Discount Amount Formula

Trade discount amount = List price × Trade discount rate

($896.53)   ($3,586.10)   (25%)

The price that the retailer (bookstore) pays the manufacturer (publisher) or wholesaler is the **net price.** The following formula for calculating the net price gives the numbers from the Figure 7.1 invoice in parentheses:

Net Price Formula

Net price   = List price − Trade discount amount

($2,689.57)   ($3,586.10)   ($896.53)

Frequently, manufacturers and wholesalers issue catalogs to retailers containing list prices of the seller's merchandise and the available trade discounts. To reduce printing costs when prices change, these sellers usually update the catalogs with new *discount sheets*. The discount sheet also gives the seller the flexibility of offering different trade discounts to different classes of retailers. For example, some retailers buy in quantity and service the products. They may receive a larger discount than the retailer who wants the manufacturer to service the products. Sellers may also give discounts to meet a competitor's price, to attract new retailers, and to reward the retailers who buy product-line products. Sometimes the ability of the retailer to negotiate with the seller determines the trade discount amount.

Retailers cannot take trade discounts on freight, returned goods, sales tax, and so on. Trade discounts may be single discounts or a chain of discounts.

Single Trade Discount

In the introduction to this unit, we showed how to use the trade discount amount formula and the net price formula to calculate the Irwin/McGraw-Hill Publishing Company textbook sale to the North Shore Community College Bookstore. Since Irwin/McGraw-Hill gave the bookstore only one trade discount, it is a **single trade discount.** In the following word problem, we use the formulas to solve another example of a single trade discount. Again, we will use a blueprint aid to help dissect and solve the word problem.

The Word Problem   The list price of a Macintosh computer is $2,700. The manufacturer offers dealers a 40% trade discount. What are the trade discount amount and the net price?

The facts	Solving for?	Steps to take	Key points
List price: $2,700. *Trade discount rate:* 40%.	Trade discount amount. Net price.	Trade discount amount = List price × Trade discount rate. Net price = List price − Trade discount amount.	(circle diagram) Trade discount amount / Portion (?) / Base ($2,700) × Rate (.40) / List price Trade discount rate

Steps to solving problem

1. Calculate the trade discount amount. $2,700 × .40 = $1,080
2. Calculate the net price. $2,700 − $1,080 = $1,620

Now let's learn how to check the dealers' net price of $1,620 with an alternate procedure using a complement.

How to Calculate the Net Price Using Complement of Trade Discount Rate

The **complement** of a trade discount rate is the difference between the discount rate and 100%. The following steps show you how to use the complement of a trade discount rate:

Calculating Net Price Using Complement of Trade Discount Rate

Step 1. To find the complement, subtract the single discount rate from 100%.
Step 2. Multiply the list price times the complement (from Step 1).

Think of a complement of any given percent (decimal) as the result of subtracting the percent from 100%.

Step 1.   100%
          − 40 ←——Trade discount rate
          ——————
          60% or .60

(circle diagram) Portion (?) / Base ($2,700) × Rate (.60) / List price

The complement means that we are spending 60 cents per dollar because we save 40 cents per dollar. Since we planned to spend $2,700, we multiply .60 by $2,700 to get a net price of $1,620.

Step 2. $1,620 = $2,700 × .60

Note how the portion ($1,620) and rate (.60) relate to the same piece of the base ($2,700). The portion ($1,620) is smaller than the base, since the rate is less than 100%.

Be aware that some people prefer to use the trade discount amount formula and the net price formula to find the net price. Other people prefer to use the complement of the trade discount rate to find the net price. The result is always the same.

Finding List Price When You Know Net Price and Trade Discount Rate

The following formula has many useful applications:

Calculating List Price When Net Price and Trade Discount Rate Are Known

$$\text{List price} = \frac{\text{Net price}}{\text{Complement of trade discount rate}}$$

Next, let's see how to dissect and solve a word problem calculating list price.

The Word Problem   A Macintosh computer has a $1,620 net price and a 40% trade discount. What is its list price?

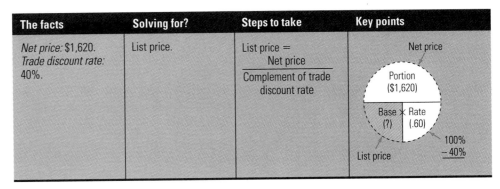

The facts	Solving for?	Steps to take	Key points
Net price: $1,620. *Trade discount rate:* 40%.	List price.	List price = $\dfrac{\text{Net price}}{\text{Complement of trade}}$ discount rate	

Steps to solving problem

1. Calculate the complement of the trade discount.

$$\begin{array}{r} 100\% \\ -\ 40 \\ \hline 60\% = .60 \end{array}$$

2. Calculate the list price.

$$\frac{\$1,620}{.60} = \boxed{\$2,700}$$

Note that the portion ($1,620) and rate (.60) relate to the same piece of the base.

Let's return to the Irwin/McGraw-Hill invoice in Figure 7.1 and calculate the list price using the formula for finding list price when net price and trade discount rate are known. The net price of the textbooks is $2,689.57. The complement of the trade discount rate is 100% − 25% = 75% = .75. Dividing the net price $2,689.57 by the complement .75 equals $3,586.09,[1] the list price shown in the Irwin/McGraw-Hill invoice. We can show this as follows:

$$\frac{\$2,689.57}{.75} = \$3,586.09, \text{ the list price}$$

Chain Discounts

✗ Frequently, manufacturers want greater flexibility in setting trade discounts for different classes of customers, seasonal trends, promotional activities, and so on. To gain this flexibility, some sellers give **chain discounts**—trade discounts in a series of two or more successive discounts.

Sellers list chain discounts as a group, for example, 20/15/10. Let's look at how Mick Company arrives at the net price of office equipment with a 20/15/10 chain discount.

EXAMPLE   The list price of the office equipment is $15,000. The chain discount is 20/15/10. The long way to calculate the net price is as follows:

Step 1	Step 2	Step 3	Step 4
$15,000	$15,000	$12,000	$10,200
× .20	− 3,000	− 1,800	− 1,020
$3,000	$12,000	$10,200	$ 9,180 net price
	× .15	× .10	
	$ 1,800	$ 1,020	

Never add the 20/15/10 together.

Note how we multiply the percent (in decimal) times the new balance after we subtract the previous trade discount amount. For example, in Step 3, we change the last discount, 10%, to decimal form and multiply times $10,200. Remember that each percent is multiplied by a successively *smaller* base. You could write the 20/15/10 discount rate in any order and still arrive at the same net price. Thus, you would get the $9,180 net price if the discount were 10/15/20 or 15/20/10. However, sellers usually give the larger discounts first. *Never try to shorten this step process by adding the discounts.* Your net price will be incorrect because, when done properly, each percent is calculated on a different base.

---

[1]Off by 1 cent due to rounding.

Net Price Equivalent Rate

In the example above, you could also find the $9,180 net price with the **net price equivalent rate**—a shortcut method. Let's see how to use this rate to calculate net price.

Calculating Net Price Using Net Price Equivalent Rate

Step 1. Subtract each chain discount rate from 100% (find the complement) and convert each percent to a decimal.

Step 2. Multiply the decimals. Do not round off decimals, since this number is the net price equivalent rate.

Step 3. Multiply the list price times the net price equivalent rate (Step 2).

The following word problem with its blueprint aid illustrates how to use the net price equivalent rate method.

The Word Problem The list price of office equipment is $15,000. The chain discount is 20/15/10. What is the net price?

The facts	Solving for?	Steps to take	Key points
List price: $15,000. *Chain discount:* 20/15/10	Net price.	Net price equivalent rate. Net price = List price × Net price equivalent rate.	Do not round net price equivalent rate.

Steps to solving problem

1. Calculate the complement of each rate and convert each percent to a decimal.

$$\begin{array}{ccc} 100\% & 100\% & 100\% \\ -20 & -15 & -10 \\ \hline 80\% & 85\% & 90\% \\ \downarrow & \downarrow & \downarrow \\ .8 & .85 & .9 \end{array}$$

2. Calculate the net price equivalent rate. (Do not round.)

$.8 \times .85 \times .9 = .612$ Net price equivalent rate For each $1, you are spending about 61 cents.

3. Calculate the net price (actual cost to buyer).

$15,000 \times .612 = \boxed{\$9,180}$

Next, we see how to calculate the trade discount amount with a simpler method.

In the previous word problem, we could calculate the trade discount amount as follows:

$$\begin{array}{rl} \$15,000 & \longleftarrow \text{List price} \\ -\ 9,180 & \longleftarrow \text{Net price} \\ \hline \boxed{\$\ 5,820} & \longleftarrow \text{Trade discount amount} \end{array}$$

Single Equivalent Discount Rate

You can use another method to find the trade discount by using the **single equivalent discount rate.**

Calculating Trade Discount Amount Using Single Equivalent Discount Rate

Step 1. Subtract the net price equivalent rate from 1. This is the single equivalent discount rate.

Step 2. Multiply the list price times the single equivalent discount rate. This is the trade discount amount.

Let's now do the calculations.

Step 1.   1.000 ⟵ If you are using a calculator, just press 1.
− .612 NPER

.388 ⟵ This is the single equivalent discount rate.

Step 2. $15,000 × .388 = **$ 5,820** ⟶ This is the trade discount amount.

Remember that when we use the net price equivalent rate, the buyer of the office equipment pays $.612 on each $1 of list price. Now with the single equivalent discount rate, we can say that the buyer saves $.388 on each $1 of list price. The .388 is the single equivalent discount rate for the 20/15/10 chain discount. Note how we use the .388 single equivalent discount rate as if it were the only discount.

It's time to try the Practice Quiz.

LU 7.1 PRACTICE QUIZ[2]

1. The list price of a dining room set with a 40% trade discount is $12,000. What are the trade discount amount and net price (use complement method for net price)?

2. The net price of a video system with a 30% trade discount is $1,400. What is the list price?

3. Lamps Outlet bought a shipment of lamps from a wholesaler. The total list price was $12,000 with a 5/10/25 chain discount. Calculate the net price and trade discount amount. (Use the net price equivalent rate and single equivalent discount rate in your calculation.)

✓   **Solutions**

1. Dining room set trade discount amount and net price:

The facts	Solving for?	Steps to take	Key points
List price: $12,000. Trade discount rate: 40%.	Trade discount amount. Net price.	Trade discount amount = List price × Trade discount rate. Net price = List price × Complement of trade discount rate.	Trade discount amount Portion (?) Base ($12,000) × Rate (.40) List price Trade discount rate

Steps to solving problem

1. Calculate the trade discount. $12,000 × .40 = **$4,800** Trade discount amount

2. Calculate the net price. $12,000 × .60 = **$7,200** (100% − 40% = 60%)

2. Video system list price:

The facts	Solving for?	Steps to take	Key points
Net price: $1,400. Trade discount rate: 30%.	List price.	List price = $\dfrac{\text{Net price}}{\text{Complement of trade discount}}$	Net price Portion ($1,400) Base (?) × Rate (.70) List price 100% −30%

Steps to solving problem

1. Calculate the complement of trade discount.

$$\begin{array}{r} 100\% \\ -\ \ 30 \\ \hline 70\% = .70 \end{array}$$

2. Calculate the list price. $\dfrac{\$1,400}{.70} =$ **$2,000**

---

[2]For all three problems we will show blueprint aids. You might want to draw them on scrap paper.

3. Lamps Outlet's net price and trade discount amount:

The facts	Solving for?	Steps to take	Key points
List price: $12,000. *Chain discount:* 5/10/25.	Net price. Trade discount amount.	Net price = List price × Net price equivalent rate. Trade discount amount = List price × Single equivalent discount rate.	Do not round off net price equivalent rate or single equivalent discount rate.

Steps to solving problem

1. Calculate the complement of each chain discount.

$$
\begin{array}{ccc}
100\% & 100\% & 100\% \\
-\ 5 & -\ 10 & -\ 25 \\
\hline
95\% & 90\% & 75\%
\end{array}
$$

2. Calculate the net price equivalent rate.   .95 × .90 × .75 = .64125

3. Calculate the net price. $12,000 × .64125 = **$7,695**

4. Calculate the single equivalent discount rate.

$$
\begin{array}{r}
1.00000 \\
-\ .64125 \\
\hline
.35875
\end{array}
$$

5. Calculate the trade discount amount. $12,000 × .35875 = **$4,305**

LEARNING UNIT 7.2   Cash Discounts, Credit Terms, and Partial Payments

Invoice No.: 5582

Irwin/McGraw-Hill Publishing Co.
1333 Burr Ridge Parkway
Burr Ridge, Illinois 60521

Date: July 8, 2001
Ship: Two-day UPS
Terms: 2/10, n/30

Sold to: North Shore Community College Bookstore
1 Ferncroft Road
Danvers, MA 01923

	Description	Unit list price	Total amount
50	Managerial Accounting—Garrison/Noreen	$59.99	$2,999.50
10	Marketing—McCarthy	58.66	586.60
	Total List Price		$3,586.10
	Less: Trade Discount 25%		− 896.53
	Net Price		$2,689.57
	Plus: Prepaid Shipping Charge		65.50
	Total Invoice Amount		$2,755.07

NSCC Bookstore
1 Ferncroft Road
Danvers, MA 01923

4418
22-70/960

July 12 20*01*

PAY TO THE
ORDER OF   *Irwin/McGraw-Hill Publishing Co.* $ *2,701 28/100*

Two thousand, seven hundred one and 28/100 ———— DOLLARS

PARK BANK
2254 Como Avenue
Danvers, MA 01924

James Casley

⑆096000700⑆ 23593100 ⑈ 0650

To introduce this learning unit, we return to the Irwin/McGraw-Hill Publishing Company textbook invoice shown in Figure 7.1. For your convenience, we have repeated the invoice.

As you can see, the terms of the Irwin/McGraw-Hill invoice are 2/10, n/30. This means that if North Shore Community College Bookstore pays the invoice within 10 days, it may deduct 2% from the net price before adding the prepaid shipping charge. The check below the invoice shows that the bookstore paid Irwin/McGraw-Hill $2,701.28.

Net price	$2,689.57
Less: Cash discount	− 53.79 ($2,689.57 × .02)
Plus: Freight	+ 65.50
	$2,701.28

In this unit we will see why the bookstore pays Irwin/McGraw-Hill $2,701.28. Before we discuss the common credit terms offered by sellers, let's look at cash discounts and how they are determined.

Cash Discounts

In the Irwin/McGraw-Hill Publishing Company invoice, the bookstore received a cash discount of $53.79. This amount is determined by the **terms of the sale,** which include the credit period, cash discount, discount period, and freight terms.

Buyers can often benefit from buying on credit. The time period that sellers give buyers to pay their invoices is the **credit period.** Frequently, buyers can sell the goods bought during this credit period. Then, at the end of the credit period, buyers can pay sellers with the funds from the sales of the goods. When buyers can do this, they can use the consumer's money to pay the invoice instead of their money.

A cash discount is for prompt payment. A trade discount is not.

Sellers can also offer a cash discount, or reduction from the invoice price, if buyers pay the invoice within a specified time. This time period is the **discount period,** which is part of the total credit period. Sellers offer this cash discount because they can use the dollars to better advantage sooner than later. Buyers who are not short of cash like cash discounts because the goods will cost them less and, as a result, provide an opportunity for larger profits.

Trade discounts should be taken before cash discounts.

Remember that buyers do not take cash discounts on freight, returned goods, sales tax, and trade discounts. Buyers take cash discounts on the *net price* of the invoice. Before we discuss how to calculate cash discounts, you should understand how companies determine freight charges.

Freight Terms

The most common **freight terms** are *FOB shipping point* and *FOB destination.* These terms determine how the freight will be paid. The key words in the terms are *shipping point* and *destination.*

FOB shipping point means free on board at shipping point; that is, the buyer pays the freight cost of getting the goods to the place of business.

For example, assume that IBM in San Diego bought goods from Argo Suppliers in Boston. Argo ships the goods FOB Boston by plane. IBM takes title to the goods when the aircraft in Boston receives the goods, so IBM pays the freight from Boston to San Diego. Frequently, the seller (Argo) prepays the freight and adds the amount to the buyer's (IBM) invoice. When paying the invoice, the buyer takes the cash discount off the net price and adds the freight cost. FOB shipping point can be illustrated as follows:

© Charles Thatcher/Tony Stone Images.

T

FOB shipping point (Boston)

FOB destination means the seller pays the freight cost until it reaches the buyer's place of business. If Argo ships its goods to IBM FOB destination or FOB San Diego, the title to the goods remains with Argo. Then it is Argo's responsibility to pay the freight from Boston to IBM's place of business in San Diego. FOB destination can be illustrated as follows:

FOB destination (San Diego)

Before you learn how to calculate cash discounts, let's look at some aids that will help you calculate credit **due dates** and **end of credit periods.**

Aids in Calculating Credit Due Dates

Sellers usually give credit for 30, 60, or 90 days. Not all months of the year have 30 days. So you must count the credit days from the date of the invoice. The trick is to remember the number of days in each month. You can choose one of the following three options to help you do this.

Option 1: Days-in-a-Month Rule   You may already know this rule. Remember that every 4 years is a leap year.

Years divisible by 4 are leap years. Leap years occur in 2000 and 2004.

> Thirty days has September, April, June, and November; all the rest have 31 except February has 28, and 29 in leap years.

Option 2: Knuckle Months   Some people like to use the knuckles on their hands to remember which months have 30 or 31 days. Note in the following diagram that each knuckle represents a month with 31 days. The short months are in between the knuckles.

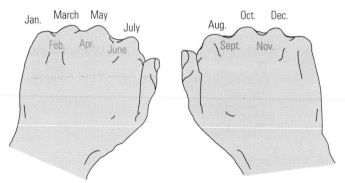

31 days: Jan., March, May, July, Aug., Oct., Dec.

Option 3: Days-in-a-Year Calendar   The days-in-a-year calendar (excluding leap year) is another tool to help you calculate dates for discount and credit periods (Table 7.1). For example, let's use Table 7.1 to calculate 90 days from August 12.

EXAMPLE   By Table 7.1: August 12 = 224 days
                                          + 90
                                      _____
                                       314 days

TABLE 7.1   Exact days-in-a-year calendar (excluding leap year)

Day of month	31 Jan.	28 Feb.	31 Mar.	30 Apr.	31 May	30 June	31 July	31 Aug.	30 Sept.	31 Oct.	30 Nov.	31 Dec.
1	1	32	60	91	121	152	182	213	244	274	305	335
2	2	33	61	92	122	153	183	214	245	275	306	336
3	3	34	62	93	123	154	184	215	246	276	307	337
4	4	35	63	94	124	155	185	216	247	277	308	338
5	5	36	64	95	125	156	186	217	248	278	309	339
6	6	37	65	96	126	157	187	218	249	279	310	340
7	7	38	66	97	127	158	188	219	250	280	311	341
8	8	39	67	98	128	159	189	220	251	281	312	342
9	9	40	68	99	129	160	190	221	252	282	313	343
10	10	41	69	100	130	161	191	222	253	283	314	344
11	11	42	70	101	131	162	192	223	254	284	315	345
12	12	43	71	102	132	163	193	224	255	285	316	346
13	13	44	72	103	133	164	194	225	256	286	317	347
14	14	45	73	104	134	165	195	226	257	287	318	348
15	15	46	74	105	135	166	196	227	258	288	319	349
16	16	47	75	106	136	167	197	228	259	289	320	350
17	17	48	76	107	137	168	198	229	260	290	321	351
18	18	49	77	108	138	169	199	230	261	291	322	352
19	19	50	78	109	139	170	200	231	262	292	323	353
20	20	51	79	110	140	171	201	232	263	293	324	354
21	21	52	80	111	141	172	202	233	264	294	325	355
22	22	53	81	112	142	173	203	234	265	295	326	356
23	23	54	82	113	143	174	204	235	266	296	327	357
24	24	55	83	114	144	175	205	236	267	297	328	358
25	25	56	84	115	145	176	206	237	268	298	329	359
26	26	57	85	116	146	177	207	238	269	299	330	360
27	27	58	86	117	147	178	208	239	270	300	331	361
28	28	59	87	118	148	179	209	240	271	301	332	362
29	29	—	88	119	149	180	210	241	272	302	333	363
30	30	—	89	120	150	181	211	242	273	303	334	364
31	31	—	90	—	151	—	212	243	—	304	—	365

If using calendar and going from one year to another, be sure to subtract the first date from 365.

Search for day 314 in Table 7.1. You will find that day 314 is November 10. In this example, we stayed within the same year. Now let's try an example in which we overlap from year to year.

EXAMPLE   What date is 80 days after December 5?

Table 7.1 shows that December 5 is 339 days from the beginning of the year. Subtracting 339 from 365 (the end of the year) tells us that we have used up 26 days by the end of the year. This leaves 54 days in the new year. Go back in the table and start with the beginning of the year and search for 54 (80 − 26) days. The 54th day is February 23.

By table

    365 days in year
− 339 days until December 5
     26 days used in year

     80 days from December 5
− 26 days used in year
     54 days in new year or February 23

Without use of table

December   31
− December   5
         26
+ 31 days in January
         57
+ 23 due date (February 23)
       80 total days

When you know how to calculate credit due dates, you can understand the common business terms sellers offer buyers involving discounts and credit periods. Remember that discount and credit terms vary from one seller to another.

Common Credit Terms Offered by Sellers

✱The common credit terms sellers offer buyers include *ordinary dating, receipt of goods (ROG),* and *end of month (EOM).* In this section we examine these credit terms. To determine the due dates, we used the exact days-in-a-year calendar (Table 7.1).

Ordinary Dating

Today, businesses frequently use the **ordinary dating** method. It gives the buyer a cash discount period that begins with the invoice date. The credit terms of two common ordinary dating methods are 2/10, n/30 and 2/10, 1/15, n/30.

2/10, n/30 Ordinary Dating Method   The 2/10, n/30 is read as "two ten, net thirty." Buyers can take a 2% cash discount off the gross amount of the invoice if they pay the bill within 10 days from the invoice date. If buyers miss the discount period, the net amount—without a discount—is due between day 11 and day 30. *Freight, returned goods, sales tax, and trade discounts must be subtracted from the gross before calculating a cash discount.*

EXAMPLE $400 invoice dated July 5: terms 2/10, n/30; no freight; paid on July 11.

Step 1.   Calculate end of 2% discount period:

> July   5 date of invoice
> + 10 days
>
> July 15   end of 2% discount period

Step 2.   Calculate end of credit period:

> July 5 by Table 7.1
> 186 days
> + 30
> 216 days

Search in Table 7.1 for 216 ⟶ August 4 ⟶ end of credit period

Step 3.   Calculate payment on July 11: *should be July 15?*
> .02 × $400 = $8 cash discount
> $400 − $8 = $392 paid

> *Note:* A 2% cash discount means that you save 2 cents on the dollar and pay 98 cents on the dollar. Thus, $.98 × $400 = $392.

The following time line illustrates the 2/10, n/30 ordinary dating method beginning and ending dates of the above example:

 Another illustration

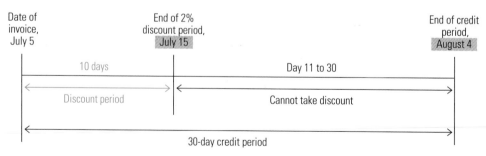

2/10, 1/15, n/30 Ordinary Dating Method   The 2/10, 1/15, n/30 is read "two ten, one fifteen, net thirty." The seller will give buyers a 2% (2 cents on the dollar) cash discount if they pay within 10 days of the invoice date. If buyers pay between day 11 and day 15 from the date of the invoice, they can save 1 cent on the dollar. If buyers do not pay on day 15, the net or full amount is due 30 days from the invoice date.

EXAMPLE $600 invoice dated May 8; $100 of freight included in invoice price; paid on May 22.

Step 1. Calculate the end of the 2% discount period:

   May   8 date of invoice
   + 10 days

   May 18 end of 2% discount period

Step 2. Calculate end of 1% discount period:

   May 18 end of 2% discount period
   + 5 days   *Note this is not 15 days* ← *Could use May 8 + 15 Days = May 23*

   May 23 end of 1% discount period

Step 3. Calculate end of credit period:

   May 8 by Table 7.1
   128 days
   + 30

   158 days

   Search in Table 7.1 for 158 ⟶ June 7 ⟶ end of credit period

Step 4. Calculate payment on May 22 (14 days after date of invoice):

   $600 invoice
   − 100 freight

   $500
   × .01

   $5.00   *Disc.*

   $500 − $5.00 + $100 freight = $595   *Another way to look at this*

   ┌──┐
   │ A 1% discount means we pay $.99 on the dollar or │
   │ $500 × $.99 = $495 + $100 freight = $595. ←   │
   │ *Note:* Freight is added back since no cash discount is taken on freight. │
   └──┘

The following time line illustrates the 2/10, 1/15, n/30 ordinary dating method beginning and ending dates of the above example:

Receipt of Goods (ROG)

3/10, n/30 ROG   With the **receipt of goods (ROG),** the cash discount period begins when buyer receives goods, *not* the invoice date. Industry often uses the ROG terms when buyers cannot expect delivery until a long time after they place the order. Buyers can take a 3% discount within 10 days *after* receipt of goods. Full amount is due between day 11 and day 30 if cash discount period is missed.

EXAMPLE $900 invoice dated May 9; no freight or returned goods; the goods were received on July 8; terms 3/10, n/30 ROG; payment made on July 20.

Step 1. Calculate the end of the 3% discount period:

   July   8 date goods arrive
   + 10 days

   July 18 end of 3% discount period

Step 2. Calculate the end of the credit period:

July 8 by Table 7.1

189 days

+ 30

219 days

Search in Table 7.1 for 219 $\longrightarrow$ August 7 $\longrightarrow$ end of credit period

Step 3. Calculate payment on July 20:

In this case

Missed discount period and paid net or full amount of $900.

The following time line illustrates 3/10, n/30 ROG beginning and ending dates of the above example:

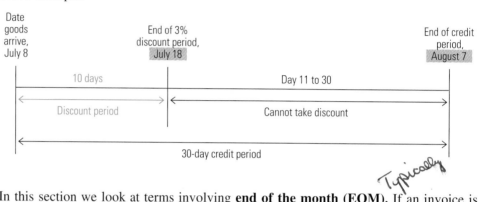

End of Month (EOM)[3]

Helps control Month end Inventory

In this section we look at terms involving **end of the month (EOM).** If an invoice is dated the *25th or earlier* of a month, we follow one set of rules. If an invoice is dated after the 25th of the month, a new set of rules is followed. Let's look at each situation.

Typically

Invoice Dated 25th or Earlier in Month, 1/10 EOM   If sellers date an invoice on the 25th or earlier in the month, buyers can take the cash discount if they pay the invoice by the first 10 days of the month following the sale (next month). If buyers miss the discount period, the full amount is due within 20 days after the end of the discount period.

EXAMPLE $600 invoice dated July 6; no freight or returns; terms 1/10 EOM; paid on August 8.

Step 1. Calculate the end of the 1% discount period:

August 10 $\longleftarrow$ First 10 days of month following sale.

Step 2. Calculate the end of the credit period:

August 10

+ 20 days

August 30 $\longleftarrow$ Credit period is 20 days after discount period.

Step 3. Calculate payment on August 8:

$.99 \times \$600 = \$594$

The following time line illustrates the beginning and ending dates of the EOM invoice of the above example:

*Even though the discount period begins with the next month following the sale, if buyers wish, they can pay before the discount period (date of invoice until the discount period).

---

[3]Sometimes the Latin term *proximo* is used. Other variations of EOM exist, but the key point is that the seller guarantees the buyer 15 days' credit. We assume a 30-day month.

Invoice Dated after 25th of Month, 2/10 EOM When sellers sell goods *after* the 25th of the month, buyers gain an additional month. The cash discount period ends on the 10th day of the second month that follows the sale. Why? This occurs because the seller guarantees the 15 days' credit of the buyer. If a buyer bought goods on August 29, September 10 would be only 12 days. So the buyer gets the extra month.

EXAMPLE $800 invoice dated April 29; no freight or returned goods; terms 2/10 EOM; payment made on June 18.

Step 1. Calculate the end of the 2% discount period:

June 10 ← First 10 days of second month following sale

Step 2. Calculate the end of the credit period:

June 10
+ 20 days
June 30 ← Credit period is 20 days after discount period.

Step 3. Calculate the payment on June 18:

No discount; $800 paid.

The following time line illustrates the beginning and ending dates of the EOM invoice of the above example:

Date of invoice, April 29	2nd month following sale, June*	End of 2% discount period, June 10	End of credit period, June 30
		10 days	20 days
		Discount period	Cannot take discount

*Even though the discount period begins with the second month following the sale, if buyers wish, they can pay before the discount date (date of invoice until the discount period).

Solving a Word Problem with Trade and Cash Discount

Now that we have studied trade and cash discounts, let's look at a combination that involves both a trade and a cash discount.

The Word Problem Hardy Company sent Regan Corporation an invoice for office equipment with a $10,000 list price. Hardy dated the invoice July 29 with terms of 2/10 EOM (end of month). Regan receives a 30% trade discount and paid the invoice on September 6. Since terms were FOB destination, Regan paid no freight charge. What was the cost of office equipment for Regan?

The facts	Solving for?	Steps to take	Key points
List price: $10,000. *Trade discount rate:* 30%. *Terms:* 2/10 EOM. *Invoice date:* 7/29. *Date paid:* 9/6.	Cost of office equipment.	Net price = List price × Complement of trade discount rate. After 25th of month for EOM. Discount period is 1st 10 days of second month that follows sale.	Trade discounts are deducted before cash discounts are taken. Cash discounts are not taken on freight or returns.

Steps to solving problem

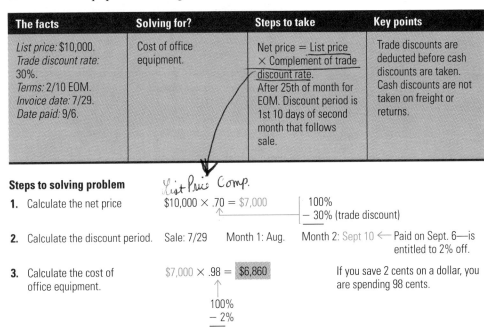

List Price Comp.

1. Calculate the net price
$10,000 × .70 = $7,000
100%
− 30% (trade discount)

2. Calculate the discount period. Sale: 7/29 Month 1: Aug. Month 2: Sept 10 ← Paid on Sept. 6—is entitled to 2% off.

3. Calculate the cost of office equipment.
$7,000 × .98 = $6,860
100%
− 2%
If you save 2 cents on a dollar, you are spending 98 cents.

Partial Payments

Often buyers cannot pay the entire invoice before the end of the discount period. To calculate partial payments and outstanding balance, use the following steps:

Calculating Partial Payments and Outstanding Balance

Step 1. Calculate the complement of a discount rate.

Step 2. Divide partial payments by the complement of a discount rate (Step 1). This gives the amount credited.

Step 3. Subtract Step 2 from the total owed. This is the outstanding balance.

EXAMPLE   Molly McGrady owed $400. Molly's terms were 2/10, n/30. Within 10 days, Molly sent a check for $80. The actual credit the buyer gave Molly is as follows:

Step 1. $100\% - 2\% = 98\% \longrightarrow .98$

Step 2. $\dfrac{\$80}{.98} = \$81.63$ $\dfrac{\$80}{1 - .02} \longleftarrow$ Discount rate

Step 3. $\$400.00$
$\underline{- \ 81.63}$ partial payment—although sent in $80
$\$318.37$ outstanding balance

Note: We do not multiply .02 × $80 because the seller did not base the original discount on $80. When Molly makes a payment within the 10-day discount period, 98 cents pays each $1 she owes. Before buyers take discounts on partial payments, they must have permission from the seller. Not all states allow partial payments.

LU 7.2 PRACTICE QUIZ

Complete the following table:

	Date of invoice	Date goods received	Terms	Last day* of discount period	End of credit period
1.	July 6		2/10, n/30		
2.	February 19	June 9	3/10, n/30 ROG		
3.	May 9		4/10, 1/30, n/60		
4.	May 12		2/10 EOM		
5.	May 29		2/10 EOM		

*If more than one discount, assume date of last discount.

6. Metro Corporation sent Vasko Corporation an invoice for equipment with an $8,000 list price. Metro dated the invoice May 26. Terms were 2/10 EOM. Vasco receives a 20% trade discount and paid the invoice on July 3. What was the cost of equipment for Vasko? (A blueprint aid will be in the solution to help dissect this problem.)

7. Complete amount to be credited and balance outstanding:

Amount of invoice: $600
Terms: 2/10, 1/15, n/30
Date of invoice: September 30
Paid October 3: $400

✓ **Solutions**

1. End of discount period: July 6 + 10 days = July 16
   End of credit period: By Table 7.1, July 6 =   187 days
                                                   + 30 days
                                                   ----
                                                    217 ⟶ search ⟶ Aug. 5

2. End of discount period: June 9 + 10 days = June 19
   End of credit period: By Table 7.1, June 9 =   160 days
                                                   + 30 days
                                                   ----
                                                    190 ⟶ search ⟶ July 9

3. End of discount period: By Table 7.1, May 9 =   129 days
                                                   + 30 days
                                                   ----
                                                    159 ⟶ search ⟶ June 8
   End of credit period: By Table 7.1, May 9 =   129 days
                                                   + 60 days
                                                   ----
                                                    189 ⟶ search ⟶ July 8

4. End of discount period: June 10
   End of credit period: June 10 + 20 = June 30

5. End of discount period: July 10
   End of credit period: July 10 + 20 = July 30

6. Vasko Corporation's cost of equipment:

The facts	Solving for?	Steps to take	Key points
List price: $8,000. *Trade discount rate:* 20%. *Terms:* 2/10 EOM. *Invoice date:* 5/26. *Date paid:* 7/3.	Cost of equipment.	Net price = List price × Complement of trade discount rate. *EOM before 25th:* Discount period is 1st 10 days of month that follows sale.	Trade discounts are deducted before cash discounts are taken. Cash discounts are not taken on freight or returns.

Steps to solving problem

1. Calculate the net price. $8,000 × .80 = $6,400 | 100% − 20%

2. Calculate the discount period.   Until July 10
3. Calculate the cost of office equipment. $6,400 × .98 = $6,272
                                             (100% − 2%)

7. $\frac{\$400}{.98} = \$408.16$, amount credited.
   $600 − $408.16 = $191.84 , balance outstanding.

Chapter Organizer and Reference Guide

Topics	Key point, procedure, formula	Example(s) to illustrate situation
Trade discount amount, p. 166	$\text{Trade discount amount} = \text{List price} \times \text{Trade discount rate}$	$600 list price 30% trade discount rate Trade discount amount = $600 × .30 = $180
Calculating net price, p. 167	$\text{Net price} = \text{List price} - \text{Trade discount amount}$ or $\text{List price} \times \text{Complement of trade discount rate}$	$600 list price 30% trade discount rate Net price = $600 × .70 = $420 $\begin{array}{r} 1.00 \\ -\ .30 \\ \hline .70 \end{array}$
Calculating list price when net price and trade discount rate are known, p. 168	$\text{List price} = \dfrac{\text{Net price}}{\text{Complement of trade discount rate}}$	40% trade discount rate Net price, $120 $\dfrac{\$120}{.60} = \$200$ list price (1.00 − .40)
Chain discounts, p. 169	Can never be added because rate is based on a successively lower base.	5/10 on a $100 list item $\begin{array}{ll} \$100 & \$\ 95 \\ \times\ .05 & \times\ .10 \\ \hline \$5.00 & \$9.50 \end{array}$ $\begin{array}{r} \$95.00 \\ -\ 9.50 \\ \hline \$85.50 \end{array}$ (running balance) $85.50 net price
Net price equivalent rate, p. 170	$\text{Actual cost to buyer} = \text{List price} \times \text{Net price equivalent rate}$ Take complement of each chain discount and multiply—do not round. $\text{Trade discount amount} = \text{List price} - \text{Actual cost to buyer}$	Given: 5/10 on $1,000 list price Take complement: .95 × .90 = .855 (net price equivalent) $1,000 × .855 = $855 (actual cost or net price) $\begin{array}{r} \$1,000 \\ -\ 855 \\ \hline \$\ \ 145 \end{array}$ trade discount amount
Single equivalent discount rate, p. 170	$\text{Trade discount amount} = \text{List price} \times 1 - \text{Net price equivalent rate}$	See example above for facts: 1 − .855 = .145 .145 × $1,000 = $145
Cash discounts, p. 173	Cash discounts, due to prompt payment, are not taken on freight, returns, etc.	Gross $1,000 (includes freight) Freight $25 Terms, 2/10, n/30 Returns $25 Purchased: Sept. 9; paid Sept 15 Cash discount = $950 × .02 = $19
Freight, p. 173	FOB shipping point—buyer pays freight. FOB destination—seller pays freight.	Moose Company of New York sells equipment to Agee Company of Oregon. Terms of shipping are FOB New York. Agee pays cost of freight since terms are FOB shipping point.
Calculating due dates, p. 174	*Option 1:* Thirty days has September, April, June, and November; all the rest have 31 except February has 28, and 29 in leap years. *Option 2:* Knuckles—31-day month; in between knuckles are short months. *Option 3:* Days-in-a-year table.	Invoice $500 on March 5; terms 2/10, n/30. *End of discount period:* $\begin{array}{r} \text{March}\ \ 5 \\ +\ 10 \\ \hline \text{March 15} \end{array}$ *End of credit period by Table 7.1:* $\begin{array}{r} \text{March 5} = 64\ \text{days} \\ +\ 30 \\ \hline 94\ \text{days} \end{array}$ Search in Table 7.1 April 4

	Chapter Organizer and Reference Guide (concluded)	
Topics	**Key point, procedure, formula**	**Example(s) to illustrate situation**
Common terms of sale **a.** Ordinary dating, p. 176	Discount period begins from date of invoice. Credit period ends 20 days from the end of the discount period unless otherwise stipulated; example, 2/10, n/60—the credit period ends 50 days from end of discount period.	Invoice $600 (freight of $100 included in price) dated March 8; payment on March 16; 3/10, n/30. March 8 + 10 End of discount period: March 18 End of credit period by Table 7.1: March 8 = 67 days +30 = 97 days Search in Table 7.1 April 7 If paid on March 16: .97 × $500 = $485 +100 freight $585
b. Receipt of goods (ROG), p. 177	Discount period begins when goods are received. Credit period ends 20 days from end of discount period.	4/10, n/30, ROG. $600 invoice; no freight; dated August 5; goods received October 2; payment made October 20. October 2 + 10 End of discount period: October 12 End of credit period by Table 7.1: October 2 = 275 + 30 = 305 Search in Table 7.1 November 1 Payment on October 20: No discount; pay $600
c. End of month (EOM), p. 178	On or before 25th of the month, discount period is 10 days after month following sale. After 25th of the month, an additional month is gained.	$1,000 invoice dated May 12; no freight or returns; terms 2/10 EOM. End of discount period → June 10 End of credit period → June 30
Partial payments, p. 180	$\text{Amount credited} = \dfrac{\text{Partial payment}}{1 - \text{Discount rate}}$	$200 invoice, terms 2/10, n/30, dated March 2; paid $100 on March 5. $\dfrac{\$100}{1-.02} = \dfrac{\$100}{.98} = \$102.04$
Key terms	Cash discount, *p. 166* Chain discounts, *p. 169* Complement, *p. 168* Credit period, *p. 173* Discount period, *p. 173* Due dates, *p. 174* End of credit period, *p. 174* End of month (EOM), *p. 178*	FOB destination, *p. 174* FOB shipping point, *p. 173* Freight terms, *p. 173* List price, *p. 166* Net price, *p. 167* Net price equivalent rate, *p. 170* Ordinary dating, *p. 176* Receipt of goods (ROG), *p. 177* Single equivalent discount rate, *p. 170* Single trade discounts, *p. 167* Terms of the sale, *p. 173* Trade discount, *p. 166* Trade discount amount, *p. 166* Trade discount rate, *p. 166*

**Critical Thinking
Discussion Questions**

1. What is the net price? June Long bought a jacket from a catalog company. She took her trade discount off the original price plus freight. What is wrong with June's approach? Who would benefit from June's approach—the buyer or the seller?

2. How do you calculate the list price when the net price and trade discount rate are known? A publisher tells the bookstore its net price of a book along with a suggested trade discount of 20%. The bookstore uses a 25% discount rate. Is this ethical when textbook prices are rising?

3. What are the steps to calculate the net price equivalent rate? Why is the net price equivalent rate *not* rounded?

4. What are the steps to calculate the single equivalent discount rate? Is this rate off the list or net price? Explain why this calculation of a single equivalent discount rate may not always be needed.

5. What is the difference between a discount and credit period? Are all cash discounts taken before trade discounts. Agree or disagree? Why?

6. Explain FOB shipping point and FOB destination. Think back to your last major purchase. Was it FOB shipping point or FOB destination? Did you get a trade or a cash discount?

7. Explain the following credit terms of sale:
   a. 2/10, n/30.
   b. 3/10, n/30 ROG.
   c. 1/10 EOM (on or before 25th of month).
   d. 1/10 EOM (after 25th of month).

8. Explain how to calculate a partial payment. Whom does a partial payment favor—the buyer or the seller?

END-OF-CHAPTER PROBLEMS   Name _____   Date _____

DRILL PROBLEMS

For all problems, round your final answer to the nearest cent. Do not round net price equivalent rates or single equivalent discount rates.

Complete the following:

Item	List price	Chain discount	Net price equivalent rate (in decimals)	Single equivalent discount rate (in decimals)	Trade discount	Net price
7–1. Dell computer	$999	8/3	.8924	.1076	$107.49	$891.51

$$\begin{array}{cc} 1.00 & 1.00 \\ -\ .08 & -\ .03 \\ \hline .92 & \times \quad .97 = .8924 \times \$999 = \$891.51 \end{array}$$

$$\begin{array}{c} 1.0000 \\ -\ .8924 \\ \hline .1076 \ \times \ \$999 = \$107.49 \end{array}$$

| **7–2.** Sony video camcorder | $349 | 20/10/10 | .648 | .352 | $122.85 | $226.15 |

$$\begin{array}{ccc} 1.00 & 1.00 & 1.00 \\ -\ .20 & -\ .10 & -\ .10 \\ \hline .80 & \times \quad .90 & \times \quad .90 = .648 \times \$349 = \$226.15 \end{array}$$

$$\begin{array}{c} 1.000 \\ -\ .648 \\ \hline .352 \times \$349 = \$122.85 \end{array}$$

| **7–3.** Cannon fax machine | $290 | 8/4/2 | .865536 | .134464 | $38.99 | $251.01 |

$$\begin{array}{ccc} 1.00 & 1.00 & 1.00 \\ -\ .08 & -\ .04 & -\ .02 \\ \hline .92 & \times \quad .96 & \times \quad .98 = .865536 \times \$290 = \$251.01 \end{array}$$

$$\begin{array}{c} 1.000000 \\ -\ .865536 \\ \hline .134464 \times \$290 = \$38.99 \end{array}$$

Complete the following:

7–4. Item	List price	Chain discount	Net price	Trade discount
Trotter treadmill	$3,000	9/4	$2,620.80	$379.20

$3,000 × .8736 = $2,620.80 (.8736 = .91 × .96)
$3,000 × .1264 = $379.20 (1 − .8736 = .1264)

| **7–5.** Maytag dishwasher | $450 | 8/5/6 | $369.70 | $80.30 |

$450 × .82156 = $369.70 (.82156 = .92 × .95 × .94)
$450 × .17844 = $80.30 (1 − .82156 = .17844)

| **7–6.** Brother word processor | $320 | 3/5/9 | $268.34 | $51.66 |

$320 × .838565 = $268.34 (.838565 = .97 × .95 × .91)
$320 × .161435 = $51.66 (1 − .838565 = .161435)

| **7–7.** Nautilus equipment | $1,850 | 12/9/6 | $1,392.59 | $457.41 |

$1,850 × .752752 = $1,392.59 (.752752 = .88 × .91 × .94)
$1,850 × .247248 = $457.41 (1 − .752752 = .247248)

7–8. Which of the following companies, A or B, gives a higher discount? Use the single equivalent discount rate to make your choice (convert your equivalent rate to the nearest hundredth percent).

Company A
8/10/15/3

$$\begin{array}{r} 1.000000 \\ A: .92 \times .90 \times .85 \times .97 = \ -\ .682686 \\ \hline .317314 \ = 31.73\% \end{array}$$

Company B
10/6/16/5 ✓

$$\begin{array}{r} 1.000000 \\ B: .90 \times .94 \times .84 \times .95 = \ -\ .675108 \\ \hline .324892 = 32.49\% \ \text{Better} \end{array}$$

Complete the following:

	Invoice	Dates when goods received	Terms	Last day* of discount period	Final day bill is due (end of credit period)	
7–9.	May 16		1/10, n/30	May 26	→June 15	
	By Table 7.1, May 16 = 136 + 30 = 166 ⟶ search in Table 7.1.					
7–10.	Nov. 27		2/10 EOM	Jan. 10	Jan. 30	Extra month since after the 25th. Credit period ends 20 days from end of discount period.
7–11.	May 15	June 5	3/10, n/30, ROG	June 15	July 5	
7–12.	April 10		2/10, 1/30, n/60	May 10	→June 9	
	By Table 7.1, April 10 = 100 + 60 = 160 ⟶ search in Table 7.1.					
7–13.	June 12		3/10 EOM	July 10	July 30	Discount and credit period begin at end of month of sale.
7–14.	Jan. 10	Feb. 3 (no leap year)	4/10, n/30, ROG	Feb. 13	→March 5	
	By Table 7.1, February 3 = 34 + 30 = 64 ⟶ search in Table 7.1.					

*If more than one discount, assume date of last discount.

Complete the following by calculating the cash discount and net amount paid:

	Gross amount of invoice (freight charge already included)	Freight charge	Date of invoice	Terms of invoice	Date of payment	Cash discount	Net amount paid
7–15.	$3,000	$100	3/6	2/10, n/60	3/15	$58 (.02 × $2,900)	$2,942 ($2,900 × .98 = $2,842 + 100 = $2,942)
7–16.	$600	None	8/1	3/10, 2/15, n/30	8/13	$12 (.02 × $600)	$588 (.98 × $600)
7–17.	$200	None	11/13	1/10 EOM	12/3	$2 (.01 × $200)	$198 (.99 × $200)
7–18.	$500	$100	11/29	1/10 EOM	1/4	$4 (.01 × $400)	$496 (.99 × $400 = $396 + $100 = $496)

Complete the following:

	Amount of invoice	Terms	Invoice date	Actual partial payment made	Date of partial payment	Amount of payment to be credited	Balance outstanding
7–19.	$450	2/10, n/60	6/6	$110	6/15	$112.24	$337.76
	$\dfrac{$110}{.98} =$	$\begin{array}{r} $450.00 \\ -\ 112.24 \\ \hline $337.76 \end{array}$					
7–20.	$600	4/10, n/60	7/5	$400	7/14	$416.67	$183.33
	$\dfrac{$400}{.96} =$	$\begin{array}{r} $600.00 \\ -\ 416.67 \\ \hline $183.33 \end{array}$					

WORD PROBLEMS (Round to nearest cent as needed)

7–21. The list price of an Eddie Bauer watch is $89.95. Pete Long receives a trade discount of 30%. Find the trade discount amount and the net price.
$89.95 × .30 = $26.99
$89.95 × .70 = $62.97

7–22. A Sony camera lists for $499 with a trade discount of 15%. What is the net price of the camera?
$499 × .85 = $424.15

7–23. On December 3, 1997, the Chicago *Sun-Times* reported that when a textbook is ordered for classroom use, college bookstores typically get a 20% discount from publishers. However, according to the National Association of College Stores, when the same book is ordered by other stores, publishers give discounts of at least 30%. If the list price is $60.30, what would be the net price to **(a)** the college bookstore and **(b)** the other stores?

a. $60.30 list

$\times$ .80 (100% − 20%)

$48.24 net price

b. $60.30

$\times$ .70 (100% − 30%)

$42.21 net price

7–24. Pacesetter Furniture buys a living room set with a $4,000 list price and a 55% trade discount. Freight (FOB shipping point) of $50 is not part of the list price. What is the delivered price (including freight) of the living room set, assuming a cash discount of 2/10, n/30, ROG? The invoice had an April 8 date. Pacesetter received the goods on April 19 and paid the invoice on April 25.

$4,000 $\times$ .45 = $1,800 $1,800 $\times$ .98 = $1,764 + $50 = $1,814

7–25. A manufacturer of in-line skates offered a 5/2/1 chain discount to many customers. Bob's Sporting Goods ordered 20 pairs of in-line skates for a total $625 list price. What was the net price of the skates? What was the trade discount amount?

Net price	**Trade discount**
.95 $\times$ .98 $\times$ .99 = .92169 $\times$ $625 = $576.05625	.07831 $\times$ $625 = $48.94
= $576.06	

7–26. Radio Shack wants to buy a new line of shortwave radios. Manufacturer A offers a 21/13 chain discount. Manufacturer B offers a 26/8 chain discount. Both manufacturers have the same list price. What manufacturer should Radio Shack buy from?

Manufacturer A

1.0000

.79 $\times$ .87 = − .6873

.3127 = 31.27%

Manufacturer B ✓

1.0000

74 $\times$ .92 = − .6808

.3192 = 31.92%

7–27. Maplewood Supply received a $5,250 invoice dated 4/15/00. The $5,250 included $250 freight. Terms were 4/10, 3/30, n/60. If Maplewood pays the invoice on April 27, what will it pay? If Maplewood pays the invoice on May 21, what will it pay?

$5,250 − $250 = $5,000 $\times$ .97 = $4,850

+ 250 freight   May 21

$5,100 $5,250

7–28. Sports-Are-Us ordered 30 pairs of Converse tennis shoes from Converse Company. The shoes were priced at $65 for each pair with the following terms: 2/10, 1/30, n/60. The invoice was dated September 15. Sports-Are-Us sent in payment on September 28. What should have been the amount of the check? Round to the nearest cent.

$ 65.00

$\times$ 30

$1,950.00

$\times$ .99

$1,930.50

7–29. Macy of New York sold Marriott of Chicago office equipment with a $6,000 list price. Sale terms were 3/10, n/30 FOB New York. Macy agreed to prepay the $30 freight. Marriott pays the invoice within the discount period. What does Marriott pay Macy?

.97 $\times$ $6,000 = $5,820 + $30 freight = $5,850

7–30. Royal Furniture bought a sofa for $800. The sofa had a $1,400 list price. What was the trade discount rate Royal received? Round to the nearest hundredth percent.

$\dfrac{\$600 \ (P)}{\$1,400 \ (B)}$ = 42.86% (R)

7–31. Dalton Bookseller paid a $4,500 net price for textbooks. The publisher offered a 25% trade discount. What was the publisher's list price?

$\dfrac{\$4,500 \ (P)}{.75 \ (R)}$ = $6,000 (B)

7–32. Heartland Manufacturing sent Sully Corporation an invoice for machinery with a $9,000 list price. Heartland dated the invoice July 23 with 2/10 EOM terms. Sully receives a 30% trade discount. Sully pays the invoice on August 5. What does Sully pay Heartland?

$9,000 $\times$ .70 = $6,300 $6,300 $\times$ .98 = $6,174

7–33. On August 1, Sully Corporation (Problem 7–32) returns $100 of the machinery due to defects. What does Sully pay Heartland on August 5?

$9,000
$\underline{-\ 100}$ returns
$8,900 \times .70 = \$6,230$ $6,230 \times .98 = \$6,105.40$

7–34. Stacy's Dress Shop received a $1,050 invoice dated July 8 with 2/10, 1/15, n/60 terms. On July 22, Stacy's sent a $242 partial payment. What credit should Stacy's receive? What is Stacy's outstanding balance?

$\dfrac{\$242}{.99} = \$244.44$ $\$1,050 - \$244.44 = \$805.56$

7–35. On March 11, Jangles Corporation received a $20,000 invoice dated March 8. Cash discount terms were 4/10, n/30. On March 15, Jangles sent an $8,000 partial payment. What credit should Jangles receive? What is Jangles' outstanding balance?

$\dfrac{\$8,000}{.96} = \$8,333.33$

$20,000.00$
$\underline{-\ 8,333.33}$
$11,666.67$ balance outstanding

ADDITIONAL SET OF WORD PROBLEMS

7–36. Master Healthcare wants to buy a new line of high-speed computers. Manufacturer A offers a 10/5 chain discount. Manufacturer B offers a 9/6 chain discount. Both manufacturers have the same list price. Which manufacturer should Master buy from?

Manufacturer A ✓

1.000
$.90 \times .95 = \underline{-\ .855}$
$.145 = 14.5\%$

Manufacturer B

1.000
$.91 \times .94 = \underline{-\ .8554}$
$.1446 = 14.46\%$

7–37. The Dalton Bookstore paid a $39.95 net price for each business math book. The publisher offered a 30% trade discount. What was the publisher's list price?

$\dfrac{\$39.95}{.70} = \$57.07$

7–38. Staples buys word processors from a wholesaler. The word processors have a $425 list price with a 40% trade discount. What is the trade discount amount? What is the net price of the word processor? Freight charges are FOB destination.

$\$425 \times .40 = \$170$ trade discount $\$425 \times .60 = \$225$ net price

7–39. Vail Ski Shop received a $1,201 invoice dated July 8 with 2/10, 1/15, n/60 terms. On July 22, Vail sent a $485 partial payment. What credit should Vail receive? What is Vail's outstanding balance?

$\dfrac{\$485}{.99} = \$489.90$

$1,201.00$
$\underline{-\ 489.90}$
$\$\ \ 711.10$ balance outstanding

7–40. Hiawatha Supply received an invoice dated 4/15/02. The invoice had a $5,500 balance that included $300 freight. Terms were 4/10, 3/30, n/60. Hiawatha pays the invoice on April 29. What amount does Hiawatha pay?

$\$5,500 - \$300 = \$5,200 \times .97 = \$5,044$
$\underline{+\ 300}$
$\$5,344$

7–41. Office Supply, Inc., purchased seven new computers for $850 each. It received a 15% discount because it purchased more than five and an additional 6% discount because it took immediate delivery. Terms of payment were 2/10, n/30. Office Supply pays the bill within the cash discount period. How much should the check be? Round to the nearest cent.

$\$\ \ 850.00$
$\underline{\times\ 7}$
$\$5,950.00$

Chain: $.85 \times .94 = .799$

$\$5,950.00$
$\underline{\times\ .799}$ chain discount
$\$4,754.05$
$\underline{\times\ .98}$ cash discount
$\$4,658.97$

7–42. On May 14, Talbots of Boston sold Forrest of Los Angeles $7,000 of fine clothes. Terms were 2/10 EOM FOB Boston. Talbots agreed to prepay the $80 freight. If Forrest pays the invoice on June 8, what will Forrest pay? If Forrest pays on June 20, what will Forrest pay?

.98 × $7,000 = $6,860 + $80 freight = $6,940

June 20: $7,080 ($7,000 + $80)

7–43. Steele Roller Skates offers 4/3/1 chain discounts to many of its customers. Bob's Sporting Goods ordered 20 pairs of roller skates with a total list price of $900. What is the net price of the roller skates? What was the trade discount amount? Round to the nearest cent.

.96 × .97 × .99 = .921888

$900	$900
× .921888	× .078112
$829.70 net price	$70.30 trade discount

7–44. Majestic Manufacturing sold Jordans Furniture a living room set for an $8,500 list price with 35% trade discount. The $100 freight (FOB shipping point) was not part of the list price. Terms were 3/10, n/30 ROG. The invoice date was May 30. Jordans received the goods on July 18 and paid the invoice on July 20. What was the final price (include cost of freight) of the living room set?

$8,500 × .35 = $2,975 TD

$8,500 − $2,975 = $5,525 × .97 = $5,359.25 + $100 = $5,459.25

 (or .65 × $8,500) ⤴

7–45. Boeing Truck Company received an invoice showing 8 tires at $110 each, 12 tires at $160 each, and 15 tires at $180 each. Shipping terms are FOB shipping point. Freight is $400, trade discount is 10/5, and a cash discount of 2/10, n/30 is offered. Assuming Boeing paid within the discount period, what did Boeing pay?

```
 8 × $110 = $  880        1.00      1.00
12 × $160 = $1,920       − .10     − .05
15 × $180 = $2,700        .90 ×     .95 =          .855
            $5,500 list                        × $5,500
                                      $4,702.50 × .98 = $4,608.45
                                                      + 400.00
                                                      $5,008.45
```

7–46. On November 1997, *Nation's Business* reported that you can sometimes cut one-half off the hotel quoted room rates by getting your reservations through a hotel broker. Hotels often designate 10% to 15% of their rooms to be sold by brokers at deeply discounted rates because these specialized travel companies can guarantee the hotel business in the low season. One major hotel in Las Vegas normally charges up to $200 a night for a room you can get through a broker for $69. Golf Pacific Coast, a small package-tour company, takes advantage of these savings. What would be the discount percent (to the nearest tenth percent) on the hotel rate of the $200 room sold by the broker for $69?

$200 list	$131 (P)
− 69 net	────── = 65.5% (R) discount percent
$131 discount	$200 (B)

7–47. Reliance Company offers to sell cellular phones listing for $99.99 with a chain discount of 15/10/5. Morgan Company offers to sell its cellular phones that list at $102.99 with a chain discount of 25/5. If Irene is to buy 6 phones, how much could she save if she buys from the lower-priced company?

Reliance: .85 × .90 × .95 = .72675

Morgan: .75 × .95 = .7125

Reliance: 6 phones × $99.99 = $599.94 × .72675 = $436.01

Morgan: 6 phones × $102.99 = $617.94 × .7125 = $440.28

Save $4.27 by buying from Reliance.

7–48. Bryant Manufacture sells its furniture to wholesalers and retailers. It offers to wholesalers a chain discount of 15/10/5 and to retailers a chain discount of 15/10. If a sofa lists for $500, how much would the wholesaler and retailer pay?

Wholesaler: .85 × .90 × .95 = .72675	**Retailer:** .85 × .90 = .765
× $500	× $500
$363.38	$382.50

CHALLENGE PROBLEMS

7–49. You are the purchasing agent for Wheeler Tire Company. You have two wholesale suppliers of tires. Major Wholesaler lists tires at $65 with a chain discount of 15/12/5 and a cash discount of 2/10, net 30. Lester Wholesaler lists the same tire at $68 with a chain discount of 14/13/9 and a cash discount of 3/10, net 30. Which wholesaler should you purchase your tires from and what would be your savings if you paid the bill within 10 days? Round to the nearest cent.

Major

.85 × .88 × .95 = .7106

$ 65.00
× .7106

$46.189= $46.19 price after discount
        × .98 cash discount

$45.27

Lester

.86 × .87 × .91 = .680862

$ 68.00
  × .680862

$46.298616 = $46.30
        × .97

$44.91

$45.27 Major
44.91 Lester

$ .36 savings with Lester

7–50. On March 30, Century Television received an invoice dated March 28 from ACME Manufacturing for 50 televisions at a cost of $125 each. Century received a 10/4/2 chain discount. Shipping terms were FOB shipping point. ACME prepaid the $70 freight. Terms were 2/10 EOM. When Century received the goods, 3 sets were defective. Century returned these sets to ACME. On April 8, Century sent a $150 partial payment. Century will pay the balance on May 6. What is Century's final payment on May 6? Assume no taxes.

List price   (50 − 3) × $125 = $5,875
Less trade discount .90 × .96 × .98 × $5,875 = $4,974.48 + Freight
April 8 pays $150 $\dfrac{\$150}{.98} = \$153.06$

$4,974.48 − $153.06 = $4,821.42 due + $70
May 6 $4,821.42 − (.02 × $4,821.42) = $96.43
       $4,821.42 − $96.43 = $4,724.99
                          + 70.00
                          $4,794.99

SUMMARY PRACTICE TEST

Complete the following: *(p. 167)*

Item	List price	Single trade discount	Net price
1. Goodyear tires	$400	20%	$320 = $400 × .80 $P = B \times R$
2. DP treadmill $\left(\dfrac{\$420\,(P)}{.60\,(R)}\right)$	$700 (B)	40%	$420

Calculate the net price and trade discount (use net price equivalent rate and single equivalent discount rate) for the following: *(p. 170)*

Item	List price	Chain discount	Net price	Trade discount
3. Kitchen Aid dishwasher	$650	9/7	$550.10 .91 × .93 = .8463 .8463 × $650 = $550.10	$99.91 1.000 − .8463 .1537 × 650 $99.91

4. From the following, what is the last date for each discount period and credit period? *(p. 176)*

Date of invoice	Terms	End of discount period	End of credit period
a. Sept. 8	2/10, n/30	Sept. 18 (Sept. 8 + 10)	Oct. 8
			(Sept. 8 ⟶ 251 days + 30 = 281)
b. Oct. 12, 2001	4/10, n/30 ROG (Goods received July 6, 2002)	July 16	Aug. 5 (July 6 ⟶ 187 + 30 = 217)
c. April 9	2/10 EOM	May 10	May 30
d. Nov. 28	2/10 EOM	Jan. 10	Jan. 30

5. Kmart buys a television from a wholesaler with an $800 list price and a 40% trade discount. What is the trade discount amount? What is the net price of the television? *(p. 167)*
$800 \times .40 = $320
$800 \times .60 = $480

6. Dee Company of Boston sold James Company of New York computer equipment with an $11,000 list price. Sale terms were 2/10, n/30 FOB Boston. Dee agreed to prepay the $100 freight. James pays the invoice within the discount period. What does James pay Dee? *(p. 173)*
$.98 \times $11,000 = $10,780 + $100 = $10,880

7. Jen Rich wants to buy a new line of stereos for her shop. Manufacturer A offers a 17/11 chain discount. Manufacturer B offers a 21/8 chain discount. Both manufacturers have the same list price. Which manufacturer should Jennifer buy from? *(p. 170)*

Manufacturer A

1.00	1.00	1.0000
− .17	− .11	− .7387
.83 ×	.89 = .7387	.2613 = 26.13% discount ✓

Manufacturer B

1.00	1.00	1.0000
− .21	− .08	− .7268
.79 ×	.92 = .7268	.2732 = 27.32% discount

8. Al's Print Shop received a $5,000 invoice dated May 10. Terms were 2/10, 1/15, n/60. On May 23, Al's Print Shop sent a $1,400 partial payment. What credit should Al's Print Shop receive? What is Al's Print Shop's outstanding balance? Round to the nearest cent. *(p. 180)*
$\frac{$1,400}{.99} = $1,414.14$ $5,000 − $1,414.14 = $3,585.86

9. Lang Company received from Lou Company an invoice dated August 28. Terms were 2/10 EOM. List price on the invoice was $7,000 (freight not included). Lang receives an 11/8 chain discount. Freight charges are Lang's responsibility, but Lou agreed to prepay the $120 freight. Lang pays the invoice on October 6. What does Lang Company pay Lou? *(p. 179)*
$.89 \times .92 = .8188 \times $7,000 = $5,731.60$
$\times .98$
$5,616.97
+ 120.00 freight
$5,736.97

A KIPLINGER APPROACH

A GROUP PROJECT Defend or reject the following business math issue based on the *Kiplinger's Personal Finance Magazine* article below:

Canine Claims and Kitty Co-pays

▸ **Veterinary HMOs are a new rival for pet health insurance.**

Pet health insurance may appeal to pet owners who would spare no expense to treat an ailing furry friend. But coverage is expensive for what you get. With Veterinary Pet Insurance (800-872-7387), you would pay $121 per year to insure a one-year-old dog or cat for up to $2,000 per "incident" (after a deductible and co-payment of $76 on the first $180 in vet bills).

But that $2,000 cap is misleading because there's a benefit schedule that sets much lower caps for most ailments—such as $490 to treat lymphosarcoma, a form of cancer. (An upgraded policy costs $206 and covers up to $1,030 in expenses, still less than it may cost to treat a pet with cancer.) Policies cost more for older pets and don't cover preexisting conditions. For $99 a year you can purchase a rider to cover routine care.

Pet HMOs are more like a dis-count plan for routine as well as critical care. Use a vet who participates in Pet Assure (888-789-7387), for example, and you get a 25% discount on all medical procedures—from routine visits and vaccinations to x-rays and surgery. Pet Assure also offers 10% to 50% discounts on food, flea products, training, grooming and boarding from participating providers. Any pet is covered, without regard to age or preexisting conditions.

At $99 a year, joining Pet Assure isn't a bad deal if you live where there are a lot of participating veterinarians and service providers (California and New York have the most participants; 22 states have none). The plan is likely to expand as HMOs for humans begin marketing the plan to their members—as Health Net in California and Capital Care in Washington, D.C., already do. ●

REPORTER: JAMES RAMAGE

Business Math Issue

Pets really do not need health insurance. It is only a fad.

1. List the key points of the article and information to support your position.
2. Write a group defense of your position using math calculations to support your view.

Ding-Dong: Fewer Salespeople Will Help Avon Come Out Ahead

BY TARA PARKER-POPE
Staff Reporter of THE WALL STREET JOURNAL

About 25,000 Avon representatives aren't calling anymore.

Almost 6% of the U.S. sales force of Avon Products Inc. has quit in the past three months. But is Avon worried? Hardly. The company says these salespeople were costing it more money than they brought in.

The exodus came after Avon ended a steep 40% discount it had offered its sales force on certain promotional lotions and potions designed for use in demonstrations. Avon representatives, virtually all of whom are women, usually qualify for discounts based on the volume of sales they generate. Some top sellers can purchase products at 50% off the retail price. Others with lower volume sales get as little as 10% off. But the 40% discount applied to promotional items regardless of sales volume.

"What we're losing are unprofitable sales," says James E. Preston, Avon's chairman and chief executive officer. "It was costing us money."

How much? Well, the departed representatives accounted for about 5% of Avon's estimated $400 million in first-quarter U.S. sales. Yet their departure actually will save Avon $6 million to $8 million, Mr. Preston says.

In the past, Avon has balked at any move that might upset its 440,000-strong U.S. sales force. Sure enough, the change did upset some high-selling representatives, who thought the new rule would cost them money as well. As a result, Avon plans to change the policy one more time. Avon representatives who order more than $50 worth of products get the old 40% discount on promotional items. Those who order less than $50 just get an extra 20% off.

Project A

What is your reaction to Avon's new proposed policy change?
Answers will vary.

Nucor Corp. Discounts Sheet Steel, Again, for Its Largest Customers

BY CHRIS ADAMS
Staff Reporter of THE WALL STREET JOURNAL

Nucor Corp. has notified large customers of a second price cut in a little over a month, dropping the price of its sheet steel products $10 a ton, or between 2% and 3%.

The move adds more downward pricing pressure on the industry, which still enjoys strong demand but faces significant competition from imports and start-up minimills.

The drop also could affect long-term contracts being negotiated between the steel industry and such major buyers as the auto industry. While such talks are continuing, PaineWebber Inc. analyst Peter Marcus says he believes that overall contract pricing for the auto makers will drop 2% to 3% in 1998 from 1997 levels.

Nucor Chairman Kenneth Iverson said the price cut applies only to the steelmaker's largest customers—those that buy at least 10,000 tons of steel a month. He said that fewer than 10 customers will enjoy the price reduction, and that it will affect less than 20% of the company's shipments of flat-rolled steel.

"It doesn't affect earnings that much, and doesn't affect distribution, but it is something we needed to do because other producers were giving these discounts," Mr. Iverson said.

For large customers, the reduction means they will pay $315 a ton for hot-rolled steel, the industry's basic commodity product, used in everything from pipe to construction applications. The price cut also applies to Nucor's more processed, and thus pricier, cold-rolled and galvanized steel products. "This really shows the price weakness in the market," said Michelle Galanter Applebaum, an analyst with Salomon Brothers Inc.

At the end of September, Charlotte, N.C.-based Nucor cut the price of hot-rolled steel $25 a ton, or 7%, one of its largest single cuts in years. Rival steelmakers haven't announced similar reductions, although the other companies usually are far less public about price changes than Nucor.

Overall, spot market prices for steel have dropped about 8% in the past four months, said PaineWebber's Mr. Marcus. That's despite healthy demand, which he estimates will top 122 million tons this year, compared with 117 million tons in 1996 and 110 million tons in 1995. The culprit is rising supply, including unusually high levels of imports, the start-up of new low-cost steel minimills, and the return to market of **WHX** Corp.'s Wheeling-Pittsburgh Steel Corp., which had been on strike for 10 months.

Mr. Marcus said Nucor's price drop for large customers is likely to affect the rest of the industry. "Unfortunately, Nucor has itself in a fish bowl where its actions are noticed by everybody else and move the market," he said.

Project B

What was the cost of steel per ton before the end of September? Prove your answer.

Nov.: $315
+ 10   2nd price drop
—————
$325
+ 25   1st price drop
—————
$350

$350 − 7% − 3% = $315.74

 See text Web site (www.mhhe.com/slater) and *The Business Math Internet Resource Guide.*

8

MARKUPS AND MARKDOWNS; INSIGHT INTO PERISHABLES

LEARNING UNIT OBJECTIVES

LU 8.1 Markups[1] Based on Cost (100%)

- Calculate dollar markup and percent markup on cost *(p. 197)*.
- Calculate selling price when you know the cost and percent markup on cost *(p. 198)*.
- Calculate cost when dollar markup and percent markup on cost are known *(p. 198)*.
- Calculate cost when you know the selling price and percent markup on cost *(p. 199)*.

LU 8.2 Markups Based on Selling Price (100%)

- Calculate dollar markup and percent markup on selling price *(p. 201)*.
- Calculate selling price when dollar markup and percent markup on selling price are known *(p. 202)*.
- Calculate selling price when cost and percent markup on selling price are known *(p. 203)*.
- Calculate cost when selling price and percent markup on selling price are known *(p. 203)*.
- Convert from percent markup on selling price to percent markup on cost and vice versa *(p. 204)*.

LU 8.3 Markdowns and Perishables

- Calculate markdowns; compare markdowns and markups *(p. 207)*.
- Price perishable items to cover spoilage loss *(p. 208)*.

---

[1]Some texts use the term *markon* (selling price minus cost).

Photo courtesy of Cotter & Company, Chicago, which is the national headquarters for the more than 6,000 True Value hardware stores nationwide.

Nancy Ford is a retailer who owns a True Value hardware store. One of the most important business decisions Nancy must make concerns the selling price of her goods. She knows that her selling price must include the cost of bringing the goods into her store, her operating expenses, and a profit. To remain in business, Nancy's selling price must also be competitive with that of other hardware retailers.

Before we study the two pricing methods available to Nancy (percent markup on cost and percent markup on selling price), we must know the following terms:

- **Selling price:** The price retailers charge consumers. Sears Roebuck sells one-third of all the appliances sold in the United States. Beginning in 1998, Sears Roebuck is also selling the Maytag brand. The total selling price of all the retailer's goods represents the retailer's total sales.

- **Cost:** The price retailers pay to a manufacturer or supplier to bring the goods into the store.

- **Markup, margin, or gross profit:** These three terms refer to the difference between the cost of bringing the goods into the store and the selling price of the goods.

- **Operating expenses or overhead:** The regular expenses of doing business such as wages, rent, utilities, insurance, and advertising.

- **Net profit or net income:** The profit remaining after subtracting the cost of bringing the goods into the store and the operating expenses from the sale of the goods (including any returns or adjustments).

From these definitions, we can conclude that **markup** represents the amount that retailers must add to the cost of the goods to cover their operating expenses and make a profit.[2]

To help you understand the basic selling price formula that follows, let's return to Nancy Ford and her True Value hardware store. Nancy has bought a Toro snowthrower from a supplier for $210. She plans to sell the snowthrower for $300.

Basic selling price formula

Selling price (S) =	Cost (C)	+	Markup (M)
↑	↑		↑
$300 =	$210	+	$90
(snowthrower)	(price paid to bring snowthrower into store)		(amount in dollars to cover operating expenses and make a profit)

Note that in this example, the markup is a dollar amount, or a **dollar markup.** Markup is also expressed in percent. When expressing markup in percent, retailers can choose a percent based on *cost* (Learning Unit 8.1) or a percent based on *selling price* (Learning Unit 8.2).

By VANESSA O'CONNELL
Staff Reporter of THE WALL STREET JOURNAL

Campbell Soup Co. is making a m'm major strategic shift to arrest a big downturn in its flagship business.

This spring, Campbell decided to forgo its usual spring price markup of 3% to 7%. Basil Anderson, chief financial officer, says the decision was part of "a major strategic shift" to "put a lot less reliance on pricing."

© 1998 Dow Jones & Company, Inc.

An example of a change in markup strategy is reported by *The Wall Street Journal* in this Campbell Soup clipping. You may not have been aware that in the spring of each year, it has been Campbell Soup Co.'s policy to increase its price from 3% to 7%. However, this spring, Campbell has made a strategic shift to put a lot less reliance on pricing.

---

[2]In this chapter we concentrate on the markup of retailers. Manufacturers and suppliers also use markup to determine selling price.

LEARNING UNIT 8.1   Markups Based on Cost (100%)

In Chapter 6 you were introduced to the portion formula, which we used to solve percent problems. We also used the portion formula in Chapter 7 to solve problems involving trade and cash discounts. In this unit you will see how we use the basic selling price formula and the portion formula to solve percent markup situations based on cost. We will be using blueprint aids to show how to dissect and solve all word problems in this chapter.

Many manufacturers mark up goods on cost because manufacturers can get cost information more easily than sales information. Since retailers have the choice of using percent markup on cost or selling price, in this unit we assume Nancy Ford has chosen percent markup on cost for her True Value hardware store. In Learning Unit 8.2 we show how Nancy Ford would determine her markup if she decided to use percent markup on selling price.

Businesses that use **percent markup on cost** recognize that cost is 100%. This 100% represents the base of the portion formula. All situations in this unit use cost as 100%.

To calculate percent markup on cost, let's use Nancy Ford's Toro snowthrower purchase and begin with the basic selling price formula given in the chapter introduction. When we know the dollar markup, we can use the portion formula to find the percent markup on cost.

Markup expressed in dollars:

Selling price ($300) = Cost ($210) + Markup ($90)

Markup expressed as percent markup on cost:

Cost	100.00% ⟶
+ Markup	+42.86
= Selling price	142.86%

> Cost is 100%—the base. Dollar markup is the portion, and percent markup on cost is the rate.

In Situation 1 (below) we show why Nancy has a 42.86% markup based on cost by presenting Nancy's snowthrower purchase as a word problem. We solve the problem with the blueprint aid used in earlier chapters. In the second column, however, you will see footnotes after two numbers. These refer to the steps we use below the blueprint aid to solve the problem. Throughout the chapter, the numbers that we are solving for are in red. Remember that cost is the base for this unit.

Situation 1: Calculating Dollar Markup and Percent Markup on Cost

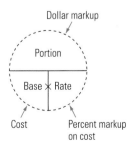

The dollar markup is calculated with the basic selling price formula $S = C + M$. When you know the cost and the selling price of the goods, you reverse the basic selling price formula to $M = S - C$. Subtract the cost from the selling price, and you have the dollar markup.

The percent markup on cost is calculated with the portion formula. For Situation 1 the *portion* (P) is the dollar markup, which you know from the selling price formula. In this unit the *rate* (R) is always the percent markup on cost and the *base* (B) is always the cost (100%). To find the percent markup on cost (R), use the portion formula $R = \frac{P}{B}$ and divide the dollar markup (P) by the cost (B). Convert your answer to a percent and round if necessary.

Now let's look at the Nancy Ford example to see how to calculate the 42.86% markup on cost.

The Word Problem   Nancy Ford bought a snowthrower that cost $210 for her True Value hardware store. She plans to sell the snowthrower for $300. What is Nancy's dollar markup? What is her percent markup on cost (round to the nearest hundredth percent)?

The facts	Solving for?			Steps to take	Key points
Snowthrower cost: $210. Snowthrower selling price: $300.		%	$	Dollar markup = $\frac{\text{Selling price}}{}$ − Cost.	Dollar markup
	C	100.00%	$210		Portion ($90)
	+ M	42.86[2]	90[1]	Percent markup on cost = $\frac{\text{Dollar markup}}{\text{Cost}}$	Base × Rate ($210) (?)
	= S	142.86%	$300		
	[1]Dollar markup. [2]Percent markup on cost.				Cost

Steps to solving problem

1. Calculate the dollar markup.

$$\text{Dollar markup} = \text{Selling price} - \text{Cost}$$
$$\boxed{\$90} \quad = \quad \$300 \quad - \$210$$

2. Calculate the percent markup on cost.

$$\text{Percent markup on cost} = \frac{\text{Dollar markup}}{\text{Cost}}$$

$$= \frac{\$90}{\$210} = \boxed{42.86\%}$$

To check the percent markup on cost. you can use the basic selling price formula $S = C + M$. Convert the percent markup on cost found with the portion formula to a decimal and multiply it by the cost. This gives the dollar markup. Then add the cost and the dollar markup to get the selling price of the goods.

You could also check the cost (B) by dividing the dollar markup (P) by the percent markup on cost (R).

Check

Selling price = Cost + Markup	**or**	$\text{Cost }(B) = \dfrac{\text{Dollar markup }(P)}{\text{Percent markup on cost }(R)}$

$$\$300 \quad = \$210 + .4286(\$210)\leftarrow$$
$$\$300 \quad = \$210 + \$90^*$$
$$\$300 \quad = \$300$$

$$= \frac{\$90}{.4286} = \$209.99^*$$

Parentheses mean that you multiply the percent markup on cost in decimal by the cost.

*Off 1 cent due to rounding of percent.

Situation 2: Calculating Selling Price When You Know Cost and Percent Markup on Cost

When you know the cost and the percent markup on cost, you calculate the selling price with the basic selling formula $S = C + M$. Remember that when goods are marked up on cost, the cost is the base (100%). So you can say that the selling price is the cost plus the markup in dollars (percent markup on cost times cost).

Now let's look at Mel's Furniture where we calculate Mel's dollar markup and selling price.

The Word Problem   Mel's Furniture bought a lamp that cost $100. To make Mel's desired profit, he needs a 65% markup on cost. What is Mel's dollar markup? What is his selling price?

The facts	Solving for?			Steps to take	Key points
Lamp cost: $100. Markup on cost: 65%.		%	$	Dollar markup: $S = C + M.$ or	Selling price
	C	100%	$100		Portion (?)
	+ M	65	65[1]	$S = \text{Cost} \times \left(1 + \dfrac{\text{Percent markup on cost}}{}\right)$	Base × Rate ($100) (1.65)
	= S	165%	$165[2]		
	[1]Dollar markup. [2]Selling price.				Cost 100% +65%

Steps to solving problem

1. Calculate the dollar markup.

$S = C + M$

$S = \$100 + .65(\$100)$ ⟵ Parentheses mean you multiply the percent markup in decimal by the cost.

$S = \$100 + \boxed{\$65}$ ⟵ Dollar markup

2. Calculate the selling price.

$S = \boxed{\$165}$

You can check the selling price with the portion formula $P = B \times R$. You are solving for portion (P)—the selling price. Rate (R) represents the 100% cost plus the 65% markup on cost. Since in this unit the markup is on cost, the base is the cost. Convert 165% to a decimal and multiply the cost by 1.65 to get the selling price of $165.

Check

Selling price = Cost × (1 + Percent markup on cost)	$= \$100 \times 1.65 = \boxed{\$165}$
(P) (B) (R)	

Situation 3: Calculating Cost When You Know Selling Price and Percent Markup on Cost

When you know the selling price and the percent markup on cost, you calculate the cost with the basic selling formula $S = C + M$. Since goods are marked up on cost, the percent markup on cost is added to the cost.

Let's see how this is done in the following Jill Sport example.

The Word Problem Jill Sport, owner of Sports, Inc., sells tennis rackets for $50. To make her desired profit, Jill needs a 40% markup on cost. What do the tennis rackets cost Jill? What is the dollar markup?

The facts	Solving for?		Steps to take	Key points
Selling price: $50.		% $	$S = C + M.$ or	Selling price
Markup on cost: 40%.	C 100% 35.71^1		$Cost = \dfrac{\text{Selling price}}{1 + \text{markup on cost}}$	Portion ($50)
	$+ M$ 40 14.29^2			Base × Rate
	$= S$ 140% 50.00		$M = S - C.$	(?) (1.40)
	¹Cost. ²Dollar markup.			100% +40% Cost

Steps to solving problem

1. Calculate the cost.

$S = C + M$

$\$50.00 = C + .40C$ ⟵ This means 40% times cost. C is the same as $1C$. Adding $.40C$ to $1C$ gives the percent markup on cost of $1.40C$ in decimal.

$\dfrac{\$50.00}{1.40} = \dfrac{\cancel{1.40}C}{\cancel{1.40}}$

$\boxed{\$35.71} = C$

2. Calculate the dollar markup.

$M = S - C$

$M = \$50.00 - \$35.71$

$M = \boxed{\$14.29}$

You can check your cost answer with the portion formula $B = \frac{P}{R}$. Portion (P) is the selling price. Rate (R) represents the 100% cost plus the 40% markup on cost. Convert the percents to decimals and divide the portion by the rate to find the base, or cost.

Check

$$\text{Cost } (B) = \frac{\text{Selling price } (P)}{1 + \text{Percent markup on cost } (R)} \quad = \frac{\$50.00}{1.40} = \boxed{\$35.71}$$

Now try the following Practice Quiz to check your understanding of this unit.

LU 8.1	PRACTICE QUIZ

Solve the following situations (markups based on cost):

1. Irene Westing bought a desk for $400 from an office supply house. She plans to sell the desk for $600. What is Irene's dollar markup? What is her percent markup on cost? Check your answer.

2. Suki Komar bought dolls for her toy store that cost $12 each. To make her desired profit. Suki must mark up each doll 35% on cost. What is the dollar markup? What is the selling price of each doll? Check your answer.

3. Jay Lyman sells calculators. His competitor sells a new calculator line for $14 each. Jay needs a 40% markup on cost to make his desired profit, and he must meet price competition. At what cost can Jay afford to bring these calculators into the store? What is the dollar markup? Check your answer.

✓ **Solutions**

1. Irene's dollar markup and percent markup on cost:

The facts	Solving for?			Steps to take	Key points
Desk cost: $400.		%	$	Dollar markup $=\dfrac{\text{Selling}}{\text{price}}-\text{Cost.}$	Dollar markup
Desk selling price: $600.	C	100%	$400		Portion ($200)
	$+M$	50^2	200^1	Percent markup on cost $=\dfrac{\text{Dollar markup}}{\text{Cost}}$	
	$=S$	150%	$600		Base × Rate ($400) (?)
	¹Dollar markup. ²Percent markup on cost.				Cost

Steps to solving problem

1. Calculate the dollar markup.

$$\text{Dollar markup} = \text{Selling price} - \text{Cost}$$
$$\boxed{\$200} = \$600 - \$400$$

2. Calculate the percent markup on cost.

$$\text{Percent markup on cost} = \dfrac{\text{Dollar markup}}{\text{Cost}}$$
$$= \dfrac{\$200}{\$400} = \boxed{50\%}$$

Check

Selling price = Cost + Markup	**or**	Cost $(B) = \dfrac{\text{Dollar markup } (P)}{\text{Percent markup on cost } (R)}$
$600 = $400 + .50($400)		
$600 = $400 + $200		$= \dfrac{\$200}{.50} = \$400$
$600 = $600		

2. Dollar markup and selling price of doll:

The facts	Solving for?			Steps to take	Key points
Doll cost: $12 each.		%	$	Dollar markup: $S = C + M.$	Selling price
Markup on cost: 35%.	C	100%	$12.00	or	Portion (?)
	$+M$	35	4.20^1	$S = \text{Cost} \times \left(1 + \dfrac{\text{Percent markup on cost}}{}\right)$	
	$=S$	135%	16.20^2		Base × Rate ($12) (1.35)
	¹Dollar markup. ²Selling price.				100% +35% Cost

Steps to solving problem

1. Calculate the dollar markup.

$$S = C + M$$
$$S = \$12.00 + .35(\$12.00)$$
$$S = \$12.00 + \boxed{\$4.20} \longleftarrow \text{Dollar markup}$$

2. Calculate the selling price.

$$S = \boxed{\$16.20}$$

Check

Selling price = Cost × (1 + Percent markup on cost) = $12.00 × 1.35 = $16.20
$\quad$ (P) $\qquad$ (B) $\qquad\qquad$ (R)

3. Cost and dollar markup:

The facts	Solving for?			Steps to take	Key points
Selling price: $14. Markup on cost: 40%.		%	$	$S = C + M.$ or $\text{Cost} = \dfrac{\text{Selling price}}{\begin{array}{c}\text{Percent}\\ 1 + \text{markup}\\ \text{on cost}\end{array}}$ $M = S - C.$	
	C	100%	$10[1]		
	$+ M$	40	4[2]		
	$= S$	140%	$14		
	[1]Cost. [2]Dollar markup.				

Steps to solving problem

1. Calculate the cost.
$$S = C + M$$
$$\$14 = C + .40C$$
$$\frac{\$14}{1.40} = \frac{1.40C}{1.40}$$
$$\boxed{\$10} = C$$

2. Calculate the dollar markup.
$$M = S - C$$
$$M = \$14 - \$10$$
$$M = \boxed{\$4}$$

Check

$$\text{Cost } (B) = \frac{\text{Selling price } (P)}{1 + \text{Percent markup on cost } (R)} = \frac{\$14}{1.40} = \$10$$

LEARNING UNIT 8.2 $\quad$ Markups Based on Selling Price (100%)

Many retailers, such as Victoria's Secret (see Business Math Scrapbook, p. 221), mark up their goods on the selling price since sales information is easier to get than cost information. These retailers use retail prices in their inventory and report their expenses as a percent of sales.

Businesses that mark up their goods on selling price recognize that selling price is 100%. We begin this unit by assuming that Nancy Ford has decided to use percent markup based on selling price for her True Value hardware store. We repeat Nancy's selling price formula expressed in dollars.

Markup expressed in dollars:

Selling price ($300) = Cost ($210) + Markup ($90)

Markup expressed as **percent markup on selling price:**

Cost	70%
+ Markup	+30
= Selling price	100%

> Selling price is 100%—the base. Dollar markup is the portion, and percent markup on selling price is the rate.

In Situation 1 (below) we show why Nancy has a 30% markup based on selling price. In the last unit, markups were on cost. In this unit, markups are on *selling price.*

Situation 1: Calculating Dollar Markup and Percent Markup on Selling Price

The dollar markup is calculated with the selling price formula used in Situation 1, Learning Unit 8.1: $M = S - C$. To find the percent markup on selling price, use the portion formula $R = \frac{P}{B}$, where rate (the percent markup on selling price) is found by dividing the portion (dollar markup) by the base (selling price). Note that when solving for percent markup on cost in Situation 1, Learning Unit 8.1, you divided the dollar markup by the cost.

The Word Problem   Nancy Ford bought a snowthrower that cost $210 for her True Value hardware store. She plans to sell the snowthrower for $300. What is Nancy's dollar markup? What is her percent markup on selling price?

The facts	Solving for?		Steps to take	Key points
Snowthrower cost: $210. Snowthrower selling price: $300.		% $ C 70% $210 $+ M$ 30^2 90^1 $= S$ 100% $300 ^{1}Dollar markup. ^{2}Percent markup on selling price.	$\text{Dollar markup} = \dfrac{\text{Selling}}{\text{price}} - \text{Cost}.$ $\text{Percent markup on selling price} = \dfrac{\text{Dollar markup}}{\text{Selling price}}$	Dollar markup Portion ($90) Base × Rate ($300) (?) Selling price

Steps to solving problem

1. Calculate the dollar markup.

    Dollar markup = Selling price − Cost

    $90   = $300   − $210

2. Calculate the percent markup on selling price.

    $\dfrac{\text{Percent markup}}{\text{on selling price}} = \dfrac{\text{Dollar markup}}{\text{Selling price}}$

    $= \dfrac{\$90}{\$300} = 30\%$

You can check the percent markup on selling price with the basic selling price formula $S = C + M$. You can also use the portion formula by dividing the dollar markup (P) by the percent markup on selling price (R).

Check

Selling price = Cost + Markup	**or**	$\text{Selling price } (B) = \dfrac{\text{Dollar markup } (P)}{\text{Percent markup on selling price } (R)}$

$300   = $210 + .30($300)

$300   = $210 + $90

$300   = $300

$= \dfrac{\$90}{.30} = \$300$

Parentheses mean you multiply the percent markup on selling price in decimal by the selling price.

Situation 2: Calculating Selling Price When You Know Cost and Percent Markup on Selling Price

When you know the cost and percent markup on selling price, you calculate the selling price with the basic selling formula $S = C + M$. Remember that when goods are marked up on selling price, the selling price is the base (100%). Since you do not know the selling price, the percent of markup is based on the unknown selling price. To find the dollar markup after you find the selling price, use the selling price formula $M = S - C$.

The Word Problem   Mel's Furniture bought a lamp that cost $100. To make Mel's desired profit, he needs a 65% markup on selling price. What are Mel's selling price and his dollar markup?

The facts	Solving for?		Steps to take	Key points
Lamp cost: $100. Markup on selling price: 65%.		% $ C 35% $100.00 $+ M$ 65 185.71^2 $= S$ 100% 285.71^1 ^{1}Selling price. ^{2}Dollar markup.	$S = C + M.$ or $S = \dfrac{\text{Cost}}{1 - \dfrac{\text{Percent markup}}{\text{on selling price}}}$	Cost Portion ($100) Base × Rate (?) (.35) Selling price 100% −65%

Steps to solving problem

1. Calculate the selling price.

$$S = C + M$$
$$S = \$100.00 + .65S$$

$$\left.\begin{array}{r} 1.00S \\ -\ .65S \\ \hline =\ .35S \end{array}\right]$$

$$\begin{array}{r} -\ .65S \qquad\qquad -\ .65S \\ \hline \dfrac{.35S}{.35} = \dfrac{\$100.00}{.35} \end{array}$$

$$S = \boxed{\$285.71}$$

Do not multiply the .65 times $100.00. The 65% is based on selling price not cost.

2. Calculate the dollar markup.

$$M = S - C$$
$$\boxed{\$185.71} = \$285.71 - \$100.00$$

You can check your selling price with the portion formula $B = \frac{P}{R}$. To find the selling price (B), divide the cost (P) by the rate (100% − percent markup on selling price).

Check

$$\text{Selling price } (B) = \dfrac{\text{Cost } (P)}{1 - \text{Percent markup on selling price } (R)}$$

$$= \dfrac{\$100.00}{1 - .65} = \dfrac{\$100.00}{.35} = \boxed{\$285.71}$$

Situation 3: Calculating Cost When You Know Selling Price and Percent Markup on Selling Price

When you know the selling price and the percent markup on selling price, you calculate the cost with the basic formula $S = C + M$. To find the dollar markup, multiply the markup percent by the selling price. When you have the dollar markup, subtract it from the selling price to get the cost.

The Word Problem   Jill Sport, owner of Sports, Inc., sells tennis rackets for $50. To make her desired profit, Jill needs a 40% markup on the selling price. What is the dollar markup? What do the tennis rackets cost Jill?

The facts	Solving for?			Steps to take	Key points
Selling price: $50. Markup on selling price: 40%.	C $+ M$ $= S$	% 60% 40 100%	$ $30² 20¹ $50	$S = C + M$. or Cost = Selling price × $\left(1 - \dfrac{\text{Percent markup}}{\text{on selling price}}\right)$	Cost / Portion (?) / Base × Rate ($50) (.60) / Selling price / 100% −40%

¹Dollar markup.
²Cost.

Steps to solving problem

1. Calculate the dollar markup.

$$S = C + M$$
$$\$50 = C + .40(\$50)$$

2. Calculate the cost.

$$\$50 = C + \boxed{\$20} \leftarrow \text{Dollar markup}$$

$$\begin{array}{r} -\ 20 \qquad\quad -\ 20 \\ \hline \boxed{\$30} = C \end{array}$$

To check your cost, use the portion formula Cost (P) = Selling price (B) × (100% selling price − Percent markup on selling price) (R).

Check

$$\underset{(P)}{\text{Cost}} = \underset{(B)}{\underset{\text{price}}{\text{Selling}}} \times \underset{(R)}{\left(1 - \underset{\text{on selling price}}{\text{Percent markup}}\right)} = \$50 \times .60 = \boxed{\$30}$$

$$(1.00 - .40)$$

In Table 8.1, we compare percent markup on cost with percent markup on retail (selling price). This table is a summary of the answers we calculated from the word problems in Learning Units 8.1 and 8.2. The word problems in the units were the same except in Learning Unit 8.1, we assumed markups were on cost, while in Learning Unit 8.2, markups were on selling price. Note that in Situation 1, the dollar markup is the same $90, but the percent markup is different.

Let's now look at how to convert from percent markup on cost to percent markup on selling price and vice versa. We will use Situation 1 from Table 8.1.

Formula for Converting Percent Markup on Selling Price to Percent Markup on Cost

To convert percent markup on selling price to percent markup on cost:

$$\frac{.30}{1 - .30} = \frac{.30}{.70} = \boxed{42.86\%}$$

$$\frac{\text{Percent markup on selling price}}{1 - \text{Percent markup on selling price}}$$

Formula for Converting Percent Markup on Cost to Percent Markup on Selling Price

To convert percent markup on cost to percent markup on selling price:

$$\frac{.4286}{1 + .4286} = \boxed{30\%}$$

$$\frac{\text{Percent markup on cost}}{1 + \text{Percent markup on cost}}$$

Key point: A 30% markup on selling price or a 42.86% markup on cost results in same dollar markup of $90.

Table 8.2 summarizes the calculations of these two formulas. As stated in the table, the rate of markup on selling price is always *lower* than the rate of markup on cost. Before you go on to the topic of markdowns and perishables, check your progress with the following Practice Quiz.

TABLE 8.1

Comparison of markup on cost versus markup on selling price

Markup based on cost— Learning Unit 8.1	Markup based on selling price— Learning Unit 8.2
Situation 1: Calculating dollar amount of markup and percent markup on cost. Snowthrower cost, $210. Snowthrower selling price, $300. $M = S - C$ $M = \$300 - \$210 = \boxed{\$90}$ markup (p. 198) $M \div C = \$90 \div \$210 = \boxed{42.86\%}$	*Situation 1: Calculating dollar amount of markup and percent markup on selling price.* Snowthrower cost, $210. Snowthrower selling price, $300. $M = S - C$ $M = \$300 - \$210 = \boxed{\$90}$ markup (p. 202) $M \div S = \$90 \div \$300 = \boxed{30\%}$
Situation 2: Calculating selling price on cost. Lamp cost, $100. 65% markup on cost $S = C \times (1 + \text{Percent markup on cost})$ $S = \$100 \times 1.65 = \boxed{\$165}$ (p. 199) $(100\% + 65\% = 165\% = 1.65)$	*Situation 2: Calculating selling price on selling price.* Lamp cost, $100. 65% markup on selling price $S = C \div (1 - \text{Percent markup on selling price})$ $S = \$100.00 \div .35$ $(100\% - 65\% = 35\% = .35)$ $S = \boxed{\$285.71}$ (p. 203)
Situation 3: Calculating cost on cost. Tennis racket selling price, $50. 40% markup on cost $C = S \div (1 + \text{Percent markup on cost})$ $C = \$50.00 \div 1.40$ $(100\% + 40\% = 140\% = 1.40)$ $C = \boxed{\$35.71}$ (p. 199)	*Situation 3: Calculating cost on selling price.* Tennis racket selling price, $50. 40% markup on selling price $C = S \times (1 - \text{Percent markup on selling price})$ $C = \$50 \times .60 = \boxed{\$30}$ (p. 203) $(100\% - 40\% = 60\% = .60)$

TABLE 8.2
Equivalent markup

Percent markup on selling price	Percent markup on cost (round to nearest tenth percent)
20	25.0
25	33.3
30	42.9
33	49.3
35	53.8
40	66.7
50	100.0

Note: Rate of markup on selling price is always lower than on cost because the cost base is always lower than the selling price base.

LU 8.2 PRACTICE QUIZ

Solve the following situations (markups based on selling price). Note numbers 1, 2, and 3 are parallel problems to those in Practice Quiz 8.1.

1. Irene Westing bought a desk for $400 from an office supply house. She plans to sell the desk for $600. What is Irene's dollar markup? What is her percent markup on selling price (round to the nearest tenth percent)? Check your answer. Selling price will be slightly off due to rounding.

2. Suki Komar bought dolls for her toy store that cost $12 each. To make her desired profit, Suki must mark up each doll 35% on the selling price. What is the selling price of each doll? What is the dollar markup? Check your answer.

3. Jay Lyman sells calculators. His competitor sells a new calculator line for $14 each. Jay needs a 40% markup on the selling price to make his desired profit, and he must meet price competition. What is Jay's dollar markup? At what cost can Jay afford to bring these calculators into the store? Check your answer.

4. Dan Flow sells wrenches for $10 that cost $6. What is Dan's percent markup at cost? Round to the nearest tenth percent. What is Dan's percent markup on selling price? Check your answer.

✓ **Solutions**

1. Irene's dollar markup and percent markup on selling price:

The facts	Solving for?			Steps to take	Key points
Desk cost: $400. Desk selling price: $600.		%	$	$\text{Dollar markup} = \dfrac{\text{Selling price}}{} - \text{Cost.}$ $\text{Percent markup on selling price} = \dfrac{\text{Dollar markup}}{\text{Selling price}}$	Markup / Portion ($200) / Base × Rate ($600) (?) / Selling price
	C	66.7%	$400		
	+ M	33.3²	200¹		
	= S	100%	$600		
	¹Dollar markup. ²Percent markup on selling price.				

Steps to solving problem

1. Calculate the dollar markup.

$$\text{Dollar markup} = \text{Selling price} - \text{Cost}$$
$$\boxed{\$200} = \$600 - \$400$$

2. Calculate the percent markup on selling price.

$$\dfrac{\text{Percent markup}}{\text{on selling price}} = \dfrac{\text{Dollar markup}}{\text{Selling price}}$$
$$= \dfrac{\$200}{\$600} = \boxed{33.3\%}$$

Check

Selling price = Cost + Markup   **or**
$600   = $400 + .333($600)
$600   = $400 + $199.80
$600   = $599.80*
*Off due to rounding.

$$\text{Selling price } (B) = \dfrac{\text{Dollar markup } (P)}{\text{Percent markup on selling price } (R)}$$
$$= \dfrac{\$200}{.333} = \$600.60*$$
(not exactly $600 due to rounding)

2. Selling price of doll and dollar markup:

The facts	Solving for?			Steps to take	Key points
Doll cost: $12 each. *Markup on selling price:* $35%.		%	$	$S = C + M.$ or $$S = \dfrac{\text{Cost}}{1 - \dfrac{\text{Percent markup}}{\text{on selling price}}}$$	Cost / Portion ($12) / Base × Rate (?) (.65) / Selling price / 100% −35%
	C	65%	$12.00		
	$+M$	35	6.46[2]		
	$=S$	100%	$18.46[1]		
	[1]Selling price. [2]Dollar markup.				

Steps to solving problem

1. Calculate the selling price.

$$S = C + M$$
$$S = \$12.00 + .35S$$
$$-.35S \qquad\qquad -.35S$$
$$\dfrac{.65S}{.65} = \dfrac{\$12.00}{.65}$$
$$S = \boxed{\$18.46}$$

2. Calculate the dollar markup.

$$M = S - C$$
$$\boxed{\$6.46} = \$18.46 - \$12.00$$

Check

$$\text{Selling price } (B) = \dfrac{\text{Cost } (P)}{1 - \text{Percent markup on selling price } (R)} = \dfrac{\$12.00}{.65} = \boxed{\$18.46}$$

3. Dollar markup and cost:

The facts	Solving for?			Steps to take	Key points
Selling price: $14. *Markup on selling price:* 40%.		%	$	$S = C + M.$ or $\text{Cost} = \text{Selling price} \times$ $\left(1 - \dfrac{\text{Percent markup}}{\text{on selling price}}\right)$	Cost / Portion (?) / Base × Rate ($14) (.60) / Selling price / 100% −40%
	C	60%	$ 8.40[2]		
	$+M$	40	5.60[1]		
	$=S$	100%	$14.00		
	[1]Dollar markup. [2]Cost.				

Steps to solving problem

1. Calculate the dollar markup.

$$S = C + M$$
$$\$14.00 = C + .40(\$14.00)$$

2. Calculate the cost.

$$\$14.00 = C + \boxed{\$5.60} \leftarrow \text{Dollar markup}$$
$$\underline{-5.60} \qquad\qquad \underline{-5.60}$$
$$\boxed{\$ 8.40} = C$$

Check

$$\text{Cost} = \text{Selling price} \times (1 - \text{Percent markup on selling price}) = \$14.00 \times .60 = \boxed{\$8.40}$$
$$\ (P) \qquad\quad (B) \qquad\qquad\qquad\qquad (R)$$
$$(1.00 - .40)$$

4. $\text{Cost} = \dfrac{\$4}{\$6} = \boxed{66.7\%}$ $\dfrac{.40}{1 - .40} = \dfrac{.40}{.60} = \dfrac{2}{3} = 66.7\%$

       $\text{Selling price} = \dfrac{\$4}{\$10} = \boxed{40\%}$ $\dfrac{.667}{1 + .667} = \dfrac{.667}{1.667} = 40\% \text{ (due to rounding)}$

LEARNING UNIT 8.3   Markdowns and Perishables

Foreign Aisles

The Wal-Mart Way Sometimes Gets Lost In Translation Overseas

Chain Changes Some Tactics To Meet Local Tastes; Competitors Are Tough

But Brazil's 'Market Is Ripe'

By JONATHAN FRIEDLAND and LOUISE LEE
Staff Reporters of THE WALL STREET JOURNAL
SAO BERNARDO, Brazil — Wal-Mart Stores Inc. is finding out that what plays in

Peoria isn't necessarily a hit in suburban Sao Paulo.

Tanks of live trout are out; sushi is in. American footballs have been replaced by soccer balls. The fixings for *feijoada*, a medley of beef and pork in black-bean stew, are now displayed on the deli counter. American-style jeans priced at $19.99 have been dropped in favor of $9.99 knockoffs.

But adapting to local tastes may have been the easy part. Three years after embarking on a blitz to bring "everyday low prices" to the emerging markets of Brazil and Argentina, Wal-Mart is finding the going tougher than expected.

Brutal competition, market conditions that don't play to Wal-Mart's ability to achieve efficiency through economies of scale and some of its own mistakes have produced red ink. Moreover, the company's insistence on doing things "the Wal-Mart way" has apparently alienated local suppliers and employees.

© 1997 Dow Jones & Company, Inc.

The Wall Street Journal clipping "The Wal-Mart Way Sometimes Gets Lost in Translation Overseas" reports that Wal-Mart is finding that the markets of Brazil and Argentina are tougher than expected. The company has experienced "red ink" as a result of brutal competition, market conditions, and some of Wal-Mart's own mistakes; and the "Wal-Mart way" has alienated local suppliers and employees. Wal-Mart must rethink its strategy, which may involve markdowns or the deletion of some products it is now selling. Evidently, what sells well in the United States doesn't guarantee success in foreign markets.

In a few moments, we'll look at how businesses price perishable items that may spoil before customers buy them. First, let's focus our attention on how to calculate markdowns.

Markdowns

Dollar markdown
Portion ($7.20)
Base ($18) × Rate (?)
Original selling price

Markdowns are reductions from the original selling price caused by seasonal changes, special promotions, style changes, and so on. We calculate the markdown percent as follows:

$$\text{Markdown percent} = \frac{\text{Dollar markdown}}{\text{Selling price (original)}}$$

Kmart has suffered from some colossal buying mistakes. Last year, the beleaguered retailer had to liquidate $700 million in merchandise that wouldn't sell. The heavy markdowns taken by Kmart contributed to the multimillion-dollar losses it reported for the third and fourth quarters.

© 1996 Dow Jones & Company, Inc.

Let's look at the following Kmart clipping and an example using Kmart:

EXAMPLE   Kmart marked down an $18 video to $10.80. What are the **dollar markdown** and the markdown percent?

$18.00   Original selling price   → $\dfrac{\text{Dollar markdown, } \$7.20}{\text{Selling price (original), } \$18.00} = \boxed{40\%}$

− 10.80   Sale price

$ 7.20   Markdown

Calculating a Series of Markdowns and Markups

Often the final selling price is the result of a series of markdowns (and possibly a markup in between markdowns). We calculate additional markdowns on the previous selling price. Note in the following example how we calculate markdown on selling price after we add a markup.

EXAMPLE   Jones Department Store paid its supplier $400 for a TV. On January 10, Jones marked the TV up 60% on selling price. As a special promotion, Jones marked the TV down 30% on February 8 and another 20% on February 28. No one purchased the TV, so Jones marked it up 10% on March 11. What was the selling price of the TV on March 11?

January 10: Selling price = Cost + Markup

$$S = \$400 + .60S$$
$$-.60S \qquad\qquad -.60S$$
$$\dfrac{.40S}{.40} = \dfrac{\$400}{.40}$$
$$S = \$1,000$$

Check $S = \dfrac{\text{Cost}}{1 - \text{Percent markup on selling price}}$

$$S = \dfrac{\$400}{1 - .60} = \dfrac{\$400}{.40} = \$1,000$$

February 8 markdown:

    100%
   − 30%
     70% → .70 × $1,000 = $700 selling price

February 28 additional markdown:

    100%
   − 20%
     80% → .80 × $700 = $560

March 11 additional markup:

    100%
   + 10%
   110% → 1.10 × $560 = $616

Pricing Perishable Items

Let's see how companies determine the price of goods that have a short shelf life such as fruit, flowers, and pastry. (We limit this discussion to obviously **perishable** items.)

The Word Problem   Audrey's Bake Shop baked 20 dozen bagels. Audrey expects 10% of the bagels to become stale and not salable. The bagels cost Audrey $1.20 per dozen. Audrey wants a 60% markup on cost. What should Audrey charge for each dozen bagels so she will make her profit? Round to the nearest cent.

The facts	Solving for?	Steps to take	Key points
Bagels cost: $1.20 per dozen. *Not salable:* 10%. *Baked:* 20 dozen. *Markup on cost:* 60%.	Price of a dozen bagels.	Total cost. Total dollar markup. Total selling price. Bagel loss. $TS = TC + TM$.	Markup is based on cost.

Steps to solving problem

1. Calculate the total cost.
2. Calculate the total dollar markup.

$TC = 20 \text{ dozen} \times \$1.20 = \$24.00$

$$\boxed{TS = TC + TM}$$

$TS = \$24.00 + .60(\$24.00)$

$TS = \$24.00 + \$14.40 \longleftarrow$ Total dollar markup

3. Calculate the total selling price.

4. Calculate the bagel loss.

5. Calculate the selling price for a dozen bagels.

$TS = \$38.40$ ←——Total selling price

20 dozen × .10 = 2 dozen

$\dfrac{\$38.40}{18} =$ $\$2.13$ per dozen $\quad \begin{array}{r} 20 \\ -2 \end{array}$

It's time to try the Practice Quiz.

LU 8.3 PRACTICE QUIZ

1. Sunshine Music Shop bought a stereo for $600 and marked it up 40% on selling price. To promote customer interest, Sunshine marked the stereo down 10% for one week. Since business was slow, Sunshine marked the stereo down an additional 5%. After a week, Sunshine marked the stereo up 2%. What is the new selling price of the stereo to the nearest cent? What is the markdown percent based on the original selling price to the nearest hundredth percent?

2. Alvin Rose owns a fruit and vegetable stand. He knows that he cannot sell all his produce at full price. Some of his produce will be markdowns, and he will throw out some produce. Alvin must put a high enough price on the produce to cover markdowns and rotted produce and still make his desired profit. Alvin bought 300 pounds of tomatoes at 14 cents per pound. He expects a 5% spoilage and marks up tomatoes 60% on cost. What price per pound should Alvin charge for the tomatoes?

✓ **Solutions**

1.

$S = C + M$

$S = \$600 + .40S$

$-.40S \qquad -.40S$

$\dfrac{.60S}{.60} = \dfrac{\$600}{.60}$

$S = \$1,000$

Check

$S = \dfrac{\text{Cost}}{1 - \text{Percent markup on selling price}}$

$S = \dfrac{\$600}{1 - .40} = \dfrac{\$600}{.60} = \$1,000$

First markdown: $.90 \times \$1,000 = \$900$ selling price

Second markdown: $.95 \times \$900 = \$855$ selling price

Markup: $1.02 \times \$855 = $ $\$872.10$ final selling price

$\$1,000 - \$872.10 = \dfrac{\$127.90}{\$1,000} = $ 12.79%

2. Price of tomatoes per pound:

The facts	Solving for?	Steps to take	Key points
300 lb. tomatoes at $.14 per pound. *Spoilage:* 5%. *Markup on cost:* 60%.	Price of tomatoes per pound.	Total cost. Total dollar markup. Total selling price. Spoilage amount. *TS* = *TC* + *TM*.	Markup is based on cost.

Steps to solving problem

1. Calculate the total cost.

2. Calculate the total dollar markup.

3. Calculate the total selling price.

4. Calculate the tomato loss.

5. Calculate the selling price per pound of tomatoes.

$TC = 300 \text{ lb.} \times \$.14 = \$42.00$

$TS = TC + TM$
$TS = \$42.00 + .60(\$42.00)$
$TS = \$42.00 + \$25.20$ ←——Total dollar markup
$TS = \$67.20$ ←——Total selling price

300 pounds × .05 = 15 pounds spoilage

$\dfrac{\$67.20}{285} = $ $\$.24$ per pound (rounded to nearest hundredth)

(300 − 15)

Chapter Organizer and Reference Guide

Topic	Key point, procedure, formula	Example(s) to illustrate situation
Markups based on cost: cost is 100% (base), p. 197	Selling price (S) = Cost (C) + Markup (M)	$\$400 = \$300 + \$100$ $S = C + M$
Percent markup on cost, p. 197 Cost, p. 198	$\dfrac{\text{Dollar markup (portion)}}{\text{Cost (base)}} = \begin{array}{l}\text{Percent markup}\\ \text{on cost (rate)}\end{array}$ $C = \dfrac{\text{Dollar markup}}{\text{Percent markup on cost}}$	$\dfrac{\$100}{\$300} = \dfrac{1}{3} = 33\frac{1}{3}\%$ $\dfrac{\$100}{.33} = \$303$ Off slightly due to rounding
Calculating selling price, p. 199	$S = C + M$ **Check** $S = \text{Cost} \times (1 + \text{Percent markup on cost})$	Cost, \$6; percent markup on cost, 20% $S = \$6 + .20(\$6)$ **Check** $S = \$6 + \$1.20$ $\downarrow$ $S = \$7.20$ $\boxed{\$6 \times 1.20 = \$7.20}$
Calculating cost, p. 199	$S = C + M$ **Check** $\text{Cost} = \dfrac{\text{Selling price}}{1 + \text{Percent markup on cost}}$	$S = \$100;\ M = 70\%$ of cost $\quad S = C + M$ $\$100 = C + .70C$ $\$100 = 1.7C$ *(Remember, C = 1.00C)* $\dfrac{\$100}{1.7} = C$ **Check** $\qquad\qquad\qquad\quad \downarrow$ $\boxed{\$58.82} = C$ $\boxed{\dfrac{\$100}{1 + .70} = \$58.82}$
Markups based on selling price: selling price is 100% (base), p. 201	Dollar markup = Selling price − Cost	$M = S - C$ $\$600 = \$1{,}000 - \$400$
Percent markup on selling price, p. 202 Selling price, p. 202	$\dfrac{\text{Dollar markup (portion)}}{\text{Selling price (base)}} = \begin{array}{l}\text{Percent markup on}\\ \text{selling price (rate)}\end{array}$ $S = \dfrac{\text{Dollar markup}}{\text{Percent markup on selling price}}$	$\dfrac{\$600}{\$1{,}000} = 60\%$ $\dfrac{\$600}{.60} = \$1{,}000$
Calculating selling price, p. 203	$S = C + M$ **Check** $\text{Selling price} = \dfrac{\text{Cost}}{1 - \text{Percent markup on selling price}}$	Cost, \$400; percent markup on S, 60% $S = C + M$ $S = \$400 + .60S$ $S - .60S = \$400 + .60S - .60S$ $\dfrac{.40S}{.40} = \dfrac{\$400}{.40}$ $S = \$1{,}000$ **Check** $\longrightarrow$ $\boxed{\dfrac{\$400}{1 - .60} = \dfrac{\$400}{.40} = \$1{,}000}$
Calculating cost, p. 203	$S = C + M$ **Check** $\text{Cost} = \text{Selling price} \times \left(1 - \begin{array}{l}\text{Percent markup}\\ \text{on selling price}\end{array}\right)$	$\$1{,}000 = C + 60\%(\$1{,}000)$ $\$1{,}000 = C + \$600$ $\$400 = C$ **Check** $\longrightarrow$ $\boxed{\begin{array}{l}\$1{,}000 \times (1 - .60)\\ \$1{,}000 \times .40 = \$400\end{array}}$
Conversion of markup percent, p. 204	$\begin{array}{l}\text{Percent markup}\\ \text{on selling price}\end{array}$ to $\begin{array}{l}\text{Percent markup}\\ \text{on cost}\end{array}$ $\boxed{\dfrac{\text{Percent markup on selling price}}{1 - \text{Percent markup on selling price}}}$ $\begin{array}{l}\text{Percent markup}\\ \text{on cost}\end{array}$ to $\begin{array}{l}\text{Percent markup}\\ \text{on selling price}\end{array}$ $\boxed{\dfrac{\text{Percent markup on cost}}{1 + \text{Percent markup on cost}}}$	*Round to nearest percent:* 35% markup on selling price $\longrightarrow$ 54% markup on cost $\dfrac{.35}{1 - .35} = \dfrac{.35}{.65} = 54\%$ 54% markup on cost $\longrightarrow$ 35% markup on selling price $\dfrac{.54}{1 + .54} = \dfrac{.54}{1.54} = 35\%$

Topic	Key point, procedure, formula	Example(s) to illustrate situation
Markdowns, p. 207	$\text{Markdown percent} = \dfrac{\text{Dollar markdown}}{\text{Selling price (original)}}$	$40 selling price 10% markdown $40 \times .10 = \$4$ markdown $\dfrac{\$4}{\$40} = $ 10%

Pricing perishables, p. 208	1. Calculate total cost and total selling price.
	2. Calculate selling price per unit by dividing total sales in Step 1 by units expected to be sold after taking perishables into account.
		50 pastries cost 20 cents each; 10 will spoil before being sold. Markup is 60% on cost.
		1. $TC = 50 \times \$.20 = \$10$
		   $TS = TC + TM$
		   $TS = \$10 + .60(\$10)$
		   $TS = \$10 + \$6$
		   $TS = $ $16
		2. $\dfrac{\$16}{40 \text{ pastries}} = $ \$.40 per pastry

Key terms	Cost, *p. 196* Dollar markdown, *p. 207* Dollar markup, *p. 196* Gross profit, *p. 196* Margin, *p. 196*	Markdowns, *p. 207* Markup, *p. 196* Net profit (net income), *p. 196* Operating expenses, *p. 196* Percent markup on cost, *p. 197* Percent markup on selling price, *p. 201* Perishables, *p. 208* Selling price, *p. 196*

Chapter Organizer and Reference Guide (concluded)

Critical Thinking Discussion Questions

1. Assuming markups are based on cost, explain how the portion formula could be used to calculate cost, selling price, dollar markup, and percent markup on cost. Pick a company and explain why it would mark goods up on cost rather than on selling price.

2. Assuming markups are based on selling price, explain how the portion formula could be used to calculate cost, selling price, dollar markup, and percent markup on selling price. Pick a company and explain why it would mark up goods on selling price rather than on cost.

3. What is the formula to convert percent markup on selling price to percent markup on cost? How could you explain that a 40% markup on selling price, which is a 66.7% markup on cost, would result in the same dollar markup?

4. Explain how to calculate markdowns. Do you think stores should run one-day-only markdown sales? Would it be better to offer the best price "all the time"?

5. Explain the five steps in calculating a selling price for perishable items. Recall a situation where you saw a store that did *not* follow the five steps. How did it sell its items?

DRILL PROBLEMS

Assume markups in Problems 8–1 to 8–6 are based on cost. Find the dollar markup and selling price for the following problems. Round answers to the nearest cent.

Item	Cost	Markup percent	Dollar markup	Selling price
8–1. Nike sneakers	$90	30%	$27	$117

$S = C + M$
$S = \$90 + .30(\$90)$ **Check** $S = \text{Cost} \times (1 + \text{Percent markup on cost})$
$S = \$90 + \$27$
$S = \$117$ $\$117 = \$90 \times 1.30$

Item	Cost	Markup percent	Dollar markup	Selling price
8–2. Lionel train set	$189	70%	$132.30	$321.30

$S = \$189 + .70(\$189)$
$S = \$189 + \$132.30$ **Check** $\$321.30 = \$189 \times 1.70$
$S = \$321.30$

Solve for cost (round to the nearest cent):

8–3. Selling price of office furniture at Staples, $6,000 $\$6,000 = C + .40C$

Percent markup on cost, 40%

Actual cost? $\dfrac{\$6,000}{1.40} = \dfrac{\cancel{1.40}C}{\cancel{1.40}}$

Check $\dfrac{\$6,000}{1.40} = \$4,285.71$ $\$4,285.71 = C$ $C = \dfrac{\text{Selling price}}{1 + \text{Percent markup on cost}}$

8–4. Selling price of lumber at Home Depot, $4,000 $\$4,000 = C + .30C$

Percent markup on cost, 30%

Actual cost? $\dfrac{\$4,000}{1.30} = \dfrac{\cancel{1.30}C}{\cancel{1.30}}$

$\$3,076.92 = C$

Check $\dfrac{\$4,000}{1.30} = \$3,076.92$

Complete the following:

Cost	Selling price	Dollar markup	Percent markup on cost*
8–5. $15.10	$22.00	? $6.90	? 45.70% $\left(\dfrac{\$6.90}{\$15.10}\right)$
8–6. ? $4.60	$ 9.30	$4.70	102.17% $C = \dfrac{\$4.70}{1.0217}$

*Round to the nearest hundredth percent.

Assume markups in Problems 8–7 to 8–12 are based on selling price.
Find the dollar markup and cost (round answers to the nearest cent):

Item	Selling price	Markup percent	Dollar markup	Cost
8–7. GE refrigerator	$595	40%	$238	$357

$\$595 = C + .40(\$595)$
$\$595 = C + \$238$ **Check** $\$357 = \$595 \times .60$
$\dfrac{- 238 \quad\quad -238}{\$357 = C}$ $C = \text{Selling price} \times (1 - \text{Percent markup on selling price})$

Item	Selling price	Markup percent	Dollar markup	Cost
8–8. Timex watch	$ 80	30%	$24	$56

$\$80 = C + .30(\$80)$ **Check**
$\$80 = C + \$24$ ←— *Note:* Markup is on $\$56 = \$80 \times .70$
$\dfrac{-\ 24 \quad\quad -24}{\$56 = C}$ selling price, not cost. $C = \text{Selling price} \times (1 - \text{Percent markup on selling price})$

Solve for the selling price (round to the nearest cent):

8–9. Selling price of a complete set of pots and pans at Wal-Mart?
40% markup on selling price
Cost, actual, $66.50

$$S = \$66.50 + .40S$$
$$-.40S \qquad\qquad -.40S$$
$$\frac{.60S}{.60} = \frac{\$66.50}{.60}$$
$$S = \$110.83$$

Check $\dfrac{\$66.50}{.60} = \$110.83$

$$S = \frac{\text{Cost}}{1 - \text{Percent markup on selling price}}$$

8–10. Selling price of a dining room set at Sears?
55% markup on selling price
Cost, actual, $800

$$S = \$800 + .55S$$
$$-.55S = \qquad -.55S$$
$$\frac{.45S}{.45} = \frac{\$800}{.45}$$

Check
$\dfrac{\$800}{.45} = \$1,777.78$

$$S = \$1,777.78$$

Complete the following:

Cost	Selling price	Dollar markup	Percent markup on selling price (round to nearest tenth percent)	
8–11. $14.80	$49.00	? $34.20	? 69.8%	$\left(\dfrac{\$34.20}{\$49.00}\right)$
8–12. $16	? $20	$4	20%	$S = \dfrac{\$4}{.20}$

By conversion of the markup formula, solve the following (round to the nearest whole percent as needed):

Percent markup on cost	**Percent markup on selling price**
8–13. 12.4%	? $11\% \quad \dfrac{.124}{1 + .124}$
8–14. ? $15\% \quad \dfrac{.13}{1 - .13}$	13%

Complete the following:

8–15. Calculate the final selling price to the nearest cent and markdown percent to the nearest hundredth percent:

Original selling price	First markdown	Second markdown	Markup	Final markdown
$5,000	20%	10%	12%	5%

$5,000 × .80 = $4,000.00
$4,000 × .90 = $3,600.00
$3,600 × 1.12 = $4,032.00
$4,032 × .95 = $3,830.40

$$\begin{array}{r} \$5,000.00 \\ -\ 3,830.40 \\ \hline \$1,169.60 \end{array}$$

$$\frac{\$1,169.60}{\$5,000.00} = 23.39\%$$

Item	Total quantity bought	Unit cost	Total cost	Percent markup on cost	Total selling price	Percent that will spoil	Selling price per brownie
8–16. Brownies	20	$.79	? $15.80	60%	? $25.28	10%	? $1.40

Total cost = 20 × $.79 = $15.80
Total selling price = $TC + TM$
$$TS = \$15.80 + .60(\$15.80)$$
$$TS = \$15.80 + \$9.48$$
$$TS = \$25.28$$

$$\frac{\$25.28}{18} = \$1.40 \text{ per brownie}$$

$(20 - 2)$

WORD PROBLEMS

8–17. At a toy convention, Kyle Hoyt bought an old Mickey Mouse poster for $700. He plans to resell it for $1,200. What are the dollar markup and the percent markup on cost (to the nearest tenth percent)? Check the cost figure.

Dollar markup $= S - C$ Percent markup on cost $= \dfrac{\$500}{\$700} = 71.4\%$
$\quad$ $\$500$ $\qquad = \$1,200 - \$700$

Check $\quad C = \dfrac{\text{Dollar markup}}{\text{Percent markup on cost}} = \dfrac{\$500}{.714} = \$700.28$ (due to rounding)

8–18. Harvey Drew, store manager for Drake Appliance, does not know how to price a refrigerator that cost $800. Harvey knows his boss wants a 38% markup on cost. Help Harvey price the refrigerator.

Note: The markup of
38% is based on cost, $S = \$800 + .38(\$800)$ **Check**
not selling price. $S = \$800 + \$304$ $S = \text{Cost} \times (1 + \text{Percent markup on cost})$
$\qquad\qquad\qquad\qquad$ $S = \$1,104$ $\$1,104 = \$800 \times 1.38$

8–19. Cecil Green sells golf hats. He knows that most people will not pay more than $20 for a golf hat. Cecil needs a 40% markup on cost. What should Cecil pay for his golf hats? Round to the nearest cent.

Note: The markup of
40% is based on cost, $\$20 = C + .40C$ **Check**
not selling price. $\dfrac{\$20}{1.40} = \dfrac{1.40C}{1.40}$ $\text{Cost} = \dfrac{\text{Selling price}}{1 + \text{Percent markup on cost}}$
$\qquad\qquad\qquad\qquad$ $\$14.29 = C$
$\qquad\qquad\qquad\qquad\qquad\qquad\qquad\qquad$ $\$14.29 = \dfrac{\$20}{1.40}$

8–20. *Kiplinger's 1998 Carbuyer's Guide* states that a 1998 Acura 2.3CL two-door sells for $22,545 with a 10.9% markup on selling price. What is the cost to the dealer? Round to the nearest dollar.

$\qquad\qquad$ $S = C + .109(\$22,545)$ **Check**
$\$22,545.00 = C + \$2,457.41$ $C = \text{Selling price} \times (1 - \text{Percent markup on selling})$
$\underline{\;-\;2,457.41 \qquad\quad -\;2,457.41\;}$ $C = \$22,545 \times (1 - .109)$
$\$20,087.59 = C$ $C = \$20,087.595 = \$20,088$
$\qquad\qquad = \$20,088$

8–21. *Kiplinger's 1998 Carbuyer's Guide* states that a 1998 BMW 740iL four-door costs the dealer $57,915. The dealer has a 12.3% markup on selling price. What is the selling price of the vehicle? Round to the nearest dollar. *Note:* Markup is on selling price, not cost.

$\qquad$ $S = \$57,915 + .123S$ $S = \$66,037.628$
$\underline{-\;.123S \qquad\qquad -\;.123S\;}$ $S = \$66,038$
$\qquad\qquad\qquad\qquad\qquad\qquad$ **Check**
$\dfrac{.877S}{.877} = \dfrac{\$57,915}{.877}$ $S = \dfrac{\text{Cost}}{1 - \text{Percent markup on selling price}} = \$66,038 = \dfrac{\$57,915}{.877}$

8–22. *Kiplinger's 1998 Carbuyer's Guide* states that a 1998 Chevrolet Cavalier two-door costs the dealer $11,355, and he plans to sell the vehicle for $12,110. What is the percent markup based on selling price? Round to the nearest tenth percent. Check the selling price (will be off due to rounding).

Dollar markup $=\quad S \quad - \quad C$ Percent markup on selling price:
$\qquad$ $\$755 \qquad = \$12,110 - \$11,355$ $\dfrac{\$755}{\$12,110} = 6.2345169\% = 6.2\%$

$\qquad\qquad\qquad\qquad\qquad\qquad\qquad$ **Check**
$\qquad\qquad$ Dollar markup $\longrightarrow \dfrac{\$755}{} $
$\dfrac{}{\text{Percent markup on selling price} \longrightarrow .062} = \$12,177$ (off due to rounding)

8–23. Misu Sheet, owner of the Bedspread Shop, knows his customers will pay no more than $120 for a comforter. Misu wants a 30% markup on selling price. What is the most that Misu can pay for a comforter?

Note: The markup is
on the selling price, $\$120 = C + .30(\$120)$ **Check**
not cost. $\$120 = C + \$36$ $C = \text{Selling price} \times (1 - \text{Percent markup on selling price})$
$\qquad\qquad\qquad\qquad$ $\underline{-\;36 \qquad\quad -\;36\;}$
$\qquad\qquad\qquad\qquad$ $\$\,84 = C$ $\$84 = \$120 \times .70$

8–24. Assume Misu Sheet (Problem 8–23) wants a 30% markup on cost instead of on selling price. What is Misu's cost? Round to the nearest cent.

Note: The markup is on the cost, not the selling price.

$$\$120 = C + .30C$$
$$\frac{\$120}{1.3} = \frac{1.3C}{1.3}$$
$$\$92.31 = C$$

Check

$$C = \frac{\text{Selling price}}{1 + \text{Percent markup on cost}}$$
$$\$92.31 = \frac{\$120}{1.30}$$

8–25. Misu Sheet (Problem 8–23) wants to advertise the comforter as "percent markup on cost." What is the equivalent rate of percent markup on cost compared to the 30% markup on selling price? Check your answer. Is this a wise marketing decision? Round to the nearest hundredth percent.

$$\frac{.30}{1 - .30} = \frac{.30}{.70} = 42.86\%$$

Check $$\frac{.4286}{1 + .4286} = \frac{.4286}{1.4286} = 30\%$$

No, customers will see 42.86% instead of 30%. They will think markup is higher, although dollar markup of $36 is the same.

8–26. DeWitt Company sells a kitchen set for $475. To promote July 4, DeWitt ran the following advertisement:

> Beginning each hour up to 4 hours we will mark down the kitchen set 10%. At the end of each hour, we will mark up the set 1%.

Assume Ingrid Swenson buys the set 1 hour 50 minutes into the sale. What will Ingrid pay? Round each calculation to the nearest cent. What is the markdown percent? Round to the nearest hundredth percent.

$475.00 × .90 = $427.50 beginning of hour 1
$427.50 × 1.01 = $431.78 end of hour 1
$431.78 × .90 = $388.60 beginning of hour 2

$$\begin{array}{r} \$475.00 \\ -\ 388.60 \\ \hline \$\ 86.40 \end{array}$$

$$\frac{\$86.40}{\$475.00} = 18.19\%$$

8–27. Angie's Bake Shop makes birthday chocolate chip cookies that cost $2 each. Angie expects that 10% of the cookies will crack and be discarded. Angie wants a 60% markup on cost and produces 100 cookies. What should Angie price each cookie? Round to the nearest cent.

Total cost = 100 × $2.00 = $200
Total selling price = TC + TM
$$TS = \$200 + .60(\$200)$$
$$TS = \$200 + \$120$$
$$TS = \$320$$

Selling price per cookie = $$\frac{\$320}{90 \text{ cookies}} = \$3.56$$

8–28. Assume that Angie (Problem 8–27) can sell the cracked cookies for $1.10 each. What should Angie price each cookie?

$$\frac{\$320 - (10 \text{ cookies} \times \$1.10)}{90 \text{ cookies}} = \frac{\$320 - \$11}{90} = \frac{\$309}{90} = \$3.43$$

The 90 cookies are sold for $320 less what is received from cracked cookies.

ADDITIONAL SET OF WORD PROBLEMS

8–29. Service Merchandise bought a treadmill for $395. Service Merchandise has a 70% markup on selling price. What is the selling price of the treadmill? Round to the nearest cent.

Note: Markup is on selling price, not cost.

$$S = \$395 + .70S$$
$$\underline{-\ .70S \qquad\qquad -\ .70S}$$
$$\frac{.30S}{.30} = \frac{\$395}{.30}$$
$$S = \$1,316.67$$

Check $$S = \frac{\text{Cost}}{1 - \text{Percent markup on selling price}}$$
$$\$1,316.67 = \frac{\$395}{.30}$$

8–30. Sachi Wong, store manager for Hawk Appliance, does not know how to price a refrigerator that cost $399. Sachi knows her boss wants a 40% markup on cost. Can you help Sachi price the refrigerator?

Note: Markup is on cost, not selling price.

$$S = \$399 + .40(\$399)$$
$$S = \$399 + \$159.60$$
$$S = \$558.60$$

Check

$$S = \text{Cost} \times (1 + \text{Percent markup on cost})$$
$$\$558.60 = \$399 \times 1.40$$

8–31. On November 30, 1997, the *Chicago Tribune* reported that a few weeks ago, an Evanston travel agency sold a $51 Amtrak ticket and charged an additional fee of $12. How much of a percent markup is $12, based on the travel agency's original selling price? Round to the nearest hundredth percent. Check the cost figure (rounded to the nearest dollar).

$$\text{Dollar markup} \longrightarrow \frac{\$12}{\$51} = 23.52941\% = 23.53\% \qquad \text{Cost} = \frac{\text{Dollar markup}}{\text{Percent markup on cost}} = \frac{\$12}{.2353} = \$51$$
$$\text{Original selling price} \longrightarrow$$

8–32. Heather Jenkins, owner of Jenkins Bed Shop, knows her customers will pay no more than $250 for a bedspread. Heather wants a 40% markup on selling price. What is the most that Heather can pay for a bedspread?

Note: Markup is on selling price, not cost.

$$\$250 = C + .40(\$250)$$
$$\$250 = C + \$100$$
$$\underline{-\ 100} \qquad \underline{-\ 100}$$
$$\$150 = C$$

Check

$$C = \text{Selling price} \times \left(1 - \begin{array}{c}\text{Percent markup} \\ \text{on selling price}\end{array}\right)$$

$$\$150 = \$250 \times .60$$

8–33. Salvador Spring sells mittens. He knows the most that people will pay for a pair of mittens is $29.95. Salvador needs a 35% markup on cost. What is the most that Salvador can pay for a pair of mittens? Round to the nearest cent.

Note: Markup is on cost, not selling price.

$$\$29.95 = C + .35C$$
$$\frac{\$29.95}{1.35} = \frac{1.35C}{1.35}$$
$$\$22.19 = C$$

Check

$$C = \frac{\text{Selling price}}{1 + \text{Percent markup on cost}} \qquad \$22.19 = \frac{\$29.95}{1.35}$$

8–34. The March 1997 issue of *Business Startups* contained an article that featured Judy Proudfoot, owner of Proudfoot Wearable Art, who was selling her dresses for $59. However, compared to her competition, the same dresses were selling for as much as $95. If Judy and her competition paid $43 for a dress, what would be Judy's percent markup based on selling price compared to that of her competition? Round to the nearest hundredth percent.

Judy

Dollar markup = Selling price − Cost
$$\$16 \quad = \quad \$59 \quad - \$43$$

$$\begin{array}{c}\text{Percent markup} \\ \text{on selling price}\end{array} = \frac{\text{Dollar markup}}{\text{Selling price}}$$

$$\frac{\$16}{\$59} = 27.118644\% = 27.12\%$$

Competition

Dollar markup = Selling price − Cost
$$\$52 \quad = \quad \$95 \quad - \$43$$

$$\frac{\$52}{\$95} = 54.73684\% = 54.74\%$$

8–35. Circuit City sells a camcorder for $799. Circuit City marked up the camcorder 45% on the selling price. What is the cost of the camcorder?

Note: Markup is on selling price, not cost.

$$\$799.00 = C + .45(\$799)$$
$$\$799.00 = C + \$359.55$$
$$\underline{-\ 359.55} \qquad \underline{-\ 359.55}$$
$$\$439.45 = C$$

Check

$$C = \text{Selling price} \times \left(1 - \begin{array}{c}\text{Percent markup} \\ \text{on selling price}\end{array}\right)$$

$$\$439.45 = \$799 \times .55$$

8–36. Arley's Bakery makes fat-free cookies that cost $1.50 each. Arley expects 15% of the cookies to fall apart and be discarded. Arley wants a 45% markup on cost and produces 200 cookies. What should Arley price each cookie? Round to the nearest cent.

Total cost = 200 × $1.50 = $300
$$TS = \$300 + .45(\$300)$$
$$TS = \$300 + \$135$$
$$TS = \$435$$

$$\frac{\$435}{170 \text{ cookies}} = \$2.56$$

8–37. Assume that Arley (Problem 8–36) can sell the broken cookies for $1.40 each. What should Arley price each cookie?

$$\frac{\$435 - (30 \text{ cookies} \times \$1.40)}{170 \text{ cookies}} = \frac{\$435 - \$42}{170} = \$2.31$$

8–38. Ron's Computer Center sells computers for $1,258.60. Assuming the computers cost $10,788 per dozen, find for each computer the **(a)** dollar markup, **(b)** percent markup on cost, and **(c)** percent markup on selling price (nearest hundredth percent).

a. $\dfrac{\$10,788}{12} = \$899$ $\begin{array}{r} \$1,258.60 \\ -\ 899.00 \\ \hline \$\ \ 359.60 \end{array}$ **b.** $\dfrac{\$359.60}{\$899} = 40\%$ **c.** $\dfrac{\$359.60}{\$1,258.60} = 28.57\%$

Prove **(b)** and **(c)** of the above problem using the equivalent formulas.

$\dfrac{.40}{1 + .40} = 28.57\%$ $\dfrac{.2857}{1 - .2857} = \dfrac{.2857}{.7143} = 39.99\% = 40\%$

CHALLENGE PROBLEMS

8–39. **Looking Back at Car Prices 10 Years Ago.** In a report dated December 1992, *Money* magazine stated that the dealer of a one-price seller Saturn sells the Saturn SL1 for $9,995, which is priced at 12.3% over the dealer's cost. The cost may look like a bargain compared with the Honda Civic DX's $10,350 selling price at a cost of $8,694. But a hard bargainer should be able to get the Honda at 4% over dealer cost.
  a. If the markup is *based on cost,* what is the Saturn's cost to the dealer? Round to the nearest dollar.
  b. What should you be able to purchase the Honda for, based on cost? Round to the nearest dollar.
  c. What is the difference between what you would pay for the Saturn and what you would pay for the Honda?

a. $C = \dfrac{\text{Selling price}}{1 + \text{Percent markup on cost}}$ **b.** $S = \text{Cost} \times (1 + \text{Percent markup on cost})$
$C = \dfrac{\$9,995}{1.123}$ $S = \$8,694.00 \times 1.04 = \$9,041.76$
$C = \$8,900$ $S = \$9,041$

c. Saturn $\$9,995$ selling price
Honda $-\ \underline{9,041}$ selling price
$\$\ 954$

8–40. On July 8, 2001, Leon's Kitchen Hut bought a set of pots with a $120 list price from Lambert Manufacturing. Leon's receives a 25% trade discount. Terms of the sale were 2/10, n/30. On July 14, Leon's sent a check to Lambert for the pots. Leon's expenses are 20% of the selling price. Leon's must also make a profit of 15% of the selling price. A competitor marked down the same set of pots 30%. Assume Leon's reduces its selling price by 30%.
  a. What is the sale price at Kitchen Hut?
  b. What was the operating profit or loss?

a. $\$120 \times .75 = \$90 \times .98 = \$88.20$ **b.** Total cost $= \$88.20 + .20(\$135.69)$ $P = SP - TC$
$S = \$88.20 + .20S + .15S$ $= \$88.20 + \$27.14$ $= \$94.98 - \$115.34$
$S = \$88.20 + .35S$ $= \$115.34$ Loss $= \$20.36$
$.65S = \$88.20$
$S = \$135.69$

Sale price: $94.98, or (.70 × $135.69)

SUMMARY PRACTICE TEST

1. Glow Electronics marks up merchandise 32% on cost. A television costs Glow $225. What is Glow's selling price? Round to the nearest cent. *(p. 198)*
$S = \$225 + .32(\$225)$ **Check** $S = \text{Cost} \times (1 + \text{Percent markup on cost})$
$S = \$225 + \$72$ $\$297 = \$225 \times 1.32$
$S = \$297$

2. Jeans, Inc., sells jeans for $42.99 that cost $19.75. What is the percent markup on cost? Round to the nearest hundredth percent. Check the cost *(p. 198)*
$\begin{array}{r} \$42.99 = \$19.75 + M \\ -\ 19.75 \quad -\ 19.75 \\ \hline \$23.24 = \quad\ \ M \end{array}$ $\dfrac{\$23.24}{\$19.75} = 117.67\%$ **Check** $C = \dfrac{\$23.24}{1.1767} = \$19.75$

3. LB's Appliance sells a disposal for $210. LB's marks up the disposal 80% on cost. What are the cost and dollar markup of the disposal? *(p. 199)*

$$\$210 = C + .80C \qquad \textbf{Check} \quad \text{Cost} = \frac{\text{Selling price}}{1 + \text{Percent markup on cost}}$$

$$\frac{\$210}{1.80} = \frac{\cancel{1.80}C}{\cancel{1.80}} \qquad \$116.67 = \frac{\$210}{1.80} \qquad \text{Markup} = \$210 - \$116.67 = \$93.33$$

$$\$116.67 = C$$

4. Al's Workshop marks up a bench $50 and sells it for $95. Markup is on cost. What are the cost and percent markup to nearest tenth percent? *(p. 198)*

$$\begin{array}{r} \$95 \\ -\ 50 \\ \hline \$45 \text{ cost} \end{array} \qquad \frac{\$50}{\$45} = 111.1\%$$

5. Bob's Shoe Barn bought deck shoes for $65. Bob marks up his deck shoes 45% on the selling price. What is the selling price of the deck shoes? Round to the nearest cent. *(p. 203)*

$$S = \$65 + .45S \qquad \textbf{Check} \quad S = \frac{\text{Cost}}{1 - \text{Percent markup on selling price}}$$

$$\begin{array}{r} -\ .45S \qquad\qquad -\ .45S \end{array}$$

$$\frac{\cancel{.55}S}{\cancel{.55}} = \frac{\$65}{.55} \qquad \$118.18 = \frac{\$65}{.55}$$

$$S = \$118.18$$

6. Logic Computer Company sells a monitor for $469.89 and marks up the monitor 40% on the selling price. What did the monitor cost Logic? Round to the nearest cent. *(p. 203)*

$$\$469.89 = C + .40(\$469.89) \qquad \textbf{Check} \quad C = \text{Selling price} \times (1 - \text{Percent markup on selling price})$$

$$\$469.89 = C + \$187.96$$

$$\begin{array}{r} -187.96 \qquad\qquad -\ 187.96 \\ \hline \$281.93 = C \end{array} \qquad \$281.93 = \$469.89 \times .60$$

7. Lite Furniture sells lamps for $89.99 that cost $52. What is Lite's percent markup on selling price? Round to the nearest hundredth percent. Check the selling price. *(p. 202)*

$$\begin{array}{r} \$89.99 \\ -\ 52.00 \\ \hline \$37.99 \end{array} \qquad \frac{\$37.99}{\$89.99} = 42.22\% \qquad \textbf{Check} \quad \frac{\$37.99}{.4222} = \$89.98 \text{ (off 1 cent due to rounding)}$$

8. Claire Montgomery, a customer of Angel Company, will pay $300 for a tea set. Angel Company has a 70% markup on selling price. What is the most that Angel can pay for this tea set? *(p. 203)*

$$\$300 = C + .70(\$300) \qquad \textbf{Check} \quad C = \text{Selling price} \times (1 - \text{Percent markup on selling price})$$

$$\$300 = C + \$210 \qquad\qquad \$90 = \$300 \times .30$$

$$\begin{array}{r} -\ 210 \qquad -\ 210 \\ \hline \$\ 90 = C \end{array}$$

9. Laurel Company marks up its merchandise 60% on cost. What is Laurel's equivalent markup on selling price? Round to the nearest tenth percent. *(p. 204)*

$$\frac{.60}{1 + .60} = 37.5\%$$

10. BJ's Bakeshop makes no-fat muffins that cost $.35 each. BJ's knows that 25% of the muffins will spoil. If BJ's wants 40% markup on cost and produces 400 muffins, what should BJ's price each muffin? Round to the nearest cent. *(p. 208)*

$$TC = \$.35 \times 400 = \$140$$
$$TS = \$140 + .40(\$140)$$
$$TS = \$140 + \$56$$
$$TS = \$196$$

$$\frac{\$196}{300} = \$.65$$

$$(400 - 25\%)$$

A KIPLINGER APPROACH

A GROUP PROJECT Defend or reject the following business math issue based on the *Kiplinger's Personal Finance Magazine* article below:

EDUCATION

Here's a college cost that's headed down

Online textbook sellers are shoehorning themselves into the niche once monopolized by college bookstores, and the result is (finally!) price competition.

Shopping for textbooks through Amazon.com (www.amazon.com) or Barnes & Noble (www.bkstore.com) can save students between $9 and $24 a class, says a study by Atlantis Technology, which develops Web sites for bookstores.

At least one online service sells only textbooks. VarsityBooks.com, which will be available this fall, offers discounts of 15% to 40% off bookstore prices to students at five colleges in the Washington, D.C., area. That could add up to a considerable savings for students, who often spend $500 on books and supplies for an academic year.

"There's also the convenience factor," says Eric Kuhn, who co-founded VarsityBooks.com with Tim Levy. "You can buy books 24 hours a day without the hassle."

To retaliate, many campus bookstores are establishing Web sites of their own (although not to offer discounts) and trying to make their meticulously compiled course booklists proprietary. But Kuhn and Levy say faculty members concerned about getting their students a better deal are increasingly inclined to supply online booksellers with booklists. And access to the lists is unrestricted at public colleges and universities, says Alroy Scott, an assistant director of the campus bookstore at the University of Maryland, College Park.
— *SHRUTI DATÉ*

AARON LEE FINEMAN

On campus: Fewer browsers at the bookstore?

Business Math Issue

In the future, the college bookstore will be replaced completely by bookstores on the internet.

1. List the key points of the article and information to support your position.

2. Write a group defense of your position using math calculations to support your view.

Stores' Demands Squeeze Apparel

By LAURA BIRD
And WENDY BOUNDS
Staff Reporters of THE WALL STREET JOURNAL

The dress business hasn't been good to Jimmy Sheak lately.

Dozens of plastic-sheathed dresses hang from pipe racks waiting to leave his

FASHION

Manhattan warehouse, but Mr. Sheak, president of apparel maker **Jeffrey Ray International** Inc., says that the more dresses he sells to department stores these days, the more money he loses.

It's basic math: Following two years of disappointing clothing sales, department stores are making greater-than-ever demands from their suppliers to cover the heavy discounts and markdowns on their own selling floors. They want suppliers to guarantee their stores' profit margins, and they insist on cash rebates if the guarantee isn't met. They are exacting fines for violations of ticketing, packing and shipping rules. Cumulatively, the demands are nearly wiping out profits for all but the very biggest suppliers, according to fashion designers and garment makers.

On Seventh Avenue, paying up is the standard cost of doing business with department stores, Mr. Sheak says. "Not so many people dare to say anything," he says. "They will wipe you from the list. We are scared."

1. Designer X creates wool women's jacket for fall. **Manufacturing Cost: $50**

2. Major Department Store orders jackets for $100 each but gets an 8% discount as 'good customer.' **Designer's Profit: $42**

3. Designer X and Department Store agree jacket will retail for $200—a 50% profit if all jackets sell at full price. But Department Store demands at least 40% profit; if margins dip below, Designer X must make up difference.

4. Designer X delivers jackets a few days late, on wrong hangers and with order numbers on wrong side of box. Miscellaneous charges deduct $5 per jacket. **Designer's Profit: $37**

5. Jackets hit selling floor at $200 but are soon marked down to $150. Designer X must make up part of the difference to Department Store—either in monthly payments or with discounts on next season's orders.

6. Cycle continues next season.

Tight Fit
How a designer's profit dwindles as a department store makes demands

Illustrations by Tom Bloom

© 1997 Dow Jones & Company, Inc.

Project A

Do department stores have the right to demand these guarantees from suppliers? Take a stand and defend your position.

Victoria's Secret mailed out a staggering 350 million catalogs this year, 8% more than last year. It sends out as many as 22 mailings a year, meaning some customers could get the catalog nearly every other week.

© 1996 Dow Jones & Company, Inc.

Project B

1. Assume you bought a new bathrobe for $29.95. Assuming a 30% markup on selling price, what was the cost to Victoria's Secret?

$$S = C + M$$
$$\$29.95 = C + .30(\$29.95)$$
$$\$29.95 = C + \$8.99$$
$$\underline{- 8.99 \qquad - 8.99}$$
$$\$20.96 = C$$

2. How many catalogs were sent out last year? Round to the nearest million.

$$B = \frac{350}{1.08}$$
$$B = 324 \text{ million}$$

Portion (350)

Base × Rate (?)   (1.08)

 See text Web site (www.mhhe.com/slater) and *The Business Math Internet Resource Guide*.

CUMULATIVE REVIEW: A Word Problem Approach—Chapters 6, 7, 8

1. Assume Kellogg's produced 715,000 boxes of Corn Flakes this year. This was 110% of the annual production last year. What was last year's annual production? *(p. 146)*

$$\frac{715,000}{1.10} = 650,000$$

Portion
(715,000)

Base × Rate
(?)   (1.10)

2. A new Sony camcorder has a list price of $420. The trade discount is 10/20 with terms of 2/10, n/30. If a retailer pays the invoice within the discount period, what is the amount the retailer must pay? *(p. 179)*

$$.9 \times .8 = .72$$
$420 \times .72 = \$302.40$ (net price)
$$\begin{array}{r} \times .98 \\ \hline \$296.35 \end{array}$$

3. JCPenney sells loafers with a markup of $40. If the markup is 30% on cost, what did the loafers cost JCPenney? Round to the nearest dollar. *(p. 198)*

$$\frac{\$40}{.30} = \$133$$

4. Aster Computers received from Ring Manufacturers an invoice dated August 28 with terms 2/10 EOM. The list price of the invoice is $3,000 (freight not included). Ring offers Aster a 9/8/2 trade chain discount. Terms of freight are FOB shipping point, but Ring prepays the $150 freight. Assume Aster pays the invoice on October 9. How much will Ring receive? *(p. 179)*

$$.91 \times .92 \times .98 = .820456 \times \$3,000 = \$2,461.37$$
$$\begin{array}{r} \times .98 \\ \hline \$2,412.14 \\ + \ 150.00 \\ \hline \$2,562.14 \end{array}$$

5. Runners World marks up its Nike jogging shoes 25% on selling price. The Nike shoe sells for $65. How much did the store pay for them? *(p. 203)*

$$\begin{aligned} S &= C + M \\ \$65.00 &= C + .25(\$65) \\ \$65.00 &= C + \$16.25 \\ - 16.25 & \quad\quad - \ 16.25 \\ \hline \$48.75 &= C \end{aligned}$$

$$C = \text{Selling price} \times \left(1 - \frac{\text{Percent markup}}{\text{on selling price}} \right)$$
$$C = \$65 \times .75$$
$$C = \$48.75$$

6. Ivan Rone sells antique sleds. He knows that the most he can get for a sled is $350. Ivan needs a 35% markup on cost. Since Ivan is going to an antiques show, he wants to know the maximum he can offer a dealer for an antique sled. *(p. 199)*

$$\begin{aligned} S &= C + M \\ \$350 &= C + .35C \\ \frac{\$350}{1.35} &= \frac{1.35C}{1.35} \\ \$259.26 &= C \end{aligned}$$

$$\text{Cost} = \frac{\text{Selling price}}{1 + \text{Percent markup on cost}}$$
$$= \frac{\$350}{1.35}$$
$$= \$259.26$$

7. Bonnie's Bakery bakes 60 loaves of bread for $1.10 each. Bonnie's estimates that 10% of the bread will spoil. Assume a 60% markup on cost. What is the selling price of each loaf? If Bonnie's can sell the old bread for one-half the cost, what is the selling price of each loaf? *(p. 208)*

$$\begin{aligned} TC &= 60 \times \$1.10 = \$66 \\ TS &= TC + TM \\ TS &= \$66 + .60(\$66) \\ TS &= \$66 + \$39.60 \\ TS &= \$105.60 \end{aligned}$$

$$\frac{\$105.60}{54} = \$1.96$$
$$\rightarrow 54$$
$$(60 \times .90)$$

$$\frac{\$105.60 - (6 \times \$.55)}{54} = \frac{\$105.60 - \$3.30}{54} = \$1.89$$

CLASSROOM NOTES

CLASSROOM NOTES

9

PAYROLL

LEARNING UNIT OBJECTIVES

LU 9.1 **Calculating Various Types of Employees' Gross Pay**

- Define, compare, and contrast weekly, biweekly, semimonthly, and monthly pay periods *(p. 227)*.
- Calculate gross pay with overtime on the basis of time *(p. 227)*.
- Calculate gross pay for piecework, differential pay scales, straight commission, and salary plus commission *(pp. 228–29)*.

LU 9.2 **Computing Payroll Deductions for Employees' Pay; Employers' Responsibilities**

- Prepare and explain the parts of a payroll register *(p. 230)*.
- Explain and calculate federal and state unemployment taxes *(p. 234)*.

Work Week

A Special News Report About Life On the Job — and Trends Taking Shape There

CALLING IN SICK? Some airlines pay their employees not to.

Bedeviled by absenteeism during heavy travel periods, airlines dole out prizes to those who don't miss a day. Northwest Airlines awards Corvettes, Ford Explorers or $18,000 cash to eligible employees whose names are picked in a drawing. United Airlines offered prize-winning workers Jeeps last year, but "everyone opted for the cash," a spokeswoman says.

Between Thanksgiving and Christmas, absenteeism triples the normal rate and airlines can't afford to let operations slip. But some unions complain the incentives are unfair to legitimately ill workers. "People who are sick as a dog crawl on board hoping they'll win a car," says Dotty Malinsky, vice president of Northwest's flight-attendants union.

Nike Cancels Pacts With Indonesia Plants Over Wage Policies

By a WALL STREET JOURNAL *Staff Reporter*

PORTLAND, Ore. – Nike Inc., facing criticism over labor practices at Asian factories run by its contractors, said it severed contracts with four factories in Indonesia where pay is below the government-set minimum wage.

Nike, the world's largest athletic-shoe maker, said in the last three months it has scrutinized its operations in China, Vietnam and Indonesia to ensure compliance with the company's code of conduct, which includes a provision that contractors pay the minimum wage set by the government. Indonesia increased the minimum wage by 11% in April, but allowed companies to seek exemptions. The four contractors had received exemptions, but Nike said that under its policy, the companies must pay the full minimum wage. Nike has more than 50 factories in Indonesia.

Have you ever gone to an airport before Christmas and wondered why so many airline employees were working during the holidays? *The Wall Street Journal* "Work Week" clipping at the left may have an answer for you. In an effort to avoid the absenteeism that occurs during heavy travel periods, airlines give prizes to those who don't miss a day of work. Eligible employees whose names are picked from a drawing can receive cars or cash as a reward for maintaining an absent-free work record. As you might expect, most employees take the cash.

Do you wear Nike athletic shoes? You probably know that Nike has factories in foreign countries. You may not know that foreign factories must follow the Nike policy to pay workers the full minimum wage. *The Wall Street Journal* Nike clipping at the right reports that Nike has severed contracts with four factories in Indonesia where the pay is below the government-set minimum wage.

This chapter discusses (1) the type of pay people work for, (2) how employers calculate paychecks and deductions, and (3) what employers must report and pay in taxes.

LEARNING UNIT 9.1   Calculating Various Types of Employees' Gross Pay

Logan Company manufactures dolls of all shapes and sizes. These dolls are sold worldwide. We study Logan Company in this unit because of the variety of methods Logan uses to pay its employees.

Companies usually pay employees **weekly, biweekly, semimonthly,** or **monthly.** How often employers pay employees can affect how employees manage their money. Some employees prefer a weekly paycheck that spreads the inflow of money. Employees who have monthly bills may find the twice-a-month or monthly paycheck more convenient. All employees would like more money to manage.

Let's assume you earn $50,000 per year. The following table shows what you would earn each pay period. Remember that 13 weeks equals one quarter. Four quarters or 52 weeks equals a year.

Salary paid	Period (based on a year)	Earnings for period (dollars)	
Weekly	52 times (once a week)	$ 961.54	($50,000 ÷ 52)
Biweekly	26 times (every two weeks)	$1,923.08	($50,000 ÷ 26)
Semimonthly	24 times (twice a month)	$2,083.33	($50,000 ÷ 24)
Monthly	12 times (once a month)	$4,166.67	($50,000 ÷ 12)

Now let's look at some pay schedule situations and examples of how Logan Company calculates its payroll for employees of different pay status.

Situation 1: Hourly Rate of Pay; Calculation of Overtime

> **COPS FIGHT FOR overtime pay but lose the latest battle.**
>
> The U.S. Supreme Court deals a blow to police, ruling that sergeants and lieutenants in the St. Louis Police Department aren't entitled to time-and-a-half pay for working overtime. The court, in a decision two weeks ago, said supervisory officers are exempt as white-collar employees from the Fair Labor Standards Act. The ruling could have implications for other cities and states.

© 1997 Dow Jones & Company, Inc.

The **Fair Labor Standards Act** sets minimum wage standards and overtime regulations for employees of companies covered by this federal law. The law provides that employees working for an hourly rate receive time-and-a-half pay for hours worked in excess of their regular 40-hour week. The current hourly minimum wage is $5.15, and it will probably increase in the future. Many managerial people, however, are exempt from the time-and-a-half pay for all hours in excess of a 40-hour week. *The Wall Street Journal* clipping "Cops Fight for Overtime Pay but Lose Latest Battle" reports that the U.S. Supreme Court ruled that the sergeants and lieutenants of the St. Louis Police Department were not entitled to time-and-a-half overtime pay.

Logan Company is calculating the weekly pay of Ramon Valdez who works in its manufacturing division. For the first 40 hours Ramon works, Logan calculates his **gross pay** (earnings before **deductions**) as follows:

© PhotoDisc.

> Gross pay = Hours employee worked × Rate per hour

Ramon works more than 40 hours in a week. For every hour over his 40 hours, Ramon must be paid an **overtime** pay of at least 1.5 times his regular pay rate. The following formula is used to determine Ramon's overtime:

> Hourly overtime pay rate = Regular hourly pay rate × 1.5

Logan Company must include Ramon's overtime pay with his regular pay. To determine Ramon's gross pay, Logan uses the following formula:

> Gross pay = Earnings for 40 hours + Earnings at time-and-a-half rate (1.5)

Let's calculate Ramon's gross pay from the following data:

EXAMPLE

Employee	M	T	W	Th	F	S	Total hours	Rate per hour
Ramon Valdez	13	$8\frac{1}{2}$	10	8	$11\frac{1}{4}$	$10\frac{3}{4}$	$61\frac{1}{2}$	$9

$61\frac{1}{2}$ total hours

$-\ 40$ regular hours

$\overline{21\frac{1}{2}}$ hours overtime[1]   Time-and-a-half pay: $9 × 1.5 = $13.50

Gross pay = (40 hours × $9) + ($21\frac{1}{2}$ hours × $13.50)

$\qquad\quad =\qquad$ $360 $\quad+\quad$ $290.25

$\qquad\quad =$ $650.25

Note that the $13.50 overtime rate came out even. However, throughout the text, *if an overtime rate is greater than two decimal places, do not round it. Round only the final answer. This gives greater accuracy.*

Situation 2: Straight Piece Rate Pay

Some companies, especially manufacturers, pay workers according to how much they produce. Logan Company pays Ryan Foss for the number of dolls he produces in a week. This gives Ryan an incentive to make more money by producing more dolls. Ryan receives $.96 per doll, less any defective units. The following formula determines Ryan's gross pay:

> Gross pay = Number of units produced × Rate per unit

Companies may also pay a guaranteed hourly wage and use a piece rate as a bonus. However, Logan uses straight piece rate as wages for some of its employees.

EXAMPLE   During the last week of April, Ryan Foss produced 900 dolls. Using the above formula, Logan Company paid Ryan $864.

Gross pay = 900 dolls × $.96

$\qquad\quad =$ $864

Situation 3: Differential Pay Schedule

Some of Logan's employees can earn more than the $.96 straight piece rate for every doll they produce. Logan Company has set up a **differential pay schedule** for these employees. The company determines the rate these employees make by the amount of units the employees produce at different levels of production.

EXAMPLE   Logan Company pays Abby Rogers on the basis of the following schedule:

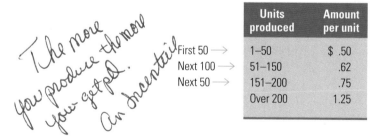

	Units produced	Amount per unit
First 50 →	1–50	$ .50
Next 100 →	51–150	.62
Next 50 →	151–200	.75
	Over 200	1.25

The more you produce the more you get pd. An incentive

Last week Abby produced 300 dolls. What is Abby's gross pay?
    Logan calculated Abby's gross pay as follows:

(50 × $.50) + (100 × $.62) + (50 × $.75) + (100 × $1.25)

$\quad$ $25 $\quad+\quad$ $62 $\quad+\quad$ $37.50 $\quad+\quad$ $125 $\qquad=$ $249.50

We are now ready to study some of the other types of employee commission payment plans.

---

[1]Some companies pay overtime for time over 8 hours in one day; Logan Company pays overtime for time over 40 hours per week.

3 Commission Rates

Situation 4: Straight Commission with Draw

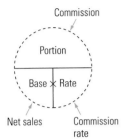

Companies frequently use **straight commission** to determine the pay of salespersons. This commission is usually a certain percentage of the amount the salesperson sells. Logan Company allows some of its salespersons to draw against this commission at the beginning of each month.

A **draw** is an advance on the salesperson's commission. Logan subtracts this advance later from the employee's commission earned based on sales. When the commission does not equal the draw, the salesperson owes Logan the difference between the draw and the commission.

EXAMPLE   Logan Company pays Jackie Okamoto a straight commission of 15% on her net sales (net sales are total sales less sales returns). In May, Jackie had net sales of $56,000. Logan gave Jackie a $600 draw in May. What is Jackie's gross pay?

Logan calculated Jackie's commission minus her draw as follows:

$$\$56,000 \times .15 = \$8,400$$
$$\underline{-\ \ \ 600}$$
$$\boxed{\$7,800}$$

Logan Company pays some people in the sales department on a variable commission scale. Let's look at this, assuming the employee had no draw.

Situation 5: Variable Commission Scale

A company with a **variable commission scale** uses different commission rates for different levels of net sales.

EXAMPLE   Last month, Jane Ring's net sales were $160,000. What is Jane's gross pay based on the following schedule?

Up to $35,000	4%
Excess of $35,000 to $45,000	6%
Over $45,000	8%

$$\text{Gross pay} = (\$35,000 \times .04) + (\$10,000 \times .06) + (\$115,000 \times .08)$$
$$= \quad \$1,400 \quad + \quad \$600 \quad + \quad \$9,200$$
$$= \boxed{\$11,200}$$

Situation 6: Salary Plus Commission

Logan Company pays Joe Roy a $3,000 monthly salary plus a 4% commission for sales over $20,000. Last month Joe's net sales were $50,000. Logan calculated Joe's gross monthly pay as follows:

$$\text{Gross pay} = \text{Salary} + (\text{Commission} \times \text{Sales over } \$20,000)$$
$$= \$3,000 + \qquad (\$.04 \times \$30,000)$$
$$= \$3,000 + \qquad\qquad \$1,200$$
$$= \boxed{\$4,200}$$

Before you take the Practice Quiz, you should know that many managers today receive **overrides.** These managers receive a commission based on the net sales of the people they supervise.

LU 9.1 PRACTICE QUIZ

1. Jill Foster worked 52 hours in one week for Delta Airlines. Jill earns $10 per hour. What is Jill's gross pay, assuming overtime is at time-and-a-half?

2. Matt Long had $180,000 in sales for the month. Matt's commission rate is 9%, and he had a $3,500 draw. What was Matt's end-of-month commission?

3. Bob Meyers receives a $1,000 monthly salary. He also receives a variable commission on net sales based on the following schedule (commission doesn't begin until Bob earns $8,000 in net sales):

$8,000–$12,000	1%	Excess of $20,000 to $40,000	5%
Excess of $12,000 to $20,000	3%	More than $40,000	8%

Assume Bob earns $40,000 net sales for the month. What is his gross pay?

✓ **Solutions**

1. 40 hours × $10.00 = $400.00
   12 hours × $15.00 = ___180.00___ ($10.00 × 1.5 = $15.00)
   $\boxed{\$580.00}$

2. $180,000 × .09 = $16,200
   − 3,500
   $\boxed{\$12,700}$

3. Gross pay = $1,000 + ($4,000 × .01) + ($8,000 × .03) + ($20,000 × .05)
   = $1,000 + $40 + $240 + $1,000
   = $\boxed{\$2,280}$

LEARNING UNIT 9.2 Computing Payroll Deductions for Employees' Pay; Employers' Responsibilities

When you get your weekly paycheck, do you take the time to check all the numbers? Do you understand the difference between Social Security and Medicare? This unit begins by dissecting a paycheck. Then we give you an insight into the tax responsibilities of employers.

Computing Payroll Deductions for Employees

Companies often record employee payroll information in a multicolumn form called a **payroll register.** The increased use of computers in business has made computerized registers a timesaver for many companies.

Gonzales Company uses a multicolumn payroll register. Below is Gonzales's partial register showing the payroll information for Dave Reilly during week 50. Let's check each column to see if Dave's take-home pay of $952.76 is correct. Note how the circled letters in the register correspond to the explanations given below the register.

GONZALES COMPANY
Payroll Register
November 11, 20XX

Week #50

Employee name	Allow. & marital status	Cum. earn.	Sal. per week	Earnings			Cum. earn.	FICA taxable earnings		Deductions					
										FICA					
				Reg.	Ovt.	Gross		S.S.	Med.	S.S.	Med.	FIT	SIT	Health ins.	Net pay
Reilly, Dave	M-2	67,375	1,375	1,375	—	1,375	68,750	1,025	1,375	63.55	19.94	220	68.75	50	952.76
	Ⓐ	Ⓑ	Ⓒ			Ⓓ	Ⓔ	Ⓕ	Ⓖ	Ⓗ	Ⓘ	Ⓙ	Ⓚ	Ⓛ	Ⓜ

Based on Taxable Earnings

Payroll Register Explanations

Ⓐ—*Allowance and marital status*

Ⓑ, Ⓒ, Ⓓ—*Cumulative earnings before payroll, salaries, earnings*

Ⓔ—*Cumulative earnings after payroll*

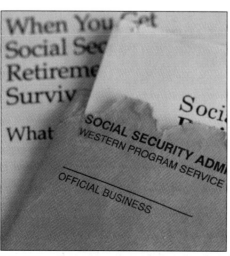

© PhotoDisc.

When Dave was hired, he completed the **W-4 (Employee's Withholding Allowance Certificate)** form shown in Figure 9.1 stating that he is married and claims an allowance (exemption) of 2. Gonzales Company will need this information to calculate the federal income tax Ⓙ.

Before this pay period, Dave has earned $67,375 (49 weeks × $1,375 salary per week). Since Dave receives no overtime, his $1,375 salary per week represents his gross pay (pay before any deductions).

After this pay period, Dave has earned $68,750 ($67,375 + $1,375).

FIGURE 9.1
Employee's W-4 form

| Form **W-4** Department of the Treasury Internal Revenue Service | **Employee's Withholding Allowance Certificate** ▶ For Privacy Act and Paperwork Reduction Act Notice, see reverse. | OMB No. 1545-0010 **20XX** |

1 Type or print your first name and middle initial   Dave   Last name   Reilly   2 Your social security number   021 36 9494

Home address (number and street or rural route)   2 Roundy Road   3 ☐ Single ☒ Married ☐ Married, but withhold at higher Single rate.
Note: *If married, but legally separated, or spouse is a nonresident alien, check the Single box.*

City or town, state, and ZIP code   Marblehead, MA 01945   4 If your last name differs from that on your social security card, check here and call 1-800-772-1213 for a new card . . . . . ▶ ☐

5 Total number of allowances you are claiming (from line G above or from the worksheets on page 2 if they apply) .   5 2

6 Additional amount, if any, you want withheld from each paycheck . . . .   6 $

7 I claim exemption from withholding for 1995 and I certify that I meet **BOTH** of the following conditions for exemption:
• Last year I had a right to a refund of **ALL** Federal income tax withheld because I had **NO** tax liability; **AND**
• This year I expect a refund of **ALL** Federal income tax withheld because I expect to have **NO** tax liability.
If you meet both conditions, enter "EXEMPT" here . . . . ▶ 7

Under penalties of perjury, I certify that I am entitled to the number of withholding allowances claimed on this certificate or entitled to claim exempt status.

Employee's signature ▶ *Dave Reilly*   Date ▶ 1/1   , 20 XX

8 Employer's name and address (Employer: Complete 8 and 10 only if sending to the IRS)   9 Office code (optional)   10 Employer identification number

Cat. No. 10220Q

The **Federal Insurance Contribution Act (FICA)** funds the **Social Security** program. The program includes Old Age and Disability, Medicare, Survivor Benefits, and so on. The FICA tax requires separate reporting for Social Security and **Medicare.** We will use the following rates for Gonzales Company:

	Rate	Base
Social Security	6.20%	$68,400*
Medicare	1.45	No base

*The 1999 rate is 6.20% on a base of $72,600.

These rates mean that Dave Reilly will pay Social Security taxes on the first $68,400 he earns this year. After earning $68,400, Dave's wages will be exempt from Social Security. Note that Dave will be paying Medicare taxes on all wages since Medicare has no base cutoff.

To help keep Gonzales's record straight, the *taxable earnings column only shows what wages will be taxed. This amount is not the tax.* For example, in week 50, only $1,025 of Dave's salary will be taxable for Social Security.

Ⓕ, Ⓖ—*Taxable earnings for Social Security and Medicare*

$68,400 Social Security base
− 67,375 Ⓑ *Earnings thru wk 49*
$ 1,025

Ⓗ—*Social Security*

Dave's entire weekly salary of $1,375 will be taxed for Medicare, since there is no base. To calculate Dave's Social Security tax, we multiply $1,025 Ⓕ by 6.2%.

$1,025 × .062 = $63.55

Ⓘ—*Medicare*

Since Dave's total salary is taxed for Medicare, we multiply $1,375 Ⓖ by 1.45%.

$1,375 × .0145 = $19.94

Ⓙ—*FIT*

Using the W-4 form Dave completed, Gonzales deducts **federal income tax withholding (FIT).** The more allowances an employee claims, the less money Gonzales deducts from the employee's paycheck. Two methods are used to determine FIT: wage bracket method and percentage method. Gonzales uses the wage bracket method. We will also show the percentage method.

1. Wage Bracket Method   The **wage bracket method** uses the tables in Circular E of the federal government's Employer's Guide. Circular E contains many tables for wages paid weekly, biweekly, semimonthly, monthly, and so on. Table 9.1 (p. 232) shows a table for married persons paid weekly. Table 9.2 (p. 233) shows a table for a single person paid monthly. (Be sure to check each year with the Internal Revenue Service for the latest tables.) Since Dave is married and his weekly pay is $1,375, we go down the left of Table 9.1 until we see at least $1,370. Then we go across to 2 withholding allowances. At the intersection, we see $220 . This is Dave's federal income tax. Note that if Dave's pay were $1,380, we would have used the next row down.

TABLE 9.1   Weekly payroll table for married persons

MARRIED Persons— WEEKLY Payroll Period

If the wages are—		And the number of withholding allowances claimed is—										
At least	But less than	0	1	2	3	4	5	6	7	8	9	10
		The amount of income tax to be withheld is—										
$740	$750	93	85	78	70	62	54	46	39	31	23	15
750	760	95	87	79	71	63	56	48	40	32	25	17
760	770	96	88	81	73	65	57	49	42	34	26	18
770	780	98	90	82	74	66	59	51	43	35	28	20
780	790	99	91	84	76	68	60	52	45	37	29	21
790	800	101	93	85	77	69	62	54	46	38	31	23
800	810	102	94	87	79	71	63	55	48	40	32	24
810	820	104	96	88	80	72	65	57	49	41	34	26
820	830	105	97	90	82	74	66	58	51	43	35	27
830	840	107	99	91	83	75	68	60	52	44	37	29
840	850	108	100	93	85	77	69	61	54	46	38	30
850	860	110	102	94	86	78	71	63	55	47	40	32
860	870	111	103	96	88	80	72	64	57	49	41	33
870	880	113	105	97	89	81	74	66	58	50	43	35
880	890	114	106	99	91	83	75	67	60	52	44	36
890	900	116	108	100	92	84	77	69	61	53	46	38
900	910	118	109	102	94	86	78	70	63	55	47	39
910	920	121	111	103	95	87	80	72	64	56	49	41
920	930	124	112	105	97	89	81	73	66	58	50	42
930	940	126	114	106	98	90	83	75	67	59	52	44
940	950	129	115	108	100	92	84	76	69	61	53	45
950	960	132	117	109	101	93	86	78	70	62	55	47
960	970	135	120	111	103	95	87	79	72	64	56	48
970	980	138	123	112	104	96	89	81	73	65	58	50
980	990	140	126	114	106	98	90	82	75	67	59	51
990	1,000	143	129	115	107	99	92	84	76	68	61	53
1,000	1,010	146	131	117	109	101	93	85	78	70	62	54
1,010	1,020	149	134	120	110	102	95	87	79	71	64	56
1,020	1,030	152	137	122	112	104	96	88	81	73	65	57
1,030	1,040	154	140	125	113	105	98	90	82	74	67	59
1,040	1,050	157	143	128	115	107	99	91	84	76	68	60
1,050	1,060	160	145	131	116	108	101	93	85	77	70	62
1,060	1,070	163	148	134	119	110	102	94	87	79	71	63
1,070	1,080	166	151	136	122	111	104	96	88	80	73	65
1,080	1,090	168	154	139	125	113	105	97	90	82	74	66
1,090	1,100	171	157	142	128	114	107	99	91	83	76	68
1,100	1,110	174	159	145	130	116	108	100	93	85	77	69
1,110	1,120	177	162	148	133	119	110	102	94	86	79	71
1,120	1,130	180	165	150	136	121	111	103	96	88	80	72
1,130	1,140	182	168	153	139	124	113	105	97	89	82	74
1,140	1,150	185	171	156	142	127	114	106	99	91	83	75
1,150	1,160	188	173	159	144	130	116	108	100	92	85	77
1,160	1,170	191	176	162	147	133	118	109	102	94	86	78
1,170	1,180	194	179	164	150	135	121	111	103	95	88	80
1,180	1,190	196	182	167	153	138	124	112	105	97	89	81
1,190	1,200	199	185	170	156	141	126	114	106	98	91	83
1,200	1,210	202	187	173	158	144	129	115	108	100	92	84
1,210	1,220	205	190	176	161	147	132	117	109	101	94	86
1,220	1,230	208	193	178	164	149	135	120	111	103	95	87
1,230	1,240	210	196	181	167	152	138	123	112	104	97	89
1,240	1,250	213	199	184	170	155	140	126	114	106	98	90
1,250	1,260	216	201	187	172	158	143	129	115	107	100	92
1,260	1,270	219	204	190	175	161	146	131	117	109	101	93
1,270	1,280	222	207	192	178	163	149	134	120	110	103	95
1,280	1,290	224	210	195	181	166	152	137	123	112	104	96
1,290	1,300	227	213	198	184	169	154	140	125	113	106	98
1,300	1,310	230	215	201	186	172	157	143	128	115	107	99
1,310	1,320	233	218	204	189	175	160	145	131	116	109	101
1,320	1,330	236	221	206	192	177	163	148	134	119	110	102
1,330	1,340	238	224	209	195	180	166	151	137	122	112	104
1,340	1,350	241	227	212	198	183	168	154	139	125	113	105
1,350	1,360	244	229	215	200	186	171	157	142	128	115	107
1,360	1,370	247	232	218	203	189	174	159	145	130	116	108
1,370	1,380	250	235	220	206	191	177	162	148	133	119	110
1,380	1,390	252	238	223	209	194	180	165	151	136	121	111

$1,390 and over

TABLE 9.2   Monthly payroll table for single persons

SINGLE Persons—MONTHLY Payroll Period

If the wages are—		And the number of withholding allowances claimed is—										
At least	But less than	0	1	2	3	4	5	6	7	8	9	10
		The amount of income tax to be withheld is—										
$2,440	$2,480	364	302	268	235	201	167	133	100	66	32	0
2,480	2,520	375	312	274	241	207	173	139	106	72	38	4
2,520	2,560	387	324	280	247	213	179	145	112	78	44	10
2,560	2,600	398	335	286	253	219	185	151	118	84	50	16
2,600	2,640	409	346	292	259	225	191	157	124	90	56	22
2,640	2,680	420	357	298	265	231	197	163	130	96	62	28
2,680	2,720	431	368	305	271	237	203	169	136	102	68	34
2,720	2,760	443	380	317	277	243	209	175	142	108	74	40
2,760	2,800	454	391	328	283	249	215	181	148	114	80	46
2,800	2,840	465	402	339	289	255	221	187	154	120	86	52
2,840	2,880	476	413	350	295	261	227	193	160	126	92	58
2,880	2,920	487	424	361	301	267	233	199	166	132	98	64
2,920	2,960	499	436	373	310	273	239	205	172	138	104	70
2,960	3,000	510	447	384	321	279	245	211	178	144	110	76
3,000	3,040	521	458	395	332	285	251	217	184	150	116	82
3,040	3,080	532	469	406	343	291	257	223	190	156	122	88
3,080	3,120	543	480	417	354	297	263	229	196	162	128	94
3,120	3,160	555	492	429	366	303	269	235	202	168	134	100
3,160	3,200	566	503	440	377	314	275	241	208	174	140	106
3,200	3,240	577	514	451	388	325	281	247	214	180	146	112
3,240	3,280	588	525	462	399	336	287	253	220	186	152	118
3,280	3,320	599	536	473	410	347	293	259	226	192	158	124
3,320	3,360	611	548	485	422	359	299	265	232	198	164	130
3,360	3,400	622	559	496	433	370	307	271	238	204	170	136
3,400	3,440	633	570	507	444	381	318	277	244	210	176	142
3,440	3,480	644	581	518	455	392	329	283	250	216	182	148
3,480	3,520	655	592	529	466	403	340	289	256	222	188	154
3,520	3,560	667	604	541	478	415	352	295	262	228	194	160
3,560	3,600	678	615	552	489	426	363	301	268	234	200	166
3,600	3,640	689	626	563	500	437	374	311	274	240	206	172
3,640	3,680	700	637	574	511	448	385	322	280	246	212	178
3,680	3,720	711	648	585	522	459	396	333	286	252	218	184
3,720	3,760	723	660	597	534	471	408	345	292	258	224	190
3,760	3,800	734	671	608	545	482	419	356	298	264	230	196
3,800	3,840	745	682	619	556	493	430	367	304	270	236	202
3,840	3,880	756	693	630	567	504	441	378	315	276	242	208
3,880	3,920	767	704	641	578	515	452	389	326	282	248	214
3,920	3,960	779	716	653	590	527	464	401	338	288	254	220
3,960	4,000	790	727	664	601	538	475	412	349	294	260	226
4,000	4,040	801	738	675	612	549	486	423	360	300	266	232
4,040	4,080	812	749	686	623	560	497	434	371	308	272	238
4,080	4,120	823	760	697	634	571	508	445	382	319	278	244
4,120	4,160	835	772	709	646	583	520	457	394	331	284	250
4,160	4,200	846	783	720	657	594	531	468	405	342	290	256
4,200	4,240	857	794	731	668	605	542	479	416	353	296	262
4,240	4,280	868	805	742	679	616	553	490	427	364	302	268
4,280	4,320	879	816	753	690	627	564	501	438	375	312	274
4,320	4,360	891	828	765	702	639	576	513	450	387	324	280
4,360	4,400	902	839	776	713	650	587	524	461	398	335	286
4,400	4,440	913	850	787	724	661	598	535	472	409	346	292
4,440	4,480	924	861	798	735	672	609	546	483	420	357	298
4,480	4,520	935	872	809	746	683	620	557	494	431	368	305
4,520	4,560	947	884	821	758	695	632	569	506	443	380	317
4,560	4,600	958	895	832	769	706	643	580	517	454	391	328
4,600	4,640	969	906	843	780	717	654	591	528	465	402	339
4,640	4,680	980	917	854	791	728	665	602	539	476	413	350
4,680	4,720	991	928	865	802	739	676	613	550	487	424	361
4,720	4,760	1,003	940	877	814	751	688	625	562	499	436	373
4,760	4,800	1,014	951	888	825	762	699	636	573	510	447	384
4,800	4,840	1,026	962	899	836	773	710	647	584	521	458	395
4,840	4,880	1,038	973	910	847	784	721	658	595	532	469	406
4,880	4,920	1,051	984	921	858	795	732	669	606	543	480	417
4,920	4,960	1,063	996	933	870	807	744	681	618	555	492	429
4,960	5,000	1,076	1,007	944	881	818	755	692	629	566	503	440
5,000	5,040	1,088	1,018	955	892	829	766	703	640	577	514	451

$5,040 and over

TABLE 9.3

Percentage method income tax withholding table

Payroll Period	One Withholding Allowance
Weekly	$ 51.92
Biweekly	103.85
Semimonthly	112.50
Monthly	225.00
Quarterly	675.00
Semiannually	1,350.00
Annually	2,700.00
Daily or miscellaneous (each day of the payroll period)	10.38

2. Percentage Method   Today, since many companies do not want to store the wage bracket tables, they use computers for their payroll. These companies use the **percentage method.** For this method we use Table 9.3 (above) and Table 9.4 (p. 235) from Circular E to calculate Dave's FIT.

Step 1. In Table 9.3, locate the weekly withholding for one allowance. Multiply this number by 2. *Claiming 2 allowances withholding*

$$\$51.92 \times 2 = \$103.84$$

Step 2. Subtract $103.84 in Step 1 from Dave's total pay.

$$\begin{array}{r} \$1,375.00 \\ -\ 103.84 \\ \hline \$1,271.16 \end{array}$$

Step 3. In Table 9.4 (p. 235), locate the married person's weekly pay table. The $1,271.16 falls between $899 and $1,855. The tax is $116.25 plus 28% of the excess over $899.

$$\begin{array}{r} \$1,271.16 \\ -\ 899.00 \\ \hline \$\ \ \ 372.16 \end{array}$$

Tax $\$116.25 + .28(\$372.16)$ *hence*

$\$116.25 + \$104.20 = $ $\boxed{\$220.45}$

Note that the percentage method results in a slightly different tax from that of the wage bracket method due to the range in table bracket intervals. If we use the middle of each range, our answer is close.

Ⓚ—*SIT*

We assume a 5% **state income tax (SIT).**

$$\$1,375 \times .05 = \$68.75$$

Ⓛ—*Health insurance*

Ⓜ—*Net pay*

Dave contributes $50 per week for health insurance.

Dave's **net pay** is his gross pay less all deductions.

$$\begin{array}{rll} \$1,375.00 & \text{gross} \\ -\ \ \ \ \ 63.55 & \text{Social Security} \\ -\ \ \ \ \ 19.94 & \text{Medicare} \\ -\ \ \ 220.00 & \text{FIT } \textit{Fed. Income Tax} \\ -\ \ \ \ \ 68.75 & \text{SIT } \textit{State Income Tax} \\ -\ \ \ \ \ 50.00 & \text{health insurance} \\ \hline =\ \$\ \ 952.76 & \text{net pay} \end{array}$$

Employers' Responsibilities[2]

In the first section of this unit, we saw that Dave Reilly contributed to Social Security and Medicare. Gonzales Company has the legal responsibility to match his contributions. Besides matching Social Security and Medicare, Gonzales must pay two important taxes that employees do not have to pay—federal and state unemployment taxes.

---

[2]Companies must deposit payroll taxes (federal income tax, Social Security, and Medicare) in a timely manner. If a business reported $50,000 or less for payroll tax liability in the prior year, deposits will be due monthly. If more than $50,000 was reported by a company in a prior year, deposits would be semiweekly. Check with the IRS for the latest details.

TABLE 9.4   Percentage method income tax withholding tables

Tables for Percentage Method of Withholding
(For Wages Paid in 1998)

TABLE 1—WEEKLY Payroll Period

(a) SINGLE person (including head of household)—

If the amount of wages (after subtracting withholding allowances) is:	The amount of income tax to withhold is:		
Not over $51	$0		
Over—	**But not over—**		**of excess over—**
$51	—$517	. 15%	—$51
$517	—$1,105	. $69.90 plus 28%	—$517
$1,105	—$2,493	. $234.54 plus 31%	—$1,105
$2,493	—$5,385	. $664.82 plus 36%	—$2,493
$5,385	. . . . .	. $1,705.94 plus 39.6%	—$5,385

(b) MARRIED person—

If the amount of wages (after subtracting withholding allowances) is:	The amount of income tax to withhold is:		
Not over $124	$0		
Over—	**But not over—**		**of excess over—**
$124	—$899	. 15%	—$124
$899	—$1,855	. $116.25 plus 28%	—$899
$1,855	—$3,084	. $383.93 plus 31%	—$1,855
$3,084	—$5,439	. $764.92 plus 36%	—$3,084
$5,439	. . . . .	. $1,612.72 plus 39.6%	—$5,439

TABLE 2—BIWEEKLY Payroll Period

(a) SINGLE person (including head of household)—

If the amount of wages (after subtracting withholding allowances) is:	The amount of income tax to withhold is:		
Not over $102	$0		
Over—	**But not over—**		**of excess over—**
$102	—$1,035	. 15%	—$102
$1,035	—$2,210	. $139.95 plus 28%	—$1,035
$2,210	—$4,987	. $468.95 plus 31%	—$2,210
$4,987	—$10,769	. $1,329.82 plus 36%	—$4,987
$10,769	. . . . .	. $3,411.34 plus 39.6%	—$10,769

(b) MARRIED person—

If the amount of wages (after subtracting withholding allowances) is:	The amount of income tax to withhold is:		
Not over $248	$0		
Over—	**But not over—**		**of excess over—**
$248	—$1,798	. 15%	—$248
$1,798	—$3,710	. $232.50 plus 28%	—$1,798
$3,710	—$6,167	. $767.86 plus 31%	—$3,710
$6,167	—$10,879	. $1,529.53 plus 36%	—$6,167
$10,879	. . . . .	. $3,225.85 plus 39.6%	—$10,879

TABLE 3—SEMIMONTHLY Payroll Period

(a) SINGLE person (including head of household)—

If the amount of wages (after subtracting withholding allowances) is:	The amount of income tax to withhold is:		
Not over $110	$0		
Over—	**But not over—**		**of excess over—**
$110	—$1,121	. 15%	—$110
$1,121	—$2,394	. $151.65 plus 28%	—$1,121
$2,394	—$5,402	. $508.09 plus 31%	—$2,394
$5,402	—$11,667	. $1,440.57 plus 36%	—$5,402
$11,667	. . . . .	. $3,695.97 plus 39.6%	—$11,667

(b) MARRIED person—

If the amount of wages (after subtracting withholding allowances) is:	The amount of income tax to withhold is:		
Not over $269	$0		
Over—	**But not over—**		**of excess over—**
$269	—$1,948	. 15%	—$269
$1,948	—$4,019	. $251.85 plus 28%	—$1,948
$4,019	—$6,681	. $831.73 plus 31%	—$4,019
$6,681	—$11,785	. $1,656.95 plus 36%	—$6,681
$11,785	. . . . .	. $3,494.39 plus 39.6%	—$11,785

TABLE 4—MONTHLY Payroll Period

(a) SINGLE person (including head of household)—

If the amount of wages (after subtracting withholding allowances) is:	The amount of income tax to withhold is:		
Not over $221	$0		
Over—	**But not over—**		**of excess over—**
$221	—$2,242	. 15%	—$221
$2,242	—$4,788	. $303.15 plus 28%	—$2,242
$4,788	—$10,804	. $1,016.03 plus 31%	—$4,788
$10,804	—$23,333	. $2,880.99 plus 36%	—$10,804
$23,333	. . . . .	. $7,391.43 plus 39.6%	—$23,333

(b) MARRIED person—

If the amount of wages (after subtracting withholding allowances) is:	The amount of income tax to withhold is:		
Not over $538	$0		
Over—	**But not over—**		**of excess over—**
$538	—$3,896	. 15%	—$538
$3,896	—$8,038	. $503.70 plus 28%	—$3,896
$8,038	—$13,363	. $1,663.46 plus 31%	—$8,038
$13,363	—$23,571	. $3,314.21 plus 36%	—$13,363
$23,571	. . . . .	. $6,989.09 plus 39.6%	—$23,571

Federal Unemployment Tax Act (FUTA)

The federal government participates in a joint federal-state unemployment program to help unemployed workers. At this writing, employers pay the government a 6.2% **FUTA** tax on the first $7,000 paid to employees as wages during the calendar year. Any wages in excess of $7,000 per worker are exempt wages and are not taxed for FUTA. If the total cumulative amount the employer owes the government is less than $100, the employer can pay the liability yearly (end of January in the following calendar year). If the tax is greater than $100, the employer must pay it quarterly.

Companies involved in a state unemployment tax fund can usually take a 5.4% credit against their FUTA tax. *In reality, then, companies are paying .8% (.008) to the federal unemployment program.* In all our calculations, FUTA is .008.

EXAMPLE   Assume a company had total wages of $19,000 in a calendar year. No employee earned more than $7,000 during the calendar year. The FUTA tax is .8% (6.2% minus the company's 5.4% credit for state unemployment tax). How much does the company pay in FUTA tax?

The company calculates its FUTA tax as follows:

$$6.2\% \text{ FUTA tax}$$
$$- 5.4\% \text{ credit for SUTA tax}$$
$$= .8\% \text{ tax for FUTA}$$

$.008 \times \$19,000 =$ $\boxed{\$152}$ FUTA tax due to federal government

State Unemployment Tax Act (SUTA)

The current **SUTA** tax in many states is 5.4% on the first $7,000 the employer pays an employee. Some states offer a merit rating system that results in a lower SUTA rate for companies with a stable employment period. The federal government still allows 5.4% credit on FUTA tax to companies entitled to the lower SUTA rate. States also charge companies with a poor employment record a higher SUTA rate. However, these companies cannot take any more than the 5.4% credit against the 6.2% federal unemployment rate.

EXAMPLE   Assume that a company has total wages of $20,000 and $4,000 of the wages are exempt from SUTA. What are the company's SUTA and FUTA taxes if the company's SUTA rate is 5.8% due to a poor employment record?

The exempt wages (over $7,000 earnings per worker) are not taxed for SUTA or FUTA. So the company owes the following SUTA and FUTA taxes:

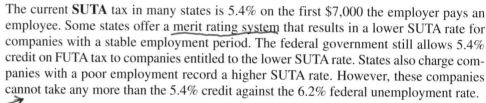

$$\$20,000$$
$$- 4,000 \text{ (exempt wages)}$$

Federal FUTA tax would then be:

$\$16,000 \times .058 =$ $\boxed{\$928}$ SUTA $\$16,000 \times .008 =$ $\boxed{\$128}$

You can check your progress with the following Practice Quiz.

LU 9.2 PRACTICE QUIZ

1. Calculate Social Security taxes, Medicare taxes, and FIT for Joy Royce. Joy's company pays her a monthly salary of $4,600. She is single and claims 1 deduction. Before this payroll, Joy's cumulative earnings were $66,000. (Social Security maximum is 6.2% on $68,400, and Medicare is 1.45%.) Calculate FIT by the wage bracket method and the percentage method.

2. Jim Brewer, owner of Arrow Company, has three employees who earn $300, $700, and $900 a week. Assume a state SUTA rate of 5.1%. What will Jim pay for state and federal unemployment taxes for the first quarter?

✓ **Solutions**

1. **Social Security**

   $$\$68,400$$
   $$- 66,000$$
   $$\$ 2,400 \times .062 = \boxed{\$148.80}$$

   Medicare

   $\$4,600 \times .0145 =$ $\boxed{\$66.70}$

   FIT

   a. Wage bracket method:
      1 withholding: $4,600 to $4,640 $\longrightarrow$ $\boxed{\$906}$ tax (Table 9.2)
   b. Percentage method: $4,600

      $$\$225 \times 1 = \quad\quad - 225 \text{ (Table 9.3)}$$
      $$\$4,375$$
      $$\$2,242 \text{ to } \$4,788 \longrightarrow \$303.15 \text{ plus } 28\% \text{ of excess over } \$2,242 \text{ (Table 9.4)}$$

      $$\$4,375$$
      $$- 2,242$$
      $$\$2,133 \times .28 = \quad \$597.24$$
      $$+ 303.15$$
      $$\boxed{\$900.39}$$

2. 13 weeks × $300 = $ 3,900
   13 weeks × $700 = 9,100 ($9,100 − $7,000) ⟶ $2,100 ⎫ Exempt wages
   13 weeks × $900 = 11,700 ($11,700 − $7,000) ⟶ 4,700 ⎬ (not taxed for
   ───── ───── ⎭ FUTA or SUTA)
   $24,700 $6,800

   $24,700 − $6,800 = $17,900 taxable wages

   SUTA = .051 × $17,900 = $912.90

   FUTA = .008 × $17,900 = $143.20

   Note: FUTA remains at .008 whether SUTA rate is higher or lower than standard.

Chapter Organizer and Reference Guide		
Topic	**Key point, procedure, formula**	**Example(s) to illustrate situation**
Gross pay, p. 227	Hours employee worked × Rate per hour	$6.50 per hour at 36 hours Gross pay = 36 × $6.50 = $234
Overtime, p. 227	Gross earnings (pay) = Regular pay + Earnings at overtime rate ($1\frac{1}{2}$)	$6 per hour; 42 hours Gross pay = (40 × $6) + (2 × $9) = $240 + $18 = $258
Straight piece rate, p. 228	Gross pay = Number of units produced × Rate per unit	1,185 units; rate per unit, $.89 Gross pay = 1,185 × $.89 = $1,054.65
Differential pay schedule, p. 228	Rate on each item is related to the number of items produced.	1–500 at $.84; 501–1,000 at $.96; 900 units produced Gross pay = (500 × $.84) + (400 × $.96) = $420 + $384 = $804
Straight commission, p. 229	Total sales × Commission rate Any draw would be subtracted from earnings.	$155,000 sales; 6% commission $155,000 × .06 = $9,300
Variable commission scale, p. 229	Sales at different levels pay different rates of commission.	Up to $5,000, 5%; $5,001 to $10,000, 8%; over $10,000, 10% Sold: $6,500 Solution: ($5,000 × .05) + ($1,500 × .08) = $250 + $120 = $370
Salary plus commission, p. 229	Regular wages (fixed) + Commissions earned	Base $400 per week + 2% on sales over $14,000 Actual sales: $16,000 $400 (base) + (.02 × $2,000) = $440
Payroll register, p. 230	Multicolumn form to record payroll. Married and paid weekly. (Table 9.1) Claims 0 allowances. FICA rates from chapter.	(see table below)
FICA, p. 231 Social Security Medicare	6.2% on $68,400 (S.S.) 1.45% (Med.) (Check IRS for latest rates.)	If John earns $70,000, what did he contribute for the year to Social Security and Medicare? S.S.: $68,400 × .062 = $4,240.80 Med.: $70,000 × .0145 = $1,015
FIT calculation (wage bracket method), p. 231	FIT has no maximum, unlike Social Security and Medicare.	Al Doy—married and 2 allowances. Paid weekly, $1,200. Table 9.1 $173 ↗ $1,200–$1,210

Payroll register example:

Earnings	Deductions			Net pay
Gross	FICA			
	SS	Med.	FIT	
1,100	68.20	15.95	174	841.85

	Chapter Organizer and Reference Guide (concluded)	
Topic	**Key point, procedure, formula**	**Example(s) to illustrate situation**
FIT calculation (percentage method), p. 234	The percentage method will produce approximately the same answer as wage bracket method. Companies with computers would utilize the percentage method.	Use same example as above. $1,200.00 − 103.84 ($51.92 × 2) Table 9.3 $1,096.16 By Table 9.4: $1,096.16 − 899.00 $ 197.16 $116.25 + .28 ($197.16) $116.25 + $55.20 = $171.45
State and federal unemployment, p. 235	Employer pays these taxes. Rates are 6.2% on $7,000 for federal and 5.4% for state on $7,000. 6.2% − 5.4% = .8% federal rate after credit. If state unemployment rate is higher than 5.4%, no additional credit is taken. If state unemployment rate is less than 5.4%, the full 5.4% credit can be taken for federal unemployment.	Cumulative pay before payroll, $6,400; this week's pay, $800. What are state and federal unemployment taxes for employer, assuming a 5.2% state unemployment rate? State → .052 × $600 = $31.20 Federal → .008 × $600 = $4.80 ($6,400 + $600 = $7,000 maximum)
Key terms	Biweekly, *p. 226* Deductions, *p. 227* Differential pay schedule, *p. 228* Draw, *p. 229* Employee's Withholding Allowance Certificate (W-4), *p. 230* Fair Labor Standards Act, *p. 227* Federal income tax withholding (FIT), *p. 231* Federal Insurance Contribution Act (FICA), *p. 231*	Federal Unemployment Tax Act (FUTA), *p. 235* Gross pay, *p. 227* Medicare, *p. 231* Monthly, *p. 226* Net pay, *p. 234* Overrides, *p. 229* Overtime, *p. 227* Payroll register, *p. 230* Percentage method, *p. 234* Semimonthly, *p. 226* Social Security, *p. 231* State income tax (SIT), *p. 234* State Unemployment Tax Act (SUTA), *p. 236* Straight commission, *p. 229* Variable commission scale, *p. 229* W-4, *p. 230* Wage bracket method, *p. 231* Weekly, *p. 226*

Critical Thinking Discussion Questions

1. Explain the difference between biweekly and semimonthly. Explain what problems may develop if a retail store hires someone on straight commission to sell cosmetics.

2. Explain what each column of a payroll register records (p. 230) and how each number is calculated. Social Security tax is based on a specific rate and base; Medicare tax is based on a rate but no base. Do you think this is fair to all taxpayers?

3. Compare and contrast the wage bracket method to the percentage method. Why would some companies choose the percentage method over the wage bracket method?

4. What taxes are the responsibility of the employer? How can an employer benefit from a merit-rating system for state unemployment?

DRILL PROBLEMS

Complete the following table:

Employee	M	T	W	Th	F	Hours	Rate per hour	Gross pay
9–1. Julie Felte	8	7	6	8	5	34	$5.60	$190.40
9–2. Pete Joll	7	9	8	8	8	40	$7.25	$290.00

Complete the following table (assume the overtime for each employee is a time-and-a-half rate after 40 hours):

Employee	M	T	W	Th	F	Sa	Total regular hours	Total overtime hours	Regular rate	Overtime rate	Gross earnings
9–3. Blue	12	9	9	9	9	3	40	11	$8.00	$12.00	$452.00

$40 \times \$8 = \$320$
$11 \times \$12 = \underline{\ 132}$
$\qquad\quad\ \$452$

Employee	M	T	W	Th	F	Sa	Total regular hours	Total overtime hours	Regular rate	Overtime rate	Gross earnings
9–4. Tagney	14	8	9	9	5	1	40	6	$7.60	$11.40	$372.40

$40 \times \$7.60 = \$304.00$
$6 \times \$11.40 = \underline{\ \ 68.40}$
$\qquad\qquad\ \ \$372.40$

Calculate gross earnings:

Worker	Number of units produced	Rate per unit	Gross earnings
9–5. Lang	510	$2.10	$1,071.00 (510 × $2.10)
9–6. Swan	846	$ .58	$ 490.68 ($.58 × 846)

Calculate the gross earnings for each apple picker based on the following differential pay scale:

1–1,000:	$.03 each	1,001–1,600	$.05 each	over 1,600	$.07 each

Apple picker	Number of apples picked	Gross earnings
9–7. Ryan	1,600	$60 = (1,000 × $.03) + (600 × $.05)
9–8. Rice	1,925	$82.75 = (1,000 × $.03) + (600 × $.05) + (325 × $.07)

Employee	Total sales	Commission rate	Draw	End-of-month commission received
9–9. Reese	$300,000	7%	$8,000	$13,000

$$\begin{pmatrix} .07 \times \$300{,}000 = \$21{,}000 \\ -\ 8{,}000 \\ \hline \$13{,}000 \end{pmatrix}$$

Ron Company has the following commission schedule:

Commission rate	Sales
2%	Up to $80,000
3.5%	Excess of $80,000 to $100,000
4%	More than $100,000

Calculate the gross earnings of Ron Company's two employees:

Employee	Total sales	Gross earnings
9–10. Bill Moore	$ 70,000	$1,400 ($70,000 × .02)
9–11. Ron Ear	$155,000	$4,500

$$\begin{pmatrix} \$80{,}000 \times .02\ = \$1{,}600 \\ \$20{,}000 \times .035 =\ \ \ \ 700 \\ \$55{,}000 \times .04\ \ =\ \underline{2{,}200} \\ \$4{,}500 \end{pmatrix}$$

239

Complete the following table, given that A Publishing Company pays its salespeople a weekly salary plus a 2% commission on all net sales over $5,000 (no commission on returned goods):

Employee	Gross sales	Return	Net sales	Given quota	Commission sales	Commission rates	Total commission	Regular wage	Total wage
9–12. Ring	$ 8,000	$25	$ 7,975	$5,000	$2,975	2%	$ 59.50	$250	$309.50
9–13. Porter	$12,000	$100	$11,900	$5,000	$6,900	2%	$138.00	$250	$388.00

Calculate the Social Security and Medicare deductions for the following employees (assume a tax rate of 6.2% on $68,400 for Social Security and 1.45% for Medicare):

Employee	Cumulative earnings before this pay period	Pay amount this period	Social Security	Medicare
9–14. Wilson	$60,000 $1,500 × .062 = $93	$1,500 $1,500 × .0145 = $21.75	$93	$21.75
9–15. Rosen	$68,200 $200 × .062 = $12.40	$1,800 $1,800 × .0145 = $26.10	$12.40	$26.10
9–16. Brown	$90,000	$1,900 $1,900 × .0145 = $27.55	0	$27.55

Complete the following payroll register. Calculate FIT by the wage bracket method for this weekly period; Social Security and Medicare are the same rates as in the previous problems. No one will reach the maximum for FICA.

Employee	Marital status	Allowances claimed	Gross pay	FIT	FICA S.S.	FICA Med.	Net pay
9–17. Al Holland	M S.S.: $910 × .062 = $56.42	2	$910 Med.: $910 × .0145 = $13.20	$103	$56.42	$13.20	$737.38
9–18. Jill West	M S.S.: $1,300 × .062 = $80.60	3	$1,300 Med.: $1,300 × .0145 = $18.85	$186	$80.60	$18.85	$1,014.55

Complete the following weekly payroll register. Calculate FIT by the percentage method. Assume the FICA maximum will not be reached by an employee. Social Security and Medicare are the same rates as in previous problems.

Employee	Marital status	Exemptions claimed	Gross pay	FIT	FICA S.S.	FICA Med.	Net pay
9–19. French	M	4	$1,900	$338.38	$117.80	$27.55	$1,416.27

$1,900.00
− 207.68   ($51.92 × 4)   S.S.: $1,900 × .062 = $117.80

$1,692.32 $116.25 + .28($793.32)   Med.: $1,900 × .0145 = $27.55
− 899.00 $116.25 + $222.13

$ 793.32 $338.38

9–20. Given the following, calculate the state (assume 5.3%) and federal unemployment taxes that the employer must pay for each of the first two quarters. The federal unemployment tax is .8% on the first $7,000.

Payroll summary		
	Quarter 1	Quarter 2
Bill Adams	$4,000	$ 8,000
Rich Haines	8,000	14,000
Alice Smooth	3,200	3,800

*Note only first $7,000 is taxed.
†Only first $3,000 is taxed since that puts Adams over $7,000 for the year.

Quarter 1

Adams	$ 4,000
Haines	7,000*
Smooth	3,200
	$14,200
	× .053

SUTA = $752.60

.008 × $14,200 = $113.60 FUTA

Quarter 2

Adams	$ 3,000†
Haines	0
Smooth	3,800
	$ 6,800
	× .053

SUTA = $360.40

FUTA = $ 54.40   ($6,800 × .008)

WORD PROBLEMS

9–21. On December 3, 1997, *Suburban Life* ran the following advertisement: "School Bus Driver CDL Driver Permit desirable. Will train if needed. $10.85 per hour." If the driver drives for 45 hours per week (time and a half for overtime), what will be the driver's gross pay?

$$\begin{array}{r} \$\ 10.85 \\ \times\ 40 \\ \hline \$434.00 \end{array}$$

+ 5 hours at 5 × $16.275 ($10.85 × 1.5) = $81.38

$$\begin{array}{r} \$434.00 \\ +\ 81.38 \\ \hline \$515.38 \end{array}$$

9–22. On December 17, 1997, *Suburban Life* ran the following help-wanted advertisement: "Building Inspector Village of Woodridge, starting salary $33,280 per year." John, who is married and claims two exemptions, is trying to determine what his weekly take-home pay would be if he took this job. The only deductions would be FIT, Social Security, Medicare, and 3% state income tax. What would John's net pay be at the end of each week? Use the percentage method of withholding. Social Security is 6.2% on $68,400; Medicare is 1.45%.

$$\begin{array}{l} \$640 \text{ per week} \\ 52)\overline{\$33,280} \end{array}$$

$$\begin{array}{r} \$640.00 \\ \times\ .03 \text{ state income tax} \\ \hline \$\ 19.20 \text{ (SIT)} \end{array}$$

$$\begin{array}{r} \$640.00 \\ \times\ .062 \text{ Social Security tax} \\ \hline \$\ 39.68 \text{ (FICA)} \end{array}$$

$$\begin{array}{r} \$640.00 \\ \times\ .0145 \text{ Medicare tax} \\ \hline \$\ 9.28 \text{ (Medicare)} \end{array}$$

FIT

$$\begin{array}{r} \$\ 51.92 \\ \times\ \ 2 \\ \hline \$103.84 \end{array}$$

$$\begin{array}{r} \$640.00 \\ -\ 103.84 \\ \hline \$536.16 \\ -\ 124.00 \\ \hline \$412.16 \\ \times\ .15 \\ \hline \$\ 61.82 \end{array}$$

$$\begin{array}{r} \$640.00 \text{ per week} \\ -\ 61.82 \text{ (FIT)} \\ -\ 39.68 \text{ (FICA)} \\ -\ 19.20 \text{ (SIT)} \\ -\ 9.28 \text{ (Medicare)} \\ \hline \$510.02 \text{ net pay} \end{array}$$

9–23. In 1996, Chicago Dartnell Corporation stated that although most firms start paying commission on the first dollar of sales, 39% pay with the following variable commission scale:

First $20,000 of sales, 4%

Next $15,000 of sales, 5%

Over $35,000 sales, 6%

Bill Murray sold $46,000 this month. What will his earnings be?

$$\begin{array}{r} \$20,000 \times .04 = \$\ \ 800 \\ \$15,000 \times .05 = \ \ 750 \\ \$11,000 \times .06 = \ \ 660 \\ \hline \$2,210 \end{array}$$

9–24. Dennis Toby is a salesclerk at Northwest Department Store. Dennis receives $8 per hour plus a commission of 3% on all sales. Assume Dennis works 30 hours and has sales of $1,900. What is his gross pay?

(30 hours × $8) + ($1,900 × .03) = $240 + $57 = $297

9–25. Blinn Corporation pays its employees on a graduated commission scale: 3% on first $40,000 sales, 4% on sales from $40,001 to $85,000, and 6% on sales greater than $85,000. Bill Burns had $87,000 sales. What commission did Bill earn?

$$\begin{array}{r} \$40,000 \times .03 = \$1,200 \\ 45,000 \times .04 = \ 1,800 \\ 2,000 \times .06 = \ \ 120 \\ \hline \$3,120 \end{array}$$

9–26. Robin Hartman earns $600 per week plus 3% of sales over $6,500. Robin's sales are $14,000. How much does Robin earn?

$600 + (.03 × $7,500) = $600 + $225 = $825

9–27. Pat Maninen earns a gross salary of $1,600 each week. What are Pat's first week's deductions for Social Security and Medicare? Will any of Pat's wages be exempt from Social Security and Medicare for the calendar year? Assume a rate of 6.2% on $68,400 for Social Security and 1.45% for Medicare.

Social Security: $1,600 × .062 = $99.20   Medicare: $1,600 × .0145 = $23.20

Yes for Social Security. 52 weeks × $1,600 =

$83,200
− 68,400

$14,800 exempt

9–28. Richard Gaziano is a manager for Health Care, Inc. Health Care deducts Social Security, Medicare, and FIT from his earnings. Assume the same Social Security and Medicare rates as in Problem 9–27. Before this payroll, Richard is $1,000 below the maximum level for Social Security earnings. Richard is married, is paid weekly, and claims 2 exemptions. Use wage bracket Table 9.1 for FIT. What is Richard's net pay for the week if he earns $1,300?

Social Security: $1,000 × .062 = $62   Medicare: $1,300 × .0145 = $18.85

$1,300 − $62 − $18.85 − $201 = $1,018.15

9–29. Len Mast earned $2,200 for the last two weeks. He is married, is paid biweekly, and claims 3 exemptions. What is Len's income tax? Use the percentage method.

$2,200.00
− 311.55 ($103.85 × 3)

$1,888.45 $232.50 + .28($90.45)
− 1,798.00 $232.50 + $25.33

$ 90.45 $257.83

9–30. Westway Company pays Suzie Chan $1,400 per week. By the end of week 50, how much did Westway deduct for Suzie's Social Security and Medicare for the year? Assume Social Security is 6.2% on $68,400 and 1.45% for Medicare. What state and federal unemployment taxes does Westway pay on Suzie's yearly salary? The state unemployment rate is 5.1%. FUTA is .8%.

50 weeks × $1,400 = $70,000

Social Security: $68,400 × .062 = $4,240.80   Medicare: $70,000 × .0145 = $1,015.00

SUTA: .051 × $7,000 = $357   FUTA: .008 × $7,000 = $56

9–31. Morris Leste, owner of Carlson Company, has three employees who earn $400, $500, and $700 per week. What are the total state and federal unemployment taxes that Morris owes for the first 11 weeks of the year and for week 30? Assume a state rate of 5.6% and a federal rate of .8%.

11 × $400 = $ 4,400   State: $16,900 × .056 = $946.40

11 × $500 =   5,500   Federal: $16,900 × .008 = $135.20

11 × $700 =   7,700 $0 for week 30

$17,600
− 700

$16,900

CHALLENGE PROBLEMS

9–32. Bill Rose is a salesperson for Boxes, Inc. He believes his $1,460.47 monthly paycheck is in error. Bill earns a $1,400 salary per month plus a 9.5% commission on sales over $1,500. Last month, Bill had $8,250 in sales. Bill believes his traveling expenses are 16% of his weekly gross earnings before commissions. Monthly deductions include Social Security, $126.56; Medicare, $29.60; FIT, $239.29; union dues, $25.00; and health insurance, $16.99. Calculate the following: **(a)** Bill's monthly take-home pay, and indicate the amount his check was under- or overstated, and **(b)** Bill's weekly traveling expenses. Round your final answer to the nearest dollar.

a. $8,250
− 1,500

$6,750 × .095 = $641.25

$1,400.00 monthly salary
+ 641.25 commission

$2,041.25
− 126.56
− 29.60
− 239.29
− 25.00
− 16.99

$1,603.81 net pay   Difference: $143.34 overstated

b. $\dfrac{\$1,400 \times 12}{52} \times .16 = \$51.69 = \$52$

9–33. John Muscle is employed as a construction worker for Chicago Bridge and Iron Company. He is married and claims 2 exemptions on his withholdings at work. He is looking at his final paycheck for the year and finds he earned $83,980. John is paid weekly; however, in checking his pay stub 6 months ago, he noticed his net pay was more than $100 less. He is worried that his employer has been withholding too much. **(a)** Recalculate John's last paycheck to verify his net pay. **(b)** Explain to John why his earnings would have been more than $100 less 6 months ago. John's only deductions are FIT, Social Security, and Medicare. Use the percentage method of withholding and the rates given in the chapter.

$$\frac{\$1,615}{52)\overline{\$83,980}}$$

FIT

$$
\begin{array}{r}
\$\ 51.92 \\
\times\ 2 \\
\hline
\$103.84
\end{array}
$$

$$
\begin{array}{r}
\$1,615.00 \\
-\ 103.84\ \text{tax} \\
\hline
\end{array}
$$

$1,511.16 = \$116.25$ plus 28% over $899

$$
\begin{array}{r}
\$1,511.16 \\
-\ 899.00 \\
\hline
\$\ \ 612.16 \\
\times\ .28 \\
\hline
\$\ \ \ \ 171.40
\end{array}
$$

Social Security: No amount taken out. Has already exceeded maximum $68,400.

Medicare:
$$
\begin{array}{r}
\$1,615.00 \\
\times\ .0145 \\
\hline
\$\ \ \ \ 23.42
\end{array}
$$

(FIT)
$116.25 + \$171.40 = \$287.65$

(FIT)   (FICA)   (Med.)
Earnings $1,615.00 − \$287.65 −   0   − \$23.42 = \$1,303.93$

Six months ago Social Security would have been taken out since the limit was not reached ($1,615 \times .062 = \$100.13$).

 SUMMARY PRACTICE TEST

1. Calculate Paul's gross pay (he is entitled to time and a half). *(p. 227)*

M	T	W	Th	F	Total hours	Rate per hour	Gross pay
$8\frac{1}{2}$	$8\frac{1}{4}$	$10\frac{1}{2}$	$7\frac{1}{4}$	$11\frac{1}{2}$	46	$8.00	$392.00

$$
\begin{array}{l}
40\ \text{hours} \times \$\ 8.00 = \$320.00 \\
\ \ 6\ \text{hours} \times \$12.00 = \ \ \underline{\ \ 72.00} \\
\ \$392.00
\end{array}
$$

2. Clair Montgomery sells shoes for Macy's. Macy pays Clair $7.50 per hour plus a 3% commission on all sales. Assume Clair works 38 hours for the week and has $5,600 sales. What is Clair's gross pay? *(p. 229)*

$$
\begin{array}{l}
38\ \text{hours} \times \$7.50 = \$285 \\
\$5,600\ \ \times\ \ \ .03 = \underline{\ 168} \\
\ \$453
\end{array}
$$

3. Haley Company pays its employees on a graduated commission scale: 3% on the first $30,000 sales; 5% on sales from $30,001 to $80,000; and 9% on sales of more than $80,000. Dan Power, an employee of Haley, has $170,000 in sales. What commission did Dan earn? *(p. 229)*

$$
\begin{array}{l}
.03 \times \$30,000 = \$\ \ \ 900 \\
.05 \times \$50,000 = \ \ 2,500 \\
.09 \times \$90,000 = \ \ \underline{8,100} \\
\ \ \ \ \ \ \ \ \ \ \ \ \ \ \ \ \ \ \$11,500
\end{array}
$$

4. Lou Chin, an accountant for Ace Corporation, earned $66,000 from January to June. In July, Lou earned $18,000. Assume a tax rate of 6.2% for Social Security on $68,400 and 1.45% on Medicare. How much are the July taxes for Social Security and Medicare? *(p. 231)*

$$
\begin{array}{lr}
\text{Social Security:} & \$68,400 \\
& \underline{-\ 66,000} \\
& \$\ 2,400 \times .062\ = \$148.80 \\
\text{Medicare:} & \$18,000 \times .0145 = \$261
\end{array}
$$

5. Maggie Kate earns $800 per week. She is married and claims 2 exemptions. What is Maggie's income tax? Use the percentage method. *(p. 234)*

   $800.00
   − 103.84 (2 × $51.92)
   ―――――
   $696.16
   − 124.00
   ―――――
   $572.16 × .15 = $85.82

6. John Toby pays his two employees $500 and $850 per week. Assume a state unemployment tax rate of 5.7% and a federal unemployment tax rate of .8%. What state and federal unemployment taxes will John pay at the end of quarter 1 and quarter 2? *(p. 236)*

   Quarter 1   13 weeks × $500 = $6,500
   　　　　　　　　13 weeks × $850 = $11,050
   Taxable $6,500 + $7,000 = $13,500 × .057 = $769.50 SUTA
   FUTA = $13,500 × .008 = $108.00

   Quarter 2 $7,000 − $6,500 = $500 × .057 = $28.50 SUTA
   　　　　　　　　　　　　　　$500 × .008 = $4.00 FUTA

A GROUP PROJECT Defend or reject the following business math issue based on the *Kiplinger's Personal Finance Magazine* article below:

CAREER

Rosy Outlook for Raises and Bonuses

▶ **Knowing what you're worth is a key to making sure you get your fair share.** By Marc L. Schulhof

Despite the shenanigans in the stock market and worries about the world economy, record-low unemployment here at home is painting an optimistic picture for this year's raise-and-bonus season.

Raises for professionals are expected to average 4.2%, the highest in seven years, according to the annual *Report on Salary Surveys* published by the Institute of Management and Administration. The word on bonuses is even more exciting: The average this year is estimated at 11.1%, compared with only (only!) 10.2% a year ago.

Will you get your fair share of the booty? That depends on lots of things, including exactly how well your company is doing, how well you are doing—and how well your boss thinks you are doing. But compensation experts say that the most convincing argument for a raise or bonus rests on solid research into the going rate for your position. In other words, what are you worth?

But how do you know that—unless you're in the enviable position of being hounded by headhunters or decide to launch a time-consuming search for a better-paying job someplace else?

TELL THE BOSS A THING OR TWO. The easiest place to start your research is the Internet. The Salary Zone (www.ioma.com/zone) charges for information, but the personalized research you'll receive from the site's compensation consultants might be worth the outlay. For $40, you'll get a report showing the average salary and bonus figures for someone in your area of the country with your kind of job and years of experience, as well as commentary on which professional designations, specialized training or job-specific responsibilities might affect the pay scale.

The Salary Zone service has recently expanded to individuals; its original clients were drawn from the opposing side of the table—managers who used the data to figure out what they should pay new hires. Now, though, the service will play both sides of the negotiations.

If you'd rather not pay to play, there are free Web sites with salary information. Recruitment Extra (recruitmentextra.com/salarysurveys.html) and the National Business Employment Weekly (careers.wsj.com/?content=cwc-salaries.htm) both offer mostly up-to-date salary surveys for different occupations. The federal government's Bureau of Labor Statistics is developing a National Compensation Survey; until it's completed, search the *Occupational Outlook Handbook*, a reliable bellwether for national average salaries (stats.bls.gov/ocohome.htm).

When you use these sites and others like them, make sure to pick out pertinent information. Avoid the gravitational pull toward surveys that show high salaries but don't distinguish among important factors such as where you live, the size of your company and your experience. Conversely, if surveys show you're being paid more than average, don't throw in the towel. Where you live and your value to the company could justify even higher pay.

Your professional association, preferably the local chapter, may have a recent salary survey as well. Again, match yourself to the salary level that most closely mirrors your own situation. Your peers, both within and outside your own company, could be a good guide, too. But should you ask co-workers what they make? Tough call. Sharing your bottom line could be like opening Pandora's cubicle, and could create a truly awful office atmosphere. There may be an easier way, too. "A lot of companies post job openings," says Michael O'Malley, a compensation consultant and author of *Are You Paid What You're Worth?* "They often print the salary range and midpoint. If you watch the company bulletin board, you can pretty much piece together the salary structure."

Finally, consider calling some recruiters. If you've developed a relationship with a few already, great. If not, try to get referrals from colleagues. Ask the headhunters for an estimate of what you could command on the open market, and factor that into your evidence.

MARC ROSENTHAL

Business Math Issue

Headhunters always can find you the best jobs.

1. List the key points of the article and information to support your position.
2. Write a group defense of your position using math calculations to support your view.

Continental's Pilot Payroll Costs to Rise By 27% in First Year of Tentative Pact

By SCOTT MCCARTNEY
Staff Reporter of THE WALL STREET JOURNAL

Continental Airlines' cockpit payroll costs will jump 27% in the first year of a new tentative pilot contract and a total of more than 50% over the life of the five-year deal, according to a union briefing to pilots.

The deal, struck last week by negotiators with help from the National Mediation Board, will put wages on par with pay rates at the five airlines larger than Continental within two years, the Independent Association of Continental Pilots said. After years of givebacks and bankruptcy reorganization, both the Houston-based airline and the union agreed Continental's pilots were underpaid compared with other large carriers.

"We will be able to look at 1999 pay rates at Delta, United, Northwest, US Airways and American and hold our heads [and our checkbooks] high," union leaders said in a letter to Continental's 5,000 pilots.

But the tentative deal, which must be approved by the union's 20-member board and then ratified by pilots, is already drawing some criticism within the rank-and-file.

The contract trades profit-sharing for higher wage rates, for example, while some pilots wanted both. Pilots will receive a 7.5% raise in 1998, but will lose a profit-sharing check of about 7% of salary. "Approval is not a slam-dunk right now, particularly without the profit-sharing," said one senior pilot. "The question is whether anyone is willing to go to war over 7% profit-sharing?"

In addition, some pilots grumble that the new contract will switch Continental from a seniority-only pay system to wage rates set by the type of airplane flown, forcing senior pilots to retrain for larger aircraft if they want to maintain higher wages. Currently, a Continental pilot is paid the same whether he flies a jumbo jet or a small 100-seat airplane, and the pilot can choose a schedule, based on seniority, that fits his lifestyle. Changing aircraft can dramatically change a pilot's schedule, but the change "was a small price to pay for wage gains," union leaders said in their letter to pilots.

In addition to a 27% hike in pilot payroll retroactive to Oct. 1 and the 7.5% hike next Oct. 1, the tentative agreement includes raises of 7.5% in 1999, 2.5% in 2000 and 1% in 2001.

Continental Chairman and Chief Executive Gordon Bethune has said he wanted to get all employees to industry-standard wages within three years, offsetting the raises with cost reductions in areas like travel-agent expenses and revenue increases resulting from a bigger mix of high-fare business travelers.

Continental currently spends about $430 million on pilots a year, but will see that increase to more than $630 million by Oct. 1, 1999. The tentative deal with pilots does preserve productivity advantages for Continental, however. "The agreement fits the economic models we have for the next five years," a company spokesman said.

The IACP also said pension benefits will increase under the tentative deal. Pensions will be calculated at a rate of 2.2% of the final average earnings, compared with the current formula at 1.45%.

Project A

How much more will the contract cost Continental for FUTA and SUTA? Assume the same rates as in the chapter.

Assume the same number of pilots. No increase for FUTA and SUTA since no tax over $7,000 base.

CLASSROOM NOTES

10

SIMPLE INTEREST

LEARNING UNIT OBJECTIVES

LU 10.1 Calculation of Simple Interest and Maturity Value

- Calculate simple interest and maturity value for months and years *(p. 250).*
- Calculate simple interest and maturity value by **(a)** exact interest and **(b)** ordinary interest *(pp. 251–52).*

LU 10.2 Finding Unknown in Simple Interest Formula

- Using the interest formula, calculate the unknown when the other two (principal, rate, or time) are given *(pp. 253–54).*

LU 10.3 U.S. Rule—Making Partial Note Payments before Due Date

- List the steps to complete the U.S. Rule *(pp. 255–56).*
- Complete the proper interest credits under the U.S. Rule *(pp. 255–56).*

DEBT SMART

When it comes to strategic borrowing investors can be pretty dumb

By KEVIN J. DELANEY

AST SUMMER Jonathan Lau came to a financial fork in the road. The 37-year-old dentist began tackling $80,000 in debt that he had generated setting up his Maui, Hawaii, practice. He was making more than $2.600 a month in payments and asking himself, "Should I just try to pay off the loan?"

Dr. Lau was torn between pooling his resources to pay down the debt and sticking it out for the rest of the loan. But a trip to the bank made his choice easier.

Without much difficulty, he persuaded the lender to refinance his loan at 9%, shaving more than two percentage points off the rate he had been paying, and with no additional costs. Dr. Lau's monthly payments dropped by more than $1,100.

© 1997 Dow Jones & Company, Inc.

We live in a credit society. For various reasons, many people and businesses use credit to "buy now and pay later." Everything has a price, and the price paid for credit is **interest,** which is a rental charge for money.

Usually, a person's largest debt is for a home or business. Once you borrow a large amount, do you have to keep paying the same rate of interest? Learn a lesson from *The Wall Street Journal* clipping on borrowing. Never be afraid to ask your lender about refinancing. As a result of refinancing, Dr. Lau's monthly business loan payment dropped more than $1,100.

This chapter is about simple interest. The principles discussed apply whether you are paying interest or receiving interest. Let's begin by learning how to calculate simple interest.

LEARNING UNIT 10.1　Calculation of Simple Interest and Maturity Value

Jan Carley, a young attorney, rented an office in a professional building. Since Jan recently graduated from law school, she was short of cash. To purchase office furniture for her new office, Jan went to her bank and borrowed $30,000 for 6 months at an 8% annual interest rate.

The original amount Jan borrowed ($30,000) is the **principal** (face value) of the loan. Jan's price for using the $30,000 is the interest rate (8%) the bank charges on a yearly basis. Since Jan is borrowing the $30,000 for 6 months, Jan's loan will have a **maturity value** of $31,200—the principal plus the interest on the loan. Thus, Jan's price for using the furniture before she can pay for it is $1,200 interest, which is a percent of the principal for a specific time period. To make this calculation, we use the following formula:

$$\text{Maturity value } (MV) = \text{Principal } (P) + \text{Interest } (I)$$

$$\$31{,}200 = \$30{,}000 + \$1{,}200$$

Jan's furniture purchase introduces **simple interest**—the cost of a loan, usually for 1 year or less. Simple interest is only on the original principal or amount borrowed. Let's examine how the bank calculated Jan's $1,200 interest.

Simple Interest Formula

To calculate interest, we use the following **simple interest formula:**

$$\text{Simple interest } (I) = \text{Principal } (P) \times \text{Rate } (R) \times \text{Time } (T)$$

Calculate Interest & Maturity Value (handwritten)

In your calculator, multiply $30,000 times .08 times 6. Divide your answer by 12. You could also use the % key—multiply $30,000 times 8% times 6 and then divide your answer by 12.

In this formula, rate is expressed as a decimal, fraction, or percent; and time is expressed in years or a fraction of a year.

EXAMPLE Jan Carley borrowed $30,000 for office furniture. The loan was for 6 months at an annual interest rate of 8%. What are Jan's interest and maturity value?

Using the simple interest formula, the bank determined Jan's interest as follows:

Step 1. Calculate the interest.

$$I = \$30,000 \times \underset{(R)}{.08} \times \underset{(T)}{\frac{6}{12}}$$
$$\underset{(P)}{}$$
$$= \$1,200$$

Step 2. Calculate the maturity value.

$$MV = \underset{(P)}{\$30,000} + \underset{(I)}{\$1,200}$$
$$= \boxed{\$31,200}$$

Now let's use the same example and assume Jan borrowed $30,000 for 1 year. The bank would calculate Jan's interest and maturity value as follows:

Step 1. Calculate the interest.

$$I = \$30,000 \times \underset{(R)}{.08} \times \underset{(T)}{1 \text{ year}}$$
$$\underset{(P)}{}$$
$$= \$2,400$$

Step 2. Calculate the maturity value.

$$MV = \underset{(P)}{\$30,000} + \underset{(I)}{\$2,400}$$
$$= \boxed{\$32,400}$$

Let's use the same example again and assume Jan borrowed $30,000 for 18 months. Then Jan's interest and maturity value would be calculated as follows:

Step 1. Calculate the interest.

$$I = \$30,000 \times \underset{(R)}{.08} \times \underset{(T)}{\frac{18^1}{12}}$$
$$\underset{(P)}{}$$
$$= \$3,600$$

Step 2. Calculate the maturity value.

$$MV = \underset{(P)}{\$30,000} + \underset{(I)}{\$3,600}$$
$$= \boxed{\$33,600}$$

Next we'll turn our attention to two common methods we can use to calculate simple interest when a loan specifies its beginning and ending dates.

Two Methods for Calculating Simple Interest and Maturity Value

on p. 175 interest (handwritten)

From the Business Math Handbook

July 6	187th day
March 4	− 63rd day
	124 days (exact time of loan)
March	31
	− 4
	27
April	30
May	31
June	30
July	+ 6
	124 days

Method 1: Exact Interest (365 Days) The Federal Reserve banks and the federal government use the **exact interest** method. The *exact interest* is calculated by using a 365-day year. For **time,** we count the exact number of days in the month that the borrower has the loan. The day the loan is made is not counted, but the day the money is returned is counted as a full day. This method calculates interest by using the following fraction to represent time in the formula:

$$\text{Time} = \frac{\text{Exact number of days}}{365} \qquad \text{Exact interest}$$

For this calculation, we use the exact days-in-a-year calendar from the *Business Math Handbook*. You learned how to use this calendar in Chapter 7, page 175.

EXAMPLE On March 4, Peg Carry borrowed $40,000 at 8% interest. Interest and principal are due on July 6. What is the interest cost and the maturity value?

Step 1. Calculate the interest.

$$I = P \times R \times T$$
$$= \$40,000 \times .08 \times \frac{124}{365}$$
$$= \$1,087.12 \text{ (rounded to nearest cent)}$$

---

[1]This is the same as 1.5 years.

Step 2.   Calculate the maturity value.
$$MV = P + I$$
$$= \$40{,}000 + \$1{,}087.12$$
$$= \boxed{\$41{,}087.12}$$

Method 2: Ordinary Interest (360 Days)   In the **ordinary interest** method, time in the formula $I = P \times R \times T$ is equal to the following:

$$\text{Time} = \frac{\text{Exact number of days}}{360} \leftarrow$$

Ordinary interest

Since banks commonly use the ordinary interest method, it is known as the **Banker's Rule.** Banks charge a slightly higher rate of interest because they use 360 days instead of 365 in the denominator. By using 360 instead of 365, the calculation is supposedly simplified. Consumer groups, however, are questioning why banks can use 360 days, since this benefits the bank and not the customer. The use of computers and calculators no longer makes the simplified calculation necessary. For example, after a court case in Oregon, banks began calculating interest on 365 days except in mortgages.

Now let's replay the Peg Carry example we used to illustrate Method 1 to see the difference in bank interest when we use Method 2.

EXAMPLE   On March 4, Peg Carry borrowed $40,000 at 8% interest. Interest and principal are due on July 6. What are the interest cost and the maturity value?

Step 1.   Calculate the interest.
$$I = \$40{,}000 \times .08 \times \frac{124}{360}$$
$$= \$1{,}102.22$$

Step 2.   Calculate the maturity value.
$$MV = P + I$$
$$= \$40{,}000 + \$1{,}102.22$$
$$= \boxed{\$41{,}102.22}$$

Note: By using Method 2, the bank increases its interest by $15.10.

$$\begin{array}{r} \$1{,}102.22 \quad \longleftarrow \text{Method 2} \\ - \ 1{,}087.12 \quad \longleftarrow \text{Method 1} \\ \hline \$ \quad 15.10 \end{array}$$

Board of Governors of the Federal Reserve System.

LU 10.1 PRACTICE QUIZ

Calculate simple interest (round to the nearest cent):

1. $14,000 at 4% for 9 months

2. $25,000 at 7% for 5 years

3. $40,000 at $10\frac{1}{2}$% for 19 months

4. On May 4, Dawn Kristal borrowed $15,000 at 8%. Dawn must pay the principal and interest on August 10. What are Dawn's simple interest and maturity value if you use the exact interest method?

5. What are Dawn Kristal's (Problem 4) simple interest and maturity value if you use the ordinary interest method?

✓   **Solutions**

1. $\$14{,}000 \times .04 \times \dfrac{9}{12} = \boxed{\$420}$

2. $\$25{,}000 \times .07 \times 5 = \boxed{\$8{,}750}$

3. $\$40{,}000 \times .105 \times \dfrac{19}{12} = \boxed{\$6{,}650}$

4.
$$\begin{array}{r} \text{August 10} \longrightarrow \quad 222 \\ \text{May 4} \quad \longrightarrow - \ 124 \\ \hline 98 \end{array}$$
$\$15{,}000 \times .08 \times \dfrac{98}{365} = \boxed{\$322.19}$

$MV = \$15{,}000 + \$322.19 = \boxed{\$15{,}322.19}$

5. $\$15{,}000 \times .08 \times \dfrac{98}{360} = \boxed{\$326.67}$ $MV = \$15{,}000 + \$326.67 = \boxed{\$15{,}326.67}$

Principal → Rate × Time

LEARNING UNIT 10.2 Finding Unknown in Simple Interest Formula

Russia Drives Up Interest Rates To Keep Investors

By BETSY McKAY

Staff Reporter of THE WALL STREET JOURNAL

MOSCOW—Russia's Central Bank boosted interest rates sharply in an attempt to stem flight from its markets after stock prices plunged, and yields on government bonds soared.

The bank raised both main interest rates to 50%, one of their highest levels since Asian market turmoil first struck Russia's financial markets last fall. Officials had already raised the Lombard lending rate to 36%-40% from 30% Friday, but it proved insufficient to keep investors from fleeing in fear of a devaluation of the ruble. The bank's benchmark refinance rate had been 30%.

© 1998 Dow Jones & Company, Inc.

© George Diebold/The Stock Market.

Interest rates fluctuate. Low interest rates at one time do not guarantee continued low interest rates. Market turmoil in a foreign market can affect interest rates in other foreign markets. *The Wall Street Journal* clipping "Russia Drives Up Interest Rates to Keep Investors" reports that Russia's Central Bank raised interest rates 50% after stock prices plunged and yields on government bonds soared.

Up to this point, we used the following simple interest formula to solve for interest:

> Interest (I) = Principal (P) × Rate (R) × Time (T)

Now we will show how to solve for principal, rate, and time. In all our calculations, we use 360 days and round only final answers.

Finding the Principal

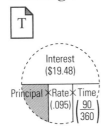

EXAMPLE Tim Jarvis paid the bank $19.48 interest at 9.5% for 90 days. How much did Tim borrow?

The following formula is used to calculate the principal of a loan:

$$\text{Principal} = \frac{\text{Interest}}{\text{Rate} \times \text{Time}}$$

$$\frac{19.48}{.095 \times \frac{90}{360}}$$

Note how we illustrated this in the margin. The shaded area is what we are solving for. When solving for principal, rate, or time, you are dividing. Interest will be in the numerator, and the denominator will be the other two elements multiplied by each other.

Step 1. Set up the formula.

$$P = \frac{\$19.48}{.095 \times \frac{90}{360}}$$

Step 2. When using a calculator, press
.095 × 90 ÷ 360 M+ .

Step 2. Multiply the denominator.

.095 times 90 divided by 360 (do not round)

$$P = \frac{\$19.48}{.02375}$$

Step 3. When using a calculator, press
19.48 ÷ MR = .

Step 3. Divide the numerator by the result of Step 2. $P = \$820.21$

Step 4. Check your answer.

$$\$19.48 = \$820.21 \times .095 \times \frac{90}{360}$$

$$(I) \qquad (P) \qquad (R) \qquad (T)$$

Finding the Rate

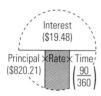

EXAMPLE   Tim Jarvis borrowed $820.21 from a bank. Tim's interest is $19.48 for 90 days. What rate of interest did Tim pay?

The following formula is used to calculate the rate of interest:

$$\text{Rate} = \frac{\text{Interest}}{\text{Principal} \times \text{Time}}$$

Step 1.   Set up the formula.

$$R = \frac{\$19.48}{\$820.21 \times \dfrac{90}{360}}$$

Step 2. When using a calculator, press
$\boxed{820.21}\boxed{\times}\boxed{90}\boxed{\div}\boxed{360}\boxed{M+}$.

Step 2.   Multiply the denominator. Do not round the answer.

$$R = \frac{\$19.48}{\$205.0525}$$

Step 3. When using a calculator, press
$\boxed{19.48}\boxed{\div}\boxed{MR}\boxed{\%}$.

Step 3.   Divide the numerator by the result of Step 2. $R = 9.5\%$

Step 4.   Check your answer.
$$\$19.48 = \$820.21 \times .095 \times \frac{90}{360}$$
$$(I) \qquad (P) \qquad (R) \qquad (T)$$

Finding the Time

EXAMPLE   Tim Jarvis borrowed $820.21 from a bank. Tim's interest is $19.48 at 9.5%. How much time does Tim have to repay the loan?

The following formula is used to calculate time:

$$\text{Time (in years)} = \frac{\text{Interest}}{\text{Principal} \times \text{Rate}}$$

Step 2. When using a calculator, press
$\boxed{820.21}\boxed{\times}\boxed{.095}\boxed{M+}$.

Step 1.   Set up the formula.

$$T = \frac{\$19.48}{\$820.21 \times .095}$$

Step 3. When using a calculator, press
$\boxed{19.48}\boxed{\div}\boxed{MR}\boxed{=}$.

Step 2.   Multiply the denominator. Do not round the answer.

$$T = \frac{\$19.48}{\$77.91995}$$

Step 3.   Divide the numerator by the result of Step 2. $T = .25$ years

Step 4.   Convert years to days (assume 360 days). $.25 \times 360 = $ 90 days

Step 5.   Check your answer.
$$\$19.48 = \$820.21 \times .095 \times \frac{90}{360}$$
$$(I) \qquad (P) \qquad (R) \qquad (T)$$

Before we go on to Learning Unit 10.3, let's check your understanding of this unit.

LU 10.2 PRACTICE QUIZ

Complete the following (assume 360 days):

	Principal	Interest rate	Time (days)	Simple interest
1.	?	5%	90 days	$8,000
2.	$7,000	?	220 days	350
3.	$1,000	8%	?	300

✓ **Solutions**

1. $\dfrac{\$8,000}{.05 \times \dfrac{90}{360}} = \dfrac{\$8,000}{.0125} = \boxed{\$640,000}$ $P = \dfrac{I}{R \times T}$

2. $\dfrac{\$350}{\$7,000 \times \dfrac{220}{360}} = \dfrac{\$350}{\$4,277.7777} = \boxed{8.18\%}$ $R = \dfrac{I}{P \times T}$

   (do not round) ⟶

3. $\dfrac{\$300}{\$1,000 \times .08} = \dfrac{\$300}{\$80} = 3.75 \times 360 = \boxed{1,350 \text{ days}}$ $T = \dfrac{I}{P \times R}$

LEARNING UNIT 10.3 U.S. Rule—Making Partial Note Payments before Due Date

Often a person may want to pay off a debt in more than one payment before the maturity date. The **U.S. Rule** allows the borrower to receive proper interest credits. This rule states that any partial loan payment first covers any interest that has built up. The remainder of the partial payment reduces the loan principal. Courts or legal proceedings generally use the U.S. Rule. The Supreme Court originated the U.S. Rule in the case of *Story v. Livingston.*

4 steps **EXAMPLE** Joe Mill owes $5,000 on an 11%, 90-day note. On day 50, Joe pays $600 on the note. On day 80, Joe makes an $800 additional payment. Assume a 360-day year. What is Joe's adjusted balance after day 50 and after day 80? What is the ending balance due?

1st *To calculate $600 payment on day 50:*

Step 1. Calculate interest on principal from date of loan to date of first principal payment. Round to nearest cent.

$I = P \times R \times T$

$I = \$5,000 \times .11 \times \dfrac{50}{360}$

$I = \$76.39$

Step 2. Apply partial payment to interest due. Subtract remainder of payment from principal. This is the **adjusted balance** (principal).

$600.00 payment
$\underline{-\ 76.39}$ interest
$523.61 ⟶

$5,000.00 principal
$\underline{-\ 523.61}$
$4,476.39 adjusted balance— principal

To calculate $800 payment on day 80:

Step 3. Calculate interest on adjusted balance that starts from previous payment date and goes to new payment date. Then apply Step 2.

Compute interest on $4,476.39 for 30 days (80 − 50)

$I = \$4,476.39 \times .11 \times \dfrac{30}{360}$

$I = \$41.03$

$800.00 payment
$\underline{-\ 41.03}$ interest
$758.97 ⟶

$4,476.39
$\underline{-\ 758.97}$
$3,717.42 adjusted balance

Step 4. At maturity, calculate interest from last partial payment. _Add_ this interest to adjusted balance.

Ten days are left on note since last payment.

$$I = \$3{,}717.42 \times .11 \times \frac{10}{360}$$

$$I = \$11.36$$

Balance owed = $\boxed{\$3{,}728.78}$ $\begin{pmatrix} \$3{,}717.42 \\ + \$11.36 \end{pmatrix}$

✴ Note that when Joe makes two partial payments, Joe's total interest is $128.78 ($76.39 + $41.03 + $11.36). If Joe had repaid the entire loan after 90 days, his interest payment would have been $137.50—a total savings of $8.72.

LU 10.3 PRACTICE QUIZ

Polly Flin borrowed $5,000 for 60 days at 8%. On day 10, Polly made a $600 partial payment. On day 40, Polly made a $1,900 partial payment. What is Polly's ending balance due under the U.S. Rule (assume a 360-day year)?

✓ **Solutions**

$$\$5{,}000 \times .08 \times \frac{10}{360} = \$11.11$$

$600.00	$5,000.00
− 11.11	− 588.89
$588.89	$4,411.11

$$\$4{,}411.11 \times .08 \times \frac{30}{360} = \$29.41$$

$1,900.00	$4,411.11
− 29.41	− 1,870.59
$1,870.59	$2,540.52

$$\$2{,}540.52 \times .08 \times \frac{20}{360} = \$11.29$$

$ 11.29 ←	
+ 2,540.52	
$\boxed{\$2{,}551.81}$	

Chapter Organizer and Reference Guide

Topic	Key point, procedure, formula	Example(s) to illustrate situation
Simple interest for months, p. 250	Interest = Principal × Rate × Time 　　(I)　　　(P)　　(R)　(T)	$2,000 at 9% for 17 months $I = \$2{,}000 \times .09 \times \frac{17}{12}$ $I = \boxed{\$255}$
Exact interest, p. 251	$T = \dfrac{\text{Exact number of days}}{365}$ $I = P \times R \times T$	$1,000 at 10% from January 5 to February 20 $I = \$1{,}000 \times .10 \times \frac{46}{365}$ Feb. 20: 51 days Jan. 5: − 5 46 days $I = \boxed{\$12.60}$
Ordinary interest (Banker's Rule), p. 252	$T = \dfrac{\text{Exact number of days}}{360}$ $I = P \times R \times T$ | Higher interest costs |	$I = \$1{,}000 \times .10 \times \frac{46}{360}$　(51 − 5) $I = \boxed{\$12.78}$
Finding unknown in simple interest formula (use 360 days), p. 253	$I = P \times R \times T$	Use this example for illustrations of simple interest formula parts: $1,000 loan at 9%, 60 days $I = \$1{,}000 \times .09 \times \frac{60}{360} = \boxed{\$15}$
Finding the principal, p. 253	$P = \dfrac{I}{R \times T}$	$P = \dfrac{\$15}{.09 \times \frac{60}{360}} = \dfrac{\$15}{.015} = \boxed{\$1{,}000}$

Topic	Key point, procedure, formula	Example(s) to illustrate situation
Chapter Organizer and Reference Guide (concluded)		
Finding the rate, p. 254	$R = \dfrac{I}{P \times T}$	$R = \dfrac{\$15}{\$1,000 \times \dfrac{60}{360}} = \dfrac{\$15}{166.66666} = .09$ $= 9\%$ *Note:* We did not round the denominator.
Finding the time, p. 254	$T = \dfrac{I}{P \times R}$ (in years) Multiply answer by 360 days to convert answer to days for ordinary interest.	$T = \dfrac{\$15}{\$1,000 \times .09} = \dfrac{\$15}{\$90} = .1666666$ $.1666666 \times 360 = 59.99 = $ 60 days

U.S. Rule (use 360 days), p. 255	Calculate interest on principal from date of loan to date of first partial payment.
	
	 Calculate adjusted balance by subtracting from principal the partial payment less interest cost. The process continues for future partial payments with the adjusted balance used to calculate cost of interest from last payment to present payment.
	
	 Balance owed equals last adjusted balance plus interest cost from last partial payment to final due date.
		12%, 120 days, $2,000
		 Partial payments:
		 On day 40; $250
		 On day 60; $200
		
		 First payment:
		 $I = \$2,000 \times .12 \times \dfrac{40}{360}$
		 $I = \$26.67$
		 $\$250.00$ payment
		 $-\ 26.67$ interest
		 $\$223.33$
		     $\$2,000.00$ principal
		     $-\ 223.33$
		     $\$1,776.67$ adjusted balance
		
		 Second payment:
		 $I = \$1,776.67 \times .12 \times \dfrac{20}{360}$
		 $I = \$11.84$
		 $\$200.00$ payment
		 $-\ 11.84$ interest
		 $\$188.16$
		     $\$1,776.67$
		     $-\ 188.16$
		     $\$1,588.51$ adjusted balance
		 60 days left:
		 $\$1,588.51 \times .12 \times \dfrac{60}{360} = \$31.77$
		 $\$1,588.51 + \$31.77 = $ $\$1,620.28$ balance due
		 Total interest = $\$26.67$
		       11.84
		     $+\ 31.77$
		     $\$70.28$

Key terms	Adjusted balance, *p. 255* Banker's Rule, *p. 252* Exact interest, *p. 251* Interest, *p. 250*	Maturity value, *p. 250* Ordinary interest, *p. 252* Principal, *p. 250* Simple interest, *p. 250* Simple interest formula, *p. 250* Time, *p. 251* U.S. Rule, *p. 255*

Critical Thinking Discussion Questions

1. What is the difference between exact interest and ordinary interest? With the increase of computers in banking, do you think that the ordinary interest method is a dinosaur in business today?

2. Explain how to use the portion formula to solve the unknowns in the simple interest formula. Why would rounding the answer of the denominator result in an inaccurate final answer?

3. Explain the U.S. Rule. Why in the last step of the U.S. Rule is the interest added, not subtracted?

DRILL PROBLEMS

Calculate the simple interest and maturity value for the following problems. Round to the nearest cent as needed.

	Principal	Interest rate	Time	Simple interest	Maturity value
10–1.	$6,000	5%	15 mo.	$375	$6,375

$$\$6,000 \times .05 \times \frac{15}{12} = \$375$$

	Principal	Interest rate	Time	Simple interest	Maturity value
10–2.	$8,000	6%	$1\frac{1}{4}$ yr.	$600	$8,600

$$\$8,000 \times .06 \times \frac{15}{12} = \$600$$

	Principal	Interest rate	Time	Simple interest	Maturity value
10–3.	$2,000	$9\frac{3}{4}$%	8 mo.	$130	$2,130

$$\$2,000 \times .0975 \times \frac{8}{12} = \$130$$

Complete the following, using ordinary interest: $T = \dfrac{\text{Exact no. of days}}{360}$

	Principal	Interest rate	Date borrowed	Date repaid	Exact time	Interest	Maturity value
10–4.	$1,000	8%	Mar. 8 67	June 9 160	93	$20.67	$1,020.67

$$\$1,000 \times .08 \times \frac{93}{360} = \$20.67$$

	Principal	Interest rate	Date borrowed	Date repaid	Exact time	Interest	Maturity value
10–5.	$585	9%	June 5 156	Dec. 15 349	193	$28.23	$613.23

$$\$585 \times .09 \times \frac{193}{360} = \$28.23$$

	Principal	Interest rate	Date borrowed	Date repaid	Exact time	Interest	Maturity value
10–6.	$1,200	12%	July 7 188	Jan. 10 10	187	$74.80	$1,274.80

$$(365 - 188 = 177 + 10) \qquad \$1,200 \times .12 \times \frac{187}{360} = \$74.80$$

Complete the following, using exact interest: $T = \dfrac{\text{Exact no. of days}}{365}$

	Principal	Interest rate	Date borrowed	Date repaid	Exact time	Interest	Maturity value
10–7.	$1,000	8%	Mar. 8 67	June 9 160	93	$20.38	$1,020.38

$$\$1,000 \times .08 \times \frac{93}{365} = \$20.38$$

	Principal	Interest rate	Date borrowed	Date repaid	Exact time	Interest	Maturity value
10–8.	$585	9%	June 5 156	Dec. 15 349	193	$27.84	$612.84

$$\$585 \times .09 \times \frac{193}{365} = \$27.84$$

	Principal	Interest rate	Date borrowed	Date repaid	Exact time	Interest	Maturity value
10–9.	$1,200	12%	July 7 188	Jan. 10 10	187	$73.78	$1,273.78

$$(365 - 188 = 177 + 10) \qquad \$1,200 \times .12 \times \frac{187}{365} = \$73.78$$

Solve for the missing item in the following (round to the nearest hundredth as needed):

	Principal	Interest rate	Time (months years)	Simple interest	
10–10.	$700	8%	?5.36	$300	

$$T = \frac{\$300}{\$700 \times .08} = \frac{\$300}{\$56} = 5.36$$

	Principal	Interest rate	Time	Simple interest	
10–11.	? $1,904.76	7%	$1\frac{1}{2}$ years	$200	

$$P = \frac{\$200}{.07 \times \frac{18}{12}} = \$1,904.76$$

	Principal	Interest rate	Time	Simple interest	
10–12.	$5,000	? 12%	6 months	$300	

$$R = \frac{\$300}{\$5,000 \times \frac{6}{12}} = .12$$

10–13. Use the U.S. Rule to solve for total interest costs, balances, and final payments (use ordinary interest).

> **Given**   Principal: $10,000, 8%, 240 days
> Partial payments: On 100th day, $4,000
> On 180th day, $2,000

8%, 100 days, $10,000

$$I = \$10,000 \times .08 \times \frac{100}{360} = \$222.22$$

$4,000.00
− 222.22 ←
$3,777.78

$10,000.00
− 3,777.78
$ 6,222.22 adjusted balance

$$\$6,222.22 \times .08 \times \frac{80}{360} = \$110.62$$

$2,000.00
− 110.62 ←
$1,889.38

$6,222.22
− 1,889.38
$4,332.84 adjusted balance

$$\$4,332.84 \times .08 \times \frac{60}{360} = \$57.77$$

$4,332.84
+ 57.77 ←
$4,390.61 balance due

Interest paid
$222.22
110.62
+ 57.77
$390.61

WORD PROBLEMS

10–14. On December 31, 1997, the Chicago *Sun-Times* announced that Dean Foods will buy Purity Dairies, which is based in Nashville, Tennessee. Dean Foods has an option of selling $5,000,000 in corporate bonds with a $5\frac{1}{2}$% interest rate payable over the next 10 years. What is the total interest Dean Foods will pay over 10 years, and what will be the maturity value?

(*P* face value)   (*R*)   (*T*)
$5,000,000   × .055 × 10 years = $2,750,000
      P   +   I   =   MV
$5,000,000 + $2,750,000 = $7,750,000

10–15. Michelle Sanchez borrowed $25,000 to pay for her child's education at Hofstra University. Michelle must repay the loan at the end of 11 months in one payment with $9\frac{1}{2}$% interest. How much interest must Michelle pay? What is the maturity value?

$$\$25,000 \times .095 \times \frac{11}{12} = \$2,177.08$$

$$\$25,000 + \$2,177.08 = \$27,177.08 \qquad MV = P + I$$

10–16. On September 12, Jody Jansen went to Sunshine Bank to borrow $2,300 at 9% interest. Jody plans to repay the loan on January 27. Assume the loan is on ordinary interest. What interest will Jody owe on January 27? What is the total amount Jody must repay at maturity?

$$\begin{array}{r} 365 \\ \text{Sept. 12} \quad - 255 \\ \hline 110 \\ + 27 \\ \hline 137 \end{array}$$

$$\$2,300 \times .09 \times \frac{137}{360} = \$78.78 \text{ interest}$$

$$\$78.78 + \$2,300 = \$2,378.78$$

10–17. Kelly O'Brien met Jody Jansen (Problem 10–16) at Sunshine Bank and suggested she consider the loan on exact interest. Recalculate the loan for Jody under this assumption.

$$\$2,300 \times .09 \times \frac{137}{365} = \$77.70 + \$2,300 = \$2,377.70 \qquad \text{Save } \$1.08$$

10–18. On August 26, 1995, an article entitled "How to Retire with Money" appeared in the Gainesville, Florida, *Sun*. The article stated that a $10,000 investment would pay $3,000 in interest after 5 years. What is the bank's rate of interest?

$$\frac{(I)\$3,000}{(P) \times (R) \times (T)} = \frac{\$3,000}{\$50,000} = 6\%$$

$$\$10,000 \times ? \times 5 \text{ years}$$

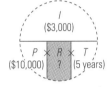

10–19. Gordon Rosel went to his bank to find out how long it will take for $1,200 to amount to $1,650 at 8% simple interest. Please solve Gordon's problem. Round time in years to the nearest tenth.

$$\frac{\$450}{\$1,200 \times .08} = \frac{\$450}{\$96} = 4.7 \text{ years}$$

10–20. Bill Moore is buying a van. His April monthly interest at 12% was $125. What was Bill's principal balance at the beginning of April? Use 360 days.

$$\frac{\$125}{.12 \times \dfrac{30}{360}} = \frac{\$125}{.01} = \$12,500$$

10–21. On March 8, 2000, Alice Clark took out a $7\frac{1}{2}$% loan for $14,000. The loan is due January 8, 2001. Use ordinary interest to calculate the interest. What total amount will Alice pay on January 8, 2001?

$$\begin{array}{r} 365 \\ - 67 \\ \hline 298 + 8 = 306 \end{array} \qquad \$14,000 \times .075 \times \frac{306}{360} = \$892.50 + \$14,000 = \$14,892.50$$

10–22. Meg Roy took out the same loan as Alice (Problem 10–21). Meg's terms, however, are exact interest. What is Meg's difference in interest? What will she pay on January 8, 2001?

$$\$14,000 \times .075 \times \frac{306}{365} = \begin{array}{r} \$ \quad 880.27 \\ + 14,000.00 \\ \hline \$14,880.27 \end{array} \qquad \begin{array}{l} \text{Difference in interest} \\ \\ \end{array} \begin{array}{r} \$892.50 \\ - 880.27 \\ \hline \$ \quad 12.23 \end{array}$$

10–23. Max Wholesaler borrowed $2,000 on a 10%, 120-day note. After 45 days, Max paid $700 on the note. Thirty days later, Max paid an additional $630. What is the final balance due? Use the U.S. Rule to determine the total interest and ending balance due. Use ordinary interest.

45 days	**75th day**	**120th day**
$\$2,000 \times .10 \times \dfrac{45}{360} = \$25.00$ interest	$\$1,325 \times .10 \times \dfrac{30}{360} = \$11.04$ interest	$\$706.04 \times .10 \times \dfrac{45}{360} = \$8.83$
$\begin{array}{r}\$2,000 \\ - 675 \;(\$700 - \$25) \\ \hline \$1,325 \text{ adjusted balance}\end{array}$	$\begin{array}{r}\$1,325.00 \\ - 618.96 \;(\$630.00 - \$11.04) \\ \hline \$ \;\;706.04 \text{ adjusted balance}\end{array}$	$\begin{array}{r}\$706.04 \\ + 8.83 \\ \hline \$714.87 \text{ ending balance due}\end{array}$

Total interest, $44.87
($25 + $11.04 + $8.83)

ADDITIONAL SET OF WORD PROBLEMS

10–24. On November 30, 1997, the Chicago *Sun-Times* reported that the credit card interest rate at Central Carolina Bank of Columbus, Georgia, was 12%. What amount of interest would you pay on a $1,500 debt when the payment is due in 80 days?

$P = \$1,500$

$R = .12$ $\$1,500 \times .12 \times \dfrac{80}{360} = \$40$ interest

$T = \dfrac{80}{360}$

10–25. Based on Problem 10–24. After 30 days, you paid $600 on the note. Twenty-five days later you paid an additional $500. Using the U.S. Rule, what is the final balance due?

30 days	**55th day or 25 days later**	**80th day or 25 days later**
$\$1,500 \times .12 \times \dfrac{30}{360} = \$15$ interest	$\$915 \times .12 \times \dfrac{25}{360} = \$7.63$ interest	$\$422.63 \times .12 \times \dfrac{25}{360} = \$3.52$ interest
$\begin{array}{r} \$1,500.00 \\ -\ 585.00 \ (\$600 - \$15) \\ \hline \$\ \ 915.00 \ \text{adjusted balance} \end{array}$	$\begin{array}{r} \$915.00 \\ -\ 492.37 \ (\$500 - \$7.63) \\ \hline \$422.63 \ \text{adjusted balance} \end{array}$	$\begin{array}{r} \$422.63 \\ +\ \ \ \ 3.52 \\ \hline \$426.15 \ \text{ending balance due} \end{array}$

10–26. On September 14, Jennifer Rick went to Park Bank to borrow $2,500 at $11\frac{3}{4}\%$ interest. Jennifer plans to repay the loan on January 27. Assume the loan is on ordinary interest. What interest will Jennifer owe on January 27? What is the total amount Jennifer must repay at maturity?

Sept. 14 $\begin{array}{r} 365 \\ -\ 257 \\ \hline 108 \\ +\ \ 27 \\ \hline 135 \end{array}$ $\$2,500 \times .1175 \times \dfrac{135}{360} = \$110.16 + \$2,500 = \$2,610.16$

10–27. Steven Linden met Jennifer Rick (Problem 10–26) at Park Bank and suggested she consider the loan on exact interest. Recalculate the loan for Jennifer under this assumption.

$\$2,500 \times .1175 \times \dfrac{135}{365} = \$108.65 + \$2,500 = \$2,608.65$

10–28. Lance Lopes went to his bank to find out how long it will take for $1,000 to amount to $1,700 at 12% simple interest. Can you solve Lance's problem? Round time in years to the nearest tenth.

$\dfrac{\$700}{\$1,000 \times .12} = \dfrac{\$700}{\$120} = 5.8$ years

10–29. Margie Pagano is buying a car. Her June monthly interest at $12\frac{1}{2}\%$ was $195. What was Margie's principal balance at the beginning of June? Use 360 days. Do not round the denominator before dividing.

$\dfrac{\$195}{.125 \times \dfrac{30}{360}} = \dfrac{\$195}{.0104166} = \$18,720.12$

10–30. Shawn Bixby borrowed $17,000 on a 120-day, 12% note. After 65 days, Shawn paid $2,000 on the note. On day 89, Shawn paid an additional $4,000. What is the final balance due? Determine total interest and ending balance due by the U.S. Rule. Use ordinary interest.

$\begin{array}{r} \$368.33 \\ +\ 122.95 \\ +\ 118.74 \\ \hline \$610.02 \ \text{total interest} \end{array}$

$\$17,000 \times .12 \times \dfrac{65}{360} = \$368.33$ interest

$\$2,000 - \$368.33 = \$1,631.67$ payment

$\$17,000 - \$1,631.67 = \$15,368.33$ adjusted balance

$\$15,368.33 \times .12 \times \dfrac{24}{360} = \$122.95$ interest

$\$4,000 - \$122.95 = \$3,877.05$ payment

$\$15,368.33 - \$3,877.05 = \$11,491.28$ adjusted balance

$\$11,491.28 \times .12 \times \dfrac{31}{360} = \$118.74$ interest

$\$11,491.28 + \$118.74 = \$11,610.02$ ending balance due

10–31. Carol Miller went to Europe and forgot to pay her $740 mortgage payment on her New Hampshire ski house. For her 59 days overdue on her payment, the bank charged her a penalty of $15. What was the rate of interest charged by the bank? Round to the nearest hundredth percent.

$$R = \frac{\$15}{\$740 \times \frac{59}{360}} = 12.37\%$$

10–32. Abe Wolf bought a new kitchen set at Sears. Abe paid off the loan after 60 days with an interest charge of $9. If Sears charges 10% interest, what did Abe pay for the kitchen set?

$$P = \frac{\$9}{.10 \times \frac{60}{360}} = \$540$$

10–33. Joy Kirby made a $300 loan to Robinson Landscaping at 11%. Robinson paid back the loan with interest of $6.60. How long in days was the loan outstanding? Check your answer.

$$T = \frac{\$6.60}{\$300 \times .11} = .2 \times 360 = 72 \text{ days} \qquad \textbf{Check} \quad \$300 \times .11 \times \frac{72}{360} = \$6.60$$

10–34. Molly Ellen, bookkeeper for Keystone Company, forgot to send in the payroll taxes due on April 15. She sent the payment November 8. The IRS sent her a penalty charge of 8% simple interest on the unpaid taxes of $4,100. Calculate the penalty. (Remember that the government uses exact interest.)

Nov. 8 → 312 $4,100 × .08 × $\frac{207}{365}$ = $186.02
Apr. 15 →− 105
――――――
         207

10–35. Oakwood Plowing Company purchased two new plows for the upcoming winter. In 200 days, Oakwood must make a single payment of $23,200 to pay for the plows. As of today, Oakwood has $22,500. If Oakwood puts the money in a bank today, what rate of interest will it need to pay off the plows in 200 days?

$$I = \$23,200 - \$22,500 = \$700 \qquad R = \frac{\$700}{\$22,500 \times \frac{200}{360}} = 5.6\%$$

CHALLENGE PROBLEMS

10–36. You work in the Santa Monica, California, Community College financial aid office. It is your responsibility to validate information that students' families have put on their financial aid applications. A student indicated that last year the family listed $635 interest income from First National Bank on their 1040 income tax form. The family has indicated a savings amount of only $300. If the bank is paying simple interest of 3% annually, what should the family have in the bank account?

$I = \$635$

$R = .03$

$T = 1$ year

$$\frac{(I)}{(R) \times (T)} = \frac{\$635}{.03} = \$21,166.67$$
$$.03 \times 1$$

10–37. Janet Foster bought a computer and printer at Computerland. The printer had a $600 list price with a $100 trade discount and 2/10, n/30 terms. The computer had a $1,600 list price with a 25% trade discount but no cash discount. On the computer, Computerland offered Janet the choice of (1) paying $50 per month for 17 months with the 18th payment paying the remainder of the balance or (2) paying 8% interest for 18 months in equal payments.

a. Assume Janet could borrow the money for the printer at 8% to take advantage of the cash discount. How much would Janet save?

b. On the computer, what is the difference in the final payment between choices 1 and 2?

a. $490 × .08 × $\frac{20}{360}$ = $2.18

($600 − $100) × .98

$10.00
− 2.18
――――
$ 7.82 (savings—worth borrowing)

b. (1) $50 × 17 = $850   Last payment $1,200 − $850 = $350
    (2) $1,200 × .08 × 1.5 = $144 $350.00
    $1,200 + $144 = $\frac{\$1,344}{18}$ = $74.67   − 74.67
                                                    ――――――
                                                    $275.33

SUMMARY PRACTICE TEST

1. Maggie Kim's real estate tax of $1,610.20 was due on December 1, 2000. Maggie lost her job and could not pay her tax bill until February 14, 2001. The penalty for late payment is $10\frac{3}{4}\%$ ordinary interest. *(p. 251)*

   a. What is the penalty Maggie must pay?

   b. What is the total amount Maggie must pay on February 14?

   Dec. 31 $\longrightarrow$ 365   **(a)** $I = P \times R \times T$
   Dec. 1 $\longrightarrow$ 335 $I = \$1,610.20 \times .1075 \times \dfrac{75}{360} = \$36.06$
   $\overline{\quad\quad\quad 30}$
   Feb. 14 $\longrightarrow$ 45   **(b)** $MV = \$1,610.20 + \$36.06$
   $\overline{\quad\quad\quad 75}$ $= \$1,646.26$

2. Jane Sullivan borrowed $120,000 to pay for her child's education. She must repay the loan at the end of 7 years in one payment with $7\frac{3}{4}\%$ interest. What is the maturity value Jane must repay? *(p. 251)*

   $\$120,000 \times .0775 \times 7 = \$65,100 + \$120,000 = \$185,100$

3. On June 10, Lee Hall borrowed $7,000 from Brass Bank at $8\frac{3}{4}\%$ interest. Lee plans to repay the loan on February 8. Assume the loan is on ordinary interest. How much will Lee repay on February 8? *(p. 252)*

   $\quad\quad\quad\quad 365$
   June 10 $\longrightarrow$ 161 $\$7,000 \times .0875 \times \dfrac{243}{360} = \$413.44 + \$7,000 = \$7,413.44$
   $\quad\quad\quad\overline{\quad 204}$
   Feb. 8 $\longrightarrow\quad 39$
   $\quad\quad\quad\overline{\quad 243}$

4. Ed Blue met Lee Hall (Problem 3) at Brass Bank. After talking with Lee, Ed decided he would like to consider the same loan on exact interest. Can you recalculate the loan for Ed under this assumption? *(p. 251)*

   $\$7,000 \times .0875 \times \dfrac{243}{365} = \$407.77 + \$7,000 = \$7,407.77$

5. Angel Wright is buying a car. Her June monthly interest was $160 at $8\frac{1}{2}\%$ interest. What is Angel's principal balance (to the nearest dollar) at the beginning of June? Use 360 days. Do not round the denominator in your calculation. *(p. 253)*

   $\dfrac{\$160}{.085 \times \dfrac{30}{360}} = \dfrac{\$160}{.0070833} = \$22,588$

6. Karen Korn borrowed $11,000 on a 7%, 60-day note. After 10 days, Karen paid $3,000 on the note. On day 40, Karen paid $2,000 on the note. What are the total interest and ending balance due by the U.S. Rule? Use ordinary interest. *(p. 255)*

   $\$11,000 \times .07 \times \dfrac{10}{360} = \$21.39$

$3,000.00	$11,000.00 principal	$21.39
− 21.39	− $2,978.61	46.79
$2,978.61	$8,021.39	23.60
		$91.78 total interest

   $\$8,021.39 \times .07 \times \dfrac{30}{360} = \$46.79$

$2,000.00	$8,021.39
− 46.79	− 1,953.21
$1,953.21	$6,068.18

   $\$6,068.18 \times .07 \times \dfrac{20}{360} = \$23.60$ $\begin{array}{r} \$6,068.18 \\ +\quad 23.60 \\ \hline \$6,091.78 \text{ ending balance due} \end{array}$

A GROUP PROJECT Defend or reject the following business math issue based on the *Kiplinger's Personal Finance Magazine* article below:

MY PERSONAL FINANCES

A Small Business You Can Bank On

▶ **Mark Young has no plans to expand his one-branch financial institution.** By Ed Henry

As president and CEO of the First National Bank of Orwell, Vt., Mark Young enjoys the ultimate in home banking. On a typical workday he gets up by 7 A.M., and one hour later he walks five feet from his front door to open the bank's one and only branch, which adjoins his house.

Originally chartered by the state legislature in 1832 as a farmers bank to serve the agricultural community in the hills of western Vermont, First National has been in Young's family for four generations. The youngest of five sons, Young, 45, took over the business because "I came along about the time my father reached retirement age."

With assets totaling $20 million, Young's bank is the third-smallest of 25 commercial banks and thrift institutions in Vermont. And it's the only one within 16 miles of Orwell, population 1,100. At a time when financial megamergers are making headlines and banks are charging customers if they want to use a teller window, Young's bank bucks the trend. "We offer very personalized, old-fashioned service," he says. "I'm a loan officer who also sweeps the walk and plows the driveway."

THE PERSONAL TOUCH. A depositor who walks into First National and forgets his account number can rest assured that a teller will look it up. The charge for a checking account is only $2 a month, no matter how many checks you write. And children can open an account with a handful of pennies; there is no minimum deposit or monthly service charge. "A savings account should not have charges of any type," says Young.

The bank has about a dozen employees and 3,000 savings accounts. It serves everyone in town, as well as former residents who have moved as far away as Australia but maintain their accounts and their ties with home.

With its self-imposed cap on fee income, First Nation-

al also keeps a tight rein on expenses and limits risk. It doesn't make loans of more than $150,000. It doesn't offer credit cards, debit cards or mutual funds. It doesn't operate ATMs (although plans are under way to offer them). "There isn't a whole lot that someone needs cash for at midnight in Orwell, Vermont," says Young.

STAYING ALIVE. Running a small bank in a big world isn't always easy. Young is particularly frustrated by paperwork associated with laws such as the Community Reinvestment Act—which, he argues, actually threatens community banking. "We have to dot our *i*'s, cross our *t*'s and go through all the hoops every couple of years just to show we're in compliance," he says. "We serve a community of 1,100 people—how could we not be in compliance?"

But in Orwell, the year 2000 won't be a problem. Earlier this year the bank spent just over $150,000 on new computers to bring it up to date, so "we're in a lot better shape than a lot of bigger banks," says Young.

First National is within 22 miles of Vermont's third-largest bank but has managed to avoid a takeover. Its directors are committed to keeping the bank the way it is; Young himself is staunchly antimerger and a proponent of the small-bank philosophy.

His own small bank has given him, his wife, Susan, who is a teacher, and their four children a comfortable living. In turn, Young has given back to the community. He's the town treasurer and is serving his fourth two-year term as a member of the Vermont legislature.

And there may even be a fifth-generation Young waiting in the wings. Mark's 22-year-old son, Russell, who graduated from Dartmouth College last year and enters law school this fall, has shown an interest in the bank. Says Mark: "We know our niche, and we stay there." •

REPORTER: JAMES RAMAGE

ED QUINN/SABA

Business Math Issue

A one-branch bank cannot survive today with all the bank mergers.

1. List the key points of the article and information to support your position.

2. Write a group defense of your position using math calculations to support your view.

IF YOUR BANK DOESN'T OFFER YOU INTEREST LIKE THIS:

	30 DAYS
$5000	10%
$100,000	12%

Annual Rates

Offer may be modified or withdrawn at any time. Interest is based on simple interest, 365-day year, and is payable at maturity. Certificates may not be redeemed before maturity dates. This offer may be modified or withdrawn at any time, without notice.

Project A

1. Find the interest on $5,000.
2. Check the $5,000 amount by formula.
3. Check the 10% by formula.
4. Check the time by formula.

1. $I = P \times R \times T$

$$\$5,000 \times .10 \times \frac{30}{365} = \$41.10$$

2. $P = \dfrac{I}{R \times T} = \dfrac{\$41.10}{.10 \times \dfrac{30}{365}} = \dfrac{\$41.10}{.0082191} = \$5,000.55$

3. $R = \dfrac{I}{P \times T} = \dfrac{\$41.10}{\$5,000 \times \dfrac{30}{365}} = \dfrac{\$41.10}{\$410.9589} = 10.001\%$

4. $T = \dfrac{I}{P \times R} = \dfrac{\$41.10}{\$5,000 \times .10} = \dfrac{\$41.10}{\$500} = .0822 \times 365 = 30.003 \text{ day}$

@ See text Web site (www.mhhe.com/slater) and *The Business Math Internet Resource Guide*.

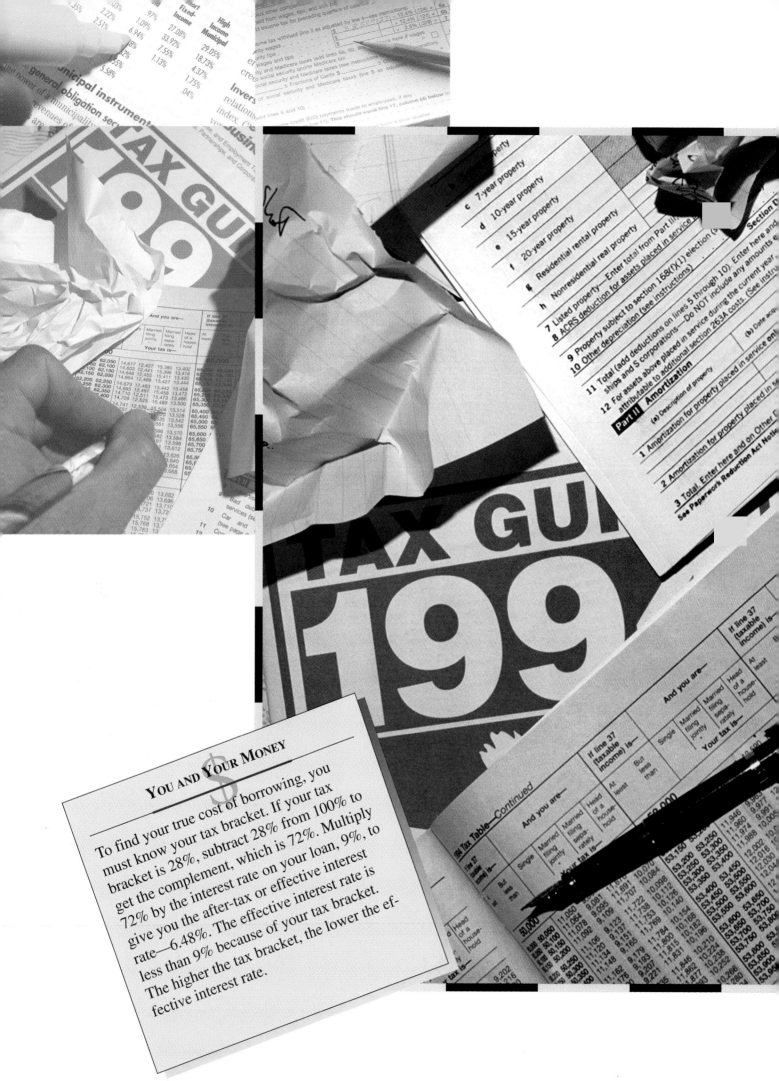

YOU AND YOUR MONEY

To find your true cost of borrowing, you must know your tax bracket. If your tax bracket is 28%, subtract 28% from 100% to get the complement, which is 72%. Multiply 72% by the interest rate on your loan, 9%, to give you the after-tax or effective interest rate—6.48%. The effective interest rate is less than 9% because of your tax bracket. The higher the tax bracket, the lower the effective interest rate.

11

PROMISSORY NOTES, SIMPLE DISCOUNT NOTES, AND THE DISCOUNT PROCESS

LEARNING UNIT OBJECTIVES

LU 11.1   Structure of Promissory Notes; the Simple Discount Note

- Differentiate between interest-bearing and noninterest-bearing notes *(pp. 270–71)*.
- Calculate bank discount and proceeds for simple discount notes *(p. 271)*.
- Calculate and compare the interest, maturity value, proceeds, and effective rate of a simple interest note with a simple discount note *(p. 272)*.
- Explain and calculate the effective rate for a Treasury bill *(p. 272)*.

LU 11.2   Discounting an Interest-Bearing Note before Maturity

- Calculate the maturity value, bank discount, and proceeds of discounting an interest-bearing note before maturity *(p. 274)*.
- Identify and complete the four steps of the discounting process *(p. 274)*.

GRAND UNION CO.

Waiver Is Sought to Avoid Default of Payment on Notes

Grand Union Co., Wayne, N.J., said it will not pay about $36 million in interest due March 2 on its 12% senior notes due 2004, putting it in default. The food-store operator said it is continuing discussions with a committee of note holders, but declined to comment on the tenor of the talks. Failure to make the interest payment also would constitute a default on its bank facility, the company said. Grand Union said it is in discussions with lenders regarding a waiver to avoid default and is "optimistic" it will obtain one. Grand Union made the announcement after markets closed. In Nasdaq Stock Market trading, Grand Union shares rose 18.75 cents, or 16%, to $1.3438.

© 1998, Dow Jones & Company, Inc.

If a company fails to pay interest on a note, it could be in default. *The Wall Street Journal* clipping "Waiver Is Sought to Avoid Default of Payment on Notes" reports that Grand Union Co. said it would not pay the interest due on its 12% notes due in 2004. If Grand Union can obtain a waiver to avoid default, it may be able to improve its financial position so that it can make future interest payments.

LEARNING UNIT 11.1 Structure of Promissory Notes; the Simple Discount Note

Although businesses frequently sign promissory notes, customers also sign promissory notes. For example, some student loans may require the signing of promissory notes. Appliance stores often ask customers to sign a promissory note when they buy large appliances on credit. As you will see in this unit, promissory notes, usually involve the payment of interest.

Structure of Promissory Notes

To borrow money, you must find a lender (a bank or a company selling goods on credit). You must also be willing to pay for the use of the money. In Chapter 10 you learned that interest is the cost of borrowing money for periods of time.

Money lenders usually require that borrowers sign a **promissory note.** This note states that the borrower will repay a certain sum at a fixed time in the future. The note often includes the charge for the use of the money, or the rate of interest. Figure 11.1 shows a sample promissory note with its terms identified and defined. Take a moment to look at each term.

In this section you will learn the difference between interest-bearing notes and noninterest-bearing notes.

Interest-Bearing versus Noninterest-Bearing Notes

A promissory note can be interest bearing or noninterest bearing. To be **interest bearing,** the note must state the rate of interest. Since the promissory note in Figure 11.1 states that its interest is 9%, it is an interest-bearing note. When the note matures, Regal Corporation

FIGURE 11.1
Interest-bearing promissory note

$10,000 a.   LAWTON, OKLAHOMA   October 2, 2001 c.

Sixty days b.   AFTER DATE we PROMISE TO PAY TO
THE ORDER OF   G.J. Equipment Company d.
Ten thousand and 00/100------------------DOLLARS.
PAYABLE AT   Able National Bank
VALUE RECEIVED WITH INTEREST AT 9% e.   REGAL CORPORATION f.
NO. 114 DUE December 1, 1997 g.   J.M. Moore
                                                    TREASURER

a. **Face value:** Amount of money borrowed—$10,000. The face value is also the principal of the note.
b. **Time:** Length of time that the money is borrowed—60 days.
c. **Date:** The date that the note is issued—October 2, 2001.
d. **Payee:** The company extending the credit—G.J. Equipment Company.
e. **Rate:** The annual rate for the cost of borrowing the money—9%.
f. **Maker:** The company issuing the note and borrowing the money—Regal Corporation.
g. **Maturity date:** The date the principal and interest are due—December 1, 2001.

will pay back the original amount (**face value**) borrowed plus interest. We use the following formulas to calculate interest and maturity value:

> Interest = Face value (principal) × Rate × Time
> Maturity value = Face value (principal) + Interest

If you sign a **noninterest-bearing** promissory note for $10,000, you pay back $10,000 at maturity. The maturity value of a noninterest-bearing note is the same as its face value. Usually, noninterest-bearing notes occur for short time periods under special conditions. For example, money borrowed from a relative could be secured by a noninterest-bearing promissory note.

Simple Discount Note

The total amount due at the end of the loan, or the **maturity value (MV),** is the sum of the face value (principal) and interest. Some banks deduct the loan interest in advance. When banks do this, the note is a **simple discount note.**

In the simple discount note, the **bank discount** is the interest that banks deduct in advance and the **bank discount rate** is the percent of interest. The amount that the borrower receives after the bank deducts its discount from the loan's maturity value is the note's **proceeds.** Sometimes we refer to simple discount notes as noninterest-bearing notes. Remember, however, that borrowers *do* pay interest on these notes.

In the example that follows, Pete Runnels has the choice of a note with a simple interest rate (Chapter 10) or a note with a simple discount rate (Chapter 11). Table 11.1 provides a summary of the calculations made in the example and gives the key points that you should remember. Now let's study the example, and then you can review Table 11.1.

EXAMPLE   Pete Runnels has a choice of two different notes that both have a face value (principal) of $14,000 for 60 days. One note has a simple interest rate of 8%, while the other note has a simple discount rate of 8%. For each type of note, calculate (**a**) interest owed, (**b**) maturity value, (**c**) proceeds, and (**d**) effective rate.

Simple interest note—Chapter 10	Simple discount note—Chapter 11
Interest	**Interest**
a. I = Face value (principal) × R × T	**a.** I = Face value (principal) × R × T
$I = \$14{,}000 \times .08 \times \dfrac{60}{360}$	$I = \$14{,}000 \times .08 \times \dfrac{60}{360}$
$I = \$186.67$	$I = \$186.67$
Maturity value	**Maturity value**
b. MV = Face value + Interest	**b.** MV = Face value
$MV = \$14{,}000 + \$186.67$	$MV = \$14{,}000$
$MV = \$14{,}186.67$	
Proceeds	**Proceeds**
c. Proceeds = Face value	**c.** Proceeds = MV − Bank discount
= $14,000	= $14,000 − $186.67
	= $13,813.33
Effective rate	**Effective rate**
d. Rate = $\dfrac{\text{Interest}}{\text{Proceeds} \times \text{Time}}$	**d.** Rate = $\dfrac{\text{Interest}}{\text{Proceeds} \times \text{Time}}$
= $\dfrac{\$186.67}{\$14{,}000 \times \dfrac{60}{360}}$	= $\dfrac{\$186.67}{\$13{,}813.33 \times \dfrac{60}{360}}$
= 8%	= 8.11%

Note that the interest of $186.67 is the same for the simple interest note and the simple discount note. The maturity value of the simple discount note is the same as the face value. In the simple discount note, interest is deducted in advance, so the proceeds are less than the face value. Note that the effective rate for a simple discount note is higher than the stated rate, since the bank calculated the rate on the face of the note and not on what Pete received.

TABLE 11.1

Comparison of simple interest note and simple discount note (Calculations from the Pete Runnels example, p. 271)

SIN   *SDN*

Simple interest note (Chapter 10)	Simple discount note (Chapter 11)
1. A promissory note for a loan with a term of usually less than 1 year. *Example:* 60 days.	**1.** A promissory note for a loan with a term of usually less than 1 year. *Example:* 60 days.
2. Paid back by one payment at maturity. Face value equals actual amount (or principal) of loan (this is not maturity value).	**2.** Paid back by one payment at maturity. Face value equals maturity value (what will be repaid).
3. Interest computed on face value or what is actually borrowed. *Example:* $186.67.	**3.** Interest computed on maturity value or what will be repaid and not on actual amount borrowed. *Example:* $186.67.
4. Maturity value = Face value + Interest. *Example:* $14,186.67.	**4.** Maturity value = Face value. *Example:* $14,000.
5. Borrower receives the face value. *Example:* $14,000.	**5.** Borrower receives proceeds = Face value − Bank discount. *Example:* $13,813.33.
6. Effective rate (true rate is same as rate stated on note). *Example:* 8%.	**6.** Effective rate is higher since interest was deducted in advance. *Example:* 8.11%.
7. Used frequently instead of the simple discount note. *Example:* 8%.	**7.** Not used as much now because in 1969 congressional legislation required that the true rate of interest be revealed. Still used where legislation does not apply, such as personal loans.

Application of Discounting—Treasury Bills

When the government needs money, it sells Treasury bills. A **Treasury bill** is a loan to the federal government for 91 days (13 weeks), 182 days (26 weeks), or 1 year. Note that *The Wall Street Journal* clipping "Treasury Sets Offering Totaling $13 Billion" states that the Treasury plans to pay down $1.15 billion on the public debt with the sale of about $13 billion in short-term bills.

Treasury Sets Offering Totaling $13 Billion

Dow Jones Newswires

WASHINGTON—The Treasury plans to pay down $1.15 billion on the public debt with the sale Tuesday of about $13 billion in short-term bills. Maturing bills outstanding total $14.15 billion.

The sale, which will take place Tuesday because of the Memorial Day holiday Monday, will include $5.75 billion of three-month bills and $7.25 billion of six-month bills, maturing Aug. 27 and Nov. 27, respectively.

© 1998 Dow Jones & Company, Inc.

Effective 1999, investors can buy Treasury bills in minimum units of $1,000. The bills can be bought over the phone or on the government Web site. The purchase price (or proceeds) of a Treasury bill is the value of the Treasury bill less the discount. For example, if you buy a $10,000, 13-week Treasury bill at 8%, you pay $9,800, since you have not yet earned your interest ($10,000 × .08 × $\frac{13}{52}$ = $200). At maturity—13 weeks—the government pays you $10,000. You calculate your effective yield (8.16% rounded to the nearest hundredth percent) as follows:

$$\text{($10,000 − $200)} \longrightarrow \frac{\$200}{\$9,800 \times \dfrac{13}{52}} = \boxed{8.16\%} \text{ effective rate}$$

Now it's time to try the Practice Quiz and check your progress.

LU 11.1 PRACTICE QUIZ

1. Warren Ford borrowed $12,000 on a noninterest-bearing, simple discount, $9\frac{1}{2}$%, 60-day note. Assume ordinary interest. What are **(a)** the maturity value, **(b)** the bank's discount, **(c)** Warren's proceeds, and **(d)** the effective rate to the nearest hundredth percent?

2. Jane Long buys a $10,000, 13-week Treasury bill at 6%. What is her effective rate? Round to the nearest hundredth percent.

✓ **Solutions**

1. **a.** Maturity value = Face value = $12,000

   b. Bank discount = MV × Bank discount rate × Time

   $$= \$12{,}000 \times .095 \times \frac{60}{360}$$

   $$= \$190$$

   c. Proceeds = MV − Bank discount

   $$= \$12{,}000 - \$190$$

   $$= \$11{,}810$$

   d. Effective rate = $\dfrac{\text{Interest}}{\text{Proceeds} \times \text{Time}}$

   $$= \dfrac{\$190}{\$11{,}810 \times \dfrac{60}{360}}$$

   $$= 9.65\%$$

2. $\$10{,}000 \times .06 \times \dfrac{13}{52} = \$150$ interest $\dfrac{\$150}{\$9{,}850 \times \dfrac{13}{52}} = 6.09\%$

LEARNING UNIT 11.2 Discounting an Interest-Bearing Note before Maturity

Manufacturers frequently deliver merchandise to retail companies and do not request payment for several months. For example, Roger Company manufactures outdoor furniture that it delivers to Sears in March. Payment for the furniture is not due until September. Roger will have its money tied up in this furniture until September. So Roger requests that Sears sign promissory notes.

If Roger Company needs cash sooner than September, what can it do? Roger Company can take one of its promissory notes to the bank, assuming the company that signed the note is reliable. The bank will buy the note from Roger. Now Roger has discounted the note and has cash instead of waiting until September when Sears would have paid Roger.

Remember that when Roger Company discounts the promissory note to the bank, the company agrees to pay the note at maturity if the maker of the promissory note fails to pay the bank. The potential liability that may or may not result from discounting a note is called a **contingent liability.**

Think of **discounting a note** as a three-party arrangement. Roger Company realizes that the bank will charge for this service. The bank's charge is a **bank discount.** The actual amount Roger receives is the **proceeds** of the note. The steps and example that follow will help you understand this discounting process.

> ### Discounting a Note
>
> **Step 1.** Calculate the interest and maturity value.
> **Step 2.** Calculate the discount period (time the bank holds note).
> **Step 3.** Calculate the bank discount.
> **Step 4.** Calculate the proceeds.

EXAMPLE Roger Company sold the following promissory note to the bank:

Date of note	Face value of note	Length of note	Interest rate	Bank discount rate	Date of discount
March 8	$2,000	185 days	10%	9%	August 9

What are Roger's (1) interest and maturity value (MV)? What are the (2) discount period and (3) bank discount? (4) What are the proceeds?

1. *Calculate Roger's interest and maturity value (MV):*

$$\text{Interest} = \$2,000 \times .10 \times \frac{185}{360}$$

$$= \$102.78$$

$$\times MV = \$2,000 + \$102.78$$

$$= \$2,102.78$$

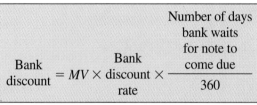

$$\boxed{MV = \text{Face value (principal)} + \text{Interest}}$$

← Exact number of days over 360

Calculating days without table:

March	31
	− 8
	23
April	30
May	31
June	30
July	31
August	9
	154

185 *days—length of note*
− 154 *days Roger held note*

31 *days bank waits*

2. *Calculate **discount period:*** Determine the number of days that the bank will have to wait for the note to come due (discount period).

August 9	221 days
March 8	− 67

154 days passed before note is discounted

185 days
− 154

31 days bank waits for note to come due

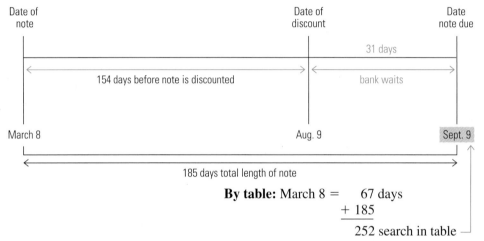

By table: March 8 =   67 days
                              + 185
                       252 search in table

3. *Calculate bank discount (bank charge):*

$$\$2,102.78 \times .09 \times \frac{31}{360} = \$16.30$$

Bank discount	$= MV \times$	Bank discount rate	$\times$	Number of days bank waits for note to come due
				$\dfrac{}{360}$

Step 1

↓

$$\text{Proceeds} = MV - \text{Bank discount (charge)}$$

Step 3

4. *Calculate proceeds:*

$$\$2,102.78$$
$$− 16.30$$
$$\$2,086.48$$

If Roger had waited until September 9, it would have received $2,102.78. Now, on August 9, Roger received $2,000 plus $86.48 interest.

FLEET FINANCIAL GROUP INC.

Major League Baseball Gets Revised Credit Agreement

Fleet Financial Group Inc. said it led a group of major banks in extending a credit agreement with Major League Baseball to the year 2005 from 2000, reflecting the league's increased television revenues. Fleet, a Boston bank holding company, said the agreement was renegotiated to allow individual teams within the league to borrow up to a total of $405 million, compared with a maximum of $250 million under the previous agreement. In addition, Patrick McAuliffe, head of Fleet's sports lending group, said the agreement includes lower interest rates. The agreement reflects improved fees that baseball will receive from recent new television contracts, he said. Others in the lending group include **J.P. Morgan** & Co. and **BankAmerica** Corp., Fleet said.

© 1998, Dow Jones & Company, Inc.

Now let's assume Roger Company received a noninterest-bearing note. Then we follow the four steps except the maturity value is the amount of the loan. No interest accumulates on a noninterest-bearing note. Today, many banks use simple interest instead of discounting. Also, instead of discounting notes, many companies set up *lines of credit* so that additional financing is immediately available.

The Wall Street Journal clipping "Major League Baseball Gets Revised Credit Agreement" reports that a renegotiated agreement to the year 2005 will allow individual baseball teams within the league to borrow up to a total of $405 million.

Now test your understanding of this unit with the following Practice Quiz.

LU 11.2 PRACTICE QUIZ

Date of note	Face value (principal) of note	Length of note	Interest rate	Bank discount rate	Date of discount
April 8	$35,000	160 days	11%	9%	June 8

From the above, calculate **(a)** interest and maturity value, **(b)** discount period, **(c)** bank discount, and **(d)** proceeds. Assume ordinary interest.

✓ **Solutions**

a. $I = \$35,000 \times .11 \times \dfrac{160}{360} = $ $\boxed{\$1,711.11}$

$MV = \$35,000 + \$1,711.11 = $ $\boxed{\$36,711.11}$

b. Discount period $= 160 - 61 = $ $\boxed{99 \text{ days.}}$

April	30
	− 8
	22
May	+ 31
	53
June	+ 8
	61

Or by table:

June 8	159
April 8	− 98
	61

c. Bank discount $= \$36,711.11 \times .09 \times \dfrac{99}{360} = $ $\boxed{\$908.60}$

d. Proceeds $= \$36,711.11 - \$908.60 = $ $\boxed{\$35,802.51}$

Chapter Organizer and Reference Guide		
Topic	**Key point, procedure, formula**	**Example(s) to illustrate situation**
Simple discount note, p. 270	Bank discount (interest) $= MV \times$ Bank discount rate $\times$ Time Interest based on amount paid back and not what received.	$\$6,000 \times .09 \times \dfrac{60}{360} = \$90$ Borrower receives \$5,910 (the proceeds) and pays back \$6,000 at maturity after 60 days. A Treasury bill is a good example of a simple discount note.
Effective rate, p. 271	$\dfrac{\text{Interest}}{\text{Proceeds} \times \text{Time}}$ ↑ What borrower receives (Face value − Discount)	*Example:* \$10,000 note, discount rate 12% for 60 days. $I = \$10,000 \times .12 \times \dfrac{60}{360} = \$200$ Effective rate: $\dfrac{\$200}{\$9,800 \times \dfrac{60}{360}} = \dfrac{\$200}{\$1,633.3333} = \boxed{12.24\%}$ ↑ Amount borrower received

Discounting an interest-bearing note, p. 273	1. Calculate interest and maturity value.
	    I = Face value × Rate × Time
	    MV = Face value + Interest
	 2. Calculate number of days bank will wait for note to come due (discount period).
	 3. Calculate bank discount (bank charge).
	
	 $MV \times \dfrac{\text{Bank discount rate}}{} \times \dfrac{\text{Number of days bank waits}}{360}$
	
	 4. Calculate proceeds.
	    MV − Bank discount (charge)
		Example: \$1,000 note, 6%, 60-day, dated November 1 and discounted on December 1 at 8%.
		 1. $I = \$1,000 \times .06 \times \dfrac{60}{360} = \$10$
		    $MV = \$1,000 + \$10 = \$1,010$
		 2. 30 days
		 3. $\$1,010 \times .08 \times \dfrac{30}{360} = \$6.73$
		 4. $\$1,010 - \$6.73 = \boxed{\$1,003.27}$

Key terms	Bank discount, *pp. 271, 273* Bank discount rate *p. 271* Contingent liability, *p. 273* Discounting a note, *p. 273* Discount period, *p. 274* Effective rate, *p. 271*	Face value, *p. 271* Interest-bearing note, *p. 270* Maker, *p. 270* Maturity date, *p. 270* Maturity value (*MV*), *p. 271* Noninterest-bearing note, *p. 271*	Payee, *p. 270* Proceeds, *pp. 271, 273* Promissory note, *p. 270* Simple discount note, *p. 271* Treasury bill, *p. 272*

Critical Thinking Discussion Questions

1. What are the differences between a simple interest note and a simple discount note? Which type of note would have a higher effective rate of interest? Why?

2. What are the four steps of the discounting process? Could the proceeds of a discounted note be less than the face value of the note?

3. What is a line of credit? What could be a disadvantage of having a large credit line?

DRILL PROBLEMS

Complete the following table for these simple discount notes. Use the ordinary interest method.

	Amount due at maturity	Discount rate	Time	Bank discount	Proceeds
11–1.	$15,000	$6\frac{1}{4}$%	210 days	$546.88	$14,453.12

$$\$15,000 \times .0625 \times \frac{210}{360} = \$546.88 \qquad \$15,000 - \$546.88 = \$14,453.12$$

11–2.	$9,000	$8\frac{1}{4}$%	220 days	$453.75	$8,546.25

$$\$9,000 \times .0825 \times \frac{220}{360} = \$453.75 \qquad \$9,000 - \$453.75 = \$8,546.25$$

Calculate the discount period for the bank to wait to receive its money:

	Date of note	Length of note	Date note discounted	Discount period	
11–3.	April 12	45 days	May 2	45 − 20 = 25	May 2 122 days
					Apr. 12 − 102
					20 days
11–4.	March 7	120 days	June 8	120 − 93 = 27	June 8 159 days
					Mar. 7 − 66
					93 days

Solve for maturity value, discount period, bank discount, and proceeds (assume for Problems 11–5 and 11–6 a bank discount rate of 9%).

	Face value (principal)	Rate of interest	Length of note	Maturity value	Date of note	Date note discounted	Discount period	Bank discount	Proceeds
11–5.	$50,000	11%	95 days	$51,451.39	June 10	July 18	57	$733.18	$50,718.21

July 18   199 days
June 10 − 161
38 days

$$\$50,000 \times .11 \times \frac{95}{360} = \$1,451.39 + \$50,000 = \$51,451.39 \; MV$$

Discount period = 95 − 38 = 57

$$\text{Bank discount} = \$51,451.39 \times .09 \times \frac{57}{360} = \$733.18$$

Proceeds = $51,451.39 − $733.18 = $50,718.21

11–6.	$25,000	9%	60 days	$25,375	June 8	July 10	28	$177.63	$25,197.37

July 10   191 days
June 8 − 159
32 days

$$\$25,000 \times .09 \times \frac{60}{360} = \$375 + \$25,000 = \$25,375 \; MV$$

Discount period = 60 − 32 = 28

$$\text{Bank discount} = \$25,375 \times .09 \times \frac{28}{360} = \$177.63$$

Proceeds = $25,375 − $177.63 = $25,197.37

11–7. Calculate the effective rate of interest (to the nearest hundredth percent) of the following Treasury bill:

Given: $10,000 Treasury bill, 7% for 13 weeks

$$\$10,000 \times .07 \times \frac{13}{52} = \$175 \qquad \$10,000 - \$175 = \$9,825 \qquad \text{Effective rate} = \frac{\$175}{\$9,825 \times \frac{13}{52}} = 7.12\%$$

WORD PROBLEMS

Use ordinary interest as needed.

11–8. Nolan Ryan borrowed $8,000 for 120 days from Marquette Bank. The bank discounted the note at 8%. What proceeds does Ryan receive? Calculate the effective rate to the nearest hundredth percent.

$$\$8,000 \times .08 \times \frac{120}{360} = \$213.33 \qquad \frac{\$213.33}{\$7,786.67 \times \frac{120}{360}} = \frac{\$213.33}{\$2,595.5566} = 8.22\%$$

$8,000 − $213.33 = $7,786.67

11–9. Jack Tripper signed a $9,000 note at Fleet Bank. Fleet charges a $9\frac{1}{4}\%$ discount rate. If the loan is for 200 days, find **(a)** the proceeds and **(b)** the effective rate charged by the bank (to the nearest tenth percent).

  a. $\$9,000 \times .0925 \times \dfrac{200}{360} = \$462.50$ **b.** $\dfrac{\$462.50}{\$8,537.50 \times \dfrac{200}{360}} = \dfrac{\$462.50}{\$4,743.0555} = 9.8\%$

  $\$9,000 - \$462.50 = \$8,537.50$

11–10. On March 1997, *Kiplinger's Personal Finance Magazine* reported on the effective rate of 1-year Treasury bills. If a $10,000 Treasury bill sold for $9,498, what is the effective rate to the nearest hundredth percent?

  $\$10,000 - \$9,498 = \$502$ discount (interest) $\dfrac{\$502}{\$9,498 \times 1} = 5.285\% = 5.29\%$

11–11. On September 5, Sheffield Company discounted at Sunshine Bank a $9,000, 120-day note dated June 5. Sunshine's discount rate was 9%. What proceeds did Sheffield Company receive?

  Sept. 5   248 days
  June 5   − 156
  　　　　　　 92 days passed $\$9,000 \times .09 \times \dfrac{28}{360} = \$63$ $\$9,000 - \$63 = \$8,937$
  120 − 92 = 28 days
  　　　(discount period)

11–12. On September 30, 1996, *Business Week* reported that at a rate-setting meeting on September 24, the Federal Reserve decided to boost the discount rate from 5% to $5\frac{1}{4}\%$. On a $150,000 loan, what would be the difference in the proceeds received?

  $\$150,000 \times .05 \times 1 = \$7,500$ discount
  $\$150,000 - \$7,500 = \$142,500$ proceeds $\$142,500$
  $\$150,000 \times .0525 \times 1 = \$7,875$ discount   Difference in proceeds: $- \ 142,125$
  $\$150,000 - \$7,875 = \$142,125$ proceeds $\$ \qquad 375$

11–13. Kim Scholten bought a $10,000, 13-week Treasury bill at 4%. What is her effective rate? Round to the nearest hundredth percent.

  $\$10,000 \times .04 \times \dfrac{13}{52} = \$100$ Effective rate $= \dfrac{\$100}{\$9,900 \times \dfrac{13}{52}} = 4.04\%$

11–14. Ron Prentice bought goods from Shelly Katz. On May 8, Shelly gave Ron a time extension on his bill by accepting a $3,000, 8%, 180-day note. On August 16, Shelly discounted the note at Roseville Bank at 9%. What proceeds does Shelly Katz receive?

  Aug. 16   228 days $\$3,000 \times .08 \times \dfrac{180}{360} = \$120$ **Bank discount**
  May 8   − 128
  　　　　 100 days passed $\$3,000 + \$120 = \$3,120$ *MV* $\$3,120.00 \times .09 \times \dfrac{80}{360} = \$62.40$
  180 − 100 = 80 days $\$3,120.00$
  　　(discount period) $- \ \ \ 62.40$
  　　　　　　　　　　　　　　　　　　　　　　　　　　　　　　　 $\$3,057.60$ proceeds

11–15. Rex Corporation accepted a $5,000, 8%, 120-day note dated August 8 from Regis Company in settlement of a past bill. On October 11, Rex discounted the note at Park Bank at 9%. What are the note's maturity value, discount period, and bank discount? What proceeds does Rex receive?

  Oct. 11   284 days $\$5,000 \times .08 \times \dfrac{120}{360} = \$133.33$ **Bank discount**
  Aug. 8   − 220
  　　　　 64 days passed $\$5,000 + \$133.33 = \$5,133.33$ *MV* $\$5,133.33 \times .09 \times \dfrac{56}{360} = \$71.87$
  120 − 64 = 56 days $\$5,133.33$
  　　(discount period) $- \ \ \ 71.87$
  　　　　　　　　　　　　　　　　　　　　　　　　　　　　　　　　 $\$5,061.46$ proceeds

11–16. On May 12, Scott Rinse accepted an $8,000, 12%, 90-day note for a time extension of a bill for goods bought by Ron Prentice. On June 12, Scott discounted the note at Able Bank at 10%. What proceeds does Scott receive?

  June 12   163 days   Maturity value $= \$8,000 \times .12 \times \dfrac{90}{360} = \$240 + \$8,000 = \$8,240$
  May 12 − 132
  　　　　 31 days passed   Discount period $= 90 - 31 = 59$

  90 − 31 = 59 days   Bank discount $= \$8,240 \times .10 \times \dfrac{59}{360} = \$135.04$
  　　(discount period)
  　　　　　　　　　　　　　　Proceeds $= \$8,240 - \$135.04 = \$8,104.96$

11–17. On May 31, 2000, Saxon Paint and Hardware sold $1,200 in paint to Reliable House Painters. Reliable signed a promissory note with terms of 6% interest due on August 3, 2000. On June 15, Saxon needed funds and turned the note over to Harris Bank whose discount rate was 8%. What proceeds will Saxon receive?

August 3 = 215; May 31 = 151; 215 − 151 = 64   64 − 15 = 49 days—bank's discount period

$$\$1,200 \times .06 \times \frac{64}{360} = \$12.80 \text{ interest}$$ $$\$1,212.80 \times .08 \times \frac{49}{360} = \$13.21 \text{ bank discount}$$

$1,200.00 (P)
+ 12.80 (I)
———————
$1,212.80 (MV)
June 15 = 166
May 31 = 151
———————
      15 days expired

$1,212.80
− 13.21
———————
$1,199.59 proceeds

 CHALLENGE PROBLEMS

11–18. Just Nuts N Bolts has a 90-day $1,200 promissory note dated April 7, 2000. The interest on the note is 5%. On May 28, Just Nuts N Bolts needed cash. In checking with First National Bank, Just Nuts N Bolts learned the bank's discount rate was $6\frac{1}{2}$%. After the note was turned over to First National Bank, it was determined the LaSalle Bank discount rate was 6%. How much more in proceeds would Just Nuts N Bolts have received by choosing LaSalle?

July 6 = 187
Apr. 7 = 97
——————
      90-day note

$$\$1,200 \times .05 \times \frac{90}{360} = \$15 \text{ interest}$$

     P   I   MV
$1,200 + $15 = $1,215

First National Bank (90 − 51)

May 28 = 148
Apr. 7 = 97
——————
      51 days expired $$\$1,215 \times .065 \times \frac{39}{360} = \$8.56 \text{ bank's discount}$$

$1,215.00
− 8.56
——————
$1,206.44 proceeds from First National

LaSalle Bank

$$\$1,215 \times .06 \times \frac{39}{360} = \$7.90 \text{ bank's discount}$$

$1,215.00
− 7.90
——————
$1,207.10 proceeds from LaSalle

$1,207.10
− 1,206.44
——————
$ .66 difference

11–19. Tina Mier must pay a $2,000 furniture bill. A finance company will loan Tina $2,000 for 8 months at a 9% discount rate. The finance company told Tina that if she wants to receive exactly $2,000, she must borrow more than $2,000. The finance company gave Tina the following formula:

$$\text{What to ask for} = \frac{\text{Amount in cash to be received}}{1 - (\text{Discount rate} \times \text{Time of loan})}$$

Calculate Tina's loan request and the effective rate of interest.

$$\frac{\$2,000}{1 - \left(.09 \times \frac{8}{12}\right)} = \frac{\$2,000}{1 - .06} = \frac{\$2,000}{.94} = \$2,127.66$$

Check

$$\$2,127.66 \times .09 \times \frac{8}{12} = \$127.66$$

$$\frac{\$127.66}{\$2,000 \times \frac{8}{12}} = 9.57\%$$

 SUMMARY PRACTICE TEST

1. On July 10, Intel Corporation accepted a $160,000, 90-day, noninterest-bearing note from Jane Corporation. What is the maturity value of the note? *(p. 270)*
$160,000

2. The face value of a simple discount note is $9,000. The discount is 8% for 130 days. Calculate the following: *(p. 271)*
   a. Amount of interest charged for each note. $260
   b. Amount borrower would receive. $8,740 ($9,000 − $260)
   c. Amount payee would receive at maturity. $9,000
   d. Effective rate (to nearest tenth percent).

$$\$9,000 \times .08 \times \frac{130}{360} = \$260 \qquad \frac{\$260}{\$8,740 \times \dfrac{130}{360}} = \frac{\$260}{\$3,156.1111} = 8.2\%$$

3. On June 9, Bill Flynn accepted a $20,000, 9%, 180-day note from Bill Boe. On August 2, Bill Flynn discounted the note at Lange Bank at 10%. What proceeds did Bill Flynn receive? *(p. 274)*

   a. $MV = \$20,000 \times .09 \times \dfrac{180}{360} = \$900 + \$20,000 = \$20,900$

   b. Aug. 2 ⟶ 214
       June 9 ⟶ $\underline{160}$
              54 days elapsed   180 − 54 = 126 days to go

   c. Bank discount = $\$20,900 \times .10 \times \dfrac{126}{360} = \$731.50$

   d. Proceeds = $20,900 − $731.50 = $20,168.50

4. Lodge Corporation accepted a $30,000, $8\frac{3}{4}$%, 90-day note on August 15. Lodge discounts the note on September 19 at Luck Bank at $8\frac{1}{2}$%. What proceeds did Lodge receive? *(p. 274)*

   a. $MV = \$30,000 \times .0875 \times \dfrac{90}{360} = \$656.25 + \$30,000 = \$30,656.25$

   b. Sept. 19 ⟶ 262
       Aug. 15 ⟶ $\underline{227}$
              35 days elapsed   90 − 35 = 55 days to go

   c. Bank discount = $\$30,656.25 \times .085 \times \dfrac{55}{360} = \$398.11$

   d. Proceeds = $30,656.25 − $398.11 = $30,258.14

5. The owner of Rick's Upholstery signed a $7,000 note at Fleet Bank. Fleet charges an $8\frac{1}{4}$% discount rate. If the loan is for 180 days, find **(a)** the proceeds and **(b)** the effective rate charged by the bank (to the nearest tenth percent). *(p. 271)*

   a. $\$7,000 \times .0825 \times \dfrac{180}{360} = \$288.75$ **b.** $\dfrac{\$288.75}{\$6,711.25 \times \dfrac{180}{360}} = 8.6\%$

       $7,000 − $288.75 = $6,711.25

6. Laune Heath buys a $10,000, 13-week Treasury bill at 7%. What is the effective rate? Round to the nearest hundredth percent. *(p. 272)*

$$\$10,000 \times .07 \times \frac{13}{52} = \$175 \qquad \frac{\$175}{\$9,825 \times \dfrac{13}{52}} = 7.12\%$$

A GROUP PROJECT   Defend or reject the following business math issue based on the *Kiplinger's Personal Finance Magazine* article below:

INVESTING
Putting T-bills within reach of the masses

The scene in the photo below may soon be nothing more than a quaint reminder of how Americans purchased government securities in the olden days. There are no plans—yet—to close the Treasury window, but new ways to invest in government debt are sure simpler. As of September 16, you can buy Treasuries online at www.publicdebt.treas.gov, and later this fall, you'll be able to use a touch-tone phone. Either way, you'll pay by authorizing a debit from your bank account.

But the Treasury's most investor-friendly innovation yet is to slash the minimum-purchase amount for T-bills from $10,000 to $1,000, putting three-, six- and 12-month securities in reach of many savers for the first time. (The $1,000 minimum also applies to longer-maturity Treasury bonds.) In addition to making it easier for small investors to buy the securities directly, the change allows big and small investors alike to redeem government notes in $1,000 increments.

The change makes owning Treasuries outright as accessible as investing in a mutual fund that buys them. You'll avoid the average 1.07% in annual expenses on government-bond funds.

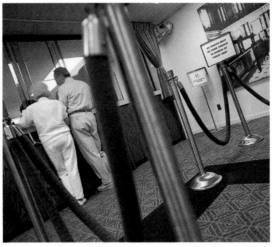

BRETON LITTLEHALES (RIGHT)

No waiting, even in short lines: It's easier than ever to buy Treasury securities.

Business Math Issue

Treasury bill minimum of $1,000 is still too high for the little investor.

1. List the key points of the article and information to support your position.
2. Write a group defense of your position using math calculations to support your view.

Dear Investor: You Won't Get Interest Promised by U.S.

By JOHN R. DORFMAN
Staff Reporter of THE WALL STREET JOURNAL

Oops.

Some 16,000 people nationwide who buy U.S. Treasury securities under the government's direct-purchase program were informed about a week ago that they would receive a fat interest check in February. Alas, it was just a computer glitch.

One sharp-eyed customer who noticed the mistake was Joseph Belth, a retired insurance professor at Indiana University. Mr. Belth had bought a $25,000, five-year Treasury note in August. His statement said that he would receive a $1,084 interest check on Feb. 28, 1995.

That seemed too generous to Mr. Belth, who was expecting to receive only $859—or half a year's interest at 6.875%.

Transposed Interest Rate

Right he was. A clerk at the Federal Reserve Bank of Philadelphia, which runs the Treasury Direct program, had transposed two digits while calculating the amount of the first interest check to be paid to buyers of the five-year Treasury notes issued in August. Instead of basing the calculation on the actual interest rate of 6.87%, the Fed's computer was misled, and applied an 8.67% rate.

"I guess you'd call it a keypunch problem," said a Treasury official.

In all, $11 billion in five-year notes were sold in the August auction. Of that total, less than $800 million was sold through the Treasury Direct program affected by the glitch, according to Lee Grandy and Chuck Andrietta of the Bureau of Public Debt. Exact dollar figures weren't available, they said.

"Dear Investor" letters were mailed last week to all 16,000 customers over the signature of Richard Koch, director of the division of consumer service for the Bureau of Public Debt. So, many people will get the bad, but correct, news today. The letter apologizes "for any inconvenience or confusion this may have caused you."

Mr. Grandy said that new procedures have been set up "to make sure it doesn't happen again."

Popular Program

The Treasury Direct program is popular with individual investors because it lets them buy Treasury bonds, notes and bills directly from the Treasury Department without paying a sales commission to a broker. Usually the mechanics are handled by the individual's bank. When interest checks are due, or when a Treasury security matures, the proceeds are deposited by the Treasury directly into the person's bank account.

Branch offices of the Federal Reserve issue applications to participate in the program, and the Federal Reserve Bank of Philadelphia handles the issuing of account statements for the whole system.

Almost all people participating in the program submit what are called "noncompetitive bids." That means they agree to accept the average price and yield that result from competitive bidding among the big boys—pension funds, mutual funds and other large institutions — that dominate each Treasury auction. The total dollar amount of noncompetitive bids submitted in the August auction was $809 million, but Treasury Direct accounts for only a portion of that.

One drawback to Treasury Direct is that — since the buyer doesn't hold the securities directly, but through an electronic entry system—it's difficult to sell on short notice. However, there are several advantages, including the availability of an automatic reinvestment program, as well as the absence of commissions.

Potential for $14 Million Mistake

Had the Treasury actually paid the extra money it mistakenly dangled in front of investors' eyes, it would have amounted to less than $14 million. But officials at both the Treasury and Federal Reserve were eager to emphasize that no one actually received any money and then had it yanked away. "Nobody was financially hurt by this," one Fed official says. "It's not like the money was actually deposited, and then had to be taken back."

How did the mistake come to light? Treasury officials said yesterday they don't know who first called it to the department's attention. Says one Treasury official: "There are a number of investors who, as soon as they get their statements, get their calculators out."

Project A

Show how the figures $1,084 and $859 were calculated.

$$\$25,000 \times .0867 \times \frac{6}{12} = \$1,083.75$$

$$\$25,000 \times .0687 \times \frac{6}{12} = \$858.75$$

 See text Web site (www.mhhe.com/slater) and *The Business Math Internet Resource Guide.*

CLASSROOM NOTES

YOU AND YOUR MONEY

Investing an amount continuously over a long time is most rewarding. For example, if you continue to invest $3,000 every year for the next 40 years and earn an average return of 10%, your nest egg will total almost $1.4 million!

12

COMPOUND INTEREST AND PRESENT VALUE

LEARNING UNIT OBJECTIVES

LU 12.1   Compound Interest (Future Value)—The Big Picture

- Compare simple interest with compound interest *(pp. 286–87).*
- Calculate the compound amount and interest manually and by table lookup *(pp. 288–90).*
- Explain and compute the effective rate (APY) *(p. 290).*

LU 12.2   Present Value—The Big Picture

- Compare present value (PV) with compound interest (FV) *(p. 292).*
- Compute present value by table lookup *(pp. 293–95).*
- Check the present value answer by compounding *(p. 295).*

Confused by Investing?

If there's something about your investment portfolio that doesn't seem to add up, maybe you should check your math.

Lots of folks are perplexed by the mathematics of investing, so I thought a refresher course might help. Here's a look at some key concepts:

■ **10 Plus 10 is 21**

Imagine you invest $100, which earns 10% this year and 10% next. How much have you made? If you answered 21%, go to the head of the class.

Here's how the math works. This year's 10% gain turns your $100 into $110. Next year, you also earn 10%, but you start the year with $110. Result? You earn $11, boosting your wealth to $121.

Thus, your portfolio has earned a *cumulative* 21% return over two years, but the *annualized* return is just 10%. The fact that 21% is more than double 10% can be attributed to the effect of investment compounding, the way that you earn money each year not only on your original investment, but also on earnings from prior years that you've reinvested.

■ **The Rule of 72**

To get a feel for compounding, try the rule of 72. What's that? If you divide a particular annual return into 72, you'll find out how many years it will take to double your money. Thus, at 10% a year, an investment will double in value in a tad over seven years.

"Confused by Investing?" asks *The Wall Street Journal* clipping. Read this clipping carefully. It explains how money increases when you invest. The important word is *compounding*.

In this chapter we look at the power of compounding—interest paid on earned interest. Let's begin by studying Learning Unit 12.1, which shows you how to calculate compound interest.

LEARNING UNIT 12.1   Compound Interest (Future Value)—The Big Picture

So far we have discussed only simple interest, which is interest on the principal alone. Simple interest is either paid at the end of the loan period or deducted in advance. From the chapter introduction, you know that interest can also be compounded.

Compounding involves the calculation of interest periodically over the life of the loan (or investment). After each calculation, the interest is added to the principal. Future calculations are on the adjusted principal (old principal plus interest). **Compound interest,** then, is the interest on the principal plus the interest of prior periods. **Future value (FV),** or the **compound amount,** is the final amount of the loan or investment at the end of the last period. In the beginning of this unit, do not be concerned with how to calculate compounding but try to understand the meaning of compounding.

Figure 12.1 shows how $1 will grow if it is calculated for 4 years at 8% annually. This means that the interest is calculated on the balance once a year. In Figure 12.1, we start with $1, which is the **present value (PV).** After year 1, the dollar with interest is worth $1.08. At the end of year 2, the dollar is worth $1.17. By the end of year 4, the dol-

FIGURE 12.1

Future value of $1 at 8% for four periods

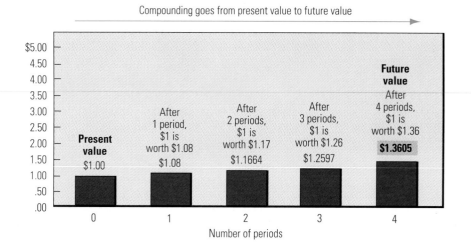

lar is worth $1.36. Note how we start with the present and look to see what the dollar will be worth in the future. *Compounding goes from present value to future value.*

Before you learn how to calculate compound interest and compare it to simple interest, you must understand the terms that follow. These terms are also used in Chapter 13.

- **Compounded annually:** Interest calculated on the balance once a year.
- **Compounded semiannually:** Interest calculated on the balance every 6 months or every $\frac{1}{2}$ year.
- **Compounded quarterly:** Interest calculated on the balance every 3 months or every $\frac{1}{4}$ year.
- **Compounded monthly:** Interest calculated on the balance each month.
- **Compounded daily:** Interest calculated on the balance each day.
- **Number of periods:**[1] Number of years multiplied by the number of times the interest is compounded per year. For example, if you compound $1 for 4 years at 8% annually, semiannually, or quarterly, the following periods will result:

      Annually: 4 years $\times$ 1 = 4 periods
      Semiannually: 4 years $\times$ 2 = 8 periods
      Quarterly: 4 years $\times$ 4 = 16 periods

- **Rate for each period:**[2] Annual interest rate divided by the number of times the interest is compounded per year. Compounding changes the interest rate for annual, semi-annual, and quarterly periods as follows:

      Annually: 8% $\div$ 1 = 8%
      Semiannually: 8% $\div$ 2 = 4%
      Quarterly: 8% $\div$ 4 = 2%

Note that both the number of periods (4) and the rate (8%) for the annual example did not change. You will see later that rate and periods (not years) will always change unless interest is compounded yearly.

Now you are ready to learn the difference between simple interest and compound interest.

Simple versus Compound Interest

Situation 1: Calculating Simple Interest and Maturity Value

The following three situations of Bill Smith will clarify the difference between simple interest and compound interest.

EXAMPLE   Bill Smith deposited $80 in a savings account for 4 years at an annual interest rate of 8%. What is Bill's simple interest?

To calculate simple interest, we use the following simple interest formula:

$$\text{Interest } (I) = \text{Principal } (P) \times \text{Rate } (R) \times \text{Time } (T)$$

$$\$25.60 \quad = \quad \$80 \quad \times \quad .08 \quad \times \quad 4$$

In 4 years Bill receives a total of $105.60 ($80.00 + $25.60)—principal plus simple interest.

Now let's look at the interest Bill would earn if the bank compounded Bill's interest on his savings.

Situation 2: Calculating Compound Amount and Interest without Tables[3]

You can use the following steps to calculate the compound amount and the interest manually:

---

[1] Periods are often expressed with the letter N for number of periods.
[2] Rate is often expressed with the letter i for interest.
[3] For simplicity of presentation, round each calculation to nearest cent before continuing the compounding process. The compound amount will be off by 1 cent.

Calculating Compound Amount and Interest Manually

Step 1. Calculate the simple interest and add it to the principal. Use this total to figure next year's interest.

Step 2. Repeat for the total number of periods.

Step 3. Compound amount − Principal = Compound interest.

EXAMPLE   Bill Smith deposited $80 in a savings account for 4 years at an annual compounded rate of 8%. What are Bill's compound amount and interest?

The following shows how the compounded rate affects Bill's interest:

	Year 1	Year 2	Year 3	Year 4
	$80.00	$86.40	$ 93.31	$100.77
	× .08	× .08	× .08	× .08
Interest	$ 6.40	$ 6.91	$ 7.46	$ 8.06
Beginning balance	+ 80.00	+ 86.40	+ 93.31	+ 100.77
Amount at year-end	$86.40	$93.31	$100.77	$108.83

Note that the beginning year 2 interest is the result of the interest of year 1 added to the principal. At the end of each interest period, we add on the period's interest. This interest becomes part of the principal we use for the calculation of the next period's interest. We can determine Bill's compound interest as follows[4]:

Compound amount	$108.83
Principal	− 80.00
Compound interest	$ 28.83

Note: In Situation 1 the interest was $25.60.

We could have used the following simplified process to calculate the compound amount and interest:

Year 1	Year 2	Year 3	Year 4
$80.00	$86.40	$ 93.31	$100.77
× 1.08	× 1.08	× 1.08	× 1.08
$86.40	$93.31	$100.77	$108.83 [5] ←—Future value

When using this simplification, you do not have to add the new interest to the previous balance. Remember that compounding results in higher interest than simple interest. Compounding is the *sum* of principal and interest multiplied by the interest rate we use to calculate interest for the next period. So, 1.08 above is 108%, with 100% as the base and 8% as the interest.

Situation 3: Calculating Compound Amount by Table Lookup

To calculate the compound amount with a future value table, use the following steps:

Calculating Compound Amount by Table Lookup

Step 1. Find the periods: Years multiplied by number of times interest is compounded in 1 year.

Step 2. Find the rate: Annual rate divided by number of times interest is compounded in 1 year.

Step 3. Go down the Period column of the table to the number of periods desired; look across the row to find the rate. At the intersection of the two columns is the table factor for the compound amount of $1.

Step 4. Multiply the table factor by the amount of the loan. This gives the compound amount.

---

[4]The formula for compounding is $A = P(1 + i)^N$, where A equals compound amount, P equals the principal, i equals interest per period, and N equals number of periods. The calculator sequence would be as follows for Bill Smith: 1 $\boxed{+}$ .08 $\boxed{y^x}$ 4 $\boxed{\times}$ 80 $\boxed{=}$ 108.84.

[5]Off 1 cent due to rounding.

Four Periods

No. of times
compounded × No. of years
in 1 year

$$1 \quad \times \quad 4$$

In Situation 2, Bill deposited $80 into a savings account for 4 years at an interest rate of 8% compounded annually. Bill heard that he could calculate the compound amount and interest by using tables. In Situation 3, Bill learns how to do this. Again, Bill wants to know the value of $80 in 4 years at 8%. He begins by using Table 12.1.

Looking at Table 12.1 below, Bill goes down the Period column to period 4, then across the row to the 8% column. At the intersection, Bill sees the number 1.3605. The marginal notes show how Bill arrived at the periods and rate. The 1.3605 table number means that $1 compounded at this rate will increase in value in 4 years to about $1.36. Do you recognize the $1.36? Figure 12.1 showed how $1 grew to $1.36. Since Bill wants to know the value of $80, he multiplies the dollar amount by the table factor as follows:

$$\$80.00 \times 1.3605 = \boxed{\$108.84}$$

Dollar amount × Table factor = Compound amount (future value)

8% Rate

$$8\% \atop rate = \frac{8\%}{1} \begin{array}{l} \rightarrow Annual\ rate \\ \rightarrow No.\ of\ times \\ \quad compounded \\ \quad in\ 1\ year \end{array}$$

Figure 12.2 illustrates this compounding procedure. We can say that compounding is a future value (FV) since we are looking into the future. Thus,

$$\$108.84 - \$80.00 = \$28.84 \text{ interest for 4 years at 8\%} \atop \text{compounded annually on \$80.00}$$

Now let's look at two examples that illustrate compounding more than once a year.

EXAMPLE Find the interest on $6,000 at 10% compounded semiannually for 5 years. We calculate the interest as follows:

Periods = 2 × 5 years = 10 $6,000 × 1.6289 = $9,773.40
Rate = 10% ÷ 2 = 5%   − 6,000.00
10 periods, 5%, in Table 12.1 = 1.6289 (table factor) $\boxed{\$3,773.40}$
                                                         interest

TABLE 12.1 Future value of $1 at compound interest

Period	1%	1½%	2%	3%	4%	5%	6%	7%	8%	9%	10%
1	1.0100	1.0150	1.0200	1.0300	1.0400	1.0500	1.0600	1.0700	1.0800	1.0900	1.1000
2	1.0201	1.0302	1.0404	1.0609	1.0816	1.1025	1.1236	1.1449	1.1664	1.1881	1.2100
3	1.0303	1.0457	1.0612	1.0927	1.1249	1.1576	1.1910	1.2250	1.2597	1.2950	1.3310
4	1.0406	1.0614	1.0824	1.1255	1.1699	1.2155	1.2625	1.3108	1.3605	1.4116	1.4641
5	1.0510	1.0773	1.1041	1.1593	1.2167	1.2763	1.3382	1.4026	1.4693	1.5386	1.6105
6	1.0615	1.0934	1.1262	1.1941	1.2653	1.3401	1.4185	1.5007	1.5869	1.6771	1.7716
7	1.0721	1.1098	1.1487	1.2299	1.3159	1.4071	1.5036	1.6058	1.7138	1.8280	1.9487
8	1.0829	1.1265	1.1717	1.2668	1.3686	1.4775	1.5938	1.7182	1.8509	1.9926	2.1436
9	1.0937	1.1434	1.1951	1.3048	1.4233	1.5513	1.6895	1.8385	1.9990	2.1719	2.3579
10	1.1046	1.1605	1.2190	1.3439	1.4802	1.6289	1.7908	1.9672	2.1589	2.3674	2.5937
11	1.1157	1.1780	1.2434	1.3842	1.5395	1.7103	1.8983	2.1049	2.3316	2.5804	2.8531
12	1.1268	1.1960	1.2682	1.4258	1.6010	1.7959	2.0122	2.2522	2.5182	2.8127	3.1384
13	1.1381	1.2135	1.2936	1.4685	1.6651	1.8856	2.1329	2.4098	2.7196	3.0658	3.4523
14	1.1495	1.2318	1.3195	1.5126	1.7317	1.9799	2.2609	2.5785	2.9372	3.3417	3.7975
15	1.1610	1.2502	1.3459	1.5580	1.8009	2.0789	2.3966	2.7590	3.1722	3.6425	4.1772
16	1.1726	1.2690	1.3728	1.6047	1.8730	2.1829	2.5404	2.9522	3.4259	3.9703	4.5950
17	1.1843	1.2880	1.4002	1.6528	1.9479	2.2920	2.6928	3.1588	3.7000	4.3276	5.0545
18	1.1961	1.3073	1.4282	1.7024	2.0258	2.4066	2.8543	3.3799	3.9960	4.7171	5.5599
19	1.2081	1.3270	1.4568	1.7535	2.1068	2.5270	3.0256	3.6165	4.3157	5.1417	6.1159
20	1.2202	1.3469	1.4859	1.8061	2.1911	2.6533	3.2071	3.8697	4.6610	5.6044	6.7275
21	1.2324	1.3671	1.5157	1.8603	2.2788	2.7860	3.3996	4.1406	5.0338	6.1088	7.4002
22	1.2447	1.3876	1.5460	1.9161	2.3699	2.9253	3.6035	4.4304	5.4365	6.6586	8.1403
23	1.2572	1.4084	1.5769	1.9736	2.4647	3.0715	3.8197	4.7405	5.8715	7.2579	8.9543
24	1.2697	1.4295	1.6084	2.0328	2.5633	3.2251	4.0489	5.0724	6.3412	7.9111	9.8497
25	1.2824	1.4510	1.6406	2.0938	2.6658	3.3864	4.2919	5.4274	6.8485	8.6231	10.8347
26	1.2953	1.4727	1.6734	2.1566	2.7725	3.5557	4.5494	5.8074	7.3964	9.3992	11.9182
27	1.3082	1.4948	1.7069	2.2213	2.8834	3.7335	4.8223	6.2139	7.9881	10.2451	13.1100
28	1.3213	1.5172	1.7410	2.2879	2.9987	3.9201	5.1117	6.6488	8.6271	11.1672	14.4210
29	1.3345	1.5400	1.7758	2.3566	3.1187	4.1161	5.4184	7.1143	9.3173	12.1722	15.8631
30	1.3478	1.5631	1.8114	2.4273	3.2434	4.3219	5.7435	7.6123	10.0627	13.2677	17.4494

Note: For more detailed tables, see your reference booklet, the *Business Math Handbook*.

FIGURE 12.2
Compounding (FV)

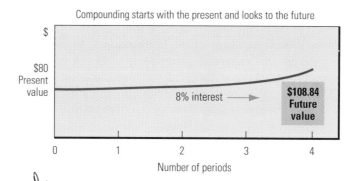

Compounding starts with the present and looks to the future

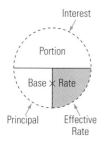

EXAMPLE   Pam Donahue deposits $8,000 in her savings account that pays 6% interest compounded quarterly. What will be the balance of her account at the end of 5 years?

Periods = 4 × 5 years = 20
Rate = 6% ÷ 4 = $1\frac{1}{2}\%$
20 periods, $1\frac{1}{2}\%$, in Table 12.1 = 1.3469 (table factor)
$8,000 × 1.3469 = **$10,775.20**

Next, let's look at bank rates and how they affect interest.

Bank Rates—Nominal versus Effective Rates (Annual Percentage Yield, or APY)

Banks often advertise their annual (nominal) interest rates and *not* their true or effective rate (annual percentage yield, or APY). This has made it difficult for investors and depositors to determine the actual rates of interest they were receiving. The Truth in Savings law forced savings institutions to reveal their actual rate of interest. The APY is defined in the Truth in Savings law as the percentage rate expressing the total amount of interest that would be received on a $100 deposit based on the annual rate and frequency of compounding for a 365-day period. As you can see from the following advertisement, banks now refer to the effective rate of interest as the annual percentage yield.

6 MONTH CD
ANNUAL PERCENTAGE YIELD
5.77%
MINIMUM DEPOSIT
$25,000

Let's study the rates of two banks to see which bank has the better return for the investor. Blue Bank pays 8% interest compounded quarterly on $8,000. Sun Bank offers 8% interest compounded semiannually on $8,000. The 8% rate is the **nominal rate,** or stated rate, on which the bank calculates the interest. To calculate the **effective rate (annual percentage yield,** or **APY),** however, we can use the following formula:

$$\frac{\text{Effective rate}}{(\text{APY})^6} = \frac{\text{Interest for 1 year}}{\text{Principal}}$$

Now let's calculate the effective rate (APY) for Blue Bank and Sun Bank.

_____
[6]Round to the nearest hundredth percent as needed. In practice, the rate is often rounded to the nearest thousandth.

Note the effective rates (APY) can be seen from Table 12.1 for $1:
1.0824 ⟵ 4 periods, 2%
1.0816 ⟵ 2 periods, 4%

Blue, 8% compounded quarterly	Sun, 8% compounded semiannually
Periods = 4 (4 × 1)	Periods = 2 (2 × 1)
Percent = $\dfrac{8\%}{4}$ = 2%	Percent = $\dfrac{8\%}{2}$ = 4%
Principal = $8,000	Principal = $8,000
Table 12.1 lookup: 4 periods, 2%	Table 12.1 lookup: 2 periods, 4%
1.0824	1.0816
× $8,000	× $8,000
Less $8,659.20	$8,652.80
principal − 8,000.00	− 8,000.00
$ 659.20	$ 652.80
Effective rate (APY) = $\dfrac{\$659.20}{\$8,000}$ = .0824	$\dfrac{\$652.80}{\$8,000}$ = .0816
= 8.24%	= 8.16%

FIGURE 12.3

Nominal and effective rates (APY) of interest compared

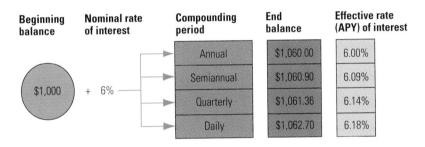

Figure 12.3 illustrates a comparison of nominal and effective rates (APY) of interest. This comparison should make you question any advertisement of interest rates before depositing your money.

Before concluding this unit, we briefly discuss compounding interest daily.

Compounding Interest Daily

Although many banks add interest to each account quarterly, some banks pay interest that is **compounded daily,** and other banks use *continuous compounding.* Remember that continuous compounding sounds great, but in fact, it yields only a fraction of a percent more interest over a year than daily compounding. Today, computers perform these calculations.

Table 12.2 (p. 292) is a partial table showing what $1 will grow to in the future by daily compounded interest, 360-day basis. For example, we can calculate interest compounded daily on $900 at 6% per year for 25 years as follows:

$900 × 4.4811 = **$4,032.99** daily compounding

Now it's time to check your progress with the following Practice Quiz.

LU 12.1 PRACTICE QUIZ

1. Complete the following without a table (round each calculation to the nearest cent as needed):

Principal	Time	Rate of compound interest	Compounded	Number of periods to be compounded	Total amount	Total interest
$200	1 year	8%	Quarterly	a.	b.	c.

2. Solve the previous problem by using compound value (FV) Table 12.1.

TABLE 12.2   Interest on a $1 deposit compounded daily—360-day basis

Number of years	6.00%	6.50%	7.00%	7.50%	8.00%	8.50%	9.00%	9.50%	10.00%
1	1.0618	1.0672	1.0725	1.0779	1.0833	1.0887	1.0942	1.0996	1.1052
2	1.1275	1.1388	1.1503	1.1618	1.1735	1.1853	1.1972	1.2092	1.2214
3	1.1972	1.2153	1.2337	1.2523	1.2712	1.2904	1.3099	1.3297	1.3498
4	1.2712	1.2969	1.3231	1.3498	1.3771	1.4049	1.4333	1.4622	1.4917
5	1.3498	1.3840	1.4190	1.4549	1.4917	1.5295	1.5682	1.6079	1.6486
6	1.4333	1.4769	1.5219	1.5682	1.6160	1.6652	1.7159	1.7681	1.8220
7	1.5219	1.5761	1.6322	1.6904	1.7506	1.8129	1.8775	1.9443	2.0136
8	1.6160	1.6819	1.7506	1.8220	1.8963	1.9737	2.0543	2.1381	2.2253
9	1.7159	1.7949	1.8775	1.9639	2.0543	2.1488	2.2477	2.3511	2.4593
10	1.8220	1.9154	2.0136	2.1168	2.2253	2.3394	2.4593	2.5854	2.7179
15	2.4594	2.6509	2.8574	3.0799	3.3197	3.5782	3.8568	4.1571	4.4808
20	3.3198	3.6689	4.0546	4.4810	4.9522	5.4728	6.0482	6.6842	7.3870
25	4.4811	5.0777	5.7536	6.5195	7.3874	8.3708	9.4851	10.7477	12.1782
30	6.0487	7.0275	8.1645	9.4855	11.0202	12.8032	14.8747	17.2813	20.0772

3. Lionel Rodgers deposits $6,000 in Victory Bank, which pays 3% interest compounded semiannually. How much will Lionel have in his account at the end of 8 years?

4. Find the effective rate (APY) for the year: principal, $7,000; interest rate, 12%; and compounded quarterly.

5. Calculate by Table 12.2 what $1,500 compounded daily for 5 years will grow to at 7%.

✓   **Solutions**

1. **a.** 4 (4 × 1)   **b.** $216.48   **c.** $16.48 ($216.48 − $200)
   $200 × 1.02 = $204 × 1.02 = $208.08 × 1.02 = $212.24 × 1.02 = $216.48

2. $200 × 1.0824 = $216.48 (4 periods, 2%)

3. 16 periods, $1\frac{1}{2}\%$, $6,000 × 1.2690 = $7,614

4. 4 periods, 3%,

$$\begin{array}{r} \$7,000 \times 1.1255 = \$7,878.50 \\ -\ 7,000.00 \\ \hline \$\ \ 878.50 \end{array} \qquad \frac{\$878.50}{\$7,000.00} = 12.55\%$$

5. $1,500 × 1.4190 = $2,128.50

LEARNING UNIT 12.2   Present Value—The Big Picture

© PhotoDisc.

Figure 12.1 (p. 286) in Learning Unit 12.1 showed how by compounding, the *future value* of $1 became $1.36. This learning unit discusses *present value*. Before we look at specific calculations involving present value, let's look at the concept of present value.

Figure 12.4 shows that if we invested 74 cents today, compounding would cause the 74 cents to grow to $1 in the future. For example, let's assume you ask this question: "If I need $1 in 4 years in the future, how much must I put in the bank *today* (assume an 8% annual interest)?" To answer this question, you must know the present value of that $1 today. From Figure 12.4, you can see that the present value of $1 is .7350. Remember that the $1 is only worth 74 cents if you wait 4 periods to receive it. This is one reason why so many athletes get such big contracts—much of the money is paid in later years when it is not worth as much.

FIGURE 12.4

Present value of $1 at 8% for four periods

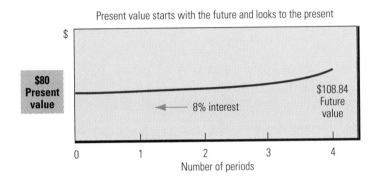

Present value goes from the future value to the present value

FIGURE 12.5

Present value

Present value starts with the future and looks to the present

Relationship of Compounding (FV) to Present Value (PV)— The Bill Smith Example Continued

In Learning Unit 12.1, our consideration of compounding started in the *present* ($80) and looked to find the *future* amount of $108.84. Present value (PV) starts with the *future* and tries to calculate its worth in the *present* ($80). For example, in Figure 12.5, we assume Bill Smith knew that in 4 years he wanted to buy a bike that cost $108.84 (future). Bill's bank pays 8% interest compounded annually. How much money must Bill put in the bank *today* (present) to have $108.84 in 4 years? To work from the future to the present, we can use a present value (PV) table. In the next section you will learn how to use this table.

How to Use Present Value (PV) Table[7]

To calculate present value with a present value table, use the following steps:

Calculating Present Value by Table Lookup

Step 1. Find the periods: Years multiplied by number of times interest is compounded in 1 year.

Step 2. Find the rate: Annual rate divided by numbers of times interest is compounded in 1 year.

Step 3. Go down the Period column of the table to the number of periods desired; look across the row to find the rate. At the intersection of the two columns is the table factor for the compound value of $1.

Step 4. Multiply the table factor times the future value. This gives the present value.

---

[7]The formula for present value is $PV = \dfrac{A}{(1 + i)^N}$, where A equals future amount (compound amount), N equals number of compounding periods, and i equals interest rate per compounding period. The calculator sequence for Bill Smith would be as follows: 1 $\boxed{+}$ $.08$ $\boxed{y^x}$ 4 $\boxed{=}$ $\boxed{M+}$ 108.84 $\boxed{\div}$ $\boxed{MR}$ $\boxed{=}$ 80.03.

Periods

$$4 \;\times\; 1 \;=\; 4$$

No. of   *No. of times*
years   *compounded*
            in 1 year

Table 12.3 (below) is a present value (PV) table that tells you what $1 is worth today at different interest rates. To continue our Bill Smith example, go down the Period column in Table 12.3 to 4. Then go across to the 8% column. At 8% for 4 periods, we see a table factor of .7350. This means that $1 in the future is worth approximately 74 cents today. If Bill invested 74 cents today at 8% for 4 periods, Bill would have $1.

Since Bill knows the bike will cost $108.84 in the future, he completes the following calculation:

$$\$108.84 \times .7350 = \boxed{\$80.00}$$

This means that $108.84 in today's dollars is worth $80.00. Now let's check this.

Comparing Compound Interest (FV) Table 12.1 with Present Value (PV) Table 12.3

We know from our calculations that Bill needs to invest $80 for 4 years at 8% compound interest annually to buy his bike. We can check this by going back to Table 12.1 and comparing it with Table 12.3. Let's do this now.

Compound value Table 12.1			Present value Table 12.3		
Table 12.1	**Present value**	**Future value**	**Table 12.3**	**Future value**	**Present Value**
1.3605	× $80.00 =	$108.84	.7350	× $108.84 =	$80.00
(4 per., 8%)			(4 per., 8%)		
We know the present dollar amount and find what the dollar amount is worth in the future.			We know the future dollar amount and find what the dollar amount is worth in the present.		

TABLE 12.3   Present value of $1 at end period

Period	1%	1½%	2%	3%	4%	5%	6%	7%	8%	9%	10%
1	.9901	.9852	.9804	.9709	.9615	.9524	.9434	.9346	.9259	.9174	.9091
2	.9803	.9707	.9612	.9426	.9246	.9070	.8900	.8734	.8573	.8417	.8264
3	.9706	.9563	.9423	.9151	.8890	.8638	.8396	.8163	.7938	.7722	.7513
4	.9610	.9422	.9238	.8885	.8548	.8227	.7921	.7629	.7350	.7084	.6830
5	.9515	.9283	.9057	.8626	.8219	.7835	.7473	.7130	.6806	.6499	.6209
6	.9420	.9145	.8880	.8375	.7903	.7462	.7050	.6663	.6302	.5963	.5645
7	.9327	.9010	.8706	.8131	.7599	.7107	.6651	.6227	.5835	.5470	.5132
8	.9235	.8877	.8535	.7894	.7307	.6768	.6274	.5820	.5403	.5019	.4665
9	.9143	.8746	.8368	.7664	.7026	.6446	.5919	.5439	.5002	.4604	.4241
10	.9053	.8617	.8203	.7441	.6756	.6139	.5584	.5083	.4632	.4224	.3855
11	.8963	.8489	.8043	.7224	.6496	.5847	.5268	.4751	.4289	.3875	.3505
12	.8874	.8364	.7885	.7014	.6246	.5568	.4970	.4440	.3971	.3555	.3186
13	.8787	.8240	.7730	.6810	.6006	.5303	.4688	.4150	.3677	.3262	.2897
14	.8700	.8119	.7579	.6611	.5775	.5051	.4423	.3878	.3405	.2992	.2633
15	.8613	.7999	.7430	.6419	.5553	.4810	.4173	.3624	.3152	.2745	.2394
16	.8528	.7880	.7284	.6232	.5339	.4581	.3936	.3387	.2919	.2519	.2176
17	.8444	.7764	.7142	.6050	.5134	.4363	.3714	.3166	.2703	.2311	.1978
18	.8360	.7649	.7002	.5874	.4936	.4155	.3503	.2959	.2502	.2120	.1799
19	.8277	.7536	.6864	.5703	.4746	.3957	.3305	.2765	.2317	.1945	.1635
20	.8195	.7425	.6730	.5537	.4564	.3769	.3118	.2584	.2145	.1784	.1486
21	.8114	.7315	.6598	.5375	.4388	.3589	.2942	.2415	.1987	.1637	.1351
22	.8034	.7207	.6468	.5219	.4220	.3418	.2775	.2257	.1839	.1502	.1228
23	.7954	.7100	.6342	.5067	.4057	.3256	.2618	.2109	.1703	.1378	.1117
24	.7876	.6995	.6217	.4919	.3901	.3101	.2470	.1971	.1577	.1264	.1015
25	.7798	.6892	.6095	.4776	.3751	.2953	.2330	.1842	.1460	.1160	.0923
26	.7720	.6790	.5976	.4637	.3607	.2812	.2198	.1722	.1352	.1064	.0839
27	.7644	.6690	.5859	.4502	.3468	.2678	.2074	.1609	.1252	.0976	.0763
28	.7568	.6591	.5744	.4371	.3335	.2551	.1956	.1504	.1159	.0895	.0693
29	.7493	.6494	.5631	.4243	.3207	.2429	.1846	.1406	.1073	.0822	.0630
30	.7419	.6398	.5521	.4120	.3083	.2314	.1741	.1314	.0994	.0754	.0573
35	.7059	.5939	.5000	.3554	.2534	.1813	.1301	.0937	.0676	.0490	.0356
40	.6717	.5513	.4529	.3066	.2083	.1420	.0972	.0668	.0460	.0318	.0221

Note: For more detailed tables, see your booklet, the *Business Math Handbook*.

FIGURE 12.6

Present value

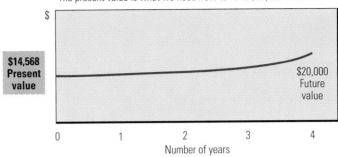

The present value is what we need *now* to have $20,000 in the future

$14,568
Present
value

$20,000
Future
value

Number of years

✗ Note that the table factor for compounding is over 1 (1.3605) and the table factor for present value is less than 1 (.7350). The compound value table starts with the present and goes to the future. The present value table starts with the future and goes to the present. Let's look at another example before trying the Practice Quiz.

EXAMPLE Rene Weaver needs $20,000 for college in 4 years. She can earn 8% compounded quarterly at her bank. How much must Rene deposit at the beginning of the year to have $20,000 in 4 years?

Remember that in this example the bank compounds the interest *quarterly*. Let's first determine the period and rate on a quarterly basis:

Periods = 4 × 4 years = 16 periods   Rate = $\frac{8\%}{4}$ = 2% Annual Rate

Now we go to Table 12.3 and find 16 under the Period column. We then move across to the 2% column and find the .7284 table factor.

$20,000   × .7284 = $14,568
(future value)   (present value)

We illustrate this in Figure 12.6.

We can check the $14,568 present value by using the compound value Table 12.1:

16 periods, 2% column = 1.3728 × $14,568 = $19,998.95[8]

Let's test your understanding of this unit with the Practice Quiz.

LU 12.2 PRACTICE QUIZ

Use the present-value Table 12.3 to complete:

Future amount desired	Length of time	Rate compounded	Table period	Rate used	PV factor	PV amount
1. $ 7,000	6 years	6% semiannually	____	____	____	____
2. $15,000	20 years	10% annually	____	____	____	____

3. Bill Blum needs $20,000 6 years from today to attend V.P.R. Tech. How much must Bill put in the bank today (12% quarterly) to reach his goal?

4. Bob Fry wants to buy his grandson a Ford Taurus in 4 years. The cost of a car will be $24,000. Assuming a bank rate of 8% compounded quarterly, how much must Bob put in the bank today?

✓ **Solutions**

1. 12 periods (6 years × 2)   3% (6% ÷ 2)   .7014 $4,909.80   ($7,000 × .7014)

2. 20 periods (20 years × 1)   10% (10% ÷ 1)   .1486 $2,229.00   ($15,000 × .1486)

3. 6 years × 4 = 24 periods $\frac{12\%}{4}$ = 3%   .4919 × $20,000 = $9,838

4. 4 × 4 years = 16 periods $\frac{8\%}{4}$ = 2%   .7284 × $24,000 = $17,481.60

---

[8]Not quite $20,000 due to rounding of table factors.

Chapter Organizer and Reference Guide

Topic	Key point, procedure, formula	Example(s) to illustrate situation
Calculating compound amount without tables (future value),* p. 286	Determine new amount by multiplying rate times new balance (that includes interest added on). Start in present and look to future. $\dfrac{\text{Compound}}{\text{interest}} = \dfrac{\text{Compound}}{\text{amount}} - \text{Principal}$ ⊢——Compounding——⊣ PV FV	$100 in savings account, compounded annually for 2 years at 8%: $100 $108 × 1.08 × 1.08 $108 $116.64 (future value)
Calculating compound amount (future value) by table lookup, p. 288	$\text{Periods} = \dfrac{\text{Number of times compounded per year}}{} \times \text{Years of loan}$ $\text{Rate} = \dfrac{\text{Annual rate}}{\text{Number of times compounded per year}}$ Multiply table factor (intersection of period and rate) times amount of loan.	*Example:* $2,000 @ 12% 5 years compounded quarterly: Periods = 4 × 5 years = 20 Rate = $\dfrac{12\%}{4}$ = 3% 20 periods, 3% = 1.8061 (table factor) $2,000 × 1.8061 = $3,612.20 (future value)
Effective rate (APY), p. 290	Effective rate (APY)= $\dfrac{\text{Interest for 1 year}}{\text{Principal}}$ or Rate can be seen in Table 12.1 factor.	$1,000 at 10% compounded semiannually for 1 year. By Table 12.1: 2 periods, 5% 1.1025 means at end of year investor has earned 110.25% of original principal. Thus the interest is 10.25%. $1,000 × 1.1025 = $1,102.50 − 1,000.00 $ 102.50 $\dfrac{\$102.50}{\$1,000}$ = 10.25% effective rate (APY)
Calculating present value (PV) with table lookup†, p. 293	Start with future and calculate worth in the present. Periods and rate computed like in compound interest. ⊢——Present value——⊣ PV FV Find periods and rate. Multiply table factor (intersection of period and rate) times amount of loan.	*Example:* Want $3,612.20 after 5 years with rate of 12% compounded quarterly: Periods = 4 × 5 = 20; % = 3% By Table 12.3: 20 periods, 3% = .5537 $3,612.20 × .5537 = $2,000.08 Invested today will yield desired amount in future
Key terms	Annual percentage yield (APY), *p. 290* Compound amount, *p. 286* Compounded annually, *p. 287* Compounded daily, *p. 287* Compounded monthly, *p. 287*	Compounded quarterly, *p. 287* Compounded semiannually, *p. 287* Compounding, *p. 286* Compound interest, *p. 286* Effective rate, *p. 290* Future value (FV), *p. 286* Nominal rate, *p. 290* Number of periods, *p. 287* Present value (PV), *p. 286* Rate for each period, *p. 287*

*$A = P(1 + i)^N$.   †$\dfrac{A}{(1 + i)^N}$ if table not used.

Critical Thinking Discussion Questions

1. Explain how periods and rates are calculated in compounding problems. Compare simple interest to compound interest.

2. What are the steps to calculate the compound amount by table? Why is the compound table factor greater than $1?

3. What is the effective rate (APY)? Why can the effective rate be seen directly from the table factor?

4. Explain the difference between compounding and present value. Why is the present value table factor less than $1?

DRILL PROBLEMS

Complete the following without using Table 12.1 (round to the nearest cent for each calculation) and then check by Table 12.1 (check will be several cents off due to rounding).

	Principal	Time (years)	Rate of compound interest	Compounded	Periods	Rate	Total amount	Total interest
12–1.	$800	2	8%	Semiannually	4	4%	$935.89	$135.89

2 years × 2 = 4 periods $\dfrac{8\%}{2} = 4\%$

$800.00	$832.00	$865.28	$899.89	$935.89	**Check** $800 × 1.1699 = $935.92
× 1.04	× 1.04	× 1.04	× 1.04	− 800.00	
$832.00	$865.28	$899.89	$935.89	$135.89	

Complete the following using compound future value Table 12.1:

	Time	Principal	Rate	Compounded	Amount	Interest
12–2.	6 years	$9,000	6%	Semiannually	$12,832.20	$3,832.20

   6 years × 2 = 12 periods $\dfrac{6\%}{2} = 3\%$ $9,000 × 1.4258 = $12,832.20
     − 9,000.00
     $ 3,832.20

12–3.	6 months	$10,000	8%	Quarterly	$10,404.00	$404.00

   $\dfrac{6}{12} × 4 = 2$ periods $\dfrac{8\%}{4} = 2\%$ $10,000 × 1.0404 = $10,404
     −10,000
     $ 404

12–4.	3 years	$2,000	12%	Semiannually	$2,837.00	$837.00

   3 years × 2 = 6 periods $\dfrac{12\%}{2} = 6\%$ $2,000 × 1.4185 = $2,837
     − 2,000
     $ 837

Calculate the effective rate (APY) of interest for 1 year.

12–5. Principal: $15,500
Interest rate: 12%
Compounded quarterly
Effective rate (APY): 12.55%

4 periods, $\dfrac{12\%}{4} = 3\%$

$15,500 × 1.1255 = $17,445.25
     − 15,500.00
     $ 1,945.25

$\dfrac{\$1,945.25}{\$15,500} = .1255 = 12.55\%$

12–6. Using Table 12.2, calculate what $700 would grow to at $6\frac{1}{2}\%$ per year compounded daily for 7 years.
$700 × 1.5761 = $1,103.27

Complete the following using present value Table 12.3:

	Amount desired at end of period	Length of time	Rate	Compounded	On PV Table 12.3 Period used	On PV Table 12.3 Rate used	PV factor used	PV of amount desired at end of period
12–7.	$ 1,200	5 years	6%	Semiannually	10	3%	.7441	$ 892.92

   $1,200 × .7441 = $892.92

12–8.	$ 7,650	2 years	12%	Monthly	24	1%	.7876	$6,025.14

   $7,650 × .7876 = $6,025.14

12–9.	$17,600	7 years	12%	Quarterly	28	3%	.4371	$7,692.96

   $17,600 × .4371 = $7,692.96

12–10.	$20,000	20 years	8%	Annually	20	8%	.2145	$4,290.00

   $20,000 × .2145 = $4,290

12–11. Check your answer in Problem 12–9 by the compound value Table 12.1. The answer will be off due to rounding.
2.2879 × $7,692.96 = $17,600.72
(28 periods, 3%)

WORD PROBLEMS

12–12. "How to Retire with Money" was the topic discussed in the financial section of the Gainesville, Florida, *Sun*, dated August 26, 1995. **(a)** How much would a $10,000 4-year Certificate of Deposit at 6% compounded monthly be worth at the end of 4 years? **(b)** How much more is this than the same at simple interest? Use tables in the *Business Math Handbook.*

a. 4 years × 12 = 48 periods $\dfrac{6\%}{12} = \dfrac{1}{2}\%$ **b.** $10,000 × .06 × 4 = $ 2,400 interest

$\begin{array}{r} \$10,000 \\ \times 1.2705 \\ \hline \$12,705 \end{array}$

$\begin{array}{r} +10,000 \\ \hline \$12,400 \end{array}$

$12,705 − $12,400 = $305 more by compounding

12–13. Alice Horn, owner of Horn's Ceramics Shop, loaned $12,000 to Pete Hall to help him open a deli. Pete plans to repay Alice at the end of 5 years with 8% interest compounded semiannually. How much will Alice receive at the end of 5 years?

5 years × 2 = 10 periods $\dfrac{8\%}{2} = 4\%$ $12,000 × 1.4802 = $17,762.40

12–14. Molly Slate deposited $35,000 at Quazi Bank at 6% interest compounded quarterly. What is the effective rate (APY) to the nearest hundredth percent?

1 year × 4 = 4 periods $\dfrac{6\%}{4} = 1.5\%$ $35,000 × 1.0614 = $37,149 − $35,000 = $\dfrac{\$2,149}{\$35,000} = 6.14\%$

12–15. Melvin Indecision has difficulty deciding whether to put his savings in Mystic Bank or Four Rivers Bank. Mystic offers 10% interest compounded semiannually. Four Rivers offers 8% interest compounded quarterly. Melvin has $10,000 to invest. He expects to withdraw the money at the end of 4 years. Which bank gives Melvin the better deal? Check your answer.

Mystic ✓

4 years × 2 = 8 periods

$\dfrac{10\%}{2} = 5\%$

$\begin{array}{r} \$10,000 \times 1.4775 = \$14,775 \\ -10,000 \\ \hline \$ 4,775 \end{array}$

Four Rivers

4 years × 4 = 16 periods

$\dfrac{8\%}{4} = 2\%$

$\begin{array}{r} \$10,000 \times 1.3728 = \$13,728 \\ -10,000 \\ \hline \$ 3,728 \end{array}$

12–16. Brian Costa deposited $20,000 in a new savings account at 12% interest compounded semiannually. At the beginning of year 4, Brian deposits an additional $30,000 at 12% interest compounded semiannually. At the end of 6 years, what is the balance in Brian's account?

3 years × 2 = 6 periods $20,000 × 1.4185 = $28,370 $58,370 × 1.4185 = $82,797.85

$\dfrac{12\%}{2} = 6\%$

$\begin{array}{r} +30,000 \\ \hline \$58,370 \end{array}$

12–17. Carol Mores loaned Jeff Sales $12,000 to open up a coffee shop. After 5 years, Jeff will repay Carol with 12% interest compounded quarterly. How much will Carol receive at the end of 5 years?

5 years × 4 = 20 periods $\dfrac{12\%}{4} = 3\%$ $12,000 × 1.8061 = $21,673.20

12–18. The title of an article that appeared in the December/January 1998 issue of *Your Money* was "Many Families Don't Think about the Future Cost of College." Today, Harvard may cost $120,000 for 4 years, but 20 years from now it may cost $385,000. How much should you put away today to send your child to Harvard in the year 2018 if Bank A is compounding interest annually at 6% and Bank B is compounding interest semiannually at 5%? Use tables in the *Business Math Handbook.*

Bank A

20 years × 1 = 20 periods $\dfrac{6\%}{1} = 6\%$

$\begin{array}{r} \$385,000 \\ \times .3118 \\ \hline \$120,043 \end{array}$

Bank B

20 years × 2 = 40 periods $\dfrac{5\%}{2} = 2\tfrac{1}{2}\%$

$\begin{array}{r} \$385,000 \\ \times .3724 \\ \hline \$143,374 \end{array}$

12–19. Kyle Wong loans $12,000 to his brother-in-law. He will be repaid at the end of 9 years with interest at 8% compounded semiannually. Find out how much will be repaid.

9 years × 2 = 18 periods   2.0258 × $12,000 = $24,309.60

8% ÷ 2 = 4%

12–20. The November 1997 issue of *Money* stated that Robert Feeney, a retired engineering professor at California State Polytechnic, has a nest egg of $92,000. He decides to put this money in his local bank, which compounds interest quarterly at an interest rate of 4%. **(a)** How much will Robert have in 10 years? **(b)** How much interest will he have earned? Use tables in the *Business Math Handbook*.

a. 10 years × 4 = 40 periods $\frac{4\%}{4} = 1\%$ $ 92,000.00

$$\times\ 1.4889$$

$$\overline{\$136,978.80}$$

$$-\ 92,000.00$$

b. $ 44,978.80

12–21. St. Paul Federal Bank is quoting 1-year Certificates of Deposits with an interest rate of 5% compounded semiannually. Joe Saver purchased a $5,000 CD. What is the CD's effective rate (APY) to the nearest hundredth percent? Use tables in the *Business Math Handbook*.

1 year × 2 = 2 periods $\frac{5\%}{2} = 2\frac{1}{2}\%$ Effective rate (APY) = $\frac{\$253}{\$5,000 \times 1} = 5.06\%$

$5,000

× 1.0506

$5,253

− 5,000

$ 253 interest

12–22. Jim Jones, an owner of a Burger King restaurant, assumes that his restaurant will need a new roof in 7 years. He estimates the roof will cost him $9,000 at that time. What amount should Jim invest today at 6% compounded quarterly to be able to pay for the roof? Check your answer.

.6591 × $9,000 = $5,931.90   7 years × 4 = 28 periods   6% ÷ 4 = 1.5%

Check $5,931.90 × 1.5172 = $8,999.88 (due to rounding)

12–23. Tony Ring wants to attend Northeast College. He will need $60,000 4 years from today. Assume Tony's bank pays 12% interest compounded semiannually. What must Tony deposit today so he will have $60,000 in 4 years?

4 years × 2 = 8 periods $\frac{12\%}{2} = 6\%$ $60,000 × .6274 = $37,644

12–24. Could you check your answer (to the nearest dollar) in Problem 12–23 by using the compound value Table 12.1? The answer will be slightly off due to rounding.

$37,644 × 1.5938 = $59,997

12–25. Pete Air wants to buy a new Jeep in 5 years. He estimates the Jeep will cost $15,000. Assume Pete invests $10,000 now at 12% interest compounded semiannually. Will Pete have enough money to buy his Jeep at the end of 5 years?

Compounding   **or**   **Present value**

5 years × 2 = 10 periods $\frac{12\%}{2} = 6\%$ 10 periods $15,000 × .5584 = $8,376

$10,000 × 1.7908 = $17,908   Yes.   6%   Yes.

12–26. Lance Jackson deposited $5,000 at Basil Bank at 9% interest compounded daily. What is Lance's investment at the end of 4 years?

$5,000 × 1.4333 = $7,166.50

12–27. Paul Havlik promised his grandson Jamie that he would give him $6,000 8 years from today for graduating from high school. Assume money is worth 6% interest compounded semiannually. What is the present value of this $6,000?

8 years × 2 = 16 periods $\frac{6\%}{2} = 3\%$ $6,000 × .6232 = $3,739.20

12–28. Earl Ezekiel wants to retire in San Diego when he is 65 years old. Earl is now 50. He believes he will need $300,000 to retire comfortably. To date, Earl has set aside no retirement money. Assume Earl gets 6% interest compounded semiannually. How much must Earl invest today to meet his $300,000 goal?

$$15 \text{ years} \times 2 = 30 \text{ periods} \qquad \frac{6\%}{2} = 3\% \qquad \$300,000 \times .4120 = \$123,600$$

12–29. Lorna Evenson would like to buy a $19,000 car in 4 years. Lorna wants to put the money aside now. Lorna's bank offers 8% interest compounded semiannually. How much must Lorna invest today?

$$4 \text{ years} \times 2 = 8 \text{ periods} \qquad \frac{8\%}{2} = 4\% \qquad \$19,000 \times .7307 = \$13,883.30$$

12–30. John Smith saw the following advertisement. Could you show him how $88.77 was calculated?

$$\$2,000 \times .06 \times \frac{270}{365} = \$88.77$$

*As of January 31, 200X, and subject to change. Interest on the 9-month CD is credited on the maturity date and is not compounded. For example, a $2,000, 9-month CD on deposit for an interest rate of 6.00% (6.05% APY) will earn $88.77 at maturity. Withdrawals prior to maturity require the consent of the bank and are subject to a substantial penalty. There is $500 minimum deposit for IRA, SEP IRA, and Keogh CDs (except for 9-month CD for which the minimum deposit is $1,000). There is $1,000 minimum deposit for all personal CDs (except for 9-month CD for which the minimum deposit is $2,000). Offer not valid on jumbo CDs.

 CHALLENGE PROBLEMS

12–31. You are the financial planner for Johnson Controls. Last year's profits were $700,000. The board of directors decided to forgo dividends to stockholders and retire high-interest outstanding bonds that were issued 5 years ago at a face value of $1,250,000. You have been asked to invest the profits in a bank. The board must know how much money you will need from the profits earned to retire the bonds in 10 years. Bank A pays 6% compounded quarterly, and Bank B pays $6\frac{1}{2}\%$ compounded annually. Which bank would you recommend, and how much of the company's profit should be placed in the bank? If you recommended that the remaining money not be distributed to stockholders but be placed in Bank B, how much would the remaining money be worth in 10 years? Use tables in the *Business Math Handbook*.* (Round final answer to nearest dollar.)

Bank A

$$10 \text{ years} \times 4 = 40 \text{ periods} \qquad \frac{6\%}{4} = 1\frac{1}{2}\% \qquad \$1,250,000 \times .5513 = \$689,125$$

Bank B

$$10 \text{ years} \times 1 = 10 \text{ periods} \qquad \frac{6\frac{1}{2}\%}{1} = 6\frac{1}{2}\% \qquad \$1,250,000 \times .5327 = \$665,875 \qquad \text{Bank B is recommended.}$$

$700,000 − $665,875 = $34,125 (remaining funds)

Bank B

10 periods, $6\frac{1}{2}\%$ = $34,125 × 1.8771 = $64,056

*Check glossary for unfamiliar terms.

12–32. Lori Jacob put $3,000 in a money market account that pays an annual rate of 8% compounded quarterly. After 2 years she withdrew $552.70 to buy a new stove. A year later she put $1,000 in the account. What will be her ending balance if she keeps the money in the account for 4 more years?

$$2 \times 4 = 8 \text{ periods}, \frac{8\%}{4} = 2\%: 1.1717 \times \$3,000 = \$3,515.10 \text{ (2 years)}$$

$$- \ 552.70 \text{ (withdrew for stove)}$$

$$4 \text{ periods}, 2\%: 1.0824 \times \$2,962.40 = \$3,206.50$$

$$+ \ 1,000.00$$

$$4 \times 4 = 16 \text{ periods}. \ 2\%: 1.3728 \times \$4,206.50 = \$5,774.68$$

SUMMARY PRACTICE TEST

1. Larry Olse, owner of The Barn Shop, loaned $16,000 to Rick Froy to help him open an art shop. Rick plans to repay Larry at the end of 7 years with 10% interest compounded semiannually. How much will Larry receive at the end of 7 years? *(p. 288)*

   7 years × 2 = 14 periods $\qquad \dfrac{10\%}{2} = 5\%$ $\qquad$ $16,000 × 1.9799 = $31,678.40

2. Dan Miller wants to attend the University of Massachusetts. Four years from today he will need $40,000. If Dan's bank pays 6% interest compounded semiannually, what must Dan deposit today to have $40,000 in 4 years? *(p. 293)*

   4 years × 2 = 8 periods $\qquad \dfrac{6\%}{2} = 3\%$ $\qquad$ $40,000 × .7894 = $31,576

3. Art Newner deposited $30,000 in a savings account at 8% interest compounded semiannually. At the beginning of year 4, Art deposits an additional $70,000 at 8% interest compounded semiannually. At the end of 6 years, what is the balance in Art's account? *(p. 288)*

   3 years × 2 = 6 periods $\qquad \dfrac{8\%}{2} = 4\%$ $\qquad$ $30,000 × 1.2653 = \$\ 37,959$
   $$\underline{+\ 70,000}$$
   $$107,959 × 1.2653 = $136,600.52$$

4. Len Glass wants to buy a new camper in 7 years. He estimates the camper will cost $8,000. If Len invests $5,200 now at 8% interest compounded semiannually, will Len have enough money to buy his camper at the end of 8 years? *(p. 288, 293)*

   Compounding $\qquad\qquad\qquad\qquad\qquad$ **Present value**

   7 years × 2 = 14 periods $\qquad \dfrac{8\%}{2} = 4\%$ $\qquad$ 14 periods, 4% $\qquad$ $8,000 × .5775 = $4,620

   $5,200 × 1.7317 = $9,004.84 $\qquad$ Yes. $\qquad$ Yes.

5. Asha Hall deposited $14,000 in Lee Bank at 8% interest compounded semiannually. What was the effective rate (APY)? Round to the nearest hundredth percent. *(p. 290)*

   1 year × 2 = 2 periods, $\dfrac{8\%}{2} = 4\%$ $\qquad$ $14,000 × 1.0816 = \begin{array}{r} \$15,142.40 \\ -\ 14,000.00 \\ \hline \$\ 1,142.40 \end{array}$ $\qquad \dfrac{\$1,142.40}{\$14,000} = 8.16\%$

6. Gene Sack, owner of Sack's Garage, estimates that he will need $30,000 for new equipment in 12 years. Gene decided to put aside the money today so it will be available in 12 years. Lone Bank offers Gene 8% interest compounded semiannually. How much must Gene invest to have $30,000 in 12 years? *(p. 293)*

   12 years × 2 = 24 periods $\qquad \dfrac{8\%}{2} = 4\%$ $\qquad$ $30,000 × .3901 = $11,703

7. Doug Millstone wants to retire to Denver when he is 65 years of age. Doug is now 50. He believes that he will need $300,000 to retire comfortably. To date, Doug has set aside no retirement money. If Doug gets 6% compounded semiannually, how much must Doug invest today to meet his $300,000 goal? *(p. 293)*

   15 years × 2 = 30 periods $\qquad \dfrac{6\%}{2} = 3\%$ $\qquad$ $300,000 × .4120 = $123,600

8. Rachel Swan deposited $9,000 in a savings account at 8% interest compounded daily. At the end of 30 years, what is the balance in Rachel's account? *(p. 292)*

   $9,000 × 11.0202 = $99,181.80

A GROUP PROJECT   Defend or reject the following business math issue based on the *Kiplinger's Personal Finance Magazine* article below:

FAMILY FINANCES

A Winning Way to Save for College

▸ **New state savings plans have an edge over prepaid plans and education IRAs.** By Stephanie Gallagher

The new education IRA has gotten all the press. But state by state, a better savings opportunity is quietly emerging for parents or grandparents saving for a youngster's future college expenses. As recently as two years ago, fewer than a dozen states offered programs to help families save for college, and most of those were prepaid-tuition plans with numerous restrictions and no more than a return of principal if the child decided not to attend college. Now 20 states have some type of state-sponsored tuition savings plan, 20 others have committed to starting one in the next year or two, and nine more are studying the idea (see the table on page 53). Georgia has a statewide scholarship program instead of a savings plan, and the District of Columbia has taken no steps toward a program.

A majority of the newer programs are *savings* plans—an improvement over the prepaid-tuition plans that many parents have found too inflexible. Among other advantages, savings plans have a gentler impact on financial-aid eligibility than prepaid plans, and many are exempt from state tax. (At least two states even let you take a state-tax deduction for your contributions.) Most also have the potential for higher returns, but at the expense of a guarantee that your payments today will cover tuition tomorrow.

WHAT'S THE DIFFERENCE? Prepaid-tuition plans let you buy up to four years' worth of tuition at current prices, either in installments or as a lump sum. The appeal is the guarantee that when your child is ready for freshman year, your account will cover tuition, no matter how much it has risen. Your return in such plans is roughly equivalent to the rate of tuition inflation at public colleges and universities in your state—which made the plans extremely attractive when tuitions were rising at 10% and more a year. Today, with the average rate of tuition inflation closer to 5%, prepaid plans are no match for investing in the stock market when you have many years before you'll need the money.

Many of the newer savings plans are basically state-run investment accounts that invest for stock- or bond-market returns. You decide how much to contribute, and the state pays you a return based on the investments it chooses for the entire pool of participants. Under federal law, you cannot choose your own investments, as you can in an education IRA or Roth IRA.

The Kentucky Educational Savings Plan Trust takes the safe road, investing primarily in Treasury securities. Since 1991 it has paid returns that range from 5.6% to 9.2%. Other plans invest in mutual funds. The Indiana Family College Savings Plan, for example, currently directs contributions into the Pegasus Managed Assets Balanced fund, a portfolio of stocks and bonds that has returned an annualized 16.9% over the past three years.

TAX BENEFITS. What gives these accounts extra *zing* is that—as with prepaid plans—your earnings are free from state tax and enjoy federal-tax-deferred growth until the money is used for college expenses. Then the student pays tax on the earnings in his or her tax bracket—usually 15%. In Mississippi and New York, parents can even take a state-tax deduction for contributions. And in Massachusetts, distributions are exempt from state *and* federal tax because your money is invested in municipal bonds.

CONTRIBUTION LIMITS. Another shortcoming of many prepaid plans is that your savings are limited to the cost of tuition at in-state public colleges—often a fraction of the expense at a private institution.

Savings plans, however, can become a home for most or all of your college savings—up to $9,405 a year in Indiana and up to $100,000 total in New York's forthcoming program (though only $5,000 a year will be state-tax-deductible). That's also a far cry from the $500 a year you can trickle into a tax-free education IRA.

Business Math Issue

State savings plans will definitely replace all prepaid plans for saving for college.

1. List the key points of the article and information to support your position.

2. Write a group defense of your position using math calculations to support your view.

BUSINESS MATH SCRAPBOOK
Putting Your Skills to Work

	When you deposit	30-month C.D. interest rate	30-month interest at maturity	If 12% interest at maturity	Interest difference
A.	$100,000	**12.28% 11.75%** _{Annual percentage yield Interest rate}	$33,578	$34,390.00	$812.00
B.	$80,001	**12.28% 11.75%** _{Annual percentage yield Interest rate}	$26,863	$27,512.34	$649.34
C.	$60,001	**12.28% 11.75%** _{Annual percentage yield Interest rate}	$20,147	$20,634.34	$487.34
D.	$40,001	**12.28% 11.75%** _{Annual percentage yield Interest rate}	$13,431	$13,756.34	$325.34
E.	$20,001	**12.28% 11.75%** _{Annual percentage yield Interest rate}	$6,716	$6,878.34	$162.34
F.	$15,001	**12.28% 11.75%** _{Annual percentage yield Interest rate}	$5,037	$5,158.84	$121.84
G.	$10,001	**12.28% 11.75%** _{Annual percentage yield Interest rate}	$3,358	$3,439.34	$81.34

This yield assumes that principal and interest remain on deposit for a full year interest compounded quarterly

Project A

Bill Smith saw this bank advertisement. He feels the interest rate may rise to 12% next month. If you use the compound interest Table 12.1 in the text, what would the interest be at maturity for each amount? By waiting until next month, how much interest could Bill gain over depositing now? Assume that Bill wants to work out the interest rate for each deposit shown. What would be the annual effective yield (APY) with an interest rate of 12%?

$$2.5 \text{ years} \times 4 = 10 \text{ periods} \qquad \frac{12\%}{4} = 3\%$$

A. $100,000 × 1.3439 = $134,390 $34,390
                             − 100,000   − 33,578
                             $ 34,390 $ 812

B. $80,001 × 1.3439 = $107,513.34 $27,512.34
                          − 80,001.00   − 26,863.00
                          $ 27,512.34 $ 649.34

C. $60,001 × 1.3439 = $80,635.34 $20,634.34
                          − 60,001.00   − 20,147.00
                          $20,634.34 $ 487.34

D. $40,001 × 1.3439 = $53,757.34 $13,756.34
                          − 40,001.00   − 13,431.00
                          $13,756.34 $ 325.34

E. $20,001 × 1.3439 = $26,879.34 $6,878.34
                          − 20,001.00   − 6,716.00
                          $ 6,878.34 $ 162.34

F. $15,001 × 1.3439 = $20,159.84 $5,158.84
                          − 15,001.00   − 5,037.00
                          $ 5,158.84 $ 121.84

G. $10,001 × 1.3439 = $13,440.34 $3,439.34
                          − 10,001.00   − 3,358.00
                          $ 3,439.34 $ 81.34

Effective rate (APY), 12.55% (3%, 4 periods)

Note: Have students visit a bank to see the current rate of CDs.

@ See text Web site (www.mhhe.com/slater) and *The Business Math Internet Resource Guide*.

13

ANNUITIES AND SINKING FUNDS

LEARNING UNIT OBJECTIVES

LU 13.1   Annuities: Ordinary Annuity and Annuity Due (Find Future Value)

- Differentiate between contingent annuities and annuities certain *(p. 307)*.
- Calculate the future value of an ordinary annuity and an annuity due manually and by table lookup *(pp. 307–11)*.

LU 13.2   Present Value of an Ordinary Annuity (Find Present Value)

- Calculate the present value of an ordinary annuity by table lookup and manually check the calculation *(pp. 311–13)*.
- Compare the calculation of the present value of one lump sum versus the present value of an ordinary annuity *(p. 313)*.

LU 13.3   Sinking Funds (Find Periodic Payments)

- Calculate the payment made at the end of each period by table lookup *(pp. 314–15)*.
- Check table lookup by using ordinary annuity table *(p. 315)*.

Make a Child a Millionaire

BY JONATHAN CLEMENTS
Staff Reporter of THE WALL STREET JOURNAL

Thanks a million.

Even if you haven't got a lot of money, you can easily give $1 million or more to your children, grandchildren or favorite charity. All it takes is a small initial investment and a lot of time.

Suppose your 16-year-old daughter plans to take a summer job, which will pay her at least $2,000. Because she has earned income, she can open an individual retirement account. If you would like to help fund her retirement, Kenneth Klegon, a financial planner in Lansing, Mich., suggests giving her $2,000 to set up the IRA. He then advises doing the same in each of the next five years, so that your daughter stashes away a total of $12,000.

Result? If the money is invested in stocks, and stocks deliver their historical average annual return of 10%, your daughter will have more than $1 million by the time she turns 65.

This *Wall Street Journal* clipping "Make a Child a Millionaire" tells you how to make a 16-year-old a millionaire at age 65. This is accomplished through the magic of compounding.

This chapter shows how to compute compound interest that results from a *stream* of payments, or an annuity. Chapter 12 showed how to calculate compound interest on a lump-sum payment deposited at the beginning of a particular time. Knowing how to calculate interest compounding on a lump sum will make the calculation of interest compounding on annuities easier to understand.

We begin the chapter by explaining the difference between calculating the future value of an ordinary annuity and an annuity due. Then you learn how to find the present value of an ordinary annuity. The chapter ends with a discussion of sinking funds.

LEARNING UNIT 13.1   Annuities: Ordinary Annuity and Annuity Due (Find Future Value)

Many parents of small children are concerned about being able to afford to pay for their children's college educations. Some parents deposit a lump sum in a financial institution when the child is in diapers. The interest on this sum is compounded until the child is 18, when the parents withdraw the money for college expenses. Parents could also fund their children's educations with annuities by depositing a series of payments for a certain time. The concept of annuities is the first topic in this learning unit.

Concept of an Annuity—The Big Picture

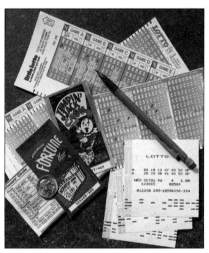

Sharon Hoogstraten.

All of us would probably like to win $1 million in a state lottery. What happens when you have the winning ticket? You take it to the lottery headquarters. When you turn in the ticket, do you immediately receive a check for $1 million? No. Lottery payoffs are not usually made in lump sums.

Lottery winners receive a series of payments over a period of time—usually years. This *stream* of payments is an **annuity.** By paying the winners an annuity, lotteries do not actually spend $1 million. The lottery deposits a sum of money in a financial institution. The continual growth of this sum through compound interest provides the lottery winner with a series of payments.

When we calculated the maturity value of a lump-sum payment in Chapter 12, the maturity value was the principal and its interest. Now we are looking not at lump-sum payments but at a series of payments (usually of equal amounts over regular **payment periods**) plus the interest that accumulates. So the **future value of an annuity** is the future *dollar amount* of a series of payments plus interest.[1] The **term of the annuity** is the time from the beginning of the first payment period to the end of the last payment period.

The concept of the future value of an annuity is illustrated in Figure 13.1. Do not be concerned about the calculations (we will do them soon). Let's first focus on the big picture of annuities. In Figure 13.1 we see the following:

At end of period 1: The $1 is still worth $1 because it was invested at the *end* of the period.

At end of period 2: An additional $1 is invested. The $2.00 is now worth $2.08. Note the $1 from period 1 earns interest but not the $1 invested at the end of period 2.

At end of period 3: An additional $1 is invested. The $3.00 is now worth $3.25. Remember that the last dollar invested earns no interest.

---

[1]The term *amount of an annuity* has the same meaning as *future value of an annuity.*

FIGURE 13.1

Future value of an annuity of $1 at 8%

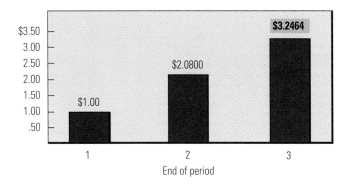

Before learning how to calculate annuities, you should understand the two classifications of annuities.

How Annuities Are Classified

Annuities have many uses in addition to lottery payoffs. Some of these uses are insurance companies' pension installments, Social Security payments, home mortgages, businesses paying off notes, bond interest, and savings for a vacation trip or college education.

Annuities are classified into two major groups: contingent annuities and annuities certain. **Contingent annuities** have no fixed number of payments but depend on an uncertain event (e.g., life insurance payments that cease when the insured dies). **Annuities certain** have a specific stated number of payments (e.g., mortgage payments on a home). Based on the time of the payment, we can divide each of these two major annuity groups into the following:

1. **Ordinary annuity**—regular deposits (payments) made at the *end* of the period. Periods could be months, quarters, years, and so on. An ordinary annuity could be salaries, stock dividends, and so on.
2. **Annuity due**—regular deposits (payments) made at the *beginning* of the period, such as rent or life insurance premiums.

The remainder of this unit shows you how to calculate and check ordinary annuities and annuities due. Remember that you are calculating the *dollar amount* of the annuity at the end of the annuity term or at the end of the last period.

Ordinary Annuities: Money Invested at End of Period (Find Future Value)

Before we explain how to use a table that simplifies calculating ordinary annuities, let's first determine how to calculate the future value of an ordinary annuity manually.

Calculating Future Value of Ordinary Annuities Manually

Remember that an ordinary annuity invests money at the *end* of each year (period). After we calculate ordinary annuities manually, you will see that the total value of the investment comes from the *stream* of yearly investments and the buildup of interest on the current balance.

Calculating Future Value of an Ordinary Annuity Manually

Step 1. For period 1, no interest calculation is necessary, since money is invested at the end of the period.

Step 2. For period 2, calculate interest on the balance and add the interest to the previous balance.

Step 3. Add the additional investment at the end of period 2 to the new balance.

Step 4. Repeat Steps 2 and 3 until the end of the desired period is reached.

EXAMPLE Find the value of an investment after 3 years for a $3,000 ordinary annuity at 8%.

We calculate this manually as follows:

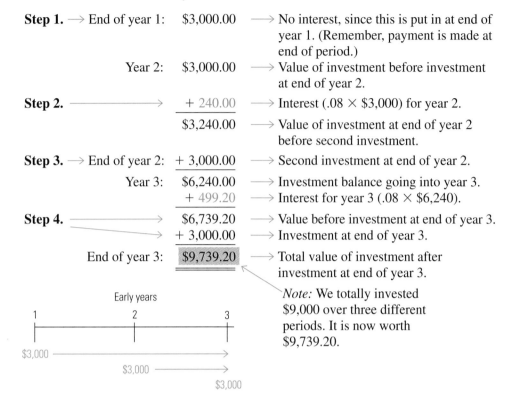

Step 1. → End of year 1: $3,000.00   ⟶ No interest, since this is put in at end of year 1. (Remember, payment is made at end of period.)

            Year 2: $3,000.00   ⟶ Value of investment before investment at end of year 2.

Step 2. ⟶   + 240.00   ⟶ Interest (.08 × $3,000) for year 2.

                     $3,240.00   ⟶ Value of investment at end of year 2 before second investment.

Step 3. → End of year 2: + 3,000.00   ⟶ Second investment at end of year 2.

            Year 3: $6,240.00   ⟶ Investment balance going into year 3.
                      + 499.20   ⟶ Interest for year 3 (.08 × $6,240).

Step 4. ⟶ $6,739.20   ⟶ Value before investment at end of year 3.
            ⟶   + 3,000.00   ⟶ Investment at end of year 3.

            End of year 3: $9,739.20   ⟶ Total value of investment after investment at end of year 3.

Note: We totally invested $9,000 over three different periods. It is now worth $9,739.20.

Early years

| 1 | 2 | 3 |

$3,000 ⟶
    $3,000 ⟶
        $3,000

When you deposit $3,000 at the end of each year at an annual rate of 8%, the total value of the annuity is $9,739.20. What we called *maturity value* in compounding is now called the *future value of the annuity*. Remember that Interest = Principal × Rate × Time, with the principal changing because of the interest payments and the additional deposits. We can make this calculation easier by using Table 13.1 (p. 309).

Calculating Future Value of Ordinary Annuities by Table Lookup

Use the following steps to calculate the future value of an ordinary annuity by table lookup.[2]

> ### Calculating Future Value of an Ordinary Annuity by Table Lookup
>
> **Step 1.** Calculate the number of periods and rate per period.
> **Step 2.** Look up the periods and rate in an ordinary annuity table. The intersection gives the table factor for the future value of $1.
> **Step 3.** Multiply the payment each period by the table factor. This gives the future value of the annuity.

EXAMPLE   Find the value of an investment after 3 years for a $3,000 ordinary annuity at 8%.

Step 1.   Periods = 3 years × 1 = 3   Rate = $\dfrac{8\%}{\text{Annually}}$ = 8%

Step 2.   Go to Table 13.1, an ordinary annuity table. Look for 3 under the Period column. Go across to 8%. At the intersection is the table factor, 3.2464. (This was the example we showed in Figure 13.1.)

---

[2]The formula for an ordinary annuity is $A = Pmt \times \dfrac{[(1 + i)^n - 1]}{i}$, where A equals future value of an ordinary annuity, Pmt equals annuity payment, i equals interest, and n equals number of periods. The calculator sequence for this example is: 1 + .08 = y^x 3 − 1 ÷ .08 × 3,000 = 9,739.20.

TABLE 13.1   Ordinary annuity table: Compound sum of an annuity of $1

Period	2%	3%	4%	5%	6%	7%	8%	9%	10%	11%	12%	13%
1	1.0000	1.0000	1.0000	1.0000	1.0000	1.0000	1.0000	1.0000	1.0000	1.0000	1.0000	1.0000
2	2.0200	2.0300	2.0400	2.0500	2.0600	2.0700	2.0800	2.0900	2.1000	2.1100	2.1200	2.1300
3	3.0604	3.0909	3.1216	3.1525	3.1836	3.2149	3.2464	3.2781	3.3100	3.3421	3.3744	3.4069
4	4.1216	4.1836	4.2465	4.3101	4.3746	4.4399	4.5061	4.5731	4.6410	4.7097	4.7793	4.8498
5	5.2040	5.3091	5.4163	5.5256	5.6371	5.7507	5.8666	5.9847	6.1051	6.2278	6.3528	6.4803
6	6.3081	6.4684	6.6330	6.8019	6.9753	7.1533	7.3359	7.5233	7.7156	7.9129	8.1152	8.3227
7	7.4343	7.6625	7.8983	8.1420	8.3938	8.6540	8.9228	9.2004	9.4872	9.7833	10.0890	10.4047
8	8.5829	8.8923	9.2142	9.5491	9.8975	10.2598	10.6366	11.0285	11.4359	11.8594	12.2997	12.7573
9	9.7546	10.1591	10.5828	11.0265	11.4913	11.9780	12.4876	13.0210	13.5795	14.1640	14.7757	15.4157
10	10.9497	11.4639	12.0061	12.5779	13.1808	13.8164	14.4866	15.1929	15.9374	16.7220	17.5487	18.4197
11	12.1687	12.8078	13.4863	14.2068	14.9716	15.7836	16.6455	17.5603	18.5312	19.5614	20.6546	21.8143
12	13.4120	14.1920	15.0258	15.9171	16.8699	17.8884	18.9771	20.1407	21.3843	22.7132	24.1331	25.6502
13	14.6803	15.6178	16.6268	17.7129	18.8821	20.1406	21.4953	22.9534	24.5227	26.2116	28.0291	29.9847
14	15.9739	17.0863	18.2919	19.5986	21.0150	22.5505	24.2149	26.0192	27.9750	30.0949	32.3926	34.8827
15	17.2934	18.5989	20.0236	21.5785	23.2759	25.1290	27.1521	29.3609	31.7725	34.4054	37.2797	40.4174
16	18.6392	20.1569	21.8245	23.6574	25.6725	27.8880	30.3243	33.0034	35.9497	39.1899	42.7533	46.6717
17	20.0120	21.7616	23.6975	25.8403	28.2128	30.8402	33.7503	36.9737	40.5447	44.5008	48.8837	53.7390
18	21.4122	23.4144	25.6454	28.1323	30.9056	33.9990	37.4503	41.3014	45.5992	50.3959	55.7497	61.7251
19	22.8405	25.1169	27.6712	30.5389	33.7599	37.3789	41.4463	46.0185	51.1591	56.9395	63.4397	70.7494
20	24.2973	26.8704	29.7781	33.0659	36.7855	40.9954	45.7620	51.1602	57.2750	64.2028	72.0524	80.9468
25	32.0302	36.4593	41.6459	47.7270	54.8644	63.2489	73.1060	84.7010	98.3471	114.4133	133.3338	155.6194
30	40.5679	47.5754	56.0849	66.4386	79.0580	94.4606	113.2833	136.3077	164.4941	199.0209	241.3327	293.1989
40	60.4017	75.4012	95.0254	120.7993	154.7616	199.6346	259.0569	337.8831	442.5928	581.8260	767.0913	1013.7030
50	84.5790	112.7968	152.6669	209.3470	290.3351	406.5277	573.7711	815.0853	1163.9090	1668.7710	2400.0180	3459.5010

Note: This is only a sampling of tables available. The *Business Math Handbook* shows tables from $\frac{1}{2}$% to 15%.

Step 3.   Multiply $3,000 × 3.2464 = $9,739.20 (the same figure we calculated manually).

Annuities Due: Money Invested at Beginning of Period (Find Future Value)

In this section we look at what the difference in the total investment would be for an annuity due. As in the previous section, we will first make the calculation manually and then use the table lookup.

Calculating Future Value of Annuities Due Manually

Use the steps that follow to calculate the future value of an annuity due manually.

Calculating Future Value of an Annuity Due Manually

Step 1.   Calculate the interest on the balance for the period and add it to the previous balance.

Step 2.   Add additional investment at the *beginning* of the period to the new balance.

Step 3.   Repeat Steps 1 and 2 until the end of the desired period is reached.

Remember that in an annuity due, we deposit the money at the *beginning* of the year and gain more interest. Common sense should tell us that the *annuity due* will give a higher final value. We will use the same example that we used before.

EXAMPLE   Find the value of an investment after 3 years for a $3,000 annuity due at 8%. We calculate this manually as follows:

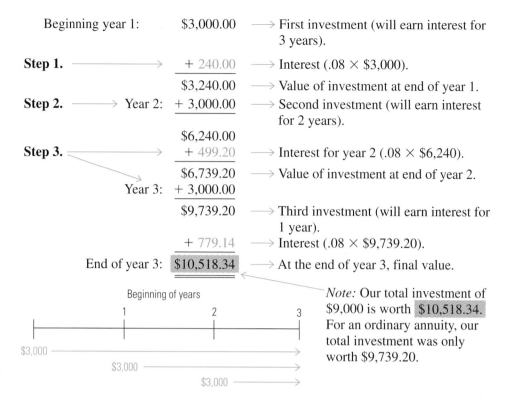

Beginning year 1: $3,000.00 $\longrightarrow$ First investment (will earn interest for 3 years).

Step 1. $\longrightarrow$ + 240.00 $\longrightarrow$ Interest (.08 × $3,000).

$3,240.00 $\longrightarrow$ Value of investment at end of year 1.

Step 2. $\longrightarrow$ Year 2:   + 3,000.00 $\longrightarrow$ Second investment (will earn interest for 2 years).

$6,240.00

Step 3. $\longrightarrow$ + 499.20 $\longrightarrow$ Interest for year 2 (.08 × $6,240).

$6,739.20 $\longrightarrow$ Value of investment at end of year 2.

Year 3:   + 3,000.00

$9,739.20 $\longrightarrow$ Third investment (will earn interest for 1 year).

+ 779.14 $\longrightarrow$ Interest (.08 × $9,739.20).

End of year 3: $10,518.34 $\longrightarrow$ At the end of year 3, final value.

Note: Our total investment of $9,000 is worth $10,518.34. For an ordinary annuity, our total investment was only worth $9,739.20.

Calculating Future Value of Annuities Due by Table Lookup

To calculate the future value of an annuity due with a table lookup, use the steps that follow.

Calculating Future Value of an Annuity Due by Table Lookup[3]

Step 1.   Calculate the number of periods and the rate per period. Add one extra period.

Step 2.   Look up in an ordinary annuity table the periods and rate. The intersection gives the table *factor* for future value of $1.

Step 3.   Multiply payment each period by the table factor.

Step 4.   Subtract 1 payment from Step 3.

Let's check the $10,518.34 by table lookup.

Step 1.   Periods = 3 years × 1 =   3 $\text{Rate} = \dfrac{8\%}{\text{Annually}} = 8\%$

+ 1 extra

4

Step 2.   Table factor, 4.5061

Step 3. $3,000 × 4.5061 = $13,518.30

Step 4.   − 3,000.00 $\longleftarrow$ Be sure to subtract 1 payment.

= $10,518.34   (off 4 cents due to rounding)

Note that the annuity due shows an ending value of $10,518.30, while the ending value of ordinary annuity was $9,739.20. We had a higher ending value with the annuity due because the investment took place at the beginning of each period.

Annuity payments do not have to be made yearly. They could be made semiannually, monthly, quarterly, and so on. Let's look at one more example with a different number of periods and rate.

---

[3]The formula for an annuity due is $A = Pmt \times \dfrac{(1 + i)^n - 1}{i} \times (1 + i)$, where A equals future value of annuity due, Pmt equals annuity payment, i equals interest, and n equals number of periods. This formula is the same as that in footnote 2 except we multiply the future value of annuity by $1 + i$ since payments are made at the beginning of the period. The calculator sequence for this example is: 1 + .08 = × 9,739.20 = 10,518.34.

Different Number of Periods and Rates

By using a different number of periods and rates, we will contrast an ordinary annuity with an annuity due in the following example:

EXAMPLE   Using Table 13.1, find the value of a $3,000 investment after 3 years made quarterly at 8%.

In the annuity due calculation, be sure to add one period and subtract one payment from the total value.

	Ordinary annuity	**Annuity due**	
Step 1.	Periods = 3 years × 4 = 12 Rate = 8% ÷ 4 = 2%	Periods = 3 years × 4 = 12 Rate = 8% ÷ 4 = 2%	**Step 1**
Step 2.	Table 13.1: 12 periods, 2% = 13.4120	Table 13.1: 13 periods, 2% = 14.6803	**Step 2**
Step 3.	$3,000 × 13.4120 = $40,236	$3,000 × 14.6803 = $44,040.90	**Step 3**
		− 3,000.00	**Step 4**
		$41,040.90	

Again, note that with annuity due, the total value is greater since you invest the money at the beginning of each period.

Now check your progress with the Practice Quiz.

LU 13.1 PRACTICE QUIZ

1. Using Table 13.1, **(a)** find the value of an investment after 4 years on an ordinary annuity of $4,000 made semiannually at 10%, and **(b)** recalculate, assuming an annuity due.

2. Wally Beaver won a lottery and will receive a check for $4,000 at the beginning of each 6 months for the next 5 years. If Wally deposits each check into an account that pays 6%, how much will he have at the end of the 5 years?

✓   **Solutions**

1. **a. Step 1.**	Periods = 4 years × 2 = 8	**b.** Periods = 4 years × 2 = 8 + 1 = 9	**Step 1**
	10% ÷ 2 = 5%	10% ÷ 2 = 5%	
Step 2.	Factor = 9.5491	Factor = 11.0265	**Step 2**
Step 3.	$4,000 × 9.5491	$4,000 × 11.0265 = $44,106	**Step 3**
	= $38,196.40	− 1 payment − 4,000	**Step 4**
		$40,106	

2. **Step 1.**   5 years × 2 = 10 $\dfrac{6\%}{2} = 3\%$
                + 1
                11 periods

    Step 2.   Table factor, 12.8078

    Step 3. $4,000 × 12.8078 = $51,231.20
    Step 4.   − 4,000.00
                  $47,231.20

LEARNING UNIT 13.2   Present Value of an Ordinary Annuity (Find Present Value)

This unit begins by presenting the concept of present value of an ordinary annuity. Then you will learn how to use a table to calculate the present value of an ordinary annuity.

Concept of Present Value of an Ordinary Annuity—The Big Picture

Let's assume that we want to know how much money we need to invest *today* to receive a stream of payments for a given number of years in the future. This is called the **present value of an ordinary annuity.**

In Figure 13.2 (p. 312) you can see that if you wanted to withdraw $1 at the end of one period, you would have to invest 93 cents *today*. If at the end of each period for three periods, you wanted to withdraw $1, you would have to put $2.58 in the bank *today* at 8% interest. (Note that we go from the future back to the present.)

Now let's look at how we could use tables to calculate the present value of annuities and then check our answer.

FIGURE 13.2

Present value of an annuity
of $1 at 8%

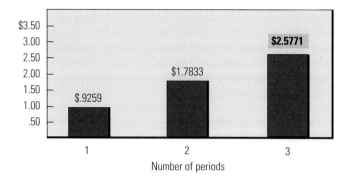

Number of periods

Calculating Present Value of an Ordinary Annuity by Table Lookup

Use the following steps to calculate by table lookup the present value of an ordinary annuity.[4]

Calculating Present Value of an Ordinary Annuity by Table Lookup

Step 1. Calculate the number of periods and rate per period.

Step 2. Look up the periods and rate in the present value of an annuity table. The intersection gives the table factor for the present value of $1.

Step 3. Multiply the withdrawal for each period by the table factor. This gives the present value of an ordinary annuity.

EXAMPLE John Fitch wants to receive an $8,000 annuity in 3 years. Interest on the annuity is 8% annually. John will make withdrawals at the end of each year. How much must John invest today to receive a stream of payments for 3 years? Use Table 13.2. Remember that interest could be earned semiannually, quarterly, and so on, as shown in the previous unit.

Step 1. 3 years $\times$ 1 = 3 periods $\quad \dfrac{8\%}{\text{Annually}} = 8\%$

Step 2. Table factor, 2.5771 (we saw this in Figure 13.2)

Step 3. $8,000 $\times$ 2.5771 = $20,616.80

If John wants to withdraw $8,000 at the end of each period for 3 years, he will have to deposit $20,616.80 in the bank *today*.

$20,616.80
+ 1,649.34 $\longrightarrow$ Interest at end of year 1 (.08 $\times$ $20,616.80)

$22,266.14
− 8,000.00 $\longrightarrow$ First payment to John

$14,266.14
+ 1,141.29 $\longrightarrow$ Interest at end of year 2 (.08 $\times$ $14,266.14)

$15,407.43
− 8,000.00 $\longrightarrow$ Second payment to John

$ 7,407.43
+ 592.59 $\longrightarrow$ Interest at end of year 3 (.08 $\times$ $7,407.43)

$ 8,000.02
− 8,000.00 $\longrightarrow$ After end of year 3 John receives his last $8,000

.02[5]

---

[4]The formula for the present value of an ordinary annuity is $P = Pmt \times \dfrac{1 - 1 \div (1 + i)^n}{i}$, where P equals present value of annuity, Pmt equals annuity payment, i equals interest, and n equals number of periods. The calculator sequence would be as follows for the John Fitch example: 1 [+] .08 [=] [Yˣ] 3 [+−] [=] [M+] 1 [−] [MR] [÷] .08 [×] 8,000 [=] 21,000.

[5]Off due to rounding.

TABLE 13.2   Present value of an annuity of $1

Period	2%	3%	4%	5%	6%	7%	8%	9%	10%	11%	12%	13%
1	0.9804	0.9709	0.9615	0.9524	0.9434	0.9346	0.9259	0.9174	0.9091	0.9009	0.8929	0.8850
2	1.9416	1.9135	1.8861	1.8594	1.8334	1.8080	1.7833	1.7591	1.7355	1.7125	1.6901	1.6681
3	2.8839	2.8286	2.7751	2.7232	2.6730	2.6243	2.5771	2.5313	2.4869	2.4437	2.4018	2.3612
4	3.8077	3.7171	3.6299	3.5459	3.4651	3.3872	3.3121	3.2397	3.1699	3.1024	3.0373	2.9745
5	4.7134	4.5797	4.4518	4.3295	4.2124	4.1002	3.9927	3.8897	3.7908	3.6959	3.6048	3.5172
6	5.6014	5.4172	5.2421	5.0757	4.9173	4.7665	4.6229	4.4859	4.3553	4.2305	4.1114	3.9975
7	6.4720	6.2303	6.0021	5.7864	5.5824	5.3893	5.2064	5.0330	4.8684	4.7122	4.5638	4.4226
8	7.3255	7.0197	6.7327	6.4632	6.2098	5.9713	5.7466	5.5348	5.3349	5.1461	4.9676	4.7988
9	8.1622	7.7861	7.4353	7.1078	6.8017	6.5152	6.2469	5.9952	5.7590	5.5370	5.3282	5.1317
10	8.9826	8.5302	8.1109	7.7217	7.3601	7.0236	6.7101	6.4177	6.1446	5.8892	5.6502	5.4262
11	9.7868	9.2526	8.7605	8.3064	7.8869	7.4987	7.1390	6.8052	6.4951	6.2065	5.9377	5.6869
12	10.5753	9.9540	9.3851	8.8632	8.3838	7.9427	7.5361	7.1607	6.8137	6.4924	6.1944	5.9176
13	11.3483	10.6350	9.9856	9.3936	8.8527	8.3576	7.9038	7.4869	7.1034	6.7499	6.4235	6.1218
14	12.1062	11.2961	10.5631	9.8986	9.2950	8.7455	8.2442	7.7862	7.3667	6.9819	6.6282	6.3025
15	12.8492	11.9379	11.1184	10.3796	9.7122	9.1079	8.5595	8.0607	7.6061	7.1909	6.8109	6.4624
16	13.5777	12.5611	11.6523	10.8378	10.1059	9.4466	8.8514	8.3126	7.8237	7.3792	6.9740	6.6039
17	14.2918	13.1661	12.1657	11.2741	10.4773	9.7632	9.1216	8.5436	8.0216	7.5488	7.1196	6.7291
18	14.9920	13.7535	12.6593	11.6896	10.8276	10.0591	9.3719	8.7556	8.2014	7.7016	7.2497	6.8399
19	15.6784	14.3238	13.1339	12.0853	11.1581	10.3356	9.6036	8.9501	8.3649	7.8393	7.3658	6.9380
20	16.3514	14.8775	13.5903	12.4622	11.4699	10.5940	9.8181	9.1285	8.5136	7.9633	7.4694	7.0248
25	19.5234	17.4131	15.6221	14.0939	12.7834	11.6536	10.6748	9.8226	9.0770	8.4217	7.8431	7.3300
30	22.3964	19.6004	17.2920	15.3724	13.7648	12.4090	11.2578	10.2737	9.4269	8.6938	8.0552	7.4957
40	27.3554	23.1148	19.7928	17.1591	15.0463	13.3317	11.9246	10.7574	9.7790	8.9511	8.2438	7.6344
50	31.4236	25.7298	21.4822	18.2559	15.7619	13.8007	12.2335	10.9617	9.9148	9.0417	8.3045	7.6752

Before we leave this unit, let's work out two examples that show the relationship of Chapter 13 to Chapter 12. Use the tables in your *Business Math Handbook*.

Lump Sums versus Annuities

EXAMPLE   John Sands made deposits of $200 semiannually to Floor Bank, which pays 8% interest compounded semiannually. After 5 years, John makes no more deposits. What will be the balance in the account 6 years after the last deposit?

Step 1.   Calculate amount of annuity: Table 13.1

   10 periods, 4% $200 × 12.0061 = $2,401.22

Step 2.   Calculate how much the final value of the annuity will grow by the compound interest table.   Table 12.1

   12 periods, 4% $2,401.22 × 1.6010 = **$3,844.35**

For John, the stream of payments grows to $2,401.22. Then this *lump sum* grows for 6 years to $3,844.35. Now let's look at a present value example.

EXAMPLE   Mel Rich decided to retire in 8 years to New Mexico. What amount should Mel invest today so he will be able to withdraw $40,000 at the end of each year for 25 years *after* he retires? Assume Mel can invest money at 5% interest (compounded annually).

Step 1.   Calculate the present value of the annuity: Table 13.2

   25 periods, 5% $40,000 × 14.0939 = $563,756

Step 2.   Find the present value of $563,756 since Mel will not retire for 8 years:

                                   Table 12.3

   8 periods, 5% (PV table) $563,756 × .6768 = **$381,550.06**

If Mel deposits $381,550 in year 1, it will grow to $563,756 after 8 years.
   It's time to try the Practice Quiz and check your understanding of this unit.

LU 13.2 PRACTICE QUIZ

(Use tables in Business Math Handbook)

1. What must you invest today to receive an $18,000 annuity for 5 years semiannually at a 10% annual rate? All withdrawals will be made at the end of each period.

2. Rase High School wants to set up a scholarship fund to provide five $2,000 scholarships for the next 10 years. If money can be invested at an annual rate of 9%, how much should the scholarship committee invest today?

3. Joe Wood decided to retire in 5 years in Arizona. What amount should Joe invest today so he can withdraw $60,000 at the end of each year for 30 years after he retires? Assume Joe can invest money at 6% compounded annually.

✓   **Solutions**

1. **Step 1.**   Periods = 5 years × 2 = 10; Rate = 10% ÷ 2 = 5%
    Step 2.   Factor, 7.7217
    Step 3. $18,000 × 7.7217 = $138,990.60

2. **Step 1.**   Periods = 10; Rate = 9%
    Step 2.   Factor, 6.4177
    Step 3. $10,000 × 6.4177 = $64,177

3. **Step 1.**   Calculate present value of annuity: 30 periods, 6%.
                  $60,000 × 13.7648 = $825,888
    Step 2.   Find present value of $825,888 for 5 years: 5 periods, 6%.
                  $825,888 × .7473 = $617,186.10

LEARNING UNIT 13.3   Sinking Funds (Find Periodic Payments)

©PhotoDisc.

A **sinking fund** is a financial arrangement that sets aside regular periodic payments of a particular amount of money. Compound interest accumulates on these payments to a specific sum at a predetermined future date. Corporations use sinking funds to discharge bonded indebtedness, to replace worn-out equipment, to purchase plant expansion, and so on.

A sinking fund is different from an annuity. In a sinking fund, you determine the amount of periodic payments you need to achieve a given financial goal. In the annuity, you know the amount of each payment and must determine its future value. Let's work with the following:

$$\text{Sinking fund payment} = \text{Future value} \times \text{Sinking fund table factor}^6$$

EXAMPLE   To retire a bond issue, Moore Company needs $60,000 in 18 years from today. The interest rate is 10% compounded annually. What payment must Moore make at the end of each year? Use Table 13.3.

We begin by looking down the Period column in Table 13.3 until we come to 18. Then we go across until we reach the 10% column. The table factor is .0219.

Now we multiply $60,000 by the factor as follows:

$60,000 × .0219 = $1,314

---

[6]Sinking fund table is the reciprocal of the ordinary annuity table.

TABLE 13.3

Sinking fund table based on $1

Period	2%	3%	4%	5%	6%	8%	10%
1	1.0000	1.0000	1.0000	1.0000	1.0000	1.0000	1.0000
2	0.4951	0.4926	0.4902	0.4878	0.4854	0.4808	0.4762
3	0.3268	0.3235	0.3203	0.3172	0.3141	0.3080	0.3021
4	0.2426	0.2390	0.2355	0.2320	0.2286	0.2219	0.2155
5	0.1922	0.1884	0.1846	0.1810	0.1774	0.1705	0.1638
6	0.1585	0.1546	0.1508	0.1470	0.1434	0.1363	0.1296
7	0.1345	0.1305	0.1266	0.1228	0.1191	0.1121	0.1054
8	0.1165	0.1125	0.1085	0.1047	0.1010	0.0940	0.0874
9	0.1025	0.0984	0.0945	0.0907	0.0870	0.0801	0.0736
10	0.0913	0.0872	0.0833	0.0795	0.0759	0.0690	0.0627
11	0.0822	0.0781	0.0741	0.0704	0.0668	0.0601	0.0540
12	0.0746	0.0705	0.0666	0.0628	0.0593	0.0527	0.0468
13	0.0681	0.0640	0.0601	0.0565	0.0530	0.0465	0.0408
14	0.0626	0.0585	0.0547	0.0510	0.0476	0.0413	0.0357
15	0.0578	0.0538	0.0499	0.0463	0.0430	0.0368	0.0315
16	0.0537	0.0496	0.0458	0.0423	0.0390	0.0330	0.0278
17	0.0500	0.0460	0.0422	0.0387	0.0354	0.0296	0.0247
18	0.0467	0.0427	0.0390	0.0355	0.0324	0.0267	0.0219
19	0.0438	0.0398	0.0361	0.0327	0.0296	0.0241	0.0195
20	0.0412	0.0372	0.0336	0.0302	0.0272	0.0219	0.0175
24	0.0329	0.0290	0.0256	0.0225	0.0197	0.0150	0.0113
28	0.0270	0.0233	0.0200	0.0171	0.0146	0.0105	0.0075
32	0.0226	0.0190	0.0159	0.0133	0.0110	0.0075	0.0050
36	0.0192	0.0158	0.0129	0.0104	0.0084	0.0053	0.0033
40	0.0166	0.0133	0.0105	0.0083	0.0065	0.0039	0.0023

This states that if Moore Company pays $1,314 at the end of each period for 18 years, then $60,000 will be available to pay off the bond issue at maturity.

We can check this by using Table 13.1 (the ordinary annuity table):

$1,314 × 45.5992 = $59,917.35[7]

It's time to try the following Practice Quiz.

LU 13.3 PRACTICE QUIZ

Today, Arrow Company issued bonds that will mature to a value of $90,000 in 10 years. Arrow's controller is planning to set up a sinking fund. Interest rates are 12% compounded semiannually. What will Arrow Company have to set aside to meet its obligation in 10 years? Check your answer. Your answer will be off due to the rounding of Table 13.3.

✓ **Solution**

10 years × 2 = 20 periods $\qquad \dfrac{12\%}{2} = 6\% \qquad $90,000 × .0272 = $2,448

Check $2,448 × 36.7855 = $90,050.90

---

[7]Off due to rounding.

Chapter Organizer and Reference Guide

Topic	Key point, procedure, formula	Example(s) to illustrate situation
Ordinary annuities (find future value), p. 306	Invest money at end of each period. Find future value at maturity. Answers question of how much money accumulates.	Use Table 13.1: 2 years, $4,000 ordinary annuity at 8% annually. Value = $4,000 × 2.0800 = $8,320 (2 periods, 8%)

Annuities due (find future value), p. 309	Invest money at beginning of each period. Find future value at maturity. Should be higher than ordinary annuity since it is invested at beginning of each period. Use Table 13.1, but add one period and subtract one payment from answer.	*Example:* Same example as above but invest money at beginning of period.
		$4,000 × 3.2464 = $12,985.60
		          − 4,000.00
		          $8,985.60 (3 periods, 8%)

Present value of an ordinary annuity (find present value), p. 311	Calculate number of periods and rate per period. Use Table 13.2 to find table factor for present value of $1. Multiply withdrawal for each period by table factor to get present value of an ordinary annuity.	*Example:* Receive $10,000 for 5 years. Interest is 10% compounded annually.
		Table 13.2: 5 periods, 10%
		                3.7908
		           × $10,000
		What you put in today = $37,908

Sinking funds (find periodic payment), p. 314	Paying a particular amount of money for a set number of periodic payments to accumulate a specific sum. We know the future and must calculate the periodic payments needed. Answer can be proved by ordinary annuity table.	*Example:* $200,000 bond to retire 15 years from now. Interest is 6% compounded annually. By Table 13.3: $200,000 × .0430 = $8,600 Check by Table 13.1: $8,600 × 23.2759 = $200,172.74
Key terms	Annuities certain, *p. 307* Annuity, *p. 306* Annuity due, *p. 307* Contingent annuities, *p. 307*	Future value of an annuity, *p. 306* Ordinary annuity, *p. 307* Payment periods, *p. 306* Present value of an annuity, *p. 311* Sinking fund, *p. 314* Term of the annuity, *p. 306*

Critical Thinking Discussion Questions

1. What is the difference between an ordinary annuity and an annuity due? If you were to save money in an annuity, which would you choose and why?
2. Explain how you would calculate ordinary annuities and annuities due by table lookup. Create an example to explain the meaning of a table factor from an ordinary annuity.
3. What is a present value of an ordinary annuity? Create an example showing how one of your relatives might plan for retirement by using the present value of an ordinary annuity. Would you ever have to use lump-sum payments in your calculation from Chapter 12?
4. What is a sinking fund? Why could an ordinary annuity table be used to check the sinking fund payment?

DRILL PROBLEMS

Complete the ordinary annuities for the following using tables in the *Business Math Handbook:*

Amount of payment	Payment payable	Years	Interest rate	Value of annuity
13–1. $2,200	Quarterly 16	4 17.9323	6% $1\frac{1}{2}$%	$39,451.06 ($2,200 × 17.9323)
13–2. $3,000	Semiannually 20	10 33.0659	10% 5%	$99,197.70 ($3,000 × 33.0659)

Redo Problem 13–1 as an annuity due:

13–3. $2,200, 17 periods, $1\frac{1}{2}$% = 19.2013 × $2,200 = $42,242.86
$$\begin{array}{r} -\ 2,200.00 \\ \hline \$40,042.86 \end{array}$$

Calculate the value of the following annuity due without a table. Check your results by Table 13.1 or *Business Math Handbook* (they will be slightly off due to rounding):

Amount of payment	Payment payable	Years	Interest rate
13–4. $2,000	Annually	3	6%

$$\begin{array}{r} \$2,000.00 \\ +\quad 120.00 \\ \hline \$2,120.00 \\ +\ 2,000.00 \\ \hline \$4,120.00 \\ +\quad 247.20 \\ \hline \$4,367.20 \end{array} \qquad \begin{array}{r} \$4,367.20 \\ +\ 2,000.00 \\ \hline \$6,367.20 \\ +\quad 382.03 \\ \hline \$6,749.23 \end{array}$$

Check   4 periods, 6%
$2,000 × 4.3746 = $8,749.20
$$\begin{array}{r} -\ 2,000.00 \\ \hline \$6,749.20 \end{array}$$

Complete the following, using Table 13.2 or the *Business Math Handbook* for the present value of an ordinary annuity:

Amount of annuity expected	Payment	Time	Interest rate	Present value (amount needed now to invest to receive annuity)
13–5. $600	Annually	3 years	8%	$1,546.26 ($600 × 2.5771) (3 periods, 8%)
13–6. $12,000	Quarterly	4 years	12%	$150,733.20 ($12,000 × 12.5611) (16 periods, 3%)

13–7. Check Problem 13–5 without the use of Table 13.2.

$$\begin{array}{r} \$1,546.26 \\ (\$1,546.26 \times .08)\quad +\ 123.70 \\ \hline \$1,669.96 \\ -\ 600.00 \\ \hline \$1,069.96 \end{array} \qquad \begin{array}{r} \$1,069.96 \\ +\quad 85.60 \\ \hline \$1,155.56 \\ -\ 600.00 \\ \hline \$\ 555.56 \end{array} \qquad \begin{array}{r} \$555.56 \\ +\quad 44.44 \\ \hline \$600.00 \\ -\ 600.00 \\ \hline \$\quad .00 \end{array}$$

Using the sinking fund Table 13.3 or the *Business Math Handbook* complete the following:

Required amount	Frequency of payment	Length of time	Interest rate	Payment amount end of each period
13–8. $25,000	Quarterly	6 years	8%	$822.50 (24 periods, 2% = .0329) $25,000 × .0329 = $822.50
13–9. $15,000	Annually	8 years	8%	$1,410 (8 periods, 8% = .0940) $15,000 × .0940 = $1,410

13–10. Check the answer in Problem 13–9 by Table 13.1.
$1,410 × 10.6366 = $14,997.61 (due to rounding of table factors)

WORD PROBLEMS (Use tables in the *Business Math Handbook*)

13–11. Leroy Santos made deposits of $800 at the end of each year for 6 years. Interest is 9% compounded annually. What is the value of Santos' annuity at the end of 6 years?
6 periods, 9% (Table 13.1)
$800 × 7.5233 = $6,018.64

13–12. Pete King promised to pay his son $300 semiannually for 9 years. Assume Pete can invest his money at 8% in an ordinary annuity. How much must Pete invest today to pay his son $300 semiannually for 9 years?
18 periods, 4% (Table 13.2)
$300 × 12.6593 = $3,797.79

13–13. On December 15, 1996, an article appeared in the *Sacramento Bee* entitled "Women Need to Save Harder for Retirement." The article discusses a 35-year-old woman who contributes $3,000 annually to a 401(k) plan with an employer match of $1,500 a year at 8% interest. How much would the woman accumulate during an uninterrupted 30-year career?
30 periods, 8% (Table 13.1)

$$\begin{array}{r} 113.2833 \\ \times\ \$4,500.00\ (\$3,000.00 + \$1,500.00) \\ \hline \$509,774.85 \end{array}$$

13–14. The following question is based on the article "Amount of College Money Available," which appeared in *Intouch*, a New York Life Insurance publication dated 1997. If you invest $200 at the beginning of each month in your 14-year-old child's education at 6% interest, how much will you have when the child is ready for college at 18 years of age?
$4 × 12 = 48$ periods $+ 1 = 49$ periods $\dfrac{6\%}{12} = \tfrac{1}{2}\%$

$$\begin{array}{r} 55.3684\ \text{(amount of annuity)} \\ \times\ \$200 \\ \hline \$11,073.68 \\ -\ 200.00 \\ \hline \$10,873.68 \end{array}$$

13–15. On February 28, 1997, the *Sun-Sentinel* reported the amount that a 31-year-old who puts $2,000 a year in an individual retirement account will have earned in 35 years if the money is compounded at 9% annually. How much will the 31-year-old woman have earned? What is the cash value of this annuity due?
$35 + 1 = 36, 9\%$

$$\begin{array}{r} \$2,000 × 236.1251 = \$472,250.20 \\ -\ 2,000.00 \\ \hline \$470,250.20\ \text{(amount of annuity)} \end{array}$$

13–16. Patricia and Joe Payne are divorced. The divorce settlement stipulated that Joe pay $525 a month for their daughter Suzanne until she turns 18 in 4 years. How much must Joe set aside today to meet the settlement? Interest is 6% a year.
$4 × 12 = 48$ periods $\dfrac{6\%}{12} = \tfrac{1}{2}\% = 42.5804$
(present value of annuity)

$$\begin{array}{r} 42.5804 \\ \times\ \$525.00 \\ \hline \$22,354.71 \end{array}$$

13–17. Josef Company borrowed money that must be repaid in 20 years. The company wants to make sure the loan will be repaid at the end of year 20. So it invests $12,500 at the end of each year at 12% interest compounded annually. What was the amount of the original loan?
20 periods, 12% (Table 13.1)
$12,500 × 72.0524 = $900,655

13–18. Jane Frost wants to receive yearly payments of $15,000 for 10 years. How much must she deposit at her bank today at 11% interest compounded annually?
10 periods, 11% (Table 13.2)
$15,000 × 5.8892 = $88,338

13–19. Toby Martin invests $2,000 at the end of each year for 10 years in an ordinary annuity at 11% interest compounded annually. What is the final value of Toby's investment at the end of year 10?
10 periods, 11%, 16.7220 (Table 13.1)
$2,000 × 16.7220 = $33,444

13–20. Alice Longtree has decided to invest $400 quarterly for 4 years in an ordinary annuity at 8%. As her financial adviser, calculate for Alice the total cash value of the annuity at the end of year 4.
16 periods, 2% (Table 13.1)
$400 × 18.6392 = $7,455.68

13–21. At the beginning of each period for 8 years, Segel Flynn invests $300 semiannually at 8%. What is the cash value of this annuity due at the end of year 8?

16 + 1, 4% (Table 13.1) $300 × 23.6975 = $7,109.25
                                        − 300.00
                                        ――――――
                                        $6,809.25

13–22. Jeff Associates borrowed $30,000. The company plans to set up a sinking fund that will repay the loan at the end of 8 years. Assume a 12% interest rate compounded semiannually. What must Jeff pay into the fund each period of time? Check your answer by Table 13.1.

Check

16 periods, 6% = .0390 (Table 13.3) $1,170 × 25.6725 = $30,036.83 (due to table rounding)
$30,000 × .0390 = $1,170   (by Table 13.1)

13–23. On Joe's graduation from college, Joe Martin's uncle promised him a gift of $12,000 in cash or $900 every quarter for the next 4 years after graduation. If money could be invested at 8% compounded quarterly, which offer is better for Joe?

16 periods, $\frac{8\%}{4}$ = 2% $900 × 13.5777 = $12,219.93   **or** $900 × 18.6392 = $16,775.28
                                     (Table 13.2)   (Table 13.1)   × .7284 (Table 12.3)

Choose the annuity. $12,219.11

13–24. The article "Will You Be Able to Retire When You Want to?" appeared in *Intouch*, a New York Life Insurance publication dated 1997. Imagine that you have saved $500,000 by the time you retire at age 65 and want to receive $4,000 a month ($48,000 a year) for living expenses for the next 14 years. If your money earns 4% compounded annually, would your $500,000 provide you with what you need? What should you have in your retirement account?

14 periods, 4%   10.5631 (Table 13.2)
                   × $48,000.00
                   ――――――――――
                   $507,028.80 (need)

13–25. GU Corporation must buy a new piece of equipment in 5 years that will cost $88,000. The company is setting up a sinking fund to finance the purchase. What will the quarterly deposit be if the fund earns 8% interest?

20 periods, 2% (Table 13.3)
.0412 × $88,000 = $3,625.60 quarterly payment

13–26. Mike Macaro is selling a piece of land. Two offers are on the table. Morton Company offered a $40,000 down payment and $35,000 a year for the next 5 years. Flynn Company offered $25,000 down and $38,000 a year for the next 5 years. If money can be invested at 8% compounded annually, which offer is better for Mike?

Morton: 5 periods, 8% (Table 13.2)   3.9927 × $35,000 = $139,744.50 + $40,000 = $179,744.50
Flynn: 5 periods, 8% (Table 13.2)   3.9927 × $38,000 = $151,722.60 + $25,000 = $176,722.60
Morton offer is the better deal.

Note: Problems 13–27 to 13–29 integrate Chapters 12 and 13 together.

13–27. Al Vincent has decided to retire to Arizona in 10 years. What amount should Al invest today so that he will be able to withdraw $28,000 at the end of each year for 15 years *after* he retires? Assume he can invest the money at 8% interest compounded annually.

PV annuity table: 15 periods, 8% (Table 13.2)   8.5595 × $28,000 = $239,666
PV table: 10 years, 8% (Table 12.3)   .4632 × $239,666 = $111,013.29

13–28. Victor French made deposits of $5,000 at the end of each quarter to Book Bank, which pays 8% interest compounded quarterly. After 3 years, Victor made no more deposits. What will be the balance in the account 2 years after the last deposit?

Amount of annuity table: 3 years × 4 = 12 periods $\frac{8\%}{4}$ = 2% (Table 13.1)
13.4120 × $5,000 = $67,060
Compound table: 2 years × 4 = 8 periods, 2% (Table 12.1)
1.1717 × $67,060 = $78,574.20

13–29. Janet Woo decided to retire to Florida in 6 years. What amount should Janet invest today so she can withdraw $50,000 at the end of each year for 20 years after she retires? Assume Janet can invest money at 6% compounded annually.

PV annuity table: 20 periods, 6% (Table 13.2)   11.4699 × $50,000 = $573,495
PV table: 6 years, 6% (Table 12.3)   .7050 × $573,495 = $404,313.97

CHALLENGE PROBLEMS

13–30. The November 17, 1997, issue of *Newsweek* discussed a situation in which a worker with $100,000 in a 401(k) plan earned 8% a year (the plan's assets are split between stocks earning 10% and bonds earning 6%). **(a)** Delaying retirement for 3 years would raise the fund to what new level if no extra money were added? **(b)** If $2,000 were added at the end of each year, what would be the total amount reached? Do not use tables.*

a.	**b.**	
$100,000.00	$100,000	$118,800
× 1.08	× 1.08	+ 2,000
$108,000.00	$108,000	$120,800
× 1.08	+ 2,000	× 1.08
$116,640.00	$110,000	$130,464
× 1.08	× 1.08	+ 2,000
$125,971.20	$118,800	$132,464

*See Chapter 21 for a discussion of stocks and bonds.

13–31. Ajax Corporation has hired Brad O'Brien as its new president. Terms included the company's agreeing to pay retirement benefits of $18,000 at the end of each semiannual period for 10 years. This will begin in 3,285 days. If the money can be invested at 8% compounded semiannually, what must the company deposit today to fulfill its obligation to Brad?

10 years × 2 = 20 periods $\qquad \dfrac{8\%}{2} = 4\%$

$18,000 × 13.5903 = $244,625.40 (Table 13.2)

$\dfrac{3{,}285\ \text{days}}{365\ \text{days per year}} = 9$ years $\qquad$ 9 years × 2 = 18 periods $\qquad \dfrac{8\%}{2} = 4\%$

$244,625.40 × .4936 = $120,747.09

Check $120,747.09 × 2.0258 = $244,609.45 (off due to rounding)

 SUMMARY PRACTICE TEST (Use tables in the *Business Math Handbook*)

1. Marcy Hall plans to deposit $1,200 at the end of every 6 months for the next 10 years at 10% interest compounded semiannually. What is the value of Marcy's annuity at the end of 10 years? *(p. 308)*
   20 periods, 5% $\qquad$ $1,200 × 33.0659 = $39,679.08
   (Table 13.1)

2. On Stan's graduation from law school, Stan Smith's uncle, Bob March, promised him a gift of $25,000 or $2,500 every quarter for the next 3 years after graduating from law school. If the money could be invested at 8% compounded quarterly, which offer should Stan choose? *(p. 312)*

   12 periods, $\dfrac{8\%}{4} = 2\%$ $\qquad$ $2,500 × 10.5753 = $26,438.25 **or** $2,500 × 13.4120 = $33,530
   (Table 13.2) $\qquad\qquad\qquad$ Choose the annuity. $\qquad\qquad$ (Table 13.1) $\qquad$ × .7885 (Table 12.3)
   $\qquad\qquad\qquad\qquad\qquad\qquad\qquad\qquad\qquad\qquad\qquad\qquad\qquad\qquad\qquad\qquad\qquad$ $26,438.41

3. Joyce Levitt wants to receive $5,000 each year for 18 years. How much must Joyce invest today at 8% interest compounded annually? *(p. 312)*
   18 periods, 8% (Table 13.2) $\qquad$ $5,000 × 9.3719 = $46,859.50

4. In 6 years, Lowell Company will have to repay a $60,000 loan. Assume an 8% interest rate compounded quarterly. How much must Lowell pay each period to have $60,000 at the end of 6 years? *(p. 314)*
   6 × 4 = 24 periods
   8% ÷ 4 = 2% $\qquad$ $60,000 × .0329 = $1,974

5. Langly Associates borrowed $40,000. The company plans to set up a sinking fund that will repay the loan at the end of 15 years. Assume a 10% interest rate compounded semiannually. What amount must Langly Associates pay into the fund each period? Check your answer by Table 13.1. *(pp. 314, 308)*
   30 periods, 5% $\qquad$ $40,000 × .0151 = $604
   Check $604 × 66.4386 = $40,128.91 (off due to rounding)

6. Lee Wong wants to receive $7,000 each year for the next 20 years. Assume a 9% interest rate compounded annually. How much must Lee invest today? *(p. 312)*
   20 periods, 9% (Table 13.2) $\qquad$ $7,000 × 9.1285 = $63,899.50

7. Twice a year for 8 years, Meg Ryan invested $1,200 compounded semiannually at 8% interest. What is the value of this annuity due? *(p. 310)*

17 periods, 4% (Table 13.1) $1,200 × 23.6975 = $28,437
                                                                    − 1,200
                                                                    ─────────
                                                                    $27,237

8. Maggie Path invested $900 semiannually for 10 years at 10% interest compounded semiannually. What is the value of this annuity due? *(p. 310)*

21 periods, 5% $900 × 35.7192 = $32,147.28
                                                                    − 900.00
                                                                    ─────────
                                                                    $31,247.28

9. Miguel Lopez decided to retire to San Antonio in 6 years. What amount should Miguel deposit so that he will be able to withdraw $70,000 at the end of each year for 20 years after he retires? Assume Miguel can invest money at 9% interest compounded annually. *(p. 312)*

Present value annuity Table 13.2; 20 periods, 9%   Present value Table 12.3 (Chapter 12); 6 periods, 9%
$70,000 × 9.1285 = $638,995 $638,995 × .5963 = $381,032.71

10. Bill Blue made deposits of $7,000 at the end of each quarter to Lee Bank, which pays 8% interest compounded quarterly. After 7 years, Bill made no more deposits. What will be the account's balance 3 years after the last deposit? *(p. 308)*

Amount of annuity table: 7 years × 4 = 28 periods, $\dfrac{8\%}{4} = 2\%$
37.0511 × $7,000 = $259,357.70
Compound table: 3 years × 4 = 12 periods, 2% (Table 12.1)
1.2682 × $259,357.70 = $328,917.44

A GROUP PROJECT   Defend or reject the following business math issue based on the *Kiplinger's Personal Finance Magazine* article below:

Making the Most of Your Roth IRA

▶ **It's not so much *whether* to use this new tax shelter, but *which way* to use it.**   By Marc L. Schulhof

Meet Keith and Lori Masterson. He's a pilot, she's a nurse. They have a 3-year-old daughter, Haley. And they are among the first on their block to have Roth IRAs. In January they converted $26,000 in traditional individual retirement accounts to the latest tax shelter offered by Congress.

The couple will pay nearly $4,000 in extra taxes—in four equal, annual chunks starting in 1999—for the privilege of transforming their old, tax-*deferred* IRAs to the brand-new tax-*free* IRAs. That doesn't bother them a bit. In fact, Keith, 32, is almost gloating over it.

"I really think they're suckers," he says of the lawmakers who created the Roth. "I realize they allow conversions so they can get more tax money now—and they'll get it now. I'll be glad to give it to them. Tax-free earnings is an incredible deal."

It's a bargain, Keith figures, because in addition to racking up tax-free earnings from now on, he expects to be in a higher tax bracket when he and Lori retire. So paying tax on the amount in the old IRAs sooner rather than later will save them money. And if they don't need all the money in their IRAs, the remainder can go to Haley income-tax-free.

The Mastersons should be proud of themselves. Their decisiveness is rare. Though IRA business is booming at many mutual funds and brokerages, it seems that many investors are imbibing information rather than opening accounts. Confusion is at least as common as enthusiasm. But

The Mastersons: Mom and Dad's Roth IRAs could grow into an enormous legacy for Haley.

why are savvy investors having such a difficult time pulling the trigger on this opportunity?

For starters, there are all the rules that govern who is eligible to open an account, when money can be withdrawn and whether it will be taxed. Beyond that, blame the head-scratching on the fact that the Roth IRA has a familiar moniker but acts in many ways like an entirely new animal.

"It takes some work to figure this out," says Bill Berger, founder of the

Berger funds, "but any savings or investment takes work. This is worth it." If inertia has prevented you from making a decision, try looking at the Roth one angle at a time. Find the approach that suits you best. Then follow through.

ROTH AS RETIREMENT PLAN. This is what it's all about, isn't it? I-R-A. Individual retirement account. The Roth plays this role well.

KRIS HUNDT

Business Math Issue

Converting to a Roth is really a good deal for everyone.

1. List the key points of the article and information to support your position.
2. Write a group defense of your position using math calculations to support your view.

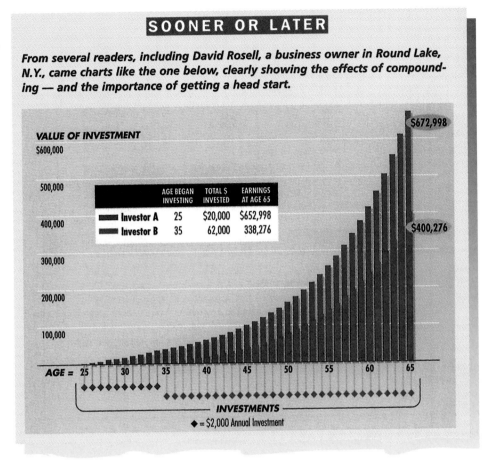

SOONER OR LATER

From several readers, including David Rosell, a business owner in Round Lake, N.Y., came charts like the one below, clearly showing the effects of compounding — and the importance of getting a head start.

VALUE OF INVESTMENT

$672,998

$400,276

	AGE BEGAN INVESTING	TOTAL $ INVESTED	EARNINGS AT AGE 65
Investor A	25	$20,000	$652,998
Investor B	35	62,000	338,276

AGE = 25 ... 30 ... 35 ... 40 ... 45 ... 50 ... 55 ... 60 ... 65

INVESTMENTS

◆ = $2,000 Annual Investment

© Fidelity Focus 1998, p. 36.

Project A

Could you explain why investor A has a greater value of investment than investor B? The chart assumes an average return of 10%. What other factors should be considered? Assume all income is reinvested in the tax-deferred account.

Solution

Investor A puts $2,000 per year for 10 years in a tax-deferred account, then stops contributing, but her money continues to grow through monthly compounding. **Investor B** postpones investing until age 35, then contributes $2,000 per year for the next 31 years. Assuming an average annual return of 10% and the reinvestment of all income, **A** will have $272,722 more in her account than **B** when they both reach age 65. These data do not account for taxes, inflation, or transaction costs. Past performance is no guarantee of future results, and your own accounts may earn more or less than this example.

Source: Ibbotson Associates, 1998.

The opinions expressed are exclusively those of the individuals noted above.

 See text Web site (www.mhhe.com/slater) and *The Business Math Internet Resource Guide.*

CUMULATIVE REVIEW   A Word Problem Approach—Chapters 10, 11, 12, 13

1. Amy O'Mally graduated from high school. Her uncle promised her as a gift a check for $2,000 or $275 every quarter for 2 years. If money could be invested at 6% compounded quarterly, which offer is better for Amy? (Use the tables in the *Business Math Handbook.*) *(p. 312)*

   2 years × 4 = 8 periods $\dfrac{6\%}{4} = 1\tfrac{1}{2}\%$

   $275 × 7.4859 = $2,058.62   **or** $275 × 8.4328 = $2,319.02
   Take the annuity   × .8877
                                        ─────────────
                                        $2,058.59

2. Alan Angel made deposits of $400 semiannually to Sag Bank, which pays 10% interest compounded semiannually. After 4 years, Alan made no more deposits. What will be the balance in the account 3 years after the last deposit? (Use the tables in the *Business Math Handbook.*) *(p. 308)*

   4 years × 2 = 8 periods $\dfrac{10\%}{2} = 5\%$ (Table 13.1)

   9.5491 × $400 = $3,819.64
   3 years × 2 = 6 periods   5%   (Table 12.1)
   1.3401 × $3,819.64 = $5,118.70

3. Roger Disney decides to retire to Florida in 12 years. What amount should Roger invest today so that he will be able to withdraw $30,000 at the end of each year for 20 years *after* he retires? Assume he can invest money at 8% interest compounded annually. (Use tables in the *Business Math Handbook.*) *(p. 313)*

   20 periods, 8%   (Table 13.2)   9.8181 × $30,000 = $294,543
   12 periods, 8%   (Table 12.3)   .3971 × $294,543 = $116,963.02

4. On September 15, Arthur Westering borrowed $3,000 from Vermont Bank at $10\tfrac{1}{2}\%$ interest. Arthur plans to repay the loan on January 25. Assume the loan is based on exact interest. How much will Arthur totally repay? *(p. 251)*

365	$I = P \times R \times T$
Sept. 15 − 258	
─────	$I = \$3{,}000 \times .105 \times \dfrac{132}{365}$
107	
+ 25	= $113.92
─────	$113.92 + $3,000 = $3,113.92
132	

5. Sue Cooper borrowed $6,000 on an $11\tfrac{3}{4}\%$, 120-day note. Sue paid $300 toward the note on day 50. On day 90, Sue paid an additional $200. Using the U.S. Rule, Sue's adjusted balance after her first payment is the following. *(p. 255)*

   $6,000 × .1175 × $\dfrac{50}{360}$ = $97.92

   $300.00
   − 97.92 $6,000 − $202.08 = $5,797.92
   ────────
   $202.08

6. On November 18, Northwest Company discounted an $18,000, 12%, 120-day note dated September 8. Assume a 10% discount rate. What will be the proceeds? Use ordinary interest. *(p. 274)*

   $MV = \$18{,}000 \times .12 \times \dfrac{120}{360}$ = $720 + $18,000 = $18,720

Nov. 18 322	120	
Sept. 8 − 251	− 71	$18,720 × .10 × $\dfrac{49}{360}$ = $254.80
───── 71	─── 49	

   Proceeds = $18,720 − $254.80 = $18,465.20

7. Alice Reed deposits $16,500 into Rye Bank, which pays 10% interest compounded semiannually. Using the appropriate table, what will Alice have in her account at the end of 6 years? *(p. 288)*

   6 years × 2 = 12 periods $\dfrac{10\%}{2} = 5\%$ (Table 12.1)

   12 periods, 5% = 1.7959 $16,500 × 1.7959 = $29,632.35

8. Peter Regan needs $90,000 in 5 years from today to retire in Arizona. Peter's bank pays 10% interest compounded semiannually. What will Peter have to put in the bank today to have $90,000 in 5 years? *(p. 293)*

   5 years × 2 = 10 periods $\dfrac{10\%}{2} = 5\%$ $90,000 × .6139 = $55,251
                                                           (Table 12.3)

CLASSROOM NOTES

14

INSTALLMENT BUYING, RULE OF 78, AND REVOLVING CHARGE CREDIT CARDS

LEARNING UNIT OBJECTIVES

LU 14.1 Cost of Installment Buying

- Calculate the amount financed, finance charge, and deferred payment *(p. 328)*.
- Calculate the estimated APR by table lookup *(p. 329)*.
- Calculate the monthly payment by formula and by table lookup *(p. 329)*.

LU 14.2 Paying Off Installment Loan before Due Date

- Calculate the rebate and payoff for Rule of 78 *(p. 332)*.

LU 14.3 Revolving Charge Credit Cards

- Calculate the finance charges on revolving charge credit card accounts *(pp. 335–37)*.

Purchasing a large-ticket item such as a car or truck usually involves obtaining a loan and paying interest. To reduce the total cost of the loan, you can either increase your down payment or shorten the life of the loan. You should also shop for the loan with the lowest interest charge. This chapter discusses the various types of installment buying and the revolving charge credit card.

LEARNING UNIT 14.1   Cost of Installment Buying

Installment buying can add a substantial amount to the cost of a purchase. To illustrate this, we follow the procedure of buying a pickup truck, including the amount financed, finance charge, and deferred payment. Then we study the effect of the Truth in Lending Act.

Amount Financed, Finance Charge, and Deferred Payment

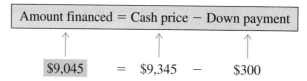

©Donald Johnston/Tony Stone Images.

This advertisement for the sale of a pickup truck appeared in a local paper. As you can see from this advertisement, after customers make a **down payment,** they can buy the truck with an **installment loan.** This loan is paid off with a series of equal periodic payments. These payments include both interest and principal. The payment process is called **amortization.** In the promissory notes of earlier chapters, the loan was paid off in one ending payment. Now let's look at the calculations involved in buying a pickup truck.

4X4 Pickup

9,345

$194³⁸ **MONTH**

With $300 down cash or trade for 60 months at Annual Percentage Rate of 10.5%. Amt. financed—$9,045.00. Finance chg.—$2,617.80. Total note—$11,662.80. Total deferred payment price—$11,962.80. Taxes, title, insurance additional.

Checking Calculations in Pickup Advertisement

Calculating Amount Financed   The **amount financed** is what you actually borrow. To calculate this amount, use the following formula:

Amount financed = Cash price − Down payment

$$\$9,045 \quad = \quad \$9,345 \quad - \quad \$300$$

Calculating Finance Charge   The words **finance charge** in the advertisement represent the **interest** charge. The interest charge resulting in the finance charge includes the cost of credit reports, mandatory bank fees, and so on. You can use the following formula to calculate the total interest on the loan:

Total finance charge (interest charge) = Total of all monthly payments − Amount financed

$$\$2,617.80 \quad = \quad \$11,662.80 \quad - \quad \$9,045$$
$$(\$194.38 \times 60 \text{ months})$$

Calculating Deferred Payment Price   The **deferred payment price** represents the total of all monthly payments plus the down payment. The following formula is used to calculate the deferred payment price:

Deferred payment price = Total of all monthly payments + Down payment

$$\$11,962.80 \quad = \quad \$11,662.80 \quad + \quad \$300$$
$$(\$194.38 \times 60)$$

Truth in Lending: APR Defined and Calculated

In 1969, the Federal Reserve Board established the **Truth in Lending Act** (Regulation Z). The law doesn't regulate interest charges; its purpose is to make the consumer aware of the true cost of credit.

The Truth in Lending Act requires that creditors provide certain basic information about the actual cost of buying on credit. Before buyers sign a credit agreement, creditors must inform them in writing of the amount of the finance charge and the **annual percentage rate (APR).** The APR represents the true or effective annual interest creditors charge. This is helpful to buyers who repay loans over different periods of time (1 month, 48 months, and so on).

To illustrate how the APR affects the interest rate, assume you borrow $100 for 1 year and pay a finance charge of $9. Your interest rate would be 9% if you waited until the end of the year to pay back the loan. Now let's say you pay off the loan and the finance charge in 12 monthly payments. Each month that you make a payment, you are losing some of the value or use of that money. So the true or effective APR is actually greater than 9%.

The APR can be calculated by formula or by tables. We will use the table method since it is more exact.

Calculating APR Rate by Table 14.1

To calculate the APR using Table 14.1, we first divide the finance charge by the amount financed and multiply by $100:

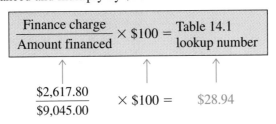

We multiply by $100, since the table is based on $100 of financing.

$$\frac{\$2,617.80}{\$9,045.00} \times \$100 = \$28.94$$

To look up $28.94 in Table 14.1 (p. 330), we go down the left side of the table until we come to 60 payments (the advertisement states 60 months). Then, moving to the right, we look for $28.94 or the two numbers closest to it. The number $28.94 is between $28.22 and $28.96. So we look at the column headings and see a rate between 10.25% and 10.5%. The Truth in Lending Act requires that when creditors state the APR, it must be accurate to the nearest $\frac{1}{4}$ of 1%.[1]

Calculating the Monthly Payment by Formula and Table 14.2

The advertisement showed a $194.38 monthly payment. We can check this by formula and by table lookup.

By Formula

$$\boxed{\frac{\text{Finance charge} + \text{Amount financed}}{\text{Number of payments of loan}}} = \frac{\$2,617.80 + \$9,045}{60} = \$194.38$$

By Table 14.2 The **loan amortization table** (many variations of this table are available) in Table 14.2 (p. 332) can be used to calculate the monthly payment for the pickup truck. To calculate a monthly payment with a table, use the following steps:

Calculating Monthly Payment by Table Lookup

Step 1. Divide the loan amount by $1,000 (since Table 14.2 is per $1,000):

$$\frac{\$9,045}{\$1,000} = 9.045$$

Step 2. Look up the rate (10.5%) and number of months (60). At the intersection is the table factor showing the monthly payment per $1,000.

Step 3. Multiply quotient in Step 1 by the table factor in Step 2:

$$9.045 \times \$21.49 = \$194.38.$$

---

[1]If we wanted an exact reading of APR when the number is not exactly in the table, we would use the process of interpolating. We do not cover this method in this course.

TABLE 14.1   Annual percentage rate table per $100

NUMBER OF PAYMENTS	ANNUAL PERCENTAGE RATE															
	10.00%	10.25%	10.50%	10.75%	11.00%	11.25%	11.50%	11.75%	12.00%	12.25%	12.50%	12.75%	13.00%	13.25%	13.50%	13.75%
	(FINANCE CHARGE PER $100 OF AMOUNT FINANCED)															
1	0.83	0.85	0.87	0.90	0.92	0.94	0.96	0.98	1.00	1.02	1.04	1.06	1.08	1.10	1.12	1.15
2	1.25	1.28	1.31	1.35	1.38	1.41	1.44	1.47	1.50	1.53	1.57	1.60	1.63	1.66	1.69	1.72
3	1.67	1.71	1.76	1.80	1.84	1.88	1.92	1.96	2.01	2.05	2.09	2.13	2.17	2.22	2.26	2.30
4	2.09	2.14	2.20	2.25	2.30	2.35	2.41	2.46	2.51	2.57	2.62	2.67	2.72	2.78	2.83	2.88
5	2.51	2.58	2.64	2.70	2.77	2.83	2.89	2.96	3.02	3.08	3.15	3.21	3.27	3.34	3.40	3.46
6	2.94	3.01	3.08	3.16	3.23	3.31	3.38	3.45	3.53	3.60	3.68	3.75	3.83	3.90	3.97	4.05
7	3.36	3.45	3.53	3.62	3.70	3.78	3.87	3.95	4.04	4.12	4.21	4.29	4.38	4.47	4.55	4.64
8	3.79	3.88	3.98	4.07	4.17	4.26	4.36	4.46	4.55	4.65	4.74	4.84	4.94	5.03	5.13	5.22
9	4.21	4.32	4.43	4.53	4.64	4.75	4.85	4.96	5.07	5.17	5.28	5.39	5.49	5.60	5.71	5.82
10	4.64	4.76	4.88	4.99	5.11	5.23	5.35	5.46	5.58	5.70	5.82	5.94	6.05	6.17	6.29	6.41
11	5.07	5.20	5.33	5.45	5.58	5.71	5.84	5.97	6.10	6.23	6.36	6.49	6.62	6.75	6.88	7.01
12	5.50	5.64	5.78	5.92	6.06	6.20	6.34	6.48	6.62	6.76	6.90	7.04	7.18	7.32	7.46	7.60
13	5.93	6.08	6.23	6.38	6.53	6.68	6.84	6.99	7.14	7.29	7.44	7.59	7.75	7.90	8.05	8.20
14	6.36	6.52	6.69	6.85	7.01	7.17	7.34	7.50	7.66	7.82	7.99	8.15	8.31	8.48	8.64	8.81
15	6.80	6.97	7.14	7.32	7.49	7.66	7.84	8.01	8.19	8.36	8.53	8.71	8.88	9.06	9.23	9.41
16	7.23	7.41	7.60	7.78	7.97	8.15	8.34	8.53	8.71	8.90	9.08	9.27	9.46	9.64	9.83	10.02
17	7.67	7.86	8.06	8.25	8.45	8.65	8.84	9.04	9.24	9.44	9.63	9.83	10.03	10.23	10.43	10.63
18	8.10	8.31	8.52	8.73	8.93	9.14	9.35	9.56	9.77	9.98	10.19	10.40	10.61	10.82	11.03	11.24
19	8.54	8.76	8.98	9.20	9.42	9.64	9.86	10.08	10.30	10.52	10.74	10.96	11.18	11.41	11.63	11.85
20	8.98	9.21	9.44	9.67	9.90	10.13	10.37	10.60	10.83	11.06	11.30	11.53	11.76	12.00	12.23	12.46
21	9.42	9.66	9.90	10.15	10.39	10.63	10.88	11.12	11.36	11.61	11.85	12.10	12.34	12.59	12.84	13.08
22	9.86	10.12	10.37	10.62	10.88	11.13	11.39	11.64	11.90	12.16	12.41	12.67	12.93	13.19	13.44	13.70
23	10.30	10.57	10.84	11.10	11.37	11.63	11.90	12.17	12.44	12.71	12.97	13.24	13.51	13.78	14.05	14.32
24	10.75	11.02	11.30	11.58	11.86	12.14	12.42	12.70	12.98	13.26	13.54	13.82	14.10	14.38	14.66	14.95
25	11.19	11.48	11.77	12.06	12.35	12.64	12.93	13.22	13.52	13.81	14.10	14.40	14.69	14.98	15.28	15.57
26	11.64	11.94	12.24	12.54	12.85	13.15	13.45	13.75	14.06	14.36	14.67	14.97	15.28	15.59	15.89	16.20
27	12.09	12.40	12.71	13.03	13.34	13.66	13.97	14.29	14.60	14.92	15.24	15.56	15.87	16.19	16.51	16.83
28	12.53	12.86	13.18	13.51	13.84	14.16	14.49	14.82	15.15	15.48	15.81	16.14	16.47	16.80	17.13	17.46
29	12.98	13.32	13.66	14.00	14.33	14.67	15.01	15.35	15.70	16.04	16.38	16.72	17.07	17.41	17.75	18.10
30	13.43	13.78	14.13	14.48	14.83	15.19	15.54	15.89	16.24	16.60	16.95	17.31	17.66	18.02	18.38	18.74
31	13.89	14.25	14.61	14.97	15.33	15.70	16.06	16.43	16.79	17.16	17.53	17.90	18.27	18.63	19.00	19.38
32	14.34	14.71	15.09	15.46	15.84	16.21	16.59	16.97	17.35	17.73	18.11	18.49	18.87	19.25	19.63	20.02
33	14.79	15.18	15.57	15.95	16.34	16.73	17.12	17.51	17.90	18.29	18.69	19.08	19.47	19.87	20.26	20.66
34	15.25	15.65	16.05	16.44	16.85	17.25	17.65	18.05	18.46	18.86	19.27	19.67	20.08	20.49	20.90	21.31
35	15.70	16.11	16.53	16.94	17.35	17.77	18.18	18.60	19.01	19.43	19.85	20.27	20.69	21.11	21.53	21.95
36	16.16	16.58	17.01	17.43	17.86	18.29	18.71	19.14	19.57	20.00	20.43	20.87	21.30	21.73	22.17	22.60
37	16.62	17.06	17.49	17.93	18.37	18.81	19.25	19.69	20.13	20.58	21.02	21.46	21.91	22.36	22.81	23.25
38	17.08	17.53	17.98	18.43	18.88	19.33	19.78	20.24	20.69	21.15	21.61	22.07	22.52	22.99	23.45	23.91
39	17.54	18.00	18.46	18.93	19.39	19.86	20.32	20.79	21.26	21.73	22.20	22.67	23.14	23.61	24.09	24.56
40	18.00	18.48	18.95	19.43	19.90	20.38	20.86	21.34	21.82	22.30	22.79	23.27	23.76	24.25	24.73	25.22
41	18.47	18.95	19.44	19.93	20.42	20.91	21.40	21.89	22.39	22.88	23.38	23.88	24.38	24.88	25.38	25.88
42	18.93	19.43	19.93	20.43	20.93	21.44	21.94	22.45	22.96	23.47	23.98	24.49	25.00	25.51	26.03	26.55
43	19.40	19.91	20.42	20.94	21.45	21.97	22.49	23.01	23.53	24.05	24.57	25.10	25.62	26.15	26.68	27.21
44	19.86	20.39	20.91	21.44	21.97	22.50	23.03	23.57	24.10	24.64	25.17	25.71	26.25	26.79	27.33	27.88
45	20.33	20.87	21.41	21.95	22.49	23.03	23.58	24.12	24.67	25.22	25.77	26.32	26.88	27.43	27.99	28.55
46	20.80	21.35	21.90	22.46	23.01	23.57	24.13	24.69	25.25	25.81	26.37	26.94	27.51	28.08	28.65	29.22
47	21.27	21.83	22.40	22.97	23.53	24.10	24.68	25.25	25.82	26.40	26.98	27.56	28.14	28.72	29.31	29.89
48	21.74	22.32	22.90	23.48	24.06	24.64	25.23	25.81	26.40	26.99	27.58	28.18	28.77	29.37	29.97	30.57
49	22.21	22.80	23.39	23.99	24.58	25.18	25.78	26.38	26.98	27.58	28.18	28.80	29.41	30.02	30.63	31.24
50	22.69	23.29	23.89	24.50	25.11	25.72	26.33	26.95	27.56	28.18	28.80	29.42	30.04	30.67	31.29	31.92
51	23.16	23.78	24.40	25.02	25.64	26.26	26.89	27.52	28.15	28.78	29.41	30.05	30.68	31.32	31.96	32.60
52	23.64	24.27	24.90	25.53	26.17	26.81	27.45	28.09	28.73	29.38	30.02	30.67	31.32	31.98	32.63	33.29
53	24.11	24.76	25.40	26.05	26.70	27.35	28.00	28.66	29.32	29.98	30.64	31.30	31.97	32.63	33.30	33.97
54	24.59	25.25	25.91	26.57	27.23	27.90	28.56	29.23	29.91	30.58	31.25	31.93	32.61	33.29	33.98	34.66
55	25.07	25.74	26.41	27.09	27.77	28.44	29.13	29.81	30.50	31.18	31.87	32.56	33.26	33.95	34.65	35.35
56	25.55	26.23	26.92	27.61	28.30	28.99	29.69	30.39	31.09	31.79	32.49	33.20	33.91	34.62	35.33	36.04
57	26.03	26.73	27.43	28.13	28.84	29.54	30.25	30.97	31.68	32.39	33.11	33.83	34.56	35.28	36.01	36.74
58	26.51	27.23	27.94	28.66	29.37	30.10	30.82	31.55	32.27	33.00	33.74	34.47	35.21	35.95	36.69	37.43
59	27.00	27.72	28.45	29.18	29.91	30.65	31.39	32.13	32.87	33.61	34.36	35.11	35.86	36.62	37.37	38.13
60	27.48	28.22	28.96	29.71	30.45	31.20	31.96	32.71	33.47	34.23	34.99	35.75	36.52	37.29	38.06	38.83

Note: For a more detailed set of tables from 2% to 21.75%, see the reference tables in the *Business Math Handbook*.

TABLE 14.1 (concluded)

NUMBER OF PAYMENTS	ANNUAL PERCENTAGE RATE															
	14.00%	14.25%	14.50%	14.75%	15.00%	15.25%	15.50%	15.75%	16.00%	16.25%	16.50%	16.75%	17.00%	17.25%	17.50%	17.75%
	(FINANCE CHARGE PER $100 OF AMOUNT FINANCED)															
1	1.17	1.19	1.21	1.23	1.25	1.27	1.29	1.31	1.33	1.35	1.37	1.40	1.42	1.44	1.46	1.48
2	1.75	1.78	1.82	1.85	1.88	1.91	1.94	1.97	2.00	2.04	2.07	2.10	2.13	2.16	2.19	2.22
3	2.34	2.38	2.43	2.47	2.51	2.55	2.59	2.64	2.68	2.72	2.76	2.80	2.85	2.89	2.93	2.97
4	2.93	2.99	3.04	3.09	3.14	3.20	3.25	3.30	3.36	3.41	3.46	3.51	3.57	3.62	3.67	3.73
5	3.53	3.59	3.65	3.72	3.78	3.84	3.91	3.97	4.04	4.10	4.16	4.23	4.29	4.35	4.42	4.48
6	4.12	4.20	4.27	4.35	4.42	4.49	4.57	4.64	4.72	4.79	4.87	4.94	5.02	5.09	5.17	5.24
7	4.72	4.81	4.89	4.98	5.06	5.15	5.23	5.32	5.40	5.49	5.58	5.66	5.75	5.83	5.92	6.00
8	5.32	5.42	5.51	5.61	5.71	5.80	5.90	6.00	6.09	6.19	6.29	6.38	6.48	6.58	6.67	6.77
9	5.92	6.03	6.14	6.25	6.35	6.46	6.57	6.68	6.78	6.89	7.00	7.11	7.22	7.32	7.43	7.54
10	6.53	6.65	6.77	6.88	7.00	7.12	7.24	7.36	7.48	7.60	7.72	7.84	7.96	8.08	8.19	8.31
11	7.14	7.27	7.40	7.53	7.66	7.79	7.92	8.05	8.18	8.31	8.44	8.57	8.70	8.83	8.96	9.09
12	7.74	7.89	8.03	8.17	8.31	8.45	8.59	8.74	8.88	9.02	9.16	9.30	9.45	9.59	9.73	9.87
13	8.36	8.51	8.66	8.81	8.97	9.12	9.27	9.43	9.58	9.73	9.89	10.04	10.20	10.35	10.50	10.66
14	8.97	9.13	9.30	9.46	9.63	9.79	9.96	10.12	10.29	10.45	10.62	10.78	10.95	11.11	11.28	11.45
15	9.59	9.76	9.94	10.11	10.29	10.47	10.64	10.82	11.00	11.17	11.35	11.53	11.71	11.88	12.06	12.24
16	10.20	10.39	10.58	10.77	10.95	11.14	11.33	11.52	11.71	11.90	12.09	12.28	12.46	12.65	12.84	13.03
17	10.82	11.02	11.22	11.42	11.62	11.82	12.02	12.22	12.42	12.62	12.83	13.03	13.23	13.43	13.63	13.83
18	11.45	11.66	11.87	12.08	12.29	12.50	12.72	12.93	13.14	13.35	13.57	13.78	13.99	14.21	14.42	14.64
19	12.07	12.30	12.52	12.74	12.97	13.19	13.41	13.64	13.86	14.09	14.31	14.54	14.76	14.99	15.22	15.44
20	12.70	12.93	13.17	13.41	13.64	13.88	14.11	14.35	14.59	14.82	15.06	15.30	15.54	15.77	16.01	16.25
21	13.33	13.58	13.82	14.07	14.32	14.57	14.82	15.06	15.31	15.56	15.81	16.06	16.31	16.56	16.81	17.07
22	13.96	14.22	14.48	14.74	15.00	15.26	15.52	15.78	16.04	16.30	16.57	16.83	17.09	17.36	17.62	17.88
23	14.59	14.87	15.14	15.41	15.68	15.96	16.23	16.50	16.78	17.05	17.32	17.60	17.88	18.15	18.43	18.70
24	15.23	15.51	15.80	16.08	16.37	16.65	16.94	17.22	17.51	17.80	18.09	18.37	18.66	18.95	19.24	19.53
25	15.87	16.17	16.46	16.76	17.06	17.35	17.65	17.95	18.25	18.55	18.85	19.15	19.45	19.75	20.05	20.36
26	16.51	16.82	17.13	17.44	17.75	18.06	18.37	18.68	18.99	19.30	19.62	19.93	20.24	20.56	20.87	21.19
27	17.15	17.47	17.80	18.12	18.44	18.76	19.09	19.41	19.74	20.06	20.39	20.71	21.04	21.37	21.69	22.02
28	17.80	18.13	18.47	18.80	19.14	19.47	19.81	20.15	20.48	20.82	21.16	21.50	21.84	22.18	22.52	22.86
29	18.45	18.79	19.14	19.49	19.83	20.18	20.53	20.89	21.23	21.58	21.94	22.29	22.64	22.99	23.35	23.70
30	19.10	19.45	19.81	20.17	20.54	20.90	21.26	21.62	21.99	22.35	22.72	23.08	23.45	23.81	24.18	24.55
31	19.75	20.12	20.49	20.87	21.24	21.61	21.99	22.37	22.74	23.12	23.50	23.88	24.26	24.64	25.02	25.40
32	20.40	20.79	21.17	21.56	21.95	22.33	22.72	23.11	23.50	23.89	24.28	24.68	25.07	25.46	25.86	26.25
33	21.06	21.46	21.85	22.25	22.65	23.06	23.46	23.86	24.26	24.67	25.07	25.48	25.88	26.29	26.70	27.11
34	21.72	22.13	22.54	22.95	23.37	23.78	24.19	24.61	25.03	25.44	25.86	26.28	26.70	27.12	27.54	27.97
35	22.38	22.80	23.23	23.65	24.08	24.51	24.94	25.36	25.79	26.23	26.66	27.09	27.52	27.96	28.39	28.83
36	23.04	23.48	23.92	24.35	24.80	25.24	25.68	26.12	26.57	27.01	27.46	27.90	28.35	28.80	29.25	29.70
37	23.70	24.16	24.61	25.06	25.51	25.97	26.42	26.88	27.34	27.80	28.26	28.72	29.18	29.64	30.10	30.57
38	24.37	24.84	25.30	25.77	26.24	26.70	27.17	27.64	28.11	28.59	29.06	29.53	30.01	30.49	30.96	31.44
39	25.04	25.52	26.00	26.48	26.96	27.44	27.92	28.41	28.89	29.38	29.87	30.36	30.85	31.34	31.83	32.32
40	25.71	26.20	26.70	27.19	27.69	28.18	28.68	29.18	29.68	30.18	30.69	31.19	31.69	32.19	32.69	33.20
41	26.39	26.89	27.40	27.91	28.41	28.92	29.44	29.95	30.46	30.97	31.49	32.01	32.52	33.04	33.56	34.08
42	27.06	27.58	28.10	28.62	29.15	29.67	30.19	30.72	31.25	31.78	32.31	32.84	33.37	33.90	34.44	34.97
43	27.74	28.27	28.81	29.34	29.88	30.42	30.96	31.50	32.04	32.58	33.13	33.67	34.22	34.76	35.31	35.86
44	28.42	28.97	29.52	30.07	30.62	31.17	31.72	32.28	32.83	33.39	33.95	34.51	35.07	35.63	36.19	36.76
45	29.11	29.67	30.23	30.79	31.36	31.92	32.49	33.06	33.63	34.20	34.77	35.35	35.92	36.50	37.08	37.66
46	29.79	30.36	30.94	31.52	32.10	32.68	33.26	33.84	34.43	35.01	35.60	36.19	36.78	37.37	37.96	38.56
47	30.48	31.07	31.66	32.25	32.84	33.44	34.03	34.63	35.23	35.83	36.43	37.04	37.64	38.25	38.86	39.46
48	31.17	31.77	32.37	32.98	33.59	34.20	34.81	35.42	36.03	36.65	37.27	37.88	38.50	39.13	39.75	40.37
49	31.86	32.48	33.09	33.71	34.34	34.96	35.59	36.21	36.84	37.47	38.10	38.74	39.37	40.01	40.65	41.29
50	32.55	33.18	33.82	34.45	35.09	35.73	36.37	37.01	37.65	38.30	38.94	39.59	40.24	40.89	41.55	42.20
51	33.25	33.89	34.54	35.19	35.84	36.49	37.15	37.81	38.46	39.12	39.79	40.45	41.11	41.78	42.45	43.12
52	33.95	34.61	35.27	35.93	36.60	37.27	37.94	38.61	39.28	39.96	40.63	41.31	41.99	42.67	43.36	44.04
53	34.65	35.32	36.00	36.68	37.36	38.04	38.72	39.41	40.10	40.79	41.48	42.17	42.87	43.57	44.27	44.97
54	35.35	36.04	36.73	37.42	38.12	38.82	39.52	40.22	40.92	41.63	42.33	43.04	43.75	44.47	45.18	45.90
55	36.05	36.76	37.46	38.17	38.88	39.60	40.31	41.03	41.74	42.47	43.19	43.91	44.64	45.37	46.10	46.83
56	36.76	37.48	38.20	38.92	39.65	40.38	41.11	41.84	42.57	43.31	44.05	44.79	45.53	46.27	47.02	47.77
57	37.47	38.20	38.94	39.68	40.42	41.16	41.91	42.65	43.40	44.15	44.91	45.66	46.42	47.18	47.94	48.71
58	38.18	38.93	39.68	40.43	41.19	41.95	42.71	43.47	44.23	45.00	45.77	46.54	47.32	48.09	48.87	49.65
59	38.89	39.66	40.42	41.19	41.96	42.74	43.51	44.29	45.07	45.85	46.64	47.42	48.21	49.01	49.80	50.60
60	39.61	40.39	41.17	41.95	42.74	43.53	44.32	45.11	45.91	46.71	47.51	48.31	49.12	49.92	50.73	51.55

TABLE 14.2   Loan amortization table (monthly payment per $1,000 to pay principal and interest on installment loan)

Terms in months	7.50%	8%	8.50%	9%	10.00%	10.50%	11.00%	11.50%	12.00%
6	$170.34	$170.58	$170.83	$171.20	$171.56	$171.81	$172.05	$172.30	$172.55
12	86.76	86.99	87.22	87.46	87.92	88.15	88.38	88.62	88.85
18	58.92	59.15	59.37	59.60	60.06	60.29	60.52	60.75	60.98
24	45.00	45.23	45.46	45.69	46.14	46.38	46.61	46.84	47.07
30	36.66	36.89	37.12	37.35	37.81	38.04	38.28	38.51	38.75
36	31.11	31.34	31.57	31.80	32.27	32.50	32.74	32.98	33.21
42	27.15	27.38	27.62	27.85	28.32	28.55	28.79	29.03	29.28
48	24.18	24.42	24.65	24.77	25.36	25.60	25.85	26.09	26.33
54	21.88	22.12	22.36	22.59	23.07	23.32	23.56	23.81	24.06
60	20.04	20.28	20.52	20.76	21.25	21.49	21.74	21.99	22.24

Remember that this $194.38 fixed payment includes interest and the reduction of the balance of the loan. As the number of payments increases, interest payments get smaller and the reduction of the principal gets larger.[2]

Now let's check your progress with the Practice Quiz.

LU 14.1   PRACTICE QUIZ

From the partial advertisement at the right calculate the following:

1. **a.** Amount financed.
    b. Finance charge.
    c. Deferred payment price.
    d. APR by Table 14.1.
    e. Monthly payment by formula.

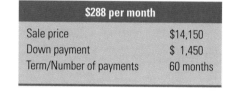

$288 per month	
Sale price	$14,150
Down payment	$ 1,450
Term/Number of payments	60 months

2. Jay Miller bought a New Brunswick boat for $7,500. Jay put down $1,000 and financed the balance at 10% for 60 months. What is his monthly payment? Use Table 14.2.

Courtesy Brunswick Corporation.

✓   **Solutions**

1. **a.** $14,150 − $1,450 = $12,700
    b. $17,280 ($288 × 60) − $12,700 = $4,580
    c. $17,280 ($288 × 60) + $1,450 = $18,730
    d. $\dfrac{\$4,580}{\$12,700} \times \$100 = \$36.06$; between 12.75% and 13%
    e. $\dfrac{\$4,580 + \$12,700}{60} = \$288$

2. $\dfrac{\$6,500}{\$1,000} = 6.5 \times \$21.25 = \$138.13$ (10%, 60 months)

LEARNING UNIT 14.2   Paying Off Installment Loan before Due Date

In Learning Unit 10.3 (p. 255), you learned about the U.S. Rule. This rule applies partial payments to the interest *first,* and then the remainder of the payment reduces the principal. Many states and the federal government use this rule.

Some states use another method for prepaying a loan, called the **Rule of 78.** It is a variation of the U.S. Rule. The Rule of 78 got its name because it bases the finance charge rebate and the payoff on a 12-month loan. (Any number of months can be used.) The Rule of 78 is used less today. However, GMAC says that about 50% of its auto loans still use the Rule of 78. For loans of 61 months or longer, the Rule of 78 is not allowed (some states have even shorter requirements).

---

[2]In Chapter 15 we give an amortization schedule for home mortgages that shows how much of each fixed payment goes to interest and how much reduces the principal. This repayment schedule also gives a running balance of the loan.

TABLE 14.2 (concluded)

Terms in months	12.50%	13.00%	13.50%	14.00%	14.50%	15.00%	15.50%	16.00%
6	$172.80	$173.04	$173.29	$173.54	$173.79	$174.03	$174.28	$174.53
12	89.08	89.32	89.55	89.79	90.02	90.26	90.49	90.73
18	61.21	61.45	61.68	61.92	62.15	62.38	62.62	62.86
24	47.31	47.54	47.78	48.01	48.25	48.49	48.72	48.96
30	38.98	39.22	39.46	39.70	39.94	40.18	40.42	40.66
36	33.45	33.69	33.94	34.18	34.42	34.67	34.91	35.16
42	29.52	29.76	30.01	30.25	30.50	30.75	31.00	31.25
48	26.58	26.83	27.08	27.33	27.58	27.83	28.08	28.34
54	24.31	24.56	24.81	25.06	25.32	25.58	25.84	26.10
60	22.50	22.75	23.01	23.27	23.53	23.79	24.05	24.32

With the Rule of 78, the finance charge earned the first month is $\frac{12}{78}$. The 78 comes from summing the 12 months. The second month, the finance charge would be $\frac{11}{78}$. We will use tables to simplify this process. Remember that the Rule of 78 charges a larger portion of the finance charges to the earlier payments.

To calculate the **rebate** amount of the finance charge and the payoff for the Rule of 78, use the steps that follow.

Calculating Rebate and Payoff for Rule of 78

Step 1. Find the balance of the loan outstanding.
Step 2. Calculate the total finance charge.
Step 3. Find the number of payments remaining.
Step 4. Set up the rebate fraction from Table 14.3.
Step 5. Calculate the rebate amount of the finance charge.
Step 6. Calculate the payoff.

Let's see what the rebate of the finance charge and payoff would be if the pickup truck loan were paid off after 27 months (instead of 60).

To find the finance charge rebate and the final payoff, we follow six specific steps listed below. Let's begin.

Step 1. Find the balance of the loan outstanding:

Total of monthly payments (60 × $194.38)	$11,662.80
Payments to date: 27 × $194.38	− 5,248.26
Balance of loan outstanding	$ 6,414.54

Step 2. Calculate the total finance charge:

$11,662.80	Total of all payments (60 × $194.38)
− 9,045.00	Amount financed ($9,345 − $300)
$ 2,617.80	Total finance charge

Step 3. Find the number of payments remaining:

$$60 - 27 = 33$$

Step 4. Set up the **rebate fraction** from Table 14.3.[3]

---

[3]If no table is available, the following formula is available:

$$\frac{\frac{N(N + 1)}{2}}{\frac{T(T + 1)}{2}} = \frac{\frac{33(33 + 1)}{2}}{\frac{60(60 + 1)}{2}} = \frac{561}{1,830}$$

In the numerator, N stands for number of months to go, and in the denominator, T is total months of the loan.

TABLE 14.3

Rebate fraction table based on Rule of 78

Months to go	Sum of digits	Months to go	Sum of digits	
1	1	31	496	
2	3	32	528	
3	6	33	561	⟶ 33 months to go
4	10	34	595	
5	15	35	630	
6	21	36	666	
7	28	37	703	
8	36	38	741	
9	45	39	780	
10	55	40	820	
11	66	41	861	
12	78	42	903	
13	91	43	946	
14	105	44	990	
15	120	45	1,035	
16	136	46	1,081	
17	153	47	1,128	
18	171	48	1,176	
19	190	49	1,225	
20	210	50	1,275	
21	231	51	1,326	
22	253	52	1,378	
23	276	53	1,431	
24	300	54	1,485	
25	325	55	1,540	
26	351	56	1,596	
27	378	57	1,653	
28	406	58	1,711	
29	435	59	1,770	
30	465	60	1,830	⟶ 60 months = 1,830

$$\frac{\text{Sum of digits based on number of months to go}}{\text{Sum of digits based on total number of months of loan}} = \frac{561}{1,830} \begin{matrix} \longleftarrow 33 \text{ months to go} \\ \longleftarrow 60 \text{ months in loan} \end{matrix}$$

Note: If this loan were for 12 months, the denominator would be 78.

Step 5. Calculate the rebate amount of the finance charge:

$$\boxed{\text{Rebate fraction} \times \text{Total finance charge} = \text{Rebate amount}}$$

$$\underset{\textbf{(Step 4)}}{\frac{561}{1,830}} \times \underset{\textbf{(Step 2)}}{\$2,617.80} = \$802.51$$

Step 6. Calculate the payoff:

$$\boxed{\text{Balance of loan outstanding} - \text{Rebate} = \text{Payoff}}$$

$$\underset{\textbf{(Step 1)}}{\$6,414.54} - \underset{\textbf{(Step 5)}}{\$802.51} = \$5,612.03$$

LU 14.2 PRACTICE QUIZ

Calculate the finance charge rebate and payoff (calculate all six steps):

Loan	Months of loan	End-of-month loan is repaid	Monthly payment	Finance charge rebate	Final payoff
$5,500	12	7	$510		

✓ **Solutions**

Step 1.
$$12 \times \$510 = \quad \$6,120$$
$$7 \times \$510 = \quad -\,3,570$$
$$\underline{}$$
$$\$2,550$$
(balance outstanding)

Step 2.
$$12 \times \$510 = \quad \$6,120$$
$$-\,5,500$$
$$\underline{}$$
$$\$\ 620$$
(total finance charge)

Step 3. $12 - 7 = 5$

Step 4. $\dfrac{15}{78}$ (by Table 14.3)

Step 5. $\dfrac{15}{78} \times \$620 = \boxed{\$119.23 \text{ rebate}}$
(Step 4)   (Step 2)

Step 6. Step 1 − Step 5
$$\$2,550 - \$119.23$$
$$= \boxed{\$2,430.77 \text{ payoff}}$$

LEARNING UNIT 14.3 Revolving Charge Credit Cards

Revolving charge credit cards are widely used today. Businesses find that consumers tend to buy more when they can use a credit card for their purchases. Consumers find credit cards convenient to use and valuable in establishing credit.

To protect consumers, Congress passed the **Fair Credit and Charge Card Disclosure Act of 1988.** This act requires that for direct-mail application or solicitation, credit card companies must provide specific details involving all fees, grace period, calculation

New Regulations for Credit Reports To Go Into Effect, Aiding Consumers

By ANDREA WEIGL
Staff Reporter of THE WALL STREET JOURNAL

WASHINGTON—Sweeping new regulations concerning credit reports go into effect tomorrow, providing consumers with protection from inaccurate information.

The law already allows consumers to see their credit reports. But there was no systematic way for consumers to get redress, nor was there a deadline for credit bureaus to respond. Consumers sometimes had to battle for years to have inaccurate information removed from the reports, said Karen Kirchgasser, press secretary for Sen. Richard Bryan (D., Nev.), a sponsor of the legislation.

Under the rules, to be issued by the Federal Trade Commission under legislation passed a year ago, credit bureaus must:

• Respond to consumer complaints about inaccurate information within 30 days.

• Provide a toll-free consumer service number, staffed with live personnel, by tomorrow.

• Tell consumers, on request, who has asked for copies of their credit history

within the past year.

• Get the subject's permission before giving a report to an employer, or before releasing a report containing medical information.

The new law also allows consumers to sue not only credit bureaus over false information, but also companies that provided the information to the bureaus, such as banks and mortgage companies.

The changes to the Fair Credit Reporting Act will be outlined today by the FTC. The act governs credit bureaus that sell information about consumers—where they live and work, how they pay their bills, and whether they have been sued, arrested or filed for bankruptcy — and those who furnish it.

When sold to creditors, employers, landlords, banks and insurance companies, credit reports can affect a person's ability to get a job, a loan, an apartment, a credit card or insurance. "Consumers with mistakes in the credit bureau's report would try to get a loan or an apartment, but were held up because their credit reports showed they were deadbeats, even though that wasn't the case," said Michelle Meier of Consumers Union, publisher of Consumer Reports.

TABLE 14.4　Schedule of payments

Monthly payment number	Outstanding balance due	$1\frac{1}{2}$% interest payment	Amount of monthly payment	Reduction in balance due	Outstanding balance due
1	$8,000.00	$120.00 (.015 × $8,000.00)	$500	$380.00 ($500 − $120.00)	$7,620.00 ($8,000 − $380)
2	7,620.00	114.30 (.015 × 7,620.00)	500	385.70 ($500 − 114.30)	7,234.30 (7,620 − 385.70)
3	7,234.30	108.51 (.015 × 7,234.30)	500	391.49 ($500 − 108.51)	6,842.81 (7,234.30 − 391.49)

of finance charges, and so on. *The Wall Street Journal* clipping "New Regulations for Credit Reports to Go into Effect, Aiding Consumers" reports on the 1997 update of the Fair Credit and Charge Card Disclosure Act of 1988.

We begin the unit by seeing how Moe's Furniture Store calculates the finance charge on Abby Jordan's previous month's credit card balance. Then we learn how to calculate the average daily balance on the partial bill of Joan Ring.

Calculating Finance Charge on Previous Month's Balance

Abby Jordan bought a dining room set for $8,000 on credit. She has a **revolving charge account** at Moe's Furniture Store. A revolving charge account gives to a buyer **open-end credit.** Abby can make as many purchases on credit as she wants until she reaches her maximum $10,000 credit limit.

Often customers do not completely pay their revolving charge accounts at the end of a billing period. When this occurs, stores add interest charges to the customers' bills. Moe's Furniture Store charges $1\frac{1}{2}$% interest on the *previous month's balance,* or 18% per year. Moe's has no minimum monthly payment (many stores require $10 or $15, or a percent of the outstanding balance).

Abby has no other charges on her revolving charge account. She plans to pay $500 per month until she completely pays off her dining room set. Abby realizes that when she makes a payment, Moe's Furniture Store first applies the money toward the interest and then reduces the **outstanding balance** due. (This is the U.S. Rule we discussed in Chapter 10.) For her own information, Abby worked out the first 3-month schedule of payments, shown in Table 14.4. Note how the interest payment is the rate times the outstanding balance.

Today, most companies with credit card accounts calculate the finance charge, or interest, as a percentage of the average daily balance. Interest on credit cards can be very expensive for consumers; however, interest is a source of income for credit card companies. Note that Dayton Hudson and Best Buy moved their credit card headquarters to South Dakota, which made it possible for Dayton Hudson to raise its rate from 16% to 21% and Best Buy to raise its rate from 16% to 23%.

Calculating Average Daily Balance

Let's look at the following steps for calculating the **average daily balance.** Remember that a **cash advance** is a cash loan from a credit card company.

Calculating Average Daily Balance

Step 1. Calculate the daily balance or amount owed at the end of each day during the billing cycle:

$$\frac{\text{Daily}}{\text{balance}} = \frac{\text{Previous}}{\text{balance}} + \frac{\text{Cash}}{\text{advances}} + \text{Purchases} - \text{Payments}$$

Step 2. When the daily balance is the same for more than one day, multiply it by the number of days the daily balance remained the same, or the number of days of the current balance. This gives a cumulative daily balance.

Step 3. Add the cumulative daily balances.

Step 4. Divide the sum of the cumulative daily balances by the number of days in the billing cycle.

Following is the partial bill of Joan Ring and an explanation of how Joan's average daily balance was calculated. Note how we calculated each **daily balance** and then multiplied each daily balance by the number of days the balance remained the same. Take a moment to study how we arrived at 8 days. The total of the cumulative daily balances was $16,390. To get the average daily balance, we divided by the number of days in the billing cycle—30.

30-day billing cycle			
6/20	Billing date	Previous balance	$450
6/27	Payment		$ 50 cr.
6/30	Charge: JCPenney		200
7/9	Payment		40 cr.
7/12	Cash advance		60

7 days had a balance of $450

	No. of days of current balance	**Current daily balance**	**Extension**	
Step 1 →	7	$450	$ 3,150	←— Step 2
	3	400 ($450 − $50)	1,200	
	9	600 ($400 + $200)	5,400	
	3	560 ($600 − $40)	1,680	
	8	620 ($560 + $60)	4,960	
	30		$16,390	←— Step 3

30-day cycle − 22 (7 + 3 + 9 + 3) equals 8 days left with a balance of $620.

$$\text{Average daily balance} = \frac{\$16,390}{30} = \$546.33 \quad \text{←—Step 4}$$

Now try the following Practice Quiz to check your understanding of this unit.

LU 14.3 PRACTICE QUIZ

1. Calculate the balance outstanding at the end of month 2 (use U.S. Rule) given the following: purchased $600 desk; pay back $40 per month; and charge of $2\frac{1}{2}\%$ interest on unpaid balance.

2. Calculate the average daily balance from the following information:

31-day billing cycle			
8/20	Billing date	Previous balance	$210
8/27	Payment		$50 cr.
8/31	Charge: Staples		30
9/5	Payment		10 cr.
9/10	Cash advance		60

✓ **Solutions**

1.

Month	**Balance due**	**Interest**	**Monthly payment**	**Reduction in balance**	**Balance outstanding**
1	$600	$15.00 (.025 × $600)	$40	$25.00 ($40 − $15)	$575.00
2	575	14.38 (.025 × $575)	40	25.62	$549.38

2. Average daily balance calculated as follows:

No. of days of current balance	**Current balance**	**Extension**
7	$210	$1,470
4	160 ($210 − $50)	640
5	190 ($160 + $30)	950
5	180 ($190 − $10)	900
10	240 ($180 + $60)	2,400
31		$6,360

31 − 21 (7 + 4 + 5 + 5) → 10

$$\text{Average daily balance} = \frac{\$6,360}{31} = \$205.16$$

Chapter Organizer and Reference Guide

Topic	Key point, procedure, formula	Example(s) to illustrate situation
Amount financed, p. 328	$$\frac{\text{Amount}}{\text{financed}} = \frac{\text{Cash}}{\text{price}} - \frac{\text{Down}}{\text{payment}}$$	60 payments at $125.67 per month; cash price $5,295 with a $95 down payment Cash price $5,295 − Down payment − 95 = Amount financed $5,200
Total finance charge (interest), p. 328	$$\begin{array}{l}\text{Total} \\ \text{finance} \\ \text{charge}\end{array} = \begin{array}{l}\text{Total of} \\ \text{all monthly} \\ \text{payments}\end{array} - \begin{array}{l}\text{Amount} \\ \text{financed}\end{array}$$	*(continued from above)* $\frac{\$125.67}{\text{per month}} \times \frac{60}{\text{months}} = \$7,540.20$ − Amount financed − $5,200.00 = Finance charge $2,340.20
Deferred payment price, p. 328	$$\frac{\text{Deferred}}{\text{payment price}} = \frac{\text{Total of all}}{\text{monthly payments}} + \frac{\text{Down}}{\text{payment}}$$	*(continued from above)* $7,540.20 + $95 = $7,635.20
Calculating APR by Table 14.1, p. 329	$$\frac{\text{Finance charge}}{\text{Amount financed}} \times \$100 = \begin{array}{l}\text{Table 14.1} \\ \text{lookup number}\end{array}$$	*(continued from above)* $\frac{\$2,340.20}{\$5,200.00} \times \$100 = \$45.004$ Search in Table 14.1 between 15.50% and 15.75% for 60 payments.

Monthly payment, p. 329	*By formula:*
	$$\frac{\text{Finance charge} + \text{Amount financed}}{\text{Number of payments of loan}}$$
	By table:
	$$\frac{\text{Loan}}{\$1,000} \times \begin{array}{l}\text{Table} \\ \text{factor}\end{array} \text{(rate, months)}$$
		(continued from above)
		$\frac{\$2,340.20 + \$5,200.00}{60} = \$125.67$
		Given: 15.5%
		        60 months
		        $5,200 loan
		$\frac{\$5,200}{\$1,000} = 5.2 \times \$24.05 = \$125.06^*$
		
		*Off due to rounding of rate.

Paying off installment loan before due date, p. 332	**1.** Find balance of loan outstanding (Total of monthly payments − Payments to date).
	2. Calculate total finance charge.
	3. Find number of payments remaining.
	4. Set up rebate fraction from Table 14.3.
	5. Calculate rebate amount of finance charge.
	6. Calculate payoff.
		Example: Loan, $8,000; 20 monthly payments of $420; end of month repaid 7.
		1. $8,400 (20 × $420)
		      − 2,940 (7 × $420)
		      $5,460 (balance of loan outstanding)
		2. $8,400 (total payments)
		      − 8,000 (amount financed)
		      $ 400 (total finance charge)
		3. 20 − 7 = 13
		4 and 5. $\frac{91}{210} \times \$400 = \$173.33$
		6. $5,460.00 (Step 1)
		   − 173.33 rebate (Step 5)
		   $5,286.67 payoff

Chapter Organizer and Reference Guide (concluded)		
Topic	**Key point, procedure, formula**	**Example(s) to illustrate situation**
Open end credit, p. 336	Monthly payment applied to interest first before reducing balance outstanding.	$4,000 purchase $250 a month payment $2\frac{1}{2}\%$ interest on unpaid balance $4,000 × .025 = $100 interest $250 − $100 = $150 to lower balance $4,000 − $150 = $3,850 Balance outstanding after month 1.
Average daily balance, p. 337	$\dfrac{\text{Daily}}{\text{balance}} = \dfrac{\text{Previous}}{\text{balance}} + \dfrac{\text{Cash}}{\text{advances}}$ $+ \text{Purchases} - \text{Payments}$ $\dfrac{\text{Average daily}}{\text{balance}} = \dfrac{\text{Sum of cumulative daily balances}}{\text{Number of days in billing cycle}}$ 30-day billing cycle less the 8 and 14. ⟵	*30-day billing cycle:* *Example:* 8/21 Balance $100 8/29 Payment $10 9/12 Charge 50 *Average daily balance equals:* 8 days × $100 = $ 800 14 days × 90 = 1,260 8 days × 140 = 1,120 $3,180 ÷ 30 Average daily balance = $106
Key terms	Amortization, *p. 328* Amount financed, *p. 328* Annual percentage rate (APR), *p. 329* Average daily balance, *p. 336* Cash advance, *p. 336* Daily balance, *p. 337* Deferred payment price, *p. 328*	Down payment, *p. 328* Fair Credit and Charge Card Disclosure Act of 1988, *p. 335* Finance charge, *p. 328* Installment loan, *p. 328* Interest, *p. 328* Loan amortization table, *p. 329* Open-end credit, *p. 336* Outstanding balance, *p. 336* Rebate, *p. 333* Rebate fraction, *p. 333* Revolving charge account, *p. 336* Rule of 78, *p. 332* Truth in Lending Act, *p. 329*

**Critical Thinking
Discussion Questions**

1. Explain how to calculate the amount financed, finance charge, and APR by table lookup. Do you think the Truth in Lending Act should regulate interest charges?

2. Explain how to use the loan amortization table. Check with a person who owns a home and find out what part of each payment goes to pay interest versus the amount that reduces the loan principal.

3. What are the six steps used to calculate the rebate and payoff for the Rule of 78? Do you think it is right for the Rule of 78 to charge a larger portion of the finance charges to the earlier payments?

4. What steps are used to calculate the average daily balance? Many credit card companies charge 18% annual interest. Do you think this is a justifiable rate? Defend your answer.

DRILL PROBLEMS

Complete the following table:

	Purchase price of product	Down payment		Amount financed	Number of monthly payments		Amount of monthly payments		Total of monthly payments	Total finance charge
14–1.	Mustang convertible $28,500	− $7,000	=	$21,500	60	×	$399	=	$23,940	$2,440 ($23,940 − $21,500)
14–2.	Sony camcorder $900	− $100	=	$800	12	×	$79.99	=	$959.88	$159.88 ($959.88 − $800)

Calculate **(a)** the amount financed, **(b)** the total finance charge, and **(c)** APR by table lookup.

	Purchase price of a used car	Down payment	Number of monthly payments	Amount financed	Total of monthly payments	Total finance charge	APR
14–3.	$5,673	$1,223	48	$4,450	$5,729.76	$1,279.76	12.75%–13%
	$5,673 −1,223 ------ $4,450	$5,729.76 −4,450.00 --------- $1,279.76	$\dfrac{\$1,279.76}{\$4,450.00} \times \$100 = \$28.76$ is between 12.75% and 13% at 48 months				
14–4.	$4,195	$95	60	$4,100	$5,944.00	$1,844.00	15.50%–15.75%
	$4,195 −95 ------ $4,100	$5,944 −4,100 ------ $1,844	$\dfrac{\$1,844}{\$4,100} \times \$100 = \$44.98$ at 60 months is between 15.50% and 15.75%				

Calculate the monthly payment for Problems 14–3 and 14–4 by table lookup and formula. (Answers will not be exact due to rounding of percents in table lookup.)

14–5. **(14–3)** (Use 13% for table lookup.)

Table: $5,673
          − 1,223

         $4,450 ÷ $1,000 =   4.45
                          × 26.83 (13%, 48 months)

                          $119.39

Formula: $\dfrac{\$1,279.76 + \$4,450}{48} = \$119.37$

14–6. **(14–4)** (Use 15.5% for table lookup.)

Table: $4,195
          − 95

         $4,100 ÷ $1,000 =   4.1
                          × 24.05 (15.5%, 60 months)

                          $98.61

Formula: $\dfrac{\$1,844 + \$4,100}{60} = \$99.07$

Calculate the finance charge rebate and payoff:

	Loan	Months of loan	End-of-month loan is repaid	Monthly payment	Finance charge rebate	Final payoff
14–7.	$6,000	48	10	$180	$1,663.47	$5,176.53

Step 1. 48 × $180 = $8,640
            10 × $180 = 1,800
            Balance outstanding $6,840

Step 2. 48 × $180 = $8,640
            Amount financed   − 6,000
            Total finance charge $2,640

Step 3. 48 − 10 = 38

Step 4. $\dfrac{741}{1,176}$ (by Table 14.3)

Step 5. $\dfrac{741}{1,176}$ × $2,640 = $1,663.47
            (Step 4)   (Step 2)   (rebate)

Step 6. $6,840 − $1,663.47 = $5,176.53
            (Step 1)   (Step 5)   (payoff)

14–8. $9,000   24   9 $440 $624.00 $5,976.00

Step 1.   **Step 2.**

Total payments   Total of all payments $10,560

$440 × 24 = $10,560   Amount financed   − 9,000

$440 × 9 =   − 3,960   Total finance charge $ 1,560

Balance outstanding $ 6,600

Step 3.   **Step 4.**

24 − 9 = 15   By Table 14.3, $\dfrac{120}{300}$ $\begin{array}{l}\to\ 15 \text{ months to go}\\ \to\ 24 \text{ months total loan}\end{array}$

Step 5.   **Step 6.**

$\dfrac{120}{300}$ × $1,560 $624 finance charge $6,600 − $624 = $5,976

(**Step 4**)   (**Step 2**)   rebate)   (**Step 1**) (**Step 5**)   (payoff)

14–9. Calculate the average daily balance:

30-day billing cycle		
9/16	Billing date Previous balance	$2,000
9/19	Payment	$ 60
9/30	Charge: Home Depot	1,500
10/3	Payment	60
10/7	Cash advance	70

No. of days of current balance	Current balance	Extension
3	$2,000	$ 6,000
11	1,940	21,340
3	3,440	10,320
4	3,380	13,520
9	3,450	31,050

$\dfrac{\$82,230}{30}$ = $2,741 average daily balance

WORD PROBLEMS

14–10. An article in the October 1996 *Consumer Reports* discussed the following: On a 1994 Lexus ES300 priced at $25,750, a $2,600 down payment was made. The loan was for 36 months with monthly payments of $767. From this information, calculate (**a**) the amount financed, (**b**) the finance charge, (**c**) the deferred payment price, and (**d**) APR using the table. (Use table in the *Business Math Handbook*.)

   a. Cash price − Down payment = Amount financed

       $25,750   − $2,600   = $23,150

   b. $\begin{array}{c}\text{Total of all monthly}\\ \text{payments}\end{array}$ − $\begin{array}{c}\text{Amount}\\ \text{financed}\end{array}$ = $\begin{array}{c}\text{Total finance}\\ \text{charge}\end{array}$

       36 × $767 = $27,612 − $23,150 = $4,462

   c. $\begin{array}{c}\text{Total of all monthly}\\ \text{payments}\end{array}$ + $\begin{array}{c}\text{Down}\\ \text{payment}\end{array}$ = $\begin{array}{c}\text{Deferred}\\ \text{payment price}\end{array}$

       $27,612   + $2,600 = $30,212

   d. $\dfrac{\$4,462 \text{ finance charge}}{\$23,150 \text{ amount financed}}$ × $100 = $19.27

               (36 months) = 11.75% to 12.00%

14–11. The *Bank Rate Monitor* reported the lowest auto rates as of October 15, 1997. The loans were based on $16,000 borrowed for 48 months. New York Citibank reported monthly payments of $390.61. Los Angeles Sanwa Bank reported monthly payments of $396.26. What would be the APR for each of these banks? Use Tables in the *Business Math Handbook*.

New York Citibank   **Los Angeles Sanwa Bank**

$390.61 × 48 = $18,749.28 $396.26 × 48 = $19,020.48

             − 16,000.00   − 16,000.00

               $ 2,749.28 finance charge $3,020.48 finance charge

$\dfrac{\$2,749.28}{\$16,000.00}$ × 100 = 17.183 = 8% to 8.25% $\dfrac{\$3,020.48}{\$16,000.00}$ × 100 = 18.878 = 8.50% to 8.75%

14–12. Lou Barmin saw the following advertisement for a used Volkswagen Jetta and decided to work out the numbers to be sure the ad had no errors. Please help Mike by calculating **(a)** the amount financed, **(b)** the finance charge, **(c)** APR by table lookup, **(d)** the monthly payment by formula, and **(e)** the monthly payment by table lookup (will be off slightly).

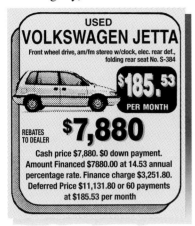

a. Amount financed: $7,880 − 0 = $7,880

$$\frac{\text{Selling}}{\text{price}} - \frac{\text{Down}}{\text{payment}} = \frac{\text{Amount}}{\text{financed}}$$

b. Finance charge: ($185.53 × 60) − $7,880 = $3,251.80

c. APR by table lookup: $\dfrac{\$3,251.80}{\$7,880.00} \times \$100 = 41.27$

Between 14.50% and 14.75%

d. Monthly payment by formula: $\dfrac{\$3,251.80 + \$7,880.00}{60} = \$185.53$

e. Monthly payment by table lookup (use 14.50%):

$$\frac{\$7,880}{\$1,000} = 7.88 \times \$23.53 = \$185.42$$

14–13. From this partial advertisement calculate:

> **$89.11 per month**
>
> #969531 Used car. Cash price $3,984. Down payment $95. For 60 months.

a. Amount financed.

b. Finance charge.

c. Deferred payment price.

d. APR by Table 14.1.

e. Check monthly payment (by formula).

a. Amount financed = $3,984 − $95 = $3,889

b. Finance charge = $5,346.60 ($89.11 × 60) − $3,889 = $1,457.60

c. Deferred payment price = $5,346.60 ($89.11 × 60) + $95 = $5,441.60

d. $\dfrac{\$1,457.60}{\$3,889.00} \times \$100 = \$37.48$ (in Table 14.1, between 13.25% and 13.50%)

e. $\dfrac{\$1,457.60 + \$3,889.00}{60} = \$89.11$

14–14. Paula Westing borrowed $6,200 to travel to Sweden to see her son Arthur. Her loan was to be paid in 48 monthly installments of $170. At the end of 9 months, Paula's daughter Irene convinced her that she should pay off the loan early. What are Paula's rebate and her payoff amount?

Step 1. Total payments $8,160 (48 × $170)   **Step 2.** $8,160 (total payments)
Payments to date − 1,530 (9 × $170)   − 6,200 (amount financed)
                  ―――――――――   ―――――――――
                  $6,630 $1,960 (total finance charge)

Step 3. 48 − 9 = 39   **Step 4.** $\dfrac{780}{1,176}$

Step 5. $\dfrac{780}{1,176} \times \$1,960 = \$1,300$ rebate   **Step 6.** $6,630 − $1,300 = $5,330 payoff

14–15. The title of an article in the October 1993 issue of *Kiplinger's Personal Finance Magazine* was "When It Pays to Pay Off an Old Loan." The article states that a 1994 Lexus ES300 priced at $25,750 with $2,600 down payment has monthly payments of $767 for 36 months. What would be the rebate and the final payoff if the automobile was paid off after 20 months?

36 × $767 = $27,612 total monthly payments
20 × $767 = − 15,340
―――――――――――――――――――――
         $12,272 balance of loan outstanding

  $27,612
− 23,150 ($25,750 − $2,600 down payment)
―――――――――
 $ 4,462 total finance charge

36 − 20 payments = 16 remaining payments

136 ⟵ 16 months to go (Table 14.3)
666 ⟵ 36 months in loan (Table 14.3)

Finance charge
$\dfrac{136}{666} \times \$4,462 = \$911.16$ rebate amount

Balance of loan
outstanding   Rebate   Payoff
  $12,272   − $911.16 = $11,360.84

14–16. Joanne Flynn bought a new boat for $14,500. She put a $2,500 down payment on it. The bank's loan was for 48 months. Finance charges totaled $4,400.16. Assume Joanne decided to pay off the loan at the end of the 28th month. What rebate would she be entitled to and what would be the actual payoff amount?

$$\text{Monthly payment} = \frac{\$4,400.16 + \$12,000}{48} = \$341.67$$

Step 1. 48 × $341.67 = $16,400.16
28 × $341.67 = − 9,566.76
$ 6,833.40 balance outstanding

Step 2. $16,400.16
− 12,000.00
$ 4,400.16

Step 3. 48 − 28 = 20

Step 4. $\frac{210}{1,176}$

Step 5. $\frac{210}{1,176}$ × $4,400.16 = $785.74 rebate

Step 6. $6,833.40
− 785.74
$6,047.66 payoff

14–17. An article entitled "Deals on Wheels, Which Loans Cost Least?" appeared in the November 1995 issue of *Working Woman*. A $15,000 loan for 5 years will run a whopping $3,240 in interest. For the same loan over a 4-year period, the total interest cost will be $2,568, which is $672 less than for the longer loan. What is the APR for the 5-year loan? Use tables in the *Business Math Handbook*.

$$\frac{\$3,240 \text{ finance charge}}{\$15,000 \text{ amount financed}} \times 100 = 21.6 \text{ (60 months) })$$
$$= 7.75\% \text{ to } 8.00\%$$

14–18. From the following facts, Molly Roe has requested you to calculate the average daily balance. The customer believes the average daily balance should be $877.67. Respond to the customer's concern.

28-day billing cycle			
3/18	Billing date	Previous balance	$800
3/24	Payment	$ 60	
3/29	Charge: Sears	250	
4/5	Payment	20	
4/9	Charge: Macys	200	

No. of days of current balance	Current balance	Extension
6	$ 800	$ 4,800
5	740	3,700
7	990	6,930
4	970	3,880
6 (28 − 22)	1,170	7,020
		$26,330 ÷ 28 = $940.36

Customer divided by 30 days instead of 28 days; should be $940.36

14–19. Jill bought a $500 rocking chair. The terms of her revolving charge are $1\frac{1}{2}\%$ on the unpaid balance from the previous month. If she pays $100 per month, complete a schedule for the first 3 months like Table 14.4. Be sure to use the U.S. Rule.

Monthly payment number	Outstanding balance due	$1\frac{1}{2}\%$ interest payment	Amount of monthly payment	Reduction in balance due	Outstanding balance due
1	$500.00	$7.50 ($500.00 × .015)	$100.00	$92.50 ($100.00 − $7.50)	$407.50 ($500.00 − $92.50)
2	$407.50	$6.11 ($407.50 × .015)	$100.00	$93.89 ($100.00 − $6.11)	$313.61 ($407.50 − $93.89)
3	$313.61	$4.70 ($313.61 × .015)	$100.00	$95.30 ($100.00 − $4.70)	$218.31 ($313.61 − $95.30)

CHALLENGE PROBLEMS

14–20. You have a $1,100 balance on your 15% credit card. You have lost your job and been unemployed for 6 months. You have been unable to make any payments on your balance. However, you received a tax refund and want to pay off the credit card. How much will you owe on the credit card, and how much interest will have accrued? What will be the effective rate of interest after the 6 months (to nearest hundredth percent)?

Interest

1 month: $1,100.00 $\times$ .15 $\times \frac{1}{12}$ = $13.75 = $1,113.75

2 months: $1,113.75 $\times$ .15 $\times \frac{1}{12}$ = $13.92 = $1,127.67

3 months: $1,127.67 $\times$ .15 $\times \frac{1}{12}$ = $14.10 = $1,141.77

4 months: $1,141.77 $\times$ .15 $\times \frac{1}{12}$ = $14.27 = $1,156.04

5 months: $1,156.04 $\times$ .15 $\times \frac{1}{12}$ = $14.45 = $1,170.49

6 months: $1,170.49 $\times$ .15 $\times \frac{1}{12}$ = $14.63 = $1,185.12

$$\frac{\$85.12 \text{ interest}}{\$1,100 \times \dfrac{6}{12}} = \frac{\$85.12}{\$550} = 15.48\%$$

14–21. Elaine Johnson saw the following advertisement and called the dealer, indicating that the $5.18 figure was not true. Does Elaine have a case or is her math incorrect?

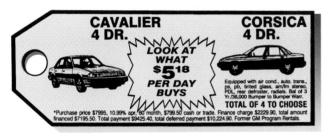

CAVALIER 4 DR.   CORSICA 4 DR.   LOOK AT WHAT **$5**18 PER DAY BUYS

Equipped with air cond., auto. trans., ps, pb, tinted glass, am/fm stereo, PDL, rear defroster, radials. Bal of 3 Yr./36,000 Bumper to Bumper Warr. **TOTAL OF 4 TO CHOOSE**

*Purchase price $7995, 10.99% apr, 60 month, $799.50 cash or trade. Finance charge $2229.90, total amount financed $7195.50. Total payment $9425.40, total deferred payment $10,224.90. Former GM Program Rentals.

If use 365 days:

60 months = 5 years $\times$ 365 days = 1,825 days

Total payments: $\dfrac{\$9,425.40}{1,825 \text{ days}}$ = $5.16

Doesn't quite match ad. Elaine has a case.

If use 52 weeks:

52 weeks $\times$ 5 = 260 weeks

260 weeks $\times$ 7 days = 1,820 days

$\dfrac{\$9,425.40}{1,820 \text{ days}}$ = $5.178 = $5.18

Elaine has no case.

 SUMMARY PRACTICE TEST

1. Bee Paul bought a Ford Expedition for $32,500. Bee made a down payment of $9,000 and paid $410 monthly for 60 months. What are the total amount financed and the total finance charge that Bee paid at the end of the 60 months? *(p. 328)*

   $32,500 − $9,000   = $23,500 amount financed

   Total finance charge = ($410 $\times$ 60) − $23,500

   = $24,600   − $23,500

   = $1,100

2. Meg Long bought a Compaq computer for $2,700. Meg put down $600 and financed the balance at 9% for 48 months. What is her monthly payment (use loan amortization table)? *(p. 329)*

   $2,700 − $600 = $\dfrac{\$2,100}{\$1,000}$ = 2.1 $\times$ $24.77 = $52.02

3. Lynn Hall read the following partial advertisement: Price, $20,000; down payment, $1,000, cash or trade; and $370.99 per month for 60 months. Calculate **(a)** the total finance charge and **(b)** the APR by Table 14.1 (use tables in *Business Math Handbook*) to the nearest hundredth percent. *(p. 329)*

   a. $20,000 $370.99 $\times$ 60 = $22,259.40

   − 1,000   − 19,000.00

   $19,000 $ 3,259.40 total finance charge

   b. Table 14.1 $\dfrac{\$3,259.40}{\$19,000} \times 100$ = 17.15 between 6.25% and 6.50%

4. Rich Hall bought a $6,000 desk at Staples. Based on his income, Rich could only afford to pay back $600 per month. The charge on the unpaid balance is $2\frac{1}{2}\%$. The U.S. Rule is used in the calculation. Calculate at the end of month 2 the balance outstanding. *(p. 336)*

Month	Balance due	Interest	Monthly payment	Reduction in balance	Balance outstanding
1	$6,000	$150	$600	$450	$5,550
		(.025 × $6,000)		($600 − $150)	($6,000 − $450)
2	$5,550	$138.75	$600	$461.25	$5,088.75
		(.025 × $5,550)		($600 − $138.75)	($5,550 − $461.25)

5. Bob Foster borrowed $10,000 to travel to France to see his son Bill. His loan was to be paid in 48 monthly installments of $240. At the end of 9 months, his daughter Fran convinced him that he should pay off the loan early. What are Bob's rebate and the payoff amount? *(p. 333)*

Step 1.
Total payments	$11,520 ($240 × 48)
Payments to date	− 2,160 ($240 × 9)
Balance of loan outstanding	$9,360

Step 2.
Total payments	$11,520
Amount financed	− 10,000
	$ 1,520

Step 3. 48 − 9 = 39

Step 4. $\dfrac{780}{1,176}$

Step 5. $\dfrac{780}{1,176} \times \$1,520 = \$1,008.16$ rebate

Step 6.
$9,360.00
− 1,008.16
$8,351.84 payoff

6. Calculate the average daily balance. *(p. 337)*

30-day billing cycle	
6/6	Balance	$300
6/14	Payment	40
6/21	Charge: Lord and Taylor	80

8 days × $300 = $2,400
7 days × $260 = $1,820
15 days (30 − 15) × $340 = $5,100
$9,320 ÷ 30 = $310.67

Defend or reject the following business math issue based on the *Kiplinger's Personal Finance Magazine* article below:

Know what you'll pay

CEDRIC RASHAD, an Atlanta leasing consultant, says many people shy away from leasing because "they think it's some kind of voodoo. But don't be put off. This "calculator," which Rashad helped us develop to demystify the lease, will help steer you to good deals.
CAPITALIZED COST. This is the cost of the car written into the lease, including title and registration fees and other costs rolled into the lease.
CAPITALIZED-COST REDUC- TION. Any down payment, the value of your trade-in and rebates that reduce the price of the car.
RESIDUAL. The estimated value of the car

at the end of the lease. Ask the dealer for this figure or use the resale values in our tables for an estimate. We show retained value after two and four years. If you want a three-year lease, split the difference.
MONEY FACTOR. This repre- sents the cost of financing the car. It is the equivalent of an interest rate divided by 24. So a money factor of 0.00375 is the equivalent of an 9% rate on an auto loan. Ask the dealer for the money factor.
SALES TAX. Some states charge this in full at the start of the lease; oth- ers add it to each payment. Ask how it works where you live.

Figuring the Lease Payment

DEPRECIATION
A. Gross capitalized cost (cap cost) .... $_____
B. Cap-cost reduction .... $_____
C. Net cap cost (A − B) .... $_____
D. Residual .... $_____
E. Depreciation (C − D) .... $_____
F. Lease term (in months) .... _____

1. MONTHLY DEPRECIATION (E ÷ F) .... $_____

FINANCE CHARGE
G. Finance base (C + D) .... $_____
H. Money factor .... _____

2. MONTHLY FINANCE CHARGE (G x H) .. $_____

SALES TAX
3. MONTHLY SALES TAX .... $_____

ESTIMATED LEASE PAYMENT (1 + 2 + 3) .. $_____

Business Math Issue

Leasing is always a bad deal.

1. List the key points of the article and information to support your position.
2. Write a group defense of your position using math calculations to support your view.

BUSINESS MATH SCRAPBOOK
Putting Your Skills to Work

American Express Credit-Card Share Increased to 18.9% in First Half of Year

By STEPHEN E. FRANK

Staff Reporter of THE WALL STREET JOURNAL

NEW YORK — **American Express** Co.'s share of the domestic credit-card market increased during the first six months of this year, indicating a turnaround in the company's card business may be gathering steam.

The numbers are significant because American Express lost market share steadily for nearly a decade. That trend seemed to reverse in 1996, when purchase volume on American Express cards increased at a slightly faster pace than volume on its rivals' credit cards.

But the new numbers are especially noteworthy because they include purchases on debit cards, the credit-card look-alikes that deduct money instantly from users' bank accounts. Unlike its biggest rivals, **Visa U.S.A.** and **MasterCard International**, American Express doesn't issue debit cards, putting it at a significant competitive disadvantage as debit-card use skyrockets. The fact that the company, which issues credit and charge cards, has been able to increase its share of the overall card market despite this obstacle suggests the reversal in its fortunes may be more dramatic than it first seemed.

American Express's gains came at the expense of MasterCard, which has been losing market share since 1994. Visa, which holds a commanding lead in the card market, saw its share essentially remain flat, suggesting the rapid growth in its business over the last decade may be slowing.

During the first six months of thi year, American Express's market share in creased to 18.90% from 18.31% at the end of 1996, according to the Nilson Report, an Oxnard, Calif., credit-card research firm. Visa's share slipped to 48.85% from 48.88%, while MasterCard's share dropped to 25.04% from 25.60%. **Morgan Stanley Dean**

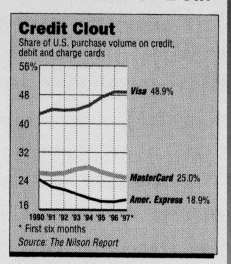

Credit Clout
Share of U.S. purchase volume on credit, debit and charge cards

Visa 48.9%
MasterCard 25.0%
Amer. Express 18.9%

1990 '91 '92 '93 '94 '95 '96 '97*
* First six months
Source: The Nilson Report

Witter Discover & Co., the fourth-ranked credit-card brand, saw its share increase to 6.11% from 6%. The numbers include only spending at merchants, and don't include cash advances, balance transfers, or debit-card withdrawals from automated-teller machines.

Credit-card analysts noted that Visa and MasterCard typically see 56% of their charge volume during the second half of the year, buoyed by holiday shopping, while much of American Express's volume comes from corporate-card users, whose spending is less seasonal. Still, the analysts called American Express's gains impressive.

"You've got to give credit to American Express for overcoming huge obstacles to growth through creative marketing and excellent customer service," said H. Spencer Nilson, publisher of the Nilson Report. "They're making all the others look a little sick.

The data elicited a defiant statement from *V*isa, which vowed its growth would pick-up during the second half of the year.

Project A

Visit a store in your community that doesn't take American Express. Find out why.

CLASSROOM NOTES

ESTOPPEL DEED
MORTGAGE OR TRUST DEED

FOR SA

YOU AND YOUR MONEY

By adding a little extra to your mortgage payment each month, you will pay your mortgage off early and slash your borrowing costs. If you took out a $100,000, 30-year loan today, you could trim about 10 years off the life of the loan and save $70,000 in interest by adding $85 a month to your monthly payment.

15

THE COST OF
HOME
OWNERSHIP

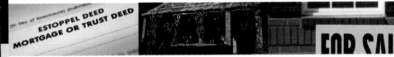

LEARNING UNIT OBJECTIVES

LU 15.1 Types of Mortgages and the Monthly Mortgage Payment

- List the types of mortgages available (*pp. 352–53*).
- Utilize an amortization chart to compute monthly mortgage payments (*p. 354*).
- Calculate the total cost of interest over the life of a mortgage (*p. 354*).

LU 15.2 Amortization Schedule—Breaking Down the Monthly Payment

- Calculate and identify the interest and principal portion of each monthly payment (*p. 355*).
- Prepare an amortization schedule (*p. 356*).

FIGURE 15.1   Types of mortgages available

Loan types	Advantages	Disadvantages
30-year fixed rate mortgage	A predictable monthly payment.	If interest rates fall, you are locked in to higher rate unless you refinance. (Application and appraisal fees along with other closing costs will result.)
15-year fixed rate mortgage	Interest rate lower than 30-year fixed (usually $\frac{1}{4}$ to $\frac{1}{2}$ of a percent). Your equity builds up faster while interest costs are cut by more than one-half.	A larger down payment is needed. Monthly payment will be higher.
Graduated-payment mortgage (GPM)	Easier to qualify for than 30- or 15-year fixed rate. Monthly payments start low and increase over time.	May have higher APR than fixed or variable rates.
Biweekly mortgage	Shortens term loan; saves substantial amount of interest; 26 biweekly payments per year. Builds equity twice as fast.	Not good for those not seeking an early loan payoff.
Adjustable rate mortgage (ARM)	Lower rate than fixed. If rates fall, could be adjusted down without refinancing. Caps available that limit how high rate could go for each adjustment period over term of loan.	Monthly payment could rise if interest rates rise. Riskier than fixed-rate mortgage in which monthly payment is stable.
Home equity loan	Cheap and reliable accessible lines of credit backed by equity in your home. Tax-deductible. Rates can be locked in. Reverse mortgages may be available to those 62 or older.	Could lose home if not paid. No annual or interest caps.

Chapter 15 could save you thousands of dollars! Read the following true story.

    This is how I was able to save $70,121.40 when I purchased my new home. Over the life of the mortgage, a 30-year **fixed rate mortgage** (Figure 15.1) of $100,000 would have cost me $207,235 in interest. My monthly payment would have been $849.99. This would not include taxes, insurance, and so on.

    I chose a **biweekly mortgage** (Figure 15.1). This meant that every two weeks (26 times a year) I would pay the bank $425. By paying every two weeks instead of once a month, my mortgage would be paid off in 23 years instead of 30, and my *savings* on interest would be $70,121.40! Why? When a payment is made every two weeks, the principal is reduced more quickly, which substantially reduces the interest cost.

LEARNING UNIT 15.1   Types of Mortgages and the Monthly Mortgage Payment

© Greg Vaughn/Tony Stone Images.

In the past several years, interest rates have been low, which has caused an increase in home sales. Today, more people are buying homes than are renting homes. The question facing prospective buyers concerns which type of **mortgage** will be best for them. Figure 15.1 lists the types of mortgages available to home buyers. Depending on how interest rates are moving when you purchase a home, you may find one type of mortgage to be the most advantageous for you.

    Have you heard that elderly people who are house-rich and cash-poor can use their home to get cash or monthly income? The Federal Housing Administration makes it possible for older homeowners to take out a **reverse mortgage** on their homes. Under reverse mortgages, senior homeowners borrow against the equity in their property, often getting fixed monthly checks. The debt is repaid only when the homeowners or their estate sells the home.

    Now let's learn how to calculate a monthly mortgage payment and the total cost of loan interest over the life of a mortgage. We will use the following example in our discussion.

EXAMPLE   Gary bought a home for $200,000. He made a 20% down payment. The 9% mortgage is for 30 years (30 × 12 = 360 payments). What are Gary's monthly payment and total cost of interest?

Computing the Monthly Payment for Principal and Interest

To calculate the principal and interest of Gary's **monthly payment,** use the amortization chart in Table 15.1 (p. 353) and the following steps. (Remember that this is the same type of amortization chart used in Chapter 14 for installment loans.)

TABLE 15.1 Amortization chart (mortgage principal and interest per $1,000)

Term in years	$6\frac{1}{2}$%	7%	$7\frac{1}{2}$%	8%	$8\frac{1}{2}$%	9%	$9\frac{1}{2}$%	10%	$10\frac{1}{2}$%	11%	$11\frac{1}{2}$%	$11\frac{3}{4}$%	12%
10	11.36	11.62	11.88	12.14	12.40	12.67	12.94	13.22	13.50	13.78	14.06	14.21	14.35
12	10.02	10.29	10.56	10.83	11.11	11.39	11.67	11.96	12.25	12.54	12.84	12.99	13.14
15	8.72	8.99	9.28	9.56	9.85	10.15	10.45	10.75	11.06	11.37	11.69	11.85	12.01
17	8.12	8.40	8.69	8.99	9.29	9.59	9.90	10.22	10.54	10.86	11.19	11.35	11.52
20	7.46	7.76	8.06	8.37	8.68	9.00	9.33	9.66	9.99	10.33	10.67	10.84	11.02
22	7.13	7.44	7.75	8.07	8.39	8.72	9.05	9.39	9.73	10.08	10.43	10.61	10.78
25	6.76	7.07	7.39	7.72	8.06	8.40	8.74	9.09	9.45	9.81	10.17	10.35	10.54
30	6.33	6.66	7.00	7.34	7.69	8.05	8.41	8.78	9.15	9.53	9.91	10.10	10.29
35	6.05	6.39	6.75	7.11	7.47	7.84	8.22	8.60	8.99	9.37	9.77	9.96	10.16

Computing Monthly Payment by Using an Amortization Chart

Step 1. Divide the amount of the mortgage by $1,000.

Step 2. Look up the rate and term in the amortization chart. At the intersection is the table factor.

Step 3. Multiply Step 1 by Step 2.

For Gary, we calculate the following:

$$\frac{\$160,000 \text{ (amount of mortgage)}}{\$1,000} = 160 \times \$8.05 \text{ (table rate)} = \boxed{\$1,288}$$

So $160,000 is the amount of the mortgage ($200,000 less 20%). The $8.05 is the table factor of 9% for 30 years per $1,000. Since Gary is mortgaging 160 units of $1,000, the factor of $8.05 is multiplied by 160. Remember that the $1,288 payment does not include taxes, insurance, and so on.

What Is the Total Cost of Interest?

We can use the following formula to calculate Gary's total interest cost over the life of the mortgage:

$$\begin{array}{ccc} \text{Total cost} & = & \text{Total of all} & - & \text{Amount of} \\ \text{of interest} & & \text{monthly payments} & & \text{mortgage} \\ \uparrow & & \uparrow & & \uparrow \\ \boxed{\$303,680} = & & \$463,680 & - & \$160,000 \\ & & (\$1,288 \times 360) \end{array}$$

Effects of Interest Rates on Monthly Payment and Total Cost

To show the effect that interest rates have on Gary's monthly payment and to determine his total cost of interest, let's look at Table 15.2. For the table, note that if interest rates rise to 11%, the 2% increase will result in Gary's paying an additional $85,248 in total interest.

For most people, purchasing a home is a major lifetime decision. Many factors must be considered before this decision is made. One of these factors is how to pay for the home. The purpose of this unit is to tell you that being informed about the types of available mortgages can save you thousands of dollars.

In addition to the mortgage payment, buying a home can include the following costs:

- *Closing costs:* When property passes from seller to buyer, **closing costs** may include fees for credit reports, recording costs, lawyer's fees, points, title search, and so on. A **point** is a one-time charge that is a percent of the mortgage. Two points means 2% of the mortgage.

TABLE 15.1 concluded

Term in years	Interest									
	$12\frac{1}{2}$%	$12\frac{3}{4}$%	13%	$13\frac{1}{2}$%	$13\frac{3}{4}$%	14%	$14\frac{1}{2}$%	$14\frac{3}{4}$%	15%	$15\frac{1}{2}$%
10	14.64	14.79	14.94	15.23	15.38	15.53	15.83	15.99	16.14	16.45
12	13.44	13.60	13.75	14.06	14.22	14.38	14.69	14.85	15.01	15.34
15	12.33	12.49	12.66	12.99	13.15	13.32	13.66	13.83	14.00	14.34
17	11.85	12.02	12.19	12.53	12.71	12.88	13.23	13.41	13.58	13.94
20	11.37	11.54	11.72	12.08	12.26	12.44	12.80	12.99	13.17	13.54
22	11.14	11.33	11.51	11.87	12.06	12.24	12.62	12.81	12.99	13.37
25	10.91	11.10	11.28	11.66	11.85	12.04	12.43	12.62	12.81	13.20
30	10.68	10.87	11.07	11.46	11.66	11.85	12.25	12.45	12.65	13.05
35	10.56	10.76	10.96	11.36	11.56	11.76	12.17	12.37	12.57	12.98

TABLE 15.2 Effect of interest rates on monthly payments

	9%	11%	Difference
Monthly payment	$1,288	$1,524.80	$236.80 per month
	(160 × $8.05)	(160 × $9.53)	
Total cost of interest	$303,680	$388,928	$85,248
	($1,288 × 360) − $160,000	($1,524.80 × 360) − $160,000	($236.80 × 360)

- *Escrow amount:* Usually, the lending institution, for its protection, requires that each month $\frac{1}{12}$ of the insurance cost and $\frac{1}{12}$ of the real estate taxes be kept in a special account called the **escrow account.** The monthly balance in this account will change depending on the cost of the insurance and taxes. Interest is paid on escrow accounts.

- *Repairs and maintenance:* This includes paint, wallpaper, landscaping, plumbing, electrical expenses, and so on.

As you can see, the cost of owning a home can be expensive. But remember that all interest costs of your monthly payment and your real estate taxes are deductible. For many, owning a home can have advantages over renting.

LU 15.1  PRACTICE QUIZ

Given: Price of home, $225,000; 20% down payment; 9% interest rate; 25-year mortgage.
Solve for:

1. Monthly payment and total cost of interest over 25 years.
2. If rate fell to 8%, what would be the total decrease in interest cost over the life of the mortgage?

✓ **Solutions**

1. $225,000 − $45,000 = $180,000
   $$\frac{\$180,000}{\$1,000} = 180 \times \$8.40 = \boxed{\$1,512}$$
   $\boxed{\$273,600} =\quad \$453,600 \quad − \$180,000$

   ($1,512 × 300) 25 years × 12 payments per year

2. 8% = $1,389.60 monthly payment
   (180 × $7.72)
   Total interest cost $236,880 = ($1,389.60 × 300) − $180,000
   Savings $\boxed{\$36,720}$ = ($273,600 − $236,880)

LEARNING UNIT 15.2 Amortization Schedule—Breaking Down the Monthly Payment

In Learning Unit 15.1, we saw that over the life of Gary's $160,000 loan, he would pay $303,680 in interest. Now let's use the following steps to determine what portion of Gary's first monthly payment reduces the principal and what portion is interest.

Calculating Interest, Principal, and New Balance of Monthly Payment

Step 1. Calculate the interest for a month (use current principal): Interest = Principal × Rate × Time.

Step 2. Calculate the amount used to reduce the principal: Principal reduction = Monthly payment − Interest (Step 1).

Step 3. Calculate the new principal: Current principal − Reduction of principal (Step 2) = New principal.

Step 1.   Interest (I) = Principal (P) × Rate (R) × Time (T)

$$\$1,200 = \$160,000 \times .09 \times \frac{1}{12}$$

Step 2.   The reduction of the $160,000 principal each month is equal to the payment less interest. So we can calculate Gary's new principal balance at the end of month 1 as follows:

Monthly payment at 9% (from Table 15.1)	$1,288 (160 × $8.05)
− Interest for first month	− 1,200
= Principal reduction	$ 88

Step 3.   As the years go by, the interest portion of the payment decreases and the principal portion increases.

Principal balance	$160,000
Principal reduction	− 88
Balance of principal	$159,912

Let's do month 2:

Step 1.   Interest = Principal × Rate × Time

$$= \$159,912 \times .09 \times \frac{1}{12}$$

$$= \$1,199.34$$

Step 2.

$1,288.00 monthly payment
− 1,199.34 interest for month 2
$ 88.66 principal reduction

Step 3.

$159,912.00 principal balance
−   88.66 principal reduction
$159,823.34 balance of principal

Note that in month 2, interest costs drop 66 cents ($1,200.00 − $1,199.34). So in 2 months, Gary has reduced his mortgage balance by $176.66 ($88.00 + $88.66). After 2 months, Gary has paid a total interest of $2,399.34 ($1,200.00 + $1,199.34).

Example of an Amortization Schedule

The partial **amortization schedule** given in Table 15.3 shows the breakdown of Gary's monthly payment. Note the amount that goes toward reducing the principal and toward payment of actual interest. Also note how the outstanding balance of the loan is reduced. After 7 months, Gary still owes $159,369.97. Often when you take out a mortgage loan, you will receive an amortization schedule from the company that holds your mortgage.

   The Wall Street Journal clipping "A 125% Solution to Card Debt Stirs Worry" (p. 356) introduces a new type of mortgage—a 125% second mortgage. Second mortgages are similar to home equity loans (see Table 15.1). Read the clipping and learn how a South Carolina couple used a 125% second mortgage loan to pay off their credit cards and sharply reduce their monthly payments. The clipping explains why this option has a serious downside.

TABLE 15.3   Partial amortization schedule

		Monthly payment, $1,288		
Payment number	Principal (current)	Interest	Principal reduction	Balance of principal
1	$160,000.00	$1,200.00	$88.00	$159,912.00
		$\left(\$160{,}000 \times .09 \times \dfrac{1}{12}\right)$	($1,288 − $1,200)	($160,000 − $88)
2	$159,912.00	$1,199.34	$88.66	$159,823.34
		$\left(\$159{,}912 \times .09 \times \dfrac{1}{12}\right)$	($1,288 − $1,199.34)	($159,912 − $88.66)
3	$159,823.34	$1,198.68	$89.32	$159,734.02
4	$159,734.02	$1,198.01	$89.99	$159,644.03
5	$159,644.03	$1,197.33	$90.67	$159,553.36
6	$159,553.36	$1,196.65	$91.35	$159,462.01
7	$159,462.01	$1,195.97*	$92.04	$159,369.97

*Off 1 cent due to rounding.

A 125% Solution to Card Debt Stirs Worry

Second-Mortgage Trend May Signal Economic Trouble

By FRED R. BLEAKLEY
Staff Reporter of THE WALL STREET JOURNAL

Vincent and Evelyn Favazzo of Moncks Corner, S.C., used their 10 credit cards for just about everything: to pay medical bills, buy presents for their new grandchild, purchase a camcorder and take a few road trips to Ohio.

Before they knew it, they owed $20,000, and the minimum monthly payments were taking a big bite out of Vincent's salary as an auto mechanic.

"We could never get those lousy things paid off," recalls Mr. Favazzo. Then he heard about a 125% second-mortgage loan that could be used to pay off credit-card debt and sharply reduce monthly payments, even for homeowners who have little or no equity in their homes.

The 125% loan — so called because most lenders allow borrowers to take a second mortgage that, when combined with a first mortgage, can total as much as 125% of a home's appraised value — reduced the Favazzo's monthly payments for card debt and another loan that also was paid off to $500 from $800.

But they also now owe $82,000 on a home valued at $70,000.

It's a sign of the times that 125% loans have become the hot product in consumer lending. After a decadelong spending spree that boosted consumer credit-card debt outstanding to an astonishing $526 billion now from $174 billion in 1988, many consumers are now tapped out and looking for some relief. According to Gary Gordon of PaineWebber, lenders are expected to make about $10 billion of 125% loans this year, up from $4 billion last year and $1 billion in 1995.

"For consumers who own homes it's

How the 125% Home Mortgage Works

SECOND MORTGAGE

Consumer has home valued at $100,000 and mortgage of $80,000. He takes out a second mortgage of $45,000 to pay off $30,000 in credit-card debt and have $13,000 in extra spending money after loan fees.

MORE THAN 100% OWED

That gives him a total mortgage of $125,000, which is 125% the value of the home.

M.E. Cohen

LOWER PAYMENTS

But it also gives him lower monthly payments ($300-$400 vs. $700) because the credit-card debt had higher interest rates and a faster paydown schedule than the new mortgage. And it gives him a zero balance on his credit cards, freeing them up for more spending.

one more way to keep spending," says Maury Harris, chief economist at Mr. Gordon's firm. Not only do they get money to pay off card debt, but also the lower monthly payments (due to the longer maturity and lower finance costs of the second mortgage) provide new buying power. Plus, there's a tax break, since most mortgage interest payments are deductible while those for credit cards are not.

But what may be good for consumers with excellent credit records like the Fa-

vazzos may be a worrisome sign of trouble brewing for the economy. For one thing, these risky loans break the time-honored mortgage-lending standards that require banks to lend no more than 80% of a home's appraised value. With the 125% loan, borrowers are, in effect, under water without enough value in the collateral to pay off the loan in case of trouble.

LU 15.2 PRACTICE QUIZ

Prepare an amortization schedule for first three periods for the following: mortgage, $100,000; 11%; 30 years.

$100,000 mortgage; monthly payment, $953 (100 × $9.53)

✓ **Solutions**

| Payment number | Principal (current) | Portion to— | | |
		Interest	Principal reduction	Balance of principal
1	$100,000	$916.67	$36.33	$99,963.67
		$\left(\$100,000 \times .11 \times \dfrac{1}{12}\right)$	($953 − $916.67)	($100,000 − $36.33)
2	$99,963.67	$916.33	$36.67	$99,927.00
		$\left(\$99,963.67 \times .11 \times \dfrac{1}{12}\right)$	($953 − $916.33)	($99,963.67 − $36.67)
3	$99,927	$916.00	$37.00	$99,890.00
		$\left(\$99,927 \times .11 \times \dfrac{1}{12}\right)$	($953 − $916)	($99,927 − $37)

Chapter Organizer and Reference Guide

Topic	Key point, procedure, formula	Example(s) to illustrate situation
Computing monthly mortgage payment, p. 353	Based on per $1,000 Table 15.1: $$\dfrac{\text{Amount of mortgage}}{\$1,000} \times \text{Table rate}$$	Use Table 15.1: 12% on $60,000 mortgage for 30 years. $$\dfrac{\$60,000}{\$1,000} = 60 \times \$10.29$$ $$= \$617.40$$
Calculating total interest cost, p. 353	Total of all monthly payments − Amount of mortgage	Using example above: 30 years = 360 (payments) × $617.40 \dfrac{}{} $222,264 − 60,000 \dfrac{}{} $162,264 (mortgage interest over life of mortgage)
Amortization schedule, p. 355	$I = P \times R \times T$ $\left(I \text{ for month} = P \times R \times \dfrac{1}{12}\right)$ $\dfrac{\text{Principal}}{\text{reduction}} = \dfrac{\text{Monthly}}{\text{payment}} - \text{Interest}$ $\dfrac{\text{New}}{\text{principal}} = \dfrac{\text{Current}}{\text{principal}} - \dfrac{\text{Reduction of}}{\text{principal}}$	Using same example:

Amortization schedule example table:

| Payment number | Portion to— | | |
	Interest	Principal reduction	Balance of principal
1	$600	$17.40	$59,982.60
	$\left(\$60,000 \times .12 \times \dfrac{1}{12}\right)$	$\left(\begin{array}{c}\$617.40 \\ -\,\$600.00\end{array}\right)$	$\left(\begin{array}{c}\$60,000.00 \\ -\,\$17.40\end{array}\right)$
2	$599.83	$17.57	$59,965.03
	$\left(\$59,982.60 \times .12 \times \dfrac{1}{12}\right)$	$\left(\begin{array}{c}\$617.40 \\ -\,\$599.83\end{array}\right)$	$\left(\begin{array}{c}\$59,982.60 \\ -\,\$17.57\end{array}\right)$

Key terms

Adjustable rate mortgage, (ARM), *p. 352*
Amortization schedule, *p. 355*
Biweekly mortgage, *p. 352*
Closing costs, *p. 353*

Escrow account, *p. 354*
Fixed rate mortgage, *p. 352*
Graduated-payment mortgages (GPM), *p. 352*
Home equity loan, *p. 352*

Monthly payment, *p. 352*
Mortgages, *p. 352*
Points, *p. 353*
Reverse mortgage, *p. 352*

**Critical Thinking
Discussion Questions**

1. Explain the advantages and disadvantages of the following loan types: 30-year fixed rate, 15-year fixed rate, graduated-payment mortgage, biweekly mortgage, adjustable rate mortgage, and home equity loan. Why might a bank require a home buyer to establish an escrow account?

2. How is an amortization schedule calculated? Is there a best time to refinance a mortgage?

3. What is a point? Is paying points worth the cost?

4. Would you ever consider a 125% solution to pay off your credit card balance? Defend your position.

DRILL PROBLEMS

Complete the following amortization chart by using Table 15.1.

	Selling price of home	Down payment	Principal (loan)	Rate of interest	Years	Payment per $1,000	Monthly mortgage payment
15–1.	$192,000	$20,000	$172,000	$7\frac{1}{2}\%$	20	$8.06	$1,386.32 (172 × $8.06)
15–2.	$ 70,000	$12,000	$ 58,000	11%	30	$9.53	$ 552.74 (58 × $9.53)
15–3.	$275,000	$50,000	$225,000	9%	35	$7.84	$1,764 (225 × $7.84)

15–4. What is total cost of interest in Problem 15–2?

$552.74 × 360 payments = $198,986.40
        − 58,000.00 (amount of mortgage)
        $140,986.40

15–5. If the interest rate rises to 13% in Problem 15–2, what is the total cost of interest?

Table factor 13%, 30 years = $ 11.07
                              × 58
                         $ 642.06
                         × 360 payments
        $231,141.60 − $58,000 = $173,141.60

At 13% $173,141.60
At 11%   − 140,986.40
          $ 32,155.20

Complete the following:

	Selling price	Down payment	Amount of mortgage	Rate	Years	Monthly payment	First payment broken down into– Interest	First payment broken down into– Principal	Balance at end of month
15–6.	$170,000	$20,000	$150,000	8%	25	$1,158	$1,000	$158	$149,842

150 × $7.72 = $1,158; $150,000 × .08 × $\frac{1}{12}$ = $1,000   ($150,000 − $158)

15–7.	$199,000	$40,000	$159,000	$12\frac{1}{2}\%$	35	$1,679.04	$1,656.25	$22.79	$158,977.21

159 × $10.56 = $1,679.04; $159,000 × .125 × $\frac{1}{12}$ = $1,656.25   ($159,000 − $22.79)

15–8. Bob Jones bought a new log cabin for $70,000 at 11% interest for 30 years. Please prepare an amortization schedule for first 3 periods.

	Payment number	Portion to– Interest	Portion to– Principal	Balance of loan outstanding
$70,000 × .11 × $\frac{1}{12}$ = $641.67	1	$641.67	$25.43 ($667.10 − $641.67)	$69,974.57 ($70,000 − $25.43)
$69,974.57 × .11 × $\frac{1}{12}$ = $641.43	2	$641.43	$25.67	$69,948.90
$69,948.90 × .11 × $\frac{1}{12}$ = $641.20	3	$641.20	$25.90	$69,923.00

Monthly payment is $667.10 by Table 15.1 (70 × $9.53)

WORD PROBLEMS

15–9. On November 30, 1997, the Chicago *Sun-Times* reported that the average price of both new and existing houses has increased. San Francisco tops the list at $295,500. Denver was number 10 at $186,800. Your company has an office in both cities, and you may be transferred to one of these cities. Both houses require 20% down, $8\frac{1}{2}\%$ interest, and a 30-year fixed rate mortgage. What would be the monthly payments in each city?

San Francisco: $295,500
              × .20
        $ 59,100 down payment

$295,500 − $59,100 = $\frac{$236,400}{$1,000}$
        = 236.40 × $7.69 = $1,817.92

Denver: $186,800
       × .20
     $ 37,360 down payment

$186,800 − $37,360 = $\frac{$149,440}{$1,000}$
        = 149.44 × $7.69 = $1,149.19

15–10. The October/November 1997 issue of *Your Money* contained an article called "Points or No Points." If you take out a 30-year $100,000 fixed rate loan at $7\frac{1}{2}$ % with no points, your monthly payment will be $700. However, if you add two points ($2,000), the rate could drop to 7%. What will be your monthly savings? What will be the total savings over the term of the loan?

$$\frac{\$100,000}{\$1,000} = 100 \times \$6.66 = \$666 \text{ monthly payment}$$

$$\begin{array}{r} \$ \quad 700 \\ - \ 666 \\ \hline \$ \quad\ 34 \text{ savings every month} \\ \times \ 360 \\ \hline \$12,240 \text{ total savings} \end{array}$$

15–11. Bill Allen bought a home in Arlington, Texas, for $108,000. He put down 25% and obtained a mortgage for 30 years at 11%. What is Bill's monthly payment? What is the total interest cost of the loan?

$$\$108,000 - \$27,000 = \frac{\$81,000}{\$1,000} = 81 \times \$9.53 = \$771.93$$

$$\$771.93 \times 360 = \$277,894.80 - \$81,000.00 = \$196,894.80 \text{ total interest}$$

15–12. If in Problem 15–11 the rate of interest is 14%, what is the difference in interest cost?

$$81 \times \$11.85 = \$959.85 \times 360 = \$345,546.00$$

$$\$345,546 - \$81,000 = \$264.546 - \$196,894.80 = \$67,651.20 \text{ difference in interest cost}$$

15–13. Mike Jones bought a new split-level home for $150,000 with 20% down. He decided to use Victory Bank for his mortgage. They were offering $13\frac{3}{4}$% for 25-year mortgages. Provide Mike with an amortization schedule for the first three periods.

Payment number	Portion to– Interest	Portion to– Principal	Balance of loan outstanding
1	$1,375.00	$47.00	$119,953.00
		($1,422 − $1,375)	($120,000 − $47.00)
2	$1,374.46	$47.54	$119,905.46
		($1,422 − $1,374.46)	($119,953 − $47.54)
3	$1,373.92	$48.08	$119,857.38

Monthly payment is:

$$\frac{\$120,000}{\$1,000} = 120 \times \$11.85 = \$1,422$$

$$\$120,000 \times .1375 \times \frac{1}{12} = \$1,375.00$$

$$\$119,953.00 \times .1375 \times \frac{1}{12} = \$1,374.46$$

$$\$119,905.46 \times .1375 \times \frac{1}{12} = \$1,373.92$$

15–14. Harriet Marcus is concerned about the financing of a home. She saw a small cottage that sells for $50,000. If she puts 20% down, what will her monthly payment be at **(a)** 25 years, $11\frac{1}{2}$%; **(b)** 25 years, $12\frac{1}{2}$%; **(c)** 25 years, $13\frac{1}{2}$%; **(d)** 25 years, 15%? What is the total cost of interest over the cost of the loan for each assumption? **(e)** What is the savings in interest cost between $11\frac{1}{2}$% and 15%? **(f)** If Harriet uses 30 years instead of 25 for both $11\frac{1}{2}$% and 15%, what is the difference in interest?

a. $40 \times \$10.17 = \$406.80 \times 300 = \$122,040 - \$40,000 = \$\ 82,040$

b. $40 \times \$10.91 = \$436.40 \times 300 = \$130,920 - \$40,000 = \$\ 90,920$

c. $40 \times \$11.66 = \$466.40 \times 300 = \$139,920 - \$40,000 = \$\ 99,920$

d. $40 \times \$12.81 = \$512.40 \times 300 = \$153,720 - \$40,000 = \$113,720$

e. $\$113,720 - \$82,040 = \$31,680$ difference

f. $40 \times \$12.65 = \$506 \quad\ \times 360 = \$182,160 - \$40,000 = \$142,160$

   $40 \times \$\ 9.91 = \$396.40 \times 360 = \$142,704 - \$40,000 = - \ 102,704$

   $\underline{\hspace{5cm}}$

   $\$\ 39,456$ difference

15–15. The August 1997 issue of *Money* reported on the leading borrowing deals in Chicago: "Dear *Money* reader, here are the leading borrowing deals in Chicago: Fixed rate 30-year mortgage from LaSalle Home Mortgage, 7.38%, 5% down, 2.75 points." What will be the amount paid for points if the home lists for $150,000?

$$\begin{array}{r} \$150,000.00 \\ \times \ \ .05 \\ \hline \$ \quad 7,500.00 \text{ down payment} \end{array}$$

$$\begin{array}{r} \$150,000.00 \\ - \ 7,500.00 \\ \hline \$142,500.00 \text{ mortgage} \\ \times \ .0275 \\ \hline \$ \quad 3,918.75 \end{array}$$

15–16. The November 1997 *Kiplinger's Personal Finance Magazine* advertised "Vacation Homes. Mammoth Lakes, California, 2-bedroom, 2-bath loft condo. Listing price $189,000 with 20% down payment and a 30-year fixed rate mortgage at $7\frac{1}{2}$%. Property taxes $189 a month and condo fee $288 a month." What will be your monthly payment, including property taxes and condo fee?

$189,000
$\underline{\times\ .20}$
$\ 37,800$ down payment

$\dfrac{\$151,200}{\$1,000} = 151.2 \times \$7.00 = \$1,058.40$
$\qquad\qquad\qquad\qquad\qquad + 189.00$
$\qquad\qquad\qquad\qquad\qquad \underline{+ 288.00}$
$\qquad\qquad\qquad\qquad\qquad \$1,535.40$

CHALLENGE PROBLEMS

15–17. The following advertisement ran in the November 29, 1997, Chicago *Sun-Times:* "New Homes, $3,490 down, 30-year fixed rate, 3% down on Calumet Park Townhouses, $7\frac{1}{2}$% mortgage." **(a)** What is the price of the townhouse (round to the nearest dollar)? **(b)** What will be your total interest when the townhouse is paid? **(c)** Provide an amortization schedule for the first two periods.

a. $\dfrac{\$3,490}{.03} = \$116,333$

b. $116,333
$\underline{- 3,490}$
$112,843$ amount of mortgage

c. $112,843 \times .075 \times \dfrac{1}{12} = \$705.27$ interest
$\$789.88$
$\underline{- 705.27}$
$\ 84.61$ to principal

$112,843.00 - \$84.61 = \$112,758.39$

$112,758.39 \times .075 \times \dfrac{1}{12} = \$704.74$
$\$789.88$
$\underline{- 704.74}$
$\ 85.14$ to principal
$112,758.39 - \$85.14 = \$112,673.25$

$\dfrac{\$112,843}{\$1,000} = \$112.84$ units $\times \$7.00 = \$\qquad 789.88$ monthly payment
$\qquad\qquad\qquad\qquad\qquad\qquad \underline{\times\ 360}$ (30 $\times$ 12)
$\qquad\qquad\qquad\qquad\qquad\qquad \$284,356.80$
$\qquad\qquad\qquad\qquad\qquad\qquad \underline{- 112,843.00}$
$\qquad\qquad\qquad\qquad\qquad\qquad \$171,513.80$ interest

15–18. Sharon Fox decided to buy a home in Marblehead, Massachusetts, for $275,000. Her bank requires a 30% down payment. Sue Willis, an attorney, has notified Sharon that besides the 30% down payment there will be the following additional costs:

Recording of the deed	$ 30.00
A credit and appraisal report	155.00
Preparation of appropriate documents	48.00

A transfer tax of 1.8% of the purchase price and a loan origination fee of 2.5% of the mortgage amount

Assume a 30-year mortgage at a rate of 10%.
a. What is the initial amount of cash Sharon will need?
b. What is her monthly payment?
c. What is the total cost of interest over the life of the mortgage?

a. Down payment $\quad$ $275,000 \times .30 = \$82,500$
$\quad$ Mortgage $\qquad\quad$ $275,000 - \$82,500 = \$192,500$
$\quad$ Transfer tax $\qquad$ $.018 \times \$275,000 = \$4,950$
$\quad$ Loan origination fee $\ .025 \times \$192,500 = \$4,812.50$
b. Monthly payment: 30-year, 10%, 8.78
$\quad \dfrac{\$192,500}{1,000} \times \$8.78 = \$1,690.15$ per month
c. $360 \times \$1,690.15 = \quad \$608,454$
$\qquad\qquad\qquad\qquad \underline{- 192,500}$
$\qquad\qquad\qquad\qquad\quad \$415.954$

Cash needed	$82,500.00
Recording of the deed	30.00
Credit and appraisal report	155.00
Document preparation	48.00
Transfer tax	4,950.00
Loan origination fee	4,812.50
	$92,495.50

SUMMARY PRACTICE TEST

1. Mike Kaminsky bought a home for $170,000 with a down payment of $10,000. His rate of interest is $8\frac{1}{2}\%$ for 35 years. Calculate his **(a)** monthly payment, **(b)** first payment, broken down into interest and principal, and **(c)** balance of mortgage at the end of the month. *(pp. 353, 354)*

   a. $\dfrac{\$160,000}{\$1,000} = 160 \times \$7.47 = \$1,195.20$

   b. $\$160,000 \times .085 \times \dfrac{1}{12} = \$1,133.33$ interest; $61.87   ($1,195.20 - $1,133.33)

   c. Balance of mortgage at end of month: $159,938.13   ($160,000 - $61.87)

2. Jay Horton bought a home in Alabama for $110,000. He put down 30% and obtained a mortgage for 30 years at 8%. What are Jay's monthly payment and the total interest cost of the loan? *(p. 353)*

   $110,000 - $33,000 = $77,000 $77 \times $7.34 = $565.18 $565.18 \times 360 = $203,464.80
    − 77,000.00
    $126,464.80

3. June Leahy is concerned about the financing of a home. She saw a small cape that sells for $70,000. If she puts 20% down, what will her monthly payment be at **(a)** 25 years, $8\frac{1}{2}\%$; **(b)** 25 years, 9%; **(c)** 25 years, 10%; and **(d)** 25 years, 11%? What is the total cost of interest over the cost of the loan for each assumption? *(p. 355)*

   a. $56 \times $8.06 = $451.36 \times 300 = $135,408 - $56,000 = $ 79,408
   b. $56 \times $8.40 = $470.40 \times 300 = $141,120 - $56,000 = $ 85,120 ⎫
   c. $56 \times $9.09 = $509.04 \times 300 = $152,712 - $56,000 = $ 96,712 ⎬ Total cost of interest
   d. $56 \times $9.81 = $549.36 \times 300 = $164,808 - $56,000 = $108,808 ⎭

4. Ann Ling bought a home for $165,000 with a down payment of $15,000. Her rate of interest is $8\frac{1}{2}\%$ for 25 years. Calculate Ling's payment per $1,000 and her monthly mortgage payment. *(p. 353)*

   $\dfrac{\$150,000}{\$1,000} = 150 \times \$8.06 = \$1,209$

5. Using Problem 4, calculate the total cost of interest for Ann Ling. *(p. 355)*

   $1,209 \times 300 = $362,700 - $150,000 = $212,700 interest cost

A GROUP PROJECT   Defend or reject the following business math issue based on the *Kiplinger's Personal Finance Magazine* article below:

HOME

It's Not Too Late to Refinance

▶ **You could still cash in even if you missed the very lowest rates.**   By Elizabeth Razzi

So you're not Quick Draw McGraw when it comes to refinancing your mortgage: Maybe you missed out on a 30-year, fixed-rate loan under 6.5% this fall. But don't hang up your holster yet—you still have a clear shot at a better deal.

Homeowners trying to refinance in mid October sampled the stressful life of a bond trader. Rates—which for weeks had been lolling about at record-low levels of 6.5% on average for a 30-year mortgage with one point—shot back up half a point in two frenzied days as the throes of the international bond market created an increase in mortgage rates here at home. "Rates were rising so fast you couldn't get your people locked in fast enough," says Lore Cook, a mortgage broker in Pleasanton, Cal.

But a week later rates were headed back down, giving brokers and borrowers some relief. "When rates are going up, people are flooding to the closing table. When rates are coming down, people are holding off, trying to find the bottom of the market," says Bob Brown, an executive vice-president at Countrywide Home Loans.

Tim Winkler, a plant comptroller in Janesville, Wis., isn't worried about missing the bottom. He's a refinancing veteran, biding his time, waiting for his next chance to come along. If it doesn't, it doesn't.

Winkler bought his house in May 1997 with a 30-year, fixed-rate mortgage at about 8.3%. In July of this year he refinanced to an 18-year loan at 7.2%. The closing costs, which he rolled over into the new loan, equaled one month's mortgage payment. His payment actually went up about $30, but he stood to build his equity much faster.

When Winkler saw rates in his area hit 6.2% this fall, he started thinking about another refinance—maybe into a 15- or even a ten-year loan. But rates started to creep up, so

he held off. "It's not keeping me awake at night," he says.

DOES IT MAKE SENSE?
Fortunately, you don't have to worry about timing the bottom, either. The numbers can still make sense—especially if your rate is above 7.5%. "Refinancing to a rate between 6.5% and 7% is still a pretty good deal," says Frank Nothaft, deputy chief economist at Freddie Mac, which buys mortgages for resale on the bond markets. He expects rates to stay in that range into the new year.

You're a candidate to refinance if you can lower your monthly payment and recover the closing costs before you move—or refinance again. Take

the total cost of the refinance and divide it by your monthly savings. That tells you how many months it will take to recover your costs. What if you have a close call—say, a $200,000 30-year loan with a fixed rate of 7.5%? Should you refinance to 6.8% with no points and $2,600 in fees, which you'll roll over into your new loan amount? Refinancing will lower your monthly payment by $77—and it will take 34 months to break even—so maybe you'll want to wait for a lower rate. (The calculators at www.kiplinger.com can help you figure out your own break-even point.)

STEPHEN WEBSTER

Business Math Issue

The lawyers are the only ones who really win in refinancing.

1. List the key points of the article and information to support your position.
2. Write a group defense of your position using math calculations to support your view.

BUSINESS MATH SCRAPBOOK
Putting Your Skills to Work

A Loan Forever? No, It May Make Sense To Use Savings to Pay Down Mortgage

Maybe this is the year to put it on the house.

Spooked by the stock market? Disenchanted with lowly bond yields? Consider taking some of your investment dollars and using them to pay down your mortgage.

Admittedly, making extra-mortgage payments won't earn you dazzling returns. If your mortgage rate is 8%, that's your effective pretax rate of return on every additional dollar you add to your mortgage check.

Doesn't seem like much? Sure, it can't compare with the 11%-a-year total return for stocks since year-end 1925, and it pales beside the 31% annual stock-market gain of the past three calendar years, as calculated by Chicago's Ibbotson Associates.

But making extra-mortgage payments can be a smart move for conservative investors who would otherwise buy bonds, money-market funds and certificates of deposit.

The case for making extra-mortgage payments has been bolstered by the recent drop in interest rates, which has squeezed yields on bonds and other conservative investments. In fact, interest rates have fallen so much that many folks are seizing the chance to refinance their mortgages and lock in lower rates.

"Anybody who has a mortgage rate above 8¼% should look at refinancing," says Keith Gumbinger, a vice president with HSH Associates, a mortgage-information provider in Butler, N.J.

What if your interest rate is 8% or below? "You really have to look very hard at the costs" that you would incur in a refinancing, Mr. Gumbinger says.

For those homeowners who find it's not worth refinancing, extra-mortgage payments offer an alternative way of eliminating costly mortgage debt. By adding just a few dollars to each monthly check, you can save thousands of dollars in interest over the life of your mortgage.

Suppose you just borrowed $200,000 using a 30-year, 7½% fixed-rate mortgage that requires a $1,400 monthly payment. By adding only $25 to each check, for a total of $8,425 over the life of the loan, you would save $22,500 in interest and pay off your mortgage almost two years early.

Adding a few dollars to the monthly check can also make sense if you have an adjustable-rate mortgage. But with an ARM, your extra $25 won't shorten the length of the loan. Instead, the additional dollars will lead to lower required monthly payments.

"It's almost always a good time to pay down your mortgage," Mr. Gumbinger argues. "It's a solid, 100%-guaranteed investment."

Still, before you tack an extra $25, $50 or $100 onto the next mortgage check, make sure you have already made the most of other options that promise a higher return. For instance, instead of paying down your mortgage, you are much better off getting rid of credit-card debt. Your cards may be costing you 18% a year and, unlike mortgage debt, the interest isn't tax-deductible.

Similarly, before you make any extra-mortgage payments, you should invest the maximum possible in your employer's retirement-savings plan and fully fund a regular or Roth individual retirement account.

Once you have paid off high-cost debt and made full use of tax-sheltered retirement accounts, you may have additional money that you want to save. At that point, you might use the extra money to pay down your mortgage or, alternatively, you could use the cash to buy investments in a regular taxable account.

So which should it be? It all depends on what investments you would buy. If the choice is between stocks in a taxable account and paying down the mortgage, I would opt for stocks. Yeah, stocks may be richly valued. But over the long haul, you should still earn higher returns than you would with extra-mortgage payments.

That's not the case, however, with bonds or CDs. If the choice is between paying down an 8% mortgage or buying a bond with a 6% yield, I would favor making extra-mortgage payments.

But what about losing all that tax-deductible mortgage interest, you cry? True, if you are in the 28% federal income-tax bracket, every $1 of interest is saving you 28 cents in taxes (and maybe more if the interest is deductible at the state level), so the real cost of that 8% mortgage is just 5.76%.

That's less than the 6% you will get on the bond. But remember, the bond is also taxable. After paying tax at 28% on the 6% interest, you will be left with just 4.32%—far less than the 5.76% you earn with extra-mortgage payments. Unless bond prices rally, you will get much better results by paying down your mortgage.

"I would rather buy paper from myself that's costing me 7% or 8% than buy paper from the government that's paying less than 6%," says Michael Maloon, a financial planner in San Ramon, Calif. "As rates drop, paying down your mortgage makes more and more sense."

Moreover, making extra-mortgage payments is remarkably easy. You don't need to conduct any investment research, as you would before buying a mutual fund or a bond. Instead, to save thousands in interest, all you have to do is write a slightly larger check next time you pay your mortgage.

Roman Scott

Project A

Do you think paying down a mortgage is really such a good idea? Defend your position.

 See text Web site (www.mhhe.com/slater) and *The Business Math Internet Resource Guide.*

16

HOW TO READ, ANALYZE, AND INTERPRET FINANCIAL REPORTS

LEARNING UNIT OBJECTIVES

LU 16.1 Balance Sheet—Report as of a Particular Date

- Explain the purpose and the key items on the balance sheet *(pp. 368–70)*.
- Explain and complete vertical and horizontal analysis *(pp. 370–73)*.

LU 16.2 Income Statement—Report for a Specific Period of Time

- Explain the purpose and the key items on the income statement *(pp. 373–75)*.
- Explain and complete vertical and horizontal analysis *(pp. 376–77)*.

LU 16.3 Trend and Ratio Analysis

- Explain and complete a trend analysis *(p. 376)*.
- List, explain, and calculate key financial ratios *(p. 378)*.

Chairman of Pepsi Bottler Quits; Accounting Errors Are Discovered

By ROBERT FRANK
Staff Reporter of THE WALL STREET JOURNAL

The chairman of **Pepsi-Cola Puerto Rico Bottling** Co. resigned after the company discovered "accounting irregularities" that will force it to restate recent earnings.

The bottling company, which makes and distributes **PepsiCo** Inc. soft drinks in Puerto Rico, said the accounting errors resulted in "substantial understatement of certain expenses" and will result in operating losses for its last two quarters.

The Wall Street Journal clipping "Chairman of Pepsi Bottler Quits; Accounting Errors Are Discovered" illustrates the importance of accounting in today's reporting process. As you will see in this chapter, an understatement of expenses overstates the reported earnings or net income of a company. This overstatement presents a false picture of the company's financial position.

In this chapter we focus our attention on analyzing financial reports. Business owners must understand their financial statements to avoid financial difficulties. This includes knowing how to read, analyze, and interpret financial reports.

The two key financial reports that we discuss in this chapter are the *balance sheet* (shows a company's financial condition at a particular date) and the *income statement* (shows a company's profitability over a time period).[1]

LEARNING UNIT 16.1   Balance Sheet—Report as of a Particular Date

The **balance sheet** gives a financial picture of what a company is worth as of a particular date, usually at the end of a month or year. This report lists (1) how much the company owns (assets), (2) how much the company owes (liabilities), and (3) how much the owner (owner's equity) is worth. So we have the following formula:

Assets − Liabilities = Owner's equity

Like all formulas, the items on both sides of the equal sign must balance.

Sharon Hoogstraten.

By reversing the above formula, we have the following common balance sheet layout:

$$\boxed{\text{Assets} = \text{Liabilities} + \text{Owner's equity}}$$

To introduce you to the balance sheet, let's assume that you collect baseball cards and decide to open a baseball card shop. As the owner of The Card Shop, your investment, or owner's equity, is called **capital.** Since your business is small, your balance sheet is short. After the first year of operation, The Card Shop balance sheet looks like this (p. 369). The heading gives the name of the company, title of the report, and date of the report. Note how the totals of both sides of the balance sheet are the same. This is true of all balance sheets.

_____

[1]The third key financial report is the statement of cash flows. We do not discuss this statement. For more information on the statement of cash flows, check your accounting text.

	THE CARD SHOP Balance Sheet December 31, 2001		Report as of a particular date	
Assets		**Liabilities**		
Cash	$ 3,000	Accounts payable		$2,500
Merchandise inventory (baseball cards)	4,000	**Owner's Equity**		
Equipment	3,000	E. Slott, capital		7,500
Total assets	$10,000	Total liabilities and owner's equity		$10,000

Capital does not mean cash. It is the owner's investment in the company.

We can take figures from the balance sheet of The Card Shop and use our first formula to determine how much the business is worth:

$$\text{Assets} - \text{Liabilities} = \text{Owner's equity (capital)}$$

$$\$10,000 - \$2,500 = \$7,500$$

Since you are the single owner of The Card Shop, your business is a **sole proprietorship.** If a business has two or more owners, it is a **partnership.** A **corporation** has many owners or stockholders, and the equity of these owners is called **stockholders' equity.** Now let's study the balance sheet elements of a corporation.

Elements of the Balance Sheet

The format and contents of all corporation balance sheets are similar. Figure 16.1 shows the balance sheet of Mool Company. As you can see, the formula Assets = Liabilities + Stockholders' equity (we have a corporation in this example) is also the framework of this balance sheet.

To help you understand the three main balance sheet groups (assets, liabilities, and stockholders' equity) and their elements, we have labeled them in Figure 16.1. An explanation of these groups and their elements follows. Do not try to memorize the elements. Just try to understand their meaning. Think of Figure 16.1 as a reference aid. You will find that the more you work with balance sheets, the easier it is for you to understand them.

1. **Assets:** Things of value *owned* by a company (economic resources of the company) that can be measured and expressed in monetary terms.

FIGURE 16.1   Balance sheet

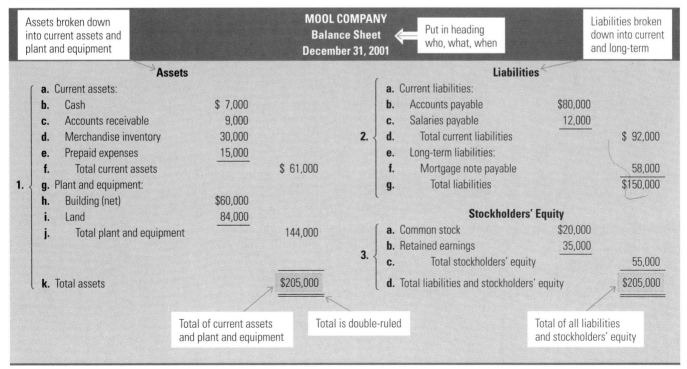

    a. **Current assets:** Assets that companies consume or convert to cash *within 1 year* or a normal operating cycle.

    b. **Cash:** Total cash in checking accounts, savings accounts, and on hand.

    c. **Accounts receivable:** Money *owed* to a company by customers from sales on account (buy now, pay later).

    d. **Merchandise inventory:** Cost of goods in stock for resale to customers.

    e. **Prepaid expenses:** The purchases of a company are assets until they expire (insurance or rent) or are consumed (supplies).

    f. **Total current assets:** Total of all assets that the company will consume or convert to cash within 1 year.

    g. **Plant and equipment:** Assets that will last longer than 1 year. These assets are used in the operation of the company.

    h. **Building (net):** The cost of the building minus the depreciation that has accumulated. Usually, balance sheets show this as "Building less accumulated depreciation." In Chapter 17 we discuss accumulated depreciation in greater detail.

    i. **Land:** An asset that does not depreciate, but it can increase or decrease in value.

    j. **Total plant and equipment:** Total of building and land, including machinery and equipment.

    k. **Total assets:** Total of current assets and plant and equipment.

2. **Liabilities:** Debts or obligations of the company.

    a. **Current liabilities:** Debts or obligations of the company that are *due within 1 year.*

    b. **Accounts payable:** A current liability that shows the amount the company owes to creditors for services or items purchased.

    c. **Salaries payable:** Obligations that the company must pay within 1 year for salaries earned but unpaid.

    d. **Total current liabilities:** Total obligations that the company must pay within 1 year.

    e. **Long-term liabilities:** Debts or obligations that the company does not have to pay within 1 year.

    f. **Mortgage note payable:** Debt owed on a building that is a long-term liability; often the building is the collateral.

    g. **Total liabilities:** Total of current and long-term liabilities.

3. **Stockholders' equity (owner's equity):** The rights or interest of the stockholders to assets of a corporation. If the company is not a corporation, the term *owner's equity* is used. The word *capital* follows the owner's name under the title *Owner's Equity.*

    a. **Common stock:** Amount of the initial and additional investment of corporation owners by the purchase of stock.

    b. **Retained earnings:** The amount of corporation earnings that the company retains, not necessarily in cash form.

    c. **Total stockholders' equity:** Total of stock plus retained earnings.

    d. **Total liabilities and stockholders' equity:** Total current liabilities, long-term liabilities, stock, and retained earnings. This total represents all the claims on assets—prior and present claims of creditors, owners' residual claims, and any other claims.

    Now that you are familiar with the common balance sheet items, you are ready to analyze a balance sheet.

Vertical Analysis and the Balance Sheet

Often financial statement readers want to analyze reports that contain data for two or more successive accounting periods. To make this possible, companies present a statement showing the data from these periods side by side. As you might expect, this statement is called a **comparative statement.**

    Comparative reports help illustrate changes in data. Financial statement readers should compare the percents in the reports to industry percents and the percents of competitors.

    Figure 16.2 shows the comparative balance sheet of Roger Company. Note that the statement analyzes each asset as a percent of total assets for a single period. The statement

FIGURE 16.2

Comparative balance sheet:
Vertical analysis

*We divide each item by
the total of assets.*

*We divide each item by
the total of liabilities and
stockholders' equity.*

	2001		2000	
ROGER COMPANY **Comparative Balance Sheet** **December 31, 2000 and 2001**				
	Amount	Percent	Amount	Percent
Assets				
Current assets:				
Cash	$22,000	25.88	$18,000	22.22
Accounts receivable	8,000	9.41	9,000	11.11
Merchandise inventory	9,000	10.59	7,000	8.64
Prepaid rent	4,000	4.71	5,000	6.17
Total current assets	$43,000	50.59	$39,000	48.15*
Plant and equipment:				
Building (net)	$18,000	21.18	$18,000	22.22
Land	24,000	28.24	24,000	29.63
Total plant and equipment	$42,000	49.41*	$42,000	51.85
Total assets	$85,000	100.00	$81,000	100.00
Liabilities				
Current liabilities:				
Accounts payable	$14,000	16.47	$ 8,000	9.88
Salaries payable	18,000	21.18	17,000	20.99
Total current liabilities	$32,000	37.65	$25,000	30.86*
Long-term liabilities:				
Mortgage note payable	12,000	14.12	20,000	24.69
Total liabilities	$44,000	51.76*	$45,000	55.56*
Stockholders' Equity				
Common stock	$20,000	23.53	$20,000	24.69
Retained earnings	21,000	24.71	16,000	19.75
Total stockholders' equity	$41,000	48.24	$36,000	44.44
Total liabilities and stockholders' equity	$85,000	100.00	$81,000	100.00

Note: All percents are rounded to the nearest hundredth percent.
*Due to rounding.

then analyzes each liability and equity as a percent of total liabilities and stockholders' equity. We call this type of analysis **vertical analysis.**

The following steps use the portion formula to prepare a vertical analysis of a balance sheet.

Preparing a Vertical Analysis of a Balance Sheet

Step 1. Divide each asset (the portion) as a percent of total assets (the base). Round as indicated.

Step 2. Round each liability and stockholders' equity (the portions) as a percent of total liabilities and stockholders' equity (the base). Round as indicated.

Horizontal Analysis and the Balance Sheet

We can also analyze balance sheets for two or more periods by using **horizontal analysis.** Horizontal analysis compares each item in one year by amount, percent, or both with the same item of the previous year. Note the Abby Ellen Company horizontal analysis shown in Figure 16.3. To make a horizontal analysis, we use the portion formula and the steps that follow.

FIGURE 16.3

Comparative balance sheet:
Horizontal analysis

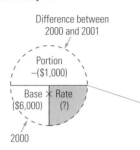

Difference between
2000 and 2001

Portion
−($1,000)

Base × Rate
($6,000)   (?)

2000

ABBY ELLEN COMPANY Comparative Balance Sheet December 31, 2000 and 2001				
			Increase (decrease)	
	2001	2000	Amount	Percent
Assets				
Current assets:				
Cash	$ 6,000	$ 4,000	$2,000	50.00*
Accounts receivable	5,000	6,000	(1,000)	− 16.67
Merchandise inventory	9,000	4,000	5,000	125.00
Prepaid rent	5,000	7,000	(2,000)	− 28.57
Total current assets	$25,000	$21,000	$4,000	19.05
Plant and equipment:				
Building (net)	$12,000	$12,000	−0−	−0−
Land	18,000	18,000	−0−	−0−
Total plant and equipment	$30,000	$30,000	−0−	−0−
Total assets	$55,000	$51,000	$4,000	7.84
Liabilities				
Current liabilities:				
Accounts payable	$ 3,200	$ 1,800	$1,400	77.78
Salaries payable	2,900	3,200	(300)	− 9.38
Total current liabilities	$ 6,100	$ 5,000	$1,100	22.00
Long-term liabilities:				
Mortgage note payable	17,000	15,000	2,000	13.33
Total liabilities	$23,100	$20,000	$3,100	15.50
Owner's Equity				
Abby Ellen, capital	$31,900	$31,000	$ 900	2.90
Total liabilities and owner's equity	$55,000	$51,000	$4,000	7.84

*The percents are not summed vertically in horizontal analysis.

Preparing a Horizontal Analysis of a Comparative Balance Sheet

Step 1. Calculate the increase or decrease (portion) in each item from the base year.
Step 2. Divide the increase or decrease in Step 1 by the old or base year.
Step 3. Round as indicated.

You can see the difference between vertical analysis and horizontal analysis by looking at the example of vertical analysis in Figure 16.2. The percent calculations in Figure 16.2 are for each item of a particular year as a percent of that year's total assets or total liabilities and stockholders' equity.

Horizontal analysis needs comparative columns because we take the difference *between* periods. In Figure 16.3, for example, the accounts receivable decreased $1,000 from 2000 to 2001. Thus, by dividing $1,000 (amount of change) by $6,000 (base year), we see that Abby's receivables decreased 16.67%.

Let's now try the following Practice Quiz.

LU 16.1 PRACTICE QUIZ

1. Complete this partial comparative balance sheet by vertical analysis. Round percents to the nearest hundredth.

	2001		2000	
	Amount	**Percent**	**Amount**	**Percent**
Assets				
Current assets:				
a. Cash	$ 42,000		$ 40,000	
b. Accounts receivable	18,000		17,000	
c. Merchandise inventory	15,000		12,000	
d. Prepaid expenses	17,000		14,000	
.	.		.	
.	.		.	
.	.		.	
Total current assets	$160,000		$150,000	

2. What is the amount of change in merchandise inventory and the percent increase?

✓ **Solutions**

	2001	2000
1. **a.** Cash	$\dfrac{\$42,000}{\$160,000} = 26.25\%$	$\dfrac{\$40,000}{\$150,000} = 26.67\%$
b. Accounts receivable	$\dfrac{\$18,000}{\$160,000} = 11.25\%$	$\dfrac{\$17,000}{\$150,000} = 11.33\%$
c. Merchandise inventory	$\dfrac{\$15,000}{\$160,000} = 9.38\%$	$\dfrac{\$12,000}{\$150,000} = 8.00\%$
d. Prepaid expenses	$\dfrac{\$17,000}{\$160,000} = 10.63\%$	$\dfrac{\$14,000}{\$150,000} = 9.33\%$

2.
$$\begin{array}{r} \$15,000 \\ - \ 12,000 \\ \hline \end{array}$$
$\text{Amount} = \boxed{\$ \ 3,000}$ $\qquad \text{Percent} = \dfrac{\$3,000}{\$12,000} = \boxed{25\%}$

LEARNING UNIT 16.2 Income Statement—Report for a Specific Period of Time

Bestfoods Earnings Climb 22% on Sales Of Its Baked Goods

By a WALL STREET JOURNAL *Staff Reporter*
ENGLEWOOD CLIFFS, N.J. — **Best-foods** reported a 22% increase in first-quarter net income on strong sales of its bagels, muffins, pizza crusts and other baked goods.

© 1998, Dow Jones & Company, Inc.

The Wall Street Journal clipping "Best-foods Earnings Climb 22% on Sales of Its Baked Goods" reports that strong sales increased Bestfoods' earnings. In this learning unit we look at the **income statement**—a financial report that tells how well a company is performing (its profitability or net profit) during a specific period of time (month, year, etc.). In general, the income statement reveals the inward flow of revenues (sales) against the outward or potential outward flow of costs and expenses.

The form of income statements varies depending on the company's type of business. However, the basic formula of the income statement is the same:

$$\boxed{\text{Revenues} - \text{Operating expenses} = \text{Net income}}$$

In a merchandising business like The Card Shop, we can enlarge on this formula:

Revenues (sales) ← ⟋ After any returns, allowances, or discounts
− Cost of merchandise or goods ⟵ Baseball cards
= Gross profit from sales
− Operating expenses
= Net income (profit)

THE CARD SHOP
Income Statement
For Month Ended December 31, 2001

Revenues (sales)	$8,000
Cost of merchandise sold	3,000
Gross profit from sales	$5,000
Operating expenses	750
Net income	$4,250

Now let's look at The Card Shop's income statement to see how much profit The Card Shop made during its first year of operation. For simplicity, we assume The Card Shop sold all the cards it bought during the year. For its first year of business, The Card Shop made a profit of $4,250.

We can now go more deeply into the income statement elements as we study the income statement of a corporation.

Elements of the Corporation Income Statement

Figure 16.4 gives the format and content of the Mool Company income statement—a corporation. The five main items of an income statement are revenues, cost of merchandise (goods) sold, gross profit on sales, operating expenses, and net income. We will follow the same pattern we used in explaining the balance sheet and define the main items and the letter-coded subitems.

1. **Revenues:** Total earned sales (cash or credit) less any sales returns and allowances or sales discounts.
   a. **Gross sales:** Total earned sales before sales returns and allowances or sales discounts.
   b. **Sales returns and allowances:** Reductions in price or reductions in revenue due to goods returned because of product defects, errors, and so on. When the buyer keeps the damaged goods, an allowance results.
   c. **Sales (not trade) discounts:** Reductions in the selling price of goods due to early customer payment. For example, a store may give a 2% discount to a customer who pays a bill within 10 days.
   d. **Net sales:** Gross sales less sales returns and allowances less sales discounts.
2. **Cost of merchandise (goods) sold:** All the costs of getting the merchandise that the company sold. The cost of all unsold merchandise (goods) will be subtracted from this item (ending inventory).
   a. **Merchandise inventory, December 1, 2001:** Cost of inventory in the store that was for sale to customers at the beginning of the month.
   b. **Purchases:** Cost of additional merchandise brought into the store for resale to customers.
   c. **Purchase returns and allowances:** Cost of merchandise returned to the store due to damage, defects, errors, and so on. Damaged goods kept by the buyer result in a cost reduction called an *allowance.*
   d. **Purchase discounts:** Savings received by the buyer for paying for merchandise before a certain date. These discounts can result in a substantial savings to a company.
   e. **Cost of net purchases:** Cost of purchases less purchase returns and allowances less purchase discounts.
   f. **Cost of merchandise (goods available for sale):** Sum of beginning inventory plus cost of net purchases.

FIGURE 16.4   Income statement

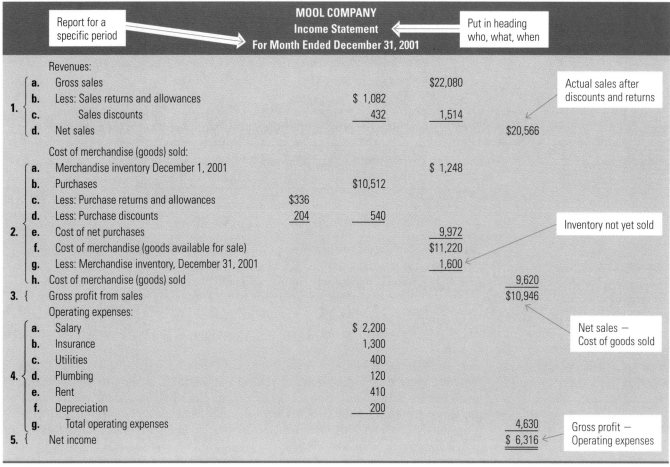

Note: Numbers are subtotaled from left to right.

    g. Merchandise inventory, December 31, 2001: Cost of inventory remaining in the store to be sold.

    h. Cost of merchandise (goods) sold: Beginning inventory plus net purchases less ending inventory.

3. Gross profit from sales: Net sales less cost of merchandise (goods) sold.

4. Operating expenses: Additional costs of operating the business beyond the actual cost of inventory sold.

    a.–f. Expenses: Individual expenses broken down.

    g. Total operating expenses: Total of all the individual expenses.

5. Net income: Gross profit less operating expenses.

    In the next section you will learn some formulas that companies use to calculate various items on the income statement.

Calculating Net Sales, Cost of Merchandise Sold, Gross Profit, and Net Income of an Income Statement

It is time to look closely at Figure 16.4 and see how each section is built. Use the previous vocabulary as a reference. We will study Figure 16.4 step by step.

Step 1.   Calculate the net sales—what Mool earned:

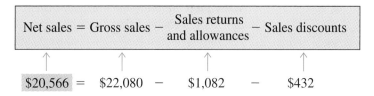

Step 2. Calculate the cost of merchandise (goods) sold:

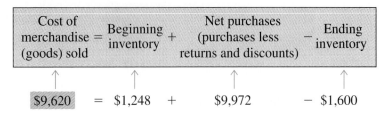

$$\begin{array}{ccc}
\text{Cost of} & & \text{Net purchases} & \\
\text{merchandise} = \text{Beginning} + (\text{purchases less} & - \text{Ending} \\
(\text{goods}) \text{ sold} & \text{inventory} & \text{returns and discounts}) & \text{inventory}
\end{array}$$

$$\$9,620 \quad = \quad \$1,248 \quad + \quad \$9,972 \quad - \quad \$1,600$$

Step 3. Calculate the gross profit from sales—profit before operating expenses:

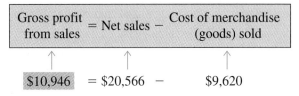

$$\begin{array}{c}
\text{Gross profit} \\
\text{from sales}
\end{array} = \text{Net sales} - \begin{array}{c}
\text{Cost of merchandise} \\
(\text{goods}) \text{ sold}
\end{array}$$

$$\$10,946 \quad = \$20,566 \quad - \quad \$9,620$$

Step 4. Calculate the net income—profit after operating expenses:

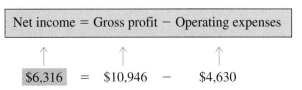

$$\text{Net income} = \text{Gross profit} - \text{Operating expenses}$$

$$\$6,316 \quad = \quad \$10,946 \quad - \quad \$4,630$$

Analyzing Comparative Income Statements

We can apply the same procedures of vertical and horizontal analysis to the income statement that we used in analyzing the balance sheet. Let's first look at the vertical analysis for Royal Company, Figure 16.5. Then we will look at the horizontal analysis of Flint Company's 2000 and 2001 income statements shown in Figure 16.6. Note in the margin how numbers are calculated.

LU 16.2 PRACTICE QUIZ

From the following information, calculate:

a. Net sales.   b. Cost of merchandise (goods) sold.

c. Gross profit from sales.   d. Net income.

Given Gross sales, $35,000; sales returns and allowances, $3,000; beginning inventory, $6,000; net purchases, $7,000; ending inventory, $5,500; operating expenses, $7,900.

✓ **Solutions**

a. $35,000 − $3,000 = $32,000 (Gross sales − Sales returns and allowances)

b. $6,000 + $7,000 − $5,500 = $7,500 (Beginning inventory + Net purchases − Ending inventory)

c. $32,000 − $7,500 = $24,500 (Net sales − Cost of merchandise sold)

d. $24,500 − $7,900 = $16,600 (Gross profit from sales − Operating expenses)

LEARNING UNIT 16.3 Trend and Ratio Analysis

Analyzing financial reports can indicate various trends. The study of these trends is valuable to businesses, financial institutions, and consumers. We begin this unit with a discussion of trend analysis.

Trend Analysis

Many tools are available to analyze financial reports. When data cover several years, we can analyze changes that occur by expressing each number as a percent of the base year. The base year is a past period of time that we use to compare sales, profits, and so on, with other years. We call this **trend analysis.**

FIGURE 16.5
Vertical analysis

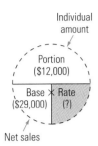

ROYAL COMPANY Comparative Income Statement For Years Ended December 31, 2000 and 2001				
	2001	Percent of net	2000	Percent of net
Net sales	$45,000	100.00	$29,000	100.00*
Cost of merchandise sold	19,000	42.22	12,000	41.38
Gross profit from sales	$26,000	57.78	$17,000	58.62
Operating expenses:				
Depreciation	$ 1,000	2.22	$ 500	1.72
Selling and advertising	4,200	9.33	1,600	5.52
Research	2,900	6.44	2,000	6.90
Miscellaneous	500	1.11	200	.69
Total operating expenses	$ 8,600	19.11†	$ 4,300	14.83
Income before interest and taxes	$17,400	38.67	$12,700	43.79
Interest expense	6,000	13.33	3,000	10.34
Income before taxes	$11,400	25.33†	$ 9,700	33.45
Provision for taxes	5,500	12.22	3,000	10.34
Net income	$ 5,900	13.11	$ 6,700	23.10†

*Net sales = 100%
†Off due to rounding.

FIGURE 16.6
Horizontal analysis

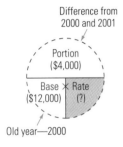

FLINT COMPANY Comparative Income Statement For Years Ended December 31, 2000 and 2001				
			Increase (decrease)	
	2001	2000	Amount	Percent
Sales	$90,000	$80,000	$10,000	
Sales returns and allowances	2,000	2,000	–0–	
Net sales	$88,000	$78,000	$10,000	+ 12.82
Cost of merchandise (goods) sold	45,000	40,000	5,000	+ 12.50
Gross profit from sales	$43,000	$38,000	$ 5,000	+ 13.16
Operating expenses:				
Depreciation	$ 6,000	$ 5,000	$ 1,000	+ 20.00
Selling and administrative	16,000	12,000	4,000	+ 33.33
Research	600	1,000	(400)	– 40.00
Miscellaneous	1,200	500	700	+ 140.00
Total operating expenses	$23,800	$18,500	$ 5,300	+ 28.65
Income before interest and taxes	$19,200	$19,500	$ (300)	– 1.54
Interest expense	4,000	4,000	–0–	
Income before taxes	$15,200	$15,500	$ (300)	– 1.94
Provision for taxes	3,800	4,000	(200)	– 5.00
Net income	$11,400	$11,500	$ (100)	– .87

Using the following example of Rose Company, we complete a trend analysis with the following steps:

Completing a Trend Analysis

Step 1. Select the base year (100%).
Step 2. Express each amount as a percent of the base year amount (rounded to the nearest whole percent).

	Given (base year 1999)			
	2002	2001	2000	1999
Sales	$621,000	$460,000	$340,000	$420,000
Gross profit	182,000	141,000	112,000	124,000
Net income	48,000	41,000	22,000	38,000

	Trend analysis			
	2002	2001	2000	1999
Sales	148%	110%	81%	100%
Gross profit	147	114	90	100
Net income	126	108	58	100

How to Calculate Trend Analysis

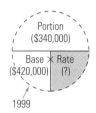

$$\frac{\text{Each item}}{\text{Base amount}} = \frac{\$340,000 \;\; \nearrow \text{Sales for 2000}}{\$420,000 \;\; \searrow \text{Sales for 1999}} = 80.95\% = \boxed{81\%}$$

What Trend Analysis Means   Sales of 2000 were 81% of the sales of 1999. Note that you would follow the same process no matter which of the three areas you were analyzing. All categories are compared to the base year—sales, gross profit, or net income.

We now will examine **ratio analysis**—another tool companies use to analyze performance.

Ratio Analysis

A *ratio* is the relationship of one number to another. Many companies compare their ratios with those of previous years and with ratios of other companies in the industry. Companies can get ratios of the performance of other companies from their bankers, accountants, local small business center, libraries, and newspaper articles.

Percentage ratios are used by companies to determine the following:

1. How well the company manages its assets—*asset management ratios.*
2. The company's debt situation—*debt management ratios.*
3. The company's profitability picture—*profitability ratios.*

Spanning the West

	NORWEST	WELLS FARGO
Headquarters	Minneapolis	San Francisco
Chief Executive	Richard Kovacevich	Paul Hazen
1997 Assets	$96.1 billion	$94.8 billion
1997 Return on assets	1.63%	1.16%
1997 Return on equity	22.1%	8.79%
1997 Net income	$1.35 billion	$1.16 billion
1997 Net income per share	$1.78	$12.77
Employees	57,036	32,414
Number of branches	960 in 16 states	1,930 in 10 states
States	Arizona, Colorado, Illinois, Indiana, Iowa, Minnesota, Montana, Nebraska, Nevada, New Mexico, N. Dakota, Ohio, S.Dakota, Texas, Wisconsin and Wyoming	Arizona, California, Colorado, Idaho, Nevada, New Mexico, Oregon, Texas, Utah and Washington

Source: the companies

The return on equity (ROE) ratio (explained in Table 16.1) is a frequently used profitability ratio. Note that in *The Wall Street Journal* clipping "Spanning the West," the 1997 return on equity for Norwest was 22.1% and for Wells Fargo it was 8.79%. So for each $1 invested in Norwest, it had a return of 22 cents (rounded); for each $1 invested in Wells Fargo, it had a return of 9 cents (rounded).

Each company must decide the true meaning of what the three types of ratios (asset management, debt management, and profitability) are saying. Table 16.1 gives a summary of the key ratios, their calculations (rounded to the nearest hundredth), and what they mean. All calculations are from Figures 16.1 and 16.4.

TABLE 16.1 Summary of key ratios: A reference guide*

Ratio	Formula	Actual calculations	What it says	Questions that could be raised
1. Current ratio†	$\dfrac{\text{Current assets}}{\text{Current liabilities}}$ (Current assets include cash, accounts receivable, and marketable securities.)	$\dfrac{\$61,000}{\$92,000} = .66{:}1$ Industry average, 2 to 1	Business has 66¢ of current assets to meet each $1 of current debt.	Not enough current assets to pay off current liabilities. Industry standard is $2 for each $1 of current debt.
2. Acid test (quick ratio) Top of fraction often referred to as *quick assets*	$\dfrac{\begin{array}{c}\text{Current assets}\\ -\text{ Inventory}\\ -\text{ Prepaid expenses}\end{array}}{\text{Current liabilities}}$ (Inventory and prepaid expenses are excluded because it may not be easy to convert these to cash.)	$\dfrac{\begin{array}{c}\$61,000 - \$30,000\\ -\ \$15,000\end{array}}{\$92,000}$ $= .17{:}1$ Industry average, 1 to 1	Business has only 17¢ to cover each $1 of current debt. This calculation excludes inventory and prepaid expenses.	Same as above but more severe.
3. Average day's collection	$\dfrac{\text{Accounts receivable}}{\dfrac{\text{Net sales}}{360}}$	$\dfrac{\$9,000}{\dfrac{\$20,566}{360}} = 158\text{ days}$ Industry average, 90–120 days	On the average, it takes 158 days to collect accounts receivable.	Could we speed up collection since industry average is 90–120 days?
4. Total debt to total assets	$\dfrac{\text{Total liabilities}}{\text{Total assets}}$	$\dfrac{\$150,000}{\$205,000} = 73.17\%$ Industry average, 50%–70%	For each $1 of assets, the company owes 73¢ in current and long-term debt.	73% is slightly higher than industry average.
5. Return on equity	$\dfrac{\text{Net income}}{\text{Stockholders' equity}}$	$\dfrac{\$6,316}{\$55,000} = 11.48\%$ Industry average, 15%–20%	For each $1 invested by the owner, a return of 11¢ results.	Could we get a higher return on money somewhere else?
6. Asset turnover	$\dfrac{\text{Net sales}}{\text{Total assets}}$	$\dfrac{\$20,566}{\$205,000} = 10\text{¢}$ Industry average, 3¢ to 8¢	For each $1 invested in assets, it returns 10¢ in sales.	Are assets being utilized efficiently?
7. Profit margin on net sales	$\dfrac{\text{Net income}}{\text{Net sales}}$	$\dfrac{\$6,316}{\$20,566} = 30.71\%$ Industry average, 25%–40%	For each $1 of sales, company produces 31¢ in profit.	Compared to competitors, are we showing enough profits versus our increased sales?

*Inventory turnover is discussed in Chapter 18.
†For example, Wal-Mart Stores, Inc., has a current ratio of 1.51.

Now you can check your knowledge with the Practice Quiz that follows.

LU 16.3 PRACTICE QUIZ

1. Prepare a trend analysis from the following sales, assuming a base year of 1999. Round to the nearest whole percent.

	2002	**2001**	**2000**	**1999**
Sales	$29,000	$44,000	$48,000	$60,000

2. **Given**   Total current assets (CA), $15,000; accounts receivable (AR), $6,000; total current liabilities (CL), $10,000; inventory (Inv.), $4,000; net sales, $36,000; total assets, $30,000; net income (NI), $7,500.

   Calculate

   a. Current ratio.

   b. Acid test.

   c. Average day's collection.

   d. Profit margin on sales (round to the nearest hundredth percent).

✓ **Solutions**

	2002	**2001**	**2000**	**1999**
1. Sales	48%	73%	80%	100%
	$\left(\dfrac{\$29,000}{\$60,000}\right)$	$\left(\dfrac{\$44,000}{\$60,000}\right)$	$\left(\dfrac{\$48,000}{\$60,000}\right)$	

2. a. $\dfrac{CA}{CL} = \dfrac{\$15,000}{\$10,000} = 1.5$

b. $\dfrac{CA - Inv}{CL} = \dfrac{\$15,000 - \$4,000}{\$10,000} = 1.1$

c. $\dfrac{AR}{\dfrac{Net\ sales}{360}} = \dfrac{\$6,000}{\dfrac{\$36,000}{360}} = 60\ days$

d. $\dfrac{NI}{Net\ sales} = \dfrac{\$7,500}{\$36,000} = 20.83\%$

Chapter Organizer and Reference Guide		
Topic	**Key point, procedure, formula**	**Example(s) to illustrate situation**
Balance sheet		
Vertical analysis, p. 370	Process of relating each figure on a financial report (down the column) to a total figure.	Current assets $520 52% Plant and equipment 480 48 Total assets $1,000 100%
Horizontal analysis, p. 371	Analyzing comparative financial reports shows rate and amount of change across columns item by item.	<table><tr><td>**2001**</td><td>**2000**</td><td>**Change**</td><td>**%**</td></tr><tr><td>Cash, $5,000</td><td>$4,000</td><td>$1,000</td><td>25% ←</td></tr></table> $\left(\dfrac{\$1,000}{\$4,000}\right)$
Income statement formulas, p. 375	(Horizontal and vertical analysis can also be done for income statements.)	
Net sales, p. 375	$\dfrac{\text{Gross}}{\text{sales}} - \dfrac{\text{Sales returns}}{\text{and allowances}} - \dfrac{\text{Sales}}{\text{discounts}}$	$200 gross sales − 10 sales returns and allowances − 2 sales discounts $188 net sales
Cost of merchandise (goods) sold, p. 375	$\dfrac{\text{Beginning}}{\text{inventory}} + \dfrac{\text{Net}}{\text{purchases}} - \dfrac{\text{Ending}}{\text{inventory}}$	$50 + $100 − $20 = $130 Beginning inventory + Net purchases − Ending inventory = Cost of merchandise (goods) sold
Gross profit from sales, p. 375	Net sales − $\dfrac{\text{Cost of merchandise}}{\text{(goods) sold}}$	$188 − $130 = $58 gross profit from sales Net sales − Cost of merchandise (goods) sold = Gross profit from sales
Net income, p. 375	Gross profit − Operating expenses	$58 − $28 = $30 Gross profit from sales − Operating expenses = Net income
Trend analysis, p. 376	Each number expressed as a percent of the base year. $\dfrac{\text{Each item}}{\text{Base amount}}$	<table><tr><td></td><td>**2002**</td><td>**2001**</td><td>**2000**</td></tr><tr><td>Sales</td><td>$200</td><td>$300</td><td>$400 ← Base year</td></tr><tr><td></td><td>50%</td><td>75%</td><td>100%</td></tr></table> $\left(\dfrac{\$200}{\$400}\right) \quad \left(\dfrac{\$300}{\$400}\right)$
Ratios, p. 378	Tools to interpret items on financial reports.	Use this example for calculating the following ratios: current assets, $30,000; accounts receivable, $12,000; total current liabilities, $20,000; inventory, $6,000; prepaid expenses, $2,000; net sales, $72,000; total assets, $60,000; net income, $15,000; total liabilities, $30,000.
Current ratio, p. 379	$\dfrac{\text{Current assets}}{\text{Current liabilities}}$	$\dfrac{\$30,000}{\$20,000} = 1.5$
Acid test (quick ratio), p. 379	Called quick assets ↙ $\dfrac{\text{Current assets} - \text{Inventory} - \text{Prepaid expenses}}{\text{Current liabilities}}$	$\dfrac{\$30,000 - \$6,000 - \$2,000}{\$20,000} = 1.1$
Average day's collection, p. 379	$\dfrac{\text{Accounts receivable}}{\dfrac{\text{Net sales}}{360}}$	$\dfrac{\$12,000}{\dfrac{\$72,000}{360}} = 60 \text{ days}$
Total debt to total assets, p. 379	$\dfrac{\text{Total liabilities}}{\text{Total assets}}$	$\dfrac{\$30,000}{\$60,000} = 50\%$

Chapter Organizer and Reference Guide (concluded)		
Topic	**Key point, procedure, formula**	**Example(s) to illustrate situation**
Return on equity, p. 379	$\dfrac{\text{Net income}}{\text{Stockholders' equity (A} - \text{L)}}$	$\dfrac{\$15,000}{\$30,000} = 50\%$
Asset turnover, p. 379	$\dfrac{\text{Net sales}}{\text{Total assets}}$	$\dfrac{\$72,000}{\$60,000} = 1.2$
Profit margin on net sales, p. 379	$\dfrac{\text{Net income}}{\text{Net sales}}$	$\dfrac{\$15,000}{\$72,000} = .2083 = 20.83\%$
Key terms	Accounts payable, *p. 370* Accounts receivable, *p. 370* Acid test, *p. 379* Assets, *p. 369* Asset turnover, *p. 379* Balance sheet, *p. 368* Capital, *p. 368* Common stock, *p. 370* Comparative statement, *p. 370* Corporation, *p. 369* Cost of merchandise (goods) sold, *p. 374* Current assets, *p. 370* Current liabilities, *p. 370* Current ratio, *p. 379* Expenses, *p. 375*	Gross profit from sales, *p. 375* Gross sales, *p. 374* Horizontal analysis, *p. 371* Income statement, *p. 373* Liabilities, *p. 370* Long-term liabilities, *p. 370* Merchandise inventory, *p. 370* Mortgage note payable, *p. 370* Net income, *p. 375* Net purchases, *p. 376* Net sales, *p. 375* Operating expenses, *p. 375* Owner's equity, *p. 370* Partnership, *p. 369* Plant and equipment, *p. 370*	Prepaid expenses, *p. 370* Purchase discounts, *p. 374* Purchase returns and allowances, *p. 374* Purchases, *p. 374* Quick assets, *p. 379* Quick ratio, *p. 379* Ratio analysis, *p. 378* Retained earnings, *p. 370* Return on equity, *p. 379* Revenues, *p. 374* Salaries payable, *p. 370* Sole proprietorship, *p. 369* Stockholders' equity, *p. 369* Trend analysis, *p. 376* Vertical analysis, *p. 371*

Critical Thinking Discussion Questions

1. What is the difference between current assets and plant and equipment? Do you think land should be allowed to depreciate?

2. What items make up stockholders' equity? Why might a person form a sole proprietorship instead of a corporation?

3. Explain the steps to complete a vertical or horizontal analysis relating to balance sheets. Why are the percents not summed vertically in horizontal analysis?

4. How do you calculate net sales, cost of goods sold, gross profit, and net income? Why do we need two separate figures for inventory in the cost of goods sold section?

5. Explain how to calculate the following: current ratios, acid test, average day's collection, total debt to assets, return on equity, asset turnover, and profit margin on net sales. How often do you think ratios should be calculated?

6. What is trend analysis? Explain how the portion formula assists in preparing a trend analysis.

DRILL PROBLEMS

16–1. From the following, prepare a balance sheet like that for The Card Shop (LU 16.1) for Bob's Hardware Shop on December 31, 2001: cash, $8,000; accounts payable, $11,000; merchandise inventory, $6,000; B. Ball, capital, $15,000; and equipment, $12,000.

BOB'S HARDWARE SHOP
Balance Sheet
December 31, 2001

Assets		Liabilities	
Cash	$ 8,000	Accounts payable	$11,000
Merchandise inventory	6,000	**Owner's Equity**	
Equipment	12,000	B. Ball, capital	15,000
Total assets	$26,000	Total liabilities and owner's equity	$26,000

16–2. From the following, prepare a classified balance sheet for Rug Company as of December 31, 2001. Ending merchandise inventory was $3,000 for the year.

Cash	$1,000	Accounts payable	$1,200
Prepaid rent	1,200	Salaries payable	1,500
Prepaid insurance	2,000	Note payable (long term)	1,000
Office equipment (net)	3,000	B. Rug, capital*	6,500

*What the owner supplies to the business. Replaces common stock and retained earnings section.

RUG COMPANY
Balance Sheet
December 31, 2001

Assets			Liabilities		
Current assets:			Current liabilities:		
Cash	$1,000		Accounts payable	$1,200	
Merchandise inventory	3,000		Salaries payable	1,500	
Prepaid insurance	2,000		Total current liabilities		$ 2,700
Prepaid rent	1,200		Long-term liabilities:		
Total current assets		$ 7,200	Notes payable		1,000
			Total liabilities		$ 3,700
Plant and equipment:					
Office equipment (net)		3,000	**Owner's Equity**		
			B. Rug, capital		6,500
Total assets		$10,200	Total liabilities and owner's equity		$10,200

16–3. Complete a horizontal analysis for Brown Company (round percents to the nearest hundredth):

BROWN COMPANY					
Comparative Balance Sheet					
December 31, 2000 and 2001					
				Increase (decrease)	
	2001	**2000**	**Amount**	**Percent**	
Assets					
Current assets:					
Cash	$ 15,750	$ 10,500	$ 5,250	+ 50.00	$\frac{\$5,250}{\$10,500} = 50\%$
Accounts receivable	18,000	13,500	4,500	+ 33.33	
Merchandise inventory	18,750	22,500	(3,750)	− 16.67	
Prepaid advertising	54,000	45,000	9,000	+ 20.00	
Total current assets	$106,500	$ 91,500	$15,000	+ 16.39	
Plant and equipment:					
Building (net)	$120,000	$126,000	$ (6,000)	− 4.76	
Land	90,000	90,000	–0–	–0–	
Total plant and equipment	$210,000	$216,000	(6,000)	− 2.78	
Total assets	$316,500	$307,500	$ 9,000	+ 2.93	
Liabilities					
Current liabilities:					
Accounts payable	$132,000	$120,000	$12,000	+ 10.00	
Salaries payable	22,500	18,000	4,500	+ 25.00	
Total current liabilities	$154,500	$138,000	$16,500	+ 11.96	
Long-term liabilities:					
Mortgage note payable	99,000	87,000	12,000	+ 13.79	
Total liabilities	$253,500	$225,000	$28,500	+ 12.67	
Owner's Equity					
J. Brown, capital	63,000	82,500	(19,500)	− 23.64	
Total liabilities and owner's equity	$316,500	$307,500	$ 9,000	+ 2.93	

16–4. Prepare an income statement for Munroe Sauce for the year ended December 31, 2001. Beginning inventory was $1,248. Ending inventory was $1,600.

Sales	$34,900
Sales returns and allowances	1,092
Sales discount	1,152
Purchases	10,512
Purchase discounts	540
Depreciation expense	115
Salary expense	5,200
Insurance expense	2,600
Utilities expense	210
Plumbing expense	250
Rent expense	180

MUNROE SAUCE	
Income Statement	
For Year Ended December 31, 2001	
Net sales	$32,656
Cost of merchandise (goods) sold	9,620
Gross profit from sales	$23,036
Operating expenses:	
Depreciation	$ 115
Salary	5,200
Insurance	2,600
Utilities	210
Plumbing	250
Rent	180
Total operating expenses	8,555
Net income	$14,481

Net sales = $34,900 − $1,092 − $1,152

Beginning inventory	$1,248
+ Net purchases	+ 9,972
− Ending inventory	− 1,600
= COGS	$9,620

16–5. Complete the following (round percents to the nearest hundredth):

RANCH COMPANY Comparative Income Statement For Years Ended December 31, 2001 and 2002				
	2002	Percent of net	2001	Percent of net
Net sales	$110,000	100.00	$68,000	100.00
Cost of merchandise sold	75,000	68.18	22,000	32.35
Gross profit from sales	$ 35,000	31.82	$46,000	67.65
Operating expenses:				
Depreciation	$ 850	.77	$450	.66
Selling and administrative	1,900	1.73	1,250	1.84
Research	2,900	2.64	1,600	2.35
Miscellaneous	3,500	3.18	150	.22
Total operating expenses	$ 9,150	8.32	$ 3,450	5.07
Income before interest and taxes	$ 25,850	23.50	$42,550	62.57
Interest expense	8,000	7.27	$ 8,500	12.50
Income before taxes	$ 17,850	16.23	$34,050	50.07
Provision for taxes	7,000	6.36	14,000	20.59
Net income	$ 10,850	9.86	$20,050	29.49

$$\frac{\$22,000}{\$68,000} = 32.35\%$$

16–6. From the Bowmar Instrument Corporation second-quarter report ended 1997, do a vertical analysis for the second quarter of 1997.

BOWMAR INSTRUMENT CORPORATION AND SUBSIDIARIES Consolidated Statements of Operation (Unaudited) (In thousands of dollars, except share data)			
	Second quarter		
	1997	1996	Percent of net
Net sales	$6,698	$6,951	100.00
Cost of sales	4,089	4,462	61.05
Gross margin	2,609	2,489	38.95
Expenses:			
Selling, general and administrative	1,845	1,783	27.55
Product development	175	165	2.61
Interest expense	98	123	1.46
Other (income), net	(172)	(99)	(2.57)
Total expenses	1,946	1,972	29.05†
Income before income taxes	663	517	9.90
Provision for income taxes	265	209	3.96
Net income	$ 398	$ 308	5.94
Net income per common share*	$ .05	$ .03	
Weighted average number of common shares and equivalents	6,673,673	6,624,184	

*Income per common share reflects the deduction of the preferred stock dividend from net income.
†Off due to rounding.

16–7. Complete the comparative income statement and balance sheet for Logic Company (round percents to the nearest hundredth):

LOGIC COMPANY Comparative Income Statement For Years Ended December 31, 2001 and 2002			Increase (decrease)	
	2002	2001	Amount	Percent
Gross sales	$19,000	$15,000	$4,000	26.67
Sales returns and allowances	1,000	100	900	900.00
Net sales	$18,000	$14,900	$3,100	+ 20.81
Cost of merchandise (goods) sold	12,000	9,000	3,000	+ 33.33
Gross profit	$ 6,000	$ 5,900	$ 100	+ 1.69
Operating expenses:				
Depreciation	$ 700	$ 600	$ 100	+ 16.67
Selling and administrative	2,200	2,000	200	+ 10.00
Research	550	500	50	+ 10.00
Miscellaneous	360	300	60	+ 20.00
Total operating expenses	$ 3,810	$ 3,400	$ 410	+ 12.06
Income before interest and taxes	$ 2,190	$ 2,500	$ (310)	− 12.40
Interest expense	560	500	60	+ 12.00
Income before taxes	$ 1,630	$ 2,000	$ (370)	− 18.50
Provision for taxes	640	800	(160)	− 20.00
Net income	$ 990	$ 1,200	$ (210)	− 17.50

$\dfrac{\$3,100}{\$14,900}$

LOGIC COMPANY Comparative Balance Sheet December 31, 2001 and 2002	2002		2001	
	Amount	Percent	Amount	Percent
Assets				
Current assets:				
Cash	$12,000	13.48	$ 9,000	13.74
Accounts receivable	16,500	18.54	12,500	19.08
Merchandise inventory	8,500	9.55	14,000	21.37
Prepaid expenses	24,000	26.97	10,000	15.27
Total current assets	$61,000	68.54	$45,500	69.47*
Plant and equipment:				
Building (net)	$14,500	16.29	$11,000	16.79
Land	13,500	15.17	9,000	13.74
Total plant and equipment	$28,000	31.46	$20,000	30.53
Total assets	$89,000	100.00	$65,500	100.00
Liabilities				
Current liabilities:				
Accounts payable	$13,000	14.61	$7,000	10.69
Salaries payable	7,000	7.87	5,000	7.63
Total current liabilities	$20,000	22.47*	$12,000	18.32
Long-term liabilities:				
Mortgage note payable	22,000	24.72	20,500	31.30
Total liabilities	$42,000	47.19	$32,500	49.62
Stockholders' Equity				
Common stock	$21,000	23.60	$21,000	32.06
Retained earnings	26,000	29.21	12,000	18.32
Total stockholders' equity	$47,000	52.81	$33,000	50.38
Total liabilities and stockholders' equity	$89,000	100.00	$65,500	100.00

$\dfrac{\$9,000}{\$65,500}$

*Due to rounding.

From Problem 16–7, your supervisor has requested that you calculate the following ratios (round to the nearest hundredth):

		2002	**2001**
16–8.	Current ratio.	3.05	3.79
16–9.	Acid test.	1.43	1.79
16–10.	Average day's collection.	330.00	302.01
16–11.	Asset turnover.	.20	.23
16–12.	Total debt to total assets.	.47	.50
16–13.	Net income (after tax) to the net sales.	.06	.08
16–14.	Return on equity (after tax).	.02	.04

		2002	**2001**
16–8.	$\dfrac{CA}{CL}$	$\dfrac{\$61,000}{\$20,000} = 3.05$	$\dfrac{\$45,500}{\$12,000} = 3.79$
16–9.	$\dfrac{CA - Inv - \substack{\text{Prepaid} \\ \text{expenses}}}{CL}$	$\dfrac{\$61,000 - \$8,500 - \$24,000}{\$20,000} = 1.43$	$\dfrac{\$45,500 - \$14,000 - \$10,000}{\$12,000} = 1.79$
16–10.	$\dfrac{AR}{\dfrac{\text{Net sales}}{360}}$	$\dfrac{\$16,500}{\dfrac{\$18,000}{360}} = 330$	$\dfrac{\$12,500}{\dfrac{\$14,900}{360}} = 302.01$
16–11.	$\dfrac{\text{Net sales}}{TA}$	$\dfrac{\$18,000}{\$89,000} = .202 = .20$	$\dfrac{\$14,900}{\$65,500} = .227 = .23$
16–12.	$\dfrac{TL}{TA}$	$\dfrac{\$42,000}{\$89,000} = .471 = .47$	$\dfrac{\$32,500}{\$65,500} = .496 = .50$
16–13.	$\dfrac{NI}{\text{Net sales}}$	$\dfrac{\$990}{\$18,000} = .055 = .06$	$\dfrac{\$1,200}{\$14,900} = .0805 = .08$
16–14.	$\dfrac{NI}{\text{Equity}}$	$\dfrac{\$990}{\$47,000} = .021 = .02$	$\dfrac{\$1,200}{\$33,000} = .036 = .04$

WORD PROBLEMS

16–15. The March 1997 issue of *ABA Banking Journal* contained an article that stated the following: "The net income for 1995 was $1,500,000 and the return on equity was 21." What was the amount of equity to the nearest dollar?

$$\text{Return on equity} = \frac{\text{Net income}}{\text{Equity}}$$

$$\frac{\$1,500,000 \text{ (net income)}}{?} = 21\%$$

$$\frac{\$1,500,000}{.21} = \$7,142,857$$

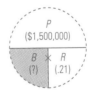

16–16. On November 17, 1997, *Newsweek* reported the sales of McDonald's domestic and overseas restaurants. Domestic sales for 1996 totaled $16.4 billion; overseas sales totaled $15.4 billion. What percent is McDonald's domestic sales of total sales, and what percent is its overseas sales of total sales? Round to the nearest hundredth percent.

$16.4 billion + $15.4 billion = $31.8 billion

Domestic

$$\frac{\$16.4 \text{ billion}}{\$31.8 \text{ billion}} = 51.57\%$$

Overseas

$$\frac{\$15.4 \text{ billion}}{\$31.8 \text{ billion}} = 48.43\%$$

16–17. On December 14, 1997, the *Chicago Tribune* ran an article on the increase in Porsche's revenue. Net income climbed to $80 million for the year ended in July from $27.6 million a year earlier. Sales rose 46% in fiscal 1996–97 to $2.35 billion. What is the ratio of profit margin to net sales? Round to the nearest hundredth percent.

$$\text{Profit margin on net sales} = \frac{\text{Net income}}{\text{Net sales}} \qquad \frac{\$80,000,000}{\$2,350,000,000} = 3.40\%$$

16–18. On October 1996, the following sentence appeared in an article in *Inc.*: "Net sales are $100,000; you have a gross margin of 30%, accounts receivable of $20,000, and cost of goods sold of $70,000." How long will you have to wait to get paid? What will be your average day's collection?

$$\frac{\text{Accounts receivable}}{\dfrac{\text{Net sales}}{360}} = \frac{\$20,000}{\dfrac{\$100,000}{360}} = \frac{\$20,000}{277.777} = 72.0, \text{ or } 72 \text{ days}$$

16–19. Don Williams received a memo requesting that he complete a trend analysis of the following numbers using 2000 as the base year and rounding each percent to the nearest whole percent. Could you help Don with the request?

	2003	2002	2001	2000
Sales	$340,000	$400,000	$420,000	$500,000
Gross profit	180,000	240,000	340,000	400,000
Net income	70,000	90,000	40,000	50,000

	2003	2002	2001	2000
Sales	68% ←	80%	84%	100%
Gross profit	45	60	85	100
Net income	140	180	80	100

$$\frac{\$340,000}{\$500,000}$$

CHALLENGE PROBLEMS

16–20. Below is Bowmar Instrument's second quarter report, which ended March 29, 1997. Complete **(a)** current ratio (round to nearest tenth), **(b)** acid test (quick ratio—round to nearest hundredth), **(c)** total debt to total assets ratio (round to nearest hundredth), and **(d)** asset turnover (to nearest tenth). Net sales were $6,698.

BOWMAR INSTRUMENT CORPORATION AND SUBSIDIARIES
Consolidated Balance Sheets
(In thousands of dollars)
(Unaudited)

	March 29, 1997	September 28, 1996
Assets		
Current assets		
Cash	$ 71	$ 108
Accounts receivable, net	4,936	3,992
Inventories	6,416	6,059
Prepaid expenses	368	402
Deferred income taxes	1,630	1,652
Total current assets	13,421	12,213
Property, plant, and equipment, net	1,244	1,122
Deferred income taxes	1,082	1,524
Other assets, net	1,618	1,679
Total assets	$17,365	$16,538
Liabilities and Shareholders' Equity		
Current liabilities		
Current portion of long-term debt	$ 607	$ 556
Accounts payable	1,696	933
Accrued expenses	1,545	2,222
Total current liabilities	3,848	3,711
Long-term debt	3,480	3,675
Other long-term liabilities	339	339
Total liabilities	7,667	7,725
Shareholders' equity	9,698	8,813
Total liabilities and shareholders' equity	$17,365	$16,538

a. Current ratio

$$\frac{\text{CA}}{\text{CL}} = \frac{\$13,421}{\$3,848} = 3.48 = 3.5$$

b. Acid test (quick ratio)

$$\frac{\begin{array}{c}\text{CA} - \text{Inventory}\\ - \text{ Prepaid expenses}\end{array}}{\text{CL}} = \frac{\$6,637}{\$3,848} = 1.72 = 1.7$$

c. Total debt to total assets

$$\frac{\text{Total liabilities}}{\text{Total assets}} = \frac{\$7,667}{\$17,365} = .44$$

d. Asset turnover

$$\frac{\text{Net sales}}{\text{Total assets}} = \frac{\$6,698}{\$17,365} = .3857 = .4$$

16–21. As the accountant for Tootsie Roll, you are asked to calculate the current ratio and the quick ratio for the following partial financial report:

Assets		Liabilities	
Current assets:		Current liabilities:	
Cash and cash equivalents (Note 1)	$ 4,224,190	Notes payable to banks	$ 672,221
Investments (Note 1)	32,533,769	Accounts payable	7,004,075
Accounts receivable, less allowances of		Dividends payable	576,607
$748,000 and $744,000	16,206,648	Accrued liabilities (Note 5)	9,826,534
Inventories (Note 1):		Income taxes payable	4,471,429
Finished goods and work in progress	12,650,955		
Raw materials and supplies	10,275,858		
Prepaid expenses	2,037,710		

$$\text{Current ratio} = \frac{\text{CA}}{\text{CL}} \quad \frac{\$77,929,130}{\$22,550,866} = 3.45 = 3.5$$

$$\text{Quick ratio} = \frac{\text{CA} - \text{Prepaid Exp.} - \text{Inventory}}{\text{CL}}$$

$$= \frac{\$77,929,130 - \$12,650,955 - \$10,275,858 - \$2,037,710}{\$22,550,866}$$

$$= \frac{\$52,964,607}{\$22,550,866}$$

$$= 2.3$$

SUMMARY PRACTICE TEST

1. **Given:** Gross sales, $90,000; sales returns and allowances, $8,000; beginning inventory, $6,600; net purchases, $7,000; ending inventory, $1,500; and operating expenses, $22,800. Calculate **(a)** net sales, **(b)** cost of merchandise (goods) sold, **(c)** gross profit from sales, and **(d)** net income. *(p. 375)*

a. Gross sales	$90,000		c. Gross profit from sales:	
− Sales discount	–0–		Net sales	$82,000
− SRA	8,000		− COGS	12,100
Net sales	$82,000		Gross profit from sales	$69,900

b. Cost of merchandise			d. Gross profit from sales	$69,900
(goods) sold:			− Operating expenses	22,800
Beginning inventory	$ 6,600		= Net income	$47,100
+ Net purchases	7,000			
− Ending inventory	1,500			
Cost of merchandise				
(goods) sold	$12,100			

2. Complete this partial comparative balance sheet by filling in the total current assets and the percent column; assume no plant and equipment (round to the nearest hundredth percent as needed). *(p. 371)*

	Amount	Percent	Amount	Percent
Assets				
Current assets:				
Cash	$ 9,000	37.50	$ 8,000	28.67
Accounts receivable	2,000	8.33	6,500	23.30
Merchandise inventory	6,000	25.00	4,400	15.77
Prepaid expenses	7,000	29.17	9,000	32.26
Total current assets	$24,000	100.00	$27,900	100.00

3. Calculate the amount of increase or decrease and the percent change of each item (round to the nearest hundredth percent as needed). *(p. 372)*

	2002	2001	Amount	Percent
Cash	$13,000	$ 8,000	$ 5,000	62.50
Land	50,000	20,000	30,000	150.00
Accounts payable	44,000	15,000	29,000	193.33

4. Complete a trend analysis for sales (round to the nearest whole percent and use 2000 as the base year). *(p. 378)*

	2003	**2002**	**2001**	**2000**
Sales	$170,000	$160,000	$140,000	$175,000
	97%	91%	80%	100%
	$\left(\dfrac{\$170,000}{\$175,000}\right)$	$\left(\dfrac{\$160,000}{\$175,000}\right)$	$\left(\dfrac{\$140,000}{\$175,000}\right)$	

5. From the following, prepare a balance sheet for Leslie Company as of December 31, 2001. *(p. 369)*

Building	$30,000	Mortgage note payable	$60,000
Merchandise inventory	14,000	Common stock	23,000
Cash	20,000	Retained earnings	16,000
Land	42,000	Accounts receivable	6,000
Accounts payable	18,000	Salaries payable	6,000
Prepaid rent	11,000		

LESLIE COMPANY
Balance Sheet
December 31, 2001

Assets			**Liabilities**		
Current assets:			Current liabilities:		
Cash	$20,000		Accounts payable	$18,000	
Accounts receivable	6,000		Salaries payable	6,000	
Merchandise inventory	14,000		Total current liabilities		$24,000
Prepaid rent	11,000		Long-term liabilities:		
Total current assets		$ 51,000	Mortgage note payable		60,000
Plant and equipment:			Total liabilities		$84,000
Land	$42,000				
Building	30,000		**Stockholders' Equity**		
Total plant and equipment		72,000	Common stock	$23,000	
			Retained earnings	16,000	
			Total stockholders' equity		39,000
Total assets		$123,000	Total liabilities and stockholders' equity		$123,000

6. Solve from the following facts (round to the nearest hundredth): *(p. 379)*

Current assets	$17,000	Net sales	$36,000
Accounts receivable	4,400	Total assets	34,000
Current liabilities	18,000	Net income	7,000
Inventory	5,000		

a. Current ratio.　　　　　　.94

b. Acid test.　　　　　　　.67

c. Average day's collection.　44 days

d. Asset turnover.　　　　　1.06

e. Profit margin on sales.　　.19

a. $\dfrac{\$17,000}{\$18,000} = .94$

b. $\dfrac{\$17,000 - \$5,000}{\$18,000} = .67$

c. $\dfrac{\dfrac{\$4,400}{\$36,000}}{360} = 44 \text{ days}$

d. $\dfrac{\$36,000}{\$34,000} = 1.06$

e. $\dfrac{\$7,000}{\$36,000} = .19$

A GROUP PROJECT   Defend or reject the following business math issue based on the *Kiplinger's Personal Finance Magazine* article below:

online consumer
The Cybersound of Music

▶ **The online music stores have plenty of differences—starting with price.** By Elizabeth Razzi

All that's missing is the sullen cashier with the pierced eyebrow. If you can do without that, you'll find a lot to like browsing music stores online. The best sites combine the joys of flipping through a good music magazine with those of wandering around a well-stocked store—without the hassle of driving to the mall. Plus, you'll often beat the prices you find at the bricks-and-mortar stores.

That helps explain the growing popularity of online music stores. Though their share of the music market is still small—about 2% of 1998 revenues, projects Jupiter Communications, a New York City research firm—online revenues will grow to 9% of the market by 2002, according to Jupiter estimates. Amazon.com, whose music department debuted in June, quickly overtook the competition in sales, another indication of pent-up demand.

But prices aren't always lower online, and the instant gratification of finding and ordering CDs from your desktop can turn into frustrating waits for the music to reach your mailbox. At the four online music stores I visited, there were also differences in how much fun it was to browse the virtual shelves.

BEST OVERALL
Music Boulevard
It was a tough call deciding which was the better site—**CDnow** (www.cdnow.com) or **Music Boulevard** (www.musicboulevard.com)—but a better browsing experience tips the scales toward Music Boulevard. The issue may become moot, anyway,

> **Amazon.com**
> www.amazon.com
> As with its books, you get other customers' reviews and star rankings.
>
> **CDnow**
> www.cdnow.com
> Its Album Advisor had some offbeat suggestions based on our purchases.
>
> **Music Boulevard**
> www.musicboulevard.com
> A better browsing experience than the others and good prices, too.
>
> **Tower Records**
> www.towerrecords.com
> Beat the other online music stores on delivery time—but not on price.

because CDnow and Music Boulevard's parent, N2K, announced a merger in October. There's no word yet on how the sites will be combined, but the companies' combined firepower is expected to give Amazon.com a run for its money.

CDnow and Music Boulevard came pretty close on prices, undercutting both Amazon.com (by a little) and Tower (by a lot). On blues great John Lee Hooker's new release, *The Best of Friends* (a socko album with Eric Clapton, Van Morrison, Bonnie Raitt and Carlos Santana), Music Boulevard offered the best price, $10.88 (plus $2.99 for shipping, which is pretty standard among the sites). The disk cost $11.88 at CDnow (and didn't come up in a search by artist), $11.88 at Amazon.com and a whopping $17.99 at Tower.

Another plus for Music Boulevard is its Frequent Buyer's Club. Signing up is free (but you have to complete a detailed survey). Then, with ten purchases, you earn credit for one free CD. I wasn't terribly impressed with CDnow's bonus plan, the Fast Forward Rewards Program. The cheapest reward, 500 points ($50 spent on music), gets you a greatest-hits CD from the MTV Video Music Awards 1984–1997. Yawn.

Music Boulevard had the best downloadable music clips, too. As at the other sites, you can hear 30-second clips of lots of tracks via RealAudio streaming, but frequently you can also choose between low-quality MPEG and high-quality MPEG format. MPEG takes longer to download than RealAudio, but it has a much better sound. Music Boulevard has music reviews from publications such as *Allstar* and *SPIN* that tend to be more substantive than the one- or two-liners on other sites.

The other sites had kids' titles, but good luck finding them. Music Boulevard has a whole kids' section, with reviews and audio clips—so you can check out *The Playground* by Tony Bennett (with Rosie O'Donnell and Sesame Street's Elmo and Kermit the Frog) before you pay $12.99 and commit to hearing it hundreds of times on your car stereo.

Business Math Issue

The Internet will hurt most corporations' bottom line in the long run.

1. List the key points of the article and information to support your position.
2. Write a group defense of your position using math calculations to support your view.

BUSINESS MATH SCRAPBOOK
Putting Your Skills to Work

Daimler-Chrysler Merger to Produce $3 Billion In Savings, Revenue Gains Within 3 to 5 Years

By STEVEN LIPIN
And BRANDON MITCHENER
Staff Reporters of THE WALL STREET JOURNAL

Daimler-Benz AG's megamerger with **Chrysler** Corp. will result in annual savings and revenue gains of at least $3 billion, and is made easier by Daimler's rich stock multiple.

At a news conference in London yesterday, Daimler formally announced its pact to merge with Chrysler in a stock-swap valued at about $38 billion. Meanwhile, U.S. labor representatives were cautiously optimistic about the merger pact, and said German works councils could be a concept that the U.S. auto industry should consider.

The combination creates a giant with a squeaky-clean balance sheet and arsenal of cash for future acquisitions. Together, DaimlerChrysler, as the new company will be called, will have $130 billion in sales, $7.1 billion in operating profit, $31 billion in stockholders equity and 421,068 employees world-wide.

In the Driver's Seat: DaimlerChrysler
1997 figures, in U.S. dollars.

	DAIMLER-BENZ	CHRYSLER	PRO-FORMA DAIMLERCHRYSLER
Revenues (in billions)	$68.92	$61.15	$130.06
Operating profit (in billions)	$2.40	$4.72	$7.13
Income excl. taxes (in billions)	$2.36	$4.56	$6.92
Net income (in billions)	$1.76*	$2.81	$4.57
Earnings per share	$3.42*	$4.15	N.A.
Stockholders' equity (in billions)	$19.49	$11.36	$30.85
Total assets (in billions)	$76.17	$60.42	$136.58
Number of employees	300,168	121,000	421,068

*Excluding non-recurring income tax benefits of $2.71 billion; including such benefits net income was $4.47 billion and 15.59 German marks per share.
NOTE: Financial figures for Daimler-Benz are converted to U.S. dollars from German marks.
Source: Chrysler, Daimler Benz

© 1998, Dow Jones & Company, Inc.

Project A

What is the asset turnover for the combined companies? Assume revenues are net sales. Round to the nearest hundredth.

$$\text{Asset turnover} = \frac{\text{Net sales}}{\text{Total assets}} = \frac{\$130.06}{\$136.58} = .95$$

Profit Slips at J.C. Penney but Climbs At Dillard, TJX Cos. and Lands' End

By LOUISE LEE
Staff Reporter of THE WALL STREET JOURNAL

J.C. Penney Co. said "heavy" markdowns contributed to a 2.1% drop in first-quarter profit from a year earlier, while retailers **Dillard Department Stores** Inc. and **TJX Cos.** and cataloger **Lands' End** Inc. posted higher profits for the period.

Penney said it used markdowns to clear out winter goods in the early part of the quarter, which ended April 26. Currently, a Penney spokesman said, inventories are still "above plan," and stores are "taking markdowns where they need to" or stocking less merchandise. However, the spokesman said the company expects sales at stores open at least a year to increase "in the low single-digits" for May.

Retailer Earnings

COMPANY	NET INCOME (millions)	PER SHARE	% CHANGE FROM YEAR AGO
J.C. Penney	$139.0	$0.53	−2.1%
Dillard	58.3	0.52	3.4
Lands' End	11.3	0.35	156.0
TJX	48.5	0.54	61.0

Project B

What was the net income for J.C. Penney 1 year ago? Round to the nearest million.

$$\frac{\$139}{.979} = \$141.98 = \$142 \text{ million}$$

© 1997, Dow Jones & Company, Inc.

 See text Web site (www.mhhe.com/slater) and *The Business Math Internet Resource Guide.*

USED CARS

17

DEPRECIATION

LEARNING UNIT OBJECTIVES

LU 17.1   Concept of Depreciation and the Straight-Line Method

- Explain the concept and causes of depreciation *(p. 396)*.
- Prepare a depreciation schedule and calculate partial-year depreciation *(p. 397)*.

LU 17.2   Units-of-Production Method

- Explain how use affects the units-of-production method *(p. 398)*.
- Prepare a depreciation schedule *(p. 399)*.

LU 17.3   Sum-of-the-Years'-Digits Method

- Explain how to use the fraction in the sum-of-the-years'-digits method *(p. 399)*.
- Prepare a depreciation schedule *(p. 400)*.

LU 17.4   Declining-Balance Method

- Explain the importance of residual value in the depreciation schedule *(p. 401)*.
- Prepare a depreciation schedule *(p. 401)*.

LU 17.5   Modified Accelerated Cost Recovery System (MACRS) with Introduction to ACRS

- Explain the goals of ACRS and MACRS and their limitations *(pp. 402–3)*.
- Calculate depreciation using the MACRS guidelines *(pp. 403–4)*.

This chapter concentrates on depreciation—a business operating expense. In Learning Units 17.1 to 17.4, we discuss methods of calculating depreciation for financial reporting. In Learning Unit 17.5, we look at how tax laws force companies to report depreciation for tax purposes. Financial reporting methods and the tax-reporting methods are both legal.

LEARNING UNIT 17.1   Concept of Depreciation and the Straight-Line Method

Companies frequently buy assets such as equipment or buildings that will last longer than 1 year. As time passes, these assets depreciate, or lose some of their market value. The total cost of these assets cannot be shown in *1 year* as an expense of running the business. In a systematic and logical way, companies must estimate the asset cost they show as an expense of a particular period. This process is called **depreciation.**

Remember that depreciation *does not* measure the amount of deterioration or decline in the market value of the asset. Depreciation is simply a means of recognizing that these assets are depreciating. For example, *The Wall Street Journal* clipping "Wendy's to Eliminate Self-Serve Salad Bars in Many Restaurants" reports that many of the salad bars that will be eliminated have been fully depreciated.

Wendy's to Eliminate Self-Serve Salad Bars In Many Restaurants

By a WALL STREET JOURNAL *Staff Reporter*

DUBLIN, Ohio — Salad bars will disappear from many **Wendy's International** Inc. restaurants in coming months.

The action reflects consumers' growing desire for prepackaged salads, as well as a line of pita sandwiches that include chopped vegetables, a spokesman said, confirming analysts' reports. "We are not lessening the importance of salads in our mix," he said.

The bars' removal from company-owned restaurants likely will lead to write-offs in the current and following two quarters, the spokesman said. He noted that since salad bars have been in hundreds of restaurants for years — the company introduced them in 1979 — many have been fully depreciated. Thus, the writeoffs aren't expected to have a major impact on earnings, he said.

While some company-owned outlets will retain the bars — decisions will reflect their popularity with local clientele — most will be taken out by next spring. The company operates more than 1,000 outlets in the U.S. and Canada.

Franchisees, who operate the bulk of the 5,100 restaurants, also are expected to decide whether to retain their salad bars in the next few months. In markets where the company removes the bars, franchisees are likely to follow suit in the name of consistency, the spokesman said.

Partly because a salad bar is labor-intensive, eliminating it could lead to slight increases in a restaurant's profit margin.

Many outlets offer five packaged salads, including a garden side, taco, grilled chicken and Caesar varieties.

Wendy's also said it is testing several other pitas, as well as a chicken sandwich with a hot, buffalo-wings sauce.

© 1997, Dow Jones & Company, Inc.

The depreciation process results in **depreciation expense** that involves three key factors: (1) **asset cost**—amount the company paid for the asset; (2) **estimated useful life**—number of years or time periods for which the company can use the asset; and (3) **residual value (salvage** or **trade-in value)**—expected cash value at the end of the asset's useful life.

Depreciation expense is listed on the income statement. The **accumulated depreciation** title on the balance sheet gives the amount of the asset's depreciation taken to date. Asset cost less accumulated depreciation is the asset's book value. The book value shows the unused amount of the asset cost that the company may depreciate in future accounting periods. At the end of the asset's life, the asset's book value is the same as its residual value—book value cannot be less than residual value.

Depending on the amount and timetable of an asset's depreciation, a company can increase or decrease its profit. If a company shows greater depreciation in earlier years, the company will have a lower reported profit and pay less in taxes. Thus, depreciation can be in indirect tax savings for the company.

Later in the chapter we will discuss the different methods of computing depreciation that spread the cost of an asset over specified periods of time. However, first let's look at some of the major causes of depreciation.

Causes of Depreciation

Photo courtesy of Hewlett-Packard Company.

As assets, all machines have an estimated amount of usefulness simply because as companies use the assets, the assets gradually wear out. The cause of this depreciation is *physical deterioration.*

The growth of a company can also cause depreciation. Many companies begin on a small scale. As the companies grow, they often find their equipment and buildings inadequate. The use of depreciation enables these businesses to "write off" their old, inadequate equipment and buildings. Companies cannot depreciate land. For example, a garbage dump can be depreciated but not the land.

Another cause of depreciation is the result of advances in technology. The computers that companies bought a few years ago may be in perfect working condition but outdated. Companies may find it necessary to replace these old computers with more sophisticated, faster, and possibly more economical machines. Thus, *product obsolescence* is a key factor contributing to depreciation.

Now we are ready to begin our study of depreciation methods. The first method we will study is straight-line depreciation. It is also the most common of the four depreciation methods (straight line, units of production, sum-of-the-years' digits, and declining balance). In a survey of 600 corporations, 81% responded that they used straight-line depreciation.

Straight-Line Method

The **straight-line method** of depreciation tries to distribute the same amount of expense to each period of time. Most large companies, such as Gillette Corporation, use the straight-line method. For example, let's assume Ajax Company bought equipment for $2,500. The company estimates that the equipment's period of "usefulness"—or *useful life*—will be 5 years. After 5 years the equipment will have a residual value (salvage value) of $500. The company decides to calculate its depreciation with the straight-line method and uses the following formula:

$$\frac{\text{Depreciation expense}}{\text{each year}} = \frac{\text{Cost} - \text{Residual value}}{\text{Estimated useful life in years}}$$

$$\frac{\$2,500 - \$500}{5 \text{ years}} = \$400 \text{ depreciation expense taken each year}$$

Table 17.1 gives a summary of the equipment depreciation that Ajax Company will take over the next 5 years. Companies call this summary a **depreciation schedule.**

TABLE 17.1

Depreciation schedule for straight-line method

$$\frac{100\%}{\text{Number of years}} = \frac{100\%}{5} = 20\%$$

Thus, the company is depreciating the equipment at a 20% rate each year.

End of year	Cost of equipment	Depreciation expense for year	Accumulated depreciation at end of year	Book value at end of year (Cost − Accumulated depreciation)
1	$2,500	$400	$ 400	$2,100 ($2,500 − $400)
2	2,500	400	800	1,700
3	2,500	400	1,200	1,300
4	2,500	400	1,600	900
5	2,500	400	2,000	500
	↑ Cost stays the same.	↑ Depreciation expense is same each year.	↑ Accumulated depreciation increases by $400 each year.	↑ Book value is lowered by $400 until residual value of $500 is reached.

Depreciation for Partial Years

If a company buys an asset before the 15th of the month, the company calculates the asset's depreciation for a full month. Companies do not take the full month's depreciation for assets bought after the 15th of the month. For example, assume Ajax Company (Table 17.1) bought the equipment on May 6. The company would calculate the depreciation for the first year as follows:

$$\frac{\$2,500 - \$500}{5 \text{ years}} = \$400 \times \frac{8}{12} = \$266.67$$

Now let's check your progress with the Practice Quiz before we look at the next depreciation method.

LU 17.1 PRACTICE QUIZ

1. Prepare a depreciation schedule using straight-line depreciation for the following:

Cost of truck	$16,000
Residual value	1,000
Life	5 years

2. If the truck were bought on February 3, what would the depreciation expense be in the first year?

✓ **Solutions**

1.

End of year	Cost of truck	Depreciation expense for year	Accumulated depreciation at end of year	Book value at end of year (Cost − Accumulated depreciation)
1	$16,000	$3,000	$ 3,000	$13,000 ($16,000 − $3,000)
2	16,000	3,000	6,000	10,000
3	16,000	3,000	9,000	7,000
4	16,000	3,000	12,000	4,000 Note that we
5	16,000	3,000	15,000	1,000 ← are down to residual value

2. $$\frac{\$16,000 - \$1,000}{5} = \$3,000 \times \frac{11}{12} = \boxed{\$2,750}$$

LEARNING UNIT 17.2   Units-of-Production Method

Unlike in the straight-line depreciation method, in the **units-of-production method** the passage of time is not used to determine an asset's depreciation amount. Instead, the company determines the asset's depreciation according to how much the company uses the asset. This use could be miles driven, tons hauled, or units that a machine produces. For example, when a company such as Ajax Company (in Learning Unit 17.1) buys equipment, the company estimates how many units the equipment can produce. Let's assume the equipment has a useful life of 4,000 units. The following formulas are used to calculate the equipment's depreciation for the units-of-production method.

$$\frac{\text{Depreciation}}{\text{per unit}} = \frac{\text{Cost} - \text{Residual value}}{\text{Total estimated units produced}} = \frac{\$2,500 - \$500}{4,000 \text{ units}} = \frac{\$.50}{\text{per unit}}$$

$$\frac{\text{Depreciation}}{\text{amount}} = \frac{\text{Unit}}{\text{depreciation}} \times \frac{\text{Units}}{\text{produced}} = \$.50 \text{ times actual number of units}$$

Now we can complete Table 17.2. Note that the table gives the units produced each year. Let's check your understanding of this unit with the Practice Quiz.

TABLE 17.2   Depreciation schedule for units-of-production method

End of year	Cost of equipment	Units produced	Depreciation expense for year	Accumulated depreciation at end of year	Book value at end of year (Cost − Accumulated depreciation)
1	$2,500	300	$ 150 (300 × $.50)	$ 150	$2,350 ($2,500 − $150)
2	2,500	400	200	350	2,150
3	2,500	600	300	650	1,850
4	2,500	2,000	1,000	1,650	850
5	2,500	700	350	2,000	500

↑ At the end of 5 years, the equipment produced 4,000 units. If in year 5 the equipment produced 1,500 units, only 700 could be used in the calculation, or it will go below the equipment's residual value.

↑ Units produced per year times $.50 equals depreciation expense.

↑ Residual value of $500 is reached. (Be sure depreciation is not taken below the residual value.)

LU 17.2 PRACTICE QUIZ

From the following facts prepare a depreciation schedule:

Machine cost $20,000
Residual value   4,000
Expected to produce 16,000 units over its expected life

	2001	2002	2003	2004	2005
Units produced:	2,000	8,000	3,000	1,800	1,600

✓ **Solutions**

$$\frac{\$20,000 - \$4,000}{16,000} = \$1$$

End of year	Cost of machine	Units produced	Depreciation expense for year	Accumulated depreciation at end of year	Book value at end of year (Cost − Accumulated depreciation)
1	$20,000	2,000	$2,000 (2,000 × $1)	$ 2,000	$18,000
2	20,000	8,000	8,000	10,000	10,000
3	20,000	3,000	3,000	13,000	7,000
4	20,000	1,800	1,800	14,800	5,200
5	20,000	1,600	1,200*	16,000	4,000

*Note that we only can depreciate 1,200 units since we cannot go below the residual value of $4,000.

LEARNING UNIT 17.3 Sum-of-the-Years'-Digits Method[1]

Now we look at the **sum-of-the-years'-digits method.** This is an **accelerated depreciation method** that computes more depreciation expense in the early years of the asset's life than in the later years. The accelerated method may more closely match the way the assets lose their value.

To calculate depreciation expense for the sum-of-the-years'-digits method, we use the following formula:

---

[1]This method is seldom used today. In a recent survey of 600 companies, only 3% use the sum-of-the-years'-digits method.

TABLE 17.3   Depreciation schedule for sum-of-the-years'-digits method

End of year	Cost − Residual value	×	Fraction for year	=	Yearly depreciation expense	Accumulated depreciation at end of year	Book value at end of year (Cost − Accumulated depreciation)
1	$2,000 ($2,500 − $500)	×	$\frac{5}{15}$	=	$666.67	$ 666.67	$1,833.33 ($2,500 − $666.67)
2	2,000	×	$\frac{4}{15}$	=	533.33	1,200.00	1,300.00 ($2,500 − $1,200)
3	2,000	×	$\frac{3}{15}$	=	400.00	1,600.00	900.00
4	2,000	×	$\frac{2}{15}$	=	266.67	1,866.67	633.33
5	2,000	×	$\frac{1}{15}$	=	133.33	2,000.00	500.00
	↑ Cost *less* residual value is multiplied by fraction for year.		↑ Large numerator occurs in early years.		↑ *Note:* Depreciation of $666.67 in year 1 is highest.	↑ Accumulated depreciation increases more slowly in later years.	↑ *Note:* We used cost of $2,500 − $2,000 accumulated depreciation to equal book value of $500.

$$\frac{\text{Depreciation}}{\text{expense}} = (\text{Cost} - \text{Residual value}) \times \frac{\text{Remaining life}}{\text{Sum-of-the-years' digits}}$$

The fraction in the formula is the key to understanding the sum-of-the-years'-digits method. We can explain this fraction by assuming an asset has 5 years of remaining life.

$\left(\dfrac{5}{15}\right)$ ⟵ Numerator of fraction is years remaining

⟵ Denominator of fraction is the sum of the asset's service life
$(5 + 4 + 3 + 2 + 1)$

We can calculate the denominator of the fraction by this formula:

$$\frac{N(N+1)}{2} = \frac{5(5+1)}{2} = \frac{30}{2} = 15$$

where N is the estimated life of the asset. Remember that the numerator of the fraction—remaining years left—changes each year as the asset gets older. The denominator of the fraction—sum-of-the-years' digits—remains the same for the life of the asset.

Now let's use the sum-of-the-years' digits method and prepare the depreciation schedule shown in Table 17.3 for Ajax Company in Learning Unit 17.2. Keep in mind that partial years for depreciation could result, as we showed in the straight-line method.

It's time for another Practice Quiz.

LU 17.3 PRACTICE QUIZ

Prepare a depreciation schedule for the sum-of-the-years'-digits method from the following:

Cost of machine, 5-year life $16,000
Residual value   1,000

✓ **Solutions**

End of year	Cost − Residual value	×	Fraction for year	=	Yearly depreciation expense	Accumulated depreciation at end of year	Book value at end of year (Cost − Accumulated depreciation)
1	$15,000	×	$\frac{5}{15}$	=	$5,000	$ 5,000	$11,000 ($16,000 − $5,000)
2	15,000	×	$\frac{4}{15}$	=	4,000	9,000	7,000
3	15,000	×	$\frac{3}{15}$	=	3,000	12,000	4,000
4	15,000	×	$\frac{2}{15}$	=	2,000	14,000	2,000
5	15,000	×	$\frac{1}{15}$	=	1,000	15,000	1,000

LEARNING UNIT 17.4 Declining-Balance Method

In the declining-balance method, we cannot depreciate below the residual value.

The **declining-balance method** is another type of accelerated depreciation that takes larger amounts of depreciation expense in the earlier years of the asset. The straight-line method, you recall, estimates the life of the asset and distributes the same amount of depreciation expense to each period. To take larger amounts of depreciation expense in the asset's earlier years, the declining-balance method uses up to *twice* the **straight-line rate** in the first year of depreciation. A key point to remember is that the declining-balance method does not deduct the residual value in calculating the depreciation expense. Today, the declining-balance method is the basis of current tax depreciation.

For all problems, we will use double the straight-line rate unless we indicate otherwise. Today, the rate is often 1.5 or 1.25 times the straight-line rate. Again we use our $2,500 equipment with its estimated useful life of 5 years. As we build the depreciation schedule in Table 17.4, note the following steps:

Step 1. Rate is equal to $\frac{100\%}{5 \text{ years}} \times 2 = 40\%$.

Or another way to look at it is that the straight-line rate is $\frac{1}{5} \times 2 = \frac{2}{5} = 40\%$.

TABLE 17.4 Depreciation schedule for declining-balance method

End of year	Cost of equipment	Accumulated depreciation at beginning of year	Book value at beginning of year (Cost − Accumulated depreciation)	Depreciation (Book value at beginning of year × Rate)	Accumulated depreciation at end of year	Book value at end of year (Cost − Accumulated depreciation)
1	$2,500	—	$2,500	$1,000 ($2,500 × .40)	$1,000	$1,500 ($2,500 − $1,000)
2	2,500	$1,000	1,500	600 ($1,500 × .40)	1,600	900
3	2,500	1,600	900	360 ($900 × .40)	1,960	540
4	2,500	1,960	540	40	2,000	500
5	2,500	2,000	500		2,000	500
	↑	↑	↑	↑	↑	↑
	Original cost of $2,500 does not change. Residual value was not subtracted.	Ending accumulated depreciation of 1 year becomes next year's beginning.	Cost less accumulated depreciation.	Note: In year 4, only $40 is taken since we cannot depreciate below residual value of $500. In year 5, no depreciation is taken.	Accumulated depreciation balance plus depreciation expense this year.	Book value now equals residual value.

Step 2.

$$\begin{array}{c}\text{Depreciation expense} \\ \text{each year}\end{array} = \begin{array}{c}\text{Book value of equipment} \\ \text{at beginning of year}\end{array} \times \begin{array}{c}\text{Depreciation} \\ \text{rate}\end{array}$$

Step 3. We cannot depreciate the equipment below its residual value ($500). The straight-line method and the sum-of-the-years'-digits method automatically reduced the asset's book value to the residual value. This is not true with the declining-balance method. So you must be careful when you prepare the depreciation schedule.

Now let's check your progress again with another Practice Quiz.

LU 17.4 PRACTICE QUIZ

Prepare a depreciation schedule from the following:

Cost of machine: $16,000   Estimated life: 5 years
Rate: 40% (this is twice the straight-line rate)   Residual value: $1,000

✓ **Solutions**

End of year	Cost of machine	Accumulated depreciation at beginning of year	Book value at beginning of year (Cost − Accumulated depreciation)	Depreciation (Book value at beginning of year × Rate)	Accumulated depreciation at end of year	Book value at end of year (Cost − Accumulated depreciation)
1	$16,000	$ −0−	$16,000.00	$6,400.00	$ 6,400.00	$9,600.00
2	16,000	6,400.00	9,600.00	3,840.00	10,240.00	5,760.00
3	16,000	10,240.00	5,760.00	2,304.00	12,544.00	3,456.00
4	16,000	12,544.00	3,456.00	1,382.40	13,926.40	2,073.60
5	16,000	13,926.40	2,073.60	829.44*	14,755.84	1,244.16

*Since we do not reach the residual value of $1,000, another $244.16 could have been taken as depreciation expense to bring it to the estimated residual value of $1,000.

LEARNING UNIT 17.5   Modified Accelerated Cost Recovery System (MACRS) with Introduction to ACRS

In Learning Units 17.1 to 17.4, we discussed the depreciation methods used for financial reporting. Since 1981, federal tax laws have been passed that state how depreciation must be taken for income tax purposes. Assets put in service from 1981 through 1986 fell under the federal **Accelerated Cost Recovery System (ACRS)** tax law enacted in 1981. The Tax Reform Act of 1986 established the **Modified Accelerated Cost Recovery System (MACRS)** for all property placed into service after December 31, 1986. Both these federal laws provide users with tables giving the useful lives of various assets and the depreciation rates. We look first at the MACRS and then at a 1989 update.

Depreciation for Tax Purposes Based on the Tax Reform Act of 1986 (MACRS)

Tables 17.5 and 17.6 give the classes of recovery and annual depreciation percentages that MACRS established in 1986. The key points of MACRS are:

1. It calculates depreciation for tax purposes.
2. It ignores residual value.
3. Depreciation in the first year (for personal property) is based on the assumption that the asset was purchased halfway through the year. (A new law adds a midquarter convention for all personal property if more than 40% is placed in service during the last 3 months of the taxable year.)
4. Classes 3, 5, 7, and 10 use a 200% declining-balance method for a period of years before switching to straight-line depreciation. You do not have to determine the year in which to switch since Table 17.6 builds this into the calculation.
5. Classes 15 and 20 use a 150% declining-balance method before switching to straight-line depreciation.
6. Classes 27.5 and 31.5 use straight-line depreciation.

TABLE 17.5

Modified Accelerated Cost Recovery System (MACRS) for assets placed in service after December 31, 1986

Class recovery period (life)	Asset types
3-year*	Racehorses more than 2 years old or any horse other than a racehorse that is more than 12 years old at the time placed into service; special tools of certain industries.
5-year*	Automobiles (not luxury); taxis; light general-purpose trucks; semiconductor manufacturing equipment; computer-based telephone central-office switching equipment; qualified technological equipment; property used in connection with research and experimentation.
7-year*	Railroad track; single-purpose agricultural (pigpens) or horticultural structures; fixtures; equipment; furniture.
10-year*	New law doesn't add any specific property under this class.
15-year†	Municipal wastewater treatment plants; telephone distribution plants and comparable equipment used for two-way exchange of voice and data communications.
20-year†	Municipal sewers.
27.5-year‡	Only residential rental property.
31.5-year‡	Only nonresidential real property.

*These classes use a 200% declining-balance method switching to the straight-line method.
†These classes use a 150% declining-balance method switching to the straight-line method.
‡These classes use a straight-line method.

TABLE 17.6   Annual recovery for MACRS

Recovery year	3-year class (200% D.B.)	5-year class (200% D.B.)	7-year class (200% D.B.)	10-year class (200% D.B.)	15-year class (150% D.B.)	20-year class (150% D.B.)
1	33.00	20.00	14.28	10.00	5.00	3.75
2	45.00	32.00	24.49	18.00	9.50	7.22
3	15.00*	19.20	17.49	14.40	8.55	6.68
4	7.00	11.52*	12.49	11.52	7.69	6.18
5		11.52	8.93*	9.22	6.93	5.71
6		5.76	8.93	7.37	6.23	5.28
7			8.93	6.55*	5.90*	4.89
8			4.46	6.55	5.90	4.52
9				6.55	5.90	4.46*
10				6.55	5.90	4.46
11				3.29	5.90	4.46
12					5.90	4.46
13					5.90	4.46
14					5.90	4.46
15					5.90	4.46
16					3.00	4.46

*Identifies when switch is made to straight line.

EXAMPLE   Using the same equipment cost of $2,500 for Ajax, prepare a depreciation schedule under MACRS assuming the equipment is a 5-year class and not part of the tax bill of 1989. Use Table 17.6. Note that percent figures from Table 17.6 have been converted to decimals.

End of year	Cost	Depreciation expense	Accumulated depreciation	Book value at end of year
1	$2,500	$500 (.20 × $2,500)	$ 500	$2,000
2	2,500	800 (.32 × $2,500)	1,300	1,200
3	2,500	480 (.1920 ×$2,500)	1,780	720
4	2,500	288 (.1152 × $2,500)	2,068	432
5	2,500	288 (.1152 × $2,500)	2,356	144
6	2,500	144 (.0576 × $2,500)	2,500	–0–

**Update on MACRS:
The 1989 Tax Bill**

Before the 1989 tax bill (**Omnibus Budget Reconciliation Act of 1989**), cellular phones and similar equipment were depreciated under MACRS. Since cellular phones are subject to personal use, the 1989 act now treats them as "listed" property. This means that unless business use is greater than 50%, the straight-line method of depreciation is required.
Let's try another Practice Quiz.

LU 17.5 PRACTICE QUIZ

1. In 1991, Rancho Corporation bought semiconductor equipment for $80,000. Using MACRS, what is the depreciation expense in year 3?
2. What would depreciation be the first year for a wastewater treatment plant that cost $800,000?

✓   **Solutions**

1. $80,000 × .1920 = $15,360

2. $800,000 × .05 = $40,000

Chapter Organizer and Reference Guide

Topic	Key point, procedure, formula	Example(s) to illustrate situation
Straight-line method, p. 397	$\dfrac{\text{Depreciation expense}}{\text{each year}} = \dfrac{\text{Cost} - \text{Residual value}}{\text{Estimated useful life in years}}$ For partial years if purchased before 15th of month depreciation is taken.	Truck, $25,000; $5,000 residual value, 4-year life. $\text{Depreciation expense} = \dfrac{\$25,000 - \$5,000}{4}$ $= \$5,000$ per year
Units-of-production method, p. 398	$\dfrac{\text{Depreciation}}{\text{per unit}} = \dfrac{\text{Cost} - \text{Residual value}}{\text{Total estimated units produced}}$ Do not depreciate below residual value even if actual units are greater than estimate.	Machine, $5,000; estimated life in units, 900; residual value, $500. Assume first year produced 175 units. $\text{Depreciation expense} = \dfrac{\$5,000 - \$500}{900}$ $= \dfrac{\$4,500}{900}$ $= \$5$ depreciation per unit 175 units $\times$ $5 = $875 depreciation expense
Sum-of-the-years'-digits method, p. 399	$\dfrac{\text{Depreciation}}{\text{expense}} = \left(\begin{array}{c}\text{Cost} - \\ \text{Residual} \\ \text{value}\end{array}\right) \times \dfrac{\text{Remaining life}}{\text{Sum-of-the-years' digits}}$ $\uparrow$ $\dfrac{N(N+1)}{2}$	Truck, $32,000; estimated life, 5 years; residual value, $2,000. <table><tr><th>Year</th><th>Cost (less residual value)</th><th>$\times$ Rate</th><th>= Depreciation expense</th></tr><tr><td>1</td><td>$30,000</td><td>$\times \frac{5}{15}$</td><td>= $10,000</td></tr><tr><td>2</td><td>30,000</td><td>$\times \frac{4}{15}$</td><td>= 8,000</td></tr></table>
Declining-balance method, p. 401	An accelerated method. Residual value not subtracted from cost in depreciation schedule. Do not depreciate below residual value. $\dfrac{\text{Depreciation}}{\text{expense}}_{\text{each year}} = \dfrac{\text{Book value of}}{\text{equipment at}}_{\text{beginning of year}} \times \dfrac{\text{Depreciation}}{\text{rate}}$	Truck, $50,000; estimated life, 5 years; residual value, $10,000. $\dfrac{1}{5} = 20\% \times 2 = 40\%$ (assume double the straight-line rate) <table><tr><th>Year</th><th>Cost</th><th>Depreciation expense</th><th>Book value at end of year</th></tr><tr><td>1</td><td>$50,000</td><td>$20,000 ($50,000 $\times$ .40)</td><td>$30,000 ($50,000 − $20,000)</td></tr><tr><td>2</td><td>50,000</td><td>12,000 ($30,000 $\times$ .40)</td><td>18,000 ($50,000 − $32,000)</td></tr></table>
MACRS/Tax Bill of 1989, p. 402	After December 31, 1986, depreciation calculation is modified. Tax Act of 1989 modifies way to depreciate cellular phones and similar equipment.	Auto: $8,000, 5 years. First year, .20 $\times$ $8,000 = $1,600 depreciation expense
Key terms	Accelerated Cost Recovery System (ACRS), *p. 402* Accelerated depreciation method, *p. 399* Accumulated depreciation, *p. 396* Asset cost, *p. 396* Book value, *p. 397* Declining-balance method, *p. 401*	Depreciation, *p. 396* Depreciation expense, *p. 396* Depreciation schedule, *p. 397* Estimated useful life, *p. 396* Modified Accelerated Cost Recovery System (MACRS), *p. 402* Omnibus Budget Reconciliation Act of 1989, *p. 404* Residual value, *p. 396* Salvage value, *p. 396* Straight-line method, *p. 397* Straight-line rate, *p. 401* Sum-of-the-years'-digits method, *p. 399* Trade-in value, *p. 396* Units-of-production method, *p. 398*

**Critical Thinking
Discussion Questions**

1. What is the difference between depreciation expense and accumulated depreciation? Why does the book value of an asset never go below the residual value?
2. Compare the straight-line method to the units-of-production method. Should both methods be based on the passage of time?
3. Explain the difference between the sum-of-the-years'-digits method and declining-balance method. Why is it possible in the declining-balance method for a person to depreciate below the residual value by mistake?
4. Explain the Modified Accelerated Cost Recovery System. Do you think this system will be eliminated in the future?

DRILL PROBLEMS

From the following facts, complete a depreciation schedule, using the straight-line method:

Given   Cost of Mercedes $80,000
Residual value   10,000
Estimated life   7 years

	End of year	Cost of Mercedes	Depreciation expense for year	Accumulated depreciation at end of year	Book value at end of year
17–1.	1	$80,000	$10,000	$10,000	$70,000 ($80,000 − $10,000)
17–2.	2	$80,000	$10,000	$20,000	$60,000
17–3.	3	$80,000	$10,000	$30,000	$50,000
17–4.	4	$80,000	$10,000	$40,000	$40,000
17–5.	5	$80,000	$10,000	$50,000	$30,000
17–6.	6	$80,000	$10,000	$60,000	$20,000
17–7.	7	$80,000	$10,000	$70,000	$10,000

$$\frac{\$80,000 - \$10,000}{7 \text{ years}} = \$10,000$$

Prepare a depreciation schedule using the sum-of-the-years'-digits method:

Given   Truck cost $11,000
Residual value   1,000
Estimated life   4 years

	End of year	Cost − Residual value	×	Fraction for year	=	Depreciation expense for year	Accumulated depreciation at end of year	Book value at end of year
17–8.	1	$10,000	×	$\frac{4}{10}$		$4,000	$ 4,000	$7,000 ($11,000 − $4,000)
17–9.	2	$10,000	×	$\frac{3}{10}$		$3,000	$ 7,000	$4,000
17–10.	3	$10,000	×	$\frac{2}{10}$		$2,000	$ 9,000	$2,000
17–11.	4	$10,000	×	$\frac{1}{10}$		$1,000	$10,000	$1,000

$$\frac{N(N + 1)}{2} = \frac{4(4 + 1)}{2} = \frac{20}{2} = 10$$

Prepare a depreciation schedule using the declining-balance method (twice the straight-line rate):

Given   Cost of truck $25,000
Residual value   5,000
Estimated life   5 years

	End of year	Cost of truck	Accumulated depreciation at beginning of year	Book value at beginning of year	Depreciation expense for year	Accumulated depreciation at end of year	Book value at end of year
17–12.	1	$25,000	–0–	$25,000	$10,000 ($25,000 × .40)	$10,000	$15,000 ($25,000 − $10,000)
17–13.	2	$25,000	$10,000	$15,000	$ 6,000 ($15,000 × .40)	$16,000	$ 9,000 ($25,000 − $16,000)
17–14.	3	$25,000	$16,000	$ 9,000	$ 3,600 ($9,000 × .40)	$19,600	$ 5,400 ($25,000 − $19,600)
17–15.	4	$25,000	$19,600	$ 5,400	$ 400* ($5,400 − $5,000)	$20,000	$ 5,000

*Cannot be depreciated below book value.

For the first 2 years, calculate the depreciation expense for a $7,000 car under MACRS. This is a nonluxury car.

<table>
<tr><td colspan="2" align="center">**MACRS**</td><td colspan="2" align="center">**MACRS**</td></tr>
<tr><td>**17–16.** Year 1</td><td>$1,400
($7,000 × .20)</td><td>**17–17.** Year 2</td><td>$2,240
($7,000 × .32)</td></tr>
</table>

Complete the following table given this information:

Cost of machine	$94,000	Estimated units machine will produce	100,000	
Residual value	4,000	Actual production:	**Year 1**	**Year 2**
Useful life	5 years		60,000	15,000

	Depreciation expense	
Method	**Year 1**	**Year 2**
17–18. Straight line	$18,000	$18,000
17–19. Units of production	54,000	13,500
17–20. Sum-of-the-years' digits	30,000	24,000
17–21. Declining balance	37,600	22,560
17–22. MACRS (5-year class)	18,800	30,080

17–18. $\dfrac{\$94,000 - \$4,000}{5} = \$18,000$

17–19. $\dfrac{\$94,000 - \$4,000}{100,000} = \$.90$ depreciation per unit

Year 1: 60,000 × $.90 = $54,000
Year 2: 15,000 × $.90 = $13,500

17–20. $\dfrac{5}{15} \times \$90,000 = \$30,000$

$\dfrac{4}{15} \times \$90,000 = \$24,000$

17–21. $\dfrac{1}{5} = .20 \times 2 = .40$

$94,000 × .40 = $37,600
$94,000 − $37,600 = $56,400
× .40
$22,560

17–22. $94,000 × .20 = $18,800

$94,000 × .32 = $30,080

WORD PROBLEMS

17–23. The April 1997 issue of *Tax Adviser* reported that a Mercedes Benz was purchased at $75,000 with a residual value of $15,000. The vehicle is used 75% for business and 25% for personal use. Using the straight-line depreciation method with a life expectancy of 3 years, how much could be charged each year as a business expense?

$75,000 − $15,000 = $60,000
× .75 business use
$45,000 total depreciation

$\dfrac{\$45,000}{3 \text{ years}} = \$15,000$ depreciation each year

17–24. Jane Hall bought a truck for $24,000 with an estimated life of 4 years. The residual value of the truck is $4,000. Assume a straight-line method of depreciation. What will be the book value of the truck at the end of year 3? If the truck was bought the first year on April 12, how much depreciation would be taken the first year?

$\dfrac{\$24,000 - \$4,000}{4 \text{ years}} = \$5,000$ depreciation expense per year

$24,000 − $15,000 = $9,000 book value

$\$5,000 \times \dfrac{9}{12} = \$3,750$

17–25. Jim Company bought a machine for $36,000 with an estimated life of 5 years. The residual value of the machine is $6,000. Calculate **(a)** the annual depreciation and **(b)** the book value at the end of year 3. Assume straight-line depreciation.

a. $\dfrac{\$36,000 - \$6,000}{5 \text{ years}} = \dfrac{\$30,000}{5 \text{ years}} = \$6,000$ depreciation expense

b. $36,000 − $18,000 = $18,000
Cost − Accumulated depreciation

17–26. Using Problem 17–25, calculate the first 2 years' depreciation, assuming the units-of-production method. This machine is expected to produce 120,000 units. In year 1, it produced 19,000 units, and in year 2, 38,000 units.

$$\frac{\$36,000 - \$6,000}{120,000 \text{ units}} = \frac{\$30,000}{120,000} = \$.25$$

Year 1: $19,000 \times \$.25 = \$4,750$
Year 2: $38,000 \times \$.25 = \$9,500$

17–27. Assume Jim Company (Problem 17–25) used the sum-of-the-years'-digits method. How much more or less depreciation expense over the first 2 years would have been taken compared to straight-line depreciation?

$$\$30,000 \times \frac{5}{15} = \$10,000$$

$$\$30,000 \times \frac{4}{15} = \underline{\quad 8,000}$$

$$\$18,000$$
$$\underline{- 12,000}$$

$\$6,000$ more using sum-of-the-years'-digits method

17–28. Quaker Oats is purchasing a 1998 Pontiac Bonneville SE four-door for salesperson Chris Yontez. The *Kiplinger's 1998 Buyer's Guide* lists the vehicle at $22,995 with a residual value of $4,600. The life expectancy of the vehicle is 5 years. Using the declining-balance method (twice the straight-line rate), what will be the depreciation expense for the first year?

$$\frac{1}{5} = 20\% \times 2 = 40\%$$

Cost $\$22,995$
$\underline{\times .40}$ double straight line
$\$\ 9,198$

17–29. The *Kiplinger's 1998 Car Buyer's Guide* lists a 1998 Lexus ES 300 four-door at $31,285. Quaker Oats is purchasing this car for the vice president of sales to be used in business. The residual value is $6,257. Using MACRS, what will be the depreciation expense for the first year?

Table 17.5, automobile (not luxury), 5 years $31,285
Table 17.6, 20%, first year $\underline{\times .20}$
                                           $\$\ 6,257$

17–30. Mr. Fix Company bought a new delivery truck for $26,000 with an estimated life of 5 years. The residual value of the truck is $1,000. As Mr. Fix's accountant, prepare depreciation schedules for straight-line, sum-of-the-years'-digits, and declining-balance ($1\frac{1}{2}$ times the straight-line rate) methods.

Straight-line method: $\dfrac{\$26,000 - \$1,000}{5} = \$5,000$ per year

End of year	Cost of truck	Depreciation expense	Accumulated depreciation
1	$26,000	$5,000	$ 5,000
2	26,000	5,000	10,000
3	26,000	5,000	15,000
4	26,000	5,000	20,000
5	26,000	5,000	25,000

Sum-of-the-years'-digits method:

End of year	Cost of truck − Residual	Depreciation expense	Accumulated depreciation
1	$25,000 \times \frac{5}{15} =$	$8,333.33	$ 8,333.33
2	$25,000 \times \frac{4}{15} =$	6,666.67	15,000.00
3	$25,000 \times \frac{3}{15} =$	5,000.00	20,000.00
4	$25,000 \times \frac{2}{15} =$	3,333.33	23,333.33
5	$25,000 \times \frac{1}{15} =$	1,666.67	25,000.00

Declining-balance method: $1.5 \times .20 = .30 = 30\%$

End of year	Cost of truck	Accumulated depreciation at beginning of year	Book value at beginning of year	Depreciation expense	Accumulated depreciation at end of year	Book value at end of year
1	$26,000	–0–	$26,000.00	$7,800.00 ($26,000 × .30)	$ 7,800.00	$18,200.00 ($26.000 − $7,800)
2	26,000	$ 7,800.00	18,200.00	5,460.00 ($18,200 × .30)	13,260.00	12,740.00
3	26,000	13,260.00	12,740.00	3,822.00	17,082.00	8,918.00
4	26,000	17,082.00	8,918.00	2,675.40	19,757.40	6,242.60
5	26,000	19,757.40	6,242.60	1,872.78*	21,630.18	4,369.82

*Since we have not reached the $1,000 residual value, another $3,369.82 ($4,369.82 − $1,000) could have been taken as depreciation expense in year 5.

CHALLENGE PROBLEMS

17–31. The April 1997 issue of *Tax Adviser* reports that Dee Company acquired a general-purpose truck with a GVW (gross vehicle weight) of 6,200 pounds (considered lightweight). The cost of the vehicle was $20,000 with a residual value of $4,000. What will be the depreciation charge each year by using MACRS versus the sum-of-the-years'-digits method?

MACRS

Sum-of-the-Years'-Digits Method

$20,000 − $4,000 = $16,000

$$N\left(\frac{N+1}{2}\right) = 5\left(\frac{6}{2}\right) = 15$$

Year

	MACRS	SYD
1	$4,000 ($20,000 × 20%)	$16,000 × \frac{5}{15} = $5,333.33
2	$6,400 ($20,000 × 32%)	$16,000 × \frac{4}{15} = $4,266.67
3	$3,840 ($20,000 × 19.20%)	$16,000 × \frac{3}{15} = $3,200.00
4	$2,304 ($20,000 × 11.52%)	$16,000 × \frac{2}{15} = $2,133.33
5	$2,304 ($20,000 × 11.52%)	$16,000 × \frac{1}{15} = $1,066.67
6	$1,152 ($20,000 × 5.76%)	

17–32. A piece of equipment was purchased July 26, 2000, at a cost of $72,000. The estimated residual value is $5,400 with a useful life of 5 years. Assume a production life of 60,000 units. Compute the depreciation for years 2000 and 2001 using **(a)** straight-line; **(b)** units-of-production (in 2000, 5,000 units produced and in 2001, 18,000 units produced); and **(c)** sum-of-the-years'-digits methods.

a. $\dfrac{\$72,000 - \$5,400}{5 \text{ years}} = \$13,320$

2000: $\$13,320 \times \dfrac{5}{12} = \$5,550$ (5/12 Aug. to Dec. 31)

2001: $13,320

b. $\dfrac{\$72,000 - \$5,400}{60,000} = \$1.11$

2000: 5,000 × $1.11 = $5,550

2001: 18,000 × $1.11 = $19,980

c. 2000: $\$66,600^{(\$72,000 - \$5,400)} \times \dfrac{5}{15} = \$22,200 \longrightarrow$ 2000: $\dfrac{5}{12} \times \$22,200 = \$9,250$

2001: $\$66,600 \times \dfrac{4}{15} = \$17,760 \longrightarrow$ 2001: $\dfrac{7}{12} \times \$22,200 = 12,950$

$\dfrac{5}{12} \times \$17,760 = \dfrac{7,400}{\$20,350}$

SUMMARY PRACTICE TEST

1. Lo Chung, owner of the Chinese Express, bought a delivery truck for $25,000. The truck has an estimated life of 4 years with a residual value of $5,000. Lo wants to know which depreciation method will be best for his truck. He asks you to prepare a depreciation schedule using the declining-balance method at twice the straight-line rate. *(p. 401)*

End of year	Cost of truck	Accumulated depreciation at beginning of year	Book value at beginning of year	Depreciation expense	Accumulated depreciation at end of year	Book value at end of year
1	$25,000	–0–	$25,000	$12,500 (.50 × $25,000)	$12,500	$12,500
2	25,000	$12,500	12,500	$ 6,250 (.50 × $12,500)	18,750	6,250

In year 3, depreciation is taken for $1,250, since we cannot go below the residual value.

2. Using MACRS, what is the depreciation for the first year on furniture costing $6,000? *(p. 403)*

$6,000 × .1428 = $856.80

3. Leah Wills bought a new delivery truck for $35,000. The truck has a life expectancy of 5 years with a residual value of $5,000. Prepare a depreciation schedule for the sum-of-the-years'-digits method. *(p. 400)*

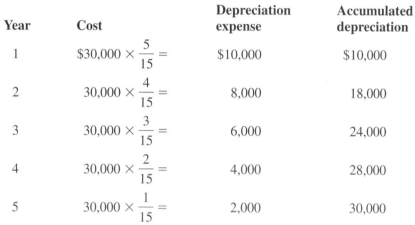

Year	Cost	Depreciation expense	Accumulated depreciation
1	$30,000 × $\frac{5}{15}$ =	$10,000	$10,000
2	30,000 × $\frac{4}{15}$ =	8,000	18,000
3	30,000 × $\frac{3}{15}$ =	6,000	24,000
4	30,000 × $\frac{2}{15}$ =	4,000	28,000
5	30,000 × $\frac{1}{15}$ =	2,000	30,000

4. Victor Corporation bought a Toyota Landcruiser for $40,000. The Toyota has a life expectancy of 10 years with a residual value of $5,000. After 2 years, the Toyota was sold for $28,000. What was the difference between the book value and the amount received from selling the car if Victor used the straight-line method of depreciation? *(p. 397)*

$$\frac{\$40,000 - \$5,000}{10 \text{ years}} = \frac{\$35,000}{10 \text{ years}} = \$3,500 \times 2 = \$7,000$$

$40,000
− 7,000
$33,000 book value
− 28,000
$ 5,000 difference (book value is greater)

5. If Victor Corporation (Problem 4) used the sum-of-the-years'-digits method, what was the difference between the book value and the price at which the Toyota was sold? Round each calculation to the nearest dollar. *(p. 400)*

$10\left(\dfrac{10 + 1}{2}\right) = 55$

$\$35,000 \times \dfrac{10}{55} = \$ 6,364$

$\$35,000 \times \dfrac{9}{55} = \dfrac{5,727}{\$12,091}$

$40,000
− 12,091
$27,909 book value
− 28,000
$ −91 difference (book value is less)

A KIPLINGER APPROACH

A GROUP PROJECT   Defend or reject the following business math issue based on the *Kiplinger's Personal Finance Magazine* article below:

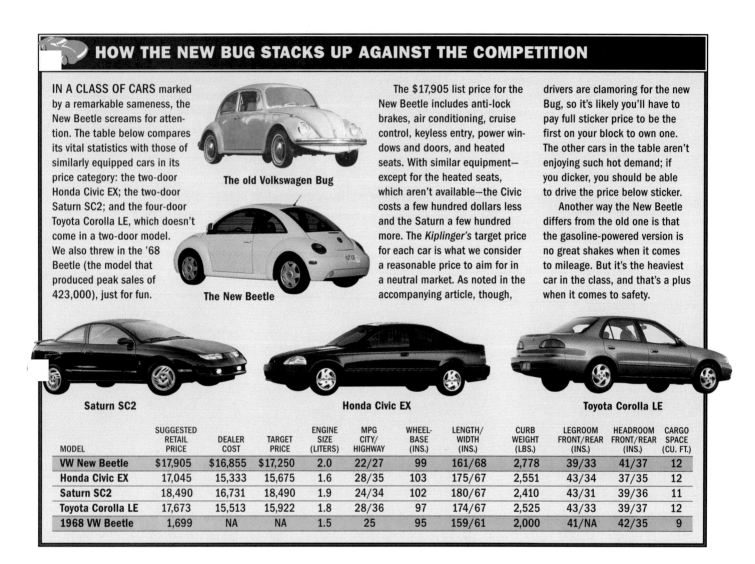

HOW THE NEW BUG STACKS UP AGAINST THE COMPETITION

IN A CLASS OF CARS marked by a remarkable sameness, the New Beetle screams for attention. The table below compares its vital statistics with those of similarly equipped cars in its price category: the two-door Honda Civic EX; the two-door Saturn SC2; and the four-door Toyota Corolla LE, which doesn't come in a two-door model. We also threw in the '68 Beetle (the model that produced peak sales of 423,000), just for fun.

The old Volkswagen Bug

The New Beetle

The $17,905 list price for the New Beetle includes anti-lock brakes, air conditioning, cruise control, keyless entry, power windows and doors, and heated seats. With similar equipment—except for the heated seats, which aren't available—the Civic costs a few hundred dollars less and the Saturn a few hundred more. The *Kiplinger's* target price for each car is what we consider a reasonable price to aim for in a neutral market. As noted in the accompanying article, though,

drivers are clamoring for the new Bug, so it's likely you'll have to pay full sticker price to be the first on your block to own one. The other cars in the table aren't enjoying such hot demand; if you dicker, you should be able to drive the price below sticker.

Another way the New Beetle differs from the old one is that the gasoline-powered version is no great shakes when it comes to mileage. But it's the heaviest car in the class, and that's a plus when it comes to safety.

Saturn SC2   **Honda Civic EX**   **Toyota Corolla LE**

MODEL	SUGGESTED RETAIL PRICE	DEALER COST	TARGET PRICE	ENGINE SIZE (LITERS)	MPG CITY/ HIGHWAY	WHEEL-BASE (INS.)	LENGTH/ WIDTH (INS.)	CURB WEIGHT (LBS.)	LEGROOM FRONT/REAR (INS.)	HEADROOM FRONT/REAR (INS.)	CARGO SPACE (CU. FT.)
VW New Beetle	$17,905	$16,855	$17,250	2.0	22/27	99	161/68	2,778	39/33	41/37	12
Honda Civic EX	17,045	15,333	15,675	1.6	28/35	103	175/67	2,551	43/34	37/35	12
Saturn SC2	18,490	16,731	18,490	1.9	24/34	102	180/67	2,410	43/31	39/36	11
Toyota Corolla LE	17,673	15,513	15,922	1.8	28/36	97	174/67	2,525	43/33	39/37	12
1968 VW Beetle	1,699	NA	NA	1.5	25	95	159/61	2,000	41/NA	42/35	9

Business Math Issue

The new Bug will not depreciate since it may be a classic in future years.

1. List the key points of the article and information to support your position.
2. Write a group defense of your position using math calculations to support your view.

Project A

Do you feel this Taxpayer Relief Act is fair? What does the $18,000 mean?

HOME OFFICE
Don't Tax Yourself Too Much at Home

Next Year Will Be Easier, But Aunt Millie Can't Use The Office as a Guest Room

By PEGGY EDERSHEIM KALB
Special to THE WALL STREET JOURNAL

FIGURING OUT HOW to take tax deductions on a home office has never been easy. Do you write off that new computer, even though your kids use it to play Tomb Raider II? What about deducting some of the housekeeper's salary if she cleans your home office?

Thanks to the new Taxpayer Relief Act, some answers are about to become simpler. For one thing, more people will qualify to write off office-related household expenses.

"The law has changed a lot over the years—loosened, tightened—and the recent changes loosened it," says Shelley Martin, an accountant with Weikart Tax Associates, New York. But since those changes aren't effective until next year, and April 15 is fast approaching, here is an overview of what you can deduct right now.

First, if you are self-employed, you may be able to deduct home-office equipment and supplies such as fax machines, computers and paper to the extent you use them for work. The Internal Revenue Service assumes that most equipment fully depreciates over five years. So if 75% of what you do on your computer is business-related, 75% of the cost of your computer is deductible over five years (though you can usually claim the full amount in the year you buy it). You can deduct up to $18,000 worth of such stuff each year, as long as you don't deduct more than you earn.

If you aren't self-employed, you may still be able to deduct equipment that is required, but not provided or reimbursed, by your employer. But make sure your boss is on board: Your company must be willing to say it's a "condition" of your employment.

That can be risky. For example, a stockbroker might feel she needs a home computer, but it's unlikely her boss would describe it as a "condition" of employment. "It's a red flag for the IRS," Ms. Martin says. "Most employers aren't willing to say they require something they won't reimburse."

Unlucky Doctor

Another big potential write-off is the deduction for office-related household expenses, such as heating and air-conditioning. But it's generally available only if you use your home office "exclusively" and regularly for business.

The home-office deduction is also typically available only if you meet patients or clients there, or if your home office is your sole office. If you have another office, it's still possible to claim this deduction, but the IRS requires that you consider your home your "principal place of business." That's obviously tough to do if your employer provides you with a desk.

Next year, the eligibility will be expanded. But now, it applies only to people who actually generate income from the work they do at home.

Too bad for the anesthesiologist who does all his administrative work at home, in his sole office, but sees patients only in the hospital. In 1993, the U.S. Supreme Court upheld the IRS's refusal of his home-office deduction. The reasoning? The home office wasn't the doctor's "principal place of business," since his income-generating

activities were essentially outside. By the same logic, an insurance agent whose sole office is at home but who spends most of her time visiting clients can't take a home-office deduction.

Next year, though, the law will expand the definition of "principal place of business" to include taxpayers like the anesthesiologist and the insurance agent. As with most tax laws, however, there are major exceptions, such as for people who use part of their home for a day-care center or to store product samples. (To learn more, check out the IRS's popular Web site at http://www.irs.ustreas.gov, and look for "Publication 587.")

So you qualify this year? Here's how to calculate your home-office deduction. Add up the square footage of the part of your home that you use for business. Then divide this area by your home's total square footage to determine the percentage your home office represents. In other words, if your home office is 200 square feet and your home is 2,000 square feet, 10% of your office-related household expenses are deductible. The space doesn't need to be partitioned off and you can even include part of a dining room or a basement, provided it is used exclusively for work activities or storage.

(Be careful: If you have another office, you can take a home-office deduction only against income you generate at home.)

You can include among your household expenses everything related to the care and maintenance of your home office, including utilities, the cost of a dedicated business phone line, and even housekeep-

What You Can, and Can't, Write Off

Here, in brief, is what the tax code generally allows home-office workers to deduct:

IF YOU ARE...	YOU ARE NOW GENERALLY ELIGIBLE TO DEDUCT....
A company employee	Depreciation of home office equipment required but not provided by your employer (to extent it's business related; limit $18,000)
Self-employed, generate income at home	Depreciation of equipment (same as above) Household expenses (on a ratio of workspace to total home square footage)
Self-employed, generate income away from home	Depreciation of equipment (same as above) **But next year....** Household expenses may also be deductible

(Note: to deduct household expenses, you must use your home office exclusively for business, and it must be considered your "primary place of business.")

See text Web site (www.mhhe.com/slater) and *The Business Math Internet Resource Guide.*

18

INVENTORY
AND
OVERHEAD

LEARNING UNIT OBJECTIVES

LU 18.1 Assigning Costs to Ending Inventory—Specific Identification; Weighted Average; FIFO; LIFO

- List the key assumptions of each inventory method *(pp. 416–21)*.
- Calculate the cost of ending inventory and cost of goods sold for each inventory method *(pp. 416–21)*.

LU 18.2 Retail Method; Gross Profit Method; Inventory Turnover; Distribution of Overhead

- Calculate the cost ratio and ending inventory at cost for the retail method *(p. 422)*.
- Calculate the estimated inventory, using the gross profit method *(p. 422)*.
- Explain and calculate inventory turnover *(p. 423)*.
- Explain overhead; allocate overhead according to floor space and sales *(p. 424)*.

Fuji Photo Ties Price Cuts To Inventories

It Says Move Doesn't Mean A War With Kodak; Analyst Is Skeptical

By LAURA JOHANNES
Staff Reporter of THE WALL STREET JOURNAL
Fuji Photo Film Co. said its rock-bottom pricing in recent months was a "temporary" measure to rid it of excess inventory and not—as several analysts believed—the opening salvo in a brutal price war aimed at wresting market share from **Eastman Kodak** Co.

GM Delays Opening Of Assembly Plant In Thailand to 2000

BANGKOK, Thailand (AP) — The opening of a **General Motors** Corp. unit's assembly plant in eastern Thailand will be delayed until the first half of 2000 because Asia's economic crisis has forced the company to reconsider what model to produce, a company spokesman said.

These two *Wall Street Journal* clippings introduce the importance of inventories for businesses in the United States and overseas. The clippings do not report the inventory method used by Fuji Photo Film Company or the Thailand General Motors Corporation assembly plant. They could use either the *perpetual inventory system* or the *periodic inventory system.*

The perpetual inventory system should be familiar to most consumers. Today, it is common for cashiers to run scanners across the product code of each item sold. These scanners read pertinent information into a computer terminal, such as the item's number, department, and price. The computer then uses the **perpetual inventory system** as it subtracts outgoing merchandise from inventory and adds incoming merchandise to inventory. However, as you probably know, the computer cannot be completely relied on to maintain an accurate count of merchandise in stock. Since some products may be stolen or lost, periodically a physical count is necessary to verify the computer count.

With the increased use of computers, many companies are changing to a perpetual inventory system of maintaining inventory records. Some small stores, however, still use the **periodic inventory system.** This system usually does not keep a running account of its inventory but relies only on a physical inventory count taken at least once a year. The store then uses various accounting methods to value the cost of its merchandise. In this chapter we discuss the periodic method of inventory.

Reproduced courtesy of International Business Machines Corporation.

You may wonder why a company should know the status of its inventory. In Chapter 16 we introduced you to the balance sheet and the income statement. Companies cannot accurately prepare these statements unless they have placed the correct value on their inventory. To do this, a company must know (1) the cost of its ending inventory (found on the balance sheet) and (2) the cost of the goods (merchandise) sold (found on the income statement).

Frequently, the same type of merchandise flows into a company at different costs. Depending on the value assumptions that a company makes about the goods it sells first, the company will assign different flows of costs to its ending inventory. Remember that different costs result in different levels of profit on a firm's financial reports. This chapter discusses four common methods that companies use to calculate costs of ending inventory and the cost of goods sold. In these methods, the flow of costs does not always match the flow of goods. Let's begin by following a case study of Blue Company.

LEARNING UNIT 18.1 Assigning Costs to Ending Inventory—Specific Identification; Weighted Average; FIFO; LIFO

Blue Company is a small artist supply store. Its beginning inventory is 40 tubes of art paint that cost $320 (at $8 a tube) to bring into the store. As shown in Figure 18.1, Blue made additional purchases in April, May, October, and December. Note that because of inflation and other competitive factors, the cost of the paint rose from $8 to $13 per tube. At the end of December, Blue had 48 unsold paint tubes. During the year, Blue had 120 paint tubes to sell. Blue wants to calculate (1) the cost of ending inventory (not sold) and (2) the cost of goods sold.

FIGURE 18.1

Blue Company—a case study

	Number of units purchased	Cost per unit	Total cost
Beginning inventory	40	$ 8	$ 320
First purchase (April 1)	20	9	180
Second purchase (May 1)	20	10	200
Third purchase (October 1)	20	12	240
Fourth purchase (December 1)	20	13	260
Goods (merchandise) available for sale	120		$1,200 ← **Step 1**
Units sold	72		
Units in ending inventory	48		

Specific Identification Method

Companies that sell high-cost items such as autos, jewelry, antiques, and so on, usually use the specific identification method.

Companies use the **specific identification method** when they can identify the original purchase cost of an item with the item. For example, Blue Company color codes its paint tubes as they come into the store. Blue can then attach a specific invoice price to each paint tube. This makes the flow of goods and flow of costs the same. Then, when Blue computes its ending inventory and cost of goods sold, it can associate the actual invoice cost with each item sold and in inventory.

To help Blue calculate its inventory with the specific identification method, use the steps that follow.

Calculating the Specific Identification Method

Step 1. Calculate the cost of goods (merchandise available for sale).
Step 2. Calculate the cost of the ending inventory.
Step 3. Calculate the cost of goods sold (Step 1 − Step 2).

First, Blue must actually count the tubes of paint on hand. Since Blue coded these paint tubes, it can identify the tubes with their purchase cost and multiply them by this cost to arrive at a total cost of ending inventory. Let's do this now.

	Cost per unit	Total cost
20 units from April 1	$ 9	$180
20 units from October 1	12	240
8 units from December 1	13	104
Cost of ending inventory		$524 ← **Step 2**

Blue uses the following cost of goods sold formula to determine its cost of goods sold:

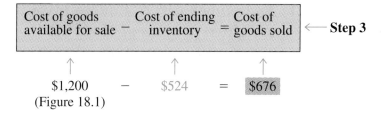

$1,200   − $524   = $676
(Figure 18.1)

Note that the $1,200 for cost of goods available for sale comes from Figure 18.1. Remember, we are focusing our attention on Blue's *purchase costs*. Blue's actual *selling price* does not concern us.

Now let's look at how Blue would use the weighted-average method.

Weighted-Average Method[1]

The **weighted-average method** prices the ending inventory by using an average unit cost. Let's replay Blue Company and use the weighted-average method to find the average unit cost of its ending inventory and its cost of goods sold. Blue would use the steps that follow.

Calculating the Weighted-Average Method

Step 1.   Calculate the average unit cost.
Step 2.   Calculate the cost of the ending inventory.
Step 3.   Calculate the cost of goods sold.

In the table that follows, Blue makes the calculation.

	Number of units purchased	Cost per unit	Total cost
Beginning inventory	40	$ 8	$ 320
First purchase (April 1)	20	9	180
Second purchase (May 1)	20	10	200
Third purchase (October 1)	20	12	240
Fourth purchase (December 1)	20	13	260
Goods (merchandise) available for sale	120		$1,200
Units sold	72		
Units in ending inventory	48		

$$\text{Weighted-average unit cost} = \frac{\text{Total cost of goods available for sale}}{\text{Total number of units available for sale}} = \frac{\$1,200}{120 \text{ units}} = \$10 \text{ average unit cost}$$ ← **Step 1**

Average cost of ending inventory: 48 units at $10 = $480   ← **Step 2**

Cost of goods available for sale − Cost of ending inventory = Cost of goods sold

$1,200   − $480   = $720   ← **Step 3**

Remember that some of the costs we used to determine the average unit cost were higher and others were lower. The weighted-average method, then, calculates an *average unit price* for goods. Companies with similar units of goods, such as rolls of wallpaper, often use the weighted-average method. Also, companies with homogeneous products such as fuels and grains may use the weighted-average method.

Now let's see how Blue Company would value its inventory with the FIFO method.

---

[1]Virtually all countries permit the use of the weighted-average method.

FIFO—First-In, First-Out Method[2]

The **first-in, first-out (FIFO)** inventory valuation method assumes that the first goods (paint tubes for Blue) brought into the store are the first goods sold. Thus, FIFO assumes that each sale is from the oldest goods in inventory. FIFO also assumes that the inventory remaining in the store at the end of the period is the most recently acquired goods. This cost flow assumption may or may not hold in the actual physical flow of the goods. An example of a corporation's using the FIFO method is Gillette Corporation.

Use the following steps to calculate inventory with the FIFO method.

Calculating the FIFO Inventory

Step 1. List the units to be included in the ending inventory and their costs.
Step 2. Calculate the cost of the ending inventory.
Step 3. Calculate the cost of goods sold.

In the table that follows, we show how to calculate FIFO for Blue using the above steps.

FIFO (bottom up)	Number of units purchased	Cost per unit	Total cost
Beginning inventory	40	$ 8	$ 320
First purchase (April 1)	20	9	180
Second purchase (May 1)	20	10	200
Third purchase (October 1)	20	12	240
Fourth purchase (December 1)	20	13	260
Goods (merchandise) available for sale	120		$1,200
Units sold	72		
Units in ending inventory	48		

20 units from December 1 purchased at $13		$260
20 units from October 1 purchased at $12	←—Step 1 —→	240
8 units from May 1 purchased at $10		80 — Step 2
48 units result in an ending inventory cost of		$580 ←

$$\text{Cost of goods available for sale} - \text{Cost of ending inventory} = \text{Cost of goods sold}$$

$$\$1,200 \quad - \quad \$580 \quad = \quad \$620 \longleftarrow \text{Step 3}$$

In FIFO, the cost flow of goods tends to follow the physical flow. For example, a fish market could use FIFO because it wants to sell its old inventory first. Note that during inflation, FIFO produces a higher income than other methods. So companies using FIFO during this time must pay more taxes.

We conclude this unit by using the LIFO method to value Blue Company's inventory.

LIFO—Last-In, First-Out Method[3]

If Blue Company chooses the **last-in, first-out (LIFO)** method of inventory valuation, then the goods sold by Blue will be the last goods brought into the store. The ending inventory would consist of the old goods that Blue bought earlier.

You can calculate inventory with the LIFO method by using the steps that follow.

---

[2]Virtually all countries permit the use of the FIFO method.
[3]Many countries, such as Australia, Hong Kong, South Africa, and the United Kingdom, do not permit the use of LIFO.

Calculating the LIFO Inventory

Step 1. List the units to be included in the ending inventory and their costs.
Step 2. Calculate the cost of the ending inventory.
Step 3. Calculate the cost of goods sold.

Now we use the above steps to calculate LIFO for Blue.

LIFO (top down)	Number of units purchased	Cost per unit	Total cost
Beginning inventory	40	$ 8	$ 320
First purchase (April 1)	20	9	180
Second purchase (May 1)	20	10	200
Third purchase (October 1)	20	12	240
Fourth purchase (December 1)	20	13	260
Goods (merchandise) available for sale	120		$1,200
Units sold	72		
Units in ending inventory	48		

40 units of beginning inventory at $8 $320
 8 units from April at $9   ←——Step 1——→   72   Step 2
48 units result in an ending inventory cost of $392

Cost of goods available for sale	−	Cost of ending inventory	=	Cost of goods sold
↑		↑		↑
$1,200	−	$392	=	$808 ←—— Step 3

Although LIFO doesn't always match the physical flow of goods, companies do still use it to calculate the flow of costs for products such as VCRs and computers, which have declining replacement costs. Also, during inflation, LIFO produces less income than other methods. This results in lower taxes for companies using LIFO.

Before we conclude this unit, let's make the following summary for the cost of ending inventory and cost of goods sold under the weighted-average, FIFO, and LIFO methods.

Inventory method	Cost of goods available for sale	Cost of ending inventory	Cost of goods sold
Weighted average	$1,200	$480 **Step 1:** Total goods, $1,200 Total units, $\frac{\$1,200}{120} = \$10$ **Step 2:** $10 × 48 = $480	$1,200 − $480 = $720
FIFO	$1,200	Bottom up to inventory level (48) 20 × $13 = $260 20 × $12 = 240 8 × $10 = 80 $580	$1,200 − $580 = $620
LIFO	$1,200	Top down to inventory level (48) 40 × $8 = $320 8 × $9 = 72 $392	$1,200 − $392 = $808

From this summary, you can see that in times of rising prices, LIFO gives the highest cost of goods sold ($808). This results in a tax savings for Blue. The weighted-average method tends to smooth out the fluctuations between LIFO and FIFO and falls in the middle.

The key to this discussion of inventory valuation is that different costing methods produce different results. So management, investors, and potential investors should understand the different inventory costing methods and should know which method a particular company uses. For example, Fruit of the Loom, Inc., changed its inventories from LIFO to FIFO due to cost reductions.

Let's check your understanding of this unit with a Practice Quiz.

LU 18.1 PRACTICE QUIZ

From the following, calculate **(a)** the cost of ending inventory and **(b)** the cost of goods sold under the assumption of (1) weighted-average method, (2) FIFO, and (3) LIFO (ending inventory shows 72 units):

	Number of books purchased for resale	Cost per unit	Total
January 1 inventory	30	$3	$ 90
March 1	50	2	100
April 1	20	4	80
November 1	60	6	360

✓ **Solutions**

1. **a.** 72 units of ending inventory × $3.94 = $283.68 cost of ending inventory
   ($630 ÷ 160)

   b.
Cost of goods available for sale	−	Cost of ending inventory	=	Cost of goods sold
↓		↓		↓
$630	−	$283.68	=	**$346.32**

2. **a.** 60 units from November 1 purchased at $6 — $360
   12 units from April 1 purchased at $4 — 48

   72 units — Cost of ending inventory — $408

   b.
Cost of goods available for sale	−	Cost of ending inventory	=	Cost of goods sold
↓		↓		↓
$630	−	$408	=	**$222**

3. **a.** 30 units from January 1 purchased at $3 — $ 90
   42 units from March 1 purchased at $2 — 84

   72 — Cost of ending inventory — $174

   b.
Cost of goods available for sale	−	Cost of ending inventory	=	Cost of goods sold
↓		↓		↓
$630	−	$174	=	**$456**

LEARNING UNIT 18.2 Retail Method; Gross Profit Method; Inventory Turnover; Distribution of Overhead

Taking a physical inventory can be time-consuming and expensive. Some stores draw up monthly financial reports but do not want to spend the time or money to take a monthly physical inventory. These stores estimate the amount of inventory on hand. Stores may also have to estimate their inventories when they have a loss of goods due to fire, theft, flood, and the like. This unit begins with two methods of estimating the value of ending inventory—the retail method and the gross profit method.

Courtesy Esprit de Corp.

FIGURE 18.2
Estimating inventory with the retail method

	Cost	Retail	
Beginning inventory	$4,000	$6,000	
Net purchases during month	2,300	3,000	
Cost of goods available for sale **(Step 1)**	$6,300	$9,000	
Less net sales for month		4,000	**(Step 3)**
Ending inventory at retail		$5,000	
Cost ratio ($6,300 ÷ $9,000) **(Step 2)**		70%	
Ending inventory at cost (.70 × $5,000) **(Step 4)**		$3,500	

Retail Method

Many companies use the **retail method** to estimate their inventory. As shown in Figure 18.2, this method does not require that a company calculate an inventory cost for each item. To calculate the $3,500 ending inventory in Figure 18.2, Green Company used the steps that follow.

Calculating the Retail Method

Step 1. Calculate the cost of goods available for sale at cost and retail: $6,300; $9,000.

Step 2. Calculate a cost ratio using the following formula:

$$\frac{\text{Cost of goods available for sale at cost}}{\text{Cost of goods available for sale at retail}} = \frac{\$6,300}{\$9,000} = .70$$

Step 3. Deduct net sales from cost of goods available for sale at retail: $9,000 − $4,000.

Step 4. Multiply the cost ratio by the ending inventory at retail: .70 × $5,000.

Now let's look at the gross profit method.

Gross Profit Method

To use the **gross profit method** to estimate inventory, the company must keep track of (1) average gross profit rate, (2) net sales at retail, (3) beginning inventory, and (4) net purchases. You can use the following steps to calculate the gross profit method:

Calculating the Gross Profit Method

Step 1. Calculate the cost of goods available for sale (Beginning inventory + Net purchases).

Step 2. Multiply the net sales at retail by the complement of the gross profit rate. This is the estimated cost of goods sold.

Step 3. Calculate the cost of estimated ending inventory (Step 1 − Step 2).

EXAMPLE   Assume Radar Company has the following information in its records:

Gross profit on sales	30%
Beginning inventory, January 1, 2001	$20,000
Net purchases	8,000
Net sales at retail for January	12,000

If you use the gross profit method, what is the company's estimated inventory?

The gross profit method calculates Radar's estimated cost of ending inventory at the end of January as follows:

Goods available for sale		
Beginning inventory, January 1, 2001		$20,000
Net purchases		8,000
Cost of goods available for sale		$28,000 ← **Step 1**
Less estimated cost of goods sold:		
Net sales at retail	$12,000	
Cost percentage (100% − 30%) **Step 2** →	.70	
Estimated cost of goods sold		8,400
Estimated ending inventory, January 31, 2001		$19,600 ← **Step 3**

Note that the cost of goods available for sale less the estimated cost of goods sold gives the estimated cost of ending inventory.

Since this chapter has looked at inventory flow, let's discuss inventory turnover—a key business ratio.

Inventory Turnover

Inventory turnover is the number of times the company replaces inventory during a specific time. Companies use the following two formulas to calculate inventory turnover:

$$\text{Inventory turnover at retail} = \frac{\text{Net sales}}{\text{Average inventory at retail}}$$

$$\text{Inventory turnover at cost} = \frac{\text{Cost of goods sold}}{\text{Average inventory at cost}}$$

You should note that inventory turnover at retail is usually lower than inventory turnover at cost. This is due to theft, markdowns, spoilage, and so on. Also, retail outlets and grocery stores usually have a higher turnover, but jewelry and appliance stores have a low turnover.

Now let's use an example to calculate the inventory turnover at retail and at cost.

EXAMPLE   The following facts are for Abby Company, a local sporting goods store (rounded to the nearest hundredth):

Net sales	$32,000	Cost of goods sold	$22,000
Beginning inventory at retail	11,000	Beginning inventory at cost	7,500
Ending inventory at retail	8,900	Ending inventory at cost	5,600

With these facts, we can make the following calculations:

$$\textbf{Average inventory} = \frac{\text{Beginning inventory} + \text{Ending inventory}}{2}$$

At retail: $\dfrac{\$32,000}{\dfrac{\$11,000 + \$8,900}{2}} = \dfrac{\$32,000}{\$9,950} = 3.22$

At cost: $\dfrac{\$22,000}{\dfrac{\$7,500 + \$5,600}{2}} = \dfrac{\$22,000}{\$6,550} = 3.36$

What Turnover Means

Novell Posts $14.6 Million Loss, Plans Layoffs, Cut in Inventories

Inventory is often a company's most expensive asset. This is reinforced by the above title from a *Wall Street Journal* article. The turnover of inventory can have important implications. Too much inventory results in the use of needed space, extra insurance coverage, and so on. A low inventory turnover could indicate customer dissatisfaction, too much tied-up capital, and possible product obsolescence. A high inventory turnover might mean insufficient amounts of inventory causing stockouts that may lead to future lost sales. If inventory is moving out quickly, perhaps the company's selling price is too low compared to that of its competitors.

In recent years the **just-in-time (JIT) inventory system** from Japan has been introduced in the United States. Under ideal conditions, manufacturers must have suppliers that will provide materials daily as the manufacturing company needs them, thus eliminating inventories. The companies that are using this system, however, have often not been able to completely eliminate the need to maintain some inventory.

Distribution of Overhead

In Chapter 16 we studied the cost of goods sold and operating expenses shown on the income statement. The operating expenses included **overhead expenses**—expenses that are *not* directly associated with a specific department or product but that contribute indirectly to the running of the business. Examples of such overhead expenses are rent, taxes, and insurance.

Companies must allocate their overhead expenses to the various departments in the company. The two common methods of calculating the **distribution of overhead** are by (1) floor space (square feet) or (2) sales volume.

Calculations by Floor Space

To calculate the distribution of overhead by floor space, use the steps that follow.

Calculating the Distribution of Overhead by Floor Space

Step 1. Calculate the total square feet in all departments.
Step 2. Calculate the ratio for each department based on floor space.
Step 3. Multiply each department's floor space ratio by the total overhead.

EXAMPLE   Roy Company has three departments with the following floor space:

Department A	6,000 square feet
Department B	3,000 square feet
Department C	1,000 square feet

The accountant's job is to allocate $90,000 of overhead expenses to the three departments. To allocate this overhead by floor space:

	Floor space in square feet	**Ratio**	
Department A	6,000	$\dfrac{6,000}{10,000} = 60\%$	
Department B	3,000	$\dfrac{3,000}{10,000} = 30\%$	← **Steps 1 and 2**
Department C	$\dfrac{1,000}{10,000}$ total square feet	$\dfrac{1,000}{10,000} = 10\%$	

Department A	$.60 \times \$90,000 =$	$54,000
Department B	$.30 \times \$90,000 =$	27,000	← **Step 3**
Department C	$.10 \times \$90,000 =$	9,000

$$\$90,000$$

Calculations by Sales

To calculate the distribution of overhead by sales, use the steps that follow.

Calculating the Distribution of Overhead by Sales

Step 1. Calculate the total sales in all departments.

Step 2. Calculate the ratio for each department based on sales.

Step 3. Multiply each department's sales ratio by the total overhead.

EXAMPLE   Morse Company distributes its overhead expenses based on the sales of its departments. For example, last year Morse's overhead expenses were $60,000. Sales of its two departments were as follows, along with its ratio calculation.

Since Department A makes 80% of the sales, it is allocated 80% of the overhead expenses.

	Sales	**Ratio**	
Department A	$ 80,000	$\dfrac{\$80,000}{\$100,000} = .80$	⎤
Department B	20,000	$\dfrac{\$20,000}{\$100,000} = .20$	⎦ ← **Steps 1 and 2**
Total sales	$100,000		

These ratios are then multiplied by the overhead expense to be allocated.

Department A   .80 × $60,000 = $48,000

Department B   .20 × $60,000 =   12,000 ← **Step 3**

$60,000

It's time to try another Practice Quiz.

LU 18.2 PRACTICE QUIZ

1. From the following facts, calculate the cost of ending inventory using the retail method (round the cost ratio to the nearest tenth percent):

January 1—inventory at cost	$ 18,000
January 1—inventory at retail	$ 58,000
Net purchases at cost	$220,000
Net purchases at retail	$376,000
Net sales at retail	$364,000

2. Given the following, calculate the estimated cost of ending inventory using the gross profit method:

Gross profit on sales	40%
Beginning inventory, January 1, 2001	$27,000
Net purchases	$ 7,500
Net sales at retail for January	$15,000

3. Calculate the inventory turnover at cost and at retail from the following (round the turnover to the nearest hundredth):

Average inventory at cost	Average inventory at retail	Net sales	Cost of goods sold
$10,590	$19,180	$109,890	$60,990

4. From the following, calculate the distribution of overhead to Departments A and B based on floor space.

Amount of overhead expense to be allocated	Square footage
$70,000	10,000 Department A
	30,000 Department B

✓   **Solutions**

		Cost	Retail
1. Beginning inventory		$ 18,000	$ 58,000
Net purchases during the month		220,000	376,000
Cost of goods available for sale		$238,000	$434,000
Less net sales for the month			364,000
Ending inventory at retail			$ 70,000
Cost ratio ($238,000 ÷ $434,000)			54.8%
Ending inventory at cost (.548 × $70,000)			$ 38,360

2. Goods available for sale

Beginning inventory, January 1, 2001		$ 27,000
Net purchases		7,500
Cost of goods available for sale		$ 34,500
Less estimated cost of goods sold:		
Net sales at retail	$ 15,000	
Cost percentage (100% − 40%)	.60	
Estimated cost of goods sold		9,000
Estimated ending inventory, January 31, 2001		$ 25,500

3. Inventory turnover at cost $= \dfrac{\text{Cost of goods sold}}{\text{Average inventory at cost}} = \dfrac{\$60,990}{\$10,590} = 5.76$

Inventory turnover at retail $= \dfrac{\text{Net sales}}{\text{Average inventory at retail}} = \dfrac{\$109,890}{\$19,180} = 5.73$

4.

		Ratio		
Department A	10,000	$\dfrac{10,000}{40,000}$	= .25 × $70,000 =	$17,500
Department B	$\dfrac{30,000}{40,000}$	$\dfrac{30,000}{40,000}$	= .75 × $70,000 =	$52,500
				$70,000

Chapter Organizer and Reference Guide		
Topic	**Key point, procedure, formula**	**Example(s) to illustrate situation**
Specific identification method, p. 417	Identification could be by serial number, physical description, or coding. The flow of goods and flow of costs are the same.	<table><tr><td></td><td>**Cost per unit**</td><td>**Total cost**</td></tr><tr><td>April 1, 3 units at</td><td>$7</td><td>$21</td></tr><tr><td>May 5, 4 units at</td><td>8</td><td>32</td></tr><tr><td></td><td></td><td>$53</td></tr></table> If 1 unit from each group is left, ending inventory is: $1 \times \$7 = \$ 7$ $+ 1 \times 8 = 8$ $\$15$ <table><tr><td>Cost of goods available for sale</td><td>−</td><td>Cost of ending inventory</td><td>=</td><td>Cost of goods sold</td></tr><tr><td>$53</td><td>−</td><td>$15</td><td>=</td><td>$38</td></tr></table>
Weighted-average method, p 418	$$\text{Weighted-average unit cost} = \frac{\text{Total cost of goods available for sale}}{\text{Total number of units available for sale}}$$	<table><tr><td></td><td>**Cost per unit**</td><td>**Total cost**</td></tr><tr><td>1/XX, 4 units at</td><td>$4</td><td>$16</td></tr><tr><td>5/XX, 2 units at</td><td>5</td><td>10</td></tr><tr><td>8/XX, 3 units at</td><td>6</td><td>18</td></tr><tr><td></td><td></td><td>$44</td></tr></table> $\text{Unit cost} = \dfrac{\$44}{9} = \$4.89$ If 5 units left, cost of ending inventory is 5 units $\times$ $4.89 = $24.45
FIFO—first-in, first-out method, p. 419	Sell old inventory first. Ending inventory is made up of last merchandise brought into store.	Using example above: 5 units left: ↓ <table><tr><td>(Last into store)</td><td>3 units at $6</td><td>$18</td></tr><tr><td></td><td>2 units at $5</td><td>10</td></tr><tr><td>Cost of ending inventory</td><td></td><td>$28</td></tr></table>
LIFO—last-in, first-out method, p. 419	Sell last inventory brought into store first. Ending inventory is made up of oldest merchandise in store.	Using weighted-average example: 5 units left: ↓ <table><tr><td>(First into store)</td><td>4 units at $4</td><td>$16</td></tr><tr><td></td><td>1 unit at $5</td><td>5</td></tr><tr><td>Cost of ending inventory</td><td></td><td>$21</td></tr></table>
Retail method, p. 421	Ending inventory at cost equals: $$\frac{\text{Cost of goods available at cost}}{\text{Cost of goods available at retail}} \times \begin{array}{c}\text{Ending}\\\text{inventory at}\\\text{retail}\end{array}$$ (This is cost ratio.)	<table><tr><td></td><td>**Cost**</td><td>**Retail**</td></tr><tr><td>Beginning inventory</td><td>$52,000</td><td>$ 83,000</td></tr><tr><td>Net purchases</td><td>28,000</td><td>37,000</td></tr><tr><td>Cost of goods available for sale</td><td>$80,000</td><td>$120,000</td></tr><tr><td>Less net sales for month</td><td></td><td>80,000</td></tr><tr><td>Ending inventory at retail</td><td></td><td>$ 40,000</td></tr></table> $\text{Cost ratio} = \dfrac{\$80,000}{\$120,000} = .67 = 67\%$ Rounded to nearest percent. Ending inventory at cost, $26,800 (.67 $\times$ $40,000)

Chapter Organizer and Reference Guide (concluded)		
Topic	**Key point, procedure, formula**	**Example(s) to illustrate situation**
Gross profit method, p. 422	$\dfrac{\text{Beginning}}{\text{inventory}} + \dfrac{\text{Net}}{\text{purchases}} - \dfrac{\text{Estimated}}{\text{cost of}} = \dfrac{\text{Estimated}}{\text{ending}}$ $\text{goods sold} \quad \text{inventory}$	**Goods available for sale** Beginning inventory $30,000 Net purchases 3,000 Cost of goods available for sale $33,000 Less: Estimated cost of goods sold: Net sales at retail $18,000 Cost percentage (100% − 30%) .70 Estimated cost of goods sold 12,600 Estimated ending inventory $20,400
Inventory turnover at retail and at cost, p. 423	$\dfrac{\text{Net sales}}{\text{Average inventory}}$ or $\dfrac{\text{Cost of goods sold}}{\text{Average inventory}}$ $\quad\text{at retail} \qquad\qquad \text{at cost}$	Inventory, January 1 at cost $20,000 Inventory, December 31 at cost 48,000 Cost of goods sold 62,000 At cost: $\dfrac{\$62,000}{\dfrac{\$20,000 + \$48,000}{2}} = 1.82$ (inventory turnover at cost)
Distribution of overhead, p. 424	Based on floor space or sales volume, calculate: 1. Ratios of department floor space or sales to the total. 2. Multiply ratios by total amount of overhead to be distributed.	Total overhead to be distributed, $10,000 **Floor space** Department A 6,000 sq. ft. Department B 2,000 sq. ft. 8,000 sq. ft. Ratio A $= \dfrac{6,000}{8,000} = .75$ Ratio B $= \dfrac{2,000}{8,000} = .25$ Dept. A = .75 × $10,000 = $7,500 Dept. B = .25 × $10,000 = $2,500
Key terms	Average inventory, *p. 423* Distribution of overhead, *p. 424* First-in, first-out (FIFO) method, *p. 419* Gross profit method, *p. 422* Inventory turnover, *p. 423*	Just-in-time (JIT) inventory system, *p. 424* Last-in, first-out (LIFO) method, *p. 419* Overhead expenses, *p. 424* Periodic inventory system, *p. 416*	Perpetual inventory system, *p. 416* Retail method, *p. 422* Specific identification method, *p. 417* Weighted-average method, *p. 418*

Critical Thinking Discussion Questions

1. Explain how you would calculate the cost of ending inventory and cost of goods sold for specific identification, FIFO, LIFO, and weighted-average methods. Explain why during inflation, LIFO results in a tax savings for a business.

2. Explain the cost ratio in the retail method of calculating inventory. What effect will the increased use of computers have on the retail method?

3. What is inventory turnover? Explain the effect of a high inventory turnover during the Christmas shopping season.

4. How is the distribution of overhead calculated by floor space or sales? Give an example of why a store in your area cut back one department to expand another. Did it work?

DRILL PROBLEMS

18–1. Using the specific identification method, calculate **(a)** the cost of ending inventory and **(b)** the cost of goods sold given the following:

Date	Units purchased	Cost per can		Ending inventory
June 1	40 cans	$ 6	$ 240	3 cans from June 1
August 1	60 cans	9	540	7 cans from August 1
October 1	70 cans	10	700	11 cans from October 1
			$1,480	

June 1	3 cans × $ 6 =	$ 18	$1,480 cost of goods available for sale
August 1	7 cans × $ 9 =	63	− 191 **(a)** cost of ending inventory
October 1	11 cans × $10 =	110	$1,289 **(b)** cost of goods sold
		$191	

From the following, calculate the cost of ending inventory (round the average unit cost to the nearest cent) and cost of goods sold using the weighted-average method, FIFO, and LIFO (ending inventory shows 61 units).

	Number purchased	Cost per unit	Total
January 1 inventory	40	$4	$ 160
April 1	60	7	420
June 1	50	8	400
November 1	55	9	495
	205		$1,475

18–2. Weighted average:

$$\frac{\$1,475}{205} = \$7.20 \text{ per unit} \times 61 = \$439.20$$
(cost of ending inventory)

$\$1,475 \quad - \quad \$439.20 \quad = \quad \$1,035.80$
Cost of goods ... Ending ... Cost of
available for sale ... inventory ... goods sold

18–3. FIFO:

$55 \times \$9 = \$495$
$6 \times 8 = \underline{\quad 48}$

Cost of ending inventory	$543	FIFO—old sold first.
Cost of goods available for sale	$1,475	
Ending inventory	− 543	
Cost of goods sold	$ 932	

18–4. LIFO:

$40 \times \$4 = \$160$
$21 \times 7 = \underline{\quad 147}$

Cost of ending inventory	$307	LIFO—new sold first.
Cost of goods available for sale	$1,475	
Ending inventory	− 307	
Cost of goods sold	$1,168	

From the following, calculate the cost of ending inventory and cost of goods sold for LIFO, FIFO, and the weighted-average methods (make sure to first find total cost to complete the table); ending inventory is 49 units:

	Beginning inventory and purchases	Units	Unit cost	Total dollar cost
18–5.	Beginning inventory, January 1	5	$2.00	$ 10.00
18–6.	April 10	10	2.50	25.00
18–7.	May 15	12	3.00	36.00
18–8.	July 22	15	3.25	48.75
18–9.	August 19	18	4.00	72.00
18–10.	September 30	20	4.20	84.00
18–11.	November 10	32	4.40	140.80
18–12.	December 15	16	4.80	76.80
		128		$493.35

18–13. LIFO:

Cost of ending inventory

$$
\begin{array}{rl}
5 \text{ at } \$2.00 = & \$\ 10.00 \\
10 \text{ at } \$2.50 = & 25.00 \\
12 \text{ at } \$3.00 = & 36.00 \\
15 \text{ at } \$3.25 = & 48.75 \\
7 \text{ at } \$4.00 = & 28.00
\end{array}
$$

Cost of ending inventory = $147.75

Cost of goods sold

$$
\begin{array}{r}
\$493.35 \\
- \ 147.75 \\
\hline
\$345.60
\end{array}
$$

18–14. FIFO:

Cost of ending inventory

$$
\begin{array}{rl}
16 \text{ at } \$4.80 = & \$\ 76.80 \\
32 \text{ at } \$4.40 = & 140.80 \\
1 \text{ at } \$4.20 = & 4.20 \\
\hline
& \$221.80
\end{array}
$$

Cost of goods sold

$$
\begin{array}{r}
\$493.35 \\
- \ 221.80 \\
\hline
\$271.55
\end{array}
$$

18–15. Weighted average:

Cost of ending inventory

$$\frac{\$493.35}{128} = \$\ 3.85$$

$49 \times \$3.85 = \$188.65$

Cost of goods sold

$$
\begin{array}{r}
\$493.35 \\
- \ 188.65 \\
\hline
\$304.70
\end{array}
$$

18–16. From the following, calculate the cost ratio (round to the nearest hundredth percent) and the cost of ending inventory to the nearest cent under the retail method.

Net sales at retail for year	$40,000	Purchases—cost	$14,000
Beginning inventory—cost	27,000	Purchases—retail	19,000
Beginning inventory—retail	49,000		

	Cost	Retail
Beginning inventory	$27,000	$49,000
Net purchases	14,000	19,000
Cost of goods available for sale	$41,000	$68,000
Less net sales at retail		40,000
Ending inventory at retail		$28,000
Cost ratio ($41,000 ÷ $68,000)		60.29%
Ending inventory at cost (.6029 × $28,000)		$16,881.20

18–17. Complete the following (round answers to the nearest hundredth):

a. Average inventory at cost	b. Average inventory at retail	c. Net sales	d. Cost of goods sold	e. Inventory turnover at cost	f. Inventory turnover at retail
$14,000	$21,540	$70,000	$49,800	3.56	3.25

$$\text{e.} = \frac{\$49,800 \text{ (d)}}{\$14,000 \text{ (a)}} = 3.56$$

$$\text{f.} = \frac{\$70,000 \text{ (c)}}{\$21,540 \text{ (b)}} = 3.25$$

Complete the following (assume $90,000 of overhead to be distributed):

	Square feet	Ratio	Amount of overhead allocated
18–18. Department A	10,000	.25 (10,000 ÷ 40,000)	$22,500 (.25 × $90,000)
18–19. Department B	30,000	.75 (30,000 ÷ 40,000)	$67,500 (.75 × $90,000)

18–20. Given the following, calculate the estimated cost of ending inventory using the gross profit method.

Gross profit on sales	55%	Net purchases	$ 3,900
Beginning inventory	$29,000	Net sales at retail	17,000

Goods available for sale

Beginning inventory	$29,000
Net purchases	3,900
Cost of goods available for sale	$32,900

Less: Estimated cost of goods sold:

Net sales at retail	$17,000
Cost percentage (100% − 55%)	.45
Estimated cost of goods sold	7,650
Estimated ending inventory	$25,250

WORD PROBLEMS

18–21. Athletic World made the following wholesale purchases of new Nike running shoes: September 1, 12 pairs at $66; November 3, 14 pairs at $52.90; and December 2, 8 pairs at $58. An inventory taken last week indicates that 13 pairs are still in stock. Calculate the cost of ending inventory by LIFO and calculate cost of goods sold.

$12 \times \$66.00 = \$ \ \ 792.00$ $12 \times \$66 \ \ \ = \$792.00$
$14 \times \$52.90 = \ \ \ \ 740.60$ $1 \times \$52.90 = + \ 52.90$
$\underline{8 \times \$58.00 = \ \ \ \ 464.00}$ $\ \ \ \ \ \ \ \ \ \ \ \ \ \ \$844.90$ (cost of ending inventory)
$\ \ \ \ \ \ \ \ \ \ \ \ \ \$1,996.60$ $\$1,996.60 − \$844.90 = \$1,151.70$

18–22. Marvin Company has a beginning inventory of 12 sets of paints at a cost of $1.50 each. During the year, the store purchased 4 sets at $1.60, 6 sets at $2.20, 6 sets at $2.50, and 10 sets at $3.00. By the end of the year, 25 sets were sold. Calculate **(a)** the number of paint sets in stock and **(b)** the cost of ending inventory under LIFO, FIFO, and the weighted-average method. Round to nearest cent for the weighted average.

	LIFO	**FIFO**
12 at $1.50 = $18.00	38 sets	10 × $3.00 = $30.00
4 at $1.60 = 6.40	− 25 sets sold	3 × $2.50 = + 7.50
6 at $2.20 = 13.20	13 inventory	$37.50 (cost of ending inventory)
6 at $2.50 = 15.00		
10 at $3.00 = 30.00	12 × $1.50 = $18.00	
38 $82.60	1 × $1.60 = + 1.60	

Weighted average $19.60 (cost of ending inventory)

$\dfrac{\$82.60}{38} = \$2.17 \times 13 = \$28.21$ (cost of ending inventory)

18–23. A *Forbes* magazine article had the following title: "Overhead Can Kill You." The article stated: "You dine with three colleagues. You skip cocktails and dessert and have a salad. The others have drinks and three courses. When the check arrives, the group divides the total by four and you get hit with $27. For a skimpy salad? Yep, that was the allocation plan." Instead of allocating the same percentage to everyone as in the above example, ABC Company bases allocation on consumption. The overhead for invoicing is $500. Division A has 20,000 customers, and division B has 500 customers. What amount of the overhead should be charged to Division A and what amount to Division B? Round to the nearest whole percent.

Division A: 20,000	
Division B: 500	
20,500	

Over-head   **A:** $\dfrac{20,000}{20,500} = .98 \times \$500 = \$490$ Over-head   **B:** $\dfrac{500}{20,500} = .02 \times \$500 = \$10$

18–24. Moose Company has a beginning inventory at a cost of $77,000 and an ending inventory costing $84,000. Sales were $302,000. Assume Moose's markup rate is 37%. Based on the selling price, what is the inventory turnover at cost? Round to the nearest hundredth.

Cost of goods sold = .63 × $302,000 = $190,260

$\dfrac{\$190,260}{\dfrac{\$77,000 + \$84,000}{2}} = \dfrac{\$190,260}{\$80,500} = 2.36$

18–25. May's Dress Shop's inventory at cost on January 1 was $39,000. Its retail value is $59,000. During the year, May purchased additional merchandise at a cost of $195,000 with a retail value of $395,000. The net sales at retail for the year were $348,000. Could you calculate May's inventory at cost by the retail method? Round the cost ratio to the nearest whole percent.

	Cost	Retail
Beginning inventory	$ 39,000	$ 59,000
Purchases	195,000	395,000
Cost of goods available for sale	$234,000	$454,000
Less net sales for year		348,000
Ending inventory at retail		$106,000
Cost ratio ($234,000 ÷ $454,000)		52%
Ending inventory at cost (.52 × $106,000)		$ 55,120

18–26. A sneaker shop has made the following wholesale purchases of new running shoes: 11 pairs at $24, 20 pairs at $2.50, and 16 pairs at $26.50. An inventory taken last week indicates that 17 pairs are still in stock. Calculate the cost of this inventory by FIFO.

FIFO

11 at $24.00 =	$264	16 × $26.50 = $424.00
20 at $2.50 =	50	1 × $ 2.50 = + 2.50
16 at $26.50 =	424	$426.50 (cost of ending inventory)
47	$738	

18–27. Over the past 3 years, the gross profit rate for Jini Company was 35%. Last week a fire destroyed all Jini's inventory. Using the gross profit method, estimate the cost of inventory destroyed in the fire, given the following facts that were recorded in a fireproof safe:

Beginning inventory	$ 6,000
Net purchases	64,000
Net sales at retail	49,000

Goods available for sale

Beginning inventory		$ 6,000
Net purchases		64,000
Cost of goods available for sale		$70,000
Less: Estimated cost of goods sold:		
Net sales at retail	$49,000	
Cost percentage (100% − 35%)	.65	
Estimated cost of goods sold		31,850
Estimated ending inventory		$38,150

CHALLENGE PROBLEMS

18–28. Dan and Alice Luna manage a Santa Monica, California, condominium. A security patrol was hired because of recent break-ins. The cost of the security patrol is $250 per month, which is to be allocated to tenants based on the number of rooms in their units. The building has 10 units: 4 units with 3 rooms, 5 units with 4 rooms, and 1 unit with 5 rooms. **(a)** What will be the cost for the 3-room units, 4-room units, and the 5-room unit? **(b)** How much must each tenant pay? In your calculations, round to the nearest whole percent.

a. 4 × 3 = 12 rooms
5 × 4 = 20 rooms
1 × 5 = 5 rooms
37 total rooms

b. 3-room units occupy 12 of 37 rooms:

	(a)	**(b)**

3-room units occupy $\frac{12}{37}$ = .32 × $250 = $ 80 ÷ 4 = $20 per unit

4-room units occupy $\frac{20}{37}$ = .54 × $250 = $135 ÷ 5 = $27 per unit

5-room unit occupies $\frac{5}{37}$ = .14 × $250 = $ 35 ÷ 1 = $35 per unit

18–29. Logan Company uses a perpetual inventory system on a FIFO basis. Assuming inventory on January 1 was 800 units at $8 each, what is the cost of ending inventory at the end of October 5?

Received			Sold		
Date	**Quantity**	**Cost per unit**	**Date**	**Quantity**	
Apr. 15	220	$5	Mar. 8	500	
Nov. 12	1,900	9	Oct. 5	200	
Jan. 1 inventory	$6,400	800 units at $8	Oct. 5 inventory	$1,900	100 units at $8
Mar. 8 inventory	2,400	300 units at $8			220 units at $5
Apr. 15 inventory	3,500	300 units at $8			
		220 units at $5			

SUMMARY PRACTICE TEST

1. Clayton Toys has a beginning inventory of 12 sets of paints at a cost of $1.75 each. During the year, the toy store purchased 8 sets at $2.10, 9 sets at $2.25, 14 sets at $2.80, and 15 sets at $3.25. By the end of the year, 30 sets were sold. Calculate **(a)** the number of paint sets in stock and **(b)** the cost of ending inventory under LIFO, FIFO, and weighted-average method. *(pp. 416–21)*

a. Ending inventory = 58 − 30 = 28

b.

		LIFO	FIFO	Weighted average
12 at $1.75 = $ 21.00		12 at $1.75 = $21.00	15 at $3.25 = $48.75	$\frac{\$146}{58} = \$2.52$
8 at $2.10 = 16.80		8 at $2.10 = 16.80	13 at $2.80 = 36.40	
9 at $2.25 = 20.25		8 at $2.25 = 18.00	$85.15	28 × $2.52 = $70.56
14 at $2.80 = 39.20		Ending inventory $55.80		
15 at $3.25 = 48.75				
58	$146.00			

2. Juno Company allocates overhead expenses to all departments on the basis of floor space (square feet) occupied by each department. The total overhead expenses for a recent year were $120,000. Department A occupied 7,000 square feet; Department B, 13,000 square feet; and Department C, 4,000 square feet. What is the overhead allocated to Department C? In your calculations, round to the nearest whole percent. *(p. 424)*

$$7,000 + 13,000 + 4,000 = 24,000 \qquad \frac{4,000}{24,000} = .17 \times \$120,000 = \$20,400$$

3. Lester Company has a beginning inventory costing $81,500 and an ending inventory costing $83,900. Sales for the year were $310,000. Assume Lester's markup rate on selling price is 70%. Based on the selling price, what is the inventory turnover at cost? Round to the nearest hundredth. *(p. 423)*

$$\text{Cost of goods sold} = .30 \times \$310,000 = \$93,000 \qquad \frac{\$93,000}{\frac{\$81,500 + \$83,900}{2}} = \frac{\$93,000}{\$82,700} = 1.12$$

4. Gracie's Dress Shop's inventory at cost on January 1 was $60,900. Its retail value is $90,200. During the year, Gracie purchased additional merchandise at a cost of $218,000 with a retail value of $329,000. The net sales at retail for the year were $298,500. Calculate Gracie's inventory at cost by the retail method. Round the cost ratio to the nearest whole percent. *(p. 422)*

	Cost	Retail	
Beginning inventory	$ 60,900	$ 90,200	Cost ratio ($278,900 ÷ $419,200) = .67 or 67%
Purchases	218,000	329,000	Ending inventory at cost
Cost of goods available for sale	$278,900	$419,200	.67 × $120,700 = $80,869
Less net sales for year		298,500	
Ending inventory at retail		$120,700	

5. On January 1, Agency Company had an inventory costing $70,000. During January, Agency had net purchases of $102,500. Over recent years, Agency's gross profit in January has averaged 38% on sales. The company's net sales in January were $175,900. Calculate the estimated cost of ending inventory using the gross profit method. *(p. 422)*

Goods available for sale

Beginning inventory, January 1		$ 70,000
Net purchases		102,500
Cost of goods available for sale		$172,500
Less: Estimated cost of goods sold:		
Net sales at retail	$175,900	
Cost percentage (100% − 38%)	.62	
Estimated cost of goods sold		109,058
Estimated ending inventory, January 31		$ 63,442

A KIPLINGER APPROACH

Defend or reject the following business math issue based on the *Kiplinger's Personal Finance Magazine* article below:

Getting Into the Antiques Business

▶ **Many dealers flounder when they set up shop too soon.** By Kimberly Lankford

After years of antiquing as a hobby, I'd like to become a dealer. Is there a good way to get started that will offer me a fighting chance to succeed in the business?
—TERRY SMITH, *Washington, D.C.*

"Get your feet wet in an antiques mall," says Ronald Barlow, author of *How to Be Successful in the Antique Business* (out of print). Antiques malls let you avoid most of the overhead costs

At Antique Station, a mall in Frederick, Md., renting 100 square feet of space costs $250 to $300 a month.

of owning a shop—such as utilities, advertising and a long-term lease. Instead, you usually pay by the space or the square foot, or pay commission to the mall's owner. The Antique Station, in Frederick, Md., for example, charges $250 to $300 per month for an average, 10- by 10-foot booth. Because you're surrounded by other dealers, you don't need much inventory to attract customers.

Some antiques malls let you use their vendor number, which allows

you to buy items for resale tax-free. Otherwise, you'd have to get your own number from your state's tax department, which usually requires a deposit based on the size of your inventory and your projected sales. You'd also need a city business license (about $25).

Getting started in an antiques mall will help you get the experience and capital you need to launch a successful stand-alone business. Barlow speculates that the failure rate for antiques businesses is higher than two out of three within the first six years—the average for small businesses—because many owners are undercapitalized, have no business background and don't buy merchandise at wholesale prices. The most difficult part of running an antiques business is knowing how to price the items and still end up with a profit, says Barlow. You also need to know how much inventory to keep. As a serious hobbyist, you've probably already learned another crucial ingredient of success: how to hunt down good deals.

PHOTOGRAPHS BY MICHAEL BOWLES

Business Math Issue

Antique shops carry too much overhead and inventory.

1. List the key points of the article and information to support your position.
2. Write a group defense of your position using math calculations to support your view.

Canadian Ice Storm Provided Stern Test Of Popular Just-in-Time Supply Method

By CHRISTOPHER J. CHIPELLO
Staff Reporter of THE WALL STREET JOURNAL

BROMONT, Quebec—The trendy "just-in-time" supply method has just survived one of its sternest tests.

In recent years, companies have saved fortunes by embracing just-in-time. Instead of gathering dust in a warehouse, supplies arrive just when they are needed, slashing inventory costs. But companies relying on just-in-time have also had to live with a gnawing fear: If a natural disaster were to strike a major supplier, would the disruption knock out the customers' operations as well?

This month's ice storm in eastern Canada was one of the worst natural disasters in the country's history. The power outages that followed closed factories day after day. Some of them had to scramble to meet just-in-time delivery obligations and keep from snarling operations of customers thousands of miles away.

It was frequently nip-and-tuck whether the factories would succeed, and customers, often in the U.S., did a lot of hand-wringing. But in the end, factory managers usually found ways to muddle through the crisis and keep their customers rolling. Consultants said their success could reassure nervous companies and ease concerns about the just-in-time approach.

"Most companies managed to cope" with the area's power debacle, says Marcel Cote, a partner at management-consulting firm Secor Inc. in Montreal. "They did a lot of little things. They subcontracted or had critical parts made in other plants," Mr. Cote says. "It's a testimony to the flexibility we find in the production system" and should reduce worries about problems with just-in-time methods, he adds.

Of course, the whole experience also

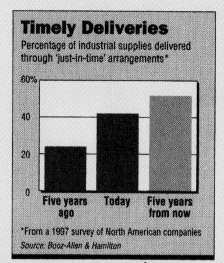

Timely Deliveries

Percentage of industrial supplies delivered through 'just-in-time' arrangements*

*From a 1997 survey of North American companies
Source: Booz-Allen & Hamilton

gave factory managers a big scare. Bertrand Masse, general manager for **Mitel** Corp.'s semiconductor plant in this town about an hour's drive east of Montreal, spent several anxious days tracking efforts to truck five huge generators here from California and western Canada. The rented generators arrived in the nick of time. The plant, which makes specialized components primarily for the fast-growing telecommunications industry, finally resumed full-scale production late last week, two weeks after it closed because of the area's power shortage.

The plant's customers, as far away as California and the United Kingdom, had been growing increasingly nervous that they might run short of chips. "We don't produce to inventory; we produce to order only," Mr. Masse says. Mitel is the sole supplier for some companies, and Mr. Masse's staff has been on the telephone daily with customers, updating them on the plant's situation.

Project A

Do you agree with the Timely Deliveries chart? Five years from now, 50% of the companies surveyed will deliver by just-in-time. Use the computer industry (IBM, Dell, Compaq, or Gateway) to support your position.

 See text Web site (www.mhhe.com/slater) and *The Business Math Internet Resource Guide.*

19

SALES, EXCISE, AND PROPERTY TAXES

House Passes Bill to Ban Taxes on Internet Sales

By a WALL STREET JOURNAL *Staff Reporter*

WASHINGTON — The House yesterday passed a bill to ban taxes on Internet sales and services for three years.

The so-called Internet Tax Freedom Act, which passed on a unanimous voice vote, would also create a temporary commission to study the myriad state and local electronic commerce tax issues.

One thorny question the commission will address is how consumers should be taxed: If a Texas shopper, for example, buys a T-shirt from a business in Maine using a Virginia-based online service provider, which state gets to tax the transaction? The new body is expected to have an answer—in the form of a legisla-tive proposal—by the end of the three-year moratorium period.

"Americans are guaranteed that for three years there won't be multiple taxes on transactions on the Internet or on your phone bill or Internet service bill," said Rep. Christopher Cox (R., Calif.), who introduced the bill with Sen. Ron Wyden (D., Ore.).

The moratorium measure overcame initial opposition. Fearing that taxation by the nation's more than 30,000 taxing entities might impede growth of Internet commerce, Messrs. Cox and Wyden initially sought a permanent tax exemption on Internet sales.

© 1998, Dow Jones & Company, Inc.

When you make a purchase at a cash register, does your state or local government collect a sales tax? Most states and some local governments collect sales taxes. Have you bought products on the Internet? Did you pay a sales tax? *The Wall Street Journal* clipping "House Passes Bill to Ban Taxes on Internet Sales" has important information for Internet consumers.

What does the greatest damage to your pocketbook, a sales tax, property tax, or state income tax? If you say "a state income tax," you are wrong. In no state does a state income tax do the greatest damage to your finances. The greatest damage is done by property taxes or sales taxes—and almost always both. Sales tax rates vary from state to state. Four state capitols (Concord, New Hampshire; Dover, Delaware; Helena, Montana; and Salem, Oregon) do not impose a sales tax. However, if you live in California, Florida, Texas, or Washington, your combined state and local tax rate reaches 7% or more.

In Learning Unit 19.1 you will learn how sales taxes are calculated. This learning unit also discusses the excise tax that is collected in addition to the sales tax. Learning Unit 19.2 explains the use of property tax.

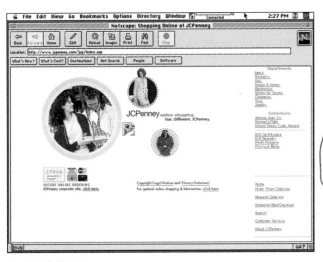

Courtesy J.C. Penney.

LEARNING UNIT 19.1   Sales and Excise Taxes

Today, many states have been raising their sales tax and excise tax. Also, states have been gradually dropping some of their sales tax exemptions. In Connecticut, a 6% sales tax was imposed on newspapers sold at newsstands but not through subscriptions. Connecticut also imposes a 6% sales tax at vending machines.

Sales Tax

In many cities, counties, and states, the sellers of certain goods and services collect **sales tax** and forward it to the appropriate government agency. Forty-five states have a sales tax. Of the 45 states, 28 states and the District of Columbia exempt food; 44 and the District of Columbia exempt prescription drugs.

Sales taxes vary from 4% to 10.75%. Would consumers purchase more goods if they did not have to pay sales taxes? You will find the answer in this *Wall Street Journal* clipping, which reports on a survey of 300 New York City stores after a week with no sales tax on clothing and shoes costing less than $500.

NEW YORKERS go on a buying spree to celebrate a week with no sales tax on clothing and shoes costing less than $500. A survey of more than 300 New York City stores showed a 77% spurt in clothing and shoe sales from Jan. 17-23, compared with a typical January week, says Charles Millard, president of the New York City Economic Development Corp.

© 1998, Dow Jones & Company, Inc.

Sales taxes are usually computed electronically by the new cash register systems and scanners. However, it is important to know how sellers calculate sales tax manually. The following example of a car battery will show you how to manually calculate sales tax.

EXAMPLE

| Selling price of a Sears battery | $32.00 | Shipping charge | $3.50 |
| Trade discount to local garage | 10.50 | Sales tax | 5% |

Amount of
sales tax

P
($1.08)

B × *R*
($21.50) (.05)

$21.50 + $1.08 = $22.58
(sale)   (tax
              amount)

Manual calculation

1. $32.00 − $10.50 = $21.50 taxable
2.   × .05
       $ 1.08 tax
     + 21.50 taxable
     + 3.50 shipping
3. $26.08 total price with tax and shipping

Check   ✓ April?

100% is base + 5% is tax = 105%

1.05 × $21.50 = $22.58
              + 3.50 shipping
              $26.08

In this example, note how the trade discount is subtracted from the selling price before any cash discounts are taken. If the buyer is entitled to a 6% cash discount, it is calculated as follows:

$$.06 \times \$21.50 = \$1.29$$

✗ Also, remember that we do not take cash discounts on the sales tax or shipping charges.

Calculating Actual Sales

Managers often use the cash register to get a summary of their total sales for the day. The total sales figure includes the sales tax. So the sales tax must be deducted from the total sales. To illustrate this, let's assume the total sales for the day were $40,000, which included a 7% sales tax. What were the actual sales?

Hint: $40,000 is 107% of actual sales

$$\text{Actual sales} = \frac{\text{Total sales}}{1 + \text{Tax rate}}$$

Total sales

$$\text{Actual sales} = \frac{\$40,000}{1.07} = \$37,383.18$$

100% sales
+ 7% tax
107% → 1.07

Thus, the store's actual sales were $37,383.18. The actual sales plus the tax equal $40,000.

Check

$37,383.18 × .07 = $ 2,616.82 sales tax
                   + 37,383.18 actual sales
                   $40,000.00 total sales including sales tax

Excise Tax

Governments (local, federal, and state) levy **excise tax** on particular products and services. This can be a sizable source of revenue for these governments.

Consumers pay the excise tax in addition to the sales tax. The excise tax is based on a percent of the *retail* price of a product or service. This tax, which varies in different states, is imposed on luxury items or nonessentials. Examples of products or services subject to the excise tax include airline travel, telephone service, alcoholic beverages, jewelry, furs, fishing rods, tobacco products, and motor vehicles. Although excise tax is often calculated as a percent of the selling price, the tax can be stated as a fixed amount per item sold. The following example calculates excise tax as a percent of the selling price.[1]

---

[1]If excise tax were a stated fixed amount per item, it would have to be added to the cost of goods or services before any sales tax were taken. For example, a $100 truck tire with a $4 excise tax would be $104 before the sales tax was calculated.

EXAMPLE   On June 1, Angel Rowe bought a fur coat for a retail price of $5,000. Sales tax is 7% with an excise tax of 8%. Her total cost is as follows:

$5,000
+ 350 sales tax (.07 × $5,000)
+ 400 excise tax (.08 × $5,000)
$5,750

Let's check your progress with a Practice Quiz.

LU 19.1 PRACTICE QUIZ

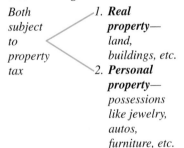

From the following shopping list, calculate the total sales tax (food items are excluded from sales tax, which is 8%):

Chicken	$6.10	Orange juice	$1.29	Shampoo	$4.10
Lettuce	$ .75	Laundry detergent	$3.65		

✓ **Solution**

Shampoo $4.10
Laundry detergent   + 3.65
                     $7.75 × .08 = $.62

LEARNING UNIT 19.2   Property Tax

When you own property, you must pay property tax. In this unit we listen in on a conversation between a property owner and a tax assessor.

Defining Assessed Value

Bill Adams was concerned when he read in the local paper that the property tax rate had been increased. Bill knows that the revenue the town receives from the tax helps pay for fire and police protection, schools, and other public services. However, Bill wants to know how the town set the new rate and the amount of the new property tax.

Bill went to the town assessor's office to get specific details. The assessor is a local official who estimates the fair market value of a house. Before you read the summary of Bill's discussion, note the following formula:

Property Can Have Two Meanings

Both subject to property tax
1. **Real property**— land, buildings, etc.
2. **Personal property**— possessions like jewelry, autos, furniture, etc.

Assessed value = Assessment rate × Market value

Bill: What does **assessed value** mean?

Assessor: *Assessed value* is the value of the property for purposes of computing property taxes. We estimated the market value of your home at $210,000. In our town, we assess property at 30% of the market value. Thus, your home has an assessed value of $63,000 ($210,000 × .30). Usually, assessed value is rounded to the nearest dollar.

Bill: I know that the **tax rate** multiplied by my assessed value ($63,000) determines the amount of my property tax. What I would like to know is how did you set the new tax rate?

Determining the Tax Rate

Assessor: In our town first we estimate the total amount of revenue needed to meet our budget. Then we divide the total of all assessed property into this figure to get the *tax rate*. The formula looks like this:

$$\text{Tax rate} = \frac{\text{Budget needed}}{\text{Total assessed value}^2}$$

Our town budget is $125,000, and we have a total assessed property value of $1,930,000. Using the formula, we have the following:

$$\frac{\$125,000}{\$1,930,000} = \$.0647668 = .0648 \text{ tax rate per dollar}$$

---

[2]Remember that exemptions include land and buildings used for educational and religious purposes and the like.

Note that the rate should be rounded up to the indicated digit, *even if the digit is less than 5.* Here we rounded to the nearest ten thousandth.

How the Tax Rate Is Expressed

Assessor: We can express the $.0648 tax rate in the following forms:

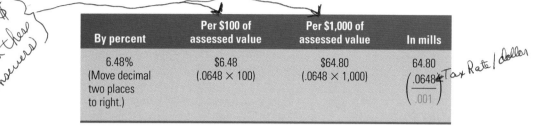

By percent	Per $100 of assessed value	Per $1,000 of assessed value	In mills
6.48% (Move decimal two places to right.)	$6.48 (.0648 × 100)	$64.80 (.0648 × 1,000)	64.80 $\left(\dfrac{.0648}{.001}\right)$

A **mill** is $\frac{1}{10}$ of a cent or $\frac{1}{1,000}$ of a dollar (.001). To represent the number of mills as a tax rate per dollar, we divide the tax rate in decimal by .001. Rounding practices vary from state to state. Colorado tax bills are now rounded to the thousandth mill. An alternative to finding the rate in mills is to multiply the rate per dollar by 1,000, since a dollar has 1,000 mills. In the problems in this text, we round the mills per dollar to nearest hundredth.

How to Calculate Property Tax Due[3]

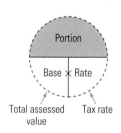

Portion

Base × Rate

Total assessed value   Tax rate

Assessor: The following formula will show you how we arrive at your **property tax:**

Total property tax due (Portion)	=	Tax rate (Rate)	×	Total assessed value (Base)

$$\$4,082.40 = .0648 \times \$63,000$$

We can use the other forms of the decimal tax rate to show you how the property tax will not change even when expressed in various forms:

By percent	Per $100	Per $1,000	Mills
6.48% × $63,000 = $4,082.40	$\dfrac{\$63,000}{\$100} = 630$ 630 × $6.48 = $4,082.40	$\dfrac{\$63,000}{\$1,000} = 63$ 63 × $64.80 = $4,082.40	Property tax due = Mills × .001 × Assessed value = 64.80 × .001 × $63,000 = $4,082.40

Now it's time to try the Practice Quiz.

LU 19.2 PRACTICE QUIZ

From the following facts: (1) calculate assessed value of Bill's home; (2) calculate the tax rate for the community in decimal (to nearest ten thousandths); (3) convert the decimal to **(a)** %, **(b)** per $100 of assessed value, **(c)** per $1,000 of assessed value, and **(d)** in mills (to nearest hundredth); and (4) calculate the property tax due on Bill's home in decimal, per $100, per $1,000, and in mills.

Given

Assessed market value	40%	Total budget needed	$ 176,000
Market value of Bill's home	$210,000	Total assessed value	$1,910,000

✓ **Solutions**

1. .40 × $210,000 = $84,000

2. $\dfrac{\$176,000}{\$1,910,000} = .0922$

3. a. .0922 = 9.22%

b. .0922 × 100 = $9.22

c. .0922 × 1,000 = $92.20

d. $\dfrac{.0922}{.001} = 92.20$ mills (or .0922 × 1,000)

---

[3]Some states have credits available to reduce what the homeowner actually pays. For example, 42 out of 50 states give tax breaks to people over age 65. In Alaska, the state's homestead exemption reduces the property tax of a $168,000 house from $1,512 to $253.

4. $.0922 \times \$84{,}000 =$ $\$7{,}744.80$

$\$9.22 \times 840 =$ $\$7{,}744.80$

$\$92.20 \times 84 =$ $\$7{,}744.80$

$92.20 \times .001 \times \$84{,}000 =$ $\$7{,}744.80$

Chapter Organizer and Reference Guide		
Topic	**Key point, procedure, formula**	**Example(s) to illustrate situation**
Sales tax, p. 438	Sales tax is not calculated on trade discounts. Shipping charges, etc., also are not subject to sales tax. $\text{Actual sales} = \dfrac{\text{Total sales}}{1 + \text{Tax rate}}$ Cash discounts are calculated on sale price before sales tax is added on.	Calculate sales tax: Purchased 12 bags of mulch at $59.40; 10% trade discount; 5% sales tax. $\$59.40 - \$5.94 = \$53.46$ $\$53.46$ Any cash discount would be $\times\ .05$ calculated on $53.46. $\$2.67$ sales tax
Excise tax, p. 439	Excise tax is calculated separately from sales tax and is an additional tax. It is based as a percent of the selling price. It could be stated as a fixed amount per item sold. In that case, the excise tax would be added to the cost of the item before any sales tax calculations. Rate for excise tax will vary.	Jewelry $4,000 retail price Sales tax 7% Excise tax 10% $4,000 + 280 sales tax + 400 excise tax $4,680
Assessed value, p. 440	Assessment rate × Market value	$100,000 house; rate, 30%; $30,000 assessed value.
Tax rate, p. 440	$\dfrac{\text{Budget needed}}{\text{Total assessed value}} = \text{Tax rate}$ (Round rate up to indicated digit even if less than 5.)	$\dfrac{\$800{,}000}{\$9{,}200{,}000} = \$.08695 = \$.0870$ tax rate per $1
Expressing tax rate in other forms, p. 441	1. Percent: Move decimal two places to right. Add % sign. 2. Per $100: Multiply by 100. 3. Per $1,000: Multiply by 1,000. 4. Mills: Divide by .001.	1. $.0870 = 8.7\%$ 2. $\$.0870 \times 100 = \$8.70$ 3. $\$.0870 \times 1{,}000 = \$87$ 4. $\dfrac{.0870}{.001} = 87$ mills

Calculating property tax, p. 441	$\begin{array}{l}\text{Total property} \\ \text{tax due}\end{array} = \text{Tax rate} \times \begin{array}{l}\text{Total assessed} \\ \text{value}\end{array}$
	Various forms:
	1. Percent × Assessed value
	2. Per $100: $\dfrac{\text{Assessed value}}{\$100} \times \text{Rate}$
	3. Per $1,000: $\dfrac{\text{Assessed value}}{\$1{,}000} \times \text{Rate}$
	4. Mills: Mills × .001 × Assessed value
		Example: Rate, $.0870 per $1;
		     $30,000 assessed value
		1. $(.087)8.7\% \times \$30{,}000 = \$2{,}610$
		2. $\dfrac{\$30{,}000}{\$100} = 300 \times \$8.70 = \$2{,}610$
		3. $\dfrac{\$30{,}000}{\$1{,}000} = 30 \times \$87 = \$2{,}610$
		4. $\dfrac{.0870}{.001} = 87$ mills
		   87 mills × .001 × $30,000 = $2,610

Key terms	Assessed value, *p. 440* Personal property, *p. 440* Sales tax, *p. 438* Excise tax, *p. 439* Property tax, *p. 441* Tax rate, *p. 440* Mill, *p. 441* Real property, *p. 440*		

Critical Thinking Discussion Questions

1. Explain sales and excise taxes. Should all states have the same tax rate for sales tax?
2. Explain how to calculate actual sales when the sales tax was included in the sales figure. Is a sales tax necessary?
3. How is assessed value calculated? If you think your value is unfair, what could you do?
4. What is a mill? When we calculate property tax in mills, why do we use .001 in the calculation?

DRILL PROBLEMS

Calculate the following:

	Retail selling price		Sales tax (6%)		Excise tax (8%)	Total price including taxes
19–1.	$ 800	+	$48 ($800 × .06)	+	$64 ($800 × .08)	$ 912
19–2.	$1,200	+	$72 ($1,200 × .06)	+	$96 ($1,200 × .08)	$1,368

Calculate the actual sales since the sales and sales tax were rung up together; assume a 6% sales tax (round your answer to the nearest cent):

19–3. $\dfrac{\$70,000}{1.06} = \$66,037.74$

19–4. $\dfrac{\$26,000}{1.06} = \$24,528.30$

Calculate the assessed value of the following pieces of property:

	Assessment rate		Market value		Assessed value
19–5.	30%	×	$160,000	=	$ 48,000
19–6.	80%	×	$210,000	=	$168,000

Calculate the tax rate in decimal form to the nearest ten thousandth:

	Required budget		Total assessed value		Tax rate per dollar
19–7.	$920,000	÷	$39,500,000	=	$.0233

Complete the following:

	Tax rate per dollar	In percent	Per $100	Per $1,000	Mills
19–8.	$.0956	9.56% (.0956)	$9.56 ($.0956 × 100)	$95.60 ($.0956 × 1,000)	95.60 $\left(\dfrac{.0956}{.001}\right)$
19–9.	$.0699	6.99% (.0699)	$6.99 ($.0699 × 100)	$69.90 ($.0699 × 1,000)	69.90 $\left(\dfrac{.0699}{.001}\right)$

Complete the amount of property tax due to the nearest cent for each situation:

	Tax rate	Assessed value	Amount of property tax due
19–10.	40 mills × .001 ×	$65,000	= $ 2,600
19–11.	$42.50 per $1,000	($105,000 ÷ $1,000) × $42.50	= $ 4,462.50
19–12.	$8.75 per $100	($125,000 ÷ $100) × $8.75	= $10,937.50
19–13.	$94.10 per $1,000	($180,500 ÷ $1,000) × 94.10	= $16,985.05

WORD PROBLEMS

19–14. Maggie Kaminsky bought a $600 treadmill that is subject to a 5% sales tax and a 10% excise tax. What is the total amount Maggie paid?

$600 + $30   + $60   = $690
   ($600 × .05)   ($600 × .10)

19–15. Don Chather bought a new computer for $1,995. This included a 6% sales tax. What is the amount of sales tax and the selling price before the tax?

$\dfrac{\$1,995}{1.06} = \$1,882.08$ actual sale $1,995 − $1,882.08 = 112.92 sales tax

19–16. On November 21, 1997, the Chicago *Sun-Times* reported "The Greatest Mansion in Kenwood up for sale. A Kenwood mansion, formerly owned by boxing legend Muhammad Ali, is on the market. The listing price $1,600,000 stings like a bee but the amenities float like a butterfly." The Chicago assessment rate is 33%, and the tax rate is .0285. What is the total property tax for the year on this property?

Market value		Assessment rate		Assessed value
$1,600,000	×	.33	=	$528,000

Tax rate (R)		Total assessed value (B)		Total property taxes due (P)
.0285	×	$528,000	=	$15,048

19–17. In the community of Ross, the market value of a home is $200,000. The assessment rate is 40%. What is the assessed value?

.40 × $200,000 = $80,000

19–18. *Kiplinger's 1998 Car Buyers Guide* lists a Mercedes-Benz S600 four-door at $135,845. Illinois has a 7% sales tax on automobiles. What will be the sales tax and the total price of the Mercedes-Benz?

$135,845.00
× .07
_____
$ 9,509.15 tax
+ 135,845.00
_____
$145,354.15 total price

19–19. Lois Clark bought a ring for $6,000. She must still pay a 5% sales tax and a 10% excise tax. The jeweler is shipping the ring, so Lois must also pay a $40 shipping charge. What is the total purchase price of Lois's ring?

$6,000
300 (.05 × $6,000) sales tax
600 (.10 × $6,000) excise tax
40 shipping
_____
$6,940

19–20. Blunt County needs $700,000 from property tax to meet its budget. The total value of assessed property in Blunt is $110,000,000. What is the tax rate of Blunt? Round to the nearest ten thousandth. Express the rate in mills.

$$\frac{\$700,000}{\$110,000,000} = .0064 \qquad \frac{.0064}{.001} = 6.40 \text{ mills}$$

19–21. Bill Shass pays a property tax of $3,200. In his community, the tax rate is 50 mills. What is Bill's assessed value?

Mills × .001 × A = $ 3,200
50 × .001 × A = $ 3,200
.05A = $ 3,200
A = $64,000

19–22. The home of Bill Burton is assessed at $80,000. The tax rate is 18.50 mills. What is the tax on Bill's home?

18.50 × .001 × $80,000 = $1,480

19–23. An article in the June 1997 issue of *Kiplinger's Personal Finance Magazine* compares property taxes in various locations. A $225,000 home in Pittsburgh, Pennsylvania, is assessed at 30% of the market value. The tax rate per dollar for the Pittsburgh home is .0800. A $225,000 home in Houston, Texas, is assessed at 30% of the market value. The tax rate per dollar for the Houston home is .0767. What is the total dollar difference in property taxes between these two homes?

Pittsburgh	Houston
$225,000	$225,000
× .30	× .30
$ 67,500 total assessed value (B)	$ 67,500

(B) (R)	(B) (R)
$67,500 × .0800 = $5,400.00	$67,500 × .0767 = $5,177.25

$5,400.00
− 5,177.25
_____
$ 222.75

19–24. Bill Blake pays a property tax of $2,500. In his community, the tax rate is 55 mills. What is Bill's assessed value? Round to the nearest dollar.

$$\text{Mills} \times .001 \times A = \$\ 2,500$$
$$55 \times .001 \times A = \$\ 2,500$$
$$.055A = \$\ 2,500$$
$$A = \$45,455$$

19–25. On November 29, 1997, the Chicago *Sun-Times* reported the following: "The City of Aurora, Illinois, will raise the city's local sales tax after the first of the year to 2% from 1.5%, although groceries, drugs, and new cars are exempted." An Aurora couple decides to purchase a $1,020 refrigerator from Sears. The couple is undecided as to when they should make this purchase. Should they buy now or wait until after the first of the year? What would be the total price of the refrigerator purchased now versus the cost after waiting until the first of the year?

Now	**After first of the year**
$1,020.00	$1,020.00
× .015	× .02
$ 15.30 city tax	$ 20.40 city tax
+ 1,020.00	+ 1,020.00
$1,035.30 total price	$1,040.40 total price

CHALLENGE PROBLEMS

19–26. The owner of a house on Hall Street in Downers Grove, Illinois, received a $3,095.41 tax bill for 1997 based on a $170,600 home. The village assessment rate is 31% of the market value, and the tax rate is .0585. The owner wants to estimate what his taxes will be for next year. The assessor told him that market values are expected to increase by 2% next year and the tax rate will remain about the same. The owner also plans to install a $10,300 swimming pool. What will be the owner's estimated taxes for 1998?

$170,600.00 present market value	$184,312.00 1998 market value ($13,712 + $170,600)
× .02 percent increase in market value	× .31 assessment rate
$ 3,412.00 increase in market value	$ 57,136.72 assessed value
+ 10,300.00 home improvement	× .0585 tax rate
$ 13,712.00	$ 3,342.50

19–27. Art Neuner, an investor in real estate, bought an office condominium. The market value of the condo was $250,000 with a 70% assessment rate. Art feels that his return should be 12% per month on his investment after all expenses. The tax rate is $31.50 per $1,000. Art estimates it will cost $275 per month to cover general repairs, insurance, and so on. He pays a $140 condo fee per month. All utilities and heat are the responsibility of the tenant. Calculate the monthly rent for Art. Round your answer to the nearest dollar (at intermediate stages).

$250,000 × .70 = $175,000 assessed value
Tax = 175 × $31.50 = $ 5,512.50 tax
 + 3,300.00 ($275 × 12) repairs and insurance
 + 1,680.00 ($140 × 12) condo fee
 $10,492.50 ÷ 12 = $874
$874 × 1.12 = $978.88 = $979

SUMMARY PRACTICE TEST

1. Bill French bought a new Compaq computer for $1,800. The price included a 6% sales tax. What are the sales tax and the selling price before the tax? *(p. 439)*

$$\frac{\$1,800}{1.06} = \$1,698.11 \text{ actual sale}$$

$1,800.00
− 1,698.11
$ 101.89 sales tax

2. Jane Sullivan bought a ring for $6,000 from Tiffany's. She must pay a 7% sales tax and a 9% excise tax. Since the jeweler is shipping the ring, Jane must also pay a $20 shipping charge. What is the total purchase price of Jane's ring? *(p. 439)*

$6,000 + $420   + $540   + $20   = $6,980
         (.07 × $6,000)   (.09 × $6,000)   (shipping charge)

3. The market value of a home in Dallas, Texas, is $170,000. The assessment rate is 32%. What is the assessed value? *(p. 440)*

   .32 × 170,000 = $54,400

4. Lang County needs $875,000 from its property tax to meet the budget. The total value of assessed property in Lang is $162,000,000. What is Lang's tax rate? Round to the nearest ten-thousandth. Express the rate in mills (to the nearest tenth). *(p. 441)*

$$\frac{\$875,000}{\$162,000,000} = .0054012 \qquad \frac{.0054}{.001} = 5.4 \text{ mills}$$
$$= .0054$$

5. The home of John Tobey is assessed at $320,000. The tax rate is 8.33 mills. What is the tax on John's home? *(p. 440)*

   8.33 mills × .001 × $320,000 = $2,665.60

6. Pete's Warehouse has a market value of $700,000. The property in Pete's area is assessed at 30% of the market value. The tax rate is $49.20 per $1,000 of assessed value. What is Pete's property tax? *(p. 441)*

$$\$700,000 \times .30 = \frac{\$210,000}{\$1,000}$$
$$= 210 \times \$49.20$$
$$= \$10,332$$

Taxing Issue for Catalog Shoppers
▶ Do you owe sales tax on out-of-state mail-order goods?

A tax tempest erupted recently on the front page of the *New York Times*—much ado about nothing, apparently.

The paper broke a big story: Major mail-order catalog companies were about to agree voluntarily with some of the biggest states to collect sales taxes on all purchases. The next day, though, the *Times* reported that the deal had collapsed after "angry customers took to the phones" to tell the mail-order companies not to become tax collectors.

A good story, perhaps, but one that nearly all the participants deny. Robert Wientzen, president of the Direct Marketing Association, which has represented the catalogs in negotiations, says an agreement was never imminent. And L.L. Bean, a catalog merchant cited as having backed off after receiving calls from customers, denies it was a big deal. "We got very few calls," says spokeswoman Mary Rose MacKinnon.

For now, it seems, the status quo remains. But what is the status quo? Do you owe sales tax on mail-order purchases or not?

TANGLED TAX WEBS. Sales taxes are supposed to be collected by companies that have a store, office or other physical presence (a "nexus," for you Scrabble players) in the state. Companies that simply mail merchandise to a state are not required to collect the tax for that state.

If there's an Eddie Bauer store in your local mall, for example, you'll have to pay sales tax when you order something from the company's catalog. But order a product from the L.L. Bean catalog and you won't have to pay tax at the time of purchase unless you live in Maine, where the company is headquartered, or in one of the few states where it has outlets.

But that doesn't mean you're off the hook for sales tax on the L.L. Bean purchase. States that impose sales taxes require residents to pay a *use* tax on goods purchased through out-of-state catalogs. Some states have a line on the income-tax form for declaring the value of such purchases. Others require that you file a separate form.

WHAT'S THE BIG DEAL? States have a big financial interest in collecting tax on catalog sales, which could amount to billions of dollars annually. Direct marketers have an interest in keeping customers happy and business simple. And for now, the merchants have the upper hand. The Supreme Court ruled in 1992 that Congress, not the states, must settle the issue; so far, Congress has left it alone.

That suits most people just fine. No sales tax at the time of purchase is widely perceived as meaning no sales tax, period. And few people look for ways to pay more taxes.

The states can't hope to track down every sweater ordered through a catalog, but some do go after big buys, such as furniture. At some point they may get a voluntary agreement from some of the big catalogs. But for now, paying sales or use tax rests primarily on the orderer's honor. ●

REPORTER: STACY STOVER

ROBERT KOPECKY

Business Math Issue

With online shopping on the Internet, the taxing issue of sales tax should be deleted from Congress's agenda.

1. List the key points of the article and information to support your position.

2. Write a group defense of your position using math calculations to support your view.

THE COMMONWEALTH OF MASSACHUSETTS
TOWN OF MARBLEHEAD
OFFICE OF THE COLLECTOR OF TAXES
FISCAL YEAR 199X REAL ESTATE TAX BILL
Based on assessments as of January 1, 199X your Real Estate Tax for the fiscal year beginning July 1, 199X and ending June 30, 199X on the parcel of real estate described below is as follows:

*** THIRD PAYMENT NOTICE ***

OFFICES AT: MARY ALLEY MUNICIPAL OFFICE BUILDING
MAIL TO: LOCKBOX 3, MARBLEHEAD, MA 01945
HOURS: WEEKDAYS 8 AM – 4:30 PM
TAX COLLECTOR: JOAN M. STACKHOUSE

TAX RATE	Class	Residential 1	Open Space 2	Commercial 3	Industrial 4
PER $1000.	Rate	10.94	10.94	10.94	10.94

BILL # 1673

Betterment or Lien Type	Amount	Committed Interest	Class	Description	Value
			1	RESID.	

TOWN OF MARBLEHEAD
DEC 3 199X
Marylou Stackhouse
COLLECTOR OF TAXES

Total Tax & Assessments	2,908.95
TOTAL PAID	1,369.26
THIRD BILL AMOUNT	769.84
FOURTH BILL AMOUNT	769.85
AMOUNT NOW DUE ✓	769.84

TOTAL ASSESSMENTS .00

TOTAL VALUE
RESIDENTIAL EXEMPTION
TAXABLE VALUATION 265,900
TOTAL TAX 2,908.95

JEFFREY SLATER
80 GARFIELD ST
MARBLEHEAD MA 01945

PAYMENTS MUST BE MADE TO THE TOWN OF MARBLEHEAD AND RECEIVED BY THE COLLECTOR BY 4:30 PM ON 2/ 1/9X

SCHOLARSHIP CONTRIBUTION

PROPERTY LOCATION	MAP	LOT	PLOT	BOOK	PAGE	CLASS	AREA	EQV.	ISSUED
80 GARFIELD ST	125	22		6985	081	101	10585		12/27/9X

INTEREST AT THE RATE OF 14% PER ANNUM WILL ACCRUE ON OVERDUE PAYMENTS FROM THE FIRST DAY THE PAYMENT IS DUE UNTIL PAYMENT IS MADE. **SEE REVERSE SIDE FOR IMPORTANT INFORMATION.**

Project A

1. Check the total tax.
2. Check the assessed value of $265,900.
3. Check the tax rate of $10.94 per $1,000.

1. $\dfrac{\$265,900}{\$1,000} = 265.9 \times \$10.94 = \$2,908.95$

2. $\dfrac{\$2,908.95}{\$10.94} = 265.9 \times \$1,000 = \$265,900$

3. $\dfrac{\$2,908.95}{\$265,900} = .01094 \times \$1,000 = \$10.94$

Fees, Fines to Go? McDonald's Is Hit In Chinese Capital

* * *

Beijing's Bureaucrats Compel The U.S. Chain to Pay Up Just to Remain in Business

By IAN JOHNSON
Staff Reporter of THE WALL STREET JOURNAL

BEIJING — The average McDonald's restaurant in this city contributes more to society than taxes. It also is forced to pay for cleaning rivers, repairing air-raid shelters and spreading Communist Party propaganda.

A surprisingly detailed list of the fines and fees — most collected illegally by bureaucrats — that the U.S. fast-food restaurant chain pays to stay in business in China's capital has quietly been made public. Gathered by municipal authorities trying to figure out why foreign investment has been dropping, the formerly secret report offers a rare glimpse of the daily travails faced by foreign business.

Project B

Can you discuss the ethics of this situation? Should McDonald's pay more than its share of taxes? What action should it take?

 See text Web site (www.mhhe.com/slater) and *The Business Math Internet Resource Guide.*

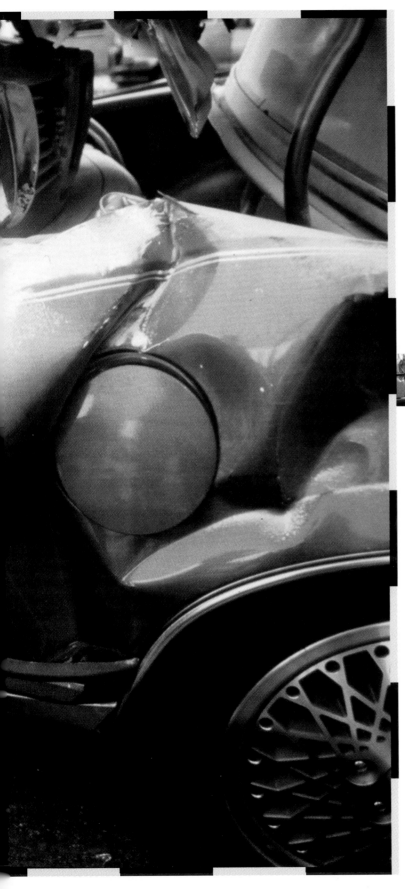

20

LIFE, FIRE, AND AUTO INSURANCE

LEARNING UNIT OBJECTIVES

LU 20.1 Life Insurance

- Explain the types of life insurance; calculate life insurance premiums *(pp. 452–54)*.
- Explain and calculate cash value and other nonforfeiture options *(pp. 455–56)*.

LU 20.2 Fire Insurance

- Explain and calculate premiums for fire insurance of buildings and their contents *(pp. 456–57)*.
- Calculate refunds when the insured and the insurance company cancel fire insurance *(pp. 457–58)*.
- Explain and calculate insurance loss when coinsurance is not met *(pp. 458–59)*.

LU 20.3 Auto Insurance

- Explain and calculate the cost of auto insurance *(pp. 458–59)*.

Living Longer

People are expected to live longer in the 21st century, putting added pressure on the Social Security and Medicare systems. Here are Census Bureau projections of life expectancy at age 65 and the growing percentage of people over 65.

Life Expectancy at 65

Year	Total	
	Male	Female
1997	15.6	19.3
2000	15.9	19.5
2010	16.8	20.0
2020	17.6	20.6
2030	18.5	21.2
2040	19.3	21.8
2050	20.3	22.4

CRINGE Even if your credit card already covers certain types of car-rental insurance, you may still have to pay. In Italy, regardless of whether your card covers auto theft, all the rental companies tack on an additional fee. According to Avis and Hertz, costs run about $100 a week for a full-size car.

© 1997, Dow Jones & Company, Inc.

© 1998, Dow Jones & Company, Inc.

Do you have enough collision coverage on your car and enough life insurance? If you rent a car, will you have to pay for car-rental insurance? The two *Wall Street Journal* clippings "Cringe" and "Living Longer" give information on planning for car-rental insurance and life insurance.

Most adults have some form of insurance. Many adults do not read or understand their insurance policies. It has been reported that half of the people in the United States who have property insurance do not read their policy and that 60% do not understand their policy. Are you one of these statistics? If you are, this chapter will help you become an informed policy reader. The chapter should answer many of your questions about life insurance, fire insurance, and auto insurance. We begin by studying life insurance.

LEARNING UNIT 20.1   Life Insurance

Courtesy State Farm Insurance Companies.

Bob Brady owns Bob's Deli. He is 40 years of age, married, and has three children. Bob wants to know what type of life insurance protection will best meet his needs. Following is a discussion between an insurance agent, Rick Jones, and Bob.

Bob: I would like to buy a life insurance policy that will pay my wife $200,000 in the event of my death. My problem is that I do not have much cash. You know, bills, bills, bills. Can you explain some types of life insurance and their costs?

Rick: Let's begin by explaining some life insurance terminology. The **insured** is you—the **policyholder** receiving coverage. The **insurer** is the company selling the insurance policy. Your wife is the **beneficiary.** As the beneficiary, she is the person named in the policy to receive the insurance proceeds at the death of the insured (that's you, Bob). The amount stated in the policy, say, $200,000, is the **face amount** of the policy. The **premium** is the periodic payments you agree to make for the cost of the insurance policy. You can pay premiums annually, semiannually, quarterly, or monthly. The more frequent the payment, the higher the total cost due to increased paperwork, billing, and so on. Now let's look at the different types of insurance.

Types of Insurance

In this section Rick explains term insurance, straight life (ordinary life), 20-payment life, 20-year endowment, and universal life insurance.

Term Insurance

Rick: The cheapest type of life insurance is **term insurance,** but it only provides *temporary* protection. Term insurance pays the face amount to your wife (beneficiary) only if you die within the period of the insurance (1, 5, 10 years, and so on).

For example, let's say you take out a 5-year term policy. The insurance company automatically allows you to renew the policy at increased rates until age 70. A new policy called **level premium term** may be less expensive than an annual term policy since each year for, say, 50 years, the premium will be fixed.

The policy of my company lets you convert to other insurance types without a medical examination. To determine your rates under 5-year term insurance, check this table (Table 20.1). The annual premium at 40 years per $1,000 of insurance is $3.52. We use the following steps to calculate the total yearly premium.

Calculating Annual Life Insurance Premiums

Step 1. Look up the age of the insured and the type of insurance in Table 20.1 (for females, subtract 3 years). This gives the premium cost per $1,000.

Step 2. Divide the amount of coverage by $1,000 and multiply the answer by the premium cost per $1,000.

$$\frac{\$200,000 \text{ (coverage)}}{\$1,000} = 200 \times \$3.52 = = \boxed{\$704}$$

Number of thousands — Cost per $1,000 for age 40 — Annual premium

Airport flight insurance is a type of term insurance.

From this formula you can see that for $704 per year for the next 5 years, we, your insurance company, offer to pay your wife $200,000 in the event of your death. At the end of the 5th year, you are not entitled to any cash from your paid premiums. If you do not renew your policy (at a higher rate) and die in the 6th year, we will not pay your wife anything. Term insurance provides protection for only a specific period of time.

TABLE 20.1

Life insurance rates for males (for females, subtract 3 years from the age)*

Age	Five-year term	Age	Straight life	Age	Twenty-payment life	Age	Twenty-year endowment
20	1.85	20	5.90	20	8.28	20	13.85
21	1.85	21	6.13	21	8.61	21	14.35
22	1.85	22	6.35	22	8.91	22	14.92
23	1.85	23	6.60	23	9.23	23	15.54
24	1.85	24	6.85	24	9.56	24	16.05
25	1.85	25	7.13	25	9.91	25	17.55
26	1.85	26	7.43	26	10.29	26	17.66
27	1.86	27	7.75	27	10.70	27	18.33
28	1.86	28	8.08	28	11.12	28	19.12
29	1.87	29	8.46	29	11.58	29	20.00
30	1.87	30	8.85	30	12.05	30	20.90
31	1.87	31	9.27	31	12.57	31	21.88
32	1.88	32	9.71	32	13.10	32	22.89
33	1.95	33	10.20	33	13.67	33	23.98
34	2.08	34	10.71	34	14.28	34	25.13
35	2.23	35	11.26	35	14.92	35	26.35
36	2.44	36	11.84	36	15.60	36	27.64
37	2.67	37	12.46	37	16.30	37	28.97
38	2.95	38	13.12	38	17.04	38	30.38
39	3.24	39	13.81	39	17.81	39	31.84
40	3.52	40	14.54	40	18.61	40	33.36
41	3.79	41	15.30	41	19.44	41	34.94
42	4.04	42	16.11	42	20.31	42	36.59
43	4.26	43	16.96	43	21.21	43	38.29
44	4.50	44	17.86	44	22.15	44	40.09

*Note that these tables are a sampling of age groups, premium costs, and insurance coverage that are available under 45 years of age.

Bob: Are you telling me that my premium does not build up any cash savings that you call **cash value?**

Rick: The term insurance policy does not build up cash savings. Let me show you a policy that does build up cash value. This policy is straight life.

Straight Life (Ordinary Life)

Rick: Straight life insurance provides *permanent* protection rather than the temporary protection provided by term insurance. The insured pays the same premium each year or until death.[1] The premium for straight life is higher than that for term insurance because straight life provides both protection and a built-in cash savings feature. According to our table (Table 20.1, p. 453), your annual premium, Bob, would be:

Face value is usually the amount paid to the beneficiary at the time of insured's death.

$$\frac{\$200,000}{\$1,000} = 200 \times \$14.54 = \boxed{\$2,908} \text{ annual premium}$$

Bob: Compared to term, straight life is quite expensive.

Rick: Remember that term insurance has no cash value accumulating, as straight life does. Let me show you another type of insurance—20-payment life—that builds up cash value.

Twenty-Payment Life

Rick: A **20-payment life** policy is similar to straight life in that 20-payment life provides permanent protection and cash value, but you (the insured) pay premiums for only the first 20 years. After 20 years you own **paid-up insurance.** According to my table (Table 20.1), your annual premium would be:

$$\frac{\$200,000}{\$1,000} = 200 \times \$18.61 = \boxed{\$3,722} \text{ annual premium}$$

Bob: The 20-payment life policy is more expensive than straight life.

Rick: This is because you are only paying for 20 years. The shorter period of time does result in increased yearly costs. Remember that in straight life you pay premiums over your entire life. Let me show you another alternative that we call 20-year endowment.

Twenty-Year Endowment

Rick: The **20-year endowment** insurance policy is the most expensive. It is a combination of term insurance and cash value. For example, from age 40 to 60, you receive term insurance protection in that your wife would receive $200,000 should you die. At age 60, your protection *ends* and you receive the face value of the policy that equals the $200,000 cash value. Let's use my table again (Table 20.1) to see how expensive the 20-year endowment is:

$$\frac{\$200,000}{\$1,000} = 200 \times \$33.36 = \boxed{\$6,672} \text{ annual premium}$$

In summary, Bob, here is a review of the costs for the various types of insurance we have talked about:

	5-year term	Straight life	20-payment life	20-year endowment
Premium cost per year	$704	$2,908	$3,722	$6,672

Before we proceed, I have another policy that may interest you—universal life.

Universal Life Insurance

Rick: Universal life is basically a **whole-life** insurance plan with flexible premium schedules and death benefits. Under whole life, the premiums and death benefits are fixed. Universal has limited guarantees with greater risk on the holder of the policy. For example, if interest rates fall, the policyholder must pay higher premiums, increase the number of payments, or switch to smaller death benefits in the future.

Bob: That policy is not for me—too much risk. I'd prefer fixed premiums and death benefits.

---

[1]In the following section on nonforfeiture values, we show how a policyholder in later years can stop making payments and still be covered by using the accumulated cash value built up.

FIGURE 20.1
Nonforfeiture options

Option 1: Cash value (cash surrender value)

a. Receive cash value of policy.
b. Policy is terminated.
The longer the policy has been in effect, the higher the cash value because more premiums have been paid in.

Option 2: Reduced paid-up insurance

a. Cash value buys protection without paying new premiums.
b. Face amount of policy is related to cash value buildup and age of insured. The **face amount is less than original policy.**
c. Policy continues for life (at a reduced face amount).

Option 3: Extended term insurance

a. Original face amount of policy continues for a certain period of time.
b. Length of policy depends on cash value built up and on insured's age.
c. This option results automatically if policyholder doesn't pay premiums and fails to elect another option.

Rick: OK, let's look at how straight life, 20-payment life, and 20-year endowment can build up cash value and provide an opportunity for insurance coverage without requiring additional premiums. We call these options **nonforfeiture values.**

Nonforfeiture Values

Rick: Except for term insurance, the other types of life insurance build up cash value as you pay premiums. These policies provide three options should you, the policyholder, ever want to cancel your policy, stop paying premiums, or collect the cash value. My company lists these options here (Figure 20.1).

For example, Bob, let's assume that at age 40 we sell you a $200,000 straight life policy. Assume that at age 55, after the policy has been in force for 15 years, you want to stop paying premiums. From this table (Table 20.2), I can show you the options that are available.

Insight into Health and Business Insurance

This unit has concentrated on personal life insurance. Before we discuss the types of insurance that business owners should consider, you should be aware of the importance of health insurance. *The Wall Street Journal* clipping "Snapshots of the Uninsured" presents some frightening statistics about health insurance. If you are one of the 55% of individuals who think that health insurance is too expensive, think again. It is too expensive *not* to have health insurance.

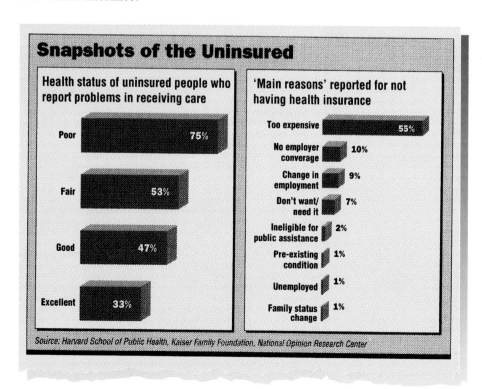

TABLE 20.2   Nonforfeiture options based on $1,000 face value

Years insurance policy in force	Straight life				20-payment life				20-year endowment			
	Cash value	Amount of paid-up insurance	Extended term Years	Extended term Day	Cash value	Amount of paid-up insurance	Extended term Years	Extended term Day	Cash value	Amount of paid-up insurance	Extended term Years	Extended term Day
5	29	86	9	91	71	220	19	190	92	229	23	140
10	96	259	18	76	186	521	28	195	319	520	30	160
15	148	371	20	165	317	781	32	176	610	790	35	300
20	265	550	21	300	475	1,000	Life		1,000	1,000	Life	

Option 1: Cash value

$$\frac{\$200,000}{\$1,000} = 200 \times \$148 = \$29,600$$

Option 2: Reduced paid-up insurance

$$\frac{\$200,000}{\$1,000} = 200 \times \$371 = \$74,200$$

Option 3: Extended term insurance

Bob could continue this $200,000 policy for 20 years and 165 days.

Some of the key types of business insurance that you may need as a business owner include the following: fire insurance, business interruption insurance (business loss until physical damages are fixed), casualty insurance (insurance against a customer's suing your business due to an accident on company property), workers' compensation (insurance against injuries or sickness from being on the job), and group insurance (life, health, and accident). For employees, company health insurance and life insurance benefits can be an important job consideration.

Although group health insurance costs have soared today, many companies still pay the major portion of the cost. Some companies also provide health insurance benefits for retirees. As health costs continue to rise, we can expect to see some changes in this employee benefit.

Companies vary in the type of life insurance benefits they provide to their employees. This insurance can be a percent of the employee's salary with the employee naming the beneficiary; or in the case of key employees, the company can be the beneficiary.

If as an employer you need any of the types of insurance mentioned in this section, be sure to shop around for the best price. If you are in the job market, consider the benefits offered by a company as part of your salary and make your decisions accordingly. In the next unit, we look specifically at fire insurance.

Let's check your understanding of this unit with a Practice Quiz.

LU 20.1 PRACTICE QUIZ

1. Bill Boot, age 39, purchased a $60,000, 5-year term life insurance policy. Calculate his annual premium from Table 20.1. After 4 years, what is his cash value?

2. Ginny Katz, age 32, purchased a $78,000, straight life policy. Calculate her annual premium. If after 10 years she wants to surrender her policy, what options and what amounts are available to her?

✓   **Solutions**

1. $$\frac{\$60,000}{\$1,000} = 60 \times \$3.24 = \boxed{\$194.40}$$ No cash value in term insurance.

2. $$\frac{\$78,000}{\$1,000} = 78 \times \$8.46^* = \boxed{\$659.88}$$

   Option 1: Cash value   78 × $96 = $7,488

   Option 2: Paid up   78 × $259 = $20,202

   Option 3: Extended term   18 years 76 days

   *For females we subtract 3 years.

LEARNING UNIT 20.2   Fire Insurance

Periodically, some areas of the United States, especially California, have experienced drought followed by devastating fires. These fires spread quickly and destroy wooded areas and homes. When the fires occur, the first thought of the owners is the adequacy of

©PhotoDisc.

Fire insurance premium equals premium for building and premium for contents.

their **fire insurance.** Homeowners are made more aware of the importance of fire insurance that provides for the replacement value of their home. Out-of-date fire insurance policies can result in great financial loss.

This unit looks at Alice Swan and the discussion with her insurance agent about her fire insurance needs for her new dress shop at 4 Park Plaza. (Alice owns the building.)

Alice: What is *extended coverage?*

Bob: Your basic fire insurance policy provides financial protection if fire or lightning damages your property. However, the extended coverage protects you from smoke, chemicals, water, or other damages that firefighters may cause to control the fire. We have many options available.

Alice: What is the cost of a fire insurance policy?

Bob: Years ago, if you bought a policy for 2, 3, 5, or more years, reduced rates were available. Today, with rising costs of reimbursing losses from fires, most insurance companies write policies for 1 to 3 years. The cost of a 3-year policy premium is 3 times the annual premium. Because of rising insurance premiums, your total costs are cheaper if you buy one 3-year policy than three 1-year policies.

Alice: For my purpose, I will need coverage for 1 year. Before you give me the premium rates, what factors affect the cost of my premium?

Bob: In your case, you have several factors in your favor that will result in a lower premium. For example, (1) your building is brick, (2) the roof is fire-resistant, (3) the building is located next to a fire hydrant, (4) the building is in a good location (not next to a gas station) with easy access for the fire department, and (5) the goods within your store are not as flammable as, say, those of a paint store. I have a table here (Table 20.3) that gives an example of typical fire insurance rates for buildings and contents (furniture, fixtures, etc.).

Let's assume your building has an insured value of $190,000 and is rated Class B, Area No. 2, and we insure your contents for $80,000. Then we calculate your total annual premium for building and contents as follows:

$$\text{Premium} = \frac{\text{Insured value}}{\$100} \times \text{Rate}$$

Building

$$\frac{\$190,000}{\$100} = 1,900 \times \$.50 = \$950$$

Contents

$$\frac{\$80,000}{\$100} = 800 \times \$.60 = \$480$$

Total premium = $950 + $480 = **$1,430**

For our purpose, we round all premiums to the nearest cent. In practice, the premium is rounded to the nearest dollar.

Canceling Fire Insurance

Alice: What if my business fails in 7 months? Do I get back any portion of my premium when I cancel?

Bob: If the insured—that's you, Alice—cancels or wants a policy for less than 1 year, we use this **short-rate table** (Table 20.4). The rates in the short-rate table will cost you more. For example, if you cancel at the end of 7 months, the premium cost is 67% of the

TABLE 20.3

Fire insurance rates per $100 of coverage for buildings and contents

	Classification of building			
	Class A		Class B	
Rating of area	Building	Contents	Building	Contents
1	.28	.35	.41	.54
2	.33	.47	.50	.60
3	.41	.50	.61	.65

TABLE 20.4

Fire insurance short-rate and cancellation table

Time policy is in force		Percent of annual rate to be charged	Time policy is in force		Percent of annual rate to be charged
Days:	5	8%	Months:	5	52%
	10	10		6	61
	20	15		7	67
	25	17		8	74
Months:	1	19		9	81
	2	27		10	87
	3	35		11	96
	4	44		12	100

annual premium. These rates are higher because it is more expensive to process a policy for a short time. We would calculate your refund as follows:

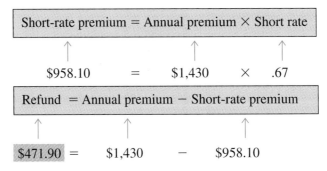

Alice: Let's say that I don't pay my premium or follow the fire codes. What happens if your insurance company cancels me?

Bob: If the insurance company cancels you, the company is *not* allowed to use the short-rate table. To calculate what part of the premium the company may keep,[2] you can prorate the premium based on the actual days that have elapsed. We can illustrate the amount of your refund by assuming you are canceled after 7 months:

Note that when the insurance company cancels the policy, the refund ($595.83) is greater than if the insured cancels ($471.90).

For insurance company: $\longrightarrow$ Charge = \$1,430 annual premium $\times \dfrac{7 \text{ months elapsed}}{12}$

Charge = \$834.17

For insured: Refund = \$1,430 annual premium $-$ \$834.17 charge

Refund = \$595.83

Coinsurance

Alice: My friend tells me that I should meet the coinsurance clause. What is coinsurance?

Bob: Usually, fire does not destroy the entire property. **Coinsurance** means that you and the insurance company *share* the risk. The reason for this coinsurance clause[3] is to encourage property owners to purchase adequate coverage.

Alice: What is adequate coverage?

Bob: In the fire insurance industry, the usual rate for coinsurance is 80% of the current replacement cost. This cost equals the value to replace what was destroyed. If your insurance coverage is 80% of the current value, the insurance company will pay all damages up to the face value of the policy.

Alice: Hold it Bob! Will you please show me how this coinsurance is figured?

Bob: Yes, Alice, I'll be happy to show you how we figure coinsurance. Let's begin by looking at the following steps so you can see what amount of the insurance the company will pay.

---

[2]Many companies use $\dfrac{\text{Days}}{365}$.

[3]In some states (including Wisconsin), the clause is not in effect for losses under \$1,000.

Calculating What Insurance Company Pays with Coinsurance Clause

Step 1. Set up a fraction. The numerator is the actual amount of the insurance carried on the property. The denominator is the amount of insurance you should be carrying on the property to meet coinsurance (80% times the replacement value).

Step 2. Multiply the fraction by the amount of loss (up to the face value of the policy).

Let's assume for this example that you carry $60,000 fire insurance on property that will cost $100,000 to replace. If the coinsurance clause in your policy is 80% and you suffer a loss of $20,000, your insurance company will pay the following:

Insurance coverage $\longrightarrow$ Loss $\swarrow$

Step 1 $\longrightarrow$ $\dfrac{\$60,000}{\$80,000} \times \$20,000 = \boxed{\$15,000}$ [4]

What you should $\longrightarrow$ have carried   ($100,000 \times .80$)   **Step 2**

Although there are many types of property and homeowner's insurance policies, they usually include fire protection.

If you had had actual insurance coverage of $80,000, then the insurance company would have paid $20,000. Remember that if the coinsurance clause is met, the most an insurance company will pay is the face value of the policy.

You are now ready for the following Practice Quiz.

LU 20.2 PRACTICE QUIZ

1. Calculate the total annual premium of a warehouse that has an area rating of 2 with a building classification of B. The value of the warehouse is $90,000 with contents valued at $30,000.

2. If insured cancels in Problem 1 at the end of month 9, what are the cost of the premium and the refund?

3. Jones insures a building for $120,000 with an 80% coinsurance clause. The replacement value is $200,000. Assume a loss of $60,000 from fire. What will the insurance company pay? If the loss was $160,000 and coinsurance *was* met, what will the insurance company pay?

✓ **Solutions**

1. $\dfrac{\$90,000}{100} = 900 \times \$.50 = \quad \$450$

   $\dfrac{\$30,000}{100} = 300 \times \$.60 = \quad \underline{180}$

                    $\boxed{\$630}$ $\longleftarrow$ total premium

2. $\$630 \times .81 = \boxed{\$510.30}$ $\$630 - \$510.30 = \boxed{\$119.70}$

3. $\dfrac{\$120,000}{\$160,000} = \dfrac{3}{4} \times \$60,000 = \boxed{\$45,000}$

    $\uparrow$

   ($.80 \times \$200,000$) $\boxed{\$160,000}$ never more than face value

---

LEARNING UNIT 20.3 Auto Insurance

If you own an auto, you have had some experience purchasing auto insurance. Often, first-time auto owners do not realize that auto insurance can be a substantial expense. Also, the cost of auto insurance varies from state to state. According to statistics, the most expensive auto insurance is in New Jersey where the average annual premium was $1,094.56. Those living in Hawaii had an annual average premium of $1,078.32; in Rhode Island, the annual average premium was $1,034.46; and in Massachusetts, the annual average premium was $1,009.56. Wherever you live, you might be interested to know that the national average premium was $730.39.

---

[4]This kind of limited insurance payment for a loss is often called an **indemnity.**

Who Wears Seat Belts

Five states with the lowest rates:		Five states with the highest rates:	
North Dakota	43%	California	87%
Mississippi	46	New Mexico	85
South Dakota	47	Washington	84
Arkansas	48	North Carolina	83
Oklahoma	48	Oregon	82

Source: National Highway Traffic Safety Administration

©1997, Dow Jones & Company, Inc.

Insurance rates often increase when a driver is involved in an accident. Some insurance companies give reduced rates to accident-free drivers, a practice that has encouraged drivers to be more safety-conscious. Many drivers now realize the importance of wearing a seat belt. *The Wall Street Journal* clipping "Who Wears Seat Belts" gives the five states with the lowest and highest rates of seat belt use. Is your state one of those mentioned? In North Carolina the increase in seat belt use from 64% to 83% has resulted in 14% fewer deaths and serious injuries. In Canada, Australia, and England, 90% of drivers use seat belts.

In this unit we follow Shirley as she learns about auto insurance. Shirley, who just bought a new auto, has never purchased auto insurance. So she called her insurance agent, Bob Long, who agreed to meet her for lunch. We will listen in on their conversation.

Shirley: Bob, where do I start?

Liability insurance includes

*1. **Bodily injury**—injury or death to people in passenger car or other cars, etc.*

*2. **Property damage**—injury to other people's autos, trees, buildings, hydrants, etc.*

Bob: Our state has two kinds of **liability insurance,** or **compulsory insurance,** that by law you must buy (regulations and requirements vary among states). Liability insurance covers any physical damages that you inflict on others or their property. You must buy liability insurance for the following:

1. **Bodily injury** to others: 10/20. This means that the insurance company will pay damages to people injured or killed by your auto up to $10,000 for injury to one person per accident or a total of $20,000 for injuries to two or more people per accident.

2. **Property damage** to someone else's property: 5. The insurance company will pay up to $5,000 for damages that you have caused to the property of others.

Now we leave Shirley and Bob for a few moments as we calculate Shirley's premium for compulsory insurance.

Calculating Premium for Compulsory Insurance[5]

The tables we use in this unit are for Territory 5. Other tables are available for different territories.

Insurance companies base auto insurance rates on the territory you live in, the class of driver (class 10 is experienced driver with driver training), whether auto is for business use, how much you drive the car, the age of the car, and the make of the car (symbol). Shirley lives in Territory 5 (suburbia). She is classified as 17 because she is an inexperienced operator licensed for less than 6 years. Her car is age 3 and symbol 4 (make of car). We use Table 20.5 to calculate Shirley's compulsory insurance. Note that the table rates in this unit are not representative of all areas of the country. In case of lawsuits, the minimum coverage may not be adequate. Some states add surcharges to the premium if the person has a poor driving record. The tables are designed to show how rates are calculated. From Table 20.5, we have the following:

$$
\begin{array}{lr}
\text{Bodily} & \$\ 98 \\
+\ \text{Property} & \underline{160} \\
& \$258
\end{array}
$$

Remember that the $258 premium represents minimum coverage. Assume Shirley hits two people and the courts award them $13,000 and $5,000, respectively. Shirley would be responsible for $3,000 because the insurance company would pay only up to $10,000 per person and a total of $20,000 per accident.

---

[5]Some states may offer medical payment insurance (a supplement to policyholders' health and accident insurance) as well as personal injury protection against uninsured or underinsured motorists.

TABLE 20.5
Compulsory insurance (based on class of driver)

Bodily injury to others		Damage to someone else's property	
Class	10/20	Class	5M*
10	$ 55	10	$129
17	98	17	160
18	80	18	160
20	116	20	186

Explanation of 10/20 and 5		
10	20	5
Maximum paid to one person per accident for bodily injury	Maximum paid for total bodily injury per accident	Maximum paid for property damage per accident

*M means thousands.

Although total damages of $18,000 are less than $20,000, the insurance company pays only $15,000.

	(1)	(2)	
	$13,000 +	$5,000 =	$18,000
Paid by insurance company →	− 10,000 −	5,000 =	− 15,000
Paid by Shirley →	$ 3,000 +	$ 0 =	$ 3,000

We return to Shirley and Bob. Bob now shows Shirley how to calculate her optional insurance coverage. Remember that optional insurance coverages (Tables 20.6 to 20.10) are added to the costs in Table 20.5.

Calculating Optional Insurance Coverage

Bob: In our state, you can add optional bodily injury to the compulsory amount. If you finance your car, the lender may require specific amounts of optional insurance to protect its investment. I have two tables (Tables 20.6 and 20.7) here that we use to calculate the option of 250/500/50. This means that in an accident the insurance company will pay $250,000 per person, up to $500,000 per accident, and up to $50,000 for property damage.

Bob then explains the tables to Shirley. By studying the tables, you can see how insurance companies figure bodily injury and damage to someone else's property. Shirley is Class 17:

Bodily
250/500 = $228

Property
50M   = + 168

$396 premium for optional bodily injury and property damage

Note: These are additional amounts to compulsory.

TABLE 20.6
Bodily injury

Class	15/30	20/40	20/50	25/50	25/60	50/100	100/300	250/500	500/1000
10	27	37	40	44	47	69	94	144	187
17	37	52	58	63	69	104	146	228	298
18	33	46	50	55	60	89	124	193	251
20	41	59	65	72	78	119	168	263	344

TABLE 20.7
Damage to someone else's property

Class	10M	25M	50M	100M
10	132	134	135	136
17	164	166	168	169
18	164	166	168	169
20	191	193	195	197

Collision and comprehensive are optional insurance types that pay only the insured. Note that Tables 20.8 and 20.9 are based on territory, age, and car symbol. The higher the symbol, the more expensive the car.

Shirley: Is that all I need?

Bob: No, I would recommend two more types of optional coverage: **collision** and **comprehensive.** Collision provides protection against damages to your car caused by a moving vehicle. It covers the cost of repairs less **deductibles** (amount of repair you cover first before the insurance company pays the rest) and depreciation.[6] In collision, insurance companies pay the resale or book value. So as the car gets older, after 5 or more years, it might make sense to drop the collision. The decision depends on how much risk you are willing to assume. Comprehensive covers damages resulting from theft, fire, falling objects, and so on. Now let's calculate the cost of these two types of coverage—assuming a $100 deductible for collision and a $200 deductible for comprehensive—with some more of my tables (Tables 20.8 and 20.9).

	Class	**Age**	**Symbol**	**Premium**	
Collision	17	3	4	$191 ($148 + $43)	Cost to
Comprehensive	17	3	4	+ 56 ($52 + $4)	reduce
				$247	deductibles

Total premium for collision and comprehensive

TABLE 20.8   Collision

Classes	Age group	Symbols 1–3 $300 ded.	Symbol 4 $300 ded.	Symbol 5 $300 ded.	Symbol 6 $300 ded.	Symbol 7 $300 ded.	Symbol 8 $300 ded.	Symbol 10 $300 ded.
10–20	1	180	180	187	194	214	264	279
	2	160	160	166	172	190	233	246
	3	148	148	154	166	183	221	233
	4	136	136	142	160	176	208	221
	5	124	124	130	154	169	196	208

These classes would use all this information.

To find the premium, use the age and symbol only.

Additional cost to reduce deductible

Class	From $300 to $200	From $300 to $100
10	13	27
17	20	43
18	16	33
20	26	55

TABLE 20.9   Comprehensive

Classes	Age group	Symbols 1–3 $300 ded.	Symbol 4 $300 ded.	Symbol 5 $300 ded.	Symbol 6 $300 ded.	Symbol 7 $300 ded.	Symbol 8 $300 ded.	Symbol 10 $300 ded.
10–25	1	61	61	65	85	123	157	211
	2	55	55	58	75	108	138	185
	3	52	52	55	73	104	131	178
	4	49	49	52	70	99	124	170
	5	47	47	49	67	94	116	163

Additional cost to reduce deductible: From $300 to $200 add $4

---

[6]In some states, repair to glass has no deductible and many insurance companies now use a $500 deductible instead of $300.

TABLE 20.10

Transportation and towing

Substitute transportation	$16
Towing and labor	4

TABLE 20.11

Worksheet for calculating Shirley's auto premium

Compulsory insurance	Limits	Deductible	Premium
Bodily injury to others	$10,000 per person	None	
	$20,000 per accident		$ 98 (Table 20.5)
Damage to someone else's property	$5,000 per accident	None	$160 (Table 20.5)
Options			
Optional bodily injury to others	$250,000 per person $500,000 per accident	None	$228 (Table 20.6)
Optional property damage	$50,000 per accident	None	$168 (Table 20.7)
Collision	Actual cash value	$100	$191 (Table 20.8) ($148 + $43)
Comprehensive	Actual cash value	$200	$ 56 (Table 20.9) ($52 + $4)
Substitute transportation	Up to $12 per day or $300 total	None	$ 16 (Table 20.10)
Towing and labor	$25 per tow	None	$ 4 (Table 20.10)
			$921 Total premium

Shirley: Anything else?

Bob: I would also recommend that you buy towing and substitute transportation coverage. The insurance company will pay up to $25 for each tow. Under substitute transportation, the insurance company will pay you $12 a day for renting a car, up to $300 total. Again, from another table (Table 20.10), we find the additional premium for towing and substitute transportation is $20 ($16 + $4).

We leave Shirley and Bob now as we make a summary of Shirley's total auto premium in Table 20.11.

Premiums for collision, property damage, and comprehensive are not reduced by no fault.

No-Fault Insurance   Some states have **no-fault insurance,** a type of auto insurance that was intended to reduce premium costs on bodily injury. With no fault, one forfeits the right to sue for *small* claims involving medical expense, loss of wages, and so on. Each person collects the bodily injury from his or her insurance company no matter who is at fault. In reality, no-fault insurance has not reduced premium costs, due to large lawsuits, fraud, and operating costs of insurance companies. Many states that were once considering no fault are no longer pursuing its adoption. Note that states with no-fault insurance require the purchase of *personal-injury protection (PIP).* The most successful no-fault law seems to be in Michigan, since it has tough restrictions on the right to sue along with unlimited medical and rehabilitation benefits.

It's time to take your final Practice Quiz in this chapter.

LU 20.3 PRACTICE QUIZ

Calculate the annual auto premium for Mel Jones who lives in Territory 5, is a driver classified 18, and has a car with age 4 and symbol 7. His state has compulsory insurance, and Mel wants to add the following options:

1. Bodily injury, 100/300.
2. Damage to someone else's property, 10M.
3. Collision, $200 deductible.
4. Comprehensive, $200 deductible.
5. Towing.

✓ **Solutions**

Compulsory

Bodily	$ 80	(Table 20.5)
Property	160	(Table 20.5)

Options

Bodily	124		(Table 20.6)
Property	164		(Table 20.7)
Collision	192	($176 + $16)	(Table 20.8)
Comprehensive	103	($99 + $4)	(Table 20.9)
Towing	4		(Table 20.10)
Total annual premium	**$827**		

Chapter Organizer and Reference Guide

Topic	Key point, procedure, formula	Example(s) to illustrate situation
Life insurance, p. 453	Using Table 20.1, per $1,000: $$\frac{\text{Coverage desired}}{\$1,000} \times \text{Rate}$$ For females, subtract 3 years.	**Given** $80,000 of insurance desired; age 34; male. 1. Five-year term: $$\frac{\$80,000}{\$1,000} = 80 \times \$2.08 \; \boxed{\$166.40}$$ 2. Straight life: $$\frac{\$80,000}{\$1,000} = 80 \times \$10.71 = \boxed{\$856.80}$$ 3. Twenty-payment life: $$\frac{\$80,000}{\$1,000} = 80 \times \$14.28 \; \boxed{\$1,142.40}$$ 4. Twenty-year endowment: $$\frac{\$80,000}{\$1,000} = 80 \times \$25.13 = \boxed{\$2,010.40}$$
Nonforfeiture values, p. 455	**By Table 20.2** Option 1: Cash surrender value. Option 2: Reduced paid-up insurance policy continues for life at reduced face amount. Option 3: Extended term—original face policy continued for a certain period of time.	A $50,000 straight-life policy was issued to Jim Rose at age 28. At age 48 Jim wants to stop paying premiums. What are his nonforfeiture options? Option 1: $$\frac{\$50,000}{\$1,000} = 50 \times \$265 = \boxed{\$13,250}$$ Option 2: $50 \times \$550 = \boxed{\$27,500}$ Option 3: $\boxed{\text{21 years 300 days}}$
Fire insurance, p. 457	Per $100 $$\text{Premium} = \frac{\text{Insurance value}}{\$100} \times \text{Rate}$$ Rate can be for buildings or contents.	**Given** Area 3; Class B; building insured for $90,000; contents, $30,000 Building: $$\frac{\$90,000}{\$100} = 900 \times \$.61 = \boxed{\$549}$$ Contents: $$\frac{\$30,000}{\$100} = 300 \times \$.65 = \boxed{\$195}$$ Total: $549 + $195 = $\boxed{\$744}$

Chapter Organizer and Reference Guide (concluded)		
Topic	**Key point, procedure, formula**	**Example(s) to illustrate situation**
Canceling fire insurance—short-rate Table 20.4 (canceling by policyholder), p. 458	$\dfrac{\text{Short-rate}}{\text{premium}} = \dfrac{\text{Annual}}{\text{premium}} \times \dfrac{\text{Short}}{\text{rate}}$ Refund = Annual premium − Short-rate premium If insurance company cancels, do not use Table 20.4.	Annual premium is $400. Short rate is .35 (cancel end of 3 months). $400 × .35 = $140 Refund = $400 − $140 = $260
Canceling by insurance company, p. 458	Annual premium × $\dfrac{\text{Months elapsed}}{12}$ (Refund is higher since company cancels.)	Using example above but if insurance company cancels at end of 3 months: $400 × $\frac{1}{4}$ = $100 Refund = $400 − $100 = $300
Coinsurance, p. 458	Amount insurance company pays: $\dfrac{\text{Actual} \longrightarrow \text{Insurance carried (Face value)}}{\text{What coverage should} \longrightarrow \text{Insurance required to meet coinsurance have been (Rate × Replacement value)}} \times \text{Loss}$ Insurance company never pays more than the face value.	**Given** Face value, $30,000; replacement value, $50,000; coinsurance rate, 80%; loss, $10,000; insurance to meet required coinsurance, $40,000. $\dfrac{\$30,000}{\$40,000} \times \$10,000 = \$7,500$ paid by insurance company ($50,000 × .80)
Auto insurance, p. 459	**Compulsory** Required insurance. **Optional** Added to cost of compulsory. Bodily injury—pays for injury to person caused by insured. Property damage—pays for property damage (not for insured auto). Collision—pays for damages to insured auto. Comprehensive—pays for damage to insured auto for fire, theft, etc. Towing. Substitute transportation.	Calculate the annual premium: Driver class 10; compulsory 10/20/5. **Optional** Bodily—100/300 Property—10M Collision—age 3, symbol 10, $100 deductible Comprehensive—$300 deductible ($55 + $129) 10/20/5 $184 Table 20.5 Bodily 94 Table 20.6 Property 132 Table 20.7 ($233 + $27) Collision 260 Table 20.8 Comprehensive 178 Table 20.9 Total premium $848
Key terms	Beneficiary, *p. 452* Bodily injury, *p. 460* Cash value, *p. 454* Coinsurance, *p. 458* Collision, *p. 462* Comprehensive insurance, *p. 462* Compulsory insurance, *p. 460* Deductibles, *p. 462* Extended term insurance, *p. 455*	Face amount, *p. 452* Fire insurance, *p. 457* Indemnity, *p. 459* Insured, *p. 452* Insurer, *p. 452* Level premium term, *p. 453* Liability insurance, *p. 460* No-fault insurance, *p. 463* Nonforfeiture values, *p. 455* Paid-up insurance, *p. 454* Policyholder, *p. 452*	Premium, *p. 452* Property damage, *p. 460* Reduced paid-up insurance, *p. 455* Short-rate table, *p. 457* Straight life insurance, *p. 454* Term insurance, *p. 452* 20-payment life, *p. 454* 20-year endowment, *p. 454* Universal life, *p. 454* Whole life, *p. 454*

**Critical Thinking
Discussion Questions**

1. Compare and contrast term insurance versus whole-life insurance. At what age do you think people should take out life insurance?

2. What is meant by *nonforfeiture values?* If you take the cash value option, should it be paid in a lump sum or over a number of years?

3. How do you use a short-rate table? Explain why an insurance company gets less in premiums if it cancels a policy than if the insured cancels.

4. What is coinsurance? Do you feel that an insurance company should pay more than the face value of a policy if a catastrophe resulted?

5. Explain compulsory auto insurance, collision, and comprehensive. If your car is stolen, explain the steps you might take with your insurance company.

6. "Health insurance is not that important. It would not be worth the premiums." Please take a stand.

DRILL PROBLEMS

Calculate the annual premium for the following policies using Table 20.1 (for females subtract 3 years from the table).

	Amount of coverage (face value of policy)	Age and sex of insured	Type of insurance policy	Annual premium
20–1.	$ 60,000	29 F	Straight life	60 × $ 7.43 = $445.80
20–2.	$100,000	30 M	20-payment life	100 × $12.05 = $1,205
20–3.	$ 75,000	38 M	5-year term	75 × $ 2.95 = $221.25
20–4.	$ 50,000	27 F	20-year endowment	50 × $16.05 = $802.50

Calculate the following nonforfeiture options for Harold Ryan, age 40, who purchased a $300,000 straight life policy. At the end of year 20, Harold stopped paying premiums.

20–5. Option 1: Cash surrender value
$$\frac{\$300,000}{\$1,000} = 300 \times \$265 = \$79,500$$

20–6. Option 2: Reduced paid-up insurance
300 × $550 − $165,000

20–7. Option 3: Extended term insurance
21 years 300 days

Calculate the total cost of a fire insurance premium for a building and contents given the following (round to nearest cent):

	Rating of area	Class	Building	Contents	Total premium cost
20–8.	3	B	$90,000	$40,000	$809 ($549 + $260)

Building $\dfrac{\$90,000}{\$100} = 900 \times \$.61 = \$549$ Contents $\dfrac{\$40,000}{\$100} = 400 \times \$.65 = \$260$

Calculate the short-rate premium and refund of the following:

	Annual premium	Canceled after	Short-rate premium	Refund
20–9.	$700	8 months by insured	$518 (.74 × $700)	$182 ($700 − $518)
20–10.	$360	4 months by insurance company	$120 $\left(\dfrac{4}{12} \times \$360\right)$	$240 ($360 − $120)

Complete the following:

	Replacement value of property	Amount of insurance	Kind of policy	Actual fire loss	Amount insurance company will pay
20–11.	$100,000	$60,000	80% coinsurance	$22,000	$16,500

($100,000 × .80) ⟶ $\dfrac{\$60,000}{\$80,000} = \dfrac{3}{4} \times \$22,000 = \$16,500$

20–12.	$60,000	$40,000	80% coinsurance	$42,000	$35,000

($60,000 × .80) ⟶ $\dfrac{\$40,000}{\$48,000} = \dfrac{5}{6} \times \$42,000 = \$35,000$

Calculate the annual auto insurance premium for the following:

20–13. Bill Burns, Territory 5
Class 17 operator
Compulsory, 10/20/5 $ 258 ($98 + $160)

Optional

a. Bodily injury, 500/1,000 $ 298

b. Property damage, 25M $ 166

c. Collision, $100 deductible $ 233 ($190 + $43)
Age of car is 2; symbol of car is 7

d. Comprehensive, $200 deductible $ 112 ($108 + $4)

Total annual premium $1,067

467

WORD PROBLEMS

20–14. The May 1997 issue of *Nation's Business* ran an advertisement for United Services Life Insurance Company. Rates were given for term life insurance for smokers and nonsmokers. The rate for a 39-year-old male smoker was $2.55 per $1,000; the rate for the same age nonsmoker was $1.54 per $1,000. What will be the cost of a $200,000 term life insurance policy for a smoker and for a nonsmoker? How much does the nonsmoker save?

Smoker

$$\frac{\$200,000 \text{ coverage}}{\$1,000} = \underset{\substack{\uparrow \\ \text{Number of} \\ \text{thousands}}}{200} \times \underset{\substack{\uparrow \\ \text{Cost per thousand,} \\ \text{age 39}}}{\$2.55} = \underset{\substack{\uparrow \\ \text{Annual premium}}}{\$510}$$

Nonsmoker

$$\frac{\$200,000}{\$1,000} = 200 \times \$1.54 = \$308$$

$$\begin{array}{r} \$510 \\ -\ 308 \\ \hline \$202 \text{ savings} \end{array}$$

20–15. Marc Sing, age 44, saw a Metropolitan Life Insurance advertisement stating that its $100,000 term policy costs $210 per year. Compare this to Table 20.1 in the text. How much would he save by going with Metropolitan?

Text $450 $\left(\dfrac{\$100,000}{\$1,000} = 100 \times \$4.50 \right)$
Metropolitan $\underline{-210}$

 $240 cheaper—it pays to shop around!

20–16. Margie Rale, age 38, a well-known actress, decided to take out a limited-payment life policy. She chose this since she expects her income to decline in future years. Margie decided to take out a 20-year payment life policy with a coverage amount of $90,000. Could you advise Margie about what her annual premium will be? If she decides to stop paying premiums after 15 years, what will be her cash value?

$$\frac{\$90,000}{\$1,000} = 90 \times \$14.92 = \$1,342.80$$

Cash value = 90 × $317 = $28,530

20–17. Joyce Gail has two young children and wants to take out an additional $400,000 of 5-year term insurance. Joyce is 34 years old. What will her additional annual premium be? In 3 years, what cash value will have been built up?

$$\frac{\$400,000}{\$1,000} = 400 \times \$1.87 = \$748$$

No cash value for term.

20–18. Roger's office building has a $320,000 value, a 2 rating, and a B building classification. The contents in the building are valued at $105,000. Could you help Roger calculate his total annual premium?

Building $\dfrac{\$320,000}{\$100} = 3,200 \times \$.50 = \$1,600$

Contents $\dfrac{\$105,000}{\$100} = 1,050 \times \$.60 = \$630$

Total premium = $1,600 + $630 = $2,230

20–19. Abby Ellen's toy store is worth $400,000 and is insured for $200,000. Assume an 80% coinsurance clause and that a fire caused $190,000 damage. What is the liability of the insurance company?

$$\frac{\$200,000}{\$320,000} \times \$190,000 = \$118,750 \qquad (.80 \times \$400,000)$$

20–20. The October/November 1996 issue of *Your Money* reported that the replacement cost of your home is the cost to rebuild it (not including the cost of the land) with like materials without depreciating them for age or wear and tear. The basic guideline is that, at the very least, your insurance coverage should be equal to 80% of your home's current replacement cost. Assume your home has a replacement value of $164,000 with an 80% coinsurance clause. You are carrying $125,000 insurance. A fire damages your property in the amount of $18,500. How much of the loss will be covered? How much must you pay out of your pocket? Round the percent to the nearest hundredth in the calculation. Round the final answer to the nearest dollar.

$164,000
$\times$ .80

$131,200 minimum needed   Carrying $125,000

$\dfrac{\$125,000}{\$131,200}$ = 95.27% coverage $\times$ $18,500 loss = $17,625 covered

$18,500 loss
$-$ 17,625 insurance company pays
$\quad$ $ 875 insured must pay

20–21. On December 30, 1997, State Farm Insurance quoted a total annual premium for a home at $369. The policy covered a $148,000 home and $11,600 for contents. Using the table in your text, what would be the cost of the home and contents? The building is rated in area 1 and class A.

Building

$\dfrac{\$148,000 \text{ insured value}}{\$100}$ = $1,480 $\times$ .28 = $414.40

Contents

$\dfrac{\$11,600}{\$100}$ $\quad$ = $\quad$ $116 $\times$ .35 = $\dfrac{\quad 40.60}{\$455.00}$

20–22. Earl Miller insured his pizza shop for $100,000 for fire insurance at an annual rate per $100 of $.66. At the end of 11 months, Earl canceled the policy since his pizza shop went out of business. What was the cost of Earl's premium and his refund?

$\dfrac{\$100,000}{\$100}$ = 1,000 $\times$ $.66
$\quad$ = $660

Cost of premium = .96 $\times$ $660
$\qquad\qquad$ = $633.60
Refund = .04 $\times$ $660 $\quad$ = $26.40

20–23. Ron Tagney insured his real estate office with a fire insurance policy for $95,000 at a cost of $.59 per $100. Eight months later the insurance company canceled his policy because of a failure to correct a fire hazard. What did Ron have to pay for the 8 months of coverage? Round to the nearest cent.

$\dfrac{\$95,000}{\$100}$ = 950 $\times$ $.59 = $560.50 $\qquad$ $\dfrac{8}{12} = \dfrac{2}{3}$ $\times$ $560.50 = $373.67

20–24. In its June 1997 issue, *Black Enterprise* ran a story on auto insurance premiums and the various discounts that may be available on insurance policies. Discounts may be given for carpoolers, driver's training or defensive driving courses, good drivers, good students, mature drivers, and multicar owners. Bill Smith of Los Angeles, California, has insurance on his 1997 Buick Century. He has 500/1,000; his class is 17, age group 4, and symbol 3 for optional collision and comprehensive; and he has 100M for damage to someone else's property. Bill's son is a B+ student, and Bill receives a 10% discount for his son. Also there have been no accidents or moving violations in the last 5 years. Good drivers in California get a mandatory 20% reduction. What is the amount of Bill Smith's annual insurance premium? Assume no compulsory insurance for this situation.

500/1,000 class 17	=	$298.00
100	=	169.00
Collision (age group 4, symbol 3) =		136.00
Comprehensive		49.00

$\overline{\qquad\quad}$ $652.00 $\times$ .70 = $456.40

20–25. Michelle Michaels bought a new Jeep and insured it with only 10/20/5 compulsory insurance. Driving up to her ski chalet one snowy evening, Michelle hit a parked van and injured the couple inside. Michelle's car had damage of $4,200, and the van she struck had damage of $5,500. After a lengthy court suit, the injured persons were awarded personal injury judgments of $16,000 and $7,900, respectively. What will the insurance company pay for this accident, and what is Michelle's responsibility?

Insurance company pays		**Michelle pays**	
Bodily	$10,000 + $7,900	$ 6,000	
Property	5,000	4,200	no collision
		500	property damage not covered by compulsory
Total	$22,900	$10,700	

20–26. Al Logan, who lives in Territory 5, carries 10/20/5 compulsory liability insurance along with optional collision that has a $300 deductible. Al was at fault in an accident that caused $3,600 damage to the other auto and $900 damage to his own. Also, the courts awarded $15,000 and $7,000, respectively, to the two passengers in the other car for personal injuries. How much will the insurance company pay, and what is Al's share of the responsibility?

Insurance company pays		Al pays
Property damage	$ 3,600	$ 300 deductible
Collision ($900 − $300)	600	5,000 bodily
Bodily	10,000	
	7,000	
	$21,200	$5,300

20–27. Alice Todd bought a new Explorer and insured it with only compulsory insurance 10/20/5. Driving up to her summer home one evening, Alice hit a parked car and injured the couple inside. Alice's car had damage of $7,500, and the car she struck had damage of $5,800. After a lengthy court suit, the couple struck were awarded personal injury judgments of $18,000 and $9,000, respectively. What will the insurance company pay for this accident, and what is Alice's responsibility?

Insurance company pays		Alice pays
Bodily	$10,000 + $9,000	$ 8,000
Property	5,000	7,500 no collision
		800 property damage not covered by compulsory
Total	$24,000	$16,300

CHALLENGE PROBLEMS

20–28. State Farm's automobile rate quote on December 30, 1997, for a 1996 Saturn was as follows: auto liability 100/300/100 premium, $381.04 (class 18); collision with a $200 deductible premium, $261.36; and comprehensive with a $200 deductible premium, $49.72. Collision and comprehensive are in age group 2, symbol 8. The total premium is $692.12. Using the same coverage and the tables in your text, what would be the difference in the annual premiums? Assume no compulsory insurance for this situation.

Bodily injury (class 18)		$692.12	
100/300	= $124	− 684.00	
Property damage		$ 8.12	
100	= 169		
Collision (age group 2, symbol 8) =	233		
Add reduce deductible	= 16		
Comprehensive	= 138		
Add reduce deductible	= 4		
	$684		

20–29. Bill, who understands the types of insurance that are available, is planning his life insurance needs. At this stage of his life (age 35), he has budgeted $200 a year for life insurance premiums. Could you calculate for Bill the amount of coverage that is available under straight life and for a 5-year term? Could you also show Bill that if he were to die at age 40, how much more his beneficiary would receive if he'd been covered under the 5-year term? Round to the nearest thousand.

Straight life

$200 ÷ $11.26 = 17.762 × $1,000 = $17,762 = $18,000

Five-year term

$200 ÷ $2.23 = 89.686 × $1,000 = $89,686 = $90,000

$90,000	
− 18,000	
$72,000	

SUMMARY PRACTICE TEST

1. Claire Montgomery, age 34, an actress, expects her income to decline in future years. She decided to take out a 20-year payment life policy with an $80,000 coverage. What will be Claire's annual premium? If she decides to stop paying premiums after 15 years, what will be her cash value? *(pp. 454, 455)*

$$\frac{\$80,000}{\$1,000} = 80 \times \$12.57 = \$1,005.60$$

Cash value = 80 × $317 = $25,360

2. Len Bright, age 39, bought a straight life insurance policy for $130,000. Calculate his annual premium. If after 20 years Len no longer pays premiums, what nonforfeiture options will be available to him? *(p. 455)*

$$\frac{\$130,000}{\$1,000} = 130 \times \$13.81 = \$1,795.30$$

Option 1:	**Option 2:**	**Option 3:**
Cash value	**Paid-up insurance**	**Extended term**
$130 \times \$265 = \$34,450$	$130 \times \$550 = \$71,500$	21 years 300 days

3. The property of Andy's Garage is worth $600,000. Andy has a $300,000 fire insurance policy that contains an 80% coinsurance clause. What will the insurance company pay on a fire that causes $340,000 damage? If Andy meets the coinsurance, how much will the insurance company pay? *(p. 459)*

$$\frac{\$300,000}{\$480,000} \times \$340,000 = \$212,500$$

($600,000 × .80)   If coinsurance is met, the company will pay $340,000.

4. Joanne Flint insured her pizza shop with an $80,000 fire insurance policy at a $.76 annual rate per $100. At the end of 7 months, Joanne's pizza shop went out of business so she canceled the policy. What were the cost of Joanne's premium and her refund? *(p. 458)*

$800 × .76 = $608 $608 × .67 = $407.36

$$\begin{array}{r} \$608.00 \\ -\ 407.36 \\ \hline \$200.64 \end{array}$$

5. Ted Williams insured his real estate office with an $80,000 fire insurance policy at an $.89 annual rate per $100. Eight months later the insurance company canceled his policy because Ted failed to correct a fire hazard. What was Ted's cost for the 8-month coverage? Round to the nearest cent. *(p. 458)*

$800 × .89 = $712 $712 × $\dfrac{8}{12}$ = $474.67

6. Pete Dell, who lives in Territory 5, carries 10/20/5 compulsory liability insurance along with optional collision that has a $1,000 deductible. Pete was at fault in an accident that caused $3,500 damage to the other car and $6,000 damage to his own car. Also, the courts awarded $15,000 and $8,000, respectively, to the two passengers in the other car for personal injuries. How much does the insurance company pay, and what is Pete's share of the responsibility? *(pp. 460–63)*

Insurance company pays		**Pete pays**
Property damage ($5,000)	$ 3,500	$1,000 deductible
Collision ($6,000 − $1,000)	5,000	5,000 ($15,000 − $10,000)
Bodily	10,000	$6,000
	8,000	
	$26,500	

A GROUP PROJECT Defend or reject the following business math issue based on the *Kiplinger's Personal Finance Magazine* article below:

Makeover: Switching to supercheap term life

With a 4-year-old daughter, Tarrah, another child on the way and 28 years left on their mortgage, Deena and Robert Stuart, both 26, of Arvada, Colo., need plenty of insurance. But with a household income of less than $50,000, they also need to be frugal.

LIFE INSURANCE. The Stuarts could cut their life insurance costs in half by switching policies—from two $150,000 annual renewable term policies that will gradually convert to whole-life starting next year (cost: $720 per year) to supercheap 30-year level-term insurance that will last until their kids graduate from college and they finish paying off their mortgage. Robert could get a $150,000 policy from First Penn-Pacific for $202; Deena's would cost $163 (see "Surfing for Policies," on page 88). Savings: $355 in the first year. They'd save even more each year after that because their old policy's

DEENA AND ROBERT STUART
Current premiums: $1,834
New premiums: $1,435
Annual savings: $399

premium is scheduled to increase.

AUTO INSURANCE. The Stuarts have been smart shoppers for auto insurance on their 1995 Ford Escort and 1985 Ford Bronco. We couldn't find any policy cheaper than their Liberty Mutual policy, at $716 per year. Allstate, Geico, Hartford, Prudential and USAA were others that charge less than $1,000 for their current coverage. And the Stuarts chose their deductible wisely—$1,000 for comprehensive and collision on the Escort. (They waived that coverage on the Bronco.)

HOMEOWNERS INSURANCE. The Stuarts also have a good deal on their homeowners insurance, paying $398 per year for their Liberty Mutual policy. They might be able to save if an agent appraises their home. They're currently insured for their house's market value, but they need to cover the house's replacement value, which could be almost $20,000 less

based on square footage and local construction costs. Savings: $44

REDIRECTING THE SAVINGS. The Stuarts could apply that $44 toward raising their auto liability coverage. Their current limits—now barely above the state minimum at $25,000 per person/$50,000 per accident/$25,000 property damage—are way too low. Destroy one new Lexus and they could be $20,000 in the hole. It would cost the Stuarts $105 a year to raise their liability coverage to $100,000/$300,000/$50,000 on both cars and another $66 to increase the uninsured-motorist coverage to the same level.

The Stuarts can use their life insurance savings to buy disability insurance for Robert, an accounting clerk whose income is essential to the family but who doesn't have coverage through work. Robert would pay $389 per year for a Provident policy that provides a $1,650 monthly benefit, after a 90-day waiting period, up to age 65. He'd receive benefits for two years if he were unable to perform his own occupation and wasn't earning money in any other occupation. After that, he'd receive benefits only if he were unable to perform any job related to his education and experience.

Robert could knock about two-thirds off that price if he bought Provident's new accident-only policy, but the benefits would be much smaller. For $136 per year, he'd get $1,125 per month for up to three years (after a 90-day waiting period) if he became disabled because of an accident. If he became disabled because of a specified illness, he'd receive a $14,000 lump sum instead.

Deena—who opened a day-care center in her home less than a year ago—would have a tough time getting disability coverage until her business produced steady income. But she should invest in liability insurance for her business. It costs $2,000 to $4,000 per year for up to $1 million in coverage, estimates Troy Sibelius, an independent agent in Denver.

JANET BELLER

Business Math Issue

Cutting insurance coverage could be risky. Full coverage provides safety for your family.

1. List the key points of the article and information to support your position.
2. Write a group defense of your position using math calculations to support your view.

John Hancock to Try Out a New Method Of Paying Commissions to Sales Agents

By LESLIE SCISM

Staff Reporter of THE WALL STREET JOURNAL

NEW YORK — **John Hancock Mutual Life Insurance** Co. is testing a change in the way it compensates sales agents, an effort expected to be closely watched as a way to curb abusive sales practices linked with the prevailing commission structure.

The effort by Hancock, the nation's eighth-biggest insurer based on assets, is one of the broadest to date by a large company. Many insurers are considering "compensation reform" to better align the interests of companies, their agents and their customers, and will be watching Hancock's test "with great interest," said Larry Mayewski, a senior vice president at A.M. Best Co., a ratings firm.

Under longstanding convention, agents reap 50% or more of a consumer's first-year premium as a commission on the sale of a new life policy, but renewal commissions drop to as little as 2% of the premium within a few years. Activists and some regulators contend that such hefty first-year payments motivate some agents to replace their customers' existing policies with new ones that can be marginally better, at best.

Hancock's pilot project, which applies to new agents in certain of its agencies nationwide, will be offered in January to certain longer-term agents on a voluntary basis. The new plan pays a commison of up to 12.5% for each of the first five years that a policy is in force, and in following years agents receive no less than 4.5%. The revised pay structure also includes new bonus plans tied to sales performance and increased training allowances. Boston-based Hancock maintains that agents, over the long term, should be better off financially with the new system.

Kevin D. Crowley, a Hancock vice president, said in an interview that so-called "levelized commissions" are being considered for use companywide as a way "to promote long-term relationships with clients" and to better reward agents for selling complex policies that require attention being paid to customers over the years.

Company officials played down any ties the new system may have to allegations by consumers that its agents have replaced existing policies with new ones for the sake of a steep commission. However, Hancock, like many of its fellow insurers, faces litigation in state and federal courts in which policyholders contend they were hurt by such actions.

Hancock's experiment comes on the heels of a decision by **Prudential Insurance Co. of America** to pay flatter commissions on a series of universal life policies with a minimum $1 million face amount. In contrast, Hancock's effort applies across all product lines.

Joseph Belth, a professor emeritus of insurance at Indiana University, said "it would be perfectly reasonable to decide one way to deal with the abuses would be to remove" the financial incentive. He noted that by reducing first-year commissions, however, the insurers also reduce incentive for legitimate sales. "It's a rather interesting and delicate balancing act going on" in Hancock's experiment, he added.

Hans G. Franz, a Hancock finance executive, said the company was initially concerned about its ability to recruit agents under the new system, but "recruiting is up from what it was a year ago, so it doesn't appear to be a stumbling block." Eighty-nine new Hancock agents have been enrolled in the pilot project since it began in April, and another 80 or so new hires will soon join them. Mr. Franz said it's too soon to judge productivity under the new arrangement.

Separately, Hancock said it agreed to sell its Freedom Securities unit to management, employees and other equity partners for $180 million.

The equity partners include Boston equity-investment firm **Thomas H. Lee** Co. and **SCP Private Equity Partners** L.P., Philadelphia. John Hancock will retain a small equity interest in Freedom Securities.

Freedom Securities consists mainly of the brokerages Tucker Anthony Inc. in Boston and Sutro & Co. in San Francisco. Tucker Anthony has more than 30 offices in the East and Sutro has 26 offices in California, Oregon, Nevada and Arizona.

John Goldsmith, president of Freedom Securities, said he plans no major changes but may be "a little more aggressive" in growing the brokerage business on the West Coast and may look for acquisitions in that region. Freedom Securities doesn't disclose its financial results, but Mr. Goldsmith said the unit has been profitable in recent years.

Project A

Could you explain the key features of this pilot project?

 See text Web site (www.mhhe.com/slater) and *The Business Math Internet Resource Guide.*

21

STOCKS, BONDS, AND MUTUAL FUNDS

LEARNING UNIT OBJECTIVES

LU 21.1 Stocks

- Read and explain stock quotations *(p. 477)*.
- Explain the difference between round and odd lots *(p. 478)*.
- Calculate dividends of preferred and common stocks; calculate return on investment *(p. 479)*.

LU 21.2 Bonds

- Read and explain bond quotations *(p. 480)*.
- Compare bond yields to bond premiums and discounts *(pp. 481–82)*.

LU 21.3 Mutual Funds

- Explain and calculate net asset value and mutual fund commissions *(p. 483)*.
- Read and explain mutual fund quotations *(p. 483)*.

Where Advice Comes From...

The percentage of surveyed investors who say they seek financial advice from each of the following

Relatives/friends	68%
Accountant	22
Banker	22
Financial planner	18
Stockbroker	15
Lawyer	15
Insurance agent	10
No one (rely on self only)	10
Don't invest in financial products	2
Don't know/refused	2

© 1997, Dow Jones & Company, Inc.

Who would you go to for financial advice? *The Wall Street Journal* clipping "Where Advice Comes From" may help you. Also, what should you know before you begin to accumulate investments? In general, (1) know your risk tolerance and the risk of the investments you are considering—determine whether you are a low-risk conservative investor or a high-risk speculative investor; (2) know your time frame—how soon you need your money; (3) know the liquidity of the investments you are considering—how easy it is to get your money; (4) know the return you can expect on your money—how much your money should earn; and (5) do not "put all your eggs in one basket"—diversify with a mixture of stocks, bonds, and cash equivalents. Most important, before you seek financial advice from others, go to the library and do some research, so you can judge the advice you receive.

This chapter introduces you to the major types of investments—stocks, bonds, and mutual funds. These investments indicate the performance of the companies they represent and the economy of the country at home and abroad.

LEARNING UNIT 21.1 Stocks

We begin this unit with an introduction to the basic stock terms. Then we explain the reason why people buy stocks, newspaper stock quotations, round and odd lots of stock, dividends on preferred and common stocks, and return on investment.

Introduction to Basic Stock Terms

If you own 50 shares of common stock, you are entitled to 50 votes in company elections. Preferred stockholders do not have this right.

Companies sell shares of ownership in their company to raise money to finance operations, plan expansion, and so on. These ownership shares are called **stocks.** The buyers of the stock (**stockholders**) receive **stock certificates** (Figure 21.1) verifying the number of shares of stock they own.

The two basic types of stock are **common stock** and **preferred stock.** Common stockholders have voting rights. Preferred stockholders do not have voting rights, but they received preference over common stockholders in **dividends** (payments from profit) and in the company's assets if the company goes bankrupt. **Cumulative preferred stock** entitles its owners to a specific amount of dividends in 1 year. Should the company fail

FIGURE 21.1
Stock certificate

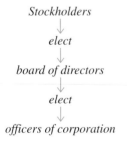

Stockholders
↓
elect
↓
board of directors
↓
elect
↓
officers of corporation

©B.D. Lamphere/Stock Boston.

to pay these dividends, the **dividends in arrears** accumulate. The company pays no dividends to common stockholders until the company brings the preferred dividend payments up to date.

Why Buy Stocks?

Some investors own stock because they think the stock will become more valuable, for example, if the company makes more profit, new discoveries, and the like. Other investors own stock to share in the profit distributed by the company in **dividends** (cash or stock).

For various reasons, investors at different times want to sell their stock or buy more stock. Strikes, inflation, or technological changes may cause some investors to think their stock will decline in value. These investors may decide to sell. Then the law of supply and demand takes over. As more people want to sell, the stock price goes down. Should more people want to buy, the stock price would go up.

How Are Stocks Traded?

Stock exchanges provide an orderly trading place for stock. You can think of these exchanges as an auction place. Only **stockbrokers** and their representatives are allowed to trade on the floor of the exchange. Stockbrokers charge commissions for stock trading—buying and selling stock for investors. As you might expect, in this age of the Internet, stock trades can also be made on the Internet. In the Business Math Scrapbook, we look at online trading on the Internet.

In 1997, the New York Stock Exchange began listing stocks in sixteenths of a dollar as well as in the traditional one-eighth, or 12.5, increment. Note in *The Wall Street Journal* clipping "Decimals Trades Are the Subject of GAO Report" that these fractions will be converted to decimals after the year 2000. In this chapter we use fractions, but please check to see when the implementation of decimals will be final. Your *Handbook of Trades* has the conversions of fractions to decimals.

Decimals Trades Are the Subject Of GAO Report

By Greg Ip *Staff Reporter of* The Wall Street Journal

Most of the country's stock markets and securities firms could be ready to trade stocks in decimals sometime in the year 2000, but still need to agree on an implementation timetable and technical standards, according to a report from the General Accounting Office.

As a result, a key congressman expects to propose a deadline of September of that year for the conversion, ending the centuries-old tradition of quoting stocks in fractions of a dollar.

© 1998, Dow Jones & Company, Inc.

How to Read Stock Quotations in the Newspaper's Financial Section

We will use Circuit City stock to learn how to read the stock quotations found in your newspaper. Note the following newspaper listing of Circuit City stock:

52 weeks										
High	Low	Stock	SYM	Div	Yld. %	PE ratio	Vol. 100s	High	Low	Close	Net change
$49\frac{5}{8}$	31	Circuit City	CC	.14	.3	37	3902	$42\frac{7}{16}$	$41\frac{1}{8}$	$41\frac{1}{8}$	$+\frac{1}{4}$

The highest price at which Circuit City stock traded during the past 52 weeks was $49.625 per share. This means that during the year someone was willing to pay $49.625 for a share of stock.

The lowest price at which Circuit City stock traded during the year was $31 per share.

The newspaper lists the company name. The symbol that Circuit City uses for trading is CC. Circuit City paid $.14 per share to stock owners last year. So if you owned 100 shares, you received a **cash dividend** of $14 (100 shares × $.14).

The **stock yield** tells stockholders that the dividend per share is returning a rate of .3% to investors. This .3% is based on the closing price. The calculation is

$$\text{Stock yield} = \frac{\text{Annual dividend per share}}{\text{Today's closing price per share}} = \frac{\$.14}{\$41.125} = .340\%, \text{ or } .3\%$$
(rounded to nearest tenth percent)

The .3% return may seem low to people who could earn a better return on their money elsewhere. Remember that if the stock price rises and you sell, your investment may result in a high rate of return.

The Circuit City stock is selling at $41.125; it is selling at 37 times its **earnings per share (EPS).**

$$\text{Earnings per share} = \text{Annual earnings} \div \text{Total number of shares outstanding}$$

The **price-earnings ratio,** or **PE ratio,** measures the relationship between the closing price per share of stock and the annual earnings per share. For Circuit City we calculate the following price-earnings ratio. (Assume Circuit City earns $1.11 per share. This is not listed in the newspaper.)

$$\text{PE ratio} = \frac{\text{Closing price per share of stock}}{\text{Annual earnings per share}} = \frac{\$41.125}{\$1.11} = 37$$

If the PE ratio column shows " . . . ," this means the company has no earnings.

The PE ratio will often vary depending on quality of stock, future expectations, economic conditions, and so on. Look at *The Wall Street Journal* clippings "Highest P/E Ratios" and "Lowest P/E Ratios" that follow. If a company is pioneering a *new* project and has little earnings, the price of the stock could be high (a high PE ratio).

HIGHEST P/E RATIOS

New England-based stocks with high stock prices relative to the past four quarters' per share earnings. (Companies that have posted a loss for the past four quarters are excluded.)

STOCK	SYMBOL	FRIDAY CLOSE	P/E RATIO
AdvancedMagnetics	AVM	10.375	1037.5
Videoserver	VSVR	11.062	553.1
InfiniumSoftware	INFM	13.750	458.3
CVS	CVS	56.250	432.7

LOWEST P/E RATIOS

New England-based stocks with low stock prices relative to the past four quarters' per share earnings. (Companies that have posted a loss for the past four quarters are excluded.)

STOCK	SYMBOL	FRIDAY CLOSE	P/E RATIO
EIS Intl	EISI	8.187	2.1
DM Management	DMMC	13.937	4.9
Learning	TLC	13.750	5.7
Transpro	TPR	10.812	5.7

©1997, Dow Jones & Company, Inc.

In the newspaper stock listing, the number in the volume column is in 100s. Thus, to 3902, you add two zeros to get 390,200. This indicates that 390,200 shares were traded on this day. Remember that shares of stock need a buyer and a seller to trade.

The highest selling price per share of Circuit City stock during the day was $42\frac{7}{16}$. (Someone was willing to pay $42.4375, and someone was willing to sell for $42.4375.)

The lowest selling price per share of Circuit City stock during the day was $41\frac{1}{8}$, or $41.125.

The last trade of the day was at $41\frac{1}{8}$, or $41.125 per share.

On the *previous day,* the closing price was $40.875 (not given). The *new* close is $41.125. The end result is that the closing price is up $\frac{1}{4}$, or $.25, from the *previous day.*

Round and Odd Lots[1]

Let's look at what it will cost to buy 200 shares of Circuit City. To keep it simple, assume the commission[2] of the stockbroker is 2% of the purchase (or selling) price. If the order is in multiples of 100 (200, 300, and so on), it is a **round lot.** If the order is an odd lot (fewer than 100 shares), the commission is an *additional* 1% on the **odd lot** portion. Keep in mind that whether you *buy* or *sell,* a commission charge results.

---
[1]The charging of odd lots has been greatly diminished today.
[2]See the Business Math Scrapbook for a discussion of online trading.

If you buy 200 shares at market (going price) for $41.125 per share, you use the following steps to calculate your total cost:

Step 1. Calculate trading cost: 200 shares $\times$ $41.125 = $8,225.00

Step 2. Calculate commission on
trading cost: $.02 \times $8,225 = \underline{+\ 164.50}$

$\boxed{$8,389.50}$ total cost
to buy 200
shares of
stock

If you buy 210 shares, the 10 shares are known as an odd lot. The steps to calculate the commission are:

Step 1. Calculate trading cost: 210 shares $\times$ $41.125 = $8,636.25

Step 2. Calculate commission: $.02 \times $8,636.25 =\ \ 172.73$

Step 3. Calculate additional commission on odd lot: $.01 \times $411.25 = \underline{+\ 4.11}$

$\boxed{$8,813.09}$

(10 shares $\times$ $41.125)

Dividends on Preferred and Common Stocks

If you own stock in a company, the company may pay out dividends. (Not all companies pay dividends.) The amount of the dividend is determined by the net earnings of the company listed in its financial report.

Earlier we stated that cumulative preferred stockholders must be paid all past and present dividends before common stockholders can receive any dividends. Following is an example to illustrate the calculation of dividends on preferred and common stocks for 2000 and 2001.

EXAMPLE The stock records of Jason Corporation show the following:

Preferred stock issued: 20,000 shares.	In 2000, Jason paid no dividends.
Preferred stock cumulative at $.80 per share.	In 2001, Jason paid $512,000 in
Common stock issued: 400,000 shares.	dividends.

Remember that common stockholders do not have the cumulative feature as preferred do.

Since Jason declared no dividends in 2000, the company has $16,000 (20,000 shares $\times$ $.80 = $16,000) dividends in arrears to preferred stockholders. The dividend of $512,000 in 2001 is divided between preferred and common stocks as follows:

	2000	2001	
Dividends paid	0	$512,000	
Preferred stockholders*	Paid: 0	Paid for 2000 (20,000 shares $\times$ $.80)	$16,000
	Owe: Preferred, $16,000 (20,000 shares $\times$ $.80)	Paid for 2001	16,000
			$32,000
Common stockholders	0	Total dividend	$512,000
		Paid preferred for 2000 and 2001	− 32,000
		To common	$480,000
		$\dfrac{$480,000}{400,000\ \text{shares}} = 1.20 per share	

*For a discussion of par value (arbitrary value placed on stock for accounting purposes) and cash and stock dividend distribution, check your accounting text.

Calculating Return on Investment

Now let's learn how to calculate a return on your investment of Circuit City stock, assuming the following:

Bought 200 shares at $41.125.
Sold at end of 1 year 200 shares at $55.
1% commission rate on buying and selling stock.
Current $.14 dividend per share in effect.

Bought		**Sold**	
200 shares at $41.125	$8,225.00	200 shares at $55	$11,000.00
+ Broker's commission		− Broker's commission	
(.01 × $8,225)	+ 82.25	(.01 × $11,000)	− 110.00
Total cost	$8,307.25	Total receipt	$10,890.00

Note: A commission is charged on both the buying and selling of stock.

Total receipt	$10,890.00
Total cost	8,307.25
Net gain	$ 2,582.75
Dividends	+ 28.00 (200 shares × $.14)
Total gain	$ 2,610.75

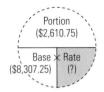

Portion
($2,610.75)

Base × Rate
($8,307.25) (?)

$$\text{Portion} \nearrow \frac{\$2,610.75}{\$8,307.25} = \boxed{31.43\%} \text{ rate of return (to nearest hundredth percent)}$$

Base

It's time for another Practice Quiz.

LU 21.1 PRACTICE QUIZ

1. From the following JC Penney stock quotation **(a)** explain the letters, **(b)** estimate the company's earnings per share, and **(c)** show how "Yld. %" was calculated.

52 weeks					Yld.	PE	Vol.				Net
High	**Low**	**Stock**	**SYM**	**Div**	**%**	**ratio**	**100s**	**High**	**Low**	**Close**	**change**
$77\frac{7}{8}$	$50\frac{1}{2}$	JCPenney	JCP	2.18	3.0	33	3663	$73\frac{7}{8}$	$72\frac{13}{16}$	$73\frac{3}{4}$	$+\frac{1}{4}$
(A)	(B)	(C)	(D)	(E)	(F)	(G)	(H)	(I)	(J)	(K)	(L)

2. **Given** 30,000 shares of preferred cumulative stock at $.70 per share; 200,000 shares of common; 2000, no dividend; 2001, $109,000. How much is paid to each class of stock in 2001?

✓ **Solutions**

1. **a.** (A) Highest price traded for year is $77.875.
   (B) Lowest price traded for year is $50.50.
   (C) Name of corporation is JCPenney.
   (D) Symbol is JCP.
   (E) Dividend per share per year is $2.18.
   (F) Yield for year is 3%.
   (G) Stock of JCPenney sells at 33 times its earnings.
   (H) Sales volume for day is 366,300 shares.
   (I) Highest price for the day is $73.875.
   (J) Lowest price for the day is $72.8125.
   (K) The last trade (closing price for the day) is at $73.75.
   (L) Stock is up $.25 from closing price yesterday.

   b. $\text{EPS} = \dfrac{\$73.75}{33} = \boxed{\$2.23}$ per share   **c.** $\dfrac{\$2.18}{\$73.75} = \boxed{3\%}$

2. **Preferred:** 30,000 × $.70 = $21,000   Arrears 2000
                                       + 21,000   2001
                                       $42,000

   Common: $67,000 ($109,000 − $42,000)

LEARNING UNIT 21.2 Bonds

Have you heard of the Rule of 115? This rule is used as a rough measure to show how quickly an investment will triple in value. To use the rule, divide 115 by the rate of return your money earns. For example, if a bond earns 5% interest, divide 115 by 5. This measure estimates that your money in the bond will triple in 23 years.

This unit begins by explaining the difference between bonds and stocks. Then you will learn how to read bond quotations and calculate bond yields.

Reading Bond Quotations

Bond quotes are stated in percents of the face value of the bond and not in dollars as stock is. Interest is paid semiannually.

Sometimes companies raise money by selling bonds instead of stock. When you buy stock, you become a part owner in the company. To raise money, companies may not want to sell more stock and thus dilute the ownership of their current stock owners, so they sell bonds. **Bonds** represent a promise from the company to pay the face amount to the bond owner at a future date, along with interest payments at a stated rate.

Once a company issues bonds, they are traded as stock is. If a company goes bankrupt, bondholders have the first claim to the assets of the corporation—before stockholders. As with stock, changes in bond prices vary according to supply and demand. Brokers also charge commissions on bond trading. These commissions vary.

How to Read the Bond Section of the Newspaper

The bond section of the newspaper shows the bonds that are traded that day. The information given on bonds differs from the information given on stocks. The newspaper states bond prices in *percents of face amount, not in dollar amounts* as stock prices are. Also, bonds are usually in denominations of $1,000 (the face amount).

When a bond sells at a price below its face value, the bond is sold at a discount. Why? The interest that the bond pays may not be as high as the current market rate. When this happens, the bond is not as attractive to investors, and it sells for a **discount.** The opposite could, of course, also occur. The bond may sell at a **premium,** which means that the bond sells for more than its face value or the bond interest is higher than the current market rate.

Let's look at this newspaper information given for IBM bonds:

Bonds	Current yield	Vol.	Close	Net change
IBM $8\frac{3}{8}$ 19	7.0	5	$120\frac{1}{2}$	+1

Note: Bond prices are stated as a percent of face amount.

The name of the company is IBM. It produces a wide range of computers. The interest on the bond is $8\frac{3}{8}\%$. The company pays the interest semiannually. The bond matures (comes due) in 2019. The total interest for the year is $83.75 (.08375 × $1,000). Remember that the face value of the bond is $1,000. Now let's show this with the following formula:

$$\frac{\text{Yearly}}{\text{interest}} = \frac{\text{Face value}}{\text{of bond}} \times \frac{\text{Stated yearly}}{\text{interest rate}}$$

$$\$83.75 = \$1,000 \times .08375$$

We calculate the 7.0% yield by dividing the total annual interest of the bond by the total cost of the bond. (For our purposes, we will omit the commission cost.) All bond yields are rounded to the nearest tenth percent.

Note this bond is selling for more than $1,000 since its interest is very attractive compared to other new offerings.

$$\frac{\text{Yearly interest}}{\text{Cost of bond at closing}} = \frac{\$83.75}{\$1,205} \frac{(.08375 \times \$1,000)}{(1.205 \times \$1,000)}$$

$$= 6.95\% = 7.0\% \quad \text{This is same as } 120.5\%.$$

Five $1,000 bonds were traded. Note that we do *not* add two zeros as we did to the sales volume of stock.

The last bond traded on this day was 120.5% of face value, or in dollars, $1,205 ($120\frac{1}{2}\% = 120.5\% = 1.205$).

The last trade of the day was up 1% of the face value from the last trade of yesterday. In dollars this is 1% = $10.

$$1\% = .01 \times \$1,000 = \$10$$

Thus, the closing price on this day, 120.5% − 1%, equals yesterday's close of 119.5% ($1,195). Note that *yesterday's close is not listed in today's quotations.*

Calculating Bond Yields

The IBM bond (selling at a premium) pays $8\frac{3}{8}\%$ interest when it is yielding investors 7%.

$$\text{Bond yield} = \frac{\text{Total annual interest of bond}}{\text{Total current cost of bond at closing*}}$$

*We assume this to be the buyer's purchase price.

The following example will show us how to calculate **bond yields.**

EXAMPLE   Jim Smith bought 5 bonds of IBM at the closing price of $120\frac{1}{2}$ (remember that in dollars $120\frac{1}{2}\%$ is $1,205). Jim's total cost excluding commission is:

$$5 \times \$1,205 = \$6,025$$

What is Jim's interest?

The yield is 7% since Jim paid more for the bonds and still receives 8 3/8% of the face value.

No matter what Jim pays for the bonds, he will still receive interest of $83.75 per bond (.08375 × $1,000). Jim bought the bonds at $1,205 each, resulting in a bond yield of 7%. Let's calculate Jim's yield to the nearest tenth percent:

$$\swarrow \text{(5 bonds} \times \$83.75 \text{ interest per bond per year)}$$

$$\frac{\$418.75}{\$6,025} = 6.95\% = \boxed{7\%}$$

Now let's try another Practice Quiz.

LU 21.2 PRACTICE QUIZ

Bonds	Yield	Sales	Close	Net change
Aetna $6\frac{3}{8}$ 03	6.4	20	$100\frac{3}{8}$	$+\frac{7}{8}$

From the above bond quotation, **(1)** calculate the cost of 5 bonds at closing (disregard commissions) and **(2)** check the current yield of 6.4%.

✓ **Solutions**

1. $100\frac{3}{8}\% = 100.375\% = 1.00375 \times \$1,000 = \$1,003.75 \times 5 = \boxed{\$5,018.75}$
2. $6.375\% = .06375 \times \$1,000 = \$63.75$ annual interest
    $$\frac{\$63.75}{\$1,003.75} = 6.35\% = \boxed{6.4\%}$$

LEARNING UNIT 21.3 Mutual Funds

Courtesy Charles Schwab & Company.

In recent years, mutual funds have increased dramatically and people in the United States have invested billions in mutual funds. Investors can choose from several fund types—stock funds, bond funds, international funds, balanced (stocks and bonds) funds, and so on. This learning unit tells you why investors choose mutual funds and discusses the net asset value of mutual funds, mutual fund commissions, and how to read a mutual fund quotation.

Why Investors Choose Mutual Funds

The main reasons investors choose mutual funds are the following:

1. **Diversification.** When you invest in a mutual fund, you own a small portion of many different companies. This protects you against the poor performance of a single company but not against a sell-off in the market (stock and bond exchanges) or fluctuations in the interest rate.
2. **Professional management.** You are hiring a professional manager to look after your money when you own shares in mutual funds. The success of a particular fund is often due to the person(s) managing the fund.
3. **Liquidity.** Most funds will buy back your fund shares whenever you decide to sell.
4. **Low fund expenses.** Competition forces funds to keep their expenses low to maximize their performance. Because stocks and bonds in a mutual fund represent thousands of shareholders, funds can trade in large blocks, reducing transaction costs.
5. **Access to foreign markets.** Through mutual funds, investors can conveniently and inexpensively invest in foreign markets.

Net Asset Value

Investing in a **mutual fund** means that you buy shares in the fund's portfolio (group of stocks and/or bonds). The value of your mutual fund share is expressed in the share's **net asset value (NAV),** which is the dollar value of one mutual fund share. You calculate the NAV by subtracting the fund's current liabilities from the current market value of the fund's investments and dividing this by the number of shares outstanding.

$$NAV = \frac{\text{Current market value of fund's investments} - \text{Current liabilities}}{\text{Number of shares outstanding}}$$

The NAV helps investors track the value of their fund investment. After the market closes on each business day, the fund uses the closing prices of the investments it owns to find the dollar value of one fund share, or NAV. This is the price investors receive if they sell fund shares on that day or pay if they buy fund shares on that day.

Commissions When Buying Mutual Funds

The following table is a quick reference for the cost of buying mutual fund shares. Commissions vary from 0% to $8\frac{1}{2}\%$, depending on how the mutual fund is classified.

Classification	Commission charge*	Offer price to buy
No-load (NL) fund	No sales charge	NAV (buy directly from investment company)
Low-load (LL) fund	3% or less	NAV + commission % (buy directly from investment company or from a broker)
Load fund	$8\frac{1}{2}\%$ or less	NAV + commission % (buy from a broker)

*On a front-end load, you pay commission when you purchase the fund shares, while on a back-end load, you pay when you redeem or sell. In general, if you hold the shares for more than 5 years, you pay no commission charge.

The offer price to buy a share for a low-load or load fund is the NAV plus the commission. Now let's look at how to read a mutual fund quotation.

How to Read a Mutual Fund Quotation

We will be studying the Putnam Mutual Funds. Cindy Joelson has invested in the Growth and Income Fund with the hope that over the years this will provide her with financial security when she retires. On May 1, Cindy turns to *The Wall Street Journal* and looks up the Putnam Growth Income Fund quotation.

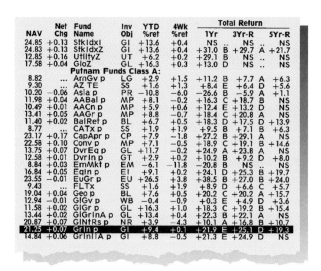

NAV	Net Chg	Fund Name	Inv Obj	YTD %ret	4Wk %ret	Total Return		
						1Yr	3Yr-R	5Yr-R
24.85	+0.13	StkIdxI	GI	+13.6	+0.4	NS ..	NS ..	NS
24.83	+0.13	StkIdxZ	GI	+13.6	+0.4	+31.0 B	+29.7 A	+21.7
12.85	+0.16	UtilityZ	UT	+6.2	+0.2	+29.1 B	NS ..	NS
17.58	+0.04	GloZ	GL	+16.3	+0.3	+13.0 D	NS ..	NS
		Putnam Funds Class A:						
8.82	...	AmGv p	LG	+2.9	+1.5	+11.2 B	+7.7 A	+6.3
9.30	...	AZ TE	SS	+1.6	+1.3	+8.4 E	+6.4 D	+5.6
10.20	−0.06	Asia p	PR	−10.8	−6.0	−26.6 B	−5.9 A	+1.1
11.98	+0.04	AABal p	MP	+8.1	−0.2	+16.3 C	+18.7 B	NS
10.49	+0.01	AACn p	MP	+5.9	+0.6	+12.4 E	+13.2 D	NS
13.41	+0.05	AAGr p	MP	+8.8	−0.7	+18.4 C	+20.8 A	NS
11.40	+0.02	BalRet p	BL	+6.7	+0.5	+18.3 D	+17.5 D	+13.9
8.77	...	CATx p	SS	+1.9	+1.9	+9.5 B	+7.1 B	+6.3
23.17	+0.17	CapApr p	CP	+7.9	−1.8	+27.2 B	+29.1 A	NS
22.58	+0.10	Conv p	MP	+7.1	−0.5	+18.9 C	+19.1 B	+14.6
13.75	+0.07	DvrEq p	GL	+11.7	−0.2	+24.9 A	+23.8 A	NS
12.58	+0.01	DvrIn p	GT	+2.9	+0.2	+10.2 B	+9.2 D	+8.0
8.84	+0.03	EmMkt p	EM	−6.1	−11.8	−20.8 B	NS ..	NS
16.84	+0.05	Eqin p	EI	+9.1	+0.2	+24.1 D	+25.3 B	+19.7
23.55	−0.01	EuGr p	EU	+26.5	+3.8	+38.5 B	+27.0 B	+24.0
9.43	...	FLTx	SS	+1.6	+1.9	+8.9 D	+6.6 C	+5.7
19.04	+0.04	Geo p	BL	+7.6	+0.5	+20.2 C	+20.2 A	+15.7
12.94	−0.01	GlGv p	WB	−0.4	−0.9	+0.3 E	+4.9 D	+3.6
11.58	+0.02	GlGr p	GL	+16.3	+1.0	+18.3 C	+19.2 B	+15.4
13.44	+0.02	GlGrInA p	GL	+13.4	+0.4	+22.3 B	+22.1 A	NS
20.87	+0.07	GlNtRs p	NR	+3.9	−4.3	+10.1 A	+16.8 B	+10.7
21.25	+0.07	**GrIn p**	GI	+9.4	+0.1	+21.9 E	+25.1 D	+19.3
14.84	+0.06	GrInIIA p	GI	+8.8	−0.5	+21.3 E	+24.9 D	NS

©1998, Dow Jones & Company, Inc.

The name of the fund is Growth and Income, which has the investment objective of growth and income securities as set forth in the fund's prospectus (document giving information about the fund). Note that this is only one fund in the Putnam family of funds.

- The $21.25 figure is the NAV plus the sales commission.
- The fund has gained 7¢ from the NAV quotation of the previous day.
- The fund has a 9.4% return this year (January through May 29). This assumes reinvestments of all distributions. Sales charges are not reflected.
- The fund for the last 4 weeks has a return of .1%.
- For the past 12 months, the fund has a 21.9% return.
- Based on performance for funds grouped in this investment objective, the fund was ranked an E (A, top 20%; B, next 20%; C, middle 20%; D, next 20%; E, bottom).

LU 21.3 PRACTICE QUIZ

From the mutual fund quotation of the Smith Barney Aggressive Growth Fund shown below, complete the following:

1. NAV
   _____

2. NAV change
   _____

3. Total return, YTD
   _____

4. Return for last 12 months
   _____

5. Ranking
   _____

✓ **Solutions**

1. 42.85
2. +$.38
3. 11.1%
4. 25.9%
5. C

NAV	Net Chg	Fund Name	Inv Obj	YTD %ret	4Wk %ret	Total Return		
						1Yr	3Yr-R	5Yr-R
		Sit Funds:						
19.08	−0.04	Intl	IL	+15.4	+0.8	+11.9 C	+11.8 C	+13.6
46.32	+0.23	LrgCpGr	GI	+15.7	−0.4	+33.0 A	+30.3 A	+21.4
15.86	+0.14	MidCpGr	MC	+8.0	−4.5	+24.1 C	+24.6 B	+18.0
10.49	...	MinnTxF	SS	+2.0	+1.1	+8.3 E	+7.0 B	NS
19.12	+0.19	SmCapGr	SC	−0.1	−7.6	+9.7 E	+18.4 D	NS
10.39	...	TxFree	GM	+2.1	+1.5	+9.7 B	+7.8 A	+7.1
10.65	−0.01	US Gov	LG	+2.4	+0.9	+9.0 E	+7.2 C	+6.4
23.46	+0.16	SkylneEq	SC	+8.3	−2.0	+30.1 B	+27.8 A	+19.6
13.81	+0.18	SkyInSmValP	SC	+8.3	−3.9	+30.3 B	+26.1 A	+18.1
		Smith Barney A:						
9.86	...	AdjGvA p	MG	+2.0	+0.7	+5.7 E	+5.5 E	+5.0
42.85	+0.38	AgGrA p	CP	+11.1	−4.1	+25.9 C	+22.2 C	+19.1
15.46	+0.04	ApprA p	GR	+11.1	+0.5	+25.3 D	+24.1 D	+17.7
10.52	...	AzMuA p	SS	+1.8	+2.1	+9.1 C	+6.9 B	+6.2
16.64	+0.11	BalancA p	UT	+2.9	+1.2	+25.0 C	+13.9 E	+9.6
15.16	+0.16	ContrarA r	GR	+6.7	−2.3	+14.4 E	NS ..	NS
17.43	+0.08	ConvA p	MP	+4.2	−0.5	+13.5 D	+14.1 D	+10.3
145.30	−0.06	TelIn	TK	+8.8	−1.8	+41.8 A	+27.7 A	+19.2
16.92	+0.01	CaMuA p	SS	+1.8	+2.1	+11.8 A	+8.4 A	+7.8
7.99	...	DvsInA p	GT	+3.3	+1.1	+9.9 C	+9.5 D	+7.9
23.48	+0.14	EuroA	EU	+37.3	+7.6	+31.1 E	+22.5 D	NS
11.02	+0.02	FdValA p	GR	+7.0	−3.9	+14.9 E	+18.5 E	+15.8
11.81	...	GlGvtA p	WB	+3.0	+1.1	+10.2 A	+8.9 B	+8.0
9.73	−0.01	GvScA	LG	+2.3	+1.5	+12.5 A	+7.5 B	+6.4
12.24	+0.04	HanGlVl p	GL	+5.9	−5.1	NS ..	NS ..	NS
11.80x	...	HiIncA t	HC	+3.8	+0.4	+12.9 C	+12.5 C	+10.2
8.70	+0.01	IntCAA	IM	+1.7	+1.4	+7.7 B	+6.4 A	+5.7

© 1998, Dow Jones & Company, Inc.

Chapter Organizer and Reference Guide

Topic	Key point, procedure, formula	Example(s) to illustrate situation
Stock yield, p. 478	$$\frac{\text{Annual dividend per share}}{\text{Today's closing price per share}}$$ (Round yield to nearest tenth percent.)	Annual dividend, $.72 Today's closing price, $42\frac{3}{8}$ $$\frac{\$.72}{\$42.375} = \boxed{1.7\%}$$
Price-earnings ratio, p. 478	$$PE = \frac{\text{Closing price per share of stock}}{\text{Annual earnings per share}}$$ (Round answer to nearest whole number.)	From example above: Closing price, $42\frac{3}{8}$ Annual earnings per share, $4.24 $$\frac{\$42.375}{\$4.24} = 9.99 = \boxed{10}$$
Dividends with cumulative preferred, p. 479	Cumulative preferred stock is entitled to all dividends in arrears before common stock receives dividend.	2000 dividend omitted; in 2001, $400,000 in dividends paid out. Preferred is cumulative at $.90 per share; 20,000 shares of preferred issued and 100,000 shares of common issued. To preferred: 20,000 shares × $.90 = $18,000 In arrears 2000: 20,000 shares × .90 = 18,000 Dividend to preferred $\boxed{\$36,000}$ To common: $364,000 ($400,000 − $36,000) $$\frac{\$364,000}{100,000 \text{ shares}} = \$3.64 \text{ dividend to common per share}$$
Cost of a bond, p. 481	Bond prices are stated as a percent of the face value. Bonds selling for less than face value result in bond discounts. Bonds selling for more than face value result in bond premiums.	Bill purchases 5 $1,000, 12% bonds at closing price of $103\frac{1}{4}$. What is his cost (omitting commissions)? $103\frac{1}{4}\% = 103.25\% = 1.0325$ in decimal $1.0325 \times \$1,000$ bond = $\boxed{\$1,032.50 \text{ per bond}}$ 5 bonds × $1,032.50 = $\boxed{\$5,162.50}$
Bond yield, p. 482	$$\frac{\text{Total annual interest of bond}}{\text{Total current cost of bond at closing}}$$ (Round to nearest tenth percent.)	Calculate bond yield from last example on one bond. ($1,000 × .12) $$\frac{\$120}{\$1,032.50} = \boxed{11.6\%}$$
NAV, p. 483	$$NAV = \frac{\text{Current market value of fund's investments} - \text{Current liabilities}}{\text{Number of shares outstanding}}$$	The NAV of the Scudder Income Bond Fund was $12.84. The NAV change was 0.01. What was the NAV yesterday? $\boxed{\$12.83}$
Key terms	Bonds, *p. 481* Bond yield, *p. 482* Cash dividend, *p. 477* Common stocks, *p. 476* Cumulative preferred stock, *p. 476* Discount, *p. 481* Dividends, *p. 476*	Dividends in arrears, *p. 477* Earnings per share (EPS), *p. 478* Mutual fund, *p. 483* Net asset value (NAV), *p. 483* Odd lot, *p. 478* PE ratio, *p. 478* Preferred stock, *p. 476*	Price-earnings ratio, *p. 478* Round lot, *p. 478* Stockbrokers, *p. 477* Stock certificate, *p. 476* Stockholders, *p. 476* Stocks, *p. 476* Stock yield, *p. 477*

**Critical Thinking
Discussion Questions**

1. Explain how to read a stock quotation. What are some of the red flags of buying stock?

2. What is the difference between odd and round lots? Explain why the commission on odd lots could be quite expensive.

3. Explain how to read a bond quote. What could be a drawback of investing in bonds?

4. Compare and contrast stock yields and bond yields. As a conservative investor, which option might be better? Defend your answer.

5. Explain what NAV means. What is the difference between a load and a no-load fund? How safe are mutual funds?

DRILL PROBLEMS

Calculate the cost (omit commission) of buying the following shares of stock:

21–1. 700 shares of Compaq at $73\frac{3}{4}$ $51,625 $(700 \times \$73.75)$

21–2. 300 shares of Citicorp at $134\frac{1}{16}$ $40,218.75 $(300 \times \$134.0625)$

Calculate the yield of each of the following stocks (round to the nearest tenth percent):

Company	Yearly dividend	Closing price per share	Yield
21–3. Maytag	$.50	$18\frac{1}{4}$	2.7% $\left(\dfrac{\$.50}{\$18.25}\right)$
21–4. Lowes Corp.	$.75	$15\frac{1}{2}$	4.8% $\left(\dfrac{\$.75}{\$15.50}\right)$

Calculate the earnings per share, price-earnings ratio, or stock price as needed:

Company	Earnings per share	Closing price per share	Price-earnings ratio
21–5. CompUSA	$2.10	$33\frac{7}{16}$ $\dfrac{\$33.4375}{\$2.10}$	16 _____
21–6. ATT	$4.50	$54 (12 \times \$4.50)$	12

21–7. Calculate the total cost of buying 350 shares of Goodyear at $54\frac{3}{4}$. Assume a 2% commission with an additional 1% commission on odd lots.

$$350 \text{ shares} \times \$54.75 = \$19,162.50$$
$$.02 \times \$19,162.50 = \quad 383.25$$
$$.01 \times 2,737.50 = \quad\quad 27.38$$
$$\overline{\hspace{3cm}}$$
$$\$19,573.13$$
(50 shares × $54.75)

21–8. If in Problem 21–1 the 700 shares of Compaq stock were sold at $66\frac{3}{16}$, what would be the loss? Commission is omitted.

Buy: 700 shares × $73.75 = $51,625.00
Sell: 700 shares × $66.1875 = − 46,331.25
$\overline{\hspace{4cm}}$
$ 5,293.75 loss

21–9. Given: 20,000 shares cumulative preferred stock ($2.25 dividend per share): 40,000 shares common stock. Dividends paid: 2000, $8,000; 2001, 0; and 2002, $160,000. How much will preferred and common receive each year?

Year	2000	2001	2002
Dividend paid	$ 8,000	–0–	$160,000
Preferred	$ 8,000 ($37,000)	–0– ($45,000)	$37,000 + $45,000 + $45,000 = $127,000
Common	–0–	–0–	$160,000 − $127,000 = $33,000

For each of these bonds, calculate the total dollar amount you would pay at the quoted price (disregard commission or any interest that may have accrued):

Company	Bond price	Number of bonds purchased	Dollar amount of purchase price
21–10. Petro	$87\frac{3}{4}$	3	$2,632.50

$87\frac{3}{4}\% = 87.75\% = .8775 \times \$1,000 = \$877.50 \times 3 = \$2,632.50$

21–11. Wang	114	2	$2,280

$114\% = 1.14 \times \$1,000 = \$1,140 \times 2 = \$2,280$

For the following bonds, calculate the total annual interest, total cost, and current yield (to the nearest tenth percent):

Bond	Number of bonds purchased	Selling price	Total annual interest	Total cost	Current yield
21–12. Sharn $11\frac{3}{4}$ 09	2	115	$235.00	$2,300	10.2%

$$\begin{array}{l} .1175 \times \$1{,}000 = \$117.50 \\ \text{interest per bond} \end{array} \qquad \dfrac{\$117.50}{\$1{,}150} \longleftarrow (115\% = 1.15 \times \$1{,}000)$$

21–13. Wang $6\frac{1}{2}$ 07	4	$68\frac{1}{8}$	$260.00	$2,725	9.5%

$$\begin{array}{l} .065 \times \$1{,}000 = \$65 \\ \text{interest per bond} \end{array} \qquad \dfrac{\$65}{\$681.25} \longleftarrow (68\frac{1}{8}\% = 68.125\% = .68125 \times \$1{,}000)$$

21–14. From the following calculate the net asset values. Round to the nearest cent.

Current market value of fund investment	Current liabilities	Number of shares outstanding	NAV
a. $ 5,550,000	$770,000	600,000	$ 7.97

$$\text{NAV} = \frac{\$5{,}550{,}000 - \$770{,}000}{600{,}000} = \$7.97$$

b. $13,560,000	$780,000	840,000	$15.21

$$\text{NAV} = \frac{\$13{,}560{,}000 - \$780{,}000}{840{,}000} = \$15.21$$

21–15. From the following mutual fund quotation, complete the blanks:

	Inv. obj.	NAV	NAV chg.	Total return			
				YTD	4 wks.	1 yr.	R
EuGr	ITL	12.04	−0.06	+8.2	+0.9	+9.6	A

NAV $12.04   NAV change −$.06

Total return, 1 year 9.6%   Rating A (top 20%)

WORD PROBLEMS

21–16. Len Albert bought 500 shares of Starbucks at 43\frac{7}{8}$ per share. Assume a commission of 2% of the purchase price. What is the total cost to Len?

500 × $43.875 = $21,937.50 × 1.02 = $22,376.25

21–17. Assume in Problem 21–16 that Len sells the stock for 59\frac{3}{16}$ with the same 2% commission rate. What is the bottom line for Len?

500 × $59.1875 = $29,593.75 × .98 = $29,001.88

Sell: $29,001.88
Buy: − 22,376.25

Gain: $ 6,625.63

21–18. Jim Corporation pays its cumulative preferred stockholders $1.60 per share. Jim has 30,000 shares of preferred and 75,000 shares of common. In 2000, 2001, and 2002, due to slowdowns in the economy, Jim paid no dividends. Now in 2003, the board of directors had decided to pay out $500,000 in dividends. How much of the $500,000 does each class of stock receive as dividends?

Preferred

30,000 shares × $1.60 = $ 48,000 per year
                              × 4 (current + 3 years in arrears)
                   $192,000

Common

$500,000 − $192,000 = $308,000

21–19. Roger Company earns $4.80 per share. Today the stock is trading at $59\frac{1}{4}$. The company pays an annual dividend of $1.40. Calculate **(a)** the price-earnings ratio (round to the nearest whole number) and **(b)** the yield on the stock (to the nearest tenth percent).

    a. $\text{PE} = \dfrac{\$59.25}{\$4.80} = 12$ **b.** $\text{Yield} = \dfrac{\$1.40}{\$59.25} = 2.4\%$

21–20. On July 28, 1997, *Forbes* reported that investors have taken a fancy to Boston Scientific (NYSE: BSX), a $1.5 billion maker of minimally invasive medical devices. Recently, the closing price per share was $69, and the annual earnings per share were $1.30. What is the price-earnings ratio for Boston Scientific?

    $\dfrac{\$69.00 \text{ closing price per share}}{\$1.30 \text{ annual earnings per share}} = 53$

21–21. The following bond was quoted in *The Wall Street Journal* on December 30, 1997:

Bonds	Curr. yld.	Vol.	Close	Net chg.
NY Tel $7\frac{1}{4}$ 11	7.2	10	$100\frac{7}{8}$	$+1\frac{1}{8}$

Five bonds were purchased yesterday, and 5 bonds were purchased today. How much more did the 5 bonds cost today (in dollars)?

Today: $5 \times \$1,008.75$ $(1.00875 \times \$1,000) = \quad \$5,043.75$

Yesterday:
$$\begin{array}{r} 100\frac{7}{8} \\ -\,1\frac{1}{8} \\ \hline 99\frac{6}{8} = 99\frac{3}{4} \end{array}$$

$5 \times \$997.50 \ (.9975 \times 1{,}000) =$ $\dfrac{-\ 4{,}987.50}{\$\quad 56.25}$

21–22. The November 1997 issue of *Kiplinger's Personal Finance Magazine* reported on the most of nifty fifty stocks. The article shows an estimate of 3- to 5-year earnings growth rates and price-earnings ratios based on 1998 earnings estimates. Below are five of these companies. What will be their projected earnings per share?

Company	Stock price	Est. PE ratio 1998	Annual earnings per share
a. General Mills (GIS)	$67	19	$3.53
b. Gillette (G)	81	27	3.00
c. H.J. Heinz (HNZ)	44	19	2.32
d. IBM (IBM)	98	14	7.00
e. Intel (INTC)	94	20	4.70

    a. $\dfrac{\$67}{19} = \$3.53$ **b.** $\dfrac{\$81}{27} = \$3.00$ **c.** $\dfrac{\$44}{19} = \$2.32$

    d. $\dfrac{\$98}{14} = \$7.00$ **e.** $\dfrac{\$94}{20} = \$4.70$

21–23. Ron bought a bond of Bee Company for $79\frac{1}{4}$. The original bond was $5\frac{3}{4}$ 08. Ron wants to know the current yield (to the nearest tenth percent). Please help Ron with the calculation.

    $79\frac{1}{4}\% = 79.25\% = .7925 \times \$1,000 = \$792.50$

    $\dfrac{\$57.50}{\$792.50} = 7.3\%$ $(5\frac{3}{4}\% = 5.75\% = .0575 \times \$1,000 = \$57.50)$

21–24. Abby Sane decided to buy corporate bonds instead of stock. She desired to have the fixed-interest payments. She purchased 5 bonds of Meg Corporation $11\frac{3}{4}$ 09 at $88\frac{1}{4}$. As the stockbroker for Abby (assume you charge her a $5 commission per bond), please provide her with the following: **(a)** the total cost of the purchase, **(b)** total annual interest to be received, and **(c)** current yield (to nearest tenth percent).

    a. $88\frac{1}{4}\% = 88.25\% = .8825 \times \$1,000 = \quad \begin{array}{r} \$\ \ 882.50 \\ \times\ 5 \\ \hline \$4{,}412.50 \\ +\ 25.00 \\ \hline \$4{,}437.50 \end{array}$

    b. $.1175 \times \$1,000 = \$117.50 \times 5 = \$587.50$

    c. $\dfrac{\$117.50}{\$882.50} = 13.3\%$

21–25. Mary Blake is considering whether to buy stocks or bonds. She has a good understanding of the pros and cons of both. The stock she is looking at is trading at $59\frac{1}{4}$, with an annual dividend of $3.99. Meanwhile, the bond is trading at $96\frac{1}{4}$, with an annual interest rate of $11\frac{1}{2}\%$. Calculate for Mary her yield (to the nearest tenth percent) for the stock and the bond.

Stock	Bond

$$\frac{\$3.99}{\$59.25} = 6.7\%$$

$$96\frac{1}{4}\% = 96.25\% = .9625 \times \$1,000 = \$962.50$$

$$.115 \times \$1,000 = \$115$$

$$\frac{\$115}{\$962.50} = 11.9\%$$

21–26. On December 31, 1997, the Chicago *Sun-Times* listed the Vanguard Growth Fund with an offer price of $22.58 and a 2% load fee. Sal Luna purchased 180 shares. What was his cost of the shares?

$22.58 + (\$22.58 \times .02) = \$23.03$
$180 \times \$23.03 = \$4,145.40$

21–27. Louis Hall read in the paper that Fidelity Growth Fund has a NAV of $16.02. He called Fidelity and asked them how the NAV was calculated. Fidelity gave him the following information:

Current market value of fund investment	$8,550,000
Current liabilities	$860,000
Number of shares outstanding	480,000

Did Fidelity provide Louis with the correct information?

Yes. $\dfrac{\$8,550,000 - \$860,000}{480,000} = \$16.02$

21–28. Lee Ray bought 130 shares of a mutual fund with a NAV of $13.10. This fund also has a load charge of $8\frac{1}{2}\%$. **(a)** What is the offer price and **(b)** what did Lee pay for his investment?

a. $\$13.10 \times .085 = \$1.11 + \$13.10 = \$14.21$ **b.** $\$14.21 \times 130 \text{ shares} = \$1,847.30$

21–29. On November 23, 1997, the *Chicago Tribune* ran an advertisement for Scottsdale Securities, Inc., in which Scottsdale compares its trading costs with those of other brokers.

Brokers	200 shares purchased at $50
Scottsdale	$ 40 fee
Schwab	110 fee
Merrill Lynch	201 fee

What is the fee percentage that each broker charged? Round to the nearest tenth percent as needed.

$200 \times \$50 = \$10,000$ cost for shares *(B)*

Schwab: $\dfrac{\$110\ (P)}{\$10,000\ (B)} = 1.1\%\ (R)$

Scottsdale: $\dfrac{\$40\ (P)}{\$10,000\ (B)} = .4\%\ (R)$

Merrill Lynch: $\dfrac{\$201\ (P)}{\$10,000\ (B)} = 2.01\%\ (R)$

CHALLENGE PROBLEMS

21–30. The June 1997 issue of *Black Enterprise* featured a story on the stock rises of Mercantile Bancorp. Inc. (NYSE: MTL), during a buying spree. The recent stock price was $56.50. Purchase price on March 1, 1996, was $44.00. Dividend was $1.72 per share. On March 1, 1996, 22 shares were purchased with a 2% commission (buying and/or selling for round lots) and an additional 1% on odd lot purchases. The 22 shares of stock were sold for $56.50. The gain is taxable at the 28% bracket. What will be the investor's net profit after taxes?

Purchased stock $44 per share $\times$ 22 = $968.00
(March 1, 1996)
+ 3% commission (odd lot)   29.04 ($968 $\times$ .03)
                                _____
                                $997.04 total purchase price

Sold at $56.50 × 22 = $1,243.00
Paid 3% commission
(odd lot)

37.29 ($1,243 × .03)

$1,205.71 cleared after commission
− 997.04 purchasing price including commission

$ 208.67 net gain
37.84 dividend collected

$ 246.51 subject to tax
× .28 (28%)

$ 69.02 taxes

$246.51 − $69.02 = $177.49 net profit

21–31. On September 6, Irene Westing purchased one bond of Mick Corporation at $98\frac{1}{2}$. The bond pays $8\frac{3}{4}$ interest on June 1 and December 1. The stockbroker told Irene that she would have to pay the accrued interest and the market price of the bond and a $6 brokerage fee. What was the total purchase price for Irene? Assume a 360-day year (each month is 30 days) in calculating the accrued interest. (*Hint:* Final cost = Cost of bond + Accrued interest + Brokerage fee. Calculate time for accrued interest.)

Cost of bond: $1,000 × .985 = $985

Time for accrued interest:		Interest: $1,000 × .0875 = $87.50			
June	30 days	$\frac{\$87.50}{360}$ = $.2430555 per day	Final cost of bond	$ 985.00
July	30 days	× 96	Accrued interest	23.33
August	30 days	$23.33	Brokerage fee	6.00
September	6 days			$1,014.33
	96 days			

SUMMARY PRACTICE TEST

1. Shelley Katz bought 600 shares of Office Depot stock at $20\frac{15}{16}$ per share. Assume a commission of 3% of the purchase price. What is the total cost to Shelley? (*p. 479*)

600 × $20.9375 = $12,562.50 × 1.03 = $12,939.38

2. Feliz Company earns $4 per share. Today, the stock is trading at $37\frac{3}{16}$. The company pays an annual dividend of $.25. Calculate **(a)** the price-earnings ratio and **(b)** the yield on the stock (to the nearest tenth percent). (*p. 478*)

a. $\frac{\$37.1875}{\$4}$ = 9   **b.** $\frac{\$.25}{\$37.1875}$ = .7%

3. The stock of IBM Corporation is trading at $99\frac{5}{8}$. The price-earnings ratio is 17 times earnings. Calculate the earnings per share (to the nearest cent) for IBM. (*p. 478*)

EPS = $\frac{\$99.625}{17}$ = $5.86

4. Molly Tram bought 6 bonds of VRT Company $6\frac{3}{4}$ 03 at 89 and 4 bonds of Lage Company $7\frac{3}{4}$ 03 at 79. Assume the commission on the bonds is $3 per bond. What was the total cost of all the purchases? (*p. 481*)

6 × $890 = $5,340
4 × $790 = 3,160
$8,500 + $30 = $8,530

5. Yvet Nah bought one bond of Ring Company for 139. The original bond was $7\frac{3}{4}$ 04. Yvet wants to know the current yield to the nearest tenth percent. Can you help Yvet with the calculation? (*p. 482*)

.0775 × $1,000 = $77.50 $\frac{\$77.50}{\$1,390}$ = 5.6%

6. Cumulative preferred stockholders of Ryan Company receive $.75 per share. The company has 90,000 shares outstanding. For the last 5 years, Ryan paid no dividends. This year, Ryan paid $295,000 in dividends. What is the amount of dividends in arrears that is still owed to preferred stockholders? (*p. 479*)

90,000 × $.75 = $ 67,500
× 6
$405,000 − $295,000 = $110,000 in arrears

7. Dan Hart bought 600 shares of a mutual fund with a NAV of $13.18. This fund has a load charge of 4%. **(a)** What is the offer price and **(b)** what did Dan pay for the investment? (*p. 483*)

a. $13.18 + ($13.18 × .04) = $13.71   **b.** $13.71 × 600 = $8,226

A GROUP PROJECT Defend or reject the following business math issue based on the *Kiplinger's Personal Finance Magazine* article below:

STOCKS
Mickey Mouse & Co. Come Down With the Asian Flu

Don't look now, but Mickey's ears are drooping. Like most international businesses, Walt Disney Co. is battling an economic malaise.

Disney's real-life kingdom is a sprawling web of entertainment fiefdoms. It owns the ABC network and cable-television staple ESPN, produces motion pictures through three studios, and counts among its assets two pro sports teams, several world-famous theme parks, a brand-new cruise line and multiple retail outlets for Disney merchandise.

So what's not to love about Disney? The Asian recession and lack of a blockbuster video hit like last year's *101 Dalmatians* have stunted sales growth for the company's Creative Content division (which handles new movies, videos and all manner of Mickey Mouse–branded gear). Overall profit growth is sluggish.

Throw in the global economic turmoil and investors are fleeing like, well, rodents from a ship in distress. The stock is down 41% from its May high, slashing the company's stock-market value from $88 billion to $49 billion.

Disney has not taken this lying down. It reduced its costly schedule of movies and will concentrate on its core strength, producing animated pictures. The company focused merchandising efforts on established characters such as Mickey Mouse and Winnie the Pooh, which account for four-fifths of all licensed goods sold. Disney launched its fledgling cruise line and is marketing its theme parks to untapped audiences. And a crown jewel of Disney's empire in the future may be its stake in the Internet search engine Infoseek—currently 42%, with plans to expand. All this should help Disney garner $2.7 billion in cash in 1999, says Prudential Securities analyst Katherine Styponias.

Earnings for fiscal 1998 (which ended September 30) were expected to be 89 cents per share, up only 3 cents from fiscal 1997. According to First Call, analysts believe fiscal 1999 can see an improvement in profits to 98 cents per share. Still, the stock trades at 26 times 1999 estimated earnings.

Walt Disney Co.

Symbol: **DIS (NYSE)**
Recent price: **$25**
Price a year ago: **$28**
Shareholder information:
818-560-1000
Web site: **www.disney.com**

Business Math Issue

The era of Disney is over. The competition knows how to beat Disney.

1. List the key points of the article and information to support your position.
2. Write a group defense of your position using math calculations to support your view.

Why Wall Street Firms Trail in On-Line Battle

By ANITA RAGHAVAN
Staff Reporter of THE WALL STREET JOURNAL

NEW YORK — On-line trading is the fastest-growing way for individuals to buy and sell stocks, yet it's increasingly clear that most of the biggest brokers in this hot market aren't on Wall Street.

As on-line trading catches fire among small investors, it is discount brokers such as San-Francisco's **Charles Schwab & Co.** and deep discounters such as **E*Trade Group**, Palo Alto, Calif., that are leading the on-line onslaught, leaving big Wall Street brokerage firms in the dust.

It's no wonder.

Unlike full-service brokerage firms such as **Merrill Lynch** & Co., which have armies of brokers who oppose on-line trading because they fear it will cannibalize their business, discounters such as Schwab and E*Trade haven't had to wrestle with such conflicts.

"It's not Merrill Lynch and PaineWebber" that are dominating the on-line channel, says Bill Burnham, who recently joined Deutsche Bank Securities Inc. as its electronic-commerce analyst. Indeed, of the top five securities firms as measured by number of brokers, only **Morgan Stanley Dean Witter** & Co.'s Discover Brokerage Direct unit ranks among the most active on-line brokers.

Mr. Burnham says about the only marquee names in the on-line arena are the traditional discount brokers, which woke up in the second part of 1997 to the fact that on-line trading "isn't just *a* channel, it is *the* channel."

Clearly the leader in the on-line trading arena is Schwab, which commands 32% of the market and handled an average 60,200 trades a day in the first quarter, compared with 34,100 in the year-earlier period, according to a report published by Mr. Burnham while he was still at Piper Jaffray Inc.

On-line trading has become such a significant component of Schwab's business that during the first quarter, Schwab said, 48% of its total average daily trades of about 126,200 were conducted via the Internet, compared with 33% in the year-ago quarter and 41% in the fourth quarter of last year.

"The Internet has now reached the mass market," says Gideon Sasson, executive vice president of electronic brokerage at Schwab. "It's no longer just for people who want to play with technology."

One of the reasons for the Internet's heady growth in the financial-services arena is its convenience. Mr. Sasson says the most popular offerings on the Internet are "sex and financial services, and in both cases, it is the most convenient way to get access to that information."

A distant second behind Schwab is E*Trade, which through its relentless price cutting has grabbed 12% of the on-line market share by handling about 23,196 average daily trades, according to Mr. Burnham's report. Waterhouse Investor Services, a unit of Canada's **Toronto Dominion Bank**, is the third-biggest player in terms of average daily trades, with 9% of market share, Mr. Burnham's Piper Jaffray report says.

Who Rules On-Line

Wall Street's biggest brokerage firms are largely absent from the top tier of on-line trading activity. Table shows first-quarter on-line trading market share.

COMPANY	SHARE
Charles Schwab	32%
E*Trade	12
Waterhouse	9
Fidelity	8
Datek Online	7
Ameritrade	6
DLJdirect	4
Quick & Reilly	4
Discover	4
Others	14

Source: Piper Jaffray

Phenomenal Growth

Frank J. Petrilli, chief executive officer of Waterhouse, says that before the firm launched personal-computer trading in January 1997, touch-tone-telephone trading accounted for 30% of the firm's business. "Now, touch-tone trading has shrunk to 7% of our business, and PC trading is the largest component of how we execute our trades," he says. Fifty-four percent of Waterhouse's trades are done electronically, and Mr. Petrilli expects that figure to climb to nearly 70% by year end.

At Boston-based **Fidelity Investments**, the growth has been equally phenomenal. Fidelity had more than one million on-line accounts as of March 31, compared with 200,000 accounts at the end of last year's first quarter. Fidelity says that through the end of April this year, 60% of all of its commissionable trades were done on-line, compared with only 17% in the year-earlier period.

Project A

Do you think online trading has any negative effects?

  See text Web site (www.mhhe.com/slater) and *The Business Math Internet Resource Guide.*

22

BUSINESS STATISTICS

QVC by the Numbers

Sales (1997)	$2.1 billion
Employees	9,000
Potential viewers (U.S.)	64 million
Viewers who bought in the past year	5.5 million
Average calls per hour	10,000
Median viewer age	43

Top products sold on QVC by category in 1997, by air time

Category	Percent
Jewelry	27%
Home decor	12%
Apparel	8%
Housewares	6%
Accessories	5%
Electronics	5%

Source: QVC Inc.

High-Fat Diet

The 10 largest quick-stop restaurant chains, by U.S. sales

RANK	CHAIN	SALES (in billions)
1	McDonald's	$16.4
2	Burger King	7.5
3	Pizza Hut*	4.9
4	Taco Bell*	4.6
5	Wendy's	4.3
6	KFC*	3.9
7	Hardee's	3.0
8	Subway	2.7
9	Dairy Queen	2.6
10	Domino's	2.3

*Part of Tricon Global Restaurants
Source: Tricon

The two *Wall Street Journal* clippings "QVC by the Numbers" and "High-Fat Diet" illustrate the importance of business statistics in today's fast-changing computerized world. Note that the median average age of QVC viewers is 43 and jewelry sales lead the products sold. When you look at the list of the 10 largest quick-stop restaurant chains, is your favorite fast-food restaurant number 1?

In this chapter we look at various techniques that analyze and graphically represent business statistics. Learning Unit 22.1 discusses the mean, median, and mode. Learning Unit 22.2 explains how to gather data by using frequency distributions and to express these data visually in graphs. Emphasis is placed on whether graphs are indeed giving accurate information. The chapter concludes with an introduction to index numbers—an application of statistics—and an optional learning unit on measures of dispersion.

LEARNING UNIT 22.1 Mean, Median, and Mode

Companies frequently use averages and measurements to guide their business decisions. The mean and median are the two most common averages used to indicate a single value that represents an entire group of numbers. The mode can also be used to describe a set of data.

Mean

The accountant of Bill's Sport Shop told Bill, the owner, that the average daily sales for the week were $150.14. The accountant stressed that $150.14 was an average and did not represent specific daily sales. Bill wanted to know how the accountant arrived at $150.14.

The accountant went on to explain that he used an arithmetic average, or **mean** (a measurement), to arrive at $150.14 (rounded to the nearest hundredth). He showed Bill the following formula:

$$\text{Mean} = \frac{\text{Sum of all values}}{\text{Number of values}}$$

The accountant used the following data:

	Sun.	Mon.	Tues.	Wed.	Thur.	Fri.	Sat.
Sport shop sales	$400	$100	$68	$115	$120	$68	$180

To compute the mean, the accountant used these data:

$$\text{Mean} = \frac{\$400 + \$100 + \$68 + \$115 + \$120 + \$68 + \$180}{7} = \boxed{\$150.14}$$

When values appear more than once, businesses often look for a **weighted mean.** The format for the weighted mean is slightly different from that for the mean. The concept, however, is the same except that you weight each value by how often it occurs (its frequency). Thus, considering the frequency of the occurrence of each value allows a weighting of each day's sales in proper importance. To calculate the weighted mean, use the following formula:

$$\text{Weighted mean} = \frac{\text{Sum of products}}{\text{Sum of frequencies}}$$

Let's change the sales data for Bill's Sport Shop and see how to calculate a weighted mean:

	Sun.	Mon.	Tues.	Wed.	Thur.	Fri.	Sat.
Sport shop sales	$400	$100	$100	$80	$80	$100	$400

Value	Frequency	Product
$400	2	$ 800
100	3	300
80	2	160
		$1,260

The weighted mean is $\dfrac{\$1,260}{7} = \boxed{\$180}$

Note how we multiply each value by its frequency of occurrence to arrive at the product. Then we divide the sum of the products by the sum of the frequencies.

When you calculate your grade point average (GPA), you are using a weighted average. The following formula is used to calculate GPA:

$$\text{GPA} = \frac{\text{Total points}}{\text{Total credits}}$$

Now let's show how Jill Rivers calculated her GPA to the nearest tenth.

Given   A = 4; B = 3; C = 2; D = 1; F = 0

Courses	Credits attempted	Grade received	Points (Credits × Grade)
Intro to Computers	4	A	16 (4 × 4)
Psychology	3	B	9 (3 × 3)
English Composition	3	B	9 (3 × 3)
Business Law	3	C	6 (2 × 3)
Business Math	3	B	9 (3 × 3)
	16		49 $\dfrac{49}{16} = \boxed{3.1}$

When high or low numbers do not significantly affect a list of numbers, the mean is a good indicator of the center of the data. If high or low numbers do have an effect, the median may be a better indicator to use.

Median

The **median** is another measurement that indicates the center of the data. The median does not distort an average that has one or more extreme values. For example, let's look at the yearly salaries of the employees of Rusty's Clothing Shop:

Alice Knight	$95,000	Jane Wang	$67,000
Jane Hess	27,000	Bill Joy	40,000
Joel Floyd	32,000		

Note how Alice's salary of $95,000 will distort an average calculated by the mean:

$$\frac{\$95,000 + \$27,000 + \$32,000 + \$67,000 + \$40,000}{5} = \boxed{\$52,200}$$

The $52,200 average salary is considerably more than the salary of three of the employees. So it is not a good representation of the store's average salary. Let's use the following steps to find the median.

Finding the Median of a Group of Values

Step 1.   Orderly arrange values from the smallest to the largest.

Step 2.   Find the middle value.

   a. *Odd number of values:* Median is the middle value. You find this by first dividing the total number of numbers by 2. The next-higher number is the median.

   b. *Even number of values:* Median is the average of the two middle values.

For Rusty's Clothing Shop, we find the median as follows:

1. Arrange values from smallest to largest:

$27,000; $32,000; $40,000; $67,000; $95,000

2. Since the middle value is an odd number, $40,000 is the median. Note that half of the salaries fall below the median and half fall above ($5 \div 2 = 2\frac{1}{2}$—next number is the median).

If Jane Hess ($27,000) were not on the payroll, we would find the median as follows:

1. Arrange values from smallest to largest:

$32,000; $40,000; $67,000; $95,000

2. Average the two middle values:

$$\frac{\$40,000 + \$67,000}{2} = \boxed{\$53,500}$$

Note that the median results in two salaries below and two salaries above the average. Now we'll look at another measurement tool—the mode.

Mode

The **mode** is a measurement that also records values. In a series of numbers, the value that occurs most often is the mode. If all the values are different, there is no mode. If two or more numbers appear most often, you may have two or more modes. Note that we do not have to arrange the numbers in the lowest-to-highest order, although this could make it easier to find the mode.

EXAMPLE   3, 4, 5, 6, 3, 8, 9, 3, 5, 3

3 is the mode since it is listed 4 times.

Now let's check your progress with a Practice Quiz.

Barton Company's sales reps sold the following last month:

Sales rep	Sales volume	Sales rep	Sales volume
A	$16,500	C	$12,000
B	15,000	D	48,900

Calculate the mean and the median. Which is the better indicator of the center of the data? Is there a mode?

✓ **Solutions**

$$\text{Mean} = \frac{\$16,500 + \$15,000 + \$12,000 + \$48,900}{4} = \boxed{\$23,100}$$

$$\text{Median} = \frac{\$15,000 + \$16,500}{2} = \$15,750$$

$12,000, $15,000, $16,500, $48,900. Note how we arrange numbers from smallest to highest to calculate median.

Median is the better indicator since in calculating the mean, the $48,900 puts the average of $23,100 much too high. There is no mode.

LEARNING UNIT 22.2 Frequency Distributions and Graphs

In this unit you will learn how to gather data and illustrate these data. Today, computer software programs can make beautiful color graphics. But how accurate are these graphics? This *Wall Street Journal* clipping gives an example of graphics that did not agree with the numbers beneath them. The clipping reminds all readers to check the numbers illustrated by the graphics.

What's Wrong With this Picture?
Utility's Glasses Are Never Empty

By KATHLEEN DEVENY
Staff Reporter of THE WALL STREET JOURNAL

When Les Waas, an investor in Philadelphia Suburban Corp., paged through the company's 1994 annual report, he was impressed by what he saw.

The water utility had used a series of charts to represent its revenues, net income and book value per share, among other results. Each figure was represented by the level of water in a glass. Each chart showed strong growth.

Then Mr. Waas looked a little more carefully. The bars in the chart seemed to indicate far more impressive growth than the numbers beneath them. A chart showing the growth in the number of Philadelphia Suburban's water customers, for ex-

1990	1991	1992	1993	1994
235	237	245	247	250

Number of Metered Water Customers (thousands)

ample, seemed to indicate the company's customer base had more than tripled since 1990. But the numbers actually increased only 6.4%.

The reason for the disparity: The charts don't begin at zero. Even an empty glass in the accompanying chart would represent a customer base of 230,000.

[handwritten note: Reason for the dramatic growth. # of customers appear to have more than tripled, in reality they have only 6.4%]

Collecting raw data and organizing the data is a prerequisite to presenting statistics graphically. Let's illustrate this by looking at the following example.

A computer industry consultant wants to know how much college freshmen are willing to spend to set up a computer in their dormitory rooms. After visiting a local college dorm, the consultant gathered the following data on the amount of money 20 students spent on computers:

$1,000	$7,000	$4,000	$1,000	$5,000	$1,000	$3,000
5,000	2,000	3,000	3,000	3,000	8,000	9,000
3,000	6,000	6,000	1,000	10,000	1,000	

Price of computer	Tally	Frequency
$ 1,000	ЖИ	5
2,000	I	1
3,000	ЖИ	5
4,000	I	1
5,000	II	2
6,000	II	2
7,000	I	1
8,000	I	1
9,000	I	1
10,000	I	1

Note that these raw data are not arranged in any order. To make the data more meaningful, the consultant made the **frequency distribution** table at the left. Think of this distribution table as a way to organize a list of numbers to show the patterns that may exist.

As you can see, 25% ($\frac{5}{20} = \frac{1}{4} = 25\%$) of the students spent $1,000 and another 25% spent $3,000. Only four students spent $7,000 or more.

Now let's see how we can use bar graphs.

Bar Graphs

© 1997, Dow Jones & Company, Inc.

Bar graphs help readers see the changes that have occurred over a period of time. This is especially true when the same type of data is repeatedly studied. The following *Wall Street Journal* clipping uses bar graphs to show the increase in millions of subscribers to the Disney Channel since 1991.

Let's return to our computer consultant example and make a bar graph of the computer purchases data collected by the consultant. Note that the height of the bar represents the frequency of each purchase. Bar graphs can be vertical or horizontal.

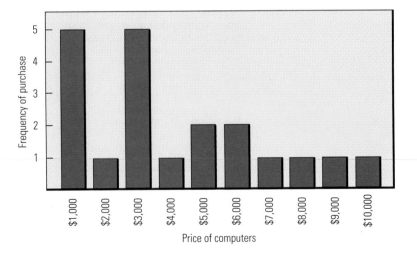

We can simplify this bar graph by grouping the prices of the computers. The grouping, or *intervals,* should be of equal sizes.

Class	Frequency
$1,000–$ 3,000.99	11
3,001– 5,000.99	3
5,001– 7,000.99	3
7,001– 9,000.99	2
9,001– 11,000.99	1

A bar graph for the grouped data follows.

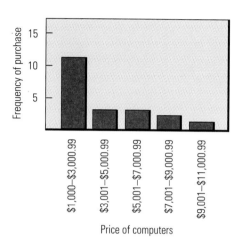

Next, let's see how we can use line graphs.

Line Graphs

A **line graph** shows trends over a period of time. Often separate lines are drawn to show the comparison between two or more trends.

The Wall Street Journal clipping "Congressional Pay Check" uses a line graph to show the increase in congressional salaries since 1960. The impact of the line graph is supported by comparing, at the right, the growing congressional salaries to the earnings of other occupations.

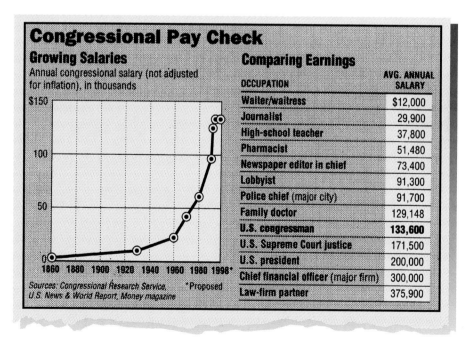

We conclude our discussion of graphics with the use of the circle graph.

Circle Graphs

Circle graphs, often called *pie charts,* are especially helpful for showing the relationship of parts to a whole. The entire circle represents 100%, or 360°; the pie-shaped pieces represent the subcategories. Note how the circle graph in *The Wall Street Journal* clipping "Age and Activity" shows the Web users by age.

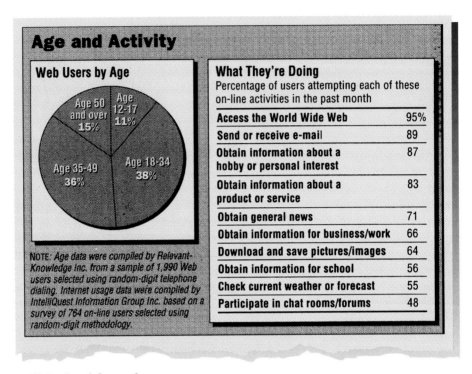

© 1998, Dow Jones & Company, Inc.

$.15 \times 360° = 54.0$
$.11 \times 360° = 39.6$
$.36 \times 360° = 129.6$
$.38 \times 360° = 136.8$
$\overline{ 360.0}$

To draw a circle graph (or pie chart), begin by drawing a circle. Then take the percentages and convert each percentage to a decimal. Next multiply each decimal by 360° to get the degrees represented by the percentage. Circle graphs must total 360°.

We conclude this unit with a brief discussion of index numbers.

An Application of Statistics: Index Numbers

The financial section of a newspaper often gives different index numbers describing the changes in business. These **index numbers** express the relative changes in a variable compared with some base, which is taken as 100. The changes may be measured from time to time or from place to place. Index numbers function as percents and are calculated like percents.

Frequently, a business will use index numbers to make comparisons of a current price relative to a given year. For example, a calculator may cost $9 today relative to a cost of $75 some 30 years ago. The **price relative** of the calculator is $\frac{\$9}{\$75} \times 100 = 12\%$. The calculator now costs 12% of what it cost some 30 years ago. A price relative, then, is the current price divided by some previous year's price—the base year—multiplied by 100.

$$\text{Price relative} = \frac{\text{Current price}}{\text{Base year's price}} \times 100$$

Index numbers can also be used to estimate current prices at various geographic locations. The frequently quoted Consumer Price Index (CPI), calculated and published monthly by the U.S. Bureau of Labor Statistics, records the price relative percentage cost of many goods and services nationwide compared to a base period. Table 22.1 gives a portion of the CPI that uses 1982–84 as its base period. Note that the table shows, for example, that the price relative for housing in Los Angeles is 139.3% of what it cost in 1982–84. Thus, Los Angeles housing costs amounting to $100.00 in 1982–84 now cost $139.30. So if you built a $90,000 house in 1982–84, it is worth $125,370 today. (Convert 139.3% to the decimal 1.393; multiply $90,000 by 1.393 = $125,370.)

Once again, we complete the unit with a Practice Quiz (p. 503).

TABLE 22.1

Consumer Price Index (in percent)

Expense	Atlanta	Chicago	New York	Los Angeles
Food	131.9	130.3	139.6	130.9
Housing	128.8	131.4	139.3	139.3
Clothing	133.8	124.3	121.8	126.4
Medical care	177.6	163.0	172.4	163.3

LU 22.2 PRACTICE QUIZ

1. The following is the number of sales made by 20 salespeople on a given day. Prepare a frequency distribution and a bar graph. Do not use intervals for this example.

5	8	9	1	4	4	0	3	2	8
8	9	5	1	9	6	7	5	9	10

2. Assuming the following market shares for diapers 5 years ago, prepare a circle graph:

Pampers	32%	Huggies	24%
Luvs	20%	Others	24%

3. Today a new Explorer costs $30,000. In 1991 the Explorer cost $19,000. What is the price relative? Round to the nearest tenth percent.

✓ **Solutions**

1.

Number of sales	Tally	Frequency
0	I	1
1	II	2
2	I	1
3	I	1
4	II	2
5	III	3
6	I	1
7	I	1
8	III	3
9	IIII	4
10	I	1

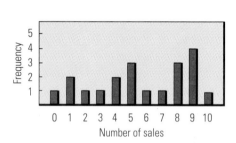

2.

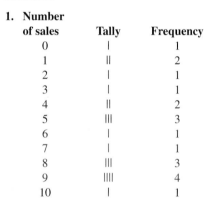

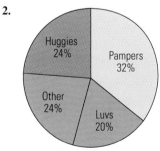

$.32 \times 360° = 115.20°$
$.20 \times 360° = 72.00°$
$.24 \times 360° = 86.40°$
$.24 \times 360° = 86.40°$

3. $\dfrac{\$30,000}{\$19,000} \times 100 = 157.9$

LEARNING UNIT 22.3 Measures of Dispersion (optional)

In Learning Unit 22.1 you learned how companies use the mean, median, and mode to indicate a single value, or number, that represents an entire group of numbers, or data. Often it is valuable to know how the information is scattered (spread or dispersed) within a data set. A **measure of dispersion** is a number that describes how the numbers of a set of data are spread out or dispersed.

This learning unit discusses three measures of dispersion—the range, standard deviation, and normal distribution. We begin with the range—the simplest measure of dispersion.

Range

The **range** is the difference between the two extreme values (highest and lowest) in a group of values or a set of data. For example, often the actual extreme values of hourly temperature readings during the past 24 hours are given but not the range or difference between the high and low readings. To find the range in a group of data, subtract the lowest value from the highest value.

> Range = Highest value − Lowest value

Thus, if the high temperature reading during the past 24 hours was 90° and the low temperature reading was 60°, the range is 90° − 60°, or 30°.

The difficulty in using the range is that this measure depends only on the values of the extremes and does not consider any other values in the data set. Also, the range depends on the number of values on which it is based; that is, the larger the number of values, the larger the range is apt to be. The range gives only a general idea of the spread of the values in a set of data.

EXAMPLE   Find the range of the following values: 83.6, 77.3, 69.2, 93.1, 85.4, 71.6.

Range = 93.1 − 69.2 = 23.9

Standard Deviation

Since the **standard deviation** is intended to measure the spread of data around the mean, the first step in finding the standard deviation of a set of data is to determine its mean. The following diagram shows two sets of data—A and B. Note that, as shown in the diagram, the means of these two data are equal. Now look at how the data in both sets are spread or dispersed.

Data set A	Data set B
X X X X X	X X X X X
0 1 2 3 4 5 6 7 8 9 10 11 12 13	0 1 2 3 4 5 6 7 8 9 10 11 12 13
Mean = (1 + 2 + 5 + 10 + 12) ÷ 5 = 6	Mean = (4 + 4 + 5 + 8 + 9) ÷ 5 = 6

You can see that although the means of data sets A and B are equal, data set A is clearly more widely dispersed; therefore, the data in set B will have a smaller standard deviation than the data in set A.

To find the standard deviation of an ungrouped set of data, use the following steps:

Finding the Standard Deviation

Step 1. Find the mean of the set of data.
Step 2. Subtract the mean from each piece of data to find each deviation.
Step 3. Square each deviation (multiply the deviation by itself).
Step 4. Sum all squared deviations.
Step 5. Divide the sum of the squared deviations by $n - 1$, where n equals the number of pieces of data.
Step 6. Find the square root ($\sqrt{}$) of the number obtained in Step 5 (use a calculator). This is the standard deviation. (The square root is a number that when multiplied by itself equals the amount shown inside the square root symbol.)

Two additional points should be made. First, Step 2 sometimes results in negative numbers. Since the sum of the deviations obtained in Step 2 should always be zero, we would not be able to find the average deviation. This is why we square each deviation—to generate positive quantities only. Second, the standard deviation we refer to is used with *sample* sets of data, that is, a collection of data from a population. The population is the *entire* collection of data. When the standard deviation for a population is calculated, the sum of the squared deviations is divided by n instead of by $n - 1$. In all problems that follow, sample sets of data are being examined.

EXAMPLE   Calculate the standard deviations for the sample data sets A and B given in the diagram above. Round the final answer to the nearest tenth. Note that Step 1—find the mean—is given in the diagram.

Standard deviation of data sets A and B:
The table on the left uses Steps 2 through 6 to find the standard deviation of data set A, and the table on the right uses Steps 2 through 6 to find the standard deviation of data set B.

Data	Step 2 Data − Mean	Step 3 (Data − Mean)^2
1	$1 - 6 = -5$	25
2	$2 - 6 = -4$	16
5	$5 - 6 = -1$	1
10	$10 - 6 = 4$	16
12	$12 - 6 = 6$	36
	Total 0	94 **(Step 4)**

Step 5: Divide by $n - 1$: $\dfrac{94}{5 - 1} = \dfrac{94}{4} = 23.5$

Step 6: The square root of $\sqrt{23.5}$ is 4.8 (rounded).

The standard deviation of data set A is 4.8.

Data	Step 2 Data − Mean	Step 3 (Data − Mean)^2
4	$4 - 6 = -2$	4
4	$4 - 6 = -2$	4
5	$5 - 6 = -1$	1
8	$8 - 6 = 2$	4
9	$9 - 6 = 3$	9
	Total 0	22 **(Step 4)**

Step 5: Divide by $n - 1$: $\dfrac{22}{5 - 1} = \dfrac{22}{4} = 5.5$

Step 6: The square root of $\sqrt{5.5}$ is 2.3.

The standard deviation of data set B is 2.3.

As suspected, the standard deviation of data set B is less than that of set A. The standard deviation value reinforces what we see in the diagram.

Normal Distribution

One of the most important distributions of data is the **normal distribution.** In a normal distribution, data are spread *symmetrically* about the mean. A graph of such a distribution looks like the bell-shaped curve in Figure 22.1. Many data sets are normally distributed. Examples are the life span of automobile engines, women's heights, and intelligence quotients.

In a normal distribution, the data are spread out symmetrically—50% of the data lie above the mean, and 50% of the data lie below the mean. Additionally, if the data are normally distributed, 68% of the data should be found within one standard deviation above and below the mean. About 95% of the data should be found within two standard deviations above and below the mean. Figure 22.1 illustrates these facts.

FIGURE 22.1

Standard deviation and the normal distribution

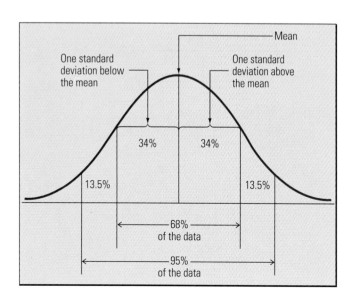

EXAMPLE Assume that the mean useful life of a particular lightbulb is 2,000 hours and is normally distributed with a standard deviation of 300 hours. Calculate the useful life of the lightbulb with **(a)** one standard deviation of the mean and **(b)** two standard deviations of the mean; also **(c)** calculate the percent of lightbulbs that will last 2,300 hours or longer.

a. The useful life of the lightbulb one standard deviation from the mean is one standard deviation above *and* below the mean.

   2,000 ± 300 = 1,700 and 2,300 hours

   The useful life is somewhere between 1,700 and 2,300 hours.

b. The useful life of the lightbulb within two standard deviations of the mean is within two standard deviations above *and* below the mean.

   2,000 ± 2(300) = 1,400 and 2,600 hours

c. Since 50% of the data in a normal distribution lie below the mean and 34% represent the amount of data one standard deviation above the mean, we must calculate the percent of data that lies beyond one standard deviation above the mean.

   100% − (50% + 34%) = 16%

   So 16% of the bulbs should last 2,300 hours or longer.

   It's time for another Practice Quiz.

LU 22.3 PRACTICE QUIZ

1. Calculate the range for the following data: 58, 13, 17, 26, 5, 41.
2. Calculate the standard deviation for the following sample set of data: 113, 92, 77, 125, 110, 93, 111. Round answers to the nearest tenth.

✓ **Solutions**

1. 58 − 5 = 53 range

2.

Data	Data − Mean	(Data − Mean)²
113	113 − 103 = 10	100
92	92 − 103 = −11	121
77	77 − 103 = −26	676
125	125 − 103 = 22	484
110	110 − 103 = 7	49
93	93 − 103 = −10	100
111	111 − 103 = 8	64
	Total	1,594

$$1{,}594 \div (7 - 1) = 265.6666667$$
$$\sqrt{265.6666667} = 16.3 \text{ standard deviation}$$

Chapter Organizer and Reference Guide		
Topics	**Key point, procedure, formula**	**Example(s) to illustrate situation**
Mean, p. 496	$$\frac{\text{Sum of all values}}{\text{Number of values}}$$	Age of basketball team: 22, 28, 31, 19, 15 $$\text{Mean} = \frac{22 + 28 + 31 + 19 + 15}{5}$$ $= \boxed{23}$
Weighted mean, p. 497	$$\frac{\text{Sum of products}}{\text{Sum of frequencies}}$$	S. M. T. W. Th. F. S. Sales $90 $75 $80 $75 $80 $90 $90 **Value** **Frequency** **Product** $90 3 $270 75 2 150 80 $\underline{2}$ $\underline{160}$ 7 $580 $\text{Mean} = \dfrac{\$580}{7} = \boxed{\$82.86}$

Median, p. 497	**1.** Arrange values from smallest to largest.
	 2. Find the middle value.
	  a. Odd number of values: median is middle value.
	  $\left(\dfrac{\text{Total number of numbers}}{2}\right)$
	  Next-higher number is median.
	  b. Even number of values: average of two middle values.
		12, 15, 8, 6, 3
		 1. 3 6 8 12 15
		 2. $\dfrac{5}{2} = 2.5$
		 Median is third number, $\boxed{8.}$

Frequency distribution, p. 499	Method of listing numbers or amounts not arranged in any particular way by columns for numbers (amounts), tally, and frequency	Number of sodas consumed in one day: 1, 5, 4, 3, 4, 2, 2, 3, 2, 0 **Number of sodas** **Tally** **Frequency** 0 I 1 1 I 1 2 III 3 3 II 2 4 II 2 5 I 1
Bar graphs, p. 500	Height of bar represents frequency. Bar graph used for grouped data. Bar graphs can be vertical or horizontal.	From soda example above:
Line graphs, p. 500	Shows trend. Helps to put numbers in order.	**Sales** 2000 $1,000 2001 2,000 2002 3,000

Chapter Organizer and Reference Guide (concluded)		
Topics	**Key point, procedure, formula**	**Example(s) to illustrate situation**
Circle graphs, p. 502	Circle = 360° % × 360° = Degrees of pie to represent percent Total should = 360°	60% favor diet soda 40% favor sugared soda .60 × 360° = 216° .40 × 360° = 144° 360°
Price relative, p. 502	$$\text{Price relative} = \frac{\text{Current price}}{\text{Base year's price}} \times 100$$	A station wagon's sticker price was \$8,799 in 1982. Today it is \$14,900. $$\text{Price relative} = \frac{\$14,900}{\$8,799} \times 100 = \boxed{169.3}$$ (rounded to nearest tenth percent)
Range (optional) p. 504	Range = Highest value − Lowest value	Calculate range of the data set consisting of 5, 9, 13, 2, 8 Range = 13 − 2 = 11
Standard deviation (optional), p. 504	**1.** Calculate mean. **2.** Subtract mean from each piece of data. **3.** Square each deviation. **4.** Sum squares. **5.** Divide sum of squares by $n - 1$, where n = number of pieces of data. **6.** Take square root of number obtained in Step 5, to find the standard deviation.	Calculate the standard deviation of this set of data: 7, 2, 5, 3, 3. **1.** Mean $= \dfrac{20}{5} = 4$ **2.** $7 - 4 = 3$ $2 - 4 = -2$ $5 - 4 = 1$ $3 - 4 = -1$ $3 - 4 = -1$ **3.** $(3)^2 = 9$ $(-2)^2 = 4$ $(1)^2 = 1$ $(-1)^2 = 1$ $(-1)^2 = 1$ **4.** $\qquad 16$ **5.** $16 \div 4 = 4$ **6.** Standard deviation = $\boxed{2}$
Key terms	Bar graph, *p. 500* Circle graph, *p. 502* Frequency distribution, *p. 500* Index numbers, *p. 502* Line graph, *p. 501*	Mean, *p. 496* Measure of dispersion, *p. 503* Median, *p. 497* Mode, *p. 498* Normal distribution, *p. 505* Price relative, *p. 502* Range, *p. 504* Standard deviation, *p. 504* Weighted mean, *p. 497*

Critical Thinking Discussion Questions

1. Explain the mean, median, and mode. Give an example that shows you must be careful when you read statistics in an article.

2. Explain frequency distributions and the types of graphs. Locate a company annual report and explain how the company shows graphs to highlight its performance. Does the company need more or fewer of these visuals? Could price relatives be used?

3. Explain the statement that standard deviations are not accurate.

DRILL PROBLEMS (*Note:* Problems for Optional Section 22.3 are after the Challenge Problem 22–23, page 513.)

Calculate the mean (to the nearest hundredth):

22–1. 7, 9, 8, 5 $= \dfrac{29}{4} = 7.25$

22–2. 9, 12, 15, 18, 14 $= \dfrac{68}{5} = 13.60$

22–3. $55.83, $66.92, $108.93 $= \dfrac{\$231.68}{3} = \$77.23$

22–4. $1,001, $68.50, $33.82, $581.95 $= \dfrac{\$1,685.27}{4} = \$421.32$

22–5. Calculate the grade-point average: A = 4, B = 3, C = 2, D = 1, F = 0 (to nearest tenth).

Courses	Credits	Grade	Units × Grade	
Computer Principles	3	B	9 (3 × 3)	
Business Law	3	C	6 (3 × 2)	
Logic	3	D	3 (3× 1)	$\dfrac{43}{16} = 2.7$
Biology	4	A	16 (4 × 4)	
Marketing	3	B	9 (3 × 3)	
	16		43	

22–6. Find the weighted mean (to the nearest tenth):

Value	Frequency	Product	
4	7	28	
8	3	24	$\dfrac{78}{21} = 3.7$
2	9	18	
4	2	8	
	21	78	

Find the median:

22–7. 55, 10, 19, 38, 100, 25 $\dfrac{25 + 38}{2} = 31.5$

10, 19, 25, 38, 55, 100

22–8. 95, 103, 98, 62, 31, 15, 82
15, 31, 62, 82, 95, 98, 103
↑

Find the mode:

22–9. 8, 9, 3, 4, 12, 8, 8, 9   8

22–10. 22, 19, 15, 16, 18, 18, 5, 18   18

22–11. **Given:**   Truck cost   1996 $30,000
                 Truck cost   1990 $21,000

Calculate the price relative (round to the nearest tenth percent).

$\dfrac{\$30,000}{\$21,000} \times 100 = 142.9$

22–12. Given the following sales of Lowe Corporation, prepare a line graph (run sales from $5,000 to $20,000).

2000	$ 8,000
2001	11,000
2002	13,000
2003	18,000

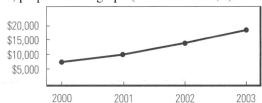

22–13. Prepare a frequency distribution from the following weekly salaries of teachers at Moore Community College. Use the following intervals:

$200–$299.99
 300– 399.99
 400– 499.99
 500– 599.99

$210	$505	$310	$380	$275
290	480	550	490	200
286	410	305	444	368

Salaries	Tally	Frequency
$200–$299.99	ЖΙ	5
300– 399.99	IIII	4
400– 499.99	IIII	4
500– 599.99	II	2

22–14. Prepare a bar graph from the frequency distribution in Problem 22–13.

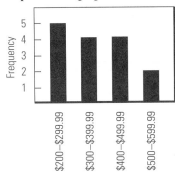

22–15. How many degrees on a pie chart would each be given from the following?

Wear digital watch	42%	.42 × 360° = 151.2°
Wear traditional watch	51%	.51 × 360° = 183.6°
Wear no watch	7%	.07 × 360° = $\underline{25.2°}$
		360°

WORD PROBLEMS

22–16. The November 1997 issue of *Money* compared flight fares. The average one-way fares for trips of more than 1,500 miles during the year ended March 31, 1997, were as follows:

Airline	Price	Airline	Price
America West	$161	Alaska Air	$279
Continental	199	Southwest	116
American	214	TWA	193
US Airways	214	Northwest	203
United	258		

What are the mean and the mode for these airlines?

Sum of all values → $\dfrac{\$1{,}837}{9}$ = $204.11 mean
Number of values →

Mode = 214 appears twice

22–17. The February 1997 issue of *Consumer Reports* rated energy costs of various refrigerators. Following are the models and energy costs:

Brand and model	Energy cost (per year)
Whirlpool	$78
Kenmore	84
GE Profile	84
GE TBX18ZAX	70
Frigidaire	74

What is the median energy cost of these refrigerators?

$70, $74, $78, $84, $84
Median = $78

22–18. The December/January 1998 issue of *Your Money* reported on the value of a $1,000 investment made 1 year ago.

Investment	How the investments fared
Blue-chip stocks	$1,381.00
Growth mutual funds	1,362.20
Small-company stocks	1,279.50
International funds	1,222.80
Long-term treasury bonds	1,125.90
High-quality corporate bonds	1,105.70
One-year CD	1,051.20

What was the mean of how these stocks fared? Round to the nearest hundredth.

$$\text{Sum of all values} \rightarrow \frac{\$8,528.30}{7} \leftarrow \text{Number of values} = \$1,218.33 \text{ mean}$$

22–19. Bill Small, a travel agent, provided Alice Hall with the following information regarding the cost of her upcoming vacation:

Transportation	35%
Hotel	28%
Food and entertainment	20%
Miscellaneous	17%

Construct a circle graph for Alice.

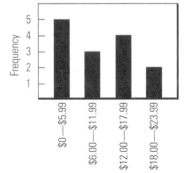

$.35 \times 360° = 126°$
$.28 \times 360° = 100.8°$
$.20 \times 360° = 72°$
$.17 \times 360° = 61.2°$

22–20. Jim Smith, a marketing student, observed how much each customer spent in a local convenience store. Based on the following results, prepare **(a)** a frequency distribution and **(b)** a bar graph. Use intervals of $0–$5.99, $6.00–$11.99, $12.00–$17.99, and $18.00–$23.99.

$18.50	$18.24	$ 6.88	$9.95
16.10	3.55	14.10	6.80
12.11	3.82	2.10	
15.88	3.95	5.50	

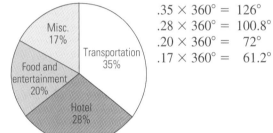

Intervals	Tally	Frequency
$ 0–$ 5.99	卌	5
$ 6.00–$11.99	|||	3
$12.00–$17.99	||||	4
$18.00–$23.99	||	2

22–21. Angie's Bakery bakes bagels. Find the weighted mean (to the nearest whole bagel) given the following daily production for June:

200	150	200	150	200
150	190	360	360	150
190	190	190	200	150
360	400	400	150	200
400	360	150	400	360
400	400	200	150	150

	Tally	Day × Bagels = Product
150	卌 ||||	9 × 150 = 1,350
190	||||	4 × 190 = 760
200	卌		6 × 200 = 1,200
360	卌	5 × 360 = 1,800
400	卌		6 × 400 = 2,400
		7,510

$$\frac{7,510}{30} = 250.33 = 250 \text{ bagels}$$

22–22. Melvin Company reported sales in 2001 of $300,000. This compared to sales of $150,000 in 2000 and $100,000 in 1999. Construct a line graph for Melvin Company.

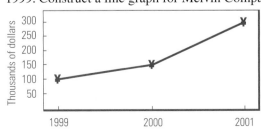

CHALLENGE PROBLEMS

22–23. The November 1997 issue of *Money* compared the number of frequent-flier miles needed for a free domestic coach ticket without a Saturday night stay-over.

Airline	Frequent-flier miles needed	Airline	Frequent-flier miles needed
Alaska Air	20,000	Northwest	25,000
American	25,000	United	40,000
America West	20,000	US Airways	25,000
Continental	50,000	TWA	20,000
Delta	25,000		

Prepare a frequency distribution. Determine the mean (to the nearest whole number), mode, and median miles needed.

Miles needed	Tally	Frequency
20,000	III	3
25,000	IIII	4
40,000	I	1
50,000	I	1

Sum of all values → $\dfrac{250,000}{9}$ = 27,777.78 or 27,778 mean   25,000 appears 4 times, mode
Number of values → 9

20,000, 20,000, 20,000, 25,000 , 25,000, 25,000, 25,000, 40,000, 50,000

25,000 median

22–24. The following circle graph is a suggested budget for Ron Rye and his family for a month:

Ron would like you to calculate the percent (to the hundredth) for each part of the circle graph along with the appropriate number of degrees.

$550 + $340 + $240 + $290 + $410 + $375 = $2,205

$\dfrac{\$550}{\$2,205} = 24.94\%$ $\dfrac{\$340}{\$2,205} = 15.42\%$ $\dfrac{\$240}{\$2,205} = 10.88\%$

$\dfrac{\$290}{\$2,205} = 13.15\%$ $\dfrac{\$410}{\$2,205} = 18.59\%$ $\dfrac{\$375}{\$2,205} = 17.01\%$

.2494 × 360° = 89.78°
.1542 × 360° = 55.51°
.1088 × 360° = 39.17°
.1315 × 360° = 47.34°
.1859 × 360° = 66.92°
.1701 × 360° = 61.24°
359.96° (due to rounding)

DRILL PROBLEMS

1. Calculate the range for the following set of data: 117, 98, 133, 52, 114, 35.
$133 - 35 = 98$

Calculate the standard deviation for the following sample sets of data. Round the final answers to the nearest tenth.

2. 83.6, 92.3, 56.5, 43.8, 77.1, 66.7

Data	Data − Mean	(Data − Mean)²
83.6	$83.6 - 70 = 13.6$	184.96
92.3	$92.3 - 70 = 22.3$	497.29
56.5	$56.5 - 70 = -13.5$	182.25
43.8	$43.8 - 70 = -26.2$	686.44
77.1	$77.1 - 70 = 7.1$	50.41
66.7	$66.7 - 70 = -3.3$	10.89
	Total	1,612.24

$1,612.24 \div (6 - 1) = 322.448$
$\sqrt{322.448} = 17.96$ standard deviation

3. 7, 3, 12, 17, 5, 8, 9, 9, 13, 15, 6, 6, 4, 5
Sum of the squared deviations $= 237.5$
$237.5 \div (14 - 1) = 18.26923077$
$\sqrt{18.2693077} = 4.3$ standard deviation

4. 41, 41, 38, 27, 53, 56, 28, 45, 47, 49, 55, 60
Sum of the squared deviations $= 1,224$
$1,224 \div (12 - 1) = 111.2727273$
$\sqrt{111.2727273} = 10.5$ standard deviation

WORD PROBLEMS

5. The mean useful life of car batteries is 48 months. They have a standard deviation of 3. If the useful life of batteries is normally distributed, calculate **(a)** the percent of batteries with a useful life of less than 45 months and **(b)** the percent of batteries that will last longer than 54 months.

a. $100\% - (50\% + 34\%) = 16\%$ **b.** $100\% - (50\% + 34\% + 13.5\%) = 2.5\%$

6. The average weight of a particular box of crackers is 24.5 ounces with a standard deviation of 0.8 ounce. The weights of the boxes are normally distributed. What percent of the boxes **(a)** weigh more than 22.9 ounces and **(b)** weigh less than 23.7 ounces?

a. 22.9 ounces is 2 standard deviations below the mean.   **b.** 23.7 is 1 standard deviation below the mean.
   $50\% + 34\% + 13.5\% = 97.5\%$ $100\% - (50\% + 34\%) = 16\%$

7. An examination is normally distributed with a mean score of 77 and a standard deviation of 6. Find the percent of individuals scoring as indicated below.

a. Between 71 and 83   **a.** $34\% + 34\% = 68\%$
b. Between 83 and 65   **b.** $34\% + 34\% + 13.5\% = 81.5\%$
c. Above 89   **c.** $100\% - (50\% + 34\% + 13.5\%) = 2.5\%$
d. Less than 65   **d.** $100\% - (50\% + 34\% + 13.5\%) = 2.5\%$
e. Between 77 and 65   **e.** $34\% + 13.5\% = 47.5\%$

8. Listed below are the sales figures in thousands of dollars for a group of insurance salespeople. Calculate the mean sales figure and the standard deviation.

$117	$350	$400	$245	$420
223	275	516	265	135
486	320	285	374	190

$\$4,601 \div 15 = \$306.73$ mean sales
The sum of the squared deviations equals 197,190.9335.
$197,190.9335 \div (15 - 1) = 14,085.066$
$\sqrt{14,085.066} = \$118.68$ standard deviation

9. The time in seconds it takes for 20 individual sewing machines to stitch a border onto a particular garment is listed below. Calculate the mean stitching time and the standard deviation to the nearest hundredth.

67	69	64	71	73
58	71	64	62	67
62	57	67	60	65
60	63	72	56	64

$1{,}292 \div 20 = 64.6$ mean time

The sum of the squared deviations equals 478.8

$478.8 \div (20 - 1) = 25.2$

$\sqrt{25.2} = 5.02$ standard deviation

 ## SUMMARY PRACTICE TEST

1. In June, Logan Realty sold 10 homes at the following prices: $135,000; $170,000; $90,000; $98,000; $185,000; $150,000; $108,000; $114,000; $142,000; and $250,000. Calculate the mean and median. *(pp. 496, 497)*

Mean $\dfrac{\begin{array}{l}\$135{,}000 + \$170{,}000 + \$90{,}000 + \$98{,}000 + \$185{,}000 \\ + \ \$150{,}000 + \$108{,}000 + \$114{,}000 + \$142{,}000 + \$250{,}000\end{array}}{10} = \$144{,}200$

Median $90,000; $108,000; $135,000; $150,000; $185,000; $\dfrac{\$135{,}000 + \$142{,}000}{2} = \$138{,}500$
  $98,000; $114,000; $142,000; $170,000; $250,000

2. Sears Hardware Store counted the number of customers entering the store for a week. The results were 1,300; 950; 1,300; 1,700; 880; 920; and 1,210. What is the mode? *(p. 498)*

   1,300

3. This semester Lee Win took four 3-credit courses at Middlesex Community College. She received an A in accounting and B's in history, psychology, and algebra. What is her cumulative grade-point average (assume A = 4 and B = 3) to the nearest hundredth? *(p. 497)*

Accounting	$3 \times 4 = 12$
History	$3 \times 3 = \ 9$
Psychology	$3 \times 3 = \ 9$
Algebra	$3 \times 3 = \ \underline{9}$
	39

$\dfrac{39}{12} = 3.25$

4. Ron's Sub Shop reported the following sales for the first 20 days of June. *(p. 500)*

$200	$400	$600	$400	$600
300	600	300	500	700
200	600	200	500	200
100	600	100	700	700

Prepare a frequency distribution for Ron.

Sales	Tally	Frequency
100	||	2
200	||||	4
300	||	2
400	||	2
500	||	2
600	⊮	5
700	|||	3

5. Star Company produced the following number of maps during the first 5 weeks of last year. Prepare a bar graph. *(p. 500)*

Week	Maps
1	800
2	700
3	300
4	750
5	400

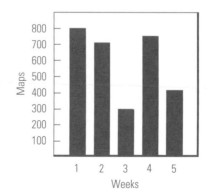

6. Leser Corporation reported record profits of 10%. It stated in the report that the cost of sales was 40% with expenses of 50%. Prepare a circle graph for Leser. *(p. 502)*

$.10 \times 360° = 36°$
$.40 \times 360° = 144°$
$.50 \times 360° = 180°$

7. Today a new LandRover costs $39,000. In 1990, the Rover cost $22,000. What is the price relative to the nearest tenth percent? *(p. 502)*

$$\frac{\$39,000}{\$22,000} \times 100 = 177.3\%$$

***8.** Calculate the standard deviation for the following set of data: 20, 32, 45, 26, 35, 42, 40. Round final answer to nearest tenth. *(p. 505)*

Data	Data − Mean	(Data − Mean)²
20	−14.28571429	204.0816328
32	−2.28571429	5.224489816
45	10.71428571	114.7959183
26	−8.28571429	68.6530613
35	0.71428571	0.5102040755
42	7.71428571	59.51020402
40	5.71428571	32.65306118
Total 240		Total 485.4285715

$240 \div 7 = 34.28571429$ mean
$485.4285715 \div (7 - 1) = 80.90476192$
$\sqrt{80.90476192} = 9.0$ standard deviation

*Optional problem.

A KIPLINGER APPROACH

A GROUP PROJECT Defend or reject the following business math issue based on the *Kiplinger's Personal Finance Magazine* article below:

STOCKS
The Mighty Coke Is Getting Beaten Up

By Brian Knestout

Imagine you're ringside at a prizefight. In one corner is the little-known challenger: a fearsome, pugnacious brute whose origins are shrouded in mystery. In the other corner is the renowned champion, a titan with a famous smile and a career followed by millions. But he's not smiling now. It's midway through the fight and he's slumped over on his stool, while his manager feverishly works to coax a little spring into his sluggish step and some power into his errant punches.

At this stage, things look bleak for our hypothetical champ. But the situation isn't so hypothetical if you're investing in **Coca-Cola**. The global economic crisis is the iron-fisted challenger, and Coke—the world's largest soft-drink company, with a globally recognized brand name and a stock-market value of $167 billion—is the struggling giant.

In addition to its flagship product, Coca-Cola produces well-known brands such as Sprite and Surge soft drinks and Fruitopia and Minute Maid juices. Sales totaled a whopping $18.9 billion in 1997 and $14.4 billion in the first nine months of 1998. But two-thirds of Coke's sales and a full three-fourths of its earnings in 1997 came from outside the U.S. Expansion into markets such as China, India and Russia figures prominently in its plans for future growth. Therein lies the problem.

Coke's dependence on overseas thirst has hurt it badly.

Coca-Cola

Symbol: KO (NYSE)
Recent share price: **$67**
Price a year ago: **$64**
Earnings per share:

'95	'96	'97	'98ᵉ	'99ᵉ
$1.18	$1.40	$1.64	$1.48	$1.65

ᵉestimate

Number of analysts who recommend:
- **Buy: 9**   ● **Hold/Sell: 8**

Shareholder information:
404-676-2121

Web site:
www.coca-cola.com

Source: Zacks Investment Research

Business Math Issue

In 1999, Coke plans to enter the bottled water business. This move will hurt sales of diet drinks.

1. List the key points of the article and information to support your position.
2. Write a group defense of your position using math calculations to support your view.

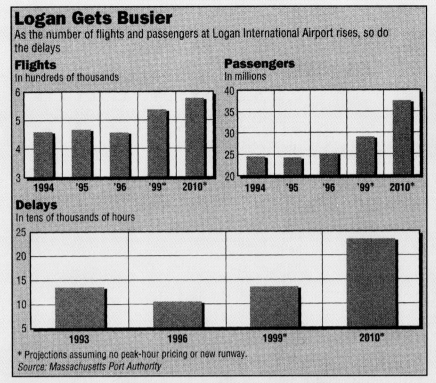

Logan Gets Busier

As the number of flights and passengers at Logan International Airport rises, so do the delays

Flights
In hundreds of thousands

Passengers
In millions

Delays
In tens of thousands of hours

* Projections assuming no peak-hour pricing or new runway.
Source: Massachusetts Port Authority

Logan Plans Peak Pricing, To Small Airlines' Dismay

By SHIRLEY LEUNG
Staff Reporter of THE WALL STREET JOURNAL

To ease increasing congestion caused by a growing armada of commuter planes, Logan International Airport is moving ahead with a plan to impose fees on take-offs and landings during peak hours.

The fees — preliminarily set between $125 and $150 for each landing and takeoff — would mark the second time Logan has attempted to use "peak period pricing" to discourage commuter planes from clogging the runways. The first effort, in 1988, ended after six months when a federal judge ruled that the policy discriminated against small aircraft by charging them higher fees than large jets. Part of the problem was also that the "peak hours" lasted most of the day instead of during the airport's busiest time.

This time, though, officials at the Massachusetts Port Authority, the agency that oversees Logan, are developing a plan that would impose a flat fee on all planes during designated peak hours. Airport planners are still trying to figure out whether a peak period will mean a block of time, an entire season or some combination.

Project A
Interpret the above graph. Will peak pricing solve the problem?

 See text Web site (www.mhhe.com/slater) and *The Business Math Internet Resource Guide.*

A ADDITIONAL HOMEWORK ASSIGNMENTS BY LEARNING UNIT

LEARNING UNIT 1.1: Reading, Writing, and Rounding Whole Numbers

DRILL PROBLEMS

1. Express the following numbers in verbal form:
   a. 8,295   Eight thousand, two hundred ninety-five _____

   b. 160,501   One hundred sixty thousand, five hundred one _____

   c. 2,098,767   Two million, ninety-eight thousand, seven hundred sixty-seven _____

   d. 58,003   Fifty-eight thousand, three _____

   e. 50,025,212,015   Fifty billion, twenty-five million, two hundred twelve thousand, fifteen _____

2. Write in numeric form:
   a. Seventy thousand, one hundred eighty-two   70,182
   b. Fifty-eight thousand, three   58,003
   c. Two hundred eighty thousand, five   280,005
   d. Three million, ten   3,000,010
   e. Sixty-seven thousand, seven hundred sixty   67,760

3. Round the following numbers:
   a. To the nearest ten:
      42   40   379   380   855   860   5,981   5,980   206   210

   b. To the nearest hundred:
      9,664   9,700   2,074   2,100   888   900   271   300   75   100

   c. To the nearest thousand:
      21,486   21,000   621   1,000   3,504   4,000   9,735   10,000

4. Round off each number to the nearest ten, nearest hundred, nearest thousand, and round all the way. (Remember that you are rounding the original number each time.)

		Nearest ten	Nearest hundred	Nearest thousand	Round all the way
a.	4,752	4,750	4,800	5,000	5,000
b.	70,351	70,350	70,400	70,000	70,000
c.	9,386	9,390	9,400	9,000	9,000
d.	4,983	4,980	5,000	5,000	5,000
e.	408,119	408,120	408,100	408,000	400,000
f.	30,051	30,050	30,100	30,000	30,000

5. Name the place position (place value) of the underlined digit.
   a. 8,348   hundreds place _____
   b. 9,734   thousands place _____
   c. 347,107   ten thousands place _____
   d. 723   tens place _____
   e. 28,200,000,121   billions place _____
   f. 706,359,005   ten millions place _____
   g. 27,563,530   hundred thousands place _____

WORD PROBLEMS

6. Ken Lawler was shopping for a computer. He went to three different stores and found the computer he wanted at three different prices. At Store A the price was $2,115, at Store B the price was $1,990, and at Store C the price was $2,050. What is the approximate price Ken will have to pay for the computer? Round to the nearest thousand. (Just one price.)

Approximately $2,000

7. Amy Parker had to write a check at the bookstore when she purchased her books for the new semester. The total cost of the books was $384. How will she write this amount in verbal form on her check?

Three hundred eighty-four

8. Matt Schaeffer was listening to the news and heard that steel production last week was one million, five hundred eighty-seven thousand tons. Express this amount in numeric form.

1,587,000 tons

9. Jackie Martin is the city clerk and must go to the aldermen's meetings and take notes on what is discussed. At last night's meeting, they were discussing repairs for the public library, which will cost three hundred seventy-five thousand, nine hundred eighty-five dollars. Write this in numeric form as Jackie would.

$375,985

10. A government survey revealed that 25,963,400 people are employed as office workers. To show the approximate number of office workers, round the number all the way.

30,000,000 office workers

11. Bob Donaldson wished to present his top student with a certificate of achievement at the end of the school year in 2001. To make it appear more official, he wanted to write the year in verbal form. How did he write the year?

Two thousand, one

12. Nancy Morrissey has a problem reading large numbers and determining place value. She asked her brother to name the place value of the 4 in the number 13,542,966. Can you tell Nancy the place value of the 4? What is the place value of the 3?

The 4 is in the ___ten thousands___ place.

The 3 is in the ___millions___ place.

LEARNING UNIT 1.2:   Adding and Subtracting Whole Numbers

DRILL PROBLEMS

1. Add by totaling each separate column:

	a.		b.		c.		d.		e.		f.		g.		h.
	695		43		493		36		716		535		751		75,730
	139		58		826		76		458		107		378		48,531
	14		96		9		43		397		778		135		15,797
	12		17		11		24		139		215		747		8
	7		18		1 2		19		478		391		368		15
	834		197		1,319		16		38		26		29		1 9
							179		25		20		25		18
									1 9		1 8		2 1		12
									2,188		2,026		2,379		140,058

2. Estimate by rounding all the way, then add the actual numbers:

	a.			b.			c.	
	580	600		1,470	1,000		475	500
	971	1,000		7,631	8,000		837	800
	548	500		4,383	4,000		213	200
	430	400		13,484	13,000		775	800
	506	500					432	400
	3,035	3,000					2,732	2,700

	d.			e.			f.	
	442	400		2,571	3,000		10,928	10,000
	609	600		3,625	4,000		9,321	9,000
	766	800		4,091	4,000		12,654	10,000
	410	400		928	900		15,492	20,000
	128	100		11,215	11,900		48,395	49,000
	2,355	2,300						

3. Estimate by rounding all the way, then subtract the actual numbers:

	a.			b.			c.	
	81	80		91	90		68	70
	− 42	− 40		− 33	− 30		− 59	− 60
	39	40		58	60		9	10

	d.			e.			f.	
	981	1,000		622	600		1,125	1,000
	− 283	− 300		− 328	− 300		− 913	− 900
	698	700		294	300		212	100

4. Subtract and check:

	a.			b.			c.	
	4,947	585		3,724	1,586		474,820	388,973
	− 4,362	+ 4,362		− 2,138	+ 2,138		− 85,847	+ 85,847
	585	4,947		1,586	3,724		388,973	474,820

	d.			e.			f.	
	50,000	28,238		65,003	40,016		15,715	12,212
	− 21,762	+ 21,762		− 24,987	+ 24,987		− 3,503	+ 3,503
	28,238	50,000		40,016	65,003		12,212	15,715

5. In the following sales report, total the rows and the columns, then check that the grand total is the same both horizontally and vertically.

Salesperson	Region 1	Region 2	Region 3	Total
a. Becker	$ 5,692	$ 7,403	$ 3,591	$16,686
b. Edwards	7,652	7,590	3,021	18,263
c. Graff	6,545	6,738	4,545	17,828
d. Jackson	6,937	6,950	4,913	18,800
e. Total	$26,826	$28,681	$16,070	$71,577

WORD PROBLEMS

6. Tom Griffin owes $4,921 on his car loan, plus interest of $541. How much will it cost him to pay off this loan?

$4,921 + $541 = $5,462 to pay off loan

7. Sales at Rich's Convenience Store were $3,587 on Monday, $3,944 on Tuesday, $4,007 on Wednesday, $3,890 on Thursday, and $4,545 on Friday. What were the total sales for the week?

$ 3,587
   3,944
   4,007
   3,890
   4,545

$19,973 total sales

8. Poor's Variety Store sold $5,000 worth of lottery tickets in the first week of August; it sold $289 less in the second week. How much were the lottery ticket sales in the second week of August?

$5,000 − $289 = $4,711 in lottery ticket sales

9. A truck weighed 9,550 pounds when it was empty. After being filled with rubbish, it was driven to the dump where it weighed in at 22,347 pounds. How much did the rubbish weigh?

22,347 − 9,550 = 12,797 pounds of rubbish

10. Lynn Jackson had $549 in her checking account when she went to the bookstore. Lynn purchased an accounting book for $62, the working papers for $28, a study guide for $25, and a mechanical pencil for $5. After Lynn writes a check for the entire purchase, how much money will remain in her checking account?

$ 62 $549
  28   − 120
  25             $429 remaining balance
   5

$120 total of purchase

11. A new hard-body truck is advertised with a base price of $6,986 delivered. However, the window sticker on the truck reads as follows: tinted glass, $210; automatic transmission, $650; power steering, $210; power brakes, $215; safety locks, $95; air conditioning, $1,056. Estimate the total price, including the accessories, by rounding all the way and *then* calculating the exact price.

$7,000 $6,986
   200   210
   700   650
   200   210
   200   215
   100   95
1,000   1,056

$9,400 $9,422

12. Four different stores are offering the same make and model of camcorder:

Store A	Store B	Store C	Store D
$1,285	$1,380	$1,440	$1,355

Find the difference between the highest price and the lowest price. Check your answer.

Check

$1,440 $ 155
− 1,285   + 1,285

$ 155 $1,440

13. The August 1997 issue of *Smart Money* compared the discounts in office supplies. A Xerox XC830 copy machine has a suggested retail price of $1,395. The net price is $649. How much is the discount on the copy machine?

$1,395
− 649

$ 746 discount

LEARNING UNIT 1.3:   Multiplying and Dividing Whole Numbers

DRILL PROBLEMS

1. In the following problems, first estimate by rounding all the way, then work the actual problems and check:

	Actual	Estimate	Check
a.	151 $\times$ 14 ‾‾‾‾ 604 151 ‾‾‾‾ 2,114	200 $\times$ 10 ‾‾‾‾ 2,000	$4 \times 151 =$ 604 $10 \times 151 = 1{,}510$ ‾‾‾‾ 2,114
b.	4,216 $\times$ 45 ‾‾‾‾ 21080 16864 ‾‾‾‾ 189,720	4,000 $\times$ 50 ‾‾‾‾ 200,000	$5 \times 4{,}216 =$ 21,080 $40 \times 4{,}216 = 168{,}640$ ‾‾‾‾ 189,720
c.	52,376 $\times$ 309 ‾‾‾‾ 471384 1571280 ‾‾‾‾ 16,184,184	50,000 $\times$ 300 ‾‾‾‾ 15,000,000	$9 \times 52{,}376 =$ 471,384 $300 \times 52{,}376 = 15{,}712{,}800$ ‾‾‾‾ 16,184,184
d.	3,106 $\times$ 28 ‾‾‾‾ 24848 6212 ‾‾‾‾ 86,968	3,000 $\times$ 30 ‾‾‾‾ 90,000	$8 \times 3{,}106 =$ 24,848 $20 \times 3{,}106 =$ 62,120 ‾‾‾‾ 86,968

2. Multiply (use the shortcut when applicable):

a. 4,072
   $\times$ 100
   ‾‾‾‾
   407,200
   $1 \times 4{,}072 + 2$ zeros $= 407{,}200$

b. 5,100
   $\times$ 40
   ‾‾‾‾
   204,000
   $4 \times 51 + 3$ zeros $= 204{,}000$

c. 76,000
   $\times$ 1,200
   ‾‾‾‾
   91,200,000
   $12 \times 76 + 5$ zeros $= 91{,}200{,}000$

d. $93 \times 100{,}000 = 9{,}300{,}000$
   $93 \times 1 + 5$ zeros $= 9{,}300{,}000$

3. Divide by rounding all the way; then do the actual calculation and check showing the remainder as a whole number.

	Actual	Estimate	Check
a.	963 R5 8)7,709 7 2 ‾‾ 50 48 ‾‾ 29 24 ‾‾ 5	1,000 8)8,000	$8 \times 963 = 7{,}704$ $+ 5$ ‾‾‾ 7,709
b.	227 R8 26)5,910 5 2 ‾‾ 71 52 ‾‾ 190 182 ‾‾ 8	200 30)6,000	$26 \times 227 = 5{,}902$ $+ 8$ ‾‾‾ 5,910

	Actual	Estimate	Check

c. $151\overline{)3{,}783}$ 25 R8

$$\frac{3\ 02}{}$$

763
755

$$\frac{}{8}$$

Estimate: $200\overline{)4{,}000}$ 20

Check: $151 \times 25 = 3{,}775$

$+\ 8$

$3{,}783$

d. $46\overline{)19{,}550}$ 425

18 4

$$\frac{}{1\ 15}$$

92

$$\frac{}{230}$$

230

Estimate: $50\overline{)20{,}000}$ 400

Check: $46 \times 425 = 19{,}550$

4. Divide by the shortcut method:

        27
a. $200\overline{)5{,}400}$
    Drop 2 zeros: $54 \div 2 = 27$

        113
b. $50\overline{)5{,}650}$
    Drop 1 zero: $565 \div 5 = 113$

        36
c. $1{,}200\overline{)43{,}200}$
    Drop 2 zeros: $432 \div 12 = 36$

        30
d. $17{,}000\overline{)510{,}000}$
    Drop 3 zeros: $510 \div 17 = 30$

WORD PROBLEMS

5. Jeanne Francis sells state lottery tickets in her variety store. If Jeanne's Variety Store sells 385 lottery tickets per day, how many tickets will be sold in a 7-day period?
$385 \times 7 = 2{,}695$ lottery tickets

6. Arlex Oil Company employs 100 people who are eligible for profit sharing. The financial manager has announced that the profits to be shared amount to $64,000. How much will each employee receive?
$\$64{,}000 \div 100 = \$640$ per employee

7. John Duncan's employer withheld $4,056 in federal taxes from his pay for the year. If equal deductions are made each week, what is John's weekly deduction?
$\$4{,}056 \div 52 = \$78$ weekly withholding

8. Anne Domingoes drives a Volvo that gets 32 miles per gallon of gasoline. How many miles can she travel on 25 gallons of gas?
$32 \times 25 = 800$ miles

9. How many 8-inch pieces of yellow ribbon can be cut from a spool of ribbon that contains 6 yards (1 yard = 36 inches)?
$6 \times 36 = 216$ total inches of ribbon $216 \div 8 = 27$ pieces of ribbon

10. The number of commercials aired per day on a local television station is 672. How many commercials are aired in 1 year?
$672 \times 365 = 245{,}280$ commercials per year

11. The computer department at City College purchased 18 computers at a cost of $2,400 each. What was the total price for the computer purchase?
$\$2{,}400 \times 18 = \$43{,}200$ total price

12. Net income for Goodwin's Partnership was $64,500. The five partners share profits and losses equally. What was each partner's share?
$\$64{,}500 \div 5 = \$12{,}900$ per partner

13. Ben Krenshaw's supervisor at the construction site told Ben to divide a load of 1,423 bricks into stacks containing 35 bricks each. How many stacks will there be when Ben has finished the job? How many "extra" bricks will there be?

       40 R23
$35\overline{)1{,}423}$ 40 stacks, and 23 "extra" bricks

1 40

$$\frac{}{23}$$

LEARNING UNIT 2.1: Types of Fractions and Conversion Procedures

DRILL PROBLEMS

1. Identify the type of fraction—proper, improper, or mixed number:

   a. $\dfrac{12}{11}$ Improper   **b.** $\dfrac{27}{29}$ Proper   **c.** $\dfrac{29}{27}$ Improper

   d. $9\dfrac{3}{11}$ Mixed number   **e.** $\dfrac{18}{5}$ Improper   **f.** $\dfrac{30}{37}$ Proper

2. Convert to a mixed number:

   a. $\dfrac{29}{4}$
   $$4\overline{)29}^{\,7\frac{1}{4}}$$
   $$\underline{28}$$
   $$1$$

   b. $\dfrac{137}{8}$
   $$8\overline{)137}^{\,17\frac{1}{8}}$$
   $$\underline{8}$$
   $$57$$
   $$\underline{56}$$
   $$1$$

   c. $\dfrac{27}{5}$
   $$5\overline{)27}^{\,5\frac{2}{5}}$$
   $$\underline{25}$$
   $$2$$

   d. $\dfrac{29}{9}$
   $$9\overline{)29}^{\,3\frac{2}{9}}$$
   $$\underline{27}$$
   $$2$$

   e. $\dfrac{71}{8}$
   $$8\overline{)71}^{\,8\frac{7}{8}}$$
   $$\underline{64}$$
   $$7$$

   f. $\dfrac{43}{6}$
   $$6\overline{)43}^{\,7\frac{1}{6}}$$
   $$\underline{42}$$
   $$1$$

3. Convert the mixed number to an improper fraction:

   a. $7\dfrac{1}{5} = \dfrac{(5 \times 7) + 1}{5} = \dfrac{36}{5}$ **b.** $12\dfrac{3}{11} = \dfrac{(11 \times 12) + 3}{11} = \dfrac{135}{11}$

   c. $4\dfrac{3}{7} = \dfrac{(7 \times 4) + 3}{7} = \dfrac{31}{7}$ **d.** $20\dfrac{4}{9} = \dfrac{(9 \times 20) + 4}{9} = \dfrac{184}{9}$

   e. $10\dfrac{11}{12} = \dfrac{(12 \times 10) + 11}{12} = \dfrac{131}{12}$ **f.** $17\dfrac{2}{3} = \dfrac{(3 \times 17) + 2}{3} = \dfrac{53}{3}$

4. Tell whether the fractions in each pair are equivalent or not:

   a. $\dfrac{3}{4}\quad\dfrac{9}{12}$ Yes   **b.** $\dfrac{2}{3}\quad\dfrac{12}{18}$ Yes   **c.** $\dfrac{7}{8}\quad\dfrac{15}{16}$ No

   d. $\dfrac{4}{5}\quad\dfrac{12}{15}$ Yes   **e.** $\dfrac{3}{2}\quad\dfrac{9}{4}$ No   **f.** $\dfrac{5}{8}\quad\dfrac{7}{11}$ No

   g. $\dfrac{7}{12}\quad\dfrac{7}{24}$ No   **h.** $\dfrac{5}{4}\quad\dfrac{30}{24}$ Yes   **i.** $\dfrac{10}{26}\quad\dfrac{12}{26}$ No

5. Find the greatest common divisor by the step approach and reduce to lowest terms:

   a. $\dfrac{36}{42}$
   $$36\overline{)42}^{\,1}$$
   $$\underline{36}$$
   $$6\nearrow$$
   $$6\overline{)36}^{\,6}$$
   $$\underline{36}$$
   $$0$$
   $$\dfrac{36 \div 6}{42 \div 6} = \dfrac{6}{7}$$

   b. $\dfrac{30}{75}$
   $$30\overline{)75}^{\,2}$$
   $$\underline{60}$$
   $$15\nearrow$$
   $$15\overline{)30}^{\,2}$$
   $$\underline{30}$$
   $$0$$
   $$\dfrac{30 \div 15}{75 \div 15} = \dfrac{2}{5}$$

   c. $\dfrac{74}{148}$
   $$74\overline{)148}^{\,2}$$
   $$\underline{148}$$
   $$0$$
   $$\dfrac{74 \div 74}{148 \div 74} = \dfrac{1}{2}$$

   d. $\dfrac{15}{600}$
   $$15\overline{)600}^{\,40}$$
   $$\underline{60}$$
   $$00$$
   $$\dfrac{15 \div 15}{600 \div 15} = \dfrac{1}{40}$$

   e. $\dfrac{96}{132}$
   $$96\overline{)132}^{\,1}$$
   $$\underline{96}$$
   $$36\nearrow$$
   $$36\overline{)96}^{\,2}$$
   $$\underline{72}$$
   $$24\nearrow$$
   $$24\overline{)36}^{\,1}$$
   $$\underline{24}$$
   $$12\nearrow$$
   $$12\overline{)24}^{\,2}$$
   $$\underline{24}$$
   $$0$$
   $$\dfrac{96 \div 12}{132 \div 12} = \dfrac{8}{11}$$

f. $\dfrac{84}{154}$ $\quad 84\overline{)154}$ $\quad 70\overline{)84}$ $\quad 14\overline{)70}$ $\quad \dfrac{84 \div 14}{154 \div 14} = \dfrac{6}{11}$

$\quad\quad\quad\quad\quad \underline{84} \quad\quad \underline{70} \quad\quad \underline{70}$

$\quad\quad\quad\quad\quad\quad 70 \quad\quad\quad\quad 14 \quad\quad\quad\quad 0$

6. Convert to higher terms:

a. $\dfrac{8}{10} = \dfrac{}{70}$ $\quad 10\overline{)70}^{\,7}$ $\quad 7 \times 8 = 56$ $\quad \dfrac{8}{10} = \dfrac{56}{70}$

b. $\dfrac{2}{15} = \dfrac{}{30}$ $\quad 15\overline{)30}^{\,2}$ $\quad 2 \times 2 = 4$ $\quad \dfrac{2}{15} = \dfrac{4}{30}$

c. $\dfrac{6}{11} = \dfrac{}{132}$ $\quad 11\overline{)132}^{\,12}$ $\quad 12 \times 6 = 72$ $\quad \dfrac{6}{11} = \dfrac{72}{132}$

d. $\dfrac{4}{9} = \dfrac{}{36}$ $\quad 9\overline{)36}^{\,4}$ $\quad 4 \times 4 = 16$ $\quad \dfrac{4}{9} = \dfrac{16}{36}$

e. $\dfrac{7}{20} = \dfrac{}{100}$ $\quad 20\overline{)100}^{\,5}$ $\quad 7 \times 5 = 35$ $\quad \dfrac{7}{20} = \dfrac{35}{100}$

f. $\dfrac{7}{8} = \dfrac{}{560}$ $\quad 8\overline{)560}^{\,70}$ $\quad 7 \times 70 = 490$ $\quad \dfrac{7}{8} = \dfrac{490}{560}$

WORD PROBLEMS

7. Ken drove to college in $3\frac{1}{4}$ hours. How many quarter-hours is that? Show your answer as an improper fraction.

$$3\frac{1}{4} = \frac{(4 \times 3) + 1}{4} = \frac{13}{4} \text{ hours}$$

8. Mary looked in the refrigerator for a dozen eggs. When she found the box, only 5 eggs were left. What fractional part of the box of eggs was left?

$\dfrac{5}{12}$ of the box

9. At a recent meeting of a local Boosters Club, 17 of the 25 members attending were men. What fraction of those in attendance were men?

$\dfrac{17}{25}$ men

10. By weight, water is two parts out of three parts of the human body. What fraction of the body is water?

$\dfrac{2}{3}$ of the body is water

11. Three out of 5 students who begin college will continue until they receive their degree. Show in fractional form how many out of 100 beginning students will graduate.

$\dfrac{3}{5} = \dfrac{60}{100}$

12. Tina and her friends came in late to a party and found only $\frac{3}{4}$ of a pizza remaining. In order for everyone to get some pizza, she wanted to divide it into smaller pieces. If she divides the pizza into twelfths, how many pieces will she have? Show your answer in fractional form.

$\dfrac{3}{4} = \dfrac{9}{12}$

13. Sharon and Spunky noted that it took them 35 minutes to do their exercise routine. What fractional part of an hour is that? Show your answer in lowest terms.

$\dfrac{35}{60} = \dfrac{35 \div 5}{60 \div 5} = \dfrac{7}{12}$

14. Norman and his friend ordered several pizzas, which were all cut into eighths. The group ate 43 pieces of pizza. How many pizzas did they eat? Show your answer as a mixed number.

$\dfrac{43}{8} = 5\dfrac{3}{8}$ $\quad 8\overline{)43}^{\,5\,R3}$

$\phantom{\dfrac{43}{8} = 5\dfrac{3}{8} \quad} \underline{40}$

$\phantom{\dfrac{43}{8} = 5\dfrac{3}{8} \quad\quad} 3$

LEARNING UNIT 2.2:   Adding and Subtracting Fractions

DRILL PROBLEMS

1. Find the least common denominator (LCD) for each of the following groups of denominators using the prime numbers:

a. 8, 16, 32

$$2\underline{/\quad 8\quad 16\quad 32}$$
$$2\underline{/\quad 4\quad 8\quad 16}$$
$$2\underline{/\quad 2\quad 4\quad 8}$$
$$\quad\quad 1\quad 2\quad 4$$

$2 \times 2 \times 2 \times 1 \times 2 \times 4 = 64$

b. 9, 15, 20

$$3\underline{/\quad 9\quad 15\quad 20}$$
$$5\underline{/\quad 3\quad 5\quad 20}$$
$$\quad\quad 3\quad 1\quad 4$$

$3 \times 5 \times 3 \times 1 \times 4 = 180$

c. 12, 15, 32

$$2\underline{/\quad 12\quad 15\quad 32}$$
$$2\underline{/\quad 6\quad 15\quad 16}$$
$$3\underline{/\quad 3\quad 15\quad 8}$$
$$\quad\quad 1\quad 5\quad 8$$

$2 \times 2 \times 3 \times 1 \times 5 \times 8 = 480$

d. 7, 9, 14, 28

$$2\underline{/\quad 7\quad 9\quad 14\quad 28}$$
$$7\underline{/\quad 7\quad 9\quad 7\quad 14}$$
$$\quad\quad 1\quad 9\quad 1\quad 2$$

$2 \times 7 \times 1 \times 9 \times 1 \times 2 = 252$

2. Add and reduce to lowest terms or change to a mixed number if needed:

a. $\dfrac{2}{7} + \dfrac{3}{7} = \dfrac{5}{7}$

b. $\dfrac{5}{12} + \dfrac{8}{15} = \dfrac{25}{60} + \dfrac{32}{60} = \dfrac{57}{60} = \dfrac{19}{20}$

$\dfrac{5}{12} = \dfrac{?}{60} = \dfrac{25}{60}$ $\dfrac{8}{15} = \dfrac{?}{60} = \dfrac{32}{60}$

c. $\dfrac{7}{8} + \dfrac{5}{12} = 1\dfrac{7}{24} = \dfrac{31}{24} = 24\overline{)31}^{\,1\,R7} = 1\dfrac{7}{24}$

$\dfrac{21}{24} + \dfrac{10}{24} = \dfrac{31}{24}$ $\dfrac{24}{7}$

$\dfrac{7}{8} = \dfrac{?}{24} = \dfrac{21}{24}$ $\dfrac{5}{12} = \dfrac{?}{24} = \dfrac{10}{24}$

d. $7\dfrac{2}{3} + 5\dfrac{1}{4} = 12\dfrac{11}{12}$

$\dfrac{2}{3} = \dfrac{?}{12} = \dfrac{8}{12}$

$\dfrac{1}{4} = \dfrac{?}{12} = \dfrac{3}{12}$

$\begin{array}{r} 7\dfrac{2}{3} \\ +\,5\dfrac{1}{4} \\ \hline \end{array}$ $\begin{array}{r} 7\dfrac{8}{12} \\ +\,5\dfrac{3}{12} \\ \hline 12\dfrac{11}{12} \end{array}$

e. $\dfrac{2}{3} + \dfrac{4}{9} + \dfrac{1}{4} = 1\dfrac{13}{36}$ $\dfrac{24}{36} + \dfrac{16}{36} + \dfrac{9}{36} = \dfrac{49}{36} = 36\overline{)49}^{\,1\,R13} = 1\dfrac{13}{36}$ $\dfrac{36}{13}$

$\dfrac{2}{3} = \dfrac{?}{36} = \dfrac{24}{36}$ $\dfrac{4}{9} = \dfrac{?}{36} = \dfrac{16}{36}$ $\dfrac{1}{4} = \dfrac{?}{36} = \dfrac{9}{36}$

3. Subtract and reduce to lowest terms:

a. $\dfrac{5}{9} - \dfrac{2}{9} = \dfrac{3}{9} = \dfrac{1}{3}$

b. $\dfrac{14}{15} - \dfrac{4}{15} = \dfrac{10}{15} = \dfrac{2}{3}$

c. $\dfrac{8}{9} - \dfrac{5}{6} = \dfrac{1}{18}$

$\dfrac{16}{18} - \dfrac{15}{18} = \dfrac{1}{18}$

d. $\dfrac{7}{12} - \dfrac{9}{16} = \dfrac{1}{48}$

$\dfrac{28}{48} - \dfrac{27}{48} = \dfrac{1}{48}$

e. $33\dfrac{5}{8} - 27\dfrac{1}{2} = 6\dfrac{1}{8}$

$\begin{array}{r} 33\dfrac{5}{8} \\ -\,27\dfrac{1}{2} \\ \hline \end{array}$ $\begin{array}{r} 33\dfrac{5}{8} \\ -\,27\dfrac{4}{8} \\ \hline 6\dfrac{1}{8} \end{array}$

f. $9 - 2\dfrac{3}{7} = 6\dfrac{4}{7}$

$\begin{array}{r} 9 \\ -\,2\dfrac{3}{7} \\ \hline \end{array}$ $\begin{array}{r} 8\dfrac{7}{7} \\ -\,2\dfrac{3}{7} \\ \hline 6\dfrac{4}{7} \end{array}$

g. $15\dfrac{1}{3} - 9\dfrac{7}{12} = 5\dfrac{3}{4}$

$\begin{array}{r} 15\dfrac{1}{3} \\ -\,9\dfrac{7}{12} \\ \hline \end{array}$ $\begin{array}{r} 15\dfrac{4}{12} \\ -\,9\dfrac{7}{12} \\ \hline \end{array}$ $\begin{array}{r} 14\dfrac{16}{12} \\ -\,9\dfrac{7}{12} \\ \hline 5\dfrac{9}{12} = 5\dfrac{3}{4} \end{array}$

h. $92\dfrac{3}{10} - 35\dfrac{7}{15} = 56\dfrac{5}{6}$

$\begin{array}{r} 92\dfrac{3}{10} \\ -\,35\dfrac{7}{15} \\ \hline \end{array}$ $\begin{array}{r} 92\dfrac{9}{30} \\ -\,35\dfrac{14}{30} \\ \hline \end{array}$ $\begin{array}{r} 91\dfrac{39}{30} \\ -\,35\dfrac{14}{30} \\ \hline 56\dfrac{25}{30} = 56\dfrac{5}{6} \end{array}$

i. $93 - 57\dfrac{5}{12} = 35\dfrac{7}{12}$

$\begin{array}{r} 93 \\ -\,57\dfrac{5}{12} \\ \hline \end{array}$ $\begin{array}{r} 92\dfrac{12}{12} \\ -\,57\dfrac{5}{12} \\ \hline 35\dfrac{7}{12} \end{array}$

j. $22\dfrac{5}{8} - 17\dfrac{1}{4} = 5\dfrac{3}{8}$

$\begin{array}{r} 22\dfrac{5}{8} \\ -\,17\dfrac{1}{4} \\ \hline \end{array}$ $\begin{array}{r} 22\dfrac{5}{8} \\ -\,17\dfrac{2}{8} \\ \hline 5\dfrac{3}{8} \end{array}$

WORD PROBLEMS

4. Dan Lund took a cross-country trip. He drove $5\frac{3}{8}$ hours on Monday, $6\frac{1}{2}$ hours on Tuesday, $9\frac{3}{4}$ hours on Wednesday, $6\frac{3}{8}$ hours on Thursday, and $10\frac{1}{4}$ hours on Friday. Find the total number of hours Dan drove in the first 5 days of his trip.

$$
\begin{array}{cc}
5\frac{3}{8} & 5\frac{3}{8} \\
6\frac{1}{2} & 6\frac{4}{8} \\
9\frac{3}{4} & 9\frac{6}{8} \\
6\frac{3}{8} & 6\frac{3}{8} \\
+10\frac{1}{4} & +10\frac{2}{8}
\end{array}
$$

$$36\frac{18}{8} = 36 + 2\frac{2}{8} = 38\frac{2}{8} = 38\frac{1}{4} \text{ hours driven}$$

5. Sharon Parker bought 20 yards of material to make curtains. She used $4\frac{1}{2}$ yards for one bedroom window, $8\frac{3}{5}$ yards for another bedroom window, and $3\frac{7}{8}$ yards for a hall window. How much material did she have left?

$$
\begin{array}{cc}
4\frac{1}{2} & 4\frac{20}{40} \\
8\frac{3}{5} & 8\frac{24}{40} \\
+3\frac{7}{8} & +3\frac{35}{40}
\end{array}
\qquad\qquad
\begin{array}{cc}
20 & 19\frac{40}{40} \\
-16\frac{39}{40} & -16\frac{39}{40} \\
& 3\frac{1}{40} \text{ yards of material left}
\end{array}
$$

$$15\frac{79}{40} = 15 + 1\frac{39}{40} = 16\frac{39}{40} \text{ material used}$$

6. On Friday, the opening stock price of MYCO Corporation was $43\frac{7}{8}$. The stock closed at $47\frac{1}{2}$. What was the amount of the increase in price?

$$
\begin{array}{ccc}
\$47\frac{1}{2} & \$47\frac{4}{8} & \$46\frac{12}{8} \\
-43\frac{7}{8} & -43\frac{7}{8} & -43\frac{7}{8} \\
& & \$\,3\frac{5}{8} \text{ increase}
\end{array}
$$

7. Bill Williams had to drive $46\frac{1}{4}$ miles to work. After driving $28\frac{5}{6}$ miles he noticed he was low on gas and had to decide whether he should stop to fill the gas tank. How many more miles does Bill have to drive to get to work?

$$
\begin{array}{ccc}
46\frac{1}{4} & 46\frac{3}{12} & 45\frac{15}{12} \\
-28\frac{5}{6} & -28\frac{10}{12} & -28\frac{10}{12} \\
& & 17\frac{5}{12} \text{ miles remaining}
\end{array}
$$

8. Albert's Lumber Yard purchased $52\frac{1}{2}$ cords of lumber on Monday and $48\frac{3}{4}$ cords on Tuesday. It sold $21\frac{3}{8}$ cords on Friday. How many cords of lumber remain at Albert's Lumber Yard?

$$
\begin{array}{cc}
52\frac{1}{2} & 52\frac{2}{4} \\
+48\frac{3}{4} & +48\frac{3}{4} \\
& 100\frac{5}{4} = 101\frac{1}{4} \text{ cords purchased}
\end{array}
\qquad
\begin{array}{ccc}
101\frac{1}{4} & 101\frac{2}{8} & 100\frac{10}{8} \\
-21\frac{3}{8} & -21\frac{3}{8} & -21\frac{3}{8} \\
& & 79\frac{7}{8} \text{ cords remain}
\end{array}
$$

9. At Arlen Oil Company, where Dave Bursett is the service manager, it took $42\frac{1}{3}$ hours to clean five boilers. After a new cleaning tool was purchased, the time for cleaning five boilers was reduced to $37\frac{4}{9}$ hours. How much time was saved?

$$
\begin{array}{ccc}
42\frac{1}{3} & 42\frac{3}{9} & 41\frac{12}{9} \\
-37\frac{4}{9} & -37\frac{4}{9} & -37\frac{4}{9} \\
& & 4\frac{8}{9} \text{ hours saved}
\end{array}
$$

LEARNING UNIT 2.3: Multiplying and Dividing Fractions

DRILL PROBLEMS

1. Multiply (use cancellation technique):

a. $\dfrac{6}{13} \times \dfrac{26}{12} = \dfrac{\overset{1}{\cancel{6}}}{\underset{1}{\cancel{13}}} \times \dfrac{\overset{2}{\cancel{26}}}{\underset{1}{\cancel{12}}} = 1$

b. $\dfrac{3}{8} \times \dfrac{2}{3} = \dfrac{\cancel{3}}{\underset{4}{\cancel{8}}} \times \dfrac{\cancel{2}}{\cancel{3}} = \dfrac{1}{4}$

c. $\dfrac{5}{7} \times \dfrac{9}{10} = \dfrac{\overset{1}{\cancel{5}}}{7} \times \dfrac{9}{\underset{2}{\cancel{10}}} = \dfrac{9}{14}$

d. $\dfrac{3}{4} \times \dfrac{9}{13} \times \dfrac{26}{27} = \dfrac{\overset{1}{\cancel{3}}}{\underset{2}{\cancel{4}}} \times \dfrac{\overset{1}{\cancel{9}}}{\cancel{13}} \times \dfrac{\overset{2}{\cancel{26}}}{\underset{\underset{1}{3}}{\cancel{27}}} = \dfrac{1}{2}$

e. $6\dfrac{2}{5} \times 3\dfrac{1}{8} = 20$

$\dfrac{\overset{4}{\cancel{32}}}{\underset{1}{\cancel{5}}} \times \dfrac{\overset{5}{\cancel{25}}}{\underset{1}{\cancel{8}}} = \dfrac{20}{1} = 20$

f. $2\dfrac{2}{3} \times 2\dfrac{7}{10} = 7\dfrac{1}{5}$

$\dfrac{\overset{4}{\cancel{8}}}{\underset{1}{\cancel{3}}} \times \dfrac{\overset{9}{\cancel{27}}}{\underset{5}{\cancel{10}}} = \dfrac{36}{5} = 7\dfrac{1}{5}$

g. $45 \times \dfrac{7}{9} = 35$

$\overset{5}{\cancel{45}} \times \dfrac{7}{\underset{1}{\cancel{9}}} = 35$

h. $3\dfrac{1}{9} \times 1\dfrac{2}{7} \times \dfrac{3}{4} = 3$

$\dfrac{\overset{\overset{4}{\cancel{28}}}{}}{\underset{1}{\cancel{9}}} \times \dfrac{\overset{1}{\cancel{9}}}{\underset{1}{\cancel{7}}} \times \dfrac{3}{\underset{1}{\cancel{4}}} = 3$

i. $\dfrac{3}{4} \times \dfrac{7}{9} \times 3\dfrac{1}{3} = 1\dfrac{17}{18}$

$\dfrac{\overset{1}{\cancel{3}}}{\underset{2}{\cancel{4}}} \times \dfrac{7}{9} \times \dfrac{\overset{5}{\cancel{10}}}{\underset{1}{\cancel{3}}} = \dfrac{35}{18} = 1\dfrac{17}{18}$

j. $\dfrac{1}{8} \times 6\dfrac{2}{3} \times \dfrac{1}{10} = \dfrac{1}{12}$

$\dfrac{1}{\underset{4}{\cancel{8}}} \times \dfrac{\overset{2}{\cancel{20}}}{3} \times \dfrac{1}{\underset{1}{\cancel{10}}} = \dfrac{1}{12}$

2. Multiply (do not use canceling; reduce by finding the greatest common divisor):

a. $\dfrac{3}{4} \times \dfrac{8}{9} = \dfrac{24 \div 12}{36 \div 12} = \dfrac{2}{3}$

$\begin{array}{r} 1 \\ 24)\overline{36} \\ 24 \\ \hline 12 \end{array} \quad \begin{array}{r} 2 \\ 12)\overline{24} \\ 24 \\ \hline 0 \end{array}$

b. $\dfrac{7}{16} \times \dfrac{8}{13} = \dfrac{56 \div 8}{208 \div 8} = \dfrac{7}{26}$

$\begin{array}{r} 3 \\ 56)\overline{208} \\ 168 \\ \hline 40 \end{array} \quad \begin{array}{r} 1 \\ 40)\overline{56} \\ 40 \\ \hline 16 \end{array} \quad \begin{array}{r} 2 \\ 16)\overline{40} \\ 32 \\ \hline 8 \end{array} \quad \begin{array}{r} 2 \\ 8)\overline{16} \\ 16 \\ \hline 0 \end{array}$

3. Multiply or divide as indicated:

a. $\dfrac{25}{36} \div \dfrac{5}{9} = \dfrac{25}{\underset{4}{\cancel{36}}} \times \dfrac{\overset{1}{\cancel{9}}}{\cancel{5}} = \dfrac{5}{4} = 1\dfrac{1}{4}$

b. $\dfrac{18}{8} \div \dfrac{12}{16} = \dfrac{\overset{3}{\cancel{18}}}{\underset{1}{\cancel{8}}} \times \dfrac{\overset{\overset{2}{\cancel{16}}}{}}{\underset{\underset{1}{2}}{\cancel{12}}} = 3$

c. $2\dfrac{6}{7} \div 2\dfrac{2}{5} = 1\dfrac{4}{21}$

$\dfrac{20}{7} \div \dfrac{12}{5} = \dfrac{\overset{5}{\cancel{20}}}{7} \times \dfrac{5}{\underset{3}{\cancel{12}}} = \dfrac{25}{21} = 1\dfrac{4}{21}$

d. $3\dfrac{1}{4} \div 16 = \dfrac{13}{64}$

$\dfrac{13}{4} \div \dfrac{16}{1} = \dfrac{13}{4} \times \dfrac{1}{16} = \dfrac{13}{64}$

e. $24 \div 1\dfrac{1}{3} = 18$

$\dfrac{24}{1} \div \dfrac{4}{3} = \dfrac{\overset{6}{\cancel{24}}}{1} \times \dfrac{3}{\underset{1}{\cancel{4}}} = 18$

f. $6 \times \dfrac{3}{2} = 9$

$\dfrac{\overset{3}{\cancel{6}}}{1} \times \dfrac{3}{\underset{1}{\cancel{2}}} = 9$

g. $3\frac{1}{5} \times 7\frac{1}{2} = 24$

$\dfrac{\overset{8}{\cancel{16}}}{\cancel{5}_1} \times \dfrac{\overset{3}{\cancel{15}}}{\cancel{2}_1} = 24$

h. $\dfrac{3}{8} \div \dfrac{7}{4} = \dfrac{3}{14}$

$\dfrac{3}{\cancel{8}_2} \times \dfrac{\overset{1}{\cancel{4}}}{7} = \dfrac{3}{14}$

i. $9 \div 3\frac{3}{4} = 2\frac{2}{5}$

$\dfrac{9}{1} \div \dfrac{15}{4} = \dfrac{\overset{3}{\cancel{9}}}{1} \times \dfrac{4}{\cancel{15}_5} = \dfrac{12}{5} = 2\frac{2}{5}$

j. $\dfrac{11}{24} \times \dfrac{24}{33} = \dfrac{1}{3}$

$\dfrac{\overset{1}{\cancel{11}}}{\cancel{24}_1} \times \dfrac{\overset{1}{\cancel{24}}}{\cancel{33}_3} = \dfrac{1}{3}$

k. $\dfrac{12}{14} \div 27 = \dfrac{2}{63}$

$\dfrac{12}{14} \div \dfrac{27}{1} = \dfrac{\overset{\overset{2}{\cancel{4}}}{\cancel{12}}}{\cancel{14}_7} \times \dfrac{1}{\cancel{27}_9} = \dfrac{2}{63}$

l. $\dfrac{3}{5} \times \dfrac{2}{7} \div \dfrac{3}{10} = \dfrac{4}{7}$

$\dfrac{\overset{1}{\cancel{3}}}{\cancel{5}_1} \times \dfrac{2}{7} \times \dfrac{\overset{2}{\cancel{10}}}{\cancel{3}_1} = \dfrac{4}{7}$

WORD PROBLEMS

4. Mary Smith plans to make 12 meatloafs to store in her freezer. Each meatloaf requires $2\frac{1}{4}$ pounds of ground beef. How much ground beef does Mary need?

$12 \times 2\frac{1}{4} = \overset{3}{\cancel{12}} \times \dfrac{9}{\cancel{4}_1} = 27$ pounds

5. Judy Carter purchased a real estate lot for $24,000. She sold it 2 years later for $1\frac{5}{8}$ times as much as she had paid for it. What was the selling price?

$\$24,000 \times 1\frac{5}{8} = \overset{3,000}{\cancel{\$24,000}} \times \dfrac{13}{\cancel{8}_1} = \$39,000$

6. Lynn Clarkson saw an ad for a camcorder that cost $980. She knew of a discount store that would sell it to her for a markdown of $\frac{3}{20}$ off the advertised price. How much is the discount she can get?

$\overset{49}{\cancel{\$980}} \times \dfrac{3}{\cancel{20}_1} = \$147$ discount

7. To raise money for their club, the members of the Marketing Club purchased 68 bushels of popcorn to resell. They plan to repackage the popcorn in bags that hold $\frac{2}{21}$ of a bushel each. How many bags of popcorn will they be able to fill?

$68 \div \dfrac{2}{21} = \overset{34}{\cancel{68}} \times \dfrac{21}{\cancel{2}_1} = 714$ bags

8. Richard Tracy paid a total of $375 for stocks costing $\$9\frac{3}{8}$ per share. How many shares did he purchase?

$\$375 \div \$9\frac{3}{8} = 375 \div \dfrac{75}{8} = \overset{5}{\cancel{375}} \times \dfrac{8}{\cancel{75}_1} = 40$ shares

9. While training for a marathon, Kristin Woods jogged $7\frac{3}{4}$ miles per hour for $2\frac{2}{3}$ hours. How many miles did Kristin jog?

$7\frac{3}{4} \times 2\frac{2}{3} = \dfrac{31}{\cancel{4}_1} \times \dfrac{\overset{2}{\cancel{8}}}{3} = \dfrac{62}{3} = 20\frac{2}{3}$ miles

10. On a map, 1 inch represents 240 miles. How many miles are represented by $\frac{3}{8}$ of an inch?

$\overset{30}{\cancel{240}} \times \dfrac{3}{\cancel{8}_1} = 90$ miles

11. In Massachusetts, the governor wants to allot $\frac{1}{6}$ of the total sales tax collections to public education. The total sales tax collected is $2,472,000; how much will go to education?

$\overset{412,000}{\cancel{\$2,472,000}} \times \dfrac{1}{\cancel{6}_1} = \$412,000$ to education

LEARNING UNIT 3.1: Rounding; Fraction and Decimal Conversions

DRILL PROBLEMS

1. Write in decimal:
   a. Sixty-five hundredths   .65 _____
   b. Three tenths   .3 _____
   c. Nine hundred fifty-three thousandths   .953 _____
   d. Four hundred one thousandths   .401 _____
   e. Six hundredths   .06 _____

2. Round each decimal to the place indicated:
   a. .4326 to the nearest thousandth   .433 _____
   b. .051 to the nearest tenth   .1 _____
   c. 8.207 to the nearest hundredth   8.21 _____
   d. 2.094 to the nearest hundredth   2.09 _____
   e. .511172 to the nearest ten thousandth   .5112 _____

3. Name the place position of the underlined digit:
   a. .8$\underline{2}$6   Hundredths place _____
   b. .91$\underline{4}$ Thousandths place _____
   c. 3.$\underline{1}$169   Tenths place _____
   d. 53.17$\underline{5}$ Thousandths place _____
   e. 1.017$\underline{4}$ Ten thousandths place _____

4. Convert to fractions (do not reduce):
   a. .83 $\dfrac{83}{100}$ _____
   b. .426 $\dfrac{426}{1,000}$ _____
   c. 2.516 $2\dfrac{516}{1,000}$ _____
   d. .62$\frac{1}{2}$ $\dfrac{625}{1,000}$ _____
   e. 13.007 $13\dfrac{7}{1,000}$ _____
   f. 5.03$\frac{1}{4}$ $5\dfrac{325}{10,000}$ _____

5. Convert to fractions and reduce to lowest terms:
   a. .4 $= \dfrac{4}{10} = \dfrac{2}{5}$
   b. .44 $= \dfrac{44}{100} = \dfrac{11}{25}$
   c. .53 $= \dfrac{53}{100}$
   d. .336 $= \dfrac{336}{1,000} = \dfrac{42}{125}$
   e. .096 $= \dfrac{96}{1,000} = \dfrac{12}{125}$
   f. .125 $= \dfrac{125}{1,000} = \dfrac{1}{8}$
   g. .3125 $= \dfrac{3,125}{10,000} = \dfrac{5}{16}$
   h. .008 $= \dfrac{8}{1,000} = \dfrac{1}{125}$
   i. 2.625 $= 2\dfrac{625}{1,000} = 2\dfrac{5}{8}$
   j. 5.75 $= 5\dfrac{75}{100} = 5\dfrac{3}{4}$
   k. 3.375 $= 3\dfrac{375}{1,000} = 3\dfrac{3}{8}$
   l. 9.04 $= 9\dfrac{4}{100} = 9\dfrac{1}{25}$

6. Convert the following fractions to decimals and round your answer to the nearest hundredth:
   a. $\dfrac{1}{8} = .125 = .13$
   b. $\dfrac{7}{16} = .4375 = .44$
   c. $\dfrac{2}{3} = .6666 = .67$
   d. $\dfrac{3}{4} = .75$

e. $\dfrac{9}{16} = .5625 = .56$

f. $\dfrac{5}{6} = .8333 = .83$

g. $\dfrac{7}{9} = .7777 = .78$

h. $\dfrac{38}{79} = .4810 = .48$

i. $2\dfrac{3}{8} = 2 + .375 = 2.38$

j. $9\dfrac{1}{3} = 9 + .3333 = 9.33$

k. $11\dfrac{19}{50} = 11 + .38 = 11.38$

l. $6\dfrac{21}{32} = 6 + .6562 = 6.66$

m. $4\dfrac{83}{97} = 4 + .8556 = 4.86$

n. $1\dfrac{2}{5} = 1 + .40 = 1.40$

o. $2\dfrac{2}{11} = 2 + .1818 = 2.18$

p. $13\dfrac{30}{42} = 13 + .7142 = 13.71$

WORD PROBLEMS

7. Alan Angel got 2 hits in his first 7 times at bat. What is his average to the nearest thousandths place?

$\dfrac{2}{7} = .2857 = .286$

8. Bill Breen earned $1,555, and his employer calculated that Bill's total FICA deduction should be $118.9575. Round this deduction to the nearest cent.

$118.9575 = $118.96

9. At the local college, .566 of the students are men. Convert to a fraction. Do not reduce.

$.566 = \dfrac{566}{1,000}$

10. The average television set is watched 2,400 hours a year. If there are 8,760 hours in a year, what fractional part of the year is spent watching television? Reduce to lowest terms.

$\dfrac{\overset{20}{\cancel{2,400}}}{\underset{73}{\cancel{8,760}}} = \dfrac{20}{73}$

11. On Saturday, the employees at the Empire Fish Company work only $\frac{1}{3}$ of a day. How could this be expressed as a decimal to nearest thousandths?

$\dfrac{1}{3} = .333$

12. The North Shore Cinema has 610 seats. At a recent film screening there were 55 vacant seats. Show as a fraction the number of filled seats. Reduce as needed.

$\begin{array}{r} 610 \\ -\ 55 \\ \hline 555 \end{array}$ $\dfrac{555}{610} = \dfrac{111}{122}$

13. Michael Sullivan was planning his marketing strategy for a new product his company had produced. He was fascinated to discover that Rhode Island, the smallest state in the United States, was only twenty thousand, five hundred seven ten millionths the size of the largest state, Alaska. Write this number in decimal.
.0020507

14. Bull Moose Company purchased a new manufacturing plant, located on an acre of land, for a total price of $2,250,000. The accountant determined that $\frac{3}{7}$ of the total price should be allocated as the price of the building. What decimal portion is the price of the building? Round to the nearest thousandth.

$\dfrac{3}{7} = .4285 = .429$

LEARNING UNIT 3.2:   Adding, Subtracting, Multiplying, and Dividing Decimals

DRILL PROBLEMS

1. Rearrange vertically and add:

a. $4.83 + 6.2 + 12.005 + 1.84$

```
   4.830
   6.200
  12.005
+  1.840
  24.875
```

b. $1.0625 + 4.0881 + .0775$

```
  1.0625
  4.0881
+  .0775
  5.2281
```

c. $.903 + .078 + .17 + .1 + .96$

```
  .903
  .078
  .170
  .100
+ .960
 2.211
```

d. $3.38 + .175 + .0186 + .2$

```
  3.3800
   .1750
   .0186
+  .2000
  3.7736
```

2. Rearrange and subtract:

a. $.86 - .43$

```
  .86
- .43
  .43
```

b. $.885 - .069$

```
  .885
- .069
  .816
```

c. $11.67 - .935$

```
  11.670
-   .935
  10.735
```

d. $261.2 - 8.08$

```
  261.20
-   8.08
  253.12
```

3. Multiply and round to the nearest tenth:

a. $13.6 \times .02$

```
   13.6
 × .02
  .272 = .3
```

b. $1.73 \times .069$

```
    1.73
  × .069
    1557
   1038
  .11937 = .1
```

c. 400×3.7

```
   400
 ×  3.7
  2800
 1 200
 1,480 = 1,480.0
```

d. 0.025×5.6

```
  0.025
 × 5.6
   150
   125
  .1400  = .1
```

4. Divide and round to the nearest hundredth:

a. $13.869 \div .6$

```
         23.115 = 23.12
    .6)13.8690
       12
       18
       18
       06
        6
       09
        6
       30
       30
```

b. $1.0088 \div .14$

```
        7.205 = 7.21
   .14)1.00880
       98
       28
       28
       080
        70
```

c. $18.7 \div 2.16$

```
           8.657 = 8.66
    2.16)18.70000
         17 28
         1 420
         1 296
          1240
          1080
          1600
          1512
```

d. $15.64 \div .34$

```
         46. = 46.00
    .34)15.64
        13 6
        204
        204
```

5. Complete by the shortcut method:

    a. $6.87 \times 1,000 = 6,870$ **b.** $927,530 \div 100 = 9,275.3$ **c.** $27.2 \div 1,000$ .0272

    d. $.21 \times 1,000 = 210$ **e.** $347 \times 100 = 34,700$ **f.** $347 \div 100 = 3.47$

    g. $.0021 \div 10 = .00021$ **h.** $85.44 \times 10,000 = 854,400$ **i.** $83.298 \times 100 = 8,329.8$

    j. $23.0109 \div 100 = .230109$

WORD PROBLEMS (Use *Business Math Handbook* **Tables as Needed.)**

6. John Sampson noted his odometer reading of 17,629.3 at the beginning of his vacation. At the end of his vacation the reading was 20,545.1. How many miles did he drive during his vacation?

    20,545.1
   − 17,629.3
       2,915.8 miles

7. Jeanne Allyn purchased 12.25 yards of ribbon for a craft project. The ribbon cost 37¢ per yard. What was the total cost of the ribbon?

     12.25
   × $.37
      8575
    3675
  $4.5325 = $4.53

8. Leo Green wanted to find out the gas mileage for his company truck. When he filled the gas tank, he wrote down the odometer reading of 9,650.7. The next time he filled the gas tank the odometer reading was 10,112.2. He looked at the gas pump and saw that he had taken 18.5 gallons of gas. Find the gas mileage per gallon for Leo's truck. Round to the nearest tenth.

     10,112.2   24.94 = 24.9 mpg
   − 9,650.7   18.5)461.500
      461.5 miles traveled   370
                            91 5
                            74 0
                          17 50
                          16 65
                           850
                           740

9. At Halley's Rent-a-Car, the cost per day to rent a medium-size car is $35.25 plus 37¢ a mile. What would be the charge to rent this car for 1 day if you drove 205.4 miles?

     205.4 $ 76.00
   × $.37   + 35.25
    14378 $111.25 charge
    6162
  $75.998 = $76.00

10. A trip to Mexico costs 6,000 pesos. What is this in U.S. dollars? Check your answer.

    $6,000 \times \$.11779 = \$706.74$
    $\$706.74 \times 8.4900 = 6,000$

11. If a commemorative gold coin weighs 7.842 grams, find the number of coins that can be produced from 116 grams of gold. Round to the nearest whole number.

            14.7 = 15 coins
   7.842)116.0000
       78 42
     37 580
     31 368
      6 2120
      5 4894
       7226

LEARNING UNIT 4.1: The Checking Account; Credit Card Transactions

DRILL PROBLEMS

1. The following is a deposit slip made out by Fred Young of the F. W. Young Company.

   a. How much cash did Young deposit? $430.64

   b. How many checks did Young deposit? 3

   c. What was the total amount deposited? $867.51

		This deposit is subject to: proof and verification, the Uniform Commercial Code, the collection and availability policy of this bank.	DESCRIPTION	DOLLARS	CENTS		ADDITIONAL CHECKS		
ᴍ Fleet Bank Checking Deposit TO THE ACCOUNT OF		DATE 3/27/02	BILLS	415	XX	DESCRIPTION 7.	DOLLARS	CENTS	
NAME (PLEASE PRINT) PLEASE ENDORSE ALL CHECKS	PLEASE ENTER CLEARLY YOUR ACCOUNT NUMBER		COIN	15	64	8.			
			LIST CHECKS 1 53-1297	188	44	9.			
			2 51-1509	98	37	10.			
			3 53-1290	150	06	11.			
			4.			12.			
			5.			13.			
			6.			14.			
			SUB TOTAL ITEMS 1-6			SUB TOTAL ITEMS 7-14			
						TOTAL			

⑆5 2 1 2000 1 7⑆

2. Blackstone Company had a balance of $2,173.18 in its checking account. Henry James, Blackstone's accountant, made a deposit that consisted of 2 fifty-dollar bills, 120 ten-dollar bills, 6 five-dollar bills, 14 one-dollar bills, $9.54 in change, plus two checks they had accepted, one for $16.38 and the other for $102.50. Find the amount of the deposit and the new balance in Blackstone's checking account.

$ 100.00 $2,173.18
1,200.00   + 1,472.42
30.00   _____
14.00 $3,645.60 new balance
9.54
16.38
+ 102.50
_____
$1,472.42 deposit

3. Answer the following questions using the illustration:

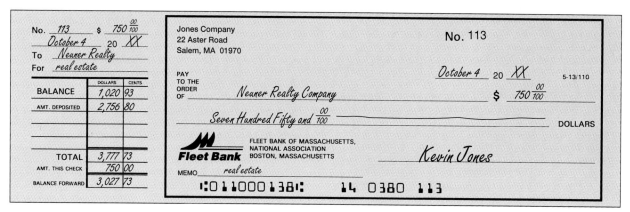

   a. Who is the payee? Neuner Realty Company

   b. Who is the drawer? Kevin Jones

   c. Who is the drawee? Fleet Bank

   d. What is the bank's identification number? 5-13/110

   e. What is Jones Company's account number? 14 0380

f. What was the balance in the account on September 30? $1,020.93

g. For how much did Jones write Check No. 113? $750.00

h. How much was deposited on October 1? $2,756.80

i. How much was left after Check No. 113 was written? $3,027.73

4. Write each of the following amounts in verbal form as you would on a check:

   a. $25   Twenty five and XX/100 --- DOLLARS

   b. $245.75   Two hundred forty-five and 75/100 --- DOLLARS

   c. $3.98   Three and 98/100 --- DOLLARS

   d. $1,205.05   One thousand, two hundred five and 05/100 --- DOLLARS

   e. $3,013   Three thousand, thirteen and XX/100 -- DOLLARS

   f. $510.10   Five hundred ten and 10/100 -- DOLLARS

5. From the following credit card transactions, calculate the net deposit that would be recorded on the merchant batch summary slip for the day.

MasterCard sales	Returns
$22.95	$ 4.09
18.51	16.50
16.92	

   $22.95 + $18.51 + $16.92 = $58.38
                             − 20.59
                        ─────────────
                          $37.79 net deposit

LEARNING UNIT 4.2:   Bank Statement and Reconciliation Process; Trends in Banking

WORD PROBLEMS

1. Find the bank balance on January 31.

Date	Checks and payments			Deposits	Balance
January 1					401.17
January 2	108.64				292.53
January 5	116.50			432.16	608.19
January 6	14.92	150.00	10.00		433.27
January 11	12.29			633.89	1,054.87
January 18	108.64	18.60			927.63
January 25	43.91	23.77		657.22	1,517.17
January 26	75.00				1,442.17
January 31	6.75 sc				1,435.42

2. Joe Madruga, of Madruga's Taxi Service, received a bank statement for the month of May showing a balance of $932.36. His records show that the bank had not yet recorded two of his deposits, one for $521.50 and the other for $98.46. There are outstanding checks in the amounts of $41.67, $135.18, and $25.30. The statement also shows a service charge of $3.38. The balance in the check register is $1,353.55. Prepare a bank reconciliation for Madruga's as of May 31.

Madruga's Taxi Service Bank Reconciliation as of May 31, 20XX			
Checkbook balance		**Bank statement balance**	
Checkbook balance	$1,353.55	Bank statement balance	$ 932.36
Less: Service charge	3.38	Add: Deposits in transit	521.50
			98.46
			$1,552.32
		Less: Outstanding checks	41.67
			135.18
			25.30
Reconciled balance	$1,350.17	Reconciled balance	$1,350.17

3. In reconciling the checking account for Nasser Enterprises, Beth Accomando found that the bank had collected a $3,000 promissory note on the company's behalf and had charged a $15 collection fee. There was also a service charge of $7.25. What amount should be added/subtracted from the checkbook balance to bring it up to date?

Add: $3,000   Deduct: $22.25

$15.00 collection fee
  7.25 service fee
$22.25

4. In reconciling the checking account for Colonial Cleaners, Steve Papa found that a check for $34.50 had been recorded in the check register as $43.50. The bank returned an NSF check in the amount of $62.55. Interest income of $8.25 was earned and a service charge of $10.32 was assessed. What amount should be added/subtracted from the checkbook balance to bring it up to date?

Add: $17.25   Deduct: $72.87

$ 9.00 recording error $62.55 returned check
  8.25 interest earned   10.32 service charge
$17.25 $72.87

5. Matthew Stokes was completing the bank reconciliation for Parker's Tool and Die Company. The check register balance was $1,503.67. Matthew found that a $76.00 check had been recorded in the check register as $67.00; that a note for $1,500 had been collected by the bank for Parker's and the collection fee was $12.00; that $15.60 interest was earned on the account; and that an $8.35 service charge had been assessed. What should the check register balance be after Matthew updates it with the bank reconciliation information?

$1,503.67 beginning balance	$1,500.00 note	$9.00 error
+ 1,515.60	15.60 interest	12.00 fee
− 29.35	$1,515.60 (add)	8.35 service charge
$2,989.92 ending balance		$29.35 (deduct)

6. Long's Video Shop had the following MasterCard sales: $44.18, $66.10, $12.50, and $24.95. Returns for the day were $13.88 and $12.99. What will be the amount of the net deposit for Long's Video Shop on the merchant batch summary slip?

$44.18 + $66.10 + $12.50 + $24.95 = $147.73
$$- 26.87\ (\$13.88 + \$12.99)$$
$120.86 net deposit

7. On May 15, 1995, *Advertising Age* ran an article entitled "Bank's $3.00 Teller Fee." Consumers, community activists, and politicians are decrying the new line of accounts because several include a $3 service charge for some customers who use bank tellers for transactions that can be done through an automated teller machine. Bill Wade banks at a local bank that charges this fee. He was having difficulty balancing his checkbook because he did not notice this fee on his bank statement. His bank statement showed a balance of $822.18. Bill's checkbook had a balance of $206.48. Check No. 406 for $116.08 and Check No. 407 for $12.50 were outstanding. A $521 deposit was not on the statement. Bill has his payroll check electronically deposited to his checking account—the payroll check was for $1,015.12 (Bill's payroll checks vary each month). There are also a $1 service fee and a teller fee of $6. Complete Bill's bank reconciliation.

Checkbook balance	$ 206.48	Bank statement balance	$ 822.18	
Direct deposit	+ 1,015.12	Check No. 406	− 116.08	
Teller fee	− 6.00	Check No. 407	− 12.50	
Service charge	− 1.00	Deposit in transit	+ 521.00	
Reconciled balance	$ 1,214.60	Reconciled balance	$1,214.60	

8. The March 1996 issue of *Consumer Reports* reported that ATMs are turning into cash machines for banks. At First National Bank in San Diego, some customers have to pay $25 each year as an ATM card fee. John Levi banks at First National Bank and just received his bank statement showing a balance of $829.25; his checkbook balance is $467.40. The bank statement shows an ATM card fee of $25.00, teller fee of $9.00, interest of $1.80, and John's $880 IRS refund check, which was processed by the IRS and deposited to his account. John has two checks that have not cleared—No. 112 for $620.10 and No. 113 for $206.05. There is also a deposit in transit for $1,312.10. Prepare John's bank reconciliation.

Checkbook balance	$ 467.40	Bank statement balance	$ 829.25	
ATM card fee	− 25.00	Check No. 112	− 620.10	
Teller fee	− 9.00	Check No. 113	− 206.05	
Interest	+ 1.80	Deposit in transit	+ 1,312.10	
IRS refund	+ 880.00	Reconciled balance	$ 1,315.20	
Reconciled balance	$1,315.20			

LEARNING UNIT 5.1:   Solving Equations for the Unknown

DRILL PROBLEMS

1. Write equations for the following situations. Use N for the unknown number. Do not solve the equations.
   a. Five times a number is 60.
   $5N = 60$
   b. A number increased by 13 equals 25.
   $N + 13 = 25$
   c. Seven less than a number is 5.
   $N - 7 = 5$
   d. Fifty-seven decreased by 3 times a number is 21.
   $57 - 3N = 21$
   e. Fourteen added to one-third of a number is 18.
   $14 + \dfrac{N}{3} = 18$
   f. Twice the sum of a number and 4 is 32.
   $2(N + 4) = 32$
   g. Three-fourths of a number is 9.
   $\dfrac{3}{4}N = 9$
   h. Two times a number plus 3 times the same number plus 8 is 68.
   $2N + 3N + 8 = 68$

2. Solve for the unknown number:

a.
$$\begin{aligned} B + 12 &= 38 \\ -12 \quad &-12 \\ \hline B &= 26 \end{aligned}$$

b.
$$\begin{aligned} 29 + M &= 44 \\ -29 \quad &-29 \\ \hline M &= 15 \end{aligned}$$

c.
$$\begin{aligned} D - 77 &= 98 \\ +77 \quad &+77 \\ \hline D &= 175 \end{aligned}$$

d. $7N = 63$
$$\frac{\cancel{7}N}{\cancel{7}} = \frac{63}{7}$$
$$N = 9$$

e. $\dfrac{X}{12} = 11$
$$(\cancel{12})\frac{X}{\cancel{12}} = 11(12)$$
$$X = 132$$

f. $3Q + 4Q + 2Q = 108$
$$\frac{\cancel{9}Q}{\cancel{9}} = \frac{108}{9}$$
$$Q = 12$$

g.
$$\begin{aligned} H + 5H + 3 &= 57 \\ 6H + 3 &= 57 \\ -3 \quad &-3 \\ \hline \frac{\cancel{6}H}{\cancel{6}} &= \frac{54}{6} \\ H &= 9 \end{aligned}$$

h.
$$\begin{aligned} 2(N - 3) &= 62 \\ 2N - 6 &= 62 \\ +6 \quad &+6 \\ \hline \frac{2N}{\cancel{2}} &= \frac{68}{2} \\ N &= 34 \end{aligned}$$

i. $\dfrac{3R}{4} = 27$
$$\cancel{4}\left(\frac{3R}{\cancel{4}}\right) = 27(4)$$
$$\frac{\cancel{3}R}{\cancel{3}} = \frac{108}{3}$$
$$R = 36$$

j.
$$\begin{aligned} E - 32 &= 41 \\ +32 \quad &+32 \\ \hline E &= 73 \end{aligned}$$

k.
$$\begin{aligned} 5(2T - 2) &= 120 \\ 10T - 10 &= 120 \\ +10 \quad &+10 \\ \hline \frac{\cancel{10}T}{\cancel{10}} &= \frac{130}{10} \\ T &= 13 \end{aligned}$$

l.
$$\begin{aligned} 12W - 5W &= 98 \\ \frac{\cancel{7}W}{\cancel{7}} &= \frac{98}{7} \\ W &= 14 \end{aligned}$$

m.
$$\begin{aligned} 49 - X &= 37 \\ +X \quad &+X \\ \hline 49 &= 37 + X \\ -37 \quad &-37 \\ \hline 12 &= X \end{aligned}$$

n.
$$\begin{aligned} 12(V + 2) &= 84 \\ 12V + 24 &= 84 \\ -24 \quad &-24 \\ \hline \frac{\cancel{12}V}{\cancel{12}} &= \frac{60}{12} \\ V &= 5 \end{aligned}$$

o.
$$\begin{aligned} 7D + 4 &= 5D + 14 \\ -5D \quad &-5D \\ \hline 2D + 4 &= \quad 14 \\ -4 \quad &-4 \\ \hline \frac{2D}{\cancel{2}} &= \frac{10}{\cancel{2}} \\ D &= 5 \end{aligned}$$

p.
$$\begin{aligned} 7(T - 2) &= 2T - 9 \\ 7T - 14 &= 2T - 9 \\ -2T \quad &-2T \\ \hline 5T - 14 &= \quad -9 \\ +14 \quad &+14 \\ \hline \frac{\cancel{5}T}{\cancel{5}} &= \frac{5}{5} \\ T &= 1 \end{aligned}$$

LEARNING UNIT 5.2: Solving Word Problems for the Unknown

WORD PROBLEMS

1. A blue denim shirt at the Gap was marked down $15. The sale price was $30. What was the original price?

Unknown(s)	Variable(s)	Relationship
Original price	P	$P - \$15 =$ Sale price
		Sale price $= \$30$

$$P - \$15 = \$30$$
$$\underline{+\ \ 15 = +\ 15}$$
$$P \qquad = \ \$45 \text{ original price of shirt}$$

2. Goodwin's Corporation found that $\frac{2}{3}$ of its employees were vested in their retirement plan. If 124 employees are vested, what is the total number of employees at Goodwin's?

Unknown(s)	Variable(s)	Relationship
Total number of employees	E	$\frac{2}{3}E =$ Vested employees
		Vested employees $= 124$

$$\frac{2}{3}E = 124$$
$$\cancel{3}\left(\frac{2E}{\cancel{3}}\right) = 124(3)$$
$$\frac{2E}{2} = \frac{372}{2}$$
$$E = 186 \text{ employees}$$

3. Eileen Haskin's utility and telephone bills for the month totaled $180. The utility bill was 3 times as much as the telephone bill. How much was each bill?

Unknown(s)	Variable(s)	Relationship
Telephone bill	B	$B + 3B =$ Total bill
Utility bill	$3B$	Total bill $= \$180$

$$B + 3B = \$180$$
$$\frac{\cancel{4}B}{\cancel{4}} = \frac{\$180}{4}$$
$$B = \ \$45 = \text{telephone bill; } 3B = \$135 \text{ utility bill}$$

4. Ryan and his friends went to the golf course to hunt for golf balls. Ryan found 15 more than $\frac{1}{3}$ of the total number of golf balls that were found. How many golf balls were found if Ryan found 75 golf balls?

Unknown(s)	Variable(s)	Relationship
Total golf balls found	G	$\frac{1}{3}G + 15 =$ Ryan found
		Ryan found $= 75$

$$\frac{1}{3}G + 15 = \ \ 75$$
$$\underline{\ \ \ \ -\ 15 = -\ 15}$$
$$\cancel{3}\left(\frac{G}{\cancel{3}}\right) \ \ \ = \ \ 60\,(3)$$
$$G \ \ \ \ = \ \ 180 \text{ total golf balls found}$$

5. Linda Mills and Sherry Somers sold 459 tickets for the Advertising Club's raffle. If Linda sold 8 times as many tickets as Sherry, how many tickets did each one sell?

Unknown(s)	Variable(s)	Relationship
Linda	$8T$	$8T + T =$ total tickets
Sherry	T	Total tickets $= 459$

$$8T + T = 459$$
$$\frac{\cancel{9}T}{\cancel{9}} = \frac{459}{9}$$
$$T = \ 51 \text{ tickets Sherry sold}$$
$$8 \times 51 = 408 \text{ tickets Linda sold}$$

6. Jason Mazzola wanted to buy a suit at Giblee's. Jason did not have enough money with him, so Mr. Giblee told him he would hold the suit if Jason gave him a deposit of $\frac{1}{5}$ of the cost of the suit. Jason agreed and gave Mr. Giblee $79. What was the price of the suit?

Unknown(s)	Variable(s)	Relationship
Price of suit	S	$\frac{1}{5}S =$ Jason's payment
		Jason's payment $= \$79$

$$\frac{1}{5}S = \$79$$
$$\cancel{5}\left(\frac{S}{\cancel{5}}\right) = 79(5)$$
$$S = \$395 \text{ price of suit}$$

7. Peter sold watches ($7) and necklaces ($4) at a flea market. Total sales were $300. People bought 3 times as many watches as necklaces. How many of each did Peter sell? What were the total dollar sales of each?

Unknown(s)	Variable(s)	Price	Relationship
Watches	$3N$	$7	$21N$
Necklaces	N	4	$+ 4N$
			$300

$21N + 4N = 300$

$\dfrac{25N}{25} = \dfrac{300}{25}$

$N = 12$

$12(\$4) + 36(\$7) = \$300$

$\$48\ +\ \$252\ = \$300$

$\$300\ = \$300$

12 necklaces
36 watches

8. Peter sold watches ($7) and necklaces ($4) at a flea market. Total sales for 48 watches and necklaces were $300. How many of each did Peter sell? What were the total dollar sales of each?

Unknown(s)	Variable(s)	Price	Relationship
Watches	W	$7	$7W$
Necklaces	$48 - W$	4	$4(48 - W)$
			$300

$7W + 4(48 - W) = \quad 300$

$7W + 192 - 4W = \quad 300$

$3W + 192 = \quad 300$

$\underline{\quad\ \ -192 \qquad\ \ -192}$

$\dfrac{3W}{3} = \dfrac{108}{3}$

$W = 36$

$36(\$7) + 12(\$4) = \$300$

$\$252 + \$48 = \$300$

$\$300 = \$300$

36 watches
$48 - 36 = 12$ necklaces

9. The September 1997 issue of *Nation's Business* ran an article on the cost of direct mailing. A 3,000 piece of mailing cost $1,435. Printing cost is $550, about $3\frac{1}{2}$ times the cost of typesetting. How much did the typesetting cost? Round to the nearest cent.

Unknown(s)	Variable(s)	Relationship	
Typesetting cost	C	Printing cost	$550
		$\times 3\frac{1}{2}C$	
		$=$ Typesetting cost	

$3\frac{1}{2}C = \$550$

$\dfrac{3\frac{1}{2}C}{3\frac{1}{2}} = \dfrac{\$550}{3\frac{1}{2}}$

$C = \$157.1428 = \$157.14$

10. The November 1997 issue of *Inc.* reported that in 1995, Tony Rigato, owner of MRM, saw an increase in sales to $13.5 million. Rigato states that since 1991, sales have more than tripled. What were his sales in 1991?

Unknown(s)	Variable(s)	Relationship
1991 sales	S	$3S = \$13.5$

$3S = \$13.5$ million

$\dfrac{3S}{3} = \dfrac{\$13.5}{3}$

$S = \$4.5$ million

LEARNING UNIT 6.1: Conversions

DRILL PROBLEMS

1. Convert the following to percents (round to the nearest tenth of a percent if needed):

a.	.06	6	%	**b.**	.875	87.5	%
c.	.002	.2	%	**d.**	8.3	830	%
e.	5.26	526	%	**f.**	6	600	%
g.	.0105	1.1	%	**h.**	.1180	11.8	%
i.	5.0375	503.8	%	**j.**	.862	86.2	%
k.	.2615	26.2	%	**l.**	.8	80	%
m.	.025	2.5	%	**n.**	.06	6	%

2. Convert the following to decimals (do not round):

a. 37% .37
b. .09% .0009
c. 4.7% .047
d. 9.67% .0967
e. .2% .002
f. $\frac{1}{4}$% .0025
g. .76% .0076
h. 110% 1.1
i. $12\frac{1}{2}$% .125
j. 5% .05
k. .004% .00004
l. $7\frac{5}{10}$% .075
m. $\frac{3}{4}$% .0075
n. 1% .01

3. Convert the following to percents (round to the nearest tenth of a percent if needed):

a. $\frac{7}{10}$ 70 %
b. $\frac{1}{5}$ 20 %
c. $1\frac{5}{8}$ 162.5 %
d. $\frac{2}{7}$ 28.6 %
e. 2 200 %
f. $\frac{14}{100}$ 14 %
g. $\frac{1}{6}$ 16.7 %
h. $\frac{1}{2}$ 50 %
i. $\frac{3}{5}$ 60 %
j. $\frac{3}{25}$ 12 %
k. $\frac{5}{16}$ 31.3 %
l. $\frac{11}{50}$ 22 %
m. $4\frac{3}{4}$ 475 %
n. $\frac{3}{200}$ 1.5 %

4. Convert the following to fractions in simplest form:

a. 40% $\frac{2}{5}$
b. 15% $\frac{3}{20}$
c. 50% $\frac{1}{2}$
d. 75% $\frac{3}{4}$
e. 35% $\frac{7}{20}$
f. 85% $\frac{17}{20}$
g. $12\frac{1}{2}$% $\frac{1}{8}$
h. $37\frac{1}{2}$% $\frac{3}{8}$
i. $33\frac{1}{3}$% $\frac{1}{3}$
j. 3% $\frac{3}{100}$
k. 8.5% $\frac{17}{200}$
l. $5\frac{3}{4}$% $\frac{23}{400}$
m. 100% 1
n. 10% $\frac{1}{10}$

5. Complete the following table by finding the missing fraction, decimal, or percent equivalent:

	Fraction	Decimal	Percent		Fraction	Decimal	Percent
a.	$\frac{1}{4}$	.25	25%	h.	$\frac{1}{6}$	$.16\overline{6}$	$16\frac{2}{3}\%$
b.	$\frac{3}{8}$	.375	$37\frac{1}{2}\%$	i.	$\frac{1}{12}$	$.083\overline{3}$	$8\frac{1}{3}\%$
c.	$\frac{1}{2}$	.5	50%	j.	$\frac{1}{9}$	$.11\overline{1}$	$11\frac{1}{9}\%$
d.	$\frac{2}{3}$	$.66\overline{6}$	$66\frac{2}{3}\%$	k.	$\frac{5}{16}$	.3125	$31\frac{1}{4}\%$
e.	$\frac{2}{5}$	.4	40%	l.	$\frac{3}{40}$	.075	$7\frac{1}{2}\%$
f.	$\frac{3}{5}$	.6	60%	m.	$\frac{1}{5}$	.20	20%
g.	$\frac{7}{10}$	.7	70%	n.	$1\frac{1}{8}$	1.125	$112\frac{1}{2}\%$

WORD PROBLEMS

6. In 2001, Mutual of New York reported an overwhelming 70% of its new sales came from existing clients. What fractional part of its new sales came from existing clients? Reduce to simplest form.

$$70\% = \frac{70}{100} = \frac{7}{10}$$

7. Six hundred ninety corporations and design firms competed for the Industrial Design Excellence Award (IDEA) in 2001. Twenty were selected as the year's best and received gold awards. Show the gold award winners as a fraction; then show what percent of the entrants received gold awards. Round to the nearest tenth of a percent.

$$\frac{20}{690} = \frac{2}{69}$$

$$\begin{array}{r} .0289 = 2.9\% \\ 69\overline{)2.0000} \\ \underline{1\ 38} \\ 620 \\ \underline{552} \\ 680 \\ \underline{621} \\ 59 \end{array}$$

8. In the first half of 2001, stock prices in the Standard & Poor's 500-stock index rose 17.5%. Show the increase in decimal.

$$17.5\% = .175$$

9. In the recent banking crisis, many banks were unable to cover their bad loans. Citicorp, the nation's largest real estate lender, was reported as having only enough reserves to cover 39% of its bad loans. What fractional part of its loan losses was covered?

$$39\% = \frac{39}{100}$$

10. Dave Mattera spent his vacation in Las Vegas. He ordered breakfast in his room, and when he went downstairs to the coffee shop, he discovered that the same breakfast was much less expensive. He had paid 1.884 times as much for the breakfast in his room. What was the percent of increase for the breakfast in his room?

$$1.884 = 188.4\%$$

11. Putnam Management Company of Boston recently increased its management fee by .09%. What is the increase as a decimal? What is the same increase as a fraction?

$$.09\% = .0009 \qquad .09\% = .0009 = \frac{9}{10,000}$$

12. Joel Black and Karen Whyte formed a partnership and drew up a partnership agreement, with profits and losses to be divided equally after each partner receives a $7\frac{1}{2}\%$ return on his or her capital contribution. Show their return on investment as a decimal and as a fraction. Reduce.

$$7\frac{1}{2}\% = 7.5\% = .075 \qquad 7\frac{1}{2}\% = 7.5\% = .075 = \frac{75}{1,000} = \frac{3}{40}$$

A-26

Name _____ Date_____

LEARNING UNIT 6.2: Application of Percents—Portion Formula

DRILL PROBLEMS

1. Fill in the amount of the base, rate, and portion in each of the following statements:
   a. The Johnsons spend $1,000 a month on food, which is $12\frac{1}{2}$% of their monthly income of $8,000.

   Base __$8,000__ Rate __$12\frac{1}{2}$%__ Portion __$1,000__

   b. Rocky Norman got a $15 discount when he purchased a new camera. This was 20% off the sticker price of $75.
   Base __$75__ Rate __20%__ Portion __$15__

   c. Mary Burns got a 12% senior citizens discount when she bought a $7.00 movie ticket. She saved $0.84.

   Base __$7.00__ Rate __12%__ Portion __$0.84__

   d. Arthur Bogey received a commission of $13,500 when he sold the Browns's house for $225,000. His commission rate is 6%.
   Base __$225,000__ Rate __6%__ Portion __$13,500__

   e. Leo Davis deposited $5,000 in a certificate of deposit (CD). A year later he received an interest payment of $450 which was a yield of 9%.
   Base __$5,000__ Rate __9%__ Portion __$450__

   f. Grace Tremblay is on a diet that allows her to eat 1,600 calories per day. For breakfast she had 600 calories, which is $37\frac{1}{2}$% of her allowance.

   Base __1,600__ Rate __$37\frac{1}{2}$%__ Portion __600__

2. Find the portion; round to the nearest hundredth if necessary:
   a. 7% of 74 __5.18 (74 × .07)__   b. 12% of 205 __24.60__   c. 16% of 630 __100.8__
   d. 7.5% of 920 __69__   e. 25% of 1,004 __251__   f. 10% of 79 __7.90__
   g. 103% of 44 __45.32__   h. 30% of 78 __23.40__   i. .2% of 50 __.10__
   j. 1% of 5,622 __56.22__   k. $6\frac{1}{4}$% of 480 __30__   l. 150% of 10 __15__
   m. 100% of 34 __34__   n. $\frac{1}{2}$% of 27 __.14__

3. Find the rate; round to the nearest tenth of a percent as needed:
   a. 30 is what percent of 90? __33.3% $\left(\frac{30}{90}\right)$__   b. 6 is what percent of 200? __3%__
   c. 275 is what percent of 1,000? __27.5%__   d. .8 is what percent of 44? __1.8%__
   e. 67 is what percent of 2,010? __3.3%__   f. 550 is what percent of 250? __220%__
   g. 13 is what percent of 650? __2%__   h. $15 is what percent of $455? __3.3%__
   i. .05 is what percent of 100? __.1%__   j. $6.25 is what percent of $10? __62.5%__

4. Find the base; round to the nearest tenth as needed:
   a. 63 is 30% of __210 $\left(\frac{63}{.30}\right)$__   b. 60 is 33% of __181.8__   c. 150 is 25% of __600__
   d. 47 is 1% of __4,700__   e. $21 is 120% of __$17.50__   f. 2.26 is 40% of __5.7__
   g. 75 is $12\frac{1}{2}$% of __600__   h. 18 is 22.2% of __81.1__   i. $37.50 is 50% of __$75.00__
   j. 250 is 100% of __250__

5. Find the percent of increase or decrease. Round to nearest tenth percent as needed:

	Last year	This year	Amount of change	Percent of change
a.	5,962	4,378	−1,584	−26.6% $\left(\frac{1,584}{5,962}\right)$
b.	$10,995	$12,250	1,255	11.4%
c.	120,000	140,000	20,000	16.7%
d.	120,000	100,000	−20,000	−16.7%

A-27

WORD PROBLEMS

6. A machine that originally cost $2,400 was sold for $600 at the end of 5 years. What percent of the original cost is the selling price?

$$\frac{\$600}{\$2,400} = .25 = 25\%$$

7. Joanne Byrne invested $75,000 in a candy shop and is making 12% per year on her investment. How much money per year is she making on her investment?

$$\$75,000 \times .12 = \$9,000$$

8. There was a fire in Bill Porper's store that caused 2,780 inventory items to be destroyed. Before the fire, 9,565 inventory items were in the store. What percent of inventory was destroyed? Round to nearest tenth percent.

$$\frac{2,780}{9,565} = 29.1\%$$

9. Elyse's Dress Shoppe makes 25% of its sales for cash. If the cash receipts on January 21 were $799, what were the total sales for the day?

$$\frac{\$799}{.25} = \$3,196$$

10. The YMCA is holding a fund-raiser to collect money for a new gym floor. So far it has collected $7,875, which is 63% of the goal. What is the amount of the goal? How much more money must the YMCA collect?

$$\frac{\$7,875}{.63} = \$12,500 \text{ goal}$$

$$\$12,500 - \$7,875 = \$4,625$$

11. Leslie Tracey purchased her home for $51,500. She sold it last year for $221,200. What percent profit did she make on the sale? Round to nearest tenth percent.

$$\begin{array}{r} \$221,200 \\ - 51,500 \\ \hline \$169,700 \end{array}$$

$$\frac{\$169,700}{\$51,500} = 329.5\%$$

Portion 7 Base

12. Maplewood Park Tool & Die had an annual production of 375,165 units this year. This is 140% of the annual production last year. What was last year's annual production?

$$\frac{375,165}{1.40} = 267,975 \text{ units}$$

Portion 7 Base

A-28

LEARNING UNIT 7.1:   Trade Discounts—Single and Chain

DRILL PROBLEMS

1. Calculate the trade discount amount for each of the following items:

Item	List price	Trade discount	Trade discount amount	
a. Dell computer	$1,500	30%	$450	**a.** $1,500 × .30 = $450
b. Sofa	$1,200	30%	$360	**b.** $1,200 × .30 = $360
c. Suit	$ 500	10%	$ 50	**c.** $500 × .10 = $50
d. Bicycle	$ 800	$12\frac{1}{2}$%	$100	**d.** $800 × .125 = $100
e. RCA television	$ 950	40%	$380	**e.** $950 × .40 = $380

2. Calculate the net price for each of the following items:

Item	List price	Trade discount amount	Net price	
a. Home Depot table	$600	$250	$350	**a.** $600 − $250 = $350
b. Bookcase	$525	$129	$396	**b.** $525 − $129 = $396
c. Rocking chair	$480	$ 95	$385	**c.** $480 − $95 = $385

3. Fill in the missing amount for each of the following items:

Item	List price	Trade discount amount	Net price	
a. Sears electric saw	$75	$19	$56.00	**a.** $56 + $19 = $75
b. Electric drill	$90	$21.50	$68.50	**b.** $90 − $68.50 = $21.50
c. Ladder	$56	$15.25	$40.75	**c.** $56 − $15.25 = $40.75

4. For each of the following, find the percent paid (complement of trade discount) and the net price:

	List price	Trade discount	Percent paid	Net price	
a.	$45	15%	85%	$38.25	**a.** 100% − 15% = 85% $45 × .85 = $38.25
b.	$195	12.2%	87.8%	$171.21	**b.** 100% − 12.2% = 87.8% $195 × .878 = $171.21
c.	$325	50%	50%	$162.50	**c.** 100% − 50% = 50% $325 × .5 = $162.50
d.	$120	18%	82%	$98.40	**d.** 100% − 18% = 82% $120 × .82 = $98.40

5. In each of the following examples, find the net price equivalent rate and the single equivalent discount rate:

	Chain discount	Net price equivalent rate	Single equivalent discount rate	
a.	25/5	.7125	.2875	**a.** .75 × .95 = .7125 1 − .7125 = .2875
b.	15/15	.7225	.2775	**b.** .85 × .85 = .7225 1 − .7225 = .2775
c.	15/10/5	.72675	.27325	**c.** .85 × .9 × .95 = .72675 1 − .72675 = .27325
d.	12/12/6	.727936	.272064	**d.** .88 × .88 × .94 = .727936 1 − .727936 = .272064

6. In each of the following examples, find the net price and the trade discount:

	List price	Chain discount	Net price	Trade discount	
a.	$5,000	10/10/5	$3,847.50	$1,152.50	
b.	$7,500	9/6/3	$6,223.04	$1,276.97	(Total is off 1¢ due to rounding)
c.	$898	20/7/2	$654.75	$243.25	
d.	$1,500	25/10	$1,012.50	$487.50	

    a. $(.9 \times .9 \times .95) \times \$5,000 = \$3,847.50$ $\$5,000 \times (1 - .7695) = \$1,152.50$

    b. $(.91 \times .94 \times .97) \times \$7,500 = \$6,223.035$ $\$7,500 \times (1 - .829738) = \$1,276.965$

    c. $(.8 \times .93 \times .98) \times \$898 = \$654.74976$ $\$898 \times (1 - .72912) = \$243.25$

    d. $(.75 \times .9) \times \$1,500 = \$1,012.50$ $\$1,500 \times (1 - .675) = \$487.50$

7. The list price of a handheld calculator is $19.50, and the trade discount is 18%. Find the trade discount amount.

$$
\begin{array}{r}
\$19.50 \\
\times\ .18 \\
\hline
15600 \\
1950 \\
\hline
3.5100 = \$3.51
\end{array}
$$

8. The list price of a silver picture frame is $29.95, and the trade discount is 15%. Find the trade discount amount and the net price.

$$
\begin{array}{r}
\$29.95 \\
\times\ .15 \\
\hline
14975 \\
2995 \\
\hline
4.4925 = \$4.49 \text{ trade discount amount}
\end{array}
\qquad
\begin{array}{r}
\$29.95 \\
-\ 4.49 \\
\hline
\$25.46 \text{ net price or } \$29.95 \times .85 = \$25.46
\end{array}
$$

9. The net price of a set of pots and pans is $65, and the trade discount is 20%. What is the list price?

$$
\frac{\$65}{1 - .20} = \frac{\$65}{.80} = \$81.25
$$

10. Jennie's Variety Store has the opportunity to purchase candy from three different wholesalers; each of the wholesalers offers a different chain discount. Company A offers 25/5/5, Company B offers 20/10/5, and Company C offers 15/20. Which company should Jennie deal with? *Hint:* Choose the company with the highest single equivalent discount rate.

    Company A: $.75 \times .95 \times .95 = .676875$ $1 - .676875 = .323125 = 32.31\%$

    Company B: $.8 \times .9 \times .95 = .684$ $1 - .684 = .316 = 31.6\%$

    Company C: $.85 \times .8 = .68$ $1 - .68 = .32 = 32\%$

    Choose Company A for the 32.31% discount.

11. The list price of a television set is $625. Find the net price after a series discount of 30/20/10.

    $(.7 \times .8 \times .9) \times \$625 = \$315$ net price

12. Mandy's Accessories Shop purchased 12 purses with a total list price of $726. What was the net price of each purse if the wholesaler offered a chain discount of 25/20?

    $(.75 \times .8) \times \$726 = \$435.60$ $\$435.60 \div 12 = \$36.30$ net price per purse

13. Kransberg Furniture Store purchased a bedroom set for $1,097.25 from Furniture Wholesalers. The list price of the set was $1,995. What trade discount rate did Kransberg receive?

    List price − Net price = Trade discount amount $\dfrac{\$1,995 - \$1,097.25}{\$1,995} = .45 = 45\%$

14. Susan Monk teaches second grade and receives a discount at the local art supply store. Recently she paid $47.25 for art supplies after receiving a chain discount of 30/10. What was the regular price of the art supplies?

    $.7 \times .9 = .63$ net price equivalent rate $\dfrac{\$47.25}{.63} = \$75$

LEARNING UNIT 7.2: Cash Discounts, Credit Terms, and Partial Payments

DRILL PROBLEMS

1. Complete the following table:

	Date of invoice	Date goods received	Terms	Last day of discount period	End of credit period
a.	February 8		2/10, n/30	February 18	March 10
b.	August 26		2/10, n/30	September 5	September 25
c.	October 17		3/10, n/60	October 27	December 16
d.	March 11	May 10	3/10, n/30, ROG	May 20	June 9
e.	September 14		2/10, EOM	October 10	October 30
f.	May 31		2/10, EOM	July 10	July 30

2. Calculate the cash discount and the net amount paid.

	Invoice amount	Cash discount rate	Discount amount	Net amount paid
a.	$75	3%	$2.25 ($75 × .03)	$72.75 ($75 × .97)
b.	$1,559	2%	$31.18	$1,527.82
c.	$546.25	2%	$10.93	$535.33 (rounded)
d.	$9,788.75	1%	$97.89	$9,690.86

3. Use the complement of the cash discount to calculate the net amount paid. Assume all invoices are paid within the discount period.

	Terms of invoice	Amount of invoice		Complement		Net amount paid
a.	2/10, n/30	$1,125	×	.98	=	$1,102.50
b.	3/10, n/30 ROG	$4,500		.97		$4,365
c.	2/10, EOM	$375.50		.98		$367.99
d.	1/15, n/45	$3,998		.99		$3,958.02

4. Calculate the amount of cash discount and the net amount paid.

	Date of invoice	Terms of invoice	Amount of invoice	Date paid	Cash discount	Amount paid
a.	January 12	2/10, n/30	$5,320	January 22	$106.40	$5,213.60
b.	May 28	2/10, n/30	$975	June 7	$19.50	$955.50
c.	August 15	2/10, n/30	$7,700	August 26	0	$7,700
d.	March 8	2/10, EOM	$480	April 10	$9.60	$470.40
e.	January 24	3/10, n/60	$1,225	February 3	$36.75	$1,188.25

5. Complete the following table:

	Total invoice	Freight charges included in invoice total	Date of invoice	Terms of invoice	Date of payment	Cash discount	Amount paid
a.	$852	$12.50	3/19	2/10, n/30	3/29	$16.79	$835.21
	[($852 − $12.50) × .02 = $16.79], ($822.71 + $12.50 = $835.21)						
b.	$669.57	$15.63	7/28	3/10, EOM	9/10	$19.62	$649.95
	[($669.57 − $15.63) × .03 = $19.62], ($634.32 + $15.63 = $649.95)						
c.	$500	$11.50	4/25	2/10, n/60	6/5	0	$500.00
	No discount, pay total invoice						
d.	$188	$9.70	1/12	2/10, EOM	2/10	$3.57	$184.43
	[($188 − $9.70) × .02 = $3.57], ($174.73 + $9.70 = $184.43)						

6. In the following table, assume that all the partial payments were made within the discount period.

Amount of invoice	Terms of invoice	Partial payment	Amount to be credited	Balance outstanding
a. $481.90	2/10, n/30	$90.00	$91.84	$390.06

($90 ÷ .98 = $91.84), ($481.90 − $91.84 = $390.06)

b. $1,000	2/10, EOM	$500.00	$510.20	$489.80

($500 ÷ .98 = $510.20), ($1,000 − $510.20 = $489.80)

c. $782.88	3/10, n/30, ROG	$275.00	$283.51	$499.37

($275 ÷ .97 = $283.51), ($782.88 − $283.51 = $499.37)

d. $318.80	2/15, n/60	$200.00	$204.08	$114.72

($200 ÷ .98 = $204.08), ($318.80 − $204.08 = $114.72)

WORD PROBLEMS

7. Northwest Chemical Company received an invoice for $12,480, dated March 12, with terms of 2/10, n/30. If the invoice was paid March 22, what was the amount due?

100% − 2% = 98% $12,480 × .98 = $12,230.40

8. On May 27, Trotter Hardware Store received an invoice for trash barrels purchased for $13,650 with terms of 3/10, EOM; the freight charge, which is included in the price, is $412. What are **(a)** the last day of the discount period and **(b)** the amount of the payment due on this date?

a. Last discount date is July 10   **b.** $13,650
                                                  − 412 freight
                                                  ─────
                                                  13,238
                                                  × .97 complement (100% − 3% = 97%)
                                                  ─────
                                                  12,840.86
                                                  + 412.00 freight
                                                  ─────
                                                  $13,252.86 total due in discount period

9. The Glass Sailboat received an invoice for $930.50 with terms 2/10, n/30 on April 19. On April 29, it sent a payment of $430.50. **(a)** How much credit will be given on the total due? **(b)** What is the new balance due?

100% − 2% = 98%   **a.** $430.50 ÷ .98 = $439.29 credit given
                       b. $930.50 − $439.29 = $491.21 balance due

10. Dallas Ductworks offers cash discounts of 2/10, 1/15, n/30 on all purchases. If an invoice for $544 dated July 18 is paid on August 2, what is the amount due?

July 18 to August 2 = 15 days
100% − 1% = 99%
$544 × .99 = $538.56 amount due

11. The list price of a compact disk player is $299.90 with trade discounts of 10/20 and terms of 3/10, n/30. If a retailer pays the invoice within the discount period, what amount must the retailer pay?

.9 × .8 = .72   100% − 3% = 97%
$299.90 × .72 = $215.928 = $215.93 net price $215.93 × .97 = $209.45 payment

12. The invoice of a sneaker supplier totaled $2,488.50, was dated February 7, and offered terms 2/10, ROG. The shipment of sneakers was received on March 7. What are **(a)** the last date of the discount period and **(b)** the amount of the discount that will be lost if the invoice is paid after that date?

a. Last discount date is March 17.
b. $2,488.50 × .02 = $49.77 discount lost after March 17

13. Starburst Toy Company receives an invoice amounting to $1,152.30 with terms of 2/10, EOM and dated November 6. If a partial payment of $750 is made on December 8, what are **(a)** the credit given for the partial payment and **(b)** the balance due on the invoice?

100% − 2% = 98%   **a.** $750 ÷ .98 = $765.31 (rounded)
                       b. $1,152.30 − $765.31 = $386.99 balance due

14. Todd's Sporting Goods received an invoice for soccer equipment dated July 26 with terms 3/10, 1/15, n/30 in the amount of $3,225.83, which included shipping charges of $375.50. If this bill is paid on August 5, what amount must be paid?

$3,225.83 − $375.50 = $2,850.33 $2,850.33 × .97 = $2,764.82 (rounded)
100% − 3% = 97% $2,764.82 + $375.50 = $3,140.32

LEARNING UNIT 8.1: Markups Based on Cost (100%)

DRILL PROBLEMS

1. Fill in the missing numbers:

Cost	Dollar markup	Selling price	
a. $7.80	$1.92	$9.72	
$S = C + M$	$S = \$7.80 + \$1.92$		
b. $8.32	$2.72	$11.04	($11.04 − $8.32 = $2.72)
c. $25.27	$4.35	$29.62	($29.62 − $25.27 = $4.35)
d. $90.00	$75.00	$165.00	($165 − $75 = $90)
e. $86.54	$29.77	$116.31	($86.54 + $29.77 = $116.31)

2. Calculate the markup based on cost (round to the nearest cent).

Cost	Markup (percent of cost)	Dollar markup	
a. $425.00	30%	$127.50	($425 × .30 = $127.50)
b. $1.52	20%	$0.30	($1.52 × .20 = $.30)
c. $9.90	$12\frac{1}{2}\%$	$1.24	($9.90 × .125 = $1.24)
d. $298.10	50%	$149.05	($298.10 × .50 = $149.05)
e. $74.25	38%	$28.22	($74.25 × .38 = $28.22)
f. $552.25	100%	$552.25	($552.25 × 1 = $552.25)

3. Calculate the dollar markup and rate of the markup as a percent of cost (round percents to nearest tenth percent). Verify your result, which may be slightly off due to rounding.

Cost	Selling price	Dollar markup	Markup (percent of cost)	Verify
a. $2.50	$4.50	$2.00	80%	$\dfrac{\$2.00}{.80} = \$2.50$
($4.50 − $2.50 = $2.00); ($2 ÷ $2.50 = .8 = 80%)				
b. $12.50	$19.00	$6.50	52%	$\dfrac{\$6.50}{.52} = \$12.50$
($19.00 − $12.50 = $6.50); ($6.50 ÷ $12.50 = .52 = 52%)				
c. $0.97	$1.25	$0.28	28.9%	$\dfrac{\$.28}{.289} = \$.97$
($1.25 − $.97 = $0.28); ($.28 ÷ $.97 = .2886 = 28.9%)				
d. $132.25	$175.00	$42.75	32.3%	$\dfrac{\$42.75}{.323} = \$132.35$
($175 − $132.25 = $42.75); ($42.75 ÷ $132.25 = .3232 = 32.3%)				
e. $65.00	$89.99	$24.99	38.4%	$\dfrac{\$24.99}{.384} = \$65.08$
($89.99 − $65 = $24.99); ($24.99 ÷ $65 = .3844 = 38.4%)				

4. Calculate the dollar markup and the selling price.

Cost	Markup (percent of cost)	Dollar markup	Selling price	
a. $2.20	40%	$0.88	$3.08	$S = C + M$
($2.20 × .40 = $.88); ($2.20 + $.88 = $3.08)				$S = \$2.20 + .40\,(\$2.20)$
b. $2.80	16%	$0.45	$3.25	
($2.80 × .16 = $.448 = $0.45); ($2.80 + $.45 = $3.25)				
c. $840.00	$12\frac{1}{2}\%$	$105.00	$945.00	
($840 × .125 = $105); ($840 + $105 = $945)				
d. $24.36	30%	$7.31	$31.67	
($24.36 × .30 = $7.31); ($24.36 + $7.31 = $31.67)				

5. Calculate the cost (round to the nearest cent).

	Selling price	Rate of markup based on cost	Cost	
a.	$1.98	30%	$1.52	$S = C + M$
	($1.98 ÷ 1.30 = $1.52)			$1.98 = C + .30C$
b.	$360.00	60%	$225.00	$S = C + M$
	($360 ÷ 1.60 = $225)			$360 = C + .60C$
c.	$447.50	20%	$372.92	
	($447.50 ÷ 1.20 = $372.92)			
d.	$1,250.00	100%	$625.00	
	($1,250 ÷ 2 = $625)			

6. Find the missing numbers. Round money to the nearest cent and percents to the nearest tenth percent.

	Cost	Dollar markup	Percent markup on cost	Selling price	
a.	$72.00	$28.80	40%	$100.80	$S = C + M$
	($72 × .40 = $28.80); ($72.00 + $28.80 = $100.80)				$S = $72 + .40 ($72)$
b.	$28.00	$7.00	25%	$35.00	$S = C + M$
	($35 − $7 = $28); ($7 ÷ $28 = .25 = 25%)				$35 = C + 7
c.	$8.80	$1.10	12.5%	$9.90	
	($1.10 ÷ $8.80 = .125 = 12.5%); ($8.80 + $1.10 = $9.90)				
d.	$15.50	$4.34	28%	$19.84	$S = C + M$
	($19.84 ÷ 1.28 = $15.50); ($19.84 − $15.50 = $4.34)				$19.84 = C + .28C$
e.	$175.00	$61.25	35%	$236.25	
	($236.25 − $175 = $61.25); ($61.25 ÷ $175 = .35 = 35%)				

WORD PROBLEMS

7. The cost of an office chair is $159.00 and the markup rate is 24% of the cost. What are **(a)** the dollar markup and **(b)** the selling price?
a. $159 × .24 = $38.16 markup $S = C + M$
b. $159 + $38.16 = $197.16 selling price $S = $159 + .24 ($159)$

8. If Barry's Furniture Store purchased a floor lamp for $120 and plans to add a markup of $90, **(a)** what will the selling price be and **(b)** what is the markup as a percent of cost?
a. $120 + $90 = $210 selling price $S = C + M$
b. $90 ÷ $120 = .75 = 75% $S = $120 + 90

9. If Lesjardin's Jewelry Store is selling a gold bracelet for $349, which includes a markup of 35% on cost, what are **(a)** Lesjardin's cost and **(b)** the amount of the dollar markup?
a. $349 ÷ 1.35 = $258.518 = $258.52 cost $S = C + M$
b. $349 − $258.52 = $90.48 markup $349 = C + .35C$

10. Toll's Variety Store sells an alarm clock for $14.75. The alarm clock cost Toll's $9.90. What is the markup amount as a percent of cost? Round to the nearest whole percent.
$14.75 − $9.90 = $4.85 $4.85 ÷ $9.90 = .4898 = 49% markup

11. Swanson's Audio Supply marks up its merchandise by 40% on cost. If the markup on a cassette player is $85, what are **(a)** the cost of the cassette player and **(b)** the selling price?

a. $85 ÷ .40 = $212.50 cost $C = \dfrac{\text{Dollar markup}}{\text{Percent markup on cost}}$ $S = C + M$

b. $212.50 + $85 = $297.50 selling price $C = \dfrac{\$85}{.40}$ $S = \$212.50 + \$85$

12. Brown's Department Store is selling a shirt for $55. If the markup is 70% on cost, what is Brown's cost (to the nearest cent)?

$55 ÷ 1.70 = $32.35 $\text{Cost} = \dfrac{\text{Selling price}}{1 + \text{Percent markup on cost}}$

13. Ward's Greenhouse purchased tomato flats for $5.75 each. Ward's has decided to use a markup of 42% on cost. Find the selling price.
$5.75 × .42 = $2.415 = $2.42 $S = C + M$
$5.75 + $2.42 = $8.17 selling price $S = $5.75 + .42 ($5.75)$

LEARNING UNIT 8.2: Markups Based on Selling Price (100%)

DRILL PROBLEMS

1. Calculate the markup based on the selling price.

	Selling price	Markup (percent of selling price)	Dollar markup	
a.	$8.00	30%	$2.40	($8.00 × .30 = $2.40)
b.	$230.00	25%	$57.50	($230 × .25 = $57.50)
c.	$81.00	42.5%	$34.43	($81 × .425 = 34.425 = $34.43)
d.	$72.88	$37\frac{1}{2}$%	$27.33	($72.88 × .375 = $27.33)
e.	$1.98	$7\frac{1}{2}$%	$0.15	($1.98 × .075 = $.148 = $0.15)

2. Calculate the dollar markup and the markup as a percent of selling price (to the nearest tenth percent). Verify your answer, which may be slightly off due to rounding.

	Cost	Selling price	Dollar markup	Markup (percent of selling price)	Verify
a.	$2.50	$4.25	$1.75	41.2%	$\dfrac{\$1.75}{.412} = \$4.25$

($4.25 − $2.50 = $1.75); ($1.75 ÷ $4.25 = .4117 = 41.2%)

b.	$16.00	$24.00	$8.00	33.3%	$\dfrac{\$8.00}{.333} = \$24.02$

($24 − $16 = $8); ($8 ÷ $24 = .3333)

c.	$45.25	$85.00	$39.75	46.8%	$\dfrac{\$39.75}{.468} = \$84.94$

($85 − $45.25 = $39.75); ($39.75 ÷ $85 = .4676 = 46.8%)

d.	$0.19	$0.25	$0.06	24%	$\dfrac{\$.06}{.24} = \$.25$

($.25 − $.19 = $.06); ($.06 ÷ $.25 = .24 = 24%)

e.	$5.50	$8.98	$3.48	38.8%	$\dfrac{\$3.48}{.388} = \$8.97$

($8.98 − $5.50 = $3.48); ($3.48 ÷ $8.98 = .3875 = 38.8%)

3. Given the *cost* and the markup as a percent of *selling price,* calculate the selling price.

	Cost	Markup (percent of selling price)	Selling price	
a.	$5.90	15%	$6.94	$S = C + M$
	[$5.90 ÷ (1 − .15) = $5.90 ÷ .85 = $6.941 = $6.94]			$S = \$5.90 + .15S$
b.	$600	32%	$882.35	$S = C + M$
	[$600 ÷ (1 − .32) = $600 ÷ .68 = $882.352 = $882.35]			$S = \$600 + .32S$
c.	$15	50%	$30	$S = C + M$
	[$15 ÷ (1 − .50) = $15 ÷ .50 = $30]			$S = \$15 + .50(S)$
d.	$120	30%	$171.43	$S = C + M$
	[$120 ÷ (1 − .30) = $120 ÷ .70 = $171.43]			$S = \$120 + .30(S)$
e.	$0.29	20%	$0.36	$S = C + M$
	[$.29 ÷ (1 − .20) = $.29 ÷ .8 = $0.362 = $0.36]			$S = \$.29 + .20(S)$

4. Given the selling price and the percent markup on selling price, calculate the cost.

	Cost	Markup (percent of selling price)	Selling price	
a.	$3.75	40%	$6.25	$S = C + M$
	[$6.25 × (1 − .40) = $6.25 × .60 = $3.75]			$6.25 = C + .40(\$6.25)$
b.	$13.00	20%	$16.25	$S = C + M$
	[$16.25 × (1 − .20) = $16.25 × .80 = $13]			$16.25 = C + .20(\$16.25)$
c.	$51.75	19%	$63.89	$S = C + M$
	[$63.89 × (1 − .19) = $63.89 × .81 = $51.75]			$63.89 = C + .19(\$63.89)$
d.	$16.50	$62\frac{1}{2}$%	$44.00	$S = C + M$
	[$44 × (1 − .625) = $44 × .375 = $16.50]			$44 = C + .625(\$44)$

5. Calculate the equivalent rate of markup (round to the nearest hundredth percent).

	Markup on cost	Markup on selling price		Markup on cost	Markup on selling price
a.	40%	<u>28.57%</u>	**b.**	50%	<u>33.33%</u>
	$(.40 \div 1.40 = .28571 = 28.57\%)$			$(.50 \div 1.50 = .3333 = 33.33\%)$	
c.	<u>100%</u>	50%	**d.**	<u>53.85%</u>	35%
	$(.50 \div .50 = 1 = 100\%)$			$(.35 \div .65 = .53846 = 53.85\%)$	
e.	<u>66.67%</u>	40%			
	$(.40 \div .60 = .66666 = 66.67\%)$				

WORD PROBLEMS

6. Fisher Equipment is selling a Wet/Dry Shop Vac for $49.97. If Fisher's markup is 40% of the selling price, what is the cost of the Shop Vac?

$$\$49.97 = C + .40(\$49.97)$$

$$\begin{array}{r} \$49.97 = C + \quad \$19.99 \\ -\ 19.99 \qquad\qquad -\ 19.99 \\ \hline \$29.98 = C \end{array}$$

or $\quad \$49.97 \times (1 - .40)$

7. Gove Lumber Company purchased a 10-inch table saw for $225 and will mark up the price 35% on the selling price. What will the selling price be?

$$\begin{array}{r} S = \$225 + \quad .35S \\ -\ .35S \qquad\qquad -\ .35S \\ \hline \end{array}$$

$$\frac{.65S}{.65} = \frac{\$225}{.65}$$

or $\quad \dfrac{\$225}{1 - .35}$

$$S = \$346.153 = \$346.15$$

8. To realize a sufficient gross margin, City Paint and Supply Company marks up its paint 27% on the selling price. If a gallon of Latex Semi-Gloss Enamel has a markup of $4.02, find **(a)** the selling price and **(b)** the cost.

a. $\dfrac{\$4.02}{.27} = \$14.89$ **b.** $\$14.89 - \$4.02 = C$ $S = \dfrac{\text{Dollar markup}}{\text{Percent markup on selling price}}$

$$\$10.87 = C$$

9. A Magnavox 20-inch color TV cost $180 and sells for $297. What is the markup based on the selling price? Round to the nearest hundredth percent.

$$\$297 - \$180 = \$117 \text{ markup} \qquad \$117 \div \$297 = .39393 = 39.39\%$$

10. Bargain Furniture sells a five-piece country maple bedroom set for $1,299. The cost of this set is $700. What are **(a)** the markup on the bedroom set, **(b)** the markup percent on cost, and **(c)** the markup percent on the selling price? Round to the nearest hundredth percent.

a. $\$1,299 - \$700 = \$599$ **b.** $\dfrac{\$599}{\$700} = 85.57\%$ **c.** $\dfrac{\$599}{\$1,299} = 46.11\%$

11. Robert's Department Store marks up its sundries by 28% on the selling price. If a 6.4-ounce tube of toothpaste costs $1.65, what will the selling price be?

$$\begin{array}{r} S = \$1.65 + \quad .28S \\ -\ .28S \qquad\qquad -\ .28S \\ \hline \end{array}$$

$$\frac{.72S}{.72} = \frac{\$1.65}{.72}$$

or $\quad \dfrac{\$1.65}{1 - .28}$

$$S = \$2.291 = \$2.29 \text{ selling price}$$

12. To be competitive, Tinker Toys must sell the Nintendo Control Deck for $89.99. To meet expenses and make a sufficient profit, Tinker Toys must add a markup on the selling price of 23%. What is the maximum amount that Tinker Toys can afford to pay a wholesaler for Nintendo?

$$\$89.99 = C + .23(\$89.99) \qquad \text{or} \qquad \$89.99 \times (1 - .23)$$

$$\begin{array}{r} \$89.99 = C + \quad \$20.70 \\ -\ 20.70 \qquad\qquad -\ 20.70 \\ \hline \$69.29 = C \ (\text{maximum cost}) \end{array}$$

13. Nicole's Restaurant charges $7.50 for a linguini dinner that cost $2.75 for the ingredients. What rate of markup is earned on the selling price? Round to the nearest hundredth percent.

$$\$7.50 - \$2.75 = \$4.75 \qquad \$4.75 \div \$7.50 = .63333 = 63.33\% \text{ on selling price}$$

LEARNING UNIT 8.3: Markdowns and Perishables

DRILL PROBLEMS

1. Find the dollar markdown and the sale price.

	Original selling price	Markdown percent	Dollar markdown	Sale price
a.	$80	20%	$16.00	$64

($80 × .20 = $16), ($80 − $16 = $64)

b.	$2,099.98	25%	$525	$1,574.98

($2,099.98 × .25 = $524.995 = $525)
($2,099.98 − $525 = $1,574.98)

c.	$729	30%	$218.70	$510.30

($729 × .30 = $218.70), ($729 − $218.70 = $510.30)

2. Find the dollar markdown and the markdown percent on original selling price.

	Original selling price	Sale price	Dollar markdown	Markdown percent
a.	$19.50	$9.75	$9.75	50%

($19.50 − $9.75 = $9.75) $\left(\dfrac{\$9.75}{\$19.50} = .050 = 50\%\right)$

b.	$250	$175	$75	30%

($250 − $175 = $75) $\left(\dfrac{\$75}{\$250} = 30\%\right)$

c.	$39.95	$29.96	$9.99	25%

($39.95 − $29.96 = $9.99) $\left(\dfrac{\$9.99}{\$39.95} = 25\%\right)$

3. Find the original selling price.

	Sale price	Markdown percent	Original selling price
a.	$328	20%	$410

(100% − 20% = 80%) $\left(\dfrac{\$328}{.80} = \$410\right)$

$\dfrac{P\ \$328}{B \times R\ .80}$

b.	$15.85	15%	$18.65

(100% − 15% = 85%) $\left(\dfrac{\$15.85}{.85} = \$18.65\right)$

4. Calculate the final selling price.

	Original selling price	First markdown	Second markdown	Final markup	Final selling price
a.	$4.96	25%	8%	5%	$3.59

[$4.96 × (1 − .25) = $3.72]
[$3.72 × (1 − .08) = $3.42]
[$3.42 × (1 + .05) = $3.59]

b.	$130	30%	10%	20%	$98.28

[$130 × (1 − .30) = $91]
[$91 × (1 − .10) = $81.90]
[$81.90 × (1 + .20) = $98.28]

5. Find the missing amounts.

	Number of units	Unit cost	Total cost	Estimated* spoilage	Desired markup (percent of cost)	Total selling price	Selling price per unit
a.	72	$3	$216	12%	50%	$324	$5.14

(72 × $3 = $216); [$216 + ($216 × .50) = $324]
(72 × .12 = 8.64 = 9 units) $TS = TC + TM$
[$324/(72 − 9) = $5.14]

b.	50	$0.90	$45	16%	42%	$63.90	$1.52

(50 × $0.90 = $45), [$45 + ($45 × .42) = $63.90]
(50 × .16 = 8 units)
[$63.90/(50 − 8) = $1.52]

*Round to the nearest whole unit as needed.

WORD PROBLEMS

6. Windom's is having a 30%-off sale on their box springs and mattresses. A queen-size, back-supporter mattress is priced at $325. What is the sale price of the mattress?
$325 × .30 = $97.50   or $325 × .70 = $227.50
$325 − $97.50 = $227.50

7. Murray and Sons sell a personal fax machine for $602.27. It is having a sale, and the fax machine is marked down to $499.88. What is the percent of the markdown?
$602.27 − $499.88 = $102.39 $\dfrac{\$102.39}{\$602.27} = 17\%$

8. Coleman's is having a clearance sale. A lamp with an original selling price of $249 is now selling for $198. Find the percent of the markdown. Round to the nearest hundredth percent.
$249 − $198 = $51 $\dfrac{\$51}{\$249} = 20.48\%$

9. Johnny's Sports Shop has advertised markdowns on certain items of 22%. A soccer ball is marked with a sale price of $16.50. What was the original price of the soccer ball?
100% − 22% = 78% $\dfrac{\$16.50}{.78} = \$21.15$ $\dfrac{P\,\$16.50}{B \times R}$
                                                          ?   .78

10. Sam Grillo sells seasonal furnishings. Near the end of the summer a five-piece patio set that was priced $349.99 had not been sold, so he marked it down by 12%. As Labor Day approached, he still had not sold the patio set, so he marked it down an additional 18%. What was the final selling price of the patio set?
$349.99 × .88 = $307.99 × .82 = $252.55

11. Calsey's Department Store sells their down comforters for a regular price of $325. During its white sale the comforters were marked down 22%. Then, at the end of the sale, Calsey's held a special promotion and gave a second markdown of 10%. When the sale was over, the remaining comforters were marked up 20%. What was the final selling price of the remaining comforters?
$325 × .78 = $253.50 $253.50 × .90 = $228.15 $228.15 × 1.2 = $273.78

12. The New Howard Bakery wants to make a 60% profit on the cost of its pies. To calculate the price of the pies, it estimated that the usual amount of spoilage is 5 pies. Calculate the selling price for each pie if the number of pies baked each day is 24 and the cost of the ingredients for each pie is $1.80.
24 × $1.80 = $43.20 total cost
$43.20 × 1.60 = $69.12 total selling price $TS = TC + TM$
24 − 5 = 19
$\dfrac{\$69.12}{19} = \$3.64$ per pie

13. Sunshine Bakery bakes 660 loaves of bread each day and estimates that 10% of the bread will go stale before it is sold and will have to be discarded. The owner of the bakery wishes to realize a 55% markup on cost on the bread. If the cost to make a loaf of bread is $0.46, what should the owner sell each loaf for?
660 × $.46 = $303.60 total cost $470.58/(660 − 66) = $.79
$303.60 × 1.55 = $470.58 total selling price
660 × .10 = 66 units spoilage

LEARNING UNIT 9.1: Calculating Various Types of Employees' Gross Pay

DRILL PROBLEMS

1. Fill in the missing amounts for each of the following employees. Do not round the overtime rate in your calculations and round your final answers to the nearest cent.

Employee	Total hours	Rate per hour	Regular pay	Overtime pay	Gross pay
a. Ben Badger	40	$7.60	$304.00	$ 0.00	$304.00
b. Casey Guitare	43	$9.00	$360.00	$40.50	$400.50
c. Norma Harris	37	$7.50	$277.50	$ 0.00	$277.50
d. Ed Jackson	45	$12.25	$490.00	$91.88	$581.88

a. $40 \times \$7.60 = \$304.00$

b. $(40 \times \$9.00 = \$360.00) + (3 \times \$13.50 = \$40.50) = \$400.50$

c. $37 \times \$7.50 = \$277.50$

d. $(40 \times \$12.25 = \$490.00) + (5 \times \$18.375 = \$91.875) = \$581.88$

2. Calculate each employee's gross from the following data. Do not round the overtime rate in your calculation but round your final answers to the nearest cent.

Employee	S	M	Tu	W	Th	F	S	Total hours	Rate per hour	Regular pay	Overtime pay	Gross pay
a. L. Adams	0	8	8	8	8	8	0	40	$8.10	$324.00	$ 0.00	$324.00
b. M. Card	0	9	8	9	8	8	4	46	$11.35	$454.00	$102.15	$556.15
c. P. Kline	2	$7\frac{1}{2}$	$8\frac{1}{4}$	8	$10\frac{3}{4}$	9	2	$47\frac{1}{2}$	$10.60	$424.00	$119.25	$543.25
d. J. Mack	0	$9\frac{1}{2}$	$9\frac{3}{4}$	$9\frac{1}{2}$	10	10	4	$52\frac{3}{4}$	$9.95	$398.00	$190.29	$588.29

a. $40 \times \$8.10 = \$324.00$

b. $(40 \times \$11.35 = \$454.00) + (6 \times \$17.025 = \$102.15) = \$556.15$

c. $(40 \times \$10.60 = \$424.00) + \left(7\frac{1}{2} \times \$15.90 = \$119.25\right) = \$543.25$

d. $(40 \times \$9.95 = \$398.00) + \left(12\frac{3}{4} \times \$14.925 = \$190.29\right) = \$588.29$

3. Calculate the gross wages of the following production workers.

Employee	Rate per unit	No. of units produced	Gross pay	
a. A. Bossie	$0.67	655	$438.85	$0.67 \times 655 = \$438.85$
b. J. Carson	$0.87\frac{1}{2}$	703	$615.13	$0.875 \times 703 = \$615.125 = \$615.13$

4. Using the given differential scale, calculate the gross wages of the following production workers.

Units produced	Amount per unit
From 1–50	$.55
From 51–100	.65
From 101–200	.72
More than 200	.95

Employee	Units produced	Gross pay
a. F. Burns	190	$124.80
b. B. English	210	$141.50
c. E. Jackson	200	$132.00

a. $(50 \times \$0.55) + (50 \times \$0.65) + (90 \times \$0.72) = \$124.80$

b. $(50 \times \$0.55) + (50 \times \$0.65) + (100 \times \$0.72) + (10 \times \$0.95) = \$141.50$

c. $(50 \times \$0.55) + (50 \times \$0.65) + (100 \times \$0.72) = \$132.00$

5. Calculate the following salespersons' gross wages.

a. Straight commission:

Employee	Net sales	Commission	Gross pay
M. Salley	$40,000	13%	$5,200

$\$40,000 \times .13 = \$5,200$

b. Straight commision with draw:

Employee	Net sales	Commission	Draw	Commission minus draw
G. Gorsbeck	$38,000	12%	$600	$3,960

($38,000 × .12) − $600 = $3,960

c. Variable commission scale:

Up to $25,000	8%
Excess of $25,000 to $40,000	10%
More than $40,000	12%

Employee	Net sales	Gross pay
H. Lloyd	$42,000	$3,740

($25,000 × .08) + ($15,000 × .10) + ($2,000 × .12) = $3,740

d. Salary plus commission:

Employee	Salary	Commission	Quota	Net sales	Gross pay
P. Floyd	$2,500	3%	$400,000	$475,000	$4,750

($475,000 − $400,000) × .03 + $2,500 = $4,750

WORD PROBLEMS

For all problems with overtime, be sure to round only the final answer.

6. In the first week of December, Dana Robinson worked 52 hours. His regular rate of pay is $11.25 per hour. What was Dana's gross pay for the week?
52 − 40 = 12 hours overtime $652.50 gross pay
(40 × $11.25) + (12 × $16.875)
$450   + $202.50

7. Davis Fisheries pays its workers for each box of fish they pack. Sunny Melanson receives $0.30 per box. During the third week of July, Sunny packed 2,410 boxes of fish. What is Sunny's gross pay?
2,410 × $.30 = $723.00 gross pay

8. Maye George is a real estate broker who receives a straight commission of 6%. What would her commission be for a house that sold for $197,500?
$197,500 × .06 = $11,850 commission

9. Devon Company pays Eileen Haskins a straight commission of $12\frac{1}{2}\%$ on net sales. In January, Devon gave Eileen a draw of $600. She had net sales that month of $35,570. What was Eileen's commission minus draw?
$35,570 × .125 = $4,446.25
                      − 600.00
                  ─────────
            $3,846.25 commission minus draw

10. Parker and Company pays Selma Stokes on a variable commission scale. In a month when Selma had net sales of $155,000, what was her gross pay based on the following schedule?

Net sales	Commission rate
Up to $40,000	5%
Excess of $40,000 to $75,000	5.5%
Excess of $75,000 to $100,000	6%
More than $100,000	7%

($40,000 × .05) + ($35,000 × .055) +($25,000 × .06) +($55,000 × .07) $9,275 gross pay
$2,000   + $1,925   + $1,500   + $3,850

11. Marsh Furniture Company pays Joshua Charles a monthly salary of $1,900 plus a commission of $2\frac{1}{2}\%$ on sales over $12,500. Last month, Joshua had net sales of $17,799. What was Joshua's gross pay for the month?
$1,900 + [($17,799 − $12,500) × .025] $2,032.48 gross pay
$1,900 + $132.48

12. Amy McWha works at Lamplighter Bookstore where she earns $7.75 per hour plus a commission of 2% on her weekly sales in excess of $1,500. Last week, Amy worked 39 hours and had total sales of $2,250. What was Amy's gross pay for the week?
($7.75 × 39) + [($2,250 − $1,500) × .02] $317.25 gross pay
$302.25   + $15.00

LEARNING UNIT 9.2: Computing Payroll Deductions for Employees' Pay; Employers' Responsibilities

DRILL PROBLEMS

Use tables in the *Business Math Handbook* (assume FICA rates in text).

Employee	Allowances and marital status	Cumulative earnings	Salary per week	Taxable earnings S.S.	Medicare
1. Pete Small	M—3	$68,200	$780	a. $200	b. $ 780
2. Alice Hall	M—1	$62,000	$1,100	c. $1,100	d. $1,100
3. Jean Rose	M—2	$130,000	$990	e. $ 0	f. $ 990

    a. $68,400
       − 68,200
       $ 200

4. What is the FIT for Pete Small by wage bracket table?
   $76

5. What is the tax for Social Security and Medicare for Pete in Problem 1?
   Social Security: .062 × $200 = $12.40   Medicare: .0145 × $780 = $11.31

6. Calculate Pete's FIT by the percentage method.
     $780.00
   − 155.76 (3 × $51.92)
     $624.24
   − 124.00
      $500.24 × .15 = $75.04

7. What would employees contribute for this week's payroll for SUTA and FUTA?
   0; wages over $7,000 are exempt

WORD PROBLEMS

8. Cynthia Pratt has earned $68,000 thus far this year. This week she earned $500. Find her total FICA tax deduction (Social Security and Medicare).

Social Security: $68,400   Total FICA: $24.80
           − 68,000   + 7.25
            $ 400 × .062 = $24.80 $32.05
Medicare: $500 × .0145 = $7.25

9. If Cynthia (Problem 8) earns $1,050 the following week, what will be her new total FICA tax deduction?
.0145 × $1,050 = $15.23 Medicare
No Social Security.

10. Martin Hartley is single and claims no withholding allowances. Use the proper wage bracket table to find his federal withholding tax if he earns $4,166.67 in May.
$846   Single monthly table

11. Roger Alley, a service dispatcher, has weekly earnings of $750. He claimed four allowances on his W-4 form and is married. Besides his FIT and FICA deductions, he has deductions of $35.16 for medical insurance and $17.25 for union dues. Calculate his net earnings for the third week in February. Use the wage bracket tables.

FIT	= $ 63.00		$750.00
Social Security	= 46.50 (.062 × $750)		− 172.79
Medicare	= 10.88 (.0145 × $750)		$577.21
Medical	= 35.16		
Union dues	= 17.25		
Total deductions	= $172.79		

12. Nicole Mariotte is unmarried and claimed one withholding allowance on her W-4 form. In the second week of February, she earned $707.35. Deductions from her pay included federal withholding, Social Security, Medicare, health insurance for $47.75, and $30.00 for the company meal plan. What is Nicole's net pay for the week? Use the percentage method.

$707.35 − $51.92 = $655.43   FIT $108.66
[($655.43 − $517.00) × .28] + $69.90   Social Security   43.86
$38.76 + $69.90 = $108.66 FIT   Medicare   10.26
Social Security: .062 × $707.35 = $43.86   Health insurance   47.75
Medicare: .0145 × $707.35 = $10.26   Meal plan   30.00

                                   Total deductions $240.53
                                   $707.35 − $240.53 = $466.82 net pay

13. Gerald Knowlton had total gross earnings of $68,100 in the last week of November. His earnings for the first week in December were $804.70. His employer uses the percentage method to calculate federal withholding. If Gerald is married, claims two allowances, and has medical insurance of $52.25 deducted each week from his pay, what is his net pay for the week?

$804.70
− 103.84 ($51.92 × 2)

$700.86 $804.70
− 124.00   − 86.53 FIT
$576.86 × .15 = $86.53 FIT   − 18.60 Social Security
                                 − 11.67 Medicare
Social Security: $68,400   − 52.25 Medical insurance
               − 68,100 $635.65 net pay
            $ 300 × .062 = $18.60
Medicare: $804.70 × .0145 = $11.67

14. An article in the September 1997 issue of *Nation's Business* discusses payroll costs. The minimum wage in the year 2002 is expected to be raised to $7.25 an hour from the present rate of $5.15 an hour. If a worker today works 6 hours a day for 5 days, how much more would the person make per week in the year 2002?

6 × 5 =   30 hours per week   30 $217.50
         × $5.15 per hour   × $7.25   − 154.50
Present: $154.50 per week   Future: $217.50 per week $ 63.00 a week more

LEARNING UNIT 10.1: Calculation of Simple Interest and Maturity Value

DRILL PROBLEMS

1. Find the simple interest for each of the following loans:

	Principal	Rate	Time	Interest	
a.	$2,000	9%	1 year	$180	a. $2,000 × .09 × 1 = $180
b.	$3,000	12%	3 years	$1,080	b. $3,000 × .12 × 3 = $1,080
c.	$18,000	$8\frac{1}{2}\%$	10 months	$1,275	c. $18,000 × .085 × $\frac{10}{12}$ = $1,275

2. Find the simple interest for each of the following loans; use the exact interest method. Use the days-in-a-year calendar in the text when needed.

	Principal	Rate	Time	Interest		
a.	$700	14%	30 days	$8.05	July 11	192
b.	$4,290	8%	250 days	$235.07	March 11	− 70
c.	$1,500	8%	Made March 11 Due July 11	$40.11		122

a. $700 × .14 × $\frac{30}{365}$ = $8.05   b. $4,290 × .08 × $\frac{250}{365}$ = $235.07   c. $1,500 × .08 × $\frac{122}{365}$ = $40.11

3. Find the simple interest for each of the following loans using the ordinary interest method (Banker's Rule).

	Principal	Rate	Time	Interest		
a.	$5,250	$7\frac{1}{2}\%$	120 days	$131.25	October 17	290
b.	$700	12%	70 days	$16.33	June 15	− 166
c.	$2,600	11%	Made on June 15 Due October 17	$98.51		124

a. $5,250 × .075 × $\frac{120}{360}$ = $131.25   b. $700 × .12 × $\frac{70}{360}$ = $16.33   c. $2,600 × .11 × $\frac{124}{360}$ = $98.51

WORD PROBLEMS

4. On October 17, Nina Verga borrowed $3,136 at a rate of 12%. She promised to repay the loan in 10 months. What are **(a)** the amount of the simple interest and **(b)** the total amount owed upon maturity?

a. $3,136 \times .12 \times \dfrac{10}{12} = \$313.60$ interest   **b.** $\$3,136 + \$313.60 = \$3,449.60$ maturity value

5. Marjorie Folsom borrowed $5,500 to purchase a computer. The loan was for 9 months at an annual interest rate of $12\frac{1}{2}\%$. What are **(a)** the amount of interest Marjorie must pay and **(b)** the maturity value of the loan?

a. $5,500 \times .125 \times \dfrac{9}{12} = \$515.63$ interest   **b.** $\$5,500 + \$515.63 = \$6,015.63$ maturity value

6. Eric has a loan for $1,200 at an ordinary interest rate of 9.5% for 80 days. Julie has a loan for $1,200 at an exact interest rate of 9.5% for 80 days. Calculate **(a)** the total amount due on Eric's loan and **(b)** the total amount due on Julie's loan.

a. $1,200 \times .095 \times \dfrac{80}{360} = \$25.33$ interest $\$1,200 + \$25.33 = \$1,225.33$ maturity value of Eric's loan

b. $1,200 \times .095 \times \dfrac{80}{365} = \$24.99$ interest $\$1,200 + \$24.99 = \$1,224.99$ maturity value of Julie's loan

7. Roger Lee borrowed $5,280 at $13\frac{1}{2}\%$ on May 24 and agreed to repay the loan on August 24. The lender calculates interest using the exact interest method. How much will Roger be required to pay on August 24?

August 24 − May 24
      $236 - 144 = 92$ days $5,280 \times .135 \times \dfrac{92}{365} = \$179.66$ interest

$\$5,280 + \$179.66 = \$5,459.66$ maturity value, due August 24

8. On March 8, Jack Faltin borrowed $10,225 at $9\frac{3}{4}\%$. He signed a note agreeing to repay the loan and interest on November 8. If the lender calculates interest using the ordinary interest method, what will Jack's repayment be?

November 8 − March 8
      $312 - 67 = 245$ days $10,225 \times .0975 \times \dfrac{245}{360} = \$678.47$ interest

$\$10,225 + \$678.47 = \$10,903.47$ maturity value, due November 8

9. Dianne Smith's real estate taxes of $641.49 were due on November 1, 2001. Due to financial difficulties, Dianne was unable to pay her tax bill until January 15, 2002. The penalty for late payment is $13\frac{3}{8}\%$ ordinary interest. What is the penalty Dianne will have to pay, and what is Dianne's total payment on January 15?

December 31 − November 1 + January 15
$365 - 305 = 60 + 15 = 75$ days $641.49 \times .13375 \times \dfrac{75}{360} = \$17.87$ penalty

$\$641.49 + \$17.87 = \$659.36$ total due on January 15

10. On August 8, Rex Eason had a credit card balance of $550, but he was unable to pay his bill. The credit card company charges interest of $18\frac{1}{2}\%$ annually on late payments. What amount will Rex have to pay if he pays his bill 1 month late?

$\$550 + \left(\$550 \times .185 \times \dfrac{1}{12}\right) = \$558.48$ (principal + interest)

11. The August/September 1996 issue of *Your Money* discusses average consumers who carry a balance of $2,000 on one credit card. If the yearly rate of interest is 18%, how much are consumers paying in interest per year?

$\qquad\qquad\qquad\qquad\quad (P) \qquad (R) \quad (T) \qquad (I)$
$P = \$2,000, R = 18\%, T = 1 \text{ year} \qquad \$2,000 \times .18 \times 1 = \$360$

12. The November 30, 1997, Chicago *Sun-Times* compared credit card interest rates across the country. AFBA Industrial Bank of Colorado Springs, Colorado, charges 11% per year. If you had a credit card debt of $1,500, what would your interest amount be after 3 months?

$P = \$1,500, R = 11\%, T = 3 \text{ months} \qquad \$1,500 \times .11 \times \dfrac{3}{12} = \$41.25$

LEARNING UNIT 10.2: Finding Unknown in Simple Interest Formula

DRILL PROBLEMS

1. Find the principal in each of the following. Round to the nearest cent. Assume 360 days. *Calculator hint:* Do denominator calculation first, do not round; when answer is displayed, save it in memory by pressing [M+]. Now key in the numerator (interest amount), [÷], [MR], [=] for the answer. Be sure to clear memory after each problem by pressing [MR] again so that the M is no longer in the display.

	Rate	Time	Interest	Principal
a.	8%	70 days	$68	$ 4,371.44
b.	11%	90 days	$125	$ 4,545.45
c.	9%	120 days	$103	$ 3,433.33
d.	$8\frac{1}{2}$%	60 days	$150	$10,588.29

a. $\dfrac{\$68}{.08 \times \dfrac{70}{360}} = \dfrac{\$68}{.0155555} = \$4,371.44$

b. $\dfrac{\$125}{.11 \times \dfrac{90}{360}} = \dfrac{\$125}{.0275} = \$4,545.45$

c. $\dfrac{\$103}{.09 \times \dfrac{120}{360}} = \dfrac{\$103}{.03} = \$3,433.33$

d. $\dfrac{\$150}{.085 \times \dfrac{60}{360}} = \dfrac{\$150}{.0141666} = \$10,588.29$

2. Find the rate in each of the following. Round to the nearest tenth of a percent. Assume 360 days.

	Principal	Time	Interest	Rate
a.	$7,500	120 days	$350	14%
b.	$975	60 days	$25	15.4%
c.	$20,800	220 days	$910	7.2%
d.	$150	30 days	$2.10	16.8%

a. $\dfrac{\$350}{\$7,500 \times \dfrac{120}{360}} = \dfrac{\$350}{\$2,500} = .14$

b. $\dfrac{\$25}{\$975 \times \dfrac{60}{360}} = \dfrac{\$25}{\$162.5} = .1538$

c. $\dfrac{\$910}{\$20,800 \times \dfrac{220}{360}} = \dfrac{\$910}{\$12,711.11} = .0716$

d. $\dfrac{\$2.10}{\$150 \times \dfrac{30}{360}} = \dfrac{\$2.10}{\$12.5} = .168$

3. Find the time (to the nearest day) in each of the following. Assuming ordinary interest, use 360 days.

	Principal	Rate	Interest	Time (days)
a.	$400	11%	$7.33	60
b.	$7,000	12.5%	$292	120
c.	$1,550	9.2%	$106.95	270
d.	$157,000	10.75%	$6,797.88	145

a. $\dfrac{\$7.33}{\$400 \times .11} = \dfrac{\$7.33}{\$44} \times 360 = 59.9$

b. $\dfrac{\$292}{\$7,000 \times .125} = \dfrac{\$292}{\$875} \times 360 = 120.1$

c. $\dfrac{\$106.95}{\$1,550 \times .092} = \dfrac{\$106.95}{\$142.6} \times 360 = 270$

d. $\dfrac{\$6,797.88}{\$157,000 \times .1075} = \dfrac{\$6,797.88}{\$16,877.50} \times 360 = 144.9$

4. Complete the following. Assume 360 days for all examples.

	Principal	Rate (nearest tenth percent)	Time (nearest day)	Simple interest
a.	$345	10%	150 days	$14.38
b.	$1,500.16	12.5%	90 days	$46.88

| c. $750 | 12.2% | 75 days | $19.06 |
| d. $20,260 | 16.7% | 110 days | $1,033.82 |

a. $\dfrac{\$14.38}{\$345 \times \dfrac{150}{360}} = \dfrac{\$14.38}{\$143.75} = .1000$

b. $\dfrac{\$46.88}{.125 \times \dfrac{90}{360}} = \dfrac{\$46.88}{.03125} = \$1,500.16$

c. $\dfrac{\$19.06}{\$750 \times .122} = \dfrac{\$19.06}{\$91.5} \times 360 = 74.9$

d. $\$20,260 \times .167 \times \dfrac{110}{360} = \$1,033.822$

WORD PROBLEMS

Use 360 days.

5. On August 27, 1997, the *Chicago Tribune* ran an article titled "Interest from Principal, Penalty of Early Withdrawal." It happened to Becky, a mother of three. In June, she opened a $20,000 bank CD paying 6% interest, but she had to withdraw the money in a few days to cover one child's college tuition. The bank charged her $600 in penalties for the withdrawal. What percent of the $20,000 was she charged?

$P = \$20,000 \qquad I \text{ (penalty)} = \$600 \qquad \dfrac{\$600 \text{ interest}}{\$20,000} = 3\%$

6. Dr. Vaccarro invested his money at $12\frac{1}{2}\%$ for 175 days and earned interest of $760. How much money did Dr. Vaccarro invest?

$\dfrac{\$760}{.125 \times \dfrac{175}{360}} = \dfrac{\$760}{.0607638} = \$12,507.446 = \$12,507.45 \text{ principal}$

7. The August/September 1996 issue of *Your Money* ran an article titled "Compounding—Which Way Is Best." If you invested $10,000 at 5% interest in a 6-month CD compounding interest daily, you would earn $252.43 in interest. How much would the same $10,000 invested in a bank paying simple interest earn?

$\begin{array}{cccc} (P) & (R) & (T) & (I) \end{array}$

$\$10,000 \times .05 \times \dfrac{6}{12} = \$250$

8. Thomas Kyrouz opened a savings account and deposited $750 in a bank that was paying 7.2% simple interest. How much were his savings worth in 200 days?

$\$750 \times .072 \times \dfrac{200}{360} = \$30 \qquad \$750 + \$30 = \$780$

9. Mary Millitello paid the bank $53.90 in interest on a 66-day loan at 9.8%. How much money did Mary borrow? Round to the nearest dollar.

$\dfrac{\$53.90}{.098 \times \dfrac{66}{360}} = \dfrac{\$53.90}{.0179666} = \$3,000$

10. If Anthony Lucido deposits $2,400 for 66 days and makes $60.72 in interest, what interest rate is he receiving?

$\dfrac{\$60.72}{\$2,400 \times \dfrac{66}{360}} = \dfrac{\$60.72}{\$440} = .138 = 13.8\%$

11. Find how long in days David Wong must invest $23,500 of his company's cash at 8.4% in order to earn $652.50 in interest.

$\dfrac{\$652.50}{\$23,500 \times .084} = \dfrac{\$652.50}{\$1,974} \times 360 = 118.99 = 119 \text{ days}$

LEARNING UNIT 10.3: U.S. Rule—Making Partial Note Payments before Due Date

DRILL PROBLEMS

1. A merchant borrowed $3,000 for 320 days at 11% (assume a 360-day year). Use the U.S. Rule to complete the following table:

Payment number	Payment day	Amount paid	Interest to date	Principal payment	Adjusted balance
					$3,000
1	75	$500	$68.75	$431.25	$2,568.75
2	160	$750	$66.72	$683.28	$1,885.47
3	220	$1,000	$34.57	$965.43	$ 920.04
4	320	$948.15	$28.11	$920.04	$ 0

1. $3,000 \times .11 \times \dfrac{75}{360} = \$68.75$; $500 - \$68.75 = \$431.25$
     $3,000 - \$431.25 = \$2,568.75$

2. $160 - 75 = 85$ days

   $2,568.75 \times .11 \times \dfrac{85}{360} = \$66.72$; $750 - \$66.72 = \$683.28$
      $2,568.75 - \$683.28 = \$1,885.47$

3. $220 - 160 = 60$ days

   $1,885.47 \times .11 \times \dfrac{60}{360} = \$34.57$; $1,000 - \$34.57 = \$965.43$
      $1,885.47 - \$965.43 = \$920.04$

4. $320 - 220 = 100$ days

   $920.04 \times .11 \times \dfrac{100}{360} = \$28.11$; $920.04 + \$28.11 = \$948.15$

2. Use the U.S. Rule to solve for total interest costs, balances, and final payments (use ordinary interest).

   Given

   Principal, $6,000, 5%, 100 days
   Partial payments on 30th day, $2,000
                 on 70th day, $1,000
   5%, 30 days, $6,000

   $I = \$6,000 \times .05 \times \dfrac{30}{360} = \$25$

$2,000	$6,000	$3,047.36
− 25	− 1,975	+ 12.70
$1,975	$4,025	$3,060.06

   $4,025 \times .05 \times \dfrac{40}{360} = \$22.36$

		Interest paid
$1,000.00	$4,025.00	$25.00
− 22.36	− 977.64	22.36
$ 977.64	$3,047.36	12.70
		$60.06

   $3,047.36 \times .05 \times \dfrac{30}{360} = \$12.70$

WORD PROBLEMS

3. John Joseph borrowed $10,800 for 1 year at 14%. After 60 days, he paid $2,500 on the note. On the 200th day, he paid an additional $5,000. Use the U.S. Rule and ordinary interest to find the final balance due.

$10,800 \times .14 \times \dfrac{60}{360} = \$252$; $\$2,500 - \$252 = \$2,248$; $\$10,800 - \$2,248 = \$8,552$

$200 - 60 = 140$ days; $\$8,552 \times .14 \times \dfrac{140}{360} = \$465.61$; $\$5,000 - \$465.61 = \$4,534.39$;

$\$8,552 - \$4,534.39 = \$4,017.61$

$360 - 200 = 160$; $\$4,017.61 \times .14 \times \dfrac{160}{360} = \$249.98$;

$\$4,017.61 + \$249.98 = \$4,267.59$ final balance due

4. Doris Davis borrowed $8,200 on March 5 for 90 days at $8\frac{3}{4}$%. After 32 days, Doris made a payment on the loan of $2,700. On the 65th day, she made another payment of $2,500. What is her final payment if you use the U.S. Rule with ordinary interest?

$\$8,200 \times .0875 \times \dfrac{32}{360} = \$63.78$; $\$2,700 - \$63.78 = \$2,636.22$

$\$8,200 - \$2,636.22 = \$5,563.78$

$65 - 32 = 33$ days; $\$5,563.78 \times .0875 \times \dfrac{33}{360} = \$44.63$;

$\$2,500 - \$44.63 = \$2,455.37$; $\$5,563.78 - \$2,455.37 = \$3,108.41$

$90 - 65 = 25$ days; $\$3,108.41 \times .0875 \times \dfrac{25}{360} = \$18.89$;

$\$3,108.41 + \$18.89 = \$3,127.30$ final payment

5. David Ring borrowed $6,000 on a 13%, 60-day note. After 10 days, David paid $500 on the note. On day 40, David paid $900 on the note. What are the total interest and ending balance due by the U.S. Rule? Use ordinary interest.

U.S. Rule

$\$6,000 \times .13 \times \dfrac{10}{360} = \$21.67$

$500.00	$6,000.00 ← Principal
− 21.67	− 478.33
$478.33	$5,521.67 ← Adjusted balance (principal)

$\$5,521.67 \times .13 \times \dfrac{30}{360} = \$59.82$

$900.00	$5,521.67
− 59.82	− 840.18
$840.18	$4,681.49

$\$4,681.49 \times .13 \times \dfrac{20}{360} = \$33.81$

$4,681.49	$21.67
+ 33.81	59.82
$4,715.30 ← Ending balance due	+ 33.81
	$115.30 ← Total interest

A-48

LEARNING UNIT 11.1: Structure of Promissory Notes; the Simple Discount Note

DRILL PROBLEMS

1. Identify each of the following characteristics of promissory notes with an **I** for simple interest note, a **D** for simple discount note, or a **B** if it is true for both.

   I   Interest is computed on face value, or what is actually borrowed.

   B   A promissory note for a loan usually less than 1 year.

   D   Borrower receives proceeds = Face value − Bank discount.

   I   Maturity value = Face value + Interest.

   D   Maturity value = Face value.

   I   Borrower receives the face value.

   B   Paid back by one payment at maturity.

   D   Interest computed on maturity value, or what will be repaid, and not on actual amount borrowed.

2. Find the bank discount and the proceeds for the following (assume 360 days):

	Maturity value	Discount rate	Time (days)	Bank discount	Proceeds
a.	$7,000	9%	60	$105	$6,895
b.	$4,550	8.1%	110	$112.61	$4,437.39
c.	$19,350	12.7%	55	$375.44	$18,974.56
d.	$63,400	10%	90	$1,585	$61,815
e.	$13,490	7.9%	200	$592.06	$12,897.94
f.	$780	$12\frac{1}{2}\%$	65	$17.60	$762.40

a. $7,000 \times .09 \times \dfrac{60}{360} = \$105$; $\$7,000 - \$105 = \$6,895$

b. $4,550 \times .081 \times \dfrac{110}{360} = \$112.61$; $\$4,550 - \$112.61 = \$4,437.39$

c. $19,350 \times .127 \times \dfrac{55}{360} = \$375.44$; $\$19,350 - \$375.44 = \$18,974.56$

d. $63,400 \times .10 \times \dfrac{90}{360} = \$1,585$; $\$63,400 - \$1,585 = \$61,815$

e. $13,490 \times .079 \times \dfrac{200}{360} = \$592.06$; $\$13,490 - \$592.06 = \$12,897.94$

f. $780 \times .125 \times \dfrac{65}{360} = \$17.60$; $\$780 - \$17.60 = \$762.40$

3. Find the effective rate of interest for each of the loans in Problem 2. Use the answers you calculated in Problem 2 to solve these problems (round to the nearest tenth percent).

	Maturity value	Discount rate	Time (days)	Effective rate
a.	$7,000	9%	60	9.1%
b.	$4,550	8.1%	110	8.3%
c.	$19,350	12.7%	55	13%
d.	$63,400	10%	90	10.3%

e. $13,490   7.9%   200   <u>8.3%</u>

f. $780 $12\frac{1}{2}\%$ 65   <u>12.8%</u>

a. $\dfrac{\$105}{\$6{,}895 \times \dfrac{60}{360}} = .0913 = 9.1\%$ **b.** $\dfrac{\$112.61}{\$4{,}437.39 \times \dfrac{110}{360}} = .0830 = 8.3\%$

c. $\dfrac{\$375.44}{\$18{,}974.56 \times \dfrac{55}{360}} = .1295 = 13\%$ **d.** $\dfrac{\$1{,}585}{\$61{,}815 \times \dfrac{90}{360}} = .1026 = 10.3\%$

e. $\dfrac{\$592.06}{\$12{,}897.94 \times \dfrac{200}{360}} = .0826 = 8.3\%$ **f.** $\dfrac{\$17.60}{\$762.40 \times \dfrac{65}{360}} = .1279 = 12.8\%$

WORD PROBLEMS

Assume 360 days.

4. Mary Smith signed a $7,500 note for 135 days at a discount rate of 13%. Find the discount and the proceeds Mary received.

   $\$7{,}500 \times .13 \times \dfrac{135}{360} = \$365.63$ discount

   $\$7{,}500 - \$365.63 = \$7{,}134.37$ proceeds

5. The Salem Cooperative Bank charges an $8\frac{3}{4}\%$ discount rate. What are the discount and the proceeds for a $16,200 note for 60 days?

   $\$16{,}200 \times .0875 \times \dfrac{60}{360} = \$236.25$ discount

   $\$16{,}200 - \$236.25 = \$15{,}963.75$ proceeds

6. Bill Jackson is planning to buy a used car. He went to City Credit Union to take out a loan for $6,400 for 300 days. If the credit union charges a discount rate of $11\frac{1}{2}\%$, what will the proceeds of this loan be?

   $\$6{,}400 \times .115 \times \dfrac{300}{360} = \$613.33;\ \$6{,}400 - \$613.33 = \$5{,}786.67$ proceeds

7. Mike Drislane goes to the bank and signs a note for $9,700. The bank charges a 15% discount rate. Find the discount and the proceeds if the loan is for 210 days.

   $\$9{,}700 \times .15 \times \dfrac{210}{360} = \$848.75$ discount

   $\$9{,}700 - \$848.75 = \$8{,}851.25$ proceeds

8. Flora Foley plans to have a deck built on the back of her house. She decides to take out a loan at the bank for $14,300. She signs a note promising to pay back the loan in 280 days. If the note was discounted at 9.2%, how much money will Flora receive from the bank?

   $\$14{,}300 \times .092 \times \dfrac{280}{360} = \$1{,}023.24$

   $\$14{,}300 - \$1{,}023.24 = \$13{,}276.76$ proceeds Flora receives

9. At the end of 280 days, Flora (Problem 8) must pay back the loan. What is the maturity value of the loan?
   $14,300 maturity value

10. Dave Cassidy signed a $7,855 note at a bank that charges a 14.2% discount rate. If the loan is for 190 days, find **(a)** the proceeds and **(b)** the effective rate charged by the bank (to the nearest tenth percent).

    a. $\$7{,}855 \times .142 \times \dfrac{190}{360} = \$588.69$ **b.** $\dfrac{\$588.69}{\$7{,}266.31 \times \dfrac{190}{360}} = .1535 = 15.4\%$ effective rate

    $\$7{,}855 - \$588.69 = \$7{,}266.31$ proceeds

11. How much money must Dave (Problem 10) pay back to the bank?
    Dave pays back $7,855.

LEARNING UNIT 11.2: Discounting an Interest-Bearing Note before Maturity

DRILL PROBLEMS

1. Calculate the maturity value for each of the following promissory notes (use 360 days):

Date of note	Principal of note	Length of note (days)	Interest rate	Maturity value
a. April 12	$4,800	135	10%	$4,980
b. August 23	$15,990	85	13%	$16,480.80
c. December 10	$985	30	11.5%	$994.44

a. $\$4,800 \times .10 \times \dfrac{135}{360} = \$180 + \$4,800 = \$4,980$

b. $\$15,990 \times .13 \times \dfrac{85}{360} = \$490.80 + \$15,990 = \$16,480.80$

c. $\$985 \times .115 \times \dfrac{30}{360} = \$9.44 + \$985 = \$994.44$

2. Find the maturity date and the discount period for the following; assume no leap years. *Hint:* See Exact Days-in-a-Year Calendar, Chapter 7.

Date of note	Length of note (days)	Date of discount	Maturity date	Discount period
a. March 11	200	June 28	September 27	91 days
b. January 22	60	March 2	March 23	21 days
c. April 19	85	June 6	July 13	37 days
d. November 17	120	February 15	March 17	30 days

a. $70 + 200 = 270 =$ September 27; $270 - 179 = 91$ days or $200 - (20 + 30 + 31 + 28) = 91$
b. $22 + 60 = 82 =$ March 23; $82 - 61 = 21$ days or $60 - (9 + 28 + 2) = 21$
c. $109 + 85 = 194 =$ July 13; $194 - 157 = 37$ days or $85 - (11 + 31 + 6) = 37$
d. $365 - 321 = 44$; $120 - 44 = 76 =$ March 17; $76 - 46 = 30$ days or $120 - (13 + 31 + 31 + 15) = 30$

3. Find the bank discount for each of the following (use 360 days):

Date of note	Principal of note	Length of note	Interest rate	Bank discount rate	Date of discount	Bank discount
a. October 5	$2,475	88 days	11%	9.5%	December 10	$14.76
b. June 13	$9,055	112 days	15%	16%	August 11	$223.25
c. March 20	$1,065	75 days	12%	11.5%	May 24	$3.49

a. Maturity value $= \$2,475 \times .11 \times \dfrac{88}{360} = \$66.55 + \$2,475 = \$2,541.55$

Discount period $= 88 - (26 + 30 + 10) = 22$ days

Bank discount $= \$2,541.55 \times .095 \times \dfrac{22}{360} = \$14.76$

b. Maturity value $= \$9,055 \times .15 \times \dfrac{112}{360} = \$422.57 + \$9,055 = \$9,477.57$

Discount period $= 112 - (17 + 31 + 11) = 53$ days

Bank discount $= \$9,477.57 \times .16 \times \dfrac{53}{360} = \$223.25$

c. Maturity value $= \$1,065 \times .12 \times \dfrac{75}{360} = \$26.63 + \$1,065 = \$1,091.63$

Discount period $= 75 - (11 + 30 + 24) = 10$ days

Bank discount $= \$1,091.63 \times .115 \times \dfrac{10}{360} = \$3.49$

4. Find the proceeds for each of the discounted notes in Problem 3.

a. $\underline{\$2,526.79}$ **a.** $2,541.55 - $14.76 = $2,526.79

b. $\underline{\$9,254.32}$ **b.** $9,477.57 - $223.25 = $9,254.32

c. $\underline{\$1,088.14}$ **c.** $1,091.63 - $3.49 = $1,088.14

WORD PROBLEMS

5. Connors Company received a $4,000, 90-day, 10% note dated April 6 from one of its customers. Connors Company held the note until May 16, when the company discounted it at a bank at a discount rate of 12%. What were the proceeds that Connors Company received?

$$\$4,000 \times .10 \times \frac{90}{360} = \$100 + \$4,000 = \$4,100$$

$$90 - (24 + 16) = 50 \text{ days} \qquad \$4,100 \times .12 \times \frac{50}{360} = \$68.33; \$4,100 - \$68.33 = \$4,031.67$$

6. Souza & Sons accepted a 9%, $22,000, 120-day note from one of its customers on July 22. On October 2, the company discounted the note at Cooperative Bank. The discount rate was 12%. What were **(a)** the bank discount and **(b)** the proceeds?

$$\$22,000 \times .09 \times \frac{120}{360} = \$660 + \$22,000 = \$22,660 \qquad \$22,660 \times .12 \times \frac{48}{360} = \$362.56 \text{ bank discount (a)}$$

$$120 - (9 + 31 + 30 + 2) = 48 \text{ days} \qquad \$22,660 - \$362.56 = \$22,297.44 \text{ proceeds (b)}$$

7. The Fargate Store accepted an $8,250, 75-day, 9% note from one of its customers on March 18. Fargate's discounted the note at Parkside National Bank at $9\frac{1}{2}\%$ on March 29. What proceeds did Fargate receive?

$$\$8,250 \times .09 \times \frac{75}{360} = \$154.69 + \$8,250 = \$8,404.69$$

$$75 - 11 = 64 \text{ days} \qquad \$8,404.69 \times .095 \times \frac{64}{360} = \$141.95; \$8,404.69 - \$141.95 = \$8,262.74$$

8. On November 1, Marjorie's Clothing Store accepted a $5,200, $8\frac{1}{2}\%$, 90-day note from Mary Rose in granting her a time extension on her bill. On January 13, Marjorie discounted the note at Seawater Bank, which charged a 10% discount rate. What were the proceeds that Majorie received?

$$\$5,200 \times .085 \times \frac{90}{360} = \$110.50 + \$5,200 = \$5,310.50$$

$$90 - (29 + 31 + 13) = 17 \qquad \$5,310.50 \times .10 \times \frac{17}{360} = \$25.08; \$5,310.50 - \$25.08 = \$5,285.42$$

9. On December 3, Duncan's Company accepted a $5,000, 90-day, 12% note from Al Finney in exchange for a $5,000 bill that was past due. On January 29, Duncan discounted the note at The Sidwell Bank at 13.1%. What were the proceeds from the note?

$$\$5,000 \times .12 \times \frac{90}{360} = \$150 + \$5,000 = \$5,150$$

$$90 - (28 + 29) = 33 \text{ days} \qquad \$5,150 \times .131 \times \frac{33}{360} = \$61.84; \$5,150 - \$61.84 = \$5,088.16$$

10. On February 26, Sullivan Company accepted a 60-day, 10% note in exchange for a $1,500 past-due bill from Tabot Company. On March 28, Sullivan Company discounted at National Bank the note received from Tabot Company. The bank discount rate was 12%. What are **(a)** the bank discount and **(b)** the proceeds?

$$\$1,500 \times .10 \times \frac{60}{360} = \$25 + \$1,500 = \$1,525 \qquad \textbf{a.} \ \$1,525 \times .12 \times \frac{30}{360} = \$15.25 \text{ bank discount}$$

$$60 - (2 + 28) = 30 \text{ days} \qquad \qquad \textbf{b.} \ \$1,525 - \$15.25 = \$1,509.75 \text{ proceeds}$$

11. On June 4, Johnson Company received from Marty Russo a 30-day, 11% note for $720 to settle Russo's debt. On June 17, Johnson discounted the note at Eastern Bank whose discount rate was 15%. What proceeds did Johnson receive?

$$\$720 \times .11 \times \frac{30}{360} = \$6.60 + \$720 = \$726.60$$

$$30 - 13 = 17 \text{ days} \qquad \$726.60 \times .15 \times \frac{17}{360} = \$5.15; \$726.60 - \$5.15 = \$721.45$$

12. On December 15, Lawlers Company went to the bank and discounted a 10%, 90-day, $14,000 note dated October 21. The bank charged a discount rate of 12%. What were the proceeds of the note?

$$\$14,000 \times .10 \times \frac{90}{360} = \$350 + \$14,000 = \$14,350$$

$$90 - (10 + 30 + 15) = 35 \text{ days} \qquad \$14,350 \times .12 \times \frac{35}{360} = \$167.42; \$14,350 - \$167.42 = \$14,182.58$$

LEARNING UNIT 12.1: Compound Interest (Future Value)—The Big Picture

DRILL PROBLEMS

1. In the following examples, calculate manually the amount at year-end for each of the deposits, assuming that interest is compounded annually. Round to the nearest cent each year.

	Principal	Rate	Number of years	Year 1	Year 2	Year 3	Year 4
a.	$530	8%	2	$572.40	$618.19		
b.	$1,980	12%	4	$2,217.60	$2,483.71	$2,781.76	$3,115.57

a. $530 × 1.08 = $572.40; $572.40 × 1.08 = $618.19

b. $1,980 × 1.12 = $2,217.60; $2,217.60 × 1.12 = $2,483.71; $2,483.71 × 1.12 = $2,781.76; $2,781.76 × 1.12 = $3,115.57

2. In the following examples, calculate the simple interest, the compound interest, and the difference between the two. Round to the nearest cent; do not use tables.

	Principal	Rate	Number of years	Simple interest	Compound interest	Difference
a.	$4,600	10%	2	$920	$966	$46
b.	$18,400	9%	4	$6,624	$7,573.10	$949.10
c.	$855	$7\frac{1}{5}$%	3	$184.68	$198.30	$13.62

a. $4,600 × .10 × 2 = $920; $4,600 × 1.1 × 1.1 = $5,566; $5,566 − $4,600 = $966; $966 − $920 = $46

b. $18,400 × .09 × 4 = $6,624; $18,400 × 1.09 × 1.09 × 1.09 × 1.09 = $25,973.10; $25,973.10 − $18,400 = $7,573.10; $7,573.10 − $6,624 = $949.10

c. $855 × .072 × 3 = $184.68; $855 × 1.072 × 1.072 × 1.072 = $1,053.30; $1,053.30 − $855 = $198.30; $198.30 − $184.68 = $13.62

3. Find the future value and the compound interest using the Future Value of $1 at Compound Interest table or the Compound Daily table. Round to the nearest cent.

	Principal	Investment terms	Future value	Compound interest
a.	$10,000	6 years at 8% compounded annually	$15,869	$5,869
b.	$10,000	6 years at 8% compounded quarterly	$16,084	$6,084
c.	$8,400	7 years at 12% compounded semiannually	$18,991.56	$10,591.56
d.	$2,500	15 years at 10% compounded daily	$11,202	$8,702
e.	$9,600	5 years at 6% compounded quarterly	$12,930.24	$3,330.24

a. $10,000 × 1.5869 = $15,869 − $10,000 = $5,869 (8%, 6 periods)

b. $10,000 × 1.6084 = $16,084; $16,084 − $10,000 = $6,084 (2%, 24 periods)

c. $8,400 × 2.2609 = $18,991.56; $18,991.56 − $8,400 = $10,591.56 (6%, 14 periods)

d. $2,500 × 4.4808 = $11,202; $11,202 − $2,500 = $8,702

e. $9,600 × 1.3469 = $12,930.24; $12,930.24 − $9,600 = $3,330.24

4. Calculate the effective rate (APY) of interest using the Future Value of $1 at Compound Interest table.

Investment terms	Effective rate (annual percentage yield)
a. 12% compounded quarterly	12.55%
b. 12% compounded semiannually	12.36%
c. 6% compounded quarterly	6.14%

a. $\dfrac{12\%}{4}$ = 3% for 4 periods; 1.1255 − 1.0000 = .1255 = 12.55% $\left(\dfrac{\$.1255}{\$1.000} = \dfrac{\text{Int. per/year}}{\text{Principal}}\right)$

b. $\dfrac{12\%}{2}$ = 6% for 2 periods; 1.1236 − 1.0000 = .1236 = 12.36%

c. $\dfrac{6\%}{4}$ = $1\dfrac{1}{2}\%$ for 4 periods; 1.0614 − 1.0000 = .0614 = 6.14%

WORD PROBLEMS

5. John Mackey deposited $5,000 in his savings account at Salem Savings Bank. If the bank pays 6% interest compounded quarterly, what will be the balance of his account at the end of 3 years?
$5,000 × 1.1960 = $5,980 (1.5%, 12 periods)

6. Pine Valley Savings Bank offers a certificate of deposit at 12% interest, compounded quarterly. What is the effective rate (APY) of interest?
1.1255 − 1.0000 = .1255 = 12.55% (3%, 4 periods)

7. Jack Billings loaned $6,000 to his brother-in-law Dan, who was opening a new business. Dan promised to repay the loan at the end of 5 years, with interest of 8% compounded semiannually. How much will Dan pay Jack at the end of 5 years?
$6,000 × 1.4802 = $8,881.20 (4%, 10 periods)

8. Eileen Hogarty deposits $5,630 in City Bank, which pays 12% interest, compounded quarterly. How much money will Eileen have in her account at the end of 7 years?
$5,630 × 2.2879 = $12,880.88 (3%, 28 periods)

9. If Kevin Bassage deposits $3,500 in Scarsdale Savings Bank, which pays 8% interest, compounded quarterly, what will be in his account at the end of 6 years? How much interest will he have earned at that time?
$3,500 × 1.6084 = $5,629.40 amount
$5,629.40 − $3,500 = $2,129.40 interest   (2%, 24 periods)

10. Arlington Trust pays 6% compounded semiannually. How much interest would be earned on $7,200 for 1 year?
$7,200 × 1.0609 = $7,638.48 (3%, 2 periods) $7,638.48 − $7,200 = $438.48 interest

11. Paladium Savings Bank pays 9% compounded quarterly. Find the amount and the interest on $3,000 after three quarters. Do not use a table.
$3,000 × 1.0225 = $3,067.50; $3,067.50 × 1.0225 = $3,136.52; $3,136.52 × 1.0225 = $3,207.09 amount
$3,207.09 − $3,000 = $207.09 interest $\dfrac{9\%}{4} = 2\dfrac{1}{4}\%$

12. David Siderski bought a $7,500 bank certificate paying 16% compounded semiannually. How much money did he obtain upon cashing in the certificate 3 years later?
$7,500 × 1.5869 = $11,901.75 (8%, 6 periods)

13. The August/September 1996 issue of *Your Money* showed that the more frequently the bank compounds your money, the better. Just how much better is a function of time. A $10,000 investment for 6% in a 5-year certificate of deposit at three different banks can result in different interest being earned.
a. Bank A (simple interest, no compounding)
b. Bank B (quarterly compounding)
c. Bank C (daily compounding)
What would be the interest for each bank?
a. $10,000 × .06 × 5 = $3,000 interest

b. 5 years × 4 = 20 periods $\dfrac{6\%}{4} = 1\dfrac{1}{2}\%$ **c.** 5 years = 1.3498
　　$10,000　　　　　　　　　　　　　　　　$10,000
　　× 1.3469　　　　　　　　　　　　　　　× 1.3498
　　――――――　　　　　　　　　　　　――――――
　　$13,469　　　　　　　　　　　　　　　$13,498
　　− 10,000　　　　　　　　　　　　　　− 10,000
　　――――――　　　　　　　　　　　　――――――
　　$ 3,469 interest　　　　　　　　　　　$ 3,498

LEARNING UNIT 12.2: Present Value—The Big Picture

DRILL PROBLEMS

1. Use the *Business Math Handbook* to find the table factor for each of the following:

	Future value	Rate	Number of years	Compounded	Table value
a.	$1.00	10%	5	Annually	.6209
b.	$1.00	12%	8	Semiannually	.3936
c.	$1.00	6%	10	Quarterly	.5513
d.	$1.00	12%	2	Monthly	.7876
e.	$1.00	8%	15	Semiannually	.3083

a. 10%, 5 periods; .6209   **b.** 6%, 16 periods; .3936
c. $1\frac{1}{2}$%, 40 periods; .5513   **d.** 1%, 24 periods; .7876
e. 4%, 30 periods; .3083

2. Use the *Business Math Handbook* to find the table factor and the present value for each of the following:

	Future value	Rate	Number of years	Compounded	Table value	Present value
a.	$1,000	14%	6	Semiannually	.4440	$444.00
b.	$1,000	16%	7	Quarterly	.3335	$333.50
c.	$1,000	8%	7	Quarterly	.5744	$574.40
d.	$1,000	8%	7	Semiannually	.5775	$577.50
e.	$1,000	8%	7	Annually	.5835	$583.50

a. 7%, 12 periods; .4440 × $1,000 = $444.00   **b.** 4%, 28 periods; .3335 × $1,000 = $333.50
c. 2%, 28 periods; .5744 × $1,000 = $574.40   **d.** 4%, 14 periods; .5775 × $1,000 = $577.50
e. 8%, 7 periods; .5835 × $1,000 = $583.50

3. Find the present value and the interest earned for the following:

	Future value	Number of years	Rate	Compounded	Present value	Interest earned
a.	$2,500	6	8%	Annually	$1,575.50	$924.50
b.	$4,600	10	6%	Semiannually	$2,547.02	$2,052.98
c.	$12,800	8	10%	Semiannually	$5,863.68	$6,936.32
d.	$28,400	7	8%	Quarterly	$16,312.96	$12,087.04
e.	$53,050	1	12%	Monthly	$47,076.57	$5,973.43

a. 8%, 6; .6302 × $2,500 = $1,575.50; $2,500 − $1,575.50 = $924.50
b. 3%, 20; .5537 × $4,600 = $2,547.02; $4,600 − $2,547.02 = $2,052.98
c. 5%, 16; .4581 × $12,800 = $5,863.68; $12,800 − $5,863.68 = $6,936.32
d. 2%, 28; .5744 × $28,400 = $16,312.96; $28,400 − $16,312.96 = $12,087.04
e. 1%, 12; .8874 × $53,050 = $47,076.57; $53,050 − $47,076.57 = $5,973.43

4. Find the missing amount (present value or future value) for each of the following:

	Present value	Investment terms	Future value
a.	$3,500	5 years at 8% compounded annually	$5,142.55
b.	$4,473	6 years at 12% compounded semiannually	$9,000
c.	$4,700	9 years at 14% compounded semiannually	$15,885.53

a. 8%, 5; 1.4693 × $3,500 = $5,142.55   **b.** 6%, 12; .4970 × $9,000 = $4,473
c. 7%, 18; 3.3799 × $4,700 = $15,885.53

WORD PROBLEMS

Solve for future value or present value.

5. Paul Palumbo assumes that he will need to have a new roof put on his house in 4 years. He estimates that the roof will cost him $18,000 at that time. What amount of money should Paul invest today at 8%, compounded semiannually, to be able to pay for the roof?
4%, 8 periods; .7307 × $18,000 = $13,152.60

6. Tilton, a pharmacist, rents his store and has signed a lease that will expire in 3 years. When the lease expires, Tilton wants to buy his own store. He wants to have a down payment of $35,000 at that time. How much money should Tilton invest today at 6% compounded quarterly to yield $35,000?

$1\frac{1}{2}$%, 12 periods; .8364 × $35,000 = $29,274

7. Brad Morrissey loans $8,200 to his brother-in-law. He will be repaid at the end of 5 years, with interest at 10% compounded semiannually. Find out how much he will be repaid.
5%, 10 periods; 1.6289 × $8,200 = $13,356.98

8. The owner of Waverly Sheet Metal Company plans to buy some new machinery in 6 years. He estimates that the machines he wishes to purchase will cost $39,700 at that time. What must he invest today at 8% compounded semiannually to have sufficient money to purchase the new machines?
4%, 12 periods; .6246 × $39,700 = $24,796.62

9. Paul Stevens' grandparents want to buy him a car when he graduates from college in 4 years. They feel that they should have $27,000 in the bank at that time. How much should they invest at 12% compounded quarterly to reach their goal?
3%, 16 periods; .6232 × $27,000 = $16,826.40

10. Gilda Nardi deposits $5,325 in a bank that pays 12% interest, compounded quarterly. Find the amount she will have at the end of 7 years.
3%, 28 periods; 2.2879 × $5,325 = $12,183.07

11. Mary Wilson wants to buy a new set of golf clubs in 2 years. They will cost $775. How much money should she invest today at 9% compounded annually so that she will have enough money to buy the new clubs?
9%, 2 periods; .8417 × $775 = $652.32

12. Jack Beggs plans to invest $30,000 at 10% compounded semiannually for 5 years. What is the future value of the investment?
5%, 10 periods; 1.6289 × $30,000 = $48,867

13. Ron Thrift has a 1991 Honda that he expects will last 3 more years. Ron does not like to finance his purchases. He went to First National Bank to find out how much money he should put in the bank to purchase a $20,300 car in 3 years. The bank's 3-year CD is compounded quarterly with a 4% rate. How much should Ron invest in the CD?

3 years × 4 = 12 periods $\frac{4\%}{4} = 1\%$ $20,300.00
  × .8874
  ────────
  $18,014.22

14. The Downers Grove YMCA had a fund-raising campaign to build a swimming pool in 6 years. Members raised $825,000; the pool is estimated to cost $1,230,000. The money will be placed in Downers Grove Bank, which pays daily interest at 6%. Will the YMCA have enough money to pay for the pool in 6 years?
$825,000 × 1.4333 = $1,182,472.50   Cost: $1,230,000.00
Earned: 1,182,472.50
────────────
Short: $ 47,527.50

LEARNING UNIT 13.1: Annuities: Ordinary Annuity and Annuity Due
(Find Future Value)

Note to instructor: All worked-out solutions for Chapters 13–22 are located in your Instructor's Resource Manual by chapter.

DRILL PROBLEMS

1. Find the value of the following ordinary annuities (calculate manually):

	Amount of each annual deposit	Rate	Value at end of year 1	Value at end of year 2	Value at end of year 3
a.	$1,000	8%	$1,000	$2,080	$3,246.40
b.	$2,500	12%	$2,500	$5,300	$8,436
c.	$7,200	10%	$7,200	$15,120	$23,832

2. Use the Ordinary Annuity Table: Compound Sum of an Annuity of $1 to find the value of the following ordinary annuities:

	Annuity payment	Payment period	Term of annuity	Rate	Value of annuity
a.	$650	Semiannually	5 years	6%	$7,451.54
b.	$3,790	Annually	13 years	12%	$106,230.28
c.	$500	Quarterly	1 year	8%	$2,060.80

3. Find the annuity due (deposits are made at beginning of period) for each of the following using the Ordinary Annuity Table:

	Amount of payment	Payment period	Rate	Time (years)	Amount of annuity
a.	$900	Annually	7%	6	$6,888.60
b.	$1,200	Annually	11%	4	$6,273.36
c.	$550	Semiannually	10%	9	$16,246.40

4. Find the amount of each annuity:

	Amount of payment	Payment period	Rate	Time (years)	Type of annuity	Amount of annuity
a.	$600	Semiannually	12%	8	Ordinary	$15,403.50
b.	$600	Semiannually	12%	8	Due	$16,327.68
c.	$1,100	Annually	9%	7	Ordinary	$10,120.44

WORD PROBLEMS

5. At the end of each year for the next 9 years, D'Aldo Company will deposit $25,000 in an ordinary annuity account paying 9% interest compounded annually. Find the value of the annuity at the end of the 9 years.
$325,525

6. David McCarthy is a professional baseball player who expects to play in the major leagues for 10 years. To save for the future, he will deposit $50,000 at the beginning of each year into an account that pays 11% interest compounded annually. How much will he have in this account at the end of 10 years?
$928,070

7. Tom and Sue plan to get married soon. Because they hope to have a large wedding, they are going to deposit $1,000 at the end of each month into an account that pays 24% compounded monthly. How much will they have in this account at the end of 1 year?
$13,412

8. Chris Dennen deposits $15,000 at the end of each year for 13 years into an account paying 7% interest compounded annually. What is the value of her annuity at the end of 13 years? How much interest will she have earned?
$302,109 value $107,109 interest

9. Amanda Blinn is 52 years old today and has just opened an IRA. She plans to deposit $500 at the end of each quarter into her account. If Amanda retires on her 62nd birthday, what amount will she have in her account if the account pays 8% interest compounded quarterly?
$30,200.85

10. Jerry Davis won the citywide sweepstakes and will receive a check for $2,000 at the beginning of each 6 months for the next 5 years. If Larry deposits each check in an account that pays 8% compounded semiannually, how much will he have at the end of 5 years?
$24,972.60

11. Mary Hynes purchased an ordinary annuity from an investment broker at 8% interest compounded semiannually. If her semiannual deposit is $600, what will be the value of the annuity at the end of 15 years?
$33,650.94

LEARNING UNIT 13.2: Present Value of an Ordinary Annuity (Find Present Value)

DRILL PROBLEMS

1. Use the Present Value of an Annuity of $1 table to find the amount to be invested today to receive a stream of payments for a given number of years in the future. Show the manual check of your answer. (Check may be a few pennies off due to rounding.)

Amount of expected payments	Payment period	Rate	Term of annuity	Present value of annuity
a. $1,500	Yearly	9%	2 years	$2,638.65
b. $2,700	Yearly	13%	3 years	$6,375.24
c. $2,700	Yearly	6%	3 years	$7,217.10

2. Find the present value of the following annuities. Use the Present Value of an Annuity of $1 table.

Amount of each payment	Payment period	Rate	Time (years)	Compounded	Present value of annuity
a. $2,000	Year	7%	25	Annually	$23,307.20
b. $7,000	Year	11%	12	Annually	$45,446.80
c. $850	6 months	12%	5	Semiannually	$6,256.09
d. $1,950	6 months	14%	9	Semiannually	$19,615.25
e. $500	Quarter	12%	10	Quarterly	$11,557.40

WORD PROBLEMS

3. Tom Hanson would like to receive $200 each quarter for the 4 years he is in college. If his bank account pays 8% compounded quarterly, how much must he have in his account when he begins college?
$2,715.54

4. Jean Reith has just retired and will receive a $12,500 retirement check every 6 months for the next 20 years. If her employer can invest money at 12% compounded semiannually, what amount must be invested today to make the semiannual payments to Jean?
$188,078.75

5. Tom Herrick will pay $4,500 at the end of each year for the next 7 years to pay the balance of his college loans. If Tom can invest his money at 7% compounded annually, how much must he invest today to make the annual payments?
$24,251.85

6. Helen Grahan is planning an extended sabbatical for the next 3 years. She would like to invest a lump sum of money at 10% interest so that she can withdraw $6,000 every 6 months while on sabbatical. What is the amount of the lump sum that Helen must invest?
$30,454.20

7. Linda Rudd has signed a rental contract for office equipment, agreeing to pay $3,200 at the end of each quarter for the next 5 years. If Linda can invest money at 12% compounded quarterly, find the lump sum she can deposit today to make the payments for the length of the contract.
$47,608

8. Sam Adams is considering lending his brother John $6,000. John said that he would repay Sam $775 every 6 months for 4 years. If money can be invested at 8%, calculate the equivalent cash value of the offer today. Should Sam go ahead with the loan?
$5,217.84   Sam should not take the deal.

9. The State Lotto Game offers a grand prize of $1,000,000 paid in 20 yearly payments of $50,000. If the state treasurer can invest money at 9% compounded annually, how much must she invest today to make the payments to the grand prize winner?
$456,425

10. Thomas Martin's uncle has promised him upon graduation a gift of $20,000 in cash or $2,000 every quarter for the next 3 years. If money can be invested at 8%, which offer will Thomas accept? (Thomas is a business major.)
$21,150.60   Choose annuity.

11. Paul Sasso is selling a piece of land. He has received two solid offers. Jason Smith has offered a $60,000 down payment and $50,000 a year for the next 5 years. Kevin Bassage offered $35,000 down and $55,000 a year for the next 5 years. If money can be invested at 7% compounded annually, which offer should Paul accept? (To make the comparison, find the equivalent cash price of each offer.)
Paul should accept Jason's offer. $265,010

12. Abe Hoster decided to retire to Spain in 10 years. What amount should Abe invest today so that he will be able to withdraw $30,000 at the end of each year for 20 years after he retires? Assume he can invest money at 8% interest compounded annually.
$136,432.31

LEARNING UNIT 13.3: Sinking Funds (Find Periodic Payments)

DRILL PROBLEMS

1. Given the number of years and the interest rate, use the Sinking Fund Table based on $1 to calculate the amount of the periodic payment.

	Frequency of payment	Length of time	Interest rate	Future amount	Sinking fund payment
a.	Annually	19 years	5%	$125,000	$4,087.50
b.	Annually	7 years	10%	$205,000	$21,607.00
c.	Semiannually	10 years	6%	$37,500	$1,395.00
d.	Quarterly	9 years	12%	$12,750	$201.45
e.	Quarterly	6 years	8%	$25,600	$842.24

2. Find the amount of each payment into the sinking fund and the amount of interest earned.

	Maturity value	Interest rate	Term (years)	Frequency of payment	Sinking fund payment	Interest earned
a.	$45,500	5%	13	Annually	$2,570.75	$12,080.25
b.	$8,500	10%	20	Semiannually	$70.55	$5,678.00
c.	$11,000	8%	5	Quarterly	$453.20	$1,936.00
d.	$66,600	12%	7 1/2	Semiannually	$2,863.80	$23,643.00

WORD PROBLEMS

3. To finance a new police station, the town of Pine Valley issued bonds totaling $600,000. The town treasurer set up a sinking fund at 8% compounded quarterly in order to redeem the bonds in 7 years. What is the quarterly payment that must be deposited into the fund?
$16,200 quarterly payment

4. Arlex Oil Corporation plans to build a new garage in 6 years. To finance the project, the financial manager established a $250,000 sinking fund at 6% compounded semianually. Find the semiannual payment required for the fund.
$17,625

5. The City Fisheries Corporation sold $300,000 worth of bonds that must be redeemed in 9 years. The corporation agreed to set up a sinking fund to accumulate the $300,000. Find the amount of the periodic payments made into the fund if payments are made annually and the fund earns 8% compounded annually.
$24,030 annual payment

6. Gregory Mines Corporation wishes to purchase a new piece of equipment in 4 years. The estimated price of the equipment is $100,000. If the corporation makes periodic payments into a sinking fund with 12% interest compounded quarterly, find the amount of the periodic payments.
$4,960 quarterly payments

7. The Best Corporation must buy a new piece of machinery in $4\frac{1}{2}$ years that will cost $350,000. If the firm sets up a sinking fund to finance this new machine, what will the quarterly deposits be assuming the fund earns 8% interest compounded quarterly?

$16,345 quarterly payments

8. The Lowest-Price-in-Town Company needs $75,500 in 6 years to pay off a debt. The company makes a decision to set up a sinking fund and make semiannual deposits. What will their payments be if the fund pays 10% interest compounded semiannually?

$4,741.40 semiannual payment

9. The WIR Company plans to renovate their offices in 5 years. They estimate that the cost will be $235,000. If they set up a sinking fund that pays 12% quarterly, what will their quarterly payments be?

$8,742 quarterly payment

LEARNING UNIT 14.1: Cost of Installment Buying

DRILL PROBLEMS

1. For the following installment problems, find the amount financed and the finance charge.

	Sale price	Down payment	Number of monthly payments	Monthly payment	Amount financed	Finance charge
a.	$1,500	$300	24	$58	$1,200	$192
b.	$12,000	$3,000	30	$340	$9,000	$1,200
c.	$62,500	$4,700	48	$1,500	$57,800	$14,200
d.	$4,975	$620	18	$272	$4,355	$541
e.	$825	$82.50	12	$67.45	$742.50	$66.90

2. For each of the above purchases, find the deferred payment price.

	Sale price	Down payment	Number of monthly payments	Monthly payment	Deferred payment price
a.	$1,500	$300	24	$58	$1,692
b.	$12,000	$3,000	30	$340	$13,200
c.	$62,500	$4,700	48	$1,500	$76,700
d.	$4,975	$620	18	$272	$5,516
e.	$825	$82.50	12	$67.45	$891.90

3. Use the Annual Percentage Rate Table per $100 to calculate the estimated APR for each of the previous purchases.

	Sale price	Down payment	Number of monthly payments	Monthly payment	Annual percentage rate
a.	$1,500	$300	24	$58	14.75%
b.	$12,000	$3,000	30	$340	10%
c.	$62,500	$4,700	48	$1,500	11.25%
d.	$4,975	$620	18	$272	15.25%
e.	$825	$82.50	12	$67.45	16.25%

4. Given the following information, calculate the monthly payment by the loan amortization table.

	Amount financed	Rate	Number of months of loan	Monthly payment
a.	$12,000	10%	18	$720.72
b.	$18,000	11%	36	$589.32
c.	$25,500	13.50%	54	$632.66

WORD PROBLEMS

5. Jill Walsh purchases a bedroom set for a cash price of $3,920. The down payment is $392, and the monthly installment payment is $176 for 24 months. Find **(a)** the amount financed, **(b)** the finance charge, and **(c)** the deferred payment price.

    a. $3,528   **b.** $696   **c.** $4,616

6. An automaker promotion loan on a $20,000 automobile and a down payment of 20% are being financed for 48 months. The monthly payments will be $367.74. What will be the APR for this auto loan? Use the table in the *Business Math Handbook*. (*Working Woman,* November 1995)

    $367.74 × 48 = $17,651.52

                − 16,000.00 (Amount financed: $20,000 × .20 down payment = $4,000; $20,000 − $4,000 = $16,000)

                $ 1,651.52 total finance charge

$$\frac{\$1{,}651.52 \text{ finance charge}}{\$16{,}000 \text{ amount financed}} \times 100 = 10.322 \text{ (48 months)} = 4.75\% \text{ to } 5.00\%$$

7. David Nason purchased a recreational vehicle for $25,000. David went to City Bank to finance the purchase. The bank required that David make a 10% down payment and monthly payments of $571.50 for 4 years. Find **(a)** the amount financed, **(b)** the finance charge, and **(c)** the deferred payment that David paid.

    a. $22,500   **b.** $4,932   **c.** $29,932

8. Calculate the estimated APR that David (Problem 7) was charged per $100 using the Annual Percentage Rate Table. Approximately 10%

9. Young's Motors advertised a new car for $16,720. They offered an installment plan of 5% down and 42 monthly payments of $470. What are **(a)** the deferred payment price and **(b)** the estimated APR for this car (use the table)?

    a. $20,576   **b.** 12.75%

10. Angie French bought a used car for $9,000. Angie put down $2,000 and financed the balance at 11.50% for 36 months. What is her monthly payment? Use the loan amortization table.
$230.86

LEARNING UNIT 14.2: Paying Off Installment Loan before Due Date

DRILL PROBLEMS

1. Find the balance of each loan outstanding and the total finance charge.

	Amount financed	Monthly payment	Number of payments	Payments to date	Balance of loan outstanding	Finance charge
a.	$1,500	$125	15	10	$625	$375
b.	$21,090	$600	40	24	$9,600	$2,910
c.	$895	$60	18	10	$480	$185
d.	$4,850	$150	42	30	$1,800	$1,450

2. For the loans in Problem 1, find the number of payments remaining and calculate the rebate amount of the finance charge (use Rebate Fraction Table Based on Rule of 78).

	Amount financed	Monthly payment	Number of payments	Payments to date	Number of payments remaining	Finance charge rebate
a.	$1,500	$125	15	10	5	$46.88
b.	$21,090	$600	40	24	16	$482.63
c.	$895	$60	18	10	8	$38.95
d.	$4,850	$150	42	30	12	$125.25

3. For the loans in Problems 1 and 2, show the remaining balance of the loan and calculate the payoff amount to retire the loan at this time.

	Amount financed	Monthly payment	Number of payments	Payments to date	Balance of loan outstanding	Final payoff
a.	$1,500	$125	15	10	$625	$578.12
b.	$21,090	$600	40	24	$9,600	$9,117.37
c.	$895	$60	18	10	$480	$441.05
d.	$4,850	$150	42	30	$1,800	$1,674.75

4. Complete the following; show all the steps.

	Loan	Months of loan	Monthly payment	End of month loan is repaid	Final payoff
a.	$6,200	36	$219	24	$2,430.77
b.	$960	12	$99	8	$366.77

WORD PROBLEMS

5. Maryjane Hannon took out a loan for $5,600 to have a swimming pool installed in her backyard. The note she signed required 21 monthly payments of $293. At the end of 15 months, Maryjane wants to know the balance of her loan outstanding and her total finance charge.
   $1,758 balance of loan outstanding $553 total finance charge

6. After calculating the above data (Problem 5), Maryjane is considering paying off the rest of the loan. To make her decision, Maryjane wants to know the finance charge rebate she will receive and the final payoff amount.
   $50.27 rebate amount $1,707.73 final payoff

7. Ben Casey decided to buy a used car for $7,200. He agreed to make monthly payments of $225 for 36 months. What is Ben's total finance charge?
   $900

8. After making 20 payments, Ben (Problem 7) wants to pay off the rest of the loan. What will be the amount of Ben's final payoff?
   $3,416.22

9. Jeremy Vagos took out a loan to buy a new boat that cost $12,440. He agreed to pay $350 a month for 48 months. After 24 monthly payments, he calculates that he has paid $8,400 on his loan and has 24 payments remaining. Jeremy's friend Luke tells Jeremy that he will pay off the rest of the loan (in a single payment) if he can be half owner of the boat. What is the amount that Luke will have to pay?
   $7,287.76

LEARNING UNIT 14.3: Revolving Charge Credit Cards

DRILL PROBLEMS

1. Use the U.S. Rule to calculate the outstanding balance due for each of the following independent situations:

Monthly payment number	Outstanding balance due	$1\frac{1}{2}\%$ interest payment	Amount of monthly payment	Reduction in balance due	Outstanding balance due
a. 1	$9,000.00	$135	$600	$465	$8,535
b. 5	$5,625.00	$84.38	$1,000	$915.62	$4,709.38
c. 4	$926.50	$13.90	$250	$236.10	$690.40
d. 12	$62,391.28	$935.87	$1,200	$264.13	$62,127.15
e. 8	$3,255.19	$48.83	$325	$276.17	$2,979.02

2. Complete the missing data for a $6,500 purchase made on credit. The annual interest charge on this revolving charge account is 18%, or $1\frac{1}{2}\%$ interest on previous month's balance. Use the U.S. Rule.

Monthly payment number	Outstanding balance due	$1\frac{1}{2}\%$ interest payment	Amount of monthly payment	Reduction in balance due	Outstanding balance due
1	$6,500	$97.50	$700	$602.50	$5,897.50
2	$5,897.50	$88.46	$700	$611.54	$5,285.96
3	$5,285.96	$79.29	$700	$620.71	$4,665.25

3. Calculate the average billing daily balance for each of the monthly statements for the following revolving credit accounts (assume a 30-day billing cycle):

	Billing date	Previous balance	Payment date	Payment amount	Charge date(s)	Charge amount(s)	Average daily balance
a.	4/10	$329	4/25	$35	4/29	$56	$332.03
b.	6/15	$573	6/25	$60	6/26	$25	
					6/30	$72	$584.83
c.	9/15	$335.50	9/20	$33.55	9/25	$12.50	
					9/26	$108	$384.28

4. Find the finance charge for each monthly statement (Problem 3) if the annual percentage rate is 15%.
   a. $4.15   b. $7.31   c. $4.80

WORD PROBLEMS

5. Niki Marshall is going to buy a new bedroom set at Scottie's Furniture Store, where she has a revolving charge account. The cost of the bedroom set is $5,500. Niki does not plan to charge anything else to her account until she has completely paid for the bedroom set. Scottie's Furniture Store charges an annual percentage rate of 18%, or $1\frac{1}{2}$% per month. Niki plans to pay $1,000 per month until she has paid for the bedroom set. Set up a schedule for Niki to show her outstanding balance at the end of each month after her $1,000 payment and also the amount of her final payment. Use the U.S. Rule.
   $784.39

6. Frances Dollof received her monthly statement from Brown's Department Store. The following is part of the information contained on that statement. Finance charge is calculated on the average daily balance.

Date	Reference	Department	Description	Amount
Dec. 15	5921	359	Petite sportswear	84.98
Dec. 15	9612	432	Footwear	55.99
Dec. 15	2600	126	Women's fragrance	35.18
Dec. 23	6247	61	Ralph Lauren towels	20.99
Dec. 24	0129	998	Payment received—thank you	100.00CR

Previous balance		Annual percentage rate	Billing date
719.04	12/13	18%	JAN 13

Brown's Charge Account Terms
Payment is required in monthly installments upon receipt of monthly statement in accordance with Brown's payment terms.

When my new balance is:	My minimum required payment is:	When my new balance is:	My minimum required payment is:
Up to $20.00	New Balance	$350.01 to $400.00	$40.00
$ 20.01 to $200.00	$20.00	$400.01 to $450.00	$45.00
$200.01 to $250.00	$25.00	$450.01 to $500.00	$50.00
$250.01 to $300.00	$30.00	More than $500.00	$50.00 plus $10.00 for each $50.00 (or fraction thereof) of New Balance over $500.00
$300.01 to $350.00	$35.00		

   a. Calculate the average daily balance for the month.
      $833.53
   b. What is Ms. Dollof's finance charge?
      $12.50
   c. What is the new balance for Ms. Dollof's account?
      $828.68
   d. What is the minimum payment Frances is required to pay according to Brown's payment terms?
      $120

7. What is the finance charge for a Brown's customer who has an average daily balance of $3,422.67?
   $51.34

8. What is the minimum payment for a Brown's customer with a new balance of $522.00?
   $60

9. What is the minimum payment for a Brown's customer with a new balance of $325.01?
   $35

10. What is the new balance for a Brown's customer with a previous balance of $309.35 whose purchases totaled $213.00, given that the customer made a payment of $75.00 and the finance charge was $4.65?
   $452.00

RECAP OF WORD PROBLEMS IN LU14.1

11. A home equity loan on a $20,000 automobile with a down payment of 20% is being financed for 48 months. The interest is tax deductible. The monthly payments will be $401.97. What is the APR on this loan? Use the table in the *Business Math Handbook*. If the person is in the 28% income tax bracket, what will be the tax savings with this type of a loan? (*Working Woman*, November 1995)

$401.97 × 48 = $19,294.56 total all monthly payments
            − 16,000.00 amount financed
            _____
            $ 3,294.56 total finance charge

$$\frac{\$3,294.56 \text{ finance charge}}{\$16,000.00 \text{ amount charged}} \times 100 = 20.591 \text{ (48 months)} = 9.50\% \text{ to } 9.75\%$$

$3,294.60
  × .28 tax bracket
  _____
$ 922.49 deductible tax savings

12. An automobile with a total transaction price of $20,000 with a down payment of 20% is being financed for 48 months. Banks and credit unions require a monthly payment of $400.36. What is the APR for this auto loan? Use the table in the *Business Math Handbook*. (*Working Woman*, November 1995)

$400.36 × 48 = $19,217.28
            − 16,000.00 amount financed
            _____
            $ 3,217.28 total finance charge

$$\frac{\$3,217.28 \text{ finance charge}}{\$16,000.00 \text{ amount financed}} \times 100 = 20.108 \text{ (48 months)} = 9.25\% \text{ to } 9.50\%$$

13. Assume you received a $2,000 rebate that brought the price of a car down to $20,000; the financing rate was for 48 months, and your total interest was $3,279. Using the table in the *Business Math Handbook*, what was your APR? (*Chicago Tribune*, August 24, 1997)

$$\frac{\$3,279 \text{ finance charge}}{\$20,000 \text{ amount financed}} \times 100 = \$16.395 \text{ (48 months)} = 7.50\% \text{ to } 7.75\%$$

LEARNING UNIT 15.1: Types of Mortgages and the Monthly Mortgage Payment

DRILL PROBLEMS

1. Use the table in the *Business Math Handbook* to calculate the monthly payment for principal and interest for the following mortgages:

Price of home	Down payment	Interest rate	Term in years	Monthly payment
a. $200,000	15%	$6\frac{1}{2}\%$	25	$1,149.20 (170 × $6.76)
b. $200,000	15%	$10\frac{1}{2}\%$	30	$1,555.50
c. $450,000	10%	$11\frac{3}{4}\%$	30	$4,090.50
d. $450,000	10%	11%	30	$3,859.65

2. For each of the mortgages in Problem 1, calculate the amount of interest that will be paid over the life of the loan.

Price of home	Down payment	Interest rate	Term in years	Total interest paid
a. $200,000	15%	$6\frac{1}{2}\%$	25	$174,760 $\left(\begin{array}{l}300 \times \$1,149.20 = \$344,760 \\ - 170,000 \\ \hline \$174,760\end{array}\right)$
b. $200,000	15%	$10\frac{1}{2}\%$	30	$389,980
c. $450,000	10%	$11\frac{3}{4}\%$	30	$1,067,580
d. $450,000	10%	11%	30	$984,474

3. Calculate the increase in the monthly mortgage payments for each of the rate increases in the following mortgages. Also calculate what percent of change the increase represents (round to the tenth percent).

Mortgage amount	Term in years	Interest rate	Increase in interest rate	Increase in monthly payment	Percent change
a. $175,000	22	9%	1%	$117.25	7.7%
b. $300,000	30	$11\frac{3}{4}\%$	$\frac{3}{4}\%$	$174	5.7%

4. Calculate the increase in total interest paid for the increase in interest rates in Problem 3.

Mortgage amount	Term in years	Interest rate	Increase in interest rate	Increase in total interest paid
a. $175,000	22	9%	1%	$30,954
b. $300,000	30	$11\frac{3}{4}\%$	$\frac{3}{4}\%$	$62,640

WORD PROBLEMS

5. The Counties are planning to purchase a new home that costs $329,000. The bank is charging them $10\frac{1}{2}\%$ interest and requires a 20% down payment. The Counties are planning to take a 25-year mortgage. How much will their monthly payment be for principal and interest?
$2,487.24

6. The MacEacherns wish to buy a new house that costs $299,000. The bank requires a 15% down payment and charges $11\frac{1}{2}\%$ interest. If the MacEacherns take out a 15-year mortgage, what will their monthly payment for principal and interest be?
$2,971.01

7. Because the monthly payments are so high, the MacEacherns (Problem 6) want to know what the monthly payments would be for **(a)** a 25-year mortgage and **(b)** a 30-year mortgage. Calculate these two payments.

   a. $2,584.71   **b.** $2,518.63

8. If the MacEacherns choose a 30-year mortgage instead of a 15-year mortgage, **(a)** how much money will they "save" monthly and **(b)** how much more interest will they pay over the life of the loan?

   a. $452.38   **b.** $371,925

9. If the MacEacherns choose the 25-year mortgage instead of the 30-year mortgage, **(a)** how much more will they pay monthly and **(b)** how much less interest will they pay over the life of the loan?

   a. $66.08   **b.** $131,293.80

10. Larry and Doris Davis plan to purchase a new home that costs $415,000. The bank that they are dealing with requires a 20% down payment and charges $12\frac{3}{4}\%$. The Davises are planning to take a 25-year mortgage. What will the monthly payment be?

    $3,685.20

11. How much interest will the Davises (Problem 10) pay over the life of the loan?

    $773,560

LEARNING UNIT 15.2: Amortization Schedule—Breaking Down the Monthly Payment

DRILL PROBLEMS

1. In the following, calculate the monthly payment for each mortgage, the portion of the first monthly payment that goes to interest, and the portion of the payment that goes toward the principal.

	Amount of mortgage	Interest rate	Term in years	Monthly payment	Portion to interest	Portion to principal
a.	$170,000	8%	22	$1,371.90	$1,133.33	$238.57
b.	$222,000	$11\frac{3}{4}\%$	30	$2,242.20	$2,173.75	$68.45
c.	$167,000	$10\frac{1}{2}\%$	25	$1,578.15	$1,461.25	$116.90
d.	$307,000	13%	15	$3,886.62	$3,325.83	$560.79
e.	$409,500	$12\frac{1}{2}\%$	20	$4,656.02	$4,265.63	$390.39

2. Prepare an amortization schedule for the first 3 months of a 25-year, 12% mortgage on $265,000.

Payment number	Monthly payment	Portion to interest	Portion to principal	Balance of loan outstanding
1	$2,793.10	$2,650.00	$143.10	$264,856.90
2	$2,793.10	$2,648.57	$144.53	$264,712.37
3	$2,793.10	$2,647.12	$145.98	$264,566.39

3. Prepare an amortization schedule for the first 4 months of a 30-year, $10\frac{1}{2}\%$ mortgage on $195,500.

Payment number	Monthly payment	Portion to interest	Portion to principal	Balance of loan outstanding
1	$1,788.83	$1,710.63	$78.20	$195,421.80
2	$1,788.83	$1,709.94	$78.89	$195,342.91
3	$1,788.83	$1,709.25	$79.58	$195,263.33
4	$1,788.83	$1,708.55	$80.28	$195,183.05

WORD PROBLEMS

4. Jim and Janice Hurst are buying a new home for $235,000. The bank which is financing the home requires a 20% down payment and charges a $13\frac{1}{2}\%$ interest rate. Janice wants to know **(a)** what the monthly payment for the principal and interest will be if they take out a 30-year mortgage and **(b)** how much of the first payment will be for interest on the loan.

   a. $2,154.48
   b. $2,115

5. The Hursts (Problem 4) thought that a lot of their money was going to interest. They asked the banker just how much they would be paying for interest over the life of the loan. Calculate the total amount of interest that the Hursts will pay.
$587,612.80

6. The banker told the Hursts (Problem 4) that they could, of course, save on the interest payments if they took out a loan for a shorter period of time. Jim and Janice decided to see if they could afford a 15-year mortgage. Calculate how much more the Hursts would have to pay each month for principal and interest if they took a 15-year mortgage for their loan.
$287.64

7. The Hursts (Problem 4) thought that they might be able to afford this, but first wanted to see **(a)** how much of the first payment would go to the principal and **(b)** how much total interest they would be paying with a 15-year mortgage.
a. $327.12 principal payment
b. $251,581.60

8. The June/July 1997 issue of *Your Money* contained the following information in an article titled "The Affordability Gap."

	1976	1996
Cost of median-priced new home	$44,200	$136,600
10% down payment	$4,420	
Fixed-rate, 30-year mortgage		
Interest rate	8.9%	$7\frac{1}{2}\%$
Total monthly principal and interest	$316	

Complete the 1996 year.

$$\begin{array}{r} \$136,600 \\ \times\ .10 \\ \hline \$\ 13,660 \text{ down payment} \end{array} \qquad \begin{array}{r} \$136,600 \\ -\ 13,660 \\ \hline \$122,940 \text{ 30-year fixed-rate mortgage} \end{array}$$

$$\frac{\$122,940}{\$1,000} = 122.94 \times \$7.00 = \$860.58$$

9. You can't count on your home mortgage lender to keep you from getting in debt over your head. The old standards of allowing 28% of your income for mortgage debt (including taxes and insurance) usually still apply (*Kiplinger's Personal Finance Magazine*, June 1997). If your total monthly payment is $1,033, what should be your annual income to buy a home (*Your Money*, June/July)?

$$\begin{array}{r} \$\ 1,033 \\ \times\ 12 \\ \hline \$12,396 \text{ per year} \end{array} \qquad \frac{\$12,396}{.28} = \$44,271.43$$

10. The January 23, 1995, issue of *U.S. News & World Report* showed that a 30-year fixed-rate mortgage for $100,000 was 9% at that date as opposed to 7% one year ago. What is the difference in monthly payments for these 2 years?

$$\frac{\$100,000}{\$1,000} = 100 \times \$8.05 = \$805 \text{ monthly payment} \qquad \frac{\$100,000}{\$1,000} = 100 \times \$6.66 = \$666 \text{ monthly payment}$$

$$\begin{array}{r} \$805 \\ -\ 666 \\ \hline \$139 \text{ per month} \end{array}$$

11. The April 19, 1997, *Dayton Daily News* ran a news article on what happens when a mortgage is increased by 10 years. If you had a $100,000 mortgage with $7\frac{1}{2}\%$ interest for 25 years and wanted a $7\frac{1}{2}\%$ loan for 35 years, what would be the change in monthly payments? How much more would you pay in interest?

$$\frac{\$100,000}{\$1,000} = 100 \times \$7.39 = \$739 \text{ monthly payment} \qquad \frac{\$100,000}{\$1,000} = 100 \times \$6.75 = \$675 \text{ monthly payment}$$

$739 - $675 = $64 less per month
$739 × 300 = $221,700 $675 × 420 = $283,500 $283,500 - $221,700 = $61,800 more interest

LEARNING UNIT 16.1: Balance Sheet—Report as of a Particular Date

DRILL PROBLEMS

1. Complete the balance sheet for David Harrison, Attorney, and show that

Assets = Liabilities + Owner's equity

Account totals are as follows: accounts receivable, $4,800; office supplies, $375; building (net), $130,000; accounts payable, $1,200; notes payable, $137,200; cash, $2,250; prepaid insurance, $1,050; office equipment (net), $11,250; land, $75,000; capital, $85,900; and salaries payable, $425.

DAVID HARRISON, ATTORNEY Balance Sheet December 31, 2001		
Assets		
Current assets:		
Cash	$ 2,250	
Accounts receivable	4,800	
Prepaid insurance	1,050	
Office supplies	375	
Total current assets		$ 8,475
Plant and equipment:		
Office equipment (net)	$ 11,250	
Building (net)	130,000	
Land	75,000	
Total plant and equipment		216,250
Total assets		$224,725
Liabilities		
Current liabilities:		
Accounts payable	$ 1,200	
Salaries payable	425	
Total current liabilities		$ 1,625
Long-term liabilities:		
Notes payable		137,200
Total liabilities		$138,825
Owner's Equity		
David Harrison, capital, December 31, 2001		85,900
Total liabilities and owner's equity		$224,725

2. Given the amounts in each of the accounts of Fisher-George Electric Corporation, fill in these amounts on the balance sheet to show that

Assets = Liabilities + Stockholders' equity

Account totals are as follows: cash, $2,500; merchandise inventory, $1,325; automobiles (net), $9,250; common stock, $10,000; accounts payable, $275; office equipment (net), $5,065; accounts receivable, $300; retained earnings, $6,895; prepaid insurance, $1,075; salaries payable, $175; and mortgage payable, $2,170.

FISHER-GEORGE ELECTRIC CORPORATION Balance Sheet December 31, 2001			
Assets			
Current assets:			
Cash	$ 2,500		
Accounts receivable	300		
Merchandise inventory	1,325		
Prepaid insurance	1,075		
Total current assets		$ 5,200	
Plant and equipment:			
Office equipment (net)	$5,065		
Automobiles (net)	9,250		
Total plant and equipment		14,315	
Total assets			$19,515
Liabilities			
Current liabilities:			
Accounts payable	$ 275		
Salaries payable	175		
Total current liabilities		$ 450	
Long-term liabilities:			
Mortgage payable		2,170	
Total liabilities			$ 2,620
Stockholders' Equity			
Common stock	$10,000		
Retained earnings	6,895		
Total stockholders' equity			16,895
Total liabilities and stockholders' equity			$19,515

3. Complete a vertical analysis of the following partial balance sheet (round all percents to the nearest hundredth percent).

THREEMAX, INC. Comparative Balance Sheet Vertical Analysis At December 31, 2000 and 2001				
	2001		**2000**	
	Amount	Percent	Amount	Percent
Assets				
Cash	$ 8,500	2.13%	$ 10,200	2.84%
Accounts receivable (net)	11,750	2.95	15,300	4.26
Merchandise inventory	55,430	13.90	54,370	15.12
Store supplies	700	0.18	532	0.15
Office supplies	650	0.16	640	0.18
Prepaid insurance	2,450	0.61	2,675	0.74
Office equipment (net)	12,000	3.01	14,300	3.98
Store equipment (net)	32,000	8.02	31,000	8.62
Building (net)	75,400	18.90	80,500	22.39
Land	200,000	50.14	150,000	41.72
Total assets	$398,880	100.00%	$359,517	100.00%

4. Complete a horizontal analysis of the following partial balance sheet (round all percents to the nearest hundredth percent).

THREEMAX, INC. Comparative Balance Sheet Horizontal Analysis At December 31, 2000 and 2001				
	2001	2000	Change	Percent
Assets				
Cash	$ 8,500	$ 10,200	$ −1,700	−16.67%
Accounts receivable (net)	11,750	15,300	−3,550	−23.20
Merchandise inventory	55,430	54,370	1,060	1.95
Store supplies	700	532	168	31.58
Office supplies	650	640	10	1.56
Prepaid insurance	2,450	2,675	−225	−8.41
Office equipment (net)	12,000	14,300	−2,300	−16.08
Store equipment (net)	32,000	31,000	1,000	3.23
Building (net)	75,400	80,500	−5,100	−6.34
Land	200,000	150,000	50,000	33.33
Total assets	$398,880	$359,517		

LEARNING UNIT 16.2: Income Statement—Report for a Specific Period of Time

DRILL PROBLEMS

1. Complete the income statement for Foley Realty, doing all the necessary addition. Account totals are as follows: office salaries expense, $15,255; advertising expense, $2,400; rent expense, $18,000; telephone expense, $650; insurance expense, $1,550; office supplies, $980; depreciation expense, office equipment, $990; depreciation expense, automobile, $2,100; sales commissions earned, $98,400; and management fees earned, $1,260.

FOLEY REALTY Income Statement For the Year Ended December 31, 2001		
Revenues:		
Sales commissions earned	$98,400	
Management fees earned	1,260	
Total revenues		$99,660
Operating expenses:		
Office salaries expense	$15,225	
Advertising expense	2,400	
Rent expense	18,000	
Telephone expense	650	
Insurance expense	1,550	
Office supplies expense	980	
Depreciation expense, office equipment	990	
Depreciation expense, automobile	2,100	
Total operating expenses		41,895
Net income		$57,765

2. Complete the income statement for Toll's, Inc., a merchandising concern, doing all the necessary addition and subtraction. Sales were $250,000, sales returns and allowances were $1,400, sales discounts were $2,100, merchandise inventory, December 31, 2000, was $42,000, purchases were $156,000, purchases returns and allowances were $1,100, purchases discounts were $3,000, merchandise inventory, December 31, 2001, was $47,000, selling expenses were $37,000, and general and administrative expenses were $29,000.

TOLL'S, INC. Income Statement For the Year Ended December 31, 2001			
Revenues:			
Sales			$250,000
Less: Sales returns and allowances		$ 1,400	
Sales discounts		2,100	3,500
Net sales			$246,500
Cost of goods sold:			
Merchandise inventory, December 31, 2000		$ 42,000	
Purchases	$156,000		
Less: Purchases returns and allowances	$1,100		
Purchase discounts	3,000	4,100	
Cost of net purchases		151,900	
Goods available for sale		$193,900	
Merchandise inventory, December 31, 2001		47,000	
Total cost of goods sold			146,900
Gross profit from sales			$ 99,600
Operating expenses:			
Selling expenses		$ 37,000	
General and administrative expenses		29,000	
Total operating expenses			66,000
Net income			$ 33,600

3. Complete a vertical analysis of the following partial income statement (round all percents to the nearest hundredth percent). Note net sales are 100%.

THREEMAX, INC. Comparative Income Statement Vertical Analysis For Periods Ended December 31, 2000 and 2001	2001		2000	
	Amount	Percent	Amount	Percent
Sales	$795,450	101.63%	$665,532	101.60%
Sales returns and allowances	−6,250	−0.80	−5,340	−0.82
Sales discounts	−6,470	−0.83	−5,125	−0.78
Net sales	$782,730	100.00	$655,067	100.00
Cost of goods sold:				
Beginning inventory	$ 75,394	9.63	$ 81,083	12.38
Purchases	575,980	73.59	467,920	71.43
Purchases discounts	−4,976	−0.64	−2,290	−0.35
Goods available for sale	$646,398	82.58	$546,713	83.46
Less ending inventory	−66,254	−8.46	−65,712	−10.03
Total costs of goods sold	$580,144	74.12	$481,001	73.43
Gross profit	$202,586	25.88	$174,066	26.57

4. Complete a horizontal analysis of the following partial income statement (round all percents to the nearest hundredth percent).

THREEMAX, INC.
Comparative Income Statement Horizontal Analysis
For Periods Ended December 31, 2001 and 2000

	2001	2000	Change	Percent
Sales	$795,450	$665,532	129,918	19.52%
Sales returns and allowances	−6,250	−5,340	−910	17.04
Sales discounts	−6,470	−5,125	−1,345	26.24
Net sales	$782,730	$655,067	127,663	19.49
Cost of goods sold:				
Beginning inventory	$ 75,394	$ 81,083	−5,689	−7.02
Purchases	575,980	467,920	108,060	23.09
Purchases discounts	−4,976	−2,290	−2,686	117.29
Goods available for sale	$646,398	$546,713	99,685	18.23
Less ending inventory	−66,254	−65,712	−542	0.82
Total costs of goods sold	$580,144	$481,001	99,143	20.61
Gross profit	$202,586	$174,066	28,520	16.38

LEARNING UNIT 16.3: Trend and Ratio Analysis

DRILL PROBLEMS

1. Express each amount as a percent of the base-year (1999) amount. Round to the nearest tenth percent.

	2002	2001	2000	1999
Sales	$562,791	$560,776	$588,096	$601,982
Percent	93.5%	93.2%	97.7%	100.0%
Gross profit	$168,837	$196,271	$235,238	$270,891
Percent	62.3%	72.5%	86.8%	100.0%
Net income	$67,934	$65,927	$56,737	$62,762
Percent	108.2%	105.0%	90.4%	100.0%

2. If current assets = $42,500 and current liabilities = $56,400, what is the current ratio (to the nearest hundredth)?
   0.75

3. In Problem 2, if inventory = $20,500 and prepaid expenses = $9,750, what is the quick ratio, or acid test (to the nearest hundredth)?
   0.22

4. If accounts receivable = $36,720 and net sales = $249,700, what is the average day's collection (to the nearest whole day)?
   53 days

5. If total liabilities = $243,000 and total assets = $409,870, what is the ratio of total debt to total assets (to the nearest hundredth percent)?
   59.29%

6. If net income = $55,970 and total stockholders' equity = $440,780, what is the return on equity (to the nearest hundredth percent)?
   12.70%

7. If net sales = $900,000 and total assets = $1,090,000, what is the asset turnover (to the nearest hundredth)?
   .83

8. In Problem 7, if the net income is $36,600, what is the profit margin on net sales (to the nearest hundredth percent)?
   4.07%

WORD PROBLEMS

9. Calculate trend percentages for the following items using 1999 as the base year. Round to the nearest hundredth percent.

	2002	2001	2000	1999
Sales	$298,000	$280,000	$264,000	$249,250
Cost of goods sold	187,085	175,227	164,687	156,785
Accounts receivable	29,820	28,850	27,300	26,250

Sales: 119.56%, 112.34%, 105.92%
Cost of goods sold: 119.33%, 111.76%, 105.04%
Accounts receivable: 113.60%, 109.90%, 104.00%

10. According to the balance sheet for Ralph's Market, current assets = $165,500 and current liabilities = $70,500. Find the current ratio (to the nearest hundredth).
2.35

11. On the balance sheet for Ralph's Market (Problem 10), merchandise inventory = $102,000. Find the quick ratio (acid test).
.90

12. The balance sheet of Moses Contractors shows cash of $5,500, accounts receivable of $64,500, an inventory of $42,500, and current liabilities of $57,500. Find Moses' current ratio and acid test ratio (both to the nearest hundredth).
1.96 current ratio   1.22 acid test

13. Moses' income statement shows gross sales of $413,000, sales returns of $8,600, and net income of $22,300. Find the profit margin on net sales (to the nearest hundredth percent).
5.51%

14. **Given:**

Cash	$ 39,000	Retained earnings	$194,000
Accounts receivable	109,000	Net sales	825,000
Inventory	150,000	Cost of goods sold	528,000
Prepaid expenses	48,000	Operating expenses	209,300
Plant and equipment (net)	487,000	Interest expense	13,500
Accounts payable	46,000	Income taxes	32,400
Other current liabilities	43,000	Net income	41,800
Long-term liabilities	225,000		
Common stock	325,000		

Calculate (to nearest hundredth or hundredth percent as needed):

a. Current ratio.
3.89

b. Quick ratio.
1.66

c. Average day's collection.
47.56 days

d. Total debt to total assets.
37.70%

e. Return on equity.
8.05%

f. Asset turnover.
$0.99

g. Profit margin on net sales.
5.07%

15. On April 1, 1997, the following story appeared in the *News and Observer.* The information was part of a 1996 year-end statement from Liggett Group, which showed the company's financial position has continued to deteriorate. The company lost $18.4 million in profits for the year as sales dropped to $401 million. Sales in 1995 were $450.6 million. What percent is the decrease in Liggett's sales? Round to the nearest hundredth percent.

1996	1995
$401 million	$450.6 million

$450.6
$-$ 401.0
$ 49.6 million decrease

$$\frac{\$49.6}{\$450.6} = 11.01\%$$

LEARNING UNIT 17.1: Concept of Depreciation and the Straight-Line Method

DRILL PROBLEMS

1. Find the annual straight-line rate of depreciation, given the following estimated lives.

Life	Annual rate	Life	Annual rate
a. 25 years	4%	**b.** 4 years	25%
c. 10 years	10%	**d.** 5 years	20%
e. 8 years	$12\frac{1}{2}\%$	**f.** 30 years	$3\frac{1}{3}\%$

2. Find the annual depreciation using the straight-line depreciation method (round to the nearest whole dollar).

	Cost of asset	Residual value	Useful life	Annual depreciation
a.	$2,460	$400	4 years	$515
b.	$24,300	$2,000	6 years	$3,717
c.	$350,000	$42,500	12 years	$25,625
d.	$17,325	$5,000	5 years	$2,465
e.	$2,550,000	$75,000	30 years	$82,500

3. Find the annual depreciation and ending hook value for the first year using the straight-line depreciation method. Round to the nearest dollar.

	Cost	Residual value	Useful life	Annual depreciation	Ending book value
a.	$6,700	$600	3 years	$2,033	$4,667
b.	$11,600	$500	6 years	$1,850	$9,750
c.	$9,980	–0–	5 years	$1,996	$7,984
d.	$36,950	$2,500	12 years	$2,871	$34,079
e.	$101,690	$3,600	27 years	$3,633	$98,057

4. Find the first-year depreciation to nearest dollar for the following assets, which were only owned for part of a year. Round to the nearest whole dollar the annual depreciation for in-between calculations.

	Date of purchase	Cost of asset	Residual value	Useful life	First year depreciation
a.	April 8	$10,500	$1,200	4 years	$1,744
b.	July 12	$23,900	$3,200	6 years	$1,725
c.	June 19	$8,880	$800	3 years	$1,347
d.	November 2	$125,675	$6,000	17 years	$1,173
e.	May 25	$44,050	–0–	9 years	$2,855

WORD PROBLEMS

5. North Shore Grinding purchased a lathe for $37,500. This machine has a residual value of $3,000 and an expected useful life of 4 years. Prepare a depreciation schedule for the lathe using the straight-line depreciation method.
$8,625 annual depreciation

6. Colby Wayne paid $7,750 for a photocopy machine with an estimated life of 6 years and a residual value of $900. Prepare a depreciation schedule using the straight-line depreciation method. Round to nearest whole dollar. (Last year's depreciation may have to be adjusted due to rounding.)
$1,142 annual depreciation

7. The Leo Brothers purchased a machine for $8,400 that has an estimated life of 3 years. At the end of 3 years the machine will have no value. Prepare a depreciation schedule for this machine.
$2,800 annual depreciation

8. Fox Realty bought a computer table for $1,700. The estimated useful life of the table is 7 years. The residual value at the end of 7 years is $370. Find **(a)** the annual rate of depreciation to the nearest hundredth percent, **(b)** the annual amount of depreciation, and **(c)** the book value of the table at the end of the *third* year using the straight-line depreciation method.
a. 14.29%   **b.** $190   **c.** $1,130

9. Cashman, Inc., purchased an overhead projector for $560. It has an estimated useful life of 6 years, at which time it will have no remaining value. Find the book value at the end of 5 years using the straight-line depreciation method. Round the annual depreciation to the nearest whole dollar.
   $95

10. Shelley Corporation purchased a new machine for $15,000. The estimated life of the machine is 12 years with a residual value of $2,400. Find **(a)** the annual rate of depreciation to the nearest hundredth percent, **(b)** the annual amount of depreciation, **(c)** the accumulated depreciation at the end of 7 years, and **(d)** the book value at the end of 9 years.
    a. 8.33%   **b.** $1,050   **c.** $7,350   **d.** $5,550

11. Wolfe Ltd. purchased a supercomputer for $75,000 on July 7, 2000. The computer has an estimated life of 5 years and will have a residual value of $15,000. Find **(a)** the annual depreciation amount, **(b)** the depreciation amount for 2000, **(c)** the accumulated depreciation at the end of 2001, and **(d)** the book value at the end of 2002.
    a. $12,000   **b.** $6,000   **c.** $18,000   **d.** $45,000

LEARNING UNIT 17.2: Units-of-Production Method

DRILL PROBLEMS

1. Find the depreciation per unit for each of the following assets. Round to three decimal places.

Cost of asset	Residual value	Estimated production	Depreciation per unit
a. $3,500	$800	9,000 units	$0.300
b. $309,560	$22,000	1,500,000 units	$0.192
c. $54,890	$6,500	275,000 units	$0.176

2. Find the annual depreciation expense for each of the assets in Problem 1.

Cost of asset	Residual value	Estimated production	Depreciation per unit	Units produced	Amount of depreciation
a. $3,500	$800	9,000 units	$0.300	3,000	$900
b. $309,560	$22,000	1,500,000 units	$0.192	45,500	$8,736
c. $54,890	$6,500	275,000 units	$0.176	4,788	$842.69

3. Find the book value at the end of the first year for each of the assets in Problems 1 and 2.

Cost of asset	Residual value	Estimated production	Depreciation per unit	Units produced	Book value
a. $3,500	$800	9,000 units	$0.300	3,000	$2,600
b. $309,560	$22,000	1,500,000 units	$0.192	45,500	$300,824
c. $54,890	$6,500	275,000 units	$0.176	4,788	$54,047.31

4. Calculate the accumulated depreciation at the end of year 2 for each of the following machines. Carry out the unit depreciation to three decimal places.

Cost of machine	Residual value	Estimated life	Hours used during year 1	Hours used during year 2	Accumulated depreciation
a. $67,900	$4,300	19,000 hours	5,430	4,856	$34,427.24
b. $3,810	$600	33,000 hours	10,500	9,330	$1,923.51
c. $25,000	$4,900	80,000 hours	7,000	12,600	$4,919.60

WORD PROBLEMS

5. Prepare a depreciation schedule for the following machine: The machine cost $63,400; it has an estimated residual value of $5,300 and expected life of 290,500 units. The units produced were:

   Year 1   95,000 units
   Year 2   80,000 units
   Year 3   50,000 units $5,300 book value at the end of year 5
   Year 4   35,500 units
   Year 5   30,000 units

6. Forsmann & Smythe purchased a new machine that cost $46,030. The machine has a residual value of $2,200 and estimated output of 430,000 hours. Prepare a units-of-production depreciation schedule for this machine (round the unit depreciation to three decimal places). The hours of use were:

Year 1   90,000 hours
Year 2   150,000 hours
Year 3   105,000 hours $2,200 book value at the end of year 4
Year 4   90,000 hours

7. Young Electrical Company depreciates its vans using the units-of-production method. The cost of its new van was $24,600, the useful life is 125,000 miles, and the trade-in value is $5,250. What are **(a)** the depreciation expense per mile (to three decimal places) and **(b)** the book value at the end of the first year if it drives 29,667 miles?
   a. $0.155   **b.** $20,001.61

8. Tremblay Manufacturing Company purchased a new machine for $52,000. The machine has an estimated useful life of 185,000 hours and a residual value of $10,000. The machine was used for 51,200 hours the first year. Find **(a)** the depreciation rate per hour (round to three decimal places), **(b)** the depreciation expense for the first year, and **(c)** the book value of the machine at the end of the first year.
   a. $0.227   **b.** $11,622.40   **c.** $40,377.60

LEARNING UNIT 17.3: Sum-of-the-Years'-Digits Method

DRILL PROBLEMS

1. Find the sum-of-the-years'-digits depreciation rate as a fraction for each year of life for the following assets:

Useful life	Year 1	Year 2	Year 3	Year 4	Year 5	Year 6	Year 7	Year 8
a. 5 years	$\frac{5}{15}$	$\frac{4}{15}$	$\frac{3}{15}$	$\frac{2}{15}$	$\frac{1}{15}$			
b. 3 years	$\frac{3}{6}$	$\frac{2}{6}$	$\frac{1}{6}$					
c. 8 years	$\frac{8}{36}$	$\frac{7}{36}$	$\frac{6}{36}$	$\frac{5}{36}$	$\frac{4}{36}$	$\frac{3}{36}$	$\frac{2}{36}$	$\frac{1}{36}$

2. Find the first year depreciation amount for the following assets using the sum-of-the-year's-digits depreciation method. Round to the nearest whole dollar.

	Cost of asset	Residual value	Useful life	First year depreciation
a.	$2,460	$400	4 years	$824
b.	$24,300	$2,000	6 years	$6,371
c.	$350,000	$42,500	12 years	$47,308
d.	$17,325	$5,000	5 years	$4,108
e.	$2,550,000	$75,000	30 years	$159,677

3. Find the depreciation expense and ending book value for the first year using the sum-of-the-years'-digits depreciation method. Round to the nearest dollar (depreciation expense as well as ending book value).

	Cost	Residual value	Useful life	First year depreciation	Ending book value
a.	$6,700	$600	3 years	$3,050	$3,650
b.	$11,600	$500	6 years	$3,171	$8,429
c.	$9,980	–0–	5 years	$3,327	$6,653
d.	$36,950	$2,500	12 years	$5,300	$31,650
e.	$101,690	$3,600	27 years	$7,006	$94,684

WORD PROBLEMS

4. North Shore Grinding purchased a lathe for $37,500. This machine has a residual value of $3,000 and an expected useful life of 4 years. Prepare a depreciation schedule for the lathe using the sum-of-the-years'-digits depreciation method.
   $3,000 book value at end of year 4

5. Colby Wayne paid $7,750 for a photocopy machine with an estimated life of 6 years and a residual value of $900. Prepare a depreciation schedule using the sum-of-the-years'-digits depreciation method. Round all amounts to the nearest whole dollar.
   $900 book value at end of year 6

6. Leo Brothers purchased a machine for $8,400 that has an estimated life of 3 years. At the end of 3 years, the machine will have no value. Prepare a depreciation schedule for this machine.
   0 book value at end of year 3

7. Fox Realty bought a computer table for $1,700. The estimated useful life of the table is 7 years. The residual value at the end of 7 years is $370. Find (a) the sum-of-the-years' denominator, (b) the amount of depreciation at the end of the *third* year, and (c) the book value of the table at the end of the *third* year using the sum-of-the-years'-digits depreciation method.
   a. 28   b. $237.50   c. $845

8. Cashman, Inc., purchased an overhead projector for $560. It has an estimated useful life of 6 years, at which time it will have no remaining value. Find the book value at the end of 5 years using the sum-of-the-years'-digits depreciation method. Round to the nearest whole dollar.
   $27

LEARNING UNIT 17.4: Declining-Balance Method

DRILL PROBLEMS

1. Find the declining-balance rate of depreciation, given the following estimated lives.

Life	Declining rate
a. 25 years	$8\% \left(\dfrac{1}{25} \times 2 = \dfrac{2}{25} \right)$
b. 10 years	$20\% \left(\dfrac{1}{10} \times 2 = \dfrac{2}{10} \right)$
c. 8 years	$25\% \left(\dfrac{1}{8} \times 2 = \dfrac{2}{8} \right)$

2. Find the first year depreciation amount for the following assets using the declining-balance depreciation method. Round to the nearest whole dollar.

Cost of asset	Residual value	Useful life	First year depreciation
a. $2,460	$400	4 years	$1,230
b. $24,300	$2,000	6 years	$8,100
c. $350,000	$42,500	12 years	$58,333
d. $17,325	$5,000	5 years	$6,930
e. $2,550,000	$75,000	30 years	$170,000

3. Find the depreciation expense and ending book value for the first year, using the declining-balance depreciation method. Round to the nearest dollar.

Cost	Residual value	Useful life	First year depreciation	Ending book value
a. $6,700	$600	3 years	$4,467	$2,233
b. $11,600	$500	6 years	$3,867	$7,733
c. $9,980	–0–	5 years	$3,992	$5,988
d. $36,950	$2,500	12 years	$6,158	$30,792
e. $101,690	$3,600	27 years	$7,533	$94,157

WORD PROBLEMS

4. North Shore Grinding purchased a lathe for $37,500. This machine has a residual value of $3,000 and an expected useful life of 4 years. Prepare a depreciation schedule for the lathe using the declining-balance depreciation method. Round to the nearest whole dollar.
Depreciation in year 4 is $1,687

5. Colby Wayne paid $7,750 for a photocopy machine with an estimated life of 6 years and a residual value of $900. Prepare a depreciation schedule using the declining-balance depreciation method. Round to the nearest whole dollar.
Depreciation in year 6 is $121

6. The Leo Brothers purchased a machine for $8,400 that has an estimated life of 3 years. At the end of 3 years, the machine will have no value. Prepare a depreciation schedule for this machine. Round to the nearest whole dollar.
Depreciation in year 3 is $933

7. Fox Realty bought a computer table for $1,700. The estimated useful life of the table is 7 years. The residual value at the end of 7 years is $370. Find **(a)** the declining depreciation rate to the nearest hundredth percent, **(b)** the amount of depreciation at the end of the *third* year, and **(c)** the book value of the table at the end of the *third* year using the declining-balance depreciation method. Round to the nearest whole dollar.
a. 28.57% **b.** $248 **c.** $619

8. Cashman, Inc., purchased an overhead projector for $560. It has an estimated useful life of 6 years, at which time it will have no remaining value. Find the book value at the end of 5 years using the declining-balance depreciation method. Round to the nearest whole dollar.
$74

9. Shelley Corporation purchased a new machine for $15,000. The estimated life of the machine is 12 years with a residual value of $2,400. Find **(a)** the declining-balance depreciation rate as a fraction and as a percent (hundredth percent), **(b)** the amount of depreciation at the end of the first year, **(c)** the accumulated depreciation at the end of 7 years, and **(d)** the book value at the end of 9 years. Round to the nearest dollar.
a. $\frac{1}{6}$; 16.67% **b.** $2,500 **c.** $10,814 **d.** $2,907

LEARNING UNIT 17.5: Modified Accelerated Cost Recovery System (MACRS) with Introduction to ACRS

DRILL PROBLEMS

1. Using the MACRS method of depreciation, find the recovery rate, first-year depreciation expense, and book value of the asset at the end of the first year. Round to the nearest whole dollar.

Cost of asset	Recovery period	Recovery rate	Depreciation expense	End-of-year book value
a. $2,500	3 years	33%	$825	$1,675
b. $52,980	3 years	33%	$17,483	$35,497
c. $4,250	5 years	20%	$850	$3,400
d. $128,950	10 years	10%	$12,895	$116,055
e. $13,775	5 years	20%	$2,755	$11,020

2. Find the accumulated depreciation at the end of the second year for each of the following assets. Round to the nearest whole dollar.

Cost of asset	Recovery period	Accumulated depreciation at end of 2nd year using MACRS	Book value at end of 2nd year using MACRS
a. $2,500	3 years	$1,950	$550
b. $52,980	3 years	$41,324	$11,656
c. $4,250	5 years	$2,210	$2,040
d. $128,950	10 years	$36,106	$92,844
e. $13,775	5 years	$7,163	$6,612

WORD PROBLEMS

3. Colby Wayne paid $7,750 for a photocopy machine that is classified as equipment and has a residual value of $900. Prepare a depreciation schedule using the MACRS depreciation method. Round all calculations to the nearest whole dollar.

Depreciation in year 8 is $346

4. Fox Realty bought a computer table for $1,700. The table is classified as furniture. The residual value at the end of the table's useful life is $370. Using the MACRS depreciation method, find **(a)** the amount of depreciation at the end of the *third* year, **(b)** the total accumulated depreciation at the end of year 3, and **(c)** the book value of the table at the end of the *third* year. Round all calculations to the nearest dollar.

a. $297   **b.** $956   **c.** $744

5. Cashman, Inc., purchased an overhead projector for $560. It is classified as office equipment and will have no residual value. Find the book value at the end of 5 years using the MACRS depreciation method. Round to the nearest whole dollar.

$125

6. Shelley Corporation purchased a new machine for $15,000. The machine is comparable to equipment used for two-way exchange of voice and data with a residual value of $2,400. Find **(a)** the amount of depreciation at the end of the first year, **(b)** the accumulated depreciation at the end of 7 years, and **(c)** the book value at the end of 9 years. Round to the nearest dollar.

a. $750   **b.** $7,470   **c.** $5,760

7.* Wolfe Ltd. purchased a supercomputer for $75,000 at the beginning of 1996. The computer is classified as a 5-year asset and will have a residual value of $15,000. Using MACRS, find **(a)** the depreciation amount for 1996, **(b)** the accumulated depreciation at the end of 1997, **(c)** the book value at the end of 1998, and **(d)** the last year that the asset will be depreciated.

a. $15,000   **b.** $39,000   **c.** $21,600   **d.** 2001

8.* Cummins Engine Company uses a straight-line depreciation method to calculate the cost of an asset of $1,200,000 with a $200,000 residual value and a life expectancy of 15 years. How much would Cummins have for depreciation expense for each of the first 2 years? Round to the nearest dollar for each year. (*Management Accounting,* July 1996)

$$\$1,200,000 - 200,000 = \frac{\$1,000,000}{15} = \$ \ 66,667 \text{ each year}$$

$$\underline{\times 2 \text{ years}}$$

$$\$133,334 \text{ depreciation for 2 years}$$

9. An article in the July 1996 issue of *Management Accounting* stated that Cummins Engine Company changed its depreciation. The cost of its asset was $1,200,000 with a $200,000 residual value (with a life expectancy of 15 years) and an estimated productive capacity of 864,000 products. Cummins produced 59,000 products this year. What would it write off for depreciation using the units-of-production method?

| | Residual | |
| Cost | value | |

$$\$1,200,000 - \$200,000 = \frac{\$1,000,000}{864,000} = \$1.16 \text{ per product}$$

$$\begin{array}{l} \$1.16 \\ \underline{\times 59,000} \\ \$68,440 \end{array} \quad \begin{array}{l} \text{(estimated units} \\ \text{of useful life} \\ \text{production)} \end{array}$$

---

*These problems are placed here for a quick review.

LEARNING UNIT 18.1: Assigning Costs to Ending Inventory—Specific Identification; Weighted Average; FIFO; LIFO

DRILL PROBLEMS

1. Given the value of the beginning inventory, purchases for the year, and ending inventory, find the cost of goods available for sale and the cost of goods sold.

	Beginning inventory	Purchases	Ending inventory	Cost of goods available for sale	Cost of goods sold
a.	$1,000	$4,120	$2,100	$5,120	$3,020
b.	$52,400	$270,846	$49,700	$323,246	$273,546
c.	$205	$48,445	$376	$48,650	$48,274
d.	$78,470	$2,788,560	$100,600	$2,867,030	$2,766,430
e.	$965	$53,799	$2,876	$54,764	$51,888

2. Find the missing amounts; then calculate the number of units available for sale and the cost of the goods available for sale.

Date	Category	Quantity	Unit cost	Total cost
January 1	Beginning inventory	1,207	$45	$ 54,315
February 7	Purchase	850	$46	$ 39,100
April 19	Purchase	700	$47	$ 32,900
July 5	Purchase	1,050	$49	$ 51,450
November 2	Purchase	450	$52	$ 23,400
Goods available for sale		4,257		$201,165

3. Using the *specific identification* method, find the ending inventory and cost of goods sold for the merchandising concern in Problem 2.

Remaining inventory	Unit cost	Total cost
20 units from beginning inventory	$45	$ 900
35 units from February 7	$46	$ 1,610
257 units from July 5	$49	$ 12,593
400 units from November 2	$52	$ 20,800
Cost of ending inventory		$ 35,903
Cost of goods sold		$165,262

4. Using the *weighted-average* method, find the average cost per unit (to the nearest cent) and the cost of ending inventory.

	Units available for sale	Cost of goods available for sale	Units in ending inventory	Weighted-average unit cost	Cost of ending inventory
a.	2,350	$120,320	1,265	$51.20	$64,768
b.	7,090	$151,017	1,876	$21.30	$39,958.80
c.	855	$12,790	989	$14.96	$14,795.44
d.	12,964	$125,970	9,542	$9.72	$92,748.24
e.	235,780	$507,398	239,013	$2.15	$513,877.95

5. Use the *FIFO* method of inventory valuation to determine the value of ending inventory, which consists of 40 units, and the cost of goods sold.

Date	Category	Quantity	Unit cost	Total cost
January 1	Beginning inventory	37	$219.00	$ 8,103.00
March 5	Purchases	18	230.60	$ 4,150.80
June 17	Purchases	22	255.70	$ 5,625.40
October 18	Purchases	34	264.00	$ 8,976.00
Goods available for sale		111		$26,855.20

Ending inventory = $10,510.20   Cost of goods sold = $16,345

6. Use the *LIFO* method of inventory valuation to determine the value of the ending inventory, which consists of 40 units, and the cost of goods sold.

Date	Category	Quantity	Unit cost	Total cost
January 1	Beginning inventory	37	$219.00	$ 8,103.00
March 5	Purchases	18	230.60	$ 4,150.80
June 17	Purchases	22	255.70	$ 5,625.40
October 18	Purchases	34	264.00	$ 8,976.00
Goods available for sale		111		$26,855.20

Ending inventory = $8,794.80   Cost of goods sold = $18,060.40

WORD PROBLEMS

7. At the beginning of September, Green's of Gloucester had 13 yellow raincoats in stock. These raincoats cost $36.80 each. During the month, Green's purchased 14 raincoats for $37.50 each and 16 raincoats for $38.40 each, and they sold 26 raincoats. Calculate (a) the average unit cost (round to the nearest cent) and (b) the ending inventory value using the weighted-average method.

a. $37.62   b. $639.54

8. If Green's of Gloucester (Problem 7) used the FIFO method, what would the value of the ending inventory be?
$651.90

9. If Green's of Gloucester (Problem 7) used the LIFO method, what would the value of the ending inventory be?
$628.40

10. Hobby Caterers purchased recycled-paper sketch pads during the year as follows:

January	350 pads for $.27 each
March	400 pads for $.31 each
July	200 pads for $.36 each
October	850 pads for $.26 each
November	400 pads for $.31 each

At the end of the year, the company had 775 of these sketch pads in stock. Find the ending inventory value using (a) the weighted-average method (round to the nearest cent), (b) the FIFO method, and (c) the LIFO method.

a. $224.75   b. $221.50   c. $227.50

11. On March 1, Sandler's Shoe Store had the following sports shoes in stock:

13 pairs running shoes for $33 a pair
22 pairs walking shoes for $29 a pair
35 pairs aerobic shoes for $26 a pair
21 pairs cross-trainers for $52 a pair

During the month Sandler's sold 10 pairs of running shoes, 15 pairs of walking shoes, 28 pairs of aerobic shoes, and 12 pairs of cross-trainers. Use the specific identification method to find (a) the cost of the goods available for sale, (b) the value of the ending inventory, and (c) the cost of goods sold.

a. $3,069   b. $952   c. $2,117

LEARNING UNIT 18.2: Retail Method; Gross Profit Method; Inventory Turnover; Distribution of Overhead

DRILL PROBLEMS

1. Given the following information, calculate (a) the goods available for sale at cost and retail, (b) the cost ratio (to the nearest thousandth), (c) the ending inventory at retail, and (d) the cost of the March 31 inventory (to the nearest dollar) by the retail inventory method.

	Cost	Retail	
Beginning inventory, March 1	$57,300	$95,500	a. $85,700; $143,500
Purchases during March	$28,400	$48,000	b. 0.597
Sales during March		$79,000	c. $64,500
			d. $38,507

2. Given the following information, use the gross profit method to calculate (a) the cost of goods available for sale, (b) the cost percentage, (c) the estimated cost of goods sold, and (d) the estimated cost of the inventory as of April 30.

Beginning inventory, April 1	$30,000	a. $111,800
Net purchases during April	81,800	b. 60%
Sales during April	98,000	c. $58,800
Average gross profit on sales	40%	d. $53,000
Inventory, April 1		$30,000
Net purchases		$81,800

3. Given the following information, find the average inventory.

Merchandise inventory, January 1, 200A	$82,000	$85,000
Merchandise inventory, December 31, 200A	$88,000	

4. Given the following information, find the inventory turnover for the company in Problem 3 to the nearest hundredth.

Cost of goods sold (12/31/0A)	$625,000	7.35

5. Given the following information, calculate the (a) average inventory at retail, (b) average inventory at cost, (c) inventory turnover at retail, and (d) inventory turnover at cost. Round to the nearest hundredth.

	Cost	Retail	
Merchandise inventory, January 1	$ 250,000	$ 355,000	a. $342,000
Merchandise inventory, December 31	$ 235,000	$ 329,000	b. $242,500
Cost of goods sold	$1,525,000		c. 5.85
Sales		$2,001,000	d. 6.29

6. Given the floor space for the following departments, find the entire floor space and the percent each department represents.

		Percent of floor space
Department A	15,000 square feet	30%
Department B	25,000 square feet	50%
Department C	10,000 square feet	20%
Total floor space	50,000 square feet	100%

7. If the total overhead for all the departments (Problem 6) is $200,000, how much of the overhead expense should be allocated to each department?

	Overhead/department
Department A	$ 60,000
Department B	$100,000
Department C	$ 40,000

WORD PROBLEMS

8. During the accounting period, Ward's Greenery sold $290,000 of merchandise at marked retail prices. At the end of the period, the following information was available from Ward's records:

	Cost	Retail
Beginning inventory	$ 53,000	$ 79,000
Net purchases	$204,000	$280,000

Use the retail method to estimate Ward's ending inventory at cost. Round the cost ratio to the nearest thousandth.
$49,404

9. On January 1, Benny's Retail Mart had a $49,000 inventory at cost. During the first quarter of the year, Benny's made net purchases of $199,900. Benny's records show that during the past several years, the store's gross profit on sales has averaged 35%. If Benny's records show $275,000 in sales for the quarter, estimate the ending inventory for the first quarter, using the gross profit method.
$70,150

10. On April 4, there was a big fire and the entire inventory of R. W. Wilson Company was destroyed. The company records were salvaged. They showed the following information:

Sales (January 1 through April 4) $127,000
Merchandise inventory, January 1   16,000
Net purchases   71,250

On January 1, the inventory was priced to sell for $38,000 and additional items bought during the period were priced to sell for $102,000. Calculate the cost of the inventory that was destroyed by the fire using the retail method. Round the cost ratio to the nearest thousandth.
$8,099

11. During the past 4 years, the average gross margin on sales for R. W. Wilson Company was 36% of net sales. Using the data in Problem 10, calculate the cost of the ending inventory destroyed by fire using the gross profit method.
$5,970

12. Chase Bank has to make a decision on whether to grant a loan to Sally's Furniture store. The lending officer is interested in how often Sally's inventory is turned over. Using selected information from Sally's income statement, calculate the inventory turnover for Sally's Furniture Store (to the nearest hundredth).

Merchandise inventory, January 1, 200A $ 43,000
Merchandise inventory, December 31, 200A   55,000
Cost of goods sold   128,000

2.61 times

13. Wanting to know more about a business he was considering buying, Jake Paige studied the business's books. He found that beginning inventory for the previous year was $51,000 at cost and $91,800 at retail, ending inventory was $44,000 at cost and $72,600 at retail, sales were $251,000, and cost of goods sold was $154,000. Using this information, calculate for Jake the inventory turnover at cost and the inventory turnover at retail.
3.24 times (at cost)
3.05 times (at retail)

14. Ralph's Retail Outlet has calculated its expenses for the year. Total overhead expenses are $147,000. Ralph's accountant must allocate this overhead to four different departments. Given the following information regarding the floor space occupied by each department, calculate how much overhead expense should be allocated to each department.

Department W   12,000 square feet $42,000
Department X   9,000 square feet $31,500
Department Y   14,000 square feet $49,000
Department Z   7,000 square feet $24,500

15. How much overhead would be allocated to each department of Ralph's Retail Outlet (Problem 14) if the basis of allocation were the sales of each department? Sales for each of the departments were:

Department W $110,000 $32,340
Department X $120,000 $35,280
Department Y $170,000 $49,980
Department Z $100,000 $29,400

LEARNING UNIT 19.1: Sales and Excise Taxes

DRILL PROBLEMS

1. Calculate the sales tax and the total amount due for each of the following:

	Total sales	Sales tax rate	Sales tax	Total amount due
a.	$536	5%	$26.80	$562.80
b.	$11,980	6%	$718.80	$12,698.80
c.	$3,090	$8\frac{1}{4}\%$	$254.93	$3,344.93
d.	$17.65	$5\frac{1}{2}\%$	$0.97	$18.62
e.	$294	7.42%	$21.81	$315.81

2. Find the amount of actual sales and amount of sales tax on the following total receipts:

	Total receipts	Sales tax rate	Actual sales	Sales tax
a.	$27,932.15	5.5%	$26,475.97	$1,456.18
b.	$35,911.53	7%	$33,562.18	$2,349.35
c.	$115,677.06	$6\frac{1}{2}\%$	$108,616.95	$7,060.11
d.	$142.96	$5\frac{1}{4}\%$	$135.83	$7.13
e.	$5,799.24	4.75%	$5,536.27	$262.97

3. Find the sales tax, excise tax, and total cost for each of the following items:

	Retail price	Sales tax, 5.2%	Excise tax, 11%	Total cost
a.	$399	$20.75	$43.89	$463.64
b.	$22,684	$1,179.57	$2,495.24	$26,358.81
c.	$7,703	$400.56	$847.33	$8,950.89

4. Calculate the amount, subtotal, sales tax, and total amount due of the following:

Quantity	Description	Unit price	Amount
3	Taxable item	$4.30	$12.90
2	Taxable item	$5.23	$10.46
4	Taxable item	$1.20	$ 4.80
		Subtotal	$28.16
		5% sales tax	1.41
		Total	$29.57

5. Given the sales tax rate and the amount of the sales tax, calculate the price of the following purchases (before tax was added):

	Tax rate	Tax amount	Price of purchase
a.	7%	$71.61	$1,023
b.	$5\frac{1}{2}\%$	$3.22	$58.55

6. Given the sales tax rate and the total price (including tax), calculate the price of the following purchases (before the tax was added):

	Tax rate	Total price	Price of purchase
a.	5%	$340.20	$324
b.	6%	$1,224.30	$1,155

WORD PROBLEMS

7. In a state with a 4.75% sales tax, what will be the sales tax and the total price of a video game marked $110?
   $5.23 sales tax $115.23 total price

8. Browning's invoice included a sales tax of $38.15. If the sales tax rate is 6%, what was the total cost of the taxable goods on the invoice?
   $635.83

9. David Bowan paid a total of $2,763 for a new computer. If this includes a sales tax of 5.3%, what was the marked price of the computer?
   $2,623.93

10. After a 5% sales tax and a 12% excise tax, the total cost of a leather jacket was $972. What was the selling price of the jacket?
    $830.77

11. A customer at the RDM Discount Store purchased four tubes of toothpaste priced at $1.88 each, six toothbrushes for $1.69 each, and three bottles of shampoo for $2.39 each. What did the customer have to pay if the sales tax is $5\frac{1}{2}$%?
    $26.20

12. Bill Harrington purchased a mountain bike for $875. Bill had to pay a sales tax of 6% and an excise tax of 11%. What was the total amount Bill had to pay for his mountain bike?
    $1,023.75

13. Donna DeCoff received a bill for $754 for a new chair she had purchased. The bill included a 6.2% sales tax and a delivery charge of $26. What was the selling price of the chair?
    $685.50

LEARNING UNIT 19.2: Property Tax

DRILL PROBLEMS

1. Find the assessed value of the following properties (round to the nearest whole dollar):

Market value	Assessment rate	Assessed value
a. $195,000	35%	$68,250
b. $1,550,900	50%	$775,450
c. $75,000	75%	$56,250
d. $2,585,400	65%	$1,680,510
e. $349,500	85%	$297,075

2. Find the tax rate for each of the following municipalities (round to the nearest tenth of a percent):

Budget needed	Total assessed value	Tax rate
a. $2,594,000	$44,392,000	5.8%
b. $17,989,000	$221,900,000	8.1%
c. $6,750,000	$47,635,000	14.2%
d. $13,540,000	$143,555,500	9.4%
e. $1,099,000	$12,687,000	8.7%

3. Express each of the following tax rates in all the indicated forms:

By percent	Per $100 of assessed value	Per $1,000 of assessed value	In mills
a. 7.45%	$7.45	$74.50	74.50
b. 14.24%	$14.24	$142.40	142.40
c. 9.08%	$9.08	$90.80	90.8
d. 6.2%	$6.20	$62.00	62

4. Calculate the property tax due for each of the following:

Total assessed value	Tax rate	Total property tax due
a. $12,900	$6.60 per $100	$851.40
b. $175,400	43 mills	$7,542.20
c. $320,500	2.7%	$8,653.50
d. $2,480,000	$17.85 per $1,000	$44,268.00
e. $78,900	59 mills	$4,655.10
f. $225,550	$11.39 per $1,000	$2,569.01
g. $198,750	$2.63 per $100	$5,227.13

WORD PROBLEMS

5. The county of Chelsea approved a budget of $3,450,000, which had to be raised through property taxation. If the total assessed value of properties in the county of Chelsea was $37,923,854, what will the tax rate be? The tax rate is stated per $100 of assessed valuation.
   $9.10

6. Linda Tawse lives in Camden and her home has a market value of $235,000. Property in Camden is assessed at 55% of its market value, and the tax rate for the current year is $64.75 per $1,000. What is the assessed valuation of Linda's home?
   $129,250

7. Using the information in Problem 6, find the amount of property tax that Linda will have to pay.
   $8,368.94

8. Mary Faye Souza has property with a fair market value of $219,500. Property in Mary Faye's city is assessed at 65% of its market value and the tax rate is $3.64 per $100. How much is Mary Faye's property tax due?
   $5,193.37

9. Cagney's Greenhouse has a fair market value of $1,880,000. Property is assessed at 35% by the city. The tax rate is 6.4%. What is the property tax due for Cagney's Greenhouse?
   $42,112

10. In Chester County, property is assessed at 40% of its market value, the residential tax rate is $12.30 per $1,000, and the commercial tax rate is $13.85 per $1,000. What is the property tax due on a home that has a market value of $205,000?
    $1,008.60

11. Using the information in Problem 10, find the property tax due on a grocery store with a market value of $5,875,000.
    $32,547.50

12. Bob Rose's home is assessed at $195,900. Last year the tax rate was 11.8 mills, and this year the rate was raised to 13.2 mills. How much more will Bob have to pay in taxes this year?
    $274.26

LEARNING UNIT 20.1: Life Insurance

DRILL PROBLEMS

1. Use the table in the *Business Math Handbook* to find the annual premium per $1,000 of life insurance and calculate the annual premiums for each policy listed. Assume the insureds are males.

Face value of policy	Type of insurance	Age at issue	Annual premium per $1,000	Number of $1,000s in face value	Annual premium
a. $25,000	Straight life	31	$9.27	25	$231.75
b. $40,500	20-year endowment	40	$33.36	40.5	$1,351.08
c. $200,000	Straight life	44	$17.86	200	$3,572
d. $62,500	20-payment life	25	$9.91	62.5	$619.38
e. $12,250	5-year term	35	$2.23	12.25	$27.32
f. $42,500	20-year endowment	42	$36.59	42.5	$1,555.08

2. Use Table 20.1 to find the annual premium for each of the following life insurance policies. Assume the insured is a 30-year-old male.

Face value of policy	Five-year term policy	Straight life policy	Twenty-payment life policy	Twenty-year endowment
a. $50,000	$93.50	$442.50	$602.50	$1,045.00
b. $1,000,000	$1,870.00	$8,850.00	$12,050.00	$20,900.00
c. $250,000	$467.50	$2,212.50	$3,012.50	$5,225.00
d. $72,500	$135.58	$641.63	$873.63	$1,515.25

3. Use the table in the *Business Math Handbook* to find the annual premium for each of the following life insurance policies. Assume the insured is a 30-year-old female.

Face value of policy	Five-year term policy	Straight life policy	Twenty-payment life policy	Twenty-year endowment
a. $50,000	$93.00	$387.50	$535.00	$916.50
b. $1,000,000	$1,860.00	$7,750.00	$10,700.00	$18,330.00
c. $250,000	$465.00	$1,937.50	$2,675.00	$4,582.50
d. $72,500	$134.85	$561.88	$775.75	$1,328.93

4. Use the table in the *Business Math Handbook* to find the nonforfeiture options for the following policies:

Years policy in force	Type of policy	Face value	Cash value	Amount of paid-up insurance	Extended term
a. 10	Straight life	$25,000	$2,400	$6,475	18 yrs 76 days
b. 20	20-year endowment	$500,000	$500,000	$500,000	Life
c. 5	20-payment life	$2,000,000	$142,000	$440,000	19 yrs 190 days
d. 15	Straight life	$750,000	$111,000	$278,250	20 yrs 165 days
e. 5	20-year endowment	$93,500	$8,602	$21,411.50	23 yrs 140 days

WORD PROBLEMS

5. If Mr. Davis, aged 39, buys a $90,000 straight life policy, what is the amount of his annual premium?
$1,242.90

6. If Miss Jennie McDonald, age 27, takes out a $65,000 20-year endowment policy, what premium amount will she pay each year?
$1,043.25

7. If Gary Thomas decides to cash in his $45,000 20-payment life insurance policy after 15 years, what cash surrender value will he receive?
$14,265

8. Mary Allyn purchased a $70,000 20-year endowment policy when she was 26 years old. Ten years later, she decided that she could no longer afford the premiums. If Mary decides to convert her policy to paid-up insurance, what amount of paid-up insurance coverage will she have?
$36,400

9. Peter and Jane Rizzo are both 28 years old and are both planning to take out $50,000 straight life insurance policies. What is the difference in the annual premiums they will have to pay?
$47.50

10. Paul Nasser purchased a $125,000 straight life policy when he was 30 years old. He is now 50 years old. Two months ago, he slipped in the bathtub and injured his back; he will not be able to return to his regular job for several months. Due to a lack of income, he feels that he can no longer continue to pay the premiums on his life insurance policy. If Paul decides to surrender his policy for cash, how much cash will he receive?
$33,125

11. If Paul Nasser (Problem 10) chooses to convert his policy to paid-up insurance, what will the face value of his new policy be?
$68,750

LEARNING UNIT 20.2: Fire Insurance

DRILL PROBLEMS

1. Use the tables in the *Business Math Handbook* to find the premium for each of the following:

	Rating of area	Building class	Building value	Value of contents	Total annual premium
a.	3	A	$80,000	$32,000	$488
b.	2	B	$340,000	$202,000	$2,912
c.	2	A	$221,700	$190,000	$1,624.61
d.	1	B	$96,400	$23,400	$521.60
e.	3	B	$65,780	$62,000	$804.26

2. Use the tables in the *Business Math Handbook* to find the short-term premium and the amount of refund due if the insured cancels.

	Annual premium	Months of coverage	Short-term premium	Refund due
a.	$1,860	3	$651	$1,209
b.	$650	7	$435.50	$214.50
c.	$1,200	10	$1,044	$156
d.	$341	12	$341	None
e.	$1,051	4	$462.44	$588.56

3. Find the amount to be paid for each of the following losses.

	Property value	Coinsurance clause	Insurance required	Insurance carried	Amount of loss	Insurance company pays (indemnity)
a.	$85,000	80%	$68,000	$70,000	$60,000	$60,000
b.	$52,000	80%	$41,600	$45,000	$50,000	$45,000
c.	$44,000	80%	$35,200	$33,000	$33,000	$30,937.50
d.	$182,000	80%	$145,600	$127,400	$61,000	$53,375

WORD PROBLEMS

4. Mary Rose wants to purchase fire insurance for her building, which is rated as Class B; the rating of the area is 2. If her building is worth $225,000 and the contents are worth $70,000, what will her annual premium be?
$1,545

5. Janet Ambrose owns a Class A building valued at $180,000. The contents of the building are valued at $145,000. The territory rating is 3. What is her annual fire insurance premium?
$1,463

6. Jack Altshuler owns a building worth $355,500. The contents are worth $120,000. The classification of the building is B, and the rating of the area is 1. What annual premium must Jack pay for his fire insurance?
$2,105.55

7. Jay Viola owns a store valued at $460,000. His fire insurance policy (which has an 80% coinsurance clause) has a face value of $345,000. A recent fire resulted in a loss of $125,000. How much will the insurance company pay?
$117,187.50

8. The building that is owned by Tally's Garage is valued at $275,000 and is insured for $225,000. The policy has an 80% coinsurance clause. If there is a fire in the building and the damages amount to $220,000, how much of the loss will be paid for by the insurance company?
$220,000

9. Michael Dannon owns a building worth $420,000. He has a fire insurance policy with a face value of $336,000 (there is an 80% coinsurance clause). There was recently a fire that resulted in a $400,000 loss. How much money will he receive from the insurance company?
$336,000

10. Rice's Rent-A-Center business is worth $375,000. He has purchased a $250,000 fire insurance policy. The policy has an 80% coinsurance clause. What will Rice's reimbursement be (a) after a $150,000 fire and (b) after a $330,000 fire?
   a. $125,000   b. $250,000

11. If Maria's Pizza Shop is valued at $210,000 and is insured for $147,000 with a policy that contains an 80% coinsurance clause, what settlement is due after a fire that causes (a) $150,000 in damages and (b) $175,000 in damages?
   a. $131,250   b. $147,000

LEARNING UNIT 20.3: Auto Insurance

DRILL PROBLEMS

1. Calculate the annual premium for compulsory coverage for each of the following.

Driver classification	Bodily	Property	Total premium
a. 17	$98	$160	$258
b. 20	$116	$186	$302
c. 10	$55	$129	$184

2. Calculate the amount of money the insurance company and the driver should pay for each of the following accidents, assuming the driver carries compulsory insurance only.

Accident and court award	Insurance company pays	Driver pays
a. Driver hit one person and court awarded $15,000.	$10,000	$5,000
b. Driver hit one person and court awarded $12,000 for personal injury.	$10,000	$2,000
c. Driver hit two people; court awarded first person $9,000 and the second person $12,000.	$19,000	$2,000

3. Calculate the additional premium payment for each of the following options.

Optional insurance coverage	Addition to premium
a. Bodily injury 50/100/25, driver class 20	$312
b. Bodily injury 25/60/10, driver class 17	$233
c. Collision insurance, driver class 10, age group 3, symbol 5, deductible $100	$181
d. Comprehensive insurance, driver class 10, age group 3, symbol 5, deductible $200	$59
e. Substitute transportation, towing, and labor; driver class 10, age group 3, symbol 5	$20

4. Compute the annual premium for compulsory insurance with optional liability coverage for bodily injury and damage to someone else's property.

	Driver classification	Bodily coverage	Premium
a.	17	50/100/25	$528
b.	20	100/300/10	$661
c.	10	25/60/25	$365
d.	18	250/500/50	$601
e.	20	25/50/10	$565

5. Calculate the annual premium for each of the following drivers with the indicated options. All drivers must carry compulsory insurance.

	Driver classification	Car age	Car symbol	Bodily injury	Collision	Comprehensive	Transportation and towing	Annual premium
a.	10	2	4	50/100/10	$100 deductible	$300 deductible	Yes	$647
b.	18	3	2	25/60/25	$200 deductible	$200 deductible	Yes	$706

WORD PROBLEMS

6. Ann Centerino's driver classification is 10. She carries only compulsory insurance coverage. What annual insurance premium must she pay?
$184

7. Gary Hines is a class 18 driver. He wants to add optional bodily injury and property damage of 250/500/50 to his compulsory insurance coverage. What will be Gary's total annual premium?
$601

8. Sara Goldberg wants optional bodily injury coverage of 50/100/25 and collision coverage with a deductible of $300 in addition to the compulsory coverage her state requires. Sara is a class 17 driver and has a symbol 4 car that is 2 years old. What annual premium must Sara pay?
$688

9. Karen Babson has just purchased a new car with a symbol of 8. She wants bodily injury and property liability of 500/1,000/100, comprehensive and collision insurance with a $200 deductible, and transportation and towing coverage. If Karen is a class 10 driver, what will be her annual insurance premium? There is no compulsory insurance requirement in her state. Assume age group 1.
$781

10. Craig Haberland is a class 18 driver. He has a 5-year-old car with a symbol of 4. His state requires compulsory insurance coverage. In addition, he wishes to purchase collision and comprehensive coverage with the maximum deductible. He also wants towing insurance. What will Craig's annual insurance premium be?
$415

11. Nancy Poland has an insurance policy with limits of 10/20. If Nancy injures a pedestrian and the judge awards damages of $18,000, (a) how much will the insurance company pay and (b) how much will Nancy pay?
a. $10,000   b. $8,000

12. Peter Bell carries insurance with bodily injury limits of 25/60. Peter is in an accident and is charged with injuring four people. The judge awards damages of $10,000 to each of the injured parties. How much will the insurance company pay? How much will Peter pay?
Company pays $40,000.   Peter pays $0.

13. Jerry Greeley carries an insurance policy with bodily injury limits of 25/60. Jerry is in an accident and is charged with injuring four people. If the judge awards damages of $20,000 to each of the injured parties, (a) how much will the insurance company pay and (b) how much will Jerry pay?
a. $60,000   b. $20,000

14. The October/November 1996 issue of *Your Money* reported that the Illinois Department of Insurance gave a typical premium for a brick house in Chicago built in 1950, assuming no policy discounts and a replacement cost estimated at $100,000. With a $100 deductible, the annual premium will be $653. Using the rate in your textbook, with a rating area 3 and class B, what would be the annual premium? (This problem reviews fire insurance.)

Insured value

$$\frac{\$100,000}{\$100} = 1,000 \times \$.61 = \$610.00$$

15. The February 1996 issue of *Money* ran a story on cutting car insurance premiums. Raising the car insurance deductible to $500 will cut the collision premium 15%. Theresa Mendex insures her car; her age group is 5 and symbol is 5. What would be her reduction if she changed her policy to a $500 deductible? What would the collision insurance now cost?

$130.00
$\times$ .15
——————
$19.50 reduction

$130.00
$-$ 19.50
——————
$110.50

16. The November 30, 1997, Chicago *Sun-Times* had a feature story on "Rides on ZIP Codes." The *Sun-Times* acquired rate manuals for three insurance companies and calculated the base rate that each company would charge to provide full coverage on a 1997 Ford Taurus in each ZIP code across the Chicago metropolitan area. The three companies often have rates that sharply differ within a specific ZIP code. The base for the Ford Taurus in the Chicago-Garfield Park area 60624 would be $720. The base for the same vehicle in Oak Brook, Illinois (suburb of Chicago) 60521, would be $364. What percent less (to the nearest hundredth percent) does an Oak Brook resident pay compared to a Chicago Garfield Park resident?

$720 Chicago ($B$)
$-$ 364 Oak Brook
——————
$356 decrease ($P$)

$$\frac{\$356}{\$720} = 49.44\%$$

17. The article "See Your Way to Lower Rates" appeared in the September 1997 issue of *Kiplinger's Personal Finance Magazine.* Robert Stuono lost his life insurance when he was downsized from an investment banking company early this year. So Stuono, age 44, enlisted the help of an independent agent who works with several insurance companies. His goal is $350,000 in term coverage with a level premium for 5 years. What will Robert's annual premium be for term insurance? (This problem reviews life insurance.)

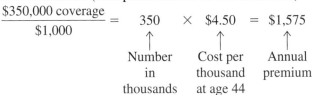

$$\frac{\$350,000 \text{ coverage}}{\$1,000} = \underset{\underset{\substack{\text{Number}\\ \text{in}\\ \text{thousands}}}{\uparrow}}{350} \times \underset{\underset{\substack{\text{Cost per}\\ \text{thousand}\\ \text{at age 44}}}{\uparrow}}{\$4.50} = \underset{\underset{\substack{\text{Annual}\\ \text{premium}}}{\uparrow}}{\$1,575}$$

LEARNING UNIT 21.1: Stocks

DRILL PROBLEMS

| 52 weeks | | | | | Yld | | Vol | | | | Net |
Hi	Lo	Stocks	SYM	Div	%	PE	100s	High	Low	Close	chg
$25\frac{7}{8}$	$18\frac{13}{16}$	BostCelts	BOS	1.00	5.0	44	75	$20\frac{1}{8}$	$19\frac{13}{16}$	$19\frac{13}{16}$	$-\frac{5}{16}$

1. From the listed information for the Boston Celtics, complete the following:
   a. $25.875 ___ was the highest price at which the Boston Celtics stock traded during the year.
   b. $18.8125 ___ was the lowest price at which the Boston Celtics stock traded during the year.
   c. $1.00 ___ was the amount of the dividend the Boston Celtics paid to shareholders last year.
   d. $100.00 ___ is the amount a shareholder with 100 shares would receive.
   e. 5% ___ is the rate of return the stock yielded to its stockholders.
   f. 44 ___ is how many times the earnings per share the stock is selling for.
   g. 4,400 ___ is the number of shares traded on the day of this stock quote.
   h. $20.125 ___ is the highest price paid for Celtics stock on this day.
   i. $19.8125 ___ is the lowest price paid for Celtics stock on this day.
   j. $.3125 dec. is the change in price from yesterday's closing price.

2. Use the Celtics information to show how the yield percent was calculated.
   $1.00 ÷ 19.8125 = 5.0%

3. Use the listed information to calculate the earnings per share for the Boston Celtics stock.
   $.45

4. What was the price of the last trade of Boston Celtics stock yesterday?
   $20.125

WORD PROBLEMS

5. Assume a stockbroker's commission of 2% for round lots plus 1% extra on odd lots. What will it cost (a) to purchase 400 shares of Boston Celtics stock at $20\frac{1}{2}$ and (b) to purchase 350 shares at the same market price?
   a. $8,364   b. $7,328.75

6. In Problem 5, the stockbroker's commission for selling stock is the same as that for buying stock. If the customer who purchased 400 shares at $20\frac{1}{2}$ sells the 400 shares of stock at the end of the year at 27, what will be the return on the investment (to the nearest tenth percent)? The dividend was the same this year as last year.
   31.3%

7. Holtz Corporation's records show 80,000 shares of preferred stock issued. The preferred dividend is $2 per share, which is cumulative. The records show 750,000 shares of common stock issued. In 2000, no dividends were paid. In 2001, the board of directors declared a dividend of $582,500. What are (a) the total amount of dividends paid to preferred stockholders, (b) the total amount of dividends paid to common stockholders, and (c) the amount of the common dividend per share?
   a. $320,000   b. $262,500   c. $0.35

8. Melissa Tucker bought 300 shares of Delta Air Lines stock listed at $59\frac{5}{8}$ per share. What is the total amount she paid if the stockbroker's commission is 2.5%?
   $18,334.69

9. A year later, Melissa (Problem 8) sold the stock she had purchased. The market price of the stock at this time was $77\frac{3}{8}$. Delta Air Lines had paid its shareholders a dividend of $1.20 per share. If the stockbroker's commission to sell stock is 2.5%, what rate of return did Melissa earn on her stock?
   25.4%

10. The board of directors of Parker Electronics, Inc., declared a $539,000 dividend. If the corporation has 70,000 shares of common stock outstanding, what is the dividend per share?
    $7.70

LEARNING UNIT 21.2: Bonds

DRILL PROBLEMS

Bond	Current yield	Sales	Close	Net change
IBM $10\frac{1}{4}$ 04	10.0	11	$102\frac{1}{2}$	$+\frac{1}{8}$

1. From the bond listing above complete the following:
   a. __IBM__ is the name of the company.
   b. __$10\frac{1}{4}$__ is the percent of interest paid on the bond.
   c. __2004__ is the year in which the bond matures.
   d. __$102.50__ is the total interest for the year. (.1025 × $1,000 = $102.50)
   e. __$102\frac{3}{8}$__ was yesterday's close on the IBM bond.

2. Show how to calculate the current yield of 10.0% for IBM. (Trade commissions have been omitted.)
   10.0%

3. Use the information for the IBM bonds to calculate (a) the amount the last bond traded for on this day and (b) the amount the last bond traded for yesterday.
   a. $1,025   b. $1,023.75

4. What will be the annual interest payment (a) to the bondholder assuming he paid $101\frac{3}{4}$ and (b) to the bondholder who purchased the bond for $102\frac{1}{2}$?
   a. $102.50   b. $102.50

5. If Terry Gambol purchased three IBM bonds at this day's closing price, (a) what will be her total cost excluding commission and (b) how much interest will she receive for the year?
   a. $3,075   b. $307.50

6. Calculate the bond yield (to the nearest tenth percent) for each of the following:

Bond interest rate	Purchase price	Bond yield
a. 7%	97	7.2%
b. $9\frac{1}{2}$%	$101\frac{5}{8}$	9.3%
c. $13\frac{1}{4}$%	$104\frac{1}{4}$	12.7%

7. For each of the following, state whether the bond sold at a premium or a discount and give the amount of the premium or discount.

Bond interest rate	Purchase price	Premium or discount
a. 7%	97	$30 discount
b. $9\frac{1}{2}$%	$101\frac{5}{8}$	$16.25 premium
c. $13\frac{1}{4}$%	$104\frac{1}{4}$	$42.50 premium

WORD PROBLEMS

8. Rob Morrisey purchased a $1,000 bond that was quoted at $102\frac{1}{4}$ and paying $8\frac{7}{8}$% interest. (a) How much did Rob pay for the bond? (b) What was the premium or discount? (c) How much annual interest will he receive?
   a. $1,022.50   b. $22.50   c. $88.75

9. Jackie Anderson purchased a bond that was quoted at $62\frac{1}{2}$ and paying interest of $10\frac{1}{2}$%. (a) How much did Jackie pay for the bond? (b) What was the premium or discount? (c) What interest will Jackie receive annually? (d) What is the bond's current annual yield (to the nearest tenth percent)?
   a. $625   b. $375   c. $105   d. 16.8%

10. Swartz Company issued bonds totaling $2,000,000 in order to purchase updated equipment. If the bonds pay interest of 11%, what is the total amount of interest the Swartz Company must pay semiannually?
   $110,000

11. The RJR and ACyan companies have both issued bonds that are paying $7\frac{3}{8}\%$ interest. The quoted price of the RJR bond is $94\frac{1}{8}$, and the quoted price of the ACyan bond is $102\frac{7}{8}$. Find the current annual yield on each (to the nearest tenth percent).

   7.8% yield for RJR bond   7.2% yield for ACyan

12. Mary Rowe purchased 25 bonds of Chrysler Corporation $8\frac{3}{8}\%$ bonds of 2001. The bonds closed at $93\frac{1}{4}$. Find **(a)** the total purchase price and **(b)** the amount of the first semiannual interest payment Mary will receive.

   a. $23,312.50   **b.** $1,046.88

13. What is the annual yield (to the nearest hundredth percent) of the bonds Mary Rowe purchased?

   8.98%

14. Mary Rowe purchased a $1,000 bond listed as ARch $10\frac{7}{8}$ 05 for $122\frac{3}{4}$. What is the annual yield of this bond (to the nearest tenth percent)?

   8.9%

LEARNING UNIT 21.3: Mutual Funds

DRILL PROBLEMS

From the following, calculate the NAV. Round to the nearest cent.

	Current market value of fund investments	Current liabilities	Number of shares outstanding	NAV
1.	$6,800,000	$850,000	500,000	$11.90
2.	$11,425,000	$690,000	810,000	$13.25
3.	$22,580,000	$1,300,000	1,400,000	$15.20

Complete the following using this information:

NAV	Net change	Fund name	Inv. obj.	YTD % Ret	Total return 1 Yr R
$23.48	+.14	EuroA	Eu	+37.3	+7.6 E

4. NAV $23.48

5. NAV change   +$.14

6. Total return year to date   37.3%

7. Return for the last 12 months   7.6%

8. What does an E rating mean?   Lowest 20%

Calculate the commission (load) charge and the offer to buy.

	NAV	% commission (load) charge	Dollar amount of commission (load) charge	Offer price
9.	$17.00	$8\frac{1}{2}\%$	$1.45	$18.45
10.	$21.55	6%	$1.29	$22.84
11.	$14.10	4%	$.56	$14.66

WORD PROBLEMS

12. Paul wanted to know how his Fidelity mutual fund $14.33 NAV in the newspaper was calculated. He called Fidelity, and he received the following information:

Current market value of fund investment	$7,500,000
Current liabilities	$910,000
Number of shares outstanding	460,000

   Please calculate the NAV for Paul. Was the NAV in the newspaper correct?
   Yes.

13. Jeff Jones bought 150 shares of Putnam Vista Fund. The NAV of the fund was $9.88. The offer price was $10.49. What did Jeff pay for these 150 shares?

   $1,573.50

14. Pam Long purchased 300 shares of the no-load Scudder's European Growth Company Fund. The NAV is $12.61. What did Pam pay for the 300 shares?

   $3,783

15. Assume in Problem 14 that 8 years later Pam sells her 300 shares. The NAV at the time of sale was $12.20. What is the amount of her profit or loss on the sale?
$123 loss

16. On December 31, 1997, the Chicago *Sun-Times* listed the following information on Disney Company stock:

52 Weeks		Stock	SYM	Div.	Yld. %	PE ratio	Vol. 100s	High	Low	Close	Net change
High	Low										
$98\frac{1}{2}$	$66\frac{3}{4}$	Disney	DIS	.05		35	20015	$100\frac{1}{4}$	98	99	+2

Complete the following:
a. High and low dollar amounts for the year.
b. Yield.
c. Annual earnings per share.
d. Shares traded.
e. Closing price yesterday.

a. $98.50, $66.75
b. Div. $\dfrac{\$.05}{\text{Close }\$99} = .05\%$
c. $\dfrac{\$99 \text{ (close)}}{35 \text{ (price-earnings ratio)}} = \$2.83$
d. 2,001,500 shares
e. $99 (increased by 2) Today
   $\dfrac{-2}{\$97}$ Yesterday

17. If you bought 150 shares of Intel at $69 with a commission of 2% on round lots and an additional 1% on odd lot portions, what would be the total purchase price?

$150 \text{ shares} \times \$69 = \$10,350.00$
$.02 \times 10,350 = \quad 207.00$
$.01 \times \$3,450 = \quad \underline{+ 34.50}$
$\nearrow \qquad \$10,591.50$
(50 shares $\times$ $69)

18. On December 1, 1997, *USA Today* ran an article on "Expert: Stock-Heavy Portfolio Needs Work." Financial planner J. Michael Martin recommended that Jim Kelly choose a long-term bond because it gives high income while Kelly waits for better stock market opportunities down the road. The bond Martin recommended matures in 2002 and was originally issued at $8\frac{1}{2}\%$ interest and the current yield is 7.9%. What would be the current selling price for this bond and how would that price appear in the bond quotations?

Bond originally paid $8\frac{1}{2}\%$ interest $\times$ $1,000 = $85 interest
$85 \div .079 = \$1,075.949 = \$1,076$
Bond would be listed as $107\frac{1}{2}$.

19. On December 30, 1997, *The Wall Street Journal* quoted the following two bonds:

Bonds	Vol.	Close	Net chg.
Comp USA $9\frac{1}{2}$ 00	70	$102\frac{3}{8}$	$-\frac{1}{8}$
GMA 7 02	5	$101\frac{5}{8}$	$-1\frac{1}{4}$

Compare these two bonds for:
a. When the bonds expire.
b. The yield of each bond.
c. The current selling price.
d. Whether the bond is selling at a discount or premium.
e. Yesterday's bond close.

a. Comp USA: Year 2000
   GMA: Year 2002

b. Comp USA: $\dfrac{\$95 \text{ interest}}{\$1,023.75 \text{ close}} = 9.28\% \text{ or } 9.3\%$

   GMA: $\dfrac{\$70 \text{ interest}}{\$1,016.25 \text{ close}} = 6.88\% \text{ or } 6.9\%$

c. Comp USA: $1.02375 \times \$1,000 = \$1,023.75$
   GMA: $1.01625 \times \$1,000 = \$1,016.25$

d. Both selling at a premium (over $1,000 face value)
   $(102\frac{3}{8} + \frac{1}{8})$

e. Comp USA: $102\frac{4}{8}$ or $102\frac{1}{2} = \$1,025$
   GMA: $101\frac{5}{8} + 1\frac{1}{4} = 102\frac{7}{8} = \$1,028.75$

LEARNING UNIT 22.1: Mean, Median, and Mode

Note: Optional problems for LU 22.3 are found on page 513.

DRILL PROBLEMS

1. Find the mean for the following lists of numbers. Round to the nearest hundredth.
   a. 12, 16, 20, 25, 29   Mean <u>20.4</u>
   b. 80, 91, 98, 82, 68, 82, 79, 90   Mean <u>83.75</u>
   c. 9.5, 12.3, 10.5, 7.5, 10.1, 18.4, 9.8, 6.2, 11.1, 4.8, 10.6   Mean <u>10.07</u>

2. Find the weighted mean for the following. Round to the nearest hundredth.
   a. 4, 4, 6, 8, 8, 13, 4, 6, 8   Weighted mean <u>6.78</u>
   b. 82, 85, 87, 82, 82, 90, 87, 63, 100, 85, 87   Weighted mean <u>84.55</u>

3. Find the median for the following:
   a. 56, 89, 47, 36, 90, 63, 55, 82, 46, 81   Median <u>59.5</u>
   b. 59, 22, 39, 47, 33, 98, 50, 73, 54, 46, 99   Median <u>50</u>

4. Find the mode for the following:
   24, 35, 49, 35, 52, 35, 52   Mode <u>35</u>

5. Find the mean, median, and mode for each of the following:
   a. 72, 48, 62, 54, 73, 62, 75, 57, 62, 58, 78
      Mean <u>63.7</u>   Median <u>62</u>   Mode <u>62</u>
   b. $0.50, $1.19, $0.58, $1.19, $2.83, $1.71, $2.21, $0.58, $1.29, $0.58
      Mean <u>$1.27</u>   Median <u>$1.19</u>   Mode <u>$0.58</u>
   c. $92, $113, $99, $117, $99, $105, $119, $112, $95, $116, $102, $120
      Mean <u>$107.42</u>   Median <u>$108.50</u>   Mode <u>$99</u>
   d. 88, 105, 120, 119, 105, 128, 160, 151, 90, 153, 107, 119, 105
      Mean <u>119.23</u>   Median <u>119</u>   Mode <u>105</u>

WORD PROBLEMS

6. The sales for the year at the 8 Bed and Linen Stores were $1,442,897, $1,556,793, $1,703,767, $1,093,320, $1,443,984, $1,665,308, $1,197,692, and $1,880,443. Find the mean earnings for a Bed and Linen Store for the year.
   $1,498,025.50

7. To avoid having an extreme number affect the average, the manager of Bed and Linen Stores (Problem 6) would like you to find the median earnings for the 8 stores.
   $1,500,388.50

8. The Bed and Linen Store in Salem sells many different towels. Following are the prices of all the towels that were sold on Wednesday: $7.98, $9.98, $9.98, $11.49, $11.98, $7.98, $12.49, $12.49, $11.49, $9.98, $9.98, $16.00, and $7.98. Find the mean price of a towel.
   $10.75

9. Looking at the towel prices, the Salem manager (Problem 8) decided that he should have calculated a weighted mean. Find the weighted mean price of a towel.
   $10.75

10. The manager of the Salem Bed and Linen Store above would like to find another measure of the central tendency called the *median*. Find the median price for the towels sold.
    $9.98

11. The manager at the Salem Bed and Linen Store would like to know the most popular towel among the group of towels sold on Wednesday. Find the mode for the towel prices for Wednesday.
    $9.98

LEARNING UNIT 22.2: Frequency Distributions and Graphs

DRILL PROBLEMS

1. A local dairy distributor wants to know how many containers of yogurt health club members consume in a month. The distributor gathered the following data:

17	17	22	14	26	23	23	15	18	16
18	15	23	18	29	20	24	17	12	15
18	19	18	20	28	21	25	21	26	14
16	18	15	19	27	15	22	19	19	13
20	17	13	24	28	18	28	20	17	16

Construct a frequency distribution table to organize this data.

18 ||||| || 7

2. Construct a bar graph for the Problem 1 data. The height of each bar should represent the frequency of each amount consumed.

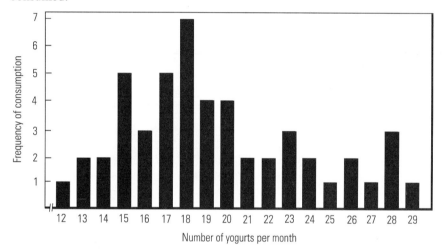

3. To simplify the amount of data concerning yogurt consumption, construct a relative frequency distribution table. The range will be from 1 to 30 with five class intervals: 1–6, 7–12, 13–18, 19–24, and 25–30.

25–30 ||||| ||| 8

4. Construct a bar graph for the grouped data.

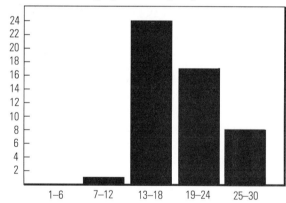

5. Prepare a pie chart to represent the above data.

7–12 $\dfrac{1}{50} \times 360° = 7.2°$

WORD PROBLEMS

6. The women's department of a local department store lists its total sales for the year: January, $39,800; February, $22,400; March, $32,500; April, $33,000; May, $30,000; June, $29,200; July, $26,400; August, $24,800; September, $34,000; October, $34,200; November, $38,400; December, $41,100. Draw a line graph to represent the monthly sales of the women's department for the year. The vertical axis should represent the dollar amount of the sales.

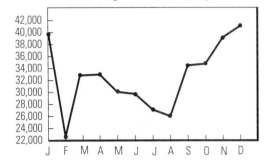

7. The following list shows the number of television sets sold in a year by the sales associates at Souza's TV and Appliance Store.

115	125	139	127	142	153	169	126	141
130	137	150	169	157	146	173	168	156
140	146	134	123	142	129	141	122	141

Construct a relative frequency distribution table to represent the data. The range will be from 115 to 174 with intervals of 10.

145–154   IIII   4

8. Use the data in the distribution table for Problem 7 to construct a bar graph for the grouped data.

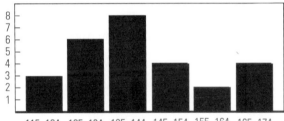

9. Expenses for Flora Foley Real Estate Agency for the month of June were as follows: salaries expense, $2,790; utilities expense, $280; rent expense, $2,000; commissions expense, $4,800; and other expenses, $340. Present this data in a circle graph. (First calculate the percent relationship between each item and the total, then determine the number of degrees that represents each item.)

98.4°   9.9°   70.5°   169.2°   11.9°

10. Today a new Jeep costs $25,000. In 1970 the Jeep cost $4,500. What is the price relative? (Round to nearest tenth percent.)

$$\frac{\$25,000}{\$4,500} \times 100 = 555.6$$

B

CHECK FIGURES

Check Figures

- Odd-Numbered Drill and Word Problems for End-of-Chapter Problems.
- Challenge Problems.
- Summary Practice Tests (all).
- Cumulative Reviews (all).
- Odd-Numbered Additional Assignments by Learning Unit from Appendix A.

Check Figures to Drill and Word Problems (Odds), Challenge Problems, Summary Practice Tests, and Cumulative Reviews

Chapter 1

End-of-chapter problems

1–1. 153
1–3. 176
1–5. 13,007
1–7. 113,690
1–9. 32
1–11. 1,700
1–13. 1,074
1–15. 31,110
1–17. 340,531
1–19. 126,000
1–21. 90
1–23. 86 R4
1–25. 205
1–27. 1,616
1–29. 24,876
1–31. 17,989; 18,000
1–33. 80
1–35. 104
1–37. 216
1–39. 19 R21
1–41. 1,735
1–43. 10,410
1–45. 2,162,000
1–47. 850
1–49. 12 R600; 12 R610
1–51. $480
1–53. 88,149
1–55. $19,780
1–57. 3,445 shares; $62,010
1–59. 84
1–61. 1 mile per gallon
1–63. 1,312; $57,728
1–65. 7,050
1–67. $182,090
1–69. 18,388
1–71. $140
1–73. $7,631
1–75. $14,300
1–77. $24
1–79. $3,710; $89; 100 shares
1–80. $12,000 difference

Summary practice test

1. 6,021,090
2. Six million, eight hundred twenty-eight thousand, four hundred ninety-one
3. **a.** 50 **b.** 700 **c.** 8,000 **d.** 20,000
4. 17,000; 16,489
5. 4,800,000; 4,594,975
6. 824,951,000
7. 288 R50
8. 10
9. $54
10. $640; no
11. $400

Chapter 2

End-of-chapter problems

2–1. Proper
2–3. Improper
2–5. $61\frac{2}{5}$
2–7. $\frac{59}{3}$
2–9. $\frac{11}{13}$
2–11. 60 (2 × 2 × 3 × 5)
2–13. 96 (2 × 2 × 2 × 2 × 2 × 3)
2–15. $\frac{13}{21}$
2–17. $15\frac{5}{12}$
2–19. $\frac{3}{4}$
2–21. $7\frac{4}{9}$
2–23. $\frac{5}{16}$
2–25. $\frac{3}{25}$
2–27. $\frac{1}{3}$
2–29. $\frac{7}{18}$
2–31. $\frac{2}{3}$
2–33. $25
2–35. $1,200
2–37. 316 miles
2–39. 8
2–41. $6\frac{1}{2}$ gallons
2–43. $525
2–45. $\frac{23}{36}$
2–47. $25
2–49. $3\frac{3}{4}$ lb apple; $8\frac{1}{8}$ cups flour; $\frac{5}{8}$ cup marg.; $5\frac{15}{16}$ cups of sugar; 5 teaspoon cin.
2–51. 300 people
2–53. 92 pieces
2–55. 5,800 books
2–57. $120\frac{1}{8}$
2–59. $\frac{103}{130}$
2–61. $62,500,000
2–63. $\frac{3}{8}$
2–65. $2\frac{3}{5}$ hours
2–67. 60 sandwiches
2–68. $74\frac{1}{4}$ inches
2–69. **a.** 400 homes **b.** $320,000 **c.** 3,000 people; 2,500 people **d.** $112.50 **e.** $8,800,000

Summary practice test

1. Mixed number
2. Proper
3. Improper
4. $18\frac{3}{7}$
5. $\frac{44}{5}$
6. 5; $\frac{23}{32}$
7. 84
8. 18 (2 × 3 × 1 × 1 × 3 × 1)
9. $7\frac{4}{5}$
10. $\frac{2}{11}$
11. $6\frac{2}{15}$
12. $\frac{2}{5}$
13. $4\frac{7}{8}$ hours
14. 3,660 chairs
15. **a.** 12,000 veggie **b.** 30,000 turkey
16. $36\frac{1}{2}$ hours
17. $26\frac{9}{16}$

Chapter 3

End-of-chapter problems

3–1. Hundredths
3–3. .9; .90; .895
3–5. 6.9; 6.92; 6.925
3–7. 6.6; 6.56; 6.556
3–9. $1,862.78
3–11. .09
3–13. .09
3–15. .64
3–17. 14.91
3–19. $\frac{62}{100}$
3–21. $\frac{125}{10,000}$

3–23. $\dfrac{825}{1,000}$

3–25. $\dfrac{7,065}{10,000}$

3–27. $28\dfrac{48}{100}$

3–29. .003

3–31. .0085

3–33. 713.8763

3–35. 3.6

3–37. 2.32

3–39. 1.2; 1.26791

3–41. 4; 4.0425

3–43. 24,526.67

3–45. 161.29

3–47. 6,824.15

3–49. .04

3–51. .63

3–53. 2.585

3–55. .0086

3–57. 486

3–59. 3.950

3–61. 7,913.2

3–63. .545

3–65. $10.03

3–67. $.185 cheaper

3–69. $119.47

3–71. $10.01

3–73. .636

3–75. $399.16

3–77. $86.88

3–79. $188.75

3–81. $73.52

3–83. $1.50

3–85. $6,465.60

3–87. $99.06

3–88. $560.45

Summary practice test

 1. 573.137
 2. .4
 3. .04
 4. .004
 5. $\dfrac{3}{10}$
 6. $5\dfrac{76}{100}$
 7. $\dfrac{795}{1,000}$
 8. .17
 9. .60
10. 3.44
11. .11
12. 273.1302
13. 13.4
14. 117.52
15. 28,325.4
16. 77,220

17. 509,916,985.2
18. $42.40
19. $435.06
20. $213.38
21. $.1516 B
22. $8.40

Cumulative review 1, 2, 3

 1. $405
 2. 200,000
 3. 50,560,000
 4. $10
 5. $225,000 savings from Boston
 6. 1¢: $500
    $1\dfrac{1}{2}$¢: $750
 7. $369.56
 8. $130,000,000
 9. $47.73; $15.91; $63.64

Chapter 4

End-of-chapter problems

 4–1. $1,362.11
 4–3. $463.40
 4–5. $9,740
 4–7. $388.44
 4–9. $711.48
 4–11. $2,637.66
 4–13. $998.86
 4–14. $1,862.03
 4–15. $3,061.67

Summary practice test

 1. $304.71
 2. $9,673.97
 3. $7,490
 4. $2,057.55
 5. $7,577.27

Chapter 5

End-of-chapter problems

 5–1. $C = 32$
 5–3. $D = 120$
 5–5. $Y = 15$
 5–7. $Y = 12$
 5–9. $P = 25$
 5–11. $P = \$59.95$
 5–13. 30 Hubert, 120 Soo
 5–15. 50 shorts; 200 T-shirts
 5–17. $B = 11$
 5–19. $N = 63$
 5–21. $Y = 7$
 5–23. $P = \$309.99$
 5–25. Pete = 90; Bill = 450
 5–27. 48 boxes paper; 240 diskettes
 5–29. $C = 98$
 5–31. $M = 60$
 5–33. $S = \$30,000$
 5–35. $W = 129$

5–37. Shift 1: 3,360; shift 2: 2,240
5–39. 22 cartons of hammers
         18 cartons of wrenches
5–40. $L = .645$
5–41. $B = 4$; $6B = 24$

Summary practice test

 1. $247.99
 2. $132
 3. Wallace 60
    K Corp 240
 4. Francis 145; Joyce 725
 5. 74 dishes; 222 pots
 6. 1,000 hamburgers; 200 pizzas

Chapter 6

End-of-chapter problems

 6–1. 86%
 6–3. 90%
 6–5. 356.1%
 6–7. .02
 6–9. .457
 6–11. 1.19
 6–13. 7.7%
 6–15. 87.5%
 6–17. $\dfrac{1}{25}$
 6–19. $\dfrac{19}{60}$
 6–21. $\dfrac{27}{400}$
 6–23. 7.2
 6–25. 102.5
 6–27. 156.6
 6–29. 114.88
 6–31. 16.2
 6–33. 115.38
 6–35. 10,000
 6–37. 17,777.78
 6–39. 108.2%
 6–41. 110%
 6–43. 400%
 6–45. 59.40
 6–47. 1,100
 6–49. 40%
 6–51. −12.50%
 6–53. 80%
 6–55. $10,000
 6–57. $105
 6–59. 677.78%
 6–61. $28,175
 6–63. 60%
 6–65. $33 million
 6–67. 39.94%
 6–69. 12.8%
 6–71. 1,000
 6–73. $400
 6–75. 25%
 6–77. $12 million

6–79. 28.69%
6–81. 13.3%
6–83. 40%
6–85. $1,160,000
6–87. $24,000
6–89. 29.79%
6–91. $41,176
6–93. $81 billion
6–95. 585,000
6–96. 69.35%; 72.99%; 65.25%; 64.75%
6–97. $55,429

Summary practice test
1. 48.1%
2. 70%
3. 1,643%
4. 600%
5. .36
6. .0485
7. 9.0
8. .0020
9. 14.3%
10. 22.2%
11. $\frac{13}{80}$
12. $\frac{31}{500}$
13. $54,400
14. $700,000
15. 95%
16. 9.33%
17. $500
18. $396
19. $275,000

Chapter 7

End-of-chapter problems
7–1. .8924; .1076; $107.49; $891.51
7–3. .865536; .134464; $38.99; $251.01
7–5. $369.70; $80.30
7–7. $1,392.59; $457.41
7–9. May 26; June 15
7–11. June 15; July 5
7–13. July 10; July 30
7–15. $58; $2,942
7–17. $2; $198
7–19. $112.24; $337.76
7–21. $26.99; $62.97
7–23. $48.24; $42.21
7–25. $576.06; $48.94
7–27. $5,100; $5,250
7–29. $5,850
7–31. $6,000
7–33. $6,105.40
7–35. $8,333.33; $11,666.67
7–37. $57.07
7–39. $489.90; $711.10
7–41. $4,658.97

7–43. $829.70; $70.30
7–45. $5,008.45
7–47. Save $4.27 with Reliance
7–49. $.36 savings with Lester
7–50. $4,794.99

Summary practice test
1. $320
2. $700
3. $550.10; $99.91
4. a. September 18; October 8
   b. July 16, 2002; August 5, 2002
   c. May 10; May 30
   d. January 10; January 30
5. $320; $480
6. $10,880
7. B: .2732 = 27.32%
8. $1,414.14; $3,585.86
9. $5,736.97

Chapter 8

End-of-chapter problems
8–1. $27; $117
8–3. $4,285.71
8–5. $6.90; 45.70%
8–7. $238; $357
8–9. $110.83
8–11. $34.20; 69.8%
8–13. 11%
8–15. $3,830.40; $1,169.60; 23.39%
8–17. $500; 71.4%
8–19. $14.29
8–21. $66,038
8–23. $84
8–25. 42.86%
8–27. $3.56
8–29. $1,316.67
8–31. $12; 23.53%
8–33. $22.19
8–35. $439.45
8–37. $2.31
8–39. $8,900; $9,041; $954
8–40. $94.98; $20.36; loss

Summary practice test
1. $297
2. 117.67%
3. $116.67; $93.33
4. $45; 111.1%
5. $118.18
6. $281.93
7. 42.22%
8. $90
9. 37.5%
10. $.65

Cumulative review 6, 7, 8
1. 650,000
2. $296.35
3. $133

4. $2,562.14
5. $48.75
6. $259.26
7. $1.96; $1.89

Chapter 9

End-of-chapter problems
9–1. $190.40
9–3. $12.00; $452
9–5. $1,071
9–7. $60
9–9. $13,000
9–11. $4,500
9–13. $11,900; $6,900; $138; $388
9–15. $12.40; $26.10
9–17. $103; $56.42; $13.20; $737.38
9–19. $338.38; $117.80; $27.55; $1,416.27
9–21. $515.38
9–23. $2,210
9–25. $3,120
9–27. $99.20 Social Security; $14,800 exempt
9–29. $257.83
9–31. $946.40; $135.20; 0 for week 30
9–32. Difference $143.34
9–33. $1,303.93

Summary practice test
1. 46; $392
2. $453
3. $11,500
4. $148.80; $261
5. $85.82
6. $769.50 SUTA; $108 FUTA; $28.50 SUTA; $4.00 FUTA

Chapter 10

End-of-chapter problems
10–1. $375; $6,375
10–3. $130; $2,130
10–5. $28.23; $613.23
10–7. $20.38; $1,020.38
10–9. $73.78; $1,273.78
10–11. $1,904.76
10–13. $4,390.61
10–15. $2,177.08; $27,177.08
10–17. $2,377.70
10–19. 4.7 years
10–21. $14,892.50
10–23. $714.87; $44.87
10–25. $426.15
10–27. $2,608.65
10–29. $18,720.12
10–31. 12.37%
10–33. 72 days
10–35. 5.6%
10–36. $21,166.67
10–37. $7.82; $275.33

Summary practice test
1. $36.06; $1,646.26
2. $185,100
3. $7,413.44
4. $7,407.77
5. $22,588
6. $6,091.78; $91.78

Chapter 11
End-of-chapter problems
11–1. $546.88; $14,453.12
11–3. 25 days
11–5. $51,451.39; 57; $733.18; $50,718.21
11–7. 7.12%
11–9. $8,537.50; 9.8%
11–11. $8,937
11–13. 4.04%
11–15. $5,133.33; 56; $71.87; $5,061.46
11–17. $1,199.59
11–18. $.66 difference
11–19. $2,127.66; 9.57%

Summary practice test
1. $160,000
2. $260; $8,740; $9,000; 8.2%
3. $20,168.50
4. $30,258.14
5. $6,711.25; 8.6%
6. 7.12%

Chapter 12
End-of-chapter problems
12–1. 4; 4%; $935.89; $135.89
12–3. $10,404; $404
12–5. 12.55%
12–7. 10; 3%; .7441; $892.92
12–9. 28; 3%; .4371; $7,692.96
12–11. 2.2879 × $7,692.96
12–13. $17,762.40
12–15. Mystic $4,775
12–17. $21,673.20
12–19. $24,309.60
12–21. 5.06%
12–23. $37,644
12–25. Yes, $17,908 or $8,376 (p. v.)
12–27. $3,739.20
12–29. $13,883.30
12–31. Bank B for $64,056
12–32. $5,774.68

Summary practice test
1. $31,678.40
2. $31,576
3. $136,600.52
4. Yes, $9,004.84 or $4,620 (p. v.)
5. 8.16%
6. $11,703

7. $123,600
8. $99,181.80

Chapter 13
End-of-chapter problems
13–1. $39,451.06
13–3. $40,042.86
13–5. $1,546.26
13–7. End of first year $1,069.96
13–9. $1,410
13–11. $6,018.64
13–13. $509,774.85
13–15. $470,250.20
13–17. $900.655
13–19. $33,444
13–21. $6,809.25
13–23. Annuity $12,219.11
13–25. $3,625.60
13–27. $111,013.29
13–29. $404,313.97
13–30. $125,971.20; $132,464
13–31. $120,747.09

Summary practice test
1. $39,679.08
2. $26,438.25 or $26,438.41
3. $46,859.50
4. $1,974
5. $604
6. $63,899.50
7. $27,237
8. $31,247.28
9. $381,032.71
10. $328,917.44

Cumulative review 10, 11, 12, 13
1. Annuity $2,058.62 or $2,058.59
2. $5,118.70
3. $116,963.02
4. $3,113.92
5. $5,797.92
6. $18,465.20
7. $29,632.35
8. $55,251

Chapter 14
End-of-chapter problems
14–1. Finance charge $2,440
14–3. Finance charge $1,279.76; 12.75%–13%
14–5. $119.39; $119.37
14–7. $1,663.47; $5,176.53
14–9. $2,741
14–11. 8%–8.25%; 8.50 to 8.75%
14–13. a. $3,889 b. $1,457.60
c. $5,441.60 d. 13.25% to 13.50% e. $89.11
14–15. $911.16; $11,360.84
14–17. 7.75%–8.00%

14–19. $218.31 outstanding balance
14–20. 15.48%
14–21. $5.16 (365 days) $5.18 (weeks)

Summary practice test
1. $23,500; $1,100
2. $52.02
3. 6.25%–6.50%
4. $5,088.75
5. $1,008.16; $8,351.84
6. $310.67

Chapter 15
End-of-chapter problems
15–1. $1,386.32
15–3. $1,764
15–5. $173,141.60
15–7. $1,679.04; $1,656.25; $22.79; $158,977.21
15–9. $1,817.92; $1,149.19
15–11. $771.93; $196,894.80
15–13. Payment 3, $119,857.38
15–15. $3,918.75
15–17. $116,333; $171,513.80; $112,673.25
15–18. $1,690.15; $415,954

Summary practice test
1. $1,195.20; $1,133.33; $61.87; $159,938.13
2. $565.18; $126,464.80
3. a. $451.36; $79,408
b. $470.40; $85,120
c. $509.04; $96,712
d. $549.36; $108,808
4. $1,209
5. $212,700

Chapter 16
End-of-chapter problems
16–1. Total assets $26,000
16–3. Inventory −16.67%; mortgage note +13.79%
16–5. Depreciation .77; .66
16–7. Depreciation $100; + 16.67%
16–9. 1.43; 1.79
16–11. .20; .23
16–13. .06; .08
16–15. $7,142,857
16–17. 3.40%
16–19. 2003 68% sales
16–20. 3.5; 1.7; .44; .4
16–21. 3.5; 2.3

Summary practice test
1. a. $82,000 b. $12,100
c. $69,900 d. $47,100
2. Acc. rec. 8.33%; 23.30%
3. Cash $5,000; +62.50%
4. 2003, 97%

5. Total assets $123,000

6. a. .94 **b.** .67 **c.** 44 days
   d. 1.06 **e.** .19

Chapter 17

End-of-chapter problems

17–1. Book value (end of year) $70,000
17–3. Book value (end of year) $50,000
17–5. Book value (end of year) $30,000
17–7. Book value (end of year) $10,000
17–9. Book value (end of year) $4,000
17–11. Book value (end of year) $1,000
17–13. Book value (end of year) $9,000
17–15. Book value (end of year) $5,000
17–17. $2,240
17–19. $54,000; $13,500
17–21. $37,600; $22,560
17–23. $15,000
17–25. $6,000; $18,000
17–27. $6,000 more
17–29. $6,257
17–31. Year 5 $2,304 versus $1,066.67
17–32. c. 2000, $9,250; 2001, $20,350

Summary practice test

1. Book value end of year 2: $6,250
2. $856.80
3. Depreciation expense, $10,000; $8,000; $6,000; $4,000; $2,000
4. $5,000 difference
5. −$91 difference

Chapter 18

End-of-chapter problems

18–1. $191; $1,289
18–3. $543; $932
18–5. $10
18–7. $36
18–9. $72
18–11. $140.80
18–13. $147.75; $345.60
18–15. $188.65; $304.70
18–17. 3.56; 3.25
18–19. .75; $67,500
18–21. $844.90; $1,151.70
18–23. $490; $10
18–25. $55,120
18–27. $38,150
18–28. 37; $27; $35
18–29. $1,900

Summary practice test

1. a. 28 **b.** $55.80
   c. $85.15 **d.** $70.56
2. $20,400
3. 1.12
4. $80,869
5. $63,442

Chapter 19

End-of-chapter problems

19–1. $912
19–3. $66,037.74
19–5. $48,000
19–7. $.0233
19–9. 6.99%; $6.99; $69.90; 69.90
19–11. $4,462.50
19–13. $16,985.05
19–15. $112.92
19–17. $80,000
19–19. $6,940
19–21. $64,000
19–23. $222.75
19–25. Now $1,035.30
19–26. $3,342.50
19–27. $979

Summary practice test

1. $101.89; $1,698.11
2. $6,980
3. $54,400
4. 5.4 mills
5. $2,665.60
6. $10,332

Chapter 20

End-of-chapter problems

20–1. $445.80
20–3. $221.25
20–5. $79,500
20–7. 21 years, 300 days
20–9. $518; $182
20–11. $16,500
20–13. $1,067
20–15. $240 cheaper
20–17. $748
20–19. $118,750
20–21. $455
20–23. $373.67
20–25. $22,900; $10,700
20–27. $24,000; $16,300
20–28. Save $8.12
20–29. $72,000

Summary practice test

1. $1,005.60, $25,360
2. $34,450, $71,500 21 years 300 days
3. $212,500; $340,000
4. $608; $200.64
5. $474.67
6. Insurance company pays $26,500; Pete pays $6,000

Chapter 21

End-of-chapter problems

21–1. $51,625
21–3. 2.7%
21–5. 16

21–7. $19,573.13
21–9. 2000   preferred $8,000
         2001   0
         2002   preferred $127,000
                 common $33,000
21–11. $2,280
21–13. $260; $2,725; 9.5%
21–15. $12.04; $−.06; 9.6%; A
21–17. Gain $6,625.63
21–19. 12; 2.4%
21–21. $5,043.75; $56.25
21–23. 7.3%
21–25. Stock 6.7%; bond 11.9%
21–27. Yes, $16.02
21–29. .4%; 1.1%; 2.01%
21–30. $177.49 net profit
21–31. $1,014.33

Summary practice test

1. $12,939.38
2. 9; .7%
3. $5.86
4. $8,530
5. 5.6%
6. $110,000 in arrears
7. $13.71; $8,226

Chapter 22

End-of-chapter problems

22–1. 7.25
22–3. $77.23
22–5. 2.7
22–7. 31.5
22–9. 8
22–11. 142.9
22–13. $200–$299.99 ⦀
22–15. Traditional watch 183.6°
22–17. $78
22–19. Transportation   126°
          Hotel   100.8°
          Food   72°
          Miscellaneous   61.2°

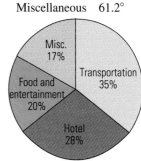

22–21. 250
22–23. 27,778 mean; $25,000 median
22–24. 24.94%

Optional Assignment

1. 98
3. 4.3
5. 16%; 2.5%
7. 68%; 81.5%; 2.5%; 2.5%; 47.5%
9. 5.02

1. $144,200; $138,500
2. 1,300
3. 3.25
4. 400; ll; 2
5. Bar 3 on horizontal axis goes up to 300 on vertical axis
6. Profits   36°
   Cost of sales   144°
   Expense   180°

7. 177.3%
8. 9.0 standard deviation

Check Figures (Odds) to Additional Assignments by Learning Unit from Appendix A

LU 1.1

1. **a.** Eight thousand, two hundred ninety-five
   d. Fifty-eight thousand, three
3. **a.** 40; 380; 860; 5,980; 210
   c. 21,000; 1,000; 4,000; 10,000
5. **a.** Hundreds place
   c. Ten thousands place
   e. Billions place
7. Three hundred eighty-four
9. $375,985
11. Two thousand, one

LU 1.2

1. **a.** 834   **c.** 1,319   **d.** 179
3. **a.** Estimated 40; 39
   c. Estimated 10; 9
5. $71,577
7. $19,973
9. 12,797 lbs
11. Estimated $9,400; $9,422
13. $746 discount

LU 1.3

1. **a.** Estimated 2,000; actual 2,114
   c. Estimated 15,000,000; actual 16,184,184
3. **a.** Estimated 1,000; actual 963 R5
   c. Estimated 20; actual 25 R8
5. 2,695
7. $78
9. 27
11. $43,200
13. 40 stacks and 23 "extra" bricks

LU 2.1

1. **a.** Improper   **b.** Proper
   c. Improper   **d.** Mixed number
   e. Improper   **f.** Proper
3. **a.** $\frac{36}{5}$ **c.** $\frac{31}{7}$ **f.** $\frac{53}{3}$
5. **a.** 6; $\frac{6}{7}$ **b.** 15; $\frac{2}{5}$ **e.** 12; $\frac{8}{11}$
7. $\frac{13}{4}$

9. $\frac{17}{25}$
11. $\frac{60}{100}$
13. $\frac{7}{12}$

LU 2.2

1. **a.** 64   **b.** 180   **c.** 480
   d. 252
3. **a.** $\frac{1}{3}$ **b.** $\frac{2}{3}$ **e.** $6\frac{1}{8}$ **h.** $56\frac{5}{6}$
5. $3\frac{1}{40}$ yards
7. $17\frac{5}{12}$ miles
9. $4\frac{8}{9}$ hours

LU 2.3

1. **a.** $\frac{\overset{1}{\cancel{6}}}{\underset{1}{\cancel{13}}} \times \frac{\overset{2}{\cancel{26}}}{\underset{2}{\cancel{12}}} = 1$

3. **a.** $1\frac{1}{4}$ **b.** 3   **g.** 24   **l.** $\frac{4}{7}$
5. $39,000
7. 714
9. $20\frac{2}{3}$ miles
11. $412,000

LU 3.1

1. **a.** .65   **b.** .3   **c.** .953
   d. .401   **e.** .06
3. **a.** Hundredths place
   d. Thousandths place
5. **a.** $\frac{2}{5}$ **b.** $\frac{11}{25}$
   g. $\frac{5}{16}$ **l.** $9\frac{1}{25}$
7. .286
9. $\frac{566}{1,000}$
11. .333
13. .0020507

LU 3.2

1. **a.** 24.875   **b.** 5.2281   **d.** 3.7736
3. **a.** .3   **b.** .1   **c.** 1,480.0   **d.** .1
5. **a.** 6,870   **c.** .0272
   e. 34,700   **i.** 8,329.8
7. $4.53
9. $111.25
11. 15

LU 4.1

1. **a.** $430.64   **b.** 3   **c.** $867.51
3. **a.** Neuner Realty Co.
   b. Kevin Jones
   h. $2,756.80
5. $37.79

LU 4.2

1. $1,435.42
3. Add $3,000; deduct $22.25
5. $2,989.92
7. $1,214.60

LU 5.1

1. **a.** $5N = 60$ **e.** $14 + \frac{N}{3} = 18$
   h. $2N + 3N + 8 = 68$

LU 5.2

1. $45
3. $45 telephone; $135 utility
5. 51 tickets—Sherry;
   408 tickets—Linda
7. 12 necklaces ($48);
   36 watches ($252)
9. $157.14

LU 6.1

1. **a.** 6%   **b.** 87.5%
   i. 503.8%   **l.** 80%
3. **a.** 70%   **c.** 162.5%
   h. 50%   **n.** 1.5%
5. **a.** $\frac{1}{4}$ **b.** .375   **c.** 50%
   d. $.66\overline{6}$ **n.** $1\frac{1}{8}$
7. 2.9%
9. $\frac{39}{100}$
11. $\frac{9}{10,000}$

LU 6.2

1. **a.** $8,000; $12\frac{1}{2}$%; $1,000
   c. $7.00; 12%; $.84
3. **a.** 33.3% **b.** 3% **c.** 27.5%
5. **a.** −1,584; −26.6%
   d. −20,000; −16.7%
7. $9,000
9. $3,196
11. 329.5%

LU 7.1

1. **a.** $450 **b.** $360 **c.** $50
   d. $100 **e.** $380
3. **a.** $75 **b.** $21.50; $40.75
5. **a.** .7125; .2875 **b.** .7225; .2775
7. $3.51
9. $81.25
11. $315
13. 45%

LU 7.2

1. **a.** February 18; March 10
   d. May 20; June 9
   e. October 10; October 30
3. **a.** .98; $1,102.50
   c. .98; $367.99
5. **a.** $16.79; $835.21
7. $12,230.40
9. **a.** $439.29 **b.** $491.21
11. $209.45
13. **a.** $765.31 **b.** $386.99

LU 8.1

1. **a.** $9.72 **b.** $2.72
   c. $4.35 **d.** $90 **e.** $116.31
3. **a.** $2; 80% **b.** $6.50; 52%
   c. $.28; 28.9%
5. **a.** $1.52 **b.** $225
   c. $372.92 **d.** $625
7. **a.** $38.16 **b.** $197.16
9. **a.** $258.52 **b.** $90.48
11. **a.** $212.50 **b.** $297.50
13. $8.17

LU 8.2

1. **a.** $2.40 **b.** $57.50
   c. $34.43 **d.** $27.33 **e.** $.15
3. **a.** $6.94 **b.** $882.35 **c.** $30
   d. $171.43
5. **a.** 28.57% **b.** 33.33%
   d. 53.85%
7. $346.15
9. 39.39%
11. $2.29
13. 63.33%

LU 8.3

1. **a.** $16.00; $64
   b. $525; $1,574.98

---

3. **a.** $410 **b.** $18.65
5. **a.** $216; $324; $5.14
   b. $45; $63.90; $1.52
7. 17%
9. $21.15
11. $273.78
13. $.79

LU 9.1

1. **a.** $304; 0; $304
   b. $360; $40.50; $400.50
3. **a.** $438.85 **b.** $615.13
5. **a.** $5,200 **b.** $3,960
   c. $3,740 **d.** $4,750
7. $723.00
9. $3,846.25
11. $2,032.48

LU 9.2

1. **a.** $200; $780
3. 0; $990
5. $12.40; $11.31 medicare
7. −0−
9. $15.23; no Social Security
11. $577.21
13. $635.65

LU 10.1

1. **a.** $180 **b.** $1,080
   c. $1,275
3. **a.** $131.25 **b.** $16.33
   c. $98.51
5. **a.** $515.63 **b.** $6,015.63
7. **a.** $5,459.66
9. $659.36
11. $360

LU 10.2

1. **a.** $4,371.44 **b.** $4,545.45
   c. $3,433.33
3. **a.** 60 **b.** 120 **c.** 270
   d. 145
5. 3%
7. $250
9. $3,000
11. 119 days

LU 10.3

1. **a.** $2,568.75; $1,885.47; $920.04
3. $4,267.59
5. $4,715.30; $115.30

LU 11.1

1. I; B; D; I; D; I; B; D
3. **a.** 9.1% **c.** 13%
5. $15,963.75
7. $848.75; $8,851.25
9. $14,300
11. $7,855

LU 11.2

1. **a.** $4,980 **b.** $16,480.80
   c. $994.44
3. **a.** $14.76 **b.** $223.25 **c.** $3.49
5. $4,031.67
7. $8,262.74
9. $5,088.16
11. $721.45

LU 12.1

1. **a.** $618.19 year 2
   b. $3,115.57 year 4
3. **a.** $15,869; $5,869
   b. $16,084; $6,084
5. $5,980
7. $8,881.20
9. $2,129.40
11. $3,207.09; $207.09
13. $3,000; $3,469; $3,498

LU 12.2

1. **a.** .6209 **b.** .3936 **c.** .5513
3. **a.** $1,575,50; $924.50
   b. $2,547.02; $2,052.98
5. $13,152.60
7. $13,356.98
9. $16,826.40
11. $652.32
13. $18,014.22

LU 13.1

1. **a.** $1,000; $2,080; $3,246.40
3. **a.** $6,888.60 **b.** $6,273.36
5. $325,525
7. $13,412
9. $30,200.85
11. $33,650.94

LU 13.2

1. **a.** $2,638.65 **b.** $6,375.24;
   $7,217.10
3. $2,715.54
5. $24,251.85
7. $47,608
9. $456,425
11. Accept Jason $265,010

LU 13.3

1. **a.** $4,087.50
3. $16,200
5. $24,030
7. $16,345
9. $8,742

LU 14.1

1. **a.** $1,200; $192
   b. $9,000; $1,200
3. **a.** 14.75% **b.** 10%
   c. 11.25%

5. a. $3,528 **b.** $696
 c. $4,616
7. a. $22,500 **b.** $4,932
 c. $29,932
9. a. $20,576 **b.** 12.75%

LU 14.2

1. a. $625; $375
 b. $9,600; $2,910
3. a. $625; $578.12
5. $1,758; $553
7. $900
9. $7,287.76

LU 14.3

1. a. $465; $8,535
 b. $915.62; $4,709.38
3. a. $332.03 **b.** $584.83
 c. $384.28
5. Final payment $784.39
7. $51.34
9. $35
11. $922.49
13. 7.50% to 7.75%

LU 15.1

1. a. $1,149.20 **b.** $1,555.50;
 $4,090.50; $3,859.65
3. a. $117.25, 7.7%
 b. $174, 5.7%
5. $2,487.24
7. $2,584.71; $2,518.63
9. a. $66.08 **b.** $131,293.80
11. $773,560

LU 15.2

1. a. $1,371.90; $1,133.33; $238.57
3. #4 balance outstanding $195,183.05
5. $587,612.80
7. $327.12; $251,581.60
9. $44,271.43
11. $61,800

LU 16.1

1. Total assets $224,725
3. Merch. inventory 13.90%; 15.12%

LU 16.2

1. Net income $57,765
3. Purchases 73.59%; 71.43%

LU 16.3

1. Sales 2002, 93.5%; 2001, 93.2%
3. .22
5. 59.29%
7. .83

9. COGS 119.33%; 111.76%; 105.04%
11. .90
13. 5.51%
15. 11.01%

LU 17.1

1. a. 4% **b.** 25% **c.** 10%
 d. 20%
3. a. $2,033; $4,667
 b. $1,850; $9,750
5. $8,625 depreciation per year
7. $2,800 depreciation per year
9. $95
11. a. $12,000 **b.** $6,000
 c. $18,000 **d.** $45,000

LU 17.2

1. a. $.300 **b.** $.192 **c.** $.176
3. a. $.300, $2,600
 b. $.192, $300,824
5. $5,300 book value end of year 5
7. a. $.155 **b.** $20,001.61

LU 17.3

1. a. $\frac{5}{15}, \frac{4}{15}, \frac{3}{15}, \frac{2}{15}, \frac{1}{15}$
3. a. $3,050; $3,650
 b. $3,171; $8,429
5. $900 book value end of year 6
7. a. 28 **b.** $237.50 **c.** $845

LU 17.4

1. a. 8% **b.** 20% **c.** 25%
3. a. $4,467; $2,233
 b. $3,867; $7,733
5. $121, year 6
7. a. 28.57% **b.** $248 **c.** $619
9. a. 16.67% **b.** $2,500
 c. $10,814 **d.** $2,907

LU 17.5

1. a. 33%; $825; $1,675
3. Depreciation year 8, $346
5. $125
7. a. $15,000 **b.** $39,000
 c. $21,600 **d.** 2001
9. $68,440

LU 18.1

1. a. $5,120; $3,020
 b. $323,246; $273,546
3. $35,903; $165,262
5. $10,510.20; $16,345
7. $37.62; $639.54
9. $628.40
11. $3,069; $952; $2,117

LU 18.2

1. a. $85,700; $143,500; .597;
 $64,500; $38,507
3. $85,000
5. $342,000; $242,500; 5.85; 6.29
7. $60,000; $100,000; $40,000
9. $70,150
11. $5,970
13. 3.24; 3.05
15. $32,340; $35,280; $49,980;
 $29,400

LU 19.1

1. a. $26.80; $562.80
 b. $718.80; $12,698.80
3. a. $20.75; $43.89; $463.64
5. Total is **(a)** $1,023; **(b)** $58.55
7. $5.23; $115.23
9. $2,623.93
11. $26.20
13. $685.50

LU 19.2

1. a. $68,250 **b.** $775,450
3. a. $7.45; $74.50; 74.50
5. $9.10
7. $8,368.94
9. $42,112
11. $32,547.50

LU 20.1

1. a. $9.27; 25; $231.75
3. a. $93.00; $387.50; $535.00;
 $916.50
5. $1,242.90
7. $14,265
9. $47.50 more
11. $68,750

LU 20.2

1. a. $488 **b.** $2,912
3. a. $68,000; $60,000
 b. $41,600; $45,000
5. $1,463
7. $117,187.50
9. $336,000
11. a. $131,250
 b. $147,000

LU 20.3

1. a. $98; $160; $258
3. a. $312 **b.** $233 **c.** $181
 d. $59; $20
5. a. $647 **b.** $706
7. $601

9. $781
11. $10,000; $8,000
13. $60,000; $20,000
15. $19.50; $110.50
17. $1,575

LU 21.1
1. a. $25.875 f. 44
3. $.45
5. a. $8,364; $7,328.75
7. a. $320,000; $262,500; $.35
9. 25.4%

LU 21.2
1. a. IBM b. $10\frac{1}{4}$ c. 2004
   d. $102.50 e. $102\frac{3}{8}$
3. a. $1,025 b. $1,023.75
5. a. $3,075 b. $307.50

7. a. $30 discount b. $16.25 premium c. $42.50 premium
9. a. $625 b. $375 discount
   c. $105 d. 16.8%
11. 7.8%; 7.2%
13. 8.98%

LU 21.3
1. $11.90
3. $15.20
5. +$.14
7. 7.6%
9. $1.45; $18.45
11. $.56; $14.66
13. $1,573.50
15. $123.00 loss
17. $10,591.50
19. a. 2000; 2002
    b. 9.3% Comp USA
       6.9% GMA

c. $1,023.75 Comp USA
   $1,016.25 GMA
d. Both at premium
e. $1,025 Comp USA
   $1,028.75 GMA

LU 22.1
1. a. 20.4 b. 83.75 c. 10.07
3. a. 59.5 b. 50
5. a. 63.7; 62; 62
7. $1,500,388.50
9. $10.75
11. $9.98

LU 22.2
1. 18: ||||| || 7
3. 25–30: ||||| ||| 8
5. 7.2°
7. 145–154: |||| 4
9. 98.4°; 9.9°; 70.5°; 169.2°; 11.9°

# GLOSSARY

The Glossary contains a comprehensive list of the key terms used in the text. In many cases, examples are also included in the definitions. Recall that key terms and their page references are listed in the Chapter Organizer and Reference Guide for each chapter.

Accelerated Cost Recovery System (ACRS)   Tax law enacted in 1981 for assets put in service from 1981 through 1986.

Accelerated depreciation method   Computes more depreciation expense in the early years of the asset's life than in the later years.

Accounts payable   Amounts owed to creditors for services or items purchased.

Accounts receivable   Amount owed by customers to a business from previous sales.

Accumulated depreciation   Amount of depreciation that has accumulated on plant and equipment assets.

Acid test   Current assets less inventory less prepaid expenses divided by current liabilities.

Addends   Numbers that are combined in the addition process. *Example:* 8 + 9 = 17, of which 8 and 9 are the addends.

Adjustable rate mortgage   Rate of mortgage is lower than a fixed rate mortgage. Rates adjusted without refinancing. Caps available to limit how high rate can go for each adjustment period over term of loan.

Adjusted bank balance   Current balance of checkbook after reconciliation process.

Amortization   Process of paying back a loan (principal plus interest) by equal periodic payments (see **amortization schedule**).

Amortization schedule   Shows monthly payment to pay back loan at maturity. Payment also includes interest. Note payment is fixed at same amount each month.

Amount financed   Cash price less down payment.

Annual percentage rate (APR)   True or effective annual interest rate charged by sellers. Required to be stated by Truth in Lending Act.

Annual percentage rate (APR) table   Effective annual rate of interest on a loan or installment purchase as shown by table lookup.

Annual percentage yield (APY)   Truth in savings law forced banks to report actual interest in form of APY. Interest yield must be calculated on actual number of days bank has the money.

Annuities certain   Annuities that have stated beginning and ending dates.

Annuity   Stream of equal payments made at periodic times.

Annuity due   Annuity that is paid (or received) at the beginning of the time period.

Assessed value   Value of a property that an assessor sets (usually a percent of property's market value) that is used in calculating property taxes.

Asset cost   Amount company paid for the asset.

Assets   Things of value owned by a business.

Asset turnover   Net sales divided by total assets.

ATM   Automatic teller machine that allows customers of a bank to transfer funds and make deposits or withdrawals.

Average daily balance   Sum of daily balances divided by number of days in billing cycle.

Average inventory   Total of all inventories divided by number of times inventory taken.

Balance sheet   Financial report that lists assets, liabilities, and equity. Report reflects the financial position of the company as of a particular date.

Bank discount   The amount of interest charged by a bank on a note. (Maturity value × Bank discount rate × Number of days bank holds note) ÷ 360.

Bank discount rate   Percent of interest.

Banker's Rule   Time is exact days/360 in calculating simple interest.

Bank reconciliation   Process of comparing the bank balance to the checkbook balance so adjustments can be made regarding checks outstanding, deposits in transit, and the like.

Bank statement   Report sent by the bank to the owner of the checking account indicating checks processed, deposits made, and so on, along with beginning and ending balances.

Bar graph   Visual representation using horizontal or vertical bars to make comparison or to show relationship on items of similar makeup.

Base   Number that represents the whole 100%. It is the whole to which something is being compared. Usually follows word *of*.

Beneficiary   Person(s) designated to receive the face value of the life insurance when insured dies.

Biweekly   Every 2 weeks (26 times in a year).

Biweekly mortgage   Mortgage payments made every 2 weeks rather than monthly. This payment method takes years off the life of the mortgage and substantially reduces the cost of interest.

Blank endorsement Current owner of check signs name on back. Whoever presents checks for payment receives the money.

Bodily injury Auto insurance that pays damages to people injured or killed by your auto.

Bond discount Bond selling for less than the face value.

Bond premium Bond selling for more than the face value.

Bonds Written promise by a company that borrows money usually with fixed-interest payment until maturity (repayment time).

Bond yield Total annual interest divided by total cost.

Book value Cost less accumulated depreciation.

Cancellation Reducing process that is used to simplify the multiplication and division of fractions. *Example:*

$$\frac{\overset{1}{\cancel{4}}}{8} \times \frac{1}{\underset{1}{\cancel{4}}}$$

Capital Owners' investment in the business.

Cash advance Money borrowed by holder of credit card. It is recorded as another purchase and is used in the calculation of the average daily balance.

Cash discount Savings that result from early payment by taking advantage of discounts offered by the seller; discount is not taken on freight or taxes.

Cash dividend Cash distribution of company's profit to owners of stock.

Cash value Except for term insurance, this indicates the value of the policy when terminated. Options fall under the heading of nonforfeiture values.

Centi- Prefix indicating .01 of a basic metric unit.

Chain discount Two or more trade discounts that are applied to the balance remaining after the previous discount is taken. Often called a **series discount.**

Check register Recordkeeping device that records checks paid and deposits made by companies using a checking account.

Checks Written documents signed by appropriate person that directs the bank to pay a specific amount of money to a particular person or company.

Check stub Provides a record of checks written. It is attached to the check.

Circle graph A visual representation of the parts to the whole.

Closing costs Costs incurred when property passes from seller to buyer such as for credit reports, recording costs, points, and so on.

CM Abbreviation for **credit memorandum.** The bank is adding to your account. The CM is found on the bank statement. *Example:* Bank collects a note for you.

Coinsurance Type of fire insurance in which the insurer and insured share the risk. Usually there is an 80% coinsurance clause.

Collision Optional auto insurance that pays for the repairs to your auto from an accident after deductible is met. Insurance company will only pay for repairs up to the value of the auto (less deductible).

Commissions Payments based on established performance criteria.

Common denominator To add two or more fractions, denominators must be the same.

Common stocks Units of ownership called shares.

Comparative statement Statement showing data from two or more periods side by side.

Complement 100% less the stated percent. *Example:* 18% → 82% is the complement (100% − 18%).

Compounding Calculating the interest periodically over the life of the loan and adding it to the principal.

Compound interest The interest that is calculated periodically and then added to the principal. The next period the interest is calculated on the adjusted principal (old principal plus interest).

Comprehensive insurance Optional auto insurance that pays for damages to the auto caused by factors other than from collision (fire, vandalism, theft, and the like).

Compulsory insurance Insurance required by law—standard coverage.

Constants Numbers such as 3 or −7. Placed on right side of equation; also called *knowns.*

Contingent annuities Beginning and ending dates of the annuity are uncertain (not fixed).

Contingent liability Potential liability that may or may not result from discounting a note.

Conversion periods How often (a period of time) the interest is calculated in the compounding process. *Example:* Daily—each day; monthly—12 times a year; quarterly—every 3 months; semiannually—every 6 months.

Corporation Company with many owners or stockholders. Equity of these owners is called stockholders' equity.

Cost Price retailers pay to manufacturer or supplier to bring merchandise into store.

Cost of goods (merchandise) sold Beginning inventory + Net purchases − Ending inventory.

Credit card A piece of plastic that allows you to buy on credit.

Credit memo (CM) Transactions of bank that increase customer's account.

Credit period (end) Credit days are counted from date of invoice. Has no relationship to the discount period.

Cumulative preferred stock Holders of preferred stock must receive current year and any dividends in arrears before any dividends are paid out to the holders of common stock.

Current assets Assets that are used up or converted into cash within 1 year or operating cycle.

Current liabilities Obligations of a company due within 1 year.

Current ratio Current assets divided by current liabilities.

Daily balance Calculated to determine customer's finance charge: Previous balance + Any cash advances + Purchases − Payments.

Daily compounding Interest calculated on balance each day.

Debit memo (DM) A debit transaction bank does for customers.

Deca- Prefix indicating 10 times basic metric unit.

Deci- Prefix indicating .1 of basic metric unit.

Decimal equivalent Decimal represents the same value as the fraction. *Example:*

$$.05 = \frac{5}{100}$$

Decimal fraction Decimal representing a fraction; the denominator has a power of 10.

Decimal point Position located between units and tenths.

Decimals Numbers written to the right of a decimal point. *Example:* 5.3, 18.22.

Declining-balance method Accelerated method of depreciation. The depreciation each year is calculated by book value beginning each year times the rate.

Deductibles Amount insured pays before insurance company pays. Usually the higher the deductible, the lower the premium will be.

Deductions Amounts deducted from gross earnings to arrive at net pay.

Deferred payment price Total of all monthly payments plus down payment.

Denominator The number of a common fraction below the division line (bar). *Example:*

$\frac{8}{9}$, of which 9 is the denominator

Deposits in transit Deposits not received or processed by bank at the time the bank statement is prepared.

Deposit slip Document that shows date, name, account number, and items making up a deposit.

Depreciation Process of allocating the cost of an asset (less residual value) over the asset's estimated life.

Depreciation causes Normal use, product obsolescence, aging, and so on.

Depreciation expense Process involving asset cost, estimated useful life, and residual value (salvage or trade-in value).

Depreciation schedule Table showing amount of depreciation expense, accumulated depreciation, and book value for each period of time for a plant asset.

Difference The resulting answer from a subtraction problem. *Example:* Minuend less subtrahend equals difference.

$$215 - 15 = 200$$

Differential pay schedule Pay rate is based on a schedule of units completed.

Digit Our decimal number system of 10 characters from 0 to 9.

Discounting a note Receiving cash from selling a note to a bank before the due date of a note. Steps to discount include: (1) calculate maturity value, (2) calculate number of days bank waits for money, (3) calculate bank discount, and (4) calculate proceeds.

Discount period Amount of time to take advantage of a cash discount.

Distribution of overhead Companies distribute overhead by floor space or sales volume.

Dividend Number in the division process that is being divided by another. *Example:* $5\overline{)15}$, in which 15 is the dividend.

Dividends Distribution of company's profit in cash or stock to owners of stock.

Dividends in arrears Dividends that accumulate when a company fails to pay dividends to cumulative preferred stockholders.

Divisor Number in the division process that is dividing into another. *Example:* $5\overline{)15}$, in which 5 is the divisor.

DM Abbreviation for **debit memorandum.** The bank is charging your account. The DM is found on the bank statement. *Example:* NSF.

Dollar markdown Original selling price less the reduction to price. Markdown may be stated as a percent of the original selling price. *Example:*

$$\frac{\text{Dollar markdown}}{\text{Original selling price}}$$

Dollar markup Selling price less cost. Difference is the amount of the markup. Markup is also expressed in percent.

Down payment Amount of initial cash payment made when item is purchased.

Drafts Written orders like checks instructing a bank, credit union, or savings and loan institution to pay your money to a person or organization.

Draw The receiving of advance wages to cover business or personal expenses. Once wages are earned, drawing amount reduces actual amount received.

Drawee One ordered to pay the check.

Drawer One who writes the check.

Due date Maturity date or when the note will be repaid.

Earnings per share Annual earnings ÷ Total number of shares outstanding.

Effective rate True rate of interest. The more frequent the compounding, the higher the effective rate.

Electronic deposits Credit card run through terminal which approves (or disapproves) the amount and adds it to company's bank balance.

Electronic funds transfer (EFT) A computerized operation that electronically transfers funds among parties without the use of paper checks.

Employee's Withholding Allowance Certificate (W-4) Completed by employee to indicate allowance claimed to determine amount of FIT that is deducted.

End of credit period Last day from date of invoice when customer can take cash discount.

End of month—EOM (also **proximo**) Cash discount period begins at the end of the month invoice is dated. After the 25th discount period, one additional month results.

Endorse Signing the back of the check; thus ownership is transferred to another party.

Endowment life Form of insurance that pays at maturity a fixed amount of money to insured or to the beneficiary. Insurance coverage would terminate when paid—similar to term life.

Equation Math statement that shows equality for expressions or numbers, or both.

Equivalent (fractional) Two or more fractions equivalent in value.

Escrow account Lending institution requires that each month $\frac{1}{12}$ of the insurance cost and real estate taxes be kept in a special account.

Exact interest Calculating simple interest using 365 days per year in time.

Excise tax Tax that government levies on particular products and services. Tax on specific luxury items or nonessentials.

Extended term insurance Resulting from nonforfeiture, it keeps the policy for the full face value going without further premium payments for a specific period of time.

Face amount Dollar amount stated in policy.

Face value Amount of insurance that is stated on the policy. It is usually the maximum amount for which the insurance company is liable.

Fair Credit and Charge Card Disclosure Act of 1988 Act that tightens controls on credit card companies soliciting new business.

Fair Labor Standards Act Federal law has minimum wage standards and the requirement of overtime pay. There are many exemptions for administrative personnel and for others.

Federal income tax (FIT) withholding Federal tax withheld from paycheck.

Federal Insurance Contribution Act (FICA) Percent of base amount of each employee's salary. FICA taxes used to fund retirement, disabled workers, Medicare, and so on. FICA is now broken down into Social Security and Medicare.

Federal Unemployment Tax Act (FUTA) Tax paid by employer. Current rate is .8% on first $7,000 of earnings.

Federal withholding tax See **Income tax.**

Finance charge Total payments − Actual loan cost.

Fire insurance Stipulated percent (normally 80%) of value that is required for insurance company to pay to reimburse one's losses.

First-in, first-out (FIFO) method This method assumes the first inventory brought into the store will be the first sold. Ending inventory is made up of goods most recently purchased.

Fixed rate mortgage Monthly payment fixed over number of years, usually 30 years.

FOB destination Seller pays cost of freight in getting goods to buyer's location.

FOB shipping point Buyer pays cost of freight in getting goods to his location.

Formula Equation that expresses in symbols a general fact, rule, or principle.

Fraction Expresses a part of a whole number. *Example:*

$\frac{5}{6}$ expresses 5 parts out of 6

Freight terms Determine how freight will be paid. Most common freight terms are **FOB shipping point** and **FOB destination.**

Frequency distribution Shows by table the number of times event(s) occurs.

Full endorsement This endorsement identifies the next person or company to whom the check is to be transferred.

Future value (FV) Final amount of the loan or investment at the end of the last period. Also called *compound amount*.

Future value of annuity Future dollar amount of a series of payments plus interest.

Graduated-payment mortgage Borrower pays less at beginning of mortgage. As years go on, the payments increase.

Graduated plans In beginning years, mortgage payment is less. As years go on, monthly payments rise.

Gram Basic unit of weight in metric system. An ounce equals about 28 grams.

Greatest common divisor The largest possible number that will divide evenly into both the numerator and denominator.

Gross pay Wages before deductions.

Gross profit Difference between cost of bringing goods into the store and selling price of the goods.

Gross profit from sales Net sales − Cost of goods sold.

Gross profit method Used to estimate value of inventory.

Gross sales Total earned sales before sales returns and allowances or sales discounts.

Hecto- Prefix indicating 100 times basic metric unit.

Higher terms Expressing a fraction with a new numerator and denominator that is equivalent to the original. *Example:*

$$\frac{2}{9} \rightarrow \frac{6}{27}$$

Home equity loan Cheap and readily accessible lines of credit backed by equity in your home; tax-deductible; rates can be locked in.

Horizontal analysis Method of analyzing financial reports where each total this period is compared by amount of percent to the same total last period.

Improper fraction Fraction that has a value equal to or greater than 1; numerator is equal to or greater than the denominator. *Example:*

$$\frac{6}{6}, \frac{14}{9}$$

Income statement Financial report that lists the revenues and expenses for a specific period of time. It reflects how well the company is performing.

Income tax or FIT Tax that depends on allowances claimed, marital status, and wages earned.

Indemnity Insurance company's payment to insured for loss.

Index numbers Express the relative changes in a variable compared with some base, which is taken as 100.

Individual retirement account (IRA) An account established for retirement planning.

Installment cost Down payment + (Number of payments × Monthly payment). Also called deferred payment.

Installment loan Loan paid off with a series of equal periodic payments.

Installment purchases Purchase of an item(s) that requires periodic payments for a specific period of time with usually a high rate of interest.

Insured Customer or policyholder.

Insurer The insurance company that issues the policy.

Interest Principal × Rate × Time.

Interest-bearing note Maturity value of note is greater than amount borrowed since interest is added on.

Inventory turnover Ratio that indicates how quickly inventory turns:

$$\frac{\text{Cost of goods sold}}{\text{Average inventory at cost}}$$

Invoice Document recording purchase and sales transactions.

Just-in-time (JIT) inventory system System that eliminates inventories. Suppliers provide materials daily as manufacturing company needs them.

Kilo- Prefix indicating 1,000 times basic metric unit.

Last-in, first-out (LIFO) method This method assumes the last inventory brought into the store will be the first sold. Ending inventory is made up of the oldest goods purchased.

Least common denominator (LCD) Smallest nonzero whole number into which all denominators will divide evenly. *Example:*

$$\frac{2}{3} \text{ and } \frac{1}{4} \qquad \text{LCD} = 12$$

Level premium term Insurance premium that is fixed, say, for 50 years.

Liabilities Amount business owes to creditors.

Liability insurance Insurance for bodily injury to others and damage to someone else's property.

Like fractions Proper fractions with the same denominators.

Like terms Terms that are made up with the same variable:

$$A + 2A + 3A = 6A$$

Limited payment life (20-payment life) Premiums are for 20 years (a fixed period) and provide paid-up insurance for the full face value of the policy.

Line graphs Graphical presentation that involves a time element. Shows trends, failures, backlogs, and the like.

Line of credit Provides immediate financing up to an approved limit.

Liquid assets Cash or other assets that can be converted quickly into cash.

List price Suggested retail price paid by customers.

Liter Basic unit of measure in metric, for volume.

Loan amortization table Table used to calculate monthly payments.

Long-term liabilities Debts or obligations that company does not have to pay within 1 year.

Lowest terms Expressing a fraction when no number divides evenly into the numerator and denominator except the number 1. *Example:*

$$\frac{5}{10} \rightarrow \frac{1}{2}$$

Maker One who writes the note.

Manual deposit Salesperson fills out charge slip and completes merchant batch header slip at end of business day.

Margin Difference between cost of bringing goods into store and selling price of goods

Markdowns Reductions from original selling price caused by seasonal changes, special promotions, and so on.

Markup Amount retailers add to cost of goods to cover operating expenses and make a profit.

Markup percent calculation Markup percent on cost × Cost = Dollar markup; or Markup percent on selling price × Selling price = Dollar markup.

Maturity date Date the principal and interest are due.

Maturity value Principal plus interest (if interest is charged). Represents amount due on the due date.

Maturity value of note Amount of cash paid on the due date. If interest-bearing maturity, value is greater than amount borrowed.

Mean Statistical term that is found by:

$$\frac{\text{Sum of all figures}}{\text{Number of figures}}$$

Measure of dispersion Number that describes how the numbers of a set of data are spread out or dispersed.

Median Statistical term that represents the central point or midpoint of a series of numbers.

Merchandise inventory Cost of goods for resale.

Merchant batch header slip Slip used by company to list and attach charge slips.

Meter Basic unit of length in metric system. A meter is a little longer than a yard.

Metric system A decimal system of weights and measures. The basic units are meters, grams, and liters.

Mill $\frac{1}{10}$ of a cent or $\frac{1}{1,000}$ of a dollar. In decimal, it is .001. *In application:*

$$\frac{\text{Property}}{\text{tax due}} = \frac{\text{Mills} \times .001 \times}{\text{Assessed valuation}}$$

Milli- Prefix indicating .001 of basic metric unit.

Minuend In a subtraction problem, the larger number from which another is subtracted. *Example:*

$$50 - 40 = 10$$

Mixed decimal Combination of a whole number and decimal, such as 59.8, 810.85.

Mixed number Sum of a whole number greater than zero and a proper fraction:

$$2\frac{1}{4}, 3\frac{3}{9}$$

Mode Value that occurs most often in a series of numbers.

Modified Accelerated Cost Recovery System (MACRS) Part of Tax Reform Act of 1986 that revised depreciation schedules of ACRS. Tax Bill of 1989 updates MACRS.

Monthly Some employers pay employees monthly.

Mortgage Cost of home less down payment.

Multiplicand The first or top number being multiplied in a multiplication problem. *Example:*

$$\begin{array}{ccccc} \text{Product} & = & \text{Multiplicand} & \times & \text{Multiplier} \\ 40 & = & 20 & \times & 2 \end{array}$$

Multiplier The second or bottom number doing the multiplication in a problem. *Example:*

$$\begin{array}{ccccc} \text{Product} & = & \text{Multiplicand} & \times & \text{Multiplier} \\ 40 & = & 20 & \times & 2 \end{array}$$

Mutual fund Investors buy shares in the fund's portfolio (group of stocks and/or bonds).

Net asset value (NAV) The dollar value of one mutual fund share; calculated by subtracting current liabilities from current market value of fund's investments and dividing this by number of shares outstanding.

Net deposits Credit card sales less returns.

Net pay See **Net wages.**

Net price List price less amount of trade discount. The net price is before any cash discount.

Net price equivalent rate When multiplied times the list price, this rate or factor produces the actual cost to the buyer. Rate is found by taking the complement of each term in the discount and multiplying them together (do not round off).

Net proceeds Maturity value less bank discount.

Net profit (net income) Gross profit − Operating expenses.

Net purchases Purchases − Purchase discounts − Purchase returns and allowances.

Net sales Gross sales − Sales discounts − Sales returns and allowances.

Net wages Gross pay less deductions.

Net worth Assets less liabilities.

No-fault insurance Involves bodily injury. Damage (before a certain level) that is paid by an insurance company no matter who is to blame.

Nominal rate Stated rate.

Nonforfeiture values When a life insurance policy is terminated (except term), it represents (1) the available cash value, (2) additional extended term, or (3) additional paid-up insurance.

Noninterest-bearing note Note where the maturity value will be equal to the amount of money borrowed since no additional interest is charged.

Nonsufficient funds (NSF) Drawer's account lacked sufficient funds to pay written amount of check.

Normal distribution Data is spread symmetrically about the mean.

Numerator Number of a common fraction above the division line (bar). *Example:*

$$\frac{8}{9}, \text{ in which 8 is the numerator}$$

Odd lot Fewer than 100 shares.

Omnibus Budget Reconciliation Act of 1989 An update of MACRS. Unless business use of equipment is greater than 50%, straight-line depreciation is required.

Open-end credit Set payment period. Also, additional credit amounts can be added up to a set limit. It is a revolving charge account.

Operating expenses Regular expenses of doing business. These are not costs.

Ordinary annuities Annuity that is paid (or received) at end of the time period.

Ordinary dating Cash discount is available within the discount period. Full amount due by end of credit period if discount is missed.

Ordinary interest Calculating simple interest using 360 days per year in time.

Ordinary life insurance See **Straight life insurance.**

Outstanding balance Amount left to be paid on a loan.

Outstanding checks Checks written but not yet processed by the bank before bank statement preparation.

Overdraft Occurs when company or person wrote a check without enough money in the bank to pay for it (NFS check).

Overhead expenses Operating expenses *not* directly associated with a specific department or product.

Override Commission that managers receive due to sales by people that they supervise.

Overtime Time-and-a-half pay for more than 40 hours of work.

Owner's equity See **Capital.**

Paid-up insurance A certain level of insurance can continue, although the premiums are terminated. This results from the nonforfeiture value (except term). Result is a reduced paid-up policy until death.

Partial products Numbers between multiplier and product.

Partial quotient Occurs when divisor doesn't divide evenly into the dividend.

Partnership Business with two or more owners.

Payee One who is named to receive the amount of the check.

Payroll register Multicolumn form to record payroll data.

Percent Stands for hundredths. *Example:*

$$4\% \text{ is 4 parts of one hundred, or } \frac{4}{100}$$

Percentage method A method to calculate withholdings. Opposite of wage bracket method.

Percent decrease Calculated by decrease in price over original amount.

Percent increase Calculated by increase in price over original amount.

Percent markup on cost Dollar markup divided by the cost; thus, markup is a percent of the cost.

Percent markup on selling price Dollar markup divided by the selling price; thus, markup is a percent of the selling price.

Periodic inventory system Physical count of inventory taken at end of a time period. Inventory records are not continually updated.

Periods Number of years times the number of times compounded per year (see **Conversion period**).

Perishables Goods or services with a limited life.

Perpetual inventory system Inventory records are continually updated; opposite of periodic.

Personal property Items of possession, like cars, home, furnishings, jewelry, and so on. These are taxed by the property tax (don't forget real property is also taxed).

Piecework Compensation based on the number of items produced or completed.

Place value The digit value that results from its position in a number.

Plant and equipment Assets that will last longer than 1 year.

Point of sale Terminal that accepts cards (like those used at ATMs) to purchase items at retail outlets. No cash is physically exchanged.

Points Percentage(s) of mortgage that represents an additional cost of borrowing. It is a one-time payment made at closing.

Policy Written insurance contract.

Policyholder The insured.

Portion Amount, part, or portion that results from multiplying the base times the rate. Not expressed as a percent; it is expressed as a number.

Preferred stock Type of stock that has a preference regarding a corporation's profits and assets.

Premium Periodic payments that one makes for various kinds of insurance protection.

Premium rates (payroll) Higher rates based on a quota system.

Prepaid expenses Items a company buys that have not been used are shown as assets.

Prepaid rent Rent paid in advance.

Present value of annuity Amount of money needed today to receive a specified stream (annuity) of money in the future.

Present value (PV) How much money will have to be deposited today (or at some date) to reach a specific amount of maturity (in the future).

Price-earnings (PE) ratio Closing price per share of stock divided by earnings per share.

Price relative The quotient of the current price divided by some previous year's price—the base year—multiplied by 100.

Prime numbers Whole number greater than 1 that is only divisible by itself and 1. *Examples:* 2, 3, 5.

Principal Amount of money that is originally borrowed, loaned, or deposited.

Proceeds Maturity value less the bank charge.

Product Answer of a multiplication process, such as:

$$\text{Product} = \text{Multiplicand} \times \text{Multiplier}$$
$$50 \quad = \quad 5 \quad \times \quad 10$$

Promissory note Written unconditional promise to pay a certain sum (with or without interest) at a fixed time in the future.

Proper fractions Fractions with a value less than 1; numerator is smaller than denominator, such as $\frac{5}{9}$.

Property damage Auto insurance covering damages that are caused to the property of others.

Property tax Tax that raises revenue for school districts, cities, counties, and the like.

Property tax due Tax rate × Assessed valuation

Proximo (prox) Same as end of month.

Purchase discounts Savings received by buyer for paying for merchandise before a certain date.

Purchase returns and allowances Cost of merchandise returned to store due to damage, defects, and so on. An *allowance* is a cost reduction that results when buyer keeps or buys damaged goods.

Pure decimal Has no whole number(s) to the left of the decimal point, such as .45.

Quick assets Current assets − Inventory − Prepaid expenses.

Quick ratio (Current assets − Inventory − Prepaid expenses) ÷ Current liabilities.

Quotient The answer of a division problem.

Range Difference between the highest and lowest values in a group of values or set of data.

Rate Percent that is multiplied times the base that indicates what part of the base we are trying to compare to. Rate is not a whole number.

Rate of interest Percent of interest that is used to compute the interest charge on a loan for a specific time.

Ratio analysis Relationship of one number to another.

Real property Land, buildings, and so on, which are taxed by the property tax.

Rebate Finance charge that a customer receives for paying off a loan early.

Rebate fraction Sum of digits based on number of months to go divided by sum of digits based on total number of months of loan.

Receipt of goods (ROG) Used in calculating the cash discount period; begins the day that the goods are received.

Reciprocal of a fraction The interchanging of the numerator and the denominator. Inverted number is the reciprocal. *Example:*

$$\frac{6}{7} \rightarrow \frac{7}{6}$$

Reduced paid-up insurance Insurance that uses cash value to buy protection, face amount is less than original policy, and policy continues for life.

Remainder Leftover amount in division.

Repeating decimals Decimal numbers that repeat themselves continuously and thus do not end.

Residual value Estimated value of a plant asset after depreciation is taken (or end of useful life).

Restrictive endorsement Check must be deposited to the payee's account. This restricts one from cashing it.

Retail method Method to estimate cost of ending inventory. The cost ratio times ending inventory at retail equals the ending cost of inventory.

Retained earnings Amount of earnings that is kept in the business.

Return on equity Net income divided by stockholders' equity.

Revenues Total earned sales (cash or credit) less any sales discounts, returns, or allowances.

Reverse mortgage Federal Housing Administration makes it possible for older homeowners to live in their homes and get cash or monthly income.

Revolving charge account Charges for a customer are allowed up to a specified maximum, a minimum monthly payment is required, and interest is charged on balance outstanding.

ROG Receipt of goods; cash discount period begins when goods are received, not ordered.

Rounding decimals Reducing the number of decimals to an indicated position, such as $59.59 \longrightarrow 59.6$ to the nearest tenth.

Rounding whole numbers all the way Process to estimate actual answer. When rounding all the way, only one nonzero digit is left. Rounding all the way gives the least degree of accuracy. *Example:* 1,251 to 1,000; 2,995 to 3,000.

Round lot One hundred shares of stock or multiples of 100.

Rule of 78 Method to compute rebates on consumer finance loans. How much of finance charge you are entitled to? Formula or table lookup may be used.

Safekeeping Bank procedure whereby a bank does not return checks. Canceled checks are photocopied.

Sales tax Tax levied on consumers for certain sales of merchandise or services by states, counties, or various local governments.

Salvage value Cost less accumulated depreciation.

Selling price   Cost plus markup equals selling price.

Semiannually   Twice a year.

Semimonthly   Some employees are paid twice a month.

Series discount   See **chain discount.**

Short-rate table   Fire insurance rate table used when insured cancels the policy.

Short-term policy   Fire insurance policy for less than 1 year.

Signature card   Information card signed by person opening a checking account.

Simple discount note   A note in which bank deducts interest in advance.

Simple interest   Interest is only calculated on the principal. In $I = P \times R \times T$, the interest plus original principal equals the maturity value of an interest-bearing note.

Simple interest formula

$$\text{Interest} = \text{Principal} \times \text{Rate} \times \text{Time}$$

$$\text{Principal} = \frac{\text{Interest}}{\text{Rate} \times \text{Time}}$$

$$\text{Rate} = \frac{\text{Interest}}{\text{Principal} \times \text{Time}}$$

$$\text{Time} = \frac{\text{Interest}}{\text{Principal} \times \text{Rate}}$$

Single equivalent discount rate   Rate or factor as a single discount that calculates the amount of the trade discount by multiplying the rate times the list price. This single equivalent discount replaces a series of chain discounts. The single equivalent rate is (1 − Net price equivalent rate).

Single trade discount   Company gives only one trade discount.

Sinking fund   An annuity in which the stream of deposits with appropriate interest will equal a specified amount in the future.

Sliding scale commissions   Different commission. Rates depend on different levels of sales.

Sole proprietorship   A business owned by one person.

Specific identification method   This method calculates the cost of ending inventory by identifying each item remaining to invoice price.

Standard deviation   Measures the spread of data around the mean.

State unemployment tax (SUTA)   Tax paid by employer. Rate varies depending on amount of unemployment the company experiences.

Stockbrokers   People who with their representatives do the trading on the floor of the stock exchange.

Stock certificate   Piece of paper that shows certificate of ownership in a company.

Stockholder   One who owns stock in a company.

Stockholders' equity   Assets less liabilities.

Stocks   Ownership shares in the company sold to buyers, who receive stock certificates.

Stock yield percent   Dividend per share divided by the closing price per share.

Straight commission   Wages calculated as a percent of the value of goods sold.

Straight life insurance (whole or ordinary)   Protection (full value of policy) results from continual payment of premiums by insured. Until death or retirement, nonforfeiture values exist for straight life.

Straight-line method   Method of depreciation that spreads an equal amount of depreciation each year over the life of the assets.

Straight-line rate (rate of depreciation)   One divided by number of years of expected life.

Subtrahend   In a subtraction problem smaller number that is being subtracted from another. *Example:* 30 in

$$150 - 30 = 120$$

Sum   Total in the adding process.

Sum-of-the-years'-digits method   Accelerated method of depreciation. Depreciation each year is calculated by multiplying cost (less residual value) times a fraction. Numerator is number of years of useful life remaining. Denominator is the sum of the years of estimated life.

Tax rate $\dfrac{\text{Budget needed}}{\text{Total assessed value}}$

Term life insurance   Inexpensive life insurance that provides protection for a specific period of time. No nonforfeiture values exist for term.

Term policy   Period of time that the policy is in effect.

Terms of the sale   Criteria on invoice showing when cash discounts are available, such as rate and time period.

Time   Expressed as years or fractional years, used to calculate the simple interest.

Trade discount   Reduction off original selling price (list price) not related to early payment.

Trade discount amount   List price less net price.

Trade discount rate   Trade discount amount given in percent.

Trade-in (scrap)   Estimated value of a plant asset after depreciation is taken (or end of useful life).

Treasury bill   Loan to the federal government for 91 days (13 weeks), 182 days (26 weeks,), or 1 year.

Trend analysis   Analyzing each number as a percentage of a base year.

Truth in Lending Act   Federal law that requires sellers to inform buyers, in writing, of (1) the finance charge and (2) the annual percentage rate. The law doesn't dictate what can be charged.

Twenty-payment life   Provides permanent protection and cash value, but insured pays premiums for first 20 years.

Twenty-year endowment   Most expensive life insurance policy. It is a combination of term insurance and cash value.

Unemployment tax   Tax paid by the employer that is used to aid unemployed persons.

Units-of-production method   Depreciation method that estimates amount of depreciation based on usage.

Universal life   Whole life insurance plan with flexible premium and death benefits. This life plan has limited guarantees.

Unknown   The variable we are solving for.

Unlike fractions   Proper fractions with different denominators.

Useful life   Estimated number of years the plant asset is used.

U.S. Rule   Method that allows the borrower to receive proper interest credits when paying off a loan in more than one payment before the maturity date.

U.S. Treasury bill   A note issued by federal government to investors.

Value of an annuity   Sum of series of payments and interest (think of this as the maturity value of compounding).

Variable commission scale   Company pays different commission rates for different levels of net sales.

Variable rate   Home mortgage rate is not fixed over its lifetime.

Variables   Letters or symbols that represent unknowns.

Vertical analysis   Method of analyzing financial reports where each total is compared to one total. *Example:* Cash is a percent of total assets.

W-4   See **Employee's Withholding Allowance Certificate.**

Wage bracket method   Tables used in Circular E to compute FIT withholdings.

Weekly Some employers pay employees weekly.

Weighted-average method Calculates the cost of ending inventory by applying an average unit cost to items remaining in inventory for that period of time.

Weighted mean Used to find an average when values appear more than once.

Whole life insurance See **Straight life insurance.**

Whole number Number that is 0 or larger and doesn't contain a decimal or fraction, such as 10, 55, 92.

Withholding Amount of deduction from one's paycheck.

Workers' compensation Business insurance covering sickness or accidental injuries to employees that result from on-the-job activities.

D

METRIC SYSTEM

Metric System Seems To Be Moving Ahead

WITH MANY STATES lowering their resistance, a plan to convert highway signs to the metric system is inching forward.

For decades, outcries from motorists and state officials have squelched efforts to switch from miles to kilometers. This month, however, the Federal Highway Administration is reviewing a new batch of comments on a proposed switch, and only a few states say they're opposed to metric. Moreover, most states say a fast conversion would be better than replacing mileage signs as they wear out (too confusing), or posting signs with both miles and kilometers for a few years (too expensive).

"We're a bit surprised to find the states as forthcoming and responsive as they've been," Rodney Slater, federal highway administrator, says. His agency may require kilometer signs as soon as 1996 to satisfy a five-year-old law requiring use of the metric system by anyone receiving federal funds.

For more detail in metric and measurement, order booklet ISBN 0-256-19088-7 from your local representative or customer service.

John Sullivan: Angie, I drove into the gas station last night to fill the tank up. Did I get upset! The pumps were not in gallons but in liters. This country (U.S.) going to metric is sure making it confusing.

Angie Smith: Don't get upset. Let me first explain the key units of measure in metric, and then I'll show you a convenient table I keep in my purse to convert metric to U.S. (also called customary system), and U.S. to metric. Let's go on.

The metric system is really a decimal system in which each unit of measure is exactly 10 times as large as the unit just smaller. In a moment, we will see how this aids in conversions. First, look at the middle column (Units) of this to see the basic units of measure:

U.S.	Thousands	Hundreds	Tens	Units	Tenths	Hundredths	Thousandths
Metric	Kilo- 1,000	Hecto- 100	Deka- 10	Gram Meter Liter 1	Deci- .1	Centi- .01	Milli- .001

- Weight: Gram (think of it as $\frac{1}{30}$ of an ounce).
- Length: Meter (think of it for now as a little more than a yard).
- Volume: Liter (a little more than a quart).

To aid you in looking at this, think of a decimeter, a centimeter, or a millimeter as being "shorter" (smaller) than a meter, whereas a dekameter, hectometer, and kilometer are "larger" than a meter. For example:

1 centimeter $= \frac{1}{100}$ of a meter; or 100 centimeters equals 1 meter.

1 millimeter $= \frac{1}{1,000}$ meter; or 1,000 millimeters equals 1 meter.

1 hectometer $= 100$ meters.

1 kilometer $= 1,000$ meters.

Remember we could have used the same setup for grams or liters. Note the summary here.

Length	Volume	Mass
1 meter:	1 liter:	1 gram:
= 10 decimeters	= 10 deciliters	= 10 decigrams
= 100 centimeters	= 100 centiliters	= 100 centigrams
= 1,000 millimeters	= 1,000 milliliters	= 1,000 milligrams
= .1 dekameter	= .1 dekaliter	= .1 dekagram
= .01 hectometer	= .01 hectoliter	= .01 hectogram
= .001 kilometer	= .001 kiloliter	= .001 kilogram

Practice these conversions and check solutions.

PRACTICE QUIZ 1

Convert the following:

1. 7.2 meters to centimeters
2. .89 meter to millimeters
3. 64 centimeters to meters
4. 350 grams to kilograms
5. 7.4 liters to centiliters
6. 2,500 milligrams to grams

✓ **Solutions**

1. 7.2 meters $= 7.2 \times 100 = 720$ centimeters (remember, 1 meter $= 100$ centimeters)
2. .89 meters $= .89 \times 1,000 = 890$ millimeters (remember, 1 meter $= 1,000$ millimeters)
3. 64 centimeters $= 64/100 = .64$ meters (remember, 1 meter $= 100$ centimeters)
4. 350 grams $= \dfrac{350}{1,000} = .35$ kilograms (remember 1 kilogram $= 1,000$ grams)
5. 7.4 liters $= 7.4 \times 100 = 740$ centiliters (remember, 1 liter $= 100$ centiliters)
6. 2,500 milligrams $= \dfrac{2,500}{1,000} = 2.5$ grams (remember, 1 gram $= 1,000$ milligrams

Angie: Look at the table of conversions and I'll show you how easy it is. Note how we can convert liters to gallons. Using the conversion from meters to U.S. (liters to gallons), we see that you multiply numbers of liters by .26, or 37.95 × .26 = 9.84 gallons.

Common conversion factors for English/metric					
A. To convert from U.S. to	**Metric**	**Multiply by**	**B. To convert from metric to**	**U.S.**	**Multiply by**
Length:			*Length:*		
Inches (in)	Meters (m)	.025	Meters (m)	Inches (in)	39.37
Feet (ft)	Meters (m)	.31	Meters (m)	Feet (ft)	3.28
Yards (yd)	Meters (m)	.91	Meters (m)	Yards (yd)	1.1
Miles	Kilometers (km)	1.6	Kilometers (km)	Miles	.62
Weight:			*Weight:*		
Ounces (oz)	Grams (g)	28	Grams (g)	Ounces (oz)	.035
Pounds (lb)	Grams (g)	454	Grams (g)	Pounds (lb)	.0022
Pounds (lb)	Kilograms (kg)	.45	Kilograms (kg)	Pounds (lb)	2.2
Volume or capacity:			*Volume or capacity:*		
Pints	Liters (L)	.47	Liters (L)	Pints	2.1
Quarts	Liters (L)	.95	Liters (L)	Quarts	1.06
Gallons (gal)	Liters (L)	3.8	Liters (L)	Gallons	.26

John: How would I convert 6 miles to kilometers?

Angie: Take the number of miles times 1.6, thus 6 miles × 1.6 = 9.6 kilometers.

John: If I weigh 120 pounds, what is my weight in kilograms?

Angie: 120 times .45 (use the conversion table) equals 54 kilograms.

John: OK. Last night, when I bought 16.6 liters of gas, I really bought 4.3 gallons (16.6 liters times .26).

PRACTICE QUIZ 2

Convert the following:

1. 10 meters to yards
2. 110 quarts to liters
3. 78 kilometers to miles
4. 52 yards to meters
5. 82 meters to inches
6. 292 miles to kilometers

✓ **Solutions**

1. 10 meters × 1.1 = 11 yards
2. 110 quarts × .95 = 104.5 liters
3. 78 kilometers × .62 = 48.36 miles
4. 52 yards × .91 = 47.32 meters
5. 82 meters × 39.37 = 3,228.34 inches
6. 292 miles × 1.6 = 467.20 kilometers

Name _____ Date _____

DRILL PROBLEMS

Convert:

1. 65 centimeters to meters — .65 meters $\left(\dfrac{65}{100}\right)$

2. 7.85 meters to centimeters — 785 centimeters (7.85×100)

3. 44 centiliters to liters — .44 liter $\left(\dfrac{44}{100}\right)$

4. 1,500 grams to kilograms — 1.5 kilograms $\left(\dfrac{1,500}{1,000}\right)$

5. 842 millimeters to meters — .842 meter $\left(\dfrac{842}{1,000}\right)$

6. 9.4 kilograms to grams — 9,400 grams $(9.4 \times 1,000)$
7. .854 kilograms to grams — 854 grams $(.854 \times 1,000)$
8. 5.9 meters to millimeters — 5,900 millimeters $(5.9 \times 1,000)$
9. 8.91 kilograms to grams — 8,910 grams $(8.91 \times 1,000)$
10. 2.3 meters to millimeters — 2,300 millimeters $(2.3 \times 1,000)$

Convert (round off to nearest tenth):

11. 50.9 kilograms to pounds — 112 pounds (50.9×2.2)
12. 8.9 pounds to grams — 4,040.6 grams (8.9×454)
13. 395 kilometers to miles — 244.9 miles $(395 \times .62)$
14. 33 yards to meters — 30.03 meters $(33 \times .91)$
15. 13.9 pounds to grams — 6,310.6 grams (13.9×454)
16. 594 miles to kilometers — 950.4 kilometers (594×1.6)
17. 4.9 feet to meters — 1.5 meters $(4.9 \text{ ft} \times .31)$
18. 9.9 feet to meters — 3.1 meters $(9.9 \times .31)$
19. 100 yards to meters — 91 meters $(100 \times .91)$
20. 40.9 kilograms to pounds — 90 pounds (40.9×2.2)
21. 895 miles to kilometers — 1,432 kilometers (895×1.6)
22. 1,000 grams to pounds — 2.2 pounds $(1,000 \times .0022)$
23. 79.1 meters to yards — 87 yards (79.1×1.1)
24. 12 liters to quarts — 12.7 quarts (12×1.06)
25. 2.92 meters to feet — 9.6 feet (2.92×3.28)
26. 5 liters to gallons — 1.3 gallons $(5 \times .26)$
27. 8.7 meters to feet — 28.5 feet (8.7×3.28)
28. 8 gallons to liters — 30.4 liters (8×3.8)
29. 1,600 grams to pounds — 3.52 pounds $(1,600 \times .0022)$
30. 310 meters to yards — 341 yards (310×1.1)

WORD PROBLEM

31. **Given:** A metric ton is 39.4 bushels of corn. Calculate number of bushels purchased from metric tons to bushels of corn.

    Problem: Soviets bought 450,000 metric tons of U.S. corn, valued at $58 million, for delivery after September 30.
    $450,000 \times 39.4 = 17,730,000$ bushels of corn

CLASSROOM NOTES

CLASSROOM NOTES

CLASSROOM NOTES

CLASSROOM NOTES

Classroom Notes

STUDENT CD-ROM

This student CD-ROM contains the following assets designed to help you succeed in the business math course:

- **Excel Spreadsheet Templates** to assist in solving end-of-chapter exercises that are indicated by a disk logo.

- **Tutorials** for each chapter in the book in true/false, multiple-choice, interactive, and key terms formats.

- **Practice Quizzes** covering key concepts in each chapter and giving you quick feedback on your responses.

- **Internet Resource Guide** providing information on using the Internet and useful Web sites for use with each chapter.

- **Web Links** to the *Practical Business Math Procedures* text Web site and other sites containing additional material to help you.